WORLD HISTORY

Educational Advisory Panel

The following educators provided ongoing review during the development of prototypes and key elements of this program.

Jose Colon

Berkeley High School
Berkeley, California

Bethany Copeland

Peach County High School
Fort Valley, Georgia

Darrel Dexter

Egyptian Community Unit School
Tamms, Illinois

Charles Dietz

Burnett Middle School
San Jose, California

John Hogan

Brevard High School
Brevard, North Carolina

Jeffrey Kaufman

Aspirations Diploma Plus High School
Brooklyn, New York

Beth E. Kuhlman

Queens Metropolitan High School
Forest Hills, New York

Beatrice Nudelman

Aptakisic Junior High School
Buffalo Grove, Illinois

Kyle Race

Greene High School
Greene, New York

Gretchen Ritter Varela

Northville High School
Northville, Michigan

Sharon Shirley

Branford High School
Branford, Connecticut

Yvette Snopkowski

Davis Junior High School
Sterling Heights, Michigan

La-Shanda West

Cutler Bay Senior High School
Cutler Bay, Florida

Contents

Videos related to each module can be accessed through your digital Student Edition.

Module 3

Module 4

Module 5

Module 6

Module 7

Module 8

🌐

Module 9

🌐

Module 10

Module 11

Module 12

Module 13

Module 14

Module 15

Reformation and Upheaval 1400–1600

Module 16

Module 17

Module 18

Module 19

🌐

Module 20

🌐

Module 21

🌐

Module 22

Module 23

Module 24

Module 25

Module 26

Module 27

Module 28

Module 29

Module 30

Module 31

Module 32

Available Online

Reading Like a Historian
World History Themes
Biographical Dictionary
Close-Read Screencasts
Economics Handbook
Geography and Map Skills Handbook
Skillbuilder Handbook

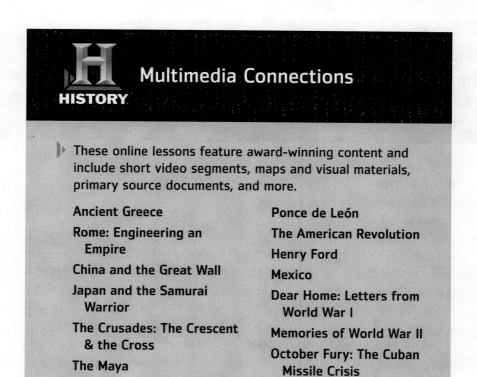

Multimedia Connections

▶ These online lessons feature award-winning content and include short video segments, maps and visual materials, primary source documents, and more.

Ancient Greece

Rome: Engineering an Empire

China and the Great Wall

Japan and the Samurai Warrior

The Crusades: The Crescent & the Cross

The Maya

Ponce de León

The American Revolution

Henry Ford

Mexico

Dear Home: Letters from World War I

Memories of World War II

October Fury: The Cuban Missile Crisis

HISTORY MADE EVERY DAY.

HISTORY® is the leading destination for revealing, award-winning, original non-fiction series and event-driven specials that connect history with viewers in an informative, immersive and entertaining manner across multiple platforms. HISTORY is part of A+E Networks, a global entertainment media company that includes, among others, A&E®, HISTORY®, Lifetime®, H2®, FYI™, and LMN®.

HISTORY programming greatly appeals to educators and young people who are drawn into the visual stories our documentaries tell. Our Education Department has a long-standing record in providing teachers and students with curriculum resources that bring the past to life in the classroom. Our content covers a diverse variety of subjects, including American and world history, government, economics, the natural and applied sciences, arts, literature and the humanities, health and guidance, and even pop culture.

The HISTORY website, located at **www.history.com**, is the definitive historical online source that delivers entertaining and informative content featuring broadband video, interactive timelines, maps, games, podcasts and more.

"We strive to engage, inspire and encourage the love of learning..."

Since its founding in 1995, HISTORY has demonstrated a commitment to providing the highest quality resources for educators. We develop multimedia resources for K–12 schools, two- and four-year colleges, government agencies, and other organizations by drawing on the award-winning documentary programming of A&E Television Networks. We strive to engage, inspire and encourage the love of learning by connecting with students in an informative and compelling manner. To help achieve this goal, we have formed a partnership with Houghton Mifflin Harcourt.

The Idea Book for Educators

Classroom resources that bring the past to life

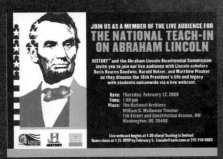
Live webcasts

HISTORY Take a Veteran to School Day

In addition to premium video-based resources, **HISTORY** has extensive offerings for teachers, parents, and students to use in the classroom and in their in-home educational activities, including:

▶ *The Idea Book for Educators* is a biannual teacher's magazine, featuring guides and info on the latest happenings in history education to help keep teachers on the cutting edge.

▶ **HISTORY Classroom (www.history.com/classroom)** is an interactive website that serves as a portal for history educators nationwide. Streaming videos on topics ranging from the Roman aqueducts to the civil rights movement connect with classroom curricula.

▶ **HISTORY email newsletters** feature updates and supplements to our award-winning programming relevant to the classroom with links to teaching guides and video clips on a variety of topics, special offers, and more.

▶ **Live webcasts** are featured each year as schools tune in via streaming video.

▶ **HISTORY Take a Veteran to School Day** connects veterans with young people in our schools and communities nationwide.

In addition to **Houghton Mifflin Harcourt**, our partners include the *Library of Congress,* the *Smithsonian Institution, National History Day, The Gilder Lehrman Institute of American History,* the Organization of American Historians, and many more. HISTORY video is also featured in museums throughout America and in over 70 other historic sites worldwide.

HMH Social Studies
Dashboard

Designed for today's digital natives, **HMH® Social Studies** offers you an informative and exciting online experience.

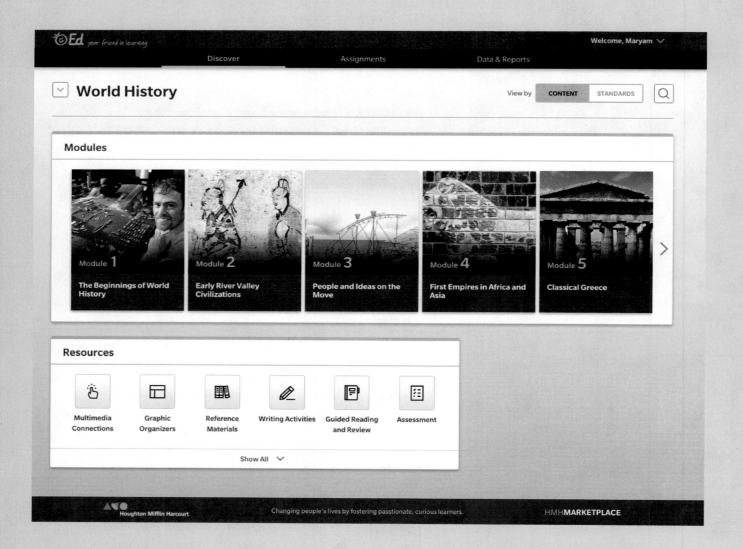

Your personalized Dashboard is organized into three main sections:

1. **Discover**—Quickly access content and search program resources

2. **Assignments**—Review your assignments and check your progress on them

3. **Data & Reports**—Monitor your progress on the course

Explore Online ▷
to **Experience** the **Power** of
World History

Houghton Mifflin Harcourt™ is changing
the way you **experience** social studies.

By delivering an immersive experience through compelling narratives
enriched with media, we're connecting you to history through experiences that are
energizing, inspiring, and memorable. The following pages highlight
some digital tools and instructional support that will help you
approach history through active inquiry, so you can connect to the past
while becoming active and informed citizens for the future.

The Student eBook is the primary learning portal.

More than just the digital version of a textbook, the Student eBook serves as the primary learning portal for you. The narrative is supported by a wealth of multimedia and learning resources to bring history to life and give you the tools you need to succeed.

Bringing Content to Life

HISTORY® videos and Multimedia Connections bring content to life through primary source footage, dramatic storytelling, and expert testimonials.

In-Depth Understanding

Close Read Screencasts model an analytical conversation about primary sources.

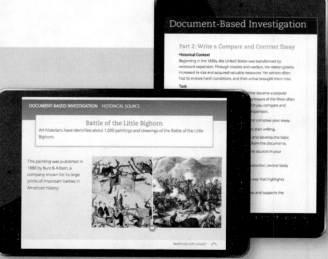

Content in a Fun Way

Interactive Features, Maps, and **Games** provide quick, entertaining activities and assessments that present important content in a fun way.

Investigate Like a Historian

Document-Based Investigations in every lesson build to end-of-module DBI performance tasks so you can examine and assess primary sources as historians do.

Full-Text Audio Support

You can listen while you read.

Skills Support

Point-of-use support is just a click away, providing instruction on critical reading and social studies skills.

Personalized Annotations

Notes encourages you to take notes while you read and allows you to customize them to your study preferences. You can easily access them to review later as you prepare for exams.

Interactive Lesson Graphic Organizers

Graphic organizers help you process, summarize, and keep track of your learning for end-of-module performance tasks.

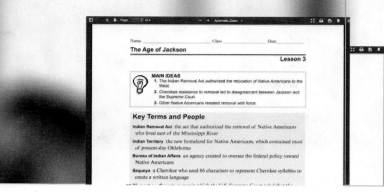

The **Guided Reading Workbook** and **Spanish/English Guided Reading Workbook** offer you lesson summaries with vocabulary, reading, and note-taking support.

Map Connections connects you with history and geography through interactive maps, games, and data.

Current Events features trustworthy articles on today's news that connect what you learn in class to the world around you.

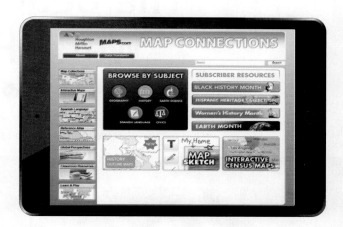

No Wi-Fi®? No problem!

With the **HMH Player®** app, you can connect to content and resources by downloading when online and accessing when offline.

HMH**PLAYER®** also allows you to:

Work Offline

Download lesson content and resources to work offline.

Communicate

"Raise a Hand" to ask or answer questions without having to be in the same room as your teacher.

Collaborate

Collaborate with your teacher via chat and in-lesson teamwork.

Module 1

The Beginnings of World History

Essential Question
How has the way that we think about and study world history changed over time?

About the Photo: A researcher examines hominid fossils from Rising Star Cave in South Africa.

In this module you will learn about how new archaeological finds and technology continue to change our understanding of early human life.

▶ Explore ONLINE!

HISTORY

VIDEOS, including...
- Little Ice Age: Big Chill
- The Vikings
- Axes, Swords, and Knives
- Stone Age Tools
- Man's Best Friend

✓ Document Based Investigations

✓ Graphic Organizers

✓ Interactive Games

✓ Image Carousel: Survival Tools in the Neolithic Age

✓ Image with Hotspots: Çatal Hüyük

What You Will Learn ...

The Big Idea The study and our understanding of world history are affected by place and time and are constantly changing.

The Big Idea Fossil evidence shows that the earliest humans originated in Africa and spread across the globe.

The Big Idea The development of agriculture caused an increase in population and the growth of a settled way of life.

The Big Idea Early cultures did not form advanced civilizations, but they left behind artifacts that have contributed greatly to our understanding of the past.

Timeline of Events, Prehistory–2500 BC

▶ Explore ONLINE!

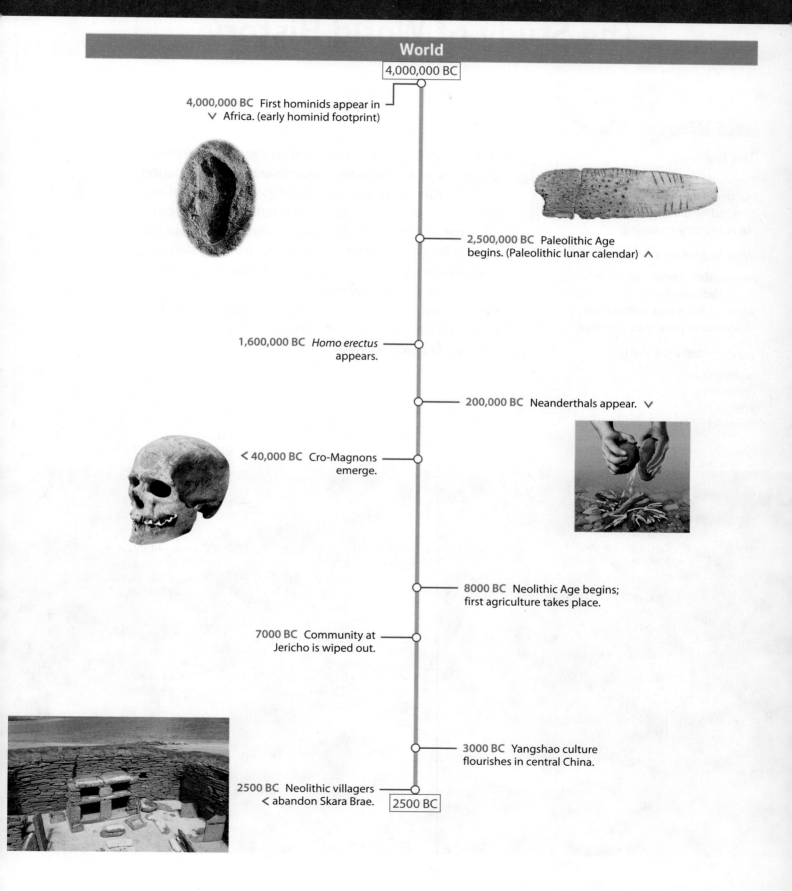

World

4,000,000 BC

4,000,000 BC First hominids appear in
∨ Africa. (early hominid footprint)

2,500,000 BC Paleolithic Age
begins. (Paleolithic lunar calendar) ∧

1,600,000 BC *Homo erectus*
appears.

200,000 BC Neanderthals appear. ∨

< **40,000 BC** Cro-Magnons
emerge.

8000 BC Neolithic Age begins;
first agriculture takes place.

7000 BC Community at
Jericho is wiped out.

3000 BC Yangshao culture
flourishes in central China.

2500 BC Neolithic villagers
< abandon Skara Brae.

2500 BC

The Study of World History

The Big Idea

The study of world history and our understanding of it are affected by place and time and are constantly changing.

Why It Matters Now

As new discoveries and technological advancements are made, what we learn and understand about world history can change.

Key Terms and People

historiography
civilization
artifact
hominid

Setting the Stage

Historiography is the study and writing of history with an emphasis on the careful examination of information or data, often from the analysis of evidence. Historians, archaeologists, and other social scientists piece together information in this way to write explanations about how people lived in the past. The writers may have different perspectives. Where they live, new interpretations of old discoveries, or new evidence can all affect their perspective. As new discoveries are made, historical interpretations and theories often change. History is constantly being revised.

An archaeologist carefully wipes away layers of dirt from artifacts at an ancient tomb site of the Ichsma culture in Lima, Peru.

Geography

Geography can affect historiography, as well as the course of events that happen throughout world history. Geography includes physical, human, and cultural characteristics. When studying history, social scientists consider these aspects of geography but also factors such as who made a discovery and the place and time where the discovery occurred. These factors are important in the study of world history and our understanding of the past because they can influence people's interpretations and theories. Not everyone understands or interprets a historical event in the same way.

The Impact of Geography Scholars have tried to address the role and impact of geography in world history. In his Pulitzer Prize–winning book *Guns, Germs, and Steel*, Jared Diamond examines the role of geography in the success and failure of **civilizations**, or complex cultures that developed at least five key characteristics. These characteristics include advanced cities, specialized workers, complex institutions, record keeping, and advanced technology. In addition, Diamond points to several factors that made Eurasian civilizations successful in conquering other civilizations. He suggests that Eurasia's location and climate provided good conditions for agriculture, resistance to certain germs that wiped out or decimated other civilizations, and the ability to develop stronger and better technology and social institutions. Other civilizations that developed outside of this geographic area were unable to surmount these challenges that many Eurasian civilizations were able to overcome.

But what other geographic factors affect the development and success of civilizations? A civilization that is landlocked and does not have access to bodies of water is posed with certain challenges for survival. On the other hand, civilizations that are surrounded entirely by water face other challenges. Yet, sometimes those challenges have been used to their advantage.

An Island Nation in the East Island nations are, for the most part, isolated, and throughout history they have developed differently. Japan, for example, was largely isolated from the West. Before the mid-1800s when Commodore Matthew Perry arrived with a fleet to "open" Japanese trade with the United States, Japan had very limited trade with the West. The Japanese had traded with the Chinese and the Dutch, but it was limited and controlled. After the Japanese began to trade with the United States and other Western countries, they wanted to modernize and Westernize their own country. By the early 1900s, the Japanese had engaged in war with the Russians and defeated them. The former isolated island nation had now entered the world stage and was considered a world power.

An Island Nation in the West The island nation of Great Britain developed differently than Japan. It also became a world power, but at a much earlier time. We can examine its interaction with Rome, for example, to better understand how geography has impacted its history. In ancient

Britain's White Cliffs of Dover were another obstacle the Romans faced in conquering the island.

times when Rome became a republic and later expanded into an empire, many lands came under its rule, including Britain. Yet, because Britain is an island, it took the Romans much longer to conquer it compared to other places that became part of its empire. Another example of how geography impacts the history and development of a place is to look at Britain's role in the Age of Exploration in the 1500s and 1600s. It joined other European nations in the quest to start colonies in the Americas, Asia, and Africa between the 1600s and 1800s. By the late 19th century, it had built a vast empire around the world. As an island nation, Britain developed into a formidable sea power. This was due in large part to its geography and its need to protect its empire, which spanned the globe.

Beyond Location In studying history, one should examine not only place and time in assessing the role of geography. Climate must also be considered. Climate can affect food availability and variety, as well as other natural resources. Along with physical features such as mountains and bodies of water, climate can enable or discourage migration. It can be a factor in wiping out a civilization if successive crop yields are poor. It can also cause involuntary migration, in which people are forced to move because a place that was once suitable for humans is no longer livable.

Scientists know from their research that a phenomenon known as the Little Ice Age started between 1100 and 1250. It had devastating effects across Europe, causing crop failures, famines, forced migration, and the failure of settlements. Even though by this time peoples and civilizations had been successfully using agriculture to meet their food needs for centuries, they could not control the weather. Cold weather over long periods of time wiped out crops. To avoid starvation, some people had to abandon growing crops and go back to relying on hunting and gathering.

One example of the effects of the Little Ice Age can be seen in the study of Greenland. In 2011, researchers presented their conclusions after examining ice cores from lakes in western Greenland. They determined that Norse Vikings may have left their settlements over time because of the plunge in temperatures, but they could have abandoned them for other reasons. The cooler weather was gradual, but it made the growing season shorter and possibly caused lower crop yields. The cooler temperatures may have also created more sea ice, which could have hampered trade.

Reading Check
Evaluate How has geography affected history? Cite two examples from the text.

Role of Archaeology

Archaeology plays a key role in historiography because it deals with the study of **artifacts**, or human-made objects, and other evidence from the past. Archaeologists use this evidence to discover clues about how people lived, developed, and interacted with their environment.

Archaeology and Perception Archaeological discoveries have revealed evidence from prehistory to the modern era, in all parts of the world. They have provided DNA evidence of the Neanderthal genome, uncovered the terra cotta soldiers of China's first emperor Shi Huangdi, and revealed clues to how the bubonic plague spread through Asia and Europe, to name just a few important discoveries.

Often archaeologists work with people from other disciplines to help piece together the past. They work with genetic scientists to describe human history. They work with environmental scientists to understand resource allocation and land degradation. People from different fields of science often work together. They show that the interpretation of history is affected not only by the perspective of various disciplines, but also by the contrasting perceptions of people living in different areas of the world. In other words, the same event or time period may be perceived in distinctive ways. For example, when discussing a war, the defeated and the victor may retell the course of events differently. In a similar way, one archaeological discovery may be interpreted differently from one discipline to another.

Archaeologists work at a site in Denisova Cave, Siberia, to uncover Paleolithic bone fragments of an early hominid.

Scientists in Madrid, Spain, use advanced technology to try to locate human remains from the past.

other scientists are able to decode or translate the language, which helps them to interpret past civilizations. For example, it took a very long time to fully decipher Mayan glyphs. Once scholars could read the language, they were able to learn and understand more about the Mayan culture and ways of life.

A Rising Star?

In November 2013, a team of scientists made up of female archaeologists, anthropologists, and paleontologists began exploring the Rising Star cave in South Africa. Over time, the team excavated some 1,550 hominid fossils.

Getting through the narrow passage to the cave's Dinaledi Chamber, where thousands of fossils still remain, is a physical challenge. The passage narrows to less than 10 inches high and the chamber sits more than 100 feet away from the cave's entrance.

Among the Rising Star fossils studied so far, a new species, called *Homo naledi,* was discovered. This has changed previously held theories about human evolution, making it more complex and puzzling than ever before.

Newer Finds Replace Old Theories One example of changing history, theories, and interpretations is based on the discovery made at Olduvai (OHL•duh•vy) Gorge in northern Tanzania, Africa. The discovery of a hominid fossil there in 1960 revealed information about the tools that early humans made and how they developed technology to survive. A **hominid** is a human or other creature that walks upright. Yet later discoveries of early human fossils or early human tools, such as points and stone blades at Chinchihuapi Creek (1977) in Monte Verde, Chile; Liang Bua Cave (2004) on Flores Island; Buttermilk Creek Complex (06) in central Texas; Denisova Cave (2008) in Siberia; and Rising Star Cave (2013) in South Africa revealed more about early humans and how they lived. These discoveries changed earlier interpretations and theories that scientists and other researchers had developed about human species after studying evidence at Olduvai Gorge.

Reading Check
Draw Conclusions
Why must history be flexible?

Lesson 1 Assessment

1. **Organize Information** Create a timeline of the Little Ice Age.

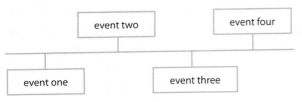

Make a mental map of the areas affected by the Little Ice Age. Write a paragraph explaining how the Little Ice Age caused people to migrate and adapt their ways of life.

2. **Key Terms and People** For each key term or the lesson, write a sentence explaining its sign

3. **Draw Conclusions** Why does history change?

4. **Analyze Effects** How has geography affected the course of history?

5. **Analyze Effects** Was the migration caused by the Little Ice Age voluntary or involuntary, and what we the consequences of the migration? Explain.

6. **Form and Support Opinions** Do you think the fact that Britain and Japan are islands enabled or deterred migration to and from those places? Explain.

7. **Analyze Effects** How might the discovery of fossils at Rising Star cave affect history?

Human Origins in Africa

The Big Idea
Fossil evidence shows that the earliest humans originated in Africa and spread across the globe.

Why It Matters Now
The study of early human remains and artifacts helps in understanding our place in human history.

Key Terms and People
culture
Paleolithic Age
Neolithic Age
technology
Homo sapiens

Setting the Stage

What were the earliest humans like? Many people have asked this question. Because there are no written records of prehistoric peoples, scientists have to piece together information about the past. Teams of scientists use a variety of research methods to learn more about how, where, and when early humans developed. Interestingly, recent discoveries provide the most knowledge about human origins and the way prehistoric people lived. Yet, the picture of prehistory is still far from complete.

Scientists Search for Human Origins

Written documents provide a window to the distant past. For several thousand years, people have recorded information about their beliefs, activities, and important events. Prehistory, however, dates back to the time before the invention of writing—roughly 5,000 years ago. Without access to written records, scientists investigating the lives of prehistoric peoples face special challenges.

Scientific Clues Archaeologists are specially trained scientists who work like detectives to uncover the story of prehistoric peoples. They learn about early people by excavating and studying the traces of early settlements. An excavated site, called an archaeological dig, provides one of the richest sources of clues to the prehistoric way of life. Archaeologists sift through the dirt in a small plot of land. They analyze all existing evidence, such as bones and artifacts. Bones might reveal what the people looked like, how tall they were, the types of food they ate, diseases they may have had, and how long they lived. Artifacts such as tools and jewelry might hint at how people dressed, what work they did, or how they worshiped.

Understanding Culture

In prehistoric times, bands of humans that lived near one another began to develop shared ways of doing things: common ways of dressing, similar hunting practices, favorite animals to eat. These shared traits were the first beginnings of what anthropologists and historians call *culture*.

Culture is the way of life of a group of people. Culture includes common practices of a society, its shared understandings, and its social organization. By overcoming individual differences, culture helps to unify the group.

COMPONENTS OF CULTURE

Common Practices	Shared Understandings	Social Organization
• what people eat • clothing and adornment • sports • tools and technology • social customs • work	• language • symbols • religious beliefs • values • the arts • political beliefs	• family • class and caste structure • relationships between individual and community • government • economic system • view of authority

HOW CULTURE IS LEARNED

People are not born knowing about culture. Instead, they must learn culture. Generally, individuals learn culture in two ways. First, they observe and imitate the behavior of people in their society. Second, people in their society directly teach the culture to them, usually through spoken or written language.

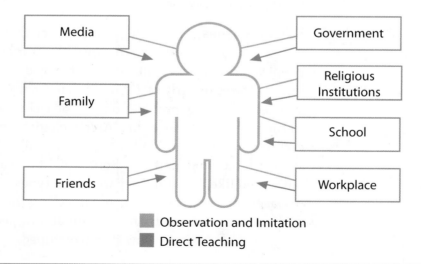

Media

Government

Family

Religious Institutions

Friends

School

Workplace

■ Observation and Imitation
■ Direct Teaching

Critical Thinking

1. **Form and Support Opinions** In U.S. culture, which shared understanding do you think is the most powerful? Why?

2. **Make Inferences** Which do you think has a greater impact on culture, observation and imitation or direct teaching? Explain your answer.

Scientists called anthropologists study **culture**, or a people's unique way of life. Anthropologists examine the artifacts at archaeological digs. From these, they re-create a picture of early people's cultural behavior. (See Analyze Key Concepts on culture on the following page.)

Other scientists, called paleontologists, study fossils—evidence of early life preserved in rocks. Human fossils often consist of small fragments of teeth, skulls, or other bones. Paleontologists use complex techniques to date ancient fossil remains and rocks. Archaeologists, anthropologists, paleontologists, and other scientists work as a team to make new discoveries about how prehistoric people lived.

Early Footprints Found In the 1970s, archaeologist Mary Leakey led a scientific expedition to the region of Laetoli in Tanzania in East Africa. (See map on page 17.) There, she and her team looked for clues about human origins. In 1978, they found prehistoric footprints that resembled those of modern humans preserved in volcanic ash. These footprints were made by humanlike beings now called australopithecines (aw•stray•loh•PIHTH•ih•synz) which lived from about 4.1 to 1.8 million years ago. The Laetoli footprints provided striking evidence about human origins.

The Discovery of "Lucy" While Mary Leakey was working in East Africa, U.S. anthropologist Donald Johanson and his team were also searching for fossils. They were exploring sites in Ethiopia, about 1,000 miles to the north. In 1974, Johanson's team made a remarkable find—an unusually complete skeleton of an adult female hominid. They nicknamed her "Lucy" after the Beatles song "Lucy in the Sky with Diamonds." She had lived around 3.5 million years ago—the oldest hominid found to that date.

DOCUMENT-BASED INVESTIGATION   Historical Source

Finding Lucy

Donald Johanson and his team had been conducting a search in Hadar, Ethiopia, when they discovered a forearm and other bones that seemed to be related.

Analyze Historical Sources
1. **Compare** How was the discovery of "Lucy" similar to Mary Leakey's discovery in Tanzania?

2. **Draw Conclusions** Do you think that Johanson and his team knew they had made a significant find when they found "Lucy"? Explain.

> *"We reluctantly headed back toward camp. Along the way, I glanced over my right shoulder. Light glinted off a bone. I knelt down for a closer look . . . Everywhere we looked on the slope around us we saw more bones lying on the surface. . . The find launched a celebration in camp."*
>
> —Donald Johanson
> from *Ancestors: In Search of Human Origins*

Louis S. B. Leakey (1903–1972) and Mary Leakey (1913–1996)

The Leakey family has had a tremendous impact on the study of human origins. British anthropologists Louis S. B. Leakey and Mary Leakey began searching for early human remains in East Africa in the 1930s. Their efforts turned what was a sideline of science into a major field of scientific inquiry. Mary became one of the world's renowned hunters of human fossils. Their son Richard; Richard's wife, Maeve; and Richard and Maeve's daughter Louise have continued the family's fossil-hunting in East Africa into the 21st century.

Hominids Walk Upright Lucy and the hominids who left their footprints in East Africa were species of australopithecines. Walking upright helped them travel distances more easily. They were also able to spot threatening animals and carry food and children.

These early hominids had already developed the opposable thumb. This means that the tip of the thumb can cross the palm of the hand. The opposable thumb was crucial for tasks such as picking up small objects and making tools. (To see its importance, try picking up a coin with just the index and middle fingers. Imagine all of the other things that cannot be done without the opposable thumb.)

Reading Check
Draw Conclusions
Why were the discoveries of hominid footprints and "Lucy" important?

The Old Stone Age Begins

The invention of tools, mastery over fire, and the development of language are some of the most impressive achievements in human history. Scientists believe these occurred during the prehistoric period known as the Stone Age. It spanned a vast length of time. The earlier and longer part of the Stone Age, called the Old Stone Age or **Paleolithic Age**, lasted from about 2.5 million to 8000 BC. The oldest stone chopping tools date back to this era. The New Stone Age, or **Neolithic Age**, began about 8000 BC and ended as early as 3000 BC in some areas. People who lived during this second phase of the Stone Age learned to polish stone tools, make pottery, grow crops, and raise animals.

Much of the Paleolithic Age occurred during the period in the earth's history known as the Ice Age. During this time, glaciers alternately advanced and retreated as many as 18 times. The last of these ice ages ended about 10,000 years ago. By the beginning of the Neolithic Age, glaciers had retreated to roughly the same area they now occupy.

Timeline: Hominid Development

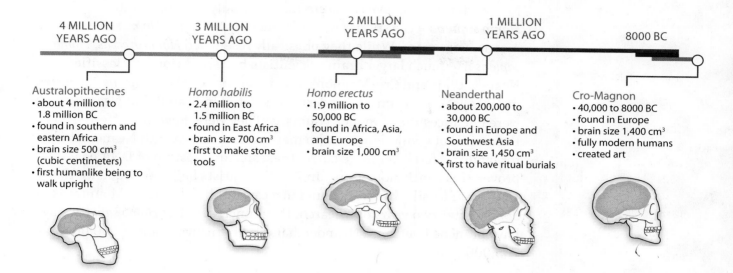

| 4 MILLION YEARS AGO | 3 MILLION YEARS AGO | 2 MILLION YEARS AGO | 1 MILLION YEARS AGO | 8000 BC |

Australopithecines
- about 4 million to 1.8 million BC
- found in southern and eastern Africa
- brain size 500 cm³ (cubic centimeters)
- first humanlike being to walk upright

Homo habilis
- 2.4 million to 1.5 million BC
- found in East Africa
- brain size 700 cm³
- first to make stone tools

Homo erectus
- 1.9 million to 50,000 BC
- found in Africa, Asia, and Europe
- brain size 1,000 cm³

Neanderthal
- about 200,000 to 30,000 BC
- found in Europe and Southwest Asia
- brain size 1,450 cm³
- first to have ritual burials

Cro-Magnon
- 40,000 to 8000 BC
- found in Europe
- brain size 1,400 cm³
- fully modern humans
- created art

***Homo habilis* May Have Used Tools** Before the australopithecines eventually vanished, new hominids appeared in East Africa around 2.4 million years ago to 1.5 million years ago. In 1960, archaeologists Louis and Mary Leakey discovered a hominid fossil at Olduvai (OHL•duh•vy) Gorge in northern Tanzania. The Leakeys named the fossil *Homo habilis,* which means "man of skill." The Leakeys and other researchers found tools made of lava rock. They believed *Homo habilis* used these tools to cut meat and crack open bones. Tools made the task of survival easier.

***Homo erectus* Develops Technology** About 1.9 million years ago to 50,000 years ago, before *Homo habilis* left the scene, another species of hominids appeared in East Africa. This species is now known as *Homo erectus,* or "upright man." Some anthropologists believe *Homo erectus* was a more intelligent and adaptable species than *Homo habilis. Homo erectus* people used intelligence to develop **technology**—ways of applying knowledge, tools, and inventions to meet their needs. These hominids gradually became skillful hunters and invented more sophisticated tools for digging, scraping, and cutting. They also eventually became the first hominids to migrate, or move, from Africa. Fossils and stone tools show that bands of *Homo erectus* hunters settled in India, China, Southeast Asia, and Europe.

According to anthropologists, *Homo erectus* was the first to use fire. Fire provided warmth in cold climates, cooked food, and frightened away attacking animals. The control of fire also probably helped *Homo erectus* settle new lands.

Homo erectus may have developed the beginnings of spoken language. Language, like technology, probably gave *Homo erectus* greater control over the environment and boosted chances for survival. The teamwork needed to plan hunts and cooperate in other tasks probably relied on language. *Homo erectus* might have named objects, places, animals, and plants and exchanged ideas.

Reading check
Recognize Effects
How did *Homo erectus* use fire to adapt to the environment?

The Dawn of Modern Humans

Many scientists believe *Homo erectus* eventually developed into *Homo sapiens*—the species name for modern humans. *Homo sapiens* means "wise men." While they physically resembled *Homo erectus*, *Homo sapiens* had much larger brains. Scientists have traditionally classified Neanderthals and Cro-Magnons as early groups of *Homo sapiens*. However, in 1997, DNA tests on a Neanderthal skeleton indicated that Neanderthals were not ancestors of modern humans. They were, however, affected by the arrival of Cro-Magnons, who may have competed with Neanderthals for land and food. Yet more current research and testing of DNA has proved this conclusion wrong. In 2013, scientists began to sequence the DNA from fossils that were found in a cave in the Atapuerca Mountains in Spain. After two years of research, they concluded that *Homo sapiens* may have branched out from Neanderthals and Denisovans about 550,000 to 765,000 years ago.

Neanderthals' Way of Life In 1856, as quarry workers were digging for limestone in the Neander Valley in Germany, they spotted fossilized bone fragments. These were the remains of Neanderthals, whose bones were discovered elsewhere in Europe and Southwest Asia. These people were powerfully built. They had heavy slanted brows, well-developed muscles,

History in Depth

Timeline of Planet Earth

Imagine the 102 stories of the Empire State Building as a scale for a timeline of the earth's history. Each story represents about 40 million years. Modern human beings have existed for just a tiny percentage of the life of this planet. Yet, since those prehistoric days of making stone tools and learning to control fire, the technology of modern humans has advanced considerably.

Cro-Magnons and Neanderthals made fire by striking flint against a stone, usually one that contained iron.

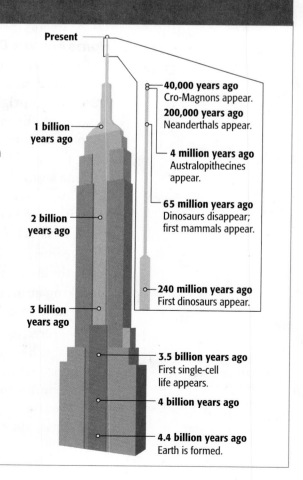

Present

1 billion years ago

2 billion years ago

3 billion years ago

40,000 years ago
Cro-Magnons appear.

200,000 years ago
Neanderthals appear.

4 million years ago
Australopithecines appear.

65 million years ago
Dinosaurs disappear; first mammals appear.

240 million years ago
First dinosaurs appear.

3.5 billion years ago
First single-cell life appears.

4 billion years ago

4.4 billion years ago
Earth is formed.

Early Human Migration, 1,600,000–10,000 BC

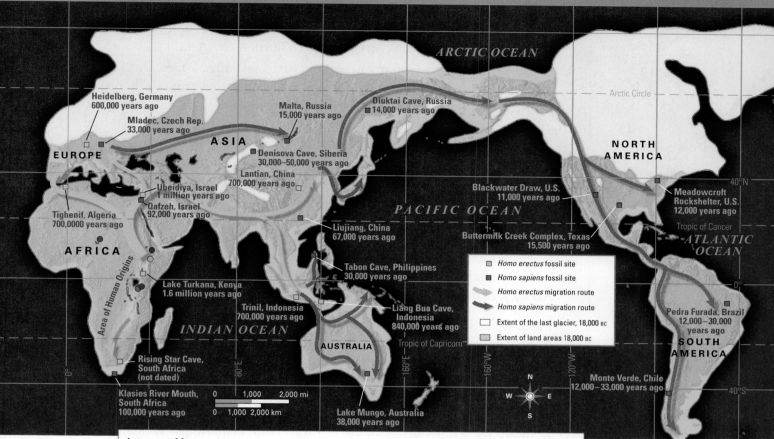

Interpret Maps

1. **Movement** To what continents did *Homo erectus* groups migrate after leaving Africa?

2. **Human-Environment Interaction** What do the migration routes of *Homo sapiens* reveal about their survival skills and ability to adapt?

and thick bones. To many people, the name "Neanderthal" calls up the comic-strip image of a club-carrying caveman. However, archaeological discoveries reveal a more realistic picture of these early hominids, who lived roughly between 200,000 and 30,000 years ago.

Evidence suggests that Neanderthals tried to explain and control their world. They developed religious beliefs and performed rituals. About 60,000 years ago, Neanderthals held a funeral for a man in Shanidar Cave, located in northeastern Iraq. Some archaeologists theorize that during the funeral, the Neanderthal's family covered his body with flowers. This funeral points to a belief in a world beyond the grave.

Neanderthals were also resourceful. They survived harsh Ice Age winters by living in caves or temporary shelters made of wood and animal skins. Animal bones found with Neanderthal fossils indicate the ability of Neanderthals to hunt in subarctic regions of Europe. To cut up and skin their prey, they fashioned stone blades, scrapers, and other tools. The Neanderthals survived for some 170,000 years and then mysteriously vanished about 30,000 years ago.

Cro-Magnons Emerge About 40,000 years ago, a group of prehistoric humans called Cro-Magnons appeared. Their skeletal remains show that they are identical to modern humans. The remains also indicate that they were probably strong and generally about five-and-one-half feet tall. Cro-Magnons migrated from North Africa to Europe and Asia.

Cro-Magnons made many new tools with specialized uses. Unlike Neanderthals, they planned their hunts. They studied animals' habits and stalked their prey. Evidently, Cro-Magnons' superior hunting strategies allowed them to survive more easily. This may have caused Cro-Magnon populations to grow at a slightly faster rate and eventually replace the Neanderthals. Cro-Magnons' advanced skill in spoken language may also have helped them to plan more difficult projects. This cooperation perhaps gave them an edge over the Neanderthals.

New Findings Add to Knowledge

Scientists are continuing to work at numerous sites in Africa. Their discoveries change our views of the still sketchy picture of human origins in Africa and of the migration of early humans out of Africa.

Fossils, Tools, and Cave Paintings Newly discovered fossils in Chad and Kenya, dating between 6 and 7 million years old, have some apelike features but also some that resemble hominids. Study of these fossils continues, but evidence suggests that they may be the earliest hominids. A 2.33-million-year-old jaw from Ethiopia is the oldest fossil belonging to the line leading to humans. Stone tools found at the same site suggest that toolmaking may have begun earlier than previously thought.

New discoveries also add to what we already know about prehistoric peoples. For example, in 1996, a team of researchers from Canada and the United States, including a high school student from New York, discovered a Neanderthal bone flute 43,000 to 82,000 years old. This discovery hints at a previously unknown talent of the Neanderthals—the gift of musical expression. The finding on cave walls of drawings of animals and people dating back as early as 35,000 years ago gives information on the daily activities and perhaps even religious practices of these peoples.

Early humans' skills and tools for surviving and adapting to the environment became more sophisticated as time passed. As you will read in the next lesson, these technological advances would help launch a revolution in the way people lived.

Discovery at Denisova Cave In 2008, a discovery of hominin artifacts was made in the Altai Mountains. They were found in Denisova Cave in Russia. At first, researchers believed the artifacts to be part of a new group of hominins, called the Denisovans. To find out if the artifacts were the remains of early modern humans or Neanderthals, a group of scientists used recent technology to sequence the DNA genome from a finger bone

Reading check
Compare
How were Neanderthals similar to people today?

Chad Discovery

In 2002, an international team of scientists announced the discovery of a 6- to 7-million-year-old skull in northern Chad. The skull is similar in size to a modern chimpanzee, with a similar brain capacity. (See photograph.)

The team reported that the skull, nicknamed *Toumai*, or "hope of life," was the earliest human ancestor so far discovered. Its date is, in fact, millions of years older than the previous oldest-known hominid. The skull dates from the time that scientists believe the ancestors of humans split from the great apes. Whether the skull is actually human or ape will require further study.

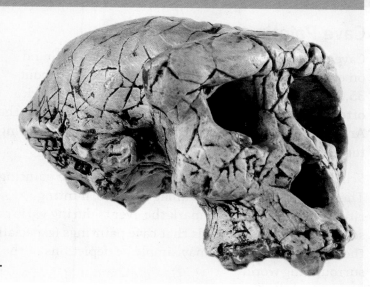

Reading Check
Analyze Effects
How has the ability to make new discoveries about how prehistoric peoples lived changed over time?

of one of the specimens found in Denisova Cave. They concluded that the Denisovans came from a common ancestor that dates back before the Neanderthal. They believe that these hominins lived in Denisova Cave some time between 50,000 and 170,000 years ago.

Later, in 2013, a group of evolutionary anthropologists drew new conclusions based on a new genome from the same cave. They said that based on this genome, they believe that the Denisovans and Neanderthals interacted.

Lesson 2 Assessment

1. **Organize Information** Complete the diagram with details about hominids and Cro-Magnons. Which advance by a hominid group do you think was the most significant? Explain.

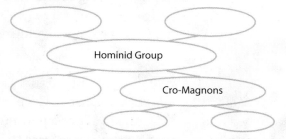

Hominid Group

Cro-Magnons

2. **Key Terms and People** For each term in the lesson, write a sentence explaining its significance.

3. **Draw Conclusions** What clues do bones and artifacts give about early peoples?

4. **Summarize** What were the major achievements in human history during the Old Stone Age?

5. **Recognize Effects** Why was the discovery of fire so important?

6. **Make Inferences** Why will specific details about the physical appearance and the customs of early peoples never be fully known?

7. **Synthesize** How do recent findings keep revising knowledge of the prehistoric past?

Cave Paintings

Cave paintings created by primitive people are found on every continent. The oldest ones were made about 35,000 years ago. Cave paintings in Europe and Africa often show images of hunting and daily activities. In the Americas and Australia, on the other hand, the paintings tend to be more symbolic and less realistic.

Scholars are not sure about the purpose of cave paintings. They may have been part of magical rites, hunting rituals, or an attempt to mark the events during various seasons. Another theory is that cave paintings (especially the more realistic ones) may simply be depictions of the surrounding world.

▼ CAVE PAINTINGS AT TASSILI N'AJER, ALGERIA

These paintings depict women, children, and cattle. Located in Algeria, the Tassili n'Ajer (tah•SEEL•ee-nah•ZHEER) site contains more than 15,000 images. They depict shifts in climate, animal migrations, and changes in human life. The oldest paintings date back to about 6000 BC. Images continued to be painted until around the second century AD.

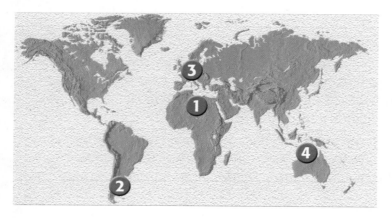

▼ CAVE PAINTINGS AT *CUEVAS DE LAS MANOS* IN ARGENTINA

Cuevas de las Manos (Cave of the Hands) is located in the Rio Pinturas ravine, northeast of Santa Cruz, Argentina. Its rock walls display numerous hand paintings in vivid colors. The Tehuelches (tuh•WEHL•cheez) people created the paintings between 13,000 and 9,500 years ago. The cave is about 78 feet deep and, at the entrance, about 48 feet wide and 32 feet high.

▲ REPLICA OF LASCAUX CAVE PAINTING, FRANCE

Discovered in 1940, the Lascaux (lah•SKOH) cave contains more than 600 painted animals and symbols. These works were probably created between 15,000 and 13,000 BC. In 1963, the cave was closed to the public. The high volume of visitors and the use of artificial lighting were damaging the paintings. A partial replica of the cave was created and is visited by about 250,000 people a year.

▲ AUSTRALIAN ABORIGINAL CAVE PAINTING

This Aboriginal cave painting is in Kakadu (KAH•kuh•doo) National Park, Australia. Aboriginal people have lived in this area for at least 25,000 years. The painting depicts a Barramundi (bahr•uh•MUHN•dee) fish and a Dreamtime spirit. In the Aboriginal culture, Dreamtime is a supernatural past in which ancestral beings shaped and humanized the natural world.

Critical Thinking

1. **Analyze Motives** Why do you think primitive peoples used the walls of caves for their paintings?

2. **Compare and Contrast** How are these paintings similar to or different from public murals created today?

Humans Try to Control Nature

The Big Idea
The development of agriculture caused an increase in population and the growth of a settled way of life.

Why It Matters Now
New methods for obtaining food and the development of technology laid the foundations for modern civilizations.

Key Terms and People
nomad
hunter-gatherer
Neolithic Revolution
slash-and-burn farming
domestication

Setting the Stage

About 40,000 years ago, Cro-Magnons began to emerge and become fully modern in their physical appearance. With a shave, a haircut, and a suit, a Cro-Magnon man would have looked like a modern business executive. However, over the following thousands of years, the way of life of early humans underwent incredible changes. People developed new technology, artistic skills, and most importantly, agriculture.

Early Advances in Technology and Art

Early modern humans quickly distinguished themselves from their ancestors, who had spent most of their time just surviving. As inventors and artists, more advanced humans stepped up the pace of cultural changes.

Tools Needed to Survive For tens of thousands of years, men and women of the Old Stone Age were nomads. **Nomads** were highly mobile people who moved from place to place foraging, or searching, for new sources of food. Nomadic groups whose food supply depends on hunting animals and collecting plant foods are called **hunter-gatherers**. Prehistoric hunter-gatherers, such as roving bands of Cro-Magnons, increased their food supply by inventing tools. For example, hunters crafted special spears that enabled them to kill game at greater distances. Digging sticks helped food gatherers pry plants loose at the roots.

Early modern humans had launched a technological revolution. They used stone, bone, and wood to fashion more than 100 different tools. These expanded tool kits included knives to kill and butcher game, and fish hooks and harpoons to catch fish. A chisel-like cutter was designed to make other tools. Cro-Magnons used bone needles to sew clothing made of animal hides.

This birch-bark container was preserved in ice near the remains of a Neolithic hunter nicknamed the "Ice Man."

Artistic Expression in the Paleolithic Age The tools of early modern humans explain how they met their survival needs. Yet their world best springs to life through their artistic creations. Necklaces of seashells, lion teeth, and bear claws adorned both men and women. People ground mammoth tusks into polished beads. They also carved small realistic sculptures of animals that inhabited their world.

As you read in the Cave Paintings feature, Stone Age peoples on all continents created cave paintings. The best known of these are the paintings on the walls and ceilings of European caves, mainly in France and Spain. There, early artists drew lifelike images of wild animals. Cave artists made colored paints from charcoal, mud, and animal blood. In Africa, early artists engraved pictures on rocks or painted scenes in caves or rock shelters. In Australia, they created paintings on large rocks.

Reading Check
Summarize
How did tools affect the food supply of Paleolithic hunters?

Vocabulary
edible safe to be eaten

The Beginnings of Agriculture

For thousands upon thousands of years, humans survived by hunting game and gathering edible plants. They lived in bands of 25 to 70 people. The men almost certainly did the hunting. The women gathered fruits, berries, roots, and grasses. They usually migrated to areas where they could find the resources that they needed to survive. Then about 10,000 years ago, some of the women may have scattered seeds near a regular campsite. When they returned the next season, they may have found new crops growing. This discovery would usher in the **Neolithic Revolution**, or the agricultural revolution—the far-reaching changes in human life resulting from the beginnings of farming. The shift from food-gathering to food-producing culture represents one of the great breakthroughs in history.

DOCUMENT-BASED INVESTIGATION **Historical Source**

Agriculture Causes Population Growth

Peter N. Stearns, Professor of History at George Mason University, explained the importance of agriculture to human population growth during the Neolithic Age.

Analyze Historical Sources
1. **Compare and Contrast** What were the costs and benefits of agriculture over hunting and gathering?
2. **Draw Conclusions** Do you think that this source is a credible secondary source? Explain your reasoning.

"The Neolithic Revolution was one of the great changes in human history. Agricultural existence had a number of drawbacks compared to hunting-gathering, including greater inequalities, more vulnerability to disease and harder work. But it had huge advantages in terms of food supply, allowing rapid population increase. Different dates describe the advent and spread of agriculture in different places. Agriculture generated some similar changes wherever it developed, including patriarchal gender systems and (usually) village clustering."

—Peter N. Stearns

Causes of the Agricultural Revolution Scientists do not know exactly why the agricultural revolution occurred during this period. Change in climate was probably a key reason. (See chart on page 26.) Rising temperatures worldwide provided longer growing seasons and drier land for cultivating wild grasses. A rich supply of grain helped support a small population boom. As populations slowly rose, hunter-gatherers felt pressure to find new food sources. Farming offered an attractive alternative. Unlike hunting, it provided a steady source of food.

Early Farming Methods Some groups practiced **slash-and-burn farming**, in which they cut trees or grasses and burned them to clear a field. The ashes that remained fertilized the soil. Farmers planted crops for a year or two, then moved to another area of land. After several years, trees and grass grew back, and other farmers repeated the process of slashing and burning.

History in Depth

The Neolithic Ice Man

In 1991, two German hikers made an accidental discovery that gave archaeologists a firsthand look at the technology of early toolmakers. Near the border of Austria and Italy, they spotted the mummified body of a prehistoric traveler, preserved in ice for some 5,000 years.

Nicknamed the "Ice Man," this early human was not empty-handed. The tool kit found near him included a six-foot longbow and a deerskin case with 14 arrows. It also contained a stick with an antler tip for sharpening flint blades, a small flint dagger in a woven sheath, a copper ax, and a medicine bag.

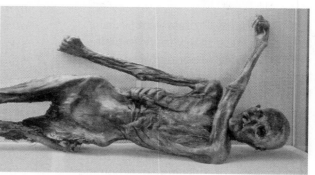

Scientific research on the body concluded that the Ice Man was in his 40s when he died in the late spring or early summer. It revealed that he was likely murdered after engaging in hand-to-hand combat two days before he bled to death. Scientists also determined that before his death, he ate wild goat, red deer, and grains. The Ice Man is housed in a museum in Bolzano, Italy.

Analyze Visuals

1. **Draw Conclusions** How do you think scientists determined the circumstances that led to the Ice Man's death?

2. **Make Inferences** Why does knowing what the Ice Man ate and the tools that he used help us better understand history?

Domestication of Animals Food gatherers' understanding of plants probably spurred the development of farming. Meanwhile, hunters' expert knowledge of wild animals likely played a key role in the **domestication**, or taming, of animals. They tamed horses, dogs, goats, and pigs. Like farming, domestication of animals came slowly. Stone Age hunters may have driven herds of animals into rocky ravines to be slaughtered. It was then a small step to drive herds into human-made enclosures. From there, farmers could keep the animals as a constant source of food and gradually tame them.

Not only farmers domesticated animals. Pastoral nomads, or wandering herders, tended sheep, goats, camels, or other animals. These herders moved their animals to new pastures and watering places.

Agriculture in Jarmo Today, the eroded and barren rolling foothills of the Zagros Mountains in northeastern Iraq seem an unlikely site for the birthplace of agriculture. According to archaeologist Robert Braidwood, thousands of years ago the environmental conditions of this region favored the development of agriculture, but not anymore. Wild wheat and barley, along with wild goats, pigs, sheep, and horses, had once thrived near the Zagros Mountains.

In the 1950s, Braidwood led an archaeological dig at a site called Jarmo. He concluded that an agricultural settlement was built there about 9,000 years ago. The Jarmo farmers, and others like them in places as far apart as Mexico and Thailand, pioneered a new way of life. Villages like Jarmo marked the beginning of a new era and laid the foundation for modern life.

Villages Grow and Prosper

The changeover from hunting and gathering to farming and herding took place not once but many times. Neolithic people in many parts of the world independently developed agriculture, as the map on the next page shows. Roles of men and women shifted with the advent of agriculture. Both men and women farmed the land, depending on the culture. Their former roles as hunters and gatherers were no longer the focus of everyday tasks.

Farming Develops in Many Places Within a few thousand years, people in many other regions, especially in fertile river valleys, turned to farming.

- **Africa** The Nile River Valley developed into an important agricultural center for growing wheat, barley, and other crops.
- **China** About 8,000 years ago, farmers along the middle stretches of the Huang He (Yellow River) cultivated a grain called millet. About 1,000 years later, farmers first domesticated wild rice in the Chang Jiang River delta.
- **Mexico and Central America** Farmers cultivated corn, beans, and squash.
- **Peru** Farmers in the Central Andes were the first to grow tomatoes, sweet potatoes, and white potatoes.

From these early and varied centers of agriculture, farming then spread to surrounding regions.

Reading Check
Compare
How did the Neolithic Revolution differ from the Paleolithic Revolution?

Agriculture Emerges, 5000–500 BC

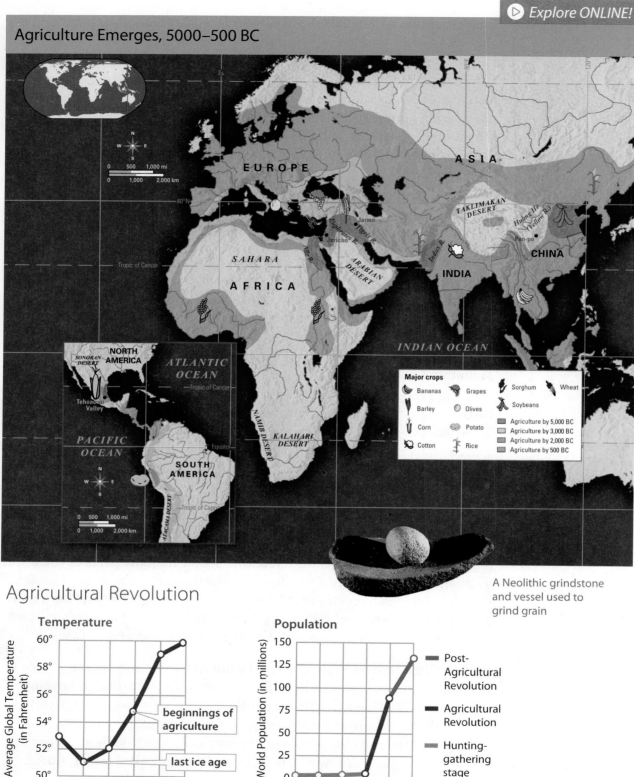

Major crops

- Bananas
- Barley
- Corn
- Cotton
- Grapes
- Olives
- Potato
- Rice
- Sorghum
- Soybeans
- Wheat

- Agriculture by 5,000 BC
- Agriculture by 3,000 BC
- Agriculture by 2,000 BC
- Agriculture by 500 BC

A Neolithic grindstone and vessel used to grind grain

Agricultural Revolution

Temperature

Average Global Temperature (in Fahrenheit)

beginnings of agriculture

last ice age

Years Ago (in thousands)

Source: *Ice Ages, Solving the Mystery*

Population

World Population (in millions)

- Post-Agricultural Revolution
- Agricultural Revolution
- Hunting-gathering stage

Years Ago (in thousands)

Source: *A Geography of Population: World Patterns*

Analyze Maps and Charts

1. **Place** What geographic feature favored the development of agricultural areas before 5000 BC?

2. **Cause and Effect** What effect did the agricultural revolution have on population growth? Why?

The town of Catal Huyuk formed a complex society with some characteristics of a civilization, such as religion.

Catal Huyuk In 1958, archaeologists discovered the agricultural village now known as Catal Huyuk (chuh•TUL hoo•YOOK), or the "forked mound." It was located on a fertile plain in south-central Turkey (about 30 miles from modern-day Konya), near a twin-coned volcano. Catal Huyuk covered an area of about 32 acres. At its peak 8,000 years ago, the village was home to 5,000 to 6,000 people who lived in about 1,000 dwellings. These rectangular-shaped houses were made of brick and were arranged side-by-side like a honeycomb.

Catal Huyuk showed the benefits of settled life. Its rich, well-watered soil produced large crops of wheat, barley, and peas. Villagers also raised sheep and cattle. Catal Huyuk's agricultural surpluses supported a number of highly skilled workers, such as potters and weavers. But the village was best known at the time for its obsidian products. This dark volcanic rock, which looks like glass, was plentiful. It was used to make mirrors, jewelry, and knives for trade.

Catal Huyuk's prosperity also supported a varied cultural life. Archaeologists have uncovered colorful wall paintings depicting animals and hunting scenes. Many religious shrines were dedicated to a mother goddess. According to her worshipers, she controlled the supply of grain.

Vocabulary
shrines places where sacred relics are kept

The new settled way of life also had its drawbacks—some of the same ones that had affected hunter-gatherer settlements. Floods, fire, drought, and other natural disasters could destroy a village. Diseases, such as malaria, spread easily among people living closely together. Jealous neighbors and roving nomadic bands might attack and loot a wealthy village like Catal Huyuk.

Despite problems, these permanent settlements provided their residents with opportunities for fulfillment—in work, in artistic pursuits, and in leisure time. Some early villages expanded into cities. These urban centers would become the setting for more complex cultures in which new tools, art, and crafts were created.

A 9,000-year-old baked-clay figurine found in Catal Huyuk

Reading Check
Make Inferences
What advantages might farming and herding have over hunting and gathering?

Lesson 3 Assessment

1. **Organize Information** Complete the details in the outline. Which effect of the development of agriculture was the most significant?

Humans Try to Control Nature

I. Early Advances in Technology and Art
   A.
   B.
II. The Beginnings of Agriculture

2. **Key Terms and People** For each term in the lesson, write a sentence explaining its significance.

3. **Make Inferences** What kinds of problems did Stone Age peoples face?

4. **Summarize** In what ways did Neolithic peoples dramatically improve their lives?

5. **Hypothesize** Why do you think the development of agriculture occurred around the same time in several different places?

6. **Form and Support Opinions** What were the most significant consequences of the Agricultural Revolution?

Neolithic Cultures

The Big Idea

Early cultures that did not form advanced civilizations have contributed greatly to our understanding of the past.

Why It Matters Now

New discoveries made about cultures from the Neolithic Age help us better understand the development of cultures from the past to the present.

Key Terms and People

excavation

This figure of a deer was uncovered at Catal Huyuk.

Setting the Stage

The discovery of Catal Huyuk changed the way scientists thought about human life in Neolithic times. It provided information about the way Neolithic people lived, including their daily activities, religion, appearance, and clothing. Other Neolithic cultures were also complex and have furthered our understanding of the development of early societies.

Pre-Civilization Cultures

Some people have the perception that early cultures are not as important as civilizations and therefore studying them is not as valuable to archaeologists, historians, and other social scientists. This is not true, since in many ways, we have learned a great deal from Neolithic cultures. For one, we can make comparisons between pre- and post-Neolithic peoples. We can also compare these societies to modern-day cultures and ways of life as scholars have done with Catal Huyuk.

Jericho The townspeople of Jericho—in the modern-day West Bank, near the Jordan River—stood back to admire their hard work. A massive stone wall with a 30-foot-high watchtower now encircled their town. Jericho's residents had every right to be proud. Around 8000 BC, when the Neolithic Age began, most people still lived as nomads, but Jericho was a walled town. It may have been the first walled town to exist. To build such a wall took engineering skill, planning, and leadership.

Located in the modern-day West Bank, near the Jordan River, ancient Jericho was an oasis in an otherwise arid land. A spring at the site provided a continuous source of water. This water allowed the people of Jericho to grow barley and wheat and herd sheep and goats. In addition, the townspeople traded across the region. Jericho's mighty wall, agriculture, and trade represented the first steps toward civilization. Yet, in the end, the wall failed to protect the town.

Sometime during the 7000s BC, the community at Jericho ceased to exist. Over time, many other groups settled at Jericho and rebuilt its wall. Even so, Jericho never developed into a civilization—the first civilization was still to come—but archaeological **excavations** have revealed important information about the people who lived here and the culture they developed.

Skara Brae More than 2,500 miles away from Jericho, in present-day Scotland, sits the remains of the ancient village of Skara Brae. This 5,000-year-old Neolithic village provides clues about the early people and cultures that lived there. Stone houses that once held roofs stand on a hillside by the Bay of Skaill.

Archaeologists first excavated four buildings in Skara Brae in the 1860s. Later excavations were made in the 1920s. The remains of a tiny village, in which people and families lived close together and relied on one another, were discovered there. Archaeologists have found flint pieces, probably from stone axes and spear points. Their research has shown that the people of Skara Brae made beautifully decorated clay pots, clothing from animal skins, and jewelry from bone beads.

DOCUMENT-BASED INVESTIGATION   Historical Source

Lasting Materials

Archaeologist Ian Hodder has led the excavation at Catal Huyuk, a Neolithic village, since 1993. In the following excerpt from the article "This Old House" in the June 2006 edition of *Natural History* magazine, Hodder describes why the Catal Huyuk site is such an archaeological gold mine.

Analyze Historical Sources
1. **Main Idea and Details** What aspect of Catal Huyuk has provided archaeologists with a wealth of information?
2. **Make Inferences** Based on what you have read about other excavations of Neolithic finds, do you think that luck plays a role in archaeological research? Explain.

"How much can be learned from what is perhaps the most intriguing feature of all about Catalhoyük: that the site was built and rebuilt over the centuries in ways that provide an unusually rich record of the minutiae [small details] of daily life? The main reason for the abundance of the archaeological record [at Catalhoyük] was that the Catalhoyükans used a particular kind of construction material. Instead of making hard, lime floors that held up for decades (as was the case at many sites in Anatolia and the Middle East), the inhabitants of Catal Huyuk made their floors mostly out of a lime-rich mud plaster, which remained soft and in need of continual resurfacing. Once a year—in some cases once a month—floors and wall plasters had to be resurfaced. Those thin layers of plaster, somewhat like the growth rings in a tree, trap traces of activity. . . . The floors even preserve such subtle tokens of daily life as the impressions of floor mats."

—Ian Hodder

These remains of stone walls and cabinets still stand in the excavated village of Skara Brae.

The excavations have shown that the people of Skara Brae buried the dead in the earth, surrounding them with stone walls. What these and other finds have revealed is a distinction between social classes in the ancient Skara Brae culture, which did not exist formally until the rise of civilizations. From this evidence we have learned about the beginnings of social institutions and how they fulfilled basic needs of the people of Skara Brae.

Early Chinese Cultures Evidence of advanced Neolithic cultures in Asia has also helped archaeologists learn about the past. Archaeologists have found painted pottery pieces from the Yangshao (yahng•show) culture in central China that date between about 5000 BC and 3000 BC. Many of the pots have geometric shapes or designs. Other kinds of pottery, which are painted red and black, have been discovered in north-central China. These have been attributed to the Banshan, Majiayao (muh•ghee•ih•yow), and Machang cultures, which came after the Yangshao. Jade has also been found as well as pottery in the form of tripod pots and thin pots, which demonstrates that these cultures may have developed a pottery wheel.

The pottery itself reveals details about the Yangshao culture, but where archaeologists uncovered the pots helps provide even more information. Archaeologists found pots and bowls buried with the dead. The dead were placed in designated graves, and the same kinds of pots and bowls were found with all of the dead. This helps archaeologists draw the conclusion that there was not a social structure that divided the wealthy from the poor or the common people.

Reading Check
Find Main Ideas
What can we learn from complex cultures?

Neolithic Cultures Leave Their Mark

Numerous monuments from cultures and civilizations have been discovered around the world, but probably one of the most recognizable is Stonehenge in present-day Wiltshire, England. Much of Stonehenge has stood in this location since construction of it began in about 3000 BC. The monument was built in several stages over a period of about 1,500 years.

Interpreting Stonehenge Stonehenge is a circle of large standing stones paired with smaller bluestones in a field in southwestern England. But what these stones mean and what they stand for are still mysteries. Some scientists believe that they helped ancient people track Earth's orbit around the sun and the change of seasons. Others say that the stones are a spiritual symbol or possibly a structure that was built to help heal the sick. Another theory is that Stonehenge was a place where leaders and other people with high status were cremated and buried.

Remote sensing technology has helped researchers better understand the meaning of the stone circle. New laser technology helps to support more recent theories that Stonehenge was built to align with the summer and winter solstices.

When scientists examined a small piece of earth near Stonehenge, they found many bluestone flakes. People may have chipped off these rock flakes from the monument, thinking they had healing properties. Scientists also discovered that many of the ancient corpses buried there died from diseases and were not from the area. From these findings, some researchers have concluded that the Neolithic people may have believed Stonehenge to be a place of healing.

Scientists used CT scanning to study the remains of more than a dozen women who were buried at Stonehenge. The women were believed to be of high status. This discovery has marked a change in our understanding of the roles of women and men. In Neolithic times, women were not given equal status to men, and female leaders were uncommon. The fact that the remains of both men and more women were found there suggests that there was some equality among men and women who held high positions.

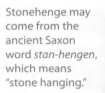

Stonehenge may come from the ancient Saxon word *stan-hengen*, which means "stone hanging."

Students from the University College London work together at the Festival of Culture in May 2016 to simulate how ancient people may have moved the heavy bluestone blocks to construct Stonehenge.

Reading Check
Summarize How has technology helped archaeologists and other scholars find out more about Neolithic cultures?

Superhenge As scientists continued to research the area in and around Stonehenge, another significant discovery was made in 2015. Using high-resolution ground-penetrating radar technology, researchers have discovered large stone monuments that are similar to Stonehenge—but the stones are underground. The new discovery has been called "Superhenge."

Archaeologists believe that "Superhenge" may have been built around the same time as Stonehenge, probably about 5,000 years ago. They think that there could be 30 to 90 large stones underground, standing in a row. Located about two miles from Stonehenge, this larger discovery may change previously held theories about Stonehenge's meaning and purpose.

Lesson 4 Assessment

1. **Organize Information** Fill in the chart with the causes and effects of three discoveries that have affected our understanding of Neolithic culture.

Cause	Effect

Which find do you think was most valuable to understanding complex Neolithic cultures?

2. **Key Terms and People** For each key term or person in the lesson, write a sentence explaining its significance.

3. **Draw Conclusions** Why is learning about complex cultures important to our understanding of history?

4. **Make Inferences** How have archaeologists learned about Neolithic social classes from excavations at Skara Brae, Stonehenge, and Yangshou sites?

5. **Summarize** What tools have archaeologists used to make new discoveries that have helped them revise history, and where have they used these tools?

6. **Evaluate** Why is the discovery of "Superhenge" an example of how new discoveries can revise past discoveries?

Module 1 Assessment

Key Terms and People

For each term below, write a sentence explaining its connection to human prehistory.

1. artifact
2. culture
3. technology
4. hunter-gatherer
5. Neolithic Revolution
6. domestication
7. civilization
8. nomad
9. excavation
10. historiography

Main Ideas

Use your notes and the information in the module to answer the following questions.

The Study of World History

1. Why is geography important to the study of world history?
2. Did the Little Ice Age cause voluntary or involuntary migration? Explain.
3. Why must the study of world history be flexible?

Human Origins in Africa

4. What kinds of evidence do archaeologists, anthropologists, and paleontologists study to find out how prehistoric people lived?
5. Why did the ability to walk upright and the development of the opposable thumb represent important breakthroughs for early hominids?
6. Why is the prehistoric period called the Stone Age?
7. What evidence supports archaeologists' beliefs that Neanderthals developed a form of religion?

Humans Try to Control Nature

8. Why do some archaeologists believe that women may have been the first farmers?
9. What role did the food supply play in shaping the nomadic life of hunter-gatherers and the settled life of farmers?
10. In what areas of the world did agriculture first develop?

Neolithic Cultures

11. What important aspects of Neolithic culture has the discovery and excavation of Catal Huyuk taught us besides early agriculture?
12. Why have scholars drawn the conclusion that there were no class divisions in the Yangshao culture?
13. Why do some historians think that Neolithic people believed Stonehenge was a place of healing?

Module 1 Assessment, continued

Critical Thinking

1. **Compare** In a chart, show the differences between Paleolithic and Neolithic cultures.

	Paleolithic	Neolithic
Source of food		
Means of living		
Technology		
Type of community		

2. **Form and Support Opinions** Which technology of the New Stone Age had the most impact on daily life? Explain.

3. **Recognize Effects** What effect did agriculture have on the roles of men and women?

4. **Synthesize** What event or development in early human history do you think is of particular significance? Why?

5. **Make Inferences** How did social institutions, such as family, religion, and social classes, fulfill the needs of Neolithic cultures?

6. **Analyze Causes** What geographic factors affected the migration of people during the Neolithic Age?

7. **Draw Conclusions** How did the geography of Japan affect its development?

8. **Make Inferences** Why do you think being a strong sea power has been important to island nations throughout history?

9. **Hypothesize** Do you think more advanced technology in the future will continue to help archaeologists dig up the past and revise history? Explain.

10. **Evaluate** How can DNA be used to advance archaeological theories?

Engage with History

You read in this module how interpretations of the past change as new discoveries are made. You also learned that these interpretations are limited because they represent the perspective of the people of the time. Discuss how these factors affect current interpretations by archaeologists and other scholars who have tried to reconstruct early human and cultural development.

Focus on Writing

Consider the religious practices of the Neanderthals and the villagers of Catal Huyuk, Skara Brae, and Yangshao. Write a two- or three- paragraph **essay** analyzing the development of religious beliefs over the course of the Stone Age. In your essay, consider the archaeological evidence that supports the conclusions about beliefs, practices, and organization.

Multimedia Activity

Write a Documentary Script

Write a documentary script and create a multimedia presentation about how the roles of women and men changed before and after the Neolithic Revolution. Then act out or film one scene from the documentary to share it with the class. Consider the following aspects as you create your script:

- introduction of agriculture
- geographic conditions
- political, social, and economic differences

Module 2
Early River Valley Civilizations

Essential Question

How did geography play a role in the development and organization of early civilizations?

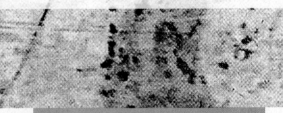

About the Photo: The photo shows a tile painting from the Chinese Shang Dynasty. Skilled artisans emerged throughout the early river valley civilizations as agricultural surplus made way for the growth of skilled workers.

▶ Explore ONLINE!

HISTORY.

VIDEOS, including...
- Egyptian Empire Is Born
- Egyptian Pyramids
- Nilometer
- Omens in China

☑ Document Based Investigations

☑ Graphic Organizers

☑ Interactive Games

☑ Image with Hotspots: The City of Ur

☑ Image Carousel: Egyptian Death Rituals

In this module you will follow the development of the earliest civilizations that formed on fertile river plains in Africa and Asia.

What You Will Learn ...

Timeline of Events 3000 BC–1000 BC

▶ *Explore ONLINE!*

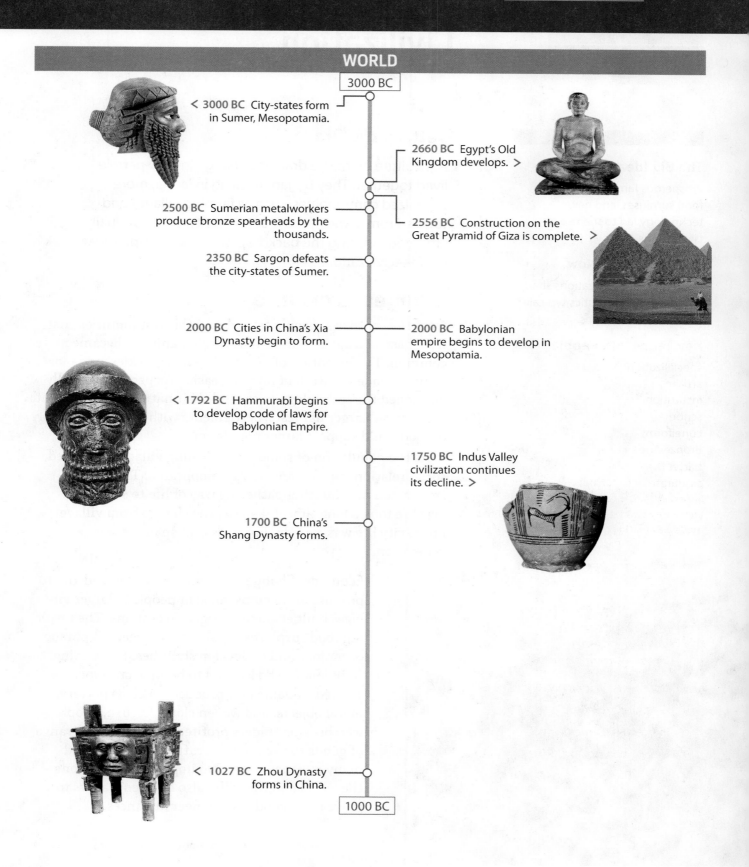

WORLD

3000 BC

< **3000 BC** City-states form in Sumer, Mesopotamia.

2660 BC Egypt's Old Kingdom develops. >

2500 BC Sumerian metalworkers produce bronze spearheads by the thousands.

2556 BC Construction on the Great Pyramid of Giza is complete. >

2350 BC Sargon defeats the city-states of Sumer.

2000 BC Cities in China's Xia Dynasty begin to form.

2000 BC Babylonian empire begins to develop in Mesopotamia.

< **1792 BC** Hammurabi begins to develop code of laws for Babylonian Empire.

1750 BC Indus Valley civilization continues its decline. >

1700 BC China's Shang Dynasty forms.

< **1027 BC** Zhou Dynasty forms in China.

1000 BC

🌐
Civilization

The Big Idea

Prosperous farming villages, food surpluses, and new technology led to the rise of civilizations.

Why It Matters Now

Contemporary civilizations share the same characteristics typical of ancient civilizations.

Key Terms and People

specialization
artisan
institution
scribe
cuneiform
Bronze Age
barter
ziggurat

Setting the Stage

Agriculture marked a dramatic change in how people lived together. They began dwelling in larger, more organized communities, such as farming villages and towns. From some of these settlements, cities gradually emerged, forming the backdrop of a more complex way of life—civilization.

Villages Grow into Cities

Over the centuries, people settled in stable communities that were based on agriculture. Domesticated animals became more common. The invention of new tools—hoes, sickles, and plow sticks—made the work of farming easier. As people gradually developed the technology to control their natural environment, they reaped larger harvests. Settlements with a plentiful supply of food could support larger populations.

As the population of some early farming villages increased, social relationships became more complicated. The change from a nomadic hunting-gathering way of life to settled village life took a long time. Likewise, the change from village life to city life was a gradual process that spanned several generations.

Economic Changes To cultivate more land and to produce extra crops, ancient people in larger villages built elaborate irrigation systems. The resulting food surpluses freed some villagers to pursue other jobs and to develop skills besides farming. Individuals who learned to become craftspeople created valuable new products, such as pottery, metal objects, and woven cloth. In turn, people who became traders profited from a broader range of goods to exchange—craftwork, grains, and many raw materials. Two important inventions—the wheel and the sail—also enabled traders to move more goods over longer distances.

The people of Sumer could find almost everything they needed in a city marketplace.

Social Changes A more complex and prosperous economy affected the social structure of village life. For example, building and operating large irrigation systems required the labor of many people. As other special groups of workers formed, social classes with varying wealth, power, and influence began to emerge. A system of social classes would become more clearly defined as cities grew.

Religion also became more organized. During the Old Stone Age, prehistoric people's religious beliefs centered around nature, animal spirits, and some idea of an afterlife. During the New Stone Age, farming peoples worshiped the many gods and goddesses who they believed had power over the rain, wind, and other forces of nature. Early city dwellers developed rituals founded on these earlier religious beliefs. As populations grew, common spiritual values became lasting religious traditions.

Reading Check
Summarize
How did the social structure of village life change as the economy became more complex?

An artist's rendering of the Sumerian city of Ur.

How Civilization Develops

Most historians believe that one of the first civilizations arose in Sumer. Sumer was located in Mesopotamia, a region that is part of modern Iraq. A civilization is often defined as a complex culture with five characteristics: (1) advanced cities, (2) specialized workers, (3) complex institutions, (4) record keeping, and (5) advanced technology. Just what set the Sumerians apart from their neighbors?

Advanced Cities Cities were the birthplaces of the first civilizations. A city is more than a large group of people living together. The size of the population alone does not distinguish a village from a city. One of the key differences is that a city is a center of trade for a larger area. Like their modern-day counterparts, ancient city dwellers depended on trade. Farmers, merchants, and traders brought goods to market in the cities. The city dwellers themselves produced a variety of goods for exchange.

Specialized Workers As cities grew, so did the need for more specialized workers, such as traders, government officials, and priests. Food surpluses provided the opportunity for **specialization**—the development of skills in a specific kind of work. An abundant food supply allowed some people to become expert at jobs besides farming. Some city dwellers became **artisans**—skilled workers who make goods by hand. Specialization helped artisans develop their skill at designing jewelry, fashioning metal tools and weapons, or making clothing and pottery. For example, early Sumerians learned how to pound wool or goat hair into felt. Some artisans who excelled at using textiles developed a sense of fashion. Fabrics were used as gifts, to design elaborate outfits, and for trading. The wide range of crafts artisans produced helped cities become centers of trade.

Complex Institutions The soaring populations of early cities made government, or a system of ruling, necessary. In civilizations, leaders emerged to maintain order among people and to establish laws. Government is an example of an **institution**—a long-lasting pattern of organization in a community. Complex institutions, such as government, religion, and the economy, are another characteristic of civilization.

With the growth of cities, religion became a formal institution. Most cities had great temples where dozens of priests took charge of religious duties. Sumerians believed that every city belonged to a god who governed the city's activities. The temple was the hub of both government and religious affairs. It also served as the city's economic center. There, food, clothing, and trade items were distributed.

Record Keeping As government, religion, and the economy became more complex, people recognized the need to keep records. In early civilizations, government officials had to document tax collections, the passage of laws, and the storage of grain. Priests needed a way to keep track of the calendar and important rituals. Merchants had to record accounts of debts and payments.

The wedge-shaped symbols of cuneiform are visible on this clay tablet.

Most civilizations developed a system of writing, though some devised other methods of record keeping. Around 3000 BC, Sumerian **scribes**—or professional record keepers—invented a system of writing called **cuneiform** (KYOO•nee•uh•fawrm), meaning "wedge-shaped." (Earlier Sumerian writing consisted of pictographs—symbols of the objects or what they represented.) The scribe's tool, called a stylus, was a sharpened reed with a wedge-shaped point. It was pressed into moist clay to create symbols. Scribes baked their clay tablets in the sun to preserve the writing.

People soon began to use writing for other purposes besides record keeping. They also wrote about their cities' dramatic events—wars, natural disasters, the reign of kings. Thus, the beginning of civilization in Sumer also signaled the beginning of written history.

Improved Technology New tools and techniques are always needed to solve problems that emerge when large groups of people live together. In early civilizations, some farmers harnessed the powers of animals and nature. For example, they used ox-drawn plows to turn the soil. They also created irrigation systems to expand planting areas.

Sumerian artisans relied on new technology to make their tasks easier. Around 3500 BC, they first used the potter's wheel to shape jugs, plates, and bowls. Sumerian metalworkers discovered that melting together certain amounts of copper and tin made bronze. After 2500 BC, metalworkers in Sumer's cities turned out bronze spearheads by the thousands. The period called the **Bronze Age** refers to the time when people began using bronze, rather than copper and stone, to fashion tools and weapons. The Bronze Age started in Sumer around 3000 BC, but the date varied in other parts of Asia and in Europe.

Reading Check
Draw Conclusions
Why were cities essential to the growth of civilizations?

Civilization Emerges in Ur

Ur, one of the earliest cities in Sumer, stood on the banks of the Euphrates River in what is now southern Iraq. Some 30,000 people once lived in this ancient city. Ur was the site of a highly sophisticated civilization.

After excavating from 1922 to 1934, English archaeologist Leonard Woolley and his team unraveled the mystery of this long-lost civilization. From archaeological evidence, Woolley concluded that around 3000 BC, Ur was a flourishing urban civilization. People in Ur lived in well-defined social classes. Rulers, as well as priests and priestesses, wielded great power. Wealthy merchants profited from foreign trade. Artists and artisans created lavish jewelry, musical instruments, and gold daggers. Woolley's finds have enabled historians to reconstruct Ur's advanced culture.

The City of Ur

1. **Ziggurat** A massive temple
2. **Court of Nanna** Sacred place of Ur's moon god
3. **Home of the High Priestess** Place where a woman with great religious authority lived
4. **Surrounding Wall** Defense for protecting Ur residents
5. **Temple and Treasury** Administrative centers in Ur
6. **Royal Cemetery** Burial site of the queen and king of Ur

The aerial photograph of Ur taken in the 1930s shows the placement of important infrastructure, such as the ziggurat. The Great Ziggurat of Ur was completely revealed in the 1920s by Leonard Woolley and his team. Woolley's excavation team found a huge, rectangular pyramidal structure made with mud and baked bricks. The ziggurat housed the temple of the city's patron god. Ur's patron god was the moon goddess, Nanna.

An Agricultural Economy Imagine a time nearly 5,000 years ago. Outside the mud-brick walls surrounding Ur, ox-driven plows cultivate the fields. People are working barefoot in the irrigation ditches that run between patches of green plants. With stone hoes, the workers widen ditches to carry water into their fields from the reservoir a mile away. This large-scale irrigation system was developed to provide Ur with food surpluses, which keep the economy thriving. The government officials who direct this public works project ensure its smooth operation.

Life in the City A broad dirt road leads from the fields to the city's wall. Inside, city dwellers go about their daily lives. Most live in windowless, one-story, boxlike houses packed tightly along the street. A few wealthy families live in two-story houses with an inner courtyard.

Down another street, artisans work in their shops. A metalworker makes bronze by mixing molten copper with just the right quantity of tin. Later, he will hammer the bronze to make spearheads—weapons to help Ur's well-organized armies defend the city. As a potter spins his potter's wheel, he expertly shapes the moist clay into a large bowl. These artisans and other craftworkers produce trade goods that help Ur prosper.

Ur's Thriving Trade The narrow streets open into a broad avenue where merchants squat under awnings and trade farmers' crops and artisans' crafts. This is the city's bazaar, or marketplace. Coins are not used to make purchases because money has not yet been invented. But merchants and their customers know roughly how many pots of grain a farmer must give to buy a jug of wine. This way of trading goods and services without money is called **barter**. More complicated trades require a scribe. He carefully forms cuneiform signs on a clay tablet. The signs may show how much barley a farmer owes a merchant for a donkey.

The Temple: Center of City Life Farther down the main avenue stands Ur's tallest and most important building—the temple. Like a city within a city, the temple is surrounded by a heavy wall. Within the temple gate, a massive, tiered structure towers over the city. This pyramid-shaped monument is called a **ziggurat** (ZIHG•uh•rat), which means "mountain of god." On the exterior of the ziggurat, a flight of perhaps 100 mud-brick stairs leads to the top. At the peak, priests conduct rituals to worship the city god who looms over Ur. Every day, priests climb these stairs. They often drag a goat or sheep to sacrifice. The temple also houses storage areas for grains, woven fabrics, and gems—offerings to the city's god. Sumerians had elaborate burial rituals and believed in an afterlife.

An early city, such as Ur, represents a model of civilizations that continued to arise throughout history. While the Sumerians were advancing their culture, civilizations were developing in Egypt, China, and elsewhere in Asia.

Reading Check
Analyze Causes
How did Ur's agricultural way of life foster the development of civilization there?

Civilization

As the history of Sumer demonstrates, civilization first developed in cities. In fact, the very word *civilization* comes from the Latin word for citizen, or city-dweller. However, the development of cities is only one aspect of civilization. Many scholars define civilization as a complex culture with five characteristics. The graphic organizer to the right shows how Sumer displayed these five characteristics.

Specialized Workers
- merchants   • teachers
- soldiers   • metalworkers
- priests   • government officials
- potters   • farmers
- scribes   • weavers

Complex Institutions
- Formal governments with officials and laws
- Priests with both religious and political power
- A rigorous education system for training of scribes

CHARACTERISTICS OF CIVILIZATION in Sumer

Record Keeping
- Cuneiform tablets— records of business transactions, historical events, customs, and traditions

Advanced Cities
- Uruk—population of about 50,000, which doubled in two centuries
- Lagash—population of about 10,000 to 50,000
- Umma—population of about 10,000 to 50,000

Advanced Technology
By around 3000 BC:
- The wheel, the plow, and the sailboat probably in daily use
- Bronze weapons and body armor that gave Sumerians a military advantage over their enemies

Critical Thinking
Make Inferences Judging from the information on this graphic, what economic activities probably took place in Sumerian cities?

Damage to Ancient Treasures

The ziggurat at Ur was damaged during the Persian Gulf War of 1991. Iraq parked military planes near the ziggurat, hoping coalition forces would not risk harming the ancient structure. While it was not attacked, bombs caused large craters nearby, and it was hit by stray machine gun fire. During the 2003 war, the Iraqi National Museum in Baghdad was damaged and then attacked by looters. Some of the treasures of the area's ancient civilizations were either stolen or destroyed.

In March 2016, Syrian government forces regained control of Palmyra, Syria, from the Islamic State of Iraq and Syria (ISIS). Experts reported mass destruction of antiquities and museums at the hands of ISIS, who claimed these ancient structures and relics promoted paganism. Videos show the militants with sledgehammers, bulldozers, and dynamite destroying temples, museums, sculptures, and other ancient treasures.

Reading Check
Analyze Events
Why do groups attack these ancient sites?

Lesson 1 Assessment

1. **Organize Information** Make a chart that lists five characteristics needed for the development of civilization. Which do you think is most important? Why?

Characteristics	
1.	
2.	
3.	
4.	
5.	

2. **Key Terms and People** For each term or name, write a sentence explaining its significance.

3. **Draw Conclusions** How did life in Sumer differ from life in a small farming community of the region?

4. **Analyze Effects** Why was writing a key invention for the Sumerians?

5. **Make Inferences** In what ways does the ziggurat of Ur reveal that Sumerians had developed an advanced civilization?

City-States in Mesopotamia

The Big Idea

The earliest civilization in Asia arose in Mesopotamia and organized into city-states.

Why It Matters Now

The development of this civilization reflects a settlement pattern that has occurred repeatedly throughout history.

Key Terms and People

Fertile Crescent
Mesopotamia
city-state
dynasty
cultural diffusion
polytheism
empire
Hammurabi

Setting the Stage

Two rivers flow from the mountains of what is now Turkey, down through Syria and Iraq, and finally to the Persian Gulf. Over six thousand years ago, the waters of these rivers provided the lifeblood that allowed the formation of farming settlements. These grew into villages and then cities.

Geography of the Fertile Crescent

A desert climate dominates the landscape between the Persian Gulf and the Mediterranean Sea in Southwest Asia. Yet within this dry region lies an arc of land that provided some of the best farming in Southwest Asia. The region's curved shape and the richness of its land led scholars to call it the **Fertile Crescent**. It includes the lands facing the Mediterranean Sea and a plain that became known as **Mesopotamia** (mehs•uh•puh•TAY•mee•uh). The word in Greek means "land between the rivers."

The rivers framing Mesopotamia are the Tigris (TY•grihs) and Euphrates (yoo•FRAY•teez). They flow southeastward to the Persian Gulf. The Tigris and Euphrates rivers flooded Mesopotamia at least once a year. As the floodwater receded, it left a thick bed of mud called silt. Farmers planted grain in this rich, new soil and irrigated the fields with river water. The results were large quantities of wheat and barley at harvest time. The surpluses from their harvests allowed villages to grow.

Environmental Challenges People first began to settle and farm the flat, swampy lands in southern Mesopotamia before 4500 BC. Around 3300 BC, the Sumerians arrived on the scene. Good soil was the advantage that attracted these settlers. However, there were three disadvantages to their new environment.

- Unpredictable flooding combined with a period of little or no rain. The land sometimes became almost a desert.

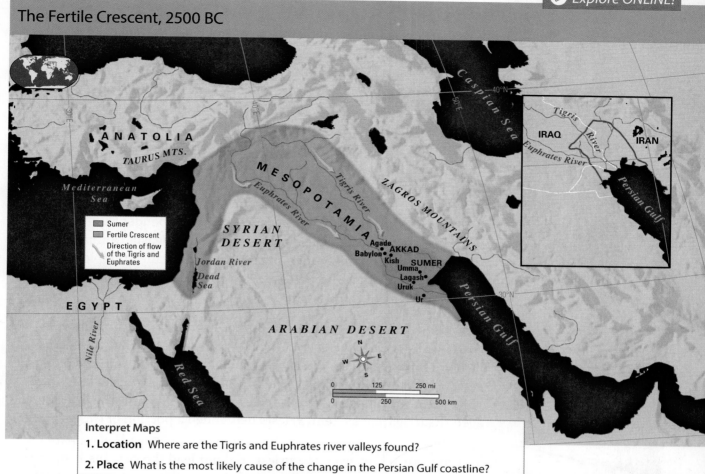

The Fertile Crescent, 2500 BC

Interpret Maps

1. **Location** Where are the Tigris and Euphrates river valleys found?

2. **Place** What is the most likely cause of the change in the Persian Gulf coastline?

- With no natural barriers for protection, a Sumerian village was nearly defenseless.
- The natural resources of Sumer were limited. Building materials and other necessary items were scarce.

Solving Problems Through Organization Over a long period of time, the people of Sumer created solutions to deal with these problems.

- To provide water, they dug irrigation ditches that carried river water to their fields and allowed them to produce a surplus of crops.
- For defense, they built city walls with mud bricks.
- Sumerians traded their grain, cloth, and crafted tools with the peoples of the mountains and the desert. In exchange, they received raw materials such as stone, wood, and metal.

These activities required organization, cooperation, and leadership. It took many people working together, for example, for the Sumerians to construct their large irrigation systems. Leaders were needed to plan the projects and supervise the digging. These projects also created a need for laws to settle disputes over how land and water would be distributed. These leaders and laws were the beginning of organized government—and eventually of civilization.

Reading Check
Summarize What are three solutions to the environmental challenges of Mesopotamia?

Sumerians Create City-States

The Sumerians stand out in history as one of the first groups of people to form a civilization. As you may have learned, five key characteristics traditionally define a civilization: (1) advanced cities, (2) specialized workers, (3) complex institutions, (4) record keeping, and (5) improved technology. All the later peoples who lived in this region of the world built upon the innovations of Sumerian civilization.

By 3000 BC, the Sumerians had built a number of cities, each surrounded by fields of barley and wheat. Although these cities shared the same culture, they developed their own governments, each with its own rulers. Each city and the surrounding land it controlled formed a **city-state**. A city-state functioned much as an independent country does today. Sumerian city-states included Uruk, Kish, Lagash, Umma, and Ur. As in Ur, the center of all Sumerian cities was the walled temple with a ziggurat in the middle. There, the priests and rulers appealed to the gods for the well-being of the city-state.

Priests and Rulers Share Control Sumer's earliest governments were controlled by the temple priests. The farmers believed that the success of their crops depended upon the blessings of the gods, and the priests acted as go-betweens with the gods. In addition to being a place of worship, the ziggurat was like a city hall. From the ziggurat the priests managed the irrigation system. Priests demanded a portion of every farmer's crop as taxes.

In time of war, however, the priests did not lead the city. Instead, the men of the city chose a tough fighter who could command the city's soldiers. At first, a commander's power ended as soon as the war was over. After 3000 BC, wars between cities became more and more frequent. Gradually, Sumerian priests and people gave commanders permanent control of standing armies.

In time, some military leaders became full-time rulers. These rulers usually passed their power on to their sons, who eventually passed it on to their own heirs. Such a series of rulers from a single family is called a **dynasty**. After 2500 BC, many Sumerian city-states came under the rule of dynasties.

The Spread of Cities Sumer's city-states grew prosperous from the surplus food produced on their farms. These surpluses allowed Sumerians to increase long-distance trade, exchanging the extra food and other goods for items they needed.

By 2500 BC, new cities were arising all over the Fertile Crescent, in what is now Syria, northern Iraq, and Turkey. Sumerians exchanged products and ideas, such as living in cities, with neighboring cultures. This process in which a new idea or a product spreads from one culture to another is called **cultural diffusion**.

Iku-Shamagen, King of Mari, a city-state in Sumer, offers prayers to the gods.

Reading Check
Analyze Causes
How did military leaders gain power in the city-states?

Sumerian Culture

The belief systems, social structure, technology, and arts of the Sumerians reflected their civilization's triumph over its dry and harsh environment.

A Religion of Many Gods Like many peoples in the Fertile Crescent, the Sumerians believed that many different gods controlled the various forces in nature. The belief in more than one god is called **polytheism** (PAHL·ee·thee·ihz·uhm). Enlil, the god of storms and air, was among the most powerful gods. Sumerians feared him as "the raging flood that has no rival." Demons known as Ugallu protected humans from the evil demons who caused disease, misfortune, and misery.

This gold and lapis ram with a shell fleece was found in a royal burial tomb.

Sumerians described their gods as doing many of the same things humans do— falling in love, having children, quarreling, and so on. Yet the Sumerians also believed that their gods were both immortal and all-powerful. Humans were nothing but their servants. At any moment, the mighty anger of the gods might strike, sending a fire, a flood, or an enemy to destroy a city. To keep the gods happy, the Sumerians built impressive ziggurats for them and offered rich sacrifices of animals, food, and wine.

Sumerians worked hard to earn the gods' protection in this life. Yet they expected little help from the gods after death. The Sumerians believed that the souls of the dead went to the "land of no return," a dismal, gloomy place between the earth's crust and the ancient sea. No joy awaited souls there. A passage in a Sumerian poem describes the fate of dead souls: "Dust is their fare and clay their food."

Some of the richest accounts of Mesopotamian myths and legends appear in a long poem called the *Epic of Gilgamesh*.

Life in Sumerian Society With civilization came the beginning of what we call social classes. Kings, landholders, and some priests made up the highest level in Sumerian society. Wealthy merchants ranked next. The vast majority of ordinary Sumerian people worked with their hands in fields and workshops. At the lowest level of Sumerian society were the slaves. Some slaves were foreigners who had been captured in war. Others were Sumerians who had been sold into slavery as children to pay the debts of their poor parents. Debt slaves could hope to eventually buy their freedom.

Social class affected the lives of both men and women. Sumerian women could work as merchants, farmers, or artisans. They could hold property in their own names. Women could also join the priesthood. Some upper-class women did learn to read and write, though Sumer's written records mention few female scribes. However, Sumerian women had more rights than women in many later civilizations.

Vocabulary
epic a long heroic poem that tells the story of a historical or legendary figure

Sumerian Science and Technology Historians believe that Sumerians invented the wheel, the sail, and the plow and that they were among the first to use bronze. Many new ideas and inventions arose from the Sumerians' practical needs.

- **Arithmetic and geometry** In order to erect city walls and buildings, plan irrigation systems, and survey flooded fields, Sumerians needed arithmetic and geometry. They developed a number system in base 60, from which stem the modern units for measuring time (60 seconds = 1 minute) and the 360 degrees of a circle.
- **Architectural innovations** Arches, columns, ramps, and the pyramid shaped the design of the ziggurat and permanently influenced Mesopotamian civilization.
- **Cuneiform** Sumerians created a system of writing. One of the first known maps was made on a clay tablet in about 2300 BC. Other tablets contain some of the oldest written records of scientific investigations in the areas of astronomy, chemistry, and medicine.

Reading check
Summarize
How did Sumerians view their gods?

The First Empire Builders

Cuneiform written in stone. Over the course of 3,000 years, cuneiform developed from a system of simple symbols to symbols representing ideas and sounds.

From 3000 to 2000 BC, the city-states of Sumer were almost constantly at war with one another. The weakened city-states could no longer ward off attacks from the peoples of the surrounding deserts and hills. Although the Sumerians never recovered from the attacks on their cities, their civilization did not die. Succeeding sets of rulers adapted the basic ideas of Sumerian culture to meet their own needs.

Sargon of Akkad About 2350 BC, a conqueror named Sargon defeated the city-states of Sumer. Sargon led his army from Akkad (AK•ad), a city-state north of Sumer. The Akkadians had long before adopted most aspects of Sumerian culture. Sargon's conquests helped to spread that culture even farther, beyond the Tigris-Euphrates Valley.

By taking control of both northern and southern Mesopotamia, Sargon created the world's first **empire**. An empire brings together several peoples, nations, or previously independent states under the control of one ruler. At its height, the Akkadian Empire loosely controlled land from the Mediterranean Coast in the west to present-day Iran in the east. Sargon's dynasty lasted only about 200 years, after which it declined due to internal fighting, invasions, and a famine.

Babylonian Empire In about 2000 BC, nomadic warriors known as Amorites invaded Mesopotamia. Gradually, the Amorites overwhelmed the Sumerians and established their capital at Babylon, on the Euphrates River. The Babylonian Empire reached its peak during the reign of **Hammurabi**, from 1792 BC to 1750 BC. Hammurabi's most enduring legacy is the code of laws he put together.

Hammurabi's Code Hammurabi recognized that a single, uniform code of laws would help to unify the diverse groups within his empire. He collected existing rules, judgments, and laws into the Code of Hammurabi. The code was engraved in stone, and copies were placed all over his empire.

The code lists 282 specific laws dealing with everything that affected the community, including family relations, business conduct, and crime. Since many people were merchants, traders, or farmers, for example, many of the laws related to property issues. Additionally, the laws sought to protect women and children from unfair treatment. The laws tell us a great deal about the Mesopotamians' beliefs and what they valued.

DOCUMENT-BASED INVESTIGATION Historical Source

Hammurabi's Code of Laws

Hammurabi's law code prescribed punishments ranging from fines to death. Often the punishments were based on the social class of the victim. Here are some examples of the laws:

> 8. If a man steal ox or sheep,...or pig, or boat – if it be from a god (temple) or a palace, he shall restore thirtyfold; if it be from a freeman, he shall render tenfold. If the thief have nothing wherewith to pay he shall be put to death.
>
> 142. If a woman hate her husband, and say: "Thou shalt not have me," they shall inquire into her antecedents for her defects; and if she have been a careful mistress and be without reproach and her husband have been going about and greatly belitting her, that woman has no blame. She shall receive her dowry and shall go to her father's house.
>
> 143. If she have not been a careful mistress, have gadded about, have neglected her house and have belitted her husband, they shall throw that woman into the water.
>
> 196. If a man destroy the eye of another man, they shall destroy his eye.
>
> 198. If one destroy the eye of a freeman or break the bone of a freeman, he shall pay one mana of silver.
>
> 199. If one destroy the eye of a man's slave or break a bone of a man's slave he shall pay one-half his price.

—The Code of Hammurabi King of Babylon About 2259 BC, translated by Robert Francis Harper

The top of a pillar that had Hammurabi's Code engraved on it.

Analyze Historical Sources

1. Why might the punishments for the crimes be based on social class?

2. What do you think the value was in making the punishments for the crimes known to all?

Hammurabi (? –1750 BC)

The noted lawgiver Hammurabi was also an able military leader, diplomat, and administrator of a vast empire. Hammurabi himself described some of his accomplishments:

As for the land of Sumer and Akkad, I collected the scattered peoples thereof, and I procured food and drink for them. In abundance and plenty I pastured them, and I caused them to dwell in peaceful habitation.

Although the code applied to everyone, it set different punishments for rich and poor and for men and women. It frequently applied the principle of retaliation (an eye for an eye and a tooth for a tooth) to punish crimes.

The prologue of the code set out the goals for this body of law. It said, "To bring about the rule of righteousness in the land, to destroy the wicked and the evil-doers; so that the strong should not harm the weak." Thus, Hammurabi's Code reinforced the principle that government had a responsibility for what occurred in society. For example, if a man was robbed and the thief was not caught, the government was required to compensate the victim.

Nearly two centuries after Hammurabi's reign, the Babylonian Empire, which had become much smaller, fell to the neighboring Kassites. Over the years, new groups dominated the Fertile Crescent. Yet the later peoples, including the Assyrians, Phoenicians, and Israelites, would adopt many ideas of the early Sumerians. Meanwhile, a similar pattern of development, rise, and fall was taking place to the west, along the Nile River in Egypt.

Reading check
Recognizing Effects
How did Hammurabi's law code advance civilization?

Lesson 2 Assessment

1. **Organize Information** Make a columned chart that lists the problems and solutions of life in Mesopotamia. The first problem has been listed for you.

Problems	Solutions
1. flooding	1.
2.	2.
3.	3.

Which of these problems required the most complex solution? Explain.

2. **Key Terms and People** For each term or name, write a sentence explaining its significance.

3. **Summarize** How was Sumerian culture spread throughout Mesopotamia?

4. **Analyze Effects** Why is the development of a written code of laws important to a society?

5. **Analyze Causes** How did the need to interact with the environment lead to advances in civilization?

Pyramids on the Nile

The Big Idea

Using mathematical knowledge and engineering skills, Egyptians built magnificent monuments to honor dead rulers.

Why It Matters Now

Many of the monuments built by the Egyptians stand as a testament to their ancient civilization.

Key Terms and People

delta
Narmer
pharaoh
theocracy
pyramid
mummification
hieroglyphics
papyrus

Setting the Stage

To the west of the Fertile Crescent in Africa, another river makes its way to the sea. While Sumerian civilization was on the rise, a similar process took place along the banks of this river, the Nile in Egypt. Yet the Egyptian civilization turned out to be very different from the collection of city-states in Mesopotamia. Early on, Egypt was united into a single kingdom, which allowed it to enjoy a high degree of unity, stability, and cultural continuity over a period of 3,000 years.

The Geography of Egypt

From the highlands of East Africa to the Mediterranean Sea, the Nile River flows northward across Africa for over 4,100 miles, making it the longest river in the world. A thin ribbon of water in a parched desert land, the great river brings its water to Egypt from distant mountains, plateaus, and lakes in present-day Burundi, Tanzania, Uganda, and Ethiopia.

Egypt's settlements arose along the Nile on a narrow strip of land made fertile by the river. The change from fertile soil to desert—from the Black Land to the Red Land—was so abrupt that a person could stand with one foot in each.

The Gift of the Nile As in Mesopotamia, yearly flooding brought the water and rich soil that allowed settlements to grow. Every year in July, rains and melting snow from the mountains of East Africa caused the Nile River to rise and spill over its banks. When the river receded in October, it left behind a rich deposit of fertile black mud called silt.

Before the scorching sun could dry out the soil, the peasants would prepare their wheat and barley fields. All fall and winter they watered their crops from a network of irrigation ditches.

In an otherwise parched land, the abundance brought by the Nile was so great that the Egyptians worshiped it as a

Explore ONLINE!

THE MIGHTY NILE

The Landsat image (left) shows the Nile flowing into its delta. An outline of the continental United States (below) shows the length of the Nile's course. The actual length of the Nile with all its twists and turns is more than 4,100 miles.

Map labels: Mediterranean Sea, Nile Delta, LOWER EGYPT, Memphis, SINAI, UPPER EGYPT, WESTERN DESERT, EASTERN DESERT, Nile River, Thebes, Red Sea, NUBIA, First Cataract, Tropic of Cancer

Legend:
- Region of Great Pyramids
- Prevailing winds
- River current
- Nile Valley

Interpret Maps

1. **Movement** In which direction does the Nile flow?

2. **Location** Describe the location of Upper Egypt and Lower Egypt.

---

god who gave life and seldom turned against them. As the ancient Greek historian Herodotus (hih•RAHD•uh•tuhs) remarked in the fifth century BC, Egypt was the "gift of the Nile."

Environmental Challenges Egyptian farmers were much more fortunate than the villagers of Mesopotamia. Compared to the unpredictable Tigris and Euphrates rivers, the Nile was as regular as clockwork. Even so, life in Egypt had its risks.

- When the Nile's floodwaters were just a few feet lower than normal, the amount of fresh silt and water for crops was greatly reduced. Thousands of people starved.
- When floodwaters were a few feet higher than usual, the unwanted water destroyed houses, granaries, and the precious seeds that farmers needed for planting.
- The vast and forbidding deserts on either side of the Nile acted as natural barriers between Egypt and other lands. They forced Egyptians to live on a very small portion of the land and reduced interaction with other people.

However, the deserts shut out invaders. For much of its early history, Egypt was spared the constant warfare that plagued the Fertile Crescent.

Upper Egypt and Lower Egypt Ancient Egyptians lived along the Nile from the mouth well into the interior of Africa. River travel was common, but it ended at the point in the Nile where boulders turn the river into churning rapids called a cataract (KAT•uh•rakt). This made it impossible for riverboats to pass this spot, known as the First Cataract, to continue upstream south to the interior of Africa.

Between the First Cataract and the Mediterranean lay two very different regions. Because its elevation is higher, the river area in the south is called Upper Egypt. It is a skinny strip of land from the First Cataract to the point where the river starts to fan out into many branches. To the north, near the sea, Lower Egypt includes the Nile **delta** region. The delta begins about 100 miles before the river enters the Mediterranean. The delta is a broad, marshy, triangular area of land formed by deposits of silt at the mouth of the river.

The Nile provided a reliable system of transportation between Upper and Lower Egypt. The Nile flows north, so northbound boats simply drifted with the current. Southbound boats hoisted a wide sail. The prevailing winds of Egypt blow from north to south, carrying sailboats against the river current. The ease of contact made possible by this watery highway helped unify Egypt's villages and promote trade.

Reading Check
What was the main difference between the flooding of the Nile and that of the rivers in Mesopotamia?

Egypt Unites into a Kingdom

Egyptians lived in farming villages as far back as 5000 BC, perhaps even earlier. Each village had its own rituals, gods, and chieftain. By 3200 BC, the villages of Egypt were under the rule of two separate kingdoms, Lower Egypt and Upper Egypt. Eventually the two kingdoms were united. There is conflicting historical evidence over who united Upper and Lower Egypt. Some evidence points to a king called Scorpion. More solid evidence points to a king named **Narmer**.

The king of Lower Egypt wore a red crown, and the king of Upper Egypt wore a tall, white crown shaped like a bowling pin. A carved piece of slate known as the Narmer Palette shows Narmer wearing the crown of Lower Egypt on one side and the crown of Upper Egypt on the other side. Some scholars believe the palette celebrates the unification of Egypt around 3000 BC.

Narmer created a double crown from the red and white crowns. It symbolized a united kingdom. He shrewdly settled his capital, Memphis, near the spot where Upper and Lower Egypt met, and established the first Egyptian dynasty. Eventually, the history of ancient Egypt would consist of 31 dynasties, spanning 2,600 years. Historians suggest that the pattern for Egypt's great civilization was set during the period from 3200 to 2700 BC. The period from 2660 to 2180 BC, known as the Old Kingdom, marks a time when these patterns became widespread.

Scorpion King

In 1999, Egyptologists discovered a series of carvings on a piece of rock about 18 by 20 inches. The tableau scene has symbols that may refer to a king named Scorpion.

The rock shows a figure carrying a staff. Near the head of the figure is a scorpion. Another artifact, a macehead, also shows a king with the scorpion symbol. Both artifacts suggest that Egyptian history may go back to around 3250 BC. Some scholars believe the Scorpion is the earliest king to begin unification of Egypt, represented by the double crown shown at far right.

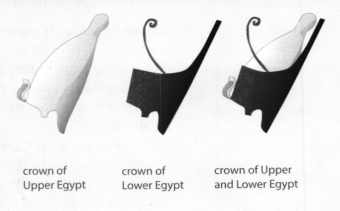

crown of Upper Egypt   crown of Lower Egypt   crown of Upper and Lower Egypt

Pharaohs Rule as Gods The role of the king was one striking difference between Egypt and Mesopotamia. In Mesopotamia, kings were considered to be representatives of the gods. To the Egyptians, kings were gods. The Egyptian god-kings, called **pharaohs** (FAIR·ohz), were thought to be almost as splendid and powerful as the gods of the heavens. This type of government in which rule is based on religious authority is called a **theocracy**.

The pharaoh stood at the center of Egypt's religion as well as its government and army. Egyptians believed that the pharaoh bore full responsibility for the kingdom's well-being. It was the pharaoh who caused the sun to rise, the Nile to flood, and the crops to grow. It was the pharaoh's duty to promote truth and justice.

Builders of the Pyramids Egyptians believed that their king ruled even after his death. He had an eternal life force, or *ka*, which continued to take part in the governing of Egypt. In the Egyptians' mind, the *ka* remained much like a living king in its needs and pleasures. Since kings expected to reign forever, their tombs were even more important than their palaces. For the kings of the Old Kingdom, the resting place after death was an immense structure called a **pyramid**. The Old Kingdom was the great age of pyramid building in ancient Egypt.

These magnificent monuments were remarkable engineering achievements, built by people who had not even begun to use the wheel. Unlike the Sumerians, however, the Egyptians did have a good supply of stone, both granite and limestone. For the Great Pyramid of Giza, for example, the limestone facing was quarried just across the Nile. Each perfectly cut stone block weighed at least 2 1/2 tons. Some weighed 15 tons. More than 2 million of these blocks were stacked with precision to a height of 481 feet. The entire structure covered more than 13 acres.

Reading Check
Make Inferences
Why were Egypt's
pharaohs unusually
powerful rulers?

The pyramids also reflect the strength of the Egyptian civilization. They show that Old Kingdom dynasties had developed the economic strength and technological means to support massive public works projects, as well as the leadership and government organization to carry them out.

Egyptian Culture

With nature so much in their favor, Egyptians tended to approach life more confidently and optimistically than their neighbors in the Fertile Crescent. Religion played an important role in the lives of Egyptians.

Religion and Life Like the Mesopotamians, the early Egyptians were polytheistic, believing in many gods. The most important gods were Re, the sun god, and Osiris (oh•SY•rihs), god of the dead. The most important goddess was Isis, who represented the ideal mother and wife. In all, Egyptians worshiped more than 2,000 gods and goddesses. They built huge temples to honor the major deities.

Vocabulary
deities gods or
goddesses

In contrast to the Mesopotamians, with their bleak view of death, Egyptians believed in an afterlife, a life that continued after death. Egyptians believed they would be judged for their deeds when they died. Anubis, god and guide of the underworld, would weigh each dead person's heart. To win eternal life, the heart could be no heavier than a feather. If the heart tipped the scale, showing that it was heavy with sin, a fierce beast known as the Devourer of Souls would pounce on the impure heart and gobble it up. But if the soul passed this test for purity and truth, it would live forever in the beautiful Other World.

People of all classes planned for their burials, so that they might safely reach the Other World. Kings and queens built great tombs, such as the pyramids, and other Egyptians built smaller tombs. Royal and elite Egyptians' bodies were preserved by **mummification**, which involves embalming and drying the corpse to prevent it from decaying.

Reading Check
Synthesize
Why did Egyptians
mummify their dead?

Attendants placed the mummy in a coffin inside a tomb. Then they filled the tomb with items the dead person could use in the afterlife, such as clothing, food, cosmetics, and jewelry. Many Egyptians purchased scrolls that contained hymns, prayers, and magic spells intended to guide the soul in the afterlife. This collection of texts is known as the *Book of the Dead*.

Life in Egyptian Society

Like the grand monuments to the kings, Egyptian society formed a pyramid. The king, queen, and royal family stood at the top. Below them were the other members of the upper class, which included wealthy landowners, government officials, priests, and army commanders. The next tier of the pyramid was the middle class, which included merchants and artisans. At the base of the pyramid was the lower class, by far the largest class. It consisted of peasant farmers and laborers.

Pyramids and Mummies

Etched into some of the stones of the pyramids are the nicknames of the teams of workers who built them—"the Vigorous Gang," "the Enduring Gang," and "the Craftsman Gang," for example. Just as construction workers today leave their marks on the skyscrapers they build, the pyramid builders scratched messages for the ages inside the pyramids.

Who were the pyramid builders? Peasants provided most of the labor. They worked for the government when the Nile was in flood and they could not farm. In return for their service, though, the country provided the workers with food and housing during this period.

◄ The ancient Egyptians mummified the body so the soul could return to it later. Egyptian embalmers were so skillful that modern archaeologists have found mummies that still have hair, skin, and teeth.

▼ This solid gold death mask of the pharaoh Tutankhamen covered the head of his mummy. The mask, which weighs 22.04 pounds, is part of a popular exhibit in the Egyptian Museum in Cairo, Egypt.

▼ The largest of the pyramids is the Great Pyramid (right background) at Giza, completed about 2556 BC. The diagram shows how the interior of a pyramid looks.

▲ These clay vessels are called Canopic jars. After preparing the mummy, embalmers placed the lungs, liver, and other internal organs of the mummy in these jars.

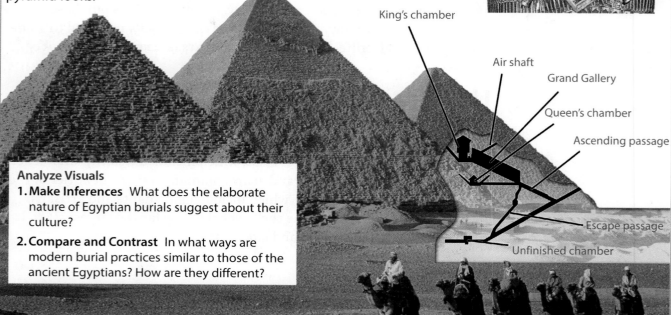

King's chamber

Air shaft

Grand Gallery

Queen's chamber

Ascending passage

Escape passage

Unfinished chamber

Analyze Visuals
1. **Make Inferences** What does the elaborate nature of Egyptian burials suggest about their culture?
2. **Compare and Contrast** In what ways are modern burial practices similar to those of the ancient Egyptians? How are they different?

Scholars still accept Herodotus's description of the process of mummification as one of the methods used by Egyptians.

Analyze Historical Sources
What does this description suggest about the Egyptians' knowledge of the human body?

"First with a crooked iron tool they draw out the brain through the nostrils, . . . and after this with a sharp stone of Ethiopia they make a cut along the side and take out the whole contents of the belly, . . . then they fill the belly with pure myrrh pounded up and with cassia and other spices except frankincense, and sew it together again. Having so done they keep it for embalming covered up in natron [a mineral salt] for seventy days, . . . and when the seventy days are past, they wash the corpse and roll its whole body up in fine linen cut into bands, smearing these beneath with gum, which the Egyptians use generally instead of glue."

—Herodotus, *The History of Herodotus*

In the later periods of Egyptian history, slavery became a widespread source of labor. Slaves, usually captives from foreign wars, served in the homes of the rich or toiled endlessly in the gold mines of Upper Egypt.

The Egyptians were not locked into their social classes. Lower- and middle-class Egyptians could gain higher status through marriage or success in their jobs. Even some slaves could hope to earn their freedom as a reward for their loyal service. To win the highest positions, people had to be able to read and write. Once a person had these skills, many careers were open in the army, the royal treasury, the priesthood, and the king's court.

Women in Egypt held many of the same rights as men. For example, a wealthy or middle-class woman could own and trade property. She could propose marriage or seek divorce. If she were granted a divorce, she would be entitled to one-third of the couple's property.

Egyptian Writing As in Mesopotamia, the development of writing was one of the keys to the growth of Egyptian civilization. Simple pictographs were the earliest form of writing in Egypt, but scribes quickly developed a more flexible writing system called **hieroglyphics** (hy•uhr•uh•GLIHF•ihks). This term comes from the Greek words *hieros* and *gluph*, meaning "sacred carving."

The Rosetta Stone

In 1799, near the delta village of Rosetta, some French soldiers found a polished black stone inscribed with a message in three languages. One version was written in hieroglyphics (top inset). A second version was in a simpler form of hieroglyphics, and the third was in Greek (both are shown in the bottom inset).

Since ancient Greek was a well-known language, it provided clues to the meaning of the hieroglyphics. Still, deciphering the Rosetta Stone took many years. In 1822, a French scholar named Jean François Champollion (shahm•paw•LYAWN) finally broke the code of the hieroglyphics.

As with Sumerian cuneiform writing, in the earliest form of hiero-glyphic writing, a picture stood for an idea. For instance, a picture of a man stood for the idea of a man. In time, the system changed so that pictures stood for sounds as well as ideas. The owl, for example, stood for an *m* sound or for the bird itself. Hieroglyphs could be used almost like let-ters of the alphabet.

Although hieroglyphs were first written on stone and clay, as in Mesopotamia, the Egyptians soon invented a better writing surface—**papyrus** (puh•PY•ruhs) reeds. These grew in the marshy delta. The Egyptians split the reeds into narrow strips, placed them crosswise in two layers, dampened them, and then pressed them. As the papyrus dried, the plant's sap glued the strips together into a paperlike sheet.

Egyptian Science and Technology Practical needs led to many Egyptian inventions. For example, the Egyptians developed a calendar to help them keep track of the time between floods and to plan their planting season. Priests observed that the same star—Sirius—appeared above the eastern horizon just before the floods came. They calculated the number of days between one rising of the star and the next as 365 days—a solar year. They divided this year into 12 months of 30 days each and added five days for holidays and feasting. This calendar was so accurate that it fell short of the true solar year by only six hours.

Egyptians developed a system of written numbers for counting, add-ing, and subtracting. The system would have helped to assess and collect taxes. Scribes used an early form of geometry to survey and reset property boundaries after the annual floods. Mathematical knowledge helped Egypt's skillful engineers and architects make accurate measurements to construct their remarkable pyramids and palaces. Egyptian architects were the first to use stone columns in homes, palaces, and temples.

Egyptian medicine was also famous in the ancient world. Egyptian doctors knew how to check a person's heart rate by feeling for a pulse in different parts of the body. They set broken bones with splints and had effective treatments for wounds and fevers. They also used surgery to treat some conditions.

Reading Check
Summarize
What were the main achievements of the ancient Egyptians?

Invaders Control Egypt

The power of the pharaohs declined about 2180 BC, marking the end of the Old Kingdom. Strong pharaohs regained control during the Middle Kingdom (2040–1640 BC) and restored law and order. They improved trade and transportation by digging a canal from the Nile to the Red Sea. They built huge dikes to trap and channel the Nile's floodwaters for irrigation. They also created thousands of new acres of farmland by draining the swamps of Lower Egypt.

The prosperity of the Middle Kingdom did not last. In about 1640 BC, a group from the area of present-day Israel moved across the Isthmus of Suez into Egypt. These people were the Hyksos (HIHK•sahs), which meant "the rulers of foreign lands." The Hyksos ruled much of Egypt from 1630 to 1523 BC.

Egypt would rise again for a new period of power and glory, the New Kingdom. During approximately the same time period as the Old Kingdom and Middle Kingdom had existed in Egypt, civilization was emerging in the Indus River Valley.

Reading Check
Summarize
Why didn't the prosperity of the Middle Kingdom last?

Lesson 3 Assessment

1. **Organize Information** Create a word web listing the most important achievements from the ancient Egyptians.

Egyptian Achievements

Which achievement do you consider the most important? Explain.

2. **Key Terms and People** For each term or name, write a sentence explaining its significance.

3. **Draw Conclusions** Which of the three natural features that served as boundaries in ancient Egypt was most important to Egypt's history? Explain.

4. **Analyze Effects** What impact did Egyptian religious beliefs have on the lives of Egyptians?

5. **Compare and Contrast** How were cuneiform and hieroglyphic writing similar? different?

Work and Play in Ancient Egypt

For ancient Egyptians, life often involved hard work. When the weather was good, most worked in the fields, producing food for their families and for export. During flood season, thousands of these farmers were called upon to help build the pharaohs' temples.

But life was not all about work. Archaeological digs offer evidence that both upper-class Egyptians and the common people found ways to enjoy themselves.

▼ GAMES

Games were popular with all classes of Egyptian society. The board shown below is for the game senet—also depicted in the painting. Players threw sticks or knuckle bones to move their pieces through squares of good or bad fortune. A player won by moving all his or her pieces off the board.

▲ FARMERS

This detail from a tomb painting shows Egyptian farmers at work. Egyptians grew enough wheat and barley to have food reserves for themselves and for export to other civilizations. They also grew fruit and vegetables in irrigated fields.

▶ COSMETICS

Ancient Egyptians used cosmetics for both work and play. They protected field workers from sun and heat and were used to enhance beauty. Egyptian men and women applied makeup, called kohl, to their eyes. They made kohl from minerals mixed with water. They also soaked flowers and fragrant woods in oil and rubbed the oil into their skin. The dark eye makeup softened the glare of the sun. The oils protected their skin from the dry air. Egyptians kept their cosmetics in chests such as the one shown at right.

▼ Temple Builders

The artist's colorful drawing of what the Karnak Temple Complex might have looked like explains why Egyptian pharaohs needed thousands of laborers to build their temples. Some historians believe the laborers may have been part of a rotating workforce drafted from the agricultural classes around Egypt. The photo at lower left shows the temple as it is today. Although faded and eroded, the temple still inspires awe.

Analyze Visuals

1. **Make Inferences** From what you have read here, what inferences can you make about Egyptian society?

2. **Compare and Contrast** How are the work and leisure activities of ancient Egypt different from those in the United States today? How are they similar?

Planned Cities on the Indus

The Big Idea

The first Indian civilization built well-planned cities on the banks of the Indus River.

Why It Matters Now

The culture of India today has its roots in the civilization of the early Indus cities.

Key Terms and People

subcontinent
monsoon
Harappan civilization

Setting the Stage

The great civilizations of Mesopotamia and Egypt rose and fell. They left behind much physical evidence about their ways of life. This is the case in what today is the area known as Pakistan and part of India where another civilization arose about 2500 BC. However, historians know less about this civilization's origins and the reasons for its eventual decline than they do about the origins and decline of Mesopotamia and Egypt. That is because the language of the culture has not been translated.

The Geography of the Indian Subcontinent

Geographers often refer to the landmass that includes India, Pakistan, and Bangladesh as the Indian **subcontinent**. A wall of the highest mountains in the world—the Hindu Kush, Karakoram, and Himalayan ranges—separates this region from the rest of the Asian continent.

Rivers, Mountains, and Plains The world's tallest mountains to the north and a large desert to the east helped protect the Indus Valley from invasion. The mountains guard an enormous flat and fertile plain formed by two rivers—the Indus and the Ganges (GAN•jeez). Each river is an important link from the interior of the subcontinent to the sea. The Indus River flows southwest from the Himalayas to the Arabian Sea. Much of the lower Indus Valley is occupied by the Thar Desert. Farming is possible only in the areas directly watered by the Indus. The Ganges drops down from the Himalayas and flows eastward across northern India. It joins the Brahmaputra River as it flows to the Bay of Bengal.

The Indus and Ganges and the lands they water make up a large area that stretches 1,700 miles across northern India and is called the Indo-Gangetic Plain. Like the Tigris, the

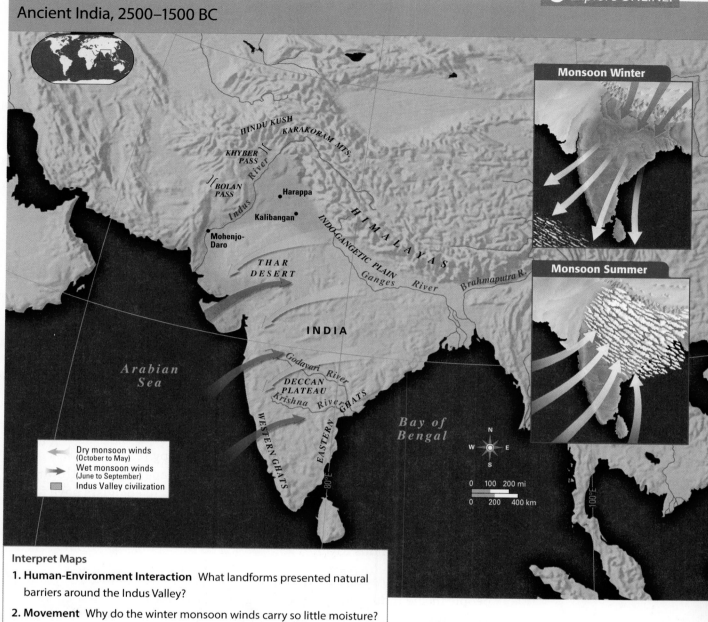

Ancient India, 2500–1500 BC

Explore ONLINE!

Monsoon Winter

Monsoon Summer

HINDU KUSH
KARAKORAM MTS.
KHYBER PASS
BOLAN PASS
Indus River
• Harappa
• Kalibangan
• Mohenjo-Daro
HIMALAYAS
INDO-GANGETIC PLAIN
Ganges River
Brahmaputra R.
THAR DESERT
INDIA
Arabian Sea
Godavari River
DECCAN PLATEAU
Krishna River
WESTERN GHATS
EASTERN GHATS
Bay of Bengal

← Dry monsoon winds (October to May)
→ Wet monsoon winds (June to September)
▨ Indus Valley civilization

0   100   200 mi
0   200   400 km

Interpret Maps

1. **Human-Environment Interaction** What landforms presented natural barriers around the Indus Valley?

2. **Movement** Why do the winter monsoon winds carry so little moisture?

Euphrates, and the Nile, these rivers carry not only water for irrigation but also silt, which produces rich land for agriculture.

Below the Indo-Gangetic Plain, the southern part of the subcontinent is a peninsula that thrusts south into the Indian Ocean. The center of the peninsula is a high plateau cut by twisting rivers. This region is called the Deccan (DEK•uhn) Plateau. The plateau is framed by low mountain ranges called the Eastern and Western Ghats. These mountains keep moist air from reaching the plateau, making it a dry region. A narrow border of lush, tropical land lies along the coasts of southern India.

Monsoons Seasonal winds called **monsoons** dominate India's climate. From October to February, winter monsoons from the northeast blow dry air westward across the country. Then, from the middle of June through

October, the winds shift. These monsoons blow eastward from the southwest, carrying moisture from the ocean in great rain clouds. The powerful storms bring so much moisture that flooding often happens. When the summer monsoons fail to develop, drought often causes crop disasters.

Environmental Challenges The civilization that emerged along the Indus River faced many of the same challenges as the ancient Mesopotamian and Egyptian civilizations.

- Yearly floods spread deposits of rich soil over a wide area. However, the floods along the Indus were unpredictable.
- The rivers sometimes changed course.
- The cycle of wet and dry seasons brought by the monsoon winds was unpredictable. If there was too little rain, plants withered in the fields and people went hungry. If there was too much rain, floods swept away whole villages.

Civilization Emerges on the Indus

Historians know less about the civilization in the Indus Valley than about those to the west. They have not yet deciphered the Indus system of writing. Evidence comes largely from archaeological digs, although many sites remain unexplored, and floods probably washed away others long ago. At its height, however, the civilization of the Indus Valley influenced an area much larger than did either Mesopotamia or Egypt.

Earliest Arrivals No one is sure how human settlement began in the Indian subcontinent. Perhaps people who arrived by sea from Africa settled the south. Northern migrants may have made their way through the Khyber Pass in the Hindu Kush mountains. Archaeologists have found evidence in the highlands of agriculture and domesticated sheep and goats dating to about 7000 BC. By about 3200 BC, people were farming in villages along the Indus River.

Planned Cities Around 2500 BC, while Egyptians were building pyramids, people in the Indus Valley were laying the bricks for India's first cities. They built strong levees, or earthen walls, to keep water out of their cities. When these were not enough, they constructed human-made islands to raise the cities above possible floodwaters. Archaeologists have found the ruins of more than 100 settlements along the Indus and its tributaries mostly in modern-day Pakistan. The largest cities were Kalibangan, Mohenjo-Daro, and Harappa. Indus Valley civilization is sometimes called **Harappan civilization**, because of the many archaeological discoveries made at that site.

One of the most remarkable achievements of the Indus Valley people was their sophisticated city planning. The cities of the early Mesopotamians were a jumble of buildings connected by a maze of winding streets. In contrast, the people of the Indus laid out their cities on a precise grid system. Cities featured a fortified area called a citadel, which contained the major buildings of the city. Buildings were constructed of

Reading Check
Contrast What environmental challenge did the farmers of the Indus Valley face that the Sumerians and Egyptians did not?

oven-baked bricks cut in standard sizes, unlike the simpler, irregular, sun-dried mud bricks of the Mesopotamians.

Early engineers also created sophisticated plumbing and sewage systems. These systems could rival any urban drainage systems built before the 19th century. The uniformity in the cities' planning and construction suggests that the Indus peoples had developed a strong central government.

Harappan Planning Harappa itself is a good example of this city planning. The city was partially built on mud-brick platforms to protect it from flooding. A thick brick wall about three and a half miles long surrounded it. Inside was a citadel, which provided protection for the royal family and also served as a temple.

The streets in its grid system were as wide as 30 feet. Walls divided residential districts from each other. Houses varied in size. Some may have been three stories high. Narrow lanes separated rows of houses, which were laid out in block units. Houses featured bathrooms where wastewater flowed out to the street and then to sewage pits outside the city walls.

Reading Check
Contrast How did the planned cities of the Indus Valley differ from other early cities?

Harappan Culture

Harappan culture spread throughout the Indus valley. Like the Egyptian and Mesopotamian civilizations, the culture was based on agriculture. Artifacts help to explain some aspects of the culture.

Language Like the other two river valley civilizations, the Harappan culture developed a written language. In contrast to cuneiform and hieroglyphics, the Harappan language has been impossible to decipher. This is because, unlike the other two languages, linguists have not found any inscriptions that are bilingual. The Harappan language is found on stamps and seals made of carved stone used for trading pottery and tools. About 400 symbols make up the language. Scientists believe the symbols, like hieroglyphs, are used both to depict an object and also as phonetic sounds. Some signs stand alone and others seem to be combined into words.

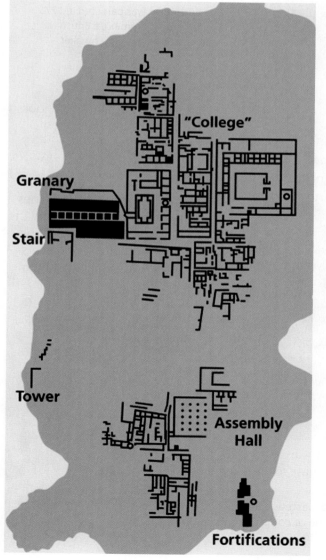

"College"

Granary

Stair

Tower

Assembly Hall

Fortifications

A map of the citadel portion of Mohenjo-Daro shows an organized pattern of buildings and streets.

Plumbing in Mohenjo-Daro

From the time people began living in cities, they have faced the problem of plumbing: how to obtain clean water and remove human wastes? In most ancient cities, people retrieved water from a river or a central well. They dumped wastes into open drainage ditches or carted them out of town. Only the rich had separate bathrooms in their homes.

By contrast, the Indus peoples built extensive and modern-looking plumbing systems. In Mohenjo-Daro, almost every house had a private bathroom and toilet. No other civilization achieved this level of convenience until the 19th and 20th centuries. The toilets were neatly built of brick with a wooden seat. Pipes connected to each house carried wastewater into an underground sewer system.

Plumbing Facts

- The ancient Romans also built sophisticated plumbing and sewage systems. Aqueducts supplied Roman cities with water.

- In the 17th century, engineers installed a series of water wheels to pump water for the fountains of Versailles, the palace of French king Louis XIV. The water was pumped from a river three miles away. This was the largest water-supply system powered by machine rather than gravity.

- The flush toilet was patented in 1775 by Alexander Cumming, a British mathematician and watchmaker.

In their private baths, people took showers by pouring pitchers of water over their head.

Wastes drained through clay pipes into brick sewers running below the streets. These sewers had manholes, through which sanitation workers could inspect the drains and clean out the muck.

Analyze Visuals

1. **Make Inferences** What does the attention the Indus people gave to the plumbing and sewer systems suggest about their culture?

2. **Compare and Contrast** Find out how water is supplied and wastewater disposed of in your home or community. How does the system in your home or community compare with what was used in Mohenjo-Daro?

Harappan seals show an elephant (top left), an Indian rhinoceros (top right), and a zebu bull (bottom).

Culture The Harappan cities show a remarkable uniformity in religion and culture. The housing suggests that social divisions in the society were not great. Artifacts such as clay and wooden children's toys suggest a relatively prosperous society that could afford to produce nonessential goods. Few weapons of warfare have been found, suggesting that conflict was limited.

The presence of animal images on many types of artifacts suggests that animals were an important part of the culture. Animals are seen on pottery, small statues, children's toys, and seals used to mark trade items. The images provide archaeologists with information about animals that existed in the region. However, some of the seals portray beasts with parts of several different animals—for example, the head of a man, an elephant trunk and tusks, horns of a bull, and the rump of a tiger. As in the case of the Harappan language, the meaning of these images has remained a mystery.

This bearded figure might represent a Harappan god or perhaps a priest king.

Role of Religion As with other cultures, the rulers of the Harappan civilization are believed to have close ties to religion. Archaeologists think that the culture was a theocracy. But no site of a temple has been found. Priests likely prayed for good harvests and safety from floods. Religious artifacts reveal links to modern Hindu culture. Figures show what may be early representations of Shiva, a major Hindu god. Other figures relate to a mother goddess, fertility images, and the worship of the bull. All of these became part of later Indian civilization.

Trade The Harappans conducted a thriving trade with peoples in the region. Gold and silver came from the north in Afghanistan. Semiprecious stones from Persia and the Deccan Plateau were crafted into jewelry. The Indus River provided an excellent means of transportation for trade goods. Brightly colored cotton cloth was a desirable trade item since few people at the time knew how to grow cotton. Overland routes moved goods from Persia to the Caspian Sea.

The Indus River provided a link to the sea. This access allowed Indus Valley inhabitants to develop trade with distant peoples, including the Mesopotamians. Seals probably used by Indus merchants to identify their goods have been found in Sumer. Ships used the Persian Gulf trade routes to bring copper, lumber, precious stones, and luxury goods to Sumer. Trading began as early as 2600 BC and continued until 1800 BC.

Reading Check
Synthesize What is the main reason Harappan language has not been deciphered?

Indus Valley Culture Ends

Around 1750 BC, the quality of building in the Indus Valley cities declined. Gradually, the great cities fell into decay. The fate of the cities remained a mystery until the 1970s. Then, satellite images of the subcontinent of India revealed evidence of shifts in tectonic plates. The plate movement probably caused earthquakes and floods and altered the course of the Indus River.

Some cities along the rivers apparently suffered through these disasters and survived. Others were destroyed. The shifts may have caused another river, the Saraswati, to dry up. Trade on this river became impossible, and cities began to die. Harappan agriculture, too, would have been influenced by these events. It is likely that these environmental changes prevented production of large quantities of food. Furthermore, Harappan agriculture may have suffered as a result of soil that was exhausted by overuse. This too, may have forced people to leave the cities in order to survive.

Other factors had an impact on the Indus Valley. The Aryans, a nomadic people from north of the Hindu Kush mountains, may have invaded the area around 1500 BC and influenced the development of Indian civilization. At the same time, farther to the east, another civilization was arising that was isolated from outside influences.

Vocabulary
tectonic plates
moving pieces of
Earth's crust

Reading Check
Analyze Causes
What factors may
have contributed
to the decline of
the Indus Valley
civilization?

Lesson 4 Assessment

1. **Organize Information** Complete the chart with facts about life in the Indus Valley.

Indus Valley	
Cities	fact
Language	fact
Trade	fact

   What is one conclusion you can draw about the Indus Valley civilization?

2. **Key Terms and People** For each term or name, write a sentence explaining its significance.

3. **Draw Conclusions** What evidence suggests Indus Valley cities were run by a strong central government?

4. **Synthesize** What skills would the construction of planned cities require? Explain.

5. **Make Inferences** How were the people of the Indus Valley connected to Mesopotamia?

River Dynasties in China

Setting the Stage

The walls of China's first cities were built 4,000 years ago. This was at least 1,000 years after the walls of Ur, the great pyramids of Egypt, and the planned cities of the Indus Valley were built. Unlike the other three river valley civilizations, the civilization that began along one of China's river systems continues to thrive today.

The Geography of China

Natural barriers somewhat isolated ancient China from all other civilizations. To China's east lies the Yellow Sea, the East China Sea, and the Pacific Ocean. Mountain ranges and deserts dominate about two-thirds of China's landmass. In west China lies the Taklimakan (tah•kluh•muh•KAHN) Desert and the icy 15,000-foot Plateau of Tibet. To the southwest are the Himalayas. And to the north are the desolate Gobi Desert and the Mongolian Plateau.

River Systems Two major river systems flow from the mountainous west to the Pacific Ocean. The Huang He (hwahng•HUH), also known as the Yellow River, is found in the north. In central China, the Chang Jiang (chang jyhang), also called Yangtze (yang•SEE), flows east to the Yellow Sea. The Huang He, whose name means "yellow river," deposits huge amounts of yellowish silt when it overflows its banks. This silt is actually fertile soil called **loess** (LOH•uhs), which is blown by the winds from deserts to the west and north.

Environmental Challenges Like the other ancient civilizations in this module, China's first civilization developed in a river valley. China, too, faced the dangers of floods—but its geographic isolation posed its own challenges.

- The Huang He's floods could be disastrous. Sometimes floods devoured whole villages, earning the river the nickname "China's Sorrow."

The Big Idea

The early rulers introduced ideas about government and society that shaped Chinese civilization.

Why It Matters Now

The culture that took root during ancient times still affects Chinese ways of life today.

Key Terms and People

loess
oracle bone
Mandate of Heaven
dynastic cycle
feudalism

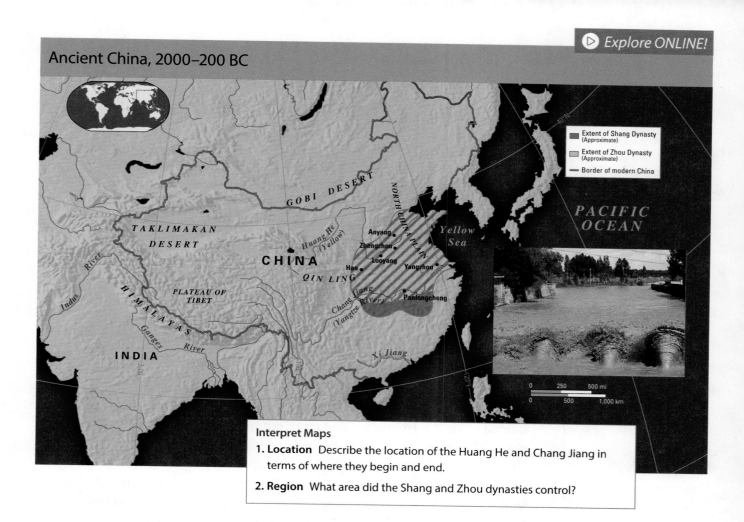

Ancient China, 2000–200 BC

▶ Explore ONLINE!

Extent of Shang Dynasty (Approximate)
Extent of Zhou Dynasty (Approximate)
Border of modern China

GOBI DESERT

TAKLIMAKAN DESERT

CHINA

Huang He (Yellow)

QIN LING

PLATEAU OF TIBET

HIMALAYAS

Indus River

Ganges River

INDIA

NORTH CHINA PLAIN

Anyang
Zhengzhou
Luoyang
Hao
Yangzhou
Panlongcheng

Chang Jiang (Yangtze River)

Xi Jiang

Yellow Sea

PACIFIC OCEAN

0   250   500 mi
0   500   1,000 km

Interpret Maps

1. **Location** Describe the location of the Huang He and Chang Jiang in terms of where they begin and end.

2. **Region** What area did the Shang and Zhou dynasties control?

- Because of China's relative geographic isolation, early settlers had to supply their own goods rather than trading with outside peoples.
- China's natural boundaries did not completely protect these settlers from outsiders. Invasions from the west and north occurred again and again in Chinese history.

China's Heartland Only about 10 percent of China's land is suitable for farming. Much of the land lies within the small plain between the Huang He and the Chang Jiang in eastern China. This plain, known as the North China Plain, is China's heartland. Throughout China's long history, its political boundaries have expanded and contracted depending on the strength or weakness of its ruling families. Yet the heartland of China remained the center of its civilization.

Reading Check
Summarize
Between which two rivers is the heartland of China found?

Civilization Emerges in Shang Times

Fossil remains show that ancestors of modern humans lived in southwest China about 1.7 million years ago. In northern China near Beijing, a *Homo erectus* skeleton was found. Known as Peking man, his remains show that the river valley attracted settlers as many as 500,000 years ago.

Lady Hao's Tomb

Lady Hao was a wife of King Wu Ding, a Shang ruler, during the 1200s BC. Her relatively small grave contained some 460 bronze artifacts, 750 jade objects, and more than 6,880 cowry shells. Also found in the tomb beside Lady Hao's coffin were the remains of 16 people and 6 dogs.

Writings found in other places reveal a remarkable figure in Lady Hao. On behalf of her husband, she led more than one military campaign, once with a force of 13,000 troops. She also took charge of rituals dedicated to the spirits of Shang ancestors, a duty reserved for the most distinguished members of the royal family.

The First Dynasties Even before the Sumerians settled in southern Mesopotamia, early Chinese cultures were building farming settlements along the Huang He. Around 2000 BC, some of these settlements grew into China's first cities. According to legend, the first Chinese dynasty, the Xia (shyah) Dynasty, emerged about this time. Its leader was an engineer and mathematician named Yu. His flood-control and irrigation projects helped tame the Huang He and its tributaries so that settlements could grow. The legend of Yu reflects the level of technology of a society making the transition to civilization.

About the time the civilizations of Mesopotamia, Egypt, and the Indus Valley fell to outside invaders, a people called the Shang rose to power in northern China. The Shang Dynasty lasted from around 1700 BC to 1027 BC. It was the first family of Chinese rulers to leave written records. The Shang kings built elaborate palaces and tombs that have been uncovered by archaeologists. The artifacts reveal much about Shang society.

Early Cities Among the oldest and most important Shang cities was Anyang (ahn•YAHNG), one of the capitals of the Shang Dynasty. Unlike the cities of the Indus Valley or Fertile Crescent, Anyang was built mainly of wood. The city stood in a forest clearing. The higher classes lived in timber-framed houses with walls of clay and straw. These houses lay inside the city walls. The peasants and craftspeople lived in huts outside the city.

The Shang surrounded their cities with massive earthen walls for protection. The archaeological remains of one city include a wall of packed earth 118 feet wide at its base that encircled an area of 1.2 square miles. It likely took 10,000 men more than 12 years to build such a structure. Like the pyramids of Egypt or the cities of the Indus Valley, these walls demonstrate the Shang rulers' ability to raise and control large forces of workers.

Shang peoples needed walled cities because they were constantly waging war. The chariot, one of the major tools of war, was probably first introduced by contact with cultures from western Asia. Professional warriors underwent lengthy training to learn the techniques of driving and shooting from horse-drawn chariots.

Reading Check
Compare
What did Shang cities have in common with those of Sumer?

The Development of Chinese Culture

In the Chinese view, people who lived outside of Chinese civilization were barbarians. Because the Chinese saw their country as the center of the civilized world, their own name for China was the Middle Kingdom.

The culture that grew up in China had strong unifying bonds. From earliest times, the group seems to have been more important than the individual. A person's chief loyalty throughout life was to the family. Beyond this, people owed obedience and respect to the ruler of the Middle Kingdom, just as they did to the elders in their family.

Family The family was central to Chinese society. The most important virtue was respect for one's parents. The elder men in the family controlled the family's property and made important decisions. Women, on the other hand, were treated as inferiors. They were expected to obey their fathers, their husbands, and later, their own sons. When a girl was between 13 and 16 years old, her marriage was arranged, and she moved into the house of her husband. Only by bearing sons for her husband's family could she hope to improve her status.

Social Classes Shang society was sharply divided between nobles and peasants. A ruling class of warrior-nobles headed by a king governed the Shang. These noble families owned the land. They governed the scattered villages within the Shang lands and sent tribute to the Shang ruler in exchange for local control.

Religious Beliefs In China, the family was closely linked to religion. The Chinese believed that the spirits of family ancestors had the power to bring good fortune or disaster to living members of the family. The Chinese did not regard these spirits as mighty gods. Rather, the spirits were more like troublesome or helpful neighbors who demanded attention and respect. Every family paid respect to the father's ancestors and made sacrifices in their honor.

Through the spirits of the ancestors, the Shang consulted the gods. The Shang worshiped a supreme god, Shang Di, as well as many lesser gods. Shang kings consulted the gods through the use of **oracle bones**, animal bones and tortoise shells on which priests had scratched questions for the gods.

Vocabulary
tribute payment made to keep peace

The earliest evidence of Chinese writing is seen on oracle bones like this one found in the city of Anyang.

Chinese Writing

The earliest writing systems in the world—including Chinese, Sumerian, and Egyptian—developed from pictographs, or simplified drawings of objects. The writing system used in China today is directly related to the pictographic writing found on Shang oracle bones. As you can see in the chart below, the ancient pictographs can still be recognized in many modern Chinese characters.

	ox	goat, sheep	tree	moon	earth	water	field	heaven	to pray
Ancient symbol									
Modern character	牛	羊	木	月	土	水	田	天	祝

After inscribing a question on the bone, a priest applied a hot poker to it, which caused it to crack. The priests then interpreted the cracks to see how the gods had answered.

Development of Writing In the Chinese method of writing, each character generally stands for one syllable or unit of language. Recall that many of the Egyptian hieroglyphs stood for sounds in the spoken language. In contrast, there were practically no links between China's spoken language and its written language. One could read Chinese without being able to speak a word of it. (This seems less strange when you think of our own number system. Both a French person and an American can understand the written equation 2 + 2 = 4. But an American may not understand the spoken statement "Deux et deux font quatre.")

The Chinese system of writing had one major advantage. People in all parts of China could learn the same system of writing, even if their spoken languages were very different. Thus, the Chinese written language helped unify a large and diverse land, and made control much easier.

The disadvantage of the Chinese system was the enormous number of written characters to be memorized—a different one for each unit of language. A person needed to know over 1,500 characters to be barely literate. To be a true scholar, one needed to know at least 10,000 characters. For centuries, this severely limited the number of literate, educated Chinese. As a general rule, a nobleperson's children learned to write, but peasant children did not.

Reading Check
Analyze Effects
How did writing help unite China?

Zhou and the Dynastic Cycle

Around 1027 BC, a people called the Zhou (joh) overthrew the Shang and established their own dynasty. The Zhou had adopted much of the Shang culture. Therefore, the change in dynasty did not bring sweeping cultural change. Nevertheless, Zhou rule brought new ideas to Chinese civilization.

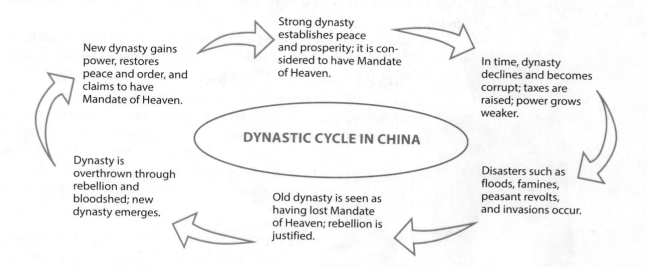

DYNASTIC CYCLE IN CHINA

New dynasty gains power, restores peace and order, and claims to have Mandate of Heaven.

Strong dynasty establishes peace and prosperity; it is considered to have Mandate of Heaven.

In time, dynasty declines and becomes corrupt; taxes are raised; power grows weaker.

Disasters such as floods, famines, peasant revolts, and invasions occur.

Old dynasty is seen as having lost Mandate of Heaven; rebellion is justified.

Dynasty is overthrown through rebellion and bloodshed; new dynasty emerges.

Mandate of Heaven To justify their conquest, the Zhou leaders declared that the final Shang king had been such a poor ruler that the gods had taken away the Shang's rule and given it to the Zhou. This justification developed over time into a broader view that royal authority came from heaven. A just ruler had divine approval, known as the **Mandate of Heaven**. A wicked or foolish king could lose the Mandate of Heaven and so lose the right to rule.

The Mandate of Heaven became central to the Chinese view of government. Floods, riots, and other calamities might be signs that the ancestral spirits were displeased with a king's rule. In that case, the Mandate of Heaven might pass to another noble family. This was the Chinese explanation for rebellion, civil war, and the rise of a new dynasty. Historians describe the pattern of rise, decline, and replacement of dynasties as the **dynastic cycle**.

Control Through Feudalism The Zhou Dynasty controlled lands that stretched far beyond the Huang He in the north to the Chang Jiang in the south. To govern this vast area, it gave control over different regions to members of the royal family and other trusted nobles. This established a system called **feudalism**. Feudalism is a political system in which nobles, or lords, are granted the use of lands that legally belong to the king. In return, the nobles owe loyalty and military service to the king and protection to the people who live on their estates. Similar systems would arise centuries later in both Japan and Europe.

At first, the local lords lived in small walled towns and had to submit to the superior strength and control of the Zhou rulers. Gradually, however, the lords grew stronger as the towns grew into cities and expanded into the surrounding territory. Peoples who had been hostile toward the lords gradually accepted their rule and adopted Zhou ways. As a result, the local lords became less dependent on the king. Over time, they increasingly fought among themselves and with neighboring peoples for wealth and territory.

Vocabulary
mandate a command or instruction from a higher authority

Improvements in Technology and Trade The Zhou Dynasty produced many innovations.

- Roads and canals were built to stimulate trade and agriculture.
- Coined money was introduced, which further improved trade.
- Blast furnaces that produced cast iron were developed.

Zhou cast iron production would not be matched in Europe until the Middle Ages. The Zhou used iron to create weapons, especially dagger-axes and swords. They also used it for common agricultural tools such as sickles, knives, and spades. Iron tools made farm work easier and more productive. The ability to grow more food helped Zhou farmers support thriving cities.

These Chinese coins are made of bronze. Their shape resembles a digging tool such as a hoe or spade.

A Period of Warring States The Zhou ruled from around 1027 to 256 BC. The Zhou empire was generally peaceful and stable. Gradually, however, Zhou rule weakened. In 771 BC, nomads from the north and west sacked the Zhou capital and murdered the Zhou monarch. A few members of the royal family escaped and set up a new capital at Luoyang.

However, the Zhou kings at Luoyang were almost powerless, and they could not control the noble families. The lords sought every opportunity to pick fights with neighboring lords. As their power grew, these warlords claimed to be kings in their own territory. As a result, the later years of the Zhou are often called "the time of the warring states."

Amid the bloodshed, traditional values collapsed. The very heart of Chinese civilization—love of order, harmony, and respect for authority—had been replaced with chaos, arrogance, and defiance. The dynastic cycle was about to bring a new start to Chinese civilization.

Reading Check
Synthesize
According to Chinese beliefs, what role did the Mandate of Heaven play in the dynastic cycle?

Sanxingdui Culture

The powerful Huang He river dynasties of ancient China were not alone in shaping Chinese culture. The river systems of southwest China, located in modern-day Sichuan Province, also nourished dynasties with large cities and distinctive cultures. Little was known, however, about the ancient kingdoms and cultures of this region and their importance until the discovery of the Sanxingdui (san•shing•dway) culture in the 20th century.

Unearthing a Lost Culture First discovered in 1929, significant archaeological findings at the Sanxingdui site, located near Sichuan's capital city Chengdu, did not occur until the site's rediscovery in 1986. Sanxingdui culture became identifiable for its bronze metalwork. The bronze artifacts discovered at the site were unlike anything unearthed before. Researchers initially had difficulty pinpointing the origins of the bronze statues and the jade and gold artifacts at the site. They later concluded that they likely

This gold-plated mask is on display at the Sanxingdui Museum. Similar masks and other artifacts surprised researchers as this style of art was unknown in Chinese art history until 1986.

belonged to the ancient Shu Kingdom. While research continues, the discovery of the Sanxingdui culture challenges the theory of Huang He river dynasties forming the cradle of Chinese civilization.

The Mysterious Sanxingdui Civilization Artifacts and some geological clues have helped archaeologists speculate about the mysterious civilization that lived in the walled city along the Minjiang River. Some archaeologists and historians believe the people of the Sanxingdui culture purposefully dismantled the city itself between 3,000 and 2,800 years ago. Historians are still trying to find out why they might have done this. Other experts believe the culture disappeared as a result of war and flood, but there isn't enough evidence to support this conclusion. How the Sanxingdui civilization came to an end still remains a mystery.

Reading Check
Summarize
What is important about the discovery of the Sanxingdui civilization?

Lesson 5 Assessment

1. **Organize Information** Create a timeline with three important events in Chinese history.

Which event do you think was a turning point in Chinese history?

2. **Key Terms and People** For each term or name, write a sentence explaining its significance.

3. **Analyze Effects** In your judgment, what are the benefits and drawbacks of the belief that the group was more important than the individual?

4. **Contrast** How did the social classes in Shang society differ from those in Egyptian society?

5. **Analyze Motives** Do you think that the Zhou Dynasty's downfall resulted from its method of control? Why or why not?

Module 2 Assessment

Key Terms and People

For each term or name below, write a sentence explaining its connection to early river valley civilizations from 3500–450 BC.

1. Fertile Crescent
2. city-state
3. polytheism
4. empire
5. pharaoh
6. hieroglyphics
7. Harappan civilization
8. Mandate of Heaven

Main Ideas

Use your notes and the information in the module to answer the following questions.

Case Study: Civilization

1. What economic changes resulted from food surpluses in agricultural villages?
2. Why did the growth of civilization make government necessary?
3. Why did a system of record-keeping develop in civilizations?

City-States in Mesopotamia

4. What is the Fertile Crescent and why is it called that?
5. Name three disadvantages of Sumer's natural environment.
6. What circumstances led to the beginning of organized government?

Pyramids on the Nile

7. Why did the Egyptians build pyramids?
8. Herodotus remarked that Egypt was the "gift of the Nile." What did he mean by that?

Planned Cities on the Indus

9. What does the uniformity of Indus Valley cities tell us about their government?
10. What evidence exists to show that Indus Valley civilizations traded with Sumer?

River Dynasties in China

11. What was the great advantage of the Chinese written language?
12. According to the dynastic cycle in China, what consequences can occur when dynasties fail to meet the basic needs of their people?

Critical Thinking

1. **Organize Information** Create a Venn diagram that compares religious beliefs among these ancient civilizations.

2. **Draw Conclusions** Why was it necessary to develop writing before civilization could advance?

3. **Make Inferences** What reasons might be suggested for the location of civilizations along river valleys?

4. **Compare** How do the archaeological and historical artifacts found in the Mesopotamian, Shang, and Indus River valley civilizations show similarities between these early civilizations?

Engage with History

Now that you have read about the development of four civilizations, think about how laws differ from place to place and how they have developed. Consider the laws written in Hammurabi's Code. Imagine you are a government official. Create talking points for a debate to support your take on the following question: What should be the main purpose of laws—to promote good behavior or to punish bad behavior? Compare your talking points with those of at least one other classmate.

Focus on Writing

Interaction with Environment Write an essay comparing the ways different geographic issues influenced settlement, trading networks, and the sustainability of each ancient civilization discussed in this module. Include details of how each civilization interacted with its environment.

Consider the following issues:

- flooding
- the junction of two rivers (Fertile Crescent)
- limited fertile lands

Multimedia Activity

Creating a Multimedia Presentation

Using the Internet, the library, or other credible resources, research the family structure in Sumer, Egypt, Indus Valley, and early Chinese civilizations in relation to their social classes.

- Explain the family structure in each of the civilizations (such as matriarchal, nuclear, extended, multiple spouses).
- Describe the social class structure of each civilization.
- Compare the differences in family structure based on social class within each civilization.

Module 3

People and Ideas on the Move

🌐

Essential Question

What ideas and innovations did ancient cultures in India and the eastern Mediterranean develop, and how were they influential?

About the Photo: Goods from as far away as Britain and western Africa were traded at Phoenician ports in the eastern Mediterranean. Phoenician port cities, such as Tyre and Sidon, became wealthy centers of trade.

▶ *Explore ONLINE!*

HISTORY.

VIDEOS, including...
- Elements of the Hindu Faith
- Jainism
- King Solomon
- Jewish Exile in Babylonia

✔ Document Based Investigations

✔ Graphic Organizers

✔ Interactive Games

✔ Image with Hotspots: Hittite Iron Making

✔ Image with Hotspots: Phoenician Shipping and Trade

In this module you will learn about how migrations and trade led to the foundations of Hinduism, Buddhism, and Judaism.

What You Will Learn ...

Timeline of Events 2000 BC–250 BC

▶ Explore ONLINE!

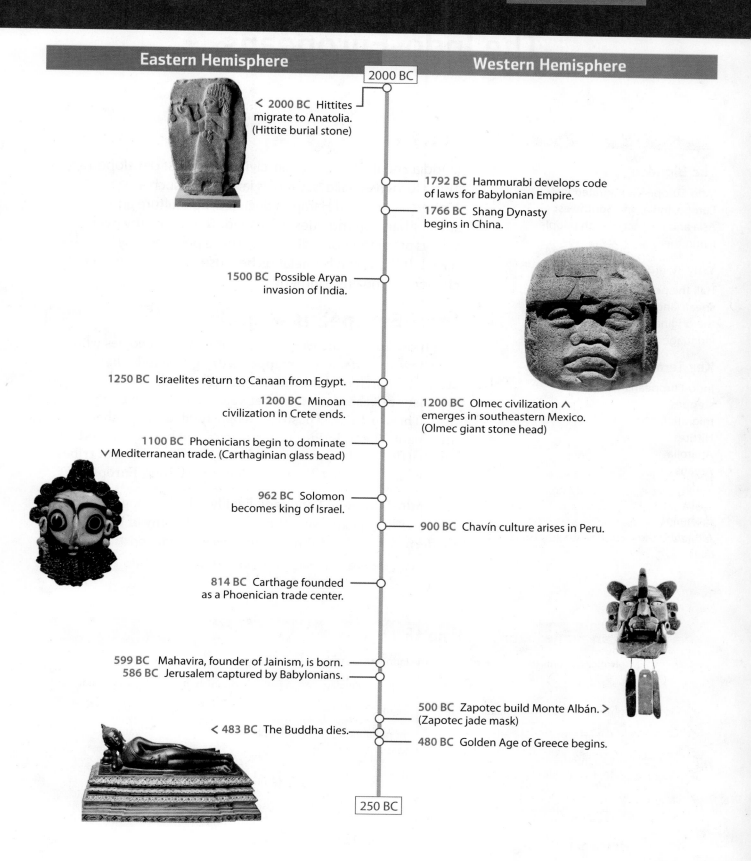

Eastern Hemisphere

2000 BC

< 2000 BC Hittites migrate to Anatolia. (Hittite burial stone)

1500 BC Possible Aryan invasion of India.

1250 BC Israelites return to Canaan from Egypt.

1200 BC Minoan civilization in Crete ends.

1100 BC Phoenicians begin to dominate ∨ Mediterranean trade. (Carthaginian glass bead)

962 BC Solomon becomes king of Israel.

814 BC Carthage founded as a Phoenician trade center.

599 BC Mahavira, founder of Jainism, is born.
586 BC Jerusalem captured by Babylonians.

< 483 BC The Buddha dies.

250 BC

Western Hemisphere

1792 BC Hammurabi develops code of laws for Babylonian Empire.

1766 BC Shang Dynasty begins in China.

1200 BC Olmec civilization ∧ emerges in southeastern Mexico. (Olmec giant stone head)

900 BC Chavín culture arises in Peru.

500 BC Zapotec build Monte Albán. **>** (Zapotec jade mask)

480 BC Golden Age of Greece begins.

The Indo-Europeans

The Big Idea

Indo-Europeans migrated into Europe, India, and Southwest Asia and interacted with peoples living there.

Why It Matters Now

Half the people living today speak languages that stem from the original Indo-European languages.

Key Terms and People

Indo-Europeans
steppes
migration
Hittites
Anatolia
Aryans
Vedas
caste
Brahmin
Mahabharata

Setting the Stage

In India and in Mesopotamia, civilizations first developed along lush river valleys. Even as large cities such as Mohenjo-Daro and Harappa declined, agriculture and small urban communities flourished. These wealthy river valleys attracted nomadic tribes. These peoples may have left their own homelands because of warfare or changes in the environment.

Indo-Europeans Migrate

The **Indo-Europeans** were a group of nomadic peoples who may have come from the **steppes**—dry grasslands that stretched north of the Caucasus (KAW•kuh•suhs). The Caucasus are the mountains between the Black and Caspian Seas. These primarily pastoral people herded cattle, sheep, and goats. The Indo-Europeans also tamed horses and rode into battle in light, two-wheeled chariots. They lived in tribes that spoke forms of a language that we call Indo-European.

The Indo-European Language Family The languages of the Indo-Europeans were the ancestors of many of the modern languages of Europe, Southwest Asia, and

Language Family Resemblances

Notice the similarities of words within the Indo-European family of languages.

English	Sanskrit	Persian	Spanish	German
mother	mātár	muhdáhr	madre	mutter
father	pitár	puhdáhr	padre	vater
daughter	duhitár	dukhtáhr	hija	tochter
new	návas	now	nuevo	neu
six	sát	shahsh	seis	sechs

South Asia. English, Spanish, Persian, and Hindi all trace their origins back to different forms of the original Indo-European language.

Historians can tell where Indo-European tribes settled by their languages. Some Slavic speakers moved north and west. Others, who spoke early Celtic, Germanic, and Italic languages, moved west through Europe. Speakers of Greek and Persian went south. The Aryans (AIR•ee•uhnz), who spoke an early form of Sanskrit, may have relocated to India.

An Unexplained Migration The origins and migrations of the Indo-European peoples are controversial topics among scholars with many differing views. There is no certainty as to why these people left their homelands in the steppes. Whatever the reason, Indo-European nomads began to migrate outward in all directions between 1700 and 1200 BC. These **migrations**, movements of a people from one region to another, happened in waves over a long period of time.

The Hittite Empire

By about 2000 BC, one group of Indo-European speakers, the **Hittites**, occupied **Anatolia** (an•uh•TOH•lee•uh), also called Asia Minor. Anatolia is a huge peninsula in modern-day Turkey that juts out into the Black and Mediterranean Seas. Anatolia is a high, rocky plateau, rich in timber and agriculture. Nearby mountains hold important mineral deposits. Separate Hittite city-states came together to form an empire there in about 1650 BC. The city of Hattusas (hah•TOO•sahs) was its capital.

The Hittite Empire went on to dominate Southwest Asia for 450 years. Hittites occupied Babylon, the chief city in the Tigris-Euphrates Valley, and struggled with Egypt for control of northern Syria. Neither the Hittites nor the Egyptians were able to get the upper hand. So, the two peoples ended their conflicts by signing a peace treaty. They each pledged to help the other fight off future invaders.

Hittites Adopt and Adapt The Hittites used their own Indo-European language with one another. However, for international use, they adopted Akkadian, the language of the Babylonians they had conquered. The Hittites borrowed ideas about literature, art, politics, and law from the

Reading Check
Find Main Ideas
Where do some historians think the Indo-Europeans lived before they arrived in India?

This illustration shows the process the Hittites used to make tools and weapons from iron.

Mesopotamians. The Hittites thus blended their own traditions with those of other, more advanced peoples.

Chariots and Iron Technology The Hittites excelled in the technology of war. They conquered an empire against Egyptian opposition—largely through their superior chariots and their iron weapons. The Hittite war chariot was light and easy to maneuver. The chariot had two wheels and a wooden frame covered with leather and was pulled by two or sometimes four horses. The Hittite chariot proved itself a superb fighting machine.

The Hittites used iron in their chariots, and they owed many of their military victories to the skill of their ironworkers. Ancient peoples had long known that iron was stronger than bronze. They also knew that it could hold a sharper edge. However, the process of purifying iron ore and working it into weapons and tools is complex. Around 1500 BC, the Hittites were the first in Southwest Asia to work with iron and harden it into weapons of war. The raw materials they needed—iron ore and wood to make charcoal—were easily available to them in the mountains of Anatolia. Knowledge of iron technology traveled widely with the Hittites—in both their trade and conquests.

Despite its military might, the powerful Hittite Empire fell quite suddenly around the year 1190 BC. As part of a great wave of invasions, tribes attacked from the north and burned the Hittite capital city.

Reading Check
Analyze Effects
How did environmental features in Anatolia help the Hittites advance technologically?

Aryans Transform India

Before 2000 BC, the Hittites began establishing themselves in Anatolia. At the same time, some scholars believe, another Indo-European people, the **Aryans**, whose homeland was probably somewhere between the Caspian and Aral Seas, crossed over the northwest mountain passes into the Indus River valley of India. Other scholars believe the Aryans originated in India. There is no archaeological evidence to prove either hypothesis.

Though they left almost no archaeological record, their sacred literature, the **Vedas** (VAY•duhz), left a picture of Aryan life. The Vedas are four collections of prayers, hymns, instructions for performing rituals, and spells and incantations. The most important of the collections is the Rig Veda. The Rig Veda contains 1,028 hymns to Aryan gods. For many years, no written form of the Vedas existed. Instead, elders of one generation passed on this tradition orally to the next generation.

A Caste System Develops According to the Rig Veda, ancient Indian society was divided into four groups called varnas. Later, in the 15th century AD, explorers from Portugal encountered this social system and called these groups **castes** (kasts). The four varnas are:

- **Brahmins**, the highest ranking, and smallest numerically, of the groups—priests and teachers
- warriors and rulers
- traders, farmers, and herders
- laborers and peasants

The Aryan Caste System

The four major castes emerged from Purusha (the first human being) shown below. Purusha is identified with the creator god Brahma. The Brahmins (priests and teachers) were his mouth; the warriors and rulers were his arms; the traders, farmers, and herders were his legs; and the laborers and peasants were his feet.

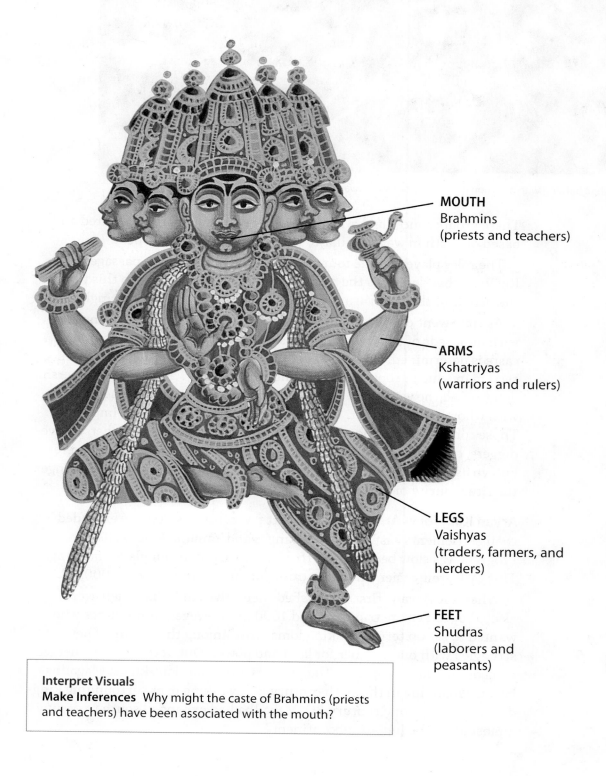

MOUTH
Brahmins
(priests and teachers)

ARMS
Kshatriyas
(warriors and rulers)

LEGS
Vaishyas
(traders, farmers, and herders)

FEET
Shudras
(laborers and peasants)

Interpret Visuals
Make Inferences Why might the caste of Brahmins (priests and teachers) have been associated with the mouth?

This painting of Krishna battling with a demon in the form of a snake was created in 1785.

These groups, once fluid and flexible, later became more structured and based on birth in ways similar to the guild system in Europe.

The roles played by the four varnas were alluded to in a passage in the Rig Veda that describes the creation of humans. According to this passage, the people of the four varnas were created from the body of a single being.

As time went on, the four basic castes gradually grew more complex—with hundreds of subdivisions. Classical texts make no mention of how caste is determined. However, over time, some communities developed a system in which people were born into their caste. Their caste membership determined the work they did, whom they could marry, and the people with whom they could eat. Cleanliness and purity became all-important. Those considered the most impure because of their work (butchers, grave-diggers, collectors of trash) lived outside the caste structure. They were known as "untouchables," since even their touch was believed to endanger the ritual purity of others.

Aryan Kingdoms Arise Over the next few centuries, Aryans extended their settlements east, along the Ganges and Yamuna River valleys. Progress was slow because of difficulties clearing the jungle for farming. This task grew easier when iron came into use in India about 1000 BC.

When the Aryans first established themselves in India, chiefs were elected by the entire tribe. Around 1000 BC, however, minor kings who wanted to set up territorial kingdoms arose among the Aryans. They struggled with one another for land and power. Out of this strife emerged a major kingdom: Magadha. Under a series of ambitious kings, Magadha began expanding in the sixth century BC by taking over surrounding king-doms. By the second century BC, Magadha had expanded south to occupy almost all of the Indian subcontinent.

The **Mahabharata** (mah•huh•BAH•ruh•tuh), one of the great epics of India, reflects the struggles that took place in India as the Aryan kings fought for control of Indian lands. One part of the *Mahabharata* is the *Bhagavad Gita*. It tells the story of a warrior prince named Arjuna, who is counseled by his chariot driver, Krishna, an incarnation of the Hindu deity Vishnu.

One of the most famous incidents in Indian literature occurs when Krishna instructs the young warrior on the proper way to live, fight, and die:

> *"He who thinks this Self [eternal spirit] to be a slayer, and he who thinks this Self to be slain, are both without discernment; the Soul slays not, neither is it slain. . . . But if you will not wage this lawful battle, then will you fail your own [caste] law and your honor, and incur sin. . . . The people will name you with dishonor; and to a man of fame dishonor is worse than death."*

—Krishna, speaking in the *Bhagavad Gita*

Reading Check
Make Inferences
How were the more physical forms of work viewed by Aryans?

The violence and confusion of the time led many to speculate about the place of the gods and human beings in the world. As a result, religion in India gradually changed. New religions were born, which you will read about in the next few lessons.

Lesson 1 Assessment

1. **Organize Information** What are some languages that originated from Indo-European roots?

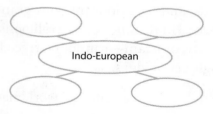
Indo-European

2. **Key Terms and People** For each key term in the lesson, write a sentence explaining its significance.

3. **Form Opinions** What important contributions did the Aryans make to the culture and way of life in India in terms of religion, literature, and roles in society?

4. **Draw Conclusions** What made the Hittite chariot an excellent fighting machine?

5. **Analyze Effect** What are the advantages and disadvantages of the varna system?

The Origins of Hinduism

The Big Idea

The religion of Hinduism developed and evolved over a long time in India, giving rise to a variety of beliefs and practices as well as other religions, such as Jainism.

Why It Matters Now

Today almost one billion people practice Hinduism in India and other parts of Asia.

Key Terms and People

reincarnation
karma
Jainism

Setting the Stage

Over time, religion in ancient India developed to include the worship of thousands of different gods. Different religious practices also led to different ways of living, and this made life more complex. This complexity led some people to question the world and their place in it. They even questioned the enormous wealth and power held by the Brahmin priests. Out of this turmoil, new religious ideas arose that have continued to influence millions of people today.

Hinduism Evolves over Centuries

Hinduism is a collection of religious beliefs that developed slowly over a long period of time. Most aspects of the religion can be traced back to ancient times. In a Hindu marriage today, for example, the bride and groom marry in the presence of the sacred fire as they did centuries ago. The faithful recite daily verses from the Vedas.

From time to time, scholars have tried to organize the many popular cults, gods, and traditions into one grand system of belief. However, Hinduism—unlike religions such as Buddhism, Christianity, or Islam—cannot be traced back to one founder with a single set of ideas.

Origins and Beliefs Hindus share a common worldview. They see religion as a way of liberating the soul from the illusions, disappointments, and mistakes of everyday existence. Sometime between 750 and 550 BC, Hindu teachers tried to interpret and explain the hidden meaning of the Vedic hymns. The teachers' comments were later written down and became known as the Upanishads (oo•PAHN•ih•shahdz).

The Upanishads are written as dialogues, or discussions, between a student and a teacher. In the course of the dialogues, the two explore how a person can achieve liberation from desires and suffering. This is described as *moksha* (MOHK•shah), a state of perfect understanding of all things. The teacher distinguishes between atman, the individual soul of a living being, and Brahman, the world soul that contains and unites all atmans. Here is how one teacher explains the unifying spirit of Brahman:

> *"Thou art woman, Thou art man, Thou art the lad and the maiden too. Thou art the old man tottering on his staff: Once born thou comest to be, thy face turned every way! A dark-blue moth art Thou, green [parrot] with red eyes. Pregnant with lightning—seasons, seas: Thyself beginningless, all things dost Thou pervade. From Thee all worlds were born."*

—Svetasvatara Upanishad. IV. 3–4

Hindus believe that everything in the world is an aspect of Brahman.

Now and Then

Hinduism Today

Hinduism originated on the Indian subcontinent and its earliest traditions date as far back as 2000 BC. Today, nearly one billion people practice some form of Hinduism, mostly in South and Southeast Asia.

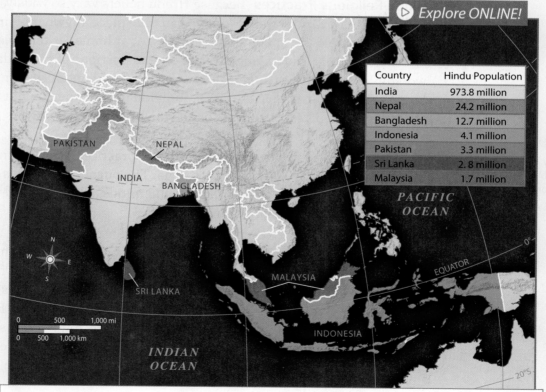

▷ Explore ONLINE!

Country	Hindu Population
India	973.8 million
Nepal	24.2 million
Bangladesh	12.7 million
Indonesia	4.1 million
Pakistan	3.3 million
Sri Lanka	2.8 million
Malaysia	1.7 million

Interpret Maps

1. **Movement** What factors likely contributed to the spread of Hinduism from India into Southeast Asia?

2. **Location** Why might Bangladesh have a large Hindu population?

When a person understands the relationship between atman and Brahman, that person achieves perfect understanding (*moksha*) and a release from life in this world. This understanding does not usually come in one lifetime. By the process of **reincarnation** (rebirth), an individual soul or spirit is born again and again until *moksha* is achieved. A soul's **karma**—good or bad deeds—follows from one reincarnation to another. Karma also influences specific life circumstances, such as one's spiritual or religious tendencies, one's state of health, one's wealth or poverty, and so on.

Hinduism Changes and Develops Hinduism has gone through many changes over the last 2,500 years. The world soul, Brahman, was sometimes seen as having the personalities of three gods: Brahma, the creator; Vishnu, the protector; and Shiva, the destroyer. Vishnu also took on many forms or personalities, for example, as Krishna, the divine cowherder, and as Rama, the perfect king. Over the centuries, Brahma gradually faded into the background, while the many forms of Devi, a great Mother Goddess, grew in importance.

Hindus today are free to choose the deity they worship or to choose none at all. Most, however, follow a family tradition that may go back centuries. They are also free to choose among three different paths for achieving *moksha*. These are the path of right thinking, the path of right action, or the path of religious devotion.

Hindu Religious Practices Because Hindu beliefs vary so widely, religious practices vary as well. Worship can take place anywhere—in large elaborate temples, in small village shrines, or at home. At temples, priests or other spiritual leaders might recite or read portions of the Vedas to worshipers. Sometimes an image of a god is carried out of the temple and brought before the people. At home, individual worshipers might offer food, drink, or gifts to a god. He or she might say special prayers, or meditate, or silently reflect upon the world and its nature.

To help them meditate, some Hindus also practice a series of integrated physical and mental exercises called yoga. The purpose of yoga is to teach people how to focus their bodies and minds, which will aid their meditation and help them attain *moksha*.

At some point during their lives, many Hindus desire to make a pilgrimage, or religious journey, to a holy location. Among the places considered sacred by many Hindus is the Ganges River, which is thought to flow from the feet of Vishnu and over the head of Shiva. Through this contact with two gods, the river's waters become holy. As a result, many Hindus believe that bathing in the Ganges will purify them and remove some of their bad karma. Huge festivals held in towns along the Ganges each year attract millions of Hindu pilgrims from around the world.

Vocabulary
integrated blended together or combined

Vishnu grew to become a major Hindu god. He is seen here as the whole universe in all its variety. He is blue, the color of infinity.

Reading Check
Make Inferences
How might the lack of a single founder result in Hinduism changing more over time than other religions?

Hinduism and Society Hindu ideas about karma and reincarnation tended to strengthen the caste system. If a person was born as an upper-caste male—a Brahmin, warrior, or merchant—his good fortune was said to come from good karma earned in a former life. However, a person who was born as a laborer or an untouchable might be getting the results of bad deeds in a former life. In the view of many people, the laws of karma worked with the same certainty as the world's other natural laws. Good karma brought good fortune and bad karma resulted in bad fortune. However, a person of any varna has the possibility of achieving *moksha* in his or her present life.

For many Hindus, caste structure dominated every aspect of their lives. These beliefs determined what one could eat and the way in which one ate it, personal cleanliness, the people one could associate with, how one dressed, and so on. Today, however, social life is far less rigid.

New Religions Arise

The same period of speculation reflected in the Upanishads also led to the rise of two other religions: Jainism (JY•nihz•uhm) and Buddhism.

Jainism Mahavira, the founder of **Jainism**, was born about 599 BC and died in 527 BC. His teachings oppose the religious rituals that most Hindus of the time emphasized. The Jains thought that ritual was unnecessary, because people could achieve *moksha* by giving up all worldly things and carefully controlling their actions.

Mahavira believed that everything in the universe has a soul and so should not be harmed. Jain monks carry the doctrine of nonviolence to its logical conclusion, carefully avoid harming any living creature, from people to insects. They sweep ants off their path and wear gauze masks over their mouths to avoid breathing in an insect accidentally. In keeping with this nonviolence, followers of Jainism looked for occupations that would not harm any creature. So they have a tradition of working in trade and commerce. Jains are usually vegetarians, refusing to eat meat from any animal.

In addition to renouncing violence, Jains promise to tell only the truth and to avoid stealing. They strive to eliminate greed, anger, prejudice, and gossip from their lives. Any of these things, they believe, can prevent a person from achieving *moksha*.

The most devout of Jains give up all of their possessions and become monks or nuns. They live outdoors, seeking shelter only during the rainy season. Jainism calls upon those who are not monks to periodically fast, especially during festivals and on holy days, and to limit their worldly possessions.

The Jains' view of other religions is much the same as the Hindu view. Jains have traditionally preached tolerance of all religions. As a result, they have made few efforts to convert followers of other faiths. Because of this tolerance, Jains have not sent out missionaries. So, almost all of the nearly five million Jains in the world today live in India. In the next lesson, you will learn about a more widespread religion in Asia that also developed from the beliefs of the Vedic Age, Buddhism.

Vocabulary
fast to eat very little

Reading Check
Synthesize How far might the Jain respect for life extend?

Lesson 2 Assessment

1. **Organize Information** Create a two-column graphic organizer similar to the one shown and fill it in with key principles of Hinduism and Jainism. What principles do the two religions share?

Hinduism	Jainism
1.	1.
2.	2.
3.	3.

2. **Key Terms and People** For each key term or person in the lesson, write a sentence explaining its significance.

3. **Make Inferences** How might the belief in reincarnation provide a form of social control?

4. **Compare** How are the Vedas and the Upanishads similar?

5. **Make Inferences** Look at the image of and caption for Vishnu in this lesson. Why might the color blue represent infinity?

The Origins of Buddhism

The Big Idea

Buddhism, which teaches people that they can escape the suffering of the world through the Buddha's teachings, developed in India and spread to other parts of Asia and the world.

Why It Matters Now

Today roughly 7% of the world's population practice Buddhism. The spread of Buddhism has had a profound influence on a variety of societies throughout the Asia-Pacific region.

Key Terms and People

Siddhartha Gautama
enlightenment
nirvana

Setting the Stage

In addition to Hinduism, another of the world's major religions developed in ancient India. That religion was Buddhism. Unlike Hinduism, which evolved over thousands of years, Buddhism can be traced back to the teachings of a single founder, **Siddhartha Gautama**, also called Buddha.

The Buddha Seeks Enlightenment

Buddhism developed out of the same period of religious questioning that shaped modern Hinduism and Jainism. The founder of Buddhism, Siddhartha Gautama (sihd•DAHR•tuh GOW•tuh•muh), was born into a noble family that lived in Kapilavastu, in the foothills of the Himalayas in Nepal. According to Buddhist legend, the baby exhibited the marks of a great man. A prophecy indicated that if the child stayed at home he was destined to become a world ruler. If the child left home, however, he would become a universal spiritual leader. To make sure the boy would be a great king and world ruler, his father isolated him in his palace. Separated from the world, Siddhartha married and had a son.

Siddhartha's Quest Siddhartha never ceased thinking about the world that lay outside, which he had never seen. When he was 29, he ventured outside the palace four times. First he saw an old man, next a sick man, then a corpse, and finally a wandering holy man who seemed at peace with himself. Siddhartha understood these events to mean that every living thing experiences old age, sickness, and death and that only a religious life offers a refuge from this inevitable suffering. Siddhartha decided to spend his life searching for religious truth and an end to life's suffering. So, soon after learning of his son's birth, he left the palace.

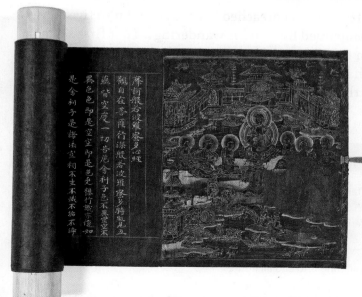

Buddhist scroll painted in Japan in the 1100s

Siddhartha Gautama
(c. 563–483 BC)

According to Buddhist tradition, Siddhartha Gautama's mother had dreamt of a beautiful elephant that was bright as silver. When asked to interpret the dream, Brahmin priests declared that the child to be born would either be a great monarch or a Buddha (an enlightened one).

Tradition also relates that at Gautama's birth, he exhibited the signs of a child destined for greatness. There were 32 such signs, including golden-tinged skin, webbed fingers and toes, a knob on the top of his skull, a long tongue, a tuft of hair between his eyebrows, and a thousand-spoked wheel on each foot. Some images of the Buddha display these traits.

Reading Check
Summarize
How did Siddhartha Gautama become the Buddha?

Siddhartha wandered through the forests of India for six years seeking **enlightenment**, or wisdom. He tried many ways of reaching an enlightened state. He first debated with other religious seekers. Then he fasted, eating only six grains of rice a day. Yet none of these methods brought him to the truth, and he continued to suffer. Finally, he sat in meditation under a large fig tree. After 49 days of meditation, he achieved an understanding of the cause of suffering in this world. From then on, he was known as the Buddha, meaning "the enlightened one."

The Teachings of Buddhism

After he achieved enlightenment, the Buddha set out to spread what he had learned to other people. His lessons became the basic teachings of Buddhism.

Origins and Beliefs The Buddha preached his first sermon to five companions who had accompanied him on his wanderings. That first sermon became a landmark in the history of the world's religions. In it, he laid out the four main ideas that he had come to understand in his enlightenment. He called those ideas the Four Noble Truths.

The Four Noble Truths	
First Noble Truth	Life is filled with suffering and sorrow.
Second Noble Truth	The cause of all suffering is people's selfish desire for the temporary pleasures of this world.
Third Noble Truth	The way to end all suffering is to end all desires.
Fourth Noble Truth	The way to overcome such desires and attain enlightenment is to follow the Eightfold Path, which is called the Middle Way between desires and self-denial.

The Eightfold Path, a guide to behavior, was like a staircase. For the Buddha, those who were seeking enlightenment had to master one step at a time. Most often, this mastery would occur over many lifetimes. Here is how he described the Middle Way and its Eightfold Path:

> *"What is the Middle Way? . . . It is the Noble Eightfold Path—Right Views, Right Resolve, Right Speech, Right Conduct, Right Livelihood, Right Effort, Right Mindfulness, and Right Concentration. This is the Middle Way."*

> —Buddha, from *Samyutta Nikaya*

By following the Eightfold Path, anyone could reach **nirvana**, the Buddha's word for release from selfishness and pain.

As in Hinduism, the Buddha accepted the idea of reincarnation. He also accepted a cyclical, or repetitive, view of history, where the world is created and destroyed over and over again. However, the Buddha rejected the many gods of Hinduism. Instead, he taught a way of enlightenment. Like many of his time, the Buddha reacted against the privileges of the Brahmin priests, and thus he rejected the caste system. The final goals of both religions—*moksha* for Hindus and nirvana for Buddhists—are similar. Both involve a perfect state of understanding and a break from the chain of reincarnations.

The Religious Community The five disciples who heard the Buddha's first sermon were the first monks admitted to the *sangha*, or Buddhist religious order. At first, the *sangha* was a community of Buddhist monks and nuns. However, *sangha* eventually referred to the entire religious community. It included Buddhist laity (those who hadn't devoted their entire lives to religion). The religious community, together with the Buddha and the *dharma* (Buddhist doctrine or teachings), make up the "Three Jewels" of Buddhism.

Buddhist tradition says that just before he died, the Buddha lay on his right side between two trees. This reclining Buddha is made of bronze.

Buddhist monks view a temple at Angkor Wat in Cambodia.

Buddhism and Society Because of his rejection of the caste system, many of the Buddha's early followers included laborers and craftspeople. He also gained a large following in northeast India, where the Aryans had less influence. The Buddha reluctantly admitted women to religious orders. He feared, however, that women's presence would distract men from their religious duties.

Monks and nuns took vows (solemn promises) to live a life of poverty, to be nonviolent, and not to marry. They wandered throughout India spreading the Buddha's teachings. Missionaries carried only a begging bowl to receive daily charity offerings from people. During the rainy season, they retreated to caves high up in the hillsides. Gradually, these seasonal retreats became permanent monasteries—some for men, others for women. One monastery, Nalanda, developed into a great university that also attracted non-Buddhists.

The teachings of the Buddha were written down shortly after his death. Buddhist sacred literature also includes commentaries, rules about monastic life, manuals on how to meditate, and legends about the Buddha's previous reincarnations (the *Jatakas*). This sacred literature was first written down in the first century BC.

The Development of Buddhism

During the centuries following the Buddha's death, missionaries were able to spread his faith over large parts of Asia. Buddhist missionaries went to Sri Lanka and Southeast Asia in the third century BC. Buddhist ideas also

Reading Check
Compare
In what ways are Buddhism and Hinduism similar?

traveled along Central Asian trade routes to China. However, Buddhism never gained a significant foothold in India, the country of its origin.

Buddhism in India Several theories exist about Buddhism's gradual disappearance in India. One theory states that Hinduism simply absorbed Buddhism. The two religions constantly influenced each other. Over time, the Buddha came to be identified by Hindus as one of the ten incarnations (reappearances on Earth) of the god Vishnu. Hindus, therefore, felt no need to convert to Buddhism.

Nonetheless, despite the small number of Buddhists in India, the region has always been an important place of pilgrimages for Buddhists. Today, as they have for centuries, Buddhist pilgrims flock to visit spots associated with the Buddha's life. These sites include his birthplace at Kapilavastu, the fig tree near Gaya, and the site of his first sermon near Varanasi. Buddhists also visit the *stupas,* or sacred mounds, that are said to contain his relics. The pilgrims circle around the sacred object or sanctuary, moving in a clockwise direction. They also lie face down on the ground as a sign of humility and leave flowers. These three actions are important rituals in Buddhist worship.

Divisions of Buddhism After the Buddha's death, differing opinions arose concerning the correct teachings and practices of Buddhism. Eventually, three main traditions formed—Theravada, Mahayana, and Tibetan Buddhism. Each sect believed that its teachings and practices most closely followed the way of the Buddha.

Theravada, meaning the Way of the Elders, is the oldest of the Buddhist traditions. It is based on the oldest known Buddhist writings. These writings are collectively called the Pali Canon, because they were written in the Pali language. Theravada teaches that the best way to attain nirvana is to become a monk or a nun and spend all of one's time in meditation. Through this meditation, each person must find his or her own path to enlightenment. As a result, Theravada is very much an individual religion. Those who do not become monks or nuns should support those who do, providing them with food and caring for temples.

In contrast, Mahayana teaches that people can help each other find enlightenment. This tradition incorporates teachings from texts that were written after the Buddha's lifetime. According to these teachings,

Vocabulary
pilgrimages travels to holy places

Now and Then

Buddhism in the West

Throughout the 20th century, large numbers of Asians have immigrated to the West, particularly to North America. Many of them brought Buddhism with them. Today, Buddhist temples are a common feature of many large cities in the West.

Since the 1950s, many non-Asians who were dissatisfied with the religions of the West have turned to Buddhism for insight into life's meaning. Today, Buddhism can claim about one million Asian and non-Asian believers in North America.

it is not necessary to be a monk or a nun to reach nirvana. Anyone can do it, with some help. That help is provided by bodhisattvas, people who have found enlightenment but have not yet passed on to nirvana. Instead, they have remained on Earth to help others find their way. Because of their wisdom and compassion, bodhisattvas are worshiped by some Mahayana Buddhists.

The third Buddhist tradition, Tibetan Buddhism, shares many teachings with Mahayana. In addition to these teachings, however, Tibetan Buddhists believe that they can use special techniques to harness spiritual energy and achieve nirvana in a single lifetime.

Trade and the Spread of Buddhism As important as missionaries were to the spread of Buddhism, traders played an even more crucial role in this process. Along with their products, traders carried Buddhism beyond India to Sri Lanka. Buddhist religion was also brought southeast along trade routes to Burma, Thailand, and the island of Sumatra. Likewise, Buddhism followed the Central Asian trade routes, called the Silk Roads, all the way to China. From China, Buddhism spread to Korea—and from Korea to Japan. As Buddhism encountered other religious traditions outside of India, it continued to change and develop. Because of this blending, various smaller traditions developed within Theravada and Mahayana. For example, a branch of Mahayana known as Zen that emphasized self-discipline and meditation developed in China and spread to Japan.

The movement of trade thus succeeded in making Buddhism the most widespread religion of East Asia. Throughout human history, trade has been a powerful force for the spread of ideas. Just as trade spread Buddhism in East Asia, it helped spread cultural influences in another major region of the world: the Mediterranean basin, as you will learn in the next lesson.

Reading Check
Find Main Ideas
How did Buddhism spread through Asia?

Lesson 3 Assessment

1. **Organize Information** Use a graphic organizer like the one below to take notes on the history of Buddhism.

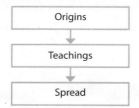

Origins

↓

Teachings

↓

Spread

2. **Key Terms and People** For each key term or person in the lesson, write a sentence explaining its significance.

3. **Evaluate** How did the experiences of Siddhartha Gautama influence his religious and ethical beliefs?

4. **Contrast** How do the three main traditions of Buddhism differ in their approach to enlightenment?

5. **Analyze Effects** Why did Buddhism grow and change as it spread out of India into other parts of Asia?

Seafaring Traders

The Big Idea
Trading societies extended the development of civilizations beyond the Fertile Crescent region.

Why It Matters Now
Traders spread knowledge of reading and writing, including an ancient form of the alphabet that we use today.

Key Terms and People
Minoans
Aegean Sea
Knossos
King Minos
Phoenicians

Setting the Stage

Buddhism spread to Southeast Asia and to East Asia mainly through Buddhist traders. In the Mediterranean, the same process took place: traders in the region carried many new ideas from one society to another. They carried new ways of writing, of governing, and of worshiping their gods.

Minoans Trade in the Mediterranean

A powerful seafaring people, the **Minoans** (mih•NOH•uhnz) dominated trade in the eastern Mediterranean from about 2000 to 1400 BC. They lived on Crete, a large island on the southern edge of the **Aegean Sea** (ee•JEE•uhn). The Minoans produced some of the finest painted pottery of the time. They traded that pottery, along with swords, figurines, and vessels of precious metals, over a large area.

Along with their goods, Minoans also exported their art and culture. These included a unique architecture, burial customs, and religious rituals. Minoan culture had a major influence on Greece, for example. Trading turned Crete into a "stepping stone" for cultural exchange throughout the Mediterranean world.

Unearthing a Brilliant Civilization Archaeologists in the late 19th and early 20th centuries excavated **Knossos**, the Minoan capital city. There, they found the remains of an advanced and thriving culture. It must have been a peaceful one as well, since Minoan cities did not seem to need fortifications to protect them. The archaeologists named the civilization they found in Crete *Minoa* after **King Minos** (MY•nuhs). According to legend, Minos was a king who owned a half-human, half-bull monster called the Minotaur (MIHN•uh•tawr). He kept the monster locked inside a labyrinth, a complicated maze from which no one could escape.

The excavation of Knossos and its painted walls produced much information about Minoans. The wall paintings, as well as the official seals and vases, show the Minoans as

BULL LEAPERS OF KNOSSOS

The wall painting captures the death-defying jump of a Minoan bull leaper in mid-flight. Many works of Minoan art show young men performing incredible acrobatic leaps over the horns of angry bulls. In one case, the gymnast jumps over the bull's horns, makes a somersault off its back, and lands behind its tail.

In another gymnastic feat, some team members hang on to the horns of a bull, using their bodies to cushion its horns and to force its head low, while another team member jumps over its back.

What was the reason for this bull leaping? Was it a sport? Just a "fun" activity? An initiation for young warriors? Or a religious ritual? Most likely it was all of these things.

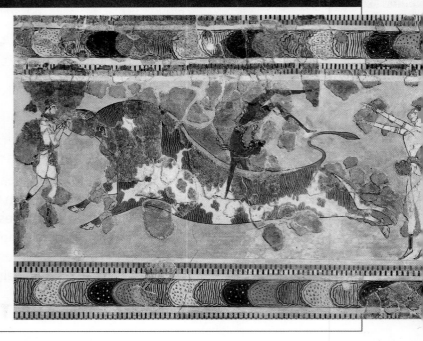

graceful, athletic people who loved nature and beautiful objects. They also enjoyed sports such as boxing, wrestling, and bull leaping.

Many Minoan artworks depict women and their role in religious ceremonies. The art suggests that women held a higher rank than in most neighboring cultures. A great Mother Earth Goddess seems to have ruled over the other gods of Crete. Also, priestesses took charge of some shrines, aided by male assistants.

Some scholars suggest that the Egyptians, through trade, may have influenced Minoan culture. For example, some Minoan religious rites, such as rituals involving bulls, were similar to those of the Egyptians. Also, the Minoan system of writing was influenced by Egyptian hieroglyphics. The Minoans even may have adopted foods, such as dates and pomegranates, from the Egyptians.

Minoan Culture's Mysterious End The Minoan civilization finally ended about 1200 BC. The reasons for its end are unclear. Could it have been the result of some natural disaster? Did the island become overpopulated? Or was it overrun by invaders?

The civilization had withstood previous disasters. In about 1700 BC, a great disaster, perhaps an earthquake, destroyed most Minoan towns and cities. The Minoans rebuilt the cities with equal richness. Then in 1470 BC a series of earthquakes rocked Crete. The quakes were followed by a violent volcanic eruption on the neighboring island of Thera. Imagine the shaking of the earth, the fiery volcanic blast, then a huge tidal wave, and finally a rain of white volcanic ash.

The disaster of 1470 BC was a blow from which the Minoans never fully recovered. This time, the Minoans had trouble rebuilding their cities. Nonetheless, Minoan civilization did linger on for almost 300 years. After that, invaders from Greece may have taken advantage of their weakened condition to destroy them. Some Minoans fled to the mountains to escape the ruin of the kingdom. Crete's influence as a major sea power and cultural force was over.

Phoenicians Spread Trade and Civilization

About 1100 BC, after Crete's decline, the most powerful traders along the Mediterranean were the **Phoenicians** (fih•NEESH•uhnz). Phoenicia was mainly the area now known as Lebanon. Phoenicians never united into a country. Instead, they founded a number of wealthy city-states around the Mediterranean that sometimes competed with one another. The first cities in Phoenicia, such as Byblos, Tyre, and Sidon, were important trading centers.

The Phoenicians were remarkable shipbuilders and seafarers. They were the first Mediterranean people to venture beyond the Strait of Gibraltar. Some scholars believe that the Phoenicians traded for tin with inhabitants of the southern coast of Britain. Some evidence exists for an even more remarkable feat—sailing around the continent of Africa by way of the Red Sea and back through the Strait of Gibraltar. Such a trip was not repeated again for 2,000 years. The Greek historian Herodotus (hih•RAHD•uh•tuhs) relates the feat:

> "The Phoenicians set out from the Red Sea and sailed the southern sea [the Indian Ocean]; whenever autumn came they would put in and sow the land, to whatever part of Libya [Africa] they might come, and there await the harvest; then, having gathered in the crop, they sailed on, so that after two years had passed, it was in the third that they rounded the Pillars of Heracles [Strait of Gibraltar] and came to Egypt. There they said (what some may believe, though I do not) that in sailing round Libya they had the sun on their right hand [in reverse position]."
>
> —Herodotus, in *History*, Book IV (fifth century BC)

Commercial Outposts Around the Mediterranean The Phoenicians' most important city-states in the eastern Mediterranean were Sidon and Tyre, both known for their production of red-purple dye, and Byblos, a trading center for papyrus. Phoenicians built colonies along the northern coast of Africa and the coasts of Sicily, Sardinia, and Spain. The colonies were about 30 miles apart—about the distance a Phoenician ship could sail in a day. The greatest Phoenician colony was at Carthage (KAHR•thihj), in North Africa. Settlers from Tyre founded Carthage in about 814 BC.

The Phoenicians traded goods they got from other lands—wine, weapons, precious metals, ivory, and slaves. They also were known as superb craftspeople who worked in wood, metal, glass, and ivory. Their red-purple dye was produced from the murex, a kind of snail that lived in the waters off Sidon and Tyre. One snail, when left to rot, produced just a drop or two

By 700 BC, Phoenician trading ships included long steering oars and a single sail.

Alphabets—Ancient and Modern

Phoenician	Greek	English
𐤀	Α	A
	Β	B
	Γ	C
	Δ	D
	Ε	E
		F
		G
	Ζ Η	H
	Θ	
	Ι	I
		J
	Κ	K
	Λ Μ	L
	Ν Ξ Ο	M
	Π	N
		O
		P
		Q
	Ρ Σ	R
		S
	Τ Υ φ	T
		U
		V
	Χ	W
	ψ	X
		Y
	Ω	Z

Interpret Charts

1. **Compare** Which letters show the most similarity across the three alphabets?

2. **Make Inferences** Why might one language have fewer letters in its alphabet than another?

of a liquid of a deep red-purple color. Some 60,000 snails were needed to produce one pound of dye, which only royalty could afford.

Phoenicia's Great Legacy: The Alphabet As merchants, the Phoenicians needed a way of recording transactions clearly and quickly. So the Phoenicians developed a writing system that used symbols to represent sounds. The Phoenician system was phonetic—that is, one sign was used for one sound. In fact, the word *alphabet* comes directly from the first two letters of the Phoenician alphabet: *aleph* and *beth*. As they traveled around the Mediterranean, the Phoenicians introduced this writing system to their trading partners. The Greeks, for example, adopted the Phoenician alphabet and changed the form of some of the letters.

Few examples of Phoenician writing exist. Most writings were on papyrus, which crumbled over time. However, the Phoenician contribution to the world was enormous. With a simplified alphabet, learning was now accessible to more people.

Phoenician trade was upset when their eastern cities were captured by Assyrians in 842 BC. However, these defeats encouraged exiles to set up city-states like Carthage to the west. The Phoenician homeland later came

Phoenician inscription from a sarcophagus.

Phoenician Trade

Phoenicia was located in a great spot for trade because it lay along well-traveled routes between Egypt and Asia. However, the Phoenicians did more than just trade with merchants who happened to pass through their region. The Phoenicians became expert sailors and went looking for opportunities to make money.

Merchant Ships Phoenician sailors developed the round boat, a ship that was very wide and had a rounded bottom. This shape created a large space for cargo.

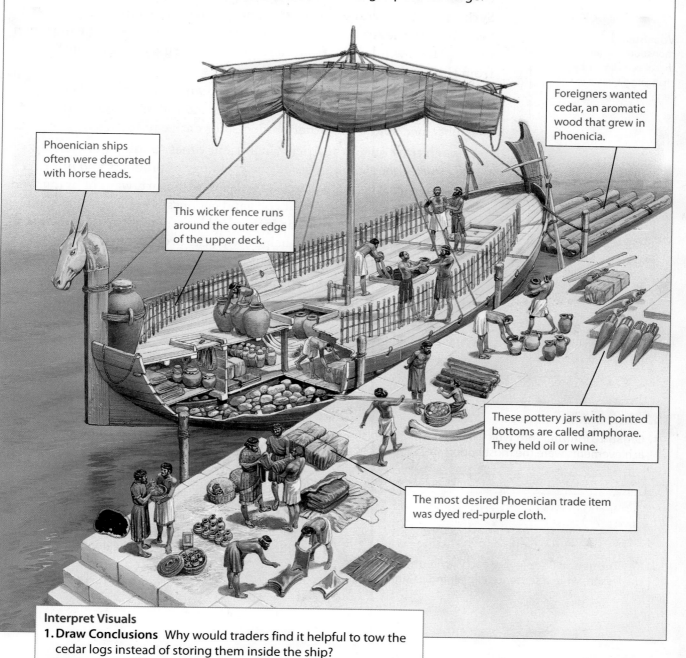

Phoenician ships often were decorated with horse heads.

This wicker fence runs around the outer edge of the upper deck.

Foreigners wanted cedar, an aromatic wood that grew in Phoenicia.

These pottery jars with pointed bottoms are called amphorae. They held oil or wine.

The most desired Phoenician trade item was dyed red-purple cloth.

Interpret Visuals
1. **Draw Conclusions** Why would traders find it helpful to tow the cedar logs instead of storing them inside the ship?
2. **Make Inferences** What purpose does the wicker fence serve?

Reading Check
Summarize What were the Phoenicians' most significant achievements?

under the control of the Babylonians and of the Persian Empire of King Cyrus I. One of their most lasting contributions remains the spread of the alphabet.

Ancient Trade Routes

Trading in ancient times also connected the Mediterranean Sea with other centers of world commerce, such as South and East Asia. Several land routes crossed Central Asia and connected to India through Afghanistan. Two sea routes began by crossing the Arabian Sea to ports on the Persian Gulf and the Red Sea. From there, traders either went over land to Egypt, Syria, and Mediterranean countries, or they continued to sail up the Red Sea. To cross the Arabian Sea, sailors learned to make use of the monsoon winds. These winds blow from the southwest during the hot months and from the northeast during the cool season.

Vocabulary
monsoon a wind that affects climate by changing direction in certain seasons

To widen the variety of their exports, Indian traders used other monsoon winds to travel to Southeast Asia and Indonesia. Once there, they obtained spices and other products not native to India.

Though traveling was difficult in ancient times, trading networks like those of the Phoenicians ensured the exchange of products and information. Along with their goods, traders carried ideas, art, ways of living, and religious beliefs. The worship of gods and goddesses in Phoenician temples, for example, influenced and was influenced by other cultures, and varied among the city-states. Traders helped with the process of cultural diffusion as well as with moving merchandise.

Phoenician traders made crucial contributions to world civilization. At the same time, another eastern Mediterranean people, the Jews, were creating a religious tradition that has lasted more than 3,000 years. This is discussed in the next lesson.

Reading Check
Summarize How did ancient trade routes in the Mediterranean and Asia impact world civilizations?

Lesson 4 Assessment

1. **Organize Information** Which Minoan and Phoenician achievements were the most important? Why?

Minoan	Phoenician
1.	1.
2.	2.
3.	3.

2. **Key Terms and People** For each key term or person in the lesson, write a sentence explaining its significance.

3. **Make Inferences** What might have caused the collapse of Minoan culture?

4. **Compare** What were some similarities between the Minoans and Phoenicians in terms of geographic location, trade, and the sustainability of their cultures?

5. **Analyze Primary Sources** Go back to Herodotus's account of a voyage around Africa on page 101. What words show his doubt? Why was he doubtful?

The Origins of Judaism

The Big Idea

The Israelites maintained monotheistic religious beliefs that were unique in the ancient world.

Why It Matters Now

From this tradition, Judaism, the religion of the Jews, evolved. Judaism is one of the world's major religions.

Key Terms and People

Canaan
Torah
Abraham
monotheism
covenant
Moses
Israel
Judah
tribute

Setting the Stage

The Phoenicians lived in a region at the eastern end of the Mediterranean Sea that was called **Canaan** (KAY•nuhn). The Phoenicians were not the only ancient people to live in the area; for example, the Philistines were another people who lived in the region. Canaan was also the ancient home of the Israelites, later called the Jews, in this area. Their history, legends, and moral laws are a major influence on Western culture, and they began a tradition also shared by Christianity and Islam.

The Search for a Promised Land

Ancient Canaan's location made it a cultural crossroads of the ancient world. By land, it connected Asia and Africa and two great empires, both eager to expand. To the east lay Assyria and Babylonia and to the west Egypt. Its seaports opened onto the two most important waterways of that time: the Mediterranean and the Red Seas. The Israelites settled in Canaan, which lay between the Jordan River and the Mediterranean Sea. In fact, the Israelites often used the word *Canaan* to refer to all of ancient Canaan. According to the Hebrew Bible, Canaan was the land God had promised to the Israelites.

From Ur to Egypt Most of what we know about the early history of the Israelites is contained in the first five books of the Hebrew Bible. Jews call these books the **Torah** (TAWR•uh) and consider them the most sacred writings in their tradition. Christians respect them as part of the Old Testament.

In the Torah, God chose **Abraham** (AY•bruh•ham) to be the "father" of the Jewish people. Abraham was a shepherd who lived in the city of Ur, in Mesopotamia. The book of

Genesis tells that God commanded him to move his people to Canaan. Around 1800 BC, Abraham, his family, and their herds made their way to Canaan. Then, around 1650 BC, the descendants of Abraham moved to Egypt.

"The Lord said to Abram, 'Go forth from your native land and from your father's house to the land that I will show you. I will make of you a great nation, and I will bless you; I will make your name great; and you shall be a blessing.'"

—Genesis 12:1-2 (Hebrew Bible)

The God of Abraham The Hebrew Bible tells how Abraham and his family migrated for many years from Mesopotamia to Canaan to Egypt and back to Canaan. All the while, God watched over them. Gods worshiped by other people were often local, and were associated with a specific place.

Unlike the other groups around them, who were polytheists, the Israelites were monotheists. They prayed to only one God. **Monotheism** (MAHN•uh•thee•ihz•uhm), a belief in a single god, comes from the Greek words *mono*, meaning "one," and *theism*, meaning "god-worship." The Israelites proclaimed that there was only one God. In their eyes, God had power over all peoples, everywhere. To the Israelites, God was not a physical being, and no physical images were to be made of him.

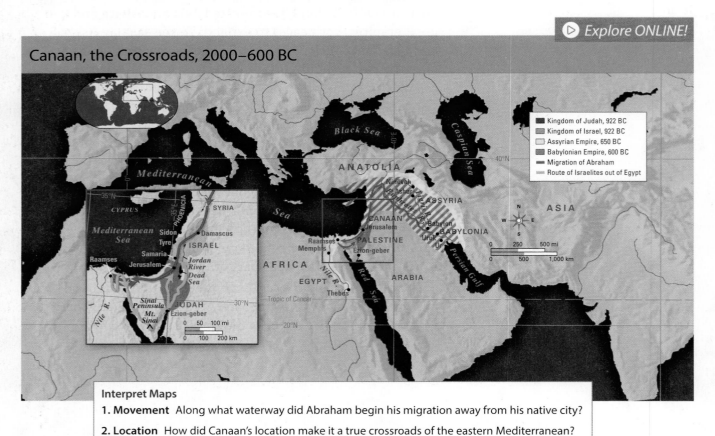

▶ Explore ONLINE!

Canaan, the Crossroads, 2000–600 BC

Legend:
- Kingdom of Judah, 922 BC
- Kingdom of Israel, 922 BC
- Assyrian Empire, 650 BC
- Babylonian Empire, 600 BC
- Migration of Abraham
- Route of Israelites out of Egypt

Interpret Maps

1. **Movement** Along what waterway did Abraham begin his migration away from his native city?

2. **Location** How did Canaan's location make it a true crossroads of the eastern Mediterranean?

Reading Check
Contrast How did the religion of the Israelites differ from many of the religions of their neighbors?

The Israelites asked God for protection from their enemies, just as other people prayed to their gods to defend them. According to the Hebrew Bible, God looked after the Israelites not so much because of ritual ceremonies and sacrifices but because Abraham had promised to obey him. In return, God had promised to protect Abraham and his descendants. This mutual promise between God and the founder of the Jewish people is called a **covenant** (KUHV•uh•nuhnt).

Moses and the Exodus

In this 14th-century painting, Moses holds a scroll inscribed with the story of God's appearance to Moses and commandment to lead the Israelites out of Egypt.

The Hebrew Bible says the Israelites migrated to Egypt because of a drought and threat of a famine. At first, the Israelites were given places of honor in the Egyptian kingdom. Later, however, they were forced into slavery.

"Let My People Go" The Israelites fled Egypt—perhaps between 1300 and 1200 BC Jews call this event "the Exodus," and they remember it every year during the festival of Passover. The Torah says that the man who led the Israelites out of slavery was **Moses**. It is told that at the time of Moses' birth, the Egyptian pharaoh felt threatened by the number of Israelites in Egypt. He thus ordered all Israelite male babies to be killed. Moses' mother hid her baby in the reeds along the banks of the Nile. There, an Egyptian princess found and adopted him. Though raised in luxury, he did not forget his Israelite birth. When God commanded him to lead the Israelites out of Egypt, he obeyed.

A New Covenant While the Israelites were traveling across the Sinai (SY•ny) Peninsula, Moses climbed to the top of Mount Sinai to pray. The Hebrew Bible says he spoke with God. When Moses came down from Mount Sinai, he brought down two stone tablets on which God had written the Ten Commandments.

These commandments and the other teachings that Moses delivered to his people became the basis for the civil and religious laws of Judaism. The Israelites believed that these laws formed a new covenant between God and the Israelites. God promised to protect them. They promised to keep God's commandments.

The Ten Commandments

Believed to have been given by God to Moses, the Ten Commandments are a code of moral laws that serve as the basis for Jewish law.

1. I the Lord am your God who brought you out of the land of Egypt, the house of bondage.
2. You shall have no other gods before Me. You shall not make for yourself a sculptured image. . . .
3. You shall not swear falsely by the name of the Lord your God. . . .
4. Remember the sabbath day and keep it holy. . . .
5. Honor your father and your mother. . . .
6. You shall not kill.
7. You shall not commit adultery.
8. You shall not steal.
9. You shall not bear false witness against your neighbor.
10. You shall not covet . . . anything that is your neighbor's.

—Exodus 20:2–14

▲ Tradition dictates that the Torah be written on a scroll and kept at the synagogue in an ornamental chest called an ark.

Analyze Historical Sources

1. **Compare** Do the first four commandments concern themselves more with the Jews' relationship with God or with one another?

2. **Contrast** What do the last six commandments have in common that distinguishes them from the first four?

The Land and People of the Bible The Torah reports that the Israelites traveled for 40 years in the Sinai Desert. Later books of the Hebrew Bible tell about the history of the Israelites after their migration. After the death of Moses, they returned to Canaan, where Abraham had lived. The Israelites made a change from a nomadic, tribal society to settled herders, farmers, and city dwellers. They learned new technologies from neighboring peoples in ancient Canaan.

When the Israelites arrived in Canaan, they were loosely organized into twelve tribes. These tribes lived in separate territories and were self-governing. In times of emergency, the Hebrew Bible tells that God would raise up judges. They would unite the tribes and provide judicial and military leadership during a crisis. In the course of time, God chose a series of judges, one of the most prominent of whom was a woman, Deborah.

Israelite Law Deborah's leadership was unusual for an Israelite woman. The roles of men and women were quite separate in most ancient societies. Women could not officiate at religious ceremonies. In general, an Israelite woman's most important duty was to raise her children and provide moral leadership for them.

The Ten Commandments were part of a code of laws delivered to Moses. The code included other rules regulating social and religious behavior. In some ways, this code resembled Hammurabi's Code with its statement "an eye for an eye and a tooth for a tooth." To Jews this meant to pay restitution and emphasize God's mercy. The code was later interpreted by religious teachers called prophets. These interpretations tended to emphasize greater equality before the law than did other codes of the time. The prophets constantly urged the Jews to stay true to their covenant with God.

The prophets taught that the Jews had a duty to worship God and live justly with one another. The goal was a moral life lived in accordance with God's laws. In the words of the prophet Micah, "He has told you, O mortal what is good; and what does the Lord require of you but to do justice, and to love kindness, and to walk humbly with your God?" This emphasis on right conduct and the worship of one God is called ethical monotheism—a Jewish idea that has influenced human behavior for thousands of years through Judaism, Christianity, and Islam.

Reading Check
Summarize What does Jewish law require of believers?

Deborah served as a judge for the Israelites and is sometimes called the "Mother of Israel."

Judaism

Judaism is the religion of the Jewish people. In Judaism, one of the most important ways for a person to please God is to study the scriptures, or sacred writings, and to live according to what they teach. Many Jews keep a scroll of an important scripture passage inside a decorative holder, such as the one shown here, that is attached to a doorpost. The scroll is known as a mezuzah.

THE SACRED WRITINGS OF JUDAISM

Sacred Writings	Contents
HEBREW BIBLE	**TORAH** • first five books of the Bible • recounts origins of humanity and Judaism • contains basic laws of Judaism **PROPHETS** • stories about and writings by Jewish teachers • divided into Former Prophets and Latter Prophets • recounts Jewish history and calls for justice, kindness, right conduct, and faithfulness to God **WRITINGS** • a collection of various other writings • includes psalms, poetry, history and stories, proverbs, and philosophical writings called wisdom literature
TALMUD	**MISHNAH** • written record of Jewish oral law **GEMARA** • explanations and interpretations of the Mishnah

Interpret Charts

1. **Contrast** What is contained in the Hebrew Bible that is not in the Talmud? What is in the Talmud that is not in the Hebrew Bible?

2. **Hypothesize** What kind of poetry would you expect to find in the Hebrew Bible? Explain what you think the subjects or themes of the poems might be.

The Kingdom of Israel

Canaan—the land that the Israelites believed had been promised them by God—combined largely harsh features such as arid desert, rocky wilderness, grassy hills, and the dry, hot valley of the Jordan River. Water was never plentiful; even the numerous limestone formations soaked up any excess rainfall. After first settling in the south-central area of ancient Canaan, the Israelites expanded south and north.

Saul and David Establish a Kingdom The judges occasionally pulled together the widely scattered tribes for a united military effort. Nonetheless, the Philistines, another people in the area, threatened the Israelites' position in ancient Canaan. The Israelites got along somewhat better with their other Canaanite neighbors.

From about 1020 to 922 BC, the Israelites united under three able kings: Saul, David, and Solomon. The new kingdom was called **Israel** (IHZ•ree•uhl). For 100 years, Israel enjoyed its greatest period of power and independence.

Saul, the first of the three kings, was chosen largely because of his success in driving out the Philistines from the central hills. Saul is portrayed in the Hebrew Bible as a tragic man, who was given to bouts of jealousy. After his death, he was succeeded by his son-in-law, David. King David, an extremely popular leader, united the tribes, established Jerusalem as the capital, and founded a dynasty.

Solomon Builds the Kingdom In about 962 BC, David was succeeded by his son Solomon, whose mother was Bathsheba. Solomon was the most powerful of the Israelite kings. He built a trading empire with the help of his friend Hiram, the king of the Phoenician city of Tyre. Solomon also

---

BIOGRAPHY

King Solomon
(962?–922? BC)

In the Bible, Solomon prays to God for "an understanding mind," which God grants him.

Soon after, the story goes, two women and a baby boy were brought before him. Each woman claimed the baby was hers. After hearing their testimony, Solomon declared, "Divide the living boy in two; then give half to the one and half to the other."

One said: "Please, my lord, give her the living boy; certainly do not kill him!" However, the other woman accepted: "It shall be neither mine nor yours; divide it."

Solomon knew that the woman who would give up the child to save it was the real mother.

Solomon's Temple in Jerusalem became the center of worship and unity for the Israelites.

beautified the capital city of Jerusalem. The crowning achievement of his extensive building program in Jerusalem was a great temple, which he built to glorify God. The temple was also a permanent home for the Ark of the Covenant, which contained the tablets of Moses' law.

The temple that Solomon built was not large, but it gleamed like a precious gem. Bronze pillars stood at the temple's entrance. The temple was stone on the outside, while its inner walls were made of cedar covered in gold. The main hall was richly decorated with brass and gold. Solomon also built a royal palace even more costly and more magnificent than the temple.

The Kingdom Divides Solomon's building projects required high taxes and badly strained the kingdom's finances. In addition, men were drafted to spend one month out of every three working on the temple. The expense and labor requirement caused much discontent. As a result, after Solomon's death, the Jews in the northern part of the kingdom, which was located far from the south, revolted. By 922 BC, the kingdom had divided in two. Israel was in the north and **Judah** (JOO•duh) was in the south. Eventually, the northern kingdom was destroyed and only the kingdom of Judah remained. As a result, the Israelites came to be called Jews, and their religion, *Judaism*.

The next 200 years were a time of upheaval for the two kingdoms of Israel and Judah. Sometimes they fought each other; sometimes they joined together to fight common enemies. Each of the kingdoms had periods of prosperity, followed by low periods of conflict and decline.

Reading Check
Draw Conclusions
How might geographical distance make the split of Israel and Judah more likely?

The Babylonian Captivity

Disaster finally struck as the two kingdoms lost their independence. In 738 BC, both Israel and Judah began paying **tribute**—peace money paid by a weaker power to a stronger—to Assyria. By paying tribute, Israel and Judah hoped to ensure that the mighty Assyrian Empire would not attack. But Israel revolted and withheld tribute and in 725 BC the Assyrians began a relentless siege of Samaria, the capital of Israel. By 722 BC, the whole northern kingdom had fallen to the Assyrians' ferocious assault.

The southern kingdom of Judah resisted for another 150 years before it too was destroyed. The destruction of Judah was to come at the hands of the Babylonians. After conquering Israel, the Assyrians rapidly lost power to a rising Babylonian Empire. The great Babylonian King Nebuchadnezzar (nehb•uh•kuhd•NEHZ•uhr) ran the Egyptians out of Syria and Judah, and he twice attacked Jerusalem. The city finally fell in 586 BC. Solomon's temple was destroyed in the Babylonian victory. Many of the survivors were exiled to Babylon. During the exile in Babylon, the Hebrew Bible describes how the prophet Ezekiel urged his people to keep their religion alive in a foreign land.

Then about 50 years after the fall of Judah, another change in fortune occurred: in 539 BC, the Persian King Cyrus the Great conquered Babylon. The next year, Cyrus allowed some 40,000 exiles to return to Jerusalem to rebuild the temple. Many, however, stayed in Babylonia.

Work on the second temple was completed in 515 BC. The walls of Jerusalem were rebuilt in 445 BC. Soon, however, other empires dominated the region—first the Persians, then the Greeks, and then the Romans. These new empires would take control both of Judah, now called Judea, and of the destiny of the Jewish people.

Reading Check
Make Inferences
The temple was rebuilt before the walls of Jerusalem. What does this fact indicate about the Jews after the Babylonian captivity?

Lesson 5 Assessment

1. **Organize Information** Use a timeline to identify the leaders of Israel from Abraham to Solomon. Which of these leaders do you think was the most important? Why?

2000 BC

Abraham:
father of
Jewish people

2. **Key Terms and People** For each key term or person in the lesson, write a sentence explaining its significance.

3. **Develop Historical Perspective** What were the main problems faced by the Israelites between 1800 BC and 700 BC?

4. **Analyze Issues** What were some of the factors that made Canaan a good place for the Israelites to settle?

5. **Compare** In what ways are the laws delivered to Moses similar to Hammurabi's Code?

Module 3 Assessment

Key Terms and People

For each term or name below, write a sentence explaining its importance in the years 2500 BC to 250 BC.

1. Indo-Europeans
2. caste
3. reincarnation
4. Siddhartha Gautama
5. nirvana
6. Minoans
7. Phoenicians
8. Abraham
9. monotheism
10. Moses

Main Ideas

Use your notes and the information in the module to answer the following questions.

The Indo-Europeans

1. What are three reasons that historians give to explain why Indo-Europeans migrated?
2. What are two technologies that helped the Hittites build their empire?
3. How was the Aryan society organized?

The Origins of Hinduism

4. What type of sacred texts helped shape Hindu beliefs?
5. How are the ideas of karma, reincarnation, and *moksha* organized?
6. Why do Hindu beliefs vary widely?

The Origins of Buddhism

7. What are the Four Noble Truths of Buddhism?
8. Why were lower castes more likely to convert to Buddhism?
9. How did Buddhism spread?

Seafaring Traders

10. What did the Minoans export?
11. Why did Phoenicia's economy revolve around trading?
12. What is Phoenicia's greatest legacy to the world?

The Origins of Judaism

13. What is ethical monotheism and why is it important?
14. What were some of the achievements of David?
15. What are two ways in which early Judaism differed from other religions of the time?

Critical Thinking

1. **Organize Information** Copy the chart into your notebook and fill in information about three world religions.

Religion	Founder	Time Originated	Area Originated
Hinduism			
Buddhism			
Judaism			

2. **Draw Conclusions** How important were the migrations of the Indo-European peoples? How lasting were the changes that they brought? Explain your conclusion.

3. **Analyze Effects** What were some of the effects of King Solomon's reign?

4. **Compare** How were the economic foundations of Minoan and Phoenician civilizations similar?

5. **Develop Historical Perspective** Why was monotheism unusual in its time and place?

Engage with History

Imagine you are in ancient times and considering leaving your homeland to find a better place to live. Your community has grown larger, grazing areas for your animals have become scarce, and there are rumors of coming invaders. Determine what kind of geographical features and climate would be suitable for you and your family. Will you adopt the customs of the people living there? What advantages and disadvantages do you expect to experience?

Focus on Writing

Some scholars believe the Aryans migrated into India. Write an expository essay describing how ironworking may have helped the Aryans carry out their migration as well as their conquering and settling of territory.

Consider the effect of ironworking technology on the following:

- weapons and tools
- transportation
- conquest
- settlement

Multimedia Activity

Introduction You are a member of a special committee commissioned by the government in ancient India to potentially end the caste system.

Task Create an electronic presentation of the issues you should consider and potential problems in restructuring the social system.

Process and Procedures Research the role that members from each caste played in ancient Indian society to help present the issues. Use this module and the Internet as resources for your research.

Evaluation and Conclusion How did this project contribute to your understanding of the caste system? What additional information would you like to know?

Module 4

First Empires in Africa and Asia

Essential Question

How effective were leaders in spreading their influence in the first large empires of Africa and Asia?

About the Photo: This lion frieze is on a brick wall that lined a street leading to a gate to the inner city of Babylon during in the late 500s BC.

In this module you will learn about the development of early empires in Africa and Asia.

▷ *Explore ONLINE!*

HISTORY

VIDEOS, including...
• Ramses' Egyptian Empire
• Seven Wonders of the World
• 110 Guards for Persia's Royal Road
• The First Emperor of China

☑ Document Based Investigations

☑ Graphic Organizers

☑ Interactive Games

☑ Image Compare: Egyptian Influence on Nubian Culture

☑ Image Carousel: Comparing Ancient Civilizations

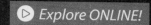
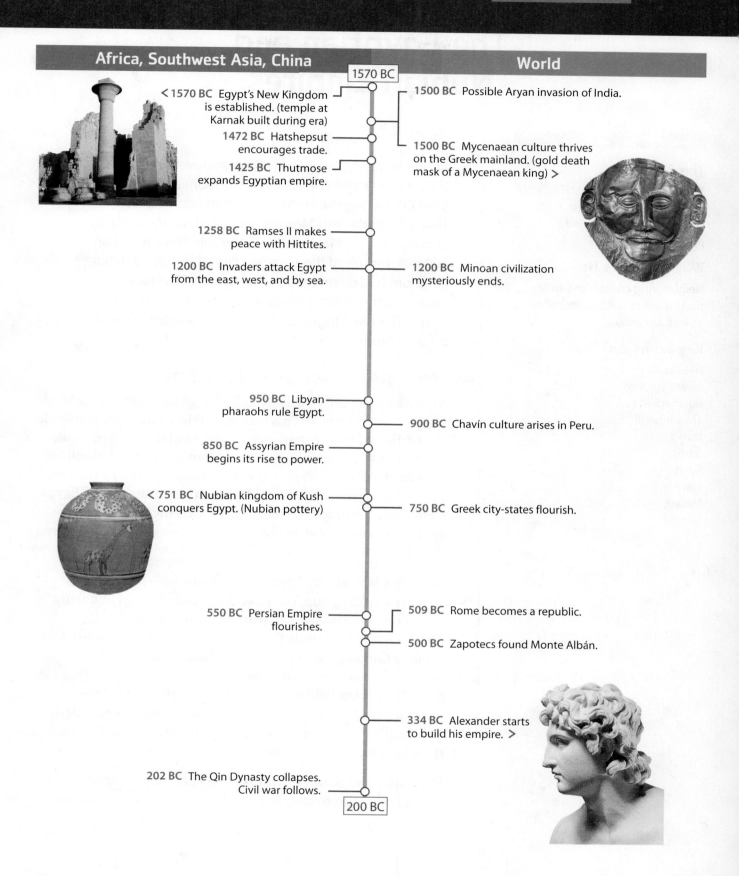

Africa, Southwest Asia, China

World

1570 BC

< 1570 BC Egypt's New Kingdom is established. (temple at Karnak built during era)

1472 BC Hatshepsut encourages trade.

1425 BC Thutmose expands Egyptian empire.

1258 BC Ramses II makes peace with Hittites.

1200 BC Invaders attack Egypt from the east, west, and by sea.

950 BC Libyan pharaohs rule Egypt.

850 BC Assyrian Empire begins its rise to power.

< 751 BC Nubian kingdom of Kush conquers Egypt. (Nubian pottery)

550 BC Persian Empire flourishes.

202 BC The Qin Dynasty collapses. Civil war follows.

200 BC

1500 BC Possible Aryan invasion of India.

1500 BC Mycenaean culture thrives on the Greek mainland. (gold death mask of a Mycenaean king) >

1200 BC Minoan civilization mysteriously ends.

900 BC Chavín culture arises in Peru.

750 BC Greek city-states flourish.

509 BC Rome becomes a republic.

500 BC Zapotecs found Monte Albán.

334 BC Alexander starts to build his empire. >

The Egyptian and Nubian Empires

The Big Idea

Two empires along the Nile, Egypt and Nubia, forged commercial, cultural, and political connections.

Why It Matters Now

Neighboring civilizations today participate in cultural exchange as well as conflict.

Key Terms and People

Hyksos
New Kingdom
Hatshepsut
Thutmose III
Nubia
Ramses II
Kush
Piankhi
Meroë

Setting the Stage

As you learned, Egyptian civilization developed along the Nile River and united into a kingdom around 3100 BC. During the Middle Kingdom (about 2080–1640 BC), trade with Mesopotamia and the Indus Valley enriched Egypt. Meanwhile, up the Nile River, less than 600 miles south of the Egyptian city of Thebes, a major kingdom had developed in the region of Nubia. For centuries, the Nubian kingdom of Kush traded with Egypt. The two kingdoms particularly influenced each other culturally.

Nomadic Invaders Rule Egypt

After the prosperity of the Middle Kingdom, Egypt descended into war and violence. This was caused by a succession of weak pharaohs and power struggles among rival nobles. The weakened country fell to invaders who swept across the Isthmus of Suez in chariots, a weapon of war unknown to the Egyptians. These Asiatic invaders, called **Hyksos** (HIHK•sohs), ruled Egypt from about 1640 to 1570 BC. The Hyksos invasion shook the Egyptians' confidence in the desert barriers that had protected their kingdom.

Israelites Migrate to Egypt Some historians believe that another Asiatic group, the Israelites, settled in Egypt during the rule of the Hyksos. According to the Hebrew Bible, Abraham and his family first crossed the Euphrates River and came to Canaan around 1800 BC. Then, around 1650 BC, the descendants of Abraham moved again—this time to Egypt. Some historians believe that the Hyksos encouraged the Israelites to settle there because the two groups were racially similar. The Egyptians resented the presence of the Hyksos in their land but were powerless to remove them.

Expulsion and Slavery Around 1600 BC, a series of warlike rulers began to restore Egypt's power. Among those who

Trade between Egypt and Nubia thrived for hundreds of years.

Reading Check
Summarize
What caused war and violence in Egypt during this period?

helped drive out the Hyksos was Queen Ahhotep (ah•HOH•tehp). She took over when her husband was killed in battle. The next pharaoh, Kamose (KAH•mohs), won a great victory over the Hyksos. His successors drove the Hyksos completely out of Egypt and pursued them across the Sinai Peninsula into Canaan. According to some Biblical scholars, the Israelites remained in Egypt and were enslaved and forced into hard labor. They would not leave Egypt until sometime between 1500 and 1200 BC, the time of the Exodus.

The New Kingdom of Egypt

After overthrowing the Hyksos, the pharaohs of the **New Kingdom** (about 1570–1075 BC) sought to strengthen Egypt by building an empire. As you may recall, an empire brings together several peoples or states under the control of one ruler. Egypt entered its third period of glory during the New Kingdom era. During this time, it was wealthier and more powerful than ever before.

Equipped with bronze weapons and two-wheeled chariots, the Egyptians became conquerors. The pharaohs of the 18th Dynasty (about 1570–1365 BC) set up an army including archers, charioteers, and infantry, or foot soldiers.

Vocabulary
dynasty a series of rulers from a single family

Hatshepsut's Prosperous Rule Among the rulers of the New Kingdom, **Hatshepsut** (hat•SHEHP•soot), who declared herself pharaoh around 1472 BC, was unique. She took over because her stepson, the male heir to the throne, was a young child at the time. Unlike other New Kingdom rulers, Hatshepsut spent her reign encouraging trade rather than just waging war.

Hatshepsut
(reigned 1472–1458 BC)

Hatshepsut was an excellent ruler of outstanding achievement who made Egypt more prosperous. As male pharaohs had done, Hatshepsut planned a tomb for herself in the Valley of the Kings. Carved reliefs on the walls of the temple reveal the glories of her reign.

The inscription from Hatshepsut's obelisk at Karnak trumpets her glory and her feelings about herself:

> *I swear as Re loves me, as my father Amon favors me, as my nostrils are filled with satisfying life, as I wear the white crown, as I appear in the red crown, . . . as I rule this land like the son of Isis.*

The trading expedition Hatshepsut ordered to the Land of Punt (poont), near present-day Somalia, was particularly successful. Hatshepsut sent a fleet of five ships down the Red Sea to Punt in search of myrrh, frankincense, and fragrant ointments used for religious ceremonies and in cosmetics. In addition to these goods, Hatshepsut's fleet brought back gold, ivory, and unusual plants and animals.

Thutmose the Empire Builder Hatshepsut's stepson, **Thutmose III** (thoot•MOH•suh), proved to be a much more warlike ruler. In his eagerness to ascend to the throne, Thutmose III may even have murdered Hatshepsut. Between the time he took power and his death around 1425 BC, Thutmose III led a number of victorious invasions eastward into Canaan and Syria. His armies also pushed farther south into **Nubia**, a region of Africa that straddled the upper Nile River. Egypt had traded with Nubia and influenced the region since the time of the Middle Kingdom.

Egypt was now a mighty empire. It controlled lands around the Nile and far beyond. In addition, it drew boundless wealth from them. Contact with other cultures brought Egypt new ideas as well as material goods. Egypt had never before—nor has it since—commanded such power and wealth as during the reigns of the New Kingdom pharaohs.

The Egyptians and the Hittites The Egyptians' conquest of parts of Syria and Canaan around 1400 BC brought them into conflict with the Hittites. The Hittites had moved into Asia Minor around 1900 BC and later expanded southward into Canaan.

After several smaller battles, the Egyptians and Hittites clashed at Kadesh around 1285 BC. The pharaoh **Ramses II** (RAM•seez) and a Hittite king later made a treaty that promised "peace and brotherhood between us forever." Their alliance lasted for the rest of the century.

An Age of Builders Like the rulers of the Old Kingdom, who built the towering pyramids, rulers of the New Kingdom erected grand buildings. In search of security in the afterlife—and protection from grave robbers—they hid their splendid tombs beneath desert cliffs. The site they chose was the remote Valley of the Kings near Thebes. Besides royal tombs, the pharaohs of this period also built great palaces and magnificent temples. Indeed, the royal title *pharaoh* means "great house" and comes from this time period.

Ramses II, whose reign extended from approximately 1290 to 1224 BC, stood out among the great builders of the New Kingdom. At Karnak, he added to a monumental temple to Amon-Re (AH•muhn•RAY), Egypt's chief god. Ramses also ordered a temple to be carved into the red sandstone cliffs above the Nile River at Abu Simbel (AH•boo SIHM•buhl). He had these temples decorated with enormous statues of himself. The ears of these statues alone measured more than three feet.

Reading Check
Recognize Effects
What were some of the political and economic effects of Egypt's conquests?

Four statues of Ramses II guarded the entrance to the Great Temple at Abu Simbel. The head of one statue was damaged in an earthquake. Near the feet of the giant statues are smaller statues of Ramses' wife, mother, and first eight children.

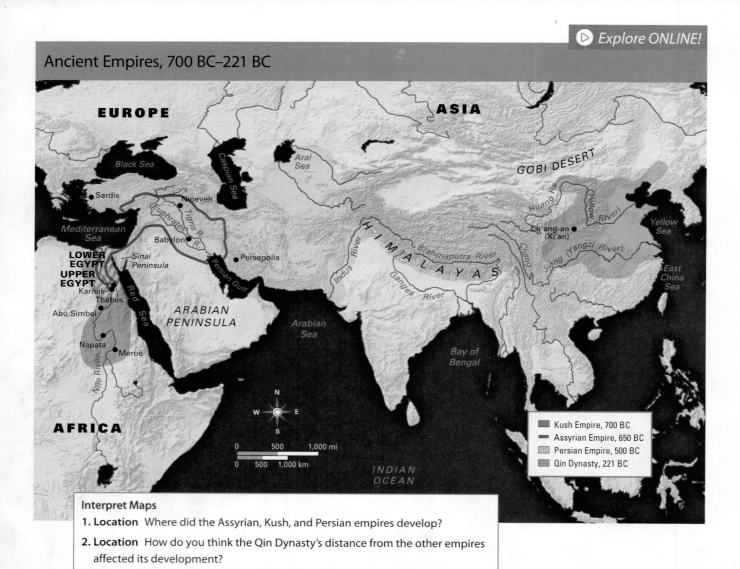

Ancient Empires, 700 BC–221 BC

EUROPE

ASIA

AFRICA

Black Sea

Caspian Sea

Aral Sea

GOBI DESERT

Sardis

Nineveh

Euphrates R.

Tigris R.

Mediterranean Sea

Babylon

LOWER EGYPT

Sinai Peninsula

Persepolis

UPPER EGYPT

Persian Gulf

Karnak

Thebes

Red Sea

Abu Simbel

ARABIAN PENINSULA

Napata

Meroë

Nile River

Arabian Sea

HIMALAYAS

Indus River

Ganges River

Brahmaputra River

Chang

Huang He (Yellow River)

Ch'ang-an (Xi'an)

Jiang (Yangzi River)

Yellow Sea

East China Sea

Bay of Bengal

N W E S

0   500   1,000 mi
0   500   1,000 km

INDIAN OCEAN

■ Kush Empire, 700 BC
■ Assyrian Empire, 650 BC
■ Persian Empire, 500 BC
■ Qin Dynasty, 221 BC

Interpret Maps

1. **Location** Where did the Assyrian, Kush, and Persian empires develop?

2. **Location** How do you think the Qin Dynasty's distance from the other empires affected its development?

The Empire Declines

The empire that Thutmose III had built and Ramses II had ruled slowly came apart after 1200 BC as other strong civilizations rose to challenge Egypt's power. Shortly after Ramses died, the entire eastern Mediterranean suffered a wave of invasions.

Invasions by Land and Sea Both the Egyptian empire and the Hittite kingdom were attacked by invaders called the "Sea Peoples" in Egyptian texts. These invaders may have included the Philistines, who are often mentioned in the Hebrew Bible. Whoever they were, the Sea Peoples caused great destruction.

The Egyptians faced other attacks. In the east, the tribes of Canaan often rebelled against their Egyptian overlords. In the west, the vast desert no longer served as a barrier against Libyan raids on Egyptian villages.

Egypt's Empire Fades After these invasions, Egypt never recovered its previous power. The Egyptian empire broke apart into regional units, and numerous small kingdoms arose. Each was eager to protect its independence.

Almost powerless, Egypt soon fell to its neighbors' invasions. Eventually, Libyans crossed the desert to the Nile Delta. There they established independent dynasties. From around 950 to 730 BC, Libyan pharaohs ruled Egypt and erected cities. But instead of imposing their own culture, the Libyans adopted Egypt's. When the Nubians came north to seize power, they too adopted Egyptian culture.

The Kushites Conquer the Nile Region

For centuries, Egypt dominated Nubia and the Nubian kingdom of **Kush**, which lasted for about a thousand years, between 2000 and 1000 BC. During this time, Egyptian armies raided and even occupied Kush for a brief period. But as Egypt fell into decline during the Hyksos period, Kush began to emerge as a regional power. Nubia now established its own Kushite dynasty on the throne of Egypt.

The People of Nubia Nubia lay south of Egypt between the first cataract of the Nile, an area of churning rapids, and the division of the river into the Blue Nile and the White Nile. Despite several cataracts around which boats had to be carried, the Nile provided the best north-south trade route. Several Nubian kingdoms, including Kush, served as a trade corridor. They linked Egypt and the Mediterranean world to the interior of Africa and to the Red Sea. Goods and ideas flowed back and forth along the river for centuries. The first Nubian kingdom, Kerma, arose shortly after 2000 BC.

The Interaction of Egypt and Nubia With Egypt's revival during the New Kingdom, pharaohs forced Egyptian rule on Kush. Egyptian governors, priests, soldiers, and artists strongly influenced the Nubians. Indeed, Kush's capital, Napata, became the center for the spread of Egyptian culture to Kush's other African trading partners.

Kushite princes went to Egypt. They learned the Egyptian language and worshiped Egyptian gods. They adopted the customs and clothing styles of the Egyptian upper class. When they returned home, the Kushite nobles brought back royal rituals and hieroglyphic writing.

With Egypt's decline, beginning about 1200 BC, Kush regained its independence. The Kushites viewed themselves as more suitable guardians of Egyptian values than the Libyans. They sought to guard these values by conquering Egypt and ousting its Libyan rulers.

Piankhi Captures the Egyptian Throne In 751 BC, a Kushite king named **Piankhi** overthrew the Libyan dynasty that had ruled Egypt for more than 200 years. He united the entire Nile Valley from the delta in the north to Napata in the south. Piankhi and his descendants became Egypt's 25th Dynasty. After his victory, Piankhi erected a monument in his homeland of Kush. He had words inscribed on it that celebrated his victory and provided a catalog of Egyptian riches, such as silver, gold, and copper.

However, Piankhi's dynasty proved short-lived. In 671 BC, the Assyrians, a warlike people from Southwest Asia, conquered Egypt.

Egyptian Influence on Nubian Culture

Nubia was heavily influenced by Egypt. This influence is particularly apparent in Nubian religious practices and burial traditions. But even though the Nubians adopted Egyptian ways, they didn't abandon their cultural identity. In many of these religious and funeral practices, the Nubians blended Egyptian customs with their own traditions.

▲ **Temples**
This stone ram, representing the Egyptian god Amen, lay at the entrance to a Nubian temple dedicated to that god. Although the Nubians worshiped many Egyptian gods, Amen's temple was located near another dedicated to Apedemak, a Nubian god.

▲ **Statues**
These figurines represented Nubian slaves. They were buried with Nubian kings and meant to serve them in death. The figurines reflect traditional Egyptian style. The human faces, however, reveal Nubian features.

▼ **Pyramids**
Unlike the Egyptian pyramids, the pyramids of Nubia had steeply sloping sides and were probably designed with a flat top.

▶ *Explore ONLINE!*

Kush Empire, 700 BC

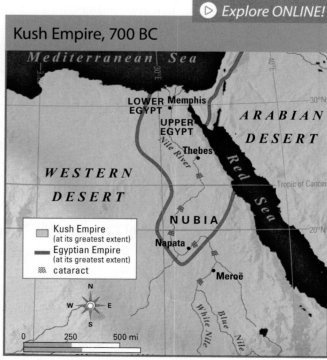

Critical Thinking
Form Opinions Why did the Nubians combine Egyptian culture with elements of their own culture?

Reading Check
Make Inferences
Why might the Kushites have viewed themselves as guardians of Egyptian values?

This ring, bearing the head of a Kushite guardian god, was found inside a Meroë queen's pyramid. It dates from the late first century BC.

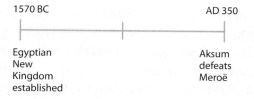

The Kushites fought bravely, but they were forced to retreat south along the Nile. There the Kushites would experience a golden age, despite their loss of Egypt.

The Golden Age of Meroë

After their defeat by the Assyrians, the Kushite royal family eventually moved south to **Meroë** (MEHR•oh•ee). Meroë lay closer to the Red Sea than Napata did, and so became active in the flourishing trade among Africa, Arabia, and India. (See map, Kush Empire, 700 BC.)

The Wealth of Kush Kush used the natural resources around Meroë and thrived for several hundred years. Unlike Egyptian cities along the Nile, Meroë enjoyed significant rainfall. And, unlike Egypt, Meroë boasted abundant supplies of iron ore. As a result, Meroë became a major center for the manufacture of iron weapons and tools.

In Meroë, ambitious merchants loaded iron bars, tools, and spearheads onto their donkeys. They then transported the goods to the Red Sea, where they exchanged these goods for jewelry, fine cotton cloth, silver lamps, and glass bottles. As the mineral wealth of the central Nile Valley flowed out of Meroë, luxury goods from India and Arabia flowed in.

The Decline of Meroë After four centuries of prosperity, from about 250 BC to AD 150, Meroë began to decline. Aksum, another kingdom located 400 miles to the southeast, contributed to Meroë's fall. With a seaport on the Red Sea, Aksum came to dominate North African trade. Aksum defeated Meroë around AD 350.

Centuries earlier, around the time the Kushite pharaoh sat on the Egyptian throne, a new empire—Assyria—had risen in the north. Like Kush, Assyria came to dominate Egypt.

Reading Check
Compare
What natural resources did Meroë have that Egypt did not?

Lesson 1 Assessment

1. **Organize Information** Use a timeline. Which empire was invaded more often? Why?

   1570 BC ———————————————— AD 350

   Egyptian New Kingdom established | Aksum defeats Meroë

2. **Key Terms and People** For each key term or person in the lesson, write a sentence explaining its significance.

3. **Evaluate** What cultural aspects of Egyptian civilization did the Kushites adopt?

4. **Analyze Effects** Why was Kush able to thrive after losing Egypt to the Assyrians?

5. **Draw Conclusions** What role did geography play in Egypt's rise and fall?

6. **Make Inferences** How did trade help both Egypt and Nubia maintain their dominance in the Nile region?

7. **Predict** What might have happened if the Kushites had imposed their own culture on Egypt?

The Assyrian Empire

The Big Idea

Assyria developed a military machine and established a well-organized administration.

Why It Matters Now

Some leaders still use military force to extend their rule, stamp out opposition, and gain wealth and power.

Key Terms and People

Assyria
Sennacherib
Nineveh
Ashurbanipal
Medes
Chaldeans
Nebuchadnezzar

Setting the Stage

For more than two centuries, the Assyrian army advanced across Southwest Asia. It overwhelmed foes with its military strength. After the Assyrians seized control of Egypt, the Assyrian King Esarhaddon proclaimed, "I tore up the root of Kush, and not one therein escaped to submit to me." The last Kushite pharaoh retreated to Napata, Kush's capital city.

A Mighty Military Machine

Beginning around 850 BC, **Assyria** (uh·SEER·ee·uh) acquired a large empire. It accomplished this by means of a highly advanced military organization and state-of-the-art weaponry. For a time, this campaign of conquest made Assyria the greatest power in Southwest Asia.

The Rise of a Warrior People The Assyrians came from the northern part of Mesopotamia. Their flat, exposed land made them easy for other people to attack. Invaders frequently swept down into Assyria from the nearby mountains. The Assyrians may have developed their warlike behavior in response to these invasions. Through constant warfare, Assyrian kings eventually built an empire that stretched from east and north of the Tigris River all the way to central Egypt. One of these Assyrian kings, **Sennacherib** (sih·NAK·uhr·ihb), bragged that he had destroyed 89 cities and 820 villages, burned Babylon, and ordered most of its inhabitants killed.

Military Organization and Conquest Assyria was a society that glorified military strength. Its soldiers were well equipped for conquering an empire. Making use of the ironworking technology of the time, the soldiers covered themselves in stiff leather and metal armor. They wore copper or iron helmets, padded loincloths, and leather skirts layered with metal scales. Their weapons were iron swords and iron-pointed spears.

Advance planning and technical skill allowed the Assyrians to lay siege to enemy cities. When deep water blocked their passage, engineers would span the rivers with pontoons, or floating structures used to support a bridge. Before attacking, the Assyrians dug beneath the city's walls to weaken them. Then, with disciplined organization, foot soldiers marched shoulder to shoulder. The foot soldiers approached the city walls and shot wave upon wave of arrows. Meanwhile, another group of troops hammered the city's gates with massive, iron-tipped battering rams. When the city gates finally splintered, the Assyrians showed no mercy. They killed or enslaved their victims. To prevent their enemies from rebelling again, the Assyrians forced captives to settle far away in the empire's distant provinces and dependent states.

Reading Check
Summarize What was the key to the success of the Assyrian Empire?

Historical Source

Assyrian Sculpture

This relief shows ferocious Assyrian warriors attacking a fortified city. A relief is a sculpture that has figures standing out from a flat background. The Assyrian war machine included a variety of weapons and methods of attack.

1 Ladders
Assyrian archers launched waves of arrows against opponents defending the city walls. Meanwhile, Assyrian troops threw their ladders up against the walls and began their climb into the enemy's stronghold.

2 Weapons
Troops were armed with the best weapons of the time, iron-tipped spears, as well as iron daggers and swords. They were also protected with armor and large shields.

3 Tactics
The Assyrians were savage in their treatment of defeated opponents. Those who were not slaughtered in the initial attack were often impaled or beheaded, while women and children were sometimes murdered or sold into slavery.

4 Tunnels
The Assyrian army used sappers—soldiers who dug tunnels to sap, or undermine, the foundations of the enemy's walls so that they would fall.

Analyze Historical Sources
1. **Make Inferences** What emotions might the relief have inspired in the Assyrian people?
2. **Form Generalizations** How might the Assyrians' enemies have reacted to the sculpture?

The Empire Expands

Between 850 and 650 BC, the kings of Assyria defeated Syria, Israel, Judah, and Babylonia. Eventually, the Assyrians ruled lands that extended far beyond the Fertile Crescent into Anatolia and Egypt.

Assyrian Rule At its peak around 650 BC, the Assyrian Empire included almost all of the old centers of civilization and power in Southwest Asia. Assyrian officials governed lands closest to Assyria as provinces and made them dependent territories. Assyrian kings controlled these dependent regions by choosing their rulers or by supporting kings who aligned themselves with Assyria. The Assyrian system of having local governors report to a central authority became the fundamental model of administration, or system of government management.

In addition, the military campaigns added new territory to the empire. These additional lands brought taxes and tribute to the Assyrian treasury. If a conquered people refused to pay, the Assyrians destroyed their cities and sent the people into exile. Such methods enabled the Assyrians to effectively govern an extended empire.

Assyrian Culture Some of Assyria's most fearsome warriors earned reputations as great builders. For example, the same King Sennacherib who had burned Babylon also established Assyria's capital at **Nineveh** (NIHN•uh•vuh) along the Tigris River. This great walled city, about three miles long and a mile wide, was the largest city of its day. In the ruins of Nineveh and other Assyrian cities, archaeologists found finely carved sculptures. Two artistic subjects particularly fascinated the Assyrians: brutal military campaigns and the lion hunt.

Nineveh also held one of the ancient world's largest libraries. In this unique library, King **Ashurbanipal** (ah•shur•BAH•nuh•pahl) collected more than 20,000 clay tablets from throughout the Fertile Crescent. The collection included the ancient Sumerian poem the *Epic of Gilgamesh* and provided historians with much information about the earliest civilizations in Southwest Asia. The library was the first to have many of the features of a modern library. For instance, the collection was organized into many rooms according to subject matter. The collection was also cataloged. Europeans would not use a library cataloging system for centuries.

Reading Check
Evaluate Why do you think modern historians value the library at Nineveh?

The Empire Crumbles

Ashurbanipal proved to be one of the last of the mighty Assyrian kings. Assyrian power had spread itself too thin. Also, the cruelty dis-played by the Assyrians had earned them many enemies. Shortly after Ashurbanipal's death, Nineveh fell.

Decline and Fall In 612 BC, a combined army of **Medes** (meedz), **Chaldeans** (kal•DEE•uhnz), and others burned and leveled Nineveh. However, because the clay writing tablets in Nineveh's library had been baked in a pottery oven, many survived the fire.

This relief shows King Ashurbanipal and his queen at a party with several servants.

Most people in the region rejoiced at Nineveh's destruction. The Jewish prophet Nahum (NAY•huhm) gave voice to the feelings of many:

> "All who see you will recoil from you and will say, 'Nineveh has been ravaged!' Who will console her? Where shall I look for anyone to comfort you? . . . Your shepherds are slumbering, O King of Assyria; your sheepmasters are lying inert; your people are scattered over the hills, and there is none to gather them."
>
> —Nahum 3:7, 18 (Hebrew Bible)

Rebirth of Babylon Under the Chaldeans After defeating the Assyrians, the Chaldeans made Babylon their capital. Around 600 BC, Babylon became the center of a new empire, more than 1,000 years after Hammurabi had ruled there. A Chaldean king named **Nebuchadnezzar** (nehb•uh•kuhd•NEHZ•uhr) restored the city. Perhaps the most impressive part of the restoration was the famous hanging gardens. Greek scholars later listed them as one of the seven wonders of the ancient world. According to legend, one of Nebuchadnezzar's wives missed the flowering shrubs of her mountain homeland. To please her, he had fragrant trees and shrubs planted on terraces that rose 75 feet above Babylon's flat, dry plain.

This is an artist's rendering of the legendary hanging gardens of Babylon. Slaves watered the plants by using hidden pumps that drew water from the Euphrates River.

Indeed, the entire city of Babylon was a wonder. Its walls were so thick that, according to one report, a four-horse chariot could wheel around on top of them. To ensure that the world knew who ruled the city, the king had the bricks inscribed with the words, "I am Nebuchadnezzar, King of Babylon."

The highest building in Babylon was a great, seven-tiered ziggurat more than 300 feet high. It was visible for miles. At night, priests observed the stars from the top of this tower and others in the city. Chaldean astronomers kept detailed records of how the stars and planets seemed to change position in the night sky. They also concluded that the sun, moon, Earth, and five other planets belonged to the same solar system. The Chaldeans' observations formed the basis for both astronomy and astrology.

Nebuchadnezzar's empire fell shortly after his death. The Persians who next came to power adopted many Assyrian military, political, and artistic inventions. The Persians would use the organization the Assyrians had developed to stabilize the region.

Reading Check
Summarize Why did the tablets in Nineveh's library survive the destruction of the city?

Lesson 2 Assessment

1. **Organize Information** Use a table. Why did the Assyrians develop into a great military power? Why did their power decline?

   Assyrian Power

Causes for Rise	Causes for Decline
Need to defend against attacks	Hated by conquered people

2. **Key Terms and People** For each key term or person in the lesson, write a sentence explaining its significance.

3. **Synthesize** What contributions to government administration and culture did the Assyrians make?

4. **Develop Historical Perspective** Why did the people in the region rejoice when the Assyrian Empire was defeated?

5. **Form Opinions** Do you think the Assyrians' almost exclusive reliance on military power was a good strategy for creating their empire? Why or why not?

6. **Make Inferences** Why might the Assyrian warrior kings have had such a great interest in writing and reading?

7. **Compare** In what ways were King Ashurbanipal and King Nebuchadnezzar similar?

The Persian Empire

The Big Idea

By governing with tolerance and wisdom, the Persians established a well-ordered empire that lasted for 200 years.

Why It Matters Now

Leaders today try to follow the Persian example of tolerance and wise government.

Key Terms and People

Cyrus
Cambyses
Darius
satrap
Royal Road
Zoroaster

Setting the Stage

The Medes, along with the Chaldeans and others, helped to overthrow the Assyrian Empire in 612 BC. The Medes marched to Nineveh from their homeland in the area of present-day northern Iran. Meanwhile, the Medes' close neighbor to the south, Persia, began to expand its horizons and territorial ambitions.

The Rise of Persia

The Assyrians employed military force to control a vast empire. In contrast, the Persians based their empire on tolerance and diplomacy. They relied on a strong military to back up their policies. Ancient Persia included what is today the country of Iran.

The Persian Homeland Indo-Europeans first migrated from Central Europe and southern Russia to the mountains and plateaus east of the Fertile Crescent around 1000 BC. This area extended from the Caspian Sea in the north to the Persian Gulf in the south. In addition to fertile farmland, ancient Iran boasted a wealth of minerals. These included copper, lead, gold, silver, and gleaming blue lapis lazuli. A thriving trade in these minerals put the settlers in contact with their neighbors to the east and the west.

At first, dozens of tiny kingdoms occupied the region. Eventually two major powers emerged: the Medes and the Persians. In time, a remarkable ruler would lead Persia to dominate the Medes and found a huge empire.

Cyrus the Great Founds an Empire The rest of the world paid little attention to the Persians until 550 BC. In that year, **Cyrus** (SY•ruhs), Persia's king, began to conquer several neighboring kingdoms. Cyrus was a military genius, leading his army from victory to victory between 550 and 539 BC. In time, Cyrus controlled an empire that spanned 2,000 miles, from the Indus River in the east to Anatolia in the west.

Even more than his military genius, though, Cyrus's most enduring legacy was his method of governing. His kindness toward conquered peoples revealed a wise and tolerant view of empire. For example, when Cyrus's army marched into a city, his generals prevented Persian soldiers from looting and burning. Unlike other conquerors, Cyrus believed in honoring local customs and religions. Instead of destroying the local temple, Cyrus would kneel there to pray. He also allowed the Jews, who had been driven from their homeland by the Babylonians, to return to Jerusalem in 538 BC. Under Persian rule, the Jews rebuilt their city and temple.

DOCUMENT-BASED INVESTIGATION   Historical Source

Cyrus's View of Empire

The Jews were grateful to Cyrus for his wise and tolerant view of empire. They considered him one of God's anointed ones. The Jewish prophet Ezra recounted Cyrus's proclamation regarding the Jewish people who had been driven from their homeland.

Analyze Historical Sources
How does this quotation show that Cyrus respected the Jews?

> "Thus said King Cyrus of Persia: The Lord God of Heaven has given me all the kingdoms of the earth and has charged me with building Him a house in Jerusalem, which is in Judah. Anyone of you of all His people—may his God be with him, and let him go up to Jerusalem that is in Judah and build the House of the Lord God of Israel, the God that is in Jerusalem."
>
> —Ezra 1: 2–3 (Hebrew Bible)

Reading Check
Summarize
What are some examples of Cyrus's tolerant method of governing?

Cyrus was killed as he fought nomadic invaders on the eastern border of his empire. According to the Greek historian Arrian, his simple, house-shaped tomb bore these words: "O man, I am Cyrus the son of Cambyses. I established the Persian Empire and was king of Asia. Do not begrudge me my memorial."

Persian Rule

The task of unifying conquered territories was left to rulers who followed Cyrus. They succeeded by combining Persian control with local self-government.

Cambyses and Darius Cyrus died in 530 BC. His son **Cambyses** (kam•BY•seez), named after Cyrus's father, expanded the Persian Empire by conquering Egypt. However, the son neglected to follow his father's wise example. Cambyses scorned the Egyptian religion. He ordered the images of Egyptian gods to be burned. After ruling for only eight years, Cambyses died. Immediately, widespread rebellions broke out across the empire. Persian control had seemed strong a decade earlier. It now seemed surprisingly fragile.

Cambyses's successor, **Darius** (duh•RY•uhs), a noble of the ruling dynasty, had begun his career as a member of the king's bodyguard. An elite group of Persian soldiers, the Ten Thousand Immortals, helped Darius seize the throne around 522 BC. Darius spent the first three years of his reign putting down revolts. He spent the next few years establishing a well-organized and efficient administration.

Having brought peace and stability to the empire, Darius turned his attention to conquest. He led his armies eastward into the mountains of present-day Afghanistan and then down into the river valleys of India. The immense Persian Empire now extended more than 2,500 miles, embracing Egypt and Anatolia in the west, part of India in the east, and the Fertile Crescent in the center. Darius's only failure was his inability to conquer Greece.

Sculpted figures bring gifts to Darius. The relief sculpture, located in the ancient Persian capital of Persepolis, dates from around the sixth century BC.

Provinces and Satraps Although Darius was a great warrior, his real genius lay in administration. To govern his sprawling empire, Darius divided it into 20 provinces. These provinces were roughly similar to the homelands of the different groups of people who lived within the Persian Empire. Under Persian rule, the people of each province still practiced their own religion. They also spoke their own language and followed many of their own laws. This administrative policy of many groups—sometimes called "nationalities"—living by their own laws within one empire was repeatedly practiced in Southwest Asia.

Although tolerant of the many groups within his empire, Darius still ruled with absolute power. In each province, Darius installed a governor called a **satrap** (SAY•trap), who ruled locally. Darius also appointed a military leader and a tax collector for each province. To ensure the loyalty of these officials, Darius sent out inspectors known as the "King's Eyes and Ears."

Two other tools helped Darius hold together his empire. An excellent system of roads allowed Darius to communicate quickly with the most distant parts of the empire. The famous **Royal Road**, for example, ran from Susa in Persia to Sardis in Anatolia, a distance of 1,677 miles. Darius borrowed the second tool, manufacturing metal coins, from the Lydians of Asia Minor. For the first time, coins of a standard value circulated throughout an extended empire. People no longer had to weigh and measure odd pieces of gold or silver to pay for what they bought. The network of roads and the wide use of standardized coins promoted trade. Trade, in turn, helped to hold together the empire.

Reading Check
Evaluate
What tools helped Darius hold together his vast empire?

The Persian Legacy

By the time of Darius's rule, about 2,500 years had passed since the first Sumerian city-states had been built. During those years, people of the Fertile Crescent had endured war, conquest, and famine. These events gave rise to a basic question: Why should so much suffering and chaos exist in the world? A Persian prophet named **Zoroaster** (ZAWR•oh•as•tuhr), who lived around 600 BC, offered an answer.

Zoroaster's Teachings Zoroaster taught that the earth is a battleground where a great struggle is fought between the spirit of good and the spirit of evil. Each person, Zoroaster preached, is expected to take part in this struggle. The Zoroastrian religion teaches a belief in one god, Ahura Mazda (ah•HUR•uh MAZ•duh). At the end of time, Ahura Mazda will judge everyone according to how well he or she fought the battle for good. Similarities to Zoroastrianism—such as the concept of Satan and a belief in angels—can be found in Judaism, Christianity, and Islam.

After the Muslim conquest of Persia in the AD 600s, the Zoroastrian religion declined. Some groups carried the faith eastward to India. Zoroastrianism was also an important influence in the development of Manichaeism (man•ih•KEE•ihz•uhm), a religious system that competed with early Christianity for believers.

The Royal Road

One of the ways in which societies build and maintain empires is by establishing systems of communication and transportation. The Royal Road, built by the rulers of the Persian Empire, connected Susa in Persia to Sardis in Anatolia.

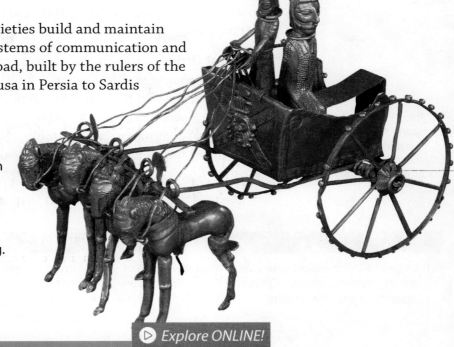

▶ This four-horse chariot dates from the sixth to fourth century BC. It is the type of vehicle that would have traveled the Royal Road in the time of Darius. The studs on the wheels prevented the chariot from slipping.

▷ *Explore ONLINE!*

A Ride Along the Royal Road

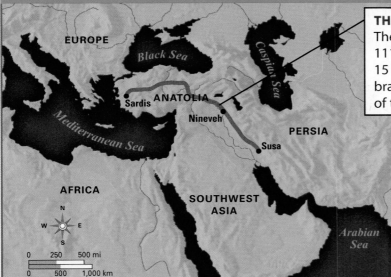

THE ROAD
The road was 1,677 miles long. There were 111 post or relay stations spaced about 15 miles apart along the road. Other roads branched off the main road to distant parts of the empire.

THE RIDE
Relay stations were equipped with fresh horses for the king's messengers. Royal messengers could cover the length of the Royal Road in seven days. Normal travel time along the road was longer. A caravan, for example, might take three months to travel the entire distance.

▲ Strong road networks like the Royal Road enabled empires to expand and maintain control over people and places. Like the Persians, the Inca of South America created a road system thousands of miles long. These roads allowed the Inca to extend their rule over as many as 16 million people. Empires throughout history have shared characteristics such as efficient communication systems, effective leaders, and powerful armies.

Critical Thinking
1. **Recognize Effects** How would the Royal Road enable a ruler to maintain power in the empire?

2. **Compare** What systems of communication and transportation today might be compared to the Royal Road of the Persians?

The followers of Mithra, a Zoroastrian god, spread westward to become a popular religion among the military legions in the Roman Empire. Today, modern Zoroastrians continue to observe the religion's traditions in several countries including Iran and India, where its followers are called Parsis.

Political Order Through their tolerance and good government, the Persians brought political order to Southwest Asia. They preserved ideas from earlier civilizations and found new ways to live and rule. Their respect for other cultures helped to preserve those cultures for the future. The powerful dynasty Cyrus established in Persia lasted 200 years and grew into a huge empire. As you will learn in Lesson 4, great empires also arose in China and dominated that region.

Reading Check
Compare What ideas and worldview did Zoroastrianism share with other religions?

Lesson 3 Assessment

1. **Organize Information** Use a Venn diagram. Which of the differences between Cyrus and Darius do you consider most important? Why?

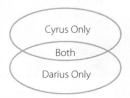

Cyrus Only

Both

Darius Only

2. **Key Terms and People** For each key term and person in the lesson, write a sentence explaining its significance.

3. **Form Generalizations** How did Cyrus treat the peoples he conquered?

4. **Synthesize** What methods and tools did Darius use to hold together his empire?

5. **Make Inferences** What do the words that appeared on Cyrus's tomb suggest about his character?

6. **Draw Conclusions** How did the Royal Road help Darius maintain control over his people?

7. **Develop Historical Perspective** What events led to the development of Zoroastrianism?

The Unification of China

The Big Idea

The social disorder of the warring states contributed to the development of three Chinese ethical systems.

Why It Matters Now

The people, events, and ideas that shaped China's early history continue to influence China's role in today's world.

Key Terms and People

Confucius
filial piety
bureaucracy
Daoism
Legalism
I Ching
yin and yang
Qin Dynasty
Shi Huangdi
autocracy

Setting the Stage

The Zhou Dynasty lasted for at least eight centuries, from approximately 1027 to 256 BC. For the first 300 years of their long reign, the Zhou kings controlled a large empire, including both eastern and western lands. Local rulers reported to the king, who had the ultimate power. By the latter years of the Zhou Dynasty, the lords of dependent territories began to think of themselves as independent kings. Their almost constant conflict, which is known as "the warring states period," led to the decline of the Zhou Dynasty.

Confucius and the Social Order

Toward the end of the Zhou Dynasty, China moved away from its ancient values of social order, harmony, and respect for authority. Chinese scholars and philosophers developed different solutions to restore these values.

Confucius Urges Harmony China's most influential scholar was **Confucius** (kuhn•FYOO•shuhs). Born in 551 BC, Confucius lived in a time when the Zhou Dynasty was in decline. He led a scholarly life, studying and teaching history, music, and moral character.

Confucius was born at a time of crisis and violence in China. He had a deep desire to restore the order and moral living of earlier times to his society. Confucius believed that social order, harmony, and good government could be restored in China if society were organized around five basic relationships. These were the relationships between: (1) ruler and subject, (2) father and son, (3) husband and wife, (4) older brother and younger brother, and (5) friend and friend. A code of proper conduct regulated each of these relationships. For example, rulers should practice kindness and virtuous living. In return, subjects should be loyal and law-abiding.

Statue of a Chinese warrior from the Qin Dynasty

Three of Confucius's five relationships were based upon the family. Confucius stressed that children should practice **filial piety**, or respect for their parents and ancestors. Filial piety, according to Confucius, meant devoting oneself to one's parents during their lifetimes. It also required honoring their memories after death through the performance of certain rituals.

In the following passage, Confucius—the "Master"—expresses his thoughts on the concept:

> *"Ziyou [a disciple of Confucius] asked about filial piety. The Master said: 'Nowadays people think they are dutiful sons when they feed their parents. Yet they also feed their dogs and horses. Unless there is respect, where is the difference?'"*

—Confucius, *Analects* 2.7

Confucius wanted to reform Chinese society by showing rulers how to govern wisely. Impressed by Confucius's wisdom, the duke of Lu appointed him minister of justice. According to legend, Confucius so overwhelmed people by his kindness and courtesy that almost overnight, crime vanished from Lu. When the duke's ways changed, however, Confucius became disillusioned and resigned.

Confucius spent the remainder of his life teaching. His students later collected his words in a book called the *Analects*. A disciple named Mencius (MEHN•shee•uhs) also spread Confucius's ideas.

Vocabulary
legend a story handed down from earlier times, especially one believed to be historical

---

BIOGRAPHY

Confucius
(551–479 BC)

Confucius was born to a poor family. As an adult, he earned his living as a teacher. But he longed to put his principles into action by advising political leaders. Finally, at around age 50, Confucius won a post as minister in his home state. According to legend, he set such a virtuous example that a purse lying in the middle of the street would be untouched for days.

After Confucius resigned his post as minister, he returned to teaching. He considered himself a failure because he had never held high office. Yet Confucius's ideas have molded Chinese thought for centuries.

Laozi
(sixth century BC)

Although a person named Laozi is credited with being the first philosopher of Daoism, no one knows for sure whether he really existed. Legend has it that Laozi's mother carried him in her womb for 62 years and that he was born with white hair and wrinkled skin. Laozi's followers claimed that he was a contemporary of Confucius.

Unlike Confucius, however, Laozi believed that government should do as little as possible and leave the people alone. Laozi thought that people could do little to influence the outcome of events. Daoism offered communion with nature as an alternative to political chaos.

Confucian Ideas About Government Confucius said that education could transform a humbly born person into a gentleman. In saying this, he laid the groundwork for the creation of a **bureaucracy**, a trained civil service, or those who run the government. According to Confucius, a gentleman had four virtues: "In his private conduct he was courteous, in serving his master he was punctilious [precise], in providing for the needs of the people, he gave them even more than their due; in exacting service from the people, he was just." Education became critically important to career advancement in the bureaucracy.

Scholars still debate whether or not Confucianism is a religion. It was, however, an ethical system, a system based on accepted principles of right and wrong. It became the foundation for Chinese government and social order. In addition, the ideas of Confucius spread beyond China and influenced civilizations throughout East Asia.

Reading Check
Summarize
How did Confucius feel about family? Explain.

Other Ethical Systems

In addition to Confucius, other Chinese scholars and philosophers developed ethical systems with very different philosophies. Some stressed the importance of nature, others, the power of government.

Daoists Seek Harmony For a Chinese thinker named Laozi (low•dzuh), who may have lived during the sixth century BC, only the natural order was important. The natural order involves relations among all living things. His book *Dao De Jing* (*The Way of Virtue*) expressed Laozi's belief. He said that a universal force called the Dao (dow), meaning "the Way," guides all things.

The philosophy of Laozi came to be known as **Daoism**. Its search for knowledge and understanding of nature led Daoism's followers to pursue scientific studies. Daoists made many important contributions to the sciences of alchemy, astronomy, and medicine.

DOCUMENT-BASED INVESTIGATION **Historical Source**

Daoist Thought

Of all the creatures of nature, according to Laozi, only humans fail to follow the Dao. They argue about questions of right and wrong, good manners or bad. According to Laozi, such arguments are pointless. In the following passage, he explains the wisdom of the Dao.

Analyze Historical Sources
What do you think is the Daoist attitude toward being a powerful person?

"The Dao never does anything,
yet through it all things are done.
    If powerful men and women
could center themselves in it,
the whole world would be transformed by
itself, in its natural rhythms.
People would be content
with their simple, everyday lives,
in harmony, and free of desire.
    When there is no desire,
all things are at peace."

—Laozi, *Dao De Jing*, Passage 37

Legalists Urge Harsh Rule In sharp contrast to the followers of Confucius and Laozi was a group of practical political thinkers called the Legalists. They believed that a highly efficient and powerful government was the key to restoring order in society. They got their name from their belief that government should use the law to end civil disorder and restore harmony. Hanfeizi and Li Si were among the founders of **Legalism**.

The Legalists taught that a ruler should provide rich rewards for people who carried out their duties well. Likewise, the disobedient should be harshly punished. In practice, the Legalists stressed punishment more than rewards. For example, anyone caught outside his own village without a travel permit should have his ears or nose chopped off.

The Legalists believed in controlling ideas as well as actions. They suggested that a ruler burn all writings that might encourage people to criticize government. After all, it was for the prince to govern and the people to obey. Eventually, Legalist ideas gained favor with a prince of a new dynasty that replaced the Zhou. That powerful ruler soon brought order to China.

I Ching and Yin and Yang People with little interest in the philosophical debates of the Confucians, Daoists, and Legalists found answers to life's questions elsewhere. Some consulted a book of oracles called **I Ching** (also spelled *Yi Jing*) to solve ethical or practical problems. Readers used the book by throwing a set of coins, interpreting the results, and then reading the appropriate oracle, or prediction.

Traditional yin-and-yang symbol.

Chinese Ethical Systems

Daoism	Confucianism	Legalism
Started around 600–500 BC.	Developed between 551 and 479 BC.	Developed during the 400s BC.
The natural order is more important than the social order.	Social order, harmony, and good government should be based on family relationships.	A highly efficient and powerful government is the key to social order.
A universal force guides all things.	Respect for parents and elders is important to a well-ordered society.	Punishments are useful to maintain social order.
Human beings should live simply and in harmony with nature.	Education is important both to the welfare of the individual and to society.	Thinkers and their ideas should be strictly controlled by the government.

Interpret Charts
1. **Compare** Which of these three systems stresses the importance of government and a well-ordered society?
2. **Synthesize** Which of these systems seems to be most moderate and balanced? Explain.

The *I Ching (The Book of Changes)* helped people to lead a happy life by offering good advice and simple common sense.

Other people turned to the ideas of ancient thinkers, such as the concept of **yin and yang**—two powers that together represented the natural rhythms of life. Yin represents all that is cold, dark, soft, and mysterious. Yang is the opposite—warm, bright, hard, and clear. The symbol of yin and yang is a circle divided into halves, as shown in the emblem on the previous page. The circle represents the harmony of yin and yang. Both forces represent the rhythm of the universe and complement each other. Both the *I Ching* and yin and yang helped Chinese people understand how they fit into the world.

Reading Check
Summarize
How did the Legalists think that a society could be made to run well?

The Qin Dynasty Unifies China

In the third century BC, the **Qin Dynasty** (chihn) replaced the Zhou Dynasty. It emerged from the western state of Qin. The ruler who founded the Qin Dynasty employed Legalist ideas to subdue the warring states and unify his country.

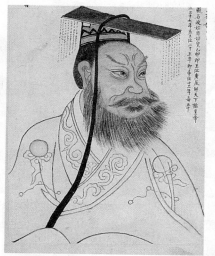

Although a tyrant, Shi Huangdi is considered the founder of unified China. The word *Qin* is the origin of *China*.

A New Emperor Takes Control In 221 BC, after ruling for more than 20 years, the Qin ruler assumed the name **Shi Huangdi** (shihr hwahng·dee), which means "First Emperor." The new emperor had begun his reign by halting the internal battles that had sapped China's strength. Next he turned his attention to defeating invaders and crushing resistance within China to his rule. Shi Huangdi's armies attacked the invaders north of the Huang He and south as far as what is now Vietnam. His victories doubled China's size. Shi Huangdi was determined to unify China.

Shi Huangdi acted decisively to crush political opposition at home. To destroy the power of rival warlords, he introduced a policy called "strengthening the trunk and weakening the branches." He commanded all the noble families to live in the capital city under his suspicious gaze. This policy, according to tradition, uprooted 120,000 noble families. Seizing their land, the emperor carved China into 36 administrative districts. He sent Qin officials to control them.

To prevent criticism, Shi Huangdi and his prime minister, the Legalist philosopher Li Si, murdered hundreds of Confucian scholars. They also ordered "useless" books burned. These books were the works of Confucian thinkers and poets who disagreed with the Legalists. Practical books about medicine and farming, however, were spared. Through measures such as these, Shi Huangdi established an **autocracy**—a government that has unlimited power and uses it in an arbitrary manner.

A Program of Centralization Shi Huangdi's sweeping program of centralization included the building of a highway network of more than 4,000 miles. Also, he set the same standards throughout China for writing, law, currency, and weights and measures—even down to the length of cart axles. This last standard made sure that all vehicles could fit into the ruts of China's main roads.

History in Depth

The Great Wall of China

From the Yellow Sea in the east to the Gobi Desert in the west, the Great Wall twisted like a dragon's tail for thousands of miles. Watch towers rose every 200 to 300 yards along the wall.

In the time of Shi Huangdi, hundreds of thousands of peasants collected, hauled, and dumped millions of tons of stone, dirt, and rubble to fill the core of the Great Wall.

Slabs of cut stone on the outside of the wall enclosed a heap of pebbles and rubble on the inside. Each section of the wall rose to a height of 20 to 25 feet.

Although Shi Huangdi built the earliest unified wall, much of the wall as it exists today dates from the later Ming Dynasty (AD 1368–1644).

▶ Explore ONLINE!

The Qin Dynasty, 221–202 BC

Legend:
- Qin Dynasty
- Extent of Zhou Dynasty (Approximate)
- Great Wall

MONGOLIA

KOREA

Anyang

Huang He

Yellow Sea

Wei He

Luoyang

Hao   Ch'ang-an (Xi'an)

East China Sea

TIBET

HIMALAYAS

Chang Jiang

Taiwan

N W E S

0   250   500 mi
0   500   1,000 km

INDIA

BURMA

Xi Jiang

VIETNAM (ANNAM)

Bay of Bengal

South China Sea

100°E   120°E   20°N

Interpret Sources

1. **Make Inferences** What were the benefits of the watch towers along the wall?

2. **Draw Conclusions** What modern structures serve the same purpose as the watch towers?

Under Shi Huangdi's rule, irrigation projects increased farm production. Trade blossomed, thanks to the new road system. Trade pushed a new class of merchants into prominence. Despite these social advances, harsh taxes and repressive government made the Qin regime unpopular. Shi Huangdi had unified China at the expense of human freedom.

Great Wall of China Scholars hated Shi Huangdi for his book burning. Poor people hated him because they were forced to work on the building of a huge defensive wall. Earlier, Zhou rulers had erected smaller walls to discourage attacks by northern nomads. Shi Huangdi determined to close the gaps and extend the wall almost the length of the empire's border. Enemies would have to gallop halfway to Tibet to get around it.

The Great Wall of China arose on the backs of hundreds of thousands of peasants. The wall builders worked neither for wages nor for love of empire. They faced a terrible choice: work on the wall or die. Many of the laborers worked on the wall and died anyway, victims of the crushing labor or the harsh winter weather. (The Great Wall, as it exists today, dates from the later Ming Dynasty, AD 1368–1644.) Besides walls, the architecture of the Qin Dynasty included a burial chamber for Shi Huangdi that was the size of a large town. It was guarded by an army of 8,000 life-sized clay soldiers, known as the terra-cotta warriors.

The Fall of the Qin The Qin Dynasty lasted only a short time. Though fully as cruel as his father, Shi Huangdi's son proved less able. Peasants rebelled just three years after the second Qin emperor took office. One of their leaders, a peasant from the land of Han, marched his troops into the capital city. By 202 BC, the harsh Qin Dynasty gave way to the Han Dynasty, one of the longest in Chinese history.

While the Chinese explored the best ways to govern, ancient Greece also was experimenting with different forms of government, as you will read about next.

Reading Check
Recognize Effects
What were the positive and negative effects of Shi Huangdi's rule?

Lesson 4 Assessment

1. **Organize Information** Use a word web. Which aspect of Chinese life was most affected by the chaos of the warring states?

2. **Key Terms and People** For each key term and person in the lesson, write a sentence explaining its significance.

3. **Synthesize** How did Confucius believe that social order, harmony, and good government could be restored in China?

4. **Evaluate** What measures did Shi Huangdi take to crush political opposition at home?

5. **Predict** How would followers of the three philosophical traditions in China react to the idea that "all men are created equal"?

6. **Analyze Causes** Why did Shi Huangdi have his critics murdered?

7. **Make Inferences** Would a ruler who followed Confucian or Daoist ideas have built the Great Wall? Why or why not?

Module 4 Assessment

Key Terms and People

For each term or person below, briefly explain its connection to the history of the first age of empires between 1570 and 200 BC.

1. Ramses II
2. Kush
3. Assyria
4. Ashurbanipal
5. Cyrus

6. Royal Road
7. Zoroaster
8. Confucius
9. Daoism
10. Shi Huangdi

Main Ideas

Use your notes and the information in the module to answer the following questions.

The Egyptian and Nubian Empires

1. How did the Kushites treat Egyptian culture after they conquered Egypt?
2. When did Kush experience a golden age?

The Assyrian Empire

3. How did Assyria acquire its empire?
4. What were the positive achievements of the Assyrian Empire?

The Persian Empire

5. What is Cyrus's enduring legacy?
6. How far did Darius extend the Persian Empire?

The Unification of China

7. Around what five basic relationships did Confucius believe society should be organized?
8. Why did Shi Huangdi have the Great Wall built?

Module 4 Assessment, continued

Critical Thinking

1. **Evaluate** Create a table, and list the successes and failures of the leaders discussed in this module.

Leader	Successes	Failures
Thutmose III		
Sennacherib		
Cyrus		

2. **Draw Conclusions** Religious and ethical systems in Persia and China arose in response to what similar conditions?

3. **Develop Historical Perspective** How have Cyrus's and Sennacherib's contrasting ruling styles probably affected their legacies?

4. **Recognize Effects** What positive results occur when cultures interact? What negative results might there be?

5. **Synthesize** What similar purpose was served by the Persians' Royal Road and by the Great Wall of China?

Engage with History

Now that you've read the module, think about the advantages and disadvantages of empire. Discuss the following questions with a small group:

- Do empires benefit conquered peoples?
- Do empires impose penalties on those they conquer?
- Which outweighs the other—the benefits or the penalties?

Focus on Writing

Study the information about the Great Wall of China. Imagine that you are one of the workers who built the Great Wall. Write three **journal entries** describing the following:

- the work you carry out on the Great Wall
- your experiences with other workers
- your impressions of daily life in China

Multimedia Activity

Create a Website

Create a website for a museum exhibit about the first empires. Choose one of these empires to research: Assyria, Kush, Persia, or Qin. Consider including the following:

- art, artifacts, and maps
- a description of the empire with dates, location, and rulers
- information on major events and conflicts
- the rise and fall of the empire
- a discussion of the empire's legacy
- a list of websites used in your research

Classical Greece

Essential Question

Why might the modern world be interested in the history, culture, and civilizations of ancient Greece?

About the Photo: The Temple of Hera II, also known as the Temple of Neptune, is a beautifully preserved example of classical Greek architecture. Its columns and pedestals demonstrate the sense of balance and symmetry typical of the classical Greek style.

> ▶ *Explore ONLINE!*

HISTORY

VIDEOS, including...
- Origins of Western Culture
- Mysteries of Troy
- Battle of Marathon

☑ Document Based Investigations

☑ Graphic Organizers

☑ Interactive Games

☑ Image Carousel: Festivals and Sports

☑ Animation: Archimedean Screw

In this module you will learn about the history and culture of classical Greece and its impact on the modern world.

What You Will Learn ...

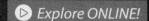

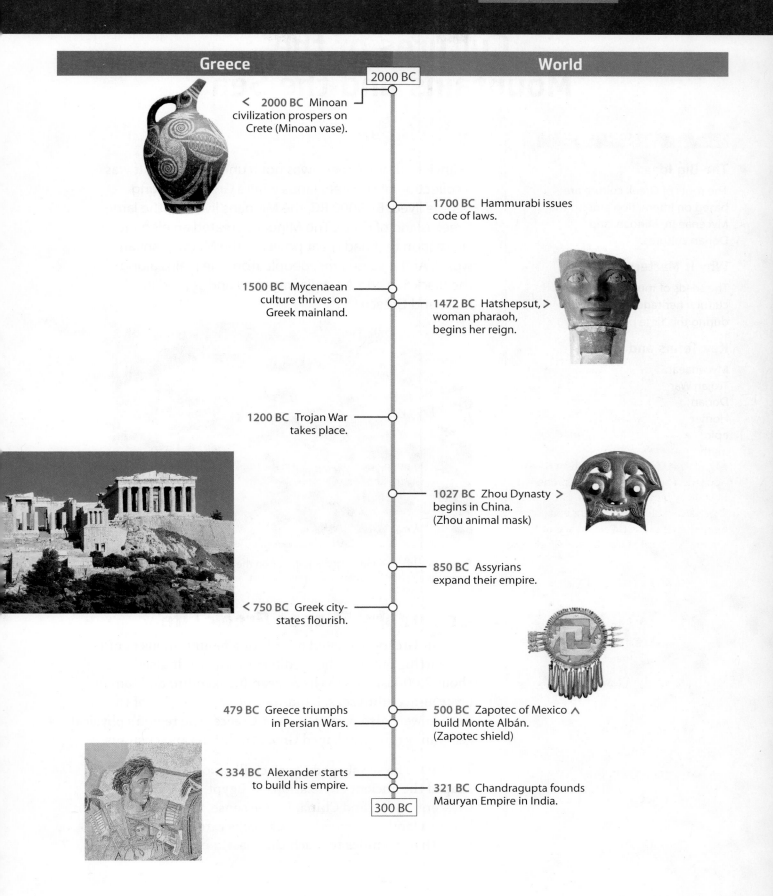

Greece	World

2000 BC

< 2000 BC Minoan civilization prospers on Crete (Minoan vase).

1700 BC Hammurabi issues code of laws.

1500 BC Mycenaean culture thrives on Greek mainland.

1472 BC Hatshepsut, **>** woman pharaoh, begins her reign.

1200 BC Trojan War takes place.

1027 BC Zhou Dynasty **>** begins in China. (Zhou animal mask)

850 BC Assyrians expand their empire.

< 750 BC Greek city-states flourish.

479 BC Greece triumphs in Persian Wars.

500 BC Zapotec of Mexico **∧** build Monte Albán. (Zapotec shield)

< 334 BC Alexander starts to build his empire.

321 BC Chandragupta founds Mauryan Empire in India.

300 BC

Cultures of the Mountains and the Sea

The Big Idea

The roots of Greek culture are based on interaction among the Mycenaean, Minoan, and Dorian cultures.

Why It Matters Now

The seeds of much of Western cultural heritage were planted during this time period.

Key Terms and People

Mycenaean
Trojan War
Dorian
Homer
epic
myth

Setting the Stage

In ancient times, Greece was not a united country. It was a collection of separate lands where Greek-speaking people lived. By 3000 BC, the Minoans lived on the large Greek island of Crete. The Minoans created an elegant civilization that had great power in the Mediterranean world. At the same time, people from the plains along the Black Sea and Anatolia migrated and settled in mainland Greece.

The palace in the Minoan city of Knossos on the island of Crete served as a center for economic, government, and religious activity.

Geography Shapes Greek Life

Ancient Greece consisted mainly of a mountainous peninsula jutting out into the Mediterranean Sea. It also included about 2,000 islands in the Aegean (ih•JEE•uhn) and Ionian (eye•OH•nee•uhn) seas. Lands on the eastern edge of the Aegean were also part of ancient Greece. The region's physical geography directly shaped Greek traditions and customs.

The Sea The sea shaped Greek civilization just as rivers shaped the ancient civilizations of Egypt, the Fertile Crescent, India, and China. In one sense, the Greeks did not live *on* a land but *around* a sea. Greeks rarely had to travel more than 85 miles to reach the coastline. The Aegean

Sea, the Ionian Sea, and the neighboring Black Sea were important transportation routes for the Greek people. These seaways linked most parts of Greece. As the Greeks became skilled sailors, sea travel connected Greece with other societies. Sea travel and trade were also important because Greece lacked natural resources, such as timber, precious metals, and usable farmland.

The Land Rugged mountains covered about three-fourths of ancient Greece. The mountain chains ran mainly from northwest to southeast along the Balkan Peninsula. Mountains divided the land into a number of different regions. This significantly influenced Greek political life. Instead of a single government, the Greeks developed small, independent communities within each little valley and its surrounding mountains. Most Greeks gave their loyalty to these local communities.

In ancient times, the uneven terrain also made land transportation difficult. Of the few roads that existed, most were little more than dirt paths. It often took travelers several days to complete a journey that might take a few hours today.

Much of the land itself was stony, and only a small part of it was arable, or suitable for farming. Tiny but fertile valleys covered about one-fourth of Greece. The small streams that watered these valleys were not suitable for large-scale irrigation projects. With so little fertile farmland or fresh water for irrigation, Greece was never able to support a large population. Historians estimate that no more than a few million people lived in ancient Greece at any given time. Even this small population could not expect the land to support a life of luxury. A desire for more living space, grassland for raising livestock, and adequate farmland may have been factors that motivated the Greeks to seek new sites for colonies.

Farmable land in Greece was—and still is—nestled into small valleys surrounded by mountains.

Reading Check
Analyze Causes
In what ways did Greece's location by the sea and its mountainous land affect its development?

The Climate Climate was the third important environmental influence on Greek civilization. Greece has a varied climate, with temperatures averaging 48 degrees Fahrenheit in the winter and 80 degrees Fahrenheit in the summer. In ancient times, these moderate temperatures supported an outdoor life for many Greek citizens. Men spent much of their leisure time at outdoor public events. They met often to discuss public issues, exchange news, and take an active part in civic life.

Mycenaean Civilization Develops

A large wave of Indo-Europeans migrated from the Eurasian steppes to Europe, India, and Southwest Asia. Some of the people who settled on the Greek mainland around 2000 BC were later known as **Mycenaeans**. The name came from their leading city, Mycenae (my·SEE·nee).

Mycenae was located in southern Greece on a steep, rocky ridge and surrounded by a protective wall more than 20 feet thick. The fortified city of Mycenae could withstand almost any attack. From Mycenae, a warrior-king ruled the surrounding villages and farms. Strong rulers controlled the areas around other Mycenaean cities, such as Tiryns and Athens. These kings dominated Greece from about 1600 to 1100 BC.

Contact with Minoans Sometime after 1500 BC, through either trade or war, the Mycenaeans came into contact with the Minoan civilization. From their contact with the Minoans, the Mycenaeans saw the value of expanded seaborne trade. Mycenaean traders soon sailed throughout the eastern Mediterranean, making stops at Aegean islands, coastal towns in Anatolia, and ports in Syria, Egypt, Italy, and Crete. These transportation routes led to an exchange of ideas and technology.

The Minoans also influenced the Mycenaeans in other ways. The Mycenaeans adapted the Minoan writing system to the Greek language and decorated vases with Minoan designs. The Minoan-influenced culture of Mycenae formed the core of Greek religious practice, art, politics, and literature. Indeed, Western civilization has its roots in these two early Mediterranean civilizations.

The Trojan War During the 1200s BC, the Mycenaeans fought a ten-year war against Troy, an independent trading city located in Anatolia. According to legend, a Greek army besieged and destroyed Troy because a Trojan prince had kidnapped Helen, the beautiful wife of a Greek king.

For many years, historians thought that the legendary stories told of the **Trojan War** were totally fictional. However, excavations conducted in northwestern Turkey during the 1870s by German archaeologist Heinrich Schliemann suggested that the stories of the Trojan War might have been

Greek stories tell of their army's capture of the legendary city of Troy by hiding soldiers in a hollow wooden horse.

The *Iliad*

The *Iliad* tells the story of the last year of the Trojan War. The heroes of the *Iliad* are warriors—the fierce Greek Achilles (uh·KIHL·eez) and the courageous and noble Hector of Troy. Near the end of the epic, Achilles kills Hector in single combat, paving the way for the Greeks' ultimate victory over Troy. In this dramatic excerpt, Hector's wife begs him not to fight Achilles. Hector's response to his wife gives insight into the Greek heroic ideal of *aretē* (ar·uh·TAY), meaning virtue and excellence. A Greek could display this ideal on the battlefield in combat or in athletic contests on the playing field.

Analyze Historical Sources
What does Hector say that demonstrates *aretē*?

> "'My dear husband, your warlike spirit will be your death. You've no compassion for your infant child, for me, your sad wife, who before long will be your widow. . . . As for me, it would be better, if I'm to lose you, to be buried in the ground. . . .'
> Great Hector . . . replied, 'Wife, all this concerns me, too. But I'd be disgraced, dreadfully shamed . . . , if I should slink away from war, like a coward. [F]or I have learned always to be brave, to fight alongside Trojans at the front, striving to win great fame for my father, for myself.'"
>
> —Homer, the *Iliad* (translated by Ian Johnston)

Reading Check
Analyze Effects
How did contact with the Minoans affect Mycenaean culture?

based on real cities, people, and events. Further archaeological studies conducted in the 20th century support Schliemann's findings. Although the exact nature of the Trojan War remains unclear, this attack on Troy was almost certainly one of the last Mycenaean battle campaigns.

Greek Culture Declines Under the Dorians

Not long after the Trojan War, Mycenaean civilization collapsed. Around 1200 BC, sea raiders attacked and burned many Mycenaean cities. According to tradition, a new group of people, the **Dorians** (DAWR·ee·uhnz), moved into the war-torn countryside. The Dorians spoke a dialect of Greek and may have been distant relatives of the Bronze Age Greeks.

The Dorians were far less advanced than the Mycenaeans. The economy collapsed and trade eventually came to a standstill soon after their arrival. Most important to historians, Greeks appear to have temporarily lost the art of writing during the Dorian Age. No written record exists from the 400-year period between 1150 and 750 BC. As a result, little is known about this period of Greek history.

Epics of Homer Lacking writing, the Greeks of this time learned about their history through the spoken word. According to tradition, the greatest storyteller was a blind man named **Homer**. Little is known of his personal life. Some historians believe that Homer composed his **epics**, narrative poems celebrating heroic deeds, sometime between 750 and 700 BC. The Trojan War forms the backdrop for one of Homer's great epic poems, the *Iliad*.

Greeks Create Myths The Greeks developed a rich set of **myths**, or traditional stories, about their gods. The works of Homer and another epic, *Theogony* by Hesiod, are the source of much of Greek mythology. Through the myths, the Greeks sought to understand the mysteries of nature and the power of human passions. Myths explained the changing of the seasons, for example.

Greeks attributed human qualities, such as love, hate, and jealousy, to their gods. The gods quarreled and competed with one another constantly. However, unlike humans, the gods lived forever. Zeus, the ruler of the gods, lived on Mount Olympus with his wife, Hera. Hera was often jealous of Zeus's relationships with other women. Athena, goddess of wisdom, was Zeus's daughter and his favorite child. The Greeks thought of Athena as the guardian of cities, especially of Athens, which was named in her honor. Athens would play a significant role in the development of Greek government.

This is a marble sculpture of Polyphemus—a cyclops, or one-eyed monster—who appears in another of Homer's epics, the *Odyssey*.

Reading Check
Synthesize
What role did mythology play in Greek culture?

Lesson 1 Assessment

1. **Organize Information** Create a two-column graphic organizer similar to the one shown. Fill it in with contributions of the three cultures.

Culture	Contribution
Minoan	Writing system; pottery designs
Mycenaean	
Dorian	

2. **Key Terms and People** For each key term or person in the lesson, write a sentence explaining its significance.

3. **Analyze Effects** What impact did nearness to the sea have on the development of Greece?

4. **Synthesize** What aspects of culture did the Mycenaeans adopt from the Minoans?

5. **Evaluate** Why were the epics of Homer important to the Greeks of the Dorian period?

6. **Draw Conclusions** How did the physical geography of Greece cause Greek-speaking peoples to develop separate, isolated communities?

7. **Analyze Causes** Other than the explanation offered in the legend, why do you think the Greeks went to war with Troy?

8. **Make Inferences** The Dorian period is often called Greece's Dark Age. Why do you think this is so?

Warring City-States

The Big Idea

The growth of city-states in Greece led to the development of several political systems, including democracy.

Why It Matters Now

Many political systems in today's world mirror the varied forms of government that evolved in Greece.

Key Terms and People

polis
acropolis
monarchy
aristocracy
oligarchy
tyrant
democracy
helot
phalanx
Persian Wars

Setting the Stage

During the Dorian period, Greek civilization experienced decline. However, two things changed life in Greece. First, Dorians and Mycenaeans alike began to identify less with the culture of their ancestors and more with the local area where they lived. Second, by the end of this period, the method of governing areas had changed from tribal or clan control to more formal governments—the city-states.

Rule and Order in Greek City-States

By 750 BC, the city-state, or **polis**, was the fundamental political unit in ancient Greece. A polis was made up of a city and its surrounding countryside, which included numerous villages. Most city-states controlled between 50 and 500 square miles of territory. They were often home to fewer than 10,000 residents. At the agora, or marketplace, or on a fortified hilltop called an **acropolis** (uh·KRAHP·uh·lihs), citizens gathered to discuss city government.

Atop the Acropolis of Athens sat the Parthenon (right), a temple built to honor the goddess Athena. The gateway (left) into the Acropolis was called the Propylaea.

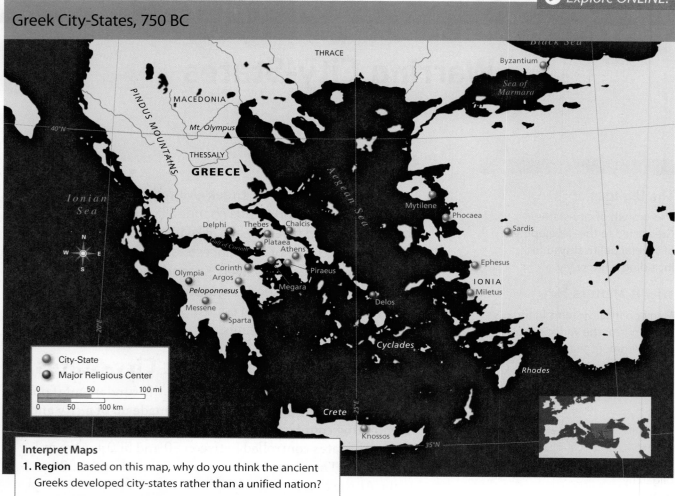

Greek City-States, 750 BC

THRACE

Byzantium

Black Sea

Sea of Marmara

MACEDONIA

PINDUS MOUNTAINS

40°N

Mt. Olympus ▲

THESSALY

GREECE

Ionian Sea

Aegean Sea

Mytilene

Phocaea

Sardis

Delphi   Thebes   Chalcis

Gulf of Corinth   Plataea
Athens

Ephesus

Olympia   Corinth
Argos   Piraeus

Megara

IONIA
Miletus

Peloponnesus

Delos

Messene

Sparta

Cyclades

Rhodes

20°E

35°E

Crete

Knossos

35°N

● City-State

● Major Religious Center

0   50   100 mi

0   50   100 km

Interpret Maps

1. **Region** Based on this map, why do you think the ancient Greeks developed city-states rather than a unified nation?

2. **Location** About how many miles was Athens from Sparta?

Greek Political Structures Greek city-states had many different forms of government. In some, a single person, called a king, ruled in a government called a **monarchy**. Others adopted an **aristocracy** (ar•ih•STAHK•ruh•see), a government ruled by a small group of noble, landowning families. These very rich families often gained political power after serving in a king's military cavalry. Later, as trade expanded, a new class of wealthy merchants and artisans emerged in some cities. When these groups became dissatisfied with aristocratic rule, they sometimes took power or shared it with the nobility. They formed an **oligarchy**, a government ruled by a few powerful people.

Tyrants Seize Power In many city-states, repeated clashes occurred between rulers and the common people. Powerful individuals, usually nobles or other wealthy citizens, sometimes seized control of the government by appealing to the common people for support. These rulers were called **tyrants**. Unlike today, tyrants generally were not considered harsh and cruel. Rather, they were looked upon as leaders who would work for the interests of the ordinary people. Once in power, for example, tyrants often set up building programs to provide jobs and housing for their supporters.

Reading Check
Form Generalizations
What were the common characteristics of Greek city-states?

Athens Builds a Limited Democracy

The idea of representative government also began to take root in some city-states, particularly Athens. Like other city-states, Athens went through power struggles between rich and poor. However, Athenians avoided major political upheavals by making timely reforms. Athenian reformers moved toward **democracy**, rule by the people. In Athens, citizens participated directly in political decision making.

Building Democracy The first step toward democracy came when a nobleman named Draco took power. In 621 BC, Draco developed a legal code that attempted to meet the needs of Athenian society. The code was based on the idea that all Athenians, rich and poor, were equal under the law. Draco's code dealt very harshly with criminals, making death the punishment for practically every crime. It also upheld such practices as debt slavery, in which debtors worked as slaves to repay their debts. The harshness of Draco's laws did not resolve the tensions between rich and poor, however. It only made things worse.

Social Structures More far-reaching democratic reforms were introduced by Solon (SOH•luhn), who came to power in 594 BC. Stating that no citizen should own another citizen, Solon outlawed debt slavery. He organized all Athenian citizens into four social classes according to wealth. Only members of the top three classes could hold political office. However, all citizens, regardless of class, could participate in the Athenian assembly. Solon also introduced the legal concept that any citizen could bring charges against wrongdoers.

Solon

Forms of Government

Monarchy	Aristocracy	Oligarchy	Direct Democracy
State ruled by a king	State ruled by nobility	State ruled by a small group of citizens	State ruled by its citizens
Rule is hereditary	Rule is hereditary and based on family ties, social rank, wealth	Rule is based on wealth or ability	Rule is based on citizenship
Some rulers claim divine right	Social status and wealth support rulers' authority	Ruling group controls military	Majority rule decides vote
Practiced in Mycenae by 2000 BC	Practiced in Athens prior to 594 BC	Practiced in Sparta by 500 BC	Practiced in Athens by about 500 BC

Interpret Charts
1. **Summarize** Which forms of government feature rule based on wealth or property ownership?
2. **Synthesize** In which form of government do citizens have the most power?

Even though Solon outlawed debt slavery, Athens continued to be a slave-owning society. Persians and other non-Greek peoples from neighboring lands were enslaved and put to work. So long as slaves toiled at labors such as working in silver mines, the Athenian aristocracy was afforded time to develop wealth and pursue cultural interests.

Further Reforms Around 500 BC, the Athenian leader Cleisthenes (KLYS•thuh•neez) introduced further reforms. He broke up the power of the nobility by organizing citizens into ten groups based on where they lived rather than on their wealth. He also increased the power of the assembly by allowing all citizens to submit laws for debate and passage. Cleisthenes then created the Council of Five Hundred. This body proposed laws and counseled the assembly. Council members were chosen by lot, or at random.

The reforms of Cleisthenes allowed Athenian citizens to participate in a limited democracy. However, citizenship was restricted to a relatively small number of Athenians. Only free adult males were considered citizens. Women, slaves, and foreigners were excluded from citizenship and had few rights.

Athenian Education For the most part, only the sons of wealthy families received formal education. Schooling began around the age of seven and largely prepared boys to be good citizens. They studied reading, grammar,

Historical Source

A Husband's Advice

In this excerpt from *The Economist*, the Greek historian Xenophon describes how a husband might respond to his wife's question about how she could remain attractive:

"I counseled her to oversee the baking woman as she made the bread; to stand beside the housekeeper as she measured out her stores; to go on tours of inspection to see if all things were in order as they should be. For, as it seemed to me, this would at once be walking exercise and supervision. And, as an excellent gymnastic, I recommended her to knead the dough and roll the paste; to shake the coverlets and make the beds; adding, if she trained herself in exercise of this sort she would enjoy her food, grow vigorous in health, and her complexion would in very truth be lovelier. The very look and aspect of the wife."

—Xenophon, *The Economist*, Book 10
(Translated by H. G. Dakyns)

Analyze Historical Sources
1. **Make Inferences** What is the husband suggesting in his advice to his wife?
2. **Synthesize** How is the husband's advice representative of Athenian attitudes toward women?

poetry, history, mathematics, and music. Because citizens were expected to debate issues in the assembly, boys also received training in logic and public speaking. And since the Greeks believed that it was important to train and develop the body, part of each day was spent in athletic activities. When they got older, boys went to military school to help them prepare for another important duty of citizenship—defending Athens.

Athenian girls did not attend school. Rather, they were educated at home by their mothers and other female members of the household. They learned about child-rearing, weaving cloth, preparing meals, managing the household, and other skills that helped them become good wives and mothers. Some women were able to take their education farther and learned to read and write. A few even became accomplished writers. Even so, most women had very little to do with Athenian life outside the boundaries of family and home.

Sparta Builds a Military State

Located in the southern part of Greece known as the Peloponnesus (pehl•uh•puh•NEE•sus), Sparta was nearly cut off from the rest of Greece by the Gulf of Corinth. In outlook and values, Sparta contrasted sharply with the other city-states, Athens in particular. Instead of a democracy, Sparta built a military state.

Sparta Dominates Messenians Around 725 BC, Sparta conquered the neighboring region of Messenia and took over the land. The Messenians became **helots** (HEHL•uhts), peasants forced to stay on the land they worked. Each year, the Spartans demanded half of the helots' crops. In about 650 BC, the Messenians, resentful of the Spartans' harsh rule, revolted. The Spartans, who were outnumbered eight to one, just barely put down the revolt. Shocked at their vulnerability, they dedicated themselves to making Sparta a strong city-state.

Sparta's Government and Society Spartan government had several branches. An assembly, which was composed of all Spartan citizens, elected officials and voted on major issues. The Council of Elders, made up of 30 older citizens, proposed laws on which the assembly voted. Five elected officials carried out the laws passed by the assembly. These men also controlled education and prosecuted court cases. In addition, two kings ruled over Sparta's military forces.

The Spartan social order consisted of several groups. The first were citizens descended from the original inhabitants of the region. This group included the ruling families who owned the land. A second group, noncitizens who were free, worked in commerce and industry. The helots, at the bottom of Spartan society, were little better than slaves. They worked in the fields or as house servants.

Spartan Daily Life From around 600 until 371 BC, Sparta had the most powerful army in Greece. However, the Spartan people paid a high price for their military supremacy. All forms of individual expression were

Reading Check
Contrast
How is Athenian democracy different from modern American democracy?

Festivals and Sports

The ancient Greeks believed that strong healthy citizens helped strengthen the city-state. They often included sporting events in the festivals they held to honor their gods. The most famous sports festival was the Olympic games, held every four years. Records of Olympics winners started in 776 BC. At first, the festival lasted only one day and had only one contest, a race called the stade. Later, many other events were added, including a long-distance race, wrestling, the long jump, the javelin, and the discus throw. The Olympics was expanded to five days in 472 BC.

WOMEN'S SPORTS ▶
Women had their own sports festival in ancient Greece. It was the festival devoted to Hera, the wife of Zeus. Like the Olympics, the Hera festival was held every four years. One of the main events was a foot race for unmarried women.

◀ DISCUS THROWER
Ancient athletes, such as this discus thrower, would be considered amateurs today because they received no pay for competing. However, they trained rigorously for months at a time. Victors were given lavish gifts and were hailed as heroes. Many athletes competed full-time.

▼ MOUNT OLYMPUS
The ancient Olympics honored Zeus, the father of all Greek gods and goddesses. According to legend, Zeus hurled a thunderbolt from Mount Olympus at a spot in rural Greece. An altar for Zeus was built on that spot. Eventually, many buildings were erected around the altar. This area was called Olympia and became the site for the Olympic games.

Critical Thinking

1. **Form Opinions** Do you think it was a good decision for the Greeks to add more sporting events to the Olympics? Explain.

2. **Compare and Contrast** How are today's Olympics similar to and different from the Olympics in ancient Greece?

discouraged. As a result, Spartans did not value the arts, literature, or other artistic and intellectual pursuits. Spartans valued duty, strength, and discipline over freedom, individuality, beauty, and learning.

Since men were expected to serve in the army until the age of 60, their daily life centered on military training. Boys left home when they were 7 and moved into army barracks, where they stayed until they reached the age of 30. They spent their days marching, exercising, and fighting. They undertook these activities in all kinds of weather, wearing only light tunics and no shoes. At night, they slept without blankets on hard benches. Their daily diet consisted of little more than a bowl of coarse black porridge. Those who wanted more to eat were encouraged to steal food. Such training produced tough, resourceful soldiers.

Spartan girls also led hardy lives. They received some military training, and they also ran, wrestled, and played sports. Like boys, girls were taught to put service to Sparta above everything—even love of family. A legend says that Spartan women told husbands and sons going to war to "come back *with* your shield or *on* it." As adults, Spartan women had considerable freedom, especially in running the family estates when their husbands were on active military service. Such freedom surprised men from other Greek city-states. This was particularly true of Athens, where women were expected to remain mostly out of sight and quietly raise children.

Reading Check
Compare
How would you compare the ideals of Spartan and Athenian societies?

The Persian Wars

Danger of a helot revolt led Sparta to become a military state. Struggles between rich and poor led Athens to become a democracy. The greatest danger of all—invasion by Persian armies—moved Sparta and Athens alike to their greatest glory.

A New Kind of Army Emerges During the Dorian Age, only the rich could afford bronze spears, shields, breastplates, and chariots. Thus, in most city-states, only the rich served in armies. Iron later replaced bronze in the manufacture of weapons. Harder than bronze, iron was more common and therefore cheaper. Soon, ordinary citizens could afford to arm and defend themselves. The shift from bronze to iron weapons made possible a new kind of army composed not only of the rich but also of merchants, artisans, and small landowners. The foot soldiers of this army, called hoplites, stood side by side, each holding a spear in one hand and a shield in the other. This fearsome formation, or **phalanx** (FAY•langks), became the most powerful fighting force in the ancient world.

This piece of Greek pottery shows a phalanx.

Battle at Marathon The **Persian Wars**, between Greece and the Persian Empire, began in Ionia on the coast of Anatolia. The Greeks had long been settled there, but around 546 BC, the Persians conquered the area. When Ionian Greeks revolted, Athens sent ships and soldiers to their aid. The Persian king Darius the Great defeated the rebels and then vowed to destroy Athens in revenge.

In 490 BC, a Persian fleet carried 25,000 men across the Aegean Sea and landed northeast of Athens on a plain called Marathon. There, 10,000 Athenians, neatly arranged in phalanxes, waited for them. Vastly outnumbered, the Greek soldiers charged. The Persians, who wore light armor and lacked training in this kind of land combat, were no match for the disciplined Greek phalanx. After several hours, the Persians fled the battlefield. The Persians lost more than 6,000 men. In contrast, Athenian casualties numbered fewer than 200.

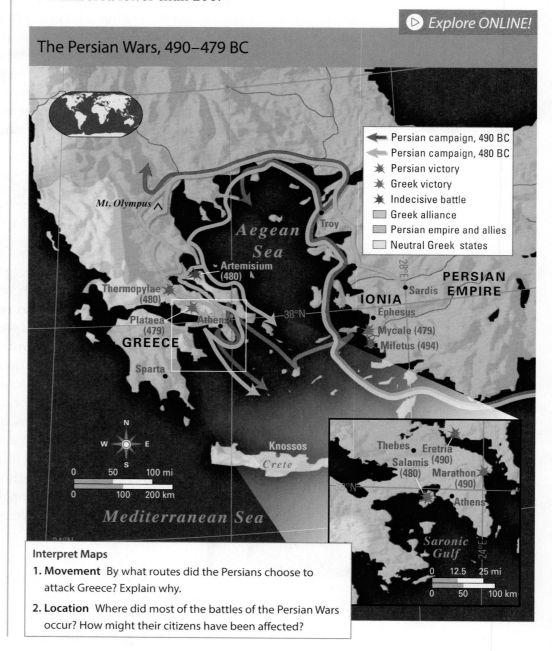

▷ Explore ONLINE!

The Persian Wars, 490–479 BC

Legend:
← Persian campaign, 490 BC
← Persian campaign, 480 BC
✳ Persian victory
✳ Greek victory
✳ Indecisive battle
☐ Greek alliance
☐ Persian empire and allies
☐ Neutral Greek states

Mt. Olympus
Aegean Sea
Troy
Artemisium (480)
Thermopylae (480)
PERSIAN EMPIRE
Sardis
IONIA
Ephesus
Plataea (479)
Athens
38°N
Mycale (479)
Miletus (494)
GREECE
Sparta
28°E

N W E S
0 50 100 mi
0 100 200 km

Knossos
Crete
Thebes
Eretria
Salamis (490)
(480)
Marathon (490)
Athens

Mediterranean Sea

Saronic Gulf
0 12.5 25 mi
0 50 100 km
24°E

Interpret Maps

1. **Movement** By what routes did the Persians choose to attack Greece? Explain why.

2. **Location** Where did most of the battles of the Persian Wars occur? How might their citizens have been affected?

Pheidippides Brings News Though the Athenians won the battle, their city now stood defenseless. According to tradition, army leaders chose a young runner to race back to Athens. In this case, a young man named Pheidippides (fy•DIP•uh•deez) brought news of the Persian defeat so that Athenians would not give up the city without a fight. After dashing the 26 miles from Marathon to Athens, he delivered his message, "Rejoice, we conquer." He then collapsed and died. Moving rapidly from Marathon, the Greek army soon arrived in Athens. When the Persians sailed into the harbor, they found the city heavily defended. They quickly went back to sea in retreat.

Thermopylae and Salamis Ten years later, in 480 BC, Darius the Great's son and successor, Xerxes (ZURK•seez), assembled an enormous invasion force to crush Athens. The Greeks were badly divided. Some city-states agreed to fight the Persians. Others thought it wiser to let Xerxes destroy Athens and return home. Some Greeks even fought on the Persian side. Consequently, Xerxes' army met no resistance as it marched down the eastern coast of Greece.

When Xerxes came to a narrow mountain pass at Thermopylae (thur•MAHP•uh•lee), 7,000 Greeks, including 300 Spartans, blocked his way. Xerxes assumed that his troops would easily push the Greeks aside. However, he underestimated their fighting ability. The Greeks stopped the Persian advance for three days. A traitor who informed the Persians about a secret path around the pass brought the Greeks' brave stand to an end. Fearing defeat, the 300 Spartan soldiers held the Persians back while the other Greek forces retreated. All of the Spartans were killed. Their valiant sacrifice made a great impression on all Greeks.

Meanwhile, the Athenians debated how best to defend their city. Themistocles, an Athenian leader, convinced them to evacuate the city and fight at sea. They positioned their fleet in a narrow channel near the island of Salamis (SAL•uh•mihs), a few miles southwest of Athens. After setting fire to Athens, Xerxes sent his warships to block both ends of the channel. However, the channel was very narrow, and the Persian ships

had difficulty turning. Smaller Greek ships armed with battering rams attacked, puncturing the hulls of many Persian warships. Xerxes watched in horror as more than one-third of his fleet sank. He faced another defeat in 479 BC, when the Greeks crushed the Persian army at the Battle of Plataea (pluh•TEE•uh). After this major setback, the Persians were always on the defensive.

The following year, several Greek city-states formed an alliance called the Delian (DEE•lee•uhn) League. (The alliance took its name from Delos, the island in the Aegean Sea where it had its headquarters.) League members continued to press the war against the Persians for several more years. In time, they drove the Persians from the territories surrounding Greece and ended the threat of future attacks.

Consequences of the Persian Wars With the Persian threat ended, all the Greek city-states felt a new sense of confidence and freedom. Athens, in particular, basked in the glory of the victory over the Persians. During the 470s, Athens emerged as the leader of the Delian League, which had grown to some 200 city-states. Soon thereafter, Athens began to use its power to control the other league members. It moved the league headquarters to Athens, and used military force against members that challenged its authority. In time, these city-states became little more than provinces of a vast Athenian empire. The prestige of victory over the Persians and the wealth of the Athenian empire set the stage for a dazzling burst of creativity in Athens. The city was entering its brief golden age.

Reading Check
Analyze Effects
How did the Persian Wars affect the Greek people, especially the Athenians?

Lesson 2 Assessment

1. **Organize Information** Create a timeline similar to the one shown. Fill it in with at least three events each for the history of Athens and Sparta between 750 BC and the end of the Persian Wars.

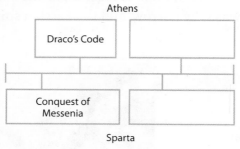

Athens

Draco's Code

Conquest of Messenia

Sparta

2. **Key Terms and People** For each key term or person in the lesson, write a sentence explaining its significance.

3. **Contrast** How does an aristocracy differ from an oligarchy?

4. **Analyze Causes** What contributions did Solon and Cleisthenes make to the development of Athenian democracy?

5. **Analyze Effects** How did Athens benefit from victory in the Persian Wars?

6. **Contrast** How was living in Athens different from living in Sparta?

7. **Make Inferences** The introduction of cheap iron weapons meant that ordinary Greek citizens could arm themselves. How might the ability to own weapons change the outlook of ordinary citizens?

8. **Analyze Motives** Why were the Spartan soldiers willing to sacrifice themselves at Thermopylae?

Democracy and Greece's Golden Age

The Big Idea
Democratic principles flourished during Greece's golden age.

Why It Matters Now
The democratic principles set forth during Greece's golden age are the foundation for modern democracies, including the United States.

Key Terms and People
direct democracy
Peloponnesian War

Setting the Stage

As the leaders in the Persian Wars, Athens and Sparta became the two most powerful and influential city-states in Greece. Because the Spartans were not popular with the rest of Greece, Athens eventually became the leading city-state. After the Persian Wars, Athens entered a golden age, an age in which it was the center of Greek culture and politics. This golden age lasted for close to 50 years, from 477 to 431 BC.

Pericles' Plan for Athens

A wise and able statesman named Pericles led Athens during much of its golden age. Honest and fair, Pericles held onto popular support for 32 years. He was a skillful politician, an inspiring speaker, and a respected general. He so dominated life in Athens from 461 to 429 BC that this period is called

Athenian and United States Democracy

ATHENIAN DEMOCRACY	BOTH	U.S. DEMOCRACY
• Citizens: male; at least 18 years old; with citizen parents	• Political power exercised by citizens	• Citizens: born in United States or completed citizenship process
• Laws voted on and proposed directly by assembly of all citizens	• Three branches of government	• Representatives elected to propose and vote on laws
• Leader chosen by lot	• Legislative branch passes laws	• Elected president
• Executive branch: a council of 500 men	• Executive branch carries out laws	• Executive branch made up of elected and appointed officials
• Juries varied in size	• Judicial branch conducts trials with paid jurors	• Juries composed of 12 jurors
• No attorneys; no appeals; one-day trials		• Defendants and plaintiffs have attorneys; long appeals process

Interpret Charts
Compare In what way was political power exercised by citizens in Athens? How is it exercised by citizens in the United States?

This stone relief panel shows democracy, represented as a person, crowning the seated Demos, who personifies the people of Athens.

the Age of Pericles. Pericles' goals included strengthening Athenian democracy as well as strengthening and holding the empire. He also worked on glorifying Athens, which you will read about in the next lesson.

Stronger Democracy To strengthen democracy, Pericles increased the number of public officials who were paid salaries. Earlier in Athens, most positions in public office were unpaid. Thus, only wealthier Athenian citizens could afford to hold public office. Now even the poorest citizen could serve if elected or chosen by lot. Consequently, Athens had more citizens engaged in self-government than any other city-state in Greece. This reform made Athens one of the most democratic governments in history.

The introduction of **direct democracy**, a form of government in which citizens rule directly and not through representatives, was an important legacy of Periclean Athens. Few other city-states practiced this style of government. In Athens, male citizens who served in the assembly established all the important government policies that affected the polis.

Athenian Empire After the defeat of the Persians, Athens helped organize the Delian League. In time, Athens took over leadership of the league and dominated all the city-states in it. Pericles used the money from the league's treasury to make the Athenian navy the strongest in the Mediterranean. A strong navy was important because it helped Athens strengthen the safety of its empire. Prosperity depended on gaining access to the surrounding waterways. Athens needed overseas trade to obtain supplies of grain and other raw materials.

DOCUMENT-BASED INVESTIGATION   Historical Source

Pericles on Democracy

Thucydides is widely considered to be the greatest historian of ancient Greece. In his *History of the Peloponnesian War*, he included excerpts of speeches from leaders on both sides, including this passage from a speech by Pericles. The speech was given as part of a funeral for Athenian soldiers who had fallen during the war. As part of honoring the Athenian war dead, Pericles expressed his great pride in Athenian democracy.

Analyze Historical Sources
How does Pericles relate the issue of class to his opinion of democracy?

"Our constitution is called a democracy because power is in the hands not of a minority but of the whole people. When it is a question of settling private disputes, everyone is equal before the law; when it is a question of putting one person before another in positions of public responsibility, what counts is not membership in a particular class, but the actual ability which the man possesses. No one, so long as he has it in him to be of service to the state, is kept in political obscurity because of poverty."

—Pericles, "The Funeral Oration," from Thucydides, *The Peloponnesian War*

Pericles (495–429 BC)

Pericles came from a rich and high-ranking noble family. His aristocratic father had led the Athenian assembly and fought at the Battle of Salamis in the Persian Wars. His mother was the niece of Cleisthenes, the Athenian noble who had introduced important democratic reforms.

Pericles was well known for his political achievements as leader of Athens. Pericles the man, however, was harder to know. One historian wrote, "[He] no doubt, was a lonely man. . . . He had no friend . . . [and] he only went out [of his home] for official business."

Reading Check
Find Main Ideas What were the key features of Athenian democracy?

Athenian military might allowed Pericles to treat other members of the Delian League as part of the empire. Some cities in the Peloponnesus, however, resisted Athens and formed their own alliances. Sparta in particular was at odds with Athens.

Athenians and Spartans Go to War

As Athens grew in wealth, prestige, and power, other city-states viewed it with hostility. Ill will was especially strong between Sparta and Athens.

The Peloponnesian League Like Athens, Sparta was the head of a league of allied city-states. It was called the Peloponnesian League. This alliance had been formed in the 500s BC to provide protection and security for its members. For decades after the Persian Wars, tension built between the Delian and Peloponnesian leagues. Athens and its allies feared the military might of the other league. In return, Sparta feared Athens' naval fleet as well as the spread of Athenian democracy.

Many people thought that war between the two was inevitable. Instead of trying to avoid conflict, leaders in Athens and Sparta pressed for a war to begin. Both groups of leaders believed their own city-state had the advantage. Eventually, Sparta declared war on Athens in 431 BC.

Peloponnesian War When the **Peloponnesian War** between the two city-states began, Athens had the stronger navy. Sparta had the stronger army, however, and its location inland meant that it could not easily be attacked by sea. Pericles' strategy was to avoid land battles with the Spartan army and wait for an opportunity to strike Sparta and its allies from the sea.

Eventually, the Spartans marched into Athenian territory. They swept over the countryside, burning the Athenian food supply. Pericles responded by bringing residents from the surrounding region inside the city walls. The city was safe from hunger as long as ships could sail into port with supplies from Athenian colonies and foreign states.

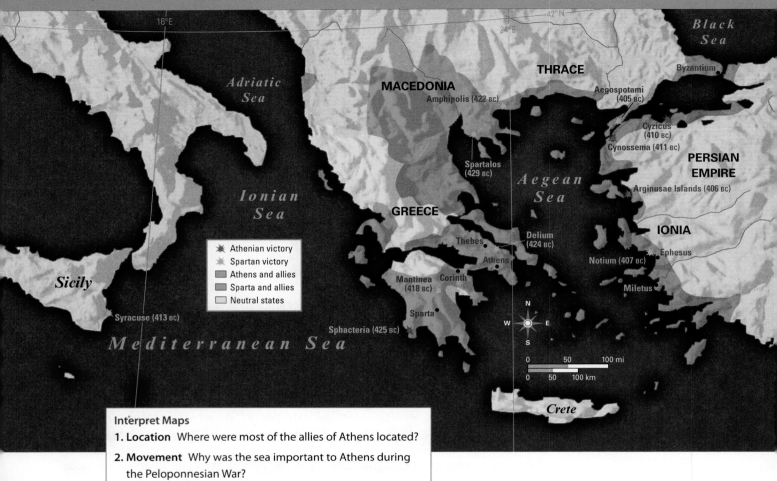

Peloponnesian War, 431–404 BC

Interpret Maps

1. **Location** Where were most of the allies of Athens located?

2. **Movement** Why was the sea important to Athens during the Peloponnesian War?

In the second year of the war, however, disaster struck Athens. A frightful plague swept through the city, killing perhaps one-third of the population, including Pericles. Although weakened, Athens continued to fight for several years. Then, in 421 BC, the two sides, worn down by the war, signed a truce.

Sparta Gains Victory The peace did not last long. In 415 BC, the Athenians sent a huge fleet carrying more than 20,000 soldiers to the island of Sicily. Their plan was to destroy the city-state of Syracuse, one of Sparta's wealthiest allies. The expedition ended with a crushing defeat in 413 BC. In his study of the Peloponnesian War, Thucydides recalled, "[The Athenians] were destroyed with a total destruction—their fleet, their army—there was nothing that was not destroyed, and few out of many returned home." Somehow, a terribly weakened Athens fended off Spartan attacks for another nine years. Finally, in 404 BC, the Athenians and their allies surrendered. Athens had lost its empire, power, and wealth. Sparta, too, was exhausted by the war. It had nearly lost several times and had suffered damage almost as great as that suffered by Athens.

CAUSES AND EFFECTS OF THE PELOPONNESIAN WAR

CAUSES

- After the Persian Wars, Athens established the Delian League. Athens took advantage of its position as the head of the Delian League to create an Athenian Empire.
- Sparta and its allies, the Peloponnesian League, resented the growing influence of Athens in Greece.
- Over decades, tensions built up between the two leagues.

EFFECTS

- Athens lost its navy and army and many lives were lost.
- Athens lost its empire, power, and wealth.
- Sparta became the supreme power in Greece. However, the Spartan army was weakened and was defeated by Thebes in 371 BC.
- In the 340s BC, after years of bitter squabbling among city-states, all of Greece was conquered by Macedonia.

Interpret Charts
Analyze Causes What caused the Peloponnesian War?

Reading Check
Analyze Motives What might have been Pericles' goals in the Peloponnesian War?

After its victory, Sparta's army tried to act as Greece's dominant power. But Sparta's wealth and resources were badly strained, and its power had worn down. As a result of this strain, the Spartans could not keep control of Greece. The city-state of Thebes defeated Sparta, but it could not maintain control either. The struggle for power in Greece led to a long cycle of warfare that left all of Greece vulnerable to attack. In the 340s BC, a Greek-speaking kingdom to the north called Macedonia swept in and took control of all of Greece.

Lesson 3 Assessment

1. **Organize Information** Create a two-column graphic organizer similar to the one shown and fill it in with details about Pericles' goals. Which of Pericles' goals do you think had the greatest impact on the modern world? Explain your choice.

Strong Democracy	Strong Empire

2. **Key Terms and People** For each key term or person in the lesson, write a sentence explaining its significance.
3. **Synthesize** What steps did Pericles take to strengthen democracy in Athens?
4. **Summarize** What were the battle strategies of Athens and Sparta in the Peloponnesian War?
5. **Draw Conclusions** Was the time of Pericles' rule a "golden age" for Athens? Explain.

Achievements of Greek Culture

The Big Idea

Classical culture flourished during Greece's golden age.

Why It Matters Now

At its height, Greece set lasting standards in art, politics, literature, and philosophy that are still influential today.

Key Terms and People

classical art
lyric poetry
tragedy
comedy
philosopher
Socrates
Plato
Aristotle

Classical Greek sculpture portrayed ideal beauty, and at a later period, moved toward realism—as shown by this Roman copy of a Greek statue.

Setting the Stage

During the golden age, trade brought great wealth to Athens. Merchants from other parts of the world moved to the city, bringing their own foods and customs. As a result, Athens was a very cosmopolitan city. Adding to its appeal were grand festivals, public celebrations, and public events. Athenians could cheer their favorite athletes in the city's religious games or watch great dramas performed in the city's theaters. Athens was the heart of Greek culture during this time as drama, sculpture, poetry, philosophy, architecture, and science reached new heights.

Glorious Art and Architecture

As leader of the Delian League, Athens controlled the money in its treasury. Pericles used the money to glorify Athens. Without the league's approval, he persuaded the Athenian assembly to allot huge sums of the league's money to buy gold, ivory, and marble. Still more money went to pay the artists, architects, and workers who used these materials. Pericles' goal was to have the greatest Greek artists and architects create magnificent sculptures and buildings to glorify Athens. At the center of his plan was what became one of architecture's noblest works—the Parthenon.

Architecture and Sculpture The Parthenon, a masterpiece of architectural design and craftsmanship, was not unique in style. Rather, Greek architects constructed the 23,000-square-foot building in the traditional style that had been used to create Greek temples for 200 years. Like most Greek temples, the Parthenon had doors but no windows. The structure was surrounded by tall, graceful columns, above which were slabs of marble carved with scenes from myths. Though the ruins of the Parthenon appear white today, parts originally were painted in vivid colors.

The Parthenon and *Athena Parthenos*

In Greek architecture, the most important type of building was the temple. The walled rooms in the center of the temple held sculptures of gods and goddesses and lavish gifts to these deities.

▲ **The Parthenon** Built between 447 and 432 BC, the Parthenon was a Greek temple dedicated to Athena. It serves as an excellent example of the Greek artistic ideals of harmony, symmetry, and balance. Just as Greek philosophers tried to understand the basic laws of nature, so Greek architects looked to nature for guidance. They discovered a ratio in nature that they believed created pleasing proportions and used that ratio to design the rectangles in the Parthenon.

◄ *Athena Parthenos* The great Athenian sculptor Phidias created a sculpture of Athena, goddess of wisdom, to stand in the Parthenon. The sculpture shown here is actually a first or second century AD Roman copy of the original *Athena Parthenos*. The original, which likely appeared quite different, has been lost. Phidias's renderings of Greek deities provided ideas of what those gods and goddesses were imagined to look like.

Analyze Historical Sources
How does the Parthenon display the Greek preference for symmetry and balance?

This temple, built to honor Athena, the goddess of wisdom and the protector of Athens, contained examples of Greek art that set standards for future generations of artists around the world. Pericles entrusted much of the work on the Parthenon to the sculptor Phidias (FIDH•ee•uhs). Within the temple, Phidias crafted a giant statue of Athena that not only contained such precious materials as gold and ivory, but also stood more than 30 feet tall.

Phidias and other sculptors during this golden age aimed to create figures that were graceful, strong, and perfectly formed. Their faces showed neither joy nor anger, only serenity. Greek sculptors also tried to capture the grace of the idealized human body in motion. They wanted to portray ideal beauty, not realism. Their values of harmony, order, balance, and

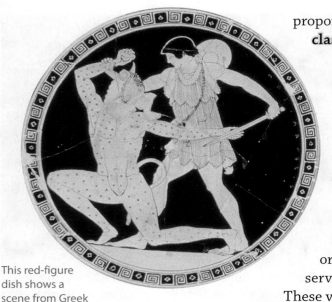

This red-figure dish shows a scene from Greek mythology in which the hero Theseus slays a creature called the Minotaur.

proportion became the standard of what is called **classical art**.

Though we know a great deal about ancient Greek sculpture, very few original works remain. Much of what we do know about Greek sculpture is based on copies of Greek statues made by the Romans a few hundred years later. Roman artists made many copies of what they considered to be the greatest Greek statues. Many of these copies survived even after the original statues were destroyed.

Painting As with Greek sculpture, only a few original Greek paintings have survived. The best preserved are paintings on vases, plates, and other vessels. These vessels are often decorated with scenes from everyday life or from myths or legends. Most of them use only two colors—red and black—for their illustrations.

The red was the natural color of the clay vessels, and the black was a glaze added to the finished pieces. Despite this limited palette, Greek artists were able to convey movement and depth in their paintings. This ability was important to the Greeks since they wanted objects to be both functional and beautiful.

Though we have little evidence of larger paintings, written sources tell us that the Greeks also created murals, or wall paintings, in many public buildings. According to these sources, the Greeks' murals often included scenes from the *Iliad* and the *Odyssey*. Such paintings often focused on the aftermath of battle rather than on the battle itself. One Athenian mural, for example, showed a scene from the day after the defeat of Troy. Fallen soldiers still dressed in full armor lay amid the ruins of once great Troy. Themes like this were very popular with the Athenian people.

Reading Check
Make Generalizations
What were some characteristics of Greek architecture and art?

Poetry, Drama, and History

While the most famous works of Greek literature are the great epic poems written by Homer, the Greeks wrote many types of poetry besides epics. For example, the poet Hesiod (HEE-see-uhd) wrote descriptive poetry. Among the subjects he described in his poems were the works of the gods and the lives of peasants.

Lyric Poetry The Greeks also created **lyric poetry**, named after a musical instrument called the lyre that was often played to accompany the reading of poems. Lyric poems do not tell stories. Instead, they deal with emotions and desires. Pindar was a lyric poet who lived from about 522 to 443 BC. He wrote poems to commemorate public events like the Olympic Games.

Drama The Greeks invented drama as an art form and built the first theaters in the West. Theatrical productions in Athens were both an

Sappho (c. 610–570 BC)

Among the earliest poets to gain fame for writing lyric poetry was Sappho (SAF•oh), one of the few Greek women to gain fame as a writer. Her poems deal with daily life, marriage, love, and relationships with her family and friends. In "Hymn to Aphrodite," Sappho begs the goddess of love to send her a new love.

> "Iridescent-throned Aphrodite, deathless
> Child of Zeus, wile-weaver, I now implore you,
> Don't—I beg you, Lady—with pains and torments
> Crush down my spirit"
>
> —Sappho, "Hymn to Aphrodite"

Analyze Historical Sources
In what way is Sappho's poem an example of lyric poetry?

expression of civic pride and a tribute to the gods. As part of their civic duty, wealthy citizens bore the cost of producing the plays. Actors used colorful costumes, masks, and sets to dramatize stories. Many plays were about leadership, justice, and the duties owed to the gods. They often included a chorus that danced, sang, and recited poetry.

Tragedy and Comedy The Greeks wrote two kinds of drama—tragedy and comedy. A **tragedy** was a serious drama about common themes such as love, hate, war, or betrayal. These dramas featured a main character, or tragic hero. The hero usually was an important person and often gifted with extraordinary abilities. A tragic flaw usually caused the hero's downfall. Often this flaw was *hubris*, or excessive pride.

In ancient times, Greece had three notable dramatists who wrote tragedies. Aeschylus (EHS•kuh•luhs) wrote more than 80 plays. His most famous work is the trilogy—a three-play series—*Oresteia* (ohr•res•TEE•uh). It is based on the family of Agamemnon, the Mycenaean king who commanded the Greeks at Troy. The plays examine the idea of justice. Sophocles (SAHFv•uh•kleez) wrote more than 100 plays,

This poster promotes an 1898 production of Euripides' *Medea*, starring the great French actress Sarah Bernhardt.

In the sixth century BC, the Greeks became the first people to use theater for its own sake and not for religious rituals. Actors wore theatrical masks like these that exaggerated human expressions. The plays were performed in outdoor theaters. The stage was partially surrounded by a semicircular seating area fitted into a hillside, such as the one shown here.

including the tragedies *Oedipus the King* and *Antigone*. Euripides (yoo•RIP•uh•deez), author of the play *Medea*, often featured strong women in his works.

In contrast to Greek tragedies, a **comedy** contained scenes filled with slapstick situations and crude humor. Playwrights often made fun of politics and respected people and ideas of the time. Aristophanes (ar•ih•STAHF•uh•neez) wrote the first great comedies for the stage, including *The Birds* and *Lysistrata*. *Lysistrata* portrayed the women of Athens forcing their husbands to end the Peloponnesian War. The fact that Athenians could listen to criticism of themselves showed the freedom and openness of public discussion that existed in democratic Athens.

History There are no written records from the Dorian period. The epic poems of Homer recount stories, but they are not accurate recordings of what took place. Herodotus, a Greek who lived in Athens for a time, pioneered the accurate reporting of events. His book on the Persian Wars is considered the first work of history. However, the greatest historian of the classical age was the Athenian Thucydides (thoo•SID•ih•deez). He believed that certain types of events and political situations recur over time. Studying those events and situations, he felt, would aid in understanding the present. The approaches Thucydides used in his work still guide historians today.

Xenophon (ZEN•uh•fuhn) is another early Greek historian whose work survives. Both a soldier and a philosopher, Xenophon had fought in Persia around 400 BC, long after the end of the Persian Wars. This service was the source for his major writing. Unlike Herodotus and Thucydides, Xenophon concentrated less on sources and debates and more on describing famous men. Despite his less critical style, Xenophon's work has helped us learn what life was like in Greece during the 300s BC.

Reading Check
Contrast
How did tragedy differ from comedy?

Philosophers Search for Truth

After the war, many Athenians lost confidence in democratic government and began to question their values. In this time of uncertainty, several great thinkers appeared. They were determined to seek the truth, no matter where the search led them. The Greeks called such thinkers **philosophers**, meaning "lovers of wisdom." These Greek thinkers based their philosophy on the following two assumptions:

- The universe (land, sky, and sea) is put together in an orderly way, subject to absolute and unchanging laws.
- People can understand these laws through logic and reason.

One group, the Sophists, questioned people's beliefs about justice and other values. One notable Sophist was Protagoras, who questioned the existence of the traditional Greek gods. He also argued that there was no universal standard of truth, saying "Man [the individual] is the measure of all things." These were radical and dangerous ideas to many Athenians.

Socrates One critic of the Sophists was **Socrates** (SAHK•ruh•teez), who believed that absolute standards did exist for truth and justice. However, he encouraged Greeks to go farther and question themselves and their moral character. Historians believe it was Socrates who said, "The unexamined life is not worth living." Socrates was admired by many who understood his ideas. However, others were puzzled by this man's viewpoints.

In 399 BC, Socrates was tried for "corrupting the youth of Athens" and "neglecting the city's gods." In his own defense, Socrates said that his

Vocabulary
unexamined not observed or inspected carefully or critically

Socrates, who was sentenced to death for his crimes, prepares to drink hemlock, a slow-acting poison.

teachings were good for Athens because they forced people to think about their values and actions. The jury disagreed and condemned him to death.

Plato A student of Socrates, **Plato** (PLAY•toh), was in his late 20s when his teacher died. Later, Plato wrote down the conversations of Socrates "as a means of philosophical investigation." Sometime in the 370s BC, Plato wrote his most famous work, *The Republic*. In it, he set forth his vision of a perfectly governed society. It was not a democracy. In his ideal society, all citizens would fall naturally into three groups: farmers and artisans, warriors, and the ruling class. The person with the greatest insight and intellect from the ruling class would be chosen philosopher-king. No one else, he argued, had the skills necessary to lead. Plato's writings dominated philosophic thought in Europe for nearly 1,500 years. His only rivals in importance were his teacher, Socrates, and his own pupil, Aristotle (AR•ih•staht•uhl).

Aristotle The philosopher **Aristotle** questioned the nature of the world and of human belief, thought, and knowledge. Aristotle came close to summarizing all of the knowledge up to his time. He invented a method for

—— BIOGRAPHY ——

Socrates
470–399 BC

Socrates encouraged his students to examine their beliefs. He asked them a series of leading questions to show that people hold many contradictory opinions. This question-and-answer approach to teaching is known as the Socratic method. Socrates devoted his life to gaining self-knowledge and once said, "There is only one good, knowledge, and one evil, ignorance."

Plato
427–347 BC

Born into a wealthy Athenian family, Plato had careers as a wrestler and a poet before he became a philosopher. After his teacher Socrates died, Plato left Greece. He later returned to Athens and founded a school called the Academy in 387 BC. The school lasted for approximately 900 years. It was Plato who once stated, "Philosophy begins in wonder."

Aristotle
384–322 BC

Aristotle, the son of a physician, was one of the brightest students at Plato's Academy. He came there as a young man and stayed for 20 years until Plato's death. In 335 BC, Aristotle opened his own school in Athens called the Lyceum. The school eventually rivaled the Academy. Aristotle once argued, "He who studies how things originated . . . will achieve the clearest view of them."

Aristotle's *Politics*

Aristotle tried to apply philosophical principles to every kind of knowledge. He used these principles to discuss politics.

"Where ought the sovereign power of the state to reside? . . . The state aims to consist as far as possible of those who are alike and equal, a condition found chiefly among the middle section. . . . The middle class is also the steadiest element, the least eager for change. They neither covet, like the poor the possessions of others, nor do others covet theirs, as the poor covet those of the rich. . . . Tyranny often emerges from an over-enthusiastic democracy or from an oligarchy, but much more rarely from middle class constitutions."

—Aristotle, quoted in *Politics*

Analyze Historical Sources
Why does Aristotle support the middle class as the location of power?

Reading Check
Make Inferences
Why would philosophers start questioning traditional beliefs at this particular time in Athenian history?

arguing according to rules of logic. He later applied his method to problems in the fields of psychology, physics, and biology. His work provides the basis of the scientific method used today. One of Aristotle's most famous pupils was Alexander, son of King Philip II of Macedonia. Around 343 BC, Aristotle accepted the king's invitation to tutor the 13-year-old prince. Alexander's status as a student abruptly ended three years later, when his father called him back to Macedonia.

Lesson 4 Assessment

1. **Organize Information** Create a graphic organizer similar to the one shown. Fill it in with characteristics, achievements, and key individuals from architecture and two other areas of classical Greek culture (philosophy, sculpture, drama, and so on). You may not be able to fill in every box. Which achievement do you think is the most enduring?

	Characteristics	Achievement(s)	Key Individual(s)
Architecture			
[other area]			
[other area]			

2. **Key Terms and People** For each key term or person in the lesson, write a sentence explaining its significance.

3. **Contrast** What are some differences between Sappho and other poets in this lesson?

4. **Make Generalizations** What was the general goal of Greek sculptors?

5. **Analyze Causes** Why do you think some Athenians found the ideas of Socrates so troubling?

6. **Make Inferences** Do you agree with Socrates that there are absolute standards for truth and justice? Why or why not?

Alexander the Great

The Big Idea

Alexander the Great conquered Persia and Egypt and extended his empire to the Indus River in northwestern India.

Why It Matters Now

Alexander's empire extended across an area that today consists of many nations and diverse cultures.

Key Terms and People

Philip II
Macedonia
Alexander the Great
Darius III

Setting the Stage

The Peloponnesian War severely weakened several Greek city-states. This caused a rapid decline in their military and economic power. In the nearby kingdom of Macedonia, King **Philip II** took note. Philip dreamed of taking control of Greece and then moving against Persia to seize its vast wealth. Philip also hoped to avenge the Persian invasion of Greece in 480 BC.

Philip Builds Macedonian Power

The kingdom of **Macedonia**, located just north of Greece, had rough terrain and a cold climate. The Macedonians were a hardy people who lived in mountain villages rather than city-states. Most Macedonian nobles thought of themselves as Greeks. The Greeks, however, looked down on the Macedonians as uncivilized foreigners who had no great philosophers, sculptors, or writers. The Macedonians did have one very important resource—their shrewd and fearless kings.

Philip's Army In 359 BC, Philip II became king of Macedonia. Though only 23 years old, he quickly proved to be a brilliant general and a ruthless politician. Philip transformed the rugged peasants under his command into a well-trained professional army. He organized his troops into phalanxes of 16 men across and 16 deep, each one armed with an 18-foot pike. Philip used this heavy phalanx formation to break through enemy lines. Then he used fast-moving cavalry to crush his disorganized opponents. After he employed these tactics successfully against northern opponents, Philip began to prepare an invasion of Greece.

Conquest of Greece Demosthenes (dee•MAHS•thuh•neez), the Athenian orator, tried to warn the Greeks of the threat Philip and his army posed. He urged them to unite against Philip. However, the Greek city-states could not agree on any single policy. Finally, in 338 BC, Athens and Thebes—a city-state in central Greece—joined forces to fight Philip. By then, however, it was too late. The Macedonians soundly defeated the Greeks at the battle of Chaeronea (kair•uh•NEE•uh). This defeat ended Greek independence. The city-states retained self-government in local affairs. However, Greece itself remained firmly under the control of a succession of foreign powers—the first of which was Philip's Macedonia.

Although Philip planned to invade Persia next, he never got the chance. At his daughter's wedding in 336 BC, he was stabbed to death by a former guardsman. Philip's son Alexander immediately proclaimed himself king of Macedonia. Because of his accomplishments over the next 13 years, he became known as **Alexander the Great**.

Alexander Defeats Persia

Although Alexander was only 20 years old when he became king, he was well prepared to lead. Under Aristotle's teaching, Alexander had learned science, geography, and literature. Alexander especially enjoyed Homer's description of the heroic deeds performed by Achilles during the Trojan War. To inspire himself, he kept a copy of the *Iliad* under his pillow.

As a young boy, Alexander learned to ride a horse, use weapons, and command troops. Once he became king, Alexander promptly demonstrated that his military training had not been wasted. When the people of Thebes rebelled, he destroyed the city. About 6,000 Thebans were killed. The survivors were sold into slavery. Frightened by his cruelty, the other Greek city-states quickly gave up any idea of rebellion.

Reading Check
Analyze Causes
How did the Peloponnesian War pave the way for Philip's conquest of Greece?

— BIOGRAPHY —

Alexander
(356–323 BC)

When Alexander was only eight or nine years old, he tamed a wild horse that none of his father's grooms could manage. Alexander calmed the horse, whose name was Bucephalus, by speaking gently. Seeing the control that Alexander had over the horse, Philip II said, "You'll have to find another kingdom; Macedonia isn't going to be big enough for you."

Alexander took his father's advice. Riding Bucephalus at the head of a great army, he conquered the lands from Greece to the Indus Valley. When the horse died in what is now Pakistan, Alexander named the city of Bucephala after it. Maybe he was tired of the name Alexandria. By that time, he had already named at least a dozen cities after himself!

Invasion of Persia With Greece now secure, Alexander felt free to carry out his father's plan to invade and conquer Persia. In 334 BC, he led 35,000 soldiers across the Hellespont into Anatolia. Persian messengers raced along the Royal Road to spread news of the invasion. An army of about 40,000 men rushed to defend Persia. The two forces met at the Granicus River. Instead of waiting for the Persians to make the first move, Alexander ordered his cavalry to attack. Leading his troops into battle, Alexander smashed the Persian defenses.

Alexander's victory at Granicus alarmed the Persian king, **Darius III**. Vowing to crush the invaders, he raised a huge army of between 50,000 and 75,000 men to face the Macedonians near Issus. Realizing that he was outnumbered, Alexander surprised his enemies. He ordered his finest troops to break through a weak point in the Persian lines. The army then charged straight at Darius. To avoid capture, the frightened king fled, followed by his panicked army. This victory gave Alexander control over Anatolia.

Conquering the Persian Empire Shaken by his defeat, Darius tried to negotiate a peace settlement. He offered Alexander all of his lands west of the Euphrates River. Alexander's advisers urged him to accept. However, the rapid collapse of Persian resistance fired Alexander's ambition. He rejected Darius's offer and confidently announced his plan to conquer the entire Persian Empire.

Bucephalus was Alexander's favorite horse until its death in 326 BC. A statue of Bucephalus and Alexander stands today in Macedonia.

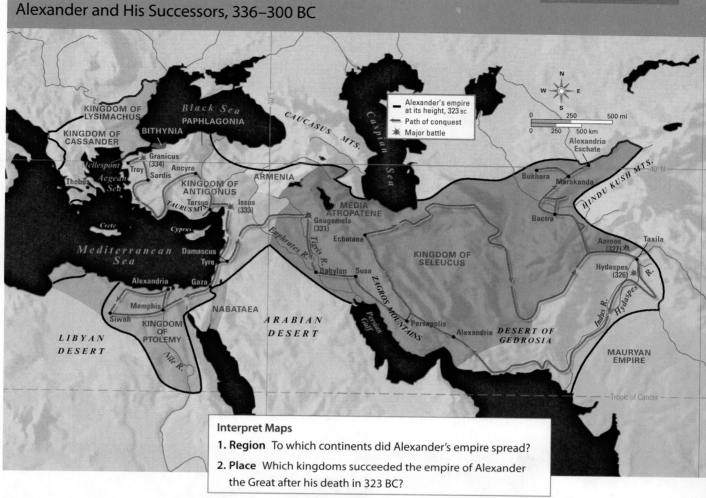

Alexander and His Successors, 336–300 BC

▷ Explore ONLINE!

Legend:
— Alexander's empire at its height, 323 BC
← Path of conquest
✳ Major battle

Interpret Maps

1. **Region** To which continents did Alexander's empire spread?

2. **Place** Which kingdoms succeeded the empire of Alexander the Great after his death in 323 BC?

Alexander marched into Egypt, a Persian territory, in 332 BC. The Egyptians welcomed him as a liberator. They crowned him pharaoh— or god-king. During his time in Egypt, Alexander founded the city of Alexandria at the mouth of the Nile River. After leaving Egypt, Alexander moved east into Mesopotamia to confront Darius. The desperate Persian king assembled a force of some 250,000 men. The two armies met at Gaugamela (gaw•guh•MEE•luh), a small village near the ruins of ancient Nineveh. Alexander launched a massive phalanx attack followed by a cavalry charge. As the Persian lines crumbled, Darius again panicked and fled. Alexander's victory at Gaugamela ended Persia's power.

Within a short time, Alexander's army occupied Babylon, Susa, and Persepolis. These cities yielded a huge treasure, which Alexander distributed among his army. A few months after it was occupied, Persepolis, Persia's royal capital, burned to the ground. Some people said Alexander left the city in ashes to signal the total destruction of the Persian Empire. The Greek historian Arrian, writing about 500 years after Alexander's time, suggested that the fire was set in revenge for the Persian burning of Athens. However, the cause of the fire remains a mystery.

Reading Check
Make Inferences
Why do you think the Egyptians viewed Alexander as a liberator?

Alexander's Other Conquests

Alexander now reigned as the unchallenged ruler of southwest Asia. But he was more interested in expanding his empire than in governing it. He left the ruined Persepolis to pursue Darius and conquer Persia's remote Asian provinces. Darius's trail led Alexander to a deserted spot south of the Caspian Sea. There he found Darius already dead, murdered by one of his provincial governors. Rather than return to Babylon, Alexander continued east. During the next three years, his army fought its way across the desert wastes and mountains of Central Asia. He pushed on, hoping to reach the farthest edge of the continent.

Alexander in India In 326 BC, Alexander and his army reached the Indus Valley. At the Hydaspes River, a powerful Indian army blocked their path. After winning a fierce battle, Alexander's soldiers marched some 200 miles farther, but their morale was low. They had been fighting for 11 years and had marched more than 11,000 miles. They had endured both scorching deserts and drenching monsoon rains. The exhausted soldiers yearned to go home. Bitterly disappointed, Alexander agreed to turn back.

By the spring of 323 BC, Alexander and his army had reached Babylon. Restless as always, Alexander announced plans to organize and unify his empire. He would construct new cities, roads, and harbors and conquer Arabia. However, Alexander never carried out his plans. He became seriously ill with a fever and died a few days later. He was just 32 years old.

Alexander the Great's army defeated Indian soldiers on elephants in the Battle of Hydaspes.

Alexander's Empire and Its Legacy, 336–306 BC

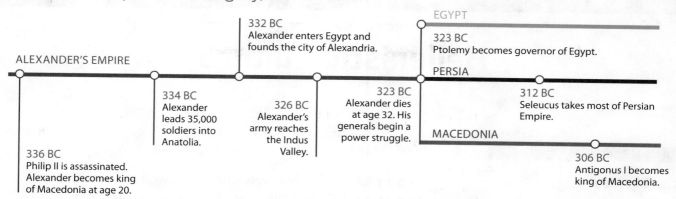

ALEXANDER'S EMPIRE

332 BC
Alexander enters Egypt and founds the city of Alexandria.

EGYPT

323 BC
Ptolemy becomes governor of Egypt.

PERSIA

334 BC
Alexander leads 35,000 soldiers into Anatolia.

326 BC
Alexander's army reaches the Indus Valley.

323 BC
Alexander dies at age 32. His generals begin a power struggle.

312 BC
Seleucus takes most of Persian Empire.

MACEDONIA

336 BC
Philip II is assassinated. Alexander becomes king of Macedonia at age 20.

306 BC
Antigonus I becomes king of Macedonia.

Alexander's Legacy After Alexander died, his Macedonian generals fought among themselves for control of his empire. Eventually, three ambitious leaders won out. Antigonus (an•TIG•uh•nuhs) became king of Macedonia and took control of the Greek city-states. Ptolemy (TAHL•uh•mee) seized Egypt, took the title of pharaoh, and established a dynasty. Seleucus (sih•LOO•kuhs) took most of the old Persian Empire, which became known as the Seleucid kingdom. Ignoring the democratic traditions of the Greek polis, these rulers and their descendants governed with complete power over their subjects.

Alexander's conquests had an interesting cultural impact. Alexander himself adopted Persian dress and customs and married a Persian woman. He included Persians and people from other lands in his army. As time passed, Greek settlers throughout the empire also adopted new ways. A vibrant new culture emerged from the blend of Greek and Eastern customs.

Reading check
Analyze Motives
Why did Alexander continue his conquests after Darius was dead?

Lesson 5 Assessment

1. **Organize Information** Create an outline that organizes information from each of the three sections of the lesson.

   > I. Philip Builds Macedonian Power
   >   A.
   >   B.
   > II. Alexander Conquers Persia

2. **Key Terms and People** For each key term or person in the lesson, write a sentence explaining its significance.

3. **Analyze Causes** How was Philip II able to conquer Greece?

4. **Synthesize** Philip II's goal was to conquer Persia. Why did Alexander continue his campaign of conquest after this goal had been achieved?

5. **Analyze Effects** What happened to Alexander's empire after his death?

6. **Form Opinions** Do you think that Alexander was worthy of the title "Great"? Explain.

7. **Predict Effects** If Alexander had lived longer, do you think he would have been as successful in ruling his empire as he was in building it? Explain.

8. **Make Inferences** Why do you think Alexander adopted Persian customs and included Persians in his army?

Hellenistic Culture

The Big Idea

Hellenistic culture, a blend of Greek and other influences, flourished throughout Greece, Egypt, and Asia.

Why It Matters Now

Western civilization today continues to be influenced by diverse cultures.

Key Terms and People

Hellenistic
Alexandria
Euclid
Archimedes
Colossus of Rhodes

Gold, coiled-snake bracelets created in Alexandria between 220 and 100 BC. The bracelets reflect a blend of cultures—paired bracelets were a Persian custom; the dual coiled snakes shows an influence from Ptolemaic Egypt.

Setting the Stage

Alexander's ambitions were cultural as well as military and political. During his wars of conquest, he actively sought to meld the conquered culture with that of the Greeks. He started new cities as administrative centers and outposts of Greek culture. These cities, from Egyptian Alexandria in the south to the Asian Alexandrias in the east, adopted many Greek patterns and customs. After Alexander's death, trade, transportation routes, a shared Greek culture, and a common language continued to link the cities together. But each region had its own traditional ways of life, religion, and government that no ruler could afford to overlook.

Hellenistic Culture in Alexandria

As a result of Alexander's policies, a vibrant new culture emerged. Greek (also known as Hellenic) culture blended with Egyptian, Persian, and Indian influences. This blending became known as **Hellenistic** culture. Koine (koy•NAY), the popular spoken language used in Hellenistic cities, was the direct result of cultural blending. The word *koine* came from the Greek word for "common." The language was a dialect of Greek. This language enabled educated people and traders from diverse backgrounds to communicate in cities throughout the Hellenistic world.

Life in the Hellenistic World The shift from Hellenic Greece to the Hellenistic world brought many drastic changes to people's lives. Perhaps the most obvious change was in how people were governed. The city-state was no longer the main political unit of the Greek world. It was replaced by the kingdom. Traditional Greek forms of government such as democracy had given way to monarchy.

The lives of women also changed significantly during the Hellenistic period. In most earlier Greek city-states, women had few rights. After Alexander, however, their lives began

Alexandria was the greatest city of the Hellenistic world. Towering above the city's busy harbor was a huge lighthouse called the Pharos, named one of the Seven Wonders of the Ancient World.

to improve. For the first time, some women gained the rights to receive an education and to own property. Legally, though, women were still not considered equal to men.

Trade and Cultural Diversity   Among the many cities of the Hellenistic world, the Egyptian city of **Alexandria** became the foremost center of commerce and Hellenistic civilization. Alexandria occupied a strategic site on the western edge of the Nile delta. Trade ships following transportation routes to and from all around the Mediterranean docked in its spacious harbor. Alexandria's thriving commerce enabled it to grow and prosper. By the third century BC, Alexandria had become an international community, with a rich mixture of customs and traditions from Egypt and from the Aegean. Its diverse population exceeded half a million people.

Alexandria's Attractions   Both residents and visitors admired Alexandria's great beauty. Broad avenues lined with statues of Greek gods divided the city into blocks. Rulers built magnificent royal palaces overlooking the harbor. A much visited tomb contained Alexander's elaborate glass coffin. Soaring more than 350 feet over the harbor stood an enormous stone lighthouse called the Pharos. This lighthouse contained a polished bronze mirror that, at night, reflected the light from a blazing fire. Alexandria's greatest attractions were its famous museum and library. The museum was a temple dedicated to the Muses, the Greek goddesses of arts and sciences. It contained art galleries, a zoo, botanical gardens, and even a dining hall. The museum was an institute of advanced study.

The Alexandrian Library stood nearby. Its collection of half a million papyrus scrolls included many of the masterpieces of ancient literature. As the first true research library in the world, it helped promote the work of a

Vocabulary
museum a building where works of art are displayed; derived from the Latin meaning "house of the muses"

gifted group of scholars. These scholars greatly respected the earlier works of classical literature and learning. They produced commentaries that explained these works.

Although Alexandria was one of the largest trading centers in the Hellenistic world, it was not the only one. Cities in Egypt, Persia, and Central Asia became trading centers. Traders went to Africa, Arabia, and India. In addition to goods from these regions, traders brought back new ideas. Among the ideas they carried were the teachings of Judaism, which influenced societies throughout the Hellenistic world. They also exchanged ideas about science and technology.

Reading Check
Analyze Effects
How did society change in the Hellenistic age?

Science and Technology

Hellenistic scholars, particularly those in Alexandria, preserved Greek and Egyptian learning in the sciences. Until the scientific advances of the 16th and 17th centuries, Alexandrian scholars provided most of the scientific knowledge available to the West.

Astronomy Alexandria's museum contained a small observatory in which astronomers could study the planets and stars. One astronomer, Aristarchus (ar·ih·STAHR·kuhs) of Samos, reached two significant scientific conclusions. In one, he estimated that the Sun was at least 300 times larger than Earth. Although he greatly underestimated the Sun's true size, Aristarchus disproved the widely held belief that the Sun was smaller than Greece. In another conclusion, he proposed that Earth and the other planets revolve around the Sun. Unfortunately for science, other astronomers refused to support Aristarchus's theory. In the second century AD, Alexandria's last renowned astronomer, Ptolemy, incorrectly placed

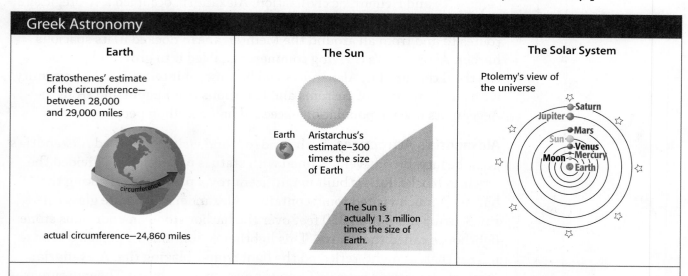

Greek Astronomy

Earth

Eratosthenes' estimate of the circumference—between 28,000 and 29,000 miles

circumference

actual circumference—24,860 miles

The Sun

Earth

Aristarchus's estimate—300 times the size of Earth

The Sun is actually 1.3 million times the size of Earth.

The Solar System

Ptolemy's view of the universe

Saturn
Jupiter
Mars
Sun
Venus
Mercury
Moon
Earth

Interpret Charts
1. **Compare** Where were Greek astronomers' ideas most incorrect compared with modern concepts?
2. **Synthesize** Which estimate is closest to modern measurements? How could the Hellenists be so accurate?

Hipparchus, who lived in Alexandria for a time, charted the position of 850 stars.

Earth at the center of the solar system. Astronomers accepted this view for the next 14 centuries.

Eratosthenes (ehr•uh•TAHS•thuh•neez), the director of the Alexandrian Library, tried to calculate Earth's true size. Using geometry, he computed Earth's circumference at between 28,000 and 29,000 miles. Modern measurements put the circumference at 24,860 miles. As well as a highly regarded astronomer and mathematician, Eratosthenes also was a poet and historian.

Mathematics and Physics In their work, Eratosthenes and Aristarchus used a geometry text compiled by **Euclid** (YOO•klihd). Euclid was a highly regarded mathematician who taught in Alexandria. His best-known book, *Elements*, contained 465 carefully presented geometry propositions and proofs. Euclid's work is still the basis for courses in geometry.

Another important Hellenistic scientist, **Archimedes** (ahr•kuh•MEE•deez) of Syracuse, studied at Alexandria. He accurately estimated the value of pi (π)—the ratio of the circumference of a circle to its diameter. In addition, Archimedes explained the law of the lever. Using Archimedes' ideas, Hellenistic scientists later built a force pump, pneumatic machines, and even a steam engine.

Reading Check
Summarize What were some of the main achievements of the scientists of the Hellenistic period?

Global Patterns

Pythagorean Theorem

The Pythagorean theorem is among the most recognized theorems in geometry. It states that the square of the hypotenuse of a right triangle equals the sum of the squared lengths of the two remaining sides—or $a^2 + b^2 = c^2$.

The theorem is attributed to Pythagoras because he is credited with providing the first mathematical proof, or deductive argument, proving the theorem. However, others knew of the theorem before Pythagoras—including Chinese mathematicians from as early as 1100 BC and ancient Egyptian surveyors. The renowned Greek mathematician Euclid (c. 300 BC) created his own proof of the theorem, which in turn spread to many other cultures. Shown at right are Arabic and Chinese translations of Euclid's proof.

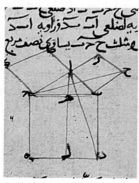
Arabic, AD 1250

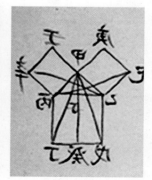
Chinese, AD 1607

Archimedes
(c. 290–c. 212 BC)

Gifted in both geometry and physics, Archimedes also put his genius to practical use. He invented the Archimedes screw, a device that raised water from the ground, and the compound pulley to lift heavy objects. The writer Plutarch described how Archimedes demonstrated to an audience of curious onlookers how something heavy can be moved by a small force.

"Archimedes took a . . . ship . . . which had just been dragged up on land with great labor and many men; in this he placed her usual complement of men and cargo, and then sitting at some distance, without any trouble, by gently pulling with his hand the end of a system of pulleys, he dragged it towards him with as smooth and even a motion as if it were passing over the sea."

—Plutarch, *Parallel Lives: Marcellus*

Analyze Historical Source
What other uses might have been found for Archimedes' invention?

Philosophy and Art

The teachings of Plato and Aristotle continued to be very influential in Hellenistic philosophy. In the third century BC, however, philosophers became concerned with how people should live their lives. Two major philosophies developed out of this concern.

Stoicism and Epicureanism A Greek philosopher named Zeno (335–263 BC) founded the school of philosophy called Stoicism (STOH·ih·sihz·uhm). Stoics proposed that people should live virtuous lives in harmony with the will of God or the natural laws that God established to run the universe. They also preached that human desires, power, and wealth were dangerous distractions that should be checked. Stoicism promoted social unity and encouraged its followers to focus on what they could control.

Epicurus (ehp·uh·KYUR·uhs) founded the school of thought called Epicureanism. He taught that gods who had no interest in humans ruled the universe. Epicurus believed that the only real objects were those that the five senses perceived. He taught that the greatest good and the highest pleasure came from virtuous conduct and the absence of pain. Epicureans proposed that the main goal of humans was to achieve harmony of body and mind. Today, the word *epicurean* means a person devoted to pursuing human pleasures, especially the enjoyment of good food. However, during his lifetime, Epicurus advocated moderation in all things.

Realism in Sculpture Like science, sculpture flourished during the Hellenistic age. Rulers, wealthy merchants, and cities all purchased statues to honor gods, commemorate heroes, and portray ordinary people in everyday situations. The largest known Hellenistic statue was created on the island of Rhodes. Known as the **Colossus of Rhodes**, this bronze statue stood more than 100 feet high. Another of the Seven Wonders of the Ancient World, this huge sculpture was toppled by an earthquake in about 225 BC. Later, the bronze was sold for scrap. Another magnificent Hellenistic sculpture found on Rhodes was the Nike, or Winged Victory, of Samothrace. It was created around 203 BC to commemorate a Greek naval victory.

Hellenistic sculpture moved away from the harmonic balance and idealized forms of the classical age. Instead of the serene face and perfect body of an idealized man or woman, Hellenistic sculptors created more natural works. They felt free to explore new subjects, carving ordinary people such as an old, wrinkled peasant woman.

By 150 BC, the Hellenistic world was in decline. A new city, Rome, was growing and gaining strength. Through Rome, Greek-style drama, architecture, sculpture, and philosophy were preserved and eventually became the core of Western civilization.

Reading Check
Draw Conclusions
What was the main concern of the Stoic and Epicurean schools of philosophy?

Discovered in 1863, the Nike, or Winged Victory, of Samothrace was probably created around 203 BC to honor a sea battle. Its exaggerated features and flowing style were common in Hellenistic art.

Lesson 6 Assessment

1. **Organize Information** Create a graphic organizer similar to the one shown and fill it in with Hellenistic achievements for each category.

Category	Achievements
astronomy	
geometry	
philosophy	
art	

2. **Key Terms and People** For each key term or person in the lesson, write a sentence explaining its significance.

3. **Analyze Effects** How did trade contribute to cultural diversity in the Hellenistic city of Alexandria?

4. **Evaluate** How did Euclid influence some of the developments in astronomy during the Hellenistic period?

5. **Compare** What did Stoicism and Epicureanism have in common?

6. **Synthesize** Describe how the growth of Alexander's empire spread Greek culture.

7. **Form Opinions** What do you think was the greatest scientific advancement of the Hellenistic period? Why?

8. **Compare** How was the purpose served by architecture and sculpture in the Hellenistic period similar to the purpose served by these arts in the golden age of Athens?

Module 5 Assessment

Key Terms and People

For each term or name below, write a sentence explaining its connection to classical Greece.

1. Trojan War
2. Homer
3. polis
4. democracy
5. direct democracy
6. classical art
7. tragedy
8. Aristotle
9. Alexander the Great
10. Hellenistic

Main Ideas

Use your notes and the information in the module to answer the following questions.

Cultures of the Mountains and the Sea
1. Why was sea travel important to early Greece?
2. Why did the Greeks develop myths?

Warring City-States
3. What were the two most powerful city-states in early Greece?
4. What were the consequences of the Persian Wars?

Democracy and Greece's Golden Age
5. What were Pericles' three goals for Athens?
6. Why did the members of the Peloponnesian League resent Athens?

Achievements of Greek Culture
7. In what forms of writing did the Greeks excel?
8. Who were the three renowned philosophers of the golden age?

Alexander the Great
9. Why was Greece so easily conquered by Macedonia?
10. What was the full extent of Alexander's empire before his death?

Hellenistic Culture
11. What four influences blended to form Hellenistic culture?
12. What are some of the scientific achievements of the Hellenistic period?

Critical Thinking

1. **Evaluate** How did Mediterranean trade routes impact the development of the Mycenaean civilization?

2. **Compare** How was education different for boys and girls in Athens?

3. **Synthesize** In a diagram, show the development of direct democracy in Athens.

4. **Draw Conclusions** "Years of uncertainty and insecurity have changed the country. It once was Athens, but now it has become Sparta." What do you think this statement means? Use information from the chapter to illustrate your answer.

5. **Form Opinions** Do you think Pericles was justified in using the Delian League's money to restore Athens? Why or why not?

6. **Develop Historical Perspective** Why might both Herodotus and Thucydides be considered fathers of history?

7. **Make Inferences** Consider Pericles and Alexander the Great. What qualifications or characteristics do you think are needed for a leader to build an empire? Why?

8. **Predict** Was the power struggle that followed Alexander's death inevitable?

Engage with History

You can learn a lot about a culture from its works of art and literature, as well as from the statements of its leaders, philosophers, and historians. Review the works of art and text excerpts you read in the module. Break into small groups and discuss what these examples suggest about classical Greek culture. Then conduct a class debate about how the art and ideals of Greece have influenced modern society.

Focus on Writing

Write a **letter** to Plato in which you either agree or disagree with his belief that one philosopher-king should rule society. Whichever position you take, use the Internet to find historical evidence to support your argument.

Multimedia Activity

Search the Internet for additional information on the Parthenon and the sculptor Phidias, who oversaw its construction. Use the information you gather to record a mock radio or television interview with Phidias. Then play it in class. Have Phidias answer questions about

- his designs for the statues and carvings that adorned the Parthenon
- the significance of the Parthenon for his fellow Athenians
- other works of art he created

ANCIENT GREECE

The Acropolis of Athens symbolizes the city and represents the architectural and artistic legacy of ancient Greece. *Acropolis* means "highest city" in Greek, and there are many such sites in Greece. Historically, an acropolis provided shelter and defense against a city's enemies. The Acropolis of Athens—the best known of them all—contained temples, monuments, and artwork dedicated to the Greek gods. Archaeological evidence indicates that the Acropolis was an important place to inhabitants from much earlier eras. However, the structures that we see today on the site were largely conceived by the statesman Pericles during the Golden Age of Athens in the 5th century B.C.

Explore the Acropolis of ancient Greece and learn about the legacy of Greek civilization. You can find a wealth of information, video clips, primary sources, activities, and more at hmhsocialstudies.com.

Go online to view these and other **HISTORY**® resources.

The Parthenon

Watch the video to see what the Parthenon, one of the most important temples on the Acropolis, might have looked like after it was completed.

The Persian Wars

Watch the video to find out how Athens emerged as the principal Greek city-state at the conclusion of the Persian Wars.

The Goddess Athena

Watch the video to learn how, according to Greek mythology, Athena became the protector of Athens.

Legacy of Greece

Watch the video to analyze The School of Athens, a painting by the Italian Renaissance artist Raphael, which pays tribute to the legacy of ancient Greece in philosophy and science.

Module 6

The Roman World and Early Christianity

Essential Question
Why is the legacy of ancient Rome still so important today?

About the Photo: This 19th-century painting by Italian artist Cesare Maccari shows Cicero, one of ancient Rome's greatest public speakers, addressing fellow members of the Roman Senate.

 Explore ONLINE!

HISTORY

VIDEOS, including...
- The Roman Republic Is Born
- The Rise of Roman Cities
- The Birth of Christianity
- The Colosseum
- Roman Roads

☑ Document Based Investigations

☑ Graphic Organizers

☑ Interactive Games

☑ Image with Hotspots: Life in a Roman Villa

☑ Animation: Aqueducts

In this module you will trace the rise, fall, and impact of the Roman Empire and the spread of Christianity.

What You Will Learn ...

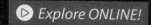
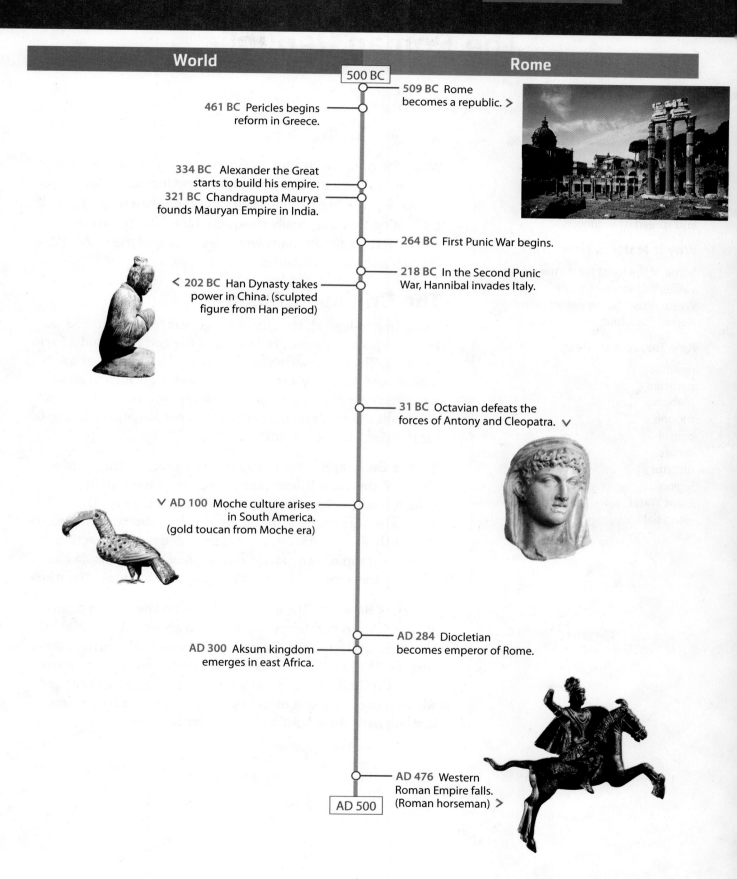

World	Rome

500 BC

509 BC Rome becomes a republic. >

461 BC Pericles begins reform in Greece.

334 BC Alexander the Great starts to build his empire.

321 BC Chandragupta Maurya founds Mauryan Empire in India.

264 BC First Punic War begins.

218 BC In the Second Punic War, Hannibal invades Italy.

< **202 BC** Han Dynasty takes power in China. (sculpted figure from Han period)

31 BC Octavian defeats the forces of Antony and Cleopatra. ∨

∨ **AD 100** Moche culture arises in South America. (gold toucan from Moche era)

AD 284 Diocletian becomes emperor of Rome.

AD 300 Aksum kingdom emerges in east Africa.

AD 476 Western Roman Empire falls. (Roman horseman) >

AD 500

The Roman Republic

The Big Idea

The early Romans established a republic, which grew powerful and spread its influence.

Why It Matters Now

Some of the most fundamental values and institutions of Western civilization began in the Roman Republic.

Key Terms and People

republic
patrician
plebeian
tribune
consul
senate
dictator
legion
Punic Wars
Hannibal

Setting the Stage

While the great civilization of Greece was in decline, a new city to the west was developing and increasing its power. Rome grew from a small settlement to a mighty civilization that eventually conquered the Mediterranean world. In time, the Romans would build one of the most famous and influential empires in history.

The Origins of Rome

According to legend, the city of Rome was founded in 753 BC by Romulus and Remus, twin sons of the god Mars and a Latin princess. The twins were abandoned on the Tiber River as infants and raised by a she-wolf. The twins decided to build a city near the spot. In reality it was humans, not immortals, who built the city, and they chose the spot largely for its strategic location and fertile soil.

Rome's Geography Rome was built on seven rolling hills at a curve on the Tiber River, near the center of the Italian peninsula. It was midway between the Alps and Italy's southern tip. Rome also was near the midpoint of the Mediterranean Sea. To the south, east, and west, the sea provided both protection and a means of rapid transportation. Much of the peninsula had rich soil and a mild climate, able to support a large population.

The First Romans The earliest settlers on the Italian peninsula arrived in prehistoric times. From about 1000 to 500 BC, three groups inhabited the region and eventually battled for control. They were the Latins, the Greeks, and the Etruscans. The Latins built the original settlement at Rome, a cluster of wooden huts atop one of its seven hills, Palatine Hill. These settlers were considered to be the first Romans.

This mosaic of Romulus and Remus with the she-wolf who raised them is from Aldborough, England, and dates back to c. AD 100.

Reading Check
Summarize What advantages did Rome's location give the city?

Between 750 and 600 BC, the Greeks established colonies along southern Italy and Sicily. The cities became prosperous and commercially active. They brought all of Italy, including Rome, into closer contact with Greek civilization.

The Etruscans were native to northern Italy. They were skilled metalworkers and engineers. The Etruscans strongly influenced the development of Roman civilization. They boasted a system of writing, for example, and the Romans adopted their alphabet. They also influenced Rome's architecture, especially the use of the arch.

The Early Republic

Around 600 BC, an Etruscan became king of Rome. In the decades that followed, Rome grew from a collection of hilltop villages to a city that covered nearly 500 square miles. Various kings ordered the construction of Rome's first temples and public centers—the most famous of which was the Forum, the heart of Roman political life.

Vincenzo Camuccini's painting *Death of Caesar* (1798) shows how Caesar's assassination was perpetrated by a conspiracy of Roman senators.

Reading Check
Analyze Motives
Why did Caesar's rivals feel they had to kill him?

Their alliance, however, ended in jealousy and violence. Octavian forced Lepidus to retire. He and Mark Antony then became rivals. While leading troops against Rome's enemies in Anatolia, Mark Antony met Queen Cleopatra of Egypt. He fell in love with her and followed her to Egypt. Octavian accused Antony of plotting to rule Rome from Egypt, and another civil war erupted. Octavian defeated the combined forces of Antony and Cleopatra at the naval battle of Actium in 31 BC. Later, Antony and Cleopatra committed suicide.

While he restored some aspects of the republic, Octavian became the unchallenged ruler of Rome. Eventually he accepted the title of **Augustus** (aw•GUHS•tuhs), or "exalted one." He also kept the title *imperator,* or "supreme military commander," a term from which *emperor* is derived. Rome was now an empire ruled by one man.

Augustus
(63 BC–AD 14)

Augustus was the most powerful ruler of the mightiest empire of the ancient world. Yet, amid the pomp of Rome, he lived a simple and frugal life. His home was modest by Roman standards. His favorite meal consisted of coarse bread, a few sardines, and a piece of cheese—the usual food of a common laborer.

Augustus was also a very religious and family-oriented man. He held to a strict moral code. He had his only child, Julia, exiled from Rome for not being faithful in her marriage.

A Vast and Powerful Empire

Rome was at the peak of its power from the beginning of Augustus's rule in 27 BC to AD 180. For 207 years, peace reigned throughout the empire, except for some fighting with tribes along the borders. This period of peace and prosperity is known as the **Pax Romana**—"Roman peace."

During this time, the Roman Empire included more than three million square miles. Its population numbered between 60 and 80 million people. About one million people lived in the city of Rome itself.

A Sound Government The Romans held their vast empire together in part through efficient government and able rulers. Augustus was Rome's ablest emperor. He stabilized the frontier and created a system of government that survived for centuries. By collecting taxes, Augustus's government had money to spend on fixing roads, building and repairing temples, and constructing numerous other splendid public buildings. He also set up a civil service. That is, he paid workers to manage the affairs of government, such as the grain supply, tax collection, and the postal system. Although the senate still functioned, civil servants drawn from plebeians and even former slaves actually administered the empire. After Augustus died in AD 14, the system of government that he established maintained the empire's stability. This was due mainly to the effectiveness of the civil service in carrying out day-to-day operations.

Vocabulary
civil service persons employed in the civil administration of government

Julio-Claudians and Flavians After the death of Augustus, for the next 54 years, relatives of Julius Caesar, called the Julio-Claudian Emperors, ruled the empire. The abilities of these emperors varied widely. Tiberius, Augustus's adopted son, was a good soldier and a competent administrator. His brutal and mentally unstable successor, Caligula, however, once supposedly demonstrated his power to the Roman Senate by appointing his favorite horse as consul.

Nero, the last of the Julio-Claudians, committed suicide in AD 68. After his death, civil wars raged in Rome, and four military leaders claimed the throne in turn. The last of them, Vespasian, reestablished order. During his reign and those of his two sons, stability returned to the empire. Together these three emperors are known as the Flavians.

The Good Emperors In AD 96 a new line of emperors established itself on the Roman throne. Called the Good Emperors, these five rulers governed Rome for almost a century. Almost all of the Good Emperors were from the provinces rather than from Rome. Consequently, they continued opening up Roman imperial society by admitting more members of the provincial elites into the Senate and the imperial administration.

Roman Emperors, AD 37–180

Bad Emperors			Good Emperors		
Caligula • 37–41 • Mentally disturbed	**Nero** • 54–68 • Good administrator but vicious • Murdered many • Persecuted Christians	**Domitian** • 81–96 • Ruled as a dictator • Feared treason everywhere and executed many	**Nerva** • 96–98 • Began custom of adopting heir **Trajan** • 98–117 • Empire reached its greatest extent • Undertook vast building program • Enlarged social welfare	**Hadrian** • 117–138 • Consolidated earlier conquests • Reorganized bureaucracy **Antoninus Pius** • 138–161 • Reign largely a period of peace and prosperity	**Marcus Aurelias** • 161–180 • Brought empire to height of economic prosperity • Defeated invaders • Wrote philosophy

Interpret Charts
What are three areas of Roman life that the good emperors improved?

Caligula

Trajan

Under the Good Emperors the empire grew tremendously. It reached the limits of its expansion under Trajan, who added present-day Romania, Armenia, Mesopotamia, and the Sinai Peninsula to the empire. Trajan's successor Hadrian, however, thought the empire had grown too large. He withdrew from almost all these eastern additions and built defensive fortifications along the frontiers to guard against invasions. In northern Britain, for example, Hadrian built a wall some 73 miles long.

Legal System Roman law also unified the empire. Stability in the Roman legal system was achieved by laws passed by assemblies, the Senate, or the emperor. These laws specified what could or could not be done and what the penalties were for breaking the law. With few exceptions, the same laws applied to all citizens in the empire, wherever they might live.

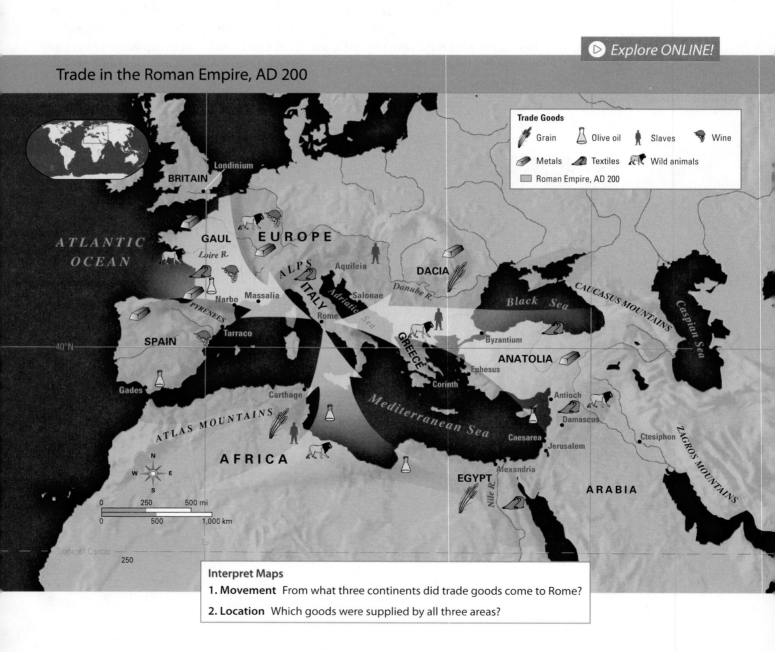

▷ Explore ONLINE!

Trade in the Roman Empire, AD 200

Trade Goods
- Grain
- Olive oil
- Slaves
- Wine
- Metals
- Textiles
- Wild animals

Roman Empire, AD 200

Interpret Maps

1. **Movement** From what three continents did trade goods come to Rome?

2. **Location** Which goods were supplied by all three areas?

Agriculture and Trade Agriculture was the most important industry in the empire. All else depended on it. About 90 percent of the people were engaged in farming. Most Romans survived on the produce from their local area. Additional food (when needed) and luxury items for the rich were obtained through trade. In Augustus's time, a silver coin called a denarius was in use throughout the empire. Having common coinage made trade between different parts of the empire much easier.

Meanwhile, manufacturing increased throughout the empire. In Italy, Gaul, and Spain, artisans made cheap pottery and textiles by hand in small shops. The most important manufacturing centers, however, were in the east, where cities such as Alexandria made products like fine glassware.

Rome had a vast trading network. Ships from the east traveled the Mediterranean protected by the Roman navy. Cities such as Corinth in Greece, Ephesus in Anatolia, and Antioch on the eastern coast of the Mediterranean grew wealthy. Rome also traded with China and India.

A complex network of roads linked the empire to such far-flung places as Persia and southern Russia. These roads were originally built by the Roman army for military purposes. Trade also brought Roman ways to the provinces and beyond.

Reading Check
Summarize
To what does the term *Pax Romana* refer?

Lesson 2 Assessment

1. **Organize Information** Create a graphic organizer similar to the one shown. Fill it in with at least three ways that Rome changed as it became an empire. What changes do you consider negative? Why?

Changes in Rome
• Dictator claims sole power
•
•

2. **Key Terms and People** For each key term or person in the lesson, write a sentence explaining its significance.

3. **Analyze Causes** What factors contributed to the fall of the Roman Republic?

4. **Summarize** What were the main reasons for the Romans' success in controlling such a large empire?

5. **Synthesize** In what way did Roman law unify the Roman empire?

6. **Analyze Causes** What role did Julius Caesar play in the decline of the republic and the rise of the empire?

7. **Analyze Issues** What aspects of Roman society remained similar from republic to empire?

8. **Form Opinions** What was Augustus's greatest contribution to Roman society? Why?

9. **Analyze Effects** What was the impact of Augustus's government spending on Rome?

Life in the Roman Empire

The Big Idea

The Romans developed a complex society in which different classes of people lived.

Why It Matters Now

Life in the Roman Empire inspired many of the social customs we have today.

Key Terms and People

villa
paterfamilias
circus
augurs

Setting the Stage

Throughout its history, Rome emphasized the values of discipline, strength, and loyalty. A person with these qualities was said to have the important virtue of *gravitas*. The Romans were a practical people. They honored strength more than beauty, power more than grace, and usefulness more than elegance.

The Roman People

Most people in the Roman Empire lived in the countryside and worked on farms. In Rome and smaller cities, merchants, soldiers, slaves, foreigners, and philosophers all shared the same crowded, noisy streets. Here, people from all walks of life came together to create a diverse society.

Rich and Poor The *Pax Romana* provided prosperity to many people, but citizens did not share equally in this wealth. Wealth and social status made huge differences in how people lived. Classes had little in common.

The rich lived extravagantly. They usually had both a city home and a country home, or **villa**, that included conveniences such as running water. They spent large sums of money on gardens, slaves, and luxuries. Wealthy Romans gave banquets that lasted for many hours and included foods that were rare and costly, such as boiled ostrich and parrot-tongue pie.

Wealthy Roman men spent much of their time embroiled in politics. Since public officials were not paid, only the wealthy could afford to hold office. Wealthy Romans could frequently be found meeting with public officials or with favored political groups. However, ties of marriage, friendship, and family alliances were as important as class interests. In addition, Roman politicians worked to perfect their public-speaking skills to better sway the opinions of members of the popular assemblies.

Unlike the wealthy, most of the nearly one million residents of Rome barely had the necessities of life. During the time of the empire, much of the city's population was unemployed. The government supported these people with daily rations of grain.

In the shadow of Rome's great temples and public buildings, poor people crowded into rickety, sprawling tenements. Fire posed a constant threat because of the torches used for light and the charcoal used for cooking. In part to keep poorer citizens from rebelling against such conditions, free food and public entertainment became a major feature of city life in Rome.

Slaves and Captivity Slavery was a significant part of Roman life. It was widespread and supported the economy. The Romans made more use of slaves than any previous civilization. Numbers of enslaved persons may have reached as high as one-third of the total population. Most slaves were conquered peoples brought back by victorious Roman armies and included men, women, and children. Children born to slaves also became slaves. Slaves could be bought and sold. According to Roman law, enslaved people were the property of their owners. They could be punished, rewarded, set free, or put to death as their masters saw fit.

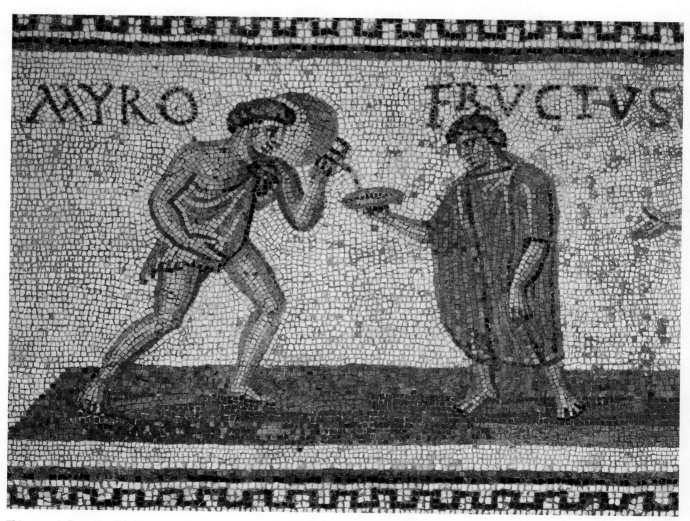

This mosaic from the third century shows a Roman man named Fructus being served a drink by his slave, Myro.

Roman families of all classes enjoyed the company of pets such as the dog portrayed in this mosaic.

Slaves worked both in the city and on farms. Many were treated cruelly and worked at hard labor all day. Some strong, healthy male slaves were forced to become gladiators, or professional fighters, who fought to the death in public contests. Other slaves, particularly those who worked in wealthy households, were better treated. Occasionally, slaves would rebel. None of the slave revolts succeeded. More than a million slaves lost their lives attempting to gain their freedom.

Family Like many other ancient peoples, Romans were patriarchal. The head of the family—the **paterfamilias**, or family father—was the oldest living male. He had extensive powers over all other family members. This included his wife, his sons with their wives and children, his unmarried daughters, and his family slaves. Within this family structure, Romans emphasized the virtues of simplicity, religious devotion, and obedience.

Adoption was an important aspect of Roman society. Some families with no sons would adopt a teenage boy or young man to serve as the heir to the paterfamilias. Adoption was one way of ensuring that the family name was carried on. Roman women could do little without the permission of their fathers or husbands. However, women could own and inherit property. Among the lower classes, though, women had more freedom. Lower-class women often worked outside of the home as shopkeepers or at similar jobs.

Reading Check
Contrast
How was life different for rich and poor citizens in Rome?

Roman Society

Roman society was highly stratified. The lives of rich and poor citizens differed greatly. Even so, there were a few common elements that most members of Roman society shared.

Public Entertainment To distract and control the masses of Romans, the government provided free games, races, mock battles, and gladiator contests. By AD 250 there were 150 holidays per year. Romans also enjoyed bloody spectacles in amphitheaters. The Colosseum, a huge arena that could hold 50,000, would be filled with the rich and the poor alike. The spectacles they watched combined bravery, cruelty, honor, and violence.

By far the most popular entertainment offered in the amphitheaters was the gladiatorial combats. Such shows often ended with the death of one or both of the professional fighters, who were usually slaves. In other contests, gladiators engaged in combat with wild animals brought from distant lands such as tigers, lions, and bears. Often, condemned criminals were thrown into the arena to be killed by ferocious beasts.

Romans of all classes also enjoyed the **circuses**, where chariot races took place. In Rome many such races were held in the Circus Maximus, a racetrack that could accommodate 250,000 spectators. Roman audiences particularly enjoyed the spectacular crashes that frequently occurred. They also liked theater, particularly comedies and satires. Performers such as mimes, jugglers, dancers, acrobats, and clowns also became quite popular.

DOCUMENT-BASED INVESTIGATION   Historical Source

Gladiator Games

Gladiator games were one of the ways that the Roman government controlled the masses of common citizens. The gladiators themselves were usually slaves; they would fight each other or a wild animal.

Thumbs-up or thumbs-down—that is how a match often ended for a gladiator (shown in the mosaic battling a tiger). When one of the combatants fell, the organizer of the games usually determined his fate. A thumbs-up sign from him meant that the fighter would live. Thumbs-down meant his death. The crowd usually played a key role in these life-and-death decisions. If the masses liked the fallen gladiator, he most likely would live to fight another day. If not, he was doomed.

Analyze Historical Sources
What do the gladiator games reveal about how slaves were regarded in Rome?

The well-preserved Roman public baths in Bath, England, are a major tourist attraction today.

Public baths were other popular places for recreation. The Romans were aware of the importance of bathing for health, but public baths offered more than just a place to get clean. After bathing in a hot pool, people could retire to a cold pool to relax and socialize. In addition to the pools, many public baths included steam rooms, exercise facilities, and meeting rooms.

Education The Romans, at least those of the upper classes, placed great value on education and literacy. Most parents taught their children at home. Some wealthy families hired expensive tutors or sent their sons to exclusive schools. In such schools, boys—and a few girls—learned Latin and Greek, law, math, and public speaking.

Gods and Goddesses The earliest Romans worshipped powerful spirits or divine forces, called *numina,* believed to reside in everything around them. Closely related to these spirits were the *Lares* (LAIR-eez), who were the guardian spirits of each family. Romans gave names to these powerful gods and goddesses. They honored them through various rituals, hoping to gain favor and avoid misfortune.

In Rome government and religion were linked. The deities were symbols of the state. Romans were expected to honor them, not only in private rituals at shrines in their homes, but also in public worship ceremonies conducted by priests in temples. Among the most important Roman gods and goddesses were Jupiter, father of the gods; Juno, who watched over women; and Minerva, goddess of wisdom and arts and crafts. During the period of empire, worship of the emperor also became part of the official religion of Rome.

This Roman painting shows the *Lares*, who protected Roman families.

The Romans adopted many elements of Greek mythology. However, the Romans did not limit their belief to only a few gods. They made offerings to any gods who might exist to ensure Roman prosperity, including gods borrowed from the Egyptians and Persians. Each Roman family also worshipped local household gods called *Penates*.

The Romans believed that the gods sent signs and warnings to human beings in the form of natural phenomena, such as the flight of birds or the color and arrangement of entrails in sacrificial animals. They paid particular respect to the priests known as **augurs**, who specialized in interpreting these signs. Nothing important was undertaken without first consulting the augurs.

During this time of *Pax Romana*, another activity slowly emerged in the Roman Empire—the practice of a new religion known as Christianity. The early followers of this new faith would suffer brutality and hardship for their beliefs. But Christianity endured and spread throughout the empire, eventually becoming one of the dominant faiths of the world.

Reading Check
Predict Effects
What present-day sport may have descended from Roman chariot racing?

Lesson 3 Assessment

1. **Organize Information** Create a word web graphic organizer and fill it in with aspects of life in the Roman world. Then write a sentence for each aspect that summarizes the Romans' views on it.

Life in the
Roman Empire

2. **Key Terms and People** For each key term or person in the lesson, write a sentence explaining its significance.

3. **Compare** In what ways was ancient Roman society patriarchal? What rights did Roman women have?

4. **Synthesize** What measures did the government take to distract and control the masses of Rome?

5. **Synthesize** What types of entertainment were held in the Circus Maximus and the Colosseum? What other types of entertainment were popular in Rome?

6. **Draw Conclusions** A Roman poet once said that the poor were only interested in "bread and circuses." What do you think he meant by that? Do you think he approved of the lifestyle he was describing? Why or why not?

Life in a Roman Villa

Much of what we know about Roman homes comes from archaeological excavations of the ancient cities of Pompeii and Herculaneum. In AD 79, Pompeii and Herculaneum were buried in volcanic ash by a tremendous eruption of Mount Vesuvius. The illustration you see here is modeled after a home in Pompeii. Notice the rich artwork and refined architecture of this home.

▼ **THE VILLA**
Very few Romans could afford to live in such luxury, but those who could left a legacy that still inspires wonder.

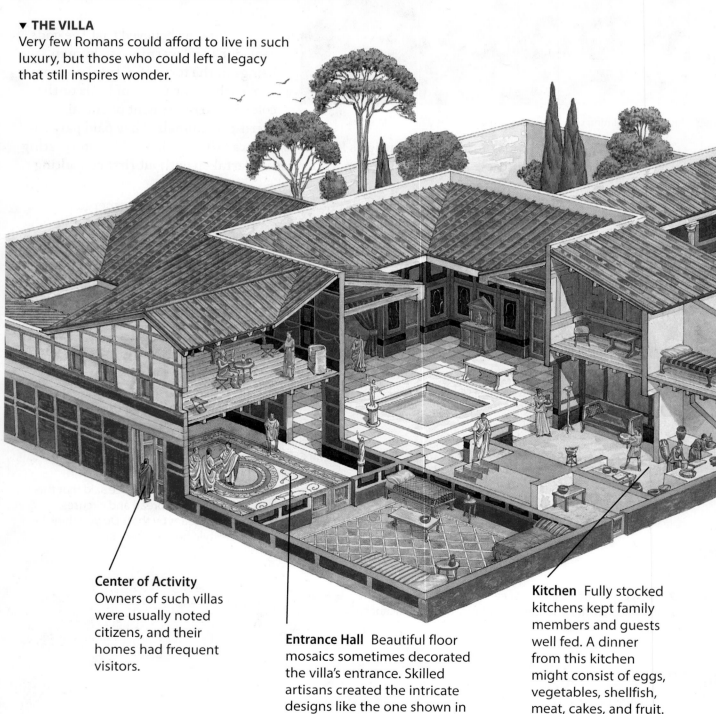

Center of Activity Owners of such villas were usually noted citizens, and their homes had frequent visitors.

Entrance Hall Beautiful floor mosaics sometimes decorated the villa's entrance. Skilled artisans created the intricate designs like the one shown in the entry of this home.

Kitchen Fully stocked kitchens kept family members and guests well fed. A dinner from this kitchen might consist of eggs, vegetables, shellfish, meat, cakes, and fruit.

▶ FRESCOES

A fresco is a painting made on damp plaster. Roman artists used this technique to brighten the walls of Roman homes. This fresco from the ruins of Pompeii reflects a couple's pride at being able to read and write—she holds tools for writing and he a scroll.

Gardens Wealthy Romans maintained gardens decorated with fountains, sculptures, and frescoes.

▶ ARCHAEOLOGICAL EXCAVATION

When Mount Vesuvius erupted, ash rained down, covered everything, and hardened. Bread (shown at right) carbonized in the bakeries. Bodies decayed under the ash leaving hollow spaces. An archaeologist developed the technique of pouring plaster into the spaces and then removing the ash. The result was a cast of the body where it fell.

Critical Thinking

1. **Make Inferences** What other types of rooms or activities can you identify in the illustration?

2. **Compare and Contrast** How are homes today similar to a Roman villa? How are they different?

The Origins of Christianity

The Big Idea

Christianity arose in Roman-occupied Judea and spread throughout the Roman Empire.

Why It Matters Now

Christianity has spread throughout the world and today has more than a billion followers.

Key Terms and People

Jesus
apostle
Paul
Diaspora
Constantine
bishop
Peter
pope

Setting the Stage

While religion played an important role in Roman society, the worship of Roman gods was impersonal and often practiced without a great deal of emotion. As the empire grew, so too did a new religion called Christianity. Born as a movement within Judaism, it emphasized a personal relationship between God and people—and attracted many Romans.

The Life and Teachings of Jesus

Roman power spread to Judea, the home of the Jews, around 63 BC. At first the Jewish kingdom remained independent, at least in name. Rome then took control of the Jewish kingdom in AD 6 and made it a province of the empire. A number of Jews, however, believed that they would once again be free. According to biblical tradition, God had promised that a savior known as the Messiah would arrive and restore the kingdom of the Jews. Roughly two decades after the beginning of Roman rule, many believed that such a savior had arrived.

Jesus of Nazareth Although the exact date is uncertain, historians estimate that sometime around 6 to 4 BC, a Jew named **Jesus** was born in Bethlehem in Judea. Historical records of the time mention very little about Jesus. The main source of information about his life and teachings is the Gospels, the first four books of the New Testament of the Christian Bible. According to the Gospels, Jesus was raised in the village of Nazareth in northern Judea. He was baptized by a prophet known as John the Baptist. As a young man, he took up the trade of carpentry.

At the age of 30, Jesus began his public ministry. For the next three years, he preached, taught, did good works, and reportedly performed miracles. His teachings contained many ideas from Jewish tradition, such as monotheism, or belief in only one God, loving others, and the principles of the Ten Commandments. Jesus emphasized God's personal relationship to each human being. He stressed the importance of people's love for God, their neighbors, their enemies, and even themselves. He also taught that God would end wickedness in the world and would establish an eternal kingdom after death for people who sincerely repented their sins.

A Growing Movement Some of the Gospels are thought to have been written by one or more of Jesus' disciples, or pupils. These 12 men later came to be called **apostles**.

As Jesus preached from town to town, his fame grew. He attracted large crowds, and many people were touched by his message. Because Jesus ignored wealth and status, his message had special appeal to the poor. "Blessed are the meek, for they shall inherit the earth," he said.

Jesus' Death Jesus' growing popularity concerned Roman leaders. According to the New Testament, when Jesus visited Jerusalem about AD 29, enthusiastic crowds greeted him as the Messiah, or king—the one whom the Bible had said would come to rescue the Jews. The Roman governor Pontius Pilate accused Jesus of defying the authority of Rome. Pilate arrested Jesus and sentenced him to be crucified, or nailed to a large wooden cross to die like thousands of other opponents of Rome.

After Jesus' death, his body was placed in a tomb. According to the Gospels, three days later his body was gone, and a living Jesus began appearing to his followers. The Gospels go on to say that he then ascended into heaven. The apostles were more convinced than ever that Jesus was the Messiah. It was from this belief that Jesus came to be referred to as Jesus Christ. *Christos* is a Greek word meaning "messiah" or "savior." The name *Christianity* is derived from "Christ."

Mary Magdalene was an important woman in Jesus' ministry.

Reading Check
Hypothesize
Why did the followers of Jesus think he was the Messiah?

Historical Source

The Gospels

Nearly all of our knowledge of Jesus comes from the Gospels—the first four books of the New Testament. The New Testament along with the books of the Hebrew Bible today make up the Christian Bible.

Jesus instructed people to repent of their sins and seek God's forgiveness. To obtain this forgiveness, he said that people must love God above all else and treat others as they would want to be treated. In addition, they should practice humility, mercy, and charity. Jesus' words, as related in the Gospels, were simple and direct.

> *"Love your enemies, do good to those who hate you, bless those who curse you, and pray for those who mistreat you. If anyone hits you on the cheek, let him hit the other one too; if someone takes your coat, let him have your shirt as well. Give to everyone who asks you for something, and when someone takes what is yours, do not ask for it back. Do for others just what you want them to do for you."*
>
> —Luke 6:27-31

Analyze Historical Sources
How does this passage support Jesus' emphasis on humility, mercy, and charity?

Christ's Charge to Saint Peter by Renaissance artist Raphael depicts Jesus calling the apostle Peter to duty as the other apostles look on.

Christianity Spreads Through the Empire

Strengthened by their conviction that he had triumphed over death, the followers of Jesus continued to spread his ideas. Jesus' teachings did not contradict Jewish law, and his first followers were Jews. Soon, however, these followers began to create a new religion based on his messages. Despite political and religious opposition, the new religion of Christianity spread slowly but steadily throughout the Roman Empire.

Paul's Mission One man, the apostle **Paul**, had enormous influence on Christianity's development. Paul was a Jew who had never met Jesus and at first was an enemy of Christianity. While traveling to Damascus in Syria, he reportedly had a vision of Christ. He spent the rest of his life spreading and interpreting Christ's teachings.

The *Pax Romana*, which made travel and the exchange of ideas fairly safe, provided the ideal conditions for Christianity to spread. Common languages—Latin and Greek—allowed the message to be easily understood. Paul wrote influential letters, called Epistles, to groups of believers. In his teaching, Paul stressed that Jesus was the son of God who died for people's sins. He also declared that Christian converts were not obligated to follow Jewish law. It was this universality that enabled Christianity to become more than just a local religion.

Paul was one of Jesus' apostles. His Epistles helped to spread Christianity.

Jewish Rebellion During the early years of Christianity, much Roman attention was focused on the land of Jesus' birth and on the Jews. In AD 66, a band of Jews rebelled against Rome. In AD 70, the Romans stormed Jerusalem and destroyed the temple complex. All that remained was a western portion of the wall, which today is the holiest Jewish shrine.

The Jewish fortress near Masada held out until AD 73. It had taken nearly 15,000 Roman soldiers almost two years to conquer the fewer than 1,000 Jewish defenders at Masada. Over the course of the rebellion against Rome, about a half million Jews were killed.

The Jews made another attempt to break free of the Romans in AD 132. Another half-million Jews died in three years of fighting. Although the Jewish religion survived, the Jewish political state ceased to exist for more than 1,800 years. Most Jews were driven from their homeland into exile. This dispersal of the Jews is called the **Diaspora**.

History in Depth

The Jewish Diaspora

Centuries of Jewish exile followed the destruction of their temple and the fall of Jerusalem in AD 70. This period is called the Diaspora, from the Greek word for "dispersal." Jews fled to many parts of the world, including Europe.

In the 1100s, many European Jews were expelled from their homes. Some moved to Turkey, Palestine, and Syria. Others went to Poland and neighboring areas.

The statelessness of the Jews did not end until the creation of Israel in 1948.

Vocabulary
Scapegoats groups
or individuals who
innocently bear the
blame for others

Reading Check
Find Main Ideas
What helped to spread
Christianity through
the Roman world?

Persecution of the Christians Christians also posed a problem for Roman rulers, mainly because they refused to worship Roman gods. This refusal was seen as opposition to Roman rule. Some Roman rulers also used Christians as scapegoats for political and economic troubles.

By the second century, as the *Pax Romana* began to crumble, persecution of the Christians intensified. Romans exiled, imprisoned, or executed Christians for refusing to worship Roman deities. Thousands were crucified, burned, or killed by wild animals in the circus arenas. Other Christians and even some non-Christians regarded persecuted Christians as martyrs. Martyrs were people willing to sacrifice their lives for the sake of a belief or a cause.

A World Religion

Despite persecution of its followers, Christianity became a powerful force. By the late third century AD, there were millions of Christians in the Roman Empire and beyond. Christianity had a widespread appeal for a variety of reasons. Christianity grew because it
- embraced all people—men and women, enslaved persons, the poor, and nobles;
- gave hope to the powerless;
- appealed to those who were repelled by the extravagances of imperial Rome;
- offered a personal relationship with a loving God;
- promised eternal life after death.

Constantine

Constantine Accepts Christianity A critical moment in Christianity occurred in AD 312, when the Roman emperor **Constantine** was fighting three rivals for leadership of Rome. He had marched to the Tiber River in Rome to battle his chief rival. On the day before the battle at Milvian Bridge, Constantine prayed for divine help. He reported that he then saw an image of a cross—a symbol of Christianity. He ordered artisans to put the Christian symbol on his soldiers' shields. Constantine and his troops were victorious in battle. He credited his success to the help of the Christian God.

In the next year, AD 313, Constantine announced an end to the persecution of Christians. In the Edict of Milan, he declared Christianity to be one of the religions approved by the emperor. Christianity continued to gain strength. In 380, the emperor Theodosius made it the empire's official religion.

Early Christian Church By this time, Christians had given their religion a structure, much as the Roman Empire had a hierarchy. At the local level, a priest led each small group of Christians. A **bishop**, who was also a priest, supervised several local churches. The apostle **Peter** had traveled to Rome from Jerusalem and became the first bishop there. According to tradition,

Vocabulary
hierarchy a group
of persons organized
in order of ranks, with
each level subject to
the authority of the
one above

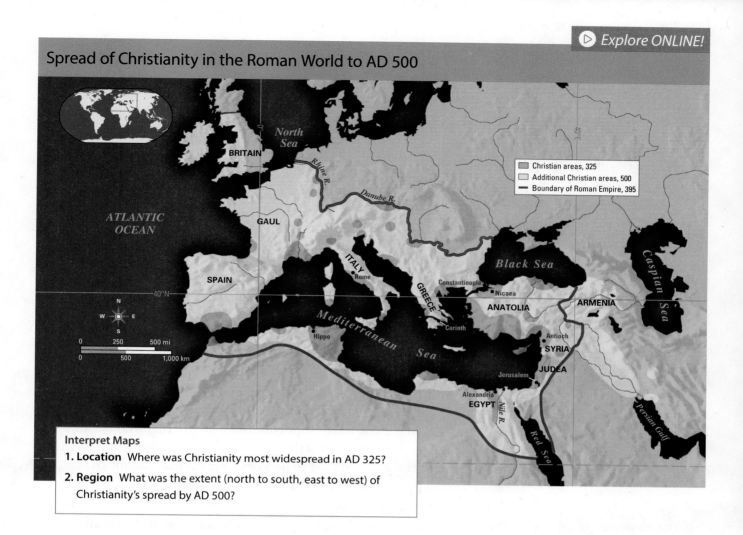

Spread of Christianity in the Roman World to AD 500

Christian areas, 325
Additional Christian areas, 500
— Boundary of Roman Empire, 395

BRITAIN
North Sea
Rhine R.
Danube R.
ATLANTIC OCEAN
GAUL
SPAIN
ITALY
Rome
GREECE
Corinth
Hippo
Mediterranean Sea
Constantinople
Nicaea
ANATOLIA
Black Sea
ARMENIA
Caspian Sea
Antioch
SYRIA
JUDEA
Jerusalem
Alexandria
EGYPT
Nile R.
Red Sea
Persian Gulf

Interpret Maps

1. **Location** Where was Christianity most widespread in AD 325?

2. **Region** What was the extent (north to south, east to west) of Christianity's spread by AD 500?

Jesus referred to Peter as the "rock" on which the Christian Church would be built. As a result, all priests and bishops traced their authority to him.

Eventually, every major city had its own bishop. However, later bishops of Rome claimed to be the heirs of Peter. These bishops said that Peter was the first **pope**, the father or head of the Christian Church. They said that whoever was bishop of Rome was also the leader of the whole Church. Also, as Rome was the capital of the empire, it seemed the logical choice to be the center of the Church.

A Single Voice As Christianity grew, disagreements about beliefs developed among its followers. Church leaders called any belief that appeared to contradict the basic teachings a heresy. Dispute over beliefs became intense. In an attempt to end conflicts, Church leaders tried to set a single, official standard of belief. These beliefs were compiled in the New Testament, which contained the four Gospels, the Epistles of Paul, and other documents. The New Testament was added to the Hebrew Bible, which Christians called the Old Testament. In AD 325, Constantine moved to solidify further the teachings of Christianity. He called Church leaders to Nicaea in Anatolia. There they wrote the Nicene Creed, which defined the basic beliefs of the Church.

Augustine and *The City of God*

One of Augustine's best-known books is *The City of God*. It was written after Rome was sacked in the fifth century AD. Augustine wrote that the fate of cities such as Rome was not important because the heavenly city, the city of God, could never be destroyed.

> "The one consists of those who live by human standards, the other of those who live according to God's will. . . . By two cities I mean two societies of human beings, one of which is predestined to reign with God for all eternity, the other is doomed to undergo eternal punishment with the Devil."
>
> —Augustine,
> *The City of God*

Analyze Historical Sources
Why would Augustine write his book after Rome had been attacked?

The Fathers of the Church Also influential in defining Church teachings were several early writers and scholars who have been called the Fathers of the Church. One of the most important was Augustine, who became bishop of the city of Hippo in North Africa in 396. Augustine taught that humans needed the grace of God to be saved. He further taught that people could not receive God's grace unless they belonged to the Church and received the sacraments.

While Christianity continued its slow but steady rise, the Roman Empire itself was gradually weakening. Under the weight of an increasing number of both foreign and domestic problems, the mighty Roman Empire eventually began to crumble.

Reading Check
Making Inferences
Why were the citizens of the Roman Empire so drawn to Christianity?

Lesson 4 Assessment

1. **Organize Information** Create a graphic organizer similar to the one shown. Fill it in with at least four events in the history of early Christianity. What event do you think had the biggest impact? Explain.

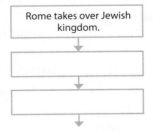

Rome takes over Jewish kingdom.

2. **Key Terms and People** For each key term or person in the lesson, write a sentence explaining its significance.

3. **Synthesize** What did Jesus emphasize in his early teachings?

4. **Analyze Causes** Why did the early Christians face persecution from the Romans?

5. **Evaluate** What was the importance of the Nicene Creed?

6. **Predict Effects** Do you think Christianity would have developed in the same way if it had arisen outside of the Roman Empire? Explain.

7. **Form Opinions** Who do you think did more to spread Christianity—Paul or Constantine? Why?

8. **Analyze Issues** Why do you think Roman leaders strongly opposed the rise of a new religion among their subjects?

The Fall of the Roman Empire

The Big Idea

Internal problems and invasions spurred the division and decline of the Roman Empire.

Why It Matters Now

The decline and fall of great civilizations is a repeating pattern in world history.

Key Terms and People

inflation
mercenary
Diocletian
Constantinople
Attila

Setting the Stage

In the third century AD, Rome faced many problems. They came both from within the empire and from outside. Only drastic economic, military, and political reforms, it seemed, could hold off collapse.

A Century of Crisis

Historians generally agree that the end of the reign of the emperor Marcus Aurelius (AD 161–180) marked the end of two centuries of peace and prosperity known as the *Pax Romana*. The rulers that followed in the next century had little or no idea how to deal with the giant empire and its growing problems. As a result, Rome began to decline.

Rome's Economy Weakens During the third century AD, several factors prompted the weakening of Rome's economy. Hostile tribes outside the boundaries of the empire and pirates on the Mediterranean Sea disrupted trade. Having reached their limit of expansion, the Romans lacked new sources of gold and silver. Desperate for revenue, the government raised taxes.

As taxes rose, however, the value of money declined. Since Rome was no longer expanding, conquests no longer brought in new sources of wealth. To maintain the money supply, emperors minted new coins with copper and lead as well as silver. It hoped to create more money with the same amount of precious metal. When people realized coins contained less silver, they refused to accept the currency at its face value. The result was growing **inflation**, a drastic drop in the value of money coupled with a rise in prices.

Agriculture faced equally serious problems. Harvests in Italy and western Europe became increasingly meager because overworked soil had lost its fertility. What's more, years of war had destroyed much farmland. Eventually, serious food shortages and the spread of disease caused the population to decline.

Military and Political Turmoil By the third century AD, the Roman military was also in disarray. Over time, Roman soldiers in general had become less disciplined and loyal. They gave their allegiance not to Rome but to their commanders, who fought among themselves for the throne. To defend against the increasing threats to the empire, the government began to recruit **mercenaries**, foreign soldiers who fought for money. While mercenaries would accept lower pay than Romans, they felt little sense of loyalty to the empire.

Feelings of loyalty eventually weakened among average citizens as well. In the past, Romans cared so deeply about their republic that they willingly sacrificed their lives for it. Conditions in the later centuries of the empire caused citizens to lose their sense of patriotism. They became indifferent to the empire's fate.

Reading Check
Summarize What problems did Rome face in the late 200s?

Emperors Attempt Reform

Remarkably, Rome survived intact for another 200 years. Reform-minded emperors and the empire's division into two parts helped to preserve it.

Diocletian Reforms the Empire In AD 284, **Diocletian**, a strong-willed army leader, became the new emperor. He ruled with an iron fist and severely limited personal freedoms. Nonetheless, he restored order to the empire and increased its strength. Diocletian doubled the size of the Roman army. To restore the prestige of the office of emperor, he claimed descent from the ancient Roman gods and created elaborate ceremonies to present himself with a godlike aura.

The imperial economy also came under state direction in a number of ways. Diocletian sought to control inflation by setting fixed prices for goods. Everywhere, commercial and manufacturing activities were geared toward the needs of imperial defense. A new tax system raised more money for the government and for the army to spend. Though drastic, these reforms were successful, saving the empire from immediate economic collapse.

Diocletian believed that the empire had grown too large and too complex for one ruler. In perhaps his most significant reform, he divided the empire into the Greek-speaking East (Greece, Anatolia, Syria, and Egypt) and the Latin-speaking West (Italy, Gaul, Britain, and Spain). He took the eastern half for himself and appointed a co-ruler for the West. While Diocletian shared authority, he kept overall control. His half of the empire, the East, included most of the empire's great cities and trade centers and was far wealthier than the West.

Because of ill health, Diocletian retired in AD 305. However, his plans for orderly succession failed. Civil war broke out immediately. By 311, four rivals were competing for power. Among them was an ambitious young commander named Constantine, the same Constantine who would later end the persecution of Christians.

Multiple Causes: Fall of the Western Roman Empire

Contributing Factors

Political	Social	Economic	Military
• Political office seen as burden, not reward • Military interference in politics • Civil war and unrest • Division of empire • Capital moved to Byzantium	• Decline in interest in public affairs • Low confidence in empire • Disloyalty, lack of patriotism, corruption • Contrast between rich and poor • Population decline due to disease and food shortage	• Poor harvests • Disruption of trade • Lack of war plunder • Gold and silver drain • Inflation • Crushing tax burden • Widening gap between rich and poor and increasingly impoverished Western Empire	• Threat from northern European tribes • Low funds for defense • Problems recruiting Roman citizens; recruiting of non-Romans • Decline of patriotism and loyalty among soldiers

Immediate Cause

Invasion by Germanic tribes and by Huns

Fall of Roman Empire

Interpreting Charts

1. **Analyze Issues** Could changes in any of the contributing factors have reversed the decline of the empire? Why or why not?

2. **Analyze Causes** Which contributing factors—political, social, economic, or military—were the most significant in the fall of the Western Roman Empire?

Constantine Moves the Capital Constantine gained control of the western part of the empire in AD 312 and continued many of the social and economic policies of Diocletian. In 324 Constantine also secured control of the East, thus restoring the concept of a single ruler.

In AD 330, Constantine took a step that would have great consequence for the empire. He moved the capital from Rome to the Greek city of Byzantium (bih•ZAN•shee•uhm), in what is now Turkey. The new capital stood on the Bosporus Strait, strategically located for trade and defense purposes on a crossroads between West and East.

With Byzantium as its capital, the center of power in the empire shifted from Rome to the East. Soon the new capital stood protected by massive walls and filled with imperial buildings modeled after those in Rome. The city eventually took a new name—**Constantinople** (kahn•stan•tuhn•OH•puhl), or the city of Constantine. After Constantine's death, the empire would again be divided. The East would survive; the West would fall.

Reading Check
Analyze Motives
Why did Constantine choose the location of Byzantium for his new capital?

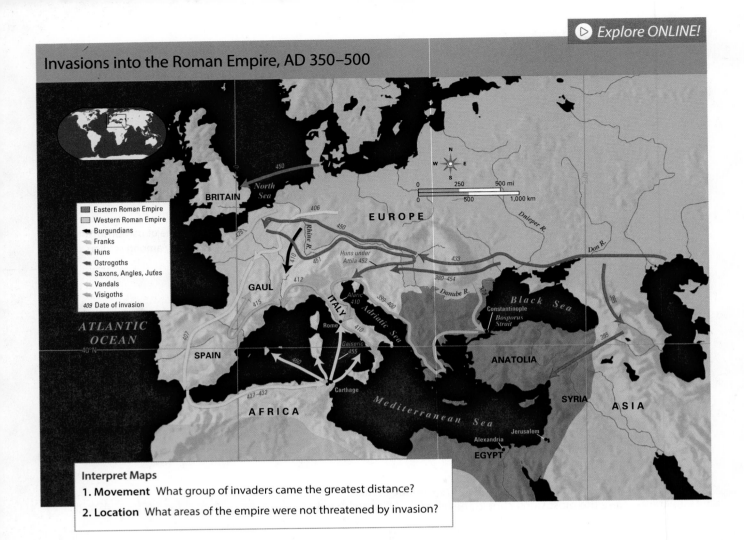

Invasions into the Roman Empire, AD 350–500

Interpret Maps

1. **Movement** What group of invaders came the greatest distance?

2. **Location** What areas of the empire were not threatened by invasion?

The Western Empire Crumbles

The decline of the Western Roman Empire took place over many years. Its final collapse was the result of worsening internal problems, the separation of the Western Empire from the wealthier Eastern part, and outside invasions.

Germanic Invasions Since the days of Julius Caesar, Germanic peoples had gathered on the northern borders of the empire and coexisted in relative peace with Rome. Around AD 370, all that changed when a fierce group of Mongol nomads from central Asia, the Huns, moved into the region and began destroying all in their path.

   In an effort to flee from the Huns, the various Germanic peoples pushed into Roman lands. (Romans called all invaders "barbarians," a term that they used to refer to non-Romans.) They kept moving through the Roman provinces of Gaul, Spain, and North Africa. The Western Empire was unable to field an army to stop them. In 410, hordes of Germanic people overran Rome itself and plundered it for three days.

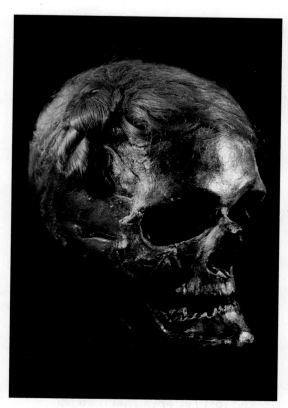

Attila the Hun Meanwhile, the Huns, who were indirectly responsible for the Germanic assault on the empire, became a direct threat. In 444, they united for the first time under a powerful chieftain named **Attila** (AT•uhl•uh). With his 100,000 soldiers, Attila terrorized both halves of the empire. In the East, his armies attacked and plundered 70 cities. (They failed, however, to scale the high walls of Constantinople.)

The Huns then swept into the West. In AD 452, Attila's forces advanced against Rome, but bouts of famine and disease kept them from conquering the city. Although the Huns were no longer a threat to the empire after Attila's death in 453, the Germanic invasions continued.

This skull, still retaining its hair, shows a kind of topknot in the hair that some Germanic peoples wore to identify themselves.

DOCUMENT-BASED INVESTIGATION Historical Source

The Fall of the Roman Empire

As part of their effort to understand the creation and development of societies over time, historians debate different historical narratives. A prominent example of this is the debate over the fall of the Roman Empire.

Since the fifth century AD, historians and others have argued over the empire's fall. They have attributed it to a variety of causes, both from within and outside the empire.

In the 1780s Edward Gibbon published *The History of the Decline and Fall of the Roman Empire*. In this passage, Gibbon explains that a major cause of the collapse was that the empire was simply too large.

Analyze Historical Sources

1. **Evaluate** Use the Internet to research opposing historical narratives about the fall of the Roman Empire. Look for more recent sources. The work of historians Arther Ferrill and Finley Hooper would be a good starting point. Evaluate how different historians' conclusions compare with Edward Gibbon's reasons for why Rome fell.

2. **Develop Historical Perspective** Formulate your own historical questions about the fall of the Roman Empire based on Gibbon's excerpt and your other research.

> "The decline of Rome was the natural and inevitable effect of immoderate greatness. Prosperity ripened the principle of decay; the causes of destruction multiplied with the extent of conquest; and, as soon as time or accident had removed the artificial supports, the stupendous fabric yielded to the pressure of its own weight. The story of its ruin is simple and obvious; and instead of inquiring why the Roman Empire was destroyed, we should rather be surprised that it had subsisted so long."

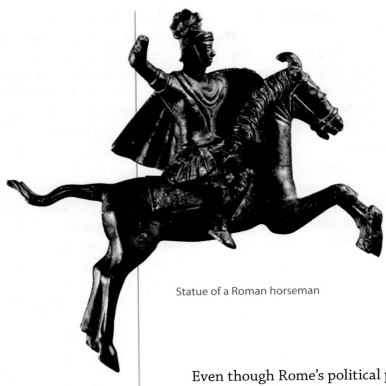

Statue of a Roman horseman

An Empire No More The last Roman emperor, a 14-year-old boy named Romulus Augustulus, was ousted by Germanic forces in 476. After that, no emperor even pretended to rule Rome and its western provinces. Roman power in the western half of the empire had disappeared.

The eastern half of the empire, which came to be called the Byzantine Empire, not only survived but flourished. It preserved the great heritage of Greek and Roman culture for another 1,000 years. The Byzantine emperors ruled from Constantinople and saw themselves as heirs to the power of Augustus Caesar. The empire endured until 1453, when it fell to the Ottoman Turks.

Even though Rome's political power in the West ended, its cultural influence did not. Its ideas, customs, and institutions influenced the development of Western civilization—and continue to do so today.

Reading Check
Predict Effects
Do you think Rome would have fallen to invaders if the Huns had not moved into the West? Explain.

Lesson 5 Assessment

1. **Organize Information** Create a graphic organizer similar to the one shown. Fill it in with the cause of each given effect regarding the fall of the Roman Empire. How did these problems open the empire to invading peoples?

Causes	Effects
	Inflation
	Untrustworthy army
	Political instability

2. **Key Terms and People** For each key term or person in the lesson, write a sentence explaining its significance.

3. **Analyze Causes** What were the main internal causes of the empire's decline?

4. **Synthesize** How did Diocletian succeed in preserving the empire?

5. **Contrast** What happened when taxes were raised during the third century AD? What happened when taxes were raised under Diocletian?

6. **Analyze Causes** Why did so many Germanic tribes begin invading the Roman Empire?

7. **Draw Conclusions** How do you think the splitting of the empire into two parts helped it survive for another 200 years?

8. **Identify Problems** Which of Rome's internal problems do you think were the most serious? Why?

9. **Analyze Issues** Why do you think the eastern half of the empire survived?

Rome and the Roots of Western Civilization

The Big Idea

The Romans developed many ideas and institutions that became fundamental to Western civilization.

Why It Matters Now

Evidence of Roman culture is found throughout Europe and North America and in Asia and Africa.

Key Terms and People

Greco-Roman culture
Pompeii
Virgil
Tacitus
aqueduct

Setting the Stage

Romans borrowed and adapted cultural elements freely, especially from the Greek and Hellenistic cultures. However, the Romans created a great civilization in their own right, whose art and architecture, language and literature, engineering, and law became its legacy to the world.

The Legacy of Greco-Roman Civilization

Under the Roman Empire, hundreds of territories were knitted into a single state. Each Roman province and city was governed in the same way. The Romans were proud of their unique ability to rule, but they acknowledged Greek leadership in the fields of art, architecture, literature, and philosophy.

By the second century BC, Romans had conquered Greece and had come to greatly admire Greek culture. Educated Romans learned the Greek language. As Horace, a Roman poet, said, "Greece, once overcome, overcame her wild conqueror." The mixing of Greek, Hellenistic, and Roman cultural elements produced a new culture, called **Greco-Roman culture**. This is often also called classical civilization.

Roman artists, philosophers, and writers did not merely copy their Greek and Hellenistic models. They adapted them for their own purposes and created a style of their own. Roman art and literature came to convey the Roman ideals of strength, permanence, and solidity.

The Roman port of Gades (GAY·deez), now Cádiz, lay on the southwestern shore of what is today Spain.

This detail of Trajan's Column is an example of bas-relief. The raised sculpture depicts military campaigns led by the emperor Trajan.

Roman Fine Arts

Roman Fine Arts Romans learned the art of sculpture from the Greeks. However, while the Greeks were known for the beauty and idealization of their sculpture, Roman sculptors created realistic portraits in stone. Much Roman art was practical in purpose, intended for public education.

The reign of Augustus was a period of great artistic achievement. At that time the Romans further developed a type of sculpture called bas-relief. In bas-relief, or low-relief, images project from a flat background. Roman sculptors used bas-relief to tell stories and to represent crowds of people, soldiers in battle, and landscapes.

Roman artists also were particularly skilled in creating mosaics. Mosaics were pictures or designs made by setting small pieces of stone, glass, or tile onto a surface. Most Roman villas, the country houses of the wealthy, had at least one colorful mosaic.

In addition, Romans excelled at the art of painting. Most wealthy Romans had bright, large murals, called frescoes, painted directly on their walls. Few have survived. The best examples of Roman painting are found in the Roman town of **Pompeii** and date from as early as the second century BC. In AD 79, nearby Mount Vesuvius erupted, covering Pompeii in a thick layer of ash and killing about 2,000 residents. The ash acted to preserve many buildings and works of art.

Learning and Literature Romans borrowed much of their philosophy from the Greeks. Stoicism, the philosophy of the Greek teacher Zeno, was especially influential. Stoicism encouraged virtue, duty, moderation, and endurance.

In literature, as in philosophy, the Romans found inspiration in the works of their Greek neighbors. While often following Greek forms and models, Roman writers promoted their own themes and ideas. The poet **Virgil** spent ten years writing the most famous work of Latin literature, the *Aeneid* (ih•NEE•ihd), the epic of the legendary Aeneas. Virgil modeled the *Aeneid*, written in praise of Rome and Roman virtues, after the Greek epics of Homer.

While Virgil's writing carries all the weight and seriousness of the Roman character, the poet Ovid wrote light, witty poetry for enjoyment. In *Amores*, Ovid relates that he can only compose when he is in love: "When I was from Cupid's passions free, my Muse was mute and wrote no elegy."

Among the fine arts that Romans mastered was the making of beautiful mosaics.

The Romans also wrote excellent prose, especially history. Livy compiled a multivolume history of Rome from its origins to 9 BC. He used legends freely, creating more of a national myth of Rome than a true history. **Tacitus** (TAS•ih•tuhs), another Roman historian, is notable among ancient historians because he presented the facts accurately. He also was concerned about the Romans' lack of morality.

Reading Check
Compare
How did Greece influence Roman learning and literature?

DOCUMENT-BASED INVESTIGATION   Historical Source

Tacitus

Tacitus was known for his criticism of Roman society and its leaders. In his *Annals* and *Histories*, he wrote about the good and bad of imperial Rome. In this selection, Tacitus shows his disgust with the actions of Emperor Nero, whom many consider to be one of Rome's cruelest rulers.

Analyze Historical Sources
How does Tacitus indicate his dislike of Nero in this passage?

"While Nero was frequently visiting the show, even amid his pleasures there was no cessation to his crimes. For during the very same period Torquatus Silanus was forced to die, because over and above his illustrious rank as one of the Junian family he claimed to be the great grandson of Augustus. Accusers were ordered to charge him with prodigality [wastefulness] in lavishing gifts, and with having no hope but in revolution. . . . Then the most intimate of his freedmen were put in chains and torn from him, till, knowing the doom which impended, Torquatus divided the arteries in his arms. A speech from Nero followed, as usual, which stated that though he was guilty and with good reason distrusted his defense, he would have lived, had he awaited the clemency of the judge."

—Tacitus, *Annals*

Western Civilization

Western civilization is generally seen as the heritage of ideas that spread to Europe and America from ancient Greece and Rome. Some historians observe, however, that Western civilization does not belong to any particular place—that it is the result of cultures coming together, interacting, and changing. Still, the legacy of Greece and Rome can be seen today.

The diagram below shows how ancient Greek and Roman ideas of government, philosophy, and literature can be traced across time. As with many cultural interactions, the links among the examples are not necessarily direct. Instead, the chart traces the evolution of an idea or theme over time.

INFLUENCE OF GREEK AND ROMAN IDEAS

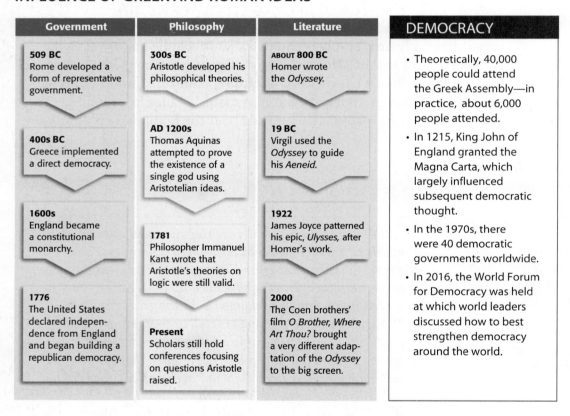

Government	Philosophy	Literature
509 BC Rome developed a form of representative government.	**300s BC** Aristotle developed his philosophical theories.	**ABOUT 800 BC** Homer wrote the *Odyssey*.
400s BC Greece implemented a direct democracy.	**AD 1200s** Thomas Aquinas attempted to prove the existence of a single god using Aristotelian ideas.	**19 BC** Virgil used the *Odyssey* to guide his *Aeneid*.
1600s England became a constitutional monarchy.	**1781** Philosopher Immanuel Kant wrote that Aristotle's theories on logic were still valid.	**1922** James Joyce patterned his epic, *Ulysses,* after Homer's work.
1776 The United States declared independence from England and began building a republican democracy.	**Present** Scholars still hold conferences focusing on questions Aristotle raised.	**2000** The Coen brothers' film *O Brother, Where Art Thou?* brought a very different adaptation of the *Odyssey* to the big screen.

DEMOCRACY

- Theoretically, 40,000 people could attend the Greek Assembly—in practice, about 6,000 people attended.
- In 1215, King John of England granted the Magna Carta, which largely influenced subsequent democratic thought.
- In the 1970s, there were 40 democratic governments worldwide.
- In 2016, the World Forum for Democracy was held at which world leaders discussed how to best strengthen democracy around the world.

Critical Thinking

1. **Form Opinions** Why do you think ancient Greek and Roman cultures have had such a lasting influence on Western civilization?

2. **Compare and Contrast** From what you know of ancient Greece and Rome, what is another element of either culture that can still be seen today? Provide an example.

water

This Roman aqueduct in modern France has survived the centuries. The cross section indicates how the water moved within the aqueduct.

The Legacy of Rome

The presence of Rome is still felt daily in the languages, the institutions, and the thought of the Western world.

The Latin Language Latin, the language of the Romans, remained the language of learning in the West long after the fall of Rome. It was the official language of the Roman Catholic Church into the 20th century.

Latin was adopted by different peoples and developed into French, Spanish, Portuguese, Italian, and Romanian. These languages are called Romance languages because of their common Roman heritage. Latin also influenced other languages. For example, more than half the words in English have a basis in Latin.

Master Builders Visitors from all over the empire marveled at the architecture of Rome. The arch, the dome, and concrete were combined to build spectacular structures, such as the Pantheon.

The Colosseum

The Colosseum was one of the greatest feats of Roman engineering and a model for the ages. The name comes from the Latin word *colossus*, meaning "gigantic." Its construction was started by the Emperor Vespasian and was completed by his sons, emperors Titus and Domitian. For centuries after its opening in AD 80, spectators, both rich and poor, cheered a variety of free, bloody spectacles—from gladiator fights to animal hunts.

▲ The Colosseum in Rome as it appears today

Elevators and ramps led from the cells and animal cages in the Colosseum basement to trapdoors concealed in the arena floor.

exits—giant staircases that allowed the building to be emptied in minutes

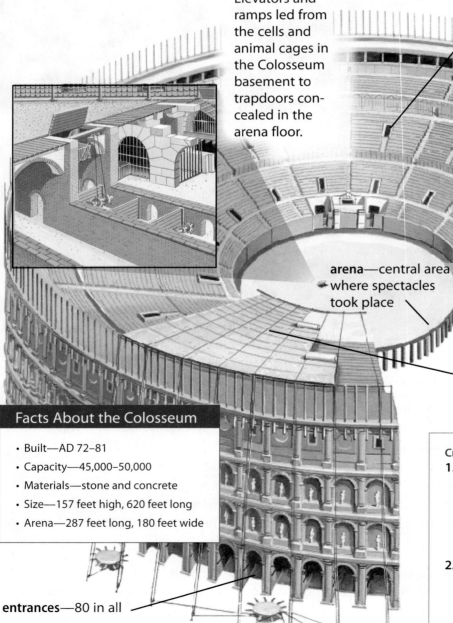

arena—central area where spectacles took place

passageways—walkways that led to seats

velarium—a retractable canvas awning that shielded spectators from sun and rain

entrances—80 in all

Facts About the Colosseum

- Built—AD 72–81
- Capacity—45,000–50,000
- Materials—stone and concrete
- Size—157 feet high, 620 feet long
- Arena—287 feet long, 180 feet wide

Critical Thinking

1. **Compare** The Colosseum has been the model for sports stadiums worldwide. How is the design of modern stadiums patterned after that of the Colosseum? What are the similarities?

2. **Draw Conclusions** What do the kind of spectacles the Romans watched tell us about them as a people and about their leaders?

Arches also supported bridges and **aqueducts**. Aqueducts were designed by Roman engineers to bring water into cities and towns. When the water channel spanned a river or ravine, the aqueduct was lifted high up on arches.

Because Roman architectural forms were so practical, they have remained popular. Thomas Jefferson began a Roman revival in the United States in the 18th century. Many large public buildings, such as the U.S. Capitol and numerous state capitols, include Roman features.

Roman roads were technological marvels. The army built a vast network of roads out of stone, concrete, and sand that connected Rome to all parts of the empire. Many lasted into the Middle Ages; some are still used.

Math, Science, Technology Although the Romans excelled in many fields, their mathematical accomplishments were somewhat limited. They did develop a number system that we know as Roman numerals—I, V, X, L, and so on. The Roman system was inspired by Etruscan numerals. Europeans used Roman numerals until the Middle Ages, and they are still used occasionally.

In pure science, also, the Romans were outshone by the Hellenistic Greeks. Three scientists deserve recognition, however. Pliny the Elder wrote *Naturalis Historia* (*Natural History*), in which he collected a vast amount of scientific knowledge from across the empire. Pliny arranged his topics in categories—plants, animals, and inorganic matter. He also made several astute observations. For example, he was the first to describe amber as fossilized tree sap. He also observed and wrote about the eruption of Mount Vesuvius.

Another important figure was the Greco-Roman Galen, a physician who lived in Rome during the AD 100s and who contributed to medicine and philosophy. Among his discoveries was a more complete understanding of the circulatory and nervous systems. Galen wrote several volumes that summarized all the medical knowledge of his day. For centuries people regarded him as the greatest authority in medicine. The third scientist is Ptolemy, who lived in Alexandria and was also of Greek heritage. Ptolemy wrote about topics as varied as astronomy, geography, the mathematics of music, and the properties of light.

The Romans' real genius, though, was in technology, or the application of knowledge to make useful things. They learned from all the peoples that they had conquered, especially the Greeks. The Romans put this knowledge to work in glassmaking, dam building, mining, sanitation, and other fields. They developed brass, soap, a harvesting machine, surgical instruments, iron tooth implants, and even a camel harness. Just as the Romans had absorbed knowledge from many lands, so their accomplishments then diffused to the far corners of the empire.

Roman System of Law Rome's most lasting and widespread contribution was its law. Early Roman law dealt mostly with strengthening the rights of Roman citizens. As the empire grew, however, the Romans came to believe that laws should be fair and apply equally to all people, rich and poor. Slowly, judges began to recognize certain standards of justice. These standards were influenced largely by the teachings of Stoic philosophers and were based on common sense and practical ideas. Some of the most important principles of Roman law were

- All persons had the right to equal treatment under the law.
- A person was considered innocent until proven guilty.
- The burden of proof rested with the accuser rather than the accused.
- A person should be punished only for actions, not thoughts.
- Any law that seemed unreasonable or grossly unfair could be set aside.

Historical Source

The Legacy of Roman Law

Secondary sources are written by people who were not present at an event and therefore did not experience it firsthand. Historians and biographers, for example, produce secondary sources. You can improve your historical research skills by identifying, analyzing, and interpreting secondary sources to make generalizations about events and life in world history.

Keep in mind that historians' interpretations of historical events are, by their nature, tentative. This means that they may change over time. The credibility, or believability, of a historian must be considered as well. For example, the credibility of a historian with a clear political bias might be worth questioning. On the other hand, the perspective of someone who specializes on a particular topic, such as the Roman Empire, is likely to be trustworthy.

In this excerpt from his book *Roman Society*, Roman historian Henry C. Boren discusses the permanent legacy of Roman law.

> "*The most imitated and studied code of law in history is the formulation by a group of lawyers . . . under the eastern Roman emperor Justinian. . . . This code served as a model for many of the nations of western Europe in the modern age and also for South Africa, Japan, and portions of Canada and the United States. Indirectly the principles of the Roman law, though perhaps not the procedures, have also strongly affected the development of the Anglo-Saxon common law, which is the basis of the legal systems in most English-speaking nations.*"
>
> —Henry C. Boren quoted in *Roman Society*

Analyze Historical Sources

1. **Draw Conclusions** According to Boren, how has Roman law affected the world?
2. **Evaluate** Why would Boren's book be considered a secondary source? Is Boren a credible authority on the legacy of Roman law? Explain.

The principles of Roman law endured to form the basis of legal systems in many European countries and of places influenced by Europe, including the United States of America.

Rome's Enduring Influence By preserving and adding to Greek civilization, Rome strengthened the Western cultural tradition. The world would be a very different place had Rome not existed. Historian R. H. Barrow has stated that Rome never fell because it turned into something even greater—an idea—and achieved immortality.

As mighty as the Roman Empire had been, however, it was not the only great civilization of its time. Around the same period that Rome was developing its enduring culture, different but equally complex empires were emerging farther east. In India, the Mauryan and Gupta empires dominated the land, while the Han Empire ruled over China.

Reading Check
Analyze Issues
How did Roman law protect those accused of crimes?

Lesson 6 Assessment

1. **Organize Information** Create a graphic organizer similar to the one shown and fill it in with Roman accomplishments for each category. Which accomplishment do you consider most important? Why?

Fine Arts	Literature
Law	Engineering

2. **Key Terms and People** For each key term or person in the lesson, write a sentence explaining its significance.

3. **Synthesize** What is Greco-Roman culture?

4. **Contrast** In what ways did Roman art differ from Greek art?

5. **Analyze Effects** What influence did Latin have on the development of Western languages?

6. **Summarize** What were some of the Romans' major achievements in math, science, and technology? How did those achievements originate and diffuse?

7. **Draw Conclusions** Which principle of law do you think has been Rome's greatest contribution?

8. **Form Opinions** Do you agree with Horace's claim that when it came to culture, Greece in essence conquered Rome? Explain.

9. **Predict Effects** Describe how the world might be different if Rome had not existed.

Module 6 Assessment

Key Terms and People

For each term or name below, write a sentence explaining its connection to ancient Rome or the rise of Christianity.

1. republic
2. senate
3. Julius Caesar
4. Augustus
5. villa
6. paterfamilias
7. Jesus
8. Constantine
9. inflation
10. Greco-Roman culture

Main Ideas

Use your notes and the information in the module to answer the following questions.

The Roman Republic

1. Name the three main parts of government under the Roman republic.
2. How did Rome treat different sections of its conquered territory?

The Roman Empire

3. How did Augustus change Roman government?
4. How did Rome's population fare during the golden age of the *Pax Romana?*

Life in the Roman Empire

5. How did wealthy Romans spend most of their time?
6. What motive did the Roman government have for providing food and entertainment for the poor?

The Origins of Christianity

7. How did the apostle Paul encourage the spread of Christianity?
8. Why did the Roman emperors persecute Christians?

The Fall of the Roman Empire

9. What was the most significant reform that the Emperor Diocletian made?
10. How did the Western Roman Empire fall?

Rome and the Roots of Western Civilization

11. Why did so much of Roman culture have a Greek flavor?
12. What aspects of Roman culture influenced future civilizations?

Module 6 Assessment, continued

Critical Thinking

1. **Synthesize** In a Venn diagram, compare the Roman Republic with the Roman Empire when both were at the peak of their power.

2. **Make Inferences** Why did patricians want to prevent plebeians from holding important positions?

3. **Analyze Issues** How did Romans' treatment of conquered people affect Rome's expansion?

4. **Analyze Issues** What type of person do you think became a martyr? Consider the personal characteristics of individuals who refused to renounce their faith even in the face of death.

5. **Summarize** Which virtues were emphasized in Roman family life?

6. **Evaluate** What do you think of Diocletian's decision to divide the Roman Empire into two parts? Was it wise? Consider Diocletian's possible motives and the results of his actions.

7. **Analyze Effects** What impact did the Romans have on the English language?

8. **Synthesize** Explain more fully what the historian R. H. Barrow meant when he said that Rome never really fell but instead achieved immortality.

Engage with History

What qualities make a successful leader? Work in small groups and discuss what you have learned about other leaders in history, such as Alexander the Great and Darius of Persia. What qualities helped them to be successful or caused them to fail? Then, consider the Roman leaders you have read about. What qualities were needed for Roman leaders to be effective? What qualities hindered their success? How would you rate the overall leadership of the Roman Empire? Finish up your discussion with this final question: Which is more important in measuring leadership—results or integrity?

Focus On Writing

Study the information about Rome's impact on the development of Western civilization in the Key Concepts feature titled Western Civilization in this module. Write an **essay** of several paragraphs summarizing the empire's impact on the Western world that developed after it. Provide information about the empire's influence on

- later governments
- philosophy
- literature

Then explain why you think Roman culture has been so enduring.

Multimedia Activity

Creating a Virtual Field Trip

Plan a two-week virtual trip through the Roman Empire. After selecting and researching the sites you'd like to visit, use the historical maps from this chapter and research contemporary maps on the Internet to determine your itinerary. Consider visiting the following places: Rome, Carthage, Pompeii, Hadrian's Wall, the Appian Way, Bath, Lepcis Magna, Horace's Villa, the Pont du Gard, and the Roman theater at Orange. You may want to include the following:

- maps of the Roman Empire
- pictures of the major sites on the field trip
- audio clips describing the sites or events that took place there
- reasons each site is an important destination

HISTORY

ROME:
ENGINEERING AN EMPIRE

The Roman Empire was one of the largest and most powerful empires in ancient history. With its strong military, the Roman Empire expanded to dominate the entire Mediterranean region, including much of western Europe and northern Africa. Keys to this expansion were the engineering and construction innovations made by Roman engineers. As the empire grew and prospered,

Roman engineers made advances in city planning, road and bridge design, water and sewage systems, and many other areas.

Explore some of the incredible monuments and engineering achievements of the Roman Empire online. You can find a wealth of information, video clips, primary sources, activities, and more at hmhsocialstudies.com.

📹 The Glory of the Colosseum

Watch the video to go inside the Colosseum, Rome's premier entertainment venue and one of the most famous buildings of the Roman Empire.

HISTORY Go online to view these and other **HISTORY®** resources.

📹 Caesar Builds an Empire

Watch the video to learn why Julius Caesar built a bridge across the Rhine River as a demonstration of Roman power.

🌐 Growth of the Roman Empire

Explore the map to analyze the growth of one of the largest empires of the ancient world.

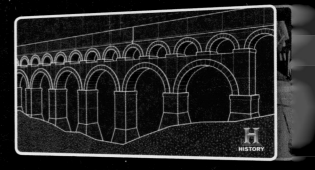

📹 Arches, Angles, Innovations

Watch the video to learn about Roman engineering advances and the construction of aqueducts.

Module 7

India and China Establish Empires

Essential Question

What role did early empires in India and China play in shaping later civilizations?

About the Photograph: This 16-inch bronze model from Han China shows an official riding in a light chariot, followed by an attendant on foot.

In this module you will learn about early empires in India and China and how their ideas spread across Asia and Europe.

▶ Explore ONLINE!

HISTORY.

VIDEOS, including...
- China's Shortest Dynasty
- The Silk Road
- Agricultural Advances in Ancient China

✓ Document Based Investigations

✓ Graphic Organizers

✓ Interactive Games

✓ Image Carousel: The Gupta Period

✓ Interactive Map: Han Dynasty, 200 BC–AD 220

What You Will Learn ...

Timeline of Events 400 BC–AD 550

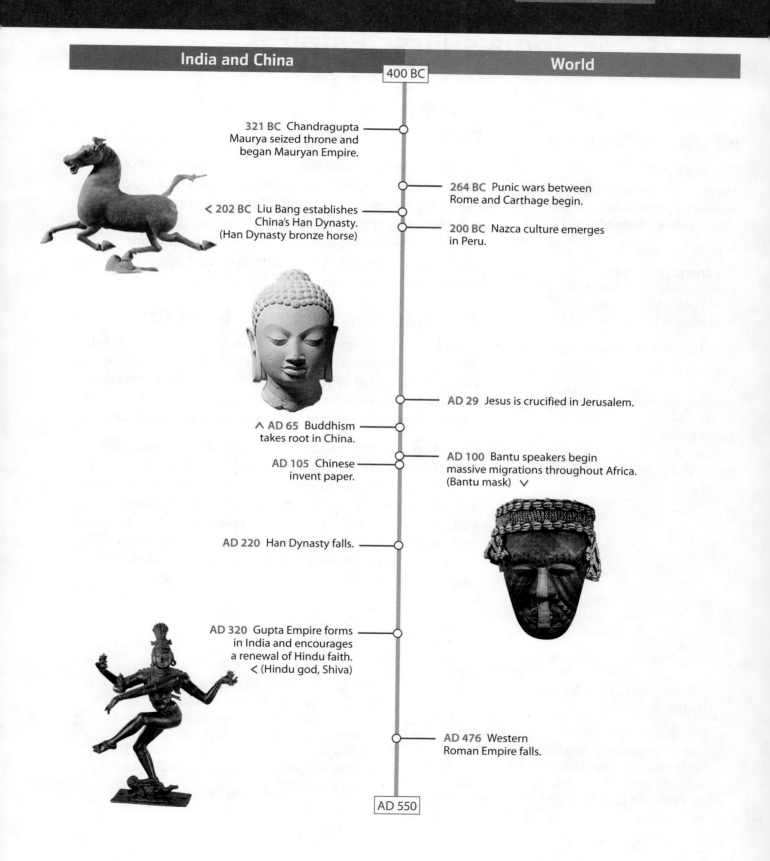

India and China	World

400 BC

321 BC Chandragupta Maurya seized throne and began Mauryan Empire.

264 BC Punic wars between Rome and Carthage begin.

< 202 BC Liu Bang establishes China's Han Dynasty. (Han Dynasty bronze horse)

200 BC Nazca culture emerges in Peru.

AD 29 Jesus is crucified in Jerusalem.

∧ AD 65 Buddhism takes root in China.

AD 105 Chinese invent paper.

AD 100 Bantu speakers begin massive migrations throughout Africa. (Bantu mask) ∨

AD 220 Han Dynasty falls.

AD 320 Gupta Empire forms in India and encourages a renewal of Hindu faith. < (Hindu god, Shiva)

AD 476 Western Roman Empire falls.

AD 550

India's First Empires

The Big Idea

The Mauryas and the Guptas established empires, but neither unified India permanently.

Why It Matters Now

The diversity of peoples, cultures, beliefs, and languages in India continues to pose challenges to Indian unity today.

Key Terms and People

Mauryan Empire
Asoka
religious toleration
Tamil
Gupta Empire
patriarchal
matriarchal

Setting the Stage

By 600 BC, almost 1,000 years after the Aryan migrations, many small kingdoms were scattered throughout India. In 326 BC, Alexander the Great brought the Indus Valley in the northwest under Macedonian control, but left almost immediately. Soon after, a great Indian military leader, Chandragupta Maurya (chuhn•druh•GUP•tuh MAH•oor•yuh), seized power.

The Mauryan Empire Is Established

Chandragupta Maurya may have been born in the powerful kingdom of Magadha. Centered on the lower Ganges River, the kingdom was ruled by the Nanda family. Chandragupta gathered an army, killed the unpopular Nanda king, and in about 321 BC claimed the throne. This began the **Mauryan Empire**.

Chandragupta Maurya Unifies North India Chandragupta moved northwest, seizing all the land from Magadha to the Indus Valley. Around 305 BC, Chandragupta began to battle Seleucus I, one of Alexander the Great's generals. Seleucus had inherited part of Alexander's empire. He wanted to reestablish Macedonian control over the Indus Valley. After several years of fighting, however, Chandragupta defeated Seleucus. By 303 BC, the Mauryan Empire stretched more

---

BIOGRAPHY

Chandragupta Maurya
(?–298 BC)

Chandragupta feared being assassinated— maybe because he had killed a king to get his throne. To avoid being poisoned, he made servants taste all his food. To avoid being murdered in bed, he slept in a different room every night.

Although Chandragupta was a fierce warrior, in 301 BC, he gave up his throne and converted to Jainism (JY•nihz•uhm). Jains taught nonviolence and respect for all life. With a group of monks, Chandragupta traveled to southern India. There he followed the Jainist custom of fasting until he starved to death.

Farmers of the Mauryan Empire

Ambassador Megasthenes described the countryside and how farmers lived.

> "[Farmers] are exempted from military service and cultivate their lands undisturbed by fear. They do not go to cities, either on business or to take part in their tumults. It therefore frequently happens that at the same time, and in the same part of the country, men may be seen marshaled for battle and risking their lives against the enemy, while other men are ploughing or digging in perfect security under the protection of these soldiers."
>
> —Megasthenes in *Geography* by Strabo

Analyze Historical Sources
What information in this quotation indicates that Mauryan India valued agriculture?

than 2,000 miles, uniting north India politically for the first time. (See map, Indian Empires, 250 BC–AD 400.)

To win his wars of conquest, Chandragupta raised a vast army: 600,000 soldiers on foot, 30,000 soldiers on horseback, and 9,000 elephants. To clothe, feed, and pay these troops, the government levied high taxes. For example, farmers had to pay up to one-half the value of their crops to the king.

Running the Empire Chandragupta relied on an adviser named Kautilya (kow•TIHL•yuh), a member of the priestly caste. Kautilya wrote a ruler's handbook called the Arthasastra (ahr•thuh•SHAHS•truh). This book proposed tough-minded policies to hold an empire together, including spying on the people and employing political assassination. Following Kautilya's advice, Chandragupta created a highly bureaucratic government. He divided the empire into four provinces, each headed by a royal prince. Each province was then divided into local districts, whose officials assessed taxes and enforced the law.

Life in the City and the Country To stay at peace, Seleucus sent an ambassador, Megasthenes (muh•GAS•thuh•neez), to Chandragupta's capital. Megasthenes wrote glowing descriptions of Chandragupta's palace, with its gold-covered pillars, many fountains, and imposing thrones. The capital city featured beautiful parks and bustling markets.

In 301 BC, Chandragupta's son assumed the throne. He ruled for 32 years. Then Chandragupta's grandson, **Asoka** (uh•SOH•kuh), brought the Mauryan Empire to its greatest heights.

Asoka Promotes Buddhism Asoka became king of the Mauryan Empire in 269 BC. At first, he followed in Chandragupta's footsteps, waging war to expand his empire. During a bloody war against the neighboring state of Kalinga, 100,000 soldiers were slain, and even more civilians perished.

Although victorious, Asoka felt sorrow over the slaughter at Kalinga. As a result, he studied Buddhism and decided to rule by the Buddha's teaching of "peace to all beings." Throughout the empire, Asoka erected huge stone pillars inscribed with his new policies. Some edicts guaranteed that Asoka would treat his subjects fairly and humanely. Others preached non-violence. Still others urged **religious toleration**—acceptance of people who held different religious beliefs.

Asoka had extensive roads built so that he could visit the far corners of India. He also improved conditions along these roads to make travel easier for his officials and to improve communication in the vast empire. For example, every nine miles he had wells dug and rest houses built. This allowed travelers to stop and refresh themselves. Such actions demonstrated Asoka's concern for his subjects' well-being.

This pillar, on which Asoka's edicts are written, is located at Vaishali.

Noble as his policies of toleration and nonviolence were, they failed to hold the empire together after Asoka died in 232 BC.

A Period of Turmoil

Asoka's death left a power vacuum. In northern and central India, regional kings challenged the imperial government. The kingdoms of central India, which had only been loosely held in the Mauryan Empire, soon regained their independence. The Andhra (AHN·druh) Dynasty arose and dominated the region for hundreds of years. Because of their central position, the Andhras profited from the extensive trade between north and south India and also with Rome, Sri Lanka, and Southeast Asia.

At the same time, northern India had to absorb a flood of new people fleeing political instability in other parts of Asia. For 500 years, beginning about 185 BC, wave after wave of Greeks, Persians, and Central Asians poured into northern India. These invaders disrupted Indian society. But they also introduced new languages and customs that added to the already rich blend of Indian culture.

Southern India also experienced turmoil. It was home to three kingdoms that had never been conquered by the Mauryans. The people who lived in this region spoke the **Tamil** (TAM·uhl) language and were called the Tamil people. These three kingdoms often were at war with one another and with other states.

Asoka
(?–232 BC)

One of Asoka's edicts states,

"If one hundredth part or one thousandth of those who died in Kalinga . . . should now suffer similar fate, [that] would be a matter of pain to His Majesty."

Even though Asoka wanted to be a loving, peaceful ruler, he had to control a huge empire. He had to balance Kautilya's methods of keeping power and Buddha's urgings to be unselfish.

Asoka softened Chandragupta's harsher policies. Instead of spies, he employed officials to look out for his subjects' welfare. He kept his army but sought to rule humanely. In addition, Asoka sent missionaries to Southeast Asia to spread Buddhism.

The grouping of Asoka's lions is used as a symbol of India.

The Gupta Empire Is Established

After 500 years of invasion and turmoil, a strong leader again arose in the northern state of Magadha. His name was Chandra Gupta (GUP•tuh), but he was no relation to India's first emperor, Chandragupta Maurya. India's second empire, the **Gupta Empire**, oversaw a great flowering of Indian civilization, especially Hindu culture.

Chandra Gupta Builds an Empire The first Gupta emperor came to power not through battle but by marrying a daughter of an influential royal family. After his marriage, Chandra Gupta I took the title "Great King of Kings" in AD 320. His empire included Magadha and the area north of it, with his power base along the Ganges River. His son, Samudra (suh•MUH•druh) Gupta, became king in AD 335. Although a lover of the arts, Samudra had a warlike side. He expanded the empire through 40 years of conquest.

Daily Life in India The Gupta era is the first period for which historians have much information about daily life in India. Most Indians lived in small villages. The majority were farmers, who walked daily from their homes to outlying fields. Craftspeople and merchants clustered in specific districts in the towns. They had shops on the street level and lived in the rooms above.

Most Indian families were **patriarchal**, headed by the eldest male. Parents, grandparents, uncles, aunts, and children all worked together to raise their crops. Because drought was common, farmers often had to irrigate their crops. There was a tax on water, and every month, people had to give a day's worth of labor to maintain wells, irrigation ditches, reservoirs, and dams. As in Mauryan times, farmers owed a large part of their earnings to the king.

Southern India followed a different cultural pattern. Some Tamil groups were **matriarchal**, headed by the mother rather than the father. Property, and sometimes the throne, was passed through the female line.

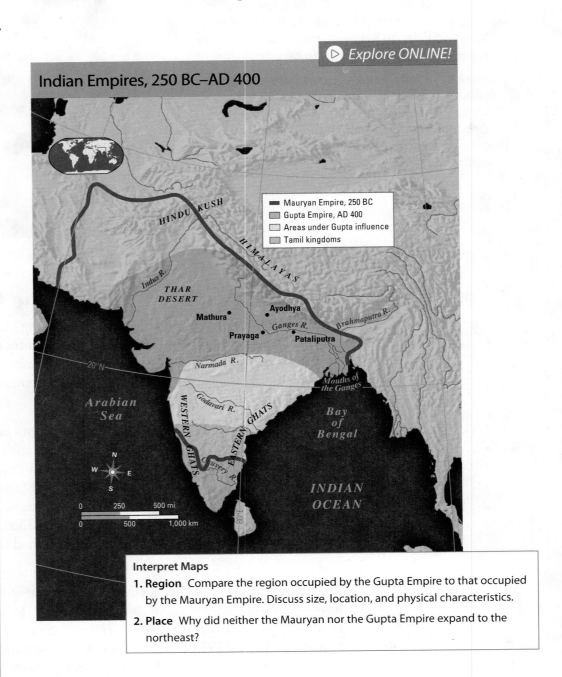

▶ Explore ONLINE!

Indian Empires, 250 BC–AD 400

Legend:
- ▬ Mauryan Empire, 250 BC
- Gupta Empire, AD 400
- Areas under Gupta influence
- Tamil kingdoms

Interpret Maps

1. **Region** Compare the region occupied by the Gupta Empire to that occupied by the Mauryan Empire. Discuss size, location, and physical characteristics.

2. **Place** Why did neither the Mauryan nor the Gupta Empire expand to the northeast?

Height of the Gupta Empire

While village life followed unchanging traditional patterns, the royal court of the third Gupta emperor was a place of excitement and growth. Indians revered Chandra Gupta II for his heroic qualities. He defeated the Shakas—enemies to the west—and added their coastal territory to his empire. This allowed the Guptas to engage in profitable trade with the Mediterranean world. Chandra Gupta II also strengthened his empire through peaceful means by negotiating diplomatic and marriage alliances. He ruled from AD 375 to 415.

This terra-cotta tile, showing a musician playing a stringed instrument, is from a Hindu temple of the Gupta period.

During the reign of the first three Guptas, India experienced a period of great achievement in the arts, religious thought, and science. These will be discussed in the next lesson. After Chandra Gupta II died, new invaders threatened northern India. These fierce fighters, called the Hunas, were related to the Huns who invaded the Roman Empire. Over the next 100 years, the Gupta Empire broke into small kingdoms. Many were overrun by the Hunas or other Central Asian nomads. The empire ended about 535.

Reading Check
Contrast How were social structures different in northern and southern India?

Lesson 1 Assessment

1. **Organize Information** Make a chart to show ways the Mauryan and Gupta Empires were similar.

   Which similarity do you think was the most significant? Explain.

Mauryan	Gupta
1.	1.
2.	2.
3.	3.

2. **Key Terms and People** For each key term or person in the lesson, write a sentence explaining its significance.

3. **Analyze Motives** Why was Asoka's first military campaign also his last campaign?

4. **Analyze Causes** What caused the fall of the Gupta Empire?

5. **Compare and Contrast** Which Indian ruler described in this lesson would you rather live under? Explain.

6. **Draw Conclusions** What impact did the Greeks, Persians, and Central Asians have on Indian life between the Mauryan and Gupta Empires?

7. **Analyze Issues** Which empire, Mauryan or Gupta, had a more significant impact on Indian history? Explain.

Trade Spreads Indian Religions and Culture

The Big Idea
Indian religions, culture, and science evolved and spread to other regions through trade.

Why It Matters Now
The influence of Indian culture and religions is very evident throughout South Asia today.

Key Terms and People
Mahayana
Theravada
stupa
Brahma
Vishnu
Shiva
Kalidasa
Silk Roads

Setting the Stage

The 500 years between the Mauryan and Gupta Empires was a time of upheaval. Invaders poured into India, bringing new ideas and customs. In response, Indians began to change their own culture.

Buddhism and Hinduism Change

By 250 BC, Hinduism and Buddhism were India's two main faiths. Hinduism is a complex polytheistic religion that blended Aryan beliefs with the many gods and cults of the diverse peoples who preceded them. Buddhism teaches that desire causes suffering and that humans should overcome desire by following the Eightfold Path. Over the centuries, both religions had become increasingly removed from the people. Hinduism became dominated by priests, while the Buddhist ideal of self-denial proved difficult for many to follow.

A More Popular Form of Buddhism The Buddha had stressed that each person could reach a state of peace called nirvana. Nirvana was achieved by rejecting the sensory world and embracing spiritual discipline. After the Buddha died, his followers developed many different interpretations of his teachings.

Although the Buddha had forbidden people to worship him, some began to teach that he was a god. Some Buddhists also began to believe that many people could become Buddhas. These potential Buddhas, called bodhisattvas (boh•dih•SUHT•vuhz), could choose to give up nirvana and work to save humanity through good works and self-sacrifice. The new ideas changed Buddhism from a religion that emphasized individual discipline to a mass religion that offered salvation to all and allowed popular worship.

By the first century AD, Buddhists had divided over the new doctrines. Those who accepted them belonged to the **Mahayana** (mah•huh•YAH•nuh) sect. Those who held to the Buddha's stricter, original teachings belonged to the

Theravada (thehr•uh•VAH•duh) sect. This is also called the Hinayana (hee•nuh•YAH•nuh) sect, but Theravada is preferred. Later, Buddhism in India was influenced by various forms of Hinduism.

These new trends in Buddhism inspired Indian art. For example, artists carved huge statues of the Buddha for people to worship. Wealthy Buddhist merchants who were eager to do good deeds paid for the construction of **stupas**— mounded stone structures built over holy relics. Buddhists walked the paths circling the stupas as a part of their meditation. Merchants also commissioned the carving of cave temples out of solid rock. Artists then adorned these temples with beautiful sculptures and paintings.

A Hindu Rebirth Like Buddhism, Hinduism had become remote from the people. By the time of the Mauryan Empire, Hinduism had developed a complex set of sacrifices that could be performed only by the priests. People who weren't priests had less and less direct connection with the religion.

Gradually, through exposure to other cultures and in response to the popularity of Buddhism, Hinduism changed. It absorbed some ideas from Buddhism. Many Hindus accepted the Buddha as an incarnation of Vishnu. Although the religion continued to embrace hundreds of gods, a trend toward monotheism was growing. Many people began to believe that there was only one divine force in the universe. The various gods represented parts of that force. The three most important Hindu gods were **Brahma** (BRAH•muh), creator of the world; **Vishnu** (VIHSH•noo), preserver of the world; and **Shiva** (SHEE•vuh), destroyer of the world. Of the three, Vishnu and Shiva were by far the favorites. Many Indians began to devote themselves to these two gods. As Hinduism evolved into a more personal religion, its popular appeal grew.

This Buddha is carved in the Gandharan artistic style, a blend of Greco-Roman and Indian styles.

Reading Check
Draw Conclusions
Why did the changes in Buddhism and Hinduism make these religions more popular?

Achievements of Indian Culture

Just as Hinduism and Buddhism underwent changes, so did Indian culture and learning. India entered a highly productive period in literature, art, science, and mathematics that continued until roughly AD 500.

Literature and the Performing Arts One of India's greatest writers was **Kalidasa** (kah•lee•DAH•suh). He may have been the court poet for Chandra Gupta II. Kalidasa's most famous play is *Shakuntala*. It tells the story of a beautiful girl who falls in love with and marries a middle-aged king. After Shakuntala and her husband are separated, they suffer tragically from a curse that keeps the king from recognizing his wife when they meet again.

Entertainment in India: Bollywood

Today, drama remains hugely popular in India. India has the largest movie industry in the world. About twice as many full-length feature films are released yearly in India as in the United States. India produces both popular and serious films. Indian popular films, such as *Monsoon Wedding*, are often love stories that blend music, dance, and drama. India's serious films have received worldwide critical praise. In 1992, the Indian director Satyajit Ray received a lifetime-achievement Academy Award for making artistic films. His films brought Indian culture to a global audience.

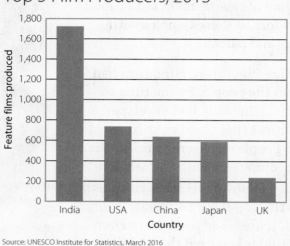

Top 5 Film Producers, 2013

Source: UNESCO Institute for Statistics, March 2016

Generations of Indians have continued to admire Kalidasa's plays because they are skillfully written and emotionally stirring.

Southern India also has a rich literary tradition. In the second century AD, the city of Madurai in southern India became a site of writing academies. More than 2,000 Tamil poems from this period still exist.

In addition to literature, drama was very popular. In southern India, traveling troupes of actors put on performances in cities across the region. Women as well as men took part in these shows, which combined drama and dance. Many of the classical dance forms in India today are based on techniques explained in a book written between the first century BC and the first century AD.

Astronomy, Mathematics, and Medicine The expansion of trade spurred the advance of science. Because sailors on trading ships used the stars to help them navigate their position at sea, knowledge of astronomy increased. From Greek invaders, Indians adapted Western methods of keeping time. They began to use a calendar based on the cycles of the sun rather than the moon. They also adopted a seven-day week and divided each day into hours.

During the Gupta Empire (AD 320 to about 500), knowledge of astronomy increased further. Almost 1,000 years before Columbus, Indian astronomers proved that the earth was round by observing a lunar eclipse. During the eclipse, the earth's shadow fell across the face of the moon. The astronomers noted that the earth's shadow was curved, indicating that the earth itself was round.

Indian mathematics was among the most advanced in the world. Modern numerals, the zero, and the decimal system were invented in India. Around AD 500, an Indian named Aryabhata (ahr•yuh•BUHT•uh) calculated the value of pi (π) to four decimal places. He also calculated the length of the solar year as 365.3586805 days. This is very close to modern calculations made with an atomic clock. In medicine, two important medical guides were compiled. They described more than 1,000 diseases and more than 500 medicinal plants. Hindu physicians performed surgery—including plastic surgery—and possibly gave injections.

Reading Check
Draw Conclusions
What achievements by Indian mathematicians are used today?

The Spread of Indian Trade

In addition to knowledge, India has always been rich in precious resources. Spices, diamonds, sapphires, gold, pearls, and beautiful woods—including ebony, teak, and fragrant sandalwood—have been valuable items

▷ Explore ONLINE!

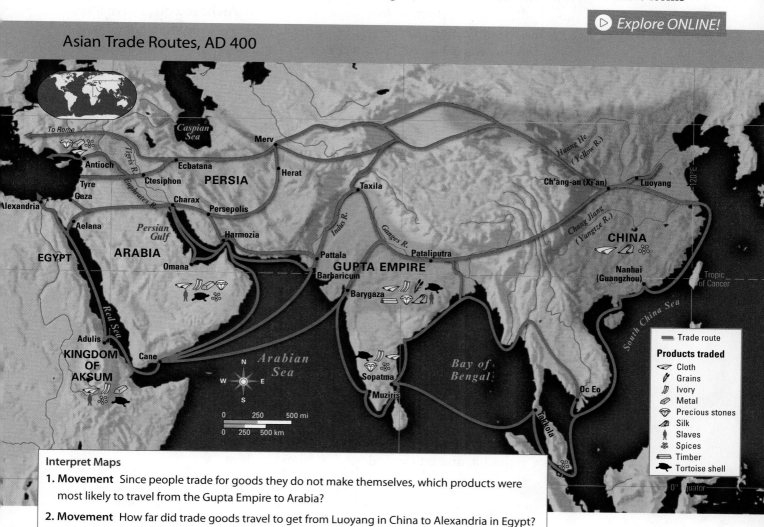

Asian Trade Routes, AD 400

Interpret Maps

1. **Movement** Since people trade for goods they do not make themselves, which products were most likely to travel from the Gupta Empire to Arabia?

2. **Movement** How far did trade goods travel to get from Luoyang in China to Alexandria in Egypt?

of exchange. Trade between India and regions as distant as Africa and Sumeria began more than 4,000 years ago. Trade expanded even after the Mauryan Empire ended around 185 BC.

Sculpture of Buddha

Overland Trade, East and West Groups who invaded India after Mauryan rule ended helped to expand India's trade to new regions. For example, Central Asian nomads told Indians about a vast network of caravan routes known as Silk Roads. These routes were called the **Silk Roads** because traders used them to bring silk from China to western Asia and then on to Rome.

Once Indians learned of the Silk Roads, they realized that they could make great profits by acting as middlemen. Middlemen are go-betweens in business transactions. For example, Indian traders would buy Chinese goods and sell them to traders traveling to Rome. To aid their role as middlemen, Indians built trading stations along the Silk Roads. They were located at oases, which are fertile spots in desert areas.

Sea Trade, East and West Sea trade also increased. Traders used coastal routes around the rim of the Arabian Sea and up the Persian Gulf to bring goods from India to Rome. In addition, traders from southern India would sail to Southeast Asia to collect spices. They brought the spices back to India and sold them to merchants from Rome. Archaeologists have found hoards of Roman gold coins in southern India. Records show that some Romans were upset about the amount of gold their countrymen spent on Indian luxuries. They believed that to foster a healthy economy, a state must collect gold rather than spend it.

Rome was not India's only sea-trading partner. India imported African ivory and gold and exported cotton cloth. Rice and wheat went to Arabia in exchange for dates and horses. After trade with Rome declined around the third century AD, India's sea trade with China and the islands of Southeast Asia increased. The Chinese, for example, imported Indian cotton cloth, monkeys, parrots, and elephants and sent India silk.

Effects of Indian Trade Increased trade led to the rise of banking in India. Commerce was quite profitable. Bankers were willing to lend money to merchants and charge them interest on the loans. Interest rates varied, depending on how risky business was. During Mauryan times, the annual interest rate on loans used for overseas trade was 240%! During the Gupta Empire, bankers no longer considered sea trade as dangerous, so they charged only 15 to 20% interest a year.

A number of Indian merchants went to live abroad and brought Indian culture with them. As a result, people throughout Asia picked up and adapted a variety of Indian traditions. For example, Indian culture affected styles in art, architecture, and dance throughout South and Southeast Asia. Indian influence was especially strong in Thailand, Cambodia, and on the Indonesian island of Java.

The Spread of Buddhism

Buddhism became a missionary religion during Asoka's reign. From his capital city (1), Asoka sent out Buddhist missionaries. After Indians began trading along the Silk Roads, Buddhist monks traveled the roads and converted people along the way.

Buddhist monks from India established their first monastery in China (2) in AD 65, and many Chinese became Buddhists. From China, Buddhism reached Korea in the fourth century AD and Japan in the sixth century AD.

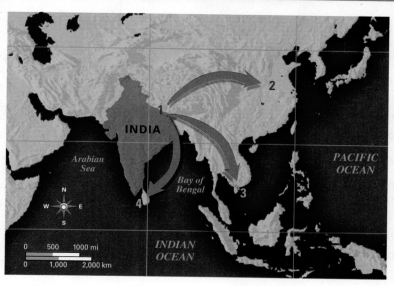

Today, Buddhism is a major religion in East and Southeast Asia. The Theravada school is strong in Myanmar, Cambodia (3), Sri Lanka (4), and Thailand. The Mahayana school is strong in Japan and Korea.

Reading Check
Make Inferences
How might the Asian trade routes have spread Indian sciences and math to other civilizations?

Traders also brought Indian religions to new regions. Hinduism spread northeast to Nepal and southeast to Sri Lanka and Borneo. Buddhism spread because of traveling Buddhist merchants and monks. In time, Buddhism even influenced China, which will be discussed in the next lesson.

Lesson 2 Assessment

1. **Organize Information** Make a chart to list achievements of the Gupta Empire.

   Which achievement had the most lasting impact? Explain.

Religion	
Arts	
Science/Math	
Trade	

2. **Key Terms and People** For each key term or person in the lesson, write a sentence explaining its significance.

3. **Draw Conclusions** Based on its achievements, can the time of the Gupta Empire's rule be called a "golden age"?

4. **Synthesize** How did Buddhism change after the Buddha's death?

5. **Summarize** What were India's main trade goods in the fifth century AD?

6. **Summarize** What were some of India's contributions to science during the Gupta period?

7. **Recognize Effects** What do you think was the most significant effect of the changes in Buddhism and Hinduism during this period? Explain.

8. **Make Inferences** Why did Indian culture flourish during the Gupta Empire?

Hindu and Buddhist Art and Architecture

The main difference between Buddhist and Hindu art and architecture in India was subject matter. Buddhist art often portrayed the Buddha or bodhisattvas, who were potential Buddhas. Hindu gods, such as Vishnu and Ganesha, were common subjects in Hindu art.

Beyond the differences in subject, Hindu and Buddhist beliefs had little influence on Indian artistic styles. For example, a Hindu sculpture and a Buddhist sculpture created at the same place and time were stylistically the same. In fact, the same artisans often created both Hindu and Buddhist art.

▼ BUDDHA

This bronze Buddha was made in India during the sixth century AD. Each detail of a Buddhist sculpture has meaning. For example, the headpiece and long earlobes shown here are lakshana, traditional bodily signs of the Buddha. The upraised hand is a gesture that means "Have no fear."

▼ THE GREAT STUPA

Built during the third to first centuries BC, the Great Stupa is a famous Buddhist monument in Sanchi, India. This stone structure is 120 feet across and 54 feet high; it has a staircase leading to a walkway that encircles the stupa. Stupas serve as memorials and often contain sacred relics. During Buddhist New Year festivals, worshipers hold images of the Buddha and move in processions around the circular walkway.

▲ DEVI JAGADAMBI TEMPLE IN KHAJURAHO

Hardly any Hindu temples from the Gupta period remain. This temple, built in the 11th century AD, shows architectural trends begun in Gupta times. These include building with stone rather than wood; erecting a high, pyramidal roof instead of a flat roof; and sculpting elaborate decorations on the walls.

▲ GANESHA

Carved in the fifth century BC, this stone sculpture represents the elephant-headed god Ganesha. According to Hindu beliefs, Ganesha is the god of success, education, wisdom, and wealth. He also is worshiped as the lifter of obstacles. The smaller picture is a recent image of Ganesha, who has gained great popularity during modern times.

Now and Then

1. **Contrast** How do the Buddhist stupa and the Hindu temple differ? What might be the reason for those differences?

2. **Make Inferences** Why do you think Ganesha is a popular god among Hindus today? Explain.

Han Emperors in China

The Big Idea

The Han Dynasty expanded China's borders and developed a system of government that lasted for centuries.

Why It Matters Now

The pattern of a strong central government has remained a permanent part of Chinese life.

Key Terms and People

Han Dynasty
centralized government
civil service
monopoly
assimilation

Setting the Stage

Under Shi Huangdi, the Qin Dynasty had unified China. Shi Huangdi established a strong government by conquering the rival kings who ruled small states throughout China. After Shi Huangdi died in 210 BC, his son proved to be a weak, ineffective leader. China's government fell apart.

The Han Restore Unity to China

Rumblings of discontent during the Qin Dynasty grew to roars in the years after Shi Huangdi's death. Peasants were bitter over years of high taxes, harsh labor quotas, and a severe penal system. They rebelled. Rival kings were eager to regain control of the regions they had held before Shi Huangdi. They raised armies and fought over territory.

Liu Bang Founds the Han Dynasty During the civil war that followed, two powerful leaders emerged. Xiang Yu (shee•ANG-yoo) was an aristocratic general who was willing to allow the warlords to keep their territories if they would acknowledge him as their feudal lord. Liu Bang (LEE•oo bahng) was one of Xiang Yu's generals.

Eventually, Liu Bang turned against Xiang Yu. The two fought their final battle in 202 BC. Liu Bang won and declared himself the first emperor of the Han Dynasty. The **Han Dynasty**, which ruled China for more than 400 years, is divided into two periods. The Former Han ruled for about two centuries, until AD 9. After a brief period when the Han were out of power, the Later Han ruled for almost another two centuries. The Han Dynasty so influenced China that even today many Chinese call themselves "people of the Han."

Emperor Liu Bang

Liu Bang's first goal was to destroy the rival kings' power. He followed Shi Huangdi's policy of establishing **centralized government**, in which a central authority controls the running of a state. Reporting to Liu Bang's central government were hundreds of local provincials called commanderies.

To win popular support, Liu Bang departed from Shi Huangdi's strict legalism. He lowered taxes and softened harsh punishments. People throughout the empire appreciated the peace and stability that Liu Bang brought to China.

The Empress Lü When Liu Bang died in 195 BC, his son became emperor, but in name only. The real ruler was his mother, Empress Lü. Although Lü had not been Liu Bang's only wife, she had powerful friends at court who helped her seize power. The empress outlived her son and retained control of the throne by naming first one infant and then another as emperor. Because the infants were too young to rule, she remained in control. When Empress Lü died in 180 BC, people who remained loyal to Liu Bang's family, rather than to Lü's family, came back into power. They rid the palace of the old empress's relatives by executing them.

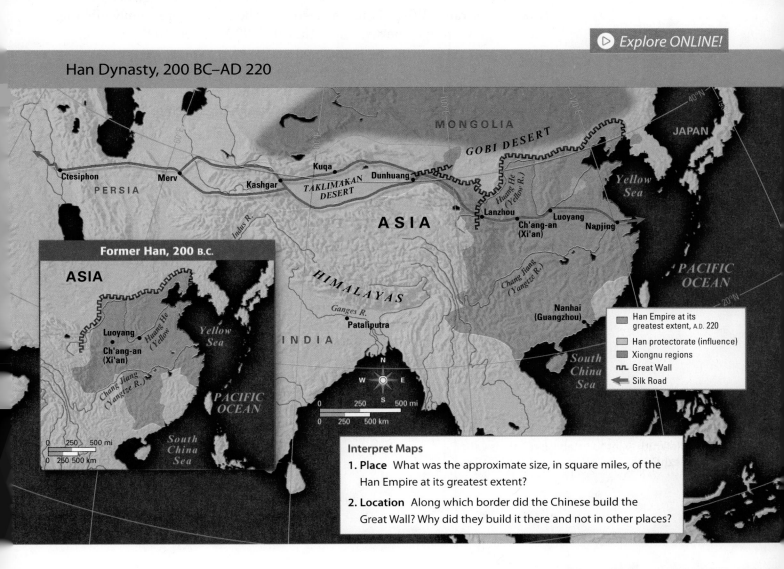

▷ Explore ONLINE!

Han Dynasty, 200 BC–AD 220

Former Han, 200 B.C.

Interpret Maps

1. **Place** What was the approximate size, in square miles, of the Han Empire at its greatest extent?

2. **Location** Along which border did the Chinese build the Great Wall? Why did they build it there and not in other places?

Such palace plots occurred often throughout the Han Dynasty. Traditionally, the emperor chose the favorite among his wives as the empress and appointed one of her sons as successor. Because of this, the palace women and their families competed fiercely for the emperor's notice. The families would make alliances with influential people in the court. The resulting power plays distracted the emperor and his officials so much that they sometimes could not govern efficiently.

The Martial Emperor When Liu Bang's great-grandson took the throne, he continued Liu Bang's centralizing policies. Wudi (woo•dee), who reigned from 141 to 87 BC, held the throne longer than any other Han emperor. He is called the "Martial Emperor" because he adopted the policy of expanding the Chinese empire through war.

Wudi's first set of enemies were the Xiongnu (shee•UNG•noo), fierce nomads known for their deadly archery skills from horseback. The Xiongnu roamed the steppes to the north and west of China. They made raids into China's settled farmland. There they took hostages and stole grain, livestock, and other valuable items. The early Han emperors tried to buy off the Xiongnu by sending them thousands of pounds of silk, rice, alcohol, and money. Usually, the Xiongnu just accepted these gifts and continued their raids. When Wudi realized that the bribes were simply making the Xiongnu stronger, he sent more than 100,000 soldiers to fight them.

After his army forced the nomads to retreat into Central Asia, Wudi attempted to make his northwest border safe by settling his troops on the Xiongnu's former pastures. Although this tactic succeeded for a time, nomadic raiders continued to cause problems during much of China's later history.

Vocabulary
martial warlike

DOCUMENT-BASED INVESTIGATION Historical Source

Fighting Nomadic Raiders

To help defeat the Xiongnu, Emperor Wudi became allies with the Yuezhi people, enemies of the Xiongnu.

Analyze Historical Source
Why did Wudi want to establish relations with the Yuezhi?

"The Xiongnu had defeated the king of the Yuezhi people and had made his skull into a drinking vessel. As a result the Yuezhi . . . bore a constant grudge against the Xiongnu, though as yet they had been unable to find anyone to join them in an attack on their enemy. . . . When the emperor [Wudi] heard this, he decided to try to send an envoy to establish relations with the Yuezhi."

—Sima Qian, *Records of the Grand Historian*

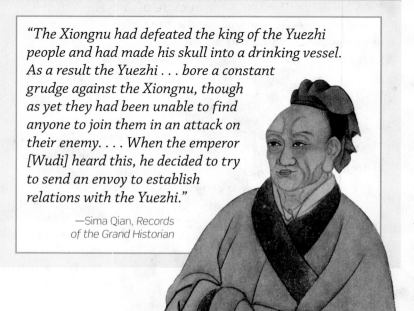

Reading Check
Synthesize
What were the main
internal and external
policies of the first
Han rulers?

Wudi also colonized areas to the northeast, now known as Manchuria and Korea. He sent his armies south, where they conquered mountain tribes and set up Chinese colonies all the way into what is now Vietnam. By the end of Wudi's reign, the empire had expanded nearly to the bounds of present-day China.

A Highly Structured Society

Chinese society under the Han Dynasty was highly structured. (See Social History below.) Just as Han emperors tried to control the people they conquered, they exerted vast control over the Chinese themselves. Because the Chinese believed their emperor to have divine authority, they accepted his exercise of power. He was the link between heaven and earth. If the emperor did his job well, China had peace and prosperity. If he failed, the heavens showed their displeasure with earthquakes, floods, and famines. However, the emperor did not rule alone.

Structures of Han Government The Chinese emperor relied on a complex bureaucracy to help him rule. The empire was divided into provinces, known as commanderies. Each commandery was run by a governor who collected taxes, recruited laborers, and dispensed justice. As Han armies advanced into present-day North Korea and Vietnam, new commanderies were established, bringing with them the structures of Han government. Running the bureaucracy and maintaining the imperial army were expensive. To raise money, the government levied taxes. Like the farmers in India, Chinese peasants owed part of their yearly crops to the government. Merchants also paid taxes.

SOCIAL HISTORY

CHINESE SOCIETY

Under the Han Dynasty, the structure of Chinese society was clearly defined. At the top was the emperor, who was considered semidivine. Next came kings and governors, both appointed by the emperor. They governed with the help of state officials, nobles, and scholars.

Peasant farmers came next. Their production of food was considered vital to the existence of the empire. Artisans and merchants were below them.

Near the bottom were the soldiers, who guarded the empire's frontiers. At the bottom were enslaved persons, who were usually conquered peoples.

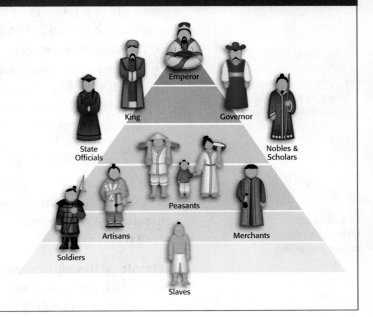

Emperor

King   Governor

State   Nobles &
Officials   Scholars

Peasants

Artisans   Merchants

Soldiers

Slaves

Besides taxes, the peasants owed the government a month's worth of labor or military service every year. With this source of labor, the Han emperors built roads and dug canals and irrigation ditches. The emperors also filled the ranks of China's vast armies and expanded the Great Wall, which stretched across the northern frontier.

Confucianism, the Road to Success Wudi's government employed more than 130,000 people. The bureaucracy included 18 different ranks of **civil service** jobs, which were government jobs that civilians obtained by taking examinations. At times, Chinese emperors rewarded loyal followers with government posts. However, another way to fill government posts evolved under the Han. This method involved testing applicants' knowledge of Confucianism—the teachings of Confucius, who had lived 400 years earlier.

The early Han emperors had employed some Confucian scholars as court advisers, but it was Wudi who actively began to favor them. Confucius had taught that gentlemen should practice "reverence [respect], generosity, truthfulness, diligence [industriousness], and kindness." Because these were exactly the qualities he wanted his government officials to have, Wudi set up a school where hopeful job applicants from all over China could come to study Confucius's works.

After their studies, job applicants took formal examinations in history, law, literature, and Confucianism. In theory, anyone could take the exams. In practice, few peasants could afford to educate their sons. So only sons of wealthy landowners had a chance at a government career. In spite of this flaw, the civil service system begun by Wudi worked so efficiently that it continued in China until 1912.

As the Han Empire expanded, it carried the Confucian tradition to its commanderies in North Korea and Vietnam. From there, Confucian ideas eventually reached Japan. Some of the key Confucian values that were important to the Han Empire are as follows:
- The family is central to the well-being of the state.
- The father, as head of the family, has complete authority.
- Rulers should govern by example rather than by force.
- In addition to providing food and security, government should educate the people.

Reading Check
Make Inferences
Why would Wudi want his officials to have qualities such as diligence?

Han Technology, Commerce, and Culture

The 400 years of Han rule saw not only improvements in education but also great advances in Chinese technology and culture. In addition, the centralized government began to exert more control over commerce and manufacturing.

Vocabulary
commerce the buying and selling of goods

Technology Revolutionizes Chinese Life Advances in technology influenced all aspects of Chinese life. Paper was invented in AD 105. Before that, books were usually written on silk. But paper was cheaper, so books became more readily available. This helped spread education in China.

The invention of paper also affected Chinese government. Formerly, all government documents had been recorded on strips of wood. Paper was much more convenient to use for record keeping, so Chinese bureaucracy expanded.

Another technological advance was the collar harness for horses. This invention allowed horses to pull much heavier loads than did the harness being used in Europe at the time. The Chinese perfected a plow that was more efficient because it had two blades. They also improved iron tools, invented the wheelbarrow, and began to use water mills to grind grain.

Agriculture Versus Commerce During the Han Dynasty, the population of China swelled to 60 million. Because there were so many people to feed, Confucian scholars and ordinary Chinese people considered agriculture the most important and honored occupation.

Although the same decree dismissed commerce as the least important occupation, manufacturing and commerce were actually very important to the Han Empire. The government established monopolies on the mining of salt, the forging of iron, the minting of coins, and the brewing of alcohol. A **monopoly** occurs when a group has exclusive control over the production and distribution of certain goods.

For a time, the government also ran huge silk mills—competing with private silk weavers in making this luxurious cloth. As contact with people from other lands increased, the Chinese realized how valuable their silk was as an item of trade. Because of this, the techniques of silk production became a closely guarded state secret. Spurred by the worldwide demand for silk, Chinese commerce expanded along the Silk Roads to most of Asia and, through India, all the way to Rome.

Reading Check
Make Inferences
Which Han Dynasty inventions helped to feed China's huge population?

History in Depth

Papermaking

People in ancient China wrote on pottery, bones, stone, silk, wood, and bamboo. Then, about 2,000 or more years ago, the Chinese invented paper. They began to use plants, such as hemp, to make thin paper. In AD 105, Ts'ai Lun, a Han official, produced a stronger paper by mixing mulberry bark and old rags with hemp fiber.

The art of papermaking slowly spread to the rest of the world. First, it moved east to Korea and Japan. Then, it spread westward to the Islamic caliphates in the 700s, and from there to Europe.

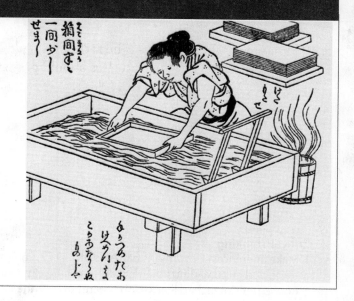

Silk Roads

Why would anyone struggle over mountains and across deserts to buy fabric? Ancient peoples valued silk because it was strong, lightweight, and beautiful. Traders made fortunes carrying Chinese silk to the West. Because of this, the caravan trails that crossed Asia were called Silk Roads, even though many other valuable trade goods were also carried along these routes. The Silk Roads also encouraged cultural diffusion.

TRADED GOLD
Gold was an important trade good. The object below is a Chinese gold dagger handle from the Zhou Dynasty. Many artifacts found along the Silk Roads show a mix of Greek, Central Asian, and Indian styles. This indicates that ideas traveled as well as objects.

CAMEL CARAVANS
No trader traveled the whole length of the Silk Roads. Mediterranean merchants went partway, then traded with Central Asian nomads—who went east until they met Chinese traders near India. Many traders traveled in camel caravans.

Critical Thinking
1. **Make Inferences** How might patterns of trade and cultural diffusion have differed if Rome, not China, had learned the secret of making silk?

2. **Compare** How did the challenges of traveling through mountains compare to the challenges of traveling through desert areas?

The Hijrah After some of his followers had been attacked, Muhammad decided to leave Mecca in AD 622. Following a small band of supporters he sent ahead, Muhammad moved to the town of Yathrib, over 200 miles to the north of Mecca. This migration became known as the **Hijrah** (HIHJ•ruh). The Hijrah to Yathrib marked a turning point for Muhammad. He attracted many devoted followers. Later, Yathrib was renamed Medina.

In Medina, Muhammad displayed impressive leadership skills. He fashioned an agreement that joined his own people with the Arabs and Jews of Medina as a single community. These groups accepted Muhammad as a political leader. As a religious leader, he drew many more converts who found his message appealing. Finally, Muhammad also became a military leader in the growing hostilities between Mecca and Medina.

The Abyssinian army set out to destroy the Ka'aba. Their elephants, however, refused to attack.

The Dome of the Rock

The Dome of the Rock, located in Jerusalem, is the earliest surviving Islamic monument. It was completed in AD 691 and is part of a larger complex, which is the third most holy place in Islam. It is situated on Mount Moriah, the site of the Jewish Temple destroyed by the Romans in AD 70, Judaism's holiest place.

The rock on the site (see photograph below, left) is the spot from which Muslims say Muhammad ascended to heaven to learn of Allah's will. With Allah's blessing, Muslims believe Muhammad returned to earth to bring God's message to all people.

▼ The ornate decorations of the exterior are also found on the interior of the building. Notice the geometric designs, a feature often found in Muslim art.

▼ This interior view shows the point at which the dome meets the circular walls, or drum. The dome is about 100 feet tall and 60 feet in diameter. It is supported by 16 pillars and columns. The drum is covered with colored glass mosaics that date back to the seventh century. The dome was redecorated later.

Interpret Visual Sources

1. **Make Inferences** If you knew nothing about this building, what elements of the building might give you the impression that it is a religious structure?

2. **Compare and Contrast** How is the Dome of the Rock similar to or different from other religious buildings you have seen?

Reading Check
Analyze Causes
Why were
Muhammad's religious
beliefs a source of
conflict in Mecca?

Returning to Mecca In AD 630, Muhammad and 10,000 of his followers marched to the outskirts of Mecca. Facing sure defeat, Mecca's leaders surrendered. Muhammad entered the city in triumph. He destroyed the idols in the Ka'aba and had the call to prayer made from its roof.

Most Meccans pledged their loyalty to Muhammad, and many converted to Islam. By doing so, they joined the *umma*, or Muslim religious community. Muhammad died two years later, at about the age of 62. However, he had taken great strides toward unifying the entire Arabian Peninsula under Islam.

Beliefs and Practices of Islam

The main teaching of Islam is that there is only one God, Allah. All other beliefs and practices follow from this teaching. Islam teaches that there is good and evil, and that each individual is responsible for the actions of his or her life.

The Five Pillars To be a Muslim, all believers have to carry out five duties. These duties are known as the Five Pillars of Islam.

- **Faith** To become a Muslim, a person has to testify to the following statement of faith: "There is no God but Allah, and Muhammad is the Messenger of Allah." This simple statement is heard again and again in Islamic rituals and in Muslim daily life.

- **Prayer** Five times a day, Muslims face toward Mecca to pray. They may assemble at a **mosque** (mahsk), an Islamic house of worship, or wherever they find themselves.

- **Alms** Muhammad taught that all Muslims have a responsibility to support the less fortunate. Muslims meet that social responsibility by giving alms, or money for the poor, through a special religious tax.

- **Fasting** During the Islamic holy month of Ramadan, Muslims fast between dawn and sunset. A simple meal is eaten at the end of the day. Fasting serves to remind Muslims that their spiritual needs are greater than their physical needs.

- **Pilgrimage** All Muslims who are physically and financially able perform the **hajj** (haj), or pilgrimage to Mecca, at least once. Pilgrims wear identical garments so that all stand as equals before Allah.

A Way of Life Carrying out the Five Pillars of Islam ensures that Muslims live their religion while serving in their community. Along with the Five Pillars, there are other customs, morals, and laws for Islamic society that affect Muslims' daily lives. Believers are forbidden to eat pork or to drink intoxicating beverages. Friday afternoons are set aside for communal worship. Unlike many other religions, Islam has no priests or central religious authority. Every Muslim is expected to worship Allah directly. Islam does, however, have a scholar class called the *ulama*. The *ulama* includes religious teachers who apply the words and deeds of Muhammad to everyday life.

Sources of Authority The original source of authority for Muslims is Allah. According to Islamic belief, Allah expressed his will through the angel Gabriel, who revealed it to Muhammad. While Muhammad lived, his followers memorized and recited the revelations he received from Gabriel. Soon after Muhammad's death, it was suggested that the revelations be collected in a book. This book is the **Qur'an** (kuh•RAN), the holy book of the Muslims.

The Qur'an is written in Arabic, and Muslims consider only the Arabic version to be the true word of Allah. Only Arabic can be used in worship. Wherever Muslims carried the Qur'an, Arabic became the language of worshipers and scholars. Thus, the Arabic language helped unite conquered peoples as Muslim control expanded.

Muslims believe that Muhammad's mission as a prophet was to receive the Qur'an and to demonstrate how to apply it in life. To them, the **Sunna** (SOON•uh), or Muhammad's example, is the best model for proper living. The guidance of the Qur'an and Sunna was assembled in a body of law known as **shari'a** (shah•REE•ah). This system of law regulates the family life, moral conduct, and business and community life of Muslims.

Artists decorate the Qur'an as a holy act. The geometric design often repeats to show the infinite quality of Allah.

MUSLIM PRAYER
Five times a day—dawn, noon, mid-afternoon, sunset, and evening—Muslims face toward Mecca to pray. Worshipers are called to prayer by a *muezzin*. The call to prayer sometimes is given from a minaret and even over public address systems or the radio in large cities.

Because they believe that standing before Allah places them on holy ground, Muslims perform a ritual cleansing before praying. They also remove their shoes.

Links to Judaism and Christianity To Muslims, Allah is the same God that is worshiped in Christianity and Judaism. However, Muslims view Jesus as a prophet, not as the Son of God. They regard the Qur'an as the word of Allah as revealed to Muhammad, in a similar way to the beliefs of Jews and Christians in their holy scriptures. Muslims believe that the Qur'an perfects the earlier revelations. To them, it is the final book, and Muhammad was the final prophet. All three religions believe in heaven and hell and a day of judgment. The Muslims trace their ancestry to Abraham, as do the Jews and Christians.

Muslims refer to Christians and Jews as "people of the book" because each religion has a holy book with teachings similar to those of the Qur'an. Shari'a law requires Muslim leaders to extend religious tolerance to Christians and Jews. A huge Muslim empire, as you will learn in Lesson 2, grew to include people of many different cultures and religions.

Reading Check
Clarify
What are the sources of authority for Muslims?

Lesson 1 Assessment

1. **Organize Information** Create a cause-and-effect chart to show what events led to the beginning of Islam.

Causes	Effects

Write a paragraph that summarizes the events that led to the beginning of Islam.

2. **Key Terms and People** For each key term or person in the lesson, write a sentence explaining its significance.

3. **Recognize Effects** How did the beliefs and practices of Islam create unity and strength among Muslims in the 600s?

4. **Compare** In what ways are the teachings of the Muslims similar to those of Christians and Jews?

5. **Draw Conclusions** How did Islam help spread Arabic culture?

Islam Expands

The Big Idea

In spite of internal conflicts, the Muslims created a huge empire that included lands on three continents.

Why It Matters Now

Muslims' influence on three continents produced cultural blending that has continued into the modern world.

Key Terms and People

caliph
Umayyads
Shi'a
Sunni
Sufi
Abbasids
al-Andalus
Fatimid

Setting the Stage

When Muhammad died in AD 632, the community faced a crisis. Muslims, inspired by the message of Allah, believed they had a duty to carry his word to the world. However, they lacked a clear way to choose a new leader. Eventually, the issue of leadership would divide the Muslim world.

Muhammad's Successors Spread Islam

Muhammad had not named a successor or instructed his followers how to choose one. Relying on ancient tribal custom, the Muslim community elected as their leader Abu-Bakr, a loyal friend of Muhammad. In AD 632, Abu-Bakr became the first **caliph** (KAY•lihf), a title that means "successor" or "deputy."

"Rightly Guided" Caliphs Abu-Bakr and the next three elected caliphs—Umar, Uthman, and Ali—all had known Muhammad. They used the Qur'an and Muhammad's actions as guides to leadership. For this, they are known as the "rightly guided" caliphs. Their rule was called a *caliphate* (KAY•lih•fayt).

Abu-Bakr had promised the Muslim community he would uphold what Muhammad stood for. Shortly after Muhammad's death, some tribes on the Arabian Peninsula abandoned Islam. Others refused to pay taxes, and a few individuals even declared themselves prophets. For the sake of Islam, Abu-Bakr invoked *jihad*. The word *jihad* means "striving" and can refer to the inner struggle against evil. However, the word is also used in the Qur'an to mean an armed struggle against unbelievers. For the next two years, Abu-Bakr applied this meaning of *jihad* to encourage and justify the expansion of Islam.

When Abu-Bakr died in AD 634, the Muslim state controlled all of Arabia. Under Umar, the second caliph, Muslim armies conquered Syria and lower Egypt, which were part of the Byzantine Empire. They also took parts of the Sassanid Empire. The next two caliphs, Uthman and Ali, continued to expand Muslim territory. By AD 750, the Muslim Empire stretched 6,000 miles from the Atlantic Ocean to the Indus River.

Reasons for Success The four "rightly guided" caliphs made great progress in their quest to spread Islam. Before his death, Muhammad had expressed a desire to spread the faith to the peoples of the north. Muslims of the day saw their victories as a sign of Allah's support and drew energy and inspiration from their faith. They fought to defend Islam and were willing to struggle to extend its word.

From AD 632 to 750, highly mobile troops mounted on camels were successful in conquering lands in the name of Allah.

The Muslim armies were well disciplined and expertly commanded. However, the success of the armies was also due to weakness in the two empires north of Arabia. The Byzantine and Sassanid empires had been in conflict for a long period of time and were exhausted militarily.

Another reason for Muslim success was the persecution suffered by people under Byzantine or Sassanid rule because they did not support the official state religions, Christianity or Zoroastrianism. The persecuted people often welcomed the invaders and their cause and chose to accept Islam. They were attracted by the appeal of the message of Islam, which offered equality and hope in this world. They were also attracted by the economic benefit for Muslims of not having to pay a poll tax.

Interaction with Conquered Peoples Muslims allowed conquered peoples to follow their own religion. Because the Qur'an forbade forced conversion of "people of the book," conquered Christians and Jews received special consideration. However, they were subject to certain restrictions. For example, they were not allowed to spread their religion. Also, they were required to a pay a poll tax each year in exchange for exemption from military duties. Before entering the newly conquered city of Damascus in the northern Arabian province of Syria, Khalid ibn al-Walid, one of Abu-Bakr's chief generals, detailed the terms of surrender:

> *"In the name of Allah, the compassionate, the merciful, this is what Khalid ibn al-Walid would grant to the inhabitants of Damascus. . . . He promises to give them security for their lives, property and churches. Their city wall shall not be demolished, neither shall any Muslim be quartered in their houses. Thereunto we give to them the pact of Allah and the protection of His Prophet, the Caliphs and the believers. So long as they pay the tax, nothing but good shall befall them."*

—Khalid ibn al-Walid, quoted in *Early Islam*

Reading Check
Analyze Causes
Why were Muslims successful conquerors?

At first, tolerance like this was practiced in Muslim territories in Africa, Asia, and Europe. Some Muslim rulers who came later, however, treated nonbelievers more harshly. In North Africa, for example, the Almohads killed Jews and Christians who refused to accept Islam.

Internal Conflict Creates a Crisis

Despite spectacular gains on the battlefield, the Muslim community had difficulty maintaining a unified rule. In AD 656, Uthman was murdered, starting a civil war in which various groups struggled for power. Ali, as Muhammad's cousin and son-in-law, was the natural choice as a successor to Uthman. However, his right to rule was challenged by Muawiya, a governor of Syria. Then, in AD 661, Ali, too, was assassinated. The elective system of choosing a caliph died with him.

A family known as the **Umayyads** (oo•MY•adz) then came to power. The Umayyads moved the Muslim capital to Damascus. This location, away from Mecca, made controlling conquered territories easier. However, the Arab Muslims felt it was too far away from their lands. In addition, the Umayyads abandoned the simple life of previous caliphs and began to surround themselves with wealth and ceremony similar to that of non-Muslim rulers. These actions, along with the leadership issue, gave rise to a fundamental division in the Muslim community.

Sunni–Shi'a Split In the interest of peace, the majority of Muslims accepted the Umayyads' rule. However, a minority continued to resist. This group developed an alternate view of the office of caliph. In this view, the caliph needed to be a descendant of Muhammad. This group was called **Shi'a**, meaning the "party" of Ali. Members of this group are called Shi'ites. Those who did not outwardly resist the rule of the Umayyads later became known as **Sunni**, meaning followers of Muhammad's example. Another group, the **Sufi** (SOO•fee), rejected the luxurious life of the Umayyads. They pursued a life of poverty and devotion to a spiritual path.

Vigorous religious and political opposition to the Umayyad caliphate led to its downfall. Rebel groups overthrew the Umayyads in the year AD 750. The most powerful of those groups, the **Abbasids** (uh•BAS•ihdz), took control of the empire.

Reading Check
Summarize
What are three groups within Islam and how do they differ?

BASIC DIFFERENCES BETWEEN SUNNI AND SHI'A MUSLIMS

Sunni	Shi'a
Believe that the first four caliphs were "rightly guided"	Believe that Ali, Muhammad's son-in-law, should have succeeded him
Believe that Muslim rulers should follow the Sunna, or Muhammad's example	Believe that all Muslim rulers should be descended from Muhammad; do not recognize the authority of the Sunna
Claim that the Shi'a have distorted the meaning of various passages in the Qur'an	Claim that the Sunni have distorted the meaning of various passages in the Qur'an

Percentage Today of Sunni and Shi'a Muslims Worldwide

Sunni 87 - 90%

Shi'a 10 - 13%

Source: The Pew Research Center

Control Extends over Three Continents

When the Abbasids came to power in AD 750, they ruthlessly murdered the remaining members of the Umayyad family. One prince named Abd al-Rahman escaped the slaughter and fled to Spain. There he set up an Umayyad caliphate. Spain had already been conquered and settled by Muslims from North Africa, who were known as Berbers. The Berber armies advanced north to within 200 miles of Paris before being halted at the Battle of Tours in AD 732. They then settled in southern Spain, where they helped form an extraordinary Muslim state in **al-Andalus** (al·an·duh·LUS).

Abbasids Consolidate Power To solidify power, the Abbasids moved the capital of the empire in AD 762 to a newly created city, Baghdad, in central Iraq. The location on key trade routes gave the caliph access to trade goods, gold, and information about the far-flung empire.

The Abbasids developed a strong bureaucracy to conduct the huge empire's affairs. A treasury kept track of the money flow. A special department managed the business of the army. Diplomats from the empire were sent to courts in Europe, Africa, and Asia to conduct imperial business. To support this bureaucracy, the Abbasids taxed land, imports and exports, and non-Muslims' wealth.

Rival Groups Divide Muslim Lands The Abbasid caliphate lasted from AD 750 to 1258. During that time, the Abbasids increased their authority by consulting religious leaders. But they failed to keep complete political control of the immense territory. Independent Muslim states sprang up, and local leaders dominated many smaller regions. The **Fatimid** (FAT·uh·mihd) caliphate was formed by Shi'a Muslims who claimed descent from Muhammad's daughter Fatima. The caliphate began in North Africa and spread across the Red Sea to western Arabia and Syria. However, the Fatimids and other smaller states were still connected to the Abbasid caliphate through religion, language, trade, and the economy.

Muslim Trade Network At this time, two major sea-trading networks existed—the Mediterranean Sea and the Indian Ocean. Through these networks, the Muslim Empire could engage in sea trade with the rest of the world. The land network connected the Silk Roads of China and India with Europe and Africa. Muslim merchants needed only a single language, Arabic, and a single currency, the Abbasid dinar, to travel in the empire.

To encourage the flow of trade, Muslim money changers set up banks in cities throughout the empire. Banks offered letters of credit, called *sakks*, to merchants. A merchant with a *sakk* from a bank in Baghdad could exchange it for cash at a bank in any other city in the empire. In Europe, *sakk* was pronounced "check." Thus, using checks dates back to the Muslim Empire.

وأثرِّهِ الصوابَ والغَلَط وانَ جلتهُ الحُكمَ عِندي فارَضوا بِقلبي ولا سُفْتُوا الحَمَل

This 13th-century miniature shows Arab traders navigating the Indian Ocean.

Reading Check
Recognize Effects
Why would a single language and a single currency be such an advantage to a trader?

At one end of the Muslim Empire was the city of Córdoba in al-Andalus. In the tenth century, this city had a population of 200,000; Paris, in contrast, had 38,000. The city attracted poets, philosophers, and scientists. Many non-Muslims adopted Muslim customs, and Córdoba became a dazzling center of Muslim culture.

In Córdoba, Damascus, Cairo, and Baghdad, a cultural blending of people fueled a period of immense achievements in the arts and the sciences.

Lesson 2 Assessment

1. **Organize Information** Create a table in which you indicate the timespan of each period of Muslim rule and indicate the developments in Islam during each period.

Rulers	Period of Rule	Developments in Islam
"Rightly guided" caliphs		
Umayyads		
Abbasids		

   Write a paragraph about which period of Muslim rule you think was most effective.

2. **Key Terms and People** For each key term or person in the lesson, write a sentence explaining its significance.

3. **Develop Historical Perspective** Do you think Muhammad should have appointed a successor? Why or why not?

4. **Draw Conclusions** What attracted non-Muslims to Islam and Islamic culture?

5. **Make Inferences** What does opposition to the luxurious life of the Umayyads suggest about what is important to most Muslims?

Muslim Culture

Setting the Stage

The Abbasids governed during a prosperous period of Muslim history. Riches flowed into the empire from all over Europe, Asia, and Africa. Rulers could afford to build luxurious cities. They supported the scientists, mathematicians, and philosophers that those cities attracted. In the special atmosphere created by Islam, the scholars preserved existing knowledge and produced an enormous body of original learning.

Muslim Society

Over time, the influence of Muslims grew as the empire attracted people from a variety of lands. The many cultural traditions combined with the Arabic culture to create an international flavor. Muslim society had a sophistication matched at that time only by the Tang Empire of China. That cosmopolitan character was most evident in urban centers.

The Rise of Muslim Cities Until the construction of Baghdad, Damascus was the leading city. It was also the

The Big Idea

Muslims combined and preserved the traditions of many peoples and also advanced learning in a variety of areas.

Why It Matters Now

Many of the ideas developed during this time became the basis of today's scientific and academic disciplines.

Key Terms and People

House of Wisdom
calligraphy

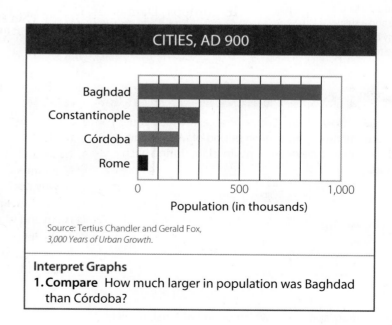

CITIES, AD 900

Source: Tertius Chandler and Gerald Fox, *3,000 Years of Urban Growth.*

Interpret Graphs
1. **Compare** How much larger in population was Baghdad than Córdoba?

cultural center of Islamic learning. Other cities grew up around power centers, such as Córdoba (the Umayyad capital), Cairo (the Fatimid capital), and Jerusalem. Cities, which symbolized the strength of the caliphate, were very impressive.

The Abbasid capital city, Baghdad, impressed all who saw it. Caliph al-Mansur chose the site for his capital on the west bank of the Tigris River in AD 762. Extensive planning went into the city's distinctive circular design, formed by three circular protective walls. The caliph's palace of marble and stone sat in the innermost circle, along with the grand mosque. Originally, the main streets between the middle wall and the palace were lined with shops. Later, the marketplace moved to a district outside the walls. Baghdad's population approached one million at its peak.

Four Social Classes Baghdad's population, made up of different cultures and social classes, was typical for a large Muslim city in the eighth and ninth centuries. Muslim society was made up of four classes. The upper class included those who were Muslims at birth. Converts to Islam were in the second class. The third class consisted of the "protected people" and included Christians, Jews, and Zoroastrians. The lowest class was composed of slaves. Many slaves were prisoners of war, and all were non-Muslim. Slaves most frequently performed household work or fought in the military.

Role of Women The Qur'an says, "Men are the managers of the affairs of women," and "Righteous women are therefore obedient." However, the Qur'an also declares that men and women, as believers, are equal. The shari'a gave Muslim women specific legal rights concerning marriage, family, and property. Thus, Muslim women had more economic and property rights than European, Indian, and Chinese women of the same time period. Nonetheless, Muslim women were still expected to submit to men. When a husband wanted to divorce his wife, all he had to do was repeat three times, "I dismiss thee." The divorce became final in three months.

In a miniature painting from Persia, women are shown having a picnic in a garden. Gardens were seen as earthly representations of paradise.

Responsibilities of Muslim women varied with the income of their husbands. The wife of a poor man would often work in the fields with her husband. Wealthier women supervised the household and its servants. They had access to education, and among them were poets and scholars. Rich or poor, women were responsible for the raising of the children. In the early days of Islam, women could also participate in public life and gain an education. However, over time, Muslim women were forced to live increasingly isolated lives. When they did go out in public, they were expected to be veiled.

Reading Check
Form Generalizations
What was the role of women in Muslim society?

Muslim Scholarship Extends Knowledge

Muslims had several practical reasons for supporting the advancement of science. Rulers wanted qualified physicians treating their ills. The faithful throughout the empire relied on mathematicians and astronomers to calculate the times for prayer and the direction of Mecca. However, their attitude also reflected a deep-seated curiosity about the world and a quest for truth. Muhammad himself believed strongly in the power of learning:

> *"Acquire knowledge. It enableth its possessor to distinguish right from wrong; it lighteth the way to Heaven; it is our friend in the desert, our society in solitude, our companion when friendless; it guideth us to happiness; it sustaineth us in misery; it is an ornament amongst friends, and an armour against enemies."*
>
> —Muhammad, quoted in *The Sayings of Muhammad*

Muhammad's emphasis on study and scholarship led to strong support of places of learning by Muslim leaders. After the fall of Rome in AD 476, Europe entered a period of upheaval and chaos, an era in which scholarship suffered. The scientific knowledge gained up to that time might have been lost. However, Muslim leaders and scholars preserved and expanded much of that knowledge. Both Umayyads and Abbasids encouraged scholars to collect and translate scientific and philosophical texts. In the early AD 800s, Caliph al-Ma'mun opened in Baghdad a combination library, academy, and translation center called the **House of Wisdom**. There, scholars of different cultures and beliefs worked side by side translating texts from Greece, India, Persia, and elsewhere into Arabic.

Reading Check
Summarize
According to Muhammad, what are the nine valuable results of knowledge?

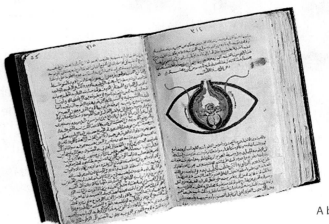

A book handwritten in Arabic.

Astronomy

Muslim interest in astronomy developed from the need to fulfill three of the Five Pillars of Islam—fasting during Ramadan, performing the hajj, and praying toward Mecca. A correct lunar calendar was needed to mark religious periods such as the month of Ramadan and the month of the hajj. Studying the skies helped fix the locations of cities so that worshipers could face toward Mecca as they prayed. Extensive knowledge of the stars also helped guide Muslim traders to the many trading cities of the ancient world.

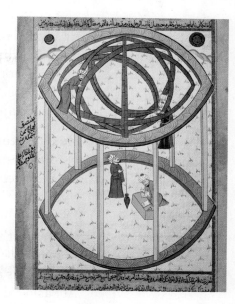

▲ The device shown here is called an **armillary sphere.** The man standing in the center is aligning the sphere, while the seated man records the observations. Astronomers calculated the time of day or year by aligning the rings with various stars. This helped Muslims set their religious calendar.

◄ **Muslim observatories** were great centers of learning. This scene depicts astronomers working at the observatory in Istanbul. They are using many instruments including an astrolabe like the one shown on this page.

◄ **The astrolabe** was an early scientific instrument. It had a fixed "plate" and a rotating "rete." The plate was a map of the sky and the rete simulated the daily movement of the earth in relation to the stars. Using this tool, one could calculate time, celestial events, and relative position. For Muslims, the astrolabe helped determine where they were in relation to Mecca.

This is the plate. The plate was etched with a map of the sky for a certain latitude.

This is the rete—it rotated over the plate. The rete was mostly cut away so the map beneath was visible.

These pointers on the rete represented different stars. At night, observers could look at the sky, position the pointers, and make their calculations.

Critical Thinking

1. **Recognize Effects** How did fulfilling religious duties lead Muslims to astronomy and a better understanding of the physical world?

2. **Compare and Contrast** Muslim astronomers developed instruments to improve their observations of the sky. We do the same thing today. Research how modern astronomers make their observations and compare their methods with early Muslim astronomers. Write two paragraphs on how their methods are similar to and different from each other.

Art and Sciences Flourish

Scholars at the House of Wisdom included researchers, editors, linguists, and technical advisers. These scholars developed standards and techniques for research that are a part of the basic methods of today's research. Some Muslim scholars used Greek ideas in fresh new ways. Others created original work of the highest quality. In these ways, Muslims in the Abbasid lands, especially in Córdoba and Baghdad, set the stage for a later revival of European learning.

Muslim Literature Literature had been a strong tradition in Arabia even before Islam. Bedouin poets, reflecting the spirit of desert life, composed poems celebrating ideals such as bravery, love, generosity, and hospitality. Those themes continued to appear in poetry written after the rise of Islam.

The Qur'an is the standard for all Arabic literature and poetry. Early Muslim poets sang the praises of Muhammad and of Islam and, later, of the caliphs and other patrons who supported them. During the age of the Abbasid caliphate, literary tastes expanded to include poems about nature and the pleasures of life and love.

Popular literature included *The Thousand and One Nights,* a collection of fairy tales, parables, and legends. The core of the collection has been linked to India and Persia, but peoples of the Muslim Empire added stories and arranged them beginning around the tenth century.

Muslim Art and Architecture As the Muslim Empire expanded, the Arabs entered regions that had rich artistic traditions. Muslims continued these traditions but often adapted them to suit Islamic beliefs and practices. For example, since Muslims believed that only Allah can create life, images of living beings were discouraged. Thus, many artists turned to **calligraphy**, or the art of beautiful handwriting. Others expressed themselves through the decorative arts, such as woodwork, glass, ceramics, and textiles.

Global Patterns

The Thousand and One Nights

The Thousand and One Nights is a collection of stories tied together using a frame story. The frame story tells of King Shahryar, who marries a new wife each day and has her killed the next. When Scheherezade marries the king, however, she tells him fascinating tales for a thousand and one nights, until the king realizes that he loves her.

The tradition of using a frame story dates back to at least 200 BC, when the ancient Indian fables of the *Panchatantra* were collected. Italian writer Giovanni Boccaccio also set his great work, *The Decameron,* within a frame story in 1335.

This illustration shows Scheherezade and King Shahryar.

Muslim Art

Muslim art is intricate and colorful but often does not contain images of living beings. Muslim leaders feared that people might worship the images rather than Allah. Thus, Muslim artists found different ways to express their creativity, as shown on this page.

▶ **CALLIGRAPHY**
Calligraphy, or ornamental writing, is important to Muslims because it is considered a way to reflect the glory of Allah. In pictorial calligraphy, pictures are formed using the letters of the alphabet. This picture of a man praying is made up of the words of the Muslim declaration of faith.

▲ **GEOMETRIC PATTERNS**
Muslim artwork sometimes focuses on strictly geometric patterns. Geometric designs can be found in everything from pottery to architecture. This mosaic is from the Jami Masjid Mosque in India (shown below) and uses intricate patterns radiating out from the central shape.

▲ **ARABESQUE**
Arabesque decoration is a complex, ornate design. It usually incorporates flowers, leaves, and geometric patterns. These arabesque tiles are from the Jami Masjid Mosque. Arabesque designs are also found in Muslim mosaics, textiles, and sculptures.

Interpret Visual Sources
Draw Conclusions What do these three artistic techniques suggest about Muslim art?

It is in architecture that the greatest cultural blending of the Muslim world can be seen. To some extent, a building reflected the culture of people of the area. For example, the Great Mosque of Damascus was built on the site of a Christian church. In many ways, the huge dome and vaulted ceiling of the mosque blended Byzantine architecture with Muslim ideas. In Syrian areas, the architecture included features that were very Roman, including baths using Roman heating systems. In Córdoba, the Great Mosque used two levels of arches in a style unknown before. The style was based on principles used in earlier mosques. These blended styles appeared in all the lands occupied by the Muslims.

Medical Advances Muslim contributions in the sciences were most recognizable in medicine, mathematics, and astronomy. A Persian scholar named al-Razi (Rhazes, according to the European pronunciation) was the greatest physician of the Muslim world and, more than likely, of world civilization between AD 500 and 1500. He wrote an encyclopedia called the *Comprehensive Book* that drew on knowledge from Greek, Syrian, Arabic, and Indian sources as well as on his own experience. Al-Razi also wrote *Treatise on Smallpox and Measles*, which was translated into several languages. He believed patients would recover more quickly if they breathed cleaner air.

Math and Science Stretch Horizons Among the ideas that Muslim scholars introduced to modern math and science, two especially stand out. They are the reliance on scientific observation and experimentation, and the ability to find mathematical solutions to old problems. As for science, Muslims translated and studied Greek texts. But they did not follow the Greek method of solving problems. Aristotle, Pythagoras, and other Greek thinkers preferred logical reasoning over uncovering facts through observation. Muslim scientists preferred to solve problems by conducting experiments in laboratory settings.

Muslim scholars believed that mathematics was the basis of all knowledge. Al-Khwarizmi, a mathematician born in Baghdad in the late AD 700s, studied Indian rather than Greek sources. He wrote a textbook in the AD 800s explaining "the art of bringing together unknowns to match a known quantity." He called this technique *al-jabr*—today called algebra.

Many of the advances in mathematics were related to the study of astronomy. Muslim observatories charted stars, comets, and planets. Ibn al-Haytham (Alhazen), a brilliant mathematician, produced a book called *Optics* that revolutionized ideas about vision. He showed that people see objects because rays pass from the objects to the eyes, not from the eyes to the objects as was commonly believed. His studies about optics were used in developing lenses for telescopes and microscopes.

Muslim Agricultural Revolution From the AD 700s to the 1200s a transformation in agriculture occurred throughout the Muslim world. This is known as the Muslim Agricultural Revolution. Muslim traders introduced a variety of new crops and farming techniques to Muslim lands.

This interior view of the Great Mosque of Córdoba showed a new architectural style. Two tiers of arches support the ceiling.

Reading Check
Find Main Ideas
What were some of the Muslim contributions in medicine, mathematics, and astronomy?

They brought sorghum from Africa, citrus fruits from China, and mangos, sugarcane, and rice from India.

Over time, agriculture in the Muslim world became more mechanized which allowed farmers to produce more crops. Muslim engineers developed new irrigation techniques that allowed farmers to grow crops in areas once too dry for agriculture. New and greater sources of food caused the population to grow. This also transformed the economy and caused urban areas to expand.

Philosophy and Religion Blend Views

In addition to scientific works, scholars at the House of Wisdom in Baghdad translated works of Greek philosophers like Aristotle and Plato into Arabic. In the 1100s, Muslim philosopher Ibn Rushd (also known as Averroës), who lived in Córdoba, was criticized for trying to blend Aristotle's and Plato's views with those of Islam. However, Ibn Rushd argued that Greek philosophy and Islam both had the same goal: to find the truth.

Moses Ben Maimon (Maimonides), a Jewish physician and philosopher, was born in Córdoba and lived in Egypt. Like Ibn Rushd, he faced strong opposition for his ideas, but he came to be recognized as the greatest Jewish philosopher in history. Writing during the same time as Ibn Rushd, Maimonides produced a book, *The Guide for the Perplexed*, that blended philosophy, religion, and science.

Ibn Rushd
1126–1198

Today Ibn Rushd is considered by many to be the most important of all Muslim philosophers. Yet his views were so offensive to Islamic conservatives that he was once stoned in the Great Mosque of Córdoba. In 1184, the philosopher began serving as physician to Caliph al-Mansur in Marrakech. Under pressure by conservatives, however, the caliph accused Ibn Rushd of heresy and ordered some of his books to be burned.

Fortunately, all of his work was not lost. Ibn Rushd's writings had a great impact on Europe in the 13th century and played a major role in the revival of Christian scholarship. In the 16th century, Italian painter Raphael placed Ibn Rushd among the ancient Greek philosophers in *School of Athens*.

The "Ideal Man" The values of many cultures were recognized by the Muslims. A ninth-century Muslim philosophical society showed that it recognized the empire's diverse nature when it described its "ideal man":

> "The ideal and morally perfect man should be of East Persian derivation, Arabic in faith, of Iraqi education, a Hebrew in astuteness, a disciple of Christ in conduct, as pious as a Greek monk, a Greek in the individual sciences, an Indian in the interpretation of all mysteries, but lastly and especially a Sufi in his whole spiritual life."
>
> —Ikhwan as-Safa, quoted in *The World of Islam*

Reading Check
Draw Conclusions
What is the advantage of blending various traditions within a culture?

Though the unified Muslim state broke up, Muslim culture continued. Three Muslim empires—the Ottoman, the Safavid, and the Mughal—would emerge that would reflect the blended nature of the culture of this time. The knowledge developed and preserved by the Muslim scholars would be drawn upon by European scholars in the Renaissance, beginning in the 14th century.

Lesson 3 Assessment

1. **Organize Information** Create an idea web that lists all of the major elements of Muslim culture.

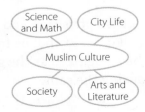

Write a paragraph describing which of these elements you think most strengthened the Abbasid rule.

2. **Key Terms and People** For each key term or person in the lesson, write a sentence explaining its significance.

3. **Evaluate** What do you consider to be the five most significant developments in scholarship and the arts during the reign of the Abbasids?

4. **Make Inferences** What united the scholars of different cultures who worked in the House of Wisdom?

5. **Synthesize** What role did cities play in the advancement of Muslim culture?

The Ottomans Build a Vast Empire

The Big Idea

The Ottomans established a Muslim empire that combined many cultures and lasted for more than 600 years.

Why It Matters Now

Many modern societies, from Algeria to Turkey, had their origins under Ottoman rule.

Key Terms and People

ghazi
Ottoman
sultan
Timur the Lame
Mehmed II
Suleyman
   the Lawgiver
devshirme
janissary

Setting the Stage

By 1300, the Byzantine Empire was declining, and the Mongols from central Asia had destroyed the Turkish Seljuk kingdom of Rum. Anatolia was inhabited mostly by the descendants of nomadic Turks. These militaristic people had a long history of invading other countries. Loyal to their own groups, they were not united by a strong central power. A small Turkish state occupied land between the Byzantine Empire and that of the Muslims. From this place, a strong leader would emerge to unite the Turks into what eventually would become an immense empire stretching across three continents.

Turks Move into Byzantium

Many Anatolian Turks saw themselves as **ghazis** (GAH•zees), or warriors for Islam. They formed military societies under the leadership of an emir, a chief commander, and followed a strict Islamic code of conduct. They raided the territories of people who lived on the frontiers of the Byzantine Empire.

Osman Establishes a State The most successful ghazi was Osman. People in the West called him Othman and named his followers **Ottomans**. Osman built a small Muslim state in Anatolia between 1300 and 1326. His successors expanded it by buying land, forming alliances with some emirs, and conquering others.

The Ottomans' military success was largely based on the use of gunpowder. They replaced their archers on horseback with musket-carrying foot soldiers. They were also among the first people to use cannons as weapons of attack. Even heavily walled cities fell to an all-out attack by the Turks.

The second Ottoman leader, Orkhan I, was Osman's son. He felt strong enough to declare himself **sultan**, meaning "overlord" or "one with power." And in 1361, the Ottomans captured Adrianople (ay•dree•uh•NOH•puhl), the second most important city in the Byzantine Empire. A new Turkish empire was on the rise.

The Ottomans acted wisely toward the people they conquered. They ruled through local officials appointed by the sultan and often improved the lives of the peasants. Most Muslims had to serve in Turkish armies and make contributions required by their faith. Non-Muslims did not have to serve in the army but had to pay for their exemption with a small tax.

Timur the Lame Halts Expansion The rise of the Ottoman Empire was briefly interrupted in the early 1400s by a rebellious warrior and conqueror from Samarkand in Central Asia. Permanently injured by an arrow in the leg, he was called Timur-i-Lang, or **Timur the Lame**. Europeans called him Tamerlane. Timur burned the powerful city of Baghdad in present-day Iraq to the ground. He crushed the Ottoman forces at the Battle of Ankara in 1402. This defeat halted the expansion of their empire.

Reading Check
Summarize By what means did the early Ottomans expand their empire?

Powerful Sultans Spur Dramatic Expansion

Soon Timur turned his attention to China. When he did, war broke out among the four sons of the Ottoman sultan. Mehmed I defeated his brothers and took the throne. His son, Murad II, defeated the Venetians, invaded Hungary, and overcame an army of Italian crusaders in the Balkans. He was the first of four powerful sultans who led the expansion of the Ottoman Empire through 1566.

Mehmed II Conquers Constantinople Murad's son **Mehmed II**, or Mehmed the Conqueror, achieved the most dramatic feat in Ottoman history. By the time Mehmed took power in 1451, the ancient city of Constantinople had shrunk from a population of a million to a mere 50,000. Although it controlled no territory outside its walls, it still dominated the Bosporus Strait. Controlling this waterway meant that it could choke off traffic between the Ottomans' territories in Asia and in the Balkans.

Mehmed II decided to face this situation head-on. "Give me Constantinople!" he thundered, shortly after taking power at age 21. Then, in 1453, he launched his attack.

Mehmed's Turkish forces began firing on the city walls with mighty cannons. One of these was a 26-foot gun that fired 1,200-pound boulders. A chain across the Golden Horn between the Bosporus Strait and the Sea of Marmara kept the Turkish fleet out of the city's harbor. Finally, one night Mehmed's army tried a daring tactic. They dragged 70 ships over a hill on greased runners from the Bosporus to the harbor. Now Mehmed's army was attacking Constantinople from two sides. The city held out for over seven weeks, but the Turks finally found a break in the wall and entered the city.

The Conquest of Constantinople

Kritovoulos, a Greek who served in the Ottoman administration, recorded the following about the Ottoman takeover of Constantinople. The second source, the French miniature at the right, shows a view of the siege of Constantinople.

"After this the Sultan entered the City and looked about to see its great size, its situation, its grandeur and beauty, its teeming population, its loveliness, and the costliness of its churches and public buildings and of the private houses and community houses and those of the officials. . . .

When he saw what a large number had been killed and the ruin of the buildings, and the wholesale ruin and destruction of the City, he was filled with compassion and repented not a little at the destruction and plundering. Tears fell from his eyes as he groaned deeply and passionately: 'What a city we have given over to plunder and destruction.'"

—Kritovoulos,
History of Mehmed the Conqueror

Document-Based Questions

1. Why do you think the sultan wept over the destruction?

2. In what details do the two sources agree? disagree?

3. Find a secondary source—an article from the Internet or a passage from a history book—that describes the Ottoman takeover of Constantinople. How does the perspective of the secondary source compare with that of the primary sources? Does the secondary source appear to have credible information based on what you have learned about the takeover?

Hagia Sophia was a Christian Orthodox church before it was converted into a mosque when the Ottomans took over Constantinople in 1453.

Mehmed the Conqueror, as he was now called, proved to be an able ruler as well as a magnificent warrior. He opened Constantinople to new citizens of many religions and backgrounds. Jews, Christians, and Muslims, Turks and non-Turks all flowed in. They helped rebuild the city, which was now called Istanbul.

Ottomans Take Islam's Holy Cities Mehmed's grandson, Selim the Grim, came to power in 1512. He was an effective sultan and a great general. In 1514, he defeated the Safavids (suh•FAH•vihdz) of Persia at the Battle of Chaldiran. Then he swept south through Syria and Palestine and into North Africa. At the same time that Cortez was toppling the Aztec Empire in the Americas, Selim's empire took responsibility for Mecca and Medina. Finally he took Cairo, the intellectual center of the Muslim world. The once-great civilization of Egypt had become just another province in the growing Ottoman Empire.

Suleyman the Lawgiver

The Ottoman Empire didn't reach its peak size and grandeur until the reign of Selim's son, Suleyman I (SOO•lay•mahn). Suleyman came to the throne in 1520 and ruled for 46 years. His own people called him **Suleyman the Lawgiver**. He was known in the West, though, as Suleyman the Magnificent. This title was a tribute to the splendor of his court and to his cultural achievements.

Reading Check
Analyze Motives
Why was taking Constantinople so important to Mehmed II?

The Empire Reaches Its Limits Suleyman was a superb military leader. He conquered the important European city of Belgrade in 1521. The next year, Turkish forces captured the island of Rhodes in the Mediterranean and now dominated the whole eastern Mediterranean.

Applying their immense naval power, the Ottomans captured Tripoli on the coast of North Africa. They continued conquering peoples along the North African coastline. Although the Ottomans occupied only the coastal cities of North Africa, they managed to control trade routes to the interior of the continent.

In 1526, Suleyman advanced into Hungary and Austria throwing central Europe into a panic. Suleyman's armies then pushed to the outskirts of Vienna, Austria. Reigning from Istanbul, Suleyman had waged war with central Europeans, North Africans, and Central Asians. He had become the most powerful monarch on earth. Only Charles V, head of the Hapsburg Empire in Europe, came close to rivaling his power.

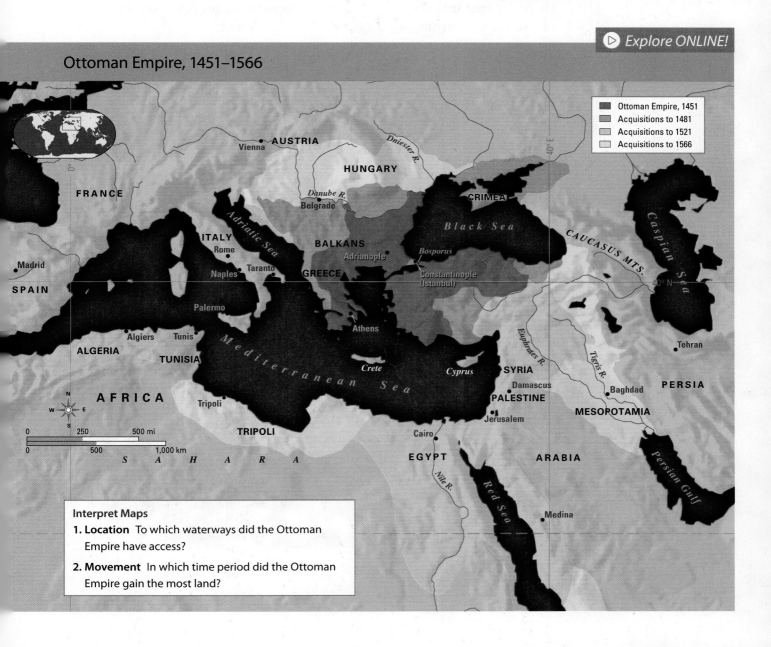

▶ Explore ONLINE!

Ottoman Empire, 1451–1566

Legend:
- Ottoman Empire, 1451
- Acquisitions to 1481
- Acquisitions to 1521
- Acquisitions to 1566

Interpret Maps

1. **Location** To which waterways did the Ottoman Empire have access?

2. **Movement** In which time period did the Ottoman Empire gain the most land?

Highly Structured Social Organization Binding the Ottoman Empire together in a workable social structure was Suleyman's crowning achievement. The massive empire required an efficient government structure and social organization. Suleyman created a law code to handle both criminal and civil actions. He also simplified and limited taxes, and systematized and reduced government bureaucracy. These changes improved the lives of most citizens and helped earn Suleyman the title of Lawgiver.

The sultan's 20,000 personal slaves staffed the palace bureaucracy. The slaves were acquired as part of a policy called *devshirme* (dehv•SHEER•meh). Under the ***devshirme*** system, the sultan's army drafted boys from the peoples of conquered Christian territories. The army educated them, converted them to Islam, and trained them as soldiers. An elite force of 30,000 soldiers known as **janissaries** was trained to be loyal only to the sultan. Their superb discipline made them the heart of the Ottoman war machine. In fact, Christian families sometimes bribed officials to take their children into the sultan's service, because the brightest ones could rise to high government posts or military positions.

BIOGRAPHY

Suleyman the Lawgiver
(1494–1566)

In the halls of the U.S. Congress are images of some of the greatest lawgivers of all time. Included in that group are such persons as Thomas Jefferson, Moses, and Suleyman.

Suleyman's law code prescribed penalties for various criminal acts and for bureaucratic and financial corruption. He also sought to reduce bribes, did not allow imprisonment without a trial, and rejected promotions that were not based on merit. He also introduced the idea of a balanced budget for governments.

Sinan's Mosque of Suleyman in Istanbul is the largest mosque in the Ottoman Empire.

As a Muslim, Suleyman was required to follow Islamic law. In accordance with Islamic law, the Ottomans granted freedom of worship to other religious communities, particularly to Christians and Jews. They treated these communities as *millets*, or nations. They allowed each *millet* to follow its own religious laws and practices. The head of the *millets* reported to the sultan and his staff. This system kept conflict among people of the various religions to a minimum.

Cultural Flowering Suleyman had broad interests, which contributed to the cultural achievements of the empire. He found time to study poetry, history, geography, astronomy, mathematics, and architecture. He employed one of the world's finest architects, Sinan, who was probably from Albania. Sinan's masterpiece, the Mosque of Suleyman, is an immense complex topped with domes and half domes. It includes four schools, a library, a bath, and a hospital.

Art and literature also flourished under Suleyman's rule. This creative period was similar to the European Renaissance. Painters and poets looked to Persia and Arabia for models. The works that they produced used these foreign influences to express original Ottoman ideas in the Turkish style. They are excellent examples of cultural blending.

Reading Check
Make Inferences
What were the advantages of the *devshirme* system to the sultan?

The Empire Declines Slowly

Despite Suleyman's magnificent social and cultural achievements, the Ottoman Empire was losing ground. Suleyman killed his ablest son and drove another into exile. His third son, the incompetent Selim II, inherited the throne.

Suleyman set the pattern for later sultans to gain and hold power. It became customary for each new sultan to have his brothers strangled. The sultan would then keep his sons prisoner in the harem, cutting them off from education or contact with the world. This practice produced a long line of weak sultans who eventually brought ruin on the empire. However, the Ottoman Empire continued to influence the world into the early 20th century.

Reading Check
Evaluate
Why do you think the Ottoman Empire continued to influence the world in the early 20th century?

Lesson 4 Assessment

1. **Organize Information** Create a table in which you list the rulers discussed in this lesson and their accomplishments.

Rulers	Successes

   Write a paragraph about which ruler's accomplishments you think were the most significant to the Ottoman Empire.

2. **Key Terms and People** For each key term or person in the lesson, write a sentence explaining its significance.

3. **Evaluate Decisions** Do you think that the Ottomans were wise in staffing their military and government with slaves? Explain.

4. **Develop Historical Perspective** How did Suleyman's selection of a successor eventually spell disaster for the Ottoman Empire?

5. **Analyze Motives** Do you think that Suleyman's religious tolerance helped or hurt the Ottoman Empire?

🌐 Cultural Blending

The Big Idea

The Safavid Empire produced a rich and complex blended culture in Persia.

Why It Matters Now

Modern Iran, which plays a key role in global politics, descended from the culturally diverse Safavid Empire.

Key Terms and People

Safavid
Isma'il
shah
Shah Abbas
Esfahan

Setting the Stage

Throughout the course of world history, cultures have interacted with each other. Often such interaction has resulted in the mixing of different cultures in new and exciting ways. This process is referred to as cultural blending. The **Safavid** Empire, a Shi'ite Muslim dynasty that ruled in Persia between the 16th and 18th centuries, provides a striking example of how interaction among peoples can produce a blending of cultures. This culturally diverse empire drew from the traditions of Persians, Ottomans, and Arabs.

Patterns of Cultural Blending

Each time a culture interacts with another, it is exposed to ideas, technologies, foods, and ways of life not exactly like its own. Continental crossroads, trade routes, ports, and the borders of countries are places where cultural blending commonly begins. Societies that are able to benefit from cultural blending are those that are open to new ways and are willing to adapt and change. The blended ideas spread throughout the culture and produce a new pattern of behavior. Cultural blending has several basic causes.

Causes of Cultural Blending Cultural change is most often prompted by one or more of the following four activities:

- migration
- pursuit of religious freedom or conversion
- trade
- conquest

The blending that contributed to the culture of the Ottomans, which you read about in Lesson 3, depended on some of these activities. Surrounded by the peoples of Byzantium, the Turks were motivated to win territory for their empire. The Ottoman Empire's location on a major trading route created many opportunities for contact with different cultures. Suleyman's interest in learning and culture prompted him to bring the best foreign artists and scholars to his court. They brought new ideas about art, literature, and learning to the empire.

Results of Cultural Blending Cultural blending may lead to changes in language, religion, styles of government, the use of technology, and military tactics. These changes often reflect unique aspects of several cultures. For example:

- **Language** Sometimes the written characters of one language are used in another, as in the case of written Chinese characters used in the Japanese language. In the Safavid Empire, the language spoken was Persian. But after the area converted to Islam, a significant number of Arabic words appeared in the Persian language.
- **Religion and ethical systems** Buddhism spread throughout Asia. Yet the Buddhism practiced by Tibetans is different from Japanese Zen Buddhism.
- **Styles of government** The concept of a democratic government spread to many areas of the globe. Although the basic principles are similar, it is not practiced exactly the same way in each country.
- **Racial or ethnic blending** One example is the mestizo, people of mixed European and Indian ancestry who live in Mexico.
- **Arts and architecture** Cultural styles may be incorporated or adapted into art or architecture. For example, Chinese artistic elements are found in Safavid Empire tiles and carpets as well as in European paintings.

The chart below shows other examples of cultural blending that have occurred over time in various areas of the world.

Reading Check
Analyze Effects
Which of the effects of cultural blending do you think is the most significant? Explain.

Cultural Blending

Location	Interacting Cultures	Reason for Interaction	Some Results of Interaction
India—1000 BC	Aryan and Dravidian Indian Arab, African, Indian	Migration	Vedic culture, forerunner of Hinduism
East Africa—AD 700	Islamic, Christian	Trade, religious conversion	New trade language, Swahili
Russia—AD 1000	Christian and Slavic	Religious conversion	Eastern Christianity, Russian identity
Mexico—AD 1500	Spanish and Aztec	Conquest	Mestizo culture, Mexican Catholicism
United States—AD 1900	European, Asian, Caribbean	Migration, religious freedom	Cultural diversity

Interpret Charts
1. **Determine Main Ideas** What are the reasons for interaction in the Americas?
2. **Hypothesize** What are some aspects of cultural diversity?

An Era of Prosperity and Innovation

During the Tang and Song dynasties, China's population nearly doubled, soaring to 100 million. By the Song era, China had at least ten cities with a population of 1 million each. China had become the most populous country in the world. It also had become the most advanced.

Science and Technology Artisans and scholars made important technological advances during the Tang and Song eras. Among the most important inventions were movable type and gunpowder. With **movable type**, a printer could arrange blocks of individual characters in a frame to make up a page for printing. Previously, printers had carved the words of a whole page into one large block. The development of gunpowder, in time, led to the creation of explosive weapons such as bombs, grenades, small rockets, and cannons. Other important inventions of this period include porcelain, the mechanical clock, paper money, and the use of the magnetic compass for sailing. (See the Social History feature Tang and Song China: People and Technology.)

The 1000s to the 1200s was a rich period for Chinese mathematics. The Chinese made advances in arithmetic and algebra. Many mathematical ideas, such as using negative numbers, spread from China southward and westward.

Agriculture The rapid growth of China resulted in part from advances in farming. Farmers especially improved the cultivation of rice. In about the year 1000, China imported a new variety of fast-ripening rice from Vietnam. This allowed the farmers to harvest two rice crops each year

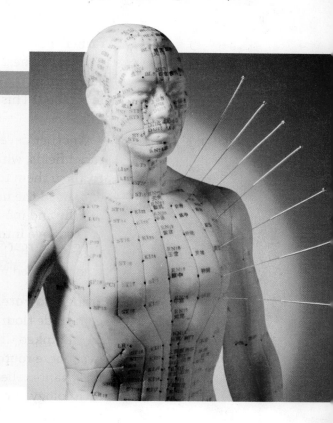

Now and Then

Acupuncture

During the Song Dynasty, the Chinese carefully studied human anatomy and created charts and models of the body. These helped to improve the practice of acupuncture, a system of treatment that involves inserting slender needles into the body at specific points, depending on the nature of the problem.

In recent years, this ancient practice has gained some acceptance in mainstream Western medicine. More and more practicing doctors are seeking training in acupuncture methods. And mainstream doctors are increasing their referrals to acupuncture specialists. In 2012, about 3.5 million people in the United States sought treatment from an acupuncturist for medical problems such as migraine headaches and drug dependency.

Rice farming probably began in China around 5000 BC. It was first practiced in southern China, where the warm, wet climate is perfect for growing rice.

rather than one. To make sure that farmers knew about this improved variety, Chinese officials distributed seedlings throughout the country. The agricultural improvements enabled China's farmers to produce more food. This was necessary to feed the rapidly expanding population in the cities.

Another development that improved rice production was the use of terraced fields, which are level platforms that farmers cut into sloping land to allow them to grow crops. During the Song Dynasty, farmers greatly expanded the number of terraced rice fields, transforming the landscape of hilly and mountainous regions. Terraced farming allowed Chinese farmers to move into sparsely populated areas that had produced little food before. But it also sometimes brought them into conflict with local people who practiced more traditional farming methods.

Trade and Foreign Contacts Under the Tang and Song emperors, foreign trade flourished. Tang imperial armies guarded the great Silk Roads, which linked China to the West. Eventually, however, China lost control over these routes during the long Tang decline. After this time, Chinese merchants relied increasingly on ocean trade. Chinese advances in sailing technology, including use of the magnetic compass, made it possible for sea trade to expand. Up and down China's long coastline, the largest port cities in the world bustled with international trade. Merchant ships carried trade goods to Korea and Japan. They sailed across the Indian Ocean to India, the Persian Gulf, and even the coast of Africa. Chinese merchants established trading colonies around Southeast Asia. Many foreign traders, mostly Arabs, resided in Chinese cities. Through trade and travel, Chinese culture spread throughout East Asia. One major cultural export was Buddhism. This religion spread from China to Vietnam, Korea, and Japan. The exchange of goods and ideas was two-way. For example, foreign religions, including Islam and some Eastern sects of Christianity, spread to China and won followers.

Revival of Confucianism Confucianism is a philosophy based on the teachings of the Chinese scholar Confucius (551–479 BC), who stressed the importance of social and civic responsibility. After the fall of the Han Dynasty, Confucianism fell into decline and Buddhism became China's most important belief system. During the late Tang and Song dynasties, scholars responded to this challenge by reinterpreting Confucian texts to address new intellectual and spiritual concerns. Their movement is known as Neo-Confucianism.

The Song Dynasty used an elaborate examination system to award government positions. This system helped promote Confucian beliefs because it required applicants to master classical texts. As trade expanded under the dynasty, Neo-Confucianism spread to Korea, Japan, and Vietnam, which developed their own distinct forms of the philosophy.

A Golden Age of Poetry and Art The prosperity of the Tang and Song dynasties nourished an age of artistic brilliance. The Tang period produced great poetry. Two of its most celebrated poets were Li Bo, who wrote about life's pleasures, and Tu Fu, who praised orderliness and Confucian virtues. Tu Fu also wrote critically about war and the hardships of soldiers. Once he himself was captured by rebels and taken to Ch'ang-an, the capital city. He had sent his family to the village of Fuzhou for safety. Here he describes their separation:

"The same moon is above Fuzhou tonight;
From the open window she will be
watching it alone,
The poor children are too little to be able
to remember Ch'ang-an.
Her perfumed hair will be dampened by
the dew, the air may be too chilly on her
delicate arms. When can we both lean
by the wind-blown curtains and see the
tears dry on each other's face?"

—Tu Fu, *"Moonlight Night"*

Birds and flowers were favorite subjects for Song painters.

Reading Check
Predict
How might the spread of mathematical ideas from China have affected other countries?

Chinese painting reached new heights of beauty during the Song Dynasty. Painting of this era shows the influence of Daoism, a philosophy that urges people to live simply and in harmony with nature. Artists emphasized the beauty of natural landscapes and objects such as a single branch or flower. The artists did not use bright colors. Black ink was their favorite paint. Said one Song artist, "Black is ten colors."

Changes in Chinese Society

China's prosperity produced many social changes during the Tang and Song periods. Chinese society became increasingly mobile. People moved to the cities in growing numbers. The Chinese also experienced greater social mobility than ever before. The most important avenue for social advancement was the civil service system.

Levels of Society During Tang and Song times, the power of the old aristocratic families began to fade. A new, much larger upper class emerged, made up of scholar-officials and their families. Such a class of powerful, well-to-do people is called the **gentry**. The gentry attained their status through education and civil service positions rather than through land ownership. Below the gentry was an urban middle class. It included merchants, shopkeepers, skilled artisans, minor officials, and others. At the bottom of urban society were laborers, soldiers, and servants. In the countryside lived the largest class by far, the peasants. They toiled for wealthy landowners as they had for centuries.

The Status of Women Women had always been subservient to men in Chinese society. Their status further declined during the Tang and Song periods. This was especially true among the upper classes in cities. There a woman's work was deemed less important to the family's prosperity and status. Changing attitudes affected peasant families less, however. Peasant women worked in the fields and helped produce their family's food and income.

One sign of the changing status of women was the new custom of binding the feet of upper-class girls. When a girl was very young, her feet were bound tightly with cloth, which eventually broke the arch and curled all but the big toe under. This produced what was admiringly called a "lily-foot." Women with bound feet were crippled for life. To others in society, such a woman reflected the wealth and prestige of her husband, who could afford such a beautiful but impractical wife.

The social, economic, and technological transformations of the Tang and Song periods permanently shaped Chinese civilization. They endured even as China fell to a group of nomadic outsiders, the Mongols, whom you will learn about in Lesson 2.

Reading Check
Make Inferences
How did the practice of foot binding reflect the changing status of Chinese women?

Lesson 1 Assessment

1. **Organize Information** Compare and contrast the Tang and Song dynasties.

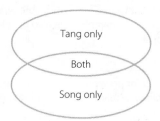

Tang only

Both

Song only

2. **Key Terms and People** For each key term or person in the lesson, write a sentence explaining its significance.

3. **Analyze Causes** What practices allowed China to feed its growing population?

4. **Analyze Effects** What impact did improvements in transportation have on Tang and Song China?

5. **Form Opinions** "Gaining power depends on merit, not birth." Do you agree with this view of China under the Tang and Song? Explain.

Tang and Song China: People and Technology

The Tang and Song dynasties were eras of major technological advancement in China. The technologies improved China as a country and, in turn, helped people conduct their daily business.

Much of China's technology spread to other parts of the world where it improved the lives of the people living there. The table on this page identifies some of that movement.

PORCELAIN ▶

Marco Polo (whom you will learn about in Lesson 2) was the first to describe the pottery found in China as porcelain. The plain piece shown here is an early example of porcelain work from the Song Dynasty. A piece like this might be used daily. Later porcelain work, such as the distinctive blue and white porcelain of the Ming Dynasty, became more decorative. Porcelain was a luxury reserved for the middle and upper classes of Chinese society.

Inventions of Tang and Song China

	Description	Impact
Porcelain Late 700s	Bone-hard, white ceramic made of a special clay and a mineral found only in China	Became a valuable export so associated with Chinese culture that it is now called china; technology remained a Chinese secret for centuries
Mechanical clock 700s	Clock in which machinery (driven by running water) regulated the movements	Early Chinese clocks short-lived; idea for mechanical clock carried by traders to medieval Europe
Printing Block printing: 700s Movable type: 1040	Block printing: one block on which a whole page is cut; movable type: individual characters arranged in frames, used over and over	Printing technology spread to Korea and Japan; Koreans first to use metal movable type in the 13th century; movable type also developed later in Europe
Explosive powder 800s	Made from mixture of saltpeter, sulfur, and charcoal	First used for fireworks, then weapons; technology spread to Korea and Japan and also west within 300 years
Paper money 1020s	Paper currency issued by Song government to replace cumbersome strings of metal cash used by merchants	Contributed to development of large-scale commercial economy in China
Magnetic compass (for navigation) 1100s	Floating magnetized needle that always points north-south; device had existed in China for centuries before it was adapted by sailors for use at sea	Helped China become a sea power; technology quickly spread west

Interpret Charts

1. **Make Inferences** Which inventions eventually affected warfare and exploration?

2. **Form Opinions** Which of these inventions do you think had the greatest impact on history? Why?

MOVABLE TYPE ▶

Traditionally, an entire page of characters was carved into a block of wood from which prints were made. Pi Sheng, a Chinese alchemist, came up with the idea of creating individual characters that could be reused whenever needed. Later, a government official created rotating storage trays for the characters.

As you have read, Tang rulers restored China's system of scholar-officials. Thus, education and printed materials became important to a larger part of Chinese society.

The trays allowed the typesetter to quickly find the characters. The typesetter would then order the characters in a tray that would be used to produce the printed pages. The two wheels held about 60,000 characters.

▼ EXPLOSIVE POWDER

Around AD 900, Chinese alchemists first discovered that the right mixture of saltpeter, sulfur, and charcoal could be explosive. The Chinese initially used the powder for fireworks, then for military applications. It is now commonly referred to as gunpowder.

This illustration shows Chinese soldiers operating ancient rocket launchers. The Chinese tied gunpowder charges to arrows and placed them in a holder. When lit, the gunpowder released hot gases that propelled the arrows toward a target.

Connect to Today
1. **Form Opinions** Of all the inventions listed on these pages, which do you think had the most lasting impact? Why?
2. **Hypothesize** What are some modern inventions that you believe will still have an impact 1,000 years from now?

LEGACY OF TANG AND SONG CHINA

PRINTING

- U.S. publishers produced over 300,000 books in 2013.
- The Library of Congress, the largest library in the world, has over 36 million books.
- The world's best-selling book is the Bible. Since 1815, around 2.5 billion copies of the Bible have been sold.

PORCELAIN

- The United States imported 423,041 one-piece toilet bowls and tanks in 2002. Of those, 302,489 came from China.
- In 2001, a Chinese newspaper reported the production of possibly the world's largest porcelain kettle—just under 10 feet tall, about 6 feet in diameter, and weighing 1.5 tons.

EXPLOSIVE POWDER

- In 2014, the United States imported about 96 percent of its fireworks from China.
- The largest single firework was used at a Japanese festival in 2014. It weighed over 1,000 pounds, and its burst was about half a mile wide.

The Mongols

The Big Idea

The Mongols, a nomadic people from the steppe, conquered settled societies across much of Asia and established the Yuan Dynasty to rule China.

Why It Matters Now

The Mongols built the largest unified land empire in world history and helped spread Chinese ideas to the West by encouraging trade.

Key Terms and People

pastoralist

clan

Genghis Khan

Pax Mongolica

Kublai Khan

Marco Polo

Setting the Stage

While the Chinese prospered during the Song Dynasty, a great people far to the north were also gaining strength. The Mongols of the Asian steppe lived their lives on the move. They prided themselves on their skill on horseback, their discipline, their ruthlessness, and their courage in battle. They also wanted the wealth and glory that came with conquering mighty empires. This desire soon exploded into violent conflict that transformed Asia and Europe forever.

Nomads of the Asian Steppe

A vast belt of dry grassland, called the steppe, stretches across the landmass of Eurasia. The significance of the steppe to neighboring civilizations was twofold. First, it served as a land trade route connecting the East and the West. Second, it was home to nomadic peoples who frequently swept down on their neighbors to plunder, loot, and conquer.

Geography of the Steppe There are two main expanses of the Eurasian steppe. The western steppe runs from Central Asia to eastern Europe. It was the original home of some ancient invaders you may have read about, including the Hittites. The eastern steppe, covering the area of present-day Mongolia, was the first home of the Huns, the Turks, and the Mongols.

Very little rain falls on the steppe, but the dry, windswept plain supports short, hardy grasses. Seasonal temperature changes can be dramatic. Temperatures in Mongolia, for example, range from −57°F in winter to 96°F in the summer. Rainfall is somewhat more plentiful and the

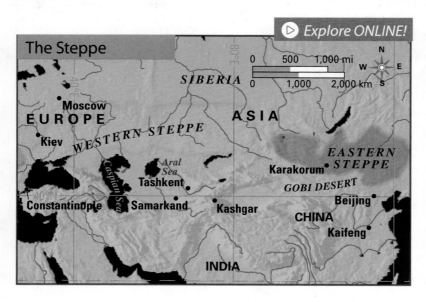

The Steppe

▶ Explore ONLINE!

0   500   1,000 mi
0   1,000   2,000 km

N
W — E
S

SIBERIA

EUROPE   ASIA

Moscow

Kiev   WESTERN STEPPE

Aral Sea

EASTERN STEPPE

Karakorum

Tashkent   GOBI DESERT

Constantinople   Samarkand   Kashgar   Beijing

CHINA

Kaifeng

INDIA

Apart from their herds, the most important possession of nomads was the portable tent called a yurt. Yurts were made of layers of felt covering wooden poles. Sheep fat applied to the outermost layer protected it from rain. Nomads furnished yurts with carpets for warmth and decoration.

Reading Check
Make Inferences
How might a strong, organized empire defend its frontier?

climate milder in the west than in the east. For this reason, movements of people have historically tended to be toward the west and the south.

The Nomadic Way of Life Nomadic peoples were **pastoralists**— that is, they herded domesticated animals. They were constantly on the move, searching for good pasture to feed their herds. But they did not wander. Rather, they followed a familiar seasonal pattern and returned on a regular basis to the same campsites. Keeping claim to land that was not permanently occupied was difficult. Battles frequently arose among nomadic groups over grassland and water rights.

Asian nomads practically lived on horseback as they followed their huge herds over the steppe. They depended on their animals for food, clothing, and housing. Their diet consisted of meat and mare's milk. They wore clothing made of skins and wool, and they lived in portable felt tents called yurts.

Steppe nomads traveled together in kinship groups called **clans**. The members of each clan claimed to be descended from a common ancestor. Different clans sometimes came together when they needed a large force to attack a common enemy or raid their settled neighbors.

Steppe Nomads and Settled Societies The differing ways of life of nomadic and settled peoples resulted in constant interaction between them. Often, they engaged in peaceful trade. The nomads exchanged horses, for example, for basic items they lacked, such as grain, metal, cloth, and tea. Nomads were accustomed to scarcity and hardship. They prided themselves on their toughness. However, they were sometimes tempted by the rich land and relative wealth of townspeople and took what they wanted by force. As a result, settled peoples lived in constant fear of raids.

Time and again in history, nomadic peoples rode out of the steppe to invade border towns and villages. When a state or empire was strong and organized, it could protect its frontier. If the state or empire became divided and weak, the nomads could increase their attacks and gain more plunder. Occasionally, a powerful nomadic group was able to conquer a whole empire and become its rulers. Over generations, these nomadic rulers often became part of the civilization they conquered.

The Rise of the Mongols

For centuries, the Mongol people had roamed the eastern steppe in loosely organized clans. It took a military and political genius to unite the Mongols into a force with a single purpose—conquest.

Genghis Khan Unites the Mongols Around 1200, a Mongol clan leader named Temujin sought to unify the Mongols under his leadership. He fought and defeated his rivals one by one. In 1206, Temujin accepted the title **Genghis Khan**, (JEHNG•gihs-KAHN), or "universal ruler" of the Mongol clans.

Over the next 21 years, Genghis led the Mongols in conquering much of Asia. His first goal was China. After invading the northern Jin Empire in 1211, however, his attention turned to the Islamic region west of Mongolia. Angered by the murder of Mongol traders and an ambassador at the hands of the Muslims, Genghis launched a campaign of terror across Central Asia. The Mongols destroyed one city after another—Utrar, Samarkand, Bukhara—and slaughtered many inhabitants. By 1225, Central Asia was under Mongol control.

Genghis the Conqueror Several characteristics lay behind Genghis Khan's stunning success as a conqueror. First, he was a brilliant organizer. He assembled his Mongol warriors into a mighty fighting force. Following the model of the Chinese military, Genghis grouped his warriors in armies of 10,000. These in turn were organized into 1,000-man brigades, 100-man companies, and 10-man squads. He put his most battle-proven and loyal men in command of these units.

Second, Genghis was a gifted strategist. He used various tricks to confuse his enemy. Sometimes, a small Mongol cavalry unit would attack, then pretend to gallop away in flight. The enemy usually gave chase. Then the rest of the Mongol army would appear suddenly and slaughter the surprised enemy forces.

Finally, Genghis Khan used cruelty as a weapon. He believed in terrifying his enemies into surrender. If a city refused to open its gates to him, he might kill the entire population when he finally captured the place. The terror the Mongols inspired spread ahead of their armies, which led many towns to surrender without a fight. As one Arab historian wrote, "In the countries that have not yet been overrun by them, everyone spends the night afraid that they may appear there too."

Reading Check
Summarize
What were some of the tactics Genghis Khan used in war?

— BIOGRAPHY —

Genghis Khan
1162?–1227

Temujin, according to legend, was born with a blood clot in his fist. In his lifetime, his hands were often covered with the blood of others.

When Temujin was about nine, the Tatars, a rival people, poisoned his father. For a time, he and his family lived in extreme poverty, abandoned by their clan. When in manhood he fought and defeated the Tatars, he slaughtered every male taller than a cart axle.

While driven by revenge, Genghis also loved conquest. He once remarked to his personal historian:

Man's greatest good fortune is to chase and defeat his enemy, seize his total possessions, leave his married women weeping and wailing, [and] ride his [horse].

The Mongol Empire, 1294

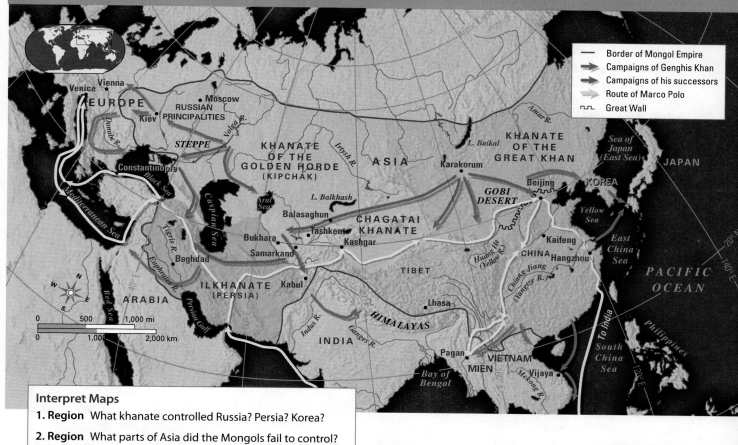

Legend:
- Border of Mongol Empire
- Campaigns of Genghis Khan
- Campaigns of his successors
- Route of Marco Polo
- Great Wall

Interpret Maps

1. **Region** What khanate controlled Russia? Persia? Korea?

2. **Region** What parts of Asia did the Mongols fail to control?

The Mongol Empire

Genghis Khan died in 1227—not from violence, but from illness. His successors continued to expand his empire. In less than 50 years, the Mongols conquered territory from China to Poland. In so doing, they created the largest unified land empire in history.

The Khanates After Genghis's death, his sons and grandsons continued the campaign of conquest. Armies under their leadership drove south, east, and west out of inner Asia. They completed their conquest of northern China and invaded Korea. They leveled the Russian city of Kiev and reached the banks of the Adriatic Sea. The cities of Venice and Vienna were within their grasp. However, in the 1250s the Mongols halted their westward campaign and turned their attention to Persia. By 1260, the Mongols had divided their huge empire into four regions, or khanates. These were the Khanate of the Great Khan (Mongolia and China), the Khanate of Chagatai (Central Asia), the Ilkhanate (Persia), and the Khanate of the Golden Horde (Russia). A descendant of Genghis ruled each khanate.

A Mighty Fighting Force

Mongol soldiers were superb horsemen, having spent all their lives in the saddle. Annual game roundups gave young men the chance to practice skills they would use in battle and gave their leaders the opportunity to spot promising warriors. When on the move, each soldier was accompanied by three extra horses. By changing mounts, soldiers could stay in the saddle for up to ten days and nights at a time. When charging toward a target, they covered as much as 120 miles a day. If food was scarce, a Mongol soldier might make a small gash in the neck of one of his horses and sustain himself by drinking the blood.

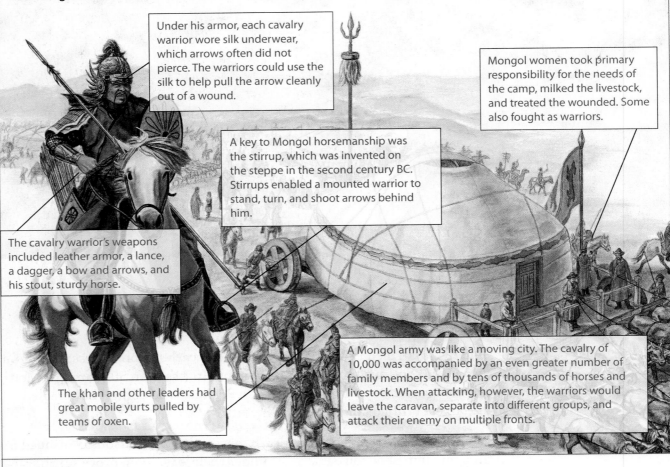

Under his armor, each cavalry warrior wore silk underwear, which arrows often did not pierce. The warriors could use the silk to help pull the arrow cleanly out of a wound.

Mongol women took primary responsibility for the needs of the camp, milked the livestock, and treated the wounded. Some also fought as warriors.

A key to Mongol horsemanship was the stirrup, which was invented on the steppe in the second century BC. Stirrups enabled a mounted warrior to stand, turn, and shoot arrows behind him.

The cavalry warrior's weapons included leather armor, a lance, a dagger, a bow and arrows, and his stout, sturdy horse.

The khan and other leaders had great mobile yurts pulled by teams of oxen.

A Mongol army was like a moving city. The cavalry of 10,000 was accompanied by an even greater number of family members and by tens of thousands of horses and livestock. When attacking, however, the warriors would leave the caravan, separate into different groups, and attack their enemy on multiple fronts.

Analyze Visuals
Name at least three things that allowed the Mongol army to be self-sufficient.

The Mongols as Rulers Many of the areas invaded by the Mongols never recovered. The populations of some cities were wiped out. In addition, the Mongols destroyed ancient irrigation systems in areas such as the Tigris and Euphrates valleys. Thus, the land could no longer support resettlement. While ferocious in war, the Mongols were quite tolerant in peace. They rarely imposed their beliefs or way of life on those they conquered. Over time, some Mongol rulers even adopted aspects of the culture of the people they ruled. The Ilkhans and the Golden Horde, for example, became Muslims. Growing cultural differences among the khanates contributed to the eventual splitting up of the empire.

The Mongol Peace From the mid-1200s to the mid-1300s, the Mongols imposed stability and law and order across much of Eurasia. This period is sometimes called the **Pax Mongolica**, or Mongol Peace. The Mongols guaranteed safe passage for trade caravans, travelers, and missionaries from one end of the empire to another.

Trade between Europe and Asia had never been more active. Ideas and inventions traveled along with the trade goods. Many Chinese innovations, such as gunpowder, reached Europe during this period.

Other things spread along with the goods and the ideas. Some historians speculate that the epidemic of bubonic plague that devastated Europe during the 1300s was first spread by the Mongols. The disease might have traveled along trade routes or have been passed to others by infected Mongol troops.

For a brief period of history, the nomadic Mongols were the lords of city-based civilizations across Asia, including China.

Reading Check
Summarize
What happened to the Mongol Empire after Genghis Khan's death?

Kublai Khan Becomes Emperor

Kublai Khan, the grandson of Genghis Khan, assumed the title Great Khan in 1260. In theory, the Great Khan ruled the entire Mongol Empire. In reality, the empire had split into four khanates. Other descendants of Genghis ruled Central Asia, Persia, and Russia as semi-independent states. So, Kublai focused instead on extending the power and range of his own khanate, which already included Mongolia, Korea, Tibet, and northern China. To begin, however, he had to fulfill the goal of his grandfather to conquer all of China.

The Chinese held off Kublai's attacks for several years. However, his armies finally overwhelmed them in 1279. Throughout China's long history, the Chinese feared and fought off invasions by northern nomads. China sometimes lost territory to nomadic groups, but no foreigner had ever ruled the whole country. With Kublai's victory, that changed.

Beginning a New Dynasty As China's new emperor, Kublai Khan founded a new dynasty called the Yuan (yoo•AHN) Dynasty. It lasted less than a century, until 1368, when it was overthrown. However, the Yuan era was an important period in Chinese history for several reasons. First, Kublai Khan united China for the first time in more than 300 years. For this he is considered one of China's great emperors. Second, the control imposed by the Mongols across all of Asia opened China to greater foreign contacts and trade. Finally, Kublai and his successors tolerated Chinese culture and made few changes to the system of government.

Unlike his Mongol ancestors, Kublai abandoned the Mongolian steppes for China. He did not share his ancestors' dislike of the settled life. On the contrary, he rather enjoyed living in the luxurious manner of a Chinese emperor. He maintained a beautiful summer palace at Shangdu, on the border between Mongolia and China. He also built a new square-walled capital at the site of modern Beijing. Kublai built this palace to enhance his

This porcelain object is known as a moon flask for its round shape. During the Yuan Dynasty, China produced delicate porcelains with elaborate painted decorations such as this.

prestige, but his new capital meant something more. Previously, the Great Khans had ruled their empire from Mongolia. Moving the capital from Mongolia to China was a sign that Kublai intended to make his mark as emperor of China.

Failure to Conquer Japan After conquering China, Kublai Khan tried to extend his rule to Japan. In 1274 and again in 1281, the Great Khan sent huge fleets against Japan. The Mongols forced Koreans to build, sail, and provide provisions for the boats, a costly task that almost ruined Korea. Both times the Japanese turned back the Mongol fleets.

The second fleet carried 150,000 Mongol, Chinese, and Korean warriors—the largest seaborne invasion force in history until World War II. After 53 days, Japanese warriors had fought the invaders to a standstill. Then, on the following day, the sky darkened and a typhoon swept furiously across the Sea of Japan. Mongol ships were upended, swamped, and dashed to bits against the rocky shore, despite their sailors' attempts to escape onto the open sea. For centuries afterward, the Japanese spoke reverently of the *kamikaze*, or "divine wind," that had saved Japan.

Mongol Rule in China

Early in Kublai Khan's reign, one of his Chinese advisers told him, "I have heard that one can conquer the empire on horseback, but one cannot govern it on horseback." This advice illustrates the problems Kublai faced as emperor. Mongol ways would not work in a sophisticated civilization like China's. Besides, the number of Mongols in China was small compared to the huge native population. Kublai would need to make use of non-Mongol officials to help him rule successfully.

The Mongols and the Chinese The Mongol rulers had little in common with their Chinese subjects. Because of their differences, the Mongols kept a separate identity. Mongols lived apart from the Chinese and obeyed different laws. They kept the Chinese out of high government offices, although they retained as many Chinese officials as possible to serve on the local level. Most of the highest government posts went to Mongols or to foreigners. The Mongols believed that foreigners were more trustworthy since they had no local loyalties.

Despite his differences with the Chinese, Kublai Khan was an able leader. He restored the Grand Canal and extended it 135 miles north to Beijing. Along its banks he built a paved highway that ran some 1,100 miles, from Hangzhou to Beijing. These land and water routes ensured the north a steady supply of grain and other goods from the southern heartland.

Foreign Trade Foreign trade increased under Kublai Khan. This was largely due to the Mongol Peace, which made the caravan routes across Central Asia safe for trade and travel. Traders transported Chinese silk and porcelain, which were greatly valued in Europe and western Asia, over

Reading Check
Evaluate Why was the Yuan Dynasty a significant period in Chinese history?

Kublai Khan
(1215–1294)

As ruler of both China and the Mongol Empire, Kublai Khan straddled two worlds. He built luxurious palaces, dressed as a Chinese emperor, and supported the work of Chinese artists. However, he remained a Mongol warrior at heart. The Great Khan is said to have planted a plot of grass from the steppe in the gardens at Beijing to remind himself of his home. He also loved to hunt and enclosed a large hunting ground at his palace at Shangdu.

Marco Polo
(1254–1324)

The man who described Kublai Khan to Europeans left behind very little information about himself. According to Polo, Kublai recognized his "merit and worth" and sent him on special missions around the empire. His impressions of China became the basis of his book, but he described few actual events about his life.

Since his book first appeared, people have debated whether Polo even visited China. He is not mentioned in Chinese accounts of this time. His tales also fail to mention such common features of China as tea, acupuncture, or foot binding. On his deathbed, Polo was asked if his travel stories were true. He replied that he had told barely half of what he had seen.

the Silk Roads and other routes. These traders also carried with them such Chinese products and inventions as printing, gunpowder, the compass, paper currency, and playing cards.

Kublai further encouraged trade by inviting foreign merchants to visit China. Most of them were Muslims from India, Central Asia, and Persia. Many European traders and travelers, including Christian missionaries, also reached China.

Marco Polo at the Mongol Court The most famous European to visit China in these years was a young Venetian trader, **Marco Polo**. He traveled by caravan on the Silk Roads with his father and uncle, arriving at Kublai Khan's court around 1275. Polo had learned several Asian languages in his travels, and Kublai Khan sent him to various Chinese cities on government missions. Polo served the Great Khan well for 17 years. In 1292, the Polos left China and made the long journey back to Venice.

Later, during a war against Venice's rival city, Genoa, Marco Polo was captured and imprisoned. In prison he had time to tell the full story of his travels and adventures. To his awed listeners, he spoke of China's fabulous cities, its fantastic wealth, and the strange things he had seen there.

Dynasties of China, 500–1400

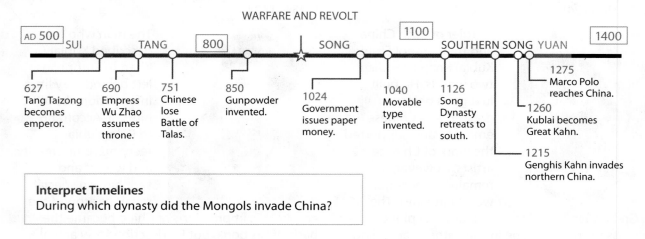

WARFARE AND REVOLT

| AD 500 | | 800 | | 1100 | | 1400 |

SUI — TANG — SONG — SOUTHERN SONG YUAN

627 Tang Taizong becomes emperor.

690 Empress Wu Zhao assumes throne.

751 Chinese lose Battle of Talas.

850 Gunpowder invented.

1024 Government issues paper money.

1040 Movable type invented.

1126 Song Dynasty retreats to south.

1275 Marco Polo reaches China.

1260 Kublai becomes Great Kahn.

1215 Genghis Kahn invades northern China.

Interpret Timelines
During which dynasty did the Mongols invade China?

He mentioned the burning of "black stones" (coal) in Chinese homes. (Coal as a fuel was little known in Europe.) He also recorded the practical workings of Kublai's government and aspects of Chinese life. Here is his description of trade in Beijing:

> "[M]ore precious and costly wares are imported into Khan-balik [Beijing] than into any other city in the world. . . . All the treasures that come from India—precious stones, pearls, and other rarities— are brought here. So too are the choicest and costliest products of Cathay [China] itself and every other province."
>
> —Marco Polo, *The Travels of Marco Polo*

A fellow prisoner gathered Polo's stories into a book. It was an instant success in Europe, but most readers did not believe a word of it. They thought Polo's account was a marvelous collection of tall tales. It was clear to Marco Polo, however, that the civilization he had visited was the greatest in the world.

The End of Mongol Rule

During the last years of Kublai Khan's reign, weaknesses began to appear in Mongol rule. In an attempt to further expand his empire, Kublai sent several expeditions into Southeast Asia. His armies and navies suffered many humiliating defeats at a huge expense of lives and equipment. Heavy spending on fruitless wars, on public works, and on the luxuries of the Yuan court burdened the treasury and created resentment among the over-taxed Chinese. This presented problems that Kublai's less able successors could not resolve.

Yuan Dynasty Overthrown Kublai Khan died in 1294. After his death, the Yuan Dynasty began to fade. Family members continually argued over who would rule. In one eight-year period, four different khans took the throne.

Reading Check
Make Inferences
How might the Chinese have felt about their lack of power in Kublai's government?

Rebellions broke out in many parts of China in the 1300s. The Chinese had long resented their Mongol rulers, and the Mongol humiliation of the Chinese only increased under Kublai Khan's successors. The rebellions were also fueled by years of famine, flood, and disease, along with growing economic problems and official corruption. In 1368, Chinese rebels finally overthrew the Mongols. The rebel leader founded a new dynasty, the Ming, which lasted until 1644.

Decline of the Mongol Empire By the time of the collapse of the Yuan Dynasty, the entire Mongol Empire had disintegrated. The government of the Ilkhanate in Persia fell apart in the 1330s. The Chagatai khans ruled Central Asia until the 1370s. Only the Golden Horde in Russia stayed in power. The Golden Horde ruled Russia for 250 years. Ivan III finally led Russia to independence from Mongol rule in 1480.

The rise and fall of Mongol rule affected civilizations from eastern Europe to China. In East Asia, the Mongols failed to conquer Japan, but they did gain control of Korea. Although Korea's ruling dynasty was not overthrown, it made peace with the Mongols under very harsh terms. You will read about this event and Korea's earlier relations with China in Lesson 3.

Reading Check
Analyze Causes
What factors contributed to the decline and fall of the Yuan Dynasty?

Lesson 2 Assessment

1. **Organize Information** Create a word web that shows key events in the life of Kublai Khan.

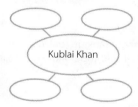

Which of the listed events do you think is the most important? Write a paragraph that explains why.

2. **Key Terms and People** For each key term or person in the lesson, write a sentence explaining its significance.

3. **Make Inferences** What characteristics of their culture do you think contributed to the Mongols' military success? Explain your response.

4. **Analyze Motives** What do you think drove Genghis Khan to conquer a great empire? Explain your answer.

5. **Evaluate Decisions** Judging from the events of the Yuan Dynasty, do you think the Mongol policies toward the Chinese were effective? Explain your answer.

6. **Analyze Effects** What impact did the Mongol Peace have on interaction between East and West?

7. **Form Opinions** Do you think that Kublai Khan was a successful ruler? Why or why not?

Korean Dynasties

The Big Idea

The Koreans adapted Chinese culture to fit their own needs but maintained a distinct way of life.

Why It Matters Now

Korea's interactions with China and Japan helped spread Buddhism and Confucianism, which remain important beliefs in East Asia today.

Key Terms and People

Silla Dynasty
Koryo Dynasty

Setting the Stage

According to a Korean legend, the first Korean state was founded by the hero Tan'gun, whose father was a god and whose mother was a bear. Another legend relates that it was founded by a royal descendant of the Chinese Shang Dynasty. These legends reflect two sides of Korean culture. On one hand, the Koreans were a distinct people who developed their own native traditions. On the other hand, their culture was shaped by Chinese influences from early dynastic times.

Tan'gun (or Dangun) is said to have founded Korea in Pyongyang in 2333 BC.

The Korean Peninsula

Korea lies between China and Japan. Because of its central location, Korea has been a bridge for the passage of people, culture, and ideas. Yet this location has also left Korea vulnerable to invasion, and both China and Japan have dominated it for periods of time.

Geography Korea is located on a peninsula that juts out from the Asian mainland toward Japan. It is about the same size as the state of Utah. Much of the peninsula is covered by mountains, which limits the amount of land for agriculture. The mountain ranges run north to south along the east coast. As a result, Korea's main population centers are in the west, where the land flattens into plains. Korea's climate is hot in the summer and very cold in the winter. The peninsula has a coastline more than 5,000 miles long, which helped the Koreans develop a long tradition of shipbuilding.

Early History The first Koreans were nomadic peoples from Northeast Asia. They formed clans or tribes that controlled different areas of the peninsula. China's Han Dynasty invaded the northern peninsula in 108 BC and established several colonies, one of which lasted four centuries. During this period, the Koreans adopted Confucianism and Buddhism as well as Chinese writing, political institutions, and agricultural methods. Korean travelers later spread Chinese culture and technology into Japan.

Reading Check
Make Inferences
Why did China have such a strong influence on Korea in its early history?

Silla and Koryo

During the period of Chinese colonization, Korean tribes began to gather together into federations. Eventually, these federations developed into three rival kingdoms: Koguryo in the north, Paekche in the southwest, and Silla in the southeast.

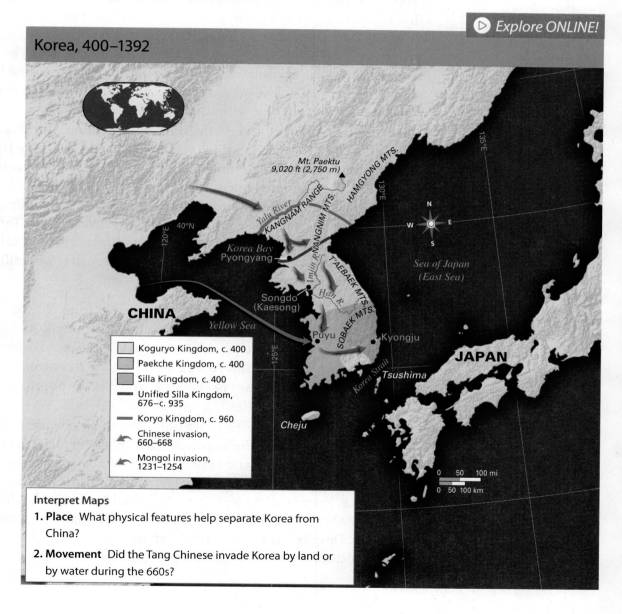

▷ Explore ONLINE!

Korea, 400–1392

Mt. Paektu
9,020 ft (2,750 m)

HAMGYONG MTS.

KANGNAM RANGE

NANGNIM MTS.

Yalu River

135°E

130°E

40°N

120°E

Korea Bay
Pyongyang

Imjin R.

T'AEBAEK MTS.

Sea of Japan
(East Sea)

Songdo
(Kaesong)

Han R.

CHINA

Yellow Sea

125°E

SOBAEK MTS.

Puyu

Kyongju

JAPAN

Korea Strait

Tsushima

Cheju

Legend:
- Koguryo Kingdom, c. 400
- Paekche Kingdom, c. 400
- Silla Kingdom, c. 400
- Unified Silla Kingdom, 676–c. 935
- Koryo Kingdom, c. 960
- Chinese invasion, 660–668
- Mongol invasion, 1231–1254

0   50   100 mi
0   50 100 km

Interpret Maps

1. **Place** What physical features help separate Korea from China?

2. **Movement** Did the Tang Chinese invade Korea by land or by water during the 660s?

Two Koreas

Since the end of World War II, Korea has been arbitrarily divided into two countries—communist North Korea and democratic South Korea. For years, many Koreans longed for their country to be reunited. Hopes for such a day rose in 2000 when the presidents of the two nations sat down to discuss reunification. In 2002, however, North Korea announced that it was developing nuclear weapons and would use them against South Korea if necessary. This greatly dimmed people's hopes for one Korea.

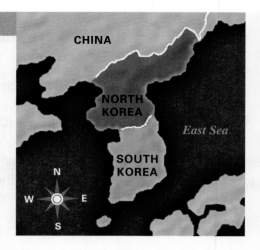

Silla's Unification of Korea In the mid-600s, the Silla defeated the other kingdoms with the help of China and then drove out the Chinese. For the first time, most of the Korean peninsula was unified as one state. The capital of the **Silla Dynasty** was Kyongju. Kyongju grew into a prosperous city with more than 175,000 households. Under the Silla, Koreans built impressive monasteries and royal tombs and created elegant stone and bronze sculptures. The economy was mainly agricultural, but Korean merchants conducted extensive trade with China and Japan.

Despite their conflict around the time of unification, the Silla established close ties with China, which was then ruled by the Tang Dynasty. The Silla made moderate payments of tribute in return for peaceful relations. Silla rulers adopted Buddhism as the official religion and also supported Confucian studies. Faced with the challenge of controlling a large territory, they tried to make some reforms modeled after the Tang government. In addition, Silla scholars developed a standard system for writing the Korean language with Chinese characters, though it was still difficult to use because the two languages are so different.

Rise and Fall of the Koryo Dynasty The Silla began to decline in the ninth century, mainly due to strife within the royal family and revolts over high taxes. In 918 a rebel officer named Wang Kon took over a region of Korea and founded the **Koryo Dynasty**. He gained control of the whole country around 935. The Koryo Dynasty, which is the origin of the name *Korea,* lasted until 1392.

Koryo's rulers continued to adopt Chinese ideas but worked to maintain distinct Korean features. For example, the dynasty modeled its central government after China's and established a civil service system. However, this system did not provide the social mobility for Koreans that it did for the Chinese. Koryo society was sharply divided between a landed aristocracy and the rest of the population, including the military, commoners, and slaves. Despite the examination system, the sons of nobles received the best positions, and these positions became hereditary.

The Koryo Dynasty faced a major threat in 1231, when the Mongols swept into Korea. The Korean government retreated to an island fortress in the Han River, where it held out for several decades before suing for peace. The Mongols demanded a crushing tribute, including 20,000 horses, clothing for a million soldiers, and many children and artisans, who were to be taken away as slaves. The harsh period of Mongol occupation lasted until the 1360s, when the Mongol Empire collapsed.

In 1392, a group of scholar-officials and military leaders overthrew the Koryo Dynasty and instituted land reforms. They established a new dynasty, called the Choson (or Yi) Dynasty, which would rule for 518 years.

Koryo Culture The Koryo period produced great achievements in Korean culture. Inspired by Song ceramic artists, Korean potters produced the much-admired celadon pottery, famous for its milky green glaze. Korean artisans produced one of the great treasures of the Buddhist world—many thousands of large wooden blocks for printing all the Buddhist scriptures. This set of blocks was destroyed by the Mongols, but the disaster sparked a national effort to re-create them. The more than 80,000 blocks in the new set remain in Korea today. In addition to wood-block printing, the Koreans experimented with movable type, creating the first printing system to use metal type.

Reading Check
Make Inferences
Why do you think the Koryo Dynasty fell in 1392 after surviving for so long during the brutal Mongol occupation?

Lesson 3 Assessment

1. **Organize Information** Create a timeline of the major events in Korea's early history.

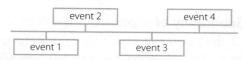

Which event was most important for the country's development? Explain.

2. **Key Terms and People** For each key term or person in the lesson, write a sentence explaining its significance.

3. **Analyze Effects** How did geography influence the history and culture of Korea? Illustrate your answer with examples.

4. **Form Opinions** How would you characterize the Tang Dynasty's behavior toward Korea?

5. **Compare and Contrast** What were some similarities and differences between the Silla and Koryo dynasties?

Feudal Powers in Japan

The Big Idea

Japanese civilization was shaped by cultural borrowing from China and the rise of feudalism and military rulers.

Why It Matters Now

An openness to adapting innovations from other cultures is still a hallmark of Japanese society.

Key Terms and People

Shinto
samurai
Bushido
shogun

Setting the Stage

Japan lies east of China, in the direction of the sunrise. In fact, the name Japan comes from the Chinese word *ri-ben*, which means "origin of the sun" or "land of the rising sun." From ancient times, Japan had borrowed ideas, institutions, and culture from the Chinese people. Japan's genius was its ability to take in new ideas and make them uniquely its own.

The Growth of Japanese Civilization

Japan's island location shaped the growth of its civilization. About 120 miles of water separates Japan from its closest neighbor, Korea, and 500 miles of water separates Japan from China. The Japanese were close enough to feel the civilizing effect of China. Yet they were far enough away to be reasonably safe from invasion.

Mount Fuji, Japan's tallest mountain, is a sacred site in the Shinto religion. Many Shinto shrines are located on the mountain's base and slopes.

The Geography of Japan About 4,000 islands make up the Japanese archipelago (ahr•kuh•PEHL•uh•goh), or island group, which extends in an arc more than 1,200 miles long. Historically, most Japanese people have lived on the four largest islands: Hokkaido (hah•KY•doh), Honshu (HAHN•shoo), Shikoku (shee•KAW•koo), and Kyushu (kee•OO•shoo).

Japan's geography has both advantages and disadvantages. With its easy access to the sea, Japan has historically relied on fishing as an important industry and food source. Southern Japan enjoys a mild climate with plenty of rainfall, which aids the cultivation of its most important crop, rice. The country is so mountainous, however, that only about 12 percent of the land is suitable for farming. This scarcity of farmland has sometimes led to internal conflict. Natural resources such as coal, oil, and iron are also in short supply. During the late summer and early fall, strong tropical storms called typhoons occur. Earthquakes and tidal waves are additional threats.

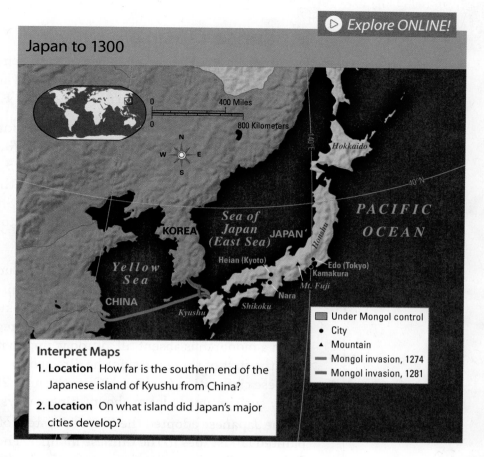

Japan to 1300

Interpret Maps

1. **Location** How far is the southern end of the Japanese island of Kyushu from China?

2. **Location** On what island did Japan's major cities develop?

Early Japan The first historic mention of Japan comes from Chinese writings of the first century BC. Japan at this time was not a united country. Instead, hundreds of clans controlled their own territories. Each clan worshiped its own nature gods and goddesses. In different parts of Japan, people honored thousands of local gods. Their varied customs and beliefs eventually combined to form Japan's earliest religion. In later times, this religion was called **Shinto** (SHIHN•toh), meaning "way of the gods."

Shinto was based on respect for the forces of nature and on the worship of ancestors. Shinto worshipers believed in *kami*, divine spirits that dwelled in nature. Any unusual or especially beautiful tree, rock, waterfall, or mountain was considered the home of a *kami*.

The Yamato Emperors By the AD 400s, the Yamato clan had established itself as the leading clan. The Yamato claimed to be descended from the sun goddess Amaterasu. By the seventh century, the Yamato chiefs called themselves the emperors of Japan. The early emperors did not control the entire country, or even much of it, but the Japanese gradually accepted the idea of an emperor.

Although many of the Yamato rulers lacked real power, the dynasty was never overthrown. When rival clans fought for power, the winning clan claimed control of the emperor and then ruled in the emperor's name. Japan had both an emperor who served as a figurehead and a ruling power who reigned behind the throne. This dual structure became an enduring characteristic of Japanese government.

Reading Check
Summarize
What are the main features of the Shinto religion?

Japanese Culture

During the 400s, the Japanese began to have more and more contact with mainland Asia. They soon came under the influence of Chinese ideas and customs, which they first learned about from Korean travelers.

Buddhism in Japan One of the most important influences brought by Korean travelers was Buddhism. In the mid-700s, the Japanese imperial court officially accepted Buddhism in Japan. By the eighth or ninth century, Buddhist ideas and worship had spread through Japanese society. The Japanese, however, did not give up their Shinto beliefs. Some Buddhist rituals became Shinto rituals, and some Shinto gods and goddesses were worshiped in Buddhist temples.

Cultural Borrowing from China Interest in Buddhist ideas at the Japanese court soon grew into an enthusiasm for all things Chinese. The most influential convert to Buddhism was Prince Shotoku (shoh•toh•ku), who served as regent for his aunt, the empress Suiko. (A regent is someone who rules when a monarch is absent, ill, or too young to rule.) In 607, Prince Shotoku sent the first of three missions he directed to China. His people studied Chinese civilization firsthand. Over the next 200 years, the Japanese sent many such groups to learn about Chinese ways.

The Japanese adopted the Chinese system of writing. Japanese artists painted landscapes in the Chinese manner. The Japanese also followed Chinese styles in the simple arts of everyday living, such as cooking, gardening, drinking tea, and hairdressing. This cultural borrowing led to an increase in trade between China and Japan, with Chinese ships bringing manufactured goods such as textiles and porcelain to Japanese ports.

For a time, Japan even modeled its government on China's. Prince Shotoku planned a strong central government like that of the Tang rulers. He also tried to introduce China's civil-service system. However, this attempt failed. In Japan, noble birth remained the key to winning a powerful position. Unlike China, Japan continued to be a country where a few great families held power.

The Japanese adapted Chinese ways to suit their own needs. While they learned much, they still retained their own traditions. Eventually, the Japanese imperial court decided it had learned enough from Tang China. In the late ninth century, it ended formal missions to the Tang Empire, which had fallen into decline. Although Chinese cultural influence would remain strong in Japan, Japan's own culture was about to bloom.

Reading Check
Synthesize
How did Chinese culture spread to Japan?

Life in the Heian Period

In the late 700s, the imperial court moved its capital from Nara to Heian (HAY•ahn), the modern Kyoto (kee•OH•toh). Many of Japan's noble families also moved to Heian. Among the upper class in Heian, a highly refined court society arose. This era in Japanese history, from 794 to 1185, is called the Heian period.

Gentlemen and ladies of the court filled their days with elaborate ritual and artistic pursuits. Rules dictated every aspect of court life—the length

Vocabulary
etiquette the code governing correct behavior and appearance

of swords, the color of official robes, forms of address, even the number of skirts a woman wore. Etiquette was also extremely important. Laughing aloud in public, for example, was frowned upon. And everyone at court was expected to write poetry and to paint.

The best accounts of Heian society come from the diaries, essays, and novels written by the women of the court. One of the finest writers of the period was Lady Murasaki Shikibu. Lady Murasaki's 11th-century masterpiece, *The Tale of Genji*, is an account of the life of a prince in the imperial court. This long prose narrative is widely considered the world's first novel.

This detail from *The Tale of the Genji* picture scroll—an illustrated version of the story— shows women at the Heian court grooming their hair and reading.

Reading Check
Summarize
What was life like at the Heian court?

Feudalism Erodes Imperial Authority

During the Heian period, Japan's central government was relatively strong. However, this strength was soon to be challenged by great landowners and clan chiefs who acted more and more as independent local rulers.

Decline of Central Power For most of the Heian period, the rich Fujiwara family held the real power in Japan. By about the middle of the 11th century, however, the power of the central government and the Fujiwaras began to slip.

Large landowners living away from the capital set up private armies. The countryside became lawless and dangerous. Armed soldiers on horseback preyed on farmers and travelers, and pirates took control of the seas. For safety, farmers and small landowners traded parts of their land to strong warlords in exchange for protection. As they acquired more land, the lords increased their power. This marked the beginning of a feudal system of localized rule like that of ancient China and medieval Europe.

Samurai Warriors Since wars between rival lords were commonplace, each lord surrounded himself with a bodyguard of loyal warriors called **samurai** (SAM•uh•ry). (*Samurai* means "one who serves.") Samurai lived according to a demanding code of behavior called **Bushido** (BUSH•ih•doh), or "the way of the warrior." A samurai was expected to show reckless courage, reverence for the gods, fairness, and generosity toward those weaker than himself. Dying an honorable death was judged more important than living a long life.

Japanese Samurai

Samurai were members of Japan's warrior class. Early samurai protected local aristocratic landowners. In the late 1100s, however, the warrior class secured national power and dominated Japanese government until 1868.

Samurai warriors followed an unwritten code that emphasized honor, bravery, and loyalty. This code came to be known as Bushido. Their reputation as fearsome warriors has become legendary.

FEMALE SAMURAI
Samurai were not always men. Here, Lady Tomoe Gozen, a famous female warrior of the 1180s, enters bravely into battle.

Helmets were made from iron plates to repel sword blows.

An iron mask was sometimes worn not only to protect the face, but to frighten the samurai's enemy as well.

Samurai swords were made by skilled artisans. The curvature of the blade makes the weapon more effective when slashing.

Individual iron plates provided protection and freedom of movement when in combat. As you can see, a samurai's armor was often richly decorated.

SAMURAI WARRIOR
In combat, a samurai's life depended on his skill and his equipment. Here you can see how the samurai's weapons and armor aided him or her in battle.

Analyze Visuals

1. **Compare and Contrast** What are some similarities or differences between Japanese samurai and European knights?

2. **Hypothesize** How might the code of the samurai have helped them in battle?

Japanese scholar

Reading Check
Summarize
What features defined Japan's feudal warrior society?

The Kamakura Shogunate During the late 1100s, Japan's two most powerful clans fought for power. After almost 30 years of war, the Minamoto family emerged victorious. In 1192, the emperor gave a Minamoto leader named Yoritomo the title of **shogun**, or "supreme general of the emperor's army." In effect, the shogun had the powers of a military dictator.

Following tradition, the emperor still reigned from Kyoto. (Kyoto was rebuilt on the ruins of Heian, which had been destroyed in war.) However, the real center of power was at the shogun's military headquarters at Kamakura (kahm·uh·KUR·uh). The 1200s are known in Japanese history as the Kamakura shogunate. The pattern of government in which shoguns ruled through puppet emperors lasted in Japan until 1868.

Although the Kamakura shogunate brought greater stability to Japan, it did not end conflict over the country's limited farmland. Disputes often arose because lords wanted to increase their land holdings at the expense of farmers and traditional landlords. The shoguns assigned a judicial board to issue rulings in such cases.

The Kamakura shoguns were strong enough to turn back the two naval invasions sent by the great Mongol ruler Kublai Khan in 1274 and 1281. However, the Japanese victory over the Mongols drained the shoguns' treasury. Loyal samurai were bitter when the government failed to pay them. The Kamakura shoguns lost prestige and power. Samurai attached themselves more closely to their local lords, who soon fought one another as fiercely as they had fought the Mongols.

Although feudal Japan no longer courted contact with China, it would continue to absorb Chinese ideas and shape them into the Japanese way. As you will read in Lesson 5, China's culture also influenced the kingdoms of Southeast Asia.

Lesson 4 Assessment

1. **Organize Information** Create a timeline of the major events in Japan's early history.

event 1 · event 2 · event 3 · event 4

What event would you consider the most important turning point in Japan's early history? Why?

2. **Key Terms and People** For each key term or person in the lesson, write a sentence explaining its significance.

3. **Analyze Effects** In what ways has Japan's geography affected its economy and society?

4. **Form Opinions** "The Japanese selectively borrowed from Chinese culture." Use information from the text to support this statement.

5. **Draw Conclusions** Why do you think the shoguns chose to rule through puppet emperors rather than simply seizing the imperial throne themselves?

6. **Evaluate** Was the rise of the shogun beneficial for Japan overall? Explain.

Kingdoms of Southeast Asia

The Big Idea

Several smaller kingdoms prospered in Southeast Asia, a region culturally influenced by China and India.

Why It Matters Now

The cultures of China and India still influence Southeast Asia today.

Key Terms and People

Pagan
Khmer Empire
Angkor Wat

Setting the Stage

To the south of China lies the region called Southeast Asia. It includes the modern countries of Myanmar (Burma), Laos, Cambodia, Vietnam, Malaysia, Indonesia, Thailand, Singapore, Brunei, and the Philippines. In the shadow of powerful China and India, many small but prosperous kingdoms rose and fell in Southeast Asia.

Influences on Southeast Asia

In Southeast Asia's river valleys and deltas and on its islands, many kingdoms had centuries of glory and left monuments of lasting beauty. The region is located between India and China. These two powerful neighbors shaped the development of societies in the region. Geography and trade were also important influences.

Geography Southeast Asia lies between the Indian and Pacific oceans and stretches from Asia almost to Australia. It consists of two main parts: (1) Indochina, the mainland peninsula that borders China to the north and India to the west, and (2) the islands, the largest of which include Sumatra, Borneo, and Java. All of Southeast Asia lies within the warm, humid tropics. Monsoon winds bring the region heavy seasonal rains.

Seas and straits separate the islands of Southeast Asia. On the mainland, five great rivers flow from the north and cut valleys to the sea. Between the valleys rise hills and mountains, making travel and communication difficult. Over time, many different peoples settled the region, so it was home to many cultures.

Trade Throughout Southeast Asia's history, the key to political power often has been control of trade routes and harbors. This is because Southeast Asia contains the most direct sea route between the Indian Ocean and the South China Sea. Two important waterways connect the two seas: the Strait of

Malacca, between the Malay Peninsula and Sumatra, and the Sunda Strait, between Sumatra and Java.

Monsoon winds, which blow northeast in summer and southwest in winter, shaped trade in Southeast Asia. Ships relied on the monsoons to sail from place to place. Once in port, ships often had to wait until the winds shifted to resume their voyage. As a result, many Southeast Asian port cities became important economic centers.

India and China Indian merchant ships, taking advantage of the monsoon winds, began arriving in Southeast Asia by the first century AD. In the period that followed, Hindu and Buddhist missionaries spread their faiths to the region. In time, kingdoms arose that followed these religions and were modeled on Indian political ideas. Gradually, Indian influence shaped many aspects of the region's culture. This early Indian influence on Southeast Asia is evident today in the region's religions, languages, and art forms.

Eventually, Indian Muslims brought Islam to Southeast Asia as well. In the early 11th century, Muslims gained control of much of northern India. Islam gradually spread into the Malay Peninsula and nearby islands through contact between Indian Muslim traders and residents of port towns. Muslim missionaries sometimes traveled with the traders and helped win converts. As a result, Islamic states formed in Sumatra, the Malay Peninsula, Borneo, and the Philippines. The spread of Islam had a lasting impact on Southeast Asia. About 40 percent of the region's population now practices Islam, and Indonesia is the most populous Muslim nation in the world.

Chinese ideas and culture spread southward in the region through migration and trade. At different times, the Chinese also exerted political influence over parts of mainland Southeast Asia, either through direct rule or by demanding tribute from local rulers.

Reading Check
Summarize
How did trade influence Southeast Asia?

Early Kingdoms and Empires

Several early kingdoms and empires arose across Southeast Asia. Although most of them were small, a few became quite powerful. As in Korea and Japan, the early kingdoms blended outside influences with their own traditions to create unique societies and cultures.

The Pagan Kingdom In the mid-800s a people called the Burmans established the kingdom of **Pagan** (puh·GAHN) in what is now Myanmar (Burma). The kingdom was located in the fertile Irrawaddy River valley, which was ideal for rice farming. Pagan's first great king was Anawrahta, who ruled from 1044 to 1077. King Anawrahta began to conquer the surrounding areas and by 1057 had united much of what is now Myanmar under his rule. His conquests provided Pagan with access to trading ports, and the kingdom prospered.

Anawrahta and his successors supported Theravada Buddhism, a sect that strictly follows the Buddha's original teachings. They built thousands of magnificent temples, and Pagan became a center of Buddhist learning.

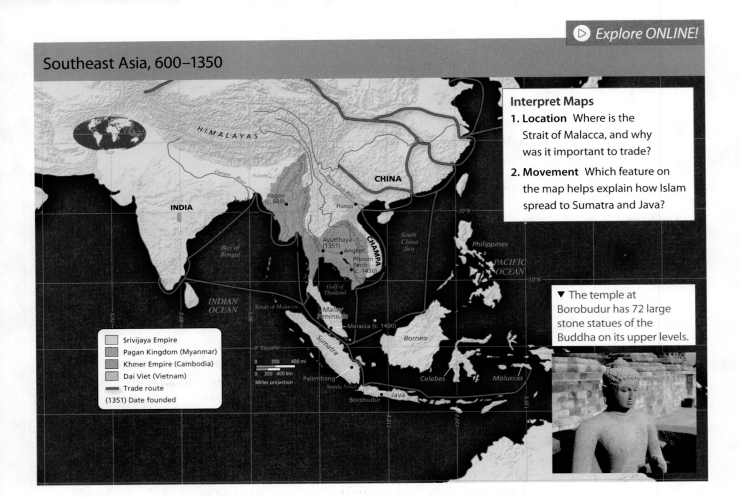

Explore ONLINE!

Interpret Maps

1. **Location** Where is the Strait of Malacca, and why was it important to trade?

2. **Movement** Which feature on the map helps explain how Islam spread to Sumatra and Java?

Srivijaya Empire
Pagan Kingdom (Myanmar)
Khmer Empire (Cambodia)
Dai Viet (Vietnam)
Trade route
(1351) Date founded

▼ The temple at Borobudur has 72 large stone statues of the Buddha on its upper levels.

The Venetian traveler Marco Polo, who visited the Mongol court in China, even mentioned the splendor of Pagan.

In the late 1200s the Mongols under the rule of Kublai Khan demanded tribute from Pagan. The king of Pagan refused and attacked the Mongols, who crushed the Pagan army. After the Pagan king fled southward, one of his sons killed him and then agreed to pay the tribute to the Mongols. Pagan survived but lost its power. Nonetheless, the people of Myanmar consider Pagan their classical age because Pagan culture established principles that continue to influence their religion and society.

The Khmer Empire The **Khmer** (kmair) **Empire**, in what is now Cambodia, was for centuries the main power on the Southeast Asian mainland. By the 800s, the Khmer had conquered neighboring kingdoms and created an empire. This empire reached the peak of its power around 1200.

Improved rice cultivation helped the Khmer become prosperous. The Khmer built elaborate irrigation systems and waterways. These advances made it possible to grow three or four crops of rice a year in an area that had previously produced only one.

At their capital, Angkor, Khmer rulers built extensive city-and-temple complexes. One of these, called **Angkor Wat**, is among the world's greatest architectural achievements. The complex, which covers nearly a square mile, was built as a symbolic mountain dedicated to the Hindu god Vishnu. The Khmer also used it as an observatory.

Island Trading Kingdoms Powerful kingdoms also developed on Southeast Asia's islands. For example, a dynasty called Sailendra ruled an agricultural kingdom on the island of Java. The Sailendra kings left behind another of the world's great architectural monuments, the Buddhist temple at Borobudur. Built around 800, this temple—like Angkor Wat—reflects strong Indian influence. The massive complex has nine terraced levels like a stepped pyramid.

The Sailendra Dynasty eventually fell under the domination of the powerful island empire of Srivijaya. At its height from the 7th to the 13th centuries, Srivijaya ruled the Strait of Malacca and other waters around the islands of Sumatra, Borneo, and Java. It grew wealthy by taxing the trade that passed through its waters. The Srivijayas established their capital, Palembang, on Sumatra. Palembang became a great center of Buddhist learning, where Chinese monks could study instead of traveling to India.

Dai Viet The people of Southeast Asia least influenced by India were the Vietnamese. Located in the coastal region just south of China, Vietnam fell under Chinese domination. Around 100 BC, during the mighty Han Dynasty, China took northern Vietnam. When China's Tang Dynasty weakened in the early AD 900s, Vietnam managed to break away. It became an independent kingdom, known as Dai Viet, in 939.

The Vietnamese absorbed many Chinese cultural influences, including Buddhism and ideas about government. However, they also preserved a strong spirit of independence and kept their own cultural identity. Vietnamese women, for example, traditionally had more freedom and influence than their Chinese counterparts.

Rulers of the Ly Dynasty (1009–1225) located their capital at Hanoi, on the Red River delta. They established a strong central government, encouraged agriculture and trade, and greatly improved road and river transportation. The changes made by the Ly continued to influence life in Vietnam long after they fell from power.

Reading Check
Analyze Effects
How was Vietnam's culture influenced by Chinese culture?

Lesson 5 Assessment

1. **Organize Information** What common themes do you notice about the mainland kingdoms? About the island kingdoms?

Kingdom	Notes
Pagan	
Khmer	
Dai Viet	
Sailendra	
Srivijaya	

2. **Key Terms and People** For each key term or person in the lesson, write a sentence explaining its significance.

3. **Recognize Effects** How did geography influence the history and culture of Southeast Asia? Illustrate your answer with examples.

4. **Compare** In what ways were the Pagan Kingdom and the Srivijaya Empire similar?

5. **Draw Conclusions** Why do you think that of all the cultures of Southeast Asia, Vietnam was the least influenced by India?

Module 9 Assessment

Key Terms and People

For each term or name below, write a sentence explaining its connection to East Asia between 600 and 1350.

1. Tang Taizong
2. Wu Zhao
3. Genghis Khan
4. Kublai Khan
5. Marco Polo
6. Silla Dynasty
7. Koryo Dynasty
8. Shinto
9. samurai
10. Angkor Wat

Main Ideas

Use your notes and the information in the module to answer the following questions.

Tang and Song China

1. Why was the reform of the civil service under the Tang so significant?
2. What were the effects of the taxation policies under the Sui and Tang dynasties?
3. How did changes in agriculture support other developments during the Song Dynasty?
4. What policies of the Song Dynasty contributed to the growth of Confucianism?

The Mongols

5. Why were nomads and settled peoples sometimes in conflict?
6. What were the positive and negative consequences of the creation of the Mongol Empire through conquest?
7. Describe how Kublai Khan treated his Chinese subjects.
8. How did Kublai Khan encourage trade?

Korean Dynasties

9. How did the nearness of Korea to China affect the development of Korean culture?
10. What were the major accomplishments of the Koryo Dynasty?

Feudal Powers in Japan

11. Describe the impact of Chinese culture on Japan.
12. How did feudalism develop in Japan?

Kingdoms of Southeast Asia

13. Describe the two sources of prosperity for Southeast Asian empires.
14. Why was control of the waterways of Southeast Asia important?

Module 9 Assessment, continued

Critical Thinking

1. **Analyze Effects** In diagrams like the one shown, identify two results from each of these developments: (a) completion of the Grand Canal under the Sui, and (b) use of the compass at sea.

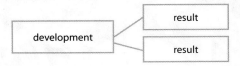

2. **Hypothesize** How might history have been different if the Mongols had conquered all or most of Europe? Discuss the possible immediate and long-term consequences for Europe and the rest of the Mongol Empire.

3. **Identify Problems and Solutions** This chapter describes the rise and fall of three Chinese dynasties. What recurring patterns appear in the decline of these dynasties? What advice, based on those patterns, might you give a Chinese emperor?

4. **Draw Conclusions** How does Japanese adaptation of Buddhism illustrate the process of selective cultural borrowing?

Engage with History

In the feature Tang and Song China: People and Technology, you read about important inventions developed during these two dynasties. Now that you have read the module, consider the impact of Chinese inventions and how they spread. If you were a European visitor to China during this period and could choose one invention to take back to your own society, which would you choose? Consider the following questions:

- Which invention would most improve the quality of life?
- Which might be the most profitable?
- What benefits and drawbacks might there be to introducing the invention into your society?

Discuss these questions with a small group.

Focus on Writing

Write a report on the Japanese religion of Shinto. Illustrate your report with photographs and sketches. In your report, consider the following:

- essential Shinto beliefs
- development of Shinto, especially the influence of Buddhism and Confucianism
- Shinto rituals and shrines

Multimedia Activity

Creating a Comparison Table

Use the Internet to learn how Chinese and Western doctors treat a variety of common illnesses and how long these treatments have been common practice. You may want to include the following illnesses in your research:

- the common cold
- influenza
- asthma
- arthritis

Create a table comparing Chinese and Western treatments for these illnesses. Display the table online or in the classroom.

Japan and the Samurai Warrior

For over a thousand years, the samurai—an elite warrior class—were a powerful force in Japanese society. The way of life of the samurai lords and warriors was, in many ways, like those of the medieval lords and knights of Europe. The great samurai warlords ruled large territories and relied on the fighting skills of their fierce samurai warriors to battle their enemies. But samurai warriors were more than just soldiers. Samurai were expected to embrace beauty and culture, and many were skilled artists. They also had a strict personal code that valued personal honor above all things—even life itself.

Explore the fascinating world of the samurai warrior online. You can find a wealth of information, video clips, primary sources, activities, and more through your online textbook.

🎥 A New Way of Life in Japan

Watch the video to learn how peace and isolation
took hold in Japan and changed the role of the
samurai in society.

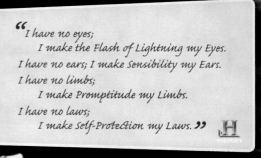

> " *I have no eyes;*
> *I make the Flash of Lightning my Eyes.*
> *I have no ears; I make Sensibility my Ears.*
> *I have no limbs;*
> *I make Promptitude my Limbs.*
> *I have no laws;*
> *I make Self-Protection my Laws.* "

📜 A Code for Samurai Living

Read the document to learn about the strict but
lyrical code of the samurai warrior.

🎥 Death of the Samurai Class

Watch the video to see how the end of Japan's
isolation from the outside world signaled the
beginning of the end of the samurai class.

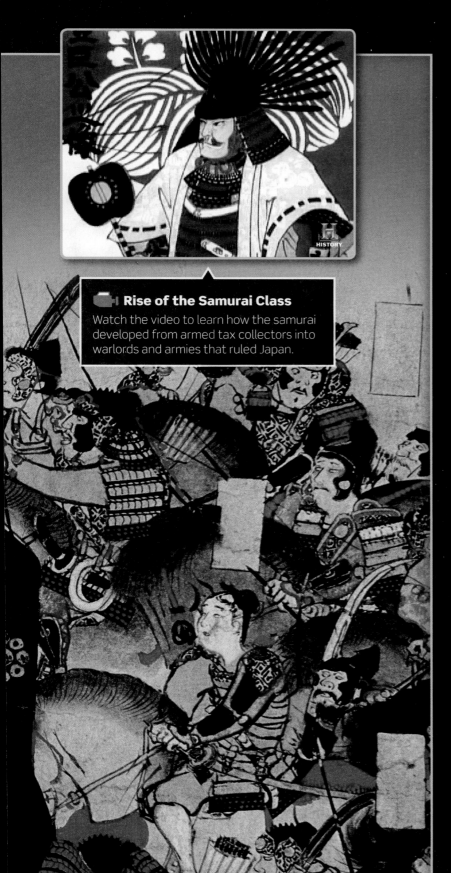

🎥 Rise of the Samurai Class

Watch the video to learn how the samurai
developed from armed tax collectors into
warlords and armies that ruled Japan.

Module 10

The Early Middle Ages

Essential Question
How did life change after the fall of Rome during the early Middle Ages?

About the Painting: This miniature is called "Month of June." It appeared in the Grimani Breviary, a Flemish illuminated manuscript. This scene shows what life was like in the European countryside during the Middle Ages.

▶ Explore ONLINE!

HISTORY

VIDEOS, including...
- Castles and Dungeons
- Hagia Sophia
- Genghis Khan
- Monasteries in Middle Ages
- Knights and Armor
- Medieval Armor

☑ Document Based Investigations

☑ Graphic Organizers

☑ Interactive Games

☑ Carousel: Russian Religious Art and Architecture

☑ Image with Hotspots: A Viking Longboat

In this module you will follow the changing political, religious, and cultural landscape of medieval Europe.

What You Will Learn ...

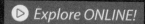
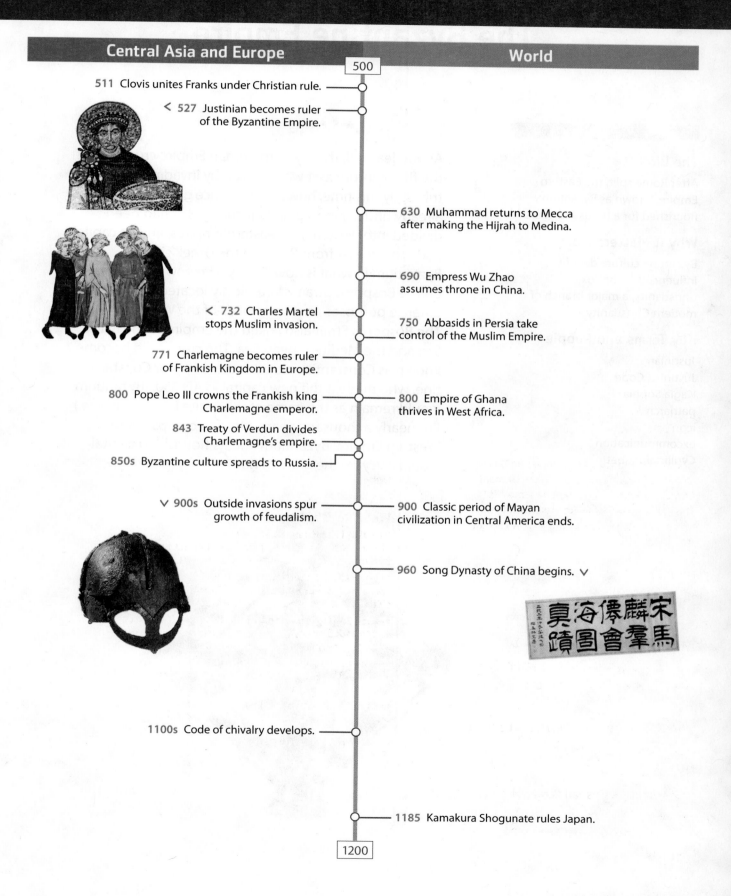

Central Asia and Europe

World

500

511 Clovis unites Franks under Christian rule.

< **527** Justinian becomes ruler of the Byzantine Empire.

630 Muhammad returns to Mecca after making the Hijrah to Medina.

690 Empress Wu Zhao assumes throne in China.

< **732** Charles Martel stops Muslim invasion.

750 Abbasids in Persia take control of the Muslim Empire.

771 Charlemagne becomes ruler of Frankish Kingdom in Europe.

800 Pope Leo III crowns the Frankish king Charlemagne emperor.

800 Empire of Ghana thrives in West Africa.

843 Treaty of Verdun divides Charlemagne's empire.

850s Byzantine culture spreads to Russia.

∨ **900s** Outside invasions spur growth of feudalism.

900 Classic period of Mayan civilization in Central America ends.

960 Song Dynasty of China begins. ∨

1100s Code of chivalry develops.

1185 Kamakura Shogunate rules Japan.

1200

The Byzantine Empire

The Big Idea

After Rome split, the Eastern Empire, known as Byzantium, flourished for a thousand years.

Why It Matters Now

Byzantine culture deeply influenced Orthodox Christianity, a major branch of modern Christianity.

Key Terms and People

Justinian
Justinian Code
Hagia Sophia
patriarch
icon
excommunication
Cyrillic alphabet

Setting the Stage

As you learned, the Western Roman Empire crumbled in the fifth century as it was overrun by invading Germanic tribes. By this time, however, the once great empire had already undergone significant changes. It had been divided into western and eastern empires, and its capital had moved east from Rome to the Greek city of Byzantium in what is now Turkey. The new capital stood on the Bosporus Strait, strategically located for trade and defense purposes on a crossroads of the West and East. The Bosporus Strait also linked the empire to the Black Sea and the Mediterranean Sea. The city would become known as Constantinople after the emperor Constantine, who made it the new capital in AD 330. (Byzantium would remain as the name of the entire Eastern Empire.) For nearly a thousand years after the collapse of the Western Empire, Byzantium and its flourishing capital would carry on the glory of Rome.

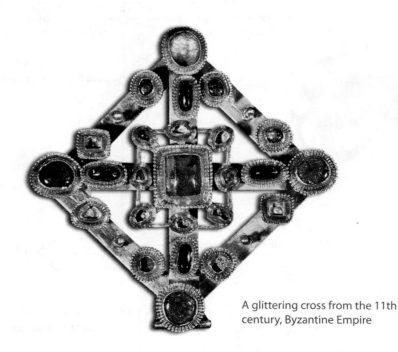

A glittering cross from the 11th century, Byzantine Empire

Emperor Justinian

A New Rome in a New Setting

Roman leaders had divided the empire in 395, largely due to difficulties in communications between the eastern and the troubled western parts of the empire. Still, rulers in the East continued to see themselves as emperors for all of Rome.

In 527, a high-ranking Byzantine nobleman named **Justinian** succeeded his uncle to the throne of the Eastern Empire. In an effort to regain Rome's fading glory and recapture the west, Justinian in 533 sent his best general, Belisarius (behl•uh•SAIR•ee•uhs), to recover North Africa from the invading Germanic tribes. Belisarius and his forces quickly succeeded.

Two years later, Belisarius attacked Rome and seized it from a group known as the Ostrogoths. But the city faced repeated attacks by other Germanic tribes. Over the next 16 years of political, economic, social, and religious transformations, Rome changed hands six times. After numerous campaigns, Justinian's armies won nearly all of Italy and parts of Spain. Justinian now ruled almost all the territory that Rome had ever ruled. He could honestly call himself a new Caesar.

Like the last of the old Caesars, the Byzantine emperors ruled with absolute power. They headed not just the state but the church as well. They appointed and dismissed bishops at will. The political turmoil was brutal—and often deadly. Emperors lived under constant risk of assassination. Of the 88 Byzantine emperors, 29 died violently, and 13 abandoned the throne to live in monasteries.

Reading Check
Compare How were the Byzantine emperors like the last of the old Caesars?

Life in the New Rome

A separate government and difficult communications with the West gave the Byzantine Empire its own character, different from that of the Western Empire. The citizens thought of themselves as sharing in the Roman tradition, but few spoke Latin anymore. Most Byzantines spoke Greek.

Having unified the two empires, Justinian set up a panel of legal experts to regulate Byzantium's increasingly complex society. The panel combed through 400 years of Roman law. It found a number of laws that were outdated and contradictory. The panel created a single, uniform code known as the **Justinian Code**. After its completion, the code consisted of four works.

Vocabulary code general system of laws; stems from the Latin word *codex,* meaning "book"

1. The *Code* contained nearly 5,000 Roman laws that were still considered useful for the Byzantine Empire.
2. The *Digest* quoted and summarized the opinions of Rome's greatest legal thinkers about the laws. This massive work ran to a total of 50 volumes.
3. The *Institutes* was a textbook that told law students how to use the laws.
4. The *Novellae* (New Laws) presented legislation passed after 534.

The Justinian Code decided legal questions that regulated whole areas of Byzantine life. Marriage, slavery, property, inheritance, women's rights, and criminal justice were just some of those areas. Although Justinian himself died in 565, his code served the Byzantine Empire for 900 years.

Resisting Mongol Rule

Although Russians by and large obeyed their Mongol rulers, pockets of resistance existed, as shown by this 1259 diary entry of a resident of Novgorod.

"The same winter the accursed raw-eating Tartars [Mongols], Berkai and Kasachik, came with their wives, and many others, and there was great tumult in Novgorod, and they did much evil in the province, taking contribution for the accursed Tartars. And the accursed ones began to fear death; they said to [Prince] Alexander: 'Give us guards, lest they kill us.' And the Knayz ordered the son of Posadnik and all the sons of the Boyars to protect them by night. The Tartars said: 'Give us your numbers for tribute or we will run away and return in greater strength.' And the common people would not give their numbers for tribute but said: 'Let us die honourably for St. Sophia and for the angelic houses.'"

—Resident of Novgorod,
from *Medieval Russia*

Rebelling Against the Mongols

Resistance against Mongol rule occasionally broke out into open rebellion, as this account of an anti-Mongol uprising in Tver in 1327 indicates.

"The lawless Shevkal, the destroyer of Christianity, . . . came to Tver, drove the Grand Prince from his court and entrenched himself there with great haughtiness and violence. . . . The entire city assembled and the uprising was in the making. The Tverians cried out and began to kill the Tartars wherever they found them until they killed Shevkal and the rest [of his men]. They missed killing the messengers who were with the horses that grazed in the meadow [outside the city]. They [the messengers] saddled their best horses and swiftly galloped to Moscow and from there to the [Golden] Horde, where they brought the news of the death of Shevkal."

—Tver Eyewitness Account,
from *Medieval Russia*

Analyze Historical Sources

1. In what way did the reasons for the uprisings in Novgorod and Tver differ?
2. Based on what you have read about the Mongols, what do you think their response was to the above events of resistance and rebellion?

The Mongols may have been forced to move out by economic or military pressures. They may have been lured by the wealth of cities to the west. Whatever their reasons for leaving, they rode their swift horses across the steppes of Asia and on into Europe. Their savage killing and burning won them a reputation for ruthless brutality. When Genghis Khan died in 1227, his successors continued the conquering that he had begun. At its fullest extent, the Mongol Empire stretched from the Yellow Sea to the Baltic Sea and from the Himalayas to northern Russia.

In 1240, the Mongols attacked and demolished Kiev. They rode under the leadership of Batu Khan, Genghis's grandson. So many inhabitants were slaughtered, a Russian historian reported, that "no eye remained to weep." A Roman Catholic bishop traveling through Kiev five years later wrote, "When we passed through that land, we found lying in the field countless heads and bones of dead people." After the fall of Kiev, Mongols ruled all of southern Russia for 200 years. The empire's official name was the "Khanate of the Golden Horde": *Khanate,* from the Mongol word for "kingdom"; *Golden,* because gold was the royal color of the Mongols; and *Horde,* from the Mongol word for "camp."

Mongol Rule in Russia Under Mongol rule, the Russians could follow all their usual customs, as long as they made no attempts to rebel. The Mongols tolerated all the religions in their realms. The Church, in fact, often acted as a mediator between the Russian people and their Mongol rulers.

The Mongols demanded just two things from Russians: absolute obedience and massive amounts of tribute, or payments. By and large, the Russian nobles agreed. Novgorod's prince and military hero **Alexander Nevsky**, for example, advised his fellow princes to cooperate with the Mongols. The Russian nobles often crushed revolts against the Mongols and collected oppressive taxes for the foreign rulers.

Mongol rule isolated the Russians more than ever from their neighbors in Western Europe. This meant that among other things, the Russians had little access to many new ideas and inventions. During this period, however, forces were at work that eventually would lead to the rise of a new center of power in the country, and to Russia's liberation.

Reading Check
Find Main Ideas
What main demands did the Mongols make on their Russian subjects?

Russia Breaks Free

The city of Moscow was first founded in the 1100s. By 1156, it was a crude village protected by a log wall. Nonetheless, it was located near three major rivers: the Volga, Dnieper, and Don. From that strategic position, a prince of Moscow who could gain control of the three rivers could control nearly all of European Russia—and perhaps successfully challenge the Mongols.

Moscow's Powerful Princes A line of Russian princes eventually emerged on the scene who would do just that. During the late 1320s, Moscow's Prince Ivan I had earned the gratitude of the Mongols by helping to crush a Russian revolt against Mongol rule. For his services, the Mongols appointed Ivan I as tax collector of all the Slavic lands they had conquered. They also gave him the title of "Grand Prince." Ivan had now become without any doubt the most powerful of all Russian princes. He also became the wealthiest and was known as "Ivan Moneybag."

Ivan convinced the Patriarch of Kiev, the leading bishop of Eastern Europe, to move to Moscow. The move improved the city's prestige and gave Moscow's princes a powerful ally: the Church. Ivan I and his successors used numerous strategies to enlarge their territory: land purchases, wars, trickery, and shrewd marriages. From generation to generation, they schemed to gain greater control over the small states around Moscow.

Ivan III
(1440–1505)

Those around him often viewed Ivan as cold, calculating, and ruthless. This may have been due in part to a difficult upbringing. Ivan came of age during a time of great civil strife in Russia. His father, Grand Prince Vasali II, was at one point imprisoned and blinded by opposition forces.

Ivan's cautious and calculating style drew criticism from Russians eager for more bold and swift action against the Mongols. Even a close aide questioned his tactics. "Would you surrender Russia to fire and sword?" he asked the prince. After Russian forces won the standoff at the Ugra River, however, such criticism turned to praise.

An Empire Emerges The Russian state would become a genuine empire during the long, 43-year reign of **Ivan III**. Upon becoming the prince of Moscow, Ivan openly challenged Mongol rule. He took the name **czar** (zahr), the Russian version of Caesar, and publicly claimed his intent to make Russia the "Third Rome." (The title "czar" became official only during the reign of Ivan IV.)

In 1480, Ivan made a final break with the Mongols. After he refused to pay his rulers further tribute, Russian and Mongol armies faced each other at the Ugra River, about 150 miles southwest of Moscow. However, neither side advanced to fight. So, after a time, both armies turned around and marched home. Russians have traditionally marked this bloodless standoff as their liberation from Mongol rule. After this liberation, the czars could openly pursue an empire.

Reading Check
Analyze Issues
What about Moscow's location was significant?

Lesson 2 Assessment

1. **Organize Information** Which group fared the worst under Mongol rule? Use a chart like the one below to organize your notes.

Nobles	Church
People	Moscow Princes

2. **Key Terms and People** For each key term or person in the lesson, write a sentence explaining its significance.

3. **Analyze Effects** How did Vladimir's conversion to Christianity affect Kiev?

4. **Form Opinions** Do you approve of Nevsky's cooperation with the Mongols? Was his policy practical or cowardly? Explain.

5. **Analyze Issues** How was Ivan I both friend and foe to the Mongol rulers?

Russian Religious Art and Architecture

Russian religious art follows an ancient tradition dating back to the early Church. At first, Christians feared that artwork showing people might lead to idol worship. Gradually, however, the Church came to accept the use of icons, or depictions of holy people. In the West, other types of art eventually replaced the icon, but the Eastern Orthodox Church still uses icons today.

Icons are painted according to strict rules. This approach also shaped other religious art in Russia. To construct a church or create a religious artifact was a sacred task, performed according to rigid guidelines. Art was not a form of self-expression.

▲ ICON
This 12th-century Russian icon is of the Archangel Gabriel. According to the Bible, Gabriel was the messenger who told the Virgin Mary that she would give birth to Jesus. In Orthodox churches, artists must follow certain rules when making icons. For example, icons are always two-dimensional because they are seen as windows through which worshipers can view heaven.

▲ CROSS AND ILLUMINATED MANUSCRIPT
The cross above was carved from ivory and shows the Archangel Michael. In Christian belief, Michael is the leader of the heavenly hosts and a spiritual warrior who helped the Israelites. That is why he is often shown with a sword, as he is here.

The illuminated manuscript was made during the 15th century and shows a scribe writing out the Gospel. Illuminated manuscripts were handwritten books decorated with gold or silver, vivid colors, elaborate designs, and small pictures. The word *illumination* originally referred to the gold or silver decoration, which made the pages seem as if light were shining on them.

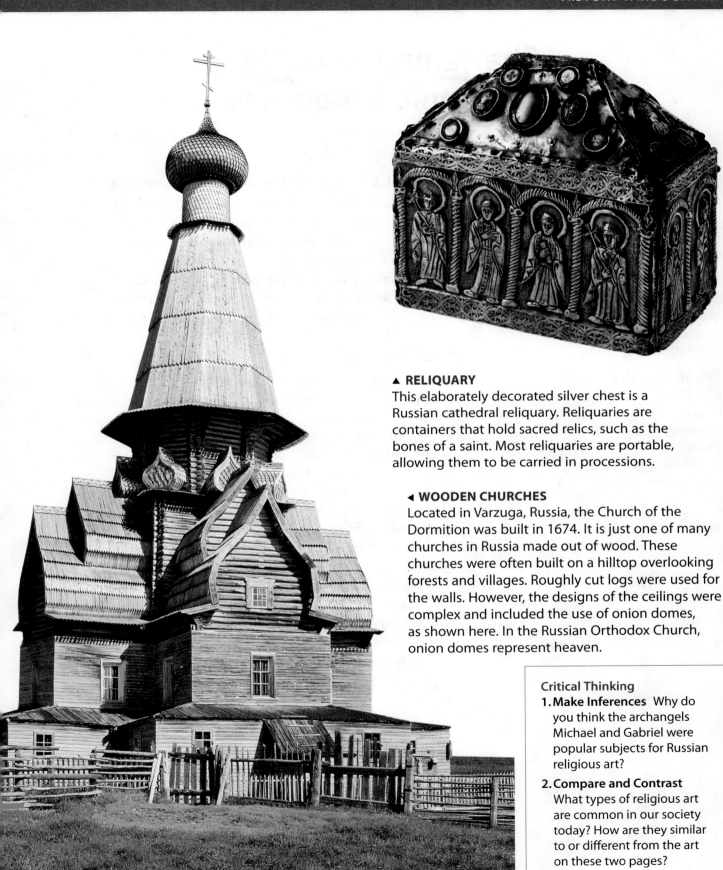

▲ RELIQUARY

This elaborately decorated silver chest is a Russian cathedral reliquary. Reliquaries are containers that hold sacred relics, such as the bones of a saint. Most reliquaries are portable, allowing them to be carried in processions.

◄ WOODEN CHURCHES

Located in Varzuga, Russia, the Church of the Dormition was built in 1674. It is just one of many churches in Russia made out of wood. These churches were often built on a hilltop overlooking forests and villages. Roughly cut logs were used for the walls. However, the designs of the ceilings were complex and included the use of onion domes, as shown here. In the Russian Orthodox Church, onion domes represent heaven.

Critical Thinking

1. **Make Inferences** Why do you think the archangels Michael and Gabriel were popular subjects for Russian religious art?

2. **Compare and Contrast** What types of religious art are common in our society today? How are they similar to or different from the art on these two pages?

Charlemagne Unites Germanic Kingdoms

The Big Idea
Many Germanic kingdoms that succeeded the Roman Empire were reunited under Charlemagne's empire.

Why It Matters Now
Charlemagne spread Christian civilization through Northern Europe, where it had a permanent impact.

Key Terms and People
Middle Ages
Franks
monastery
secular
Carolingian Dynasty
Charlemagne

Setting the Stage

The gradual decline of the Roman Empire ushered in an era of European history called the **Middle Ages**, or the medieval period. It spanned the years from about 500 to 1500. During these centuries, a new society slowly emerged in Europe impacted by the collapse of the Western Roman Empire. It had roots in: (1) the classical heritage of Rome, (2) the beliefs of the Roman Catholic Church, and (3) the customs of various Germanic tribes.

Invasions of Western Europe

In the fifth century, Germanic invaders overran the western half of the Roman Empire. Repeated invasions and constant warfare caused a series of changes that altered the economy, government, and culture:

- **Disruption of Trade** Merchants faced invasions from both land and sea. Their businesses collapsed. The breakdown of trade destroyed Europe's cities as economic centers. Money became scarce.
- **Downfall of Cities** With the fall of the Roman Empire, cities were abandoned as centers of administration.
- **Population Shifts** As Roman centers of trade and government collapsed, nobles retreated to the rural areas. Roman cities were left without strong leadership. Other city dwellers also fled to the countryside, where they grew their own food. The population of western Europe became mostly rural.

Population of Three Roman Cities

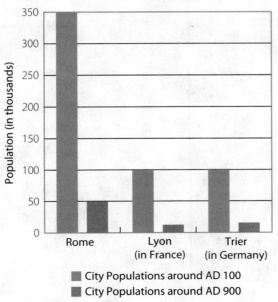

Population (in thousands)

350
300
250
200
150
100
50
0

Rome　　　Lyon　　　Trier
(in France)　(in Germany)

■ City Populations around AD 100
■ City Populations around AD 900

Sources: Man and History; 3,000 Years of Urban Growth

Interpret Graphs

1. **Find Main Ideas** What is the most important point this graph is making?

2. **Make Inferences** How does this graph show a real-world situation?

The Decline of Learning The Germanic invaders who stormed Rome could not read or write. Among Romans themselves, the level of learning sank sharply as more and more families left for rural areas. Few people except priests and other church officials were literate. Knowledge of Greek, long important in Roman culture, was almost lost. Few people could read Greek works of literature, science, and philosophy. The Germanic tribes, though, had a rich oral tradition of songs and legends.

Loss of a Common Language As German-speaking peoples mixed with the Roman population, Latin changed. While it was still an official language, it was no longer understood. Different dialects developed as new words and phrases became part of everyday speech. By the 800s, French, Spanish, and other Roman-based languages had evolved from Latin. The development of various languages mirrored the continued breakup of a once-unified empire.

Germanic Kingdoms Emerge

In the years of upheaval between 400 and 600, small Germanic kingdoms replaced Roman provinces. The borders of those kingdoms changed constantly with the fortunes of war. But the Church as an institution survived the fall of the Roman Empire. During this time of political chaos, the Church provided order and security.

The Concept of Government Changes Along with shifting boundaries, the entire concept of government changed. Loyalty to public government and written law had unified Roman society. Family ties and personal loyalty, rather than citizenship in a public state, held Germanic society together. Unlike Romans, Germanic peoples lived in small communities that were governed by unwritten rules and traditions.

Reading Check
Find Main Ideas
What are three ways that civilization in western Europe declined after the Roman Empire fell?

An army leaves after sacking a town. Illustration from a 14th-century manuscript

Every Germanic chief led a band of warriors who had pledged their loyalty to him. In peacetime, these followers lived in their lord's hall. He gave them food, weapons, and treasure. In battle, warriors fought to the death at their lord's side. They considered it a disgrace to outlive him. But Germanic warriors felt no obligation to obey a king they did not even know. Nor would they obey an official sent to collect taxes or administer justice in the name of an emperor they had never met. The Germanic stress on personal ties made it impossible to establish orderly government for large territories.

Clovis Rules the Franks In the Roman province of Gaul (mainly what is now France and Switzerland), a Germanic people called the **Franks** held power. Their leader was Clovis (KLOH•vihs). He would bring Christianity to the region. According to legend, his wife, Clothilde, had urged him to convert to her faith, Christianity. In 496, Clovis led his warriors against another Germanic army. Fearing defeat, he appealed to the Christian God. "For I have called on my gods," he prayed, "but I find they are far from my aid. . . . Now I call on Thee. I long to believe in Thee. Only, please deliver me from my enemies." The tide of the battle shifted and the Franks won. Afterward, Clovis and 3,000 of his warriors asked a bishop to baptize them.

The Church in Rome welcomed Clovis's conversion and supported his military campaigns against other Germanic peoples. By 511, Clovis had united the Franks into one kingdom. The strategic alliance between Clovis's Frankish kingdom and the Church marked the start of a partnership between two powerful forces.

Reading Check
Summarize
What replaced Roman provinces in the years between 400 and 600?

Germans Adopt Christianity

Politics played a key role in spreading Christianity. By 600, the Church, with the help of Frankish rulers, had converted many Germanic peoples. These new converts had settled in Rome's former lands. Missionaries also spread Christianity. These religious travelers often risked their lives to bring religious beliefs to other lands. During the 300s and 400s, they worked among the Germanic and Celtic groups that bordered the Roman Empire. In southern Europe, the fear of coastal attacks by Muslims also spurred many people to become Christians in the 600s.

Monasteries, Convents, and Manuscripts To adapt to rural conditions, the Church built religious communities called **monasteries**. There, Christian men called monks gave up their private possessions and devoted their lives to serving God. Women who followed this way of life were called nuns and lived in convents. The missionary activities of monks played a key role in the spread of Christianity. For example, in the fifth century, monks established monasteries in Ireland, eventually Christianizing much of the country. In turn, Irish monks established monasteries in Scotland, England, and Wales, helping to Christianize the peoples there. Monks and nuns also participated in charitable activities. For example, they housed travelers, nursed the sick, and assisted the poor.

Around 520, an Italian monk named Benedict began writing a book describing a strict yet practical set of rules for monasteries. Benedict's sister, Scholastica (skuh•LAS•tik•uh), headed a convent and adapted the same rules for women. These guidelines became a model for many other religious communities in western Europe. Monks and nuns devoted their lives to prayer and good works.

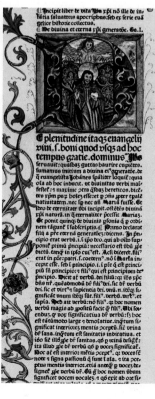

Illuminated manuscripts such as the one shown here were usually the work of monks.

Monasteries and convents served as centers of education. Monasteries became Europe's best-educated communities. Monks opened schools, maintained libraries, and copied books. In 731, the Venerable Bede, an English monk, wrote a history of England. Scholars still consider it the best historical work of the early Middle Ages. In the 600s and 700s, monks made beautiful copies of religious writings, decorated with ornate letters and brilliant pictures. These illuminated manuscripts preserved at least part of Rome's intellectual heritage.

Over time, the economic and political power of the monasteries grew as they increasingly drew their members from aristocratic families. With these aristocratic members came grants of money and land, swelling the accounts of the monasteries. Accumulated lands were farmed by peasants, and the monasteries ran them carefully to maximize

Benedict
(480?–543)

At 15, Benedict left school and hiked up to the Sabine Hills, where he lived in a cave as a hermit. After learning about Benedict's deep religious conviction, a group of monks persuaded him to lead their monastery. Benedict declared:

"We must prepare our hearts and bodies for combat under holy obedience to the divine commandments. . . . We are therefore going to establish a school in which one may learn the service of the Lord."

In his book describing the rules for monastic life, Benedict emphasized a balance between work and study. Such guidelines turned monasteries into centers of stability and learning.

Scholastica
(480?–543)

Scholastica is thought to be the twin sister of Benedict. She was born into a wealthy Italian family in the late Roman Empire. Little is known of her early life, except that she and Benedict were inseparable.

Like her brother, Scholastica devoted her life to the Church. She is thought to have been the abbess of a convent near the monastery founded by Benedict and is considered the first nun of the Benedictine order. She was a strong influence on her brother as he developed rules that guide Benedictine monasteries to this day. They died in the same year and are buried in one grave.

income and economic productivity. Aristocratic connections also meant political power and connections. For example, a number of Benedictine monks served as advisors, judges, and even military leaders for kings.

Papal Power Expands Under Gregory I In 590, Gregory I, also called Gregory the Great, became pope. As head of the Church in Rome, Gregory broadened the authority of the papacy, or pope's office, beyond its spiritual role. Under Gregory, the papacy also became a **secular**, or worldly, power involved in politics. The pope's palace was the center of Roman government. Gregory used church revenues to raise armies, repair roads, and help the poor. He also negotiated peace treaties with invaders such as the Lombards.

According to Gregory, the region from Italy to England and from Spain to Germany fell under his responsibility. Gregory strengthened the vision of Christendom. It was a spiritual kingdom fanning out from Rome to the most distant churches. The changing role of the church along with this idea of a churchly kingdom, ruled by a pope, would be a central theme of the Middle Ages. Meanwhile, secular rulers expanded their political kingdoms.

Reading Check
Make Inferences
What role did monasteries play during this time of chaos?

An Empire Evolves

After the Roman Empire dissolved, small kingdoms sprang up all over Europe. For example, England splintered into seven tiny kingdoms. Some of them were no larger than the state of Connecticut. The Franks controlled the largest and strongest of Europe's kingdoms, the area that was formerly the Roman province of Gaul. When the Franks' first Christian king, Clovis, died in 511, he had extended Frankish rule over most of what is now France.

This painting shows Charles Martel (with ax) in the Battle of Tours.

Charles Martel Emerges By 700, an official known as the *major domo,* or mayor of the palace, had become the most powerful person in the Frankish kingdom. Officially, he had charge of the royal household and estates. Unofficially, he led armies and made policy. In effect, he ruled the kingdom.

The mayor of the palace in 719, Charles Martel (Charles the Hammer), held more power than the king. Charles Martel extended the Franks' reign to the north, south, and east. He also defeated Muslim raiders from Spain at the Battle of Tours in 732. This battle was highly significant for Christian Europeans. If the Muslims had won, western Europe might have become part of the Muslim Empire. Charles Martel's victory at Tours made him a Christian hero.

At his death, Charles Martel passed his power to his son, Pepin the Short. Pepin wanted to be king. He shrewdly cooperated with the pope. On behalf of the Church, Pepin agreed to fight the Lombards, who had invaded central Italy and threatened Rome. In exchange, the pope anointed Pepin "king by the grace of God." Thus began the **Carolingian** (KAR•uh•LIHN•juhn) **Dynasty**, the family that would rule the Franks from 751 to 987.

Reading Check
Analyze Events
What pivotal battle did Charles Martel and his forces win?

Charlemagne Becomes Emperor

Pepin the Short died in 768. He left a greatly strengthened Frankish kingdom to his two sons, Carloman and Charles. After Carloman's death in 771, Charles, who was known as **Charlemagne** (SHAHR•luh•MAYN), or Charles the Great, ruled the kingdom. An imposing figure, he stood six feet four inches tall. His admiring secretary, a monk named Einhard, described Charlemagne's achievements:

"[Charlemagne] was the most potent prince with the greatest skill and success in different countries during the forty-seven years of his reign. Great and powerful as was the realm of Franks, Karl [Charlemagne] received from his father Pippin, he nevertheless so splendidly enlarged it . . . that he almost doubled it."

—Einhard, *Life of Charlemagne*

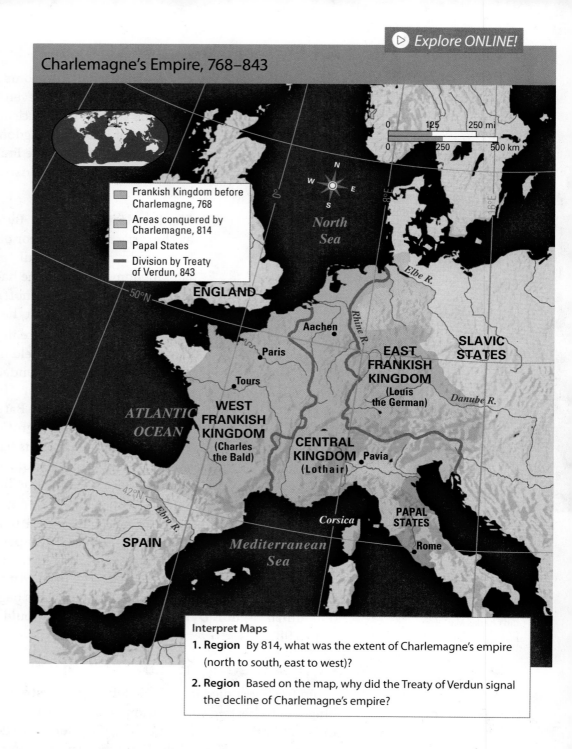

▶ Explore ONLINE!

Charlemagne's Empire, 768–843

Frankish Kingdom before Charlemagne, 768

Areas conquered by Charlemagne, 814

Papal States

Division by Treaty of Verdun, 843

North Sea

Elbe R.

ENGLAND

Aachen

Rhine R.

EAST FRANKISH KINGDOM (Louis the German)

SLAVIC STATES

Paris

Tours

WEST FRANKISH KINGDOM (Charles the Bald)

ATLANTIC OCEAN

CENTRAL KINGDOM (Lothair)

Pavia

Danube R.

50°N

42°N

Ebro R.

SPAIN

Mediterranean Sea

Corsica

PAPAL STATES

Rome

0   125   250 mi
0   250   500 km

Interpret Maps

1. **Region** By 814, what was the extent of Charlemagne's empire (north to south, east to west)?

2. **Region** Based on the map, why did the Treaty of Verdun signal the decline of Charlemagne's empire?

Charlemagne Extends Frankish Rule Charlemagne built an empire greater than any known since ancient Rome. Each summer he led his armies against enemies that surrounded his kingdom. He fought Muslims in Spain and tribes from other Germanic kingdoms. He conquered new lands to both the south and the east. Through these conquests, Charlemagne spread Christianity. He reunited western Europe for the first time since the Roman Empire. By 800, Charlemagne's empire was larger than the Byzantine Empire. He had become the most powerful king in western Europe.

Emperor Charlemagne

In 800, Charlemagne traveled to Rome to crush an unruly mob that had attacked the pope. In gratitude, Pope Leo III crowned him emperor. The coronation was historic. A pope had claimed the political right to confer the title "Roman Emperor" on a European king. This event signaled the joining of Germanic power, the Church, and the heritage of the Roman Empire.

Charlemagne Leads a Revival Charlemagne strengthened his royal power by limiting the authority of the nobles. To govern his empire, he sent out royal agents. They made sure that the powerful landholders, called counts, governed their counties justly. Charlemagne regularly visited every part of his kingdom. He also kept a close watch on the management of his huge estates—the source of Carolingian wealth and power. One of his greatest accomplishments was the encouragement of learning. He surrounded himself with English, German, Italian, and Spanish scholars. For his many sons and daughters and other children at the court, Charlemagne opened a palace school. He also ordered monasteries to open schools to train future monks and priests.

Charlemagne's Heirs A year before Charlemagne died in 814, he crowned his only surviving son, Louis the Pious, as emperor. Louis was a devoutly religious man but an ineffective ruler. He left three sons: Lothair (loh•THAIR), Charles the Bald, and Louis the German. They fought one another for control of the empire. In 843, the brothers signed the Treaty of Verdun, dividing the empire into three kingdoms. As a result, Carolingian kings lost power and central authority broke down. The lack of strong rulers led to a new system of governing and landholding—feudalism.

Reading Check
Draw Conclusions
What were Charlemagne's most notable achievements?

Lesson 3 Assessment

1. **Organize Information** Create a timeline like the one below to trace the unification of the Germanic kingdoms. What was the most important event? Why?

500

1200

2. **Key Terms and People** For each key term or person in the lesson, write a sentence explaining its significance.

3. **Draw Conclusions** How was the relationship between a Frankish king and the pope beneficial to both?
4. **Analyze Effects** Why was Charles Martel's victory at the Battle of Tours so important for Christianity?
5. **Evaluate** What was Charlemagne's greatest achievement? Give reasons for your answer.

Feudalism and Manorialism

The Big Idea

Feudalism, a political and economic system based on land-holding and protective alliances, emerged in Europe.

Why It Matters Now

The rights and duties of feudal relationships helped shape today's forms of representative government.

Key Terms and People

lord
fief
vassal
knight
serf
manor
tithe

Setting the Stage

After the Treaty of Verdun, Charlemagne's three feuding grandsons broke up the kingdom even further. Part of this territory also became a battleground as new waves of invaders attacked Europe. The political turmoil and constant warfare led to the rise of European feudalism, which is a political and economic system based on land ownership and personal loyalty.

Invaders Attack Western Europe

From about 800 to 1000, invasions destroyed the Carolingian Empire. Muslim invaders from the south seized Sicily and raided Italy. In 846, they sacked Rome. Magyar invaders struck from the east. Like the earlier migratory groups the Huns and Avars, they terrorized Germany and Italy. And from the north came the fearsome Vikings.

The Vikings Invade from the North The Vikings set sail from Scandinavia (SKAN•duh•NAY•vee•uh), a wintry, wooded region in northern Europe. (The region is now the countries of Denmark, Norway, and Sweden.) The Vikings, also called Northmen or Norsemen, were a Germanic people. In the culture of northern European peoples, they worshiped warlike gods and took pride in nicknames like Eric Bloodaxe and Thorfinn Skullsplitter.

The Vikings carried out their raids with terrifying speed. Clutching swords and heavy wooden shields, these helmeted seafarers beached their ships, struck quickly, and then moved out to sea again. They were gone before locals could mount a defense. Viking warships were awe-inspiring. The largest of these long ships held 300 warriors, who took turns rowing the ship's 72 oars. The prow of each ship swept grandly upward, often ending with the carved head of a sea monster. A ship might weigh 20 tons when fully loaded. Yet, it could sail in a mere three feet of water. Rowing up shallow creeks, the Vikings looted inland villages and monasteries.

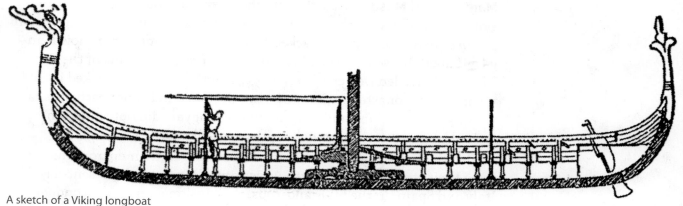

A sketch of a Viking longboat

The Vikings were not only warriors but also traders, farmers, and explorers. They ventured far beyond western Europe. Vikings journeyed down rivers into the heart of Russia, to Constantinople, and even across the icy waters of the North Atlantic. A Viking explorer named Leif (leef) Ericson reached North America around 1000, almost 500 years before Columbus. About the same time, the Viking reign of terror in Europe faded away. As Vikings gradually accepted Christianity, they stopped raiding monasteries. Also, a warming trend in Europe's climate made farming and settlement easier in Scandinavia. As a result, fewer Scandinavians adopted the sea-faring life of Viking warriors.

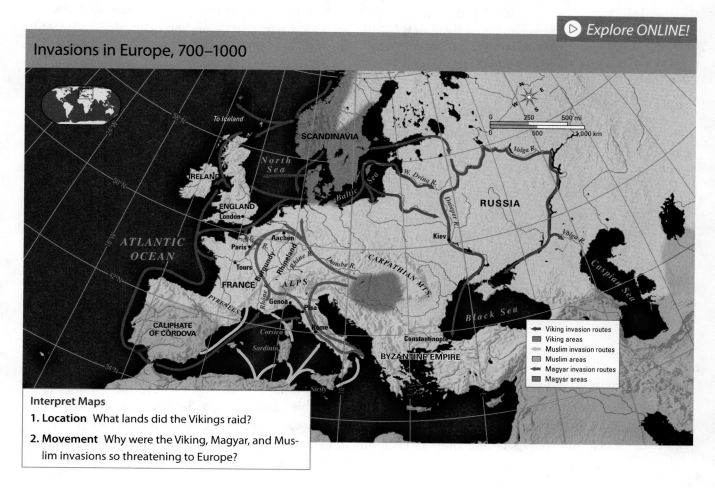

▶ Explore ONLINE!

Invasions in Europe, 700–1000

Viking invasion routes
Viking areas
Muslim invasion routes
Muslim areas
Magyar invasion routes
Magyar areas

Interpret Maps

1. **Location** What lands did the Vikings raid?

2. **Movement** Why were the Viking, Magyar, and Muslim invasions so threatening to Europe?

Magyars and Muslims Attack from the East and South As Viking invasions declined, Europe became the target of new assaults. The Magyars, a group of nomadic people, attacked from the east, from what is now Hungary. Superb horsemen, the Magyars swept across the plains of the Danube River and invaded western Europe in the late 800s. They attacked isolated villages and monasteries. They overran northern Italy and reached as far west as the Rhineland and Burgundy. The Magyars did not settle conquered land. Instead, they took captives to sell as slaves.

The Muslims struck from the south. They began their encroachments from their strongholds in North Africa, invading through present-day Italy and Spain. In the 600s and 700s, the Muslim plan was to conquer and settle in Europe. By the 800s and 900s, their goal was also to plunder. Because the Muslims were expert seafarers, they were able to attack settlements on the Atlantic and Mediterranean coasts. They also struck as far inland as Switzerland.

The invasions by Vikings, Magyars, and Muslims caused widespread disorder and suffering. Most western Europeans lived in constant danger. Kings could not effectively defend their lands from invasion. As a result, people no longer looked to a central ruler for security. Instead, many turned to local rulers who had their own armies. Any leader who could fight the invaders gained followers and political strength.

Reading Check
Analyze Effects
What was the impact of Viking, Magyar, and Muslim invasions on medieval Europe?

A New Social Order: Feudalism

In 911, two former enemies faced each other in a peace ceremony. Rollo was the head of a Viking army. Rollo and his men had been plundering the rich Seine (sayn) River valley for years. Charles the Simple was the king of France but held little power. Charles granted the Viking leader a huge piece of French territory. It became known as Northmen's land, or Normandy. In return, Rollo swore a pledge of loyalty to the king.

Feudalism Structures Society The worst years of the invaders' attacks were roughly from 850 to 950. During this time, rulers and warriors like Charles and Rollo made similar agreements in many parts of Europe. The system of governing and landholding known as feudalism had emerged in Europe. A similar feudal system existed in China under the Zhou Dynasty, which ruled from around the 11th century BC until 256 BC. Feudalism in Japan began in AD 1192 and ended in the 19th century.

The feudal system was based on rights and obligations. In exchange for military protection and other services, a **lord**, or landowner, granted an area of land called a **fief**. The person receiving a fief was called a **vassal**. Charles the Simple, the lord, and Rollo, the vassal, showed how this two-sided bargain worked. Feudalism depended on the control of land.

The Feudal Pyramid The structure of feudal society was much like a pyramid. At the peak reigned the king. Next came the most powerful vassals—wealthy landowners such as nobles and bishops. Serving beneath these vassals were knights. **Knights** were mounted horsemen who pledged to defend their lord's lands in exchange for fiefs. At the base of the pyramid were landless peasants who toiled in the fields.

Vocabulary
status social ranking

Reading Check
Synthesize What were the three social classes of the feudal system, and how were they connected?

Social Classes Are Well Defined In the feudal system, status determined a person's prestige and power. Medieval writers classified people into three groups: those who fought (nobles and knights), those who prayed (men and women of the Church), and those who worked (the peasants). Social class was usually inherited.

In Europe in the Middle Ages, the vast majority of people were peasants. Most peasants were serfs. **Serfs** were people who could not lawfully leave the place where they were born. Though bound to the land, serfs were not slaves. Their lords could not sell or buy them. But what their labor produced belonged to the lord.

Manors: The Economic Side of Feudalism

The **manor** was the lord's estate. During the Middle Ages, the manor system was the basic economic arrangement. The manor system rested on a set of rights and obligations between a lord and his serfs. The lord provided the serfs with housing, farmland, and protection from bandits. In return, serfs tended the lord's lands, cared for his animals, and performed other tasks to maintain the estate. Private property as a legal distinction was centuries away, but the manor system built upon the idea that land was power. Peasant women shared in the farm work with their husbands. All peasants, whether free or serf, owed the lord certain duties. These included at least a few days of labor each week and a certain portion of their grain.

A Self-Contained World Peasants rarely traveled more than 25 miles from their own manor. By standing in the center of a plowed field, they could see their entire world at a glance. A manor usually covered only a few square miles of land. It typically consisted of the lord's manor house, a church, and workshops. Generally, 15 to 30 families lived in the village on a manor. Fields, pastures, and woodlands surrounded the village. Sometimes a stream wound through the manor. Streams and ponds provided fish, which served as an important source of food. The mill for grinding the grain was often located on the stream.

The manor was largely a self-sufficient community based on thoughtful land use. The serfs and peasants raised or produced nearly everything that they and their lord needed for daily life—crops, milk and cheese, fuel, cloth, leather goods, and lumber. The only outside purchases were salt, iron, and a few unusual objects such as millstones. These were huge stones used to grind flour. Crops grown on the manor usually included grains, such as wheat, rye, barley, and oats, and vegetables, such as peas, beans, onions, and beets.

New Tools for Farmers One area where independent thought occurred in manor life was engineering and invention for use on farms. People invented new tools for farmers. During this time, the metal horseshoe was invented. A new type of horse harness came into use that was better than what the Romans had. The pitchfork was used for the first time to turn over plowed earth. This type of thinking kept alive original thought. This eventually led to the Scientific Revolution.

The Harshness of Manor Life For the privilege of living on the lord's land, peasants paid a high price. They paid a tax on all grain ground in the lord's mill. Any attempt to avoid taxes by baking bread elsewhere was treated as a crime. Peasants also paid a tax on marriage. Weddings could take place only with the lord's consent. After all these payments to the lord, peasant families owed the village priest a tithe, or church tax. A **tithe** represented one-tenth of their income.

Serfs lived in crowded cottages, close to their neighbors. The cottages had only one or two rooms. If there were two rooms, the main room was used for cooking, eating, and household activities. The second was the family bedroom. Peasants warmed their dirt-floor houses by bringing pigs inside. At night, the family huddled on a pile of straw that often crawled with insects. Peasants' simple diet consisted mainly of vegetables, coarse brown bread, grain, cheese, and soup.

Piers Plowman, written by William Langland in 1362, reveals the hard life of English peasants:

> *"What they can put aside from what they make spinning*
> *   they spend on housing*
> *Also on milk and meal to make porridge with*
> *   To sate their children who cry out for food.*
> *And they themselves also suffer much hunger,*
> *   And woe in wintertime, and waking up nights*
> *   To rise on the bedside to rock the cradle."*
>
> —William Langland, *Piers Plowman*

This 14th century drawing shows two men flailing grain.

For most serfs, both men and women, life was work and more work. Their days revolved around raising crops and livestock and taking care of home and family. As soon as children were old enough, they were put to work in the fields or in the home. Many children did not survive to adulthood. Illness and malnutrition were constant afflictions for medieval peasants. Average life expectancy was about 35 years.

Yet despite the hardships they endured, serfs accepted their lot in life as part of the Church's teachings. They, like most Christians during medieval times, believed that God determined a person's place in society.

Reading Check
Analyze Causes
How might the decline of trade during the early Middle Ages have contributed to the self-sufficiency of the manor system?

Feudalism

Feudalism was a political system, or institution, in which nobles were granted the use of land that legally belonged to the king. In return, the nobles agreed to give their loyalty and military services to the king. Feudalism developed not only in Europe but also in countries like Japan.

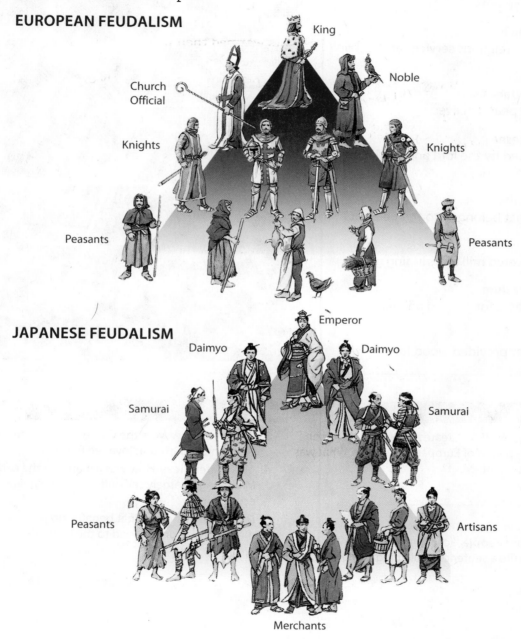

EUROPEAN FEUDALISM

King
Noble
Church Official
Knights
Knights
Peasants
Peasants

JAPANESE FEUDALISM

Emperor
Daimyo
Daimyo
Samurai
Samurai
Peasants
Artisans
Merchants

Critical Thinking

1. Compare
What are the similarities between feudalism in Europe and feudalism in Japan?

2. Form Opinions
Today, does the United States have a system of social classes? Support your answer with evidence.

The Medieval Manor

The medieval manor varied in size. The illustration is a plan of a typical English manor.

1. **Manor House**
   Dwelling place of the lord and his family and their servants

2. **Village Church**
   Site of both religious services and public meetings

3. **Peasant Cottages**
   Where the peasants lived

4. **Lord's Demesne**
   Fields owned by the lord and worked by the peasants

5. **Peasant Crofts**
   Gardens that belonged to the peasants

6. **Mill**
   Water-powered mill for grinding grain

7. **Common Pasture**
   Common area for grazing animals

8. **Woodland**
   Forests that provided wood for fuel

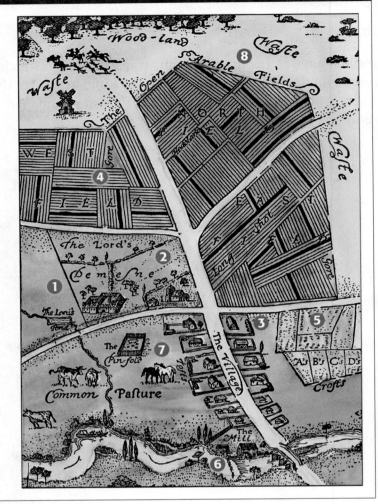

Lesson 4 Assessment

1. **Organize Information** Create a timeline like the one below for the period of European invasions. What was the most important event?

2. **Key Terms and People** For each key term or person in the lesson, write a sentence explaining its significance.

3. **Compare** How were the Vikings different from earlier Germanic groups that invaded Europe?

4. **Make Inferences** How was a manor in the early Middle Ages largely self-sufficient both militarily and economically?

5. **Draw Conclusions** What benefits do you think a medieval manor provided to the serfs who lived there?

Society in the Feudal Era

The Big Idea

The code of chivalry for knights glorified both combat and romantic love.

Why It Matters Now

The code of chivalry has shaped modern ideas of romance in Western cultures.

Key Terms and People

chivalry
tournament
troubadour

Setting the Stage

During the Middle Ages, nobles constantly fought one another. Their feuding kept Europe in a fragmented state for centuries. Through warfare, feudal lords defended their estates, seized new territories, and increased their wealth. Lords and their armies lived in a violent society that prized combat skills. By the 1100s, though, a code of behavior began to arise. High ideals guided warriors' actions and glorified their roles.

Knights: Warriors on Horseback

Soldiers mounted on horseback became valuable in combat during the reign of Charlemagne's grandfather, Charles Martel, in the 700s. Charles Martel had observed that the Muslim cavalry often turned the tide of battles. As a result, he organized Frankish troops of armored horsemen, or knights.

The Technology of Warfare Changes Leather saddles and stirrups changed the way warfare was conducted in Europe during the 700s. Both had been developed in Asia around 200 BC.

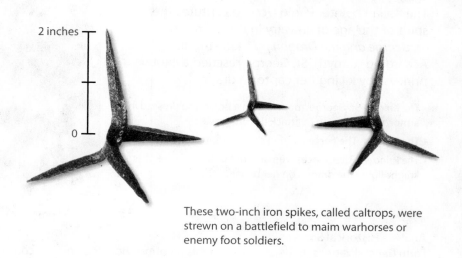

2 inches

0

These two-inch iron spikes, called caltrops, were strewn on a battlefield to maim warhorses or enemy foot soldiers.

The saddle kept a warrior firmly seated on a moving horse. Stirrups enabled him to ride and handle heavier weapons. Without stirrups to brace him, a charging warrior was likely to topple off his own horse. Frankish knights, galloping full tilt, could knock over enemy foot soldiers and riders on horseback. Gradually, mounted knights became the most important part of an army. Their warhorses played a key military role.

The Warrior's Role in Feudal Society By the 11th century, western Europe was a battleground of warring nobles vying for power. To defend their territories, feudal lords raised private armies of knights. In exchange for military service, feudal lords used their most abundant resource—land. They rewarded knights, their most skilled warriors, with fiefs from their sprawling estates. Wealth from these fiefs allowed knights to devote their lives to war. Knights could afford to pay for costly weapons, armor, and warhorses.

As the lord's vassal, a knight's main obligation was to serve in battle. A lord typically demanded about 40 days of combat a year from his knights. Knights' pastimes often revolved around training for war. Wrestling and hunting helped them gain strength and practice the skills they would need on the battlefield.

Reading Check
Find Main Ideas
What were two inventions from Asia that changed the technology of warfare in western Europe?

Knighthood and the Code of Chivalry

Knights were expected to display courage in battle and loyalty to their lord. By the 1100s, the code of **chivalry** (SHIHV·uhl·ree), a complex set of ideals, demanded that a knight fight bravely in defense of three masters. He devoted himself to his earthly feudal lord, his heavenly Lord, and his chosen lady. The chivalrous knight also protected the weak and the poor.

Historical Source

Chivalry

The Italian painter Paolo Uccello captures the spirit of the age of chivalry in this painting, *St. George and the Dragon* (c. 1455–1460). According to myth, St. George rescued a captive princess by killing her captor, a dragon.

- **The Knight** St. George, mounted on a horse and dressed in armor, uses his lance to attack the dragon.
- **The Dragon** The fierce-looking dragon represents evil.
- **The Princess** The princess remains out of the action as her knight fights the dragon on her behalf.

Analyze Historical Sources
Form Generalizations In what way does this painting show the knight's code of chivalry?

The ideal knight was loyal, brave, and courteous. Most knights, though, failed to meet all of these high standards. For example, they treated the lower classes brutally.

A Knight's Training Sons of nobles began training for knighthood at an early age and learned the code of chivalry. At age 7, a boy would be sent off to the castle of another lord. As a page, he waited on his hosts and began to practice fighting skills. At around age 14, the page reached the rank of squire. A squire acted as a servant to a knight. At around age 21, a squire became a full-fledged knight.

After being dubbed a knight, most young men traveled for a year or two. The young knights gained experience fighting in local wars. Some took part in mock battles called **tournaments**. Tournaments combined recreation with combat training. Two armies of knights charged each other. Trumpets blared, and lords and ladies cheered. Like real battles, tournaments were fierce and bloody competitions. Winners could usually demand large ransoms from defeated knights.

Brutal Reality of Warfare The small-scale violence of tournaments did not match the bloodshed of actual battles, especially those fought at castles. By the 1100s, massive walls and guard towers encircled stone castles. These castles dominated much of the countryside in western Europe. Lord and lady, their family, knights and other men-at-arms, and servants made their home in the castle. The castle was also a fortress, designed for defense.

A castle under siege was a gory sight. Attacking armies used a wide range of strategies and weapons to force castle residents to surrender. Defenders of a castle poured boiling water, hot oil, or molten lead on enemy soldiers. Expert archers were stationed on the roof of the castle. Armed with crossbows, they fired deadly bolts that could pierce full armor.

The Literature of Chivalry

In the 1100s, the themes of medieval literature downplayed the brutality of knighthood and feudal warfare. Many stories idealized castle life. They glorified knighthood and chivalry, tournaments and battles. Songs and poems about a knight's undying love for a lady were also very popular.

Epic Poetry Feudal lords and their ladies enjoyed listening to epic poems. These poems recounted a hero's deeds and adventures. Many epics retold stories about legendary heroes such as King Arthur and Charlemagne.

**Reading Check
Compare** How are tournaments like modern sports competitions?

**Vocabulary
siege** a military blockade staged by enemy armies trying to capture a fortress

Castles and Siege Weapons

Attacking armies carefully planned how to capture a castle. Engineers would inspect the castle walls for weak points in the stone. Then, enemy soldiers would try to ram the walls, causing them to collapse. At the battle site, attackers often constructed the heavy and clumsy weapons shown here.

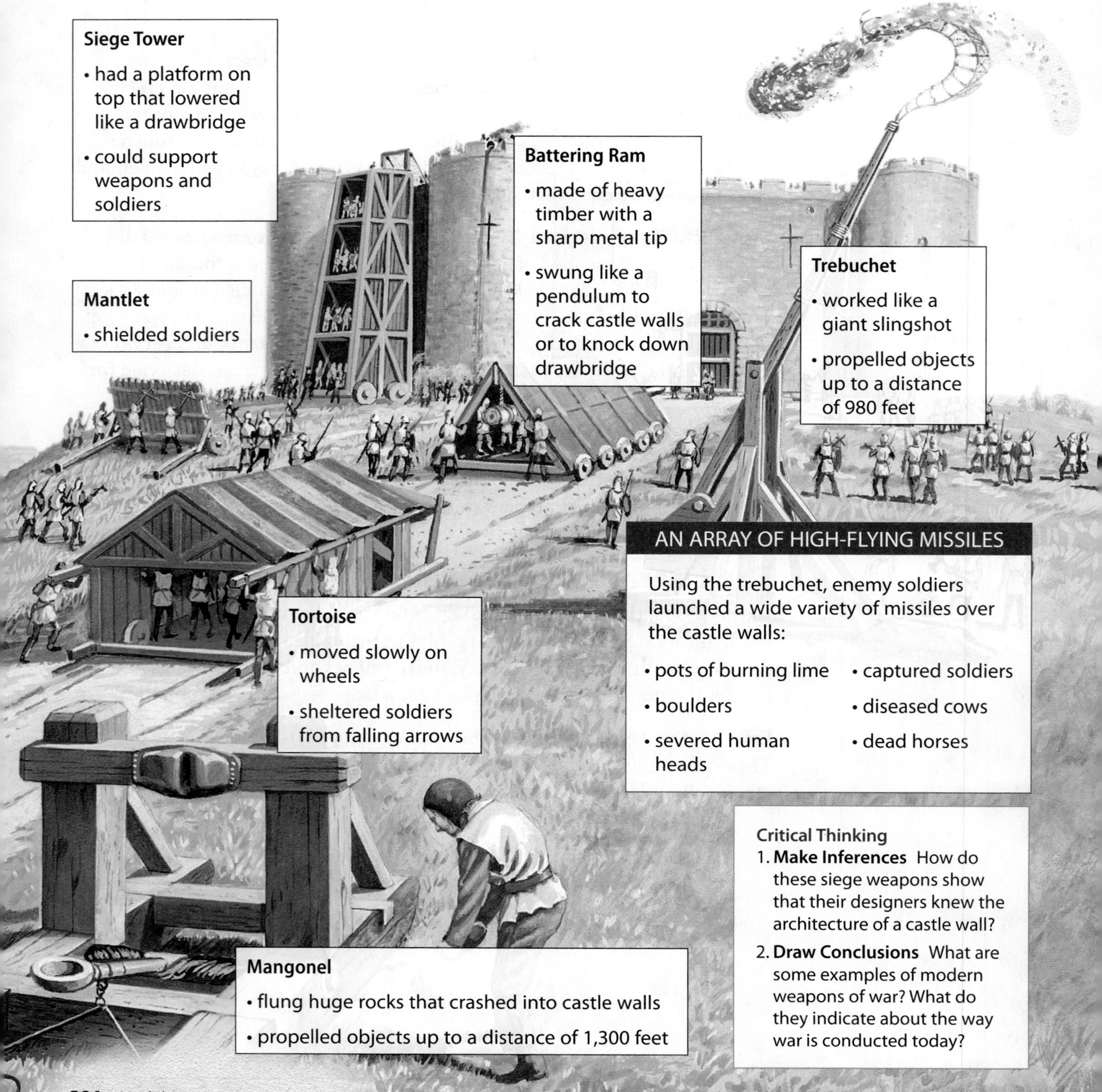

Siege Tower

- had a platform on top that lowered like a drawbridge
- could support weapons and soldiers

Mantlet

- shielded soldiers

Battering Ram

- made of heavy timber with a sharp metal tip
- swung like a pendulum to crack castle walls or to knock down drawbridge

Trebuchet

- worked like a giant slingshot
- propelled objects up to a distance of 980 feet

Tortoise

- moved slowly on wheels
- sheltered soldiers from falling arrows

AN ARRAY OF HIGH-FLYING MISSILES

Using the trebuchet, enemy soldiers launched a wide variety of missiles over the castle walls:

- pots of burning lime
- boulders
- severed human heads
- captured soldiers
- diseased cows
- dead horses

Mangonel

- flung huge rocks that crashed into castle walls
- propelled objects up to a distance of 1,300 feet

Critical Thinking

1. **Make Inferences** How do these siege weapons show that their designers knew the architecture of a castle wall?
2. **Draw Conclusions** What are some examples of modern weapons of war? What do they indicate about the way war is conducted today?

The Song of Roland is one of the earliest and most famous medieval epic poems. It praises a band of French soldiers who perished in battle during Charlemagne's reign. The poem transforms the event into a struggle. A few brave French knights led by Roland battle an overwhelming army of Muslims from Spain. Roland's friend, Turpin the Archbishop, stands as a shining example of medieval ideals. Turpin represents courage, faith, and chivalry:

> *"And now there comes the Archbishop.*
> *He spurs his horse, goes up into a mountain,*
> *summons the French; and he preached them a sermon:*
> *'Barons, my lords, [Charlemagne] left us in this place.*
> *We know our duty: to die like good men for our King.*
> *Fight to defend the holy Christian faith.'"*

—from *The Song of Roland*

Love Poems and Songs Under the code of chivalry, a knight's duty to his lady became as important as his duty to his lord. In many medieval poems, the hero's difficulties resulted from a conflict between those two obligations.

Troubadours were traveling poet-musicians at the castles and courts of Europe. They composed short verses and songs about the joys and sorrows of romantic love. Sometimes troubadours sang their own verses in the castles of their lady. They also sent roving minstrels to carry their songs to courts.

A troubadour might sing about love's disappointments: "My loving heart, my faithfulness, myself, my world she deigns to take. Then leave me bare and comfortless to longing thoughts that ever wake."

Other songs told of lovesick knights who adored ladies they would probably never win: "Love of a far-off land/For you my heart is aching/And I can find no relief." The code of chivalry promoted a false image of knights, making them seem more romantic than brutal. In turn, these love songs created an artificial image of women. In the troubadour's eyes, noblewomen were always beautiful and pure.

The most celebrated woman of the age was Eleanor of Aquitaine (1122–1204). Troubadours flocked to her court in the French duchy of Aquitaine. Later, as queen of England, Eleanor was the mother of two kings, Richard the Lion-Hearted and John. Richard himself composed romantic songs and poems.

Reading Check
Synthesize
What were some of the themes of medieval literature?

Women's Role in Feudal Society

Most women in feudal society were powerless, just as most men were. But women had the added burden of being thought inferior to men. This was the view of the Church and was generally accepted in feudal society. Nonetheless, women played important roles in both noble and peasant families.

Noblewomen Under the feudal system, a noblewoman could inherit an estate from her husband. Upon her lord's request, she could also send his knights to war. When her husband was off fighting, the lady of a medieval castle might act as military commander and a warrior. At times, noblewomen played a key role in defending castles. They hurled rocks and fired arrows at attackers.

Historical Source

Daily Life of a Noblewoman

This excerpt describes the daily life of an English noblewoman of the Middle Ages, Cicely Neville, Duchess of York. A typical noblewoman is pictured.

"She gets up at 7 a.m., and her chaplain is waiting to say morning prayers . . . and when she has washed and dressed . . . she has breakfast, then she goes to the chapel, for another service, then has dinner. . . . After dinner, she discusses business . . . then has a short sleep, then drinks ale or wine. Then . . . she goes to the chapel for evening service, and has supper. After supper, she relaxes with her women attendants. . . . After that, she goes to her private room, and says nighttime prayers. By 8 p.m. she is in bed."
—**Daily Routine of Cicely, Duchess of York**, quoted in *Women in Medieval Times* by Fiona Macdonald

Daily Life of a Peasant Woman

This excerpt describes the daily life of a medieval peasant woman like the one shown.

"I get up early . . . milk our cows and turn them into the field. . . . Then I make butter. . . . Afterward I make cheese. . . . Then the children need looking after. . . . I give the chickens food . . . and look after the young geese. . . . I bake, I brew. . . . I twist rope. . . . I tease out wool, and card it, and spin it on a wheel. . . . I organize food for the cattle, and for ourselves. . . . I look after all the household."
—**From a Ballad First Written Down in About 1500**, quoted in *Women in Medieval Times* by Fiona Macdonald

Analyze Historical Sources

1. What seem to be the major concerns in the noblewoman's life? How do they compare with those of the peasant woman?

2. What qualities would you associate with the peasant woman and the life she lived?

In reality, however, the lives of most noblewomen were limited. Whether young or old, females in noble families generally were confined to activities in the home or the convent. Also, noblewomen held little property because lords passed down their fiefs to sons and not to daughters.

Peasant Women For the vast majority of women of the lower classes, life had remained unchanged for centuries. Peasant women performed endless labor around the home and often in the fields, bore children, and took care of their families. Young peasant girls learned practical household skills from their mother at an early age, unlike daughters in rich households who were educated by tutors. Females in peasant families were poor and powerless. Yet, the economic contribution they made was essential to the survival of the peasant household.

As you have read, the Church significantly influenced the status of medieval women. The Church was a far-reaching influence in the Middle Ages.

Reading Check
Summarize What privileges did a noblewoman have in medieval society?

The noblewomen depicted in this manuscript show their courage and combat skills in defending a castle against enemies.

Lesson 5 Assessment

1. **Organize Information** Which ideas associated with chivalry have remnants in today's society? Explain. Use a web like the one below to organize your notes.

Chivalry

2. **Key Terms and People** For each key term or person in the lesson, write a sentence explaining its significance.

3. **Develop Historical Perspective** How important a role did knights play in the feudal system?

4. **Make Inferences** How was the code of chivalry like the idea of romantic love?

5. **Compare and Contrast** In what ways were the lives of a noblewoman and a peasant woman similar and different?

Module 10 Assessment

Key Terms and People

For each term or name below, write a sentence explaining its significance during the early Middle Ages.

1. Justinian Code
2. Hagia Sophia
3. patriarch
4. Slavs
5. monastery
6. Charlemagne
7. vassal
8. serf
9. manor
10. chivalry

Main Ideas

Use your notes and the information in the module to answer the following questions.

The Byzantine Empire

1. What were the names and characteristics of the four parts of the Justinian Code?
2. What were some important features of life in Constantinople?
3. Which peoples attacked the Byzantine Empire? What part of the empire did they invade?
4. What two main religions emerged out of the split in the Christian Church?

Early Russia

5. What does the *Primary Chronicle* say about Rurik and the origin of Novgorod?
6. According to the *Primary Chronicle,* how did Vladimir choose Byzantine Christianity?
7. How did Moscow's location contribute to its growth?
8. What event marked Russia's liberation from Mongol rule?

Charlemagne Unites Germanic Kingdoms

9. How did Gregory I increase the political power of the pope?
10. What was the outcome of the Battle of Tours?
11. What was the significance of the pope's declaring Charlemagne emperor?

Feudalism and Manorialism

12. Which invading peoples caused turmoil in Europe during the 800s?
13. What exchange took place between lords and vassals under feudalism?
14. What duties did the lord of a manor and his serfs owe one another?

Society in the Feudal Era

15. What were the stages of becoming a knight?
16. What were common subjects of troubadours' songs?
17. What role did women play under feudalism?

Critical Thinking

1. **Compare and Contrast** In a chart like the one shown below, compare the Byzantine Empire and feudal western Europe. Consider institutions, such as government and religion, as well as social roles.

	Byzantine Empire	Feudal Western Europe
government		
religion		
social roles		

2. **Analyze Issues** What were Justinian's goals in creating his law code? Why might a leader want to organize the laws?

3. **Draw Conclusions** Why do you think the ownership of land became an increasing source of power for feudal lords?

4. **Synthesize** What generalizations could you make about the relationship between politics and religion in the Middle Ages?

Engage with History

Imagine you are living in the countryside of western Europe during the 1100s. Like about 90 percent of the population, you are a peasant working the land. Your family's hut is located in a small village on your lord's estate. The lord provides all your basic needs, including housing, food, and protection. Especially important is his protection from invaders who repeatedly strike Europe. Write an essay about the issue of the freedoms you would give up for protection. How important is security? Is it worth not having certain basic freedoms? Discuss your ideas in a small group.

Focus on Writing

Write a three-paragraph character sketch of a historical figure described in this module. Consider the following:

- why the figure was important
- how the figure performed his or her role

Multimedia Activity

Use technological tools, such as the Internet, to find out more, research data, and verify facts about medieval tournaments. Then create a video game that imitates a medieval tournament between knights. Use a computer, tablet, or other technological tool to communicate your findings in a proposal. In your proposal describe the ideas for the game that you might send to a video game company.

Think about video games that are based on contests. You might adapt some of the rules to your game. Consider the following:

- the rules of the game
- the system of keeping score of wins and losses
- weapons that should be used

Module 11

Church and Society in Western Europe

Essential Question

What would Europe look like today if the Crusades had not happened?

About the Photo: Exterior view of Notre Dame cathedral in Paris, France.

▷ *Explore ONLINE!*

HISTORY.

VIDEOS, including...
- The Spiritual Life of Europe
- Byzantium's Call for Help
- Crusades' Aftermath

☑ Document Based Investigations

☑ Graphic Organizers

☑ Interactive Games

☑ Image with Hotspots:
Gothic Architecture

☑ Carousel: The Longbow

In this module, you will learn how the effects of the Crusades, the Hundred Years' War, and the plague transformed medieval society.

What You Will Learn ...

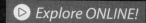
Explore ONLINE!

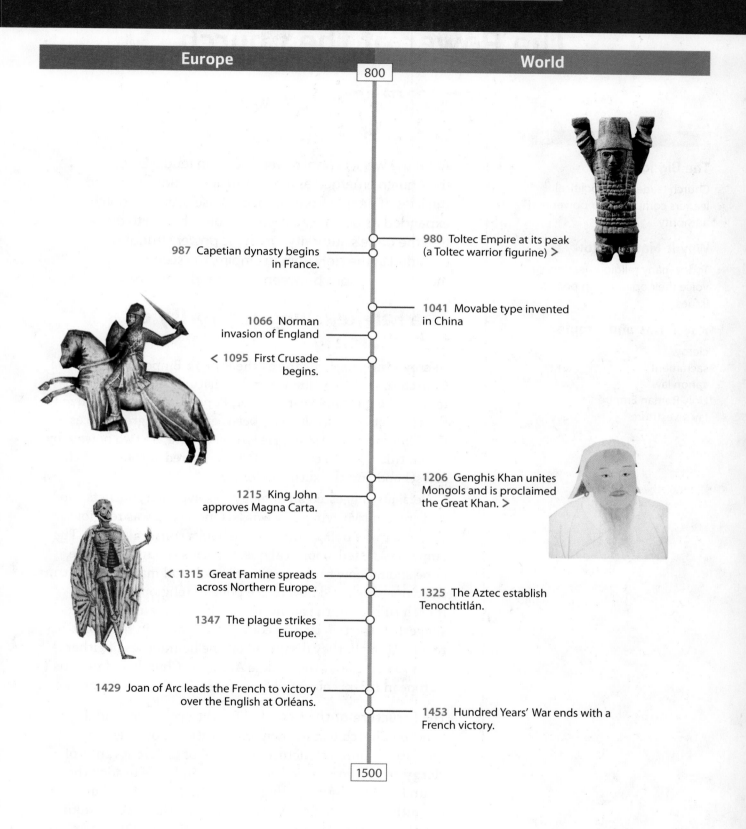

Europe		World
	800	

980 Toltec Empire at its peak (a Toltec warrior figurine) >

987 Capetian dynasty begins in France.

1041 Movable type invented in China

1066 Norman invasion of England

< **1095** First Crusade begins.

1206 Genghis Khan unites Mongols and is proclaimed the Great Khan. >

1215 King John approves Magna Carta.

< **1315** Great Famine spreads across Northern Europe.

1325 The Aztec establish Tenochtitlán.

1347 The plague strikes Europe.

1429 Joan of Arc leads the French to victory over the English at Orléans.

1453 Hundred Years' War ends with a French victory.

1500

The Power of the Church

The Big Idea
Church leaders and political leaders competed for power and authority.

Why It Matters Now
Today many religious leaders still voice their opinions on political issues.

Key Terms and People
clergy
sacrament
canon law
Holy Roman Empire
lay investiture

Setting the Stage

Amid the weak central governments in feudal Europe, the Church emerged as a powerful institution. It shaped the lives of people from all social classes. As the Church expanded its political role, strong rulers began to question the pope's authority. Dramatic power struggles unfolded in the Holy Roman Empire, the scene of mounting tensions between popes and emperors.

The Far-Reaching Authority of the Church

In crowning Charlemagne as the Roman Emperor in 800, the Church sought to influence both spiritual and political matters. Three hundred years earlier, Pope Gelasius I recognized the conflicts that could arise between the two great forces—the Church and the state. He wrote, "There are two powers by which this world is chiefly ruled: the sacred authority of the priesthood and the authority of kings."

Gelasius suggested an analogy to solve such conflicts. God had created two symbolic swords. One sword was religious. The other was political. The pope held a spiritual sword. The emperor wielded a political one. Gelasius thought that the pope should bow to the emperor in political matters. In turn, the emperor should bow to the pope in religious matters. If each ruler kept the authority in his own realm, Gelasius suggested, the two leaders could share power in harmony. In reality, though, they disagreed on the boundaries of either realm. Throughout the Middle Ages, the Church and various European rulers competed for power.

The Structure of the Church Like the system of feudalism, the Church had its own organization. Power was based on status. Church structure consisted of different ranks of **clergy**, or religious officials. The pope in Rome headed the Church. All clergy, including bishops and priests, fell under his authority. Bishops supervised priests, the lowest ranking members of the clergy. Bishops also settled disputes over

Church teachings and practices. For most people, local priests served as the main contact with the Church.

Religion as a Unifying Force Feudalism and the manor system created divisions among people. But the shared beliefs in the teachings of the Church bonded people together. The Church was a stable force during an era of constant warfare and political turmoil. It provided Christians with a sense of security and of belonging to a religious community. In the Middle Ages, religion occupied center stage. Medieval Christians' everyday lives were harsh. Still, they could all follow the same path to salvation—everlasting life in heaven. Priests and other clergy administered the **sacraments**, or important religious ceremonies. These rites paved the way for achieving salvation. For example, through the sacrament of baptism, people became part of the Christian community.

At the local level, the village church was a unifying force in the lives of most people. It served as a religious and social center. People worshiped together at the church. They also met with other villagers. Religious holidays, especially Christmas and Easter, were occasions for festive celebrations.

The Law of the Church The Church's authority was both religious and political. It provided a unifying set of spiritual beliefs and rituals. The Church also created a system of justice to guide people's conduct. All medieval Christians, kings and peasants alike, were subject to **canon law**, or Church law, in matters such as marriage and religious practices. The Church also established courts to try people accused of violating canon law. Two of the harshest punishments that offenders faced were excommunication and the interdict.

Popes used the threat of excommunication, or banishment from the Church, to wield power over political rulers. For example, a disobedient king's quarrel with a pope might result in his excommunication. This punishment meant the king would be denied salvation. Excommunication also freed all the king's vassals from their duties to him. If an excommunicated king continued to disobey the pope, the pope, in turn, could use an even more frightening weapon, the interdict.

Under an interdict, many sacraments and religious services could not be performed in the king's lands. As Christians, the king's subjects believed that without such sacraments they might be doomed to hell. In the 11th century, excommunication and the possible threat of an interdict would force a German emperor to submit to the pope's commands.

A pope's tiara symbolized his power.

Reading Check
Analyze Motives
Why did medieval peasants support the Church?

An Age of Superstition

Lacking knowledge of the laws of nature, many people during the Middle Ages were led to irrational beliefs. They expected the dead to reappear as ghosts. A friendly goblin might do a person a good deed, but an evil witch might cause great harm. Medieval people thought an evil witch had the power to exchange a healthy child for a sickly one.

The medieval Church frowned upon superstitions such as these:
- preparing a table with three knives to please good fairies
- making a vow by a tree, a pond, or any place but a church
- believing that a person could change into the shape of a wolf
- believing that meeting a priest or the croak of a raven would bring a person good or bad luck

According to medieval superstitions, ravens were thought to bring bad luck.

Critical Thinking
1. **Draw Conclusions** Why were people during the Middle Ages more likely to believe in superstitions?

2. **Make Inferences** Why do you think the medieval Church frowned upon many superstitions?

The Church and the Holy Roman Empire

When Pope Leo III crowned Charlemagne emperor in 800, he unknowingly set the stage for future conflicts between popes and emperors. These clashes would go on for centuries.

Otto I Allies with the Church The most effective ruler of medieval Germany was Otto I, known as Otto the Great. Otto, crowned king in 936, followed the policies of his hero, Charlemagne. Otto formed a close alliance with the Church. To limit the nobles' strength, he sought help from the clergy. He built up his power base by gaining the support of the bishops and abbots, the heads of monasteries. He dominated the Church in Germany. He also used his power to defeat German princes. Following in Charlemagne's footsteps, Otto also invaded Italy on the pope's behalf. In 962, the pope rewarded Otto by crowning him emperor.

Signs of Future Conflicts The German-Italian empire Otto created was first called the Roman Empire of the German Nation. It later became the **Holy Roman Empire**. It remained the strongest state in Europe until about 1100. However, Otto's attempt to revive Charlemagne's empire caused trouble for future German leaders. Popes and Italian nobles, too, resented German power over Italy.

Reading Check
Summarize
What three groups vied for power during this time?

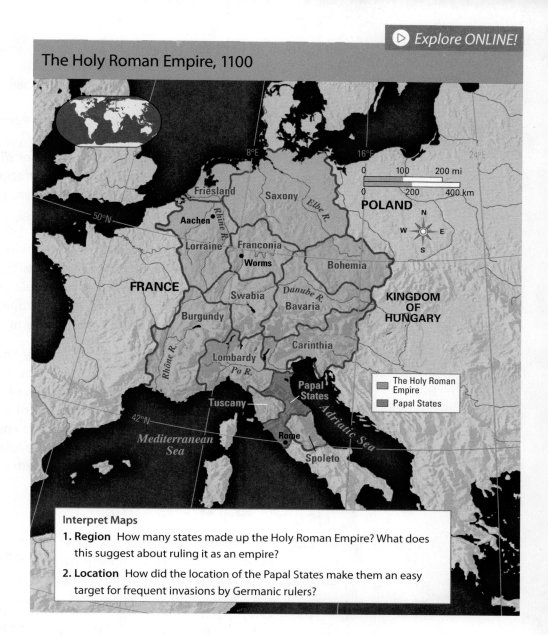

The Holy Roman Empire, 1100

POLAND

Friesland

Saxony

Elbe R.

Aachen

Rhine R.

Lorraine

Franconia

Worms

Bohemia

FRANCE

Swabia

Danube R.

Bavaria

Burgundy

KINGDOM OF HUNGARY

Carinthia

Lombardy

Po R.

Papal States

Tuscany

Adriatic Sea

Rome

Mediterranean Sea

Spoleto

The Holy Roman Empire

Papal States

Interpret Maps

1. **Region** How many states made up the Holy Roman Empire? What does this suggest about ruling it as an empire?

2. **Location** How did the location of the Papal States make them an easy target for frequent invasions by Germanic rulers?

The Emperor Clashes with the Pope

The Church was not happy that kings, such as Otto, had control over clergy and their offices. It especially resented the practice of **lay investiture**, a ceremony in which kings and nobles appointed church officials. Whoever controlled lay investiture held the real power in naming bishops, who were very influential clergy that kings sought to control. Church reformers felt that kings should not have that power. In 1075, Pope Gregory VII banned lay investiture.

The furious young German emperor, Henry IV, immediately called a meeting of the German bishops he had appointed. With their approval, the emperor ordered Gregory to step down from the papacy. In response, Gregory then excommunicated Henry. German bishops and princes feared losing salvation. By Church law, they no longer had an obligation to serve Henry, so they sided with the pope. To save his throne, Henry tried to win the pope's forgiveness.

Showdown at Canossa In January 1077, Henry crossed the snowy Alps to the Italian town of Canossa (kuh•nAHs•uh). He approached the castle where Gregory was a guest. Gregory later described the scene:

> *"There, having laid aside all the belongings of royalty, wretchedly, with bare feet and clad in wool, he [Henry IV] continued for three days to stand before the gate of the castle. Nor did he desist from imploring with many tears the aid and consolation of the apostolic mercy until he had moved all of those who were present there."*

Pope Gregory, in *Basic Documents in Medieval History*

The pope was obligated to forgive any sinner who begged so humbly. Still, Gregory kept Henry waiting in the snow for three days before ending his excommunication. Their meeting actually solved nothing. The pope had humiliated Henry, the proudest ruler in Europe. Yet, Henry felt triumphant and rushed home to punish the rebellious nobles.

Concordat of Worms The successors of Gregory and Henry continued to fight over lay investiture until 1122. That year, representatives of the Church and the emperor met in the German city of Worms (wurms). They reached a compromise known as the Concordat of Worms. By its terms, the Church alone could appoint a bishop, but the emperor could veto the appointment. As a result of Henry's struggle, German princes regained power they lost under Otto. But a later king, Frederick I, would resume the battle to build royal authority.

Disorder in the Empire

By 1152, the seven princes who elected the German king realized that Germany needed a strong ruler to keep the peace. They chose Frederick I, nicknamed "**barbarossa**" for his red beard.

The Reign of Frederick I Frederick I was the first ruler to call his lands the Holy Roman Empire. However, this region was actually a patchwork of feudal territories. His forceful personality and military skills enabled him to dominate the German princes. Yet, whenever he left the country, disorder returned. Following Otto's example, Frederick I repeatedly invaded the rich cities of Italy to assert his Imperial dominance. His brutal tactics spurred Italian merchants to unite against him. He also angered the pope, who joined the merchants in an alliance called the Lombard League.

In 1176, the foot soldiers of the Lombard League faced Frederick's army of mounted knights at the Battle of Legnano (lay•NYAHN•oh). In an astonishing victory, the Italian foot soldiers used crossbows to defeat feudal knights for the first time in history. In 1177, Frederick made peace with the pope and returned to Germany. His defeat, though, had undermined his authority with the German princes. After he drowned in 1190, his empire fell to pieces.

Reading Check
Make Inferences
Why was Henry's journey to Canossa a political act?

Vocabulary
barbarossa means "red beard" in Italian

German States Remain Separate German kings after Frederick I, including his grandson Frederick II, continued their attempts to revive Charlemagne's empire and his alliance with the Church. This policy led to wars with Italian cities and to further clashes with the pope. These conflicts were one reason why the feudal states of Germany did not unify during the Middle Ages. Another reason was that the system of German princes electing the king weakened royal authority. German rulers controlled fewer royal lands to use as a base of power. In contrast, the French and English kings of the same period were establishing a strong central authority.

Reading Check
Analyze Causes
What political trend kept German states separate during the Middle Ages?

This manuscript shows Frederick I at the height of his imperial power.

Lesson 1 Assessment

1. **Organize Information** List the major events and dates of the power struggles between the Church and rulers. What do these power struggles have in common?

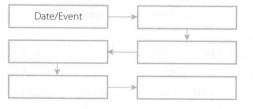

2. **Key Terms and People** For each key term or person in the lesson, write a sentence explaining its significance.

3. **Summarize** What were some of the matters covered by canon law?

4. **Analyze Effects** How did Otto the Great make the crown stronger than the German nobles?

5. **Analyze Motives** Why did lay investiture cause a struggle between kings and popes?

6. **Compare** How was the structure of the Church like that of the feudal system?

7. **Evaluate** Was the Concordat of Worms a fair compromise for both the emperor and the Church? Why or why not?

8. **Draw Conclusions** Why did German kings fail to unite their lands?

Church Reform and the Crusades

The Big Idea
The Catholic Church underwent reform and launched Crusades against Muslims.

Why It Matters Now
The Crusades left a legacy of distrust between Christians and Muslims that continues to the present.

Key Terms and People
simony
Gothic
Urban II
Crusade
Saladin
Richard the Lion-Hearted

Setting the Stage

Some historians have called the period in Western Europe between 500 and 1000 a "dark age." Magyars seeking plunder pushed up from the Danube River region. Vikings raided western European church monasteries. These groups destroyed many of these centers of learning. Around the 900s, however, a new spirit invaded the Church and brought about a spiritual revival in the clergy. Filled with new energy, the Church began restructuring itself and started massive building programs to create new places of worship.

The Age of Faith

Monasteries led the spiritual revival. The monastery founded at Cluny in France in 910 was especially important. The reformers there wanted to return to the basic principles of Christianity. To do so they established new religious orders. Influenced by the devotion and reverence for God shown by the new monasteries, the popes began to reform the Church. They restored and expanded its power and authority. A new age of religious feeling was born—the Age of Faith. Still, many problems troubled the Church.

Problems in the Church Some priests were nearly illiterate and could barely read their prayers. Some of the popes were men of questionable morals. Many bishops and abbots cared more about their positions as feudal lords than about their duties as spiritual leaders. Reformers were most distressed by three main issues.

- Many village priests married and had families. Such marriages were against Church rulings.
- Bishops sold positions in the Church, a practice called **simony** (SY•muh•nee).
- Using the practice of lay investiture, kings appointed church bishops. Church reformers believed the Church alone should appoint bishops.

This illustration depicts monks farming at their monastery.

Reform and Church Organization Pope Leo IX and Pope Gregory VII enforced Church laws against simony and the marriage of priests. The popes who followed Leo and Gregory reorganized the Church to continue the policy of reform. In the 1100s and 1200s, the Church was restructured to resemble a kingdom, with the pope at its head. The pope's group of advisers was called the papal Curia. The Curia also acted as a court. It developed canon law (the law of the Church) on matters such as marriage, divorce, and inheritance. The Curia also decided cases based on these laws. Diplomats for the pope traveled through Europe dealing with bishops and kings. In this way the popes established their authority throughout Europe.

The Church collected taxes in the form of tithes. These consumed one-tenth the yearly income from every Christian family. The Church used some of the money to perform social services such as caring for the sick and the poor. In fact, the Church operated most hospitals in medieval Europe.

New Religious Orders The Cluniac Reforms of the early 900s renewed interest in monastic life. In the early 1200s, wandering friars traveled from place to place preaching and spreading the Church's ideas. Like monks, friars took vows of chastity, poverty, and obedience. Unlike monks, friars did not live apart from the world in monasteries. Instead they preached to the poor throughout Europe's towns and cities. Friars owned nothing and lived by begging.

Dominic, a Spanish priest, founded the Dominicans, one of the earliest orders of friars. Because Dominic emphasized the importance of study, many Dominicans were scholars. Francis of Assisi (uh•SEE•zee), an Italian, founded another order of friars, the Franciscans. Francis treated all creatures, including animals, as if they were his spiritual brothers and sisters.

Women played an important role in the spiritual revival. Women joined the Dominicans, Benedictines, and Franciscans. In 1212, a woman named Clare and her friend Francis of Assisi founded the Franciscan order for women. It was known as the Poor Clares. In Germany, Hildegard of Bingen founded a Benedictine convent in 1147. Like friars, these women lived in poverty and worked to help the poor and sick. Unlike the friars, however, women were not allowed to travel from place to place as preachers.

Reading Check
Evaluate
How did the popes increase their power and authority?

Cathedrals—Cities of God

During the medieval period, most people worshiped in small churches near their homes. Larger churches called cathedrals were built in city areas. The cathedral was viewed as the representation of the City of God. As such, it was decorated with all the richness that Christians could offer. Between about 800 and 1100, churches were built in the Romanesque (ROH•muh•NEHSK) style. The churches had round arches and a heavy roof held up by thick walls and pillars. The thick walls had tiny windows that let in little light.

Gothic Architecture

The master builders in France, where the Gothic style originated, developed techniques of structural engineering that were key to Gothic architecture: (1) ribbed vaults that supported the roof's weight, (2) flying buttresses that transferred weight to thick, exterior walls, (3) pointed arches that framed huge, stained-glass windows, and (4) tall spires that seemed to be pointing to heaven.

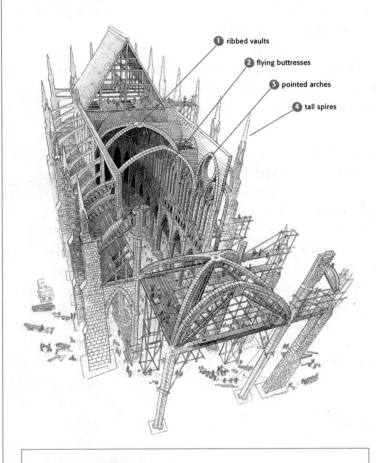

1 ribbed vaults
2 flying buttresses
3 pointed arches
4 tall spires

Chartres Cathedral
The cathedral of Chartres (shahrt) is a masterpiece of Gothic architecture. The cathedral has hundreds of sculptures. The stone carvings that frame every door illustrate Bible stories. The cathedral has not one, but two bell towers.

Stained Glass
In addition to its sculpture and soaring towers, Chartres Cathedral has some of the most beautiful stained-glass windows of any Gothic cathedral in Europe. The windows illustrate stories from the Bible. As illiterate peasants walked past the 176 windows, they could view those stories. The window above depicts the parable of the Good Samaritan.

Interpret Visual Sources

1. **Draw Conclusions** Think about elements in the style and engineering of Gothic architecture.
   a. What features enabled a cathedral to be built several stories high?
   b. What elements made the building seem even higher that it was?
   c. How did light get into the church?
2. **Compare and Contrast** Think about stained-glass windows you have seen. Do they tell a story? What figures or events do they illustrate?

A New Style of Church Architecture A new spirit in the church and access to more money from the growing wealth of towns and from trade helped fuel the building of churches in several European countries. In the early 1100s, a new style of architecture, known as **Gothic**, evolved throughout medieval Europe. The term *Gothic* comes from a Germanic tribe named the Goths. Unlike the heavy, gloomy Romanesque buildings, Gothic cathedrals thrust upward as if reaching toward heaven. Light streamed in through huge stained-glass windows. Other arts of the medieval world were incorporated around or in the Gothic cathedral—sculpture, wood-carvings, and stained-glass windows. These elements were meant to inspire the worshiper with the magnificence of God. Soon Gothic cathedrals were built in many French towns. In Paris, the vaulted ceiling of the Cathedral of Notre Dame (NOH•truh-DAHM) rose to more than 100 feet. In all, nearly 500 Gothic churches were built between 1170 and 1270.

Reading Check
Summarize
How did the architecture of Gothic cathedrals inspire reverence for God?

The Crusades

The Age of Faith also inspired wars of conquest. In 1093, the Byzantine emperor Alexius Comnenus sent an appeal to Robert, Count of Flanders. The emperor asked for help against the Muslim Turks. They were threatening to conquer his capital, Constantinople:

> *"Come then, with all your people and give battle with all your strength, so that all this treasure shall not fall into the hands of the Turks. . . . Therefore act while there is still time lest the kingdom of the Christians shall vanish from your sight and, what is more important, the Holy Sepulchre [the tomb where Jesus was buried] shall vanish. And in your coming you will find your reward in heaven, and if you do not come, God will condemn you."*
>
> —Emperor Alexius Comnenus, quoted in *The Dream and the Tomb* by Robert Payne

The red cross on his tunic identifies this knight as a crusader.

Pope **Urban II** also read that letter. Shortly after this appeal, he issued a call for what he termed a "holy war," a **Crusade**, to gain control of the **Holy Land**. Over the next 300 years, a number of such Crusades were launched and fought.

Goals of the Crusades The Crusades had economic, social, and political goals as well as religious motives. Muslims controlled Palestine (the Holy Land) and threatened Constantinople. The Byzantine emperor in Constantinople appealed to Christians to stop Muslim attacks. In addition, the pope wanted to reclaim Palestine and reunite Christendom, which had split into Eastern and Western branches in 1054.

Kings and the Church both saw the Crusades as an opportunity to get rid of quarrelsome knights who fought each other. These knights threatened the peace of the kingdoms, as well as Church property.

Others who participated in the Crusades were younger sons who, unlike eldest sons, did not stand to inherit their father's property. They were looking for land and a position in society, or for adventure.

Vocabulary
Holy Land Palestine; the area where Jesus lived and preached

Pope Urban II

In 1095, Pope Urban II issued a plea that resulted in the First Crusade. The pope assured his listeners that God was on their side.

Analyze Historical Sources
What reasons does Pope Urban II give to his listeners to undertake a holy war?

> "*Let the holy sepulcher of our Lord and Saviour, which is possessed by the unclean nations, especially arouse you. . . . This royal city [Jerusalem], situated at the center of the earth, is now held captive by the enemies of Christ and is subjected, by those who do not know God, to the worship of the heathen. Accordingly, undertake this journey eagerly for the remission of your sins, with the assurance of the reward of imperishable glory in the kingdom of heaven.*"

In the later Crusades, merchants profited by making cash loans to finance the journey. They also leased their ships for a hefty fee to transport armies over the Mediterranean Sea. At the same time, the merchants of Pisa, Genoa, and Venice hoped to win control of key trade routes to India, Southeast Asia, and China from Muslim traders.

The First and Second Crusades Pope Urban's call brought a tremendous outpouring of religious feeling and support for the Crusade. According to the pope, those who died on Crusade were assured of a place in heaven. With red crosses sewn on tunics worn over their armor and the battle cry of "God wills it!" on their lips, knights and commoners were fired up by religious zeal and became Crusaders.

By early 1097, three armies of knights and people of all classes had gathered outside Constantinople. Most of the Crusaders were French, but Bohemians, Germans, Englishmen, Scots, Italians, and Spaniards came as well. The Crusaders were ill prepared for war in this First Crusade. Many knew nothing of the geography, climate, or culture of the Holy Land. They had no grand strategy to capture Jerusalem. The nobles argued among themselves and couldn't agree on a leader. Finally an army of 12,000 (less than one-fourth of the original army) approached Jerusalem. The Crusaders besieged the city for over a month. On July 15, 1099, they captured the city.

All in all, the Crusaders had won a narrow strip of land. It stretched about 650 miles from Edessa in the north to Jerusalem in the south. Four feudal Crusader states were carved out of this territory, each ruled by a European noble.

The Crusaders' states were extremely vulnerable to Muslim counterattack. In 1144, Edessa was reconquered by the Turks. The Second Crusade was organized to recapture the city. But its armies straggled home in defeat. In 1187, Europeans were shocked to learn that Jerusalem itself had fallen to a Kurdish warrior and Muslim leader **Saladin** (SAL•uh•dihn).

Reading Check
Summarize
What, if anything, had the Crusaders gained by the end of the Second Crusade?

What are the dangers and rewards of going on a Crusade?

You are a squire in England. The knight you serve has decided to join a Christian Crusade (a holy war) to capture the city of Jerusalem from the Muslims. He has given you the choice of joining or staying home to look after his family and manor. On an earlier Crusade, the knight and his friends looted towns and manors, taking jewels and precious objects. But some of the knights were also held for ransom, robbed, and murdered. You are torn between the desire for adventure and possible riches that you might find on the Crusade, and fear of the hazards that await you on such a dangerous journey.

Richard the Lion-Hearted leads a group of Crusaders on the Third Crusade to regain Jerusalem from the Muslims.

❶

❷ Servants and women sometimes accompanied the Crusaders as they made their way toward the Holy Land.

Critical Thinking
1. **Analyze Motives** What reasons might an individual have to join a Crusade?
2. **Evaluate** What might be the advantages and disadvantages of staying home to defend the knight's family and estate?

William of Tyre

A Christian bishop, William of Tyre, drew upon eyewitness accounts of the capture of Jerusalem by Crusaders.

> "It was impossible to look upon the vast numbers of the slain without horror; everywhere lay fragments of human bodies, and the very ground was covered with the blood of the slain. It was not alone the spectacle of headless bodies and mutilated limbs strewn in all directions that roused horror in all who looked upon them. Still more dreadful was it to gaze upon the victors themselves, dripping with blood from head to foot, an ominous sight which brought terror to all who met them. It is reported that within the Temple enclosure alone about ten thousand infidels perished, in addition to those who lay slain everywhere throughout the city in the streets and squares, the number of whom was estimated as no less."

Saladin

This is an excerpt of Saladin's reply to a letter from Frederick I (Barbarossa) threatening Saladin. Saladin wrote the letter after he recaptured Jerusalem.

> "Whenever your armies are assembled . . . we will meet you in the power of God. We will not be satisfied with the land on the seacoast, but we will cross over with God's good pleasure and take from you all your lands in the strength of the Lord. . . . And when the Lord, by His power, shall have given us victory over you, nothing will remain for us to do but freely to take your lands by His power and with His good pleasure. . . . By the virtue and power of God we have taken possession of Jerusalem and its territories; and of the three cities that still remain in the hands of the Christians . . . we shall occupy them also."

Analyze Historical Sources
How did the brutal battles for Jerusalem affect each side? Explain.

The Third Crusade The Third Crusade to recapture Jerusalem was led by three of Europe's most powerful monarchs. They were Philip II (Augustus) of France, German emperor Frederick I (Barbarossa), and the English king, **Richard the Lion-Hearted**. Philip argued with Richard and went home. Barbarossa drowned on the journey. So Richard was left to lead the Crusaders in an attempt to regain the Holy Land from Saladin. Both Richard and Saladin were brilliant warriors. After many battles, the two agreed to a truce in 1192. Jerusalem remained under Muslim control. In return, Saladin promised that unarmed Christian pilgrims could freely visit the city's holy places.

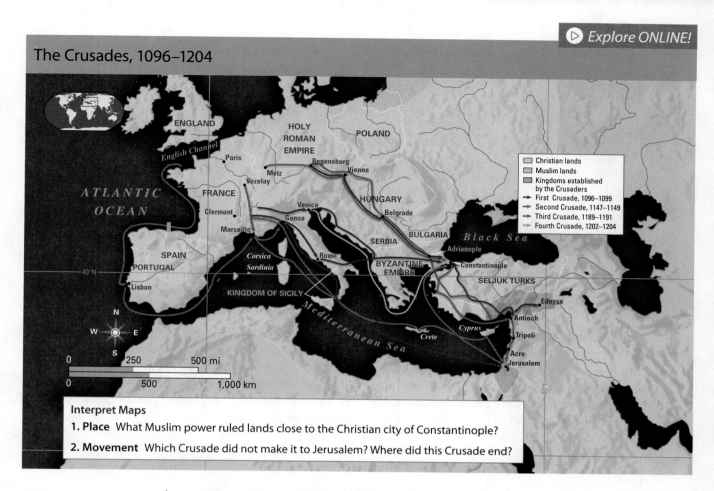

The Crusades, 1096–1204

▶ Explore ONLINE!

Christian lands
Muslim lands
Kingdoms established by the Crusaders
→ First Crusade, 1096–1099
→ Second Crusade, 1147–1149
→ Third Crusade, 1189–1191
→ Fourth Crusade, 1202–1204

Interpret Maps

1. **Place** What Muslim power ruled lands close to the Christian city of Constantinople?

2. **Movement** Which Crusade did not make it to Jerusalem? Where did this Crusade end?

The Crusading Spirit Dwindles

In 1204, the Fourth Crusade to capture Jerusalem failed. The knights did not reach the Holy Land. Instead, they ended up looting the city of Constantinople. In the 1200s, four more Crusades to free the holy land were also unsuccessful. The religious spirit of the First Crusade faded, and the search for personal gain grew. In two later Crusades, armies marched not to the Holy Land but to Egypt. The Crusaders intended to weaken Muslim forces there before going to the Holy Land. But none of these attempts conquered much land.

Historical Source

Luttrell Psalter

This illustration from a Latin text shows Richard the Lion-Hearted unhorsing Saladin during the Third Crusade. However, the two men never actually met in personal combat.

Analyze Historical Sources
What evidence reveals the artist's bias about the confrontation between Islam and Christianity?

Richard the Lion-Hearted
(1157–1199)

Richard was noted for his good looks, charm, courage, grace—and ruthlessness. When he heard that Jerusalem had fallen to the Muslims, he was filled with religious zeal. He joined the Third Crusade, leaving others to rule England in his place.

Richard mounted a siege on the city of Acre. Saladin's army was in the hills overlooking the city, but it was not strong enough to defeat the Crusaders. When finally the city fell, Richard had the Muslim survivors—some 3,000 men, women, and children—slaughtered. The Muslim army watched helplessly from the hills.

Saladin
(1138–1193)

Saladin was the most famous Muslim leader of the 1100s. His own people considered him a most devout man. Even the Christians regarded him as honest and brave.

He wished to chase the Crusaders back into their own territories. He said:

I think that when God grants me victory over the rest of Palestine, I shall divide my territories, make a will stating my wishes, then set sail on this sea for their far-off lands and pursue the Franks there, so as to free the earth from anyone who does not believe in Allah, or die in the attempt.

The Strange Story of the Children's Crusade Some stories of the Crusades mention that in 1212, thousands of children set out to conquer Jerusalem. From France, Stephen of Cloyes led as many as 30,000 children south to the Mediterranean. From Germany, Nicholas of Cologne marched about 20,000 young people over the Alps to the sea. Many died of cold and starvation on the journey. Thousands more were sold into slavery or drowned at sea after boarding ships for the Holy Land. Perhaps as few as one-tenth of those who set out on this Children's Crusade returned home.

Historians doubt that this Children's Crusade happened. The "children" probably were landless peasants and laborers searching for a better life. There certainly were young people in the crowds who took to the road in 1212, and some may have intended to travel to the Holy Land. However, the story of pious young people taking up the crusaders' banner is more fiction than fact.

Reading Check
Summarize
Why did the fervor of the Crusades end?

Cause	>	Effect
Crusaders travel to Holy Land		Increased trade and commerce More jobs for women and others left behind
Failure of Crusades		Weakened feudal nobility; increased power of kings Weakened pope and Byzantine Empire
Christian/Muslim interaction		Increased trade and shared knowledge Left legacy of hatred because of Christian intolerance

The Effects of the Crusades

The Crusades are a forceful example of the power of the Church during the medieval period. The call to go to the Holy Land encouraged thousands to leave their homes and travel to faraway lands. For those who stayed home, especially women, it meant a chance to manage affairs on the estates or to operate shops and inns.

European merchants who lived and traded in the Crusader states expanded trade between Europe and Southwest Asia. The goods imported from Southwest Asia included spices, fruits, and cloth. This trade with the West benefited both Christians and Muslims.

However, the failure of later Crusades also lessened the power of the pope. The Crusades weakened the feudal nobility and increased the power of kings. Thousands of knights and other participants lost their lives and fortunes. The fall of Constantinople weakened the Byzantine Empire.

For Muslims, the intolerance and prejudice displayed by Christians in the Holy Land left behind a legacy of bitterness and hatred. This legacy continues to the present. For Christians and Jews who remained in the Muslim-controlled region after the fall of the Crusader states, relations with the Muslim leadership worsened. The Crusades grew out of religious fervor, feudalism, and chivalry, which came together with explosive energy. This same energy led to the growth of trade, towns, and universities in medieval Europe.

Reading Check
Develop Historical Perspective
In what way did the Crusades benefit people of all faiths?

Lesson 2 Assessment

1. **Organize Information** Fill in a timeline like the one below to organize key events.
   Which of the events of the Age of Faith do you think were most important to the Church? Explain.

   900 — 1500

2. **Key Terms and People** For each key term or person in the lesson, write a sentence explaining its significance.
3. **Summarize** What were the three main causes for the need to reform the Church?
4. **Evaluate** Which Crusade was the only successful one?

5. **Develop Historical Perspective** How did the goals of the Crusades change over the years?
6. **Form and Support Opinions** Which of the following do you think best represents the spirit of the Age of Faith—Church reform, the Crusades, or the Gothic cathedrals? Explain.
7. **Make Inferences** What evidence supports the idea that the Church functioned like a kingdom?
8. **Analyze Effects** How did the Crusades change the history of Europe? Give reasons for your answer.

Changes in Medieval Society

The Big Idea

The feudal system declined as agriculture, trade, finance, towns, and universities developed.

Why It Matters Now

The changes in the Middle Ages laid the foundations for modern Europe.

Key Terms and People

three-field system
guild
Commercial Revolution
burgher
vernacular
Thomas Aquinas
scholastics

Setting the Stage

While Church reform, cathedral-building, and the Crusades were taking place, other important changes were occurring in medieval society. Between 1000 and 1300, agriculture, trade, and finance made significant advances. Towns and cities grew. This was in part due to the growing population and to territorial expansion of western Europe. Cultural interaction with the Muslim and Byzantine worlds sparked the growth of learning and the birth of an institution new to Europe—the university.

A Growing Food Supply

Europe's great revival would have been impossible without better ways of farming. Expanding civilization required an increased food supply. A warmer climate, which lasted from about 800 to 1200, brought improved farm production. Farmers began to cultivate lands in regions once too cold to grow crops. They also developed new methods to take advantage of more available land.

Switch to Horsepower For hundreds of years, peasants had depended on oxen to pull their plows. Oxen lived on the poorest straw and stubble, so they were easy to keep. Horses needed better food, but a team of horses could plow three times as much land in a day as a team of oxen.

Before farmers could use horses, however, a better harness was needed. Sometime before 900, farmers in Europe began using a harness that fitted across the horse's chest, enabling it to pull a plow. As a result, horses gradually replaced oxen for plowing and for pulling wagons. All over Europe, axes rang as the great forests were cleared for new fields.

The Three-Field System Around AD 800, some villages began to organize their lands into three fields instead of two. Two of the fields were planted, and the other lay fallow

Reading Check
Analyze Effects How did farmers take advantage of the warming climate during the Middle Ages?

(resting) for a year. Under this new **three-field system**, farmers could grow crops on two-thirds of their land each year, not just on half of it. As a result, food production increased. Villagers had more to eat. Well-fed people, especially children, could better resist disease and live longer, and as a result the European population grew dramatically.

The Guilds

A second change in the European economy was the development of the guild. A **guild** was an organization of individuals in the same business or occupation working to improve the economic and social conditions of its members. The first guilds were merchant guilds. Merchants banded together to control the number of goods being traded and to keep prices up. They also provided security in trading and reduced losses.

About the same time, skilled artisans, such as wheelwrights, glassmakers, winemakers, tailors, and druggists, began craft guilds. In most crafts, both husband and wife worked at the family trade. In a few crafts, especially for cloth making, women formed the majority. The guilds set standards for quality of work, wages, and working conditions. For example, bakers were required to sell loaves of bread of a standard size and weight. The guilds also created plans for supervised training of new workers.

By the 1000s, artisans and craftspeople were manufacturing goods by hand for local and long-distance trade. More and better products were now available to buyers in small towns, in bigger cities, and at trade fairs. Guilds became powerful forces in the medieval economy. The wealth they accumulated helped them establish influence over the government and the economy of towns and cities.

Reading Check
Summarize How did guilds change the way business was conducted and products were made?

SOCIAL HISTORY

Surnames

Many people can trace their last names, or surnames, back to a medieval occupation in Europe. The name Smith, for example, refers to someone who "smites," or works, metal. The surname Silversmith would belong to a person who works silver. In German-speaking areas, a smith was named Schmidt.

Someone who made goods out of wood was often surnamed Carpenter. In French-speaking areas, a carpenter was called Charpentier, while in German areas, the same person would be called Zimmerman.

The last name of Boulanger indicated a baker in France. A baker in Germany often had the surname Becker.

Critical Thinking
1. **Synthesize** What kind of information did a surname relay in medieval times?

2. **Make Inferences** What occupation do you think someone with the surname Taylor might have had in the Middle Ages?

Craft Guilds

Craft guilds formed an important part of town life during the medieval period. They trained young people in a skilled job, regulated the quality of goods sold, and were major forces in community life.

Guild Services	
To members:	To the community:
Set working conditions	Built almshouses for victims of misfortune
Covered members with a type of health insurance	Guaranteed quality work
Provided funeral expenses	Took turns policing the streets
Provided dowries for poor girls	Donated windows to the Church

Apprentice
- Parents paid for training
- Lived with a master and his family
- Required to obey the master
- Trained 2–7 years
- Was not allowed to marry during training
- When trained progressed to journeyman

Journeyman
(Day Worker)
- Worked for a master to earn a salary
- Worked 6 days a week
- Needed to produce a masterpiece (his finest work) to become a master
- Had to be accepted by the guild to become a master

Master
- Owned his own shop
- Worked with other masters to protect their trade
- Sometimes served in civic government

Critical Thinking
Analyze Effects How did craft guilds affect community life?

Commercial Revolution

Just as agriculture was expanding and craftsmanship changing, so were trade and finance. Increased availability of trade goods and new ways of doing business changed life in Europe. Taken together, this expansion of trade and business is called the **Commercial Revolution**.

Fairs and Trade Most trade took place in towns. Peasants from nearby manors traveled to town on fair days, hauling items to trade. Great fairs were held several times a year, usually during religious festivals, when many people would be in town. People visited the stalls set up by merchants from all parts of Europe.

Cloth was the most common trade item. Other items included bacon, salt, honey, cheese, wine, leather, dyes, knives, and ropes. Such local markets met all the needs of daily life for a small community. No longer was everything produced on a self-sufficient manor.

More goods from foreign lands became available. Trade routes spread across Europe from Flanders to Italy. Italian merchant ships traveled the Mediterranean to ports in Byzantium such as Constantinople. They also traveled to Muslim ports along the North African coast. Trade routes were opened to Asia, in part by the Crusades.

Increased business at markets and fairs made merchants willing to take chances on buying merchandise that they could sell at a profit. Merchants then reinvested the profits in more goods.

This fish market expanded the variety of food available in a medieval town.

Business and Banking As traders moved from fair to fair, they needed large amounts of cash or credit and ways to exchange many types of currencies. Enterprising merchants found ways to solve these problems. For example, bills of exchange established exchange rates between different coinage systems. **Letters of credit** between merchants eliminated the need to carry large amounts of cash and made trading easier. Trading firms and associations formed to offer these services to their groups.

Merchants looked for new markets and opportunities to make a profit. Merchants first had to purchase goods from distant places. To do so they had to borrow money, but the Church forbade Christians from lending money at interest, a sin called usury. Over time, the Church relaxed its rule on usury and Christians entered the banking business. Banking became an important business, especially in Italy.

Vocabulary
Letters of credit
a letter issued by a bank allowing the bearer to withdraw a specific amount of money from the bank or its branches

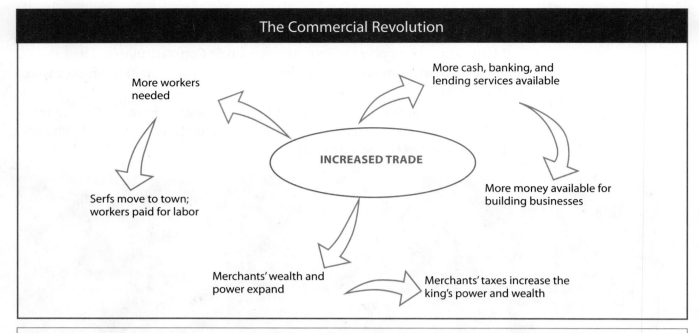

The Commercial Revolution

More workers needed

More cash, banking, and lending services available

INCREASED TRADE

Serfs move to town; workers paid for labor

More money available for building businesses

Merchants' wealth and power expand

Merchants' taxes increase the king's power and wealth

Interpret Graphics
1. **Draw Conclusions** How did increased trade increase the power of the king?
2. **Make Inferences** Why would workers now have to be paid?

Reading Check
Draw Conclusions
Why were changes in financial services necessary to expand trade?

Society Changes The changes brought about by the Commercial Revolution were slow, yet they had a major effect on the lives of Europeans. Increased trade brought many changes to aspects of society. Two of the most important changes involved what people did to earn a living and where they lived. As towns attracted workers, the towns grew into cities. Life in the cities was different from life in the sleepy villages or on manors.

Urban Life Flourishes

Scholars estimate that between 1000 and 1150, the population of western Europe rose from around 30 million to about 42 million. Towns grew and flourished. Compared to great cities like Constantinople, European towns were unsophisticated and tiny. Europe's largest city, Paris, probably had no more than 60,000 people by the year 1200. A typical town in medieval Europe had only about 1,500 to 2,500 people. Even so, these small communities became a powerful force for change in Europe.

Trade and Towns Grow Together By the later Middle Ages, trade was the very lifeblood of the new towns, which sprung up at ports and crossroads, on hilltops, and along rivers. As trade grew, towns all over Europe swelled with people. The excitement and bustle of towns drew many people. But there were some drawbacks to living in a medieval town. Streets were narrow, filled with animals and their waste. With no sewers, most people dumped household and human waste into the street in front of the house. Most people never bathed, and their houses lacked fresh air, light, and clean water. Because houses were built of wood with thatched roofs, they were a constant fire hazard. Nonetheless, many people chose to move to towns to pursue the economic and social opportunities they offered.

People were no longer content with their old feudal existence on manors or in tiny villages. Even though legally bound to their lord's manor, many serfs ran away. According to custom, a serf could now become free by living within a town for a year and a day. A saying of the time went, "Town air makes you free." Many of these runaway serfs, now free people, made better lives for themselves in towns.

Merchant Class Shifts the Social Order The merchants and craftspeople of medieval towns did not fit into the traditional medieval social order of noble, clergy, and peasant. At first, towns came under the authority of feudal lords, who used their authority to levy fees, taxes, and rents. As trade expanded, the **burghers**, or merchant-class town dwellers, resented this interference in their trade and commerce. They organized themselves and demanded privileges. These rights included freedom from certain kinds of tolls and the right to govern the town. At times they fought against their landlords and won these rights by force.

Reading Check
Draw Conclusions
Why were changes in financial services necessary to expand trade?

The Revival of Learning

During the Crusades, European contact with Muslims and Byzantines greatly expanded. This contact brought a new interest in learning, especially in the works of Greek philosophers. The Muslim and Byzantine libraries housed copies of these writings. Most had disappeared during the centuries following the fall of Rome and the invasions of western Europe.

The Muslim Connection In the 1100s, Christian scholars from Europe began visiting Muslim libraries in Spain. Few Western scholars knew Greek, but most did know Latin. So Jewish scholars living in Spain translated the Arabic versions of works by Aristotle and other Greek writers into Latin. All at once, Europeans acquired a huge new body of knowledge. This included science, philosophy, law, mathematics, and other fields. In addition, the Crusaders brought back to Europe superior Muslim technology in ships, navigation, and weapons.

Scholars and the University At the center of the growth of learning stood a new European institution—the university. The word *university* originally referred to a group of scholars meeting wherever they could. People, not buildings, made up the medieval university. Universities arose in Paris and in Bologna, Italy, by the end of the 1100s. Others followed in the English town of Oxford and in Salerno, Italy. Most students were the sons of burghers or well-to-do artisans. For most students, the goal was a job in government or the Church. Earning a bachelor's degree in theology might take five to seven years in school; becoming a master of theology took at least twelve years of study.

History in Depth

Muslim Scholars

A number of Islamic scholars had a great influence on European thought. This image shows Ibn Sina, known in the West as Avicenna. He was a Persian philosopher, astronomer, poet, and physician. His book, *The Cure*, an interpretation of Aristotle's philosophy, greatly affected Western thought. This work, translated into Latin, influenced the scholastics.

New ideas and forms of expression began to flow out of the universities. At a time when serious scholars and writers were writing in Latin, a few remarkable poets began using a lively **vernacular**, or the everyday language of their homeland. Some of these writers wrote masterpieces that are still read today. Dante Alighieri wrote *The Divine Comedy* (1308–1314) in Italian. Geoffrey Chaucer wrote *The Canterbury Tales* (about 1386–1400) in English. Christine de Pisan wrote *The Book of The City of Ladies* (1405) in French. Since most people couldn't read or understand Latin, these works written in the vernacular brought literature to many people.

Aquinas and Medieval Philosophy Christian scholars were excited by the ideas of Greek philosophers. They wondered if a Christian scholar could use Aristotle's logical approach to truth and still keep faith with the Bible.

In the mid-1200s, the scholar **Thomas Aquinas** (uh·KWY·nuhs) argued that the most basic religious truths could be proved by logical argument. Between 1267 and 1273, Aquinas wrote the *Summa Theologicae*. Aquinas's great work, influenced by Aristotle, combined ancient Greek thought with the Christian thought of his time.

Reading Check
Analyze Effects
How did the Crusades contribute to the expansion of trade and learning?

Aquinas and his fellow scholars who met at the great universities were known as schoolmen, or **scholastics**. The scholastics used their knowledge of Aristotle to debate many issues of their time. Their teachings on law and government influenced the thinking of western Europeans, particularly the English and French. Accordingly, they began to develop democratic institutions and traditions.

Thomas Aquinas's writings focused on questions of faith versus reason and logic.

Lesson 3 Assessment

1. **Organize Information** Use an outline like the one below to organize your notes.

Changes in Medieval Society

How did medieval society change between 1000 and 1500?

2. **Key Terms and People** For each key term or person in the lesson, write a sentence explaining its significance.

3. **Evaluate** How did guilds influence business practices in medieval towns?

4. **Analyze Effects** How were Muslim scholars linked to the revival of learning in Europe?

5. **Synthesize** In what ways did burghers expand their freedom from landlords?

6. **Analyze Effects** What was the effect of the development of towns on the feudal system?

7. **Analyze Motives** Why would writers choose to produce works in the vernacular instead of in Latin?

8. **Draw Conclusions** How did the Commercial Revolution lay the foundation for the economy of modern Europe?

England and France Develop

The Big Idea

As the kingdoms of England and France began to develop into nations, certain democratic traditions evolved.

Why It Matters Now

Modern concepts of jury trials, common law, and legal rights developed during this period.

Key Terms and People

William the Conqueror
Henry II
common law
Magna Carta
parliament
Hugh Capet
Philip II
Estates-General

Setting the Stage

By the early 800s, small Anglo-Saxon kingdoms covered the former Roman province of Britain. In Europe, the decline of the Carolingian Empire in the 900s left a patchwork of feudal states controlled by local lords. Gradually, the growth of towns and villages and the breakup of the feudal system were leading to more centralized government and the development of nations. The earliest nations in Europe to develop a strong unified government were England and France. Both would take similar paths.

England Absorbs Waves of Invaders

For centuries, invaders from various regions in Europe landed on English shores. The Angles and the Saxons stayed, bringing their own ways and creating an Anglo-Saxon culture.

Early Invasions In the 800s, Britain was battered by fierce raids of Danish Vikings. These invaders were so feared that a special prayer was said in churches: "God, deliver us from the fury of the Northmen." Only Alfred the Great, Anglo-Saxon king from 871 to 899, managed to turn back the Viking invaders. Gradually he and his successors united the kingdom under one rule, calling it England, "land of the Angles." The Angles were one of the Germanic tribes that had invaded the island of Britain.

In 1016, the Danish king Canute (kuh•NOOT) conquered England, molding Anglo-Saxons and Vikings into one people. In 1042, King Edward the Confessor, a descendant of Alfred the Great, took the throne. Edward died in January 1066 without an heir. A great struggle for the throne erupted, leading to one last invasion.

The Bayeux Tapestry uses embroidered scenes on linen panels to tell the story of the conquest of England by William the Conqueror.

The Norman Conquest The invader was William, duke of Normandy, who became known as **William the Conqueror**. Normandy is a region in the north of France that had been conquered by the Vikings. Its name comes from the French term for the Vikings—North men, or Norman. The Normans were descended from the Vikings, but they were French in language and in culture. As King Edward's cousin, William claimed the English crown and invaded England with a Norman army.

William's rival was Harold Godwinson, the Anglo-Saxon who claimed the throne. Harold was equally ambitious. On October 14, 1066, Normans and Anglo-Saxons fought the battle that changed the course of English history—the Battle of Hastings. After Harold was killed by an arrow that pierced his eye, the Normans won a decisive victory.

After his victory, William declared all England his personal property. William kept about one-fifth of England for himself. The English lords who supported Harold lost their lands. William then granted their lands to about 200 Norman lords who swore oaths of loyalty to him personally. By doing this, William unified control of the lands and laid the foundation for centralized government in England.

Reading Check
Summarize How did William the Conqueror begin the unification of England?

England's Evolving Government

Over the next centuries, English kings tried to achieve two goals. First, they wanted to hold and add to their French lands. Second, they wanted to strengthen their own power over the nobles and the Church.

William the Conqueror's descendants owned land both in Normandy and in England. The English king **Henry II** added to these holdings by marrying Eleanor of Aquitaine from France.

The marriage brought Henry a large territory in France called Aquitaine. He added Aquitaine to the lands in Normandy he had already inherited from William the Conqueror. Because Henry held lands in France, he was a vassal to the French king. But he was also a king in his own right.

Juries and Common Law Henry ruled England from 1154 to 1189. He strengthened the royal courts of justice by sending royal judges to every part of England at least once a year. They collected taxes, settled lawsuits, and punished crimes. Henry also introduced the use of the jury in English

--- BIOGRAPHY ---

Eleanor of Aquitaine
(1122–1204)

Eleanor of Aquitaine was one of the most remarkable women in history. She was wife to two kings and mother to two kings. She married Louis VII of France when the Second Crusade began. In 1147, she accompanied him to the Holy Land. Shortly afterward their marriage was annulled. Eleanor then married Henry Plantagenet, who was to become Henry II of England. Their marriage produced eight children. Two became English kings, Richard the Lion-Hearted and John.

courts. A jury in medieval England was a group of local people—usually 12 neighbors of the accused—who answered a royal judge's questions about the facts of a case. Jury trials became a popular means of settling disputes. Only the king's courts were allowed to conduct them.

Over the centuries, case by case, the rulings of England's royal judges formed a unified body of law that became known as **common law**. Today the principles of English common law are the basis for law in many English-speaking countries, including the United States.

The Magna Carta Henry was succeeded first by his son Richard the Lion-Hearted, hero of the Third Crusade. When Richard died, his younger brother John took the throne. John ruled from 1199 to 1216. He failed as a military leader, earning the nickname John Softsword. John lost Normandy and all his lands in northern France to the French under Philip Augustus. This loss forced a confrontation with his own nobles.

Some of John's problems stemmed from his own personality. He was cruel to his subjects and tried to squeeze money out of them. He alienated the Church and threatened to take away town charters guaranteeing self-government. John raised taxes to an all-time high to finance his wars. His nobles revolted. On June 15, 1215, they forced John to agree to the most celebrated document in English history, the **Magna Carta** (Great Charter). This document, drawn up by English nobles and reluctantly approved by King John, guaranteed certain basic political rights. The nobles wanted to safeguard their own feudal rights and limit the king's powers. In later years, however, English people of all classes argued that certain clauses in the Magna Carta applied to every citizen. Guaranteed rights included no taxation without representation, a jury trial, and the protection of the law. The Magna Carta guaranteed what are now considered basic legal rights both in England and in the United States.

The Model Parliament Another important step toward democratic government came during the rule of the next English king, Edward I. Edward needed to raise taxes for a war against the French, the Welsh, and the Scots. In 1295, Edward summoned two burgesses (citizens of wealth and property) from every **borough** and two knights from every county to serve as a **parliament**, or legislative group. In November 1295, knights, burgesses, bishops, and lords met together at Westminster in London. This is now called the Model Parliament because its new makeup (commoners, or nonnobles, as well as lords) served as a model for later kings.

Over the next century, from 1300 to 1400, the king called the knights and burgesses whenever a new tax was needed. In Parliament, these two groups gradually formed an assembly of their own called the House of Commons. Nobles and bishops met separately as the House of Lords. Under Edward I, Parliament was in part a royal tool that weakened the great lords. As time went by, Parliament became strong. Like the Magna Carta, it provided a check on royal power.

Vocabulary
borough a self-governing town

Reading Check
Analyze Effects
What is the significance of the Magna Carta?

The Magna Carta

The Magna Carta is considered one of the cornerstones of democratic government. The underlying principle of the document is the idea that all must obey the law, even the king. Its guaranteed rights are an important part of modern liberties and justice.

> "**38.** *No bailiff [officer of the court] for the future shall, upon his own unsupported complaint, put anyone to his "law," without credible witnesses brought for this purposes.*
> **39.** *No freeman shall be taken or imprisoned . . . or exiled or in any way destroyed, nor will we [the king] go upon him nor send upon him, except by the lawful judgement of his peers or by the law of the land.*
> **40.** *To no one will we sell, to no one will we refuse or delay, right or justice.*
> **45.** *We will appoint as justices, constables, sheriffs, or bailiffs only such as know the law of the realm and mean to observe it well.*"

Analyze Historical Sources

1. Why might the English nobles have insisted on the right listed in number 45?

2. Which of the statements is a forerunner to the right to a speedy public trial guaranteed in the Sixth Amendment of the U.S. Constitution?

Capetian Dynasty Rules France

The kings of France, like those of England, looked for ways to increase their power. After the breakup of Charlemagne's empire, French counts and dukes ruled their lands independently under the feudal system. By the year 1000, France was divided into about 47 feudal territories. In 987, the last member of the Carolingian family—Louis the Sluggard—died. **Hugh Capet** (kuh•PAY), an undistinguished duke from the middle of France, succeeded him. The Capet family ruled only a small territory, but at its heart stood Paris. Hugh Capet began the Capetian dynasty of French kings that ruled France from 987 to 1328.

France Becomes a Separate Kingdom Hugh Capet, his son, and his grandson all were weak rulers, but time and geography favored the Capetians. Their territory, though small, sat astride important trade routes in northern France. For 300 years, Capetian kings tightened their grip on this strategic area. The power of the king gradually spread outward from Paris. Eventually, the growth of royal power would unite France.

Philip II Expands His Power One of the most powerful Capetians was **Philip II**, called Philip Augustus, who ruled from 1180 to 1223. As a child, Philip had watched his father lose land to King Henry II of England.

The coronation of Philip II in Reims Cathedral

When Philip became king at the age of 15, he set out to weaken the power of the English kings in France. Philip was crafty, unprincipled, and willing to do whatever was necessary to achieve his goals.

Philip had little success against Henry II or Henry's son, Richard the Lion-Hearted. However, when King John, Richard's brother, gained the English throne, it was another matter. Philip earned the name Augustus (from the Latin word meaning "majestic"), probably because he greatly increased the territory of France. He seized Normandy from King John in 1204 and within two years had gained other territory. By the end of Philip's reign, he had tripled the lands under his direct control. For the first time, a French king had become more powerful than any of his vassals.

Philip II not only wanted more land, he also wanted a stronger central government. He established royal officials called bailiffs. They were sent from Paris to every district in the kingdom to preside over the king's courts and to collect the king's taxes.

Philip II's Heirs France's central government became even stronger during the reign of Philip's grandson, Louis IX, who ruled from 1226 to 1270. Unlike his grandfather, Louis was pious and saintly. He was known as the ideal king. After his death, he was made a saint by the Catholic Church. Louis created a French appeals court, which could overturn the decisions of local courts. These royal courts of France strengthened the monarchy while weakening feudal ties.

In 1302, Philip IV, who ruled France from 1285 to 1314, was involved in a quarrel with the pope. The pope refused to allow priests to pay taxes to the king. Philip disputed the right of the pope to control Church affairs

The Development of England and France

England	France
William the Conqueror invades England in 1066.	Hugh Capet increases the territory of France.
Henry II (1154–1189) introduces the use of the jury in English courts.	Philip II (1180–1223) establishes bailiffs to preside over courts and collect taxes.
Edward I (1272–1307) calls the Model Parliament in 1295.	Philip IV (1285–1314) adds Third Estate to the Estates-General.

Interpret Charts
1. **Clarify** What aspects of courts were developed during the rule of Henry II and Philip II?
2. **Develop Historical Perspective** Which aspect of centralized government developed about the same time in both England and France?

in his kingdom. As in England, the French king usually called a meeting of his lords and bishops when he needed support for his policies. To win wider support against the pope, Philip IV decided to include commoners in the meeting.

Estates-General In France, the Church leaders were known as the First Estate, and the great lords as the Second Estate. The commoners, wealthy landholders or merchants who Philip invited to participate in the council, became known as the Third Estate. The whole meeting was called the **Estates-General**.

Like the English Parliament in its early years, the Estates-General helped to increase royal power against the nobility. Unlike Parliament, however, the Estates-General never became an independent force that limited the king's power. However, centuries later, the Third Estate would play a key role in overthrowing the French monarchy during the French Revolution.

Beginnings of Democracy England and France were just beginning to establish a democratic tradition. This tradition rested on setting up a centralized government that would be able to govern widespread lands. The creation of common law and court systems was a first step toward increased central government power. Including commoners in the decision-making process of government was also an important step in the direction of democratic rule. Before England and France could move forward in this direction, however, they had to contend with a century of turmoil that included religious disputes, plague, and war.

Reading Check
Summarize
What three estates made up the Estates-General?

Lesson 4 Assessment

1. **Organize Information** Use an outline like the one below to organize your notes.

List four steps toward democratic government you read about in this lesson that are similar to U.S. practices. Explain.

2. **Key Terms and People** For each key term or person in the lesson, write a sentence explaining its significance.

3. **Summarize** What two legal practices date back to Henry II?

4. **Synthesize** What are some basic rights guaranteed by the Magna Carta?

5. **Analyze Causes** Why did Philip II call the Estates-General together?

6. **Compare** Compare the way in which England and France began developing as nations.

7. **Analyze Effects** Which of the changes in English government is reflected in the government of the United States today?

8. **Evaluate** What steps were necessary to centralize governments in England and France?

Troubles of the 14th Century

The Big Idea

In the 1300s, Europe was torn apart by religious strife, famine, the bubonic plague, and the Hundred Years' War.

Why It Matters Now

Events of the 1300s led to a change in attitudes toward religion and the state, a change reflected in modern attitudes.

Key Terms and People

Avignon
Great Schism
John Wycliffe
Jan Hus
Great Famine
Black Death
bubonic plague
Hundred Years' War
Joan of Arc

Setting the Stage

The 1300s were filled with disasters, both natural and human made. The Church seemed to be thriving but soon would face a huge division. Europe's booming population experienced a devastating famine. Then a deadly epidemic claimed millions of lives. So many people died in the epidemic that the structure of the economy changed. Claims to thrones in France and England led to wars in those lands. The wars would result in changes in the governments of both France and England. By the end of the century, the medieval way of life was beginning to disappear.

A Church Divided

At the beginning of the 1300s, the Age of Faith still seemed strong. Soon, however, both the pope and the Church were in desperate trouble.

Pope and King Collide In 1300, Pope Boniface VIII attempted to enforce papal authority on kings as previous popes had. When King Philip IV of France asserted his authority over French bishops, Boniface responded with an official document. It stated that kings must always obey popes.

Philip merely sneered at this statement. In fact, one of Philip's ministers is said to have remarked that "my master's sword is made of steel, the pope's is made of [words]." Instead of obeying the pope, Philip had him held prisoner in September 1303. The king planned to bring him to France for trial. The pope was rescued, but the elderly Boniface died a month later. Never again would a pope be able to force monarchs to obey him.

Avignon and the Great Schism In 1305, Philip IV persuaded the College of Cardinals to choose a French archbishop as the new pope. Clement V, the newly selected pope, moved from Rome to the city of **Avignon** (av•vee•NYAWN) in France. Popes would live there for the next 69 years.

The move to Avignon badly weakened the Church. When reformers finally tried to move the papacy back to Rome, however, the result was even worse. In 1378, Pope Gregory XI died while visiting Rome. The College of Cardinals then met in Rome to choose a successor. As they deliberated, they could hear a mob outside screaming, "A Roman, a Roman, we want a Roman for pope, or at least an Italian!" Finally, the cardinals announced to the crowd that an Italian had been chosen: Pope Urban VI. Many cardinals regretted their choice almost immediately. Urban VI's passion for reform and his arrogant personality caused the cardinals to elect a second pope a few months later. They chose Robert of Geneva who spoke French. He took the name Clement VII.

Now there were two popes. Each declared the other to be a false pope, excommunicating his rival. The French pope lived in Avignon, while the Italian pope lived in Rome. This began the split in the Church known as the **Great Schism** (SIHZ•uhm), or division.

In 1414, the Council of Constance attempted to end the Great Schism by choosing a single pope. By now, there were a total of three popes: the Avignon pope, the Roman pope, and a third pope elected by an earlier council at Pisa. With the help of the Holy Roman Emperor, the council forced all three popes to resign. In 1417, the Council chose a new pope, Martin V. The Great Schism finally had ended, but it left the papacy greatly weakened.

Scholars Challenge Church Authority The papacy was further challenged by an Englishman named **John Wycliffe** (WIHK•lihf). He preached that Jesus Christ, not the pope, was the true head of the Church. He was much offended by the worldliness and wealth many clergy displayed. Wycliffe believed that the clergy should own no land or wealth. Wycliffe also taught that the Bible alone—not the pope—was the final authority for Christian life. He helped spread this idea by inspiring an English translation of the New Testament of the Bible.

Influenced by Wycliffe's writings, **Jan Hus**, a professor in Bohemia (now part of the Czech Republic), taught that the authority of the Bible was higher than that of the pope. Hus was excommunicated in 1412. In 1414 he was seized by Church leaders, tried as a heretic, and then burned at the stake in 1415.

Reading Check
Contrast
According to the different beliefs of the time, what was the true source of religious authority?

The Great Famine and Bubonic Plague Strike

By 1300, Europe's population was booming. Then a series of disasters struck, beginning with the **Great Famine**. From 1315 to 1317, abnormally severe winters and torrential rains throughout the spring and summer growing seasons ruined crop yields across northern Europe. Grains were the main staple of the European diet, but soggy fields became difficult, if not impossible, to plow. In addition, the inclement weather limited the ability to dry or cure hay to feed livestock. In desperation, starving people ate the grain seeds they needed to plant more crops and killed the animals they used to plow the fields. The famine devastated the population and damaged the social network. Its lingering effects were felt until the early 1320s. However, the longer-term impact on this population whose immune systems were weakened by famine would prove costly.

The Plague Strikes During the 1300s an epidemic struck parts of Asia, North Africa, and Europe. Approximately one-third of the population of Europe, and millions more in Asia and Africa, died of the deadly disease known as the **Black Death**. It got this name because of the purplish or black spots it produced on the skin. This devastating plague swept across Europe between 1347 and 1351. Historians are still not sure what disease the Black Death was, or even if it was a single disease. One theory is that the disease took two different forms. One, called **bubonic plague**, was spread by fleas that lived on rats and other animals. The other, pneumonic plague, could be spread through the air from person to person through coughs and sneezes. Pneumonic plague spread more quickly.

An illustration representing the Black Death.

Unlike catastrophes that pull communities together, this epidemic was so terrifying that it ripped apart the very fabric of society. Giovanni Boccaccio, an Italian writer of the time, described its effect:

> *"This scourge had implanted so great a terror in the hearts of men and women that brothers abandoned brothers, uncles their nephews, sisters their brothers, and in many cases wives deserted their husbands. But even worse, . . . fathers and mothers refused to nurse and assist their own children."*

—Giovanni Boccaccio, *The Decameron*

Origins and Impact of the Plague In 1346, plague struck Mongol armies laying siege to Kaffa, a port on the Black Sea. From there rats infested with fleas carrying the disease made their way onto ships. Infected fleas bit humans transferring the disease to them. As merchants traveled, so did the plague. It spread quickly throughout Europe, first striking coastal regions of Italy. From there it moved inland along trade routes to Spain, France, Germany, England, and beyond. By 1351, almost no part of Europe remained untouched by the Black Death. Remarkably, some communities escaped the plague relatively unharmed. In others, two-thirds to three-quarters of those who caught the disease died.

The Black Death

The plague, or Black Death, was a killer disease that swept repeatedly through many areas of the world. It wiped out two-thirds of the population in some areas of China, destroyed populations of Muslim and Byzantine towns in North Africa and Southwest Asia, and then decimated one-third of the population of Europe, almost 25 million people.

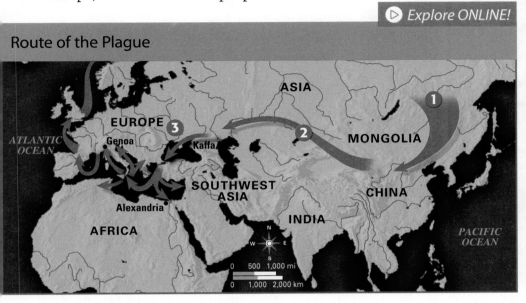

▷ *Explore ONLINE!*

Route of the Plague

1. The horse-riding Mongols likely carried infected fleas and rats in their food supplies as they swooped into China.

2. The disease traveled with merchants along the Asian trade routes to southern Asia, southwest Asia, and Africa.

3. From 1345–1346, a Mongol army besieged Kaffa. A year later, when Italian merchants returned to Italy, they unknowingly brought the plague with them.

Disease Spreads

Black rats carried fleas that were infested with a bacillus called *Yersinia pestis*. Because people did not bathe, almost all had fleas and lice. In addition, medieval people threw their garbage and sewage into the streets. These unsanitary streets became breeding grounds for more rats. The fleas carried by rats leapt from person to person, thus spreading the bubonic plague with incredible speed.

Symptoms of the Bubonic Plague

- Painful swellings called buboes (BOO•bohz) in the lymph nodes, particularly those in the armpits and groin

- Sometimes purplish or blackish spots on the skin

- Extremely high fever, chills, delirium, and in most cases, death

Death Tolls, 1300s

Western Europe	💀💀💀💀💀💀 20–25 million
China, India, other Asians	💀💀💀💀💀💀 25 million
	💀 = 4 million

Critical Thinking

1. **Hypothesize** Had people known the cause of the plague, what might they have done to slow its spread?

2. **Compare** What diseases of today might be compared to the bubonic plague? Why?

This painting, titled *The Triumph of Death*, depicts the effect of the plague.

Reading Check
Analyze Effects
Which of the effects of the plague do you think most changed life in the medieval period?

The plague returned every few years, though it never struck as severely as in the first outbreak. However, the periodic attacks further reduced the population.

Effects of the Plague The economic and social effects of the plague were enormous. The old manorial system began to crumble. Some of the effects included:

- Town populations fell.
- Trade declined. Prices rose.
- Serfs left manors in search of better wages.
- Nobles fiercely resisted peasant demands for higher wages, causing peasant revolts in England, France, Italy, and Belgium.
- Jews were falsely blamed for bringing on the plague. All over Europe, Jews were driven from their homes or, worse, massacred.
- The Church suffered a loss of prestige when its prayers failed to stop the onslaught of the bubonic plague and priests abandoned their duties.

The plague and its aftermath disrupted medieval society, hastening changes that were already in the making. The society of the Middle Ages was collapsing. The century of war between England and France was that society's final death struggle.

Now and Then

If the Plague Struck America Today

The bubonic plague reportedly wiped out about one-third of Europe's population in the 1300s. In the United States today, a one-third death toll would equal over 96 million people, or the number living in the states represented by the color red.

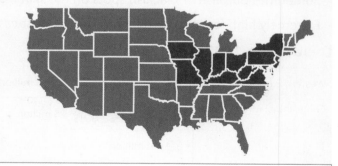

Interpret Charts
1. **Summarize** How many states on the chart would have lost their entire population to the plague?

2. **Draw Conclusions** How might the chart help explain why many Europeans thought the world was ending?

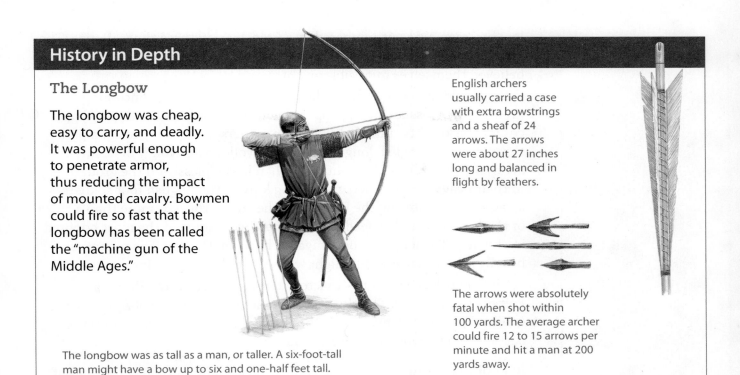

The Longbow

The longbow was cheap, easy to carry, and deadly. It was powerful enough to penetrate armor, thus reducing the impact of mounted cavalry. Bowmen could fire so fast that the longbow has been called the "machine gun of the Middle Ages."

English archers usually carried a case with extra bowstrings and a sheaf of 24 arrows. The arrows were about 27 inches long and balanced in flight by feathers.

The arrows were absolutely fatal when shot within 100 yards. The average archer could fire 12 to 15 arrows per minute and hit a man at 200 yards away.

The longbow was as tall as a man, or taller. A six-foot-tall man might have a bow up to six and one-half feet tall.

The Hundred Years' War

Not only did the people in Europe during the 1300s have to deal with epidemic disease, but they also had to deal with war. England and France battled with each other on French soil for just over a century. The century of war between England and France marked the end of medieval Europe's society.

When the last Capetian king died without a successor, England's Edward III, as grandson of Philip IV, claimed the right to the French throne. The war that Edward III launched for that throne continued on and off from 1337 to 1453. It became known as the **Hundred Years' War**. Victory passed back and forth between the two countries. Finally, between 1421 and 1453, the French rallied and drove the English out of France entirely, except for the port city of Calais.

The Hundred Years' War brought a change in the style of warfare in Europe. At this time some combatants were still operating under medieval ideals of chivalry. They looked with contempt on the common foot soldiers and archers who fought alongside them. This contempt would change as the longbow changed warfare.

The Longbow Changes Warfare The English introduced the longbow and demonstrated its power in three significant battles: Crécy, Poitiers, and Agincourt. The first and most spectacular battle was the Battle of Crécy (KREHS•ee) on August 26, 1346. The English army, including longbowmen, was outnumbered by a French army three times its size. The French army included knights and archers with crossbows. French knights believed themselves invincible and attacked.

English longbowmen let fly thousands of arrows at the oncoming French. The crossbowmen, peppered with English arrows, retreated in panic. The knights trampled their own archers in an effort to cut a path through them. English longbowmen sent volley after volley of deadly arrows. They unhorsed knights who then lay helplessly on the ground in their heavy armor. Then, using long knives, the English foot soldiers attacked, slaughtering the French. At the end of the day, more than a third of the French force lay dead. Among them were some of the most honored in chivalry. The longbow, not chivalry, had won the day. The mounted, heavily armored medieval knight was soon to become extinct.

The English repeated their victory ten years later at the Battle of Poitiers (pwah•TYAY). The third English victory, the Battle of Agincourt (AJ•ihn•kawrt), took place in 1415. The success of the longbow in these battles spelled doom for chivalric warfare.

Joan of Arc In 1420, the French and English signed a treaty stating that Henry V would inherit the French crown upon the death of the French king Charles VI. Then, in 1429, a teenage French peasant girl named **Joan of Arc** felt moved by God to rescue France from its English conquerors. When Joan was just 13 she began to have visions and hear what she believed were voices of the saints. They urged her to drive the English from France and give the French crown to France's true king, Charles VII, son of Charles VI.

On May 7, 1429, Joan led the French army into battle at a fort city near Orléans. The fort blocked the road to Orléans. It was a hard-fought battle for both sides. The French finally retreated in despair. Suddenly, Joan and a few soldiers charged back toward the fort. The entire French army stormed after her. The siege of Orléans was broken. Joan of Arc guided the French onto the path of victory.

After that victory, Joan persuaded Charles to go with her to Reims. There he was crowned king on July 17, 1429. In 1430, the Burgundians, England's allies, captured Joan in battle. They turned her over to the English. The English, in turn, handed her over to Church authorities to stand trial. Although the French king Charles VII owed his crown to Joan, he did nothing to rescue her. Condemned as a witch and a heretic because of her claim to hear voices, Joan was burned at the stake on May 30, 1431.

The Impact of the Hundred Years' War The long, exhausting war finally ended in 1453. Each side experienced major changes.

- A feeling of nationalism emerged in England and France. Now people thought of the king as a national leader, fighting for the glory of the country, not simply a feudal lord.
- The power and prestige of the French monarch increased.
- The English suffered a period of internal turmoil known as the War of the Roses, in which two noble houses fought for the throne.

Joan of Arc
(1412–1431)

In the 1420s, rumors circulated among the French that a young woman would save France from the English. So when Joan arrived on the scene she was considered the fulfillment of that prophecy. Joan cut her hair short and wore a suit of armor and carried a sword.

Her unusual appearance and extraordinary confidence inspired French troops. Eventually she was given command of troops that broke the siege of Orléans. In 1430, she was turned over to a Church court for trial. In truth, her trial was more political than religious. The English were determined to prove her a fake and to weaken her image.

Reading Check
Draw Conclusions
How did the Hundred Years' War change the perception of people toward their king?

Some historians consider the end of the Hundred Years' War in 1453 as the end of the Middle Ages. The twin pillars of the medieval world, religious devotion and the code of chivalry, both crumbled. The Age of Faith died a slow death. This death was caused by the Great Schism, the scandalous display of wealth by the Church, and the discrediting of the Church during the bubonic plague. The Age of Chivalry died on the battlefields of Crécy, Poitiers, and Agincourt.

Lesson 5 Assessment

1. **Organize Information** Use an outline like the one below to organize your notes.
   Which event had some economic effects?

	Cause & Effect
Split in Church	
Plague	
100 Years' War	

2. **Key Terms and People** For each key term or person in the lesson, write a sentence explaining its significance.

3. **Summarize** What was the Great Schism?

4. **Analyze Effects** What were the three effects of the bubonic plague?

5. **Draw Conclusions** What impact did Joan of Arc have on the Hundred Years' War?

6. **Form Opinions** Which event do you think diminished the power of the Church more—the Great Schism or the bubonic plague?

7. **Identify Problems** What problems did survivors face after the bubonic plague swept through their town?

8. **Analyze Effects** How did the Hundred Years' War encourage a feeling of nationalism in both France and England?

Module 11 Assessment

Key Terms and People

For each term or name below, write a sentence explaining its connection to western Europe during the medieval period.

1. clergy
2. Holy Roman Empire
3. Crusades
4. Commercial Revolution
5. Magna Carta
6. parliament
7. Great Schism
8. Great Famine
9. bubonic plague
10. Hundred Years' War

Main Ideas

Use your notes and the information in the module to answer the following questions.

The Power of the Church

1. What was Gelasius's two-swords theory?
2. Why was Otto I the most effective ruler of Medieval Germany?
3. How was the conflict between Pope Gregory VII and Henry IV resolved?

Church Reform and the Crusades

4. Explain the three main abuses that most distressed Church reformers.
5. What were the effects of the Crusades?

Changes in Medieval Society

6. How did trade and finance change in the period from 1000 to 1500?
7. How did the growth of towns hurt the feudal system?
8. What role did Muslims play in Europe's revival of learning?

England and France Develop

9. How did English kings increase their power and reduce the power of the nobles?
10. Why was Philip II called Augustus?

Troubles of the 14th Century

11. Summarize the main ideas of John Wycliffe.
12. Why did the bubonic plague cause people to turn away from the Church?
13. How did the Hundred Years' War change warfare in Europe?

Critical Thinking

1. **Summarize** Use a chart like the one below to list ways in which governments became more centralized in France and in England.

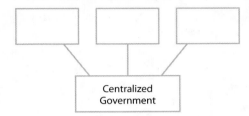

Centralized Government

2. **Compare and Contrast** How did Otto I and Frederick I try to imitate Charlemagne's approach to empire building?

3. **Analyze** Why did the appointment of bishops become the issue in a struggle between kings and popes?

4. **Synthesize** What generalizations could you make about the relationship between politics and religion in the Middle Ages?

5. **Summarize** What role did Jews and Muslims play in Christian Europe's financial revolution?

6. **Analyze Causes** Identify and discuss the events that led to the decline of the power of the Church in the period from 1000 to 1500.

7. **Analyze Effects** In what ways did the guilds change business and employment practices?

Engage with History

Consider what you learned in this module about the Crusades and what sort of rewards and dangers they entailed. Would you join a Crusade? What might a Crusader bring home from his travels? What problems might a Crusader encounter on his adventures? Discuss your opinions with a small group.

Focus on Writing

Write a brief **biography** about Joan of Arc. Be sure to include information about her influence on Charles and on the nation of France.

Consider the following:

- What are the major events in her life?
- Why did Charles value her advice?
- How is she viewed in France today?

Multimedia Activity

Work with a partner to find examples on the Internet of the impact of the bubonic plague and the Hundred Years' War on the economy of medieval Europe. Consider changes in population, working conditions, and the volume of trade. Present the results of your research in a well-organized paper.

Be sure to

- apply a search strategy when using directories and search engines to locate web resources.
- judge the usefulness and reliability of each website.
- correctly cite your web sources.
- peer-edit for organization and correct use of language.

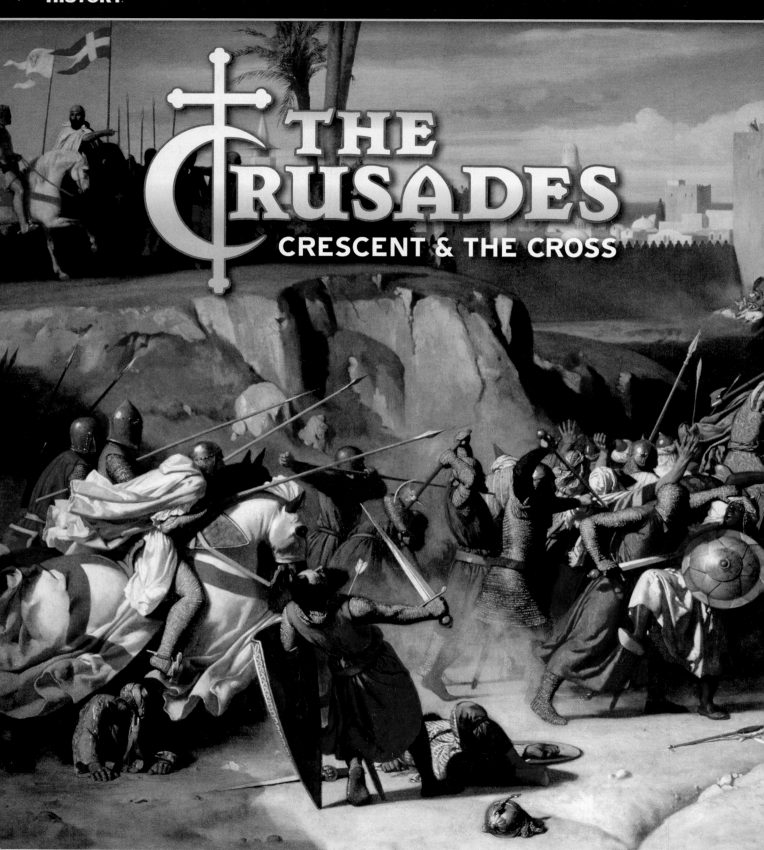

THE CRUSADES
CRESCENT & THE CROSS

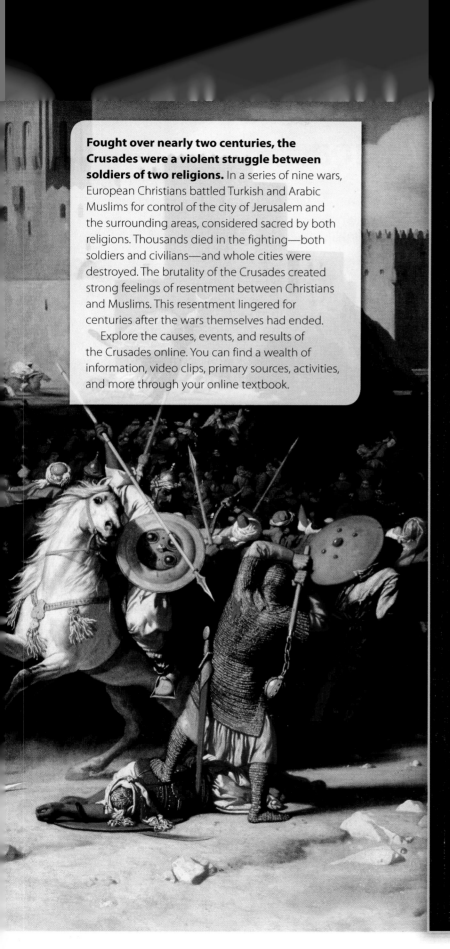

Fought over nearly two centuries, the Crusades were a violent struggle between soldiers of two religions. In a series of nine wars, European Christians battled Turkish and Arabic Muslims for control of the city of Jerusalem and the surrounding areas, considered sacred by both religions. Thousands died in the fighting—both soldiers and civilians—and whole cities were destroyed. The brutality of the Crusades created strong feelings of resentment between Christians and Muslims. This resentment lingered for centuries after the wars themselves had ended.

Explore the causes, events, and results of the Crusades online. You can find a wealth of information, video clips, primary sources, activities, and more through your online textbook.

Siege of Jerusalem

Watch the video to learn how the Christian army captured Jerusalem from the Turks in 1099.

The First Four Crusades

Explore the map to see the different routes followed by Crusaders from Europe to the Holy Land.

Defeat of the Crusaders

Watch the video to understand how Muslim leaders rallied after the Second Crusade to drive Christians out of the Holy Land.

Module 12

Societies and Empires of Africa

Essential Question

How did interactions with other cultures shape African societies?

About the Photo: This rock painting in northwestern Africa shows a line of calves tied to a rope in a pastoralist camp.

▶ *Explore ONLINE!*

HISTORY

VIDEOS, including...
- The Sahara
- Masai People of Africa
- Trans-Saharan Trade
- Timbuktu: Thriving Songhai Empire Metropolis

☑ Document Based Investigations

☑ Graphic Organizers

☑ Interactive Games

☑ Image with Hotspots: African Ironworking

☑ Carousel: The Ruins of Great Zimbabwe

In this module you will learn how African civilizations adapted to various environments and developed complex civilizations and trading networks.

What You Will Learn ...

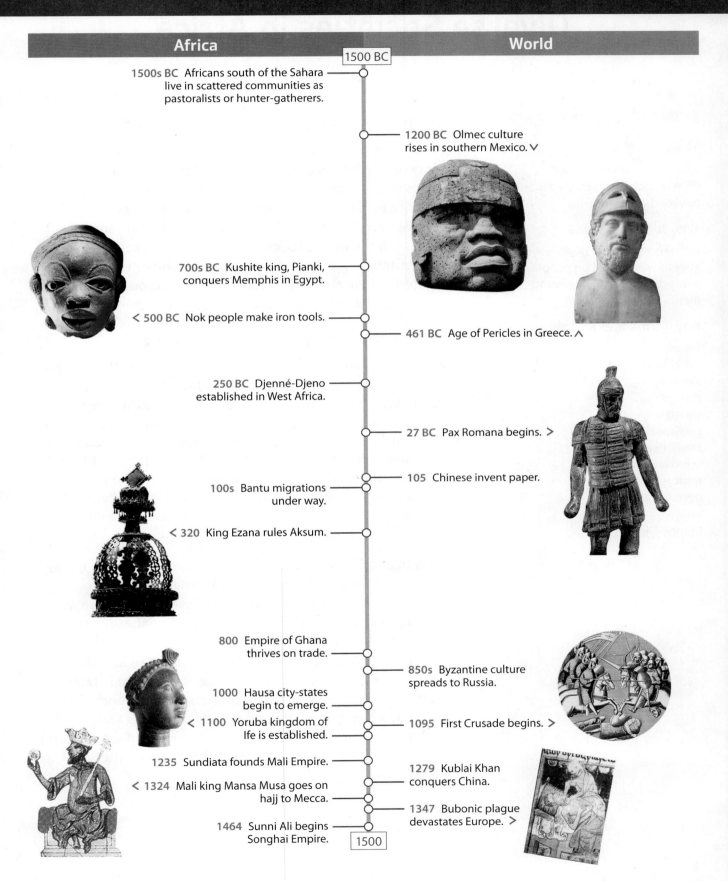

Africa | **World**

1500 BC

1500s BC Africans south of the Sahara live in scattered communities as pastoralists or hunter-gatherers.

1200 BC Olmec culture rises in southern Mexico. ∨

700s BC Kushite king, Pianki, conquers Memphis in Egypt.

< **500 BC** Nok people make iron tools.

461 BC Age of Pericles in Greece. ∧

250 BC Djenné-Djeno established in West Africa.

27 BC Pax Romana begins. >

100s Bantu migrations under way.

105 Chinese invent paper.

< **320** King Ezana rules Aksum.

800 Empire of Ghana thrives on trade.

850s Byzantine culture spreads to Russia.

1000 Hausa city-states begin to emerge.

< **1100** Yoruba kingdom of Ife is established.

1095 First Crusade begins. >

1235 Sundiata founds Mali Empire.

1279 Kublai Khan conquers China.

< **1324** Mali king Mansa Musa goes on hajj to Mecca.

1347 Bubonic plague devastates Europe. >

1464 Sunni Ali begins Songhai Empire.

1500

Diverse Societies in Africa

Setting the Stage

Africa spreads across the equator. It includes a broad range of Earth's environments—from steamy coastal plains to snow-capped mountain peaks. Some parts of Africa suffer from constant drought, while others receive over 200 inches of rain a year. Vegetation varies from sand dunes and rocky wastes to dense green rain forests. Interaction with the African environment has created unique cultures and societies. Each group found ways to adapt to the land and the resources it offers.

A Land of Geographic Contrasts

Africa is the second largest continent in the world. It stretches 4,600 miles from east to west and 5,000 miles from north to south. With a total of 11.7 million square miles, it occupies about one-fifth of Earth's land surface. Narrow coastlines (50 to 100 miles) lie on either side of a central plateau. Waterfalls and rapids often form as rivers drop down to the coast from the plateau, making navigation impossible to or from the coast. Africa's coastline has few harbors, ports, or inlets. Because of this, the coastline is actually shorter than that of Europe, which is one-third Africa's size.

Challenging Environments Each African environment offers its own challenges. The deserts are largely unsuitable for human life and also hamper people's movement to more welcoming climates. The largest deserts are the **Sahara** in the north and the Kalahari (kahl•uh•HAHR•ee) in the south.

Stretching from the Atlantic Ocean to the Red Sea, the Sahara covers an area roughly the size of the United States. Only a small part of the Sahara consists of sand dunes. The rest is mostly a flat, gray wasteland of scattered rocks and gravel. Each year the desert takes over more and more of the semiarid region at the southern edge of the Sahara Desert, the **Sahel** (suh•HAYL).

The Big Idea

African peoples developed diverse societies as they adapted to varied environments.

Why It Matters Now

Differences among modern societies are also based on people's interactions with their environments.

Key Terms and People

Sahara
Sahel
savanna
lineage
stateless society
patrilineal
matrilineal
animism
griot
desertification
Nok
Djenné-Djeno

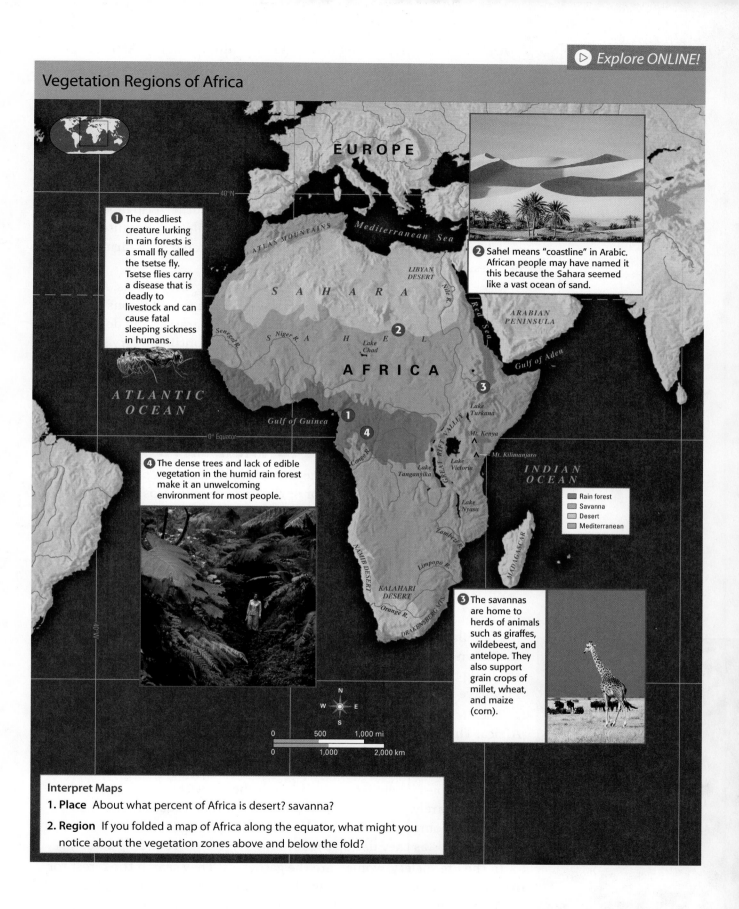

Vegetation Regions of Africa

▶ *Explore ONLINE!*

EUROPE

Mediterranean Sea

ATLAS MOUNTAINS

S A H A R A

LIBYAN DESERT

Nile R.

ATLANTIC OCEAN

Senegal R.

Niger R.

S A H E L

Lake Chad

A F R I C A

Red Sea

ARABIAN PENINSULA

Gulf of Aden

Gulf of Guinea

0° Equator

Congo R.

GREAT RIFT VALLEY

Lake Turkana

Mt. Kenya

Mt. Kilimanjaro

Lake Victoria

Lake Tanganyika

Lake Nyasa

INDIAN OCEAN

NAMIB DESERT

Zambezi R.

MADAGASCAR

KALAHARI DESERT

Limpopo R.

Orange R.

DRAKENSBERG MTS.

40°N

40°W

1 The deadliest creature lurking in rain forests is a small fly called the tsetse fly. Tsetse flies carry a disease that is deadly to livestock and can cause fatal sleeping sickness in humans.

2 Sahel means "coastline" in Arabic. African people may have named it this because the Sahara seemed like a vast ocean of sand.

4 The dense trees and lack of edible vegetation in the humid rain forest make it an unwelcoming environment for most people.

3 The savannas are home to herds of animals such as giraffes, wildebeest, and antelope. They also support grain crops of millet, wheat, and maize (corn).

Rain forest
Savanna
Desert
Mediterranean

N W E S

| 0 | 500 | 1,000 mi |
| 0 | 1,000 | 2,000 km |

Interpret Maps

1. Place About what percent of Africa is desert? savanna?

2. Region If you folded a map of Africa along the equator, what might you notice about the vegetation zones above and below the fold?

Another very different—but also partly uninhabitable—African environment is the rain forest. Sometimes called "nature's greenhouse," it produces mahogany and teak trees up to 150 feet tall. Their leaves and branches form a dense canopy that keeps sunlight from reaching the forest floor. The tsetse (TSET•see) fly is found in the rain forest. Its presence prevented Africans from using cattle, donkeys, and horses to farm near the rain forests. This deadly insect also prevented invaders—especially Europeans—from colonizing fly-infested territories.

Welcoming Lands The northern coast and the southern tip of Africa have welcoming Mediterranean-type climates and fertile soil. Because these coastal areas are so fertile, they are densely populated with farmers and herders.

Most people in Africa live on the **savannas**, or grassy plains. Africa's savannas are not just endless plains. They include mountainous highlands and swampy tropical stretches. Covered with tall grasses and dotted with trees, the savannas cover over 40 percent of the continent. Dry seasons alternate with rainy seasons—often, two of each a year. Unfortunately, the topsoil throughout Africa is thin, and heavy rains strip away minerals. In most years, however, the savannas support abundant agricultural production.

Reading Check
Find Main Ideas
Why do most people in Africa live on the savannas?

Early Humans Adapt to Their Environments

The first humans appeared in the Great Rift Valley, a deep gash in Earth's crust that runs through the floor of the Red Sea and across eastern Africa. People moved outward from this area in the world's first migration. They developed technologies and social systems that helped them survive in—and then alter—their surroundings.

Hunting-Gathering Societies Nomadic hunting-gathering societies—the oldest form of social organization in the world—began in Africa. In Africa today, hunting-gathering societies form an extremely small percentage of the population. Scattered throughout the continent, these groups speak their own languages and often use their own hunting techniques. By studying these groups, scholars learn clues about how hunter-gatherers may have lived in the past.

The Efe (AY•fay) are one of several hunting-gathering societies in Africa. They live in the Ituri Forest in the Democratic Republic of Congo (formerly Zaire). Like their ancestors, the modern-day Efe live in small groups of between 10 and 100 members, all of whom are related. Each family occupies its own grass-and-brush shelter within a camp, but their homes are rarely permanent. Their search for food causes them to be somewhat nomadic. As a result, the Efe collect few possessions and move to new camps as they use up the resources in the surrounding area.

In the Efe society, women are the gatherers. They search the forest for roots, yams, mushrooms, and wild seeds. Efe men and older boys do all the hunting. Sometimes they gather in groups to hunt small antelope called duikers. At other times, hunters go solo and use poison-tipped arrows to

An Efe camp

The first mention of Aksum was in a Greek guidebook written around AD 100, *Periplus of the Erythraean Sea*. It describes Zoskales (ZAHS•kuh•leez), thought to be the first king of Aksum. He was "a stickler about his possessions and always [greedy] for getting more, but in other respects a fine person and well versed in reading and writing Greek." Under Zoskales and other rulers, Aksum seized areas along the Red Sea and the Blue Nile in Africa. The rulers also crossed the Red Sea and took control of lands on the southwestern Arabian Peninsula.

Aksum Controls International Trade Aksum's location and expansion made it a hub for caravan routes to Egypt and Meroë. Access to sea trade on the Mediterranean Sea and the Indian Ocean helped Aksum become an international trading power. Traders from Egypt, Arabia, Persia, India, and the Roman Empire crowded Aksum's chief seaport, **Adulis** (AHD•uh•luhs), near present-day Massawa.

Aksumite merchants traded necessities such as salt and luxuries such as rhinoceros horns, tortoise shells, ivory, emeralds, and gold. In return, they chose from items such as cloth, glass, olive oil, wine, brass, iron, and

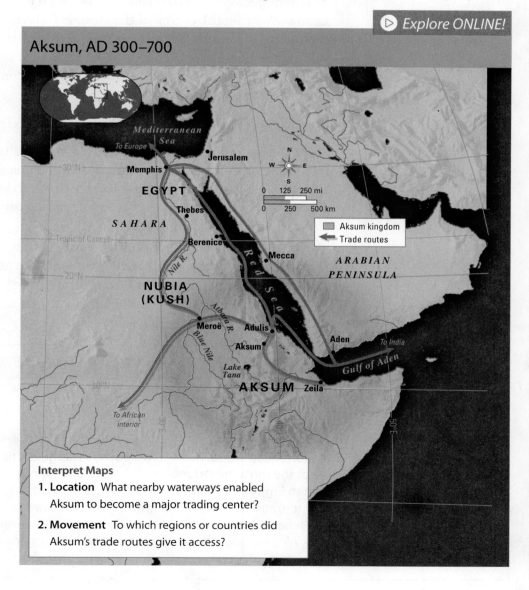

Explore ONLINE!

Aksum, AD 300–700

Interpret Maps

1. **Location** What nearby waterways enabled Aksum to become a major trading center?

2. **Movement** To which regions or countries did Aksum's trade routes give it access?

copper. Around AD 550, an Egyptian merchant named Cosmas described how Aksumite agents bargained for gold from the people in southern Ethiopia:

> *"They take along with them to the mining district oxen, lumps of salt, and iron, and when they reach its neighborhood they . . . halt . . . and form an encampment, which they fence round with a great hedge of thorns. Within this they live, and having slaughtered the oxen, cut them in pieces and lay the pieces on top of the thorns along with the lumps of salt and the iron. Then come the natives bringing gold in nuggets like peas . . . and lay one or two or more of these upon what pleases them. . . . Then the owner of the meat approaches, and if he is satisfied he takes the gold away, and upon seeing this its owner comes and takes the flesh or the salt or the iron."*

—Cosmas, quoted in *Travellers in Ethiopia*

Reading Check
Analyze Effects
How did Aksum's location and interactions with other regions affect its development?

A Strong Ruler Expands the Kingdom The kingdom of Aksum reached its height between AD 325 and 360, when an exceptionally strong ruler, **Ezana** (AY•zah•nah), occupied the throne. Determined to establish and expand his authority, Ezana first conquered the part of the Arabian peninsula that is now Yemen. Then, in 330, Ezana turned his attention to Kush, which had already begun to decline. In 350, he conquered the Kushites and burned Meroë to the ground.

An International Culture Develops

From the beginning, Aksumites had a diverse cultural heritage. This blend included traditions of the Arab peoples who crossed the Red Sea into Africa and those of the Kushite peoples they settled among. As the kingdom expanded and became a powerful trading center, it attracted people from all over the ancient world.

The port city of Adulis was particularly cosmopolitan. It included people from Aksum's widespread trading partners such as Egypt, Arabia, Greece, Rome, Persia, India, and even Byzantium. In the babble of tongues heard in Aksum, Greek stood out as the international language of the time, much as English does in the world today.

Global Patterns

A Road Paved with Gold: Aksum to Rome

The kingdom of Aksum had a tremendous impact on the ancient Mediterranean world. It particularly influenced one of the most important powers of the time, the Roman Empire. Roman ships came to Adulis weekly to trade with the Aksumites. Many Roman merchants lived in Adulis and in the capital city, Aksum.

One of the chief commodities that linked the two powers was gold. The Aksumites had access to it from inland gold mines, and the Romans needed it to support the monetary system of their growing empire. Rome and Aksum were linked not only by gold, however. They also shared a spiritual link in Christianity.

Aksumite Religion Early Aksumite religion probably resembled the polytheistic religion practiced in southern Arabia at the time. Aksumite gods included Astar, Mahrem, Beher, and Medr. Aksumites were also animists, however, and worshiped the spirits of nature and honored their dead ancestors. They offered sacrifices—often as many as a dozen oxen at a time—to those spirits, to Mahrem, and often to the Greek god of war, Ares.

Merchants exchanged more than raw materials and finished goods in Aksum. They shared ideas as well. One of these ideas was a new religion, Christianity. Based on the teachings of Jesus and a belief in one God—monotheism—Christianity began in Judea about AD 30. It spread throughout the Roman Empire and then to Africa, and eventually to Aksum.

Aksum Becomes Christian Ezana succeeded to the throne as an infant after the death of his father. While his mother ruled the kingdom, a young Christian man from Syria who had been captured and taken into the court educated him. When Ezana finally became ruler of Aksum, he converted to Christianity and established it as the kingdom's official religion. He vowed, "I will rule the people with righteousness and justice and will not oppress them, and may they preserve this Throne which I have set up for the Lord of Heaven." King Ezana's conversion led to the conversion of the royal court, but for many years people outside of the court continued to practice indigenous religions. As Christianity spread amongst the Aksumite people, they blended the new beliefs and practices with traditional religious practices, such as dancing ceremonies and use of the sistrum during worship, to form a unique expression of Christianity. The establishment of Christianity was the longest-lasting achievement of the Aksumites. Today, the land of Ethiopia, where Aksum was located, is home to millions of Christians.

Vocabulary
sistrum a handheld percussion instrument that includes a frame with rods or loops attached to it and is shaken to make sound

This mural depicting Bible stories is located on the wall of one of the oldest Christian churches in Aksum.

Aksumite Innovations The inscription on Ezana's stele is written in Ge'ez, the language brought to Aksum by its early Arab inhabitants. Aside from Egypt and Meroë, Aksum was the only ancient African kingdom known to have developed a written language. It was also the first state south of the Sahara to mint its own coins. Made of bronze, silver, and gold, these coins were imprinted with the saying, "May the country be satisfied." Ezana apparently hoped that this inscription would make him popular with the people. Every time they used a coin, it would remind them that he had their interests at heart.

In addition to these cultural achievements, the Aksumites adapted creatively to their rugged, hilly environment. They created a new method of agriculture, terrace farming. This enabled them to greatly increase the productivity of their land. **Terraces**, or steplike ridges constructed on mountain slopes, helped the soil retain water and prevented it from being washed downhill in heavy rains. The Aksumites dug canals to channel water from mountain streams into the fields. They also built dams and cisterns, or holding tanks, to store water.

Reading Check
Analyze Causes
What conditions led to Aksum's becoming Christian?

DOCUMENT-BASED INVESTIGATION   Historical Source

Pillars of Aksum

Aksumites developed a unique architecture. They put no mortar on the stones used to construct vast royal palaces and public buildings. Instead, they carved stones to fit together tightly. Huge stone pillars were erected as monuments or tomb markers. The carvings on the pillars are representations of the architecture of the time.

This towering stone pillar, or stele, was built to celebrate Aksum's achievements. Still standing today, its size and elaborate inscriptions make it an achievement in its own right. The pillars have many unique features:

- False doors, windows, and timber beams are carved into the stone.
- Typically, the top of the pillar is a rounded peak.
- The tallest stele was about 100 feet high. Of those steles left standing, one is 75 feet tall and is among the largest structures in the ancient world.
- The stone for the pillar was quarried and carved two to three miles away and then brought to the site.
- Ezana dedicated one soaring stone pillar to the Christian God, "the Lord of heaven, who in heaven and upon earth is mightier than everything that exists."

Analyze Historical Sources
How would constructing these pillars be similar to constructing the pyramids in Egypt?

The Fall of Aksum

Aksum's cultural and technological achievements enabled it to last for 800 years. The kingdom finally declined, however, under invaders who practiced the religion called Islam (ihs•LAHM). Its founder was Muhammad; by his death in 632, his followers had conquered all of Arabia. This territory included Aksum's lands on the Arabian coast of the Red Sea.

Islamic Invaders Between 632 and 750 Islamic invaders conquered vast territories in the Mediterranean world, spreading their religion as they went. Aksum protected Muhammad's family and followers during their rise to power. As a result, initially the invaders did not seize Aksum's territories on the African coast of the Red Sea. Retaining control of that coastline enabled Aksum to remain a trading power.

Before long, though, the invaders seized footholds on the African coast as well. In 710 they destroyed Adulis. This conquest cut Aksum off from the major ports along both the Red Sea and the Mediterranean. As a result, the kingdom declined as an international trading power. But it was not only Aksum's political power that weakened. Its spiritual identity and environment were also endangered.

Aksum Isolated As the invaders spread Islam to the lands they conquered, Aksum became isolated from other Christian settlements. To escape the advancing wave of Islam, Aksum's rulers moved their capital over the mountains into what is now northern Ethiopia. Aksum's new geographic isolation—along with depletion of the forests and soil erosion—led to its decline as a world power.

Although the kingdom of Aksum reached tremendous heights and left a lasting legacy in its religion, architecture, and agriculture, it never expanded outside a fairly small area. This is a pattern found in other cultures, both in Africa and around the world.

Reading Check
Analyze Effects
How did the Muslim conquest of Africa affect the kingdom of Aksum?

Lesson 3 Assessment

1. **Organize Information** Use a web like the one below to record the significant achievements of Aksum.

Aksum's Achievements

In your opinion, which of Aksum's achievements was most impressive? Why?

2. **Key Terms and People** For each key term or person in the lesson, write a sentence explaining its significance.

3. **Draw Conclusions** How did Aksum's location and interaction with other regions affect its development?

4. **Analyze Causes** Why did the kingdom of Aksum decline?

5. **Evaluate Decisions** What impact did Ezana's decision to become a Christian have on the kingdom of Aksum?

6. **Form Opinions** Write a two-paragraph opinion on the following statement: The kingdom of Aksum would have reached the same heights even if Ezana had not become king.

North and West African Civilizations

Setting the Stage

In the seventh century, the new religion Islam appeared in Arabia and quickly spread through Egypt and into North Africa. Many African rulers converted and established strong states based on Islamic law. While these states developed in North Africa, three powerful empires flourished in West Africa. These ancient African empires arose in the Sahel, the savanna region just south of the Sahara. They grew strong by controlling trade. In this section you will learn about the Almoravid and Almohad empires of North Africa and the West African empires of Ghana, Mali, and Songhai.

Muslim States

While stateless societies developed south of the Sahara and the Christian state of Aksum developed in the Horn of Africa, Islam played a vital role in North Africa. After Muhammad's death in 632, Muslims swept across the northwest part of the continent. They converted many by the sword of conquest and others peacefully. By 670, Muslims ruled Egypt and had entered the **Maghrib**, the part of North Africa that is today the Mediterranean coast of Libya, Tunisia, Algeria, and Morocco.

As Islam spread, some African rulers converted to Islam. These African Muslim rulers then based their government upon Islamic law. Muslims believe that God's law is a higher authority than any human law. Therefore, Muslim rulers often relied on religious scholars as government advisers.

Islamic Law In Islam, following the law is a religious obligation. Muslims do not separate their personal life from their religious life, and Islamic law regulates almost all areas of human life. Islamic law helped to bring order to Muslim states.

However, various Muslim states had ethnic and cultural differences. Further, these states sometimes had differing

The Big Idea

North and West Africa contained several rich and powerful states, including Muslim states in the north and Ghana, Mali, and Songhai in the west.

Why It Matters Now

These civilizations demonstrate the richness of African culture before European colonization.

Key Terms and People

Maghrib
Almoravids
Almohads
Ghana
Mali
Sundiata
Mansa Musa
Ibn Battuta
Songhai
Hausa
Yoruba
Benin

interpretations, or schools, of Islamic law. Nonetheless, Islamic law has been such a significant force in history that some states, especially in North Africa, are still influenced by it today.

Among those who converted to Islam were the Berbers. Fiercely independent desert and mountain dwellers, the Berbers were the original inhabitants of North Africa. While they accepted Islam as their faith, many maintained their Berber identities and loyalties. Two Berber groups, the Almoravids and the Almohads, founded empires that united the Maghrib under Muslim rule.

Almoravid Reformers In the 11th century, Muslim reformers founded the Almoravid (al•muh•RAHV•uhd) Empire. Its members came from a Berber group living in the western Sahara in what is today Mauritania. The movement began after devout Berber Muslims made a hajj, or pilgrimage, to Mecca. On their journey home, they convinced a Muslim scholar from Morocco named Abd Allah Ibn Yasin to return with them to teach their people about Islam. Ibn Yasin's teachings soon attracted followers, and he founded a strict religious brotherhood, known as the **Almoravids**.

▷ Explore ONLINE!

Selected African Societies, 800–1500

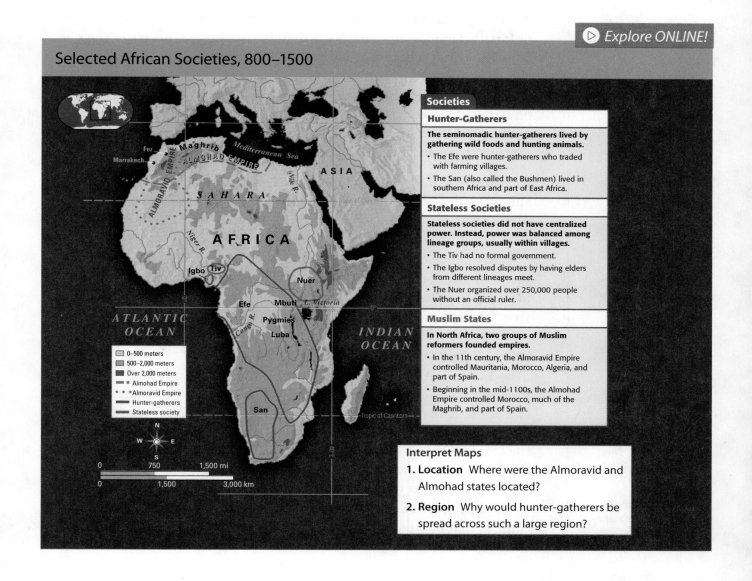

Societies

Hunter-Gatherers

The seminomadic hunter-gatherers lived by gathering wild foods and hunting animals.

- The Efe were hunter-gatherers who traded with farming villages.
- The San (also called the Bushmen) lived in southern Africa and part of East Africa.

Stateless Societies

Stateless societies did not have centralized power. Instead, power was balanced among lineage groups, usually within villages.

- The Tiv had no formal government.
- The Igbo resolved disputes by having elders from different lineages meet.
- The Nuer organized over 250,000 people without an official ruler.

Muslim States

In North Africa, two groups of Muslim reformers founded empires.

- In the 11th century, the Almoravid Empire controlled Mauritania, Morocco, Algeria, and part of Spain.
- Beginning in the mid-1100s, the Almohad Empire controlled Morocco, much of the Maghrib, and part of Spain.

0–500 meters
500–2,000 meters
Over 2,000 meters
Almohad Empire
Almoravid Empire
Hunter-gatherers
Stateless society

0 750 1,500 mi
0 1,500 3,000 km

Interpret Maps

1. **Location** Where were the Almoravid and Almohad states located?

2. **Region** Why would hunter-gatherers be spread across such a large region?

Carpets for sale in Marrakech, Morocco

According to one theory about the name's origin, the group lived in a *ribat*, or fortified monastery. They were therefore called the "people of the *ribat*," or *al-Murabitun*. This eventually became "Almoravid."

In the 1050s, Ibn Yasin led the Almoravids in an effort to spread Islam through conquest. After Ibn Yasin's death in 1059, the Almoravids went on to take Morocco and found Marrakech. It became their capital. They overran the West African empire of Ghana by 1076. The Almoravids also captured parts of southern Spain, where they were called Moors.

Almohads Take Over In the mid-1100s, the **Almohads** (AL•moh•HADZ), another group of Berber Muslim reformers, seized power from the Almoravids. The Almohads began as a religious movement in the Atlas Mountains of Morocco.

The Almohads followed the teachings of Ibn Tumart. After a pilgrimage to Mecca, Ibn Tumart criticized the later Almoravid rulers for moving away from the traditional practice of Islam. He urged his followers to strictly obey the teachings of the Qur'an and Islamic law. The Almohads, led by Abd al-Mumin, fought to overthrow the Almoravids and remain true to their view of traditional Islamic beliefs.

By 1148 the Almohads controlled most of Morocco and ended Almoravid rule. The new Muslim reformers kept Marrakech as their capital. By the end of the 12th century, they had conquered much of southern Spain. In Africa, their territory stretched from Marrakech to Tripoli and Tunis on the Mediterranean. The Almohad Empire broke up into individual Muslim dynasties. While the Almohad Empire lasted just over 100 years, it united the Maghrib under one rule for the first time.

Stronger empires were about to emerge. Societies in West Africa created empires that boasted economic and political power and strong links to trade routes.

Reading Check
Analyze Effects
What was the main effect of Almohad rule on the Maghrib?

Empire of Ghana

By AD 200, trade across the Sahara had existed for centuries. However, this trade remained infrequent and irregular because of the harsh desert conditions. Most pack animals—oxen, donkeys, and horses—could not travel very far in the hot, dry Sahara without rest or water. Then, in the third century AD, Berber nomads began using camels. The camel could plod steadily over much longer distances than other pack animals, covering as much as 60 miles in a day. In addition, it could travel more than ten days without water, twice as long as most pack animals. With the camel, nomads blazed new routes across the desert and trade increased.

Other technologies and developments also facilitated interregional trade between North and West Africa. The ironmaking technologies that had developed by 500 BC in West Africa enabled trade as people manufactured agricultural tools, weaponry, and other implements. The iron weapons helped West African empires keep order on the trade routes, providing safe passage to merchants. Iron tools also helped increase agricultural production, and agricultural surplus could be traded. Plentiful food also meant that more people could specialize in areas such as metalworking, trading, or administration. By the 11th century, Arabic writing became important for recording contracts, sharing information, and keeping other records. Pottery made locally could be used to store and transport goods, and canoes were used to carry materials and goods along the Niger (NY·juhr) River to trading towns.

The trans-Saharan trade routes crossed the savanna through the region farmed by the Soninke (soh·NIHN·keh) people. The Soninke people called their ruler *ghana,* or war chief. Muslim traders began to use the word to refer to the Soninke region. By the 700s, **Ghana** was a kingdom, and its rulers were growing rich by taxing the goods that traders carried through their territory.

Gold-Salt Trade The two most important trade items were gold and salt. Gold came from a forest region south of the savanna between the Niger and Senegal (SEHN·ih·GAWL) rivers. Miners dug gold from shafts as deep as 100 feet or sifted it from fast-moving streams. Some sources estimate that until about 1350, at least two-thirds of the world's supply of gold came from West Africa. Although rich in gold, West Africa's savanna and forests lacked salt, a material essential to human life. The Sahara contained deposits of salt. In fact, in the Saharan village of Taghaza, workers built their houses from salt blocks because it was the only material available.

Arab and Berber traders crossed the desert with camel caravans loaded down with salt. They also carried cloth, weapons, and manufactured goods from ports on the Mediterranean. After a long journey, they reached the market towns of the savanna. Meanwhile, African traders brought gold north from the forest regions. African traders also exported spices, kola nuts, shea butter, animal hides, leather goods, cloth (starting in the 11th century), and slaves.

Slaves were a part of the trans-Saharan trade from the sixth century to the 19th century. Slaves taken from West Africa were sold in North Africa, Egypt, Arabia, what is now Iraq, and India, although most African slaves in Arabia, Iraq, and India came from east African societies and were traded along the Indian Ocean routes.

Merchants met in trading cities, where they exchanged goods under the watchful eye of the king's tax collector. In addition to taxing trade, royal officials made sure that all traders weighed goods fairly and did business according to the law. Royal guards also provided protection from bandits.

Land of Gold By the year 800, Ghana had become an empire. Because Ghana's king controlled trade and commanded a large army, he could demand taxes and gifts from the chiefs of surrounding lands. As long as the chiefs made their payments, the king left them in peace to rule their own people.

In his royal palace, the king stored gold nuggets and slabs of salt (collected as taxes). Only the king had the right to own gold nuggets, although gold dust freely circulated in the marketplace. By this means, the king limited the supply of gold and kept its price from falling. Ghana's African ruler acted as a religious leader, chief judge, and military commander. He headed a large bureaucracy and could call up a huge army. In 1067, a Muslim geographer and scholar named al-Bakri wrote a description of Ghana's royal court:

"The king adorns himself . . . wearing necklaces and bracelets. . . . The court of appeal is held in a domed pavilion around which stand ten horses with gold embroidered trappings. Behind the king stand ten pages holding shields and swords decorated with gold, and on his right are the sons of the subordinate [lower] kings of his country, all wearing splendid garments and with their hair mixed with gold."

—al-Bakri, quoted in *Africa in the Days of Exploration*

Social Organization At its height, the Empire of Ghana included many peoples, some of which had their own customs and language. However, as Ghana's rule strengthened and trade continued to connect peoples and communities, the empire's cities, at least, began to develop similarities. In all of Ghana, the king was considered the supreme ruler. An administrative class helped the king run the government. Other segments that emerged in Ghana's society included miners, agricultural laborers, metalworkers, and leather crafters. Skilled craftsmen such as blacksmiths and leather crafters enjoyed a privileged place in society. Some were supported by the king's court.

Ghana was a matrilineal society, meaning that ancestry was traced through the mother's lineage. Inheritances also passed through the mother's lineage. For example, the king's son was not the king's heir. The son of the king's sister was the heir.

Islamic Influences While Islam spread through North Africa by conquest, south of the Sahara, Islam spread through trade. Muslim merchants and teachers settled in the states south of the Sahara and introduced their faith there.

Eventually, Ghana's rulers converted to Islam. By the end of the 11th century, Muslim advisers were helping the king run his kingdom. While Ghana's African rulers accepted Islam, many people in the empire clung to their animistic beliefs and practices. Animism is the belief that spirits living in animals, plants, and natural forces play an important role in daily life. Much of the population never converted. Those who did kept many of their former beliefs, which they observed along with Islam. For example, people might celebrate both Islamic festivals and festivals of local African religions. Among the upper class, Islam's growth encouraged the spread of literacy. To study the Qur'an, converts to Islam had to learn Arabic.

In 1076 the Muslim Almoravids of North Africa completed their conquest of Ghana. Although the Almoravids eventually withdrew from Ghana, the war had badly disrupted the gold-salt trade. Ghana never regained its power, but it had helped Islam to gain a foothold in the region, and the West African–North African trade that Ghana developed would continue for centuries, although the trade routes would shift.

Reading Check
Analyze Causes
Why would the disruption of trade destroy Ghana's power?

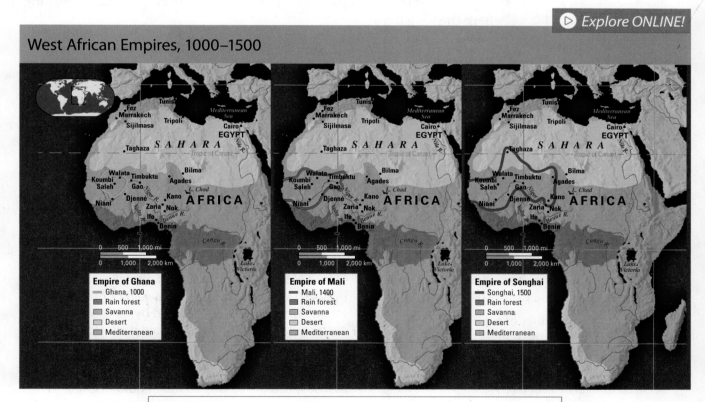

▶ Explore ONLINE!

West African Empires, 1000–1500

Empire of Ghana
- Ghana, 1000
- Rain forest
- Savanna
- Desert
- Mediterranean

Empire of Mali
- Mali, 1400
- Rain forest
- Savanna
- Desert
- Mediterranean

Empire of Songhai
- Songhai, 1500
- Rain forest
- Savanna
- Desert
- Mediterranean

Interpret Maps

1. **Region** Compare the regions occupied by the Ghana, Mali, and Songhai empires in terms of size and location.

2. **Human-Environment Interaction** How did the environment both contribute resources to and cause problems for traders?

Empire of Mali

By 1235 the kingdom of **Mali** had emerged. Its founders were Mande-speaking people who lived south of Ghana. Mali's wealth, like Ghana's, was built on gold. As Ghana remained weak, people who had been under its control began to act independently. In addition, miners found new gold deposits farther east. This caused the most important trade routes to shift eastward, which made a new group of people—the people of Mali—wealthy. With this wealth they acquired horses and crafted iron weapons and leather goods, all of which enabled them to seize power.

Sundiata Conquers an Empire Mali's first great leader, **Sundiata** (sun•JAHT•ah), came to power by crushing a cruel, unpopular leader. Then, in the words of a Mande oral tradition, "the world knew no other master but Sundiata." Sundiata became Mali's *mansa,* or emperor. Through a series of military victories, he took over the kingdom of Ghana and the trading cities of Koumbi Saleh and Walata. A period of peace and prosperity followed.

Sundiata proved to be as great a leader in peace as he had been in war. He put able administrators in charge of Mali's finances, defense, and foreign affairs. From his new capital at Niani, he promoted agriculture and reestablished the gold-salt trade. Niani became an important center of commerce and trade. People began to call Sundiata's empire Mali, meaning "where the king lives."

Mansa Musa Expands Mali Sundiata died in 1255. Some of Mali's next rulers became Muslims. These African Muslim rulers built mosques, attended public prayers, and supported the preaching of Muslim holy men. The most famous of them was **Mansa Musa** (MAHN•sah moo•SAH), who

---

BIOGRAPHY

Sundiata
(?–1255)

Sundiata came from the kingdom of Kangaba near the present-day Mali-Guinea border. According to tradition, he was one of 12 brothers who were heirs to the throne of Kangaba.

When Sumanguru, ruler of a neighboring state, overran Kangaba in the early 1200s, he wanted to eliminate rivals, so he murdered all of Sundiata's brothers. He spared Sundiata, who was sickly and seemed unlikely to survive.

However, as Sundiata grew up, he gained strength and became a popular leader of many warriors. In 1235, Sundiata's army defeated Sumanguru and his troops.

Mansa Musa
(?–1332?)

Mansa Musa, the strongest of Sundiata's successors, was a devout Muslim. On his hajj, Mansa Musa stopped in Cairo, Egypt. Five hundred slaves, each carrying a staff of gold, arrived first. They were followed by 80 camels, each carrying 300 pounds of gold dust. Hundreds of other camels brought supplies. Thousands of servants and officials completed the procession.

Mansa Musa gave away so much gold in Cairo that the value of this precious metal declined in Egypt for 12 years.

Major Trans-Saharan Trade Routes and Goods

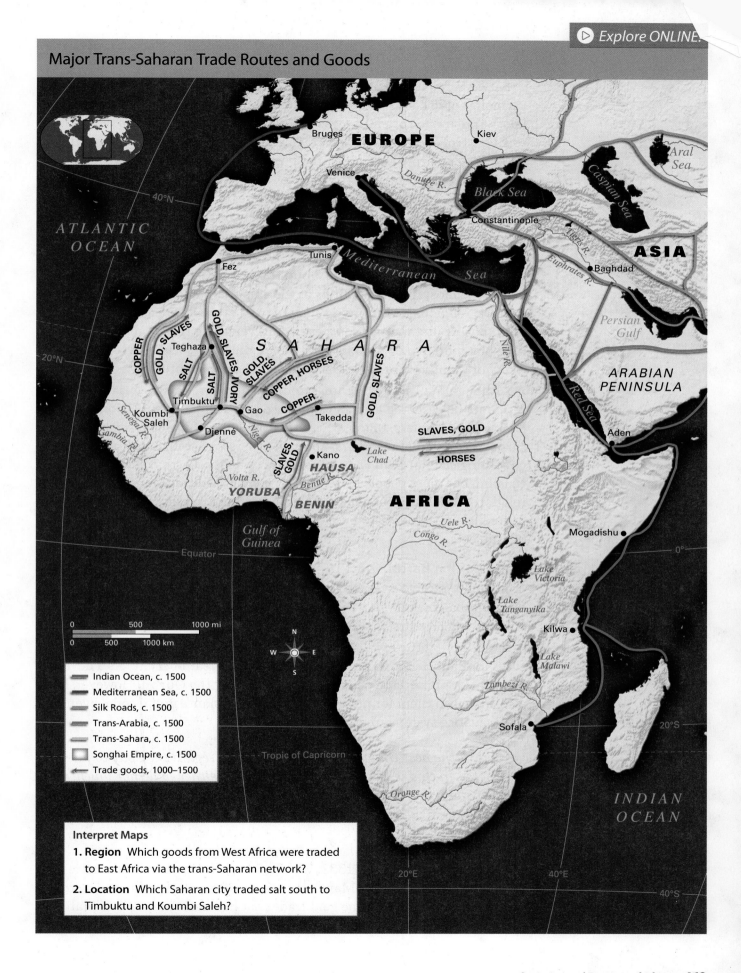

Interpret Maps

1. **Region** Which goods from West Africa were traded to East Africa via the trans-Saharan network?

2. **Location** Which Saharan city traded salt south to Timbuktu and Koumbi Saleh?

Legend:
- Indian Ocean, c. 1500
- Mediterranean Sea, c. 1500
- Silk Roads, c. 1500
- Trans-Arabia, c. 1500
- Trans-Sahara, c. 1500
- Songhai Empire, c. 1500
- Trade goods, 1000–1500

may have been Sundiata's grandnephew. Mansa Musa ruled from about 1312 to 1332.

Between the reigns of Sundiata and Mansa Musa, Mali had experienced turmoil. There had been seven different rulers in approximately 50 years. Like Sundiata, Mansa Musa was a skilled military leader who exercised royal control over the gold-salt trade and put down every rebellion. His 100,000-man army kept order and protected Mali from attack. Under Mansa Musa, the empire expanded to roughly twice the size of the Empire of Ghana. To govern his far-reaching empire, Mansa Musa divided it into provinces and appointed governors, who ruled fairly and efficiently.

A devout Muslim, Mansa Musa went on a hajj to Mecca from 1324 to 1325. When he returned, he ordered the building of new mosques at the trading cities of Timbuktu (TIHM•buhk•TOO) and Gao. Timbuktu became one of the most important cities of the empire. It attracted Muslim judges, doctors, religious leaders, and scholars from far and wide. They attended Timbuktu's outstanding mosques and universities. These intellectual and religious centers helped to integrate Islam into the society of Mali, an effect of Mansa Musa's rule that would endure for centuries.

Although Mali's urban centers flourished under Mansa Musa, their residents represented a small minority of the empire's population. Most people were farmers. Many others were skilled craftspeople, such as carpenters and metalworkers, and still others were religious leaders. The governing class of Mali and the scholars of its intellectual centers were Muslim, but most people believed in and practiced traditional African religions, especially outside of the urban centers. While Mansa Musa supported Islamic studies and religious practices, he did not force the faith on his subjects.

Travels of Ibn Battuta In 1352, one of Mansa Musa's successors prepared to receive a traveler and historian named **Ibn Battuta** (IHB•uhn-ba•TOO•tah). A native of Tangier in North Africa, Ibn Battuta had traveled for 27 years, visiting most of the countries in the Islamic world.

After leaving the royal palace, Ibn Battuta visited Timbuktu and other cities in Mali. He found he could travel without fear of crime. As a devout Muslim, he praised the people for their study of the Qur'an. However, he also criticized them for not strictly practicing Islam's moral code. Even so, Mali's justice system greatly impressed him:

> *"One of the best things in these parts is, the regard they pay to justice; for, in this respect, the Sultan regards neither little nor much. The safety, too, is very great; so that a traveller may proceed alone among them, without the least fear of a thief or robber."*

—Ibn Battuta, *The Travels of Ibn Batūta, 1829*

Reading Check
Analyze Effects
Why did Islam flourish in urban centers of West Africa?

Ibn Battuta left Mali in 1353. Within 50 years, the powerful empire began to weaken. Most of Mansa Musa's successors lacked his ability to govern well. In addition, the gold trade that had been the basis of Mali's wealth shifted eastward as new goldfields were developed elsewhere.

Mansa Musa's Kingdom

In 1324, Mansa Musa left Mali for the hajj to Mecca. On the trip, he gave away enormous amounts of gold. Because of this, Europeans learned of Mali's wealth. In 1375, a Spanish mapmaker created an illustrated map showing Mansa Musa's kingdom in western Africa. Drawn on the map is Mansa Musa holding a gold nugget.

At the top of the map is Spain. At the bottom of Spain, the Mediterranean meets the Atlantic Ocean at the Strait of Gibraltar. South of Gibraltar is Africa. Filling most of the map is North Africa, with the Mediterranean extending east and the Atlantic west of Gibraltar.

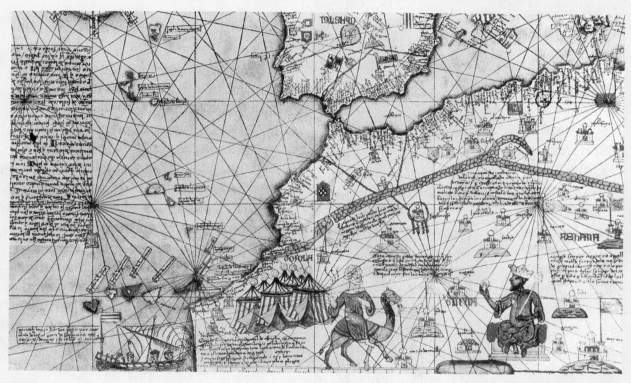

Analyze Historical Sources

1. What was a major source of wealth for the Empire of Mali?

2. How might Mali's (and Africa's) wealth have influenced interactions between Africans and Europeans?

Empire of Songhai

As Mali declined in the 1400s, people who had been under its control began to break away. Among them were the **Songhai** (SAWNG·HY) people to the east. They built up an army and extended their territory to the large bend in the Niger River near Gao. They gained control of the all-important trade routes. Gao was the capital of their empire.

Sunni Ali, a Conquering Hero   The Songhai had two extraordinary rulers, both of whom were Muslims. One was Sunni Ali, who built a vast empire by military conquest. Sunni Ali's rule began in 1464 and lasted almost 30 years.

Sunni Ali built a professional army that had a riverboat fleet of war canoes and a mobile fighting force on horseback. He expanded Songhai into an empire through his skill as a military commander and his aggressive leadership. In 1468, Sunni Ali achieved his first major military triumph. He captured the city of Timbuktu, which had been an important part of Mali's empire.

Five years later, he took Djenné, also a trade city that had a university. To take Djenné, Sunni Ali surrounded the city with his army for seven years before it fell in 1473. Sunni Ali completed the takeover of Djenné by marrying its queen.

Askia Muhammad Governs Well After Sunni Ali's death in 1492, his son succeeded him as ruler. Almost at once, the son faced a major revolt by Muslims who were angry that he did not practice their religion faithfully. The leader of the revolt was a devout Muslim named Askia Muhammad. He drove Sunni Ali's son from power and replaced him.

Askia Muhammad conquered the Mossi people, whose territory bordered Songhai to the south. Then he turned west, to the Hausa kingdoms, and conquered them. He permitted the king of the Hausa city-state Kano to remain on his throne as a vassal. In some lands that he annexed, Askia established a Songhai colony to ensure efficient governance and collection of taxes and tribute. Annexing neighboring kingdoms increased the power and wealth of the Songhai Empire by expanding control of trade routes, increasing tax revenues, and increasing receipt of tribute.

During his 37-year rule, Askia Muhammad proved to be an excellent administrator. He set up an efficient tax system and chose able officials. Adding to the centralized government created by Sunni Ali, he appointed officials to serve as ministers of the treasury, army, navy, and agriculture. In addition to the king and the elites who worked in his government, Songhai society included a class of artisans such as metalworkers, farmers, and slaves. Under his rule, the well-governed empire thrived.

Despite its wealth and learning, the Songhai Empire lacked modern weapons. The Chinese had invented gunpowder in the ninth century. About 1304, Arabs developed the first gun, which shot arrows. In 1591, a

---

SOCIAL HISTORY

Islam in West Africa

South of the Sahara, many converts to Islam also kept their African beliefs. They found ways to include traditional rituals and customs in their new religion.

The status of women in West African societies demonstrates how local custom altered Muslim practice. In many 15th-century Muslim societies, women seldom left their homes. When they did, they veiled their faces. Muslim women in West Africa, however, did not wear veils. They mingled freely with men in public, which shocked visiting Muslim religious leaders.

Reading Check
Make Inferences
Why might the
people who had been
conquered by Mali
want to break away?

Moroccan fighting force of several thousand men equipped with gunpowder and cannons crossed the Sahara and invaded Songhai. The Moroccan troops quickly defeated the Songhai warriors, who were armed only with swords and spears. The collapse of the Songhai Empire ended a 1,000-year period in which powerful kingdoms and empires ruled the central region of West Africa.

Other Peoples of West Africa

While empires rose and fell, city-states developed in other parts of West Africa. As in Ghana, Mali, and Songhai, Muslim traditions influenced some of these city-states. Other city-states held to their traditional African beliefs.

Hausa City-States Compete The **Hausa** (HOW•suh) were a group of people named after the language they spoke. The city-states of the Hausa people first emerged between the years 1000 and 1200 in the savanna area east of Mali and Songhai in what is today northern Nigeria. Songhai briefly ruled the Hausa city-states, but they soon regained their independence. In such city-states as Kano, Katsina, and Zazzau (later Zaria), local rulers built walled cities for their capitals. From their capitals, Hausa rulers governed the farming villages outside the city walls.

Each ruler depended on the crops of the farmers and on a thriving trade in salt, grain, and cotton cloth made by urban weavers. Because they were located on trade routes that linked other West African states with the Mediterranean, Kano and Katsina became major trading states. They profited greatly from supplying the needs of caravans. Kano was noted for its woven and dyed cloth and for its leather goods.

Zazzau, the southernmost state, conducted a vigorous trade in enslaved people. Zazzau's traders raided an area to take captives and then sold them to traders in other Hausa states. These traders sold the captives to other North or West African societies in exchange for horses, harnesses, and

History in Depth

Queen Amina's Reign

In the 1500s, the Hausa city-state of Zazzau (later called Zaria) was governed by Queen Amina. She was remembered as the "headdress among the turbans." Her rule was distinguished for its military conquests.

The *Kano Chronicle,* a history of the city-state of Kano, records:

> *"At this time Zaria, under Queen Amina, conquered all the towns as far as Kawarajara and Nupe. Every town paid tribute to her. . . . Her conquests extended over 34 years."*

Queen Amina's commitment to her Muslim faith also led her to encourage Muslim scholars, judges, and religious leaders from religious centers at Kano and Timbuktu to come to Zazzau.

guns. The Hausa kept some enslaved captives to build and repair city walls and grow food for the cities.

All the Hausa city-states had similar forms of government. Rulers held great power over their subjects, but ministers and other officials acted to check this power. For protection, each city-state raised an army of mounted horsemen. Although rulers often schemed and fought to gain control over their neighbors, none succeeded for long. The constant fighting among city-states prevented any one of them from building a Hausa empire.

This Yoruba crown made of glass beads and grass cloth stands about 20 inches high.

Yoruba Kings and Artists Like the Hausa, the **Yoruba** (YAWR•uh•buh) people all spoke a common language. Originally the Yoruba-speaking people belonged to a number of small city-states in the forests on the southern edge of the savanna in present-day Benin and southwestern Nigeria. In these communities most people farmed. Over time, some of these smaller communities joined together under strong leaders. This led to the formation of several Yoruba kingdoms.

Considered divine, Yoruba kings served as the most important religious and political leaders in their kingdoms. All Yoruba chiefs traced their descent from the first ruler of Ife (EE•fay). According to legend, the creator sent this first ruler down to earth at Ife, where he founded the first Yoruba state. His many sons became the heads of other Yoruba kingdoms. All Yoruba chiefs regarded the king of Ife as their highest spiritual authority. A secret society of religious and political leaders limited the king's rule by reviewing the decisions he made.

Ife and Oyo were the two largest Yoruba kingdoms. Ife, developed by 1100, was the most powerful Yoruba kingdom until the late 1600s, when Oyo became more prosperous. As large urban centers, both Ife and Oyo had high walls surrounding them. Most rural farms in the surrounding areas produced surplus food, which was sent to the cities. This enabled city dwellers to become both traders and craftspeople.

The Ife were gifted artists who carved in wood and ivory. They produced terra cotta sculptures and cast in metal. Some scholars believe that the rulers supported artists. Many clay and metal casts portray Ife rulers in an idealistic way.

Vocabulary
terra cotta a reddish-brown clay, hard ceramic

This ivory mask is one of four taken from the king of Benin in 1897. It was worn on the belt of a ceremonial costume.

Kingdom of Benin To the south and west of Ife, near the delta of the Niger River, lay the kingdom of **Benin** (buh•NIHN). Like the Yoruba people of Ife and Oyo, the people of Benin made their homes in the forest. The first kings of Benin date from the 1200s. Like the Yoruba kings, the oba, or ruler, of Benin based his right to rule on claims of descent from the first king of Ife.

In the 1400s, an oba named Ewuare made Benin into a major West African state. He did so by building a powerful army. He used it to control an area that by 1500 stretched from the Niger River delta in the east to what is today Lagos, Nigeria. Ewuare also strengthened Benin City by building walls around it. Inside the city, broad streets were lined by neat rows of houses.

The huge palace contained many courtyards and works of art. Artists working for the oba created copper figurines and magnificent brass heads of the royal family. Brass plaques on the walls and columns of the royal palace of the oba showed legends, historical scenes, and the deeds of the oba and his nobles. According to tradition, Benin artists learned their craft from an Ife artist brought to Benin by the oba to teach them.

In the 1480s, Portuguese trading ships began to sail into Benin's port at Gwatto. The Portuguese traded with Benin merchants for pepper, leopard skins, ivory, and enslaved persons. This began several centuries of European interference in Africa, during which Europeans enslaved Africans and seized African territories for colonies. Meanwhile, East Africans prospered from trade and developed thriving cities and empires.

Reading Check
Analyze Causes
What was the main reason that the Hausa did not develop an empire?

Lesson 4 Assessment

1. **Organize Information** Create a timeline like the one below to trace the growth and decline of the empires you read about in this lesson.

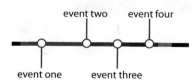

event two   event four

event one   event three

Write a paragraph describing how any two of these events are related.

2. **Key Terms and People** For each key term or person in the lesson, write a sentence explaining its significance.

3. **Analyze Motives** Why did Berber leaders want to make changes to their society?

4. **Summarize** How did the trans-Saharan trade practiced by Ghana, Mali, and Songhai work?

5. **Compare** What are some of the similarities between Sundiata and Mansa Musa?

6. **Evaluate Impact** How did the expansion of the Songhai Empire affect the people and the economy of West Africa?

7. **Compare** What are some of the similarities between the Hausa city-states and other city-states you have read about?

Benin Bronzes

Benin is famous for its bronze and brass sculptures. Benin sculpture was made by guilds controlled by the king. One of the main functions of Benin art was to please the ruler by recording his history or by displaying his power. For instance, brass plaques commemorating the ruler's great achievements adorned the palace walls. Busts of the ruler and his family showed them as idealized figures.

▶ **QUEEN MOTHER**
Perhaps the most widely known type of Benin sculpture was the royal head, such as this one. In Benin, the Queen Mother held a lot of power. To symbolize that power, she wore a woven crown called a "chicken's beak."

◀ **PLAQUE**
Plaques such as this decorated the palace of the oba, or ruler, of Benin.

▼ LEOPARD

Admired for its power, fierceness, and intelligence, the leopard was depicted on many royal objects. This snarling leopard is a symbol of the king's power. It is also a water vessel that was used on ceremonial occasions.

▲ MUSICIAN

This figure was probably made in the late 16th or early 17th century. It shows an attendant of the king blowing a horn or flute. This type of figure was often found on altars.

THE LOST-WAX PROCESS

Many of the Benin sculptures were made using the lost-wax process.

1. The artist forms a core of clay that is roughly the shape of the planned sculpture.

2. The artist applies a layer of wax over the core, then carves fine details into the surface of the wax.

3. A layer of fine clay is spread over the wax surface. This creates a smooth finish and captures the small details.

4. Several layers of coarse clay are applied to create the mold.

5. The entire object is fired in a kiln (oven). The clay hardens and the wax melts away, leaving a clay mold. (The melted wax is the origin of the name "lost-wax.")

6. Melted bronze is poured into the mold and left to harden.

7. The clay mold is broken off, revealing the finished bronze sculpture.

Now and Then

1. **Make Inferences** Why do you think the figure of a servant blowing a horn was found on an altar?

2. **Compare and Contrast** Use library resources or the Internet to identify a sculpture of a U.S. leader. What quality about that leader does the sculpture portray? How is it similar to or different from Benin's royal sculptures?

Eastern City-States and Southern Empires

The Big Idea
African city-states and empires gained wealth through developing and trading resources.

Why It Matters Now
The country of Zimbabwe and cities such as Mogadishu and Mombasa have their roots in this time period.

Key Terms and People
Swahili
Great Zimbabwe
Mutapa

Ruins of the Great Mosque at Kilwa

Setting the Stage

By the third century AD, Aksum was part of an extensive trade network. From its Red Sea port, Aksum traded with Arabia, Persia, India, and Rome. In the 600s, Muslim forces gained control of Arabia, the Red Sea, and North Africa. They cut off the Aksumites from their port. The Aksumites moved their capital south from Aksum to Roha (later called Lalibela) before 1100. Meanwhile, other cities on the east coast were thriving because of Indian Ocean trade. In this lesson, you will learn about East African trade, Islamic influences in East Africa, and the peoples of southern Africa.

East Coast Trade Cities

Villages along the east coast began to develop into important trade cities. By 1100, waves of Bantu-speaking people had migrated across central Africa to the east coast. There they established farming and fishing villages. Slowly, the coastal villages grew into bustling seaports, built on trade between East African merchants and traders from Arabia, Persia, and India. As trade increased, many Muslim Arab and Persian traders settled in the port cities. Arabic blended with the Bantu language to create **Swahili** (swah·HEE·lee).

Persian traders moved south from the Horn of Africa, a triangular peninsula near Arabia. They brought Asian manufactured goods to Africa and African raw materials to Asia. In the coastal markets, Arab traders sold porcelain bowls from China and jewels and cotton cloth from India. They bought African ivory, gold, tortoiseshell, ambergris, leopard skins, and rhinoceros horns to carry to Arabia.

By 1300, more than 35 trading cities dotted the coast from Mogadishu in the north to Kilwa and Sofala in the south. These seaports grew wealthy by controlling trade. Some cities also manufactured trade goods for export. For example, weavers in Mogadishu and Sofala made cloth. Workers in Mombasa and Malindi made iron tools.

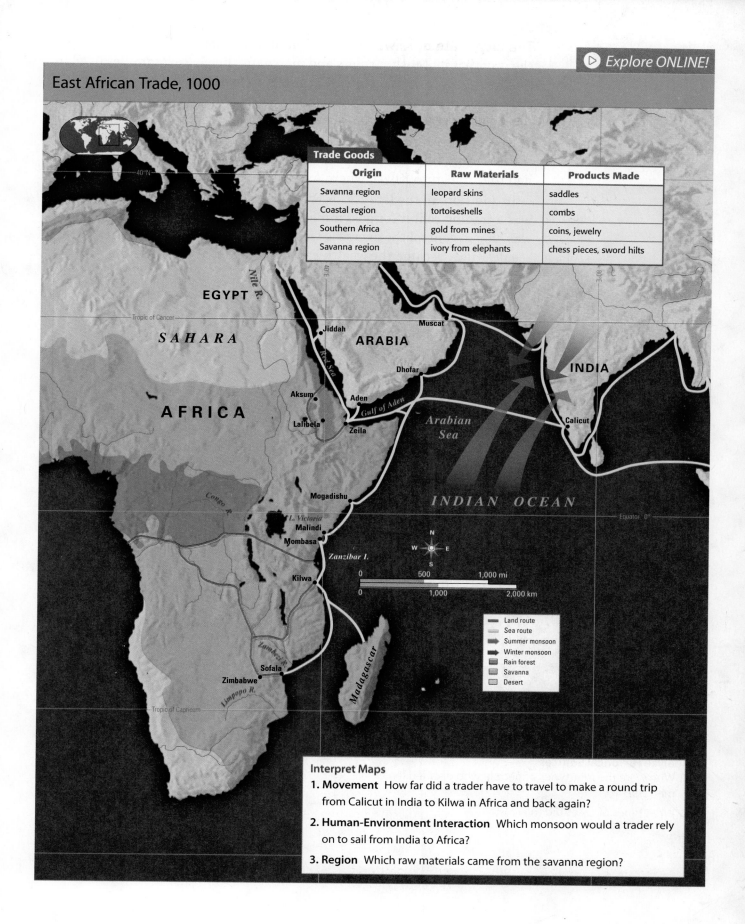

East African Trade, 1000

Trade Goods

Origin	Raw Materials	Products Made
Savanna region	leopard skins	saddles
Coastal region	tortoiseshells	combs
Southern Africa	gold from mines	coins, jewelry
Savanna region	ivory from elephants	chess pieces, sword hilts

Land route
Sea route
Summer monsoon
Winter monsoon
Rain forest
Savanna
Desert

Interpret Maps

1. **Movement** How far did a trader have to travel to make a round trip from Calicut in India to Kilwa in Africa and back again?

2. **Human-Environment Interaction** Which monsoon would a trader rely on to sail from India to Africa?

3. **Region** Which raw materials came from the savanna region?

The City-State of Kilwa In 1331, Ibn Battuta visited Kilwa. He admired the way that its Muslim rulers and merchants lived. Rich families lived in fine houses of coral and stone. They slept in beds inlaid with ivory, and their meals were served on porcelain. Wealthy Muslim women wore silk robes and gold and silver bracelets.

Kilwa grew rich because it was as far south as a ship from India could sail in one monsoon season. Therefore, trade goods from southerly regions had to funnel into Kilwa, where Asian merchants could buy them.

In addition, in the late 1200s Kilwa had seized the port of Sofala, which was a trading center for gold mined inland. By controlling Sofala, Kilwa was able to control the overseas trade of gold from southern Africa. As a result, Kilwa became the wealthiest, most powerful coastal city-state.

Portuguese Conquest In 1488, the first Portuguese ships rounded the southern tip of Africa and sailed north, looking for a sea route to India.

Historical Source

Islamic Law in Mogadishu

In 1331, Ibn Battuta, traveling by caravan, visited the African city of Mogadishu. He described how Muslim officials decided legal matters.

Analyze Historical Sources

1. Who were the four types of people who decided legal matters?

2. What types of cases did they judge?

"The Shaikh [sultan] takes his place in his hall of audience and sends for the Qadi [judge]. He takes his place on the Shaikh's left and then the lawyers come in and the chief of them sit in front of the Shaikh. . . . Then food is brought and . . . those who are in the audience chamber eat in the presence of the Shaikh. . . . After this the Shaikh retires to his private apartments and the Qadi, the wazirs [government ministers] . . . and . . . chief amirs [military commanders] sit to hear causes and complaints. Questions of religious law are decided by the Qadi, other cases are judged by the . . . wazirs and amirs. If a case requires the views of the [Shaikh], it is put in writing for him. He sends back an immediate reply."

—Ibn Battuta, *Travels of Ibn Battuta*

Reading Check
Analyze Causes
What were the two main reasons Kilwa became so wealthy?

They wanted to gain profits from the Asian trade in spices, perfumes, and silks. When the Portuguese saw the wealth of the East African city-states, they decided to conquer those cities and take over the trade themselves.

Using their shipboard cannon, the Portuguese took Sofala, Kilwa, and Mombasa. They burned parts of Kilwa and built forts on the sites of Kilwa and Mombasa. The Portuguese kept their ports and cities on the East African coast for the next two centuries.

Islamic Influences

Muslim traders introduced Islam to the East African coast, and commerce caused the religion to spread. Even the smallest towns had a mosque for the faithful. A Muslim sultan, or ruler, governed most cities. Most government officials and wealthy merchants were Muslims. However, the vast majority of people along the eastern coast held on to their traditional religious beliefs. This was also true of the people who lived in inland villages.

Enslavement of Africans Along with luxury goods, Arab Muslim traders exported enslaved persons from the East African coast. Traders sent Africans acquired through kidnapping to markets in Arabia, Persia, and

An Arab slave market in Yemen, 1237

Iraq. Wealthy people in these countries often bought slaves to do domestic tasks. Muslim traders shipped enslaved Africans across the Indian Ocean to India, where Indian rulers employed them as soldiers. Enslaved Africans also worked on docks and ships at Muslim-controlled ports and as household servants in China.

Although Muslim traders had been enslaving East Africans and selling them overseas since about the ninth century, the numbers remained small—perhaps about 1,000 a year. The trade in slaves did not increase dramatically until the 1700s. At that time, Europeans started to buy captured Africans for their colonial plantations.

Reading Check
Summarize
How extensive was the trade in enslaved persons from East Africa before 1700?

Southern Africa and Great Zimbabwe

The gold and ivory that helped the coastal city-states grow rich came from the interior of southern Africa. In southeastern Africa, the Shona people established a city called **Great Zimbabwe** (zihm·BAHB·way), which grew into an empire built on the gold trade.

Great Zimbabwe By 1000, the Shona people had settled the fertile, well-watered plateau between the Zambezi and Limpopo rivers in present-day Zimbabwe. The area was well suited to farming and cattle raising. The location also had other economic advantages. The city of Great Zimbabwe stood near an important trade route linking the goldfields with the coastal trading city of Sofala. Sometime after 1000, Great Zimbabwe gained control of these trade routes. From the 1200s through the 1400s, it became the capital of a thriving state. Its leaders taxed the traders who traveled these routes. They also demanded payments from less powerful chiefs. Because of this growing wealth, Great Zimbabwe became the economic, political, and religious center of an empire.

Almost everything that is known about Great Zimbabwe comes from its impressive ruins, which include a complex of walled enclosures on a large hill, another group of enclosures south of the hill, called the Great Enclosure, and more recent ruins in the valley between. In addition to the stone walls of the enclosures, there are ruins of many huts that were constructed of mud or stone, both within and without the walls of the enclosures. Most of the stone structures in Great Zimbabwe were probably built between 1250 and 1450.

Excavations of the ruins suggest that Great Zimbabwe's society included multiple social and economic classes. Huts outside of the city's enclosures were very close together, but inside the enclosures, they were not—showing that those living inside the enclosures enjoyed elite status. Some huts inside the hill enclosure seemed to be for special purposes, such as religious ceremonies. Additionally, most cattle bones on the site were found near the wall of the Great Enclosure, an indication that the elite of the

Great Zimbabwe

Great Zimbabwe was an important city in southern Africa. The word *zimbabwe* comes from a Shona phrase meaning "stone houses." The ruins consist of two complexes of stone buildings that once housed the royal palace of Great Zimbabwe's rulers. There are great curving walls around the ruins. Because there was no way for soldiers to climb to the top of the walls, archaeologists theorize that they were not used primarily as defenses. The massive walls were probably built to impress visitors with the strength of Zimbabwe and its ruler.

Inside the walls stands a cone-shaped tower. Among the ruins were found tall figures of birds, carved from soapstone. Archaeologists believe the construction of Great Zimbabwe may have taken about 400 years.

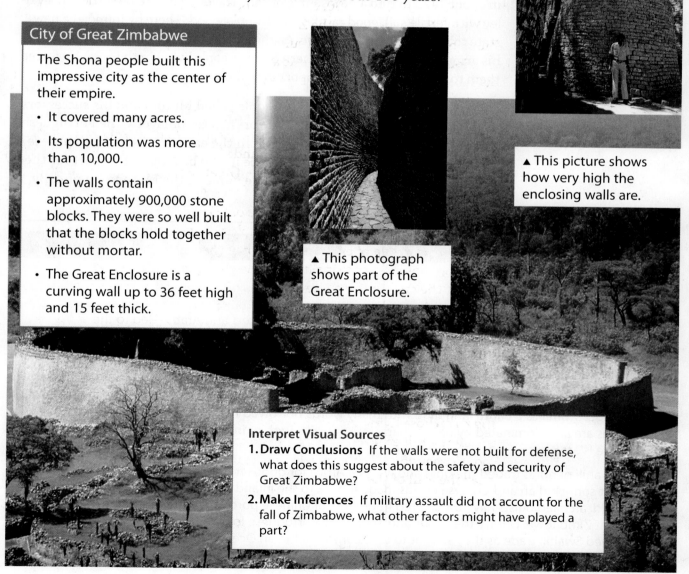

City of Great Zimbabwe

The Shona people built this impressive city as the center of their empire.

- It covered many acres.

- Its population was more than 10,000.

- The walls contain approximately 900,000 stone blocks. They were so well built that the blocks hold together without mortar.

- The Great Enclosure is a curving wall up to 36 feet high and 15 feet thick.

▲ This picture shows how very high the enclosing walls are.

▲ This photograph shows part of the Great Enclosure.

Interpret Visual Sources

1. **Draw Conclusions** If the walls were not built for defense, what does this suggest about the safety and security of Great Zimbabwe?

2. **Make Inferences** If military assault did not account for the fall of Zimbabwe, what other factors might have played a part?

community were probably the only ones who ate beef; commoners may have eaten goat or mutton, if they ate meat at all.

The people of Great Zimbabwe probably practiced a traditional religion similar to the Shona religion of today. This religion's dominant feature is devotion to the spirits of ancestors, who the Shona believe protect and guide the community.

By 1450, Great Zimbabwe was abandoned. No one knows for sure why it happened. According to one theory, cattle grazing had worn out the grasslands. In addition, farming had worn out the soil, and people had used up the salt and timber. The area could no longer support a large population.

Portuguese explorers knew about the site in the 1500s. Karl Mauch, a German explorer, was one of the first Europeans to discover the remains of these stone dwellings in 1871.

Reading Check
Analyze Events
Why did the people of Great Zimbabwe settle on the plateau between the Limpopo and Zambezi rivers?

The Mutapa Empire

According to Shona oral tradition, a man named Mutota left Great Zimbabwe in about 1420 to find a new source of salt. Traveling north, he settled in a valley with fertile soil, good rainfall, and ample wood. There he founded a new state to replace Great Zimbabwe. As the state grew, its leader, Mutota, used his army to dominate the northern Shona people living in the area. He forced them to make payments to support him and his army.

Mutapa Rulers These conquered people called Mutota and his successors *mwene mutapa*, meaning "conqueror" or "master pillager." The Portuguese who arrived on the East African coast in the early 1500s believed *mwene mutapa*—or *monomotapa,* as they wrote it—to be a title of respect for the ruler. The term is also the origin of the name of the **Mutapa** Empire. By

Global Patterns

Swahili

Over the centuries, contacts between two peoples—Bantu speakers and Arabs—led to the creation of a new people and a new language. Many Arab traders married African women. People of mixed Arab and African ancestry came to be called Swahili. The word comes from an Arabic term meaning "people of the coast" and refers to the East African coast.

Although Swahili peoples do not share a single culture, they do speak a common language. Swahili is a Bantu language with many words borrowed from Arabic. Swahili cultures are also dominated by Bantu characteristics, although many Swahili peoples practice Islam.

The Swahili peoples traded the gold and ivory of Africa for goods from India and China. At least some Indian and Chinese goods made it back to the inland Africans who supplied the gold: archaeologists have discovered fragments of Chinese porcelain in sites related to Great Zimbabwe. During the 1500s and 1600s, the Portuguese looted Swahili cities and damaged Swahili trade as they sought to take control of Indian Ocean trade.

Modern ships such as this are similar to those historically used in trading along the East African coast.

the time of Mutota's death, the Mutapa Empire had conquered all but the eastern portion of what is now Zimbabwe. By 1480 Mutota's son Matope claimed control of the area along the Zambezi River to the Indian Ocean coast. Matope established vassal states in the southern areas that he conquered.

The Mutapa Empire controlled most of the gold mines in this region of Africa and the trade routes to and from the coast. Its people were able to mine gold deposited in nearby rivers and streams. In addition, Mutapa rulers forced people in conquered areas to mine gold for them. The rulers sent gold to the coastal city-states in exchange for luxuries. Even before the death of Matope, the southern vassal states of his empire broke away. However, the Mutapa Dynasty remained in control of the smaller empire.

In the 1500s, the Portuguese tried to conquer the empire. When they failed to do so, they resorted to interfering in Mutapa politics. They helped to overthrow one ruler and replace him with one they could control. This signaled increasing European interference in Africa in centuries to come.

Reading Check
Make Inferences
Why do you think the Portuguese wanted to conquer the Mutapa Empire?

Lesson 5 Assessment

1. **Organize Information** Create a chart to list the effects of intercultural interactions between two groups of people discussed in this lesson.

cultural group	cultural group

resulting interaction

Write a paragraph analyzing the results of the cultural interaction. Were the effects mostly positive or mostly negative?

2. **Key Terms and People** For each key term or person in the lesson, write a sentence explaining its significance.

3. **Compare** Compare the Portuguese who arrived in East Africa with the rulers of the Mutapa Empire.

4. **Synthesize** What were some of the effects of East African trade on different cultural groups?

5. **Draw Conclusions** How is Swahili an example of cultural interaction?

6. **Summarize** Based on the archaeological evidence, what was the society of Great Zimbabwe like?

Module 12 Assessment

Key Terms and People

For each term or person below, write a sentence explaining its connection to Africa in the period from 1500 BC to AD 1500.

1. Sahara
2. animism
3. push-pull factors
4. Bantu-speaking peoples
5. Aksum
6. Ghana
7. Mali
8. Songhai
9. Swahili
10. Great Zimbabwe

Main Ideas

Use your notes and the information in the module to answer the following questions.

Diverse Societies in Africa

1. How did geographic features affect the settlement of Africa?
2. What technology did the Nok introduce to West Africa?
3. What circumstances enabled Djenné-Djeno to become a bustling trade center?
4. How is a dispute settled in Efe society?
5. What is an age-set system?

Case Study: Migration

6. What are three general causes of migration?
7. How are push-pull factors related to migration?
8. What caused the Bantu-speaking peoples to migrate?
9. Why were the migrations of Bantu speakers so extensive and successful?

The Kingdom of Aksum

10. Why was Aksum able to control international trade?
11. In what ways did Ezana contribute to the rise of his kingdom?
12. Why did Aksum fall?

North and West African Civilizations

13. How were the beginnings of the Almovarid and Almohad empires similar?
14. What accounted for Ghana's financial success?
15. What were two ways that Islam spread through Africa?
16. How did Sunni Ali build an empire?
17. What was the economy of the Hausa city-states like?

Eastern City-States and Southern Empires

18. How did the Swahili language evolve?
19. Why was it important for Kilwa to control Sofala?
20. Who was most affected by the introduction of Islam to East Africa?
21. What was the relationship of Great Zimbabwe to the Mutapa Empire?

Critical Thinking

1. **Compare** Use a chart like the one below to describe and compare the social, economic, and political aspects of African societies you read about in this module.

Description of Society or Empire	How They're Alike

2. **Make Inferences** How are the spread of ironmaking technology to East and South Africa and the Bantu migrations related?

3. **Evaluate** What were some of Ezana's most crucial leadership decisions?

4. **Form Opinions** Do you think cultural characteristics or personal qualities determine how individuals act toward migrating people who settle among them? Explain.

5. **Compare and Contrast** What are some positive and negative effects of migration?

6. **Recognize Effects** In what way did Islam encourage the spread of literacy?

7. **Recognize Effects** How did people adapt to the harsh conditions of the Sahara? Discuss traders who crossed the Sahara and people who lived in the Saharan village of Teghaza.

8. **Summarize** How are group membership, inheritance rights, and positions of authority usually decided in a matrilineal society?

9. **Synthesize** Why was the location of Great Zimbabwe advantageous?

10. **Compare and Contrast** In what ways was Great Zimbabwe's growth similar to and different from that of Kilwa?

Engage with History

Consider what you learned in this module about trading states in both West and East Africa. How might trade benefit both sides? Now that you've read the module, reevaluate what makes trade beneficial. How did environmental conditions affect which items had value in Africa? Did government policies have any effect on value?

Focus on Writing

Review the causes for migration you learned about in this module. Think about which of the causes might affect you personally. Write a paragraph describing a cause that would force you to migrate to another part of the country or the world. Be sure to identify either the push or pull factor that might influence your decision. Consider the environmental conditions in the area in which you live and the economic or political factors that might have a direct effect on your life.

Multimedia Activity

Today, much of eastern Africa still relies heavily on trade. Work with a group to create an electronic presentation about trade in Africa. Have each member choose one East African country to research in terms of its trade and culture. Use this module and the Internet as resources for your research. Issues to investigate might include what goods present-day East African nations trade and who their trading partners are. Remember to confirm your information by checking multiple sources. Next, create an electronic presentation of information on exports and imports, quantities shipped, where the goods are going, and how they are being transported. How did this project contribute to your understanding of the interrelationship between prosperity and trade?

Module 13

People and Empires in the Americas

Essential Question

How did early American civilizations influence future societies and cultures before the arrival of Europeans?

About the Photograph: This photograph shows the ruins of Machu Picchu, an ancient Inca city high in the Andes Mountains. It was all but forgotten for hundreds of years before its rediscovery in 1911.

▷ *Explore ONLINE!*

HISTORY.

VIDEOS, including...
• Secret Mounds of Pre-Historic America

☑ Document Based Investigations

☑ Graphic Organizers

☑ Interactive Games

☑ Image Compare: Comparing Nazca Lines

☑ Carousel: Aztec Calendar

In this module you will learn about the first Americans and the complex cultures that arose in Mesoamerica, the Andes, and North America in the period before contact with Europeans.

What You Will Learn ...

Timeline of Events 30,000 BC–AD 1500

Americas	World

30,000 BC

17,000 BC Pre-Clovis blades used at Meadowcraft Rockshelter in what is today Pennsylvania.

10,000 BC Last Ice Age ends; land bridge to Asia disappears.

< 7000 BC Agriculture begins in central Mexico.

1200 BC Olmec Civilization emerges in southeast Mexico.

1200 BC Egyptian Empire begins to decline. ∧

900 BC Chavín culture arises in Peru.

500 BC Zapotec build Monte Albán.

< 200 BC Nazca civilization arises in southern Peru.

480 BC Golden Age of Greece begins.

202 BC Han Dynasty begins in China.

AD 120 Roman Empire reaches its height. >

< AD 500s. Teotihuacán reaches population peak in central Mexico.

618 Tang Dynasty begins 289-year rule in China.

800 Anasazi culture develops in the Southwest.

800 Charlemagne crowned Holy Roman Emperor by the pope. >

900 Classic period of Maya civilization ends.

1066 Normans invade England.

1100 Mississippian culture thrives at Cahokia.

1300 Renaissance begins in Italy. >

1324 Mansa Musa, king of Mali, goes on hajj to Mecca.

< 1325 Aztecs build Tenochtitlán.

1438 Pachacuti becomes Incan emperor.

1492 Columbus makes first voyage to the Americas.

1502 Montezuma II crowned Aztec emperor.

AD 1500

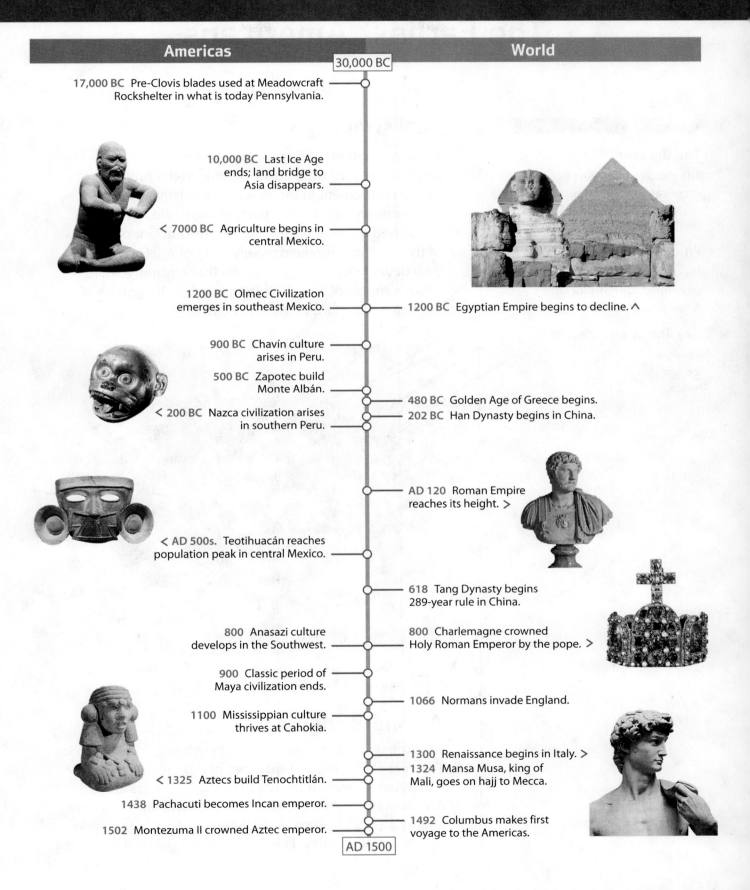

The Earliest Americans

Setting the Stage

While civilizations were developing in Africa, Asia, and Europe, they were also emerging in the Americas. Human settlement in the Americas is relatively recent compared to that in other parts of the world. However, it followed a similar pattern. At first the ancient people of the Americas survived mainly by hunting. Over time, they developed farming methods that ensured a more reliable supply of food. This in turn led to the growth of the first civilizations in the Americas.

This illustration shows what some of the earliest people to migrate to the Americas may have looked like.

A Land Bridge

The American continents include North and South America. They are connected and span two hemispheres, from the frigid Arctic Circle in the north to the icy waters around Antarctica in the south. Although this land mass narrows greatly around modern-day Panama, it stretches unbroken for about 9,000 miles. This large and rugged land is isolated from the rest of the world by vast oceans. Yet, thousands of years ago, the Americas were connected by a land bridge to Asia, called **Beringia**. Hardy Ice Age people migrated from Asia to the Americas over this land bridge. However, the Americas were not unoccupied. Recent evidence shows that people had arrived much earlier, possibly by boat.

Peopling the Americas The first Americans arrived sometime toward the end of the last **Ice Age**, which lasted from roughly 1.9 million years ago to about 10,000 BC. Huge sheets of moving ice, called glaciers, spread southward from the Arctic Circle. They covered large portions of North America. The buildup of glaciers locked up huge amounts of the earth's water. It lowered sea levels and created a land corridor between Asia and Alaska across what is now the Bering Strait.

Herds of wild animals from Siberia, including mammoths, migrated across the plains of the Beringia land bridge. Gradually, Siberian hunters followed these animals into North America. They most likely were unaware that they were entering a new continent. These migrants became the first Americans.

No one knows for sure when the first Americans arrived because there are no written records or other available sources to consult. Some scholars contend that the migration across the land bridge began as early as 30,000 BC. Others argue it occurred as late as 10,000 BC. For years, many researchers have regarded the discovery of spearheads dating back to 9500 BC near Clovis, New Mexico, to be the earliest evidence of humankind in the Americas.

Hunters killed mammoths and other large mammals using a spear-throwing device that gave them greater force and accuracy in hurling the spear from a distance.

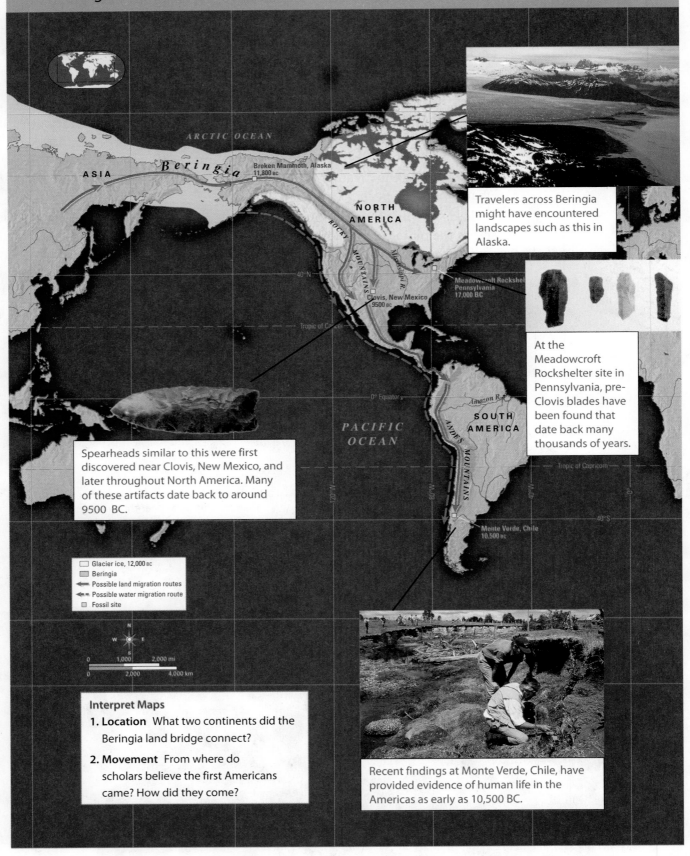

Possible Migration Routes, 30,000–10,000 BC

ARCTIC OCEAN

Beringia

ASIA

Broken Mammoth, Alaska
11,800 BC

NORTH AMERICA

ROCKY MOUNTAINS

Mississippi R.

Clovis, New Mexico
9500 BC

Meadowcroft Rockshelter
Pennsylvania
17,000 BC

40°N

Tropic of Cancer

0° Equator

PACIFIC OCEAN

Amazon R.

SOUTH AMERICA

ANDES MOUNTAINS

Tropic of Capricorn

40°S

Monte Verde, Chile
10,500 BC

Travelers across Beringia might have encountered landscapes such as this in Alaska.

At the Meadowcroft Rockshelter site in Pennsylvania, pre-Clovis blades have been found that date back many thousands of years.

Spearheads similar to this were first discovered near Clovis, New Mexico, and later throughout North America. Many of these artifacts date back to around 9500 BC.

- ☐ Glacier ice, 12,000 BC
- ☐ Beringia
- ← Possible land migration routes
- ◄-- Possible water migration route
- ☐ Fossil site

0 1,000 2,000 mi
0 2,000 4,000 km

Interpret Maps

1. **Location** What two continents did the Beringia land bridge connect?

2. **Movement** From where do scholars believe the first Americans came? How did they come?

Recent findings at Monte Verde, Chile, have provided evidence of human life in the Americas as early as 10,500 BC.

Many other pre-Clovis sites, from Texas to Brazil, reinforce what archaeologists learned at Monte Verde, Chile, near the southern tip of the Americas. Researchers there have found evidence of human life dating back to 10,500 BC. Underneath this site—a sandy bank near a creek—archaeologists discovered pieces of animal hide and various tools. They also found a preserved chunk of meat and a single child's footprint. The evidence at Monte Verde suggests that the first Americans arrived well before the Clovis era. To reach southern Chile at such an early date, some experts believe, humans would have had to cross the land bridge at least 20,000 years ago.

As more archaeological finds are examined, new theories emerge about the peopling of the Americas. Some scholars have proposed that people may have paddled from Asia to the Pacific Coast in small boats. A skull discovered near Mexico City has recently been dated to about 11,000 BC, making it the oldest skull ever found in the Americas. Some scientists studying the skull believe that it is related to the Ainu people of Japan and that these descendants of the Ainu reached the Americas by island-hopping on boats.

Reading Check
Analyze Issues
Why do scholars disagree about when the first Americans arrived?

Historical Source

A Bison Kill Site

The first hunters roaming North America hunted mammoths, deer, and bison. Researchers found the bones of bison at a kill site near Calgary, Alberta, in Canada. This kill site is believed to have been in use for more than 8,000 years.

Different layers of remains and artifacts have been found at the kill site, with different kinds of points—spears, arrows, knives, and so forth. The different styles of points can tell archaeologists about the age of a site and its various layers. Weapons and tools such as those shown here were used to kill and butcher animals for the hunters and their families to consume.

Analyze Historical Sources
What resources besides food might animals have provided to early hunters and their families?

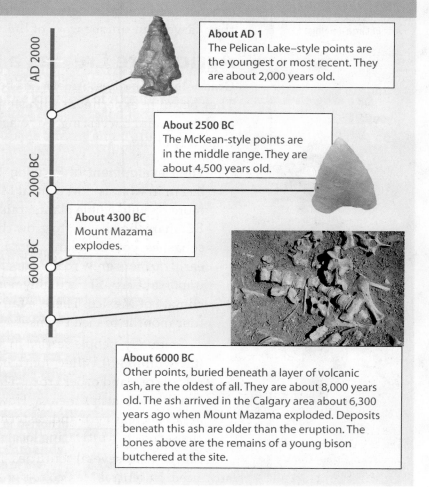

About AD 1
The Pelican Lake–style points are the youngest or most recent. They are about 2,000 years old.

About 2500 BC
The McKean-style points are in the middle range. They are about 4,500 years old.

About 4300 BC
Mount Mazama explodes.

About 6000 BC
Other points, buried beneath a layer of volcanic ash, are the oldest of all. They are about 8,000 years old. The ash arrived in the Calgary area about 6,300 years ago when Mount Mazama exploded. Deposits beneath this ash are older than the eruption. The bones above are the remains of a young bison butchered at the site.

Hunters and Gatherers

Questions remain about how and when the first Americans arrived. What appears more certain—from the discovery of chiseled spearheads and charred bones at ancient sites—is that the earliest Americans lived as hunters. Perhaps their most challenging and rewarding prey was the mammoth. Weighing more than seven tons, this animal provided meat, hide, and bones for food, clothing, shelters, and tools.

Following the Game Eventually, large animals like the mammoth were overhunted and became extinct. Hunters soon turned to smaller prey, such as deer and rabbits, for their survival. They also fished and gathered edible plants and fruits. Because they were hunters, the earliest Americans found it necessary to move regularly in search of food. Whenever they did settle in one place for a short time, prehistoric Americans lived in caves or temporary shelters in the open air.

With the end of the Ice Age, around 12,000 to 10,000 years ago, came the end of land travel across Beringia. As the great glaciers melted, sea levels rose. The ancient land bridge disappeared under the Bering Strait. By this time, however, humans inhabited most regions of the Americas. Wherever they roamed, from the grassy plains of the modern-day United States to the steamy tropical forests of Central America, the first Americans adapted to the variety of environments they inhabited. In doing so, they carved out unique ways of life.

Reading Check
Analyze Effects
How did the earliest Americans adapt to the loss of large animals?

Agriculture Creates a New Way of Life

Gradually, the earliest Americans became more familiar with plant foods. They began to experiment with simple methods of farming. Their efforts at planting and harvesting led to agriculture. This dramatically changed their way of life.

Maize, or corn, was one of the most important crops in the Americas.

The Development of Farming Around 7000 BC, a revolution quietly began in what is now central Mexico. There, people began to rely more on wild edible plants, raising some of them from seeds. By 5000 BC, many had begun to grow these preferred plants. They included squashes, gourds, beans, avocados, and chilies. By 3400 BC, these early farmers grew **maize**, or corn. Maize soon became the most important crop. This highly nourishing crop flourished in the tropical climate of Mexico. There, a family of three could raise enough corn in four months to feed themselves for a long time.

Gradually, people settled in permanent villages in the Tehuacan (tay•wuh•KAHN) Valley, south of present-day Mexico City. These people raised corn and other crops. The techniques of agriculture spread over North and South America. However, it is believed that people in some areas, such as Peru and eastern North America, may have discovered the secrets of cultivating local edible plants independently.

Over the next several centuries, farming methods became more advanced. In central Mexico native farmers created small islands in swamps and shallow lakes by stacking layers of vegetation, dirt, and mud.

The Effects of Agriculture

Before Agriculture	After Agriculture
People hunted or gathered what they ate.	People enjoyed a more reliable and steady source of food.
Families continually moved in search of big game.	Families settled down and formed larger communities.
Groups remained small due to the scarcity of reliable sources of food.	Humans concentrated on new skills: arts and crafts, architecture, and social organization.
Humans devoted much of their time to obtaining food.	Complex societies eventually arose.

Interpret Charts
How might the establishment of agriculture have helped humans to develop new skills and interests?

They then planted crops on top of the island soil. The surrounding water provided irrigation. These floating gardens were very productive, yielding up to three harvests a year.

Farming Brings Great Change In the Americas, as in other regions of the world, agriculture brought great and lasting change to people's way of life. The cultivation of corn and other crops provided a more reliable and expanding food supply. This encouraged population growth and the establishment of large, settled communities. As the population grew, and as farming became more efficient and productive, more people turned their attention to nonagricultural pursuits. They developed specialized skills in arts and crafts, building trades, and other fields. Differences between social classes—between rich and poor, ruler and subject—began to emerge. With the development of agriculture, society became more complex. The stage was set for the rise of more advanced civilizations.

Reading Check
Make Inferences
Why might the development of agriculture be characterized as a turning point in human history?

Lesson 1 Assessment

1. **Organize Information** Complete the chart with the effects. Which effect do you think had the greatest impact on the Americas?

Beringia land bridge forms.	→	

Experiments with farming begin.	→	

2. **Key Terms and People** For each key term or person in the lesson, write a sentence explaining its significance.

3. **Make Inferences** What can you infer about the development of early farming?

4. **Summarize** How did human beings come to the Americas?

5. **Analyze Effects** What sorts of changes did farming bring?

6. **Evaluate** Why do you think early Americans, isolated from the rest of the world, developed in ways similar to other early humans?

Early Mesoamerican Civilizations

The Big Idea

The Olmec created the Americas' first civilization, which in turn influenced later civilizations.

Why It Matters Now

Later American civilizations relied on the technology and achievements of earlier cultures to make advances.

Key Terms and People

Mesoamerica
Olmec
Zapotec
Monte Albán

Setting the Stage

The story of developed civilizations in the Americas begins in a region called **Mesoamerica**. This area stretches south from central Mexico to northern Honduras. It was here, more than 3,000 years ago, that the first complex societies in the Americas arose.

The Olmec

Mesoamerica's first known civilization builders were a people known as the **Olmec**. They began carving out a society around 1200 BC in the jungles of southern Mexico. The Olmec influenced neighboring groups as well as the later civilizations of the region. They often are called Mesoamerica's "mother culture."

Many large carved heads such as this one have been found by archaeologists in two major Olmec centers along the Gulf Coast of southern Mexico.

The Rise of Olmec Civilization Around 1860, a worker clearing a field in the hot coastal plain of southeastern Mexico uncovered an extraordinary stone sculpture. It stood five feet tall and weighed an estimated eight tons. The sculpture was of an enormous head wearing a headpiece. (See History Through Art.) The head was carved in a strikingly realistic style, with thick lips, a flat nose, and large oval eyes. Archaeologists had never seen anything like it in the Americas.

This head, along with others that were discovered later, was a remnant of the Olmec civilization. The Olmec emerged about 1200 BC and thrived from approximately 800 to 400 BC. They lived along the Gulf Coast of Mexico, in the modern-day Mexican states of Veracruz and Tabasco.

Gulf Coast Geography On the surface, the Gulf Coast seemed an unlikely site for a high culture to take root. The region was hot and humid and covered with swamps and jungle. In some places, giant trees formed a thick cover that prevented most sunlight from reaching the ground. Up to 100 inches of rain fell every year. The rainfall swelled rivers and caused severe flooding.

However, the region also had certain advantages. There were abundant deposits of salt and tar, as well as fine clay used in making pottery. There were also wood and rubber from the rain forest. The hills to the north provided hard stone from which the Olmec could make tools and monuments. The rivers that laced the region provided a means of transport. Most important, the flood plains of these rivers provided fertile land for farming.

The Olmec used their resources to build thriving communities. The oldest site, San Lorenzo, dates back to around 1150 BC. Here archaeologists uncovered important clues that offered a glimpse into the Olmec world.

The Olmec ball game was one of the first team sports in history.

Olmec Society At San Lorenzo, archaeologists discovered earthen mounds, courtyards, and pyramids. Set among these earthworks were large stone monuments. They included columns, altars, and more colossal sculpted heads, which may have represented particular Olmec rulers. These giant monuments weigh as much as 44 tons. Some scholars think that Olmec workers may have moved these sculptures over land on rolling logs to the river banks. From there, they may have rafted the monuments along waterways to various sites.

To the east of San Lorenzo, another significant Olmec site, La Venta, rose around 900 BC. Here, researchers discovered a 100-foot-high mound

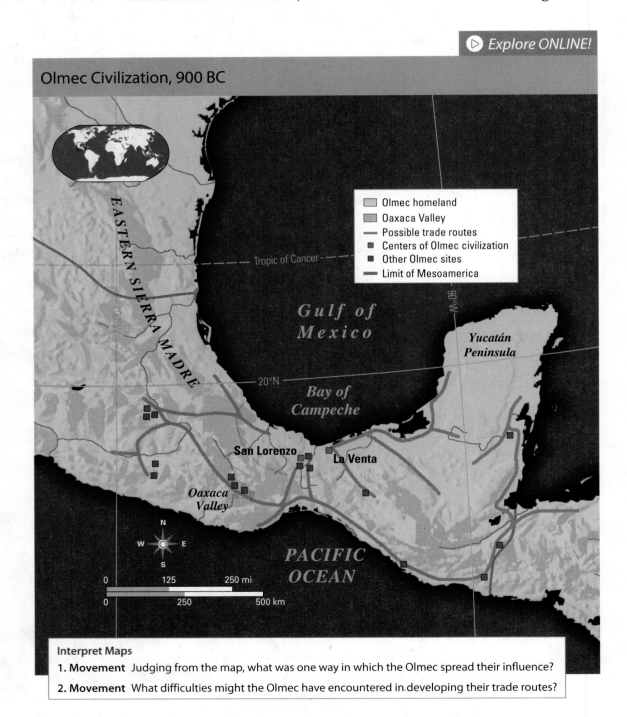

▶ Explore ONLINE!

Olmec Civilization, 900 BC

Interpret Maps

1. **Movement** Judging from the map, what was one way in which the Olmec spread their influence?

2. **Movement** What difficulties might the Olmec have encountered in developing their trade routes?

of earth and clay. This structure may have served as the tomb of a great Olmec ruler. Known as the Great Pyramid, the mound also may have been the center of the Olmec religion. Experts believe the Olmec prayed to a variety of nature gods.

Most of all, they probably worshiped the jaguar spirit. Numerous Olmec sculptures and carvings depict a half-human, half-jaguar creature. Some scholars believe that the jaguar represented a powerful rain god. Others contend that there were several jaguar gods, representing the earth, fertility, and maize.

Trade and Commerce Archaeologists once believed that sites such as La Venta were ceremonial centers where important rituals were performed but few people lived. In recent years, however, experts have begun to revise that view. The Olmec appear to have been a prosperous people who directed a large trading network throughout Mesoamerica. Olmec goods traveled as far as Mexico City to the north and Honduras to the south. In addition, raw materials—including iron ore and various stones—reached San Lorenzo from faraway regions. This trade network helped boost the Olmec economy and spread Olmec influence.

Decline of the Olmec For reasons that are not fully understood, Olmec civilization eventually collapsed. Scholars believe San Lorenzo was destroyed around 900 BC. La Venta may have fallen sometime around 400 BC. Some experts speculate that outside invaders caused the destruction. Others believe the Olmec may have destroyed their own monuments upon the death of their rulers.

Reading Check
Make Inferences
In what ways did the Olmecs' environment help in the creation of their civilization?

Zapotec Civilization Arises

By the time Olmec civilization had collapsed, another people—the **Zapotec**—were developing an advanced society to the southwest, in what is now the Mexican state of Oaxaca (wuh•HAH•kah). Though they showed traces of Olmec influence, the Zapotec built a unique civilization.

Peoples of the Oaxaca Valley Oaxaca is a rugged region of mountains and valleys in southern Mexico. In the center of the state, three valleys meet to form a large open area known as the Oaxaca Valley. This valley has fertile soil, a mild climate, and enough rainfall to support agriculture. As a result, various peoples have made the Oaxaca Valley their home, including the ancient Zapotec.

For centuries the Zapotec lived in scattered villages throughout the valley. By 1000 BC, however, one site—San José Mogote—was emerging as the main power in the region. At this site, the Zapotec constructed stone platforms. They also built temples and began work on monumental sculptures. By 500 BC they had developed early forms of writing and a calendar system.

The Zapotec Flourish at Monte Albán Around 500 BC, Zapotec civilization took a major leap forward. High atop a mountain at the center of the Oaxaca Valley, the Zapotec built the first real urban center in the Americas, **Monte Albán**. This city, with its commanding view of the entire valley, grew and prospered over the next several centuries. By 200 BC, Monte Albán was home to around 15,000 people. The city eventually would reach a peak population of almost 25,000.

From AD 250 to AD 700, Monte Albán was truly impressive. At the heart of the city was a giant plaza paved with stones. Towering pyramids, temples, and palaces, all made out of stone, surrounded this plaza. There was even an observatory for observing the stars to establish a calendar. Nearby was a series of stone carvings of corpses. Their facial features show an Olmec influence.

Global Patterns

Pyramids

A number of ancient peoples used pyramids for temples, tombs, and observatories. The Egyptians built pyramids as tombs. Their pyramids had smooth sides and came to a point. In contrast, the pyramids built by the Zapotec at Monte Albán have stepped sides, with flat tops that served as platforms for temples.

Reading Check
Compare How does Monte Albán's population compare to the populations of today's major cities?

For more than a thousand years the Zapotec controlled the Oaxaca Valley and the surrounding region. Sometime after AD 600, the Zapotec began to decline. Some scholars believe they may have suffered a loss of trade or other economic difficulties. As with the Olmec, the fall of Zapotec civilization remains a puzzle.

The Early Mesoamericans' Legacy

Although both the Zapotec and Olmec civilizations eventually collapsed, each culture influenced the Mesoamerican civilizations that followed.

The Olmec Leave Their Mark The Olmec contributed much to later Mesoamerican civilizations. They influenced the powerful Maya. Olmec art styles, especially the use of the jaguar motif, can be seen in the pottery and sculpture of later peoples in the region. In addition, future Mesoamerican societies copied the Olmec pattern of urban design.

The Olmec also left behind the notions of planned ceremonial centers, ritual ball games, and an elite ruling class. And while there is no clear evidence that the Olmec used a written language, their descendants or a related people carved out stone symbols that may have influenced later glyph writing.

Zapotec Contributions The Zapotec left behind their own legacy. It included a hieroglyphic writing system and a calendar system based on the movement of the sun. In addition, the Zapotec are noted as the Americas' first city builders. Monte Albán combined ceremonial grandeur with residential living space. This style influenced the development of future urban centers and became a hallmark of Mesoamerican civilizations.

As the Zapotec and Olmec flourished and then declined, civilizations were also taking shape in South America. Along the rough and mountainous terrain in what is now Peru, ancient peoples came together. There, they created more advanced and complex societies.

Reading Check
Summarize What do you consider to be the Olmecs' most important contributions to later cultures?

Lesson 2 Assessment

1. **Organize Information** Use a Venn diagram to record the characteristics that were similar and different among the Olmec and Zapotec. What was one of the most important characteristics that they shared?

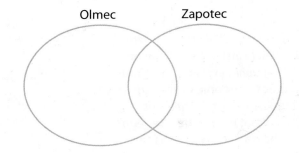

Olmec   Zapotec

2. **Key Terms and People** For each key term or person in the lesson, write a sentence explaining its significance.

3. **Analyze Causes** Why did Olmec civilization collapse?

4. **Analyze Effects** What were some important Zapotec contributions to later cultures?

5. **Analyze Causes** What factors made the Oaxaca Valley a likely place for civilization to develop?

6. **Compare** What were some similarities between the Olmec and Zapotec cultures?

Olmec Sculpture

Around 1200 BC, the Olmec civilization appeared in southeastern Mexico. Over the next several hundred years, its culture spread into the Valley of Mexico and into parts of Central America. The Olmec are especially known for their huge sculptures of heads and their small, finely crafted stone carvings. Much of their art reflects a fascination with the jaguar.

OLMEC HEAD ▶
The Olmec Center at San Lorenzo, Honduras, contains several huge carved heads. Some of them are 9 feet high and weigh about 40 tons. The heads may be portraits of Olmec leaders or of players in a sacred ball game. The stone used for the sculptures came from a site more than 250 miles away. The Olmec transported this stone over mountain ranges, rivers, and swamps.

◀ JAGUAR FIGURE
The Olmec created many carvings of beings that were part human, part jaguar. Peter Furst, in "New Light on the Olmec" in *National Geographic,* explains why: "You can almost call the Olmec the people of the jaguar. In tropical America, jaguars were the shamans [medicine men] of the animal world, the alter ego [other identity] of the shaman." Olmec jaguar art greatly influenced later Mesoamerican cultures.

▲ OLMEC ALTAR
This Olmec altar has a carved figure at the base situated at the mouth of a cave. This figure's elaborate headdress shows that he is a ruler. The ruler holds a rope that winds around the base of the altar and binds a carved figure at the back. Scholars believe that the altar was used as a throne.

◄ JADE FIGURE
Many Olmec figurines are made of this beautiful blue-green stone, a fact that puzzled scientists for decades because they believed that no jade deposits existed in the Americas. However, in May 2002, a scientist discovered what he believes to be an ancient Olmec jade mine in Guatemala.

Critical Thinking

1. **Hypothesize** The Olmec probably did not use the wheel. How do you think the Olmec transported the stone for the huge head sculptures?

2. **Compare and Contrast** Mount Rushmore in the United States also shows giant stone heads of leaders. Use an encyclopedia to find out how Mount Rushmore was created. What are similarities and differences between the way Mount Rushmore was made and the way the Olmec heads were made?

Early Civilizations of the Andes

The Big Idea

In the Andes Mountains, various groups created flourishing civilizations.

Why It Matters Now

Like the early Andean civilizations, people today must adapt to their environment in order to survive.

Key Terms and People

Chavín
Nazca
Moche

Setting the Stage

While civilizations were emerging in Mesoamerica, advanced societies were independently developing in South America. The early cultures of South America arose in a difficult environment, the rugged terrain of the Andes Mountains.

Societies Arise in the Andes

The Andes Mountains stretch about 4,500 miles down the western edge of South America, from Colombia in the north to Chile in the south. After the Himalayas in southern Asia, the Andes is the next highest mountain range in the world. The Andes has a number of peaks over 20,000 feet in elevation. South America's first civilizations emerged in the northern Andes region, in Peru.

Settlements on the Coastal Plain Peru was a harsh place to develop a civilization. The Andes are steep and rocky, with generally poor soil. Ice and snow cover the highest elevations year-round. Overland travel often is difficult. The climate is also severe: hot and dry during the day, and often freezing at night.

Between the mountains and the Pacific Ocean lies a narrow coastal plain. Most of this plain is harsh desert where rain seldom falls. In some places, however, rivers cross the desert on their path from the mountains to the sea. It was in these river valleys that the first settlements occurred.

Between 3600 and 2500 BC, people began to establish villages along the Pacific coast. These first inhabitants were hunter-gatherers who relied on seafood and small game for their survival. Around 3000 BC, these people began to farm. By 1800 BC, a number of thriving communities existed along the coast.

The Chavín Period The first influential civilization in South America arose not on the coast, however, but in the mountains. This culture, known as the **Chavín** (chah•VEEN), flourished from around 900 BC to 200 BC. Archaeologists named the culture after a major ruin, Chavín de Huántar, in the northern highlands of Peru. This site features pyramids, plazas, and massive earthen mounds.

Chavín culture spread quickly across much of northern and central Peru. Archaeologists have found no evidence of political or economic organization within the culture. Thus, they conclude that the Chavín were primarily a religious civilization. Nevertheless, the spread of Chavín art styles and religious images—as seen in stone carvings, pottery, and textiles—shows the powerful influence of this culture. Ancient Peruvians may have visited Chavín temples to pay their respects. They then carried ideas back to their communities. The Chavín are believed to have established certain patterns that helped unify Andean culture and lay the foundation for later civilizations in Peru. Thus, like the Olmec in Mesoamerica, the Chavín may have acted as a "mother culture" in South America.

Reading Check
Contrast
How did the environment of the Andes region differ from that of much of Mesoamerica?

History in Depth

Headhunters

The striking images on their pottery indicate that the Nazca may have been headhunters. In numerous ceramic and textile designs, Nazca artisans depict the taking of human heads, probably from enemies in combat. Taking and displaying the head of an enemy was considered a way of increasing the strength and well-being of a community.

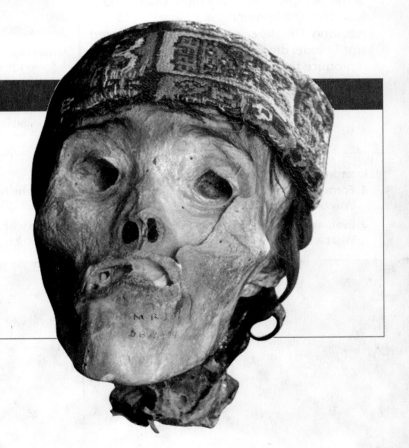

Nazca Lines

Etched on the plains of southeastern Peru are more than 1,000 drawings of animals, plants, humans, and geometric shapes. Most of them are so large that they can be recognized only from the air. Scientists believe that the Nazca people made the drawings between 200 BC and AD 600. Since the lines were discovered in 1927, people have proposed many theories about their purpose, including the following:

- The Nazca people worshiped mountain or sky gods and created the drawings to please them.

- The lines indicated where surface water entered the plain and marked elevated land between ancient riverbeds.

- The lines are a huge map that marks the course of underground aquifers, or water sources. (This is the most recent theory.)

Size of the Nazca Lines

Many of the Nazca drawings are huge. Some of the wedges (below) are more than 2,500 feet long. The hummingbird (right) is 165 feet long. The Nazca people probably created small model drawings and used math to reproduce them at such a vast scale.

Durability of the Nazca Lines
This spider was created more than 1,000 years ago. It survived because the region has little erosion. The plains are one of the driest regions on earth with only 20 minutes of rain a year. Also, the ground is flat and stony, so wind rarely carries away the soil.

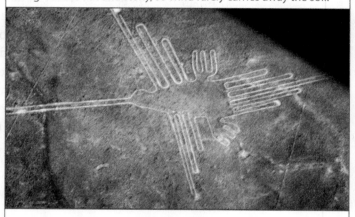

Nazca Water Cult
Some scholars think the lines were linked to a Nazca water cult, or religion. The straight lines may have led to ceremonial sites. The animals may have been symbols. For example, according to traditional beliefs, the hummingbird (above) represents the mountain gods. The mountains were a main source of water.

Interpret Visual Sources

1. **Form and Support Opinions** Do you think the purpose of the Nazca lines had something to do with water? Why or why not?

2. **Evaluate** What might be the next step for researchers who wish to prove or disprove the aquifer theory? What are potential positive and negative consequences of such an action?

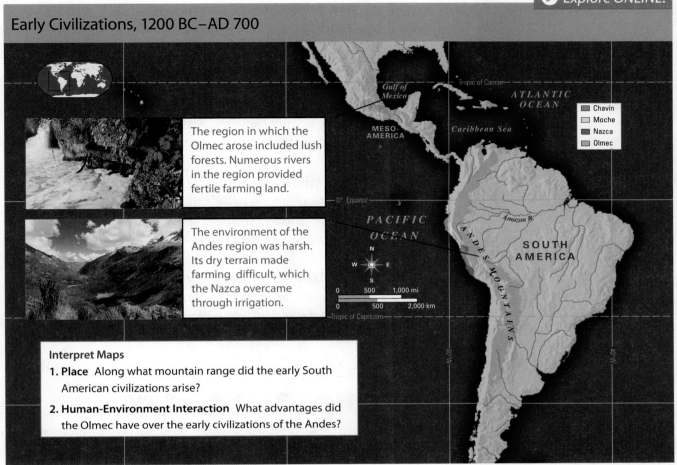

Explore ONLINE!

The region in which the Olmec arose included lush forests. Numerous rivers in the region provided fertile farming land.

The environment of the Andes region was harsh. Its dry terrain made farming difficult, which the Nazca overcame through irrigation.

Chavín
Moche
Nazca
Olmec

Interpret Maps

1. **Place** Along what mountain range did the early South American civilizations arise?

2. **Human-Environment Interaction** What advantages did the Olmec have over the early civilizations of the Andes?

Other Andean Civilizations Flourish

Around the time Chavín culture declined, other civilizations were emerging in Peru. First the Nazca and then the Moche (MOH•chay) built societies that flourished in the Andes.

Nazca Achievements The **Nazca** culture flourished along the southern coast of Peru from around 200 BC to AD 600. This area is extremely dry. The Nazca developed extensive irrigation systems, including underground canals, that allowed them to farm the land. The Nazca are known for their beautiful textiles and pottery. Both feature images of animals and mythological beings. They are even more famous, however, for an extraordinary but puzzling set of creations known as the Nazca Lines.

Moche Culture Meanwhile, on the northern coast of Peru, another civilization was reaching great heights. This was the **Moche** culture, which lasted from about AD 100 to AD 700.

The Moche took advantage of the rivers that flowed from the Andes Mountains. They built impressive irrigation systems to water their wide range of crops, which included corn, beans, potatoes, squash, and peanuts. According to Peruvian archaeologist Walter Alva, the Moche enjoyed a variety of foods. These included both fish and game.

Moche tombs uncovered in the recent past have revealed a civilization with enormous wealth. Archaeologists have found beautiful jewelry crafted from gold, silver, and semiprecious stones. The Moche were also brilliant ceramic artists. They created pottery that depicted scenes from everyday life. Moche pots show doctors healing patients, women weaving cloth, and musicians playing instruments. They also show fierce soldiers, armed with spears, leading enemy captives. Although the Moche never developed a written language, their pottery provides a wealth of detail about Moche life.

Nevertheless, many questions about the Moche remain. Experts still do not fully understand Moche religious beliefs. Nor do they know why the Moche fell. Like many early cultures of the Americas, the Moche remain something of a mystery awaiting further archaeological discoveries.

Unlike the lands you will read about in the next module—which were unified by the spread of Islam—the Americas would remain a patchwork of separate civilizations until the early 16th century. Around that time, the Europeans would begin to arrive and bring dramatic and lasting changes to the American continents.

Reading Check
Analyze Issues
How were archaeologists able to gain so much information about the Moche without the help of a written language?

Lesson 3 Assessment

1. **Organize Information** Use the chart to show the achievements that the early Mesoamerican cultures shared.

Chavín	Nazca	Moche

Did they have any similar achievements?

2. **Key Terms and People** For each key term or person in the lesson, write a sentence explaining its significance.

3. **Analyze** Why was Peru a difficult place for a civilization to develop?

4. **Compare** How was the Chavín culture like the Olmec culture?

5. **Draw Conclusions** How did the Nazca and the Moche adapt to their environment in order to build flourishing societies? Give evidence.

North American Societies

The Big Idea
Complex North American societies were linked to each other through culture and economics.

Why It Matters Now
Traditions and ideas from these cultures became part of the cultures of North America.

Key Terms and People
potlatch
Anasazi
pueblo
Mississippian
Iroquois
totem

This headdress was used by the Kwakiutl in religious ceremonies. Carved of red cedar and painted, it shows a thunderbird, the highest of the spirits in the Kwakiutl religion. Like a huge eagle, the thunderbird flew high in the sky. When it was hungry, it swooped down to catch and eat killer whales.

Setting the Stage

Between 30,000 and 12,000 years ago, hunter-gatherers migrated across the Bering Strait land bridge from Asia and began to populate the Americas. Migrating southward, those first Americans reached the southern tip of South America by somewhere between 12,000 and 7000 BC At the same time, they began to spread out east and west across North America. Over the centuries, the early North American peoples adapted to their environment, creating a very diverse set of cultures.

Complex Societies in the West

In some ways, the early North American cultures were less developed than those of South America and Mesoamerica. The North American groups created no great empires. They left few ruins as spectacular as those of ancient Mexico or Peru. Nevertheless, the first peoples of North America did create complex societies. These societies were able to conduct long-distance trade and construct magnificent buildings.

Cultures of Abundance The Pacific Northwest—from Oregon to Alaska—was rich in resources and supported a sizable population. To the Kwakiutl, Nootka, and Haida peoples, the most important resource was the sea. They hunted whales in canoes. Some canoes were large enough to carry at least 15 people. In addition to the many resources of the sea, the coastal forest provided plentiful food. In this abundant environment, the Northwest Coast tribes developed societies in which differences in wealth created social classes. Families displayed their rank and prosperity in an elaborate ceremony called the **potlatch** (PAHT•lach). In this ceremony, they gave food, drink, and gifts to the community.

Accomplished Builders The dry, desert lands of the Southwest were a much harsher environment than the temperate Pacific coastlands. However, as early as 1500 BC, the peoples of the Southwest were beginning to farm the land. Because of the climate, competition for farmland sometimes

North American Culture Areas, c. 1400

Explore ONLINE!

Inuit
Arctic Circle
Kutchin
Aleut
Dogrib
Tlingit
Slave
Haida
Kwakiutl
Nootka
Salish
Chinook
Nez Perce
Coos
Shoshone
Pomo
Miwok
Chumash
Hopi
Tohono O'odham
Cochimi

Blackfeet
Mandan
Crow
Lakota
Cheyenne
Ute
Arapaho
Navajo
Zuni
Comanche
Apache
Kiowa

Inuit
Cree
Ojibwa
Illinois
Miami
Shawnee
Natchez

Hudson Bay
Inuit
Montagnais
Algonquin
Huron
Abenaki
Iroquois
Delaware
Cherokee
Muskogee (Creek)
Timucua

Cayuga, Mohawk, Oneida, Onondaga, Seneca

Mississippi R.
Rio Grande

PACIFIC OCEAN

ATLANTIC OCEAN

Gulf of Mexico

Aztec
Mixtec
Maya

Caribbean Sea

N
W E
S

0   500   1,000 mi
0   1,000   2,000 km

Native American Cultures
- Arctic
- Subarctic
- Northwest Coast
- Plateau
- Great Basin
- California
- Southwest
- Great Plains
- Northeast
- Southeast
- Mesoamerica

Kiowa Tribe name

Interpret Maps

1. **Region** Which Native American culture group had the largest number of tribes?

2. **Human–Environment Interaction** In which culture areas would movement of trade goods be made easier by river and lake connections?

Cliff Palace, Mesa Verde, had 217 rooms and 23 kivas.

led to conflicts. Among the most successful of the early farmers in this area were the Hohokam (huh•HOH•kuhm) of central Arizona. They used irrigation to produce harvests of corn, beans, and squash. Their use of pottery rather than baskets, as well as certain religious rituals, showed contact with Mesoamerican peoples to the south.

A people to the north—the **Anasazi** (ah•nuh•SAH•zee)—also influenced the Hohokam. They lived in the Four Corners region, where the present-day states of Utah, Arizona, Colorado, and New Mexico meet. The Anasazi built impressive cliff dwellings, such as the ones at Mesa Verde, Colorado. These large houses were built on top of mesas—flat-topped hills—or in shallow caves in the sheer walls of deep canyons. By the AD 900s, the Anasazi were living in **pueblos** (PWEHB•lohs), villages of large, apartment-style compounds made of stone and adobe, or sun-baked clay.

The largest Anasazi pueblo, begun around AD 900, was Pueblo Bonito, a Spanish name meaning "beautiful village." Its construction required a high degree of social organization and inventiveness. The Anasazi relied on human labor to quarry sandstone from the canyon walls and move it to the site. Skilled builders then used a mudlike mortar to construct walls up to five stories high. Windows were small to keep out the burning sun. When completed, Pueblo Bonito probably housed about 1,000 people and contained more than 600 rooms. In addition, a number of underground or partly underground ceremonial chambers called kivas (KEE•vuhs) were used for a variety of religious practices.

Reading Check
Hypothesize
Why do you think
no great empires
developed in North
America?

Many Anasazi pueblos were abandoned around 1200, possibly because of a prolonged drought. The descendants of the Anasazi, the pueblo peoples, continued many of their customs. Pueblo groups like the Hopi and Zuni used kivas for religious ceremonies. They also created beautiful pottery and woven blankets. They traded these, along with corn and other farm products, with plains Indians to the east, who supplied bison meat and hides. These nomadic plains tribes eventually became known by such names as the Comanche, Kiowa, and Apache.

Mound Builders and Other Woodland Cultures

Beyond the Great Plains, in the woodlands east of the Mississippi River, other ancient peoples—the Mound Builders—were creating their own unique traditions. Beginning around 700 BC, a culture known as the Adena began to build huge earthen mounds in which they buried their dead. Mounds that held the bodies of tribal leaders were often filled with gifts, such as finely crafted copper and stone objects.

Some 500 years later, the Hopewell culture also began building burial mounds. Their mounds were much larger and more plentiful than those of the Adena. Some of the Hopewell mounds may have been used for purposes other than burials. For example, the Great Serpent Mound, near Hillsboro, Ohio, may have played a part in Hopewell religious ceremonies.

The last Mound Builder culture, the **Mississippian**, lasted from around AD 800 until the arrival of Europeans in the 1500s. These people created thriving villages based on farming and trade. Between 1000 and 1200, perhaps as many as 30,000 people lived at Cahokia (kuh•HOH•kee•uh), the leading site of Mississippian culture. Cahokia was led by priest-rulers, who regulated farming activities. The heart of the community was a 100-foot-high, flat-topped earthen pyramid, which was crowned by a wooden temple.

These Mississippian lands were located in a crossroads region between east and west. They enjoyed easy transportation on the Mississippi and Ohio rivers. Items found in burial mounds show that the Mississippians had traded with peoples in the West and, possibly, Mesoamerica. Similar evidence shows that they also came into contact with peoples from the Northeast.

Eastern Woodland Tribes Build Alliances The eastern woodlands tribes developed a variety of cultures. These peoples often clashed with each other over land. In some areas, tribes formed political alliances to ensure protection of tribal lands. The best example of a political alliance was the **Iroquois** (IHR•uh•kwoy), a group of tribes speaking related languages living in the eastern Great Lakes region. In the late 1500s, five of these tribes in upper New York—the Mohawk, Oneida, Onondaga, Cayuga, and Seneca—formed the Iroquois League. According to legend, Chief Hiawatha helped to create this league. His goal was to promote joint defense and cooperation among the tribes.

Reading Check
Draw Conclusions
Of what value would a
political alliance be to
an individual tribe?

Great Serpent Mound runs some 1,300 feet along its coils and is between 4 and 5 feet high.

Cultural Connections

The Iroquois alliance was a notable example of a political link among early North American peoples. For the most part, however, the connections between native North Americans were economic and cultural. They traded, had similar religious beliefs, shared social patterns, and spread ideas.

Trading Networks Tie Tribes Together Trade was a major factor linking the peoples of North America. Along the Columbia River in Oregon, the Chinook people established a lively marketplace that brought together trade goods from all over the West. And the Mississippian trade network stretched from the Rocky Mountains to the Atlantic coast and from the Great Lakes to the Gulf of Mexico.

Religion Shapes Views of Life Another feature that linked early Americans was their religious beliefs. Nearly all native North Americans believed that the world around them was filled with nature spirits. Most Native Americans recognized a number of sacred spirits. Some groups held up one supreme being, or Great Spirit, above all others. North American peoples believed that the spirits gave them rituals and customs to guide them in their lives and to satisfy their basic needs. If people practiced these rituals, they would live in peace and harmony.

Native American religious beliefs also included great respect for the land as the source of life. Native Americans used the land but tried to alter it as little as possible. The land was sacred, not something that could be bought and sold. Later, when Europeans claimed land in North America, the issue of land ownership created conflict.

Shared Social Patterns The family was the basis for social organization for Native Americans. Generally, the family unit was the extended family, including parents, children, grandparents, and other close relatives. Some tribes further organized families into clans, or groups of families descended from a common ancestor. In some tribes, clan members lived together in large houses or groups of houses.

Iroquois Women

Iroquois society was matrilineal. This means that all Iroquois traced their descent through their female ancestors. Clans of the mother controlled property, held ceremonies, and determined official titles.

The ability to grant titles to men was handed down from mother to daughter. The most important title given to men was that of "sachem," the peace, or civil, chief.

A council of sachems met once a year to decide on war and peace and other important matters. Since sachems could not go to war, they appointed warriors to lead a war party. Thus, in a way women had a say in warfare in the Iroquois tribes.

Common among Native American clans was the use of **totems** (TOH•tuhmz). The term refers to a natural object with which an individual, clan, or group identifies itself. The totem was used as a symbol of the unity of a group or clan. It also helped define certain behaviors and the social relationships of a group. The term comes from an Ojibwa word but refers to a cultural practice found throughout the Americas. For example, Northwestern peoples displayed totem symbols on masks, boats, and huge poles set in front of their houses. Others used totem symbols in rituals or dances associated with important group events such as marriages, the naming of children, or the planting or harvesting of crops.

There were hundreds of different patterns of Native American life in North America. Some societies were small and dealt with life in a limited region of the vast North American continent. Other groups were much larger and were linked by trade and culture to other groups in North America and Mesoamerica. Peoples in Mesoamerica and South America also lived in societies that varied from simple to complex. You will read about three of these cultures—the Maya, the Aztec, and the Inca—in the next three lessons. They would develop very sophisticated ways of life.

Reading Check
Make Inferences
What artificial symbols are used by nations or organizations in a way similar to totems?

Lesson 4 Assessment

1. **Organize Information** Use the chart to compare the effect of the environment on the development of the cultures of the Northwest Coast and the Southwest.

   Northwest Coast   Southwest

   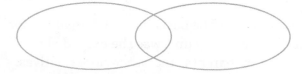

   Write a paragraph to explain how the effects were different.

2. **Key Terms and People** For each key term or person in the lesson, write a sentence explaining its significance.

3. **Summarize** For what purpose did the Mound Builder cultures use earthen mounds?

4. **Analyze Causes** Why might location have been important to the power and wealth of the Mississippian culture?

5. **Compare** In what ways did the peoples of North America share similar cultural patterns?

6. **Develop Historical Perspectives** Why did societies in North America interact with each other?

Maya Kings and Cities

The Big Idea

The Maya developed a highly complex civilization based on city-states and elaborate religious practices.

Why It Matters Now

Descendants of the Maya still occupy the same territory.

Key Terms and People

Tikal
Pacal
glyph
codex
Popol Vuh

Maya jade death mask, seventh century AD

Setting the Stage

In the early centuries AD, most North American peoples were beginning to develop complex societies. Further south, the peoples of Mexico and Central America were entering into the full flower of civilization. A prime example of this cultural flowering were the Maya, who built an extraordinary civilization in the heart of Mesoamerica.

Maya Create City-States

The homeland of the Maya stretched from southern Mexico into northern Central America. This area includes a highland region and a lowland region. The lowlands lie to the north. They include the dry scrub forest of the Yucatán (yoo•kuh•TAN) Peninsula and the dense, steamy jungles of southeastern Mexico and northern Guatemala. The highlands are further south—a range of cool, cloud-wreathed mountains that stretch from southern Mexico to El Salvador.

While the Olmec were building their civilization along the Gulf Coast in the period from 1200 to 400 BC, the Maya were also evolving. They took on Olmec influences, blending these with local customs. By AD 250, Maya culture had developed into a flourishing civilization. Over time the Maya established cultural patterns and political and economic structures that were similar to those of later civilizations, such as the Aztecs and the Incas.

Urban Centers The period from AD 250 to 900 is known as the Classic Period of Maya civilization. During this time, the Maya built spectacular cities such as **Tikal** (tee•KAHL), a major center in northern Guatemala. Other important sites included Copán, Palenque, Uxmal, and Chichén Itzá (chee•CHEHN-ee•TSAH). Each of these was an independent city-state, ruled by a god-king and serving as a center for religious ceremonies and trade. For example, **Pacal** the Great ruled Palenque in the 600s. During his reign many great buildings were constructed, such as the Temple of

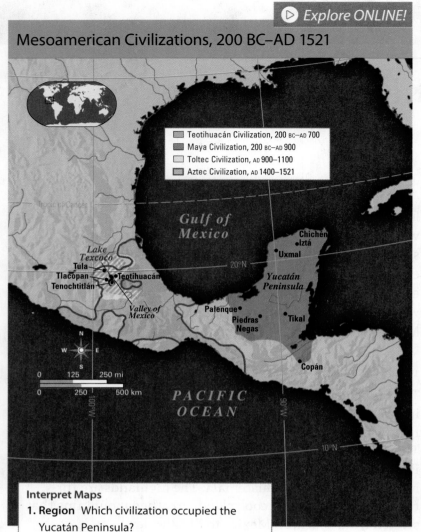

Mesoamerican Civilizations, 200 BC–AD 1521

▶ Explore ONLINE!

Teotihuacán Civilization, 200 BC–AD 700
Maya Civilization, 200 BC–AD 900
Toltec Civilization, AD 900–1100
Aztec Civilization, AD 1400–1521

Gulf of Mexico

Chichén Iztá
Uxmal
Lake Texcoco
Tula
Tlacopan
Tenochtitlán
Teotihuacán
Valley of Mexico
Yucatán Peninsula
Palenque
Piedras Negas
Tikal
Copán

PACIFIC OCEAN

0   125   250 mi
0   250   500 km

Interpret Maps

1. **Region** Which civilization occupied the Yucatán Peninsula?

2. **Region** What other civilization areas were eventually incorporated into the Aztec area?

Inscriptions, where he was laid to rest. Many other Maya cities featured giant pyramids, temples, palaces, and elaborate stone carvings dedicated to the gods and to important rulers. Tens of thousands of people lived in residential areas around the bustling city center.

Archaeologists have identified at least 50 major Maya sites, all with monumental architecture. For example, the Temple IV pyramid at Tikal stretched 212 feet into the jungle sky. In addition to temples and pyramids, each Maya city featured a ball court. In this stone-sided playing field, the Maya played a game that had religious and political significance. The Maya believed the playing of this game would maintain the cycles of the sun and moon and bring life-giving rains.

Agriculture and Trade Support Cities

Although the Maya city-states were independent of each other, they were linked through alliances and trade. Cities exchanged their local products such as salt, flint, feathers, shells, and honey. They also traded craft goods like cotton textiles and jade ornaments. While the Maya did not have a uniform currency, cacao (chocolate) beans sometimes served as one.

As in the rest of Mesoamerica, agriculture—particularly the growing of maize, beans, and squash—provided the basis for Maya life. For years, experts assumed that the Maya practiced slash-and-burn agriculture. This method involves farmers clearing the land by burning existing vegetation and planting crops in the ashes. Evidence now shows, however, that the Maya also developed more sophisticated methods, including planting on raised beds above swamps and on hillside terraces.

Kingdoms Built on Dynasties
Successful farming methods led to the accumulation of wealth and the development of social classes. The noble class, which included priests and the leading warriors, occupied the top rung of Maya society. Below them came merchants and those with specialized knowledge, such as skilled artisans. Finally, at the bottom, came the peasant majority.

Reading Check
Draw Conclusions
What does the ability
to construct complex
buildings reveal about
a society?

The Maya king sat at the top of this class structure. He was regarded as a holy figure, and his position was hereditary. When he died, he passed the throne on to his eldest son. Other sons of the ruler might expect to join the priesthood.

Religion Shapes Maya Life

Religion influenced most aspects of Maya life. The Maya believed in many gods, and they considered their rulers to be godlike. There were gods of corn, of death, of rain, and of war. Gods could be good or evil, and sometimes both. Gods also were associated with the four directions and with different colors: white for north, black for west, yellow for south, red for east, and green in the center. The Maya believed that each day was a living god whose behavior could be predicted with the help of a system of calendars. The Maya depicted their gods or rulers in art such as through carved statues and bowls, which were made of wood, stone, obsidian, or jade.

Stone panel carved by Maya artists, 8th century BC.

Religious Practices The Maya worshiped their gods in various ways. They prayed and made offerings of food, flowers, and incense. They also pierced and cut their bodies and offered their blood, believing that this would nourish the gods. Sometimes the Maya even carried out human sacrifice, usually of captured enemies. At Chichén Itzá, they threw captives into a deep sinkhole lake, called a *cenote* (say•NO•tay), along with gold, jade, and other offerings. The Maya believed that human sacrifice pleased the gods and kept the world in balance. Nevertheless, the Maya's use of sacrifice never reached the extremes of some other Mesoamerican peoples.

Math and Religion Maya religious beliefs also led to the development of the calendar, mathematics, and astronomy. The Maya believed that time was a burden carried on the back of a god. At the end of a day, month, or year, one god would lay the burden down and another would pick it up. A day would be lucky or unlucky, depending on the nature of the god, so it was very important to have an accurate calendar to know which god was in charge of the day.

The Maya developed a 260-day religious calendar, which consisted of thirteen 20-day months. A second 365-day solar calendar consisted of eighteen 20-day months, with a separate period of 5 days at the end. The two calendars were linked together like meshed gears so that any given day could be identified in both cycles. The calendar helped identify the best times to plant crops, attack enemies, and crown new rulers.

The Maya based their calendar on careful observation of the planets, sun, and moon. Highly skilled Maya astronomers and mathematicians calculated the solar year at 365.2420 days. This is only .0002 of a day short of the figure generally accepted today! The Maya astronomers were able to attain such great precision by using a math system that included the concept of zero. The Maya used a shell symbol for zero, dots for the numbers one to four, and a bar for five. The Maya number system was a base-20 system. They used the numerical system primarily for calendar and astronomical work.

A detail from the Maya *Codex Troano*

Written Language Preserves History The Maya also developed the most advanced writing system in the ancient Americas. Maya writing consisted of about 800 hieroglyphic symbols, or **glyphs** (glihfs). Some of these glyphs stood for whole words, and others represented syllables. The Maya used their writing system to record important historical events, carving their glyphs in stone or recording them in a bark-paper book known as a **codex** (KOH•dehks). Only three of these ancient books have survived.

Other original books telling of Maya history and customs do exist, however. Maya peoples wrote down their history after the arrival of the Spanish. The most famous of these books, the *Popol Vuh* (POH•pohl Voo), recounts the Highland Maya's version of the story of creation. "Before the world was created, Calm and Silence were the great kings that ruled," reads the first sentence in the book. "Nothing existed, there was nothing."

Reading Check
Make Inferences
How are math, astronomy, and calendars related?

Mysterious Maya Decline

The remarkable history of the Maya ended in mystery. Unlike the Han dynasty and the Roman Empire, evidence does not show that social unrest caused the Mayan Empire to end. Yet, like the Han dynasty and Roman Empire, the Mayan Empire did face invaders. In the late 800s, the Maya suddenly abandoned many of their cities. Invaders from the north, the Toltec, moved into the lands occupied by the Maya. These war-like peoples from central Mexico changed the culture. The high civilization of Maya cities like Tikal and Copán disappeared.

No one knows exactly why this happened, though experts offer several overlapping theories. By the 700s, warfare had broken out among the various Maya city-states. Increased warfare disrupted trade and produced

---

DOCUMENT-BASED INVESTIGATION Historical Source

The *Popul Vuh*

"Then let the emptiness fill! they said. Let the water weave its way downward so the earth can show its face! Let the light break on the ridges, let the sky fill up with the yellow light of dawn! Let our glory be a man walking on a path through the trees! "Earth!" the Creators called. They called only once, and it was there, from a mist, from a cloud of dust, the mountains appeared instantly."

—From the *Popol Vuh*

Analyze Historical Sources
What beliefs did the Maya have about the creation of the earth?

Rise and Fall of the Maya

Traits of Civilization	Strength Leading to Power	Weakness Leading to Decline
Religious beliefs and theocracy	United culture that is loyal to the king	Many physical and human resources funneled into religious activities
Independent city-states with their own power	Wealthy and prosperous urban centers	Frequent warfare occurs between city-states
Intensive agriculture	Production of more food feeds a larger population	Population growth creates need for more land

Interpret Charts

1. **Analyze Effects** Which trait aids in building a sense of loyalty to the ruler?
2. **Draw Conclusions** How can intensive agriculture be both a strength and a weakness?

economic hardship. In addition, population growth and overfarming may have damaged the environment, and this led to food shortages, famine, and disease. By the time the Spanish arrived in the early 1500s, the Maya were divided into small, weak city-states that gave little hint of their former glory.

As the Maya civilization faded, other peoples of Mesoamerica were growing in strength and sophistication. Like the Maya, these peoples would trace some of their ancestry to the Olmec. Eventually, these people would dominate the Valley of Mexico and lands beyond it, as you will learn in Lesson 6.

Reading Check
Analyze Causes
Why did the Maya civilization decline?

Lesson 5 Assessment

1. **Organize Information** Use the web diagram to describe the characteristics of Maya civilization.

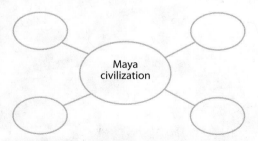

Maya civilization

How are the characteristics of Maya civilization like those of a typical civilization?

2. **Key Terms and People** For each key term or person in the lesson, write a sentence explaining its significance.
3. **Evaluate** What was the basis of Maya life?
4. **Contrast** What three explanations have been given for the collapse of the Maya civilization, and how were they different from those of the Roman Empire and Han dynasty?
5. **Analyze Effects** Why was trade important to the Maya civilization?
6. **Draw Conclusions** How important do you think the development of advanced mathematics was in the creation of the Maya calendar, and why was it important to Mayan religion?

Maya Architecture

Mayan architects created beautiful and monumental structures. The buildings are artistic in structure, as well as in ornamentation. The style and complexity of the ornamentation varies by region, but narrative, ceremonial, and celestial themes are common. Archaeologists and tourists alike are still awed by Maya architecture.

These large structures seem to be designed for ceremonial or religious purposes and dominate the landscapes of the cities. The most recognizable structures are the pyramids, but there is much more to the artful Maya architecture.

▲ DETAILING
One characteristic of Maya architecture is the exterior and interior ornamental detailing. This two-headed jaguar throne was found at Uxmal. It represents the jaguar god of the underworld, one of the many Maya gods. An ancient Maya manuscript lists over 160 gods.

▼ STELE
Another form of Maya art was the stele (STEE•lee), which is an inscribed or carved marker that is often used to mark special dates or as a building marker. This stele is in the Maya city of Copán and is part of a series of finely carved commemorative steles in the great plaza. The 13th king is represented on most of the steles in ceremonial clothing.

BALL COURT ▲

Ball courts were a feature of ancient Maya cities. The games held deep religious significance, and the same artistic detail is found in the ball courts as in other religious structures. The court shown here is at Chichén Itzá in modern Mexico. It is 545 feet long and 223 feet wide, and it is the largest in the Americas. The ornate hoop is 20 feet off the ground.

The exact rules and method of scoring the game are unknown. However, inscriptions indicate that players could not use their hands or feet to move a solid rubber ball, and that members of the losing team might be sacrificed by beheading.

◄ PYRAMID

Archaeologists have found pyramids at many Maya cities. Pyramids were religious structures and, as in Egypt, could be used as tombs. The pyramid shown here is known as Temple I in the Maya city of Tikal. It is the tomb of Ha Sawa Chaan K'awil, a Tikal ruler. The pyramid is about 160 feet tall. Another pyramid in the city is 212 feet tall. In fact, the Tikal pyramids were the tallest structures in the Americas until 1903, when the Flatiron Building was built in New York City.

Critical Thinking

1. **Make Inferences** What does the size and ornamentation of Maya architecture indicate about their society?

2. **Compare and Contrast** What are some examples of large-scale architecture in the United States? What do they indicate about our culture?

The Aztecs Control Central Mexico

The Big Idea

Through alliances and conquest, the Aztecs created a powerful empire in Mexico.

Why It Matters Now

This time period saw the origins of one of the 20th century's most populous cities, Mexico City.

Key Terms and People

obsidian
Quetzalcoatl
Triple Alliance
Montezuma I
Montezuma II

This wall hanging is a replica of the Aztec sun stone.

Setting the Stage

While the Maya were developing their civilization to the south, other high cultures were evolving in central Mexico. Some of the most important developments took place in and around the Valley of Mexico. This valley, where modern Mexico City is located, eventually became the site of the greatest empire of Mesoamerica, the Aztec. The Aztecs were preceded by two other important civilizations that traced their ancestry to the Olmec and Zapotec. You learned about the Olmec and Zapotec in Lesson 5.

The Valley of Mexico

The Valley of Mexico, a mountain basin about 7,500 feet above sea level, served as the home base of several powerful cultures. The valley had several large, shallow lakes at its center, accessible resources, and fertile soil. These advantages attracted the people of Teotihuacán (tay•oh•tee•wah•KAHN) and the Toltecs. They settled in the valley and developed advanced civilizations that controlled much of the area.

An Early City-State The first major civilization of central Mexico was Teotihuacán, a city-state whose ruins lie just outside Mexico City. In the first century AD, villagers at this site began to plan and construct a monumental city even larger than Monte Albán, in Oaxaca.

At its peak in the sixth century, Teotihuacán had a population of between 150,000 and 200,000 people, making it one of the largest cities in the world at the time. The heart of the city was a central avenue lined with more than 20 pyramids dedicated to various gods. The biggest of these was the giant Pyramid of the Sun. This imposing building stood more than 200 feet tall and measured close to 3,000 feet around its base. The people of Teotihuacán lived in apartment-block buildings in the area around the central avenue.

Teotihuacán became the center of a thriving trade network that extended far into Central America. The city's most valuable trade item was **obsidian** (ahb·SIHD·ee·uhn), a green or black volcanic glass found in the Valley of Mexico and used to make razor-sharp weapons. There is no evidence that Teotihuacán conquered its neighbors or tried to create an empire. However, evidence of art styles and religious beliefs from Teotihuacán have been found throughout Mesoamerica.

After centuries of growth, the city abruptly declined. Historians believe this decline was due either to an invasion by outside forces or conflict among the city's ruling classes. Regardless of the causes, the city was virtually abandoned by 750. The vast ruins astonished later settlers in the area, who named the site Teotihuacán, which means "City of the Gods."

Quetzalcoatl was a god for many ancient Mexican civilizations.

Reading Check
Make Inferences
Why might the followers of the war god rebel against Topiltzin?

Toltecs Take Over After the fall of Teotihuacán, no single culture dominated central Mexico for decades. Then around 900, a new people—the Toltecs—rose to power. For the next three centuries, the Toltecs ruled over the heart of Mexico from their capital at Tula. Like other Mesoamericans, they built pyramids and temples. They also carved tall pillars in the shape of armed warriors.

In fact, the Toltecs were an extremely warlike people whose empire was based on conquest. They worshiped a fierce war god who demanded blood and human sacrifice from his followers. Sometime after 1000, a Toltec ruler named Topiltzin (toh·PEELT·zeen) tried to change the Toltec religion. He called on the Toltec people to end the practice of human sacrifice. He also encouraged them to worship a different god, **Quetzalcoatl** (keht·sahl·koh·AHT·uhl), or the Feathered Serpent. Followers of the war god rebelled, however, forcing Topiltzin and his followers into exile on the Yucatán peninsula. There, they greatly influenced late Mayan culture. After Topiltzin's exile, Toltec power began to decline. By the early 1200s, their reign over the Valley of Mexico had ended.

In time, Topiltzin and Quetzalcoatl became one in the legends of the people of the Valley of Mexico. According to these legends, after his exile from Tula, the god traveled east, crossing the sea on a raft of snakes. He would return one day, bringing a new reign of light and peace. The story of Quetzalcoatl would come back to haunt the greatest empire of Mexico, the Aztecs.

The Pyramid of the Sun dominates Teotihuacán's main highway, the Avenue of the Dead.

The Aztec Empire

The Aztecs arrived in the Valley of Mexico around AD 1200. The valley contained a number of small city-states that had survived the collapse of Toltec rule. The Aztecs, who were then called the Mexica, were a poor, nomadic people from the harsh deserts of northern Mexico. Fierce and ambitious, they soon adapted to local ways, finding work as soldiers-for-hire to local rulers.

According to one of the Aztec legends, the god of the sun and warfare, Huitzilopochtli (wee•tsee•loh•POHCH•tlee), told them to found a city of their own. He said to look for a place where an eagle perched on a cactus, holding a snake in its mouth.

Historical Source

An Aztec Legend

These words capture part of the Aztec legend of Huitzilopochtli.

A statue of an Aztec eagle warrior

> *"The place where the eagle screams,*
> *where he spreads his wings;*
> *the place where he feeds,*
> *where the fish jump,*
> *where the serpents*
> *coil up and hiss!*
> *This shall be Mexico Tenochtitlán*
> *and many things shall happen!"*
>
> —*Crónica Mexicayotl*

Analyze Historical Sources
Based on what you read from the legend, what geographic feature would be in close proximity to Tenochtitlán?

They found such a place on a small island in Lake Texcoco, at the center of the valley. There, in 1325, they founded their city, which they named Tenochtitlán (teh•noch•tee•TLAHN).

Aztecs Grow Stronger Over the years, the Aztecs gradually increased in strength and number. In 1428, they joined with two other city-states—Texcoco and Tlacopan—to form the **Triple Alliance**. This alliance became the leading power in the Valley of Mexico and soon gained control over neighboring regions. By the early 1500s, they controlled a vast empire that covered some 80,000 square miles stretching from central Mexico to the Atlantic and Pacific coasts and south into Oaxaca. This empire was divided into 38 provinces. Its population may have been between 5 and 15 million people.

The Aztecs based their power on military conquest and the tribute they gained from their conquered subjects. The Aztecs generally exercised loose control over the empire, often letting local rulers govern their own regions. They did demand tribute, however, in the form of gold, maize, cacao beans, cotton, jade, and other products. If local rulers failed to pay tribute or offered any other kind of resistance, the Aztecs responded brutally. They destroyed the rebellious villages and captured or slaughtered the inhabitants.

Nobles Rule Aztec Society At the height of the Aztec Empire, military leaders held great power in Aztec society. Along with government officials and priests, these military leaders made up the noble class. Many nobles owned vast estates, which they ruled over like lords, living a life of great wealth and luxury.

There were two other broad classes in Aztec society, commoners and enslaved persons. Commoners included merchants, artisans, soldiers, and farmers who owned their own land. The merchants formed a special type of elite. They often traveled widely, acting as spies for the emperor and gaining great wealth for themselves. The lowest class, enslaved persons, were captives who did many different jobs.

The emperor sat atop the Aztec social pyramid. Although he sometimes consulted with top generals or officials, his power was absolute. The emperor lived in a magnificent palace, surrounded by servants and his wives. Visitors—even nobles—entered his presence in bare feet and cast their eyes down so as not to look at him.

Reading Check
Compare
How were the Aztecs' methods of controlling the empire like those of other empires you have read about?

Global Patterns

Warriors and Animal Symbols

Some of the highest-ranking Aztec leaders were eagle warriors. In battle, they wore eagle costumes in honor of the sun god, Huitzilopochtli, who often took the form of an eagle.

The use of animal symbols by warriors was a widespread practice in ancient times. The eagle was a favorite among Roman soldiers because they thought it symbolized victory. In many cultures, warriors adopted an animal so that they would inherit the animal's qualities. Celtic fighters, for example, wore boars' heads on their helmets so that they, like the boar, would be strong and fearless. Similarly, many African warriors adopted the lion for its fighting ferocity.

Tenochtitlán: A Planned City

By the early 1500s, Tenochtitlán had become an extraordinary urban center. Much of the building up of the city and some of its growth were achieved under **Montezuma I** (mahn·tih·ZOO·muh). With a population of between 200,000 and 400,000 people, it was larger than London or any other European capital of the time. Tenochtitlán remained on its original island site. To connect the island to the mainland, Aztec engineers built three raised roads, called causeways, over the water and marshland. Other smaller cities ringed the lake, creating a dense concentration of people in the Valley of Mexico.

Streets and broad avenues connected the city center with outlying residential districts. The canals that intersected with these roadways allowed canoes to bring people directly into the city center. Canoes also brought goods from the farthest reaches of the empire to the economic heart of the city, the huge market of Tlatelolco (tlah·tehl·AWL·koh). Visitors to the market also found a great deal of local agricultural produce on display, including avocados, beans, chili peppers, corn, squash, and tomatoes. Most of the fruits and vegetables sold at the market were grown on *chinampas,* farm plots built on the marshy fringes of the lake. These plots, sometimes called floating gardens, were extremely productive, providing the food needed for a huge urban population.

Reading Check
Draw Conclusions
How strong do you think the economy of the Aztec Empire was, based on the descriptions of Tenochtitlán? Explain your response.

At the center of the city was a massive walled complex filled with palaces, temples, and government buildings. The main structure in the complex was the Great Temple. This giant pyramid with twin temples at the top, one dedicated to the sun god and the other to the rain god, served as the center of Aztec religious life.

Religion Rules Aztec Life

Religion played a major role in Aztec society. Tenochtitlán contained hundreds of temples and religious structures dedicated to the approximately 1,000 gods that the Aztecs worshiped. The Aztecs adopted many of these gods, and religious practices related to them, from other Mesoamerican peoples. For example, the Aztecs worshiped the Toltec god Quetzalcoatl in many forms. They saw him as the god of learning and books, the god of the wind, and a symbol of death and rebirth. The Aztecs pictured Quetzalcoatl not only as a feathered serpent, but also as a pale-skinned man with a beard.

Religious Practices Aztec religious practices centered on elaborate public ceremonies designed to communicate with the gods and win their favor. At these ceremonies, priests made offerings to the gods and presented ritual dramas, songs, and dances featuring masked performers. The Aztec ceremonial calendar was full of religious festivals, which varied according to the god being honored.

Sacrifices for the Sun God The most important rituals involved a sun god, Huitzilopochtli. According to Aztec belief, Huitzilopochtli made the sun rise every day. When the sun set, he had to battle the forces of evil to

The Market at Tlatelolco

Hernando Cortés, the Spanish conqueror of Mexico, noted that the market at Tlatelolco was twice the size of the market at Salamanca, the Spanish city where he had attended university.

> "... [T]here are daily more than sixty thousand souls, buying and selling, and where are found all the kinds of merchandise produced in these countries, including food products, jewels of gold and silver, lead, brass, copper, zinc, stone, bones, shells, and feathers.... Everything is sold by a kind of measure, and, until now, we have not seen anything sold by weight. There is in this, square a very large building, like a Court of Justice, where there are always ten or twelve persons, sitting as judges, and delivering their decisions upon all cases which arise in the markets."
>
> —Hernando Cortés,
> from *Hernando Cortés his five letters of Relation to the Emperor Charles V,
> Volume I*

Tenochtitlán—a Bustling City

Bernal Díaz, one of Cortés's soldiers, was amazed to find a bustling urban center in the heart of Mexico.

> "When we saw all those cities and villages built in the water, and other great towns on dry land, and that straight and level causeway leading to Mexico, we were astounded. These great towns and cues [pyramids] and buildings rising from the water, all made of stone, seemed like an enchanted vision.... Indeed, some of our soldiers asked whether it was not all a dream."
>
> —Bernal Díaz,
> *The Conquest of New Spain*

Analyze Historical Sources
How do the descriptions by Cortés and Díaz of city life in the Aztec Empire differ? Are they both credible sources? Explain.

get to the next day. To make sure that he was strong enough for this ordeal, he needed the nourishment of human blood. Without regular offerings of human blood, Huitzilopochtli would be too weak to fight. The sun would not rise, the world would be plunged into darkness, and all life would perish. For this reason, Aztec priests practiced human sacrifice on a massive scale. Each year, thousands of victims were led to the altar atop the Great Temple, where priests carved out their hearts using obsidian knives.

Sacrificial victims included enslaved persons, criminals, and people offered as tribute by conquered provinces. Prisoners of war, however, were

This mural, in the National Palace in Mexico City, shows Quetzalcoatl in many forms.

Reading Check
Summarize
Why did the Aztecs take so many war captives?

the preferred victims. As a result, the priests required a steady supply of war captives. This in turn pushed the Aztec military to carry out new conquests. In fact, the Aztecs often went to war not to conquer new lands but simply to capture prisoners for sacrifice. They even adapted their battle tactics to ensure that they took their opponents alive.

Problems in the Aztec Empire

In 1502, a new ruler, **Montezuma II**, was crowned emperor. Under Montezuma II, the Aztec Empire began to weaken. For nearly a century, the Aztecs had been demanding tribute and sacrificial victims from the provinces under their control. Now, with the population of Tenochtitlán growing ever greater, Montezuma II called for even more tribute and sacrifice. A number of provinces rose up against Aztec oppression. This began a period of unrest and rebellion, which the military struggled to put down.

Over time, Montezuma II tried to lessen the pressure on the provinces. For example, he reduced the demand for tribute payment by cutting the number of officials in the Aztec government. But resentment continued to grow. Many Aztecs began to predict that terrible things were about to happen. They saw bad omens in every unusual occurrence—lightning striking

The Aztec Calendar

The Aztec system of tracking the days was very intricate. Archaeologists believe that the Aztec calendar system was derived from the Maya system. The Aztecs followed two main calendars: a sacred one with 13 months of 20 days and an agricultural or solar one with 18 months of 20 days. (Notice that this comes to 360 days. The Aztecs then had an unlucky five-day period known as *nemontemi*, making their solar calendar 365 days long.) Every 52 years, the two calendars would start on the same day, and a great ceremony of fire marked the occasion.

Aztec Gods
The Aztecs worshiped many different gods. They were a vital part of the Aztec calendar and daily life. The Aztecs paid tribute to different gods depending, in part, on the day, week, month, year, and religious cycle of the Aztec calendars. The god shown here is a sun god, Tonatiuh.

Aztec Sunstone
Originally located in the main ceremonial plaza of Tenochtitlán, the Aztec calendar stone measures 13 feet in diameter and weighs 24 tons. It was uncovered in Mexico City in 1790. The Sunstone, as it is called, contains a wealth of information about the days that began and ended the Aztec months, the gods associated with the days, and many other details.

This is an artist's rendition of the inner circle of the Sunstone. In the center is the god Tonatiuh.

The four squares that surround Tonatiuh are glyphs, or symbols, of the four ages preceding the time of the Aztecs: Tiger, Water, Wind, and Rain.

In the ring just outside the symbols of the previous ages, 20 segments represent the 20 days that made up an Aztec month. Each day had its own symbol and a god who watched over the day. The symbol pointed to here is Ocelotl, the jaguar.

Interpret Visual Sources

1. **Hypothesize** Why do you think the Aztecs put Tonatiuh, a sun god, in the center of the Sunstone? Explain your reasons.

2. **Compare and Contrast** How is the Aztec calendar different from the calendar we use today? How is it similar?

Rise and Fall of the Aztecs

Traits of Civilization	Strength Leading to Power	Weakness Leading to Decline
Religious beliefs and theocracy	United culture that is loyal to the emperor	Many physical and human resources funneled into religious activities
Powerful army	More land, power, and prisoners for religious sacrifices	Need for prisoners changes warfare style to less deadly and less aggressive
Empire of tribute states	Provides wealth and power and prisoners for religious sacrifice	Tribute states are rebellious and need to be controlled

Interpret Charts

1. **Draw Conclusions** How was the tribute system both a strength and a weakness?
2. **Clarifying** How are the army and religious beliefs linked in the Aztec Empire?

a temple in Tenochtitlán, or a partial eclipse of the sun, for example. The most worrying event, however, was the arrival of the Spanish. For many Aztecs, these fair-skinned, bearded strangers from across the sea brought to mind the legend of the return of Quetzalcoatl.

Further south in the high mountain valleys of the Andes, another empire was developing, one that would transcend the Aztec Empire in land area, power, and wealth. Like the Aztecs, the people of this Andean empire worshiped the sun and had large armies. However, the society they built was much different from that of the Aztecs, as you will see in Lesson 7.

Reading Check
Make Inferences
Why would cutting the number of government officials reduce the need for tribute money?

Lesson 6 Assessment

1. **Organize Information** What steps did the Aztecs take to establish an extensive empire in such a relatively short period of time?

2. **Key Terms and People** For each key term or person in the lesson, write a sentence explaining its significance.
3. **Evaluate** How did the Aztecs rule their empire, and do you think it was effective?
4. **Find Main Ideas** On what was Teotihuacán's power and wealth based?
5. **Summarize** How were the Aztecs able to overcome the problems associated with Tenochtitlán's island location?
6. **Analyze Effects** How did the Aztecs' growing empire and need for victims for sacrifice lead to problems?

The Inca Create a Mountain Empire

The Big Idea

The Inca built a vast empire supported by taxes, governed by a bureaucracy, and linked by extensive road systems.

Why It Matters Now

The Incan system of government was similar to some socialist governments in the 20th century.

Key Terms and People

Pachacuti
ayllu
mita
quipu

Setting the Stage

While the Aztecs ruled in the Valley of Mexico, another people—the Inca—created an equally powerful state in South America. From Cuzco, their capital in southern Peru, the Inca spread outward in all directions. They brought various Andean peoples under their control and built an empire that stretched from Ecuador in the north to Chile in the south. It was the largest empire ever seen in the Americas.

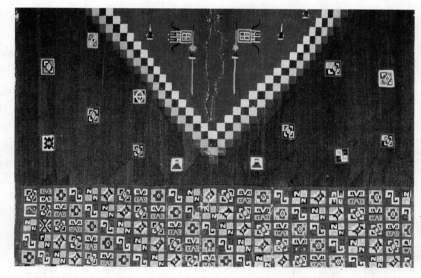

Incan textiles such as this one were a common form of art among early cultures in South America.

The Inca Build an Empire

Like the Aztecs, the Inca built their empire on cultural foundations thousands of years old. Ancient civilizations such as the Chavín, Moche, and Nazca had established a tradition of high culture in Peru. They were followed by the Huari and Tiahuanaco cultures of southern Peru and Bolivia. The Chimú, an impressive civilization of the 1300s based in the northern coastal region once controlled by the Moche, came next. The Inca would create an even more powerful state, however, extending their rule over the entire Andean region.

Incan Beginnings The Inca originally lived in a high plateau of the Andes. After wandering the highlands for years, the Inca finally settled on fertile lands in the Valley of Cuzco. By the 1200s, they had established their own small kingdom in the valley.

During this early period, the Inca developed traditions and beliefs that helped launch and unify their empire. One of these traditions was the belief that the Incan ruler was descended from the sun god, Inti, who would bring prosperity and greatness to the Incan state. Only men from one of 11 noble lineages believed to be descendants of the sun god could be selected as Incan leaders.

Pachacuti Builds an Empire At first the Incan kingdom grew slowly. In 1438, however, a powerful and ambitious ruler, **Pachacuti** (pah·chah·KOO·tee), took the throne. Under his leadership, the Inca conquered all of Peru and then moved into neighboring lands. By 1500, the Inca ruled an empire that stretched 2,500 miles along the western coast of South America. The Inca called this empire "Land of the Four Quarters." It included about 80 provinces and was home to as many as 16 million people.

Pachacuti and his successors accomplished this feat of conquest through a combination of diplomacy and military force. The Inca had a powerful military but used force only when necessary. They were also clever diplomats. Before attacking, they typically offered enemy states an honorable surrender. They would allow them to keep their own customs and rulers in exchange for loyalty to the Incan state. Because of this treatment, many states gave up without resisting. Even when force was used, the Inca took a similar approach. Once an area was defeated, they made every effort to gain the loyalty of the newly conquered people.

Reading Check
Evaluate
Do you think that Pachacuti's methods for unifying conquered lands were effective? Explain.

BIOGRAPHY

Pachacuti
(c. 1391–c. 1473)

As the second son of the Incan ruler Viracocha, Pachacuti did not expect to succeed to the throne. However, when Cuzco was attacked in 1438, Viracocha and Pachacuti's older brother fled the city. Pachacuti stayed and drove off the attackers. He then proclaimed himself the new Incan ruler.

Pachacuti, whose name means "World Transformer" or "Earthshaker," ruled for 33 years. During that time, he drew up the plans for the rebuilding of Cuzco and established the Incan system of government.

Incan Government Creates Unity

To control the huge empire, the rulers divided their territory and its people into manageable units governed by a central bureaucracy. The Inca created an efficient economic system to support the empire and an extensive road system to tie it together. They also imposed a single official language, Quechua (KEHCH•wuh), and founded schools to teach Incan ways. Certain social groups were identified by officially dictated patterns on clothing. All of these actions were calculated to unify the variety of people controlled by the Inca.

Incan Cities Show Government Presence To exercise control over their empire, the Inca built many cities in conquered areas. The architecture of government buildings was the same all over the empire, making the presence of the government apparent. As in Rome, all roads led to the capital, Cuzco. The heart of the Incan empire, Cuzco was a splendid city of temples, plazas, and palaces. "Cuzco was grand and stately," wrote Cieza de León. "It had fine streets, . . . and the houses were built of solid stones, beautifully joined." Like the Romans, the Inca were masterful engineers and stonemasons. Though they had no iron tools and did not use the wheel, Incan builders carved and transported huge blocks of stone, fitting them together perfectly without mortar. Many Incan walls still stand in Cuzco today, undisturbed by the region's frequent earthquakes.

Incan Government The Incan state exercised almost total control over economic and social life. It controlled most economic activity, regulating the production and distribution of goods. Unlike the Maya and the Aztecs, the Inca allowed little private commerce or trade. Yet the Inca network of internal trade routes helped unite and strengthen the vast empire.

The Incan social system was based on an age-old form of community cooperation—the ayllu (EYE•loo). The **ayllu,** or extended family group, undertook tasks too big for a single family. These tasks included building irrigation canals or cutting agricultural terraces into steep hillsides. The ayllu also stored food and other supplies to distribute among members during hard times.

The Inca incorporated the ayllu structure into a governing system based on the decimal system. They divided families into groups of 10, 100, 1,000, and 10,000. A chief led each group. He was part of a chain of command. That chain stretched from the community and regional levels all the way to Cuzco, where the Incan ruler and his council of state held court. In general, local administration was left in the hands of local rulers, and villages were allowed to continue their traditional ways. If a community resisted Incan control, however, the Inca might relocate the whole group to a different territory. The resisters would be placed under the control of rulers appointed by the government in Cuzco.

The main demand the Incan state placed on its subjects was for tribute, usually in the form of labor. The labor tribute was known as **mita** (MEE•tuh). It required all able-bodied citizens to work for the state a certain number of days every year. Mita workers might labor on state farmlands, produce craft goods for state warehouses, or help with public works projects. Later, the Spanish adopted the mita labor practice but changed it to a system of forced labor.

Historians have compared the Incan system to a type of socialism or a modern welfare state. Citizens were expected to work for the state and were cared for in return. For example, the aged and disabled were often supported by the state. The state also made sure that the people did not go hungry when there were bad harvests. Freeze-dried potatoes, called *chuño,* were stored in huge government warehouses for distribution in times of food shortages.

Public Works Projects The Inca had an ambitious public works program. The most spectacular project was the Incan road system. A marvel of engineering, this road system symbolized the power of the Incan state. The 14,000-mile-long network of roads and bridges spanned the empire, traversing rugged mountains and harsh deserts. The roads ranged from paved stone to simple paths. Along the roads, the Inca built guesthouses to provide shelter for weary travelers. A system of runners, known as *chasquis* (SHAH•skeys), traveled these roads as a kind of postal service, carrying messages from one end of the empire to the other. The road system also allowed the easy movement of troops to bring control to areas of the empire where trouble might be brewing.

Government Record-Keeping Despite the sophistication of many aspects of Incan life, the Inca never developed a writing system. History and literature were memorized as part of an oral tradition. For numerical information, the Inca created an accounting device known as **quipu**, a set of knotted strings that could be used to record data. The knots and their position on the string indicated numbers. They also used a device that functioned almost like a calculator that may have made division and using fractions possible. Additionally, the colors of the strings represented different categories of information important to the government. For example, red strings were used to count warriors; yellow strings

> ▷ *Explore ONLINE!*

South American Culture Areas, 100–1535

80°W

0° Equator

Amazon R.

10°S

A N D E S

Chan Chan

Machu Picchu
Cuzco

Lake Titicaca

M O U N T A I N S

Tropic of Capricorn

PACIFIC OCEAN

30°S

40°S

Legend:
- Moche, 100–700
- Chimú, 1000–1470
- Inca, 1438–1535
- Inca roads

N W E S

0   250   500 mi
0   500   1,000 km

Interpret Maps

1. **Place** The lands of which earlier South American cultures were included in the Incan Empire?

2. **Human–Environment Interaction** Look at the shape and terrain of the Incan Empire. What problems related to geography might occur in controlling the land?

Reading Check
Make Inferences
Of all of the methods used to create unity, which do you think would be most successful? Why?

were used to count gold. However, the meanings of the colors changed depending on the general purpose of the quipu.

Some historians believe that the Inca also developed an elaborate calendar system with two types of calendars, one for night and one for day. They were used primarily for religious purposes. Like the calendars of the Maya and the Aztecs, the two calendars provided information about the gods whom the Inca believed ruled the day and time.

Religion Supports the State

As with the Aztecs, religion was important to the Inca and helped reinforce the power of the state. The Inca worshiped fewer gods than the Aztecs. The Inca focused on key nature spirits such as the moon, the stars, and thunder. In the balance of nature, the Inca saw patterns for the way humans should relate to each other and to the earth. The primary Incan god was a creator god called Viracocha. Next in importance was the sun god, Inti. Because the Incan ruler was considered a descendant of Inti, sun worship amounted to worship of the king.

Machu Picchu lies some 8,000 feet above sea level on a ridge between two mountain peaks.

People and Empires in the Americas **529**

Rise and Fall of the Inca

Traits of Civilization	Strength Leading to Power	Weakness Leading to Decline
Religious beliefs and theocracy	United culture that is loyal to the emperor	Many physical and human resources funneled into religious activities
Major road systems	An interconnected empire that is easier to control	Enemy could also use roads to move troops
Type of welfare state with huge bureaucracy	Able to care for all people during good and bad times	People struggled to care for themselves with the elimination of the welfare state

Interpret Charts

1. **Form and Support Opinions** In your opinion, which of the three traits leading to power was the most valuable? Briefly discuss your reasons.

2. **Compare** Which trait did you find repeated in the Maya and Aztec empires?

Religious Practices Incan priests led the sun-worship services, assisted by young women known as *mamakuna,* or "virgins of the sun." These women, all unmarried, were drafted by the Inca for a lifetime of religious service. The young women were trained in religious activities, as teachers, spinners, weavers, and beer makers. Young men, known as *yamacuna,* also served as full-time workers for the state and in religious activities. Sacrifice of llamas and exchange of goods were a part of the religious activities. The goods were distributed by the priests to the people as gifts from the gods.

Great Cities The Temple of the Sun in Cuzco was the most sacred of all Incan shrines. It was heavily decorated in gold, a metal the Inca referred to as "sweat of the sun." According to some sources, the temple even had a garden with plants and animals crafted entirely from gold and silver. In fact, gold was a common sight throughout Cuzco. The walls of several buildings had a covering of thin gold sheeting.

Although Cuzco was the religious capital of the Incan Empire, other Incan cities also may have served a ceremonial purpose. For example, Machu Picchu, excavated by Hiram Bingham in 1912, was isolated and mysterious. Like Cuzco, Machu Picchu also had a sun temple, public buildings, and a central plaza. Some sources suggest it was a religious center. Others think it was an estate of Pachacuti. Still others believe it was a retreat for Incan rulers or the nobility.

Reading Check
Compare and Contrast How were the Inca and Aztecs alike?

Discord in the Empire

The Incan Empire reached the height of its glory in the early 1500s during the reign of Huayna Capac. Trouble was brewing, however. In the 1520s, Huayna Capac undertook a tour of Ecuador, a newly conquered area of the empire. In the city of Quito, he received a gift box. When he opened it, out flew butterflies and moths, considered an evil omen. A few weeks later, while still in Quito, Huayna Capac died of disease—probably smallpox.

After his death, the empire was split between his sons, Atahualpa (ah•tah•WAHL•pah) and Huascar (WAHS•kahr). Atahualpa received Ecuador, about one-fifth of the empire. The rest went to Huascar. At first, this system of dual emperors worked. Soon, however, Atahualpa laid claim to the whole of the empire. A bitter civil war followed. Atahualpa eventually won, but the war tore apart the empire. As you will learn, the Spanish arrived in the last days of this war. Taking advantage of Incan weakness, they would soon divide and conquer the empire.

Reading Check
Evaluate
Do you think that splitting the Incan Empire led to its fall? Explain

Lesson 7 Assessment

1. **Organize Information** Use the web diagram to show how the Inca unified the people they conquered.

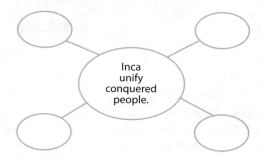

Inca unify conquered people.

Which of the Inca's methods were accepted by the conquered people?

2. **Key Terms and People** For each key term or person in the lesson, write a sentence explaining its significance.

3. **Draw Conclusions** How were the Inca able to conquer such a vast empire, and how did they create unity among diverse peoples in their empire?

4. **Form Generalizations** What role did the mita play in building the Incan Empire?

5. **Analyze Motives** Why do you think the Inca used the ayllu system as the basis for governing in the empire?

6. **Compare and Contrast** How were Incan and Aztec religious practices similar? How were they different?

Incan Mummies

For the Inca, death was an important part of life. The Inca worshiped the spirits and the bodies of their ancestors. They believed in an afterlife, and tombs and the mummies they held were considered holy.

Like the Egyptians, the Inca embalmed their dead to preserve the body. The mummies were bundled with offerings of food, tools, and precious items to help them in the afterlife. These "mummy bundles" were then buried or put in an aboveground tomb to be worshiped. Mummies have been found from many different social classes, and, as you will read, not all of them died natural deaths.

ROYAL TREATMENT ▶

The mummies of Incan rulers were among the holiest objects of Incan religion. The mummies were actually treated as if they were still alive. They had servants, maintained ownership of their property, were consulted as oracles, and were taken to major festivals or to visit other mummies. The mummy shown at right in a 16th-century Spanish codex is being transported in the same manner as the living royalty.

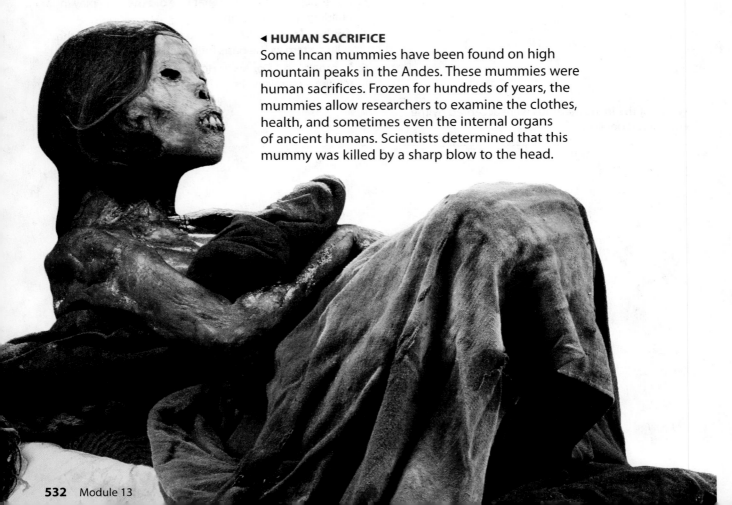

◀ HUMAN SACRIFICE

Some Incan mummies have been found on high mountain peaks in the Andes. These mummies were human sacrifices. Frozen for hundreds of years, the mummies allow researchers to examine the clothes, health, and sometimes even the internal organs of ancient humans. Scientists determined that this mummy was killed by a sharp blow to the head.

MUMMY BUNDLES ▶

At a site known as Puruchuco, just outside of Lima, Peru, archaeologists discovered a huge Incan cemetery. Some of the mummies unearthed were wrapped in layers of cotton. The outside of the bundle might have a false head made of cloth like the one shown on the right. Inside the bundle were the mummy, religious offerings, and personal items. The illustration shown below re-creates the inside of an actual bundle that archaeologists unwrapped.

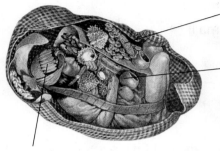

Corn, or maize, was the Inca's most important crop and is often found in Incan burials.

The Inca used gourds as bowls and containers. The gourds found in this bundle held food and cotton.

This man wears a feathered headdress that indicates high social standing.

▲ GIFTS FOR THE DEAD

The Inca sometimes placed mummies in aboveground tombs called *chullpas*. Descendants of the mummy would bring offerings of food and precious goods to honor their ancestor. This mummy is shown as it might have appeared in its tomb.

Critical Thinking
1. **Make Inferences** What do Incan mummification practices suggest about Incan culture?
2. **Form and Support Opinions** Why do you think mummification is not a common practice in the United States today?

AN INCAN GRAVEYARD

The Puruchuco graveyard lies beneath a shantytown in Peru called Tupac Amaru. in 1999, when archaeologists discovered the extent of the site, it was about to be bulldozed. Archaeologists began an emergency recovery effort.

- The remains of over 2,000 men, women, and children were recovered.
- The site may contain as many as 10,000 individuals.
- Some bundles contained up to seven bodies and weighed as much as 400 pounds.
- Between 50,000 and 60,000 artifacts were recovered.
- One of the mummy bundles became known as the "Cotton King." The mummy was wrapped in about 300 pounds of raw cotton.
- The Cotton King's bundle contained 70 artifacts, including food, pottery, animal skins, and sandals. Footwear was not common among the Inca, and sandals were a status symbol.

Module 13 Assessment

Key Terms and People

For each term or name below, briefly explain its connection to the early peoples and civilizations of the Americas.

1. Beringia
2. Olmec
3. Zapotec
4. Chavín
5. Moche
6. Mississippian
7. Iroquois
8. Montezuma I
9. Montezuma II
10. mita

Main Ideas

The Earliest Americans

1. Why was corn an important crop to early peoples?
2. What were the main differences between hunter-gatherer societies and those based primarily on agriculture?

Early Mesoamerican Civilizations

3. How did the Olmec influence the Zapotec civilization?
4. How did the Olmecs' location contribute to the development of their civilization?

Early Civilizations of the Andes

5. In what ways did the Chavín influence other peoples?
6. How did the Nazca and Moche develop rich farmland?

North American Societies

7. Why were Native American societies in North America so diverse?
8. What were the three things that most Native Americans in North America had in common?

Maya Kings and Cities

9. What role did religion play in Maya life?
10. What were three major achievements of the Maya civilization?

The Aztecs Control Central Mexico

11. How did the Aztecs build and control their empire?
12. Why did the Aztecs sacrifice human beings to their gods?

The Inca Create a Mountain Empire

13. List three ways in which the Incan government involved itself in people's lives.
14. How did Incan religion reinforce the power of the state?

Module 13 Assessment, continued

Critical Thinking

1. **Compare** In a sequence diagram, show how the early Americans' way of life developed through several stages.

2. **Summarize** What environmental challenges did the first Americans face?

3. **Draw Conclusions** Why do you think the Olmec or Zapotec civilizations might have declined?

4. **Make Inferences** What geographic factors would have made interactions between early Mesoamerican and Andean civilizations difficult?

5. **Formulate Historical Questions** Study the information on the Mound Builders again. What questions might you ask to gain a better understanding of these cultures?

6. **Compare and Contrast** Compare the religious beliefs of the Maya, the Aztecs, and the Inca. How were they similar? How were they different?

7. **Make Inferences** What can you infer about the values of the Inca from the fact that the government provided care for citizens who were aged or unable to care for themselves?

8. **Evaluate** The Maya, Aztecs, and Inca had very similar cultures but also were unique. Do you think that this statement is accurate? Consider their government, economy, art, and religion. Give reasons for your answer.

Engage with History

In this module you examined how killing a mammoth would help you survive and discussed the difficulties of living in a hunter-gatherer society. Now that you have read the module, discuss why the early Americans moved from a hunting to a farming existence. In what ways was food gathering easier in an agricultural society?

Focus on Writing

Write a three-paragraph essay comparing and contrasting American Indian civilizations in North, Central, and South America, such as the Maya, Aztecs, Inca, Pueblo, and Eastern Woodland peoples.

As you plan your essay, consider the following:

- government
- interactions with the environment
- economy
- social life

Multimedia Activity

Write a documentary film script about the Mayan, Aztec, and Incan civilizations, describing cultural patterns, the spread of American cultures, and political and economic structures. Compare and contrast these elements for each group. Provide a definition of *cultural pattern* in your script, and include examples of the following:

- cultural patterns among the Aztec, Maya, Inca, and other peoples of the Americas
- how American cultures spread
- ways in which their political and economic structures were similar and different

THE Maya

The Maya developed one of the most advanced civilizations in the Americas, but their story is shrouded in mystery. Around AD 250, the Maya began to build great cities in southern Mexico and Central America. They developed a writing system, practiced astronomy, and built magnificent palaces and pyramids with little more than stone tools. Around AD 900, however, the Maya abandoned their cities, leaving their monuments to be reclaimed by the jungle and, for a time, forgotten.

Explore some of the incredible monuments and cultural achievements of the ancient Maya online. You can find a wealth of information, video clips, primary sources, activities, and more through your online textbook.

Destroying the Maya's Past
Watch the video to learn how the actions of one Spanish missionary nearly destroyed the written record of the Maya world.

Finding the City of Palenque
Watch the video to learn about the great Maya city of Palenque and the European discovery of the site in the eighteenth century.

"Thus let it be done! Let the emptiness be filled! Let the water recede and make a void, let the earth appear and become solid; let it be done . . . "Earth!" they said, and instantly it was made."

The Popol Vuh
Read the document to learn how the Maya believed the world was created.

Pakal's Tomb
Watch the video to explore how the discovery of the tomb of a great king helped archaeologists piece together the Maya past.

The Renaissance

Essential Question
Do art and literature reflect culture, or do they shape it?

About the Painting: *The Madonna of Chancellor Rollin*, painted by Jan van Eyck in about 1435, shows the infant Jesus and his mother Mary in a 15th-century European setting. It is painted with oil paints, which were developed during the Renaissance, and uses the technique of perspective.

▷ Explore ONLINE!

VIDEOS, including...
- Da Vinci's World
- Da Vinci: Inventive Genius

HISTORY.

☑ Document Based Investigations

☑ Graphic Organizers

☑ Interactive Games

☑ Image Compare: Perspective

☑ Image with Hotspots: Printing Press

In this module you will learn how European society was revitalized as classical art and ideas were embraced and improved upon.

What You Will Learn ...

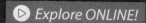
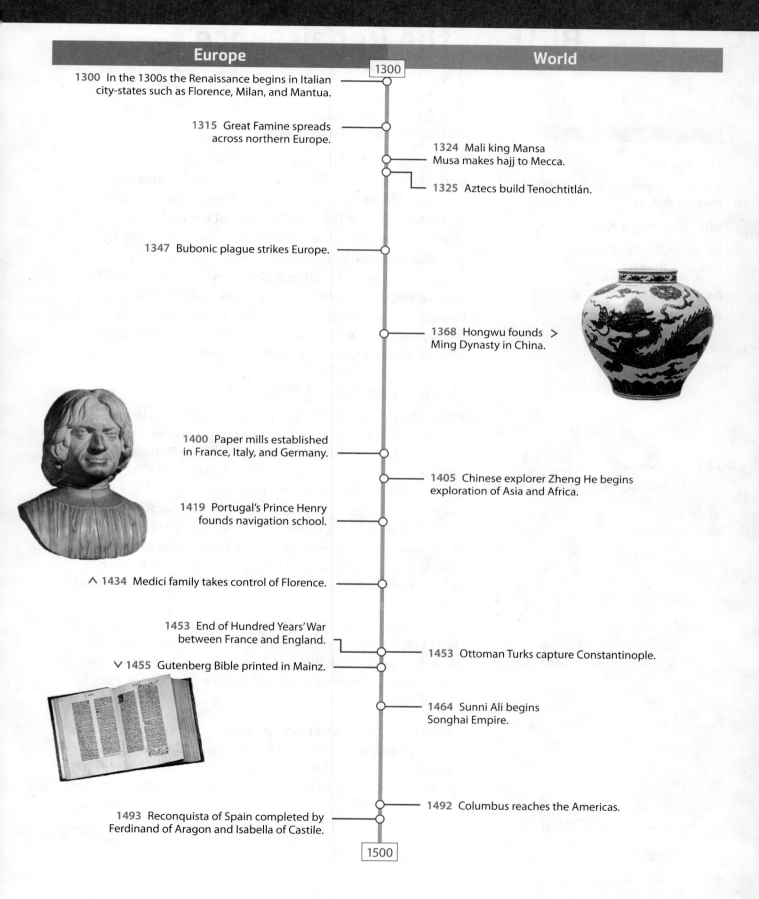

Europe	World

1300

1300 In the 1300s the Renaissance begins in Italian city-states such as Florence, Milan, and Mantua.

1315 Great Famine spreads across northern Europe.

1324 Mali king Mansa Musa makes hajj to Mecca.

1325 Aztecs build Tenochtitlán.

1347 Bubonic plague strikes Europe.

1368 Hongwu founds > Ming Dynasty in China.

1400 Paper mills established in France, Italy, and Germany.

1405 Chinese explorer Zheng He begins exploration of Asia and Africa.

1419 Portugal's Prince Henry founds navigation school.

∧ **1434** Medici family takes control of Florence.

1453 End of Hundred Years' War between France and England.

1453 Ottoman Turks capture Constantinople.

∨ **1455** Gutenberg Bible printed in Mainz.

1464 Sunni Ali begins Songhai Empire.

1492 Columbus reaches the Americas.

1493 Reconquista of Spain completed by Ferdinand of Aragon and Isabella of Castile.

1500

Birth of the Renaissance

Setting the Stage

During the late Middle Ages, Europe suffered from both war and plague. Those who survived wanted to celebrate life and the human spirit. They began to question institutions of the Middle Ages, which had been unable to prevent war or to relieve suffering brought by the plague. Some people questioned the Church, which taught Christians to endure suffering while they awaited their rewards in heaven. Some writers and artists began to express this new spirit and to experiment with different styles. These men and women would greatly change how Europeans saw themselves and their world.

The Big Idea

The Renaissance was a rebirth of learning and art.

Why It Matters Now

Renaissance art and ideas still influence thought today.

Key Terms and People

Renaissance
humanism
secular
patron

A Time of Change

From approximately 1300 to 1600, Europe experienced an explosion of creativity in art, architecture, writing, and thought. Historians call this period the **Renaissance** (rehn•ih•SAHNS). The term means "rebirth," and in this context, it refers to a revival of art and learning. People of the Renaissance hoped to bring back the culture of classical Greece and Rome. Yet in striving to revive the past, they created something new. The contributions made during this period led to innovative styles of art and literature. They also led to new values, such as individualism, or a belief in the importance of the individual.

Although the developments of the Renaissance may seem to be a complete departure from the medieval era, they grew out of several important changes in society, politics, economics, and learning. These changes laid the foundation for the Renaissance.

Shifts in Society As a result of waves of famine and disease, Europe's population in 1450 was much smaller than it had been in 1300. With far fewer people to feed, the general standard of living was much higher. People were also generally better educated. Schools in the growing towns provided at least a basic education, which was extended by recently developed universities. As literacy rates increased, so did the demand for books.

Increased trade led to the development of a new class of people between the nobility at the top and the peasants at the bottom: the middle class. The merchants, bankers, and tradespeople in the middle class had more than enough income to meet their basic needs. They had extra money to buy luxury goods and fine homes, which helped to expand the economy still further.

New Sources of Knowledge After the fall of Rome, knowledge of Greek language and learning all but disappeared in Europe. It was maintained in the Byzantine Empire, which lay at the crossroads of Europe and Asia. In 1453, when the Ottomans captured Constantinople, the capital of the Byzantine Empire, many eminent Byzantine scholars fled to Italy. With their knowledge of the language and learning of classical Greece, they contributed to the new ways of thinking that helped lead to the Renaissance.

Many Greek texts, along with the knowledge to read them, were also preserved in the libraries of the Islamic Empire. The capital of Islamic Spain, Córdoba, was a center of classical learning. Scholars there wrote commentaries in Arabic on the works of Greek writers such as Aristotle and Plato. Jewish scholars in Spain translated these commentaries into Hebrew. Later, these scholars translated into Latin both the original Greek texts and the commentaries. As a result, Western scholars visiting the libraries of Islamic Spain were able to read the works of Greek writers.

Islamic influences in Córdoba include the Moorish-style Alcazar and the cathedral, formerly an Islamic mosque.

This painting by Vicente Lopez y Portana shows King Ferdinand II of Aragon and Queen Isabella of Castile receiving Boabdil, the last Muslim ruler of Granada, in 1492.

New Technology Western Europeans also learned the technology of papermaking from Islamic Spain. Paper was first manufactured in China around 105 AD. In 751, technicians in the Abbasid caliphate learned the process. Because paper made it easier to create and store books, its use contributed to the growth of libraries. Papermaking soon spread through the Islamic world. By 1400, paper mills were to be found in France, Italy, and Germany. The availability of paper later helped make possible the development of printing.

A Changing Political Landscape Along with famine and disease, Europe had experienced almost constant warfare. Over the course of the 15th century, peace returned to much of the continent. The Hundred Years' War between France and England ended in 1453. The victory against England confirmed the French king's authority. A period of civil war followed in England, but when Henry VII came to power in 1485, England was again ruled by a strong central power. In Spain, the Reconquista, or Reconquest, was completed in 1493 by Ferdinand of Aragon and Isabella of Castile. This ended Islamic rule and brought to a close 200 years of war on the peninsula.

Reading Check
Analyze Effects
How did increasing global contact affect Europe?

The Rise of Italian City-States

The final major factor that contributed to the Renaissance was the rise of city-states in Italy. At a time when most of Europe was rural, agricultural, and manorial, Italy was much more urban and commercial. Since cities are often places where people exchange ideas, they were an ideal breeding ground for an intellectual revolution.

Economic Factors Overseas trade, spurred by the Crusades, led to the growth of large city-states in northern Italy. By the year 1000, Italian cities were at the forefront of an impressive economic expansion that would carry on into the Renaissance some 300 years later. Two decades into the 11th century, this financial success would allow Italian cities to begin to

▲ THE IMPORTANCE OF ANCIENT GREECE

Raphael The painting *School of Athens* (1508) was created for the pope's apartments in the Vatican. It shows how highly regarded the scholars of ancient Greece were during the Renaissance. Plato and Aristotle stand under the center arch. To their right, Socrates argues with several young men. Toward the front, Pythagoras draws a lesson on a slate and Ptolemy holds a globe.

RENAISSANCE SCIENCE AND TECHNOLOGY ▶

Leonardo Da Vinci Leonardo filled his notebooks with observations and sketches of new inventions. This drawing from his notebooks shows a design for a spiral screw to achieve vertical flight. Leonardo's drawing anticipated the helicopter.

Critical Thinking

1. **Draw Conclusions** How do the works of Renaissance artists and architects reflect Renaissance ideas? Explain.

2. **Synthesize** Look through books on architecture to find examples of American architects who were influenced by the architects and buildings of the Italian Renaissance. Share your findings with the class.

The Northern Renaissance

The Big Idea

In the 1400s, the ideas of the Italian Renaissance began to spread to northern Europe.

Why It Matters Now

Renaissance ideas such as the importance of the individual are an important part of modern thought.

Key Terms and People

utopia
William Shakespeare
Johann Gutenberg

Setting The Stage

The work of such artists as Leonardo da Vinci, Michelangelo, and Raphael showed the Renaissance spirit. All three artists demonstrated an interest in classical culture, a curiosity about the world, and a belief in human potential. Humanist writers expanded ideas about individuality. These ideas impressed scholars, students, and merchants who visited Italy. By the late 1400s, Renaissance ideas had spread to northern Europe—especially England, France, Germany, and Flanders (now part of France and the Netherlands).

The Northern Renaissance Begins

By 1450 the population of northern Europe, which had declined due to bubonic plague, was beginning to grow again. When the destructive Hundred Years' War between France and England ended in 1453, many cities grew rapidly. Urban merchants became wealthy enough to sponsor artists. This happened first in Flanders, which was rich from long-distance trade and the cloth industry. Then, as wealth increased in other parts of northern Europe, patronage of artists increased as well.

Unlike Italy, which was divided into city-states, England and France were unified under strong monarchs. These rulers often sponsored the arts by purchasing paintings and by supporting artists and writers. For example, Francis I of France invited Leonardo da Vinci to retire in France, and hired Italian artists and architects to rebuild and decorate his castle at Fontainebleau (fahn•tihn•BLOH). The castle became a showcase for Renaissance art.

As Renaissance ideas spread out of Italy, they mingled with northern traditions. As a result, the northern Renaissance developed its own character. For example, the Renaissance ideal of human dignity inspired some northern humanists to develop plans for social reform based on Judeo-Christian values.

Reading Check
Contrast How did the Northern Renaissance differ from the Italian Renaissance?

Artistic Ideas Spread

In 1494, a French king claimed the throne of Naples in southern Italy and launched an invasion through northern Italy. As the war dragged on, many Italian artists and writers left for a safer life in northern Europe. They brought with them the styles and techniques of the Italian Renaissance. In addition, northern European artists who studied in Italy carried Renaissance ideas back to their homelands.

German Painters Perhaps the most famous person to do this was the German artist Albrecht Dürer (DYUR·uhr). He traveled to Italy to study in 1494. After returning to Germany, Dürer produced woodcuts and engravings. Many of his prints portray religious subjects. Others portray classical myths or realistic landscapes. The popularity of Dürer's work helped to spread Renaissance styles.

Dürer's emphasis upon realism influenced the work of another German artist, Hans Holbein (HOHL·byn) the Younger. Holbein specialized in painting portraits that are almost photographic in detail. He emigrated to England where he painted portraits of King Henry VIII and other members of the English royal family.

Flemish Painters The support of wealthy merchant families in Flanders helped to make Flanders the artistic center of northern Europe. The first great Flemish Renaissance painter was Jan van Eyck (yahn van YK). Van Eyck used recently developed oil-based paints to develop techniques that painters still use. By applying layer upon layer of paint, van Eyck was able to create a variety of subtle colors in clothing and jewels. Oil painting became popular and spread to Italy.

In addition to new techniques, van Eyck's paintings display unusually realistic details and reveal the personality of their subjects. His work influenced later artists in northern Europe.

DOCUMENT-BASED INVESTIGATION   Historical Source

Peasant Wedding

The Flemish painter Pieter Bruegel's paintings provide information about peasant life in the 1500s. *Peasant Wedding* (1568) portrays a wedding feast.

- **The Bride** The bride sits under the paper crown hanging on the green cloth.

- **The Servers** Men who may be her brothers are passing out plates.

- **The Guests** Several children have come to the party.

- **The Musicians** They are carrying bagpipes. One glances hungrily at the food.

Analyze Historical Sources
In what ways does this painting present a snapshot of peasant life?

Reading Check
Summarize
What techniques did
Bruegel use to give life
to his paintings?

Flemish painting reached its peak after 1550 with the work of Pieter Bruegel (BROY•guhl) the Elder. Bruegel was also interested in realistic details and individual people. He was very skillful in portraying large numbers of people. He captured scenes from everyday peasant life such as weddings, dances, and harvests. Bruegel's rich colors, vivid details, and balanced use of space give a sense of life and feeling.

Northern Writers Try to Reform Society

Italian humanists were very interested in reviving classical languages and classical texts. When the Italian humanist ideas reached the north, people used them to examine the traditional teachings of the Church. The northern humanists were critical of the failure of the Christian Church to inspire people to live a Christian life. This criticism produced a new movement known as Christian humanism. The focus of Christian humanism was the reform of society. Of particular importance to humanists was education. The humanists promoted the education of women and founded schools attended by both boys and girls.

Christian Humanists The best known of the Christian humanists were Desiderius Erasmus (dehz•ih•DEER•ee•uhs ih•RAZ•muhs) of Holland and Thomas More of England. The two were close friends.

In 1509, Erasmus wrote his most famous work, *The Praise of Folly*. This book poked fun at greedy merchants, heartsick lovers, quarrelsome scholars, and pompous priests. Erasmus believed in a Christianity of the heart, not one of ceremonies or rules. He thought that in order to improve society, all people should study the Bible.

Thomas More tried to show a better model of society. In 1516, he wrote the book *Utopia*. In Greek, **utopia** means "no place." In English it has come to mean an ideal place as depicted in More's book. The book is about an imaginary land where greed, corruption, and war have been weeded out. In Utopia, because there was little greed, Utopians had little use for money:

"Gold and silver, of which money is made, are so treated . . . that no one values them more highly than their true nature deserves. Who does not see that they are far inferior to iron in usefulness since without iron mortals cannot live any more than without fire and water?"

—Thomas More, *Utopia*

More wrote in Latin. Eventually, his writing was translated into a variety of languages including French, German, English, Spanish, and Italian, making his ideas widely available.

Women's Reforms During this period the vast majority of Europeans were unable to read or write. Those families who could afford formal schooling usually sent only their sons. One woman spoke out against this practice. Christine de Pizan was highly educated for the time and was one

Christian humanist
Thomas More

Christine de Pizan is best known for her works defending women.

Reading Check
Analyze Issues
What kind of reform does de Pizan argue for?

of the first women to earn a living as a writer. Writing in French, she produced many books, including short stories, biographies, novels, and manuals on military techniques. She frequently wrote about the objections men had to educating women. In one book, *The Book of the City of Ladies*, she wrote:

> *"I am amazed by the opinion of some men who claim that they do not want their daughters, wives, or kinswomen to be educated because their mores [morals] would be ruined as a result. . . . Here you can clearly see that not all opinions of men are based on reason and that these men are wrong."*
>
> —Christine De Pizan, *The Book of the City of Ladies*

Christine de Pizan was one of the first European writers to question different treatment of boys and girls. However, her goal of formal education for children of both sexes would not be achieved for several centuries.

The Elizabethan Age

The Renaissance spread to England in the mid-1500s. The period was known as the Elizabethan Age, after Queen Elizabeth I. Elizabeth reigned from 1558 to 1603. She was well educated and spoke French, Italian, Latin, and Greek. She also wrote poetry and music. As queen she did much to support the development of English art and literature.

William Shakespeare The most famous writer of the Elizabethan Age was **William Shakespeare**. Many people regard him as the greatest playwright of all time. Shakespeare was born in 1564 in Stratford-upon-Avon, a small town about 90 miles northwest of London. By 1592 he was living in London and writing poems and plays, and soon he would be performing at the Globe Theater.

Like many Renaissance writers, Shakespeare revered the classics and drew on them for inspiration and plots. His works display a masterful command of the English language and a deep understanding of human beings. He revealed the souls of men and women through scenes of dramatic conflict. Many of these plays examine human flaws. However, Shakespeare also had one of his characters deliver a speech that expresses the Renaissance's high view of human nature:

> *"What a piece of work is a man, how noble in reason, how infinite in faculties, in form and moving, how express and admirable; in action how like an angel, in apprehension [understanding] how like a god: the beauty of the world, the paragon of animals."*
>
> —William Shakespeare, *Hamlet* (Act 2, Scene 2)

Reading Check
Summarize What are two ways in which Shakespeare's work showed Renaissance influences?

Shakespeare's most famous plays include the tragedies *Macbeth, Hamlet, Othello, Romeo and Juliet,* and *King Lear,* and the comedies *A Midsummer Night's Dream* and *The Taming of the Shrew.*

Shakespeare's Popularity

Even though he has been dead for about 400 years, Shakespeare remains a favorite with filmmakers. His themes have been adapted for many films, including some in foreign languages. These photos are from movie versions of some of Shakespeare's plays including *Othello* and *Romeo and Juliet* (in period costume); a Japanese film, *Ran*, an adaptation of *King Lear*; and *10 Things I Hate About You*, an adaptation of *The Taming of the Shrew* in a modern setting.

Printing Spreads Renaissance Ideas

The Chinese invented block printing in which a printer carved words or letters on a wooden block, inked the block, and then used it to print on paper. Around 1045, Bi Sheng invented movable type, which uses a separate piece of type for each character in the language. The Chinese writing system contains thousands of different characters, so most Chinese printers found movable type impractical. However, the method would prove practical for Europeans because their languages can be written using a small number of letters.

By the early 1400s in Europe, paper had replaced parchment, a writing material made from animal hides. Parchment was expensive and could not be mass-produced. Paper could be produced quickly and inexpensively. Its availability helped facilitate the printing of whole books.

Gutenberg Improves the Printing Process During the 13th century, block-printed items reached Europe from China. European printers began to use block printing to create whole pages to bind into books. However, this process was too slow to satisfy the Renaissance demand for knowledge, information, and books.

Around 1440 **Johann Gutenberg**, a craftsman from Mainz, Germany, developed a printing press that incorporated a number of technologies in a new way. The process made it possible to produce books quickly and cheaply. Using this improved process, Gutenberg printed a complete Bible, the Gutenberg Bible, in about 1455. It was the first full-sized book printed with movable type.

The printing press enabled a printer to produce hundreds of copies of a single work. For the first time, books were cheap enough that many people could buy them. At first printers produced mainly religious works. Soon they began to provide books on other subjects such as travel guides and medical manuals.

Reading Check
Analyze Effects
How did the invention of the printing press affect the dissemination of knowledge and ideas?

The Printing Press

Many inventions are creative combinations of known technologies. In 1452, Johann Gutenberg combined known technologies from Europe and Asia with his idea for molding movable type to create a printing press that changed the world.

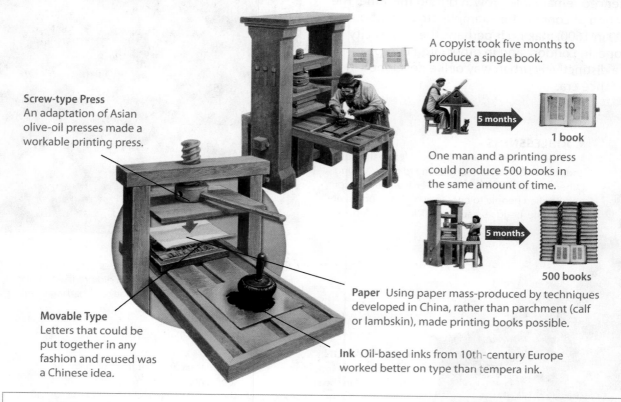

Screw-type Press
An adaptation of Asian olive-oil presses made a workable printing press.

Movable Type
Letters that could be put together in any fashion and reused was a Chinese idea.

A copyist took five months to produce a single book.

5 months → 1 book

One man and a printing press could produce 500 books in the same amount of time.

5 months → 500 books

Paper Using paper mass-produced by techniques developed in China, rather than parchment (calf or lambskin), made printing books possible.

Ink Oil-based inks from 10th-century Europe worked better on type than tempera ink.

Critical Thinking

1. **Draw Conclusions** About how many books could a printing press produce in a month?

2. **Make Inferences** Which areas of the world contributed ideas that were used in developing Gutenberg's printing press?

Lesson 3 Assessment

1. **Organize Information** Create a timeline showing key events of the Northern Renaissance.

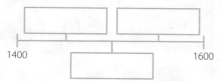

1400   1600

Which of the events listed do you think was most important? Explain.

2. **Key Terms and People** For each key term or person in the lesson, write a sentence explaining its significance.

3. **Form Generalizations** How did Albrecht Dürer's work reflect the influence of the Italian Renaissance?

4. **Analyze Effects** What was one way the Renaissance changed society?

5. **Compare** How were the paintings of the northern painters different from those of Flemish painters? Give examples.

6. **Analyze Motives** What reasons did humanists give for wanting to reform society? Explain.

CITY LIFE IN RENAISSANCE EUROPE

Throughout the 1500s, the vast majority of Europeans—more than 75 percent—lived in rural areas. However, the capital and port cities of most European countries experienced remarkable growth during this time. The population of London, for example, stood at about 200,000 in 1600, making it perhaps the largest city in Europe. In London, and in other large European cities, a distinctively urban way of life developed in the Renaissance era.

▼ JOBLESSNESS

Many newcomers to London struggled to find jobs and shelter. Some turned to crime to make a living. Others became beggars. However, it was illegal for able-bodied people to beg. To avoid a whipping or prison time, beggars had to be sick or disabled.

▲ ENTERTAINMENT

In Renaissance England, performances at playhouses were often wild affairs. If audiences did not like the play, they booed loudly, pelted the stage with garbage, and sometimes attacked the actors.

▼ SANITATION

This small pomander (POH•man•durh), a metal container filled with spices, was crafted in the shape of orange segments. Well-to-do Londoners held pomanders to their noses to shield themselves from the stench of the rotting garbage that littered the streets.

▼ FOOD

A typical meal for wealthy Londoners might include fish, several kinds of meat, bread, and a variety of vegetables, served on silver or pewter tableware. The diet of the poor was simpler. They rarely ate fish, meat, or cheese. Usually, their meals consisted of a pottage—a kind of soup—of vegetables. And the poor ate their meals from a trencher, a hollowed-out slab of stale bread or wood.

Critical Thinking

1. **Make Inferences** Study the images and captions, as well as the information in the tables. What inferences about the standard of living of London's wealthy citizens can you make from this information? How did it compare to the standard of living of London's common people?

2. **Compare** How does diet in the United States today compare to the diet of Renaissance Europeans? Cite specific examples in your answer.

▼ TRANSPORTATION

Many of London's streets were so narrow that walking was the only practical means of transportation. Often, however, the quickest way to get from here to there in the city was to take the river. Boat traffic was especially heavy when the playhouses were open. On those days, as many as 4,000 people crossed the Thames from the city to Southwark, where most of the theaters were located.

COST OF LIVING IN RENAISSANCE LONDON

These tables show what typical Londoners earned and spent in the late 1500s. The basic denominations in English currency at the time were the pound (£), the shilling, and the penny (12 pence equaled 1 shilling, and 20 shillings equaled 1 pound). The pound of the late 1500s is roughly equivalent to $400 in today's U.S. currency.

Typical Earnings

Merchant	£100 per year
Skilled Worker	£13 per year (about 5 shillings/week)
Unskilled Worker	£5 per year (about 4 pence/day)
Servant	£1 to £2 per year (plus food and lodging)

Typical Prices

Lodging	4 to 8 pence a week
Beef	3 pence per lb
Chickens	1 penny each
Eggs	2 pence per dozen
Apples	1 penny per dozen
Onions	1/2 penny a sack
Various Spices	10 to 11 shillings per lb

Renaissance Achievements

Setting the Stage

The ideas and innovations introduced during the Renaissance had far-reaching effects. The way people interacted with their world was profoundly altered. Some Renaissance innovations laid the foundation for global changes in the years that followed.

The Main Idea

The Renaissance was a period of striking achievements in many areas.

Why It Matters Now

The achievements of Renaissance artists, writers, scientists, and thinkers continue to affect people around the world today.

Key Terms and People

vernacular
skepticism

Cultural and Social Achievements

The European Renaissance was a period of great artistic and social change. It marked a break with the medieval ideals that were focused around the Church. The Renaissance belief in the dignity of the individual played a key role in the gradual rise of democratic ideas. Furthermore, the impact of the movable-type printing press was tremendous. Some historians have suggested that its effects were even more dramatic than the arrival of personal computers in the 20th century.

Changes in Art During the Renaissance, artistic styles changed as artists incorporated humanistic ideas in their work. Medieval artists had used religious subjects to convey a spiritual ideal, often arranging saints and Biblical figures in stiff groups. Renaissance painters often portrayed religious subjects, but they used a realistic style copied from classical models. They used light and shadow (called *chiaroscuro*) to give scenes added depth and fullness. As well as creating religious works, painters created secular works. Greek and Roman subjects also became popular.

New techniques and media also changed art. One important change was the introduction of paint that used oils as a binding agent. Earlier types of paint used binders such as eggs, which dry quickly. The longer drying time of oil paint meant artists could continue to add detail to a work for a longer period of time. A key technique was the use of perspective to show three dimensions on a flat surface.

Following the new emphasis on the individual, painters began to paint prominent citizens. These realistic portraits revealed what was distinctive about each person. In addition,

La Primavera, by Italian Renaissance painter Sandro Botticelli

artists used a realistic style when depicting the human body. Sculptors made sculpture more realistic by carving natural postures and expressions that reveal personality.

Changes in Literature Renaissance writers produced works that reflected their time, but they also used techniques that writers rely on today. Some followed the example of the medieval writer Dante. He wrote in the **vernacular**, or his native language, instead of Latin. Dante's native language was Italian. Writing in the vernacular meant that books could be read by anyone, not just people who had been taught Latin.

In addition, Renaissance writers wrote either for self-expression or to portray the individuality of their subjects. In these ways, writers of the Renaissance began trends that modern writers still follow.

Changes in Architecture The study of classical texts showed that the Greeks and Romans used ratios and proportions to give structure to their art. By focusing on ratios, or the relationships between numbers, Renaissance architects created designs that feel balanced and harmonious. Many cities, especially in Italy, are dominated by the impressive domes of Renaissance architecture. The Palladian style, inspired by the work of Andrea Palladio, influenced architecture throughout Europe and in the United States.

As the classical style spread to other countries, it was combined with local traditions. In France, architects combined classical style and French traditions to create a more elaborate French Renaissance style. This style

The dome on Florence's cathedral, built by Filippo Brunelleschi, is a marvel of engineering.

spread from western Europe through northern and central Europe. In Russia, which was strongly influenced by the Byzantines, the new ruler hired Italian architects and builders to rebuild Moscow. The resulting style was a blend of Italian, Byzantine, and Russian traditions. In Spain, during the centuries of Islamic rule, a style known as Moorish had developed. Elements of Moorish and classical style were combined to create a distinctive Spanish style, with intricately detailed surface ornamentation.

Changes in Society   The development of moveable type had a profound effect on society. Within a few years of the introduction of the printing press, the cost of books had fallen dramatically. More people had access to books, which prompted an increase in literacy rates. Also, printing made it easy for people to share new ideas. This facilitated some important changes and reforms in the early modern age as people began to challenge some of the structures of established religion and government.

Printing also made it easier to share new information and discoveries, which often led to further discoveries as other people built on what they read. The ability to print maps and charts made it possible for others to follow in the tracks of explorers.

Reading Check
Analyze Effects
How is the influence of Renaissance architecture seen today?

The Legacy of the Renaissance

The artists, writers, and thinkers of the Renaissance produced many extraordinary works that still command attention today. However, the Renaissance spirit led to still more advances in the decades that followed.

The Spirit of Inquiry One of the hallmarks of the Renaissance was a questioning attitude. People were no longer willing to blindly follow tradition and accept authority. They wanted to form their own opinions and make up their own minds. As Renaissance humanists rediscovered Greek philosophy, some were drawn by the tradition of **skepticism**. Where medieval thinkers accepted many ideas without questioning them, skepticism questioned everything. The practice of examining everything to check assumptions became part of the scientific method that transformed medicine, physics, and other branches of science. It also led to questions about religion and faith and prompted an upheaval within Christianity.

There was also an increased curiosity about the world. Over the course of the Crusades, thousands of Europeans traveled to the eastern Mediterranean. Crusaders who returned with silk and spices created a market for these items. Merchants addressed this market by extending their trade networks still further. Stories about far-away places made some people wonder what else was out there. As navigational tools improved, this curiosity led to the Age of Exploration.

Because of these fundamental changes, Renaissance ideas continued to have a profound influence on European thought in the decades that followed.

Reading Check
Draw Conclusions
How is the Renaissance emphasis on the individual connected to the renewed interest in skepticism?

Lesson 4 Assessment

1. **Organize Information** Use a cause-and-effect diagram like this one to identify three effects that developed from the Renaissance sense of inquiry.

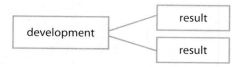

   Which effect do you consider most important? Explain.

2. **Key Terms and People** For each key term or person in the lesson, write a sentence explaining its significance.

3. **Form Generalizations** Explain how the increased availability of books affected the behavior of individuals and groups.

4. **Analyze Effects** What factors combined to make Europeans curious about other places?

5. **Contrast** How did Renaissance artists treat religious subjects differently from medieval painters?

Module 14 Assessment

Key Terms and People

For each term or name below, write a sentence explaining its connection to European history from 1300 to 1500.

1. Renaissance
2. vernacular
3. humanism
4. secular
5. patron
6. perspective
7. William Shakespeare
8. Johann Gutenberg

Main Ideas

Use your notes and the information in the module to answer the following questions.

Birth of the Renaissance

1. What economic factor promoted the growth of city-states in northern Italy?
2. What form of government dominated in western Europe during the Renaissance era?

The Italian Renaissance

3. How did merchants and nobles in northern Italy influence the Renaissance?
4. In what ways did literature and the arts change during the Renaissance?

The Northern Renaissance

5. How did the end of the Hundred Years' War and the French invasion of Italy promote the spread of Renaissance ideas?
6. How were the Christian humanist writers of the Northern Renaissance different from the humanist writers of the Italian Renaissance?

Renaissance Achievements

7. How did the intellectual and philosophical ideas of the Renaissance affect the way people viewed themselves and their place in the world?
8. How was European society as a whole affected by the development of the printing press?

Module 14 Assessment, continued

Critical Thinking

1. **Categorize** Create a web diagram to show the major influences on Renaissance thought.

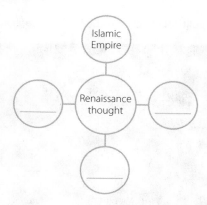

Which one do you think had the greatest influence? Explain.

2. **Analyze Effects** How did the Renaissance expand cultural interaction?

3. **Develop Historical Perspective** What conditions needed to exist before the Renaissance could occur?

4. **Synthesize** How did views of the role of women change in the Renaissance period?

Engage With History

Reread the quotation in Lesson 2 from Machiavelli's *The Prince*. Now that you have read the module, consider the quotation in the context of 15th-century Florence. Machiavelli saw a succession of rulers come and go in Florence. He lost his government position after the Medicis returned to power.

Think about the following questions:

- What opinion does Machiavelli present about people in general?
- Are these statements based on observations of human behavior, or are they assumptions?
- Do you think his advice would be useful to a ruler like Lorenzo de Medici?
- One reason Machiavelli wrote *The Prince* was in the hope of receiving a new post. Does this affect your opinion?

Discuss these questions with a small group.

Focus on Writing

How did the Renaissance revolutionize European art and thought? Support your opinions in a three-paragraph essay.

Multimedia Activity

Use the Internet to find information on the number of books published in print and those published electronically last year. Create a pie graph showing the results of your research.

Module 15

Reformation and Upheaval

Essential Question

What new ideas and values led to the Reformation, and what social and political effects did the Reformation cause?

About the Photo: In 1517 a Catholic monk named Martin Luther posted his "Ninety-Five Theses," criticizing the Roman Catholic Church.

In this module you will learn how the Protestant Reformation altered European society, how the Catholic Church responded to the Reformation, and how political and social unrest ensued.

▶ Explore ONLINE!

VIDEOS, including...
• Martin Luther Sparks a Revolution

HISTORY.

☑ Document Based Investigations

☑ Graphic Organizers

☑ Interactive Games

☑ Interactive Map: Religions in Europe, 1560

☑ Causes and Effects of the Reformation

What You Will Learn ...

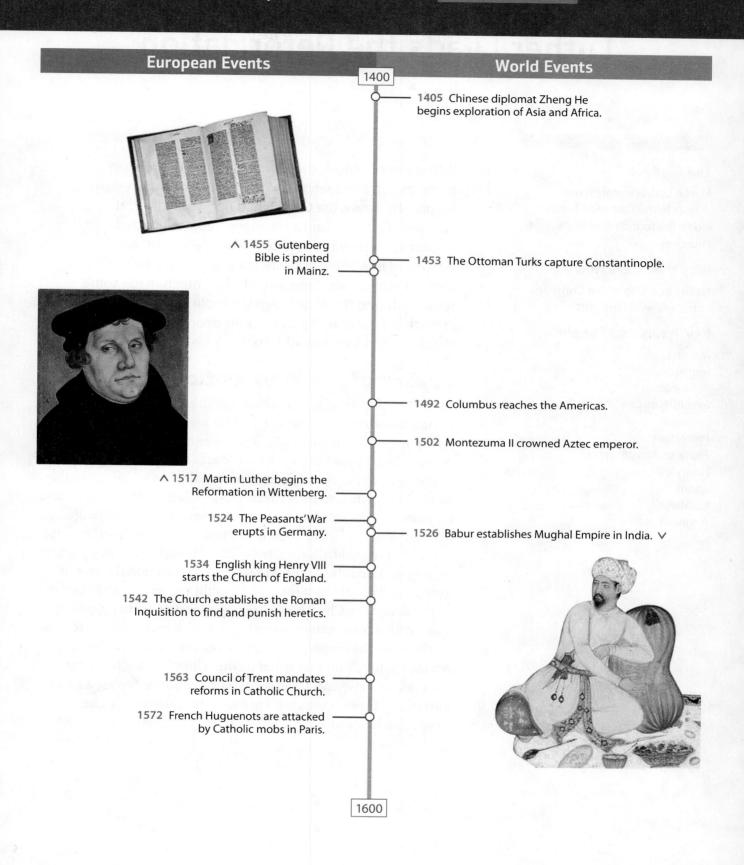

European Events | **World Events**

1400

1405 Chinese diplomat Zheng He begins exploration of Asia and Africa.

∧ **1455** Gutenberg Bible is printed in Mainz.

1453 The Ottoman Turks capture Constantinople.

1492 Columbus reaches the Americas.

1502 Montezuma II crowned Aztec emperor.

∧ **1517** Martin Luther begins the Reformation in Wittenberg.

1524 The Peasants' War erupts in Germany.

1526 Babur establishes Mughal Empire in India. ∨

1534 English king Henry VIII starts the Church of England.

1542 The Church establishes the Roman Inquisition to find and punish heretics.

1563 Council of Trent mandates reforms in Catholic Church.

1572 French Huguenots are attacked by Catholic mobs in Paris.

1600

Luther Leads the Reformation

Martin Luther's protest over abuses in the Catholic Church led to the founding of Protestant churches.

Why It Matters Now

Nearly one-fifth of the Christians in today's world are Protestants.

Key Terms and People

Martin Luther
indulgence
Reformation
excommunicate
Lutheran
Protestant
Peace of Augsburg
Henry VIII
annul
Elizabeth I
Anglican

Setting the Stage

By the tenth century, the Roman Catholic Church had come to dominate religious life in northern and western Europe. However, the Church had not won universal approval. Over the centuries, many people criticized its practices. They felt that Church leaders were too interested in worldly pursuits, such as gaining wealth and political power. Even though the Church made some reforms during the Middle Ages, people continued to criticize it. Prompted by the actions of one man, that criticism would lead to rebellion.

Causes of the Reformation

By 1500, additional forces weakened the Church. The Renaissance emphasis on the secular and the individual challenged Church authority. The invention of the printing press helped spread these secular ideas. The printing press was a new device that made printed material more widely available. At the same time, more writers and scholars began to write and translate works into the local vernacular, or common language, instead of using Latin. Together, these changes helped increase literacy, spiritual thinking, individual thought, and perspective among individuals. As individuals found commonalities, new groups of like thinkers formed. In addition, some rulers began to challenge the Church's political power. In Germany, which was divided into many competing states, it was difficult for the pope or the emperor to impose central authority. Finally, northern merchants resented paying church taxes to Rome. Spurred by these social, political, and economic forces, a new movement for religious reform began in Germany. It then swept much of Europe.

Causes of the Reformation

Social	Political	Economic	Religious
The Renaissance values of humanism and secularism led people to question the Church.	Powerful monarchs challenged the Church as the supreme power in Europe.	European princes and kings were jealous of the Church's wealth.	Some Church leaders had become worldly and corrupt.
The printing press was an effective tool that helped to spread ideas critical of the Church.	Many leaders viewed the pope as a foreign ruler and challenged his authority.	Merchants and others resented having to pay taxes to the Church.	Many people found Church practices such as the sale of indulgences unacceptable.

Criticisms of the Catholic Church Critics of the Church claimed that its leaders were corrupt. The popes who ruled during the Renaissance patronized the arts, spent extravagantly on personal pleasure, and fought wars. Pope Alexander VI, for example, admitted that he had fathered several children. Many popes were too busy pursuing worldly affairs to have much time for spiritual duties.

The lower clergy had problems as well. Many priests and monks were so poorly educated that they could scarcely read, let alone teach people. Others broke their priestly vows by marrying, and some drank to excess or gambled.

Early Calls for Reform Influenced by reformers, people had come to expect higher standards of conduct from priests and church leaders. In the late 1300s and early 1400s, John Wycliffe of England and Jan Hus of Bohemia had advocated Church reform. They denied that the pope had the right to worldly power. They also taught that the Bible had more authority than Church leaders did. In the 1500s, Christian humanists like Desiderius Erasmus and Thomas More added their voices to the chorus of criticism. In addition, many Europeans were reading religious works and forming their own opinions about the Church. The atmosphere in Europe was ripe for reform by the early 1500s.

Reading Check
Summarize
What practices of the Catholic Church in the 1500s might have disturbed ordinary churchgoers?

Luther Challenges the Church

Martin Luther's parents wanted him to be a lawyer. Instead, he became a monk and a teacher. From 1512 until his death, he taught scripture at the University of Wittenberg in the German state of Saxony. All he wanted was to be a good Christian, not to lead a religious revolution.

The 95 Theses In 1517, Luther decided to take a public stand against the actions of a friar named Johann Tetzel. Tetzel was raising money to rebuild St. Peter's Cathedral in Rome. He did this by selling indulgences. An **indulgence** was a pardon. It released a sinner from performing the

Martin Luther
(1483–1546)

In one way, fear led Luther to become a monk. At the age of 21, Luther was caught in a terrible thunderstorm. Convinced he would die, he cried out, "Saint Anne, help me! I will become a monk."

Even after entering the monastery, Luther felt fearful, lost, sinful, and rejected by God. He confessed his sins regularly, fasted, and did penance. However, by studying the Bible, Luther came to the conclusion that faith alone was the key to salvation. Only then did he experience peace.

penalty that a priest imposed for sins. Indulgences were not supposed to affect God's right to judge. Tetzel gave people the impression that by buying indulgences, they could buy their way into heaven.

Luther was troubled by Tetzel's tactics. In response, he wrote 95 theses, or formal statements, attacking the "pardon-merchants." On October 31, 1517, he posted these statements on the door of the castle church in Wittenberg and invited other scholars to debate him. Someone copied Luther's words and took them to a printer. With the support of the printing press, Luther's name and ideas soon were advertised to people and groups all over Germany. His actions began the **Reformation**, a movement for religious reform. It led to the founding of Christian churches that did not accept the pope's authority.

Luther's Teachings Soon Luther went beyond criticizing indulgences. He wanted full reform of the Church. His teachings rested on three main ideas:

- People could win salvation only by faith in God's gift of forgiveness. The Church taught that faith and "good works" were needed for salvation.
- All Church teachings should be clearly based on the words of the Bible. Both the pope and Church traditions were false authorities.
- All people with faith were equal. Therefore, people did not need priests to interpret the Bible for them.

The Response to Luther

Luther was astonished at how rapidly his ideas spread and attracted followers. Many people had been unhappy with the Church for political and economic reasons. They saw Luther's protests as a way to challenge Church control.

Reading Check
Summarize What were the main points of Luther's teachings?

The Pope's Threat Initially, Church officials in Rome viewed Luther simply as a rebellious monk who needed to be punished by his superiors. However, as Luther's ideas became more popular, the pope realized that this monk was a serious threat. In one angry reply to Church criticism, Luther actually suggested that Christians drive the pope from the Church by force.

In 1520, Pope Leo X issued a decree threatening Luther with excommunication unless he took back his statements. Luther did not take back a word. Instead, his students at Wittenberg gathered around a bonfire and cheered as he threw the pope's decree into the flames. Leo **excommunicated** Luther.

The Emperor's Opposition Holy Roman Emperor Charles V, a devout Catholic, also opposed Luther's teaching. Charles controlled a vast empire, including the German states. He summoned Luther to the town of Worms (vawrmz) in 1521 to stand trial. Charles V told Luther to recant, or take back his statements, but Luther refused:

> *"I am bound by the Scriptures I have quoted and my conscience is captive to the Word of God. I cannot and I will not retract anything, since it is neither safe nor right to go against conscience. I cannot do otherwise, here I stand, may God help me. Amen."*
>
> —Martin Luther, quoted in *The Protestant Reformation* by Lewis W. Spitz

A month after Luther made that speech, Charles issued an imperial order, the Edict of Worms. It declared Luther an outlaw and a heretic because what he believed went against the teachings of the Church. According to this edict, no one in the empire was to give Luther food or shelter. All his books were to be burned. However, Prince Frederick the Wise of Saxony disobeyed the emperor. For almost a year after the trial, he sheltered Luther in one of his castles. While there, Luther translated the New Testament into German.

Luther returned to Wittenberg in 1522. There he discovered that many of his ideas were already being put into practice. Instead of continuing to seek reforms in the Catholic Church, Luther and his followers had become a separate religious group, called **Lutherans**.

Many northern German princes supported Lutheranism. While some princes genuinely shared Luther's beliefs, others liked Luther's ideas for selfish reasons. They saw his teachings as a good excuse to seize Church property and to assert their independence from Charles V.

In 1529, German princes who remained loyal to the pope agreed to join forces against Luther's ideas. Those princes who supported Luther signed a protest against that agreement. These protesting princes came to be known as Protestants. Eventually, the term **Protestant** was applied to Christians who were not Roman Catholic or Eastern Orthodox.

Reading Check
Analyze Causes
Why did Luther's ideas appeal to many northern German princes?

Protestantism

Protestantism is a branch of Christianity that developed out of the Reformation. Three distinct branches of Protestantism emerged at first: Lutheranism, based on the teachings of Martin Luther in Germany; Calvinism, based on the teachings of John Calvin in Switzerland; and Anglicanism, established by King Henry VIII in England. Protestantism spread throughout Europe in the 16th century and, later, the world. As differences in beliefs developed, new denominations formed.

THE DIVISION OF CHRISTIANITY

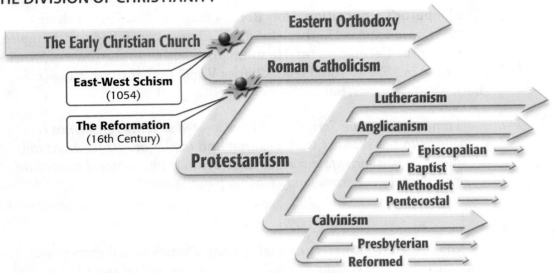

Religious Beliefs and Practices in the 16th Century

	Roman Catholicism	Lutheranism	Calvinism	Anglicanism
Leadership	Pope is head of the Church	Ministers lead congregations	Council of elders govern each church	English monarch is head of the Church
Salvation	Salvation by faith and good works	Salvation by faith alone	God has predetermined who will be saved	Salvation by faith alone
Bible	Church and Bible tradition are sources of revealed truth	Bible is sole source of revealed truth	Bible is sole source of revealed truth	Bible is sole source of revealed truth
Worship Service	Worship service based on ritual	Worship service focused on preaching and ritual	Worship service focused on preaching	Worship service based on ritual and preaching
Interpretation of Beliefs	Priests interpret Bible and Church teachings for believers	Believers interpret the Bible for themselves	Believers interpret the Bible for themselves	Believers interpret the Bible using tradition and reason

Critical Thinking

1. **Compare and Contrast** Which of the branches on the chart are most different and which are most similar?

2. **Analyze Effects** Select a Protestant denomination not shown on this page. Research it and write a paragraph tracing its roots to the Reformation.

Religious Adherents in the United States:

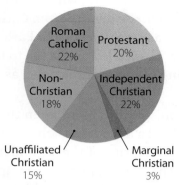

Roman Catholic 22%
Protestant 20%
Non-Christian 18%
Independent Christian 22%
Unaffiliated Christian 15%
Marginal Christian 3%

Sources: *Britannica Book of the Year 2010*

MEMBERSHIP:

- Nearly 400 million Protestants worldwide
- About 65 million Protestants in the United States

BRANCHES:

- More than 465 major Protestant denominations worldwide
- Major denominational families worldwide: Anglican, Assemblies of God, Baptist, Methodist, Lutheran, and Presbyterian
- More than 250 denominations in the United States
- About 40 denominations with more than 400,000 members each in the United States

Still determined that his subjects should remain Catholic, Charles V went to war against the Protestant princes. Even though he defeated them in 1547, he failed to force them back into the Catholic Church. In 1555, Charles, weary of fighting, ordered all German princes, both Protestant and Catholic, to assemble in the city of Augsburg. There the princes agreed that each ruler would decide the religion of his state. This famous religious settlement was known as the **Peace of Augsburg**.

England Becomes Protestant

The Catholic Church soon faced another great challenge to its authority, this time in England. Unlike Luther, the man who broke England's ties to the Roman Catholic Church did so for political and personal reasons, not religious ones.

Henry VIII Wants a Son When **Henry VIII** became king of England in 1509, he was a devout Catholic. Indeed, in 1521, Henry wrote a stinging attack on Luther's ideas. In recognition of Henry's support, the pope gave him the title "Defender of the Faith." Political needs, however, soon tested his religious loyalty. He needed a male heir. Henry's father had become king after a long civil war. Henry feared that a similar war would start if he died without a son as his heir. He and his wife, Catherine of Aragon, had one living child—a daughter, Mary—but no woman had ever successfully claimed the English throne.

By 1527, Henry was convinced that the 42-year-old Catherine would have no more children. He wanted to divorce her and take a younger queen. Church law did not allow divorce. However, the pope could **annul**, or set aside, Henry's marriage if proof could be found that it had never been legal in the first place. In 1527, Henry asked the pope to annul his marriage, but the pope turned him down. The pope did not want to offend Catherine's powerful nephew, the Holy Roman Emperor Charles V.

The Reformation Parliament Henry took steps to solve his marriage problem himself. In 1529, he called Parliament into session and asked it to pass a set of laws that ended the pope's power in England. This Parliament is known as the Reformation Parliament.

In 1533, Henry secretly married Anne Boleyn (BUL·ihn), who was in her twenties. Shortly after, Parliament legalized Henry's divorce from Catherine. In 1534, Henry's break with the pope was completed when Parliament voted to approve the Act of Supremacy. This called on people to take an oath recognizing the divorce and accepting Henry, not the pope, as the official head of England's Church.

The Act of Supremacy met some opposition. Thomas More, even though he had strongly criticized the Church, remained a devout Catholic. His faith, he said, would not allow him to accept the terms of the act and he refused to take the oath. In response, Henry had him arrested and imprisoned in the Tower of London. In 1535, More was found guilty of high treason and executed.

Consequences of Henry's Changes Henry did not immediately get the male heir he sought. After Anne Boleyn gave birth to a daughter, Elizabeth, she fell out of Henry's favor. Eventually, she was charged with treason. Like Thomas More, she was imprisoned in the Tower of London. She was found guilty and beheaded in 1536. Almost at once, Henry took a third wife, Jane Seymour. In 1537, she gave him a son named Edward. Henry's happiness was tempered by his wife's death just two weeks later. Henry married three more times. None of these marriages, however, produced children.

After Henry's death in 1547, each of his three children ruled England in turn. This created religious turmoil. Henry's son, Edward, became king when he was just nine years old. Too young to rule alone, Edward VI was

Henry VIII Causes Religious Turmoil

Henry's many marriages led to conflict with the Catholic Church and the founding of the Church of England.

1529
Henry summons the Reformation Parliament; dismantling of pope's power in England begins.

1534
Act of Supremacy names Henry and his successors supreme head of the English Church.

1509
Henry VIII becomes king; marries Catherine of Aragon.

1516
Daughter Mary is born.

1527
Henry asks the pope to end his first marriage; the pope refuses.

1510

1520

1530

1531
Parliament recognizes Henry as head of the Church.

1533
Parliament places clergy under Henry's control; Henry divorces Catherine, marries Anne Boleyn (at left); daughter Elizabeth born.

guided by adult advisers. These men were devout Protestants, and they introduced Protestant reforms to the English Church. Almost constantly in ill health, Edward reigned for just six years. Mary, the daughter of Catherine of Aragon, took the throne in 1553. She was a Catholic who returned the English Church to the rule of the pope. Her efforts met with considerable resistance, and she had many Protestants executed. When Mary died in 1558, Elizabeth, Anne Boleyn's daughter, inherited the throne.

Elizabeth Restores Protestantism **Elizabeth I** was determined to return her kingdom to Protestantism. In 1559, Parliament followed Elizabeth's wishes and set up the Church of England, or **Anglican** Church, with Elizabeth as its head. This was to be the only legal church in England.

Elizabeth decided to establish a state church that moderate Catholics and moderate Protestants might both accept. To please Protestants, priests in the Church of England were allowed to marry. They could deliver sermons in English, not Latin. To please Catholics, the Church of England kept some of the trappings of the Catholic service such as rich robes. In addition, church services were revised to be somewhat more acceptable to Catholics.

Elizabeth Faces Other Challenges By taking this moderate approach, Elizabeth brought a level of religious peace to England. Religion, however, remained a problem. Some Protestants pushed for Elizabeth to make more far-reaching church reforms. At the same time, some Catholics tried to overthrow Elizabeth and replace her with her cousin, the Catholic Mary, Queen of Scots. Elizabeth also faced threats from Philip II, the Catholic king of Spain.

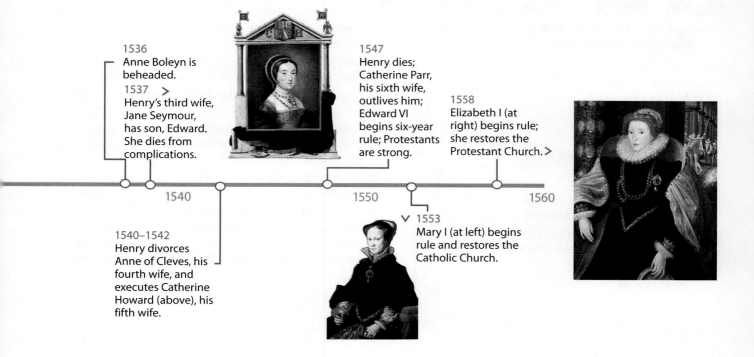

1536
Anne Boleyn is beheaded.

1537 >
Henry's third wife, Jane Seymour, has son, Edward. She dies from complications.

1540–1542
Henry divorces Anne of Cleves, his fourth wife, and executes Catherine Howard (above), his fifth wife.

1547
Henry dies; Catherine Parr, his sixth wife, outlives him; Edward VI begins six-year rule; Protestants are strong.

1558
Elizabeth I (at right) begins rule; she restores the Protestant Church. >

1553
Mary I (at left) begins rule and restores the Catholic Church.

1540   1550   1560

Reading Check
Analyze Effects
How did Henry VIII's marriages and divorces cause religious turmoil in England?

Elizabeth faced other difficulties. Money was one problem. In the late 1500s, the English began to think about building an American empire as a new source of income. While colonies strengthened England economically, they did not enrich the queen directly. Elizabeth's constant need for money would carry over into the next reign and lead to bitter conflict between the monarch and Parliament. In the meantime, the Reformation gained ground in other European countries.

— BIOGRAPHY —

Elizabeth I
(1533–1603)

Elizabeth I, like her father, had a robust nature and loved physical activity. She had a particular passion for dancing. Her fondness for exercise diminished little with age, and she showed amazing energy and strength well into her sixties.

Elizabeth resembled her father in character and temperament. She was stubborn, strong-willed, and arrogant, and she expected to be obeyed without question. Elizabeth also had a fierce and unpredictable temper. To her subjects, Elizabeth was an object of both fear and love. She was their "most dread sovereign lady."

Lesson 1 Assessment

1. **Organize Information** Make a chart and record the effects of Martin Luther's protests.

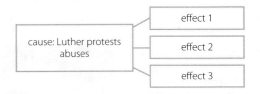

Which effect do you think had the greatest impact? Why?

2. **Key Terms and People** For each key term or person in the lesson, write a sentence explaining its significance.

3. **Summarize** What political, economic, and social factors helped bring about the Reformation?

4. **Find the Main Ideas** From where did the term *Protestantism* originate?

5. **Analyze Effects** What impact did Henry VIII's actions have on England in the second half of the 1500s?

6. **Draw Conclusions** Explain how Elizabeth I was able to bring a level of religious peace to England.

7. **Compare** Do you think Luther or Henry VIII had a better reason to break with the Church? Provide details to support your answer.

8. **Analyze Motives** How did the Catholic Church respond to Luther's teachings? Explain your answer.

9. **Develop Historical Perspective** Imagine Martin Luther and a leader of the Catholic Church are squaring off in a public debate about the Protestant Reformation. Write a brief **dialogue** between the two.

The Reformation Continues

The Big Idea

Protestant reformers were divided over beliefs, and split into several new Protestant groups.

Why It Matters Now

Many Protestant churches began during this period.

Key Terms and People

Huldrych Zwingli
John Calvin
predestination
Calvinism
theocracy
John Knox
Presbyterian
Anabaptist

Setting the Stage

Under the leadership of Queen Elizabeth I, the Anglican Church, though Protestant, remained similar to the Catholic Church in many of its doctrines and ceremonies. Meanwhile, other forms of Protestantism were developing elsewhere in Europe. Martin Luther had launched the Reformation in northern Germany, but reformers were at work in other countries. In Switzerland, another major branch of Protestantism emerged. Based mainly on the teachings of John Calvin, a French follower of Luther, it promoted unique ideas about the relationship between people and God.

Calvin Continues the Reformation

Religious reform in Switzerland was begun by **Huldrych Zwingli** (HUL•drykh-ZWIHNG•lee), a Catholic priest in Zurich. He was influenced both by the Christian humanism of Erasmus and by the reforms of Luther. In 1520, Zwingli openly attacked abuses in the Catholic Church. He called for a return to the more personal faith of early Christianity. He also wanted believers to have more control over the Church.

Zwingli's reforms were adopted in Zurich and other cities. In 1531, a bitter war between Swiss Protestants and Catholics broke out. During the fighting, Zwingli met his death. Meanwhile, **John Calvin**, then a young law student in France with a growing interest in Church doctrine, began to clarify his religious beliefs.

John Calvin (1509–1564)

A quiet boy, Calvin grew up to study law and philosophy at the University of Paris. In the 1530s, he was influenced by French followers of Luther. When King Francis I ordered Protestants arrested, Calvin fled. Eventually, he moved to Geneva.

Because Calvin and his followers rigidly regulated morality in Geneva, Calvinism is often described as strict and grim. But Calvin taught that people should enjoy God's gifts. He wrote that it should not be "forbidden to laugh, or to enjoy food, or to add new possessions to old."

Calvin Formalizes Protestant Ideas When Martin Luther posted his 95 theses in 1517, John Calvin had been only eight years old. But Calvin grew up to have as much influence in the spread of Protestantism as Luther did. He would give order to the faith Luther had begun.

In 1536, Calvin published *Institutes of the Christian Religion*. This book expressed ideas about God, salvation, and human nature. It was a summary of Protestant theology, or religious beliefs. Calvin wrote that men and women are sinful by nature. Taking Luther's idea that humans cannot earn salvation, Calvin went on to say that God chooses a very few people to save. Calvin called these few the "elect." He believed that God has known since the beginning of time who will be saved. This doctrine is called **predestination**. The religion based on Calvin's teachings is called **Calvinism**.

Calvin Leads the Reformation in Switzerland Calvin believed that the ideal government was a **theocracy**, a government controlled by religious leaders. In 1541, Protestants in Geneva, Switzerland, asked Calvin to lead their city.

When Calvin arrived there in the 1540s, Geneva was a self-governing city of about 20,000 people. He and his followers ran the city according to strict rules. Everyone attended religion class. No one wore bright clothing or played card games. Authorities would imprison, excommunicate, or banish those who broke such rules. Anyone who preached different doctrines might be burned at the stake. Yet, to many Protestants, Calvin's Geneva was a model city of highly moral citizens.

Spreading Ideas

In *Reformation Europe*, published in 1963, historian G. R. Elton noted the role of geography and trade in the spread of Reformation ideas.

Analyze Historical Sources
Why was Germany's location important to the spread of Reformation ideas?

> "Could the Reformation have spread so far and so fast if it had started anywhere but in Germany? The fact that it had its beginnings in the middle of Europe made possible a very rapid radiation in all directions. . . . Germany's position at the center of European trade also helped greatly. German merchants carried not only goods but Lutheran ideas and books to Venice and France; the north German Hanse [a trade league] transported the Reformation to the Scandinavian countries."
>
> —G. R. Elton, from *Reformation Europe*

Calvinism Spreads One admiring visitor to Geneva was a Scottish preacher named **John Knox**. When he returned to Scotland in 1559, Knox put Calvin's ideas to work. Each community church was governed by a group of laymen called elders or presbyters (PREHZ•buh•tuhrs). Followers of Knox became known as **Presbyterians**. In the 1560s, Protestant nobles led by Knox made Calvinism Scotland's official religion. They also deposed their Catholic ruler, Mary, Queen of Scots, in favor of her infant son, James.

Elsewhere, Swiss, Dutch, and French reformers adopted the Calvinist form of church organization. One reason Calvin is considered so influential is that many Protestant churches today trace their roots to Calvin. Over the years, however, many of them have softened Calvin's strict teachings.

Reading Check
Compare
How did Calvin's ideas about salvation differ from those of Luther?

Other Protestant Reformers

Protestants taught that the Bible is the source of all religious truth and that people should read it to discover those truths. As Christians interpreted the Bible for themselves, new Protestant groups formed over differences in belief.

The Anabaptists One such group baptized only those persons who were old enough to decide to be Christian. They said that persons who had been baptized as children should be rebaptized as adults. These believers were called **Anabaptists**, from a Greek word meaning "baptize again." The Anabaptists also taught that church and state should be separate, and they refused to fight in wars. They shared their possessions.

Viewing Anabaptists as radicals who threatened society, both Catholics and Protestants persecuted them. In 1533, some fled and settled in Münster, Westphalia, in Germany. Among them were Jan Mathijs and

Religions in Europe, 1560

Dominant Religion
- Roman Catholic
- Lutheran
- Anglican
- Calvinist
- Eastern Orthodox
- Islam
- Mixture of Calvinist, Lutheran, and Roman Catholic

Minority Religion
- Roman Catholic
- Lutheran
- Calvinist
- Islam
- Anabaptist

Spread of Protestantism

Spread of Religion
- Lutheran
- Anglican
- Calvinist

Interpret Maps

1. **Region** Which European countries became mostly Protestant and which remained mostly Roman Catholic?

2. **Location** Judging from the way the religions were distributed, where would you expect religious conflicts to take place? Explain.

John of Leiden, who led the persecution of all non-Anabaptists there. An army comprised of Catholics and Protestants surrounded and later captured the city in 1535. But the Anabaptists survived and became the forerunners of the Mennonites and the Amish. Later, descendants of these people settled in Pennsylvania. Their teaching influenced the later Quakers and Baptists, groups who split from the Anglican Church.

Women's Role in the Reformation Many women played prominent roles in the Reformation, especially during the early years. For example, the sister of King Francis I, Marguerite of Navarre, protected John Calvin from being executed for his beliefs while he lived in France. Other noblewomen also protected reformers. The wives of some reformers, too, had influence. Katherina Zell, married to Matthew Zell of Strasbourg, once scolded a minister for speaking harshly of another reformer. The minister responded by saying that she had "disturbed the peace." Katherina Zell answered the minister's criticism toward the reformer sharply:

> *"Do you call this disturbing the peace that instead of spending my time in frivolous amusements I have visited the plague-infested and carried out the dead? I have visited those in prison and under sentence of death. Often for three days and three nights I have neither eaten nor slept. I have never mounted the pulpit, but I have done more than any minister in visiting those in misery."*
>
> —Katherina Zell, quoted in *Women of the Reformation*

Although Catholic, Marguerite of Navarre supported the call for reform in the Church.

Katherina von Bora played a more typical, behind-the-scenes role as Luther's wife. Katherina had been sent to a convent at about age ten and became a nun. Inspired by Luther's teaching, she fled the convent. After marrying Luther, Katherina had six children. She also managed the family finances, fed all who visited their house, and supported her husband's work. She respected Luther's position but argued with him about woman's equal role in marriage.

As Protestant religions became more firmly established, their organization became more formal. Male religious leaders narrowly limited women's activities to the home and discouraged them from being leaders in the church. In fact, it was Luther who said, "God's highest gift on earth is a pious, cheerful, God-fearing, home-keeping wife."

Now and Then

Martin Luther's criticisms of the Catholic Church grew sharper over time. In recent times, historians have focused more on analyzing the political, social, and economic conditions that contributed to the Reformation. Read the primary source from Martin Luther in Lesson 1 and this secondary source. Discuss them with a partner to evaluate their credibility and perspective based on when they were written.

"*Beginning as a protest against arbitrary, self-aggrandizing, hierarchical authority in the person of the pope, the Reformation came to be closely identified in the minds of contemporaries with what we today might call states' rights or local control. To many townspeople and villagers, Luther seemed a godsend for their struggle to remain politically free and independent; they embraced his Reformation as a conserving political force, even though they knew it threatened to undo traditional religious beliefs and practices.*"

—Steven Ozment in *Protestants: The Birth of a Revolution* (1992)

Lesson 2 Assessment

1. **Organize Information** How did ideas of reformers who came after Luther help shape beliefs during the Protestant Reformation?

Zwingli	
Calvin	
Knox	
Anabaptists	

2. **Key Terms and People** For each key term or person in the lesson, write a sentence explaining its significance.

3. **Draw Conclusions** How did the Reformation set the stage for the modern world? Give examples.

4. **Find Main Ideas** What was Calvin's idea of the "elect" and their place in society?

5. **Contrast** How were the Anabaptists different from other Protestant groups in their political views?

6. **Summarize** What role did noblewomen play in the Reformation?

The Catholic Reformation

The Big Idea

The Catholic Church made reforms in response to the Protestant Reformation.

Why It Matters Now

Many Catholic schools are the result of reforms in the Church.

Key Terms and People

Catholic Reformation
Ignatius of Loyola
Jesuits
Council of Trent
heretic
nation-state

Setting the Stage

Protestant reformers were not the only ones who were dissatisfied with the state of the Catholic Church. Even before Martin Luther posted his 95 Theses, some Catholics had been working toward reform of the Church itself.

Early Reformers

While Protestant churches won many followers, millions remained true to Catholicism. Helping Catholics to remain loyal was a movement within the Catholic Church to reform itself. This movement is now known as the **Catholic Reformation**. Historians once referred to it as the Counter-Reformation. Important leaders in this movement included reformers such as Girolamo Savonarola (sahv•oh•nuh•ROH•luh) and **Ignatius of Loyola** (ihg•NAY•shuhs), who founded new religious orders. Two popes, Paul III and Paul IV, took actions to reform and renew the Church from within.

Girolamo Savonarola and Ignatius of Loyola A monk named Girolamo Savonarola was one of the first reformers to try to change the church from within. During the late 1400s, he preached fiery sermons against the abuses of the church. He called for churches to melt down their gold and silver ornaments to buy bread for the hungry and poor members of the church. Savonarola convinced people to gather and burn jewelry and trinkets. This enormous fire was known as "the bonfire of the vanities." Pope Alexander at first allowed Savonarola's work but eventually excommunicated him for spreading ideas that the pope considered dangerous. In 1498, Savonarola was executed in Florence.

Church leaders consult on reforms at the Council of Trent in this 16th-century painting.

Ignatius grew up in his father's castle in Loyola, Spain. The great turning point in his life came in 1521 when he was injured in a war. While recovering, he thought about his past sins and about the life of Jesus. His daily devotions, he believed, cleansed his soul. In 1522, Ignatius began writing a book called *Spiritual Exercises* that laid out a day-by-day plan of meditation, prayer, and study.

For the next 18 years, Ignatius gathered followers. In 1540, the pope created a religious order for his followers called the Society of Jesus. Members were called **Jesuits** (JEHZH•oo•ihts). The Jesuits focused on three activities. First, they founded schools throughout Europe. Jesuit teachers were well trained in both classical studies and theology. The Jesuits' second mission was to convert non-Christians to Catholicism. So they sent out missionaries around the world. Their third goal was to stop the spread of Protestantism. The zeal of the Jesuits overcame the drift toward Protestantism in Poland and southern Germany.

Reforming Popes Two popes took the lead in reforming the Catholic Church. Paul III, pope from 1534 to 1549, took four important steps. First, he directed a council of cardinals to investigate indulgence selling and other abuses in the Church. Second, he approved the Jesuit order. Third, he used the Inquisition to seek out heresy in papal territory. The Inquisition was a Roman Catholic tribunal for investigating and prosecuting charges of heresy. This sometimes extended to targeting specific groups such as Jews. Fourth, and most important, he called a council of Church leaders to meet in Trent, in northern Italy.

From 1545 to 1563, at the **Council of Trent**, Catholic bishops and cardinals agreed on several doctrines:

- The Church's interpretation of the Bible was final. Any Christian who substituted his or her own interpretation was a **heretic** (a person accused of having a religious belief that was contrary to the official teachings of the Church).
- Christians needed faith and good works for salvation. They were not saved by faith alone, as Luther argued.
- The Bible and Church tradition were equally powerful authorities for guiding Christian life.
- Indulgences were valid expressions of faith, but the selling of indulgences was banned.

The next pope, Paul IV, vigorously carried out the council's decrees. In 1559, he had officials draw up a list of books considered dangerous to the Catholic faith. This list was known as the Index of Forbidden Books. Catholic bishops throughout Europe were ordered to gather up the offensive books (including Protestant Bibles) and burn them in bonfires. In Venice alone, followers burned 10,000 books in one day.

Reading Check
Summarize What reforms were passed by the Council of Trent?

Global Patterns

Jesuit Missionaries

The work of Jesuit missionaries has had a lasting impact around the globe. By the time Ignatius died in 1556, about a thousand Jesuits had brought his ministry to Europe, Africa, Asia, and the Americas. Two of the most famous Jesuit missionaries of the 1500s were Francis Xavier, who worked in India and Japan, and Matteo Ricci, who worked in China.

One reason the Jesuits had such an impact is that they founded schools throughout the world. For example, the Jesuits today run about 45 high schools and 28 colleges and universities in the United States. Four of these are Georgetown University, Boston College, Marquette University, and Loyola University of Chicago.

Women Reformers

During the Renaissance, many women in religious orders began to take on more active roles in the Church. Most of them lived together in convents that were secluded, but by the late Middle Ages it was acceptable for nuns to help and work among the poor, orphaned, or sick.

Teresa of Avila Perhaps the most famous female spiritual leader was Teresa of Avila. Born in Spain in 1515, Teresa decided to become a nun around the age of 20. Her father opposed her plan, but Teresa ran away to a convent around 1536. At the convent, after deciding that the practices were too lax, she followed her own strict rules regarding fasting, prayer, and sleep. Eventually the church gave her permission to reform the Carmelite order. Teresa's deep spirituality, reported visions of Jesus, and fervor for the Catholic faith inspired many would-be Protestants to remain in the church.

Other Women Leaders Many other women had a profound and important influence during the Catholic Reformation through their work with the Church. In 1535 Italian nun Angela Merici began the Company of Saint Ursula, an order of women dedicated to teaching girls. Jane of Chantal and Francis of Sales cofounded the Visitation of Holy Mary order, which trained women to be teachers. Mary Ward of England began a network of schools for girls throughout Europe. At first her work was denounced by anti-Jesuits and the church because Ward's ideas about women were considered dangerously new. Later, however, her missionary influence was formally recognized by the Church.

Teresa of Avila

**Reading Check
Compare and
Contrast** How did
the influence of
women and men
differ during the
Catholic Reformation?

The Legacy of the Reformation

The Reformation had an enduring impact. Through its religious, social, and political effects, the Reformation set the stage for the modern world. It also ended the Christian unity of Europe and left it culturally divided.

Religious and Social Effects of the Reformation Despite religious wars and persecutions, Protestant churches flourished and new denominations developed. The Roman Catholic Church itself became more unified as a result of the reforms started at the Council of Trent. Both Catholics and Protestants realized the role that education served as a way to promote their beliefs. This led to the founding of parish schools and new colleges and universities throughout Europe.

Some women reformers had hoped to see the status of women in the Church and society improve as a result of the Reformation. But their status remained the same under both Protestantism and Roman Catholicism. Women were still mainly limited to the concerns of home and family.

Political Effects of the Reformation As the Catholic Church's moral and political authority declined, individual monarchs and states gained power. This led to the development of modern **nation-states**. In the 1600s, rulers of nation-states would seek more power for themselves and their countries through warfare, exploration, and expansion.

Questioning of beliefs and authority during the Reformation also laid the groundwork for the Enlightenment. This intellectual movement would sweep Europe in the late 18th century. It led some to reject all religions and others to call for the overthrow of existing governments.

Reading Check
Analyze Effects
What were the effects of the Reformation, and which one had the most lasting impact?

Lesson 3 Assessment

1. **Organize Information** Make a chart similar to the one below. Show key Catholic reforms that were made during the Catholic Reformation and their effects.

Catholic Reform	Effect

2. **Key Terms and People** For each key term or person in the lesson, write a sentence explaining its significance.

3. **Analyze Effects** How did the Council of Trent help to reform the Catholic Church?

4. **Summarize** What were the goals of the Jesuits?

5. **Compare** How did the steps taken by Paul III and Paul IV to reform the Catholic Church differ from Protestant reforms? Support your answer with details from the text.

6. **Analyze Causes** What caused women's roles to change in the Catholic Church during and after the Counter-Reformation?

7. **Evaluate** Were the effects of the Protestant and Catholic reformations mostly positive or negative with regard to their social, religious, and political impact? Explain your answer.

Social Unrest

The Big Idea

The Protestant and Catholic reformations caused tremendous political and social unrest throughout Europe.

Why It Matters Now

Nation-states that rose as a result of the Protestant Reformation became many of the leading countries in Europe today.

Key Terms and People

Inquisition
heresy
Huguenots

Setting the Stage

Religious turmoil increased after the Protestant and Catholic Reformations. Catholics persecuted non-Catholics and non-Catholics persecuted both Catholics and non-Catholics of denominations other than their own. Catholics and Protestants persecuted Jews, Muslims, and other non-Christian religious groups. Those who did not convert were forced out of parts of Europe.

Social and Political Impact

The Catholic Reformation affected the whole world. Although the Roman Catholic Church continued to take measures to stop the spread of Protestantism, it was no longer the only religious authority in Europe. Still, its policies influenced governments and societies wherever the Church existed.

The Inquisition To fight Protestantism, the Catholic Church established a Church court called the Roman **Inquisition** in 1542. The main purpose of the Inquisition was to impose religious uniformity, especially on converted Jews and Muslims, and later, on Protestants. The Roman Inquisition used harsh methods, including torture, to force confessions and punish **heresy**, or a denial of Church teachings. The Inquisition tried people who were accused of being Protestants, of practicing witchcraft, or of breaking Church law.

In Spain, Muslims (called Moors) controlled most of the country until 1100. In 1492, the Christian army conquered the last Muslim kingdom in Spain at Granada. Then, Spanish monarchs Ferdinand and Isabella used an Inquisition to increase their power. Jews were forced to convert to Catholic Christianity or leave Spain. In 1500, Muslims faced the same choice. Many Jews resettled in eastern and southern Europe. The majority of the Jews who had earlier converted to Christianity and were members of the educated elite stayed in Spain. In many areas of Europe where Jews were allowed

This scene depicts torture used in the Inquisition.

to stay, they were not as restricted as they had been during the Middle Ages. However, some places forced them to live in a particular part of the city, called a ghetto. The ghettos were walled and their gates closed at a certain time each evening.

In time, accounts of torture and executions by the courts damaged the church's image. The Inquisition's actions during the Catholic Reformation are still seen as an abuse of the Church's power.

Witch Trials Across Europe, many people feared that witches roamed the land, killing children and cattle and working with the devil. Their fears increased in times of poor harvests or other hardships. The fears inspired hysteria in which accused witches were rounded up and tried for their alleged wrongdoing.

The penalty for practicing witchcraft at this time was often death, and many innocent victims were executed for alleged witchcraft. The majority of executions for witchcraft occurred between 1580 and 1660. Thousands of people, most of them women or poor, were killed.

Political Effects A rising sense of national identity was interwoven with a decline in the power of the Catholic Church. The Protestant Reformation indirectly encouraged the formation of independent states and nations. Both rulers and merchants wanted the Church to be less involved in state and business affairs, which they sought to control on their own. Political power became separated from churches, although nations and churches often aligned themselves with one another to increase their own influence in a region. As a result, modern nation-states began to emerge, with their own independent governments and populations united by a shared culture, language, and national pride. Nation-states, such as Spain and Portugal, would extend their power in the 1600s.

Reading Check
Evaluate How did religious turmoil affect European society during the late 1500s and early 1600s?

THE REFORMATION

CAUSES	EFFECTS
• Humanist values led people to question Church authority.	• Many Protestant sects developed.
• Some clergy were corrupt, worldly, or poorly educated.	• Church leaders reformed the Catholic Church.
• Martin Luther posted his 95 Theses.	• Religious intolerance and anti-Semitism increased.
• The printing press helped spread Reformation ideas.	• Religious conflicts spread across Europe.

Religious Wars and Unrest

Trade, which had begun to flourish during the Renaissance, better connected regions of Europe through extensive trade routes and trading partners in the East. Italy, England, France, and Germany specialized in making certain products and traded for the products they could not produce. Through trade, ideas spread and daily life improved.

In the years after Luther published the 95 Theses, religious wars erupted within and between countries in Europe. These wars changed historic alliances, pitting against each other countries that had fought together in the Crusades.

Italy In 1494 King Charles VII of France invaded Italy. This began a series of wars in which France and Spain vied for control of the Italian Peninsula. During the Italian Wars, control of Italy bounced between these two powers. England also eventually became involved, as did several popes. The fighting finally culminated in the sack of Rome by the Spaniards and Holy Roman Emperor Charles V, who was a devout Catholic, in 1527. The Italian Wars officially ended in 1559. The most significant impact of the Italian Wars was that they helped expose the rest of Europe to the ideas of the Italian Renaissance. Troops returned home filled with ideas they had encountered in Italy. In addition, artists from Italy fled to the north, bringing new techniques and styles with them.

Germany With new ideas circulating among a growing population, peasants were becoming more disgruntled by high taxes and a lack of power. At the same time, Reformation preachers supported the idea of freedom. Stirred by these factors, tens of thousands of German peasants stormed castles and monasteries in 1524, a rebellion known as the Peasants' War. The nobles harshly suppressed the uprising. Martin Luther, accused of beginning the unrest, denounced it. The peasants, he wrote, "rob and rage and act like mad dogs." Luther's refusal to side with the peasants prevented the Reformation from spilling over into a social revolution that encouraged social equality.

France In France, Calvin's followers were called **Huguenots**. Hatred between Catholics and Huguenots frequently led to violence. The most violent clash occurred in Paris on August 24, 1572—the Catholic feast of St. Bartholomew's Day. At dawn, Catholic mobs began hunting for Protestants and murdering them. The massacres spread to other cities and lasted six months. Scholars believe that as many as 12,000 Huguenots were killed.

Huguenots fought for years against the Catholics. The fighting ended when their leader, Henry of Navarre, became Catholic. His conversion led to political stability by encouraging Catholics to accept him as king. In 1598 Henry's Edict of Nantes granted religious freedom to Protestants.

Reading Check
Analyze Causes
What factors led to the Peasants' War?

Lesson 4 Assessment

1. **Organize Information** Create a timeline of the major events that caused social and political unrest in Europe in the 1500s and early 1600s. Write a paragraph indicating how any two of these events are related.

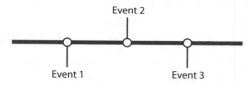

Event 2

Event 1

Event 3

2. **Key Terms and People** For each key term or person in the lesson, write a sentence explaining its significance.

3. **Analyze Causes** What led to the persecution of witches across Europe in the 1500s?

4. **Find Main Ideas** What were the Italian Wars, and how did they end?

5. **Analyze Effects** How did Luther's reaction to the Peasants' War affect the Catholic Reformation?

6. **Summarize** Who were the Huguenots, and how did France achieve political stability after years of fighting between the Huguenots and Catholics?

7. **Evaluate** How did the Protestant and Catholic reformations affect politics and government?

8. **Analyze Causes** What cause most influenced the spread of ideas and the improvement in daily life?

Module 15 Assessment

Key Terms and People

For each term or name below, briefly explain its connection to European history from 1400 to 1600.

1. indulgence
2. Reformation
3. Protestant
4. predestination
5. theocracy
6. Catholic Reformation
7. Elizabeth I
8. Henry VIII
9. Council of Trent
10. Inquisition

Main Ideas

Use your notes and the information in the module to answer the following questions.

Luther Leads the Reformation

1. On what three teachings did Martin Luther rest his Reformation movement?
2. Why did the Holy Roman Emperor go to war against Protestant German princes?
3. Why did Henry VIII create his own church?

The Reformation Continues

4. In what ways was John Calvin's church different from the Lutheran Church?
5. How did Protestant teaching lead to the forming of new groups?
6. Why did Catholics and Protestants persecute Anabaptists?

The Catholic Reformation

7. What was the goal of the Catholic Reformation?
8. What was the Council of Trent?
9. What are three legacies of the Reformation?

Social Unrest

10. Why did the Catholic Church convict Protestants of heresy?
11. What were the political effects of the Reformation on Europe?
12. After studying the religious wars in Europe during this time, what do you think might happen next on this continent?

Critical Thinking

1. **Analyze Effects** How did the Reformation lead to great changes in European ideas and institutions?

2. **Draw Conclusions** How did the printing press help spread the Reformation and democracy to individuals and groups?

3. **Analyze Effects** How did the Reformation expand cultural interaction within Europe?

4. **Make Inferences** How were the Jesuits effective in areas where people were not Christians?

5. **Analyze Motives** Why did the Catholic Church create a list of forbidden books?

6. **Develop Historical Perspective** Why did the Catholic Church want to punish Protestants as heretics?

7. **Synthesize** How did views of women and the role of women change as a result of the Reformation?

Engage with History

In the module, you reviewed several primary and secondary sources that criticized the Catholic Church from different points of view. Now, consider the context of each criticism and answer the following questions:

- How does the time period in which the source was written affect its criticism?
- Which criticism was best supported with evidence?
- Which criticism had the greatest impact?

Discuss these questions with a small group.

Focus on Writing

Review the information about Protestantism in the Analyze Key Concepts and other features in this module. Write a three-page essay that analyzes the effects of Protestantism on the Christian Church.

- Examine its impact on the number of denominations.
- Explain the different beliefs and practices it promoted.

Multimedia Activity

Work with a partner to use the Internet to research major religious reforms of the 20th century. You might search for information on changes in the Catholic Church as a result of Vatican II or major shifts in the practices or doctrines of a branch of Hinduism, Islam, Judaism, or Protestantism.

Compare the 20th-century reforms with those of the Protestant Reformation. Present the results of your research in a well-organized paper. Be sure to

- apply a search strategy when using directories and search engines to locate Internet resources
- judge the usefulness and reliability of each website
- correctly cite your Internet sources
- peer-edit for organization and correct use of language

Module 16

Expansion, Exploration, and Encounters

Essential Question

Why were peoples of the Age of Exploration willing to risk lives and fortunes to expand the influence of their homelands?

About the Painting: Japanese merchants and Jesuit missionaries await the arrival of a Portuguese ship at Nagasaki in the 1500s in this painting on wood panels.

▶ *Explore ONLINE!*

HISTORY.

VIDEOS, including...
• Life in Jamestown
• The Mughals of India: Taj Mahal
• Ancient China: Masters of the Wind and Waves
• African Slave Trade

☑ Document Based Investigations

☑ Graphic Organizers

☑ Interactive Games

☑ Carousel: Women Leaders of the Indian Subcontinent

☑ Image with Text Slider: Henry Hudson Arrives

In this module you will learn about the era of exploration and colonization and how lands and empires in both the Eastern and Western hemispheres were forever changed.

What You Will Learn ...

▶ *Explore ONLINE!*

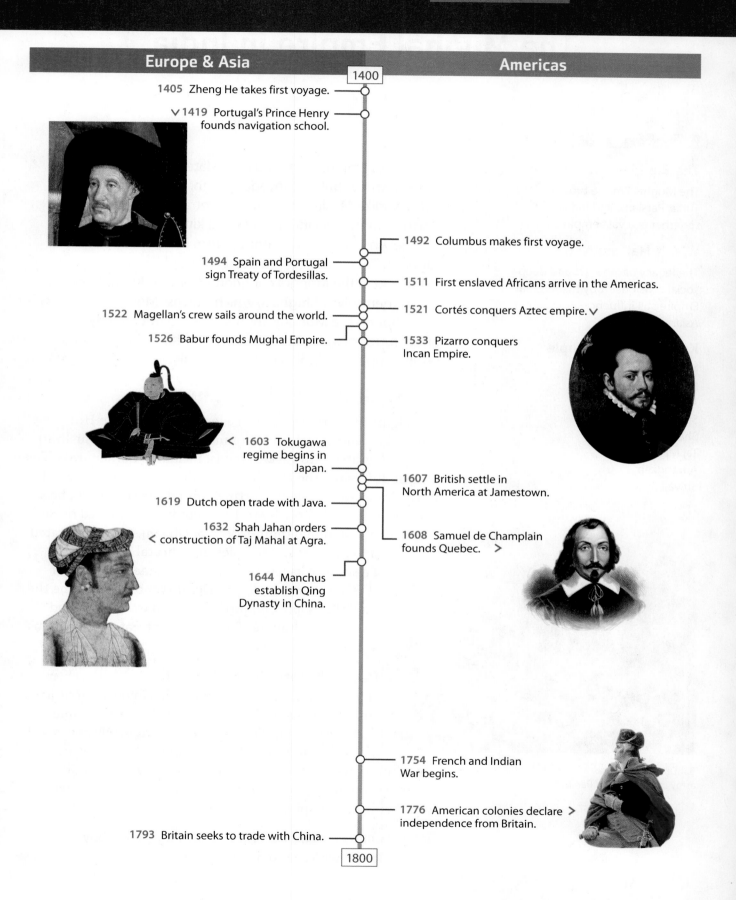

Europe & Asia

Americas

1400

1405 Zheng He takes first voyage.

∨ 1419 Portugal's Prince Henry founds navigation school.

1492 Columbus makes first voyage.

1494 Spain and Portugal sign Treaty of Tordesillas.

1511 First enslaved Africans arrive in the Americas.

1522 Magellan's crew sails around the world.

1521 Cortés conquers Aztec empire. ∨

1526 Babur founds Mughal Empire.

1533 Pizarro conquers Incan Empire.

< 1603 Tokugawa regime begins in Japan.

1607 British settle in North America at Jamestown.

1619 Dutch open trade with Java.

1632 Shah Jahan orders < construction of Taj Mahal at Agra.

1608 Samuel de Champlain founds Quebec. >

1644 Manchus establish Qing Dynasty in China.

1754 French and Indian War begins.

1776 American colonies declare > independence from Britain.

1793 Britain seeks to trade with China.

1800

The Mughal Empire in India

The Big Idea
The Mughal Empire brought Turks, Persians, and Indians together in a vast empire.

Why It Matters Now
The legacy of great art and deep social division left by the Mughal Empire still influences southern Asia.

Key Terms and People
Mughal
Babur
Akbar
Sikh
Shah Jahan
Taj Mahal
Aurangzeb
Shivaji

Babur's army clashes with the Indian army in the Battle of Panipat.

Setting the Stage

The Gupta Empire crumbled in the late 400s. First, Huns from Central Asia invaded. Then, beginning in the 700s, warlike Muslim tribes from Central Asia carved northwestern India into many small kingdoms. The people who invaded descended from Muslim Turks and Afghans. Their leader was a descendant of Timur the Lame and of the Mongol conqueror Genghis Khan. They called themselves **Mughals**, which means "Mongols." So, although the Mongols themselves did not directly affect much of India, their descendants had a long-lasting impact on Indian history and culture.

Early History of the Mughals

The eighth century began with a long clash between Hindus and Muslims in this land of many kingdoms, as Muslim groups migrated into various lands, including border areas. For almost 300 years, the Muslims were able to advance only as far as the Indus River valley. Starting around the year 1000, however, well-trained Turkish armies swept into India. Led by Sultan Mahmud (muh•MOOD) of Ghazni, they devastated Indian cities and temples in 17 brutal campaigns. These attacks left the region weakened and vulnerable to other conquerors. Delhi eventually became the capital of a loose empire of Turkish warlords called the Delhi Sultanate. These sultans treated the Hindus as conquered people.

Delhi Sultanate Between the 13th and 16th centuries, 33 different sultans ruled this divided territory from their seat in Delhi. In 1398, Timur the Lame destroyed Delhi. The city was so completely devastated that according to one witness, "for months, not a bird moved in the city." Delhi eventually was rebuilt. But it was not until the 16th century that a leader arose who would unify the empire.

Babur Founds an Empire In 1494, an 11-year-old boy named **Babur**, who counted both Timur the Lame and

Reading Check
Analyze Effects
What might have happened to the Mughal Empire if Babur had not been such a brilliant general?

Genghis Khan as ancestors, inherited a kingdom in Central Asia. It was only a tiny kingdom, and his elders soon took it away and drove him south. But Babur built up an army. In the years that followed, he swept down into India and laid the foundation for the vast Mughal Empire.

Babur was a skillful general. In 1526, for example, he led 12,000 troops to victory against an army of 100,000 commanded by a sultan of Delhi. A year later, Babur also defeated a massive Rajput army—soldiers who belonged to regional warrior clans. After Babur's death, his incompetent son, Humayun, lost most of the territory Babur had gained. Babur's 13-year-old grandson followed Humayun.

Akbar's Golden Age

Babur's grandson was called **Akbar**, which means "Great." Akbar certainly lived up to his name, ruling India with wisdom and tolerance from 1556 to 1605.

A Military Conqueror Akbar recognized military power as the root of his strength. In his opinion, a king must always be aggressive so that his neighbors will not try to conquer him.

Like the Safavids and the Ottomans, Akbar equipped his armies with heavy artillery. Cannons enabled him to break into walled cities and extend his rule into much of the Deccan plateau. In a brilliant move, he appointed some Rajputs as officers. In this way he turned potential enemies into allies. This combination of military power and political wisdom enabled Akbar to unify a land of at least 100 million people—more than in all of Europe put together.

A Liberal Ruler Akbar was a genius at cultural blending. He continued the Islamic tradition of religious freedom. He permitted people of other religions to practice their faiths. He proved his tolerance by marrying Hindu princesses without forcing them to convert. He allowed his wives to practice their religious rituals in the palace. He proved his tolerance again by abolishing both the tax on Hindu pilgrims and the hated *jizya,* or tax on non-Muslims. He even appointed a Spanish Jesuit to tutor his second son.

Akbar governed through a bureaucracy of officials. Natives and foreigners, Hindus and Muslims, could all rise to high office. This approach contributed to the quality of his government. Akbar's chief finance minister, Todar Mal, a Hindu, created a clever—and effective—taxation policy. He levied a tax similar to the present-day graduated income tax of the United States, calculating it as a percentage of the value of the peasants' crops. Because this tax was fair and affordable, the number of peasants who paid it increased. This payment brought in much needed money for the empire.

Akbar's land policies had more mixed results. He gave generous land grants to his bureaucrats. After they died, however, he reclaimed the lands and distributed them as he saw fit. On the positive side, this policy prevented the growth of feudal aristocracies. On the other hand, it did not encourage dedication and hard work by the Mughal officials. Their

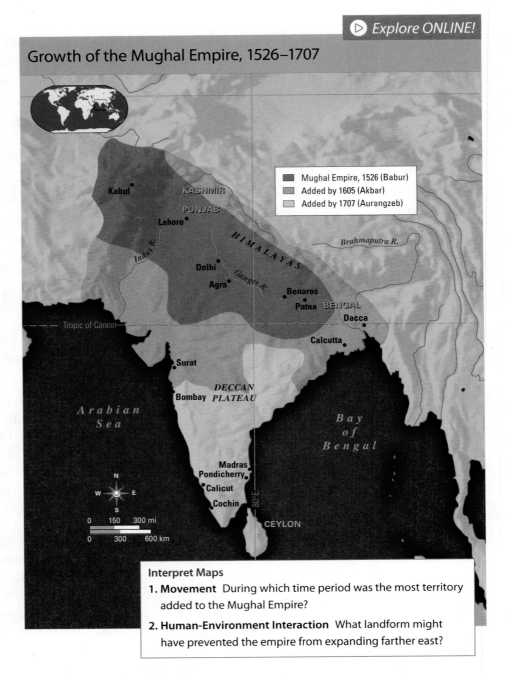

Growth of the Mughal Empire, 1526–1707

Legend:
- Mughal Empire, 1526 (Babur)
- Added by 1605 (Akbar)
- Added by 1707 (Aurangzeb)

Map labels: Kabul, KASHMIR, PUNJAB, Lahore, Indus R., HIMALAYAS, Brahmaputra R., Delhi, Agra, Ganges R., Benares, Patna, BENGAL, Dacca, Tropic of Cancer, Calcutta, Surat, DECCAN PLATEAU, Bombay, Arabian Sea, Bay of Bengal, Madras, Pondicherry, Calicut, Cochin, CEYLON

Scale: 0 150 300 mi / 0 300 600 km

Interpret Maps

1. **Movement** During which time period was the most territory added to the Mughal Empire?

2. **Human-Environment Interaction** What landform might have prevented the empire from expanding farther east?

children would not inherit the land or benefit from their parents' work. So the officials apparently saw no point in devoting themselves to their property.

Blended Cultures As Akbar extended the Mughal Empire, he welcomed influences from the many cultures in the empire. This cultural blending affected art, education, politics, and language. Persian was the language of Akbar's court and of high culture. The common people, however, spoke Hindi, a language derived from Sanskrit. Hindi remains one of the most widely spoken languages in India today. Out of the Mughal armies, where soldiers of many backgrounds rubbed shoulders, came yet another new language. This language was Urdu, which means "from the soldier's camp." A blend of Arabic, Persian, and Hindi, Urdu is today the official language of Pakistan.

Vocabulary
Sanskrit ancient Indian language from which multiple modern Indian languages evolved

Akbar
(1542–1605)

Akbar was brilliant and curious, especially about religion. He even invented a religion of his own—the "Divine Faith"—after learning about Hinduism, Jainism, Christianity, and Sufism. The religion attracted few followers, however, and offended Muslims so much that they attempted a brief revolt against Akbar in 1581. When he died, so did the "Divine Faith."

Surprisingly, despite his wisdom and his achievements, Akbar could not read. He hired others to read to him from his library of 24,000 books.

The Arts and Literature The arts flourished at the Mughal court, especially in the form of book illustrations. These small, highly detailed, and colorful paintings were called miniatures. Mughal miniatures combined Persian and Hindu influences. They were brought to a peak of perfection in the Safavid Empire. Babur's son, Humayun, brought two masters of this art to his court to teach it to the Mughals. Some of the most famous Mughal miniatures adorned the *Akbarnamah* ("Book of Akbar"), the story of the great emperor's campaigns and deeds.

Hindu literature also enjoyed a revival in Akbar's time. The poet Tulsi Das, for example, was a contemporary of Akbar's. He retold the epic love story of Rama and Sita from the fourth century BC Sanskrit poem the *Ramayana* (rah•MAH•yuh•nuh) in Hindi. This retelling, the *Ramcaritmanas*, is now even more popular than the original.

Architecture Akbar devoted himself to architecture too. The style developed under his reign is still known as Akbar period architecture. Its massive but graceful structures are decorated with intricate stonework that portrays Hindu themes. The capital city of Fatehpur Sikri is one of the most important examples of this type of architecture. Akbar had this red-sandstone city built to thank a Sufi saint, Sheik Salim Chisti, who had predicted the birth of his first son.

Akbar's Successors

With Akbar's death in 1605, the Mughal court changed to deal with the changing times. The next three emperors each left his mark on the Mughal Empire.

Jahangir and Nur Jahan Akbar's son called himself Jahangir (juh•hahn•GEER), or "Grasper of the World." However, for most of his reign, he left the affairs of state to his wife, who ruled with an iron hand.

Reading Check
Draw Conclusions
How was Akbar able to build such an immense empire?

Jahangir's wife was the Persian princess Nur Jahan. She was a brilliant politician who perfectly understood the use of power. As the real ruler of India, she installed her father as prime minister in the Mughal court. She saw Jahangir's son Khusrau as her ticket to future power. But when Khusrau rebelled against his father, Nur Jahan removed him. She then shifted her favor to another son.

This rejection of Khusrau affected more than the political future of the empire. It was also the basis of a long and bitter religious conflict that fostered future disputes over authority and power. Jahangir tried to promote Islam in the Mughal state, but was tolerant of other religions. When Khusrau rebelled, he turned to the **Sikhs**. Sikhism had emerged as a major religion and was gaining followers because of its egalitarian message. It was this message of equality between human beings regardless of their religion, gender, or caste that had drawn Khusrau to the Sikhs. Their prophet, Guru Arjun, sheltered Khusrau and defended him. In response, the Mughal rulers had Guru Arjun arrested and tortured to death. The Sikhs became the target of the Mughals' particular hatred.

Shah Jahan Jahangir's son and successor, **Shah Jahan**, could not tolerate competition and secured his throne by assassinating all his possible rivals.

Vocabulary
caste general term for one of four specific classes of people in the social systems of India

---

Now and Then

Women Leaders of the Indian Subcontinent

Since World War II, the subcontinent of India has seen the rise of several powerful women. Unlike Nur Jahan, however, they achieved power on their own—not through their husbands.

Indira Gandhi headed the Congress Party and dominated Indian politics for almost 30 years. She was elected prime minister in 1966 and again in 1980. She suspended democracy during an era known as "The Emergency." Gandhi was assassinated in 1984 by her Sikh bodyguards.

Benazir Bhutto took charge of the Pakistan People's Party after her father was assassinated.

She became prime minister in 1988, the first woman to run a modern Muslim state. Reelected in 1993, she was dismissed from office in 1996 and went into exile. She returned from exile in 2007 but was killed by a suicide bomb attack just months later.

Chandrika Bandaranaike Kumaratunga was the fifth president of Sri Lanka. She was first elected in 1994 and served until 2005. She survived an assassination attempt in 1999 and was reelected.

Khaleda Zia became Bangladesh's first woman prime minister in 1991. She was reelected several times, the last time in 2001.

Pratibha Patil, elected in 2007, was India's first female president. She retired from office in 2012.

Indira Gandhi

Chandrika Bandaranaike Kumaratunga

Khaleda Zia

Pratibha Patil

He had a great passion for two things: beautiful buildings and his wife Mumtaz Mahal (moom•TAHZ mah•HAHL). Nur Jahan had arranged this marriage between Jahangir's son and her niece for political reasons. Shah Jahan, however, fell genuinely in love with his Persian princess.

In 1631, Mumtaz Mahal died at age 39 while giving birth to her 14th child. To enshrine his wife's memory, he ordered that a tomb be built "as beautiful as she was beautiful." Fine white marble and fabulous jewels were gathered from many parts of Asia. This memorial, the **Taj Mahal**, has been called one of the most beautiful buildings in the world. Its towering marble dome and slender minaret towers look like lace and seem to change color as the sun moves across the sky.

The People Suffer But while Shah Jahan was building gardens, monuments, and forts, his country was suffering. There was famine in the land. Furthermore, farmers needed tools, roads, and ways of irrigating their crops and dealing with India's harsh environment. What they got instead were taxes and more taxes to support the building of monuments, their rulers' extravagant lifestyles, and war.

All was not well in the royal court either. When Shah Jahan became ill in 1657, his four sons scrambled for the throne. The third son, **Aurangzeb** (AWR•uhng•zehb), moved first and most decisively. In a bitter civil war, he executed his older brother, who was his most serious rival. Then he arrested his father and put him in prison, where he died several years later. After Shah Jahan's death, a mirror was found in his room, angled so that he could look out at the reflection of the Taj Mahal.

History in Depth

Building the Taj Mahal

The Taj Mahal in Agra, India, is one of the world's architectural marvels. Some 20,000 workers from all over India and central Asia labored for 22 years to build the famous tomb. It is made of white marble brought from 250 miles away. The minaret towers are about 130 feet high. The spires atop the building guide one's eyes upward.

The design of the building is a blend of Hindu and Muslim styles. The pointed arches are of Muslim design, and the perforated marble windows and doors are typical of a style found in Hindu temples.

The main structure is a dazzling white marble mausoleum that overlooks a garden. The inside of the building is a glittering garden of thousands of carved marble flowers inlaid with tiny precious stones. One tiny flower has 60 different inlays.

Often called the most beautiful building in the world, the Taj Mahal is a monument to love and the Mughal Empire.

The Mughal and Ottoman Empires in 1750

By the mid-1700s the Mughal and Ottoman empires were two powerful Muslim states that faced many challenges.

After Suleyman's rule ended in 1566, the Ottoman Empire went through two centuries of economic challenges, social unrest, and, later, limited reform. By the 18th century, Europe loomed powerfully over the Ottoman Empire. Through war, European states won back certain Ottoman territories that had separated from the empire. Other regions became independent when local officials took control. There was a religious angle to the growing European influence as well. Austria and Russia, after defeating the Ottomans in numerous wars, were in a position to provide needed legal support to Christians living under Ottoman rule. Additionally, whereas trade with Europe had once been quite profitable, by the 18th century European colonies were producing sugar, tobacco, cotton, and other goods that Europeans once received through trade with the Ottomans. All of these changes resulted in an Ottoman Empire that saw its power greatly reduced by 1750.

By contrast, the Mughal Empire found itself near collapse by 1750. The splintered, weakened empire that existed at the end of Aurangzeb's reign in 1707 was riddled with political rivalries. Aurangzeb's lack of religious and ethnic tolerance had led to the rise of various factions, including the Marathas and the Sikhs. Both claimed their own state. By the mid-1700s, the Marathas in particular wielded considerable power over much of northern and central India. Another challenge around this time emerged from a collision of politics and trade. Britain's English East India Company had been engaged in commerce with India since 1611. By 1750, the company built an army and assumed control of India's Bengal region, establishing Britain's political seat of imperialist power. By 1803 the Mughal Empire was controlled by the British.

Compare
What impact did commercial activity have on the Ottoman Empire? the Mughal Empire?

Aurangzeb's Reign A master at military strategy and an aggressive empire builder, Aurangzeb ruled from 1658 to 1707. He expanded the Mughal holdings to their greatest size. However, the power of the empire weakened during his reign.

This loss of power was due largely to Aurangzeb's oppression of the people. He rigidly enforced Islamic laws by outlawing drinking, gambling, and other activities viewed as vices. He appointed censors to police his subjects' morals and make sure they prayed at the appointed times. He also tried to erase all the gains Hindus had made under Akbar. For example, he brought back the hated tax on non-Muslims and dismissed Hindus from high positions in his government. He banned the construction of new temples and had Hindu monuments destroyed. Not surprisingly, these actions outraged the Hindus.

The Hindu Rajputs, whom Akbar had converted from potential enemies to allies, rebelled. Aurangzeb defeated them repeatedly, but never completely. In the southwest, a Hindu warrior community called Marathas founded their own state. Their greatest leader was **Shivaji**, an influential warrior king whose government included modern concepts, such as a cabinet of advisers. Aurangzeb captured Shivaji, but he escaped, and the Marathas remained unconquered. Meanwhile, the Sikhs continued

Reading Check
Recognize Effects
How did Aurangzeb's personal qualities and political policies affect the Mughal Empire?

to develop and transformed themselves into a brotherhood of warriors, emerging as a major power. Sikhism was concentrated in the Punjab, an area in northwest India. A series of military conflicts between the Sikhs and Mughal forces took place there in the early 17th century. Punjab is still the center of Sikhism today.

Aurangzeb levied oppressive taxes to pay for these wars against increasing numbers of enemies. He had done away with all taxes not authorized by Islamic law, so he doubled the taxes on Hindu merchants. This increased tax burden deepened the Hindus' bitterness and led to further rebellion. As a result, Aurangzeb needed to raise more money to increase his army. The more territory he conquered, the more desperate his situation became.

The Empire's Decline and Decay

By the end of Aurangzeb's reign, he had drained the empire of its resources. More than 2 million people died in a famine while Aurangzeb was away waging war. Most of his subjects felt little or no loyalty to him. Meanwhile, the power of local lords grew. After Aurangzeb's death, his sons fought a war of succession. In fact, three emperors reigned in the first 12 years after Aurangzeb died. The Mughal emperor was nothing but a wealthy figurehead. He did not rule a united empire, but a patchwork of independent states.

Reading Check
Analyze Effects
What was the effect of the growth of the local lords' power?

As the Mughal Empire rose and fell, Western traders slowly built their own power in the region. The Portuguese were the first Europeans to reach India. In fact, they arrived just before Babur did. Next came the Dutch, who in turn gave way to the French and the English. However, the great Mughal emperors did not feel threatened by the European traders. In 1661, Aurangzeb responded to these outsiders by casually handing them the port of Bombay. Aurangzeb had no idea that he had given India's next conquerors their first foothold in a future empire.

Lesson 1 Assessment

1. **Organize Information** Create a timeline similar to the one shown and fill it in with the names and key dates for the following Mughal emperors: Babur (given for you), Humayun, Akbar, Jahangir (and Nur Jahan), Shah Jahan, and Aurangzeb.

1494
Babur

Which of the emperors on your timeline had a positive effect on the empire? Which had negative effects?

2. **Key Terms and People** For each key term or person in the lesson, write a sentence explaining its significance.

3. **Compare** How did Akbar demonstrate tolerance in his empire, and how did his policy compare to earlier interactions between Muslims and Hindus?

4. **Draw Conclusions** What pattern is seen in the ways individuals came to power in the Mughal Empire?

5. **Analyze Causes** Why did the empire weaken under the rule of Aurangzeb?

6. **Summarize** Why were Akbar's tax policies so successful?

7. **Make Inferences** Why was Nur Jahan able to hold so much power in Jahangir's court?

Cultural Blending in Mughal India

Mughal India enjoyed a golden age under Akbar. Part of Akbar's success—indeed, the success of the Mughals—came from his religious tolerance. India's population was largely Hindu, and the incoming Mughal rulers were Muslim. The Mughal emperors encouraged the blending of cultures to create a united India.

This cultural integration can be seen in the art of Mughal India. Muslim artists focused heavily on art with ornate patterns of flowers and leaves, called arabesque or geometric patterns. Hindu artists created naturalistic and often ornate artworks. These two artistic traditions came together and created a style unique to Mughal India. As you can see, the artistic collaboration covered a wide range of art forms.

DECORATIVE ARTS ▶
Decorative work on items from dagger handles to pottery exhibits the same cultural blending as other Mughal art forms. This dagger handle shows some of the floral and geometric elements common in Muslim art, but the realistic depiction of the horse comes out of the Hindu tradition.

▲ ARCHITECTURE
Mughal emperors brought to India a strong Muslim architectural tradition. Indian artisans were extremely talented with local building materials—specifically, marble and sandstone. Together, they created some of the most striking and enduring architecture in the world, like Humayun's Tomb shown here.

▲ PAINTING

Mughal painting was largely a product of the royal court. Persian artists brought to court by Mughal emperors had a strong influence, but Mughal artists quickly developed their own characteristics. The Mughal style kept aspects of the Persian influence—particularly the flat aerial perspective, which demonstrated an artistic ideal. But, as seen in this colorful painting, the Indian artists incorporated more naturalism and detail from the world around them.

▼ FABRICS

Mughal fabrics included geometric patterns found in Persian designs, but Mughal weavers, like other Mughal artisans, also produced original designs. Common themes in Mughal fabrics included landscapes, animal chases, floral latticeworks, and central flowering plants like the one on this tent hanging.

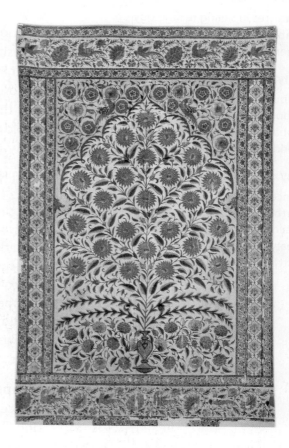

Critical Thinking
1. **Clarify** What does the art suggest about the culture of Mughal India?
2. **Form Opinions** What are some modern examples of cultural blending in art? What elements of each culture are represented in the artwork? Consider other art forms, such as music and literature, as well.

Europeans Explore the East

The Big Idea

Advances in sailing technology enabled Europeans to explore other parts of the world.

Why It Matters Now

European exploration was an important step toward the global interaction existing in the world today.

Key Terms and People

Prince Henry
Bartolomeu Dias
Vasco da Gama
Treaty of Tordesillas
Dutch East India Company

Setting the Stage

By the early 1400s, Europeans were ready to venture beyond their borders. The Renaissance encouraged, among other things, a new spirit of adventure and curiosity. This spirit of adventure, along with several other important factors, prompted Europeans to explore the world around them. This module describes how these explorations began a long process that would bring together the peoples of many different lands and permanently change the world.

For "God, Glory, and Gold"

Europeans had not been completely isolated from the rest of the world before the 1400s. Beginning around 1100, European crusaders battled Muslims for control of the Holy Lands in Southwest Asia. In 1275, the Italian trader Marco Polo reached the court of Kublai Khan in China. For the most part, however, Europeans had neither the interest nor the ability to explore foreign lands. That changed by the early 1400s. The desire to grow rich and to spread Christianity, coupled with advances in sailing technology, spurred an age of European exploration.

Europeans Seek New Trade Routes The desire for new sources of wealth was the main reason for European exploration. Through overseas exploration, merchants and traders hoped ultimately to benefit from what had become a profitable business in Europe: the trade of spices and other luxury goods from Asia. The people of Europe had been introduced to these items during the Crusades, the wars fought between Christians and Muslims from 1096 to 1270. After the Crusades ended, Europeans continued to demand such spices as nutmeg, ginger, cinnamon, and pepper, all of which added flavor to the bland foods of Europe. Because demand for these goods was greater than the supply, merchants could charge high prices and thus make great profits.

This early globe depicts the Europeans' view of Europe and Africa around 1492.

The Muslims and the Italians controlled trade from East to West. Muslims sold Asian goods to Italian merchants, who controlled trade across the land routes of the Mediterranean region. The Italians resold the items at increased prices to merchants throughout Europe.

Other European traders did not like this arrangement. Paying such high prices to the Italians severely cut into their own profits. By the 1400s, European merchants—as well as the new monarchs of England, Spain, Portugal, and France—sought to bypass the Italian merchants. This meant finding a sea route directly to Asia.

The Spread of Christianity The desire to spread Christianity also motivated Europeans to explore. The Crusades had left Europeans with a taste for spices, but more significantly with feelings of hostility between Christians and Muslims. European countries believed that they had a sacred duty not only to continue fighting Muslims, but also to convert non-Christians throughout the world.

Europeans hoped to obtain popular goods directly from the peoples of Asia. They also hoped to Christianize them. Bernal Díaz del Castillo, an early Spanish explorer, explained his motives: "To serve God and His Majesty, to give light to those who were in darkness and to grow rich as all men desire to do."

Technology Makes Exploration Possible While "God, glory, and gold" were the primary motives for exploration, advances in technology made the voyages of discovery possible. During the 1200s, it would have been nearly impossible for a European sea captain to cross 3,000 miles of ocean and return again. The main problem was that European ships could not sail against the wind. In the 1400s, shipbuilders designed a new vessel, the caravel. The caravel was sturdier than earlier vessels. In addition, triangular sails adopted from the Arabs allowed it to sail effectively against the wind.

Europeans also improved their navigational techniques. To better determine their location at sea, sailors used the astrolabe, which Islamic astronomers and mathematicians had perfected. The astrolabe was a brass circle with carefully adjusted rings marked off in degrees. Using the rings to sight the stars, a sea captain could calculate latitude, or how far north or south of the equator the ship was. Explorers were also able to more accurately track direction by using a magnetic compass, a Chinese invention. Some historians believe the magnetic compass was exchanged between the Chinese and other groups during journeys that ran along various transportation routes.

The Portuguese are credited with perfecting a 16-point wind rose, a tool that showed from which direction the wind was blowing. Captains wrote down the measurements obtained from these tools, as well as observed ocean current patterns, in pilot books, or navigation charts, for use during future voyages.

Reading Check
Summarize How might the phrase "God, glory, and gold" summarize the Europeans' motives for exploration?

Prince Henry
(1394–1460)

For his role in promoting Portuguese exploration, historians call Prince Henry "the Navigator." Although he never went on voyages of discovery, Henry was consumed by the quest to find new lands and to spread Christianity. A devout Catholic, he wanted "to make increase in the faith of our lord Jesus Christ and bring to him all the souls that should be saved."

To that end, Henry used his own fortune to organize more than 14 voyages along the western coast of Africa, which was previously unexplored by Europeans. As a result, Henry died in debt. The Portuguese crown spent more than 60 years paying off his debts.

Portugal Leads the Way

The leader in developing and applying these sailing innovations was Portugal. Located on the Atlantic Ocean at the southwest corner of Europe, Portugal was the first European country to establish trading outposts along the west coast of Africa. Eventually, Portuguese explorers pushed farther east into the Indian Ocean.

The Portuguese Explore Africa Portugal took the lead in overseas exploration in part due to strong government investment. The nation's most enthusiastic supporter of exploration was **Prince Henry**, the son of Portugal's king. Henry's dreams of overseas exploration began in 1415 when he helped conquer the Muslim city of Ceuta in North Africa. There, he had his first glimpse of the dazzling wealth that lay beyond Europe. In Ceuta, the Portuguese invaders found exotic stores filled with pepper, cinnamon, cloves, and other spices. In addition, they encountered large supplies of gold, silver, and jewels.

Henry returned to Portugal determined to reach the source of these treasures in the East. The prince also wished to spread the Christian faith. In 1419, Henry founded a navigation school on the southwestern coast of Portugal. Mapmakers, instrument makers, shipbuilders, scientists, and sea captains gathered there to perfect their trade.

Within several years, and with considerable investment from the monarchy, Portuguese ships began sailing down the western coast of Africa. By the time Henry died in 1460, the Portuguese had established a series of trading posts along western Africa's shores. There, they traded with Africans for such profitable items as gold and ivory. Eventually, they traded for African captives to be used as slaves. Having established their presence along the African coast, Portuguese explorers plotted their next move. They would attempt to find a sea route to Asia.

The Tools of Exploration

Out on the open seas, winds easily blew ships off course. With only the sun, moon, and stars to guide them, few sailors willingly ventured beyond the sight of land. In order to travel to distant places, European inventors and sailors experimented with new tools for navigation and new designs for sailing ships, often borrowing from other cultures.

▲ Here, a French mariner uses an early navigation instrument that he has brought ashore to fix his ship's position. It was difficult to make accurate calculations aboard wave-tossed vessels.

1. The average caravel was between 65 and 75 feet long. This versatile ship had triangular sails for maneuverability and square sails for power.

2. The large cargo area could hold the numerous supplies needed for long voyages.

3. Its shallow draft (depth of the ship's keel below the water) allowed it to explore close to the shore.

▲ This 17th-century compass is typical of those taken by navigators on voyages of exploration. The compass was invented by the Chinese.

◄ The sextant replaced the astrolabe in the mid-1700s as the instrument for measuring the height of the stars above the horizon to determine latitude and longitude.

Critical Thinking

1. **Analyze Motives** Why did inventors and sailors develop better tools for navigation?

2. **Summarize** What types of navigational or other tools do sailors use today? Choose one type of tool and write a brief explanation of what it does.

A Ship's Rations

The captain of a 17th-century sailing vessel, with a crew of 190 sailors, would normally order the following food items for a three-month trip:

- 8,000 pounds of salt beef; 2,800 pounds of salt pork; 600 pounds of salt cod; a few beef tongues
- 15,000 brown biscuits; 5,000 white biscuits
- 30 bushels of oatmeal, 40 bushels of dried peas, 1 1/2 bushels of mustard seed
- 1 barrel of salt, 1 barrel of flour
- 11 small wooden casks of butter, 1 large cask of vinegar
- 10,500 gallons of beer; 3,500 gallons of water; 2 large casks of cider

Portuguese Sailors Reach Asia The Portuguese believed that to reach Asia by sea, they would have to sail around the southern tip of Africa. In 1488, Portuguese captain **Bartolomeu Dias** ventured far down the coast of Africa until he and his crew reached the tip. As they arrived, a huge storm rose and battered the fleet for days. When the storm ended, Dias realized his ships had been blown around the tip to the other side. Dias explored the southeast coast of Africa and then considered sailing to India. However, his crew was exhausted and food supplies were low. As a result, the captain returned home.

With the tip of Africa finally rounded, the Portuguese continued pushing east. In 1497, Portuguese explorer **Vasco da Gama** began exploring the east African coast. In 1498, he reached the port of Calicut, on the southwestern coast of India. Da Gama and his crew were amazed by the spices, rare silks, and precious gems that filled Calicut's shops. The Portuguese sailors filled their ships with such spices as pepper and cinnamon and returned to Portugal in 1499. Their cargo was worth 60 times the cost of the voyage. Da Gama's remarkable voyage of 27,000 miles had given Portugal a direct sea route to India.

Reading Check
Analyze Effects
How did Prince Henry's experiences in Africa impact his decision to open a navigation school?

Spain Also Makes Claims

As the Portuguese were establishing trading posts along the west coast of Africa, Spain watched with increasing envy. The Spanish monarchs also desired a direct sea route to Asia.

In 1492, an Italian sea captain, Christopher Columbus, convinced Spain to finance a bold plan: finding a route to Asia by sailing west across the Atlantic Ocean. In October of that year, Columbus reached an island in the

Caribbean. He was mistaken in his thought that he had reached the East Indies. But his voyage would open the way for European colonization of the Americas—a process that would forever change the world. The immediate impact of Columbus's voyage, however, was to increase tensions between Spain and Portugal.

The Portuguese believed that Columbus had indeed reached Asia. Portugal suspected that Columbus had claimed for Spain lands that Portuguese sailors might have reached first. The rivalry between Spain and Portugal grew more tense. In 1493, Pope Alexander VI stepped in to keep peace between the two nations. He suggested an imaginary dividing line, drawn north to south, through the Atlantic Ocean. All lands to the west of the line, known as the Line of Demarcation, would be Spain's. These lands included most of the Americas. All lands to the east of the line would belong to Portugal.

Pope Alexander VI

Portugal complained that the line gave too much to Spain. So it was moved farther west to include parts of modern-day Brazil for the Portuguese. In 1494, Spain and Portugal signed the **Treaty of Tordesillas**, in which they agreed to honor the line. The era of exploration and colonization was about to begin in earnest.

Trading Empires in the Indian Ocean

With da Gama's voyage, Europeans had finally opened direct sea trade with Asia. They also opened an era of violent conflict in the East. European nations scrambled to establish profitable trading outposts along the shores of South and Southeast Asia. All the while, they battled the region's inhabitants, as well as each other.

Portugal's Trading Empire In the years following da Gama's voyage, the Portuguese monarchy's investment in global exploration began to pay off. Portugal built a bustling trading empire throughout the Indian Ocean. As the Portuguese moved into the region, they took control of the spice trade from Muslim merchants. In 1509, Portugal extended its control over the area when it defeated a Muslim fleet off the coast of India, a victory made possible by the cannons they had added aboard their ships.

Portugal strengthened its hold on the region by building a fort at Hormuz in 1514. It established control of the Straits of Hormuz, connecting the Persian Gulf and Arabian Sea, and helped stop Muslim traders from reaching India.

In 1510, the Portuguese captured Goa, a port city on India's west coast. They made it the capital of their trading empire. They then sailed farther east to Indonesia, also known as the East Indies. In 1511, a Portuguese fleet attacked the city of Malacca on the west coast of the Malay Peninsula. In capturing the town, the Portuguese seized control of the Strait of Malacca. Seizing this waterway gave them control of the Moluccas. These were islands so rich in spices that they became known as the Spice Islands.

Reading Check
Analyze Issues How did the Treaty of Tordesillas ease tensions between Spain and Portugal?

In convincing his crew to attack Malacca, Portuguese sea captain Afonso de Albuquerque stressed his country's intense desire to crush the Muslim-Italian domination over Asian trade:

"If we deprive them [Muslims] of this their ancient market there, there does not remain for them a single port in the whole of these parts, where they can carry on their trade in these things. . . . I hold it as very certain that if we take this trade of Malacca away out of their hands, Cairo and Mecca are entirely ruined, and to Venice will no spiceries . . . [be] . . . conveyed except that which her merchants go and buy in Portugal."

—Afonso de Albuquerque, from *The Commentaries of the Great Afonso Dalboquerque*

Portugal did break the old Muslim-Italian domination on trade from the East, much to the delight of European consumers. Portuguese merchants brought back goods from Asia at about one-fifth of what they cost when purchased through the Arabs and Italians. As a result, more Europeans could afford these items.

In time, Portugal's success in Asia attracted the attention of other European nations. As early as 1521, a Spanish expedition led by Ferdinand Magellan arrived in the Philippines. Spain claimed the islands and began settling them in 1565. By the early 1600s, the rest of Europe had begun to descend upon Asia. They wanted to establish their own trade empires in the East.

Other Nations Challenge the Portuguese Beginning around 1600, the English and Dutch began to challenge Portugal's dominance over the Indian Ocean trade. The Dutch Republic, also known as the Netherlands, was a small country situated along the North Sea in northwestern Europe. Since the early 1500s, Spain had ruled the area. In 1581, the people of the region declared their independence from Spain and established the Dutch Republic.

In a short time, the Netherlands became a leading sea power. By 1600, the Dutch owned the largest fleet of ships in the world—20,000 vessels. Pressure from Dutch and also English fleets eroded Portuguese control of the Asian region. The Dutch and English then battled one another for dominance of the area.

Both countries had formed an East India Company to establish and direct trade throughout Asia. These companies had the power to mint money, make treaties, and even raise their own armies. The **Dutch East India Company** was richer and more powerful than England's company. As a result, the Dutch eventually drove out the English and established their dominance over the region.

Europeans in the East, 1487–1700

Interpret Maps

1. **Place** Why would a fort at Hormuz help the Portuguese to stop trade between the Arabian Peninsula and India?

2. **Location** How many miles was the trade route between the Portuguese trading post on the Cape Verde Islands and the Cape of Good Hope?

While the Dutch were similar to Spain and Portugal in their desire to develop profitable trade, they were different in other ways. For one, the Dutch East India Company was founded by the government, not a monarch. Another difference was that the Dutch were not seeking to spread the Christian faith. They were only interested in expanding economically.

Dutch Trade Outposts In 1619, the Dutch established their trading headquarters at Batavia on the island of Java. From there, they expanded west to conquer several nearby islands. In addition, the Dutch seized both the port of Malacca and the valuable Spice Islands from Portugal. Throughout the 1600s, the Netherlands increased its control over the Indian Ocean trade. With so many goods from the East traveling to the Netherlands, the nation's capital, Amsterdam, became a leading commercial center. By 1700, the Dutch ruled much of Indonesia and had trading posts in several Asian countries. They also controlled the Cape of Good Hope on the southern tip of Africa, which was used as a resupply stop.

British and French Traders Also by 1700, Britain and France had gained a foothold in the region. Having failed to win control of the larger area, the

Now and Then

Trading Partners

Global trade is important to the economies of Asian countries now just as it was when the region first began to export spices, silks, and gems centuries ago. Today, a variety of products, including automobiles, electronic goods, tea, and textiles, are shipped around the world. (Hong Kong harbor is pictured.)

Regional trade organizations help to strengthen economic cooperation among Asian nations and promote international trade. They include the Association of Southeast Asian Nations (ASEAN) and the South Asian Association for Regional Cooperation (SAARC).

English East India Company focused much of its energy on establishing outposts in India. There, the English developed a successful business trading Indian cloth in Europe. In 1664, France also entered the Asia trade with its own East India Company. It struggled at first, as it faced continual attacks by the Dutch. Eventually, the French company established an outpost in India in the 1720s. However, it never showed much of a profit.

As the Europeans battled for a share of the profitable Indian Ocean trade, their influence inland in Southeast Asia remained limited. European traders did take control of many port cities in the region. But their impact rarely spread beyond the ports. From 1500 to about 1800, when Europeans began to conquer much of the region, the peoples of Asia remained largely unaffected by European contact. European traders who sailed farther east to seek riches in China and Japan had even less success in spreading Western culture.

Reading Check
Recognize Effects How did the arrival of the Europeans affect the peoples of the East in general?

Lesson 2 Assessment

1. **Organize Information** Create a timeline similar to the one shown and write on it the names and dates of the following key events in the European exploration of the East: Portuguese gain control of Strait of Malacca; Dias sails around tip of Africa; Prince Henry founds navigation school; Da Gama reaches Calicut. Which event is the most significant?

    1400 ———○——— 1800

2. **Key Terms and People** For each key term or person in the lesson, write a sentence explaining its significance.

3. **Synthesize** What was Prince Henry's goal and who actually achieved it?

4. **Make Inferences** What did the Treaty of Tordesillas reveal about Europeans' attitudes toward non-European lands and peoples?

5. **Analyze Motives** What were the motives behind European exploration in the 1400s? Explain.

6. **Recognize Effects** In what ways did Europeans owe some of their sailing technology to other peoples?

China and Japan Reject Expansion

The Big Idea

China under the Ming and Qing dynasties and Japan under the Tokugawa regime were uninterested in European contact.

Why It Matters Now

China and Japan's economic independence from the West continues today, though China is pursuing new economic ties with the outside world.

Key Terms and People

Ming Dynasty
Hongwu
Yonglo
Zheng He
Manchus
Qing Dynasty
Kangxi
daimyo
Oda Nobunaga
Toyotomi Hideyoshi
Tokugawa Shogunate
haiku
kabuki

Setting the Stage

The European voyages of exploration had led to opportunities for trade. Europeans made healthy profits from trade in the Indian Ocean region. They began looking for additional sources of wealth. Soon, European countries were seeking trade relationships in East Asia, first with China and later with Japan. By the time Portuguese ships dropped anchor off the Chinese coast in 1514, the Chinese had driven out their Mongol rulers and had united under a new dynasty.

China Under the Powerful Ming Dynasty

China had become the dominant power in Asia under the **Ming Dynasty** (1368–1644). In recognition of China's power, vassal states from Korea to Southeast Asia paid their Ming overlords regular tribute, which is a payment by one country to another to acknowledge its submission. China expected Europeans to do the same. Ming rulers were not going to allow outsiders from distant lands to threaten the peace and prosperity the Ming had brought to China when they ended Mongol rule.

The Rise of the Ming A peasant's son, **Hongwu**, commanded the rebel army that drove the Mongols out of China in 1368. That year, he became the first Ming emperor. Hongwu continued to rule from the former Yuan capital of Nanjing in the south. He began reforms designed to restore agricultural lands devastated by war, erase nearly all traces of the Mongol past, and promote China's power and prosperity. Hongwu's agricultural reforms increased rice production and improved irrigation. He also encouraged fish farming and growing commercial crops, such as cotton and sugar cane.

Hongwu used respected traditions and institutions to bring stability to China. For example, he encouraged a return to Confucian moral standards. He improved imperial administration by restoring the merit-based civil service examination system. Later in his rule, however, when problems developed, Hongwu became a ruthless tyrant. Suspecting plots against his rule everywhere, he conducted purges of the government, killing thousands of officials.

Porcelain vase from the Ming Dynasty

Yonglo Hongwu's death in 1398 led to a power struggle. His son **Yonglo** (yung•lu) emerged victorious. Yonglo continued many of his father's policies, although he moved the royal court to Beijing.

Yonglo also had a far-ranging curiosity about the outside world. In 1405, before Europeans began to sail beyond their borders, he launched the first of seven voyages of exploration. He hoped they would impress the world with the power and splendor of Ming China. He also wanted to expand China's tribute system.

The Voyages of Zheng He A Chinese Muslim admiral named **Zheng He** (jung-huh) led all of the seven voyages. His expeditions were remarkable for their size. Everything about them was large—distances traveled, fleet size, and ship measurements. The voyages ranged from Southeast Asia to eastern Africa. From 40 to 300 ships sailed in each expedition. Among them were fighting ships, storage vessels, and huge "treasure" ships measuring more than 400 feet long. The fleet's crews numbered over 27,000 on some voyages. They included sailors, soldiers, carpenters, interpreters, accountants, doctors, and religious leaders. Like a huge floating city, the fleet sailed from port to port along the Indian Ocean.

Everywhere Zheng He went, he distributed gifts such as silver and silk to show Chinese superiority. As a result, more than 16 countries sent tribute to the Ming court. Even so, Chinese scholar-officials complained that the voyages wasted valuable resources that could be used to defend against barbarians' attacks on the northern frontier. After the seventh voyage, in 1433, China withdrew into isolation.

Zheng He's treasure ship compared with Christopher Columbus's *Santa Maria*

The Forbidden City

When Yonglo moved the Chinese capital to Beijing, he ordered the building of a great palace complex to symbolize his power and might. Construction took 14 years, from 1406 to 1420. Red walls 35 feet in height surrounded the complex, which had dozens of buildings, including palaces and temples. The complex became known as the Forbidden City because commoners and foreigners were not allowed to enter.

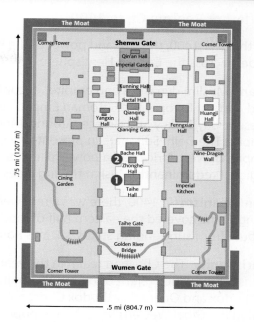

Hall of Supreme Harmony
Taihe Hall, or the Hall of Supreme Harmony, is the largest building in the compound. It measures 201 by 122 feet and stands about 125 feet high. This hall was used for important ceremonies, such as those marking the emperor's birthday or the day the crown prince took the throne.

Hall of Central Harmony
Zhonge Hall, or the Hall of Central Harmony, was a smaller square building between the two main halls. It was a sort of private office where the emperor could stop to rest on his way to ceremonies.

Nine-Dragon Wall
This wall, or screen, of glazed tiles shows nine dragons playing with pearls against a background of sea and sky. From ancient times, the dragon was the symbol of the imperial family. This is the largest of three famous nine-dragon screens in China.

Interpret Visuals
1. **Analyze Motives** Why do you think the emperor wanted to keep common people out of the Forbidden City?
2. **Draw Conclusions** What aspects of the Forbidden City helped to convey the power of the emperor?

Different Realms Circa 1400

By the year 1400, the size and power of the world's Muslim, Confucian, and Christian realms varied widely across the Eastern Hemisphere.

Islam Muslim dynasties and empires occupied lands across the Middle East, large portions of Africa, and parts of Europe. The Ottoman Empire controlled land around the Mediterranean Sea, including present-day Turkey and Greece. Around 1400, it was expanding into territories of the Byzantine Empire. The Delhi Sultanate in present-day India had begun breaking up by 1400. The wealthy Songhai Empire of West Africa had a powerful military that controlled the trans-Saharan trade routes in the region. Predominantly Muslim trading cities like Mogadishu and Kilwa dotted Africa's east coast.

Confucianism In 1400, there was a renewed focus on Confucianism in China under the Ming dynasty. Ming China covered the eastern half of modern-day China and was powerful enough to demand tribute from surrounding states, such as Korea. Korea, too, was a Confucian state in 1400.

Christianity The Christian realm in the year 1400 could be divided into two broad parts: Western Christianity, which referred to Catholicism in Europe, and Eastern Christianity, which included Eastern Orthodox and Oriental Orthodox Christian populations. Catholicism was in the midst of a division called the Great Western Schism. Two popes had been elected and their followers were split along national lines. This exacerbated rivalries between various European Christian states. Eastern Orthodoxy was prevalent in Russia, Hungary, Greece, and parts of Turkey, but the Byzantine Empire had already suffered more than 100 years of decline and lost much territory. Oriental Orthodoxy was found in Egypt, Ethiopia, pockets of the Middle East, and a region of India.

Ming Relations with Foreign Countries China's official trade policies in the 1500s reflected its isolation. To keep the influence of outsiders to a minimum, only the government was to conduct foreign trade, and only through three coastal ports: Canton, Macao, and Ningbo. In reality, trade flourished up and down the coast. Profit-minded merchants smuggled cargoes of silk, porcelain, and other valuable goods out of the country into the eager hands of European merchants. Usually, Europeans paid for purchases with silver, much of it from mines in the Americas.

Demand for Chinese goods had affected the economy. Industries such as silk-making and ceramics grew rapidly. Manufacturing and commerce increased. But China did not become highly industrialized for two main reasons. First, the idea of commerce offended Confucian beliefs. Second, Chinese economic policies traditionally favored agriculture. Taxes on agriculture stayed low. Taxes on manufacturing and trade skyrocketed.

Christian missionaries accompanied European traders into China. They brought Christianity and knowledge of European science and technology, such as the clock. The first missionary to have an impact was an Italian Jesuit named Matteo Ricci. He gained special favor at the Ming court through his intelligence and fluency in Chinese.

Still, many educated Chinese opposed the European and Christian presence.

"But I was careful not to refer to these Westerners as 'Great Officials,' and corrected Governor Liu Yin-shu when he referred to the Jesuits Regis and Fridelli . . . as if they were honored imperial commissioners. For even though some of the Western methods are different from our own, and may even be an improvement, there is little about them that is new. The principles of mathematics all derive from the Book of Changes, and the Western methods are Chinese in origin: this algebra—'A-erh-chu-pa-erh'—springs from an Eastern word. And though it was indeed the Westerners who showed us something our ancient calendar experts did not know—namely how to calculate the angles of the northern pole—this but shows the truth of what Chu Hsi arrived at through his investigation of things: the earth is like the yolk within an egg."

—Kangxi, quoted in *Emperor of China: Self-Portrait of K'ang-Hsi*

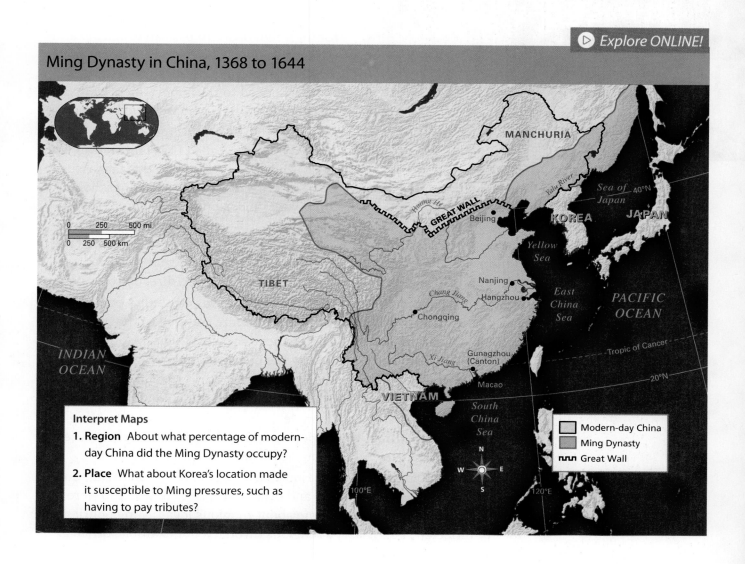

▶ Explore ONLINE!

Ming Dynasty in China, 1368 to 1644

Interpret Maps

1. **Region** About what percentage of modern-day China did the Ming Dynasty occupy?

2. **Place** What about Korea's location made it susceptible to Ming pressures, such as having to pay tributes?

Legend:
- Modern-day China
- Ming Dynasty
- Great Wall

The Great Wall of China was begun during the Qin Dynasty, but it was during the Ming Dynasty that it was rebuilt and extended into the wall that we see today.

Ming China's relationship to its neighbors was reflected in its expansion of the Great Wall. The wall had been repaired during previous dynasties, including the Song, but during the Ming, it saw its greatest extension. Fearing a Mongol invasion, Ming leaders ordered the wall to be maintained and strengthened.

A Stable and Diverse Society After Hongwu expelled the Mongols, he reorganized the government, replaced the Yuan laws with new codes based on Confucian teachings, and established the emperor as the head of the state. Because he was a strong leader, this arrangement created a stable government. It would work less well for later, ineffectual leaders.

The Ming government required candidates for high civil office to pass an official examination based on Confucian traditional texts. This ensured that administrators were highly literate and led to the appointment of many competent officials who were well versed in the Confucian ideals promoted by the Ming.

An institution called the Hanlin Academy, established during the Tang dynasty, issued the official interpretation of primary Confucian books. Hanlin scholars advised the Chinese emperor on history and Confucian thought. Under Hongwu, this Tang-era institution became more political. In his effort to exert direct control over Chinese provinces, Hongwu transformed the Hanlin Academy into an institution of six secretaries that governed various aspects of the empire. These secretaries reported directly to Hongwu.

By 1430, a department called the Censorate was created to enforce anti-corruption laws. Officials of the Censorate traveled to the provinces to complete inspections and could remove corrupt officials from office. Knowing they could be punished by the Censorate encouraged officials to obey the laws and deal honestly with others.

In more diverse provinces, Ming leaders used the military to manage China's ethnic diversity. For example, in hopes of strengthening Ming control of Yunnan province, whose population included both Han Chinese and non-Han Chinese, the military pushed more Han into the area.

During the Ming era, religion flourished, particularly Buddhism, Confucianism, and Taoism. Temples and other new places of worship were built, and monks taught and wrote about religious ideas. Ming politics and society reflected the dynasty's religious diversity. For example, officials had Daoist priests perform rituals at the imperial court and for common

Reading Check
Make Inferences
What do you think the people of other countries thought about China after one of Zheng He's visits?

people. Daoist priests also composed official hymns at the request of the emperor. The Jesuit missionaries arriving from Europe blended into Chinese society and served as musicians, astronomers, and cartographers at the imperial court. Buddhist monks were officially sanctioned to perform rituals for common people. Many Buddhist and Daoist sects integrated Confucian ideals into their own teachings.

Manchus Found the Qing Dynasty

By 1600, the Ming had ruled for more than 200 years, and the dynasty was weakening. Its problems grew—ineffective rulers, corrupt officials, and a government that was out of money. Higher taxes and bad harvests pushed millions of peasants toward starvation. Civil strife and rebellion followed.

Northeast of the Great Wall lay Manchuria. In 1644, the **Manchus** (MAN·chooz), the people of that region, invaded China and the Ming Dynasty collapsed. The Manchus seized Beijing, and their leader became China's new emperor. As the Mongols had done in the 1300s, the Manchus took a Chinese name for their dynasty, the **Qing** (chihng) **Dynasty**. They would rule for more than 260 years and expand China's borders to include Taiwan, Chinese Central Asia, Mongolia, and Tibet.

China Under the Qing Many Chinese resisted rule by the non-Chinese Manchus. Rebellions flared up periodically for decades. The Manchus, however, slowly earned the people's respect. They upheld China's traditional Confucian beliefs and social structures. They made the country's frontiers safe and restored China's prosperity. Two powerful Manchu rulers contributed greatly to the acceptance of the new dynasty.

The first, **Kangxi** (kahng·shee), became emperor in 1661 and ruled for some 60 years. He reduced government expenses and lowered taxes. A scholar and patron of the arts, Kangxi gained the support of intellectuals by offering them government positions. He also enjoyed the company of the Jesuits at court. They told him about developments in science, medicine, and mathematics in Europe.

BIOGRAPHY

Kangxi
(1654–1722)

The emperor Kangxi had too much curiosity to remain isolated in the Forbidden City. To calm the Chinese in areas devastated by the Manchu conquest, Kangxi set out on a series of "tours."

"On tours I learned about the common people's grievances by talking with them. . . . I asked peasants about their officials, looked at their houses, and discussed their crops."

In 1696, with Mongols threatening the northern border, Kangxi exhibited leadership unheard of in later Ming times. Instead of waiting in the palace for reports, he personally led 80,000 troops to victory over the Mongols.

Under his grandson Qian-long (chyahn•lung), who ruled from 1736 to 1795, China reached its greatest size and prosperity. An industrious emperor like his grandfather, Qian-long often rose at dawn to work on the empire's problems. These included armed nomads on its borders and the expanding presence of European missionaries and merchants in China.

Manchus Continue Chinese Isolation To the Chinese, their country—called the Middle Kingdom—had been the cultural center of the universe for 2,000 years. If foreign states wished to trade with China, they would have to follow Chinese rules. These rules included trading only at special ports and paying tribute.

The Dutch were masters of the Indian Ocean trade by the time of Qian-long. They accepted China's restrictions. Their diplomats paid tribute to the emperor through gifts and by performing the required "kowtow" ritual. This ritual involved kneeling in front of the emperor and touching one's head to the ground nine times. As a result, the Chinese accepted the Dutch as trading partners. The Dutch returned home with traditional porcelains and silk, as well as a new trade item, tea. By 1800, tea would make up 80 percent of shipments to Europe.

Great Britain also wanted to increase trade with China. But the British did not like China's trade restrictions. In 1793, Lord George Macartney delivered a letter from King George III to Qian-long. It asked for a better trade arrangement, including Chinese acceptance of British manufactured goods. Macartney refused to kowtow, and Qian-long denied Britain's request. China, in the emperor's view, was self-sufficient.

In the 1800s, the British, Dutch, and others would attempt to chip away at China's trade restrictions until the empire itself began to crack.

Korea Under the Manchus In 1636, even before they came to power in China, the Manchus invaded Korea and made the country change its allegiance from the Ming to the Manchus. Although Korea remained independent, it existed in China's shadow. Koreans organized their government according to Confucian principles. They also adopted China's technology, its culture, and especially its policy of isolation.

When the Manchus established the Qing dynasty, Korea's political relationship with China did not change. But Korea's attitude did. The Manchu invasion, combined with a Japanese attack in the 1590s, provoked strong feelings of nationalism in the Korean people. This sentiment was most evident in their art. Instead of traditional Chinese subjects, many artists chose to show popular Korean scenes.

Reading Check
Make Inferences
Why do you think the kowtow ritual was so important to the Chinese emperor?

Life in Ming and Qing China

In the 1600s and 1700s, there was general peace and prosperity in China. Life improved for most Chinese.

Families and the Role of Women Most Chinese families had farmed the land the same way their ancestors had. However, during the Qing Dynasty, irrigation and fertilizer use increased. Farmers grew rice and new crops,

China's Population Boom

China's population grew dramatically from 1650 to 1900. General peace and increased agricultural productivity were the causes.

The Growth of Early Modern China

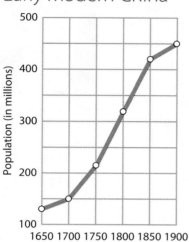

A Chinese family prepares for a wedding in the 1800s.

Interpret Graphs
Compare By what percentage did China's population increase between 1650 and 1900?

such as corn and sweet potatoes, brought by Europeans from the Americas. As food production increased, nutrition improved and families expanded. A population explosion followed.

These expanded Chinese families favored sons over daughters. Only a son was allowed to perform vital religious rituals. A son also would raise his own family under his parents' roof, assuring aging parents of help with the farming. As a result, females were not valued, and many female infants were killed. Although men dominated the household and their wives, women had significant responsibilities. Besides working in the fields, they supervised the children's education and managed the family's finances. While most women were forced to remain secluded in their homes, some found outside jobs such as working as midwives or textile workers.

Vocabulary
midwife a woman trained to assist women in childbirth

Cultural Developments The culture of early modern China was based mainly on traditional forms, and these traditions were apparent in all areas of the humanities. The great masterpiece of traditional Chinese fiction was written during this period. *Dream of the Red Chamber* by Cao Zhan examines upper class Manchu society in the 1700s. Most artists of the time painted in traditional styles, which valued technique over creativity. In pottery, technical skill as well as experimentation led to the production of high-quality ceramics, including porcelain. Drama was a popular entertainment, especially in rural China where literacy rates were low. Plays that presented Chinese history and cultural heroes entertained and also helped unify Chinese society by creating a national culture.

Comparing Renaissance and Ming Cultures

The cultural expansion that occurred under the Ming and Qing dynasties can be compared to the European Renaissance in a few general ways. The movements were similar in that they both sought to connect to their own cultural traditions. The subject matter of these traditions, however, was different.

For example, the Ming court asked painters to imitate the styles and subjects of earlier dynasties. In Italy, Renaissance thinkers and artists focused on classical Roman and Greek topics like astronomy and philosophy for inspiration. Interest in Christianity, which was held by Northern European Renaissance figures, was not shared by Chinese thinkers, who looked instead to traditional Confucian teachings and texts.

These 12th-century Chinese women work outside the home, making silk.

One shared value was a focus on individual artistic expression. For example, many Chinese artists developed their own style of calligraphy. In calligraphy, the painting of Chinese characters attains great beauty. The personal style of a calligrapher was not unlike a Renaissance artist's own painterly style.

A deep exploration of human nature was characteristic of both movements, as well, especially in works of literature. *Dream of the Red Chamber* has been praised for its rich characters as much as Shakespeare's plays have. Chinese writers, like their Renaissance counterparts, also excelled at writing in the vernacular.

Architecture was an area where China and Europe diverged. Achievements in European Renaissance architecture centered largely on Christian churches and cathedrals. The main notable work of Chinese architecture is the Forbidden City, built for the glory of the emperor. One more area in which the two cultures differed was patronage. Wealthy patrons supported Renaissance artists, but in China, the court directed all cultural activities.

A New Feudalism Under Strong Japanese Leaders

In the 1300s, the unity that had been achieved in Japan in the previous century broke down. Shoguns, or military leaders, in the north and south fiercely fought one another for power. Although these rival courts came back together, a series of politically weak shoguns lost control of the country. The whole land was torn by factional strife and economic unrest.

Local Lords Rule In 1467, civil war shattered Japan's old feudal system. The country collapsed into chaos. Centralized rule ended. Power drained away from the shogun to territorial lords in hundreds of separate domains. A violent era of disorder followed. This time in Japanese history, which lasted from 1467 to 1568, is known as the Sengoku, or "Warring States,"

Vocabulary
calligraphy the art of writing

Reading Check
Make Inferences
What was the effect of the emphasis on tradition in early modern China?

A samurai warrior

Vocabulary
shogunate the administration or rule of a shogun

period. Powerful samurai seized control of old feudal estates. They offered peasants and others protection in return for their loyalty. These warrior-chieftains, called **daimyo** (DY•mee•OH), became lords in a new kind of Japanese feudalism. *Daimyo meant* "great name." Under this system, security came from this group of powerful war-lords. The emperor at Kyoto became a figurehead who had a leader-ship title but no actual power.

The new Japanese feudalism resembled European feudalism in many ways. The daimyo built fortified castles and created small armies of samurai on horses. Later they added foot soldiers with muskets (guns) to their ranks. Rival daimyo often fought each other for territory. This led to disorder throughout the land.

New Leaders Restore Order A number of ambitious daimyo hoped to gather enough power to take control of the entire country. One, the brutal and ambitious **Oda Nobunaga** (oh•dah-noh•boo•nah•gah), defeated his rivals and seized the imperial capital Kyoto in 1568.

Following his own motto "Rule the empire by force," Nobunaga sought to eliminate his remaining enemies. These included rival daimyo as well as wealthy Buddhist monasteries aligned with them. In 1575, Nobunaga's 3,000 soldiers armed with muskets crushed an enemy force of samurai cavalry. This was the first time firearms had been used effectively in battle in Japan. However, Nobunaga was not able to unify Japan. He committed *seppuku,* the ritual suicide of a samurai, in 1582, when one of his own generals turned on him.

Nobunaga's best general, **Toyotomi Hideyoshi** (toh•you•toh•mee-hee•deh•yoh•shee), continued his fallen leader's mission. Hideyoshi set out to destroy the daimyo who remained hostile. By combining brute force with shrewd political alliances, he controlled most of the country by 1590. Hideyoshi did not stop with Japan. With the idea of eventually conquering China, he invaded Korea in 1592 and began a long campaign against the Koreans and their Ming Chinese allies. When Hideyoshi died in 1598, his troops withdrew from Korea.

Tokugawa Shogunate Unites Japan One of Hideyoshi's strongest daimyo allies, Tokugawa Ieyasu (toh•koo•gah•wah-ee•yeh•yah•soo), completed the unification of Japan. In 1600, Ieyasu defeated his rivals at the Battle of Sekigahara. His victory earned him the loyalty of daimyo throughout Japan. Three years later, Ieyasu became the sole ruler, or shogun. He then moved Japan's capital to his power base at Edo, a small fishing village that would later become the city of Tokyo.

Japan was unified, but the daimyo still governed at the local level. To keep them from rebelling, Ieyasu required that they spend every other year in the capital. Even when they returned to their lands, they had to leave their families behind as hostages in Edo. Through this "alternate attendance policy" and other restrictions, Ieyasu tamed the daimyo. This was a major step toward restoring centralized government to Japan. As a result, the rule of law overcame the rule of the sword.

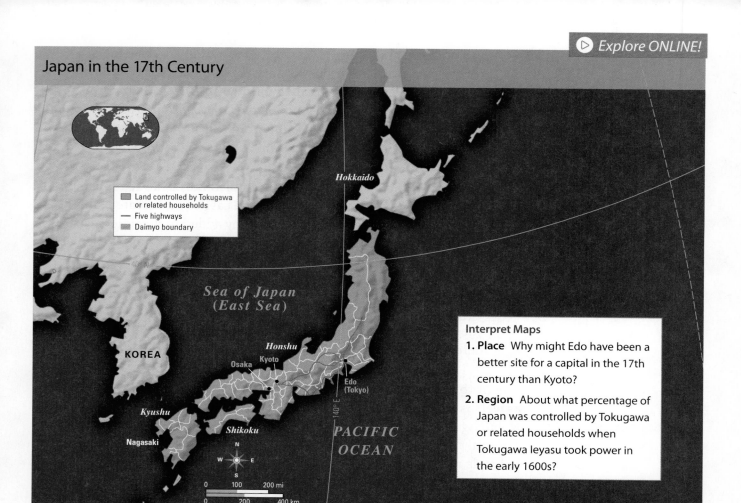

Japan in the 17th Century

▶ Explore ONLINE!

Legend:
- Land controlled by Tokugawa or related households
- Five highways
- Daimyo boundary

Hokkaido

Sea of Japan (East Sea)

KOREA

Honshu

Kyoto

Osaka

Kyushu

Shikoku

Nagasaki

Edo (Tokyo)

PACIFIC OCEAN

N W E S

0   100   200 mi
0   200   400 km

Interpret Maps

1. **Place** Why might Edo have been a better site for a capital in the 17th century than Kyoto?

2. **Region** About what percentage of Japan was controlled by Tokugawa or related households when Tokugawa Ieyasu took power in the early 1600s?

Reading Check
Draw Conclusions
How would the "alternate attendance policy" restrict the daimyo?

Ieyasu founded the **Tokugawa Shogunate**, which would hold power until 1867. On his deathbed in 1616, Ieyasu advised his son, Hidetada, "Take care of the people. Strive to be virtuous. Never neglect to protect the country." Most Tokugawa shoguns followed that advice. Their rule brought a welcome order to Japan.

Life in Tokugawa Japan

Japan enjoyed more than two and a half centuries of stability, prosperity, and isolation under the Tokugawa shoguns. Farmers produced more food, and the population rose. Still, the vast majority of peasants, weighed down by heavy taxes, led lives filled with misery. The people who prospered in Tokugawa society were the merchant class and the wealthy. However, everyone, rich and poor alike, benefited from a flowering of Japanese culture during this era.

Society in Tokugawa Japan Tokugawa society was very structured. The emperor had the top rank but was just a figurehead. The actual ruler was the shogun, who was the supreme military commander. Below him were the daimyo, the powerful landholding samurai. Samurai warriors came next. The peasants and artisans followed them. Peasants made up about four-fifths of the population. Merchants were at the bottom, but they gradually became more important as the Japanese economy expanded.

The Tokugawa era was marked by a return to Confucian values and ideas. This philosophy came to Japan in the medieval age from China. In Japan, as in China, Confucian values influenced ideas about society. According to Confucius, the ideal society depended on agriculture, not commerce. Farmers, not merchants, made ideal citizens. In the real world of Tokugawa Japan, however, peasant farmers bore the main tax burden and faced more difficulties than any other class. Many of them abandoned farm life and headed for the expanding towns and cities. There, they mixed with samurai, artisans, and merchants.

By the mid-1700s, Japan began to shift from a rural to an urban society. Edo had grown from a small village in 1600 to perhaps the largest city in the world. Its population was more than 1 million. As Japan's urban population grew, social structures changed. In these rapidly growing cities, people worked as manufacturers and wholesalers. Eventually, a class of wealthy merchants emerged. In turn, the daimyo and samurai, dependent on taxing a shrinking farmer class, saw their influence wane.

The rise of large commercial centers also increased employment opportunities for women. Women found jobs in entertainment, textile manufacturing, and publishing. Still, the majority of Japanese women led sheltered and restricted lives as peasant wives. They worked in the fields, managed the household, cared for the children, and each woman obeyed her husband without question.

Culture Under the Tokugawa Shogunate Traditional culture continued to thrive. Samurai attended ceremonial *noh* dramas, which were based on tragic themes. They read tales of ancient warriors and their courage in battle. In their homes, they hung paintings that showed scenes from classical literature. But traditional entertainment faced competition in the cities from new styles of literature, drama, and art.

Townspeople read a new type of fiction, realistic stories about self-made merchants or the hardships of life. The people also read **haiku** (HY•koo), 3-line verse poetry with a 5-7-5-syllable pattern. This poetry presents images rather than ideas.

Historical Source

Haiku

Matsuo Basho, the greatest haiku poet, wrote this poem before his death in 1694.

On a journey, ailing—
My dreams roam about
Over a withered moor.

        —Matsuo Basho, from
        Matsuo Basho

Tabi ni yande
Yume wa Kareno o
Kakemeguru

        —Matsuo Basho,
        in Japanese

Analyze Historical Sources
How is Matsuo Basho's haiku a poem about death?

Kabuki Theater

Kabuki is a traditional form of Japanese theater. It makes use of extravagant costumes, masklike makeup, and exaggerated postures and gestures. The illustrations show a contemporary actor and a 19th-century performer playing warriors.

Although kabuki was created by a woman, all roles, both male and female, are performed by men. Kabuki plays are about grand historical events or the everyday life of people in Tokugawa Japan.

For 400 years, kabuki has provided entertainment for the Japanese people. More recently, kabuki has been performed for audiences around the world, including the United States. Major centers for kabuki theater in Japan are Tokyo, Kyoto, and Osaka.

Reading Check
Summarize How did the Japanese express themselves culturally under the Tokugawa shoguns?

Townspeople also attended **kabuki** theater. Actors in elaborate costumes, using music, dance, and mime, performed skits about modern life. The paintings people enjoyed were often woodblock prints showing city life.

Contact Between Europe and Japan

Europeans began coming to Japan in the 16th century, during the Warring States period. Despite the severe disorder in the country, the Japanese welcomed traders and missionaries, first from Portugal and, later, other European countries. These newcomers introduced fascinating new technologies and ideas. Within a century, however, the aggressive Europeans had worn out their welcome.

Portugal Sends Ships, Merchants, and Technology to Japan The Japanese first encountered Europeans in 1543, when shipwrecked Portuguese sailors washed up on the shores of southern Japan. Portuguese merchants soon followed. They hoped to involve themselves in Japan's trade with China and Southeast Asia. The Portuguese brought clocks, eyeglasses, tobacco, firearms, and other unfamiliar items from Europe. Japanese merchants eager to expand their markets were happy to receive the newcomers and their goods.

Back in Japan, the daimyo, too, welcomed the strangers. The daimyo felt that European goods could provide an advantage over their rivals. For example, they were particularly interested in the Portuguese muskets and cannons. One of these warlords listened intently to a Japanese observer's description of a musket:

"In their hands they carried something two or three feet long, straight on the outside with a passage inside, and made of a heavy substance. . . . This thing with one blow can smash a mountain of silver and a wall of iron. If one sought to do mischief in another man's domain and he was touched by it, he would lose his life instantly."

—Anonymous Japanese Writer, quoted in *Sources of Japanese Tradition* (1958)

The Japanese purchased weapons from the Portuguese and soon began their own production. Firearms forever changed the time-honored tradition of the Japanese warrior, whose principal weapon had been the sword. Some daimyo recruited and trained corps of peasants to use muskets. Many samurai, who retained the sword as their principal weapon, would lose their lives to musket fire in future combat.

The cannon also had an impact on life in Japan. Daimyo had to build fortified castles, like the Himeji Castle, to withstand the destructive force of cannonballs. The castles attracted merchants, artisans, and others to surrounding lands. Many of these lands were to grow into the towns and cities of modern Japan, including Edo (Tokyo), Osaka, Himeji, and Nagoya.

Christian Missionaries in Japan In 1549, Christian missionaries began arriving in Japan. The Japanese accepted the missionaries in part because they associated them with the muskets and other European goods that they wanted to purchase. However, the religious orders of Jesuits, Franciscans, and Dominicans came to convert the Japanese.

Francis Xavier, a Jesuit, led the first mission to Japan. He wrote that the Japanese were "very sociable. . . and much concerned with their honor, which they prize above everything else." Francis Xavier baptized about a hundred converts before he left Japan. By the year 1600, other European missionaries had converted about 300,000 Japanese to Christianity.

The success of the missionaries upset Tokugawa Ieyasu. He found aspects of the Christian invasion troublesome. Missionaries scorned traditional Japanese beliefs and involved themselves in local politics. At first, Ieyasu did not take any action. He feared driving off the Portuguese, English, Spanish, and Dutch traders who spurred Japan's economy. By 1612, however, the shogun had come to fear religious uprisings more. He banned Christianity and focused on ridding his country of all Christians.

Ieyasu died in 1616, but repression of Christianity continued off and on for the next two decades under his successors. In 1637, the issue came to a head. An uprising in southern Japan of some 30,000 peasants, led by dissatisfied samurai, shook the Tokugawa shogunate. Because so many of the rebels were Christian, the shogun decided that Christianity was at the root of the rebellion. After that, the shoguns ruthlessly persecuted Christians. European missionaries were killed or driven out of Japan. All Japanese were forced to demonstrate faithfulness to some branch of Buddhism. These policies eventually eliminated Christianity in Japan and led to the formation of an exclusion policy.

Reading Check
Compare and Contrast How was the treatment of Europeans different in Japan and China? How was it similar?

The Closed Country Policy

The persecution of Christians was part of an attempt to control foreign ideas. When Europeans first arrived, no central authority existed to contain them. The strong leaders who later took power did not like the introduction of European ideas and ways, but they valued European trade. As time passed, the Tokugawa shoguns realized that they could safely exclude both the missionaries and the merchants. By 1639, they had sealed Japan's borders and instituted a "closed country policy."

Japan in Isolation Most commercial contacts with Europeans ended. One port, Nagasaki, remained open to foreign traders. But only Dutch and Chinese merchants were allowed into the port. Earlier, the English had left Japan voluntarily, while the Spanish and the Portuguese had been expelled. Since the Tokugawa shoguns controlled Nagasaki, they now had a monopoly on foreign trade, which continued to be profitable.

This painting on wood panels depicts Japanese merchants and Jesuit missionaries awaiting the arrival of a Portuguese ship at Nagasaki in the 1500s.

History in Depth

Zen Buddhism

The form of Buddhism that had the greatest impact on Japanese culture was Zen Buddhism. It especially influenced the samurai.

Zen Buddhists sought spiritual enlightenment through meditation. Strict discipline of mind and body was the Zen path to wisdom. Zen monks would sit in meditation for hours, as shown in the sculpture. If they showed signs of losing concentration, a Zen master might shout at them or hit them with a stick.

Reading Check
Form Generalizations
Do you think Japan's closed country policy effectively kept Western ideas and customs out of Japan?

For more than 200 years, Japan remained basically closed to Europeans. In addition, the Japanese were forbidden to leave, so they would not bring back foreign ideas. Japan continued to develop, but as a self-sufficient country, free from European attempts to colonize or establish their presence.

Europeans had met with much resistance in their efforts to open the East to trade. But expansion to the West, in the Americas, would prove much more successful for European traders, missionaries, and colonizers.

Lesson 3 Assessment

1. **Organize Information** Create a two-column graphic organizer similar to the one shown. Fill it in with the names of the Chinese emperors you learned about and a fact or two from the text about each. Which emperor was most influential? Explain by using your facts.

Emperor	Facts
1.	1.
2.	2.
3.	3.

2. **Key Terms and People** For each key term or person in the lesson, write a sentence explaining its significance.

3. **Analyze Effects** What did Christian missionaries bring to China?

4. **Summarize** What was the structure of society in Tokugawa Japan?

5. **Analyze Causes** How did Beijing become the capital of China?

6. **Compare and Contrast** In what ways was the European Renaissance similar to and different from the flowering of Chinese culture during the Ming and Qing dynasties?

7. **Draw Conclusions** Why do you think that the emperor had less power than a shogun?

Spain Builds an American Empire

The Big Idea

The voyages of Columbus prompted the Spanish to establish colonies in the Americas.

Why It Matters Now

Throughout the Americas, Spanish culture, language, and descendants are the legacy of this period.

Key Terms and People

Christopher Columbus
colony
Hernando Cortés
conquistador
Francisco Pizarro
Atahualpa
mestizo
encomienda

Setting the Stage

Competition for wealth in Asia among European nations was fierce. This competition prompted a Genoese sea captain named **Christopher Columbus** to make a daring voyage from Spain in 1492. Instead of sailing south around Africa and then east, Columbus sailed west across the Atlantic in search of an alternate trade route to Asia and its riches. Columbus never reached Asia. Instead, he stepped onto an island in the Caribbean. That event would bring together the peoples of Europe, Africa, and the Americas.

The Voyages of Columbus

The *Niña*, *Pinta*, and *Santa María* sailed out of a Spanish port around dawn on August 3, 1492. In a matter of months, Columbus's fleet would reach the shores of what Europeans saw as an astonishing new world.

First Encounters In the early hours of October 12, 1492, the long-awaited cry came. A lookout aboard the *Pinta* caught sight of a shoreline in the distance. *"Tierra! Tierra!"* he shouted. "Land! Land!" By dawn, Columbus and his crew were ashore. Thinking he had successfully reached the East Indies, Columbus called the surprised inhabitants who greeted him *los indios*. The term translated into "Indian," a word mistakenly applied to all the native peoples of the Americas. In his journal, Columbus recounted his first meeting with the native peoples:

> *"I presented them with some red caps, and strings of glass beads to wear upon the neck, and many other trifles of small value, wherewith they were much delighted, and became wonderfully attached to us. Afterwards they came swimming to the boats where we were, bringing parrots, balls of cotton thread,*

javelins, and many other things which they exchanged for articles we gave them . . . In fact they accepted anything and gave what they had with the utmost good will."

—Christopher Columbus, *Journal of Columbus*

Portrait of a Man Called Christopher Columbus (1519) by Sebastiano del Piombo

Columbus had miscalculated where he was. He had not reached the East Indies. Scholars believe he landed instead on an island in the Bahamas in the Caribbean Sea. The natives there were not Indians, but a group who called themselves the Taino. Nonetheless, Columbus claimed the island for Spain. He named it San Salvador, or "Holy Savior."

Columbus, like other explorers, was interested in gold. Finding none on San Salvador, he explored other islands, staking his claim to each one. "It was my wish to bypass no island without taking possession," he wrote.

In early 1493, Columbus returned to Spain. The reports he relayed about his journey delighted the Spanish monarchs. King Ferdinand and Queen Isabella, who had funded his first voyage, agreed to finance three more trips. Their sponsorship was a major motivation for Columbus to continue his explorations.

Columbus embarked on his second voyage to the Americas in September 1493. He journeyed no longer as an explorer, but as an empire builder. He commanded a fleet of some 17 ships that carried over 1,000 soldiers, crewmen, and colonists. The Spanish intended to transform the islands of the Caribbean into **colonies**, or lands that are controlled by another nation. Over the next two centuries, other European explorers began sailing across the Atlantic in search of new lands to claim.

Other Explorers Take to the Seas By the 15th century, the political systems in Portugal, headed by King John II, gave strong support to exploration of the Americas. Portugal had already established trading outposts in Africa and Asia, and the Treaty of Tordesillas allowed the king to claim Brazil. In 1500, the Portuguese explorer Pedro Álvares Cabral reached the shores of modern-day Brazil and claimed the land for his country. A year later, Amerigo Vespucci (vehs•POO•chee), an Italian in the service of Portugal, also traveled along the eastern coast of South America. Upon his return to Europe, he claimed that the land was not part of Asia, but a "new" world. In 1507, a German mapmaker named the new continent "America" in honor of Amerigo Vespucci.

In 1519, Portuguese explorer Ferdinand Magellan led the boldest exploration yet. Several years earlier, Spanish explorer Vasco Núñez de Balboa had marched through modern-day Panama and had become the first European to gaze upon the Pacific Ocean. Soon after, Magellan convinced the king of Spain to fund his voyage into the newly discovered ocean.

European Exploration of the Americas, 1492–1682

GREENLAND

ICELAND

Hudson 1610

Hudson 1609

Cabot 1497

Cartier 1534–35

ENGLAND

EUROPE

FRANCE

Smith 1606–07, Mayflower 1620

PORTUGAL

SPAIN

NORTH AMERICA

Hudson Bay

Marquette 1673

Plymouth

LaSalle 1682

Jamestown

40° N

Coronado 1540–42

Santa Fe

De Soto 1539–42

ATLANTIC OCEAN

CANARY ISLANDS

MADEIRA

Cabrillo 1542–43

St. Augustine

Ponce de León 1512–13

Verrazzano 1524

Cabeza de Vaca 1535–36

HISPANIOLA

Columbus 1492

AFRICA

Gulf of Mexico

Cortés 1519

CUBA

Santo Domingo

Columbus 1493–95

Veracruz

Tenochtitlán (Mexico City)

Caribbean Sea

Columbus 1502–03

PACIFIC OCEAN

Balboa 1510–13

Cabral 1500

Pizarro 1530–33

Columbus 1498

Magellan's Crew 1522

0° Equator

N W E S

Vespucci 1499

SOUTH AMERICA

Magellan 1519

500   1,000 mi

1,000   2,000 km

Explorers' Routes
- Spanish
- Portuguese
- French
- English
- Dutch

Magellan 1519

120° W   80° W   40° W

40° S

Interpret Maps

1. **Movement** How many different voyages did Columbus make to the Americas?

2. **Region** Which general region did the Spanish and Portuguese explore? Where did the English, Dutch, and French explore?

With about 250 men and five ships, Magellan sailed around the southern end of South America and into the waters of the Pacific. The fleet sailed for months without seeing land, except for some small islands. Food supplies soon ran out.

After exploring the island of Guam, Magellan and his crew eventually reached the Philippines. Unfortunately, Magellan became involved in a local war there and was killed. His crew, greatly reduced by disease and starvation, continued sailing west toward home. Out of Magellan's original crew, only 18 men and one ship arrived back in Spain in 1522, nearly three years after they had left. They were the first persons to circumnavigate, or sail around, the world.

Reading Check
Make Inferences
What was the significance of Magellan's voyage?

Spanish Conquests in Mexico

In 1519, as Magellan embarked on his historic voyage, a Spaniard named **Hernando Cortés** landed on the shores of Mexico. After colonizing several Caribbean islands, the Spanish had turned their attention to the American mainland. Cortés marched inland, looking to claim new lands for Spain. Cortés and the many other Spanish explorers who followed him were known as **conquistadors** (conquerors). Lured by rumors of vast lands filled with gold and silver, conquistadors carved out colonies in regions that would become Mexico, South America, and the United States. The Spanish were the first European settlers in the Americas. As a result of their colonization, the Spanish greatly enriched their empire and left a mark on the cultures of North and South America that exists today.

Cortés Conquers the Aztecs Soon after landing in Mexico in 1519, Cortés learned of the vast and wealthy Aztec Empire in the region's interior. After marching for weeks through difficult mountain passes, Cortés and his force of roughly 600 men finally reached the magnificent Aztec capital of Tenochtitlán (teh•NAWCH•tee•TLAHN). The Aztec emperor, Montezuma II, was convinced at first that Cortés was an armor-wearing god. He agreed to give the Spanish explorer a share of the empire's existing gold supply. Though Montezuma hoped that would satisfy Cortés, it did not. Cortés admitted that he and his comrades had a "disease of the heart that only gold can cure." In both the political and economic sense, Cortés wanted more power.

The Aztecs controlled hundreds of smaller surrounding cities. They gained economic power by demanding periodic payments from these conquered communities. The Spaniards disrupted this system of tribute as they invaded areas that had been under Aztec control. Many peoples from these areas were willing to ally themselves with Cortés as he sought to conquer Tenochtitlán.

The Spaniards largely destroyed Aztec culture. For example, the Aztecs maintained a series of painted books called codices. Codices described Aztec history, economy, religious beliefs, and daily life. They were written in a largely pictorial language, and Aztec cultural tradition dictated that a codex was to be read aloud to others. The Spaniards destroyed almost all of the Aztec codices. They also razed temples and other significant places.

Native Population of Central Mexico, 1500–1620

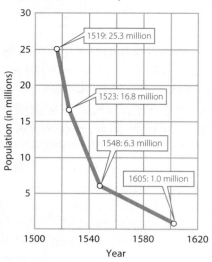

1519: 25.3 million

1523: 16.8 million

1548: 6.3 million

1605: 1.0 million

Source: *The Population of Latin America: A History*

Interpret Graphs
1. **Draw Conclusions** By what percentage did the native population decrease between 1519 and 1605?
2. **Make Inferences** How did the sharp decline in the native population, mainly from disease, affect the Spaniards' attempts to conquer the region?

Reading Check
Summarize What factors enabled the Spanish to defeat the Aztecs?

In November 1519, Cortés captured Montezuma II. The following spring, some of Cortés's men killed many Aztec warriors and chiefs while they were celebrating a religious festival. Then, in June 1520, the Aztecs rebelled against the Spanish intruders and drove out Cortés's forces.

The Spaniards, however, struck back. Despite being greatly outnumbered, Cortés and his men conquered the Aztecs in 1521. Several factors played a key role in the stunning victory. First, the Spanish had the advantage of superior weaponry. Aztec arrows were no match for the Spaniards' muskets and cannons.

Second, Cortés was able to enlist the help of various native groups. With the aid of a native woman interpreter named Malinche, Cortés learned that some natives resented the Aztecs. They hated their harsh practices, including human sacrifice. Through Malinche, Cortés convinced these natives to fight on his side.

Finally, and most important, the natives could do little to stop the invisible warrior that marched alongside the Spaniards—disease. Measles, mumps, smallpox, and typhus were just some of the diseases Europeans brought with them to the Americas. Native Americans had never been exposed to these diseases. Thus, they had developed no natural immunity to them. As a result, they died by the hundreds of thousands. By the time Cortés launched his counterattack, the Aztec population had been greatly reduced by smallpox and measles. In time, European disease would truly devastate the natives of central Mexico, killing millions of them.

Spanish Conquests in Peru

In 1532, another Spanish conquistador, **Francisco Pizarro**, marched a small force into South America. He conquered the Incan Empire and destroyed its culture, economy, and society.

Pizarro Subdues the Inca Pizarro and his army of about 200 met the Incan ruler, **Atahualpa** (AH•tuh•WAHL•puh), near the city of Cajamarca. Atahualpa, who commanded a force of about 30,000, brought several thousand mostly unarmed men for the meeting. The Spaniards waited in ambush, crushed the Incan force, and kidnapped Atahualpa.

The Spaniards then moved into the smaller surrounding cities that were under Incan control and plundered them of gold and silver. Not only was this economically devastating for the Incan Empire, but it was also a cultural blow: the gold and silver had adorned Incan temples and buildings that were destroyed during the looting.

While in captivity, Atahualpa offered to fill a room once with gold and twice with silver in exchange for his release. However, after receiving the ransom, the Spanish strangled the Incan king and burned his body, which was culturally forbidden by the Inca.

With these acts, the Spanish debilitated the Incan political organization. It signaled the beginning of the end of Incan culture. The remaining Incan force, demoralized by their leader's death, retreated from Cajamarca. Pizarro then marched on the Incan capital, Cuzco. He captured it without a struggle in 1533. From Cuzco, Pizarro established a new government that offered Incan lands to Spanish conquerors.

As Cortés and Pizarro conquered the civilizations of the Americas, fellow conquistadors defeated other native peoples. Spanish explorers also conquered the Maya in Yucatan and Guatemala. By the middle of the 16th century, Spain had created an American empire. It included New Spain (Mexico and parts of Guatemala), as well as other lands in Central and South America and the Caribbean.

Spain's Pattern of Conquest In building their new American empire, the Spaniards drew from techniques used during the *reconquista* of Spain. When conquering the Muslims, the Spanish lived among them and imposed their Spanish culture upon them. Spanish settlers in the Americas, known as *peninsulares*, were mostly men. As a result,

---

BIOGRAPHY

Francisco Pizarro
(1475?–1541)

Pizarro was the son of an infantry captain and a young peasant woman. His parents never married. Raised by his mother's poor family, he never learned to read. Ambitious, brave, and ruthless, he intended to make his fortune as an explorer and conqueror.

As Pizarro embarked on a voyage of conquest down the west coast of South America, the governor of Panama ordered him to abandon the expedition to prevent the loss of lives. Pizarro took his sword and drew a line in the dust, inviting those of his followers who desired wealth and fame to cross the line and follow him. Thus began the conquest of Peru.

Pizarro founded the city of Lima, Peru's capital, in 1535. He became governor of Peru and encouraged settlers from Spain.

Atahualpa
(1502?–1533)

Atahualpa was the last ruler of the Incan empire in Peru. After Atahualpa was captured and held for ransom by the Spanish, Incan people throughout the empire brought gold and silver that the Spanish then melted down into bullion and ingots. They accumulated 24 tons of gold and silver, the richest ransom in history.

The Spanish executed Atahualpa despite the ransom paid by his people. As he was about to be burned at the stake, the Spanish offered him a more merciful death by strangulation if he agreed to convert to Christianity, which he did. Thus died the last emperor of the Inca.

relationships between Spanish settlers and native women were common. These relationships created a large **mestizo**—or mixed Spanish and Native American—population.

Although the Spanish conquerors lived among the native people, they also oppressed them. In their effort to exploit the land for its precious resources, the Spanish enslaved Native Americans, forcing them to work within a system known as *encomienda*. Under this system, natives farmed, ranched, or mined for Spanish landlords. These landlords had received the rights to the natives' labor from Spanish authorities. The holders of *encomiendas* promised the Spanish rulers that they would act fairly and respect the workers. However, many abused the natives and worked laborers to death, especially inside dangerous mines.

The Portuguese in Brazil One area of South America that remained outside of Spanish control was Brazil. In 1500, the Portuguese king ordered Pedro Álvares Cabral to further explore Africa and Asia, but Cabral landed in Brazil instead. Portugal promptly claimed the land for itself.

Colonization of Brazil took decades to develop because Portugal's political systems there were very poor. Portugal was then at the height of its world power and had bigger concerns than establishing permanent colonies in Brazil.

During the 1530s, however, the Portuguese began settling the country's coastal region. Finding little gold or silver, the colonists grew sugar. Clearing out huge swaths of forest land, the Portuguese built giant sugar plantations. The demand for sugar in Europe was great, and the colony soon enriched Portugal.

By the year 1600, thousands of Portuguese were living in Brazil. Economic and political power was held by a small number of wealthy plantation owners. The plantations required extensive labor, and the Portuguese colonists enslaved both Native Americans and Africans to work them. In time, the Portuguese colonists pushed farther west. They settled even more land for the production of sugar, increasing demand for more native and African slaves.

To find more natives, large groups of Portuguese settlers were organized into *bandeiras*. *Bandeiras* were slave-hunting expeditions that explored western Brazil, searching for natives who could be captured and put to work on sugar plantations. Naturally, the natives resisted, and violent skirmishes often broke out. The *bandeiras* had the dual effect of settling more of Brazil's land for Portugal and destroying the lives and cultures of many native peoples.

Spain's Influence Expands

Spain's American colonies helped make it the richest, most powerful nation in the world during much of the 16th century. Ships filled with treasures from the Americas continually sailed into Spanish harbors. This newfound wealth helped usher in a golden age of art and culture in Spain.

Throughout the 16th century, Spain also increased its military might. To protect its treasure-filled ships, Spain built a powerful navy. The

Reading Check
Form Generalizations
What was the effect of Portuguese sugar plantations on native peoples in Brazil?

Spanish also strengthened their other military forces, creating a skillful and determined army. For a century and a half, Spain's army seldom lost a battle. Meanwhile, Spain enlarged its American empire by settling in parts of what is now the United States.

Conquistadors Push North Dreams of new conquests prompted Spain to back a series of expeditions into the southwestern United States. The Spanish actually had settled in parts of the United States before they even dreamed of building an empire on the American mainland. In 1513, Spanish explorer Juan Ponce de León landed on the coast of modern-day Florida and claimed it for Spain.

This U.S. postage stamp was issued in 1940 to celebrate the 400th anniversary of the Coronado expedition.

By 1540, after building an empire that stretched from Mexico to Peru, the Spanish once again looked to the land that is now the United States. In 1540–1541, Francisco Vásquez de Coronado led an expedition throughout much of present-day Arizona, New Mexico, Texas, Oklahoma, and Kansas. He was searching for another wealthy empire to conquer. Coronado found little gold amidst the dry deserts of the Southwest. As a result, the Spanish monarchy assigned mostly priests to explore and colonize the future United States.

Catholic priests had accompanied conquistadors from the very beginning of American colonization. The conquistadors had come in search of wealth. The priests who accompanied them had religious motives. The priests had come in search of converts, and they found such converts among the native people.

A group's spiritual beliefs are an essential part of its culture. As the priests converted Native Americans to the Catholic religion and Christianity spread, indigenous cultures faced significant consequences. For example, many Native Americans were forced to leave their homes and move somewhere else. Still others were forcefully put to work.

In the winter of 1609–1610, Pedro de Peralta, governor of Spain's northern holdings in New Mexico, led settlers to a tributary on the upper Rio Grande. They built a capital called Santa Fe, or "Holy Faith." In the next two decades, a string of Christian missions arose among the Pueblo, the native inhabitants of the region. Scattered missions, forts, and small ranches dotted the lands of New Mexico. These became the headquarters for advancing the Catholic religion.

Reading Check
Contrast How did Spain's colony in New Mexico differ from its colonies in New Spain?

Opposition to Spanish Rule

Spanish priests worked to spread Christianity in the Americas. They also pushed for better treatment of Native Americans. Priests spoke out against the cruel treatment of natives. In particular, they criticized the harsh pattern of labor that emerged under the *encomienda* system. "There is nothing more detestable or more cruel," Dominican monk Bartolomé de Las Casas wrote, "than the tyranny which the Spaniards use toward the Indians for the getting of pearl [riches]."

Legacy of Columbus

Historical and contemporary perspectives on Christopher Columbus's voyages have evolved, and the legacy of the voyages is debated. By their nature, interpretations of historical events are limited because they arise from a person's particular frame of reference.

The credibility, or believability, of the participants must be considered as well. For example, you might question the credibility of someone whose writing betrays a clear political bias. Conversely, you may be likely to trust the perspective of someone who lived through a historical event.

Some historians argue that Columbus took heroic first steps in the creation of great and democratic societies, while others claim that Columbus launched an era of widespread cruelty, bloodshed, and epidemic disease.

Samuel Eliot Morison, a supporter of Columbus writing in the 1940s, laments that Columbus died without realizing the true greatness of his deeds.

"One only wishes that the Admiral might have been afforded the sense of fulfillment that would have come from foreseeing all that flowed from his discoveries; that would have turned all the sorrows of his last years to joy. The whole history of the Americas stems from the Four Voyages of Columbus; and as the Greek city-states looked back to the deathless gods as their founders, so today a score of independent nations and dominions unite in homage to Christopher, the stout-hearted son of Genoa, who carried Christian civilization across the Ocean Sea."

—Samuel Eliot Morison, *Admiral of the Ocean: A Life of Christopher Columbus*

In 1892, historian Justin Winsor was one of the first American writers to criticize Columbus. William D. Phillips summarized Winsor's critique.

"He [Winsor] portrayed Columbus as a daring mariner with great powers of persuasion and extraordinary dedication to his goals. Winsor also revealed Columbus as an inept administrator, so sure of his own rectitude that he openly disobeyed royal instructions and brought many of his troubles on himself. Among his other failings, Columbus unashamedly waged war against the native inhabitants of the Caribbean and enslaved hundreds of them, hoping to profit from a transatlantic slave trade."

—William D. Phillips, *The Worlds of Christopher Columbus*

Analyze Historical Sources

1. From Samuel Eliot Morison's perspective, is the legacy of Columbus positive or negative?

2. How does Justin Winsor's opinion show that perspectives about Columbus have evolved over time? What is meant by Columbus's *rectitude*? How does that word support Winsor's perspective?

African Slavery and Native Resistance The Spanish government abolished the *encomienda* system in 1542. To meet the colonies' need for labor, Las Casas suggested Africans. "The labor of one [African] . . . [is] more valuable than that of four Indians," he said. The priest later changed his view and denounced African slavery. However, others promoted it.

Opposition to the Spanish method of colonization came not only from Spanish priests, but also from the natives themselves. Resistance to Spain's attempt at domination began shortly after the Spanish arrived in the Caribbean. In November 1493, Columbus encountered resistance in his attempt to conquer the present-day island of St. Croix. Before finally surrendering, the inhabitants defended themselves by firing poison arrows.

As late as the end of the 17th century, natives in New Mexico fought Spanish rule. Although they were not risking their lives in silver mines, the natives still felt the weight of Spanish force. In converting the natives, Spanish priests and soldiers burned their sacred objects and prohibited native rituals. The Spanish also forced natives to work for them and sometimes abused them physically.

Sculpture of Pueblo leader Popé

In 1680, Popé, a Pueblo ruler, led a well-organized rebellion against the Spanish. The rebellion involved more than 8,000 warriors from villages all over New Mexico. The native fighters drove the Spanish back into New Spain. For the next 12 years, until the Spanish regained control of the area, the southwest region of the future United States once again belonged to its original inhabitants.

By this time, however, the rulers of Spain had far greater concerns. The other nations of Europe had begun to establish their own colonies in the Americas.

Reading Check
Analyze Causes
Why did the natives of New Mexico revolt against Spanish settlers?

Lesson 4 Assessment

1. **Organize Information** Create a graphic organizer similar to the one below and place the following events in chronological order: Pizarro conquers the Inca; Columbus's arrival; conquistadors explore and colonize the southwest United States; Cortés defeats the Aztecs. Which event do you think had the greatest impact?

> Columbus arrives in Americas, 1492
>
> ↓
>
> [ ]
>
> ↓
>
> [ ]

2. **Key Terms and People** For each key term or person in the lesson, write a sentence explaining its significance.

3. **Summarize** Why were most of the Spanish explorers drawn to the Americas?

4. **Synthesize** Which country was the richest and most powerful in the 16th century, and why?

5. **Analyze Primary Sources** Reread the excerpt from the *Journal of Columbus*. When Columbus described the Taino, what part of his description might have convinced the Spanish that they could take advantage of the natives?

6. **Compare and Contrast** What might have been some similarities in character between Cortés and Pizarro?

European Nations Settle North America

The Big Idea

Several European nations fought for control of North America, and England emerged victorious.

Why It Matters Now

The English settlers in North America left a legacy of law and government that guides the United States today.

Key Terms and People

New France
Jamestown
Pilgrims
Puritans
New Netherland
French and Indian War
Metacom

Setting the Stage

Spain's successful colonization efforts in the Americas did not go unnoticed. Other European nations, such as England, France, and the Netherlands, soon became interested in obtaining their own valuable colonies. The Treaty of Tordesillas, signed in 1494, had divided the newly discovered lands between Spain and Portugal. However, other European countries ignored the treaty. They set out to build their own empires in the Americas. This resulted in a struggle for North America.

Competing Claims in North America

Magellan's voyage showed that ships could reach Asia by way of the Pacific Ocean. Spain claimed the route around the southern tip of South America. Other European countries hoped to find an easier and more direct route to the Pacific. If it existed, a northwest trade route through North America to Asia would become highly profitable. Not finding the route, the French, English, and Dutch instead established colonies in North America.

Explorers Establish New France The early French explorers sailed west with dreams of reaching the East Indies. One explorer was Giovanni da Verrazzano (VEHR•uh•ZAHN•noh), an Italian in the service of France. In 1524, he sailed to North America in search of a sea route to the Pacific. While he did not find the route, Verrazzano did discover what is today New York harbor. Ten years later, the Frenchman Jacques Cartier (kahr•TYAY) reached a gulf off the eastern coast of Canada that led to a broad river. Cartier named it the St. Lawrence. Cartier followed the river inward

Jacques Marquette explores the Mississippi River in 1673.

until he reached a large island dominated by a mountain. He named the island Mont Real (Mount Royal), which later became known as Montreal. In 1608, another French explorer, Samuel de Champlain, sailed up the St. Lawrence with about 32 colonists. They founded Quebec, which became the base of France's colonial empire in North America, known as **New France**.

Then the French moved further into the North American continent. In 1673, French Jesuit priest Jacques Marquette and trader Louis Joliet explored the Great Lakes and the upper Mississippi River. Nearly 10 years later, Sieur de La Salle explored the lower Mississippi. He claimed the entire river valley for France. He named it Louisiana in honor of the French king, Louis XIV. By the early 1700s, New France covered much of what is now the midwestern United States and eastern Canada.

A Trading Empire France's North American empire was immense. But it was sparsely populated. By 1760, the European population of New France had grown to only about 65,000. A large number of French colonists had no desire to build towns or raise families. These settlers included Catholic priests who sought to convert Native Americans. They also included young, single men engaged in what had become New France's main economic activity, the fur trade. Unlike the English, the French were less interested in occupying territories than they were in making money off the land.

Reading Check
Summarize Why were France's North American holdings so sparsely populated?

The English Arrive in North America

The explorations of the Spanish and French inspired the English. In 1606, a company of London investors received a charter from King James to found a colony in North America. In late 1606, the company's three ships, with more than 100 settlers, pushed out of an English harbor. About four months later, in 1607, they reached the coast of Virginia. The colonists claimed the land as theirs. They named the settlement **Jamestown** in honor of their king.

The Settlement at Jamestown The colony's start was disastrous. The settlers were more interested in finding gold than in planting crops. During the first few years, seven out of every ten people died of hunger, disease, or battles with the Native Americans.

Despite their nightmarish start, the colonists eventually gained a foothold in their new land. Jamestown became England's first permanent settlement in North America. The colony's outlook improved greatly after farmers there discovered tobacco. High demand for tobacco in England turned it into a profitable cash crop.

Henry Hudson's ship arrives in the bay of New York on September 12, 1609.

Puritans Create a "New England" In 1620, a group known as **Pilgrims** founded a second English colony, Plymouth, in Massachusetts. Persecuted for their religious beliefs in England, these colonists sought religious freedom. Ten years later, a group known as **Puritans** also sought religious freedom from England's Anglican Church. They established a larger colony at nearby Massachusetts Bay.

The Puritans wanted to build a model community that would set an example for other Christians to follow. Although the colony experienced early difficulties, it gradually began to prosper. This was due in large part to the numerous families in the colony, unlike the mostly single, male population in Jamestown.

The Dutch Found New Netherland The Dutch followed the English and French into North America. In 1609, Henry Hudson, an Englishman in the service of the Netherlands, sailed west. He was searching for a northwest sea route to Asia. Hudson did not find a route. He did, however, explore three waterways that were later named for him—the Hudson River, Hudson Bay, and Hudson Strait.

The Dutch claimed the region along these waterways. They established a fur trade with the Iroquois Indians. They built trading posts along the Hudson River at Fort Orange (now Albany) and on Manhattan Island. Dutch merchants formed the Dutch West India Company. In 1621, the Dutch government granted the company permission to colonize the region

Pirates

The battle for colonial supremacy occurred not only on land, but also on the sea. Acting on behalf of their governments, privately owned armed ships, known as privateers, attacked merchant ships of enemy nations and sank or robbed them.

Pirates also roamed the high seas. They attacked ships for their valuables and did not care what nation the vessels represented. One of the best-known pirates was Edward B. Teach, whose prominent beard earned him the nickname Blackbeard. According to one account, Blackbeard attempted to frighten his victims by sticking "lighted matches under his hat, which appeared on both sides of his face and eyes, naturally fierce and wild."

and expand the fur trade. The Dutch holdings in North America became known as **New Netherland**.

Although the Dutch company profited from its fur trade, it was slow to attract Dutch colonists. To encourage settlers, the colony opened its doors to a variety of peoples. Gradually more Dutch, as well as Germans, French, Scandinavians, and other Europeans, settled the area.

Colonizing the Caribbean During the 1600s, the nations of Europe also colonized the Caribbean. The French seized control of present-day Haiti, Guadeloupe, and Martinique. The English settled Barbados and Jamaica. In 1634, the Dutch captured what are now the Netherlands Antilles and Aruba from Spain.

On these islands, the Europeans built huge cotton and sugar plantations. These products, although profitable, demanded a large and steady supply of labor. Enslaved Africans eventually would supply this labor.

The Struggle for North America

As they expanded their settlements in North America, the nations of France, England, and the Netherlands battled one another for colonial supremacy.

The English Oust the Dutch To the English, New Netherland separated their northern and southern colonies. In 1664, the English king, Charles II, granted his brother, the Duke of York, permission to drive out the Dutch. When the duke's fleet arrived at New Netherland, the Dutch surrendered without firing a shot. The Duke of York claimed the colony for England and renamed it New York.

Reading Check
Contrast
How were the Dutch and French colonies different from the English colonies in North America?

Europeans in North America

▷ Explore ONLINE!

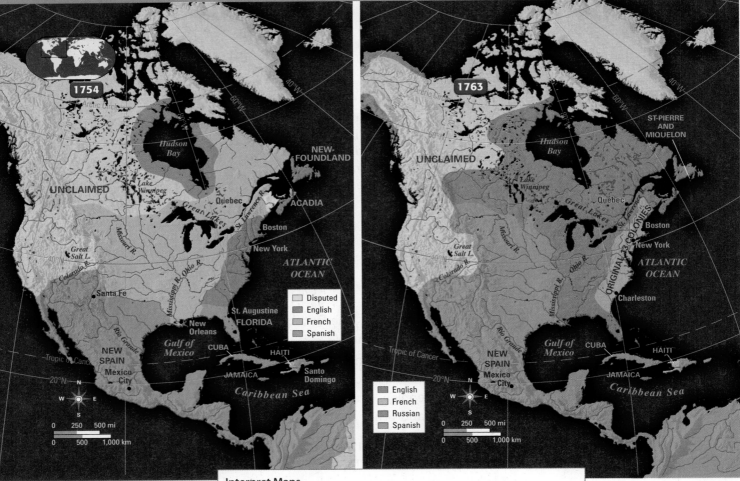

Interpret Maps

1. **Region** Which nation claimed the largest area of the present-day United States in 1754?

2. **Place** How did Britain's North American empire change by 1763?

With the Dutch gone, the English colonized the Atlantic coast of North America. By 1750, about 1.2 million English settlers lived in 13 colonies from Maine to Georgia.

England Battles France The English soon became hungry for more land for their colonial population. This economic motive led them to push farther west into the continent. By doing so, they collided with France's North American holdings. As their colonies expanded, France and England began to interfere with each other. It seemed that a major conflict was on the horizon.

In 1754 a dispute over land claims in the Ohio Valley led to a war between the British and French on the North American continent. The conflict became known as the **French and Indian War**. The war became

Reading Check
Analyze Issues
How did the larger issue of European expansion around the world play out in North America?

part of a larger conflict known as the Seven Years' War. Britain and France, along with their European allies, also battled for supremacy in Europe, the West Indies, and India.

In North America, the British colonists, with the help of the British Army, defeated the French in 1763. The French surrendered their North American holdings. As a result of the war, the British seized control of the eastern half of North America.

Native Americans Respond

As in Mexico and South America, the migration of Europeans to the present-day United States had a great impact on Native American cultures. European colonization brought mostly disaster for the land's original inhabitants.

A Strained Relationship French and Dutch settlers developed a mostly cooperative relationship with the Native Americans. This was mainly due to the mutual benefits of the fur trade. Native Americans did most of the trapping and then traded the furs to the French for such items as guns, hatchets, mirrors, and beads. The Dutch also cooperated with Native Americans in an effort to establish a fur-trading enterprise.

The groups did not live together in complete harmony. Dutch settlers fought with various Native American groups over land claims and trading rights. For the most part, however, the French and Dutch colonists lived together peacefully with their North American hosts.

The same could not be said of the English. Early relations between English settlers and Native Americans were cooperative. However, they quickly worsened over the issues of land and religion. Unlike the French and Dutch, the English sought to populate their colonies in North America. This meant pushing the natives off their land. The English colonists seized more land for their population and their tobacco crops.

Religious differences also heightened tensions. The English settlers considered Native Americans heathens, people without a faith. Over time, many Puritans viewed Native Americans as agents of the devil and as a threat to their godly society. Native Americans developed a similarly harsh view of the European invaders.

Settlers and Native Americans Battle The hostility between the English settlers and Native Americans led to warfare. As early as 1622, the Powhatan tribe attacked colonial villages around Jamestown and killed about 350 settlers. During the next few years, the colonists struck back and massacred hundreds of Powhatan.

One of the bloodiest conflicts between colonists and Native Americans was known as King Philip's War. It began in 1675 when the Native American ruler **Metacom** (also known as King Philip) led an attack on colonial villages throughout Massachusetts. In the months that followed, both sides massacred hundreds of victims. After a year of fierce fighting, the colonists were victorious. During the 17th century, many skirmishes erupted throughout North America.

Diseases Strike Native Americans More destructive than the Europeans' weapons were their diseases. Like the Spanish in Central and South America, the Europeans who settled North America brought with them several diseases. The diseases devastated the native population in North America.

In 1616, for example, an epidemic of smallpox ravaged Native Americans living along the New England coast. The population of one tribe, the Massachusett, dropped from 24,000 to 750 by 1631. From South Carolina to Missouri, nearly whole tribes fell to smallpox, measles, and other diseases.

One of the effects of this loss was a severe shortage of labor in the colonies. In order to meet their growing labor needs, European colonists soon turned to another group: Africans, whom they would enslave by the millions.

Reading Check
Identify Problems
Why did the issues of land and religion cause strife between Native Americans and settlers?

Lesson 5 Assessment

1. **Organize Information** Fill in the graphic organizer below with what the given settlements had in common.

Name of Settlement	General Location	Reasons Settled
New France		
New Netherland		
Massachusetts Bay		

2. **Key Terms and People** For each key term or person in the lesson, write a sentence explaining its significance.

3. **Contrast** What was a basic difference between French and English attitudes about the land they acquired in North America?

4. **Analyze Effects** What were some effects of European colonization of North America for Native Americans?

5. **Draw Conclusions** What need drove the English farther west into the North American continent?

6. **Contrast** In what ways did the colonies at Jamestown and Massachusetts Bay differ?

prompted a wave of new business and trade practices in Europe during the 16th and 17th centuries. These practices, many of which served as the root of today's financial dealings, dramatically changed the economic atmosphere of Europe. This economic atmosphere was not dissimilar to the economic issues experienced by Europeans trading with Japan during the 16th century. Just as Portuguese merchants conducted trade with Japan, so too were goods exchanged between colonies in the Americas and European nations.

The Rise of Capitalism One aspect of the European economic revolution was the growth of **capitalism**. Capitalism is an economic system based on private ownership and the investment of resources, such as money, for profit. No longer were governments the sole owners of great wealth. Numerous merchants obtained great wealth from overseas colonization and trade.

Investing in global exploration was important for the development of international trade. A group of investors might fund a transatlantic journey in hopes that a new market might be found with which they could exchange goods and services. The European colonies in the Americas, for example, had become important capital markets in which merchants invested their money. Profits from these investments enabled merchants and traders to reinvest even more money in other enterprises. As a result, businesses across Europe grew and flourished.

The increase in economic activity in Europe led to an overall increase in many nations' money supply. This in turn brought on inflation, or the steady rise in the price of goods. Inflation occurs when people have more money to spend and thus demand more goods and services. Because the supply of goods is less than the demand for them, the goods become both scarce and more valuable. Prices then rise. At this time in Europe, the costs of many goods rose. Spain, for example, endured a crushing bout of inflation during the 1600s, as boatloads of gold and silver from the Americas greatly increased the nation's money supply.

Joint-Stock Companies Another business venture that developed during this period was the **joint-stock company**. A joint-stock company was a partnership of investors who bought shares of stock in the company. In this type of company, a number of people combined their wealth for a common purpose.

In Europe during the 1500s and 1600s, that common purpose was American colonization. It took large amounts of money to establish overseas colonies. Moreover, while profits may have been great, so were risks. Many ships, for instance, never completed the long and dangerous ocean voyage. Because joint-stock companies involved numerous investors, the individual members paid only a fraction of the total colonization cost. If the colony failed, investors lost only their small share. If the colony thrived, the investors shared in the profits. It was a joint-stock company that was responsible for establishing Jamestown, England's first North American colony. As joint-stock companies grew and became more profitable, they adopted characteristics of modern-day corporations.

Reading Check
Make Inferences
Why would a joint-stock company be popular with investors in overseas colonies?

Mercantilism

As you have read, mercantilism was an economic theory practiced in Europe from the 16th to 18th centuries. Economists of the period believed that a country's power came from its wealth. Thus, a country would do everything possible to acquire more gold, preferably at the expense of its rivals. A mercantilist country primarily sought gold in two ways: establishing and exploiting colonies, and establishing a favorable balance of trade with a rival country. In the example, England is the home country, America is England's colony, and France is England's rival.

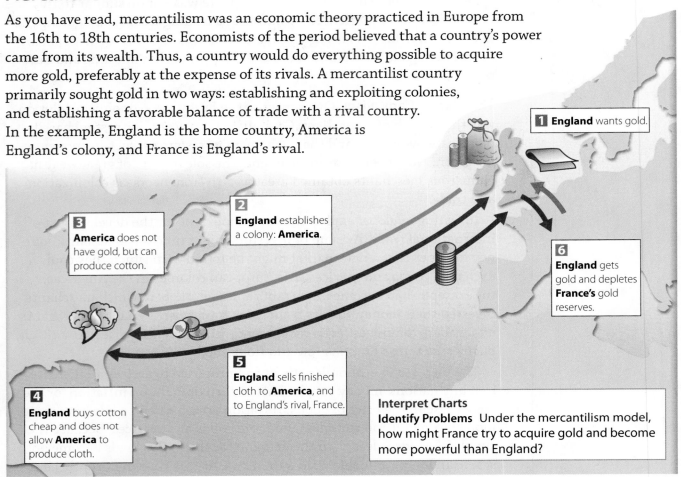

1 **England** wants gold.

2 **England** establishes a colony: **America**.

3 **America** does not have gold, but can produce cotton.

4 **England** buys cotton cheap and does not allow **America** to produce cloth.

5 **England** sells finished cloth to **America**, and to England's rival, France.

6 **England** gets gold and depletes **France's** gold reserves.

Interpret Charts
Identify Problems Under the mercantilism model, how might France try to acquire gold and become more powerful than England?

The Growth of Mercantilism

During this time, the nations of Europe adopted a new economic policy known as **mercantilism**. The theory of mercantilism held that a country's power mainly depended on its wealth. Wealth, after all, allowed nations to build strong navies and purchase vital goods. As a result, the goal of every nation became the attainment of as much wealth as possible.

Balance of Trade According to the theory of mercantilism, a nation could increase its wealth and power in two ways. First, it could obtain as much gold and silver as possible. Second, it could establish a **favorable balance of trade**, in which it sold more goods than it bought. A nation's ultimate goal under mercantilism was to become self-sufficient, not dependent on other countries for goods. An English author of the time wrote about the new economic idea of mercantilism:

> "Although a Kingdom may be enriched by gifts received, or by purchases taken from some other Nations . . . these are things uncertain and of small consideration when they happen. The ordinary means

therefore to increase our wealth and treasure is by Foreign Trade, wherein we must ever observe this rule: to sell more to strangers yearly than we consume of theirs in value."

—Thomas Mun, quoted in *World Civilizations*

Mercantilism went hand in hand with colonization because colonies played a vital role in this new economic practice. Aside from providing silver and gold, colonies provided raw materials that could not be found in the home country, such as wood or furs. In addition to playing the role of supplier, the colonies also provided a market. The home country could sell its goods to its own colonies.

Economic Revolution Changes European Society The economic changes that swept through much of Europe during the age of American colonization also led to changes in European society. The economic revolution spurred the growth of towns and the rise of a class of merchants who controlled great wealth.

The changes in European society, however, only went so far. While towns and cities grew in size, much of Europe's population continued to live in rural areas. Although merchants and traders enjoyed social mobility, the majority of Europeans remained poor. More than anything else, the economic revolution increased the wealth of European nations. In addition, mercantilism contributed to the creation of a national identity. Also, the new economic practices helped expand the power of European monarchs, who became powerful rulers.

Reading Check
Summarize
What role did colonies play in mercantilism?

Lesson 7 Assessment

1. **Organize Information** Create a three-column chart like the one shown. For each item in the first column, fill in the chart with its place of origin and its effect on the Americas and Europe. Which effect do you think had the greatest impact on history?

Food/ Livestock/ Disease	Place of Origin	Effect
Potato		
Horse		
Smallpox		

2. **Key Terms and People** For each key term or person in the lesson, write a sentence explaining its significance.

3. **Summarize** What were some of the food items that traveled from the Americas to the rest of the world?

4. **Summarize** What food and livestock from the rest of the world traveled to the Americas?

5. **Cause and Effect** What were some of the effects on European society of the economic revolution that took place in the 16th and 17th centuries?

6. **Make Inferences** Why were colonies considered so important to the nations of Europe?

7. **Compare and Contrast** What were some of the positive and negative consequences of the Columbian Exchange?

Module 16 Assessment

Key Terms and People

For each term or name below, write a sentence explaining how it relates to the era of expansion, exploration, and encounters.

1. Akbar
2. Aurangzeb
3. Bartolomeu Días
4. Dutch East India Company
5. Ming dynasty
6. Tokugawa Shogunate
7. conquistador
8. *encomienda*
9. triangular trade
10. Columbian Exchange

Main Ideas

Use your notes and the information in the module to answer the following questions.

The Mughal Empire in India

1. In what ways did Akbar defend religious freedom during his reign?
2. How did Akbar's successors promote religious conflict in the empire?

Europeans Explore the East

3. What factors helped spur European exploration?
4. Why were the Dutch so successful in establishing a trading empire in the Indian Ocean?

China and Japan Reject Expansion

5. What are five reasons the Ming Dynasty fell to civil disorder?
6. Why was the time between 1467 and 1568 called the period of the "Warring States"?

Spain Builds an American Empire

7. Why did Columbus set sail westward?
8. What were three goals of the Spanish in the Americas?

European Nations Settle North America

9. What did the Europeans mostly grow in their Caribbean colonies?
10. What was the result of the French and Indian War?

The Atlantic Slave Trade

11. What factors led European colonists to use Africans to resupply their labor force?
12. How did enslaved Africans resist their treatment in the Americas?

The Columbian Exchange and Global Trade

13. Why was the introduction of corn and potatoes to Europe and Asia so significant?
14. What was the economic policy of mercantilism?

Module 16 Assessment, continued

Critical Thinking

1. **Compare and Contrast** How were the Spanish and Portuguese colonial empires similar to and different from northern European trading empires? Consider their organization and how they were founded as part of your answer.

2. **Evaluate** Why were the policies of Aurangzeb so destructive to the Mughal Empire?

3. **Make Inferences** Conquest of new territories contributed to the growth of Muslim empires. How might it have also hindered this growth?

4. **Analyze Effects** How might a Chinese emperor's leadership be affected by living in the Forbidden City? Explain and support your opinion.

5. **Develop Historical Perspective** Of the technological advances that helped spur European exploration, which do you think was the most important? Why?

6. **Analyze Causes** What caused Japan to institute a policy of isolation? Defend your viewpoint with evidence from the text.

7. **Draw Conclusions** What factors helped the Europeans conquer the Americas? Which was the most important? Why?

8. **Analyze Effects** Explain the statement, "Columbus's voyage began a process that changed the world forever." Consider all the peoples and places American colonization affected economically.

9. **Compare and Contrast** What might have been some of the differences in the Europeans' and Native Americans' views of colonization?

10. **Compare and Contrast** How was the economic atmosphere of the colonial period similar to that of the Warring States period?

Engage with History

Think about whether or not you would sail into the unknown like the various explorers you read about. Based on what you have read, what are the reasons why you would go? If you would choose not to go, explain your feelings. Discuss your answers with a small group.

Focus on Writing

An English colony would have looked strange and different to a Native American of the time. Conduct historical research on an English colony of the 17th century. Consult at least one primary source and one secondary source. Then write an **essay** describing it, in which you provide details about the following:

- clothes
- food
- shelter
- weapons

Be sure to begin your paragraph with a thesis statement.

Multimedia Activity

Use the Internet, books, and other reference materials to create a multimedia pitch for a television special called "The Voyages of Zheng He." Your pitch should address the historical context of Zheng He's voyages, along with their impact on China and the lands he visited. Be sure to include text, images, audio, and, if possible, video as part of your pitch. During your research, consider the following:

- biographical data on Zheng He
- information about the ships, crews, and cargo
- descriptions of the voyages
- appropriate music and visuals

Ponce de León

The Spanish conquistador Juan Ponce de León was the first European to set foot on land that later became part of the United States. Ponce de León first sailed to the Americas with Christopher Columbus on his second voyage in 1493. Once in the Caribbean region, he helped conquer what is now Puerto Rico and was named ruler of the island. According to legend, Ponce de León learned about a Fountain of Youth, whose waters could make old people young again. He may have been searching for this fountain when, in 1513, he made landfall on the coast of what today is the southeastern United States. He named the area Florida and claimed it for Spain.

Explore important events in the life of Ponce de León online. You can find a wealth of information, video clips, primary sources, activities, and more through your online textbook.

🎥 Caribbean Island Encounters

Watch the video to learn about the first encounters between Spanish explorers and the people of the Caribbean.

🎥 Claiming Florida for Spain

Watch the video to learn about Ponce de León's first landing on the coast of what is now Florida.

🌎 Ponce de León's 1513 Route

Study the map to learn about the region of the Americas that Ponce de León explored in 1513.

Module 17

Absolute Monarchs in Europe

Essential Question

Why do you think absolute monarchs came to power in many different regions, and what caused their demise?

About the Painting: The absolute ruler, Louis XIV of France, imposed taxes to pay for the construction of a magnificent palace and to finance wars. His government provided security and enforced laws, but the people had no say in what the laws were. In this painting, you can see Louis's lavish clothing, which demonstrated to others his power and status. The gold flowers on his robe are the symbol of French kings.

In this module you will learn about absolute monarchs in Europe. Absolute rulers wanted to control their countries' economies so that they could free themselves from limitations imposed by the nobility.

What You Will Learn ...

▶ Explore ONLINE!

HISTORY.

VIDEOS, including...
- The Magnificent Palace of Versailles
- Peter the Great: The Tyrant Reformer
- Cromwell: Conqueror of Ireland

☑ Document Based Investigations

☑ Graphic Organizers

☑ Interactive Games

☑ Carousel: Absolute Grandeur: Versailles

☑ Carousel: A Winter Culture

Timeline of Events 1500–1800

 ▶ *Explore ONLINE!*

European Events	World Events

1500

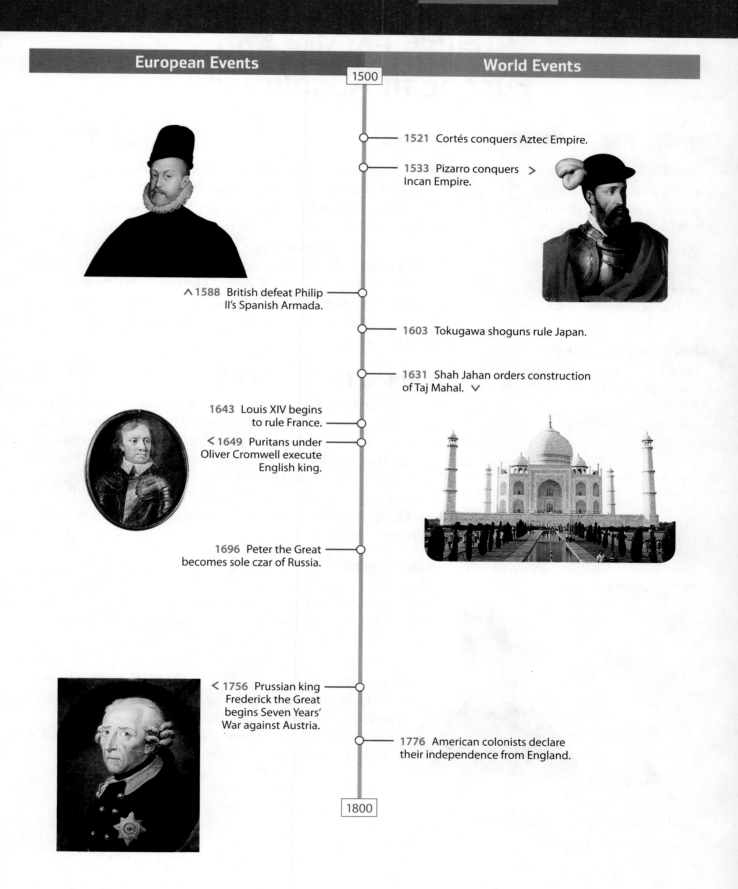

1521 Cortés conquers Aztec Empire.

1533 Pizarro conquers Incan Empire. >

∧ **1588** British defeat Philip II's Spanish Armada.

1603 Tokugawa shoguns rule Japan.

1631 Shah Jahan orders construction of Taj Mahal. ∨

1643 Louis XIV begins to rule France.

< **1649** Puritans under Oliver Cromwell execute English king.

1696 Peter the Great becomes sole czar of Russia.

< **1756** Prussian king Frederick the Great begins Seven Years' War against Austria.

1776 American colonists declare their independence from England.

1800

Spain's Empire and European Absolutism

The Big Idea

During a time of religious and economic instability, Philip II ruled Spain with a strong hand.

Why It Matters Now

When faced with crises, many heads of government take on additional economic or political powers.

Key Terms and People

Philip II
absolute monarch
divine right

Setting the Stage

As you have already learned, from 1520 to 1566, Suleyman I exercised great power as sultan of the Ottoman Empire. A European monarch of the same period, Charles V, came close to matching Suleyman's power. As the Hapsburg king, Charles inherited Spain, Spain's American colonies, parts of Italy, and lands in Austria and the Netherlands. As the elected Holy Roman emperor, he ruled much of Germany. It was the first time since Charlemagne that a European ruler controlled so much territory.

A Powerful Spanish Empire

A devout Catholic, Charles not only fought Muslims but also opposed Lutherans. In 1555, he unwillingly agreed to the Peace of Augsburg, which allowed German princes to choose the religion for their territory. The following year, Charles V divided his immense empire and retired to a monastery. To his brother Ferdinand, he left Austria and the Holy Roman Empire. His son, **Philip II**, inherited Spain, the Spanish Netherlands, and the American colonies.

Philip II's Empire Philip was shy, serious, and—like his father—deeply religious. He was also very hardworking. Yet Philip would not allow anyone to help him. Deeply suspicious, he trusted no one for long. As his own court historian wrote, "His smile and his dagger were very close."

Perhaps above all, Philip could be aggressive for the sake of his empire. In 1580, the king of Portugal died without an heir. Because Philip was the king's nephew, he seized the Portuguese kingdom. Counting Portuguese strongholds in Africa, India, and the East Indies, he now had an empire that circled the globe.

Philip II of Spain

Defeat of the Spanish Armada, 1588

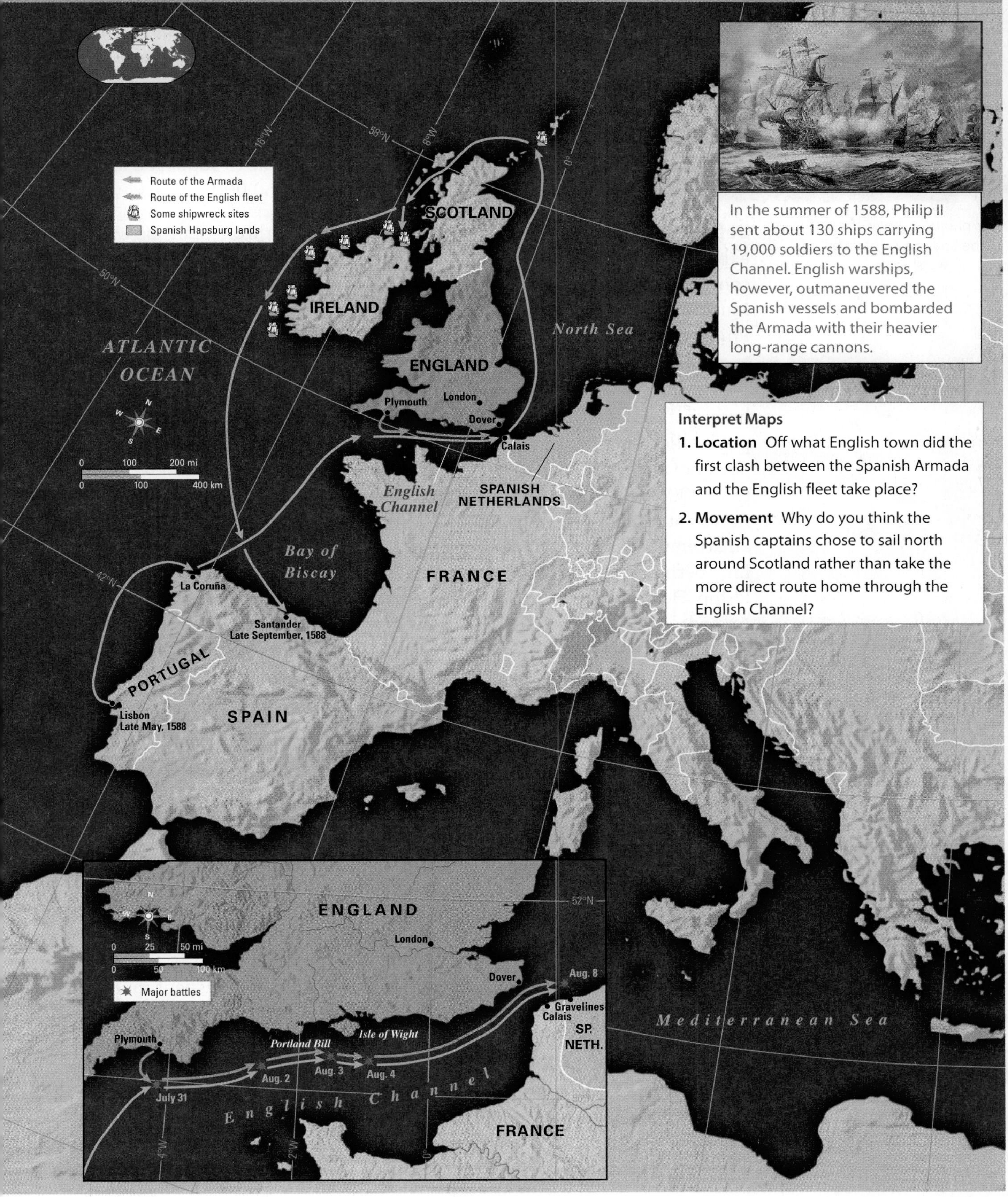

▶ Explore ONLINE!

Legend:
- → Route of the Armada
- → Route of the English fleet
- 🚢 Some shipwreck sites
- ⬛ Spanish Hapsburg lands

ATLANTIC OCEAN

SCOTLAND

IRELAND

ENGLAND

North Sea

Plymouth

London

Dover

Calais

English Channel

SPANISH NETHERLANDS

Bay of Biscay

FRANCE

La Coruña

Santander
Late September, 1588

PORTUGAL

SPAIN

Lisbon
Late May, 1588

0   100   200 mi
0   100   400 km

In the summer of 1588, Philip II sent about 130 ships carrying 19,000 soldiers to the English Channel. English warships, however, outmaneuvered the Spanish vessels and bombarded the Armada with their heavier long-range cannons.

Interpret Maps

1. **Location** Off what English town did the first clash between the Spanish Armada and the English fleet take place?

2. **Movement** Why do you think the Spanish captains chose to sail north around Scotland rather than take the more direct route home through the English Channel?

Inset map:

ENGLAND

London

Dover

Aug. 8

Gravelines
Calais

SP. NETH.

Mediterranean Sea

0   25   50 mi
0   50   100 km

✹ Major battles

Plymouth

Portland Bill

Isle of Wight

Aug. 2   Aug. 3   Aug. 4

July 31

English Channel

FRANCE

This painting shows the defeat of the Spanish Armada by English warships.

Philip's empire provided him with incredible wealth. By 1600, American mines had supplied Spain with an estimated 339,000 pounds of gold. Between 1550 and 1650, roughly 16,000 tons of silver bullion were unloaded from Spanish galleons, or ships. The king of Spain claimed between a fourth and a fifth of every shipload of treasure as his royal share. With this wealth, Spain was able to support a large standing army of about 50,000 soldiers.

Defender of Catholicism When Philip assumed the throne, Europe was experiencing religious wars caused by the Reformation. However, religious conflict was not new to Spain. The Reconquista, the campaign to drive Muslims from Spain, had been completed only 64 years before. In addition, Philip's great-grandparents Isabella and Ferdinand had used the Inquisition to investigate suspected heretics, or nonbelievers in Christianity.

Philip believed it was his duty to defend Catholicism against the Muslims of the Ottoman Empire and the Protestants of Europe. In 1571, the pope called on all Catholic princes to take up arms against the mounting power of the Ottoman Empire. Philip responded like a true crusader. More than 200 Spanish and Venetian ships defeated a large Ottoman fleet in a fierce battle near Lepanto. In 1588, Philip launched the Spanish Armada in an attempt to punish Protestant England and its queen, Elizabeth I. Elizabeth had supported Protestant subjects who had rebelled against Philip. However, his fleet was defeated. (See map, "Defeat of the Spanish Armada, 1588.")

Although this setback seriously weakened Spain, its wealth gave it the appearance of strength for a while longer. Philip's gray granite palace, the Escorial, had massive walls and huge gates that demonstrated his power. The Escorial also reflected Philip's faith. Within its walls stood a monastery as well as a palace.

Reading Check
Make Inferences
What did Philip want his palace to demonstrate about his monarchy?

Golden Age of Spanish Art and Literature

Spain's great wealth did more than support navies and build palaces. It also allowed monarchs and nobles to become patrons of artists. During the 16th and 17th centuries, Spain experienced a golden age in the arts. The works of two great painters show both the faith and the pride of Spain during this period.

El Greco and Velázquez Born in Crete, El Greco (GREHK•oh) spent much of his adult life in Spain. His real name was Domenikos Theotokopoulos, but Spaniards called him El Greco, meaning "the Greek." El Greco's art often puzzled the people of his time. He chose brilliant, sometimes clashing colors, distorted the human figure, and expressed emotion symbolically in his paintings. Although unusual, El Greco's techniques showed the deep Catholic faith of Spain. He painted saints and martyrs as huge, long-limbed figures that have a supernatural air.

In *Las Meninas (The Maids of Honor)*, Velázquez depicts King Philip IV's daughter and her attendants.

The paintings of Diego Velázquez (vuh·LAHS·kehs), on the other hand, reflected the pride of the Spanish monarchy. Velázquez, who painted 50 years after El Greco, was the court painter to Philip IV of Spain. He is best known for his portraits of the royal family and scenes of court life. Like El Greco, he was noted for using rich colors.

Don Quixote The publication of *Don Quixote de la Mancha* in 1605 is often called the birth of the modern European novel. In this book, Miguel de Cervantes (suhr·VAN·teez) wrote about a poor Spanish nobleman who went a little crazy after reading too many books about heroic knights.

Hoping to "right every manner of wrong," Don Quixote rode forth in a rusty suit of armor, mounted on a feeble horse. At one point, he mistook some windmills for giants:

> "He rushed with [his horse's] utmost speed upon the first windmill he could come at, and, running his lance into the sail, the wind whirled about with such swiftness, that the rapidity of the motion presently broke the lance into shivers, and hurled away both knight and horse along with it, till down he fell, rolling a good way off in the field."
>
> —Miguel De Cervantes, *Don Quixote de la Mancha*

Reading Check
Develop Vocabulary
Look again at the excerpt from *Don Quixote de la Mancha*. Use context clues to explain what *shivers* most likely means.

Some critics believe that Cervantes was mocking chivalry, the knightly code of the Middle Ages. Others maintain that the book is about an idealistic person who longs for the romantic past because he is frustrated with his materialistic world.

The Spanish Empire Weakens

Certainly, the age in which Cervantes wrote was a materialistic one. The gold and silver coming from the Americas made Spain temporarily wealthy. However, such treasure helped to cause long-term economic problems.

Inflation and Taxes One of these problems was severe inflation, which is a decline in the value of money, accompanied by a rise in the prices of goods and services. Inflation in Spain had two main causes. First, Spain's population was growing. As more people demanded food and goods, merchants were able to raise prices. Second, as silver bullion flooded the market, its value dropped. People needed more and more silver to buy things.

Spain's economic decline also had other causes. When Spain expelled the Jews and Moors (Muslims) around 1500, it lost many valuable artisans and businesspeople. In addition, Spain's nobles did not have to pay taxes.

The tax burden fell on the lower classes. That burden prevented them from accumulating enough wealth to start their own businesses. As a result, Spain never developed a middle class.

Making Spain's Enemies Rich Guilds that had emerged in the Middle Ages still dominated business in Spain. Such guilds used old-fashioned methods. This made Spanish cloth and manufactured goods more expensive than those made elsewhere. As a result, Spaniards bought much of what they needed from France, England, and the Netherlands. Spain's great wealth flowed into the pockets of foreigners, who were mostly Spain's enemies.

To finance their wars, Spanish kings borrowed money from German and Italian bankers. When shiploads of silver came in, the money was sent abroad to repay debts. The economy was so feeble that Philip had to declare the Spanish state bankrupt three times.

The Dutch Revolt In the Spanish Netherlands, Philip had to maintain an army to keep his subjects under control. The Dutch had little in common with their Spanish rulers. While Spain was Catholic, the Netherlands had many Calvinist congregations. Also, Spain had a sluggish economy, while the Dutch had a prosperous middle class.

Philip raised taxes in the Netherlands and took steps to crush Protestantism. In response, in 1566, angry Protestant mobs swept through Catholic churches. Philip then sent an army under the Spanish duke of Alva to punish the rebels. On a single day in 1568, the duke executed 1,500 Protestants and suspected rebels.

The Dutch continued to fight the Spanish for another 11 years. Finally, in 1579, the seven northern provinces of the Netherlands, which were largely Protestant, united and declared their independence from Spain. They became the United Provinces of the Netherlands. The ten southern provinces (present-day Belgium) were Catholic and remained under Spanish control.

Reading Check
Identify Problems
Why didn't Spain's economy benefit from the gold and silver from the Americas?

The Independent Dutch Prosper

The United Provinces of the Netherlands was different from other European states of the time. For one thing, the people there practiced religious toleration. In addition, the United Provinces was not a kingdom but a republic. Each province had an elected governor, whose power depended on the support of merchants and landholders.

Global Patterns

Tulip Mania

Tulips came to Europe from Turkey around 1550. People went wild over the flowers and began to buy rare varieties. However, the supply of tulips could not meet the demand, and prices began to rise. Soon people were spending all their savings on bulbs and taking out loans so that they could buy more.

Tulip mania reached a peak between 1633 and 1637. Soon after, tulip prices sank rapidly. Many Dutch families lost property and were left with bulbs that were nearly worthless.

Dutch Art During the 1600s, the Netherlands became what Florence had been during the 1400s. It boasted not only the best banks but also many of the best artists in Europe. As in Florence, wealthy merchants sponsored many of these artists.

Rembrandt van Rijn (REHM•brant vahn RYN) was the greatest Dutch artist of the period. Rembrandt painted portraits of wealthy middle-class merchants. He also produced group portraits. In *The Night Watch*, he portrayed a group of city guards. Rembrandt used sharp contrasts of light and shadow to draw attention to his focus.

In *The Night Watch*, Rembrandt showed the individuality of each man by capturing distinctive facial expressions and postures.

Another artist fascinated with the effects of light and dark was Jan Vermeer (YAHN vuhr•MEER). Like many other Dutch artists, he chose domestic, indoor settings for his portraits. He often painted women doing such familiar activities as pouring milk from a jug or reading a letter. The work of both Rembrandt and Vermeer reveals how important merchants, civic leaders, and the middle class in general were in 17th-century Netherlands.

Dutch Trading Empire The stability of the government allowed the Dutch people to concentrate on economic growth. The merchants of Amsterdam bought surplus grain in Poland and crammed it into their warehouses. When they heard about poor harvests in southern Europe, they shipped the grain south while prices were highest. The Dutch had the largest fleet of ships in the world—perhaps 4,800 ships in 1636. This fleet helped the Dutch East India Company (a trading company controlled by the Dutch government) to dominate the Asian spice trade and the Indian Ocean trade. Gradually, the Dutch replaced the Italians as the bankers of Europe.

Reading Check
Draw Conclusions
Why did the Dutch prosper during this period?

Absolutism

Absolutism was the political belief that one ruler should hold all of the power within the boundaries of a country. Although practiced by several monarchs in Europe during the 16th through 18th centuries, absolutism has been used in many regions throughout history. In ancient times, Shi Huangdi in China, Darius in Persia, and the Roman caesars were all absolute rulers.

CAUSES

- Religious and territorial conflicts created fear and uncertainty.
- The growth of armies to deal with conflicts caused rulers to raise taxes to pay troops.
- Heavy taxes led to additional unrest and peasant revolts.

EFFECTS

- Rulers regulated religious worship and social gatherings to control the spread of ideas.
- Rulers increased the size of their courts to appear more powerful.
- Rulers created bureaucracies to control their countries' economies.

Interpret Charts

1. **Make Inferences** Why do you think absolute rulers controlled social gatherings?

2. **Hypothesize** Today several nations of the world (such as Saudi Arabia) have absolute rulers. Judging from what you know of past causes of absolutism, why do you think absolute rulers still exist today?

Absolutism in Europe

Even though Philip II lost his Dutch possessions, he was a forceful ruler in many ways. He tried to control every aspect of his empire's affairs. During the next few centuries, many European monarchs would also claim the authority to rule without limits on their power.

The Theory of Absolutism These rulers wanted to be **absolute monarchs**, kings or queens who held all of the power within their states' boundaries. Their goal was to control every aspect of society. Absolute monarchs believed in **divine right**, the idea that God created the monarchy and that the monarch acted as God's representative on Earth. An absolute monarch answered only to God, not to his or her subjects.

Growing Power of Europe's Monarchs As Europe emerged from the Middle Ages, monarchs grew increasingly powerful. The decline of feudalism, the rise of cities, and the growth of national kingdoms all helped to centralize authority. In addition, the growing middle class usually backed monarchs, because they promised a peaceful, supportive climate for business. Monarchs used the wealth of colonies to pay for their ambitions. Church authority also broke down during the late Middle Ages and the Reformation. That opened the way for monarchs to assume even greater control. In 1576, Jean Bodin, an influential French writer, defined absolute rule. Bodin stated that a ruler has the power to make laws without the consent of anyone else. He said that if a ruler needs to consult superiors, then he is a subject himself. If a ruler needs to consult peers, he is an equal, not a ruler. If he needs to consult his subjects, he is not a ruler.

Crises Lead to Absolutism The 17th century was a period of great upheaval in Europe. Religious and territorial conflicts between states led to almost continuous warfare. This caused governments to build huge armies and to levy even heavier taxes on an already suffering population. These pressures in turn brought about widespread unrest. Sometimes peasants revolted.

In response to these crises, monarchs tried to impose order by increasing their own power. As absolute rulers, they regulated everything from religious worship to social gatherings. They created new government bureaucracies to control their countries' economic life. Their goal was to free themselves from the limitations imposed by the nobility and by representative bodies such as Parliament. Only with such freedom could they rule absolutely, as did the most famous monarch of his time, Louis XIV of France. You'll learn more about him later.

Reading Check
Draw Conclusions
How was Philip II typical of an absolute monarch?

Lesson 1 Assessment

1. **Organize Information** Use a graphic organizer to show conditions needed for a monarch to gain power.

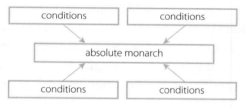

2. **Key Terms and People** For each key term or person in the lesson, write a sentence explaining its significance.

3. **Synthesize** What is the significance of England's defeat of the Spanish Armada?

4. **Analyze Motives** Why did the Dutch revolt against Spain?

5. **Draw Conclusions** What does the art described in this section reveal about the cultures of Spain and the Netherlands?

6. **Analyze Causes** What role did religion play in the struggle between the Spanish and the Dutch?

7. **Make Inferences** How did the lack of a middle class contribute to the decline of Spain's economy?

The Reign of Louis XIV

The Big Idea

After a century of war and riots, France was ruled by Louis XIV, the most powerful monarch of his time.

Why It Matters Now

Louis's abuse of power led to revolution that would inspire the call for democratic government throughout the world.

Key Terms and People

Edict of Nantes
Cardinal Richelieu
skepticism
Louis XIV
intendant
Jean Baptiste Colbert
War of the Spanish Succession

Setting the Stage

In 1559, King Henry II of France died, leaving four young sons. Three of them ruled, one after the other, but all proved incompetent. The real power behind the throne during this period was their mother, Catherine de Médicis. Catherine tried to preserve royal authority, but growing conflicts between Catholics and Huguenots—French Protestants—rocked the country. Between 1562 and 1598, Huguenots and Catholics fought eight religious wars. Chaos spread through France.

Religious Wars and Power Struggles

In 1572, the St. Bartholomew's Day Massacre in Paris sparked a six-week, nationwide slaughter of Huguenots. The massacre occurred when many Huguenot nobles were in Paris. They were attending the marriage of Catherine's daughter to a Huguenot prince, Henry of Navarre. Most of these nobles died, but Henry survived.

Henry of Navarre Descended from the popular medieval king Louis IX, Henry was robust, athletic, and handsome. In 1589, when both Catherine and her last son died, Prince Henry inherited the throne. He became Henry IV, the first king of the Bourbon dynasty in France. As king, he showed himself to be decisive, fearless in battle, and a clever politician.

Many Catholics, including the people of Paris, opposed Henry. For the sake of his war-weary country, Henry chose to give up Protestantism and become a Catholic. Explaining his conversion, Henry reportedly declared, "Paris is well worth a mass."

In 1598, Henry took another step toward healing France's wounds. He declared that the Huguenots could live in peace in France and set up their own houses of worship in some cities. This declaration of religious toleration was called the **Edict of Nantes**.

Aided by an adviser who enacted wise financial policies, Henry devoted his reign to rebuilding France and its prosperity. He restored the French monarchy to a strong position. After a generation of war, most French people welcomed peace. Some people, however, hated Henry for his religious compromises. In 1610, a fanatic leaped into the royal carriage and stabbed Henry to death.

Louis XIII and Cardinal Richelieu After Henry IV's death, his son Louis XIII reigned. Louis was a weak king, but in 1624, he appointed a strong minister who made up for all of Louis's weaknesses.

Cardinal Richelieu probably had himself portrayed in a standing position in this painting to underscore his role as ruler.

Reading Check
Make Inferences
How did Richelieu's actions toward Huguenots and the nobility strengthen the monarchy?

Cardinal Richelieu (RIHSH•uh•loo) became, in effect, the ruler of France. For several years, he had been a hardworking leader of the Catholic church in France. Although he tried sincerely to lead according to moral principles, he was also ambitious and enjoyed exercising authority. As Louis XIII's minister, he was able to pursue his ambitions in the political arena.

Richelieu took two steps to increase the power of the Bourbon monarchy. First, he moved against Huguenots. He believed that Protestantism often served as an excuse for political conspiracies against the Catholic king. Although Richelieu did not take away the Huguenots' right to worship, he forbade Protestant cities to have walls. He did not want them to be able to defy the king and then withdraw behind strong defenses.

Second, he sought to weaken the nobles' power. Richelieu ordered nobles to take down their fortified castles. He increased the power of government agents who came from the middle class. The king relied on these agents, so there was less need to use noble officials.

Richelieu also wanted to make France the strongest state in Europe. The greatest obstacle to this, he believed, were the Hapsburg rulers, whose lands surrounded France. The Hapsburgs ruled Spain, Austria, the Netherlands, and parts of the Holy Roman Empire. To limit Hapsburg power, Richelieu involved France in the Thirty Years' War.

Writers Turn Toward Skepticism

As France regained political power, a new French intellectual movement developed. French thinkers had witnessed the religious wars with horror. What they saw turned them toward **skepticism**, the idea that nothing can ever be known for certain. These thinkers expressed an attitude of doubt toward churches that claimed to have the only correct set of doctrines. To doubt old ideas, skeptics thought, was the first step toward finding truth.

Montaigne and Descartes Michel de Montaigne lived during the worst years of the French religious wars. After the death of a dear friend, Montaigne thought deeply about life's meaning. To communicate his ideas, Montaigne developed a new form of literature, the essay. An essay is a brief work that expresses a person's thoughts and opinions.

In one essay, Montaigne pointed out that whenever a new belief arose, it replaced an old belief that people once accepted as truth. In the same way, he went on, the new belief would also probably be replaced by some different idea in the future. For these reasons, Montaigne believed that humans could never have absolute knowledge of what is true.

Another French writer of the time, René Descartes, was a brilliant thinker. In his *Meditations on First Philosophy*, Descartes examined the skeptical argument that one could never be certain of anything. Descartes used his observations and his reason to answer such arguments. In doing so, he created a philosophy that influenced modern thinkers and helped to develop the scientific method. Because of this, he became an important figure in the Enlightenment, which you will read about later.

Reading Check
Compare
What made Montaigne and Descartes skeptics?

Louis XIV Comes to Power

The efforts of Henry IV and Richelieu to strengthen the French monarchy paved the way for the most powerful ruler in French history—**Louis XIV**. In Louis's view, he and the state were one and the same. He reportedly boasted, *"L'état, c'est moi,"* meaning "I am the state." Although Louis XIV became the strongest king of his time, he was only a four-year-old boy when he began his reign.

Pictured: (L) Marriage of Louis XIV to Marie Thérèse of Austria. Artist unknown; (R) Statue of Louis XIV, Lyon, France

Louis, the Boy King When Louis became king in 1643 after the death of his father, Louis XIII, the true ruler of France was Richelieu's successor, Cardinal Mazarin (MAZ•uh•RAN). Mazarin's greatest triumph came in 1648, with the ending of the Thirty Years' War.

Many people in France, particularly the nobles, hated Mazarin because he increased taxes and strengthened the central government. From 1648 to 1653, violent anti-Mazarin riots tore France apart. At times, the nobles who led the riots threatened the young king's life. Even after the violence was over, Louis never forgot his fear or his anger at the nobility. He was determined to become so strong that they could never threaten him again.

In the end, the nobles' rebellion failed for three reasons. Its leaders distrusted one another even more than they distrusted Mazarin. In addition, the government used violent repression. Finally, peasants and townspeople grew weary of disorder and fighting. For many years afterward, the people of France accepted the oppressive laws of an absolute king. They were convinced that the alternative—rebellion—was even worse.

Louis Weakens the Nobles' Authority When Cardinal Mazarin died in 1661, the 22-year-old Louis took control of the government himself. He weakened the power of the nobles by excluding them from his councils. In contrast, he increased the power of the government agents called **intendants**, who collected taxes and administered justice. To keep power under central control, he made sure that local officials communicated regularly with him.

Economic Growth Louis devoted himself to helping France attain economic, political, and cultural brilliance. No one assisted him more in achieving these goals than his minister of finance, **Jean Baptiste Colbert** (kawl•BEHR). Colbert believed in the theory of mercantilism. To prevent wealth from leaving the country, Colbert tried to make France self-sufficient. He wanted it to be able to manufacture everything it needed instead of relying on imports.

To expand manufacturing, Colbert gave government funds and tax benefits to French companies. To protect France's industries, he placed a high tariff on goods from other countries. Colbert also recognized the importance of colonies, which provided raw materials and a market for manufactured goods. The French government encouraged people to migrate to France's colony in Canada. There the fur trade added to French trade and wealth.

After Colbert's death, Louis announced a policy that slowed France's economic progress. In 1685, he canceled the Edict of Nantes, which protected the religious freedom of Huguenots. In response, thousands of Huguenot artisans and businesspeople fled the country. Louis's policy thus robbed France of many skilled workers.

Vocabulary
mercantilism the economic theory that nations should protect their home industries and export more than they import

Reading Check
Recognize Effects What effects did the years of riots have on Louis XIV? on his subjects?

— BIOGRAPHY —

Louis XIV
(1638–1715)

Although Louis XIV stood only 5 feet 5 inches tall, his erect and dignified posture made him appear much taller. (It also helped that he wore high-heeled shoes.)

Louis had very strong likes and dislikes. He hated cities and loved to travel through France's countryside. The people who traveled with him were at his mercy, however, for he allowed no stopping except for his own comfort.

It is small wonder that the vain Louis XIV liked to be called the Sun King. He believed that, as with the sun, all power radiated from him.

The Sun King's Grand Style

In his personal finances, Louis spent a fortune to surround himself with luxury. For example, each meal was a feast. An observer claimed that the king once devoured four plates of soup, a whole pheasant, a partridge in garlic sauce, two slices of ham, a salad, a plate of pastries, fruit, and hard-boiled eggs in a single sitting! Nearly 500 cooks, waiters, and other servants worked to satisfy his tastes.

Louis Controls the Nobility Every morning, the chief valet woke Louis at 8:30. Outside the curtains of Louis's canopy bed stood at least 100 of the most privileged nobles at court. They were waiting to help the great king dress. Only four would be allowed the honor of handing Louis his slippers or holding his sleeves for him.

Meanwhile, outside the bedchamber, lesser nobles waited in the palace halls and hoped Louis would notice them. A kingly nod, a glance of approval, a kind word—these marks of royal attention determined whether a noble succeeded or failed. A duke recorded how Louis turned against nobles who did not come to court to flatter him:

Though full of errors, Saint-Simon's memoirs provide valuable insight into Louis XIV's character and life at Versailles.

> *"He looked to the right and to the left, not only upon rising but upon going to bed, at his meals, in passing through his apartments, or his gardens. . . . He marked well all absentees from the Court, found out the reason of their absence, and never lost an opportunity of acting toward them as the occasion might seem to justify. . . . When their names were in any way mentioned,*
> *"I do not know them," the King would reply haughtily."*
>
> —Duke of Saint-Simon, *Memoirs of Louis XIV and the Regency*

Having the nobles at the palace increased royal authority in two ways. It made the nobility totally dependent on Louis. It also took them from their homes, thereby giving more power to the intendants. Louis required hundreds of nobles to live with him at the splendid palace he built at Versailles, about 11 miles southwest of Paris.

As you can see from the pictures, everything about the Versailles palace was immense. It faced a huge royal courtyard dominated by a statue of Louis XIV. The palace itself stretched for a distance of about 500 yards. Because of its great size, Versailles was like a small royal city. Its rich decoration and furnishings clearly showed Louis's wealth and power to everyone who came to the palace.

The Palace at Versailles

Louis XIV's palace at Versailles was proof of his absolute power. Only a ruler with total control over his country's economy could afford such a lavish palace. It cost an estimated $2.5 billion in 2003 dollars. Louis XIV was also able to force 36,000 laborers and 6,000 horses to work on the project.

Many people consider the Hall of Mirrors the most beautiful room in the palace. Along one wall are 17 tall mirrors. The opposite wall has 17 windows that open onto the gardens. The hall has gilded statues, crystal chandeliers, and a painted ceiling.

It took so much water to run all the fountains at once that it was done only for special events. On other days, when the king walked in the garden, servants would turn on fountains just before he reached them. The fountains were turned off after he walked away.

The gardens at Versailles remain beautiful today. Originally, Versailles was built with 1,400 fountains on 5,000 acres of gardens, lawns, and woods.

Interpret Visuals

1. **Analyze Motives** Why do you think Louis XIV believed he needed such a large and luxurious palace? Explain what practical and symbolic purposes Versailles might have served.

2. **Develop Historical Perspective** Consider the amount of money and effort that went into the construction of this extravagant palace. What does this reveal about the way 17th-century French society viewed its king?

3. **Compare** How were Edo and Versailles similar to the people of each region?

Reading Check
Analyze How did Louis's treatment of the nobles reflect his belief in his absolute authority? How was his treatment similar to and different from Tokugawa's treatment of the daimyo?

Patron of the Arts Versailles was a center of the arts during Louis's reign. Louis made opera and ballet more popular. He even danced the title role in the ballet *The Sun King*. One of his favorite writers was Molière (mohl•YAIR), who wrote some of the funniest plays in French literature. Molière's comedies include *Tartuffe*, which mocks religious hypocrisy.

Not since Augustus of Rome had there been a European monarch who supported the arts as much as Louis. Under Louis, the chief purpose of art was no longer to glorify God, as it had been in the Middle Ages. Nor was its purpose to glorify human potential, as it had been in the Renaissance. Now the purpose of art was to glorify the king and promote values that supported Louis's absolute rule.

Louis Fights Disastrous Wars

Under Louis, France was the most powerful country in Europe. In 1660, France had about 20 million people. This was four times as many as England and ten times as many as the Dutch Republic. The French army was far ahead of other states' armies in size, training, and weaponry.

Attempts to Expand France's Boundaries In 1667, just six years after Mazarin's death, Louis invaded the Spanish Netherlands in an effort to expand France's boundaries. Through this campaign, he gained 12 towns. Encouraged by his success, he personally led an army into the Dutch Netherlands in 1672. The Dutch saved their country by opening the dikes and flooding the countryside. This was the same tactic they had used in their revolt against Spain a century earlier. The war ended in 1678 with the Treaty of Nijmegen. France gained several towns and a region called Franche-Comté.

Louis decided to fight additional wars, but his luck had run out. By the end of the 1680s, a European-wide alliance had formed to stop France. By banding together, weaker countries could match France's strength. This defensive strategy was meant to achieve a balance of power in which no single country or group of countries could dominate others.

In 1689, the Dutch prince William of Orange became the king of England. He joined the League of Augsburg, which consisted of the Austrian Hapsburg emperor, the kings of Sweden and Spain, and the leaders of several smaller European states. Together, these countries equaled France's strength.

France at this time had been weakened by a series of poor harvests. That, added to the constant warfare, brought great suffering to the French people. So, too, did new taxes, which Louis imposed to finance his wars.

The painting shows the Battle of Denain, one of the last battles fought during the War of the Spanish Succession.

War of the Spanish Succession Tired of hardship, the French people longed for peace. What they got was another war. In 1700, the childless king of Spain, Charles II, died after promising his throne to Louis XIV's 16-year-old grandson, Philip of Anjou. The two greatest powers in Europe, enemies for so long, were now both ruled by the French Bourbons.

Other countries felt threatened by this increase in the Bourbon dynasty's power. In 1701, England, Austria, the Dutch Republic, Portugal, and several German and Italian states joined together to prevent the union of the French and Spanish thrones. The long struggle that followed is known as the **War of the Spanish Succession**.

The costly war dragged on until 1714. The Treaty of Utrecht was signed in that year. Under its terms, Louis's grandson was allowed to remain king of Spain so long as the thrones of France and Spain were not united.

The big winner in the war was Great Britain. From Spain, Britain took Gibraltar, a fortress that controlled the entrance to the Mediterranean. Spain also granted a British company an *asiento*, permission to send enslaved Africans to Spain's American colonies. This increased Britain's involvement in trading enslaved Africans.

In addition, France gave Britain the North American territories of Nova Scotia and Newfoundland, and abandoned claims to the Hudson Bay region. The Austrian Hapsburgs took the Spanish Netherlands and other Spanish lands in Italy. Prussia and Savoy were recognized as kingdoms.

Louis's Death and Legacy Louis's last years were more sad than glorious. Realizing that his wars had ruined France, he regretted the suffering he had brought to his people. He died in bed in 1715. News of his death prompted rejoicing throughout France. The people had had enough of the Sun King.

Louis left a mixed legacy to his country. On the positive side, France was certainly a power to be reckoned with in Europe. France ranked above all other European nations in art, literature, and statesmanship during Louis's reign. In addition, France was considered the military leader of Europe. This military might allowed France to develop a strong empire of colonies, which provided resources and goods for trade.

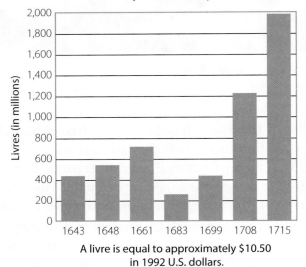

Debt of the Royal Family, 1643–1715

A livre is equal to approximately $10.50 in 1992 U.S. dollars.

Source: *Early Modern France 1560–1715*

Interpret Charts
1. **Compare** How many times greater was the royal debt in 1715 than in 1643?
2. **Synthesize** What was the royal debt of 1715 equal to in 1992 dollars?

On the negative side, constant warfare and the construction of the Palace of Versailles plunged France into staggering debt. Also, resentment over the tax burden imposed on the poor and Louis's abuse of power would plague his heirs—and eventually lead to revolution.

Absolute rule didn't die with Louis XIV. His enemies in Prussia and Austria had been experimenting with their own forms of absolute monarchy, as you will learn later.

Lesson 2 Assessment

1. **Organize Information** Create a time line that shows events that strengthened or weakened the French monarchy.

2. **Key Terms and People** For each key term or person in the lesson, write a sentence explaining its significance.

3. **Hypothesize** What impact did the French religious wars likely have on French thinkers?

4. **Draw Conclusions** What was the result of the War of the Spanish Succession?

5. **Support Opinions** Many historians think of Louis XIV as the perfect example of an absolute monarch. Do you agree? Explain why or why not.

6. **Recognize Effects** How did the policies of Colbert and Louis XIV affect the French economy? Explain both positive and negative effects.

7. **Synthesize** To what extent did anti-Protestantism contribute to Louis's downfall?

Central European Monarchs Clash

The Big Idea
After a period of turmoil, absolute monarchs ruled Austria and the Germanic state of Prussia.

Why It Matters Now
Prussia built a strong military tradition in Germany that contributed in part to world wars in the twentieth century.

Key Terms and People
Thirty Years' War
Maria Theresa
Frederick the Great
Seven Years' War

Setting the Stage

For a brief while, the German rulers appeared to have settled their religious differences through the Peace of Augsburg (1555). They had agreed that the faith of each prince would determine the religion of his subjects. Churches in Germany could be either Lutheran or Catholic, but not Calvinist. The peace was short-lived, soon to be replaced by a long war. After the Peace of Augsburg, the Catholic and Lutheran princes of Germany watched each other suspiciously.

The Thirty Years' War

Both the Lutheran and the Catholic princes tried to gain followers. In addition, both sides felt threatened by Calvinism, which was spreading in Germany and gaining many followers. As tension mounted, the Lutherans joined together in the Protestant Union in 1608. The following year, the Catholic princes formed the Catholic League. Now, it would take only a spark to set off a war.

Bohemian Protestants Revolt That spark came in 1618. The future Holy Roman emperor, Ferdinand II, was head of the Hapsburg family. As such, he ruled the Czech kingdom of Bohemia. The Protestants in Bohemia did not trust Ferdinand, who was a foreigner and a Catholic. When he closed some Protestant churches, the Protestants revolted. Ferdinand sent an army into Bohemia to crush the revolt. Several German Protestant princes took this chance to challenge their Catholic emperor.

Thus began the **Thirty Years' War**, a conflict over religion and territory and for power among European ruling families. The war can be divided into two main phases: the phase of Hapsburg triumphs and the phase of Hapsburg defeats.

Hapsburg Triumphs The Thirty Years' War lasted from 1618 to 1648. During the first 12 years, Hapsburg armies from Austria and Spain crushed the troops hired by the

Protestant princes. They succeeded in putting down the Czech uprising. They also defeated the German Protestants who had supported the Czechs.

Ferdinand II paid his army of 125,000 men by allowing them to plunder, or rob, German villages. This huge army destroyed everything in its path.

Hapsburg Defeats The Hapsburg triumph would not last. In 1630, the Protestant Gustavus Adolphus of Sweden and his army shifted the tide of war. They drove the Hapsburg armies out of northern Germany. However, Gustavus Adolphus was killed in battle in 1632.

Cardinal Richelieu and Cardinal Mazarin of France dominated the remaining years of the war. Although Catholic, these two cardinals feared the Hapsburgs more than the Protestants. They did not want other European rulers to have as much power as the French king. Therefore, in 1635, Richelieu sent French troops to join the German and Swedish Protestants in their struggle against the Hapsburg armies.

Peace of Westphalia The war did great damage to Germany. Its population dropped from 20 million to about 16 million. Both trade and agriculture were disrupted, and Germany's economy was ruined. Germany had a long, difficult recovery from this devastation. That is a major reason it did not become a unified state until the 1800s.

The Peace of Westphalia (1648) ended the war. The treaty had these important consequences:
- weakened the Hapsburg states of Spain and Austria
- strengthened France by awarding it German territory
- made German princes independent of the Holy Roman emperor
- ended religious wars in Europe
- introduced a new method of peace negotiation whereby all participants meet to settle the problems of a war and decide the terms of peace. This method is still used today.

Beginning of Modern States The treaty thus abandoned the idea of a Catholic empire that would rule most of Europe. It recognized Europe as a group of equal, independent states, sometimes called *nation-states*. This marked the beginning of the modern state system and was the most important result of the Thirty Years' War. A nation-state is the only power within its borders that can have an army, and it governs on behalf of all of its people.

Reading Check
Draw Conclusions
Judging from their actions, do you think the two French cardinals were motivated more by religion or politics? Why?

States Form in Central Europe

Strong states formed more slowly in central Europe than in western Europe. The major powers of this region were the kingdom of Poland, the Holy Roman Empire, and the Ottoman Empire. None of them was very strong in the mid-1600s.

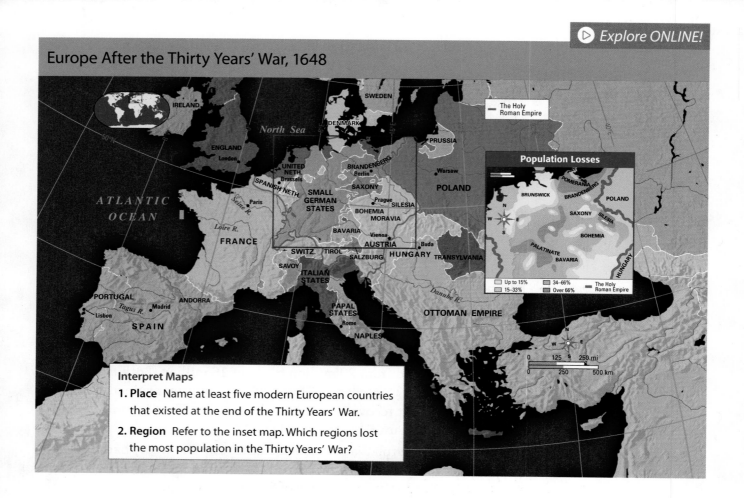

Europe After the Thirty Years' War, 1648

Explore ONLINE!

The Holy Roman Empire

SWEDEN

IRELAND

North Sea

DENMARK

ENGLAND
London

PRUSSIA

Warsaw

UNITED NETH.
Brussels

BRANDENBERG
Berlin

SPANISH NETH.

SAXONY

POLAND

SMALL GERMAN STATES

Prague SILESIA
BOHEMIA
MORAVIA

ATLANTIC OCEAN

Seine R.
Paris

Loire R.

FRANCE

BAVARIA

Vienna

SWITZ.   TIROL

AUSTRIA

Buda

SALZBURG   HUNGARY   TRANSYLVANIA

SAVOY

ITALIAN STATES

Danube R.

OTTOMAN EMPIRE

PORTUGAL   ANDORRA

Tagus R.   Madrid

Lisbon

SPAIN

PAPAL STATES
Rome

NAPLES

Population Losses

POMERANIA
BRUNSWICK   BRANDENBERG   POLAND

SAXONY   SILESIA

BOHEMIA

PALATINATE
BAVARIA

HUNGARY

☐ Up to 15%   ☐ 34–66%   — The Holy
☐ 15–33%   ☐ Over 66%   Roman Empire

0   125   250 mi
0   250   500 km

Interpret Maps

1. **Place** Name at least five modern European countries that existed at the end of the Thirty Years' War.

2. **Region** Refer to the inset map. Which regions lost the most population in the Thirty Years' War?

Economic Contrasts with the West One reason for this is that the economy of central Europe developed differently from that of western Europe. During the late Middle Ages, serfs in western Europe slowly won freedom and moved to towns. There, they joined middle-class towns-people, who gained economic power because of the commercial revolution and the development of capitalism.

By contrast, the landowning aristocracy in central Europe passed laws restricting the ability of serfs to gain freedom and move to cities. These nobles wanted to keep the serfs on the land, where they could produce large harvests. The nobles could then sell the surplus crops to western European cities at great profit.

Several Weak Empires The landowning nobles in central Europe not only held down the serfs but also blocked the development of strong kings. For example, the Polish nobility elected the Polish king and sharply limited his power. They allowed the king little income, no law courts, and no standing army. As a result, there was not a strong ruler who could form a unified state.

The two empires of central Europe were also weak. Although Suleyman the Magnificent had conquered Hungary and threatened Vienna in 1529, the Ottoman Empire could not take its European conquest any farther. From then on, the Ottoman Empire declined from its peak of power.

In addition, the Holy Roman Empire was seriously weakened by the Thirty Years' War. No longer able to command the obedience of the German states, the Holy Roman Empire had no real power. These old, weakened empires and kingdoms left a power vacuum in central Europe. In the late 1600s, two German-speaking families decided to try to fill this vacuum by becoming absolute rulers themselves.

Austria Grows Stronger One of these families was the Hapsburgs of Austria. The Austrian Hapsburgs took several steps to become absolute monarchs. First, during the Thirty Years' War, they reconquered Bohemia. The Hapsburgs wiped out Protestantism there and created a new Czech nobility that pledged loyalty to them. Second, after the war, the Hapsburg ruler centralized the government and created a standing army. Third, by 1699, the Hapsburgs had retaken Hungary from the Ottoman Empire.

In 1711, Charles VI became the Hapsburg ruler. Charles's empire was a difficult one to rule. Within its borders lived a diverse assortment of people—Czechs, Hungarians, Italians, Croatians, and Germans. Only the fact that one Hapsburg ruler wore the Austrian, Hungarian, and Bohemian crowns kept the empire together.

Maria Theresa Inherits the Austrian Throne How could the Hapsburgs make sure that they continued to rule all those lands? Charles VI spent his entire reign working out an answer to this problem. With endless arm-twisting, he persuaded other leaders of Europe to sign an agreement that declared they would recognize Charles's eldest daughter as the heir to all his Hapsburg territories. That heir was a young woman named Maria Theresa. In theory, this agreement guaranteed

The imperial crest of the Hapsburgs shows a double-headed eagle with a crown.

Maria Theresa a peaceful reign. Instead, she faced years of war. Her main enemy was Prussia, a state to the north of Austria. (See map: "Europe After the Thirty Years' War, 1648.")

Prussia Challenges Austria

Like Austria, Prussia rose to power in the late 1600s. Like the Hapsburgs of Austria, Prussia's ruling family, the Hohenzollerns, also had great ambitions. Those ambitions threatened to upset central Europe's delicate balance of power.

The Rise of Prussia The Hohenzollerns built up their state from a number of small holdings, beginning with the German states of Brandenburg and Prussia. In 1640, a 20-year-old Hohenzollern named Frederick William inherited the title of elector of Brandenburg. After seeing the destruction of the Thirty Years' War, Frederick William, later known as

Reading Check
Draw Conclusions
Why might ruling an empire with a vastly diverse assortment of people be difficult?

the Great Elector, decided that having a strong army was the only way to ensure safety.

To protect their lands, the Great Elector and his descendants moved toward absolute monarchy. They created a standing army, the best in Europe. They built it to a force of 80,000 men. To pay for the army, they introduced permanent taxation. Beginning with the Great Elector's son, they called themselves kings. They also weakened the representative assemblies of their territories.

Prussia's landowning nobility, the Junkers (YUNG·kuhrz), resisted the king's growing power. However, in the early 1700s, King Frederick William I bought their cooperation. He gave the Junkers the exclusive right to be officers in his army. As a result, Prussia became a rigidly controlled, highly militarized society.

Frederick the Great

Frederick the Great Frederick William worried that his son, Frederick, was not military enough to rule. The prince loved music, philosophy, and poetry. In 1730, when he and a friend tried to run away, they were caught. To punish Frederick, the king ordered him to witness his friend's beheading. Despite such bitter memories, Frederick II, known as **Frederick the Great**, followed his father's military policies when he came to power. However, he also softened some of his father's laws. With regard to domestic affairs, he encouraged religious toleration and legal reform. According to his theory of government, Frederick believed that a ruler should be like a father to his people, for he is the head of a family of citizens.

War of the Austrian Succession In 1740, Maria Theresa succeeded her father, just five months after Frederick II became king of Prussia. Frederick wanted the Austrian land of Silesia, which bordered Prussia. Silesia produced iron ore, textiles, and food products. Frederick underestimated Maria Theresa's strength. He assumed that because she was a woman, she would not be forceful enough to defend her lands. In 1740, he sent his army to occupy Silesia, beginning the War of the Austrian Succession.

Even though Maria Theresa had recently given birth, she journeyed to Hungary. There she held her infant in her arms as she asked the Hungarian nobles for aid. Even though the nobles resented their Hapsburg rulers, they pledged to give Maria Theresa an army. Great Britain also joined Austria to fight its longtime enemy France, which was Prussia's ally. Although Maria Theresa did stop Prussia's aggression, she lost Silesia in the Treaty of Aix-la-Chapelle in 1748. With the acquisition of Silesia, Prussia became a major European power.

The Seven Years' War Maria Theresa decided that the French kings were no longer Austria's chief enemies. She made an alliance with them. The result was a diplomatic revolution. When Frederick heard of her actions, he signed a treaty with Britain—Austria's former ally. Now, Austria, France, Russia, and others were allied against Britain and Prussia. Not only had Austria and Prussia switched allies, but for the first time, Russia was playing a role in European affairs.

Maria Theresa
(1717–1780)

An able ruler, Maria Theresa also devoted herself to her children, whom she continued to advise even after they were grown. Perhaps her most famous child was Marie Antoinette, wife of Louis XVI of France.

As the Austrian empress, Maria Theresa decreased the power of the nobility. She also limited the amount of labor that nobles could force peasants to do. She argued, "The peasantry must be able to sustain itself."

Frederick the Great
(1712–1786)

Although they reigned during the same time, Frederick the Great and Maria Theresa were very different. Where Maria was religious, Frederick was practical and atheistic. Maria Theresa had a happy home life and a huge family, while Frederick died without a son to succeed him.

An aggressor in foreign affairs, Frederick once wrote that "the fundamental role of governments is the principle of extending their territories." Frederick earned the title "the Great" by achieving his goals for Prussia.

Reading Check
Clarify What steps did the Prussian monarchs take to become absolute monarchs?

In 1756, Frederick attacked Saxony, an Austrian ally. Soon every great European power was involved in the war. Fought in Europe, India, and North America, the war lasted until 1763. It was called the **Seven Years' War**. The war did not change the territorial situation in Europe.

It was a different story on other continents. Both France and Britain had colonies in North America and the West Indies. Both were competing economically in India. The British emerged as the real victors in the Seven Years' War. France lost its colonies in North America, and Britain gained sole economic domination of India. This set the stage for further British expansion in India in the 1800s.

Lesson 3 Assessment

1. **Organize Information** Make a table to show the ways Maria Theresa and Frederick the Great were similar rulers.

Maria Theresa	Frederick the Great

2. **Key Terms and People** For each key term or person in the lesson, write a sentence explaining its significance.
3. **Synthesize** What were the major conflicts in the Thirty Years' War?
4. **Recognize Effects** How did the Peace of Westphalia lay the foundations of modern Europe?
5. **Analyze Motives** Why did Maria Theresa make an alliance with the French kings, Austria's chief enemies?
6. **Draw Conclusions** Based on Frederick's assumption about Maria Theresa at the outset of the War of the Austrian Succession, what conclusions can you draw about how men viewed women in 1700s Europe?

Absolute Rulers of Russia

The Big Idea

Peter the Great made many changes in Russia to try to make it more like western Europe.

Why It Matters Now

Many Russians today debate whether to model themselves on the West or to focus on traditional Russian culture.

Key Terms and People

Ivan the Terrible
boyar
Peter the Great
westernization

Setting the Stage

Ivan III of Moscow, who ruled Russia from 1462 to 1505, accomplished several things. First, he conquered much of the territory around Moscow. Second, he liberated Russia from the Mongols. Third, he began to centralize the Russian government. Ivan III was succeeded by his son, Vasily, who ruled for 28 years. Vasily continued his father's work of adding territory to the growing Russian state. He also increased the power of the central government. This trend continued under his son, Ivan IV, who would become an absolute ruler.

The First Czar

Ivan IV, called **Ivan the Terrible**, came to the throne in 1533 when he was only three years old. His young life was disrupted by struggles for power among Russia's landowning nobles, known as **boyars**. The boyars fought to control young Ivan. When he was 16, Ivan seized power and had himself crowned czar. This title meant "caesar," and Ivan was the first Russian ruler to use it officially. He also married Anastasia, related to an old boyar family, the Romanovs.

The years from 1547 to 1560 are often called Ivan's "good period." He won great victories, added lands to Russia, gave Russia a code of laws, and ruled justly.

Rule by Terror Ivan's "bad period" began in 1560 after Anastasia died. Accusing the boyars of poisoning his wife, Ivan turned against them. He organized his own police force, whose chief duty was to hunt down and murder people Ivan considered traitors. The members of this police force dressed in black and rode black horses.

Using these secret police, Ivan executed many boyars, their families, and the peasants who worked their lands. Thousands of people died. Ivan seized the boyars' estates and gave them to a new class of nobles, who had to remain loyal to him or lose their land.

Eventually, Ivan committed an act that was both a personal tragedy and a national disaster. In 1581, during a violent quarrel, he killed his oldest son and heir. When Ivan died three years later, only his weak second son was left to rule.

Rise of the Romanovs Ivan's son proved to be physically and mentally incapable of ruling. After he died without an heir, Russia experienced a period of turmoil known as the Time of Troubles. Boyars struggled for power, and heirs of czars died under mysterious conditions. Several impostors tried to claim the throne.

Finally, in 1613, representatives from many Russian cities met to choose the next czar. Their choice was Michael Romanov, grandnephew of Ivan the Terrible's wife, Anastasia. Thus began the Romanov dynasty, which ruled Russia for 300 years (1613–1917).

Reading Check
Recognize Effects
What were the long-term effects of Ivan's murder of his oldest son?

Peter the Great Comes to Power

Over time, the Romanovs restored order to Russia. They strengthened government by passing a law code and putting down a revolt. This paved the way for the absolute rule of Czar Peter I. At first, Peter shared the throne with his half-brother. However, in 1696, Peter became sole ruler of Russia. He is known to history as **Peter the Great**, because he was one of Russia's greatest reformers. He also continued the trend of increasing the czar's power.

—— BIOGRAPHY ——

Peter the Great
(1672–1725)

Peter the Great had the mind of a genius, the body of a giant, and the ferocious temper of a bear. He was so strong that he was known to take a heavy silver plate and roll it up as if it were a piece of paper. If someone annoyed him, he would knock the offender unconscious.

The painting represents Peter as he looked when he traveled through western Europe. He dressed in the plain clothes of an ordinary worker to keep his identity a secret.

Russia Contrasts with Europe When Peter I came to power, Russia was still a land of boyars and serfs. Serfdom in Russia lasted into the mid-1800s, much longer than it did in western Europe. Russian landowners wanted serfs to stay on the land and produce large harvests. The landowners treated the serfs like property. When a Russian landowner sold a piece of land, he sold the serfs with it. Landowners could give away serfs as presents or to pay debts. It was also against the law for serfs to run away from their owners.

Most boyars knew little of western Europe. In the Middle Ages, Russia had looked to Constantinople, not to Rome, for leadership. Then Mongol rule had cut Russia off from the Renaissance and the Age of Exploration. Geographic barriers also isolated Russia. Its only seaport, Archangel in northern Russia, was choked with ice much of the year. The few travelers who reached Moscow were usually Dutch or German, and they had to stay in a separate part of the city.

Religious differences widened the gap between western Europe and Russia. The Russians had adopted the Eastern Orthodox branch of Christianity. Western Europeans were mostly Catholics or Protestants, and the Russians viewed them as heretics and avoided them.

Peter Visits the West In the 1680s, people in the German quarter of Moscow were accustomed to seeing the young Peter striding through their neighborhood on his long legs. (Peter was more than six and a half feet tall.) He was fascinated by the modern tools and machines in the foreigners' shops. Above all, he had a passion for ships and the sea. The young czar believed that Russia's future depended on having a warm-water port. Only then could Russia compete with the more modern states of western Europe.

Peter was 24 years old when he became the sole ruler of Russia. In 1697, just one year later, he embarked on the "Grand Embassy," a long visit to western Europe. One of Peter's goals was to learn about European customs and manufacturing techniques. Never before had a czar traveled among Western "heretics."

Reading Check
Summarize Why was Russia culturally different from western Europe?

Peter Rules Absolutely

Inspired by his trip to the West, Peter resolved that Russia would compete with Europe on both military and commercial terms. Peter's goal of **westernization**, of using western Europe as a model for change, was not an end in itself. Peter saw it as a way to make Russia stronger.

Peter's Reforms Although Peter believed Russia needed to change, he knew that many of his people disagreed. As he said to one official, "For you know yourself that, though a thing be good and necessary, our people will not do it unless forced to." To force change upon his state, Peter increased his powers as an absolute ruler.

Peter brought the Russian Orthodox Church under state control. He abolished the office of patriarch, head of the Church. He set up a group called the Holy Synod to run the Church under his direction.

Like Ivan the Terrible, Peter reduced the power of the great landowners. He recruited men from lower-ranking families. He then promoted them to positions of authority and rewarded them with grants of land.

To modernize his army, Peter hired European officers, who drilled his soldiers in European tactics with European weapons. Being a soldier became a lifetime job. By the time of Peter's death, the Russian army numbered 200,000 men. To pay for this huge army, Peter imposed heavy taxes.

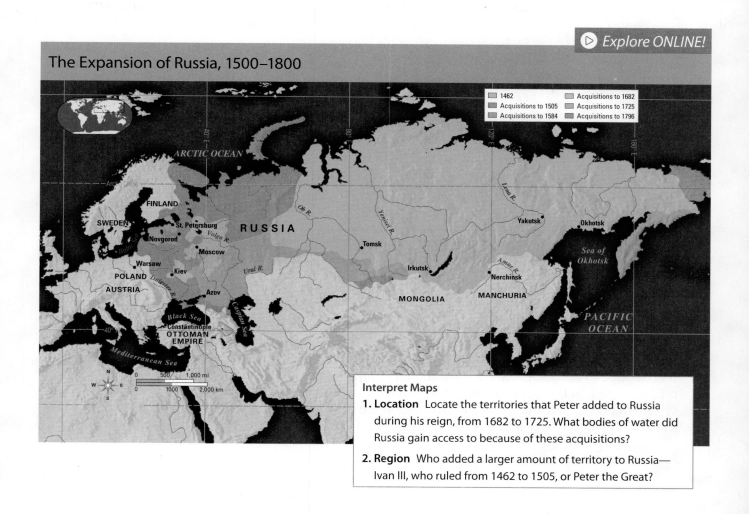

▶ Explore ONLINE!

The Expansion of Russia, 1500–1800

Legend:
- 1462
- Acquisitions to 1505
- Acquisitions to 1584
- Acquisitions to 1682
- Acquisitions to 1725
- Acquisitions to 1796

Interpret Maps

1. **Location** Locate the territories that Peter added to Russia during his reign, from 1682 to 1725. What bodies of water did Russia gain access to because of these acquisitions?

2. **Region** Who added a larger amount of territory to Russia—Ivan III, who ruled from 1462 to 1505, or Peter the Great?

Westernizing Russia As part of his attempts to westernize Russia, Peter undertook the following:

- introduced potatoes, which became a staple of the Russian diet
- started Russia's first newspaper and edited its first issue himself
- raised women's status by having them attend social gatherings
- ordered the nobles to give up their traditional clothes for Western fashions
- advanced education by opening a school of navigation and introducing schools for the arts and sciences

Peter believed that education was a key to Russia's progress. In former times, subjects were forbidden under pain of death to study the sciences in foreign lands. Now subjects were not only permitted to leave the country, but many were forced to do it.

Establishing St. Petersburg To promote education and growth, Peter wanted a seaport that would make it easier to travel to the West. Therefore, Peter fought Sweden to gain a piece of the Baltic coast. After 21 long years of war, Russia finally won the "window on Europe" that Peter had so desperately wanted.

Actually, Peter had secured that window many years before Sweden officially surrendered it. In 1703, he began building a new city on Swedish lands occupied by Russian troops. Although the swampy site was unhealthful, it seemed ideal to Peter. Ships could sail down the Neva River into the Baltic Sea and on to western Europe. Peter called the city St. Petersburg, after his patron saint.

To build a city on a desolate swamp was no easy matter. Every summer, the army forced thousands of luckless serfs to leave home and work in St. Petersburg. An estimated 25,000 to 100,000 people died from the terrible working conditions and widespread diseases. When St. Petersburg was finished, Peter ordered many Russian nobles to leave the comforts of Moscow and settle in his new capital. In time, St. Petersburg became a busy port.

Global Patterns

East Meets West

In the East, Western influence would not only affect Russia. Other eastern nations would give way—not always willingly—to the West and Western culture. In 1854, Japan was forced to open its doors to the United States. By 1867, however, Japan had decided to embrace Western civilization. The Japanese modernized their military based on the German and British models. They also adopted the American system of public education. China and Korea, on the other hand, would resist foreign intervention well into the 1900s.

For better or for worse, Peter the Great had tried to westernize and reform the culture and government of Russia. To an amazing extent he had succeeded. By the time of his death in 1725, Russia was a power to be reckoned with in Europe. Meanwhile, another great European power, England, had been developing a form of government that limited the power of absolute monarchs, as you will see later.

Lesson 4 Assessment

1. **Organize Information** Use a web to show important events that had an impact on modern Russia.

Peter the Great

2. **Key Terms and People** For each key term or person in the lesson, write a sentence explaining its significance.

3. **Analyze Motives** Why did Peter the Great believe that Russia's future depended on having a warm-water port?

4. **Synthesize** What were some of the ways Peter tried to westernize Russia?

5. **Support Opinions** Who do you think was more of an absolute monarch: Ivan the Terrible or Peter the Great? Explain.

6. **Draw Conclusions** Which class of Russian society probably didn't benefit from Peter's reforms? Why?

7. **Hypothesize** How might Peter's attempts at westernization have affected his people's opinion of Christians in western Europe?

Surviving the Russian Winter

Much of Russia has severe winters. In Moscow, snow usually begins to fall in mid-October and lasts until mid-April. Siberia has been known to have temperatures as low as -90°F. Back in the 18th century, Russians did not have down parkas or high-tech insulation for their homes. But they had other ways to cope with the climate.

For example, in the 18th century, Russian peasants added potatoes and corn to their diet. During the winter, these nutritious foods were used in soups and stews. Such dishes were warming and provided plenty of calories to help fight off the cold.

SILVER SAMOVAR ▶
In the mid-18th century, samovars were invented in Russia. These large, often elaborately decorated urns were used to boil water for tea. Fire was kept burning in a tube running up the middle of the urn—keeping the water piping hot.

◀ CRIMEAN DRESS
These people are wearing the traditional dress of tribes from the Crimean Peninsula, a region that Russia took over in the 1700s. Notice the heavy hats, the fur trim on some of the robes, and the leggings worn by those with shorter robes. All these features help to conserve body heat.

▲ TROIKA
To travel in winter, the wealthy often used sleighs called troikas. *Troika* means "group of three"; the name comes from the three horses that draw this kind of sleigh. The middle horse trotted while the two outside horses galloped.

◄ **WINTER FESTIVAL**

Russians have never let their climate stop them from having fun outdoors. Here, they are shown enjoying a Shrovetide festival, which occurs near the end of winter. Vendors sold food such as blinis (pancakes with sour cream). Entertainments included ice skating, dancing bears, and magic shows.

The people in the foreground are wearing heavy fur coats. Otter fur was often used for winter clothing. This fur is extremely thick and has about one million hairs per square inch.

▲ **WOODEN HOUSES**

Wooden houses, made of logs, were common in Russia during Peter the Great's time. To insulate the house from the wind, people stuffed moss between the logs. Russians used double panes of glass in their windows. For extra protection, many houses had shutters to cover the windows. The roofs were steep so snow would slide off.

Now and Then

1. **Make Inferences** In the 18th century, how did Russians use their natural resources to help them cope with the climate?

2. **Compare and Contrast** How has coping with winter weather changed from 18th-century Russia to today's world? How has it stayed the same?

FROSTY FACTS

- According to a 2001 estimate, Russian women spend about $500 million a year on fur coats and caps.
- The record low temperature in Asia of -90°F was reached twice, first in Verkhoyansk, Russia, in 1892 and then in Oimekon, Russia, in 1933.
- The record low temperature in Europe of -67°F was recorded in Ust'Shchugor, Russia.
- One reason for Russia's cold climate is that most of the country lies north of the 45° latitude line, closer to the North Pole than to the Equator.

Average High Temperature for January, Russian Cities

Moscow, Russia	Perm, Russia	Rostov, Russia
21°F	12°F	29°F

Source: *Worldclimate.com*

Average High Temperature for January, U.S. Cities

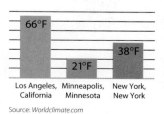

Los Angeles, California	Minneapolis, Minnesota	New York, New York
66°F	21°F	38°F

Source: *Worldclimate.com*

Parliament Limits the English Monarchy

The Big Idea

Absolute rulers in England were overthrown, and Parliament gained power.

Why It Matters Now

Many of the government reforms of this period contributed to the democratic tradition of the United States.

Key Terms and People

Charles I
English Civil War
Oliver Cromwell
Restoration
habeas corpus
Glorious Revolution
constitutional monarchy
cabinet

Setting the Stage

During her reign, Queen Elizabeth I of England had had frequent conflicts with Parliament. Many of the arguments were over money because the treasury did not have funds to pay the queen's expenses. By the time Elizabeth died in 1603, she had left a huge debt for her successor. Parliament's financial power was one obstacle to English rulers' becoming absolute monarchs. The resulting struggle between Parliament and the monarchy would have serious consequences for England.

Monarchs Defy Parliament

Elizabeth had no child, and her nearest relative was her cousin, James Stuart. Already king of Scotland, James Stuart became King James I of England in 1603. Although England and Scotland were not united until 1707, they now shared a ruler.

James's Problems James inherited the unsettled issues of Elizabeth's reign. His worst struggles with Parliament were over money. In addition, James offended the Puritan members of Parliament. The Puritans hoped he would enact reforms to purify the English church of Catholic practices. Except for agreeing to a new translation of the Bible, however, he refused to make Puritan reforms.

Charles I Fights Parliament In 1625, James I died. **Charles I**, his son, took the throne. Charles always needed money, in part because he was at war with both Spain and France. Several times when Parliament refused to give him funds, he dissolved it.

By 1628, Charles was forced to call Parliament again. This time it refused to grant him any money until he signed a document that is known as the Petition of Right. In this petition, the king agreed to four points:

- He would not imprison subjects without due cause.
- He would not levy taxes without Parliament's consent.

Reading Check
Summarize Why
did Charles defy
Parliament again and
again?

- He would not house soldiers in private homes.
- He would not impose martial law in peacetime.

After agreeing to the petition, Charles ignored it. Even so, the petition was important. It set forth the idea that the law was higher than the king. This idea contradicted theories of absolute monarchy. In 1629, Charles dissolved Parliament and refused to call it into session. To get money, he imposed fees and fines on the people. His popularity decreased yearly.

English Civil War

Charles offended Puritans by upholding the rituals of the Anglican Church. In addition, in 1637, Charles tried to force the Presbyterian Scots to accept a version of the Anglican prayer book. He wanted both his kingdoms to follow one religion. The Scots rebelled, assembled a huge army, and threatened to invade England. To meet this danger, Charles needed money—money he could get only by calling Parliament into session. This gave Parliament a chance to oppose him.

War Topples a King During the autumn of 1641, Parliament passed laws to limit royal power. Furious, Charles tried to arrest Parliament's leaders in January 1642, but they escaped. Equally furious, a mob of Londoners raged outside the palace. Charles fled London and raised an army in the north of England, where people were loyal to him.

From 1642 to 1649, supporters and opponents of King Charles fought the **English Civil War**. Those who remained loyal to Charles were called Royalists or Cavaliers. On the other side were Puritan supporters of Parliament. Because these men wore their hair short over their ears, Cavaliers called them Roundheads.

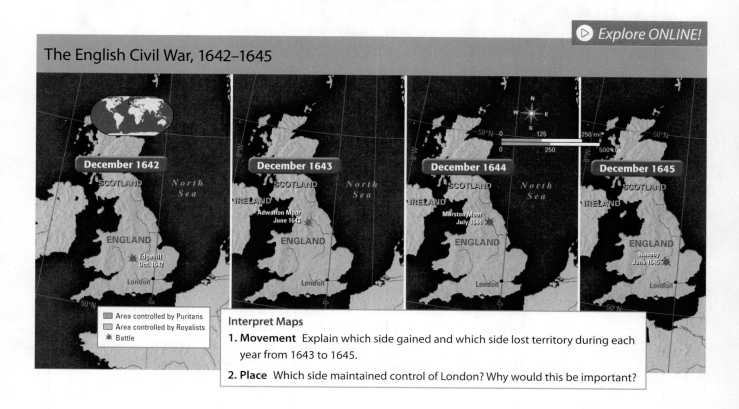

> Explore ONLINE!

The English Civil War, 1642–1645

Area controlled by Puritans
Area controlled by Royalists
Battle

Interpret Maps

1. **Movement** Explain which side gained and which side lost territory during each year from 1643 to 1645.

2. **Place** Which side maintained control of London? Why would this be important?

At first neither side could gain a lasting advantage. However, by 1644 the Puritans found a general who could win—**Oliver Cromwell**. In 1645, Cromwell's New Model Army began defeating the Cavaliers, and the tide turned toward the Puritans. In 1647, they held the king prisoner.

In 1649, Cromwell and the Puritans brought Charles to trial for treason against Parliament. They found him guilty and sentenced him to death. The execution of Charles was revolutionary. Kings had often been overthrown, killed in battle, or put to death in secret. Never before, however, had a reigning monarch faced a public trial and execution.

This engraving depicts the beheading of Charles I.

Cromwell's Rule Cromwell now held the reins of power. In 1649, he abolished the monarchy and the House of Lords. He established a commonwealth, a republican form of government. Cromwell almost immediately had to put down a rebellion in Ireland. English colonization of Ireland had begun in the 1100s under Henry II. Henry VIII and his children had brought the country firmly under English rule in the 1500s. In 1649, Cromwell landed on Irish shores with an army and crushed the uprising. He seized the lands and homes of the Irish and gave them to English soldiers. Fighting, plague, and famine killed hundreds of thousands.

In 1653, Cromwell sent home the remaining members of Parliament. Cromwell's associate John Lambert drafted a constitution, the first written constitution of any modern European state. This new government was called a protectorate. Oliver Cromwell became the head of state, called the Lord Protector. The government united England, Wales, Scotland, and Ireland under a single government, and gave all the nations a seat in the new British parliament. Under Cromwell, the protectorate provided for a large army and navy.

Puritan Morality In England, Cromwell and the Puritans sought to reform society. They made laws that promoted Puritan morality and abolished activities they found sinful, such as the theater, sporting events, and dancing. Although he was a strict Puritan, Cromwell favored religious toleration for all Christians except Catholics. He even allowed Jews to return; they had been expelled from England in 1290. Cromwell also promoted education, setting up many new schools, and he reduced punishments for minor crimes.

Reading Check
Compare What did Cromwell's rule have in common with an absolute monarchy?

Restoration and Revolution

Oliver Cromwell ruled until his death in 1658. Shortly afterward, the government he had established collapsed, and a new Parliament was selected. The English people were sick of military rule. In 1659, Parliament voted to ask the older son of Charles I to rule England.

Charles II Reigns When Prince Charles entered London in 1660, crowds shouted joyfully and bells rang. On this note of celebration, the reign of Charles II began. Because he restored the monarchy, the period of his rule is called the **Restoration**.

During Charles II's reign, Parliament passed an important guarantee of freedom, ***habeas corpus***. *Habeas corpus* is Latin meaning "to have the body." This 1679 law gave every prisoner the right to obtain a writ or document ordering that the prisoner be brought before a judge to specify the charges against the prisoner. The judge would decide whether the prisoner should be tried or set free. Because of the Habeas Corpus Act, a monarch could not put someone in jail simply for opposing the ruler. Also, prisoners could not be held indefinitely without trials.

In addition, Parliament debated who should inherit Charles's throne. Because Charles had no legitimate child, his heir was his brother James, who was Catholic. A group called the Whigs opposed James, and a group called the Tories supported him. These two groups were the ancestors of England's first political parties.

James II and the Glorious Revolution In 1685, Charles II died, and James II became king. James soon offended his subjects by displaying his Catholicism. Violating English law, he appointed several Catholics to high office. When Parliament protested, James dissolved it. In 1688, James's second wife gave birth to a son. English Protestants became terrified at the prospect of a line of Catholic kings.

King James II

James had an older daughter, Mary, who was Protestant. She was also the wife of William of Orange, a prince of the Netherlands. Seven members of Parliament invited William and Mary to overthrow James for the sake of Protestantism. When William led his army to London in 1688, James fled to France. This bloodless overthrow of King James II is called the **Glorious Revolution**.

Limits on Monarchs Power

At their coronation, William and Mary vowed to recognize Parliament as their partner in governing. England had become not an absolute monarchy but a **constitutional monarchy**, where laws limited the ruler's power.

Bill of Rights To make clear the limits of royal power, Parliament drafted a Bill of Rights in 1689. This document listed many things that a ruler could not do:

- no suspending of Parliament's laws
- no levying of taxes without a specific grant from Parliament
- no interfering with freedom of speech in Parliament
- no penalizing a citizen who petitions the king about grievances

William and Mary consented to these and other limits on their royal power.

Cabinet System Develops After 1688, no British monarch could rule without the consent of Parliament. At the same time, Parliament could not rule without the consent of the monarch. If the two disagreed, government came to a standstill.

DOCUMENT-BASED INVESTIGATION   Historical Source

The English Bill of Rights

The English Bill of Rights, passed in 1689, placed limits on a monarch's powers.

"That the pretended power of suspending [canceling] of laws or the execution [carrying out] of laws by regal authority without consent of Parliament is illegal; . . .That it is the right of the subjects to petition [make requests of] the king, and all commitments [imprisonments] and prosecutions for such petitioning are illegal; That the raising or keeping a standing army within the kingdom in time of peace, unless it be with consent of Parliament, is against the law; . . . That election of members of Parliament ought to be free [not restricted]."

—English Bill of Rights

Analyze Historical Sources
What was the purpose of the English Bill of Rights?

U.S. Democracy

Today, the United States still relies on many of the government reforms and institutions that the English developed during this period.

These include the following:

- the right to obtain *habeas corpus*, a document that prevents authorities from holding a person in jail without being charged

- a Bill of Rights, guaranteeing such rights as freedom of speech and freedom of worship

- a strong legislature and strong executive, which act as checks on each other

- a cabinet, made up of heads of executive departments, such as the Department of State

- two dominant political parties

During the 1700s, this potential problem was remedied by the development of a group of government ministers, or officials, called the **cabinet**. These ministers acted in the ruler's name but in reality represented the major party of Parliament. Therefore, they became the link between the monarch and the majority party in Parliament.

Over time, the cabinet became the center of power and policymaking. Under the cabinet system, the leader of the majority party in Parliament heads the cabinet and is called the prime minister. This system of English government continues today.

Reading Check
Analyze Effects
What effect did the British Cabinet system have on U.S. democracy?

Lesson 5 Assessment

1. **Organize Information** Use a table to show the patterns you find in the causes of conflicts with parliament.

Monarch	Conflicts with Parliament
James I	
Charles I	
James II	

2. **Key Terms and People** For each key term or person in the lesson, write a sentence explaining its significance.

3. **Draw Conclusions** Why was the death of Charles I revolutionary?

4. **Evaluate Decisions** In your opinion, which decisions by Charles I made his conflict with Parliament worse? Explain.

5. **Make Inferences** Why do you think James II fled to France when William of Orange led his army to London?

6. **Synthesize** What conditions in England made the execution of one king and the overthrow of another possible?

7. **Contrast** How might Cromwell's rule be viewed differently by the Irish and the English?

Module 17 Assessment

Key Terms and People

For each term or name below, write a sentence explaining its connection to European history from 1500 to 1800.

1. absolute monarch
2. divine right
3. Louis XIV
4. War of the Spanish Succession
5. Thirty Years' War
6. Seven Years' War
7. Peter the Great
8. English Civil War
9. Glorious Revolution
10. constitutional monarchy

Main Ideas

Spain's Empire and European Absolutism

1. What three actions demonstrated that Philip II of Spain saw himself as a defender of Catholicism?
2. According to French writer Jean Bodin, should a prince share power with anyone else? Explain why or why not.

The Reign of Louis XIV

3. What strategies did Louis XIV use to control the French nobility?
4. In what ways did Louis XIV cause suffering to the French people?

Central European Monarchs Clash

5. What were six results of the Peace of Westphalia?
6. Why did Maria Theresa and Frederick the Great fight two wars against each other?
7. Critique the successes and failures of initiatives to establish international peace, such as the War of Spanish Succession, The War of Austrian Succession, and the Seven Years' War.

Absolute Rulers of Russia

8. What were three differences between Russia and western Europe?
9. What was Peter the Great's primary goal for Russia?

Parliament Limits the English Monarchy

10. List the causes, participants, and outcome of the English Civil War.
11. How did Parliament try to limit the power of the English monarchy?
12. A nation-state has three components: all citizen are members, it is the only power that can have armies, and its government acts on behalf of the people. According to this definition, was England, after its Civil War, a nation-state? Why or why not?

Critical Thinking

1. **Use Your Notes** In a table, list actions that absolute monarchs took to increase their power. Then identify the monarchs who took these actions.

Actions of Absolute Rulers	Monarchs Who Took Them

2. **Draw Conclusions** What benefits might absolute monarchs hope to gain by increasing their countries' territory?

3. **Develop Historical Perspective** What conditions fostered the rise of absolute monarchs in Europe?

4. **Compare and Contrast** Compare the reign of Louis XIV with that of Peter the Great. Which absolute ruler had a more lasting impact on his country? Explain. Compare these absolute rulers with the rule of Tokugawa Ieyasu in Japan. How are they similar and different?

5. **Hypothesize** Would Charles I have had a different fate if he had been king of another country in western or central Europe? Why or why not?

6. **Develop Historical Perspective** What steps did the Austrian Hapsburgs take toward becoming absolute monarchs?

7. **Compare and Contrast** How does a constitutional monarchy differ from an absolute monarchy? How is it similar?

8. **Hypothesize** How did Ivan the Terrible deal with his enemies during his "bad period"?

9. **Analyze** What rights were guaranteed by the Habeas Corpus Act?

Engage with History

Now that you have read about absolute rulers, what do you consider to be the main advantage and the main disadvantage of being an absolute ruler?

Focus on Writing

Reread the information on Oliver Cromwell. Then write a **Biography**, like the ones you've seen throughout this program, on Cromwell as a leader of a successful revolution. Be sure to include the following:

- his successes and failures as a leader
- biographical information about Cromwell
- vivid language to hold the reader's attention

Multimedia Activity

Make a Video

Yet another revolution threatens the monarchy today in Great Britain. Some people would like to see the monarchy ended altogether. Find out what you can about this issue and choose a side. Present your findings—including images, tables, and an original political cartoon—in a video.

Module 18

Enlightenment and Revolution

Essential Question

In what ways were the ideas introduced by European scientists and thinkers between the 1500s and 1700s revolutionary?

About the Map: This 1660 map drawn by Dutch-German cartographer Andreas Cellarius shows the solar system as described by Polish astronomer Nicolaus Copernicus. Copernicus's concept of a heliocentric universe helped to set off the Scientific Revolution.

▷ Explore ONLINE!

HISTORY

VIDEOS, including...
• A Revolutionary Thinker
• Lessons of a Revolution

☑ Document Based Investigations

☑ Graphic Organizers

☑ Interactive Games

☑ Image with Hotspots: Enlightenment Thinking in Art

☑ Image with Text Slider: Enlightenment Ideas

In this module you will learn how Enlightenment scientists and thinkers challenged old ideas in science, the arts, government, and religion.

What You Will Learn ...

Timeline of Events 1500–1800

▶ Explore ONLINE!

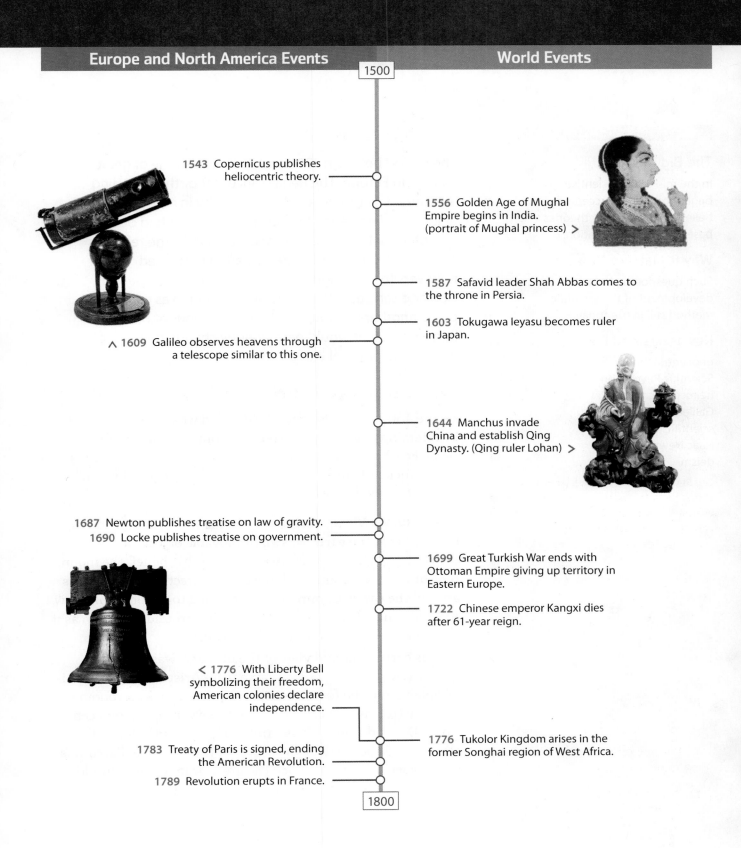

Europe and North America Events

1500

1543 Copernicus publishes heliocentric theory.

∧ **1609** Galileo observes heavens through a telescope similar to this one.

1687 Newton publishes treatise on law of gravity.
1690 Locke publishes treatise on government.

< **1776** With Liberty Bell symbolizing their freedom, American colonies declare independence.

1783 Treaty of Paris is signed, ending the American Revolution.
1789 Revolution erupts in France.

1800

World Events

1556 Golden Age of Mughal Empire begins in India. (portrait of Mughal princess) >

1587 Safavid leader Shah Abbas comes to the throne in Persia.

1603 Tokugawa Ieyasu becomes ruler in Japan.

1644 Manchus invade China and establish Qing Dynasty. (Qing ruler Lohan) >

1699 Great Turkish War ends with Ottoman Empire giving up territory in Eastern Europe.

1722 Chinese emperor Kangxi dies after 61-year reign.

1776 Tukolor Kingdom arises in the former Songhai region of West Africa.

The Scientific Revolution

The Big Idea

In the mid-1500s, scientists began to question accepted beliefs and make new theories based on experimentation.

Why It Matters Now

Such questioning led to the development of the scientific method still in use today.

Key Terms and People

geocentric theory
Scientific Revolution
heliocentric theory
Galileo Galilei
scientific method
Isaac Newton
deism

Setting the Stage

The period between 1300 and 1600 was a time of great change in Europe. The Renaissance, a rebirth of learning and the arts, inspired a spirit of curiosity in many fields. Scholars began to question ideas that had been accepted for hundreds of years. Meanwhile, the religious movement known as the Reformation prompted followers to challenge accepted ways of thinking about God and salvation. While the Reformation was taking place, another revolution in European thought had begun, one that would permanently change how people viewed the physical world.

The Roots of Modern Science

Before 1500, scholars generally decided what was true or false by referring to an ancient Greek or Roman author or to the Bible. Few European scholars challenged the scientific ideas of the ancient thinkers or the church by carefully observing nature for themselves.

The Medieval View During the Middle Ages, most scholars believed that the earth was an immovable object located at the center of the universe. According to that belief, the moon, the sun, and the planets all moved in perfectly circular paths around the earth. Common sense seemed to support this view. After all, the sun appeared to be moving around the earth as it rose in the morning and set in the evening.

This earth-centered view of the universe was called the **geocentric theory**. The idea came from Aristotle, a Greek philosopher from the fourth century BC. The Greek astronomer Ptolemy (TOL•a•mee) expanded the theory in the second century AD. In addition, Christianity taught that God had deliberately placed the earth at the center of the universe. Earth was thus a special place on which the great drama of life unfolded.

A New Way of Thinking Beginning in the mid-1500s, a few scholars published works that challenged the ideas of the ancient thinkers and the church. As these scholars replaced old assumptions with new theories, they launched a change in European thought that historians call the **Scientific Revolution**. The Scientific Revolution was a new way of thinking about the natural world. That way was based upon careful observation and a willingness to question accepted beliefs.

A combination of discoveries and circumstances led to the Scientific Revolution and helped spread its impact. During the Crusades, Europeans came in contact with the Muslim world. They learned about many advancements in mathematics and science developed by Muslim scholars, such as Arabic numerals, algebra, astronomical charts, and human anatomy. Then, during the Renaissance, European explorers traveled to Africa, Asia, and the Americas. They encountered peoples and animals previously unknown in Europe. These discoveries opened Europeans to the possibility that there were new truths to be found. The invention of the printing press during this period helped spread challenging ideas—both old and new—more widely among Europe's thinkers.

The age of European exploration also fueled a great deal of scientific research, especially in astronomy and mathematics. Navigators needed better instruments and geographic measurements, for example, to determine their location in the open sea. As scientists began to look more closely at the world around them, they made observations that did not match the ancient beliefs. They found they had reached the limit of the classical world's knowledge. Yet, they still needed to know more.

Reading Check
Analyze Effects
What impact did travel by Europeans have on the launching of the Scientific Revolution?

A Revolutionary Model of the Universe

An early challenge to accepted scientific thinking came in the field of astronomy. It started when a small group of scholars began to question the geocentric theory.

The Heliocentric Theory Although backed by authority and common sense, the geocentric theory did not accurately explain the movements of the sun, moon, and planets. This problem troubled a Polish cleric and astronomer named Nicolaus Copernicus (nik•uh•LAY•uhs koh•PUR•nuh•kuhs). In the early 1500s, Copernicus became interested in an old Greek idea that the sun stood at the center of the universe.

After studying planetary movements for more than 25 years, Copernicus reasoned that the stars, the earth, and the other planets revolved around the sun.

Copernicus's **heliocentric**, or sun-centered, **theory** still did not completely explain why the planets orbited the way they did. He also knew that most scholars and clergy

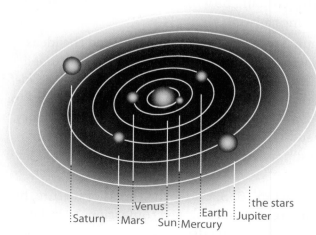

Saturn Mars Venus Sun Mercury Earth Jupiter the stars

This model shows how Copernicus saw the planets revolving around the sun.

would reject his theory because it contradicted their religious views. Fearing ridicule or persecution, Copernicus did not publish his findings until 1543, the last year of his life. He received a copy of his book, *On the Revolutions of the Heavenly Bodies,* on his deathbed.

Even though it was revolutionary, Copernicus's book caused little stir at first. Over the next century and a half, other scientists built on the foundations Copernicus had laid. A Danish astronomer, Tycho Brahe (TEE·koh-brah), carefully recorded the movements of the planets for many years, noting their positions in the sky over time. Brahe produced mountains of accurate data based on his observations. However, it was left to his followers to make mathematical sense of them.

After Brahe's death in 1601, his assistant, a brilliant mathematician named Johannes Kepler (yo·HAHN·uhs-KEP·ler), continued his work. After studying Brahe's data, Kepler concluded that certain mathematical laws govern planetary motion. One of these laws showed that the planets must revolve around the sun in elliptical orbits instead of circles, as Copernicus had thought. Kepler's laws showed that Copernicus's basic ideas were true, however. They demonstrated mathematically that the planets revolve around the sun.

Galileo's Discoveries Italian scientist **Galileo Galilei** built on the new theories about astronomy. As a young man, Galileo learned that a Dutch lens maker had built an instrument that could enlarge far-off objects. Galileo built his own telescope in 1609 and used it to study the heavens.

Then, in 1610, he published a small book called *Starry Messenger,* which described his astonishing observations. Galileo announced that Jupiter had four moons and that the sun had dark spots. He also noted that the earth's moon had a rough, uneven surface. This shattered Aristotle's theory that the moon and stars were made of a pure, perfect substance. Galileo's observations, as well as his laws of motion, also clearly supported the theories of Copernicus.

Conflict with the Church Galileo's findings frightened both Catholic and Protestant leaders because they went against church teaching and authority. If people believed the church could be wrong about this, they might question other church teachings as well.

In 1616, the Catholic Church warned Galileo not to defend the ideas of Copernicus. Although Galileo remained publicly silent, he continued his studies. Then, in 1632, he published *Dialogue Concerning the Two Chief World Systems.* This book presented the ideas of both Copernicus and Ptolemy, but it clearly showed that Galileo supported the Copernican theory. The pope angrily summoned Galileo to Rome to stand trial before the Inquisition, a court held to suppress ideas and beliefs that conflicted with Catholic teachings.

Galileo stood before the court in 1633. Under the threat of torture, he knelt before the cardinals and read aloud a signed confession. In it, he agreed that the ideas of Copernicus were false.

Galileo's Confession

When he was called before a papal court, Galileo had to make a difficult decision. Should he continue to support the heliocentric theory and anger the Church or confess to wrongdoing and stop publishing his work? He chose the latter.

"With sincere heart and unpretended faith I abjure, curse, and detest the aforesaid errors and heresies [of Copernicus] and also every other error . . . contrary to the Holy Church, and I swear that in the future I will never again say or assert . . . anything that might cause a similar suspicion toward me."

—Galileo Galilei, quoted in *The Discoverers*

Analyze Historical Sources
In what two ways does Galileo seek to appease the Church in his confession?

Reading Check
Find Main Ideas
How did Kepler's findings support the heliocentric theory?

Galileo was never again a free man. He lived under house arrest and died in 1642 at his villa near Florence. However, his books and ideas still spread all over Europe. (In 1992, the Catholic Church officially acknowledged that Galileo had been right.)

The Scientific Method

The revolution in scientific thinking that Copernicus, Kepler, and Galileo began eventually developed into a new approach to science called the **scientific method**. The scientific method is a logical procedure for gathering and testing ideas. It begins with a problem or question arising from an observation. Scientists next form a hypothesis, or unproved assumption. The hypothesis is then tested in an experiment or on the basis of data. In the final step, scientists analyze and interpret their data to reach a new conclusion. That conclusion either confirms or disproves the hypothesis.

The scientific method emphasizes two different types of thinking—deductive and inductive reasoning. Using deductive reasoning, scientists start with a theory and test the theory with experiments and observations. This is sometimes called "going from the top down." When they look for patterns in data from experiments and observation and come up with conclusions, they are using inductive reasoning. This sometimes called "going from the bottom up."

Major Steps in the Scientific Revolution

Nicolaus Copernicus began the Scientific Revolution with his heliocentric theory.

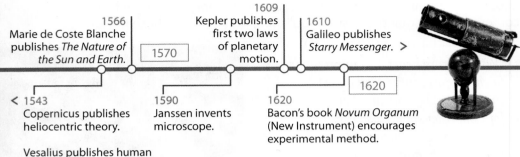

1566 Marie de Coste Blanche publishes *The Nature of the Sun and Earth.*

1570

1609 Kepler publishes first two laws of planetary motion.

1610 Galileo publishes *Starry Messenger.* >

< 1543 Copernicus publishes heliocentric theory.

Vesalius publishes human anatomy textbook.

1590 Janssen invents microscope.

1620 Bacon's book *Novum Organum* (New Instrument) encourages experimental method.

1620

Bacon and Descartes The scientific method did not develop overnight. The work of two important thinkers of the 1600s, Francis Bacon and René Descartes, helped to advance the new approach.

Francis Bacon, an English statesman and writer, had a passionate interest in science. He believed that by better understanding the world, scientists would generate practical knowledge that would improve people's lives. In his writings, Bacon attacked medieval scholars for relying too heavily on the conclusions of Aristotle and other ancient thinkers. Instead of reasoning from abstract theories, he urged scientists to experiment and then draw conclusions. This approach is called empiricism, or the experimental method.

In France, René Descartes also took a keen interest in science. He developed analytical geometry, which linked algebra and geometry. This provided an important new tool for scientific research.

Like Bacon, Descartes believed that scientists needed to reject old assumptions and teachings. As a mathematician, however, he approached gaining knowledge differently from Bacon. Rather than using experimentation, Descartes relied on mathematics and logic. He believed that everything should be doubted until proved by reason. The only thing he knew for certain was that he existed—because, as he wrote, "I think, therefore I am." From this starting point, he followed a train of strict reasoning to arrive at other basic truths.

The methodologies followed by modern sciences are based on the ideas of Bacon and Descartes. Scientists from the 1700s to the present have determined that observation and experimentation, together with general laws that can be expressed mathematically, can lead people to a better understanding of the natural world.

Reading Check
Contrast How did Descartes's approach to science differ from Bacon's?

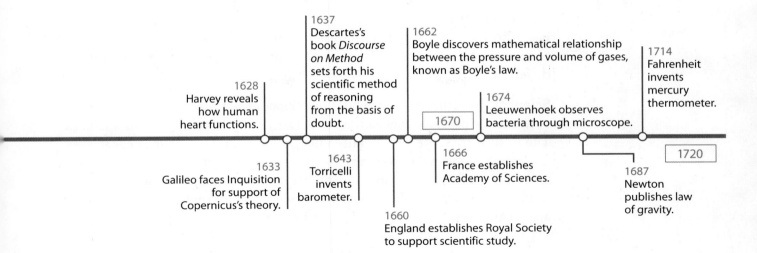

1628 Harvey reveals how human heart functions.

1637 Descartes's book *Discourse on Method* sets forth his scientific method of reasoning from the basis of doubt.

1662 Boyle discovers mathematical relationship between the pressure and volume of gases, known as Boyle's law.

1670

1674 Leeuwenhoek observes bacteria through microscope.

1714 Fahrenheit invents mercury thermometer.

1633 Galileo faces Inquisition for support of Copernicus's theory.

1643 Torricelli invents barometer.

1666 France establishes Academy of Sciences.

1720

1687 Newton publishes law of gravity.

1660 England establishes Royal Society to support scientific study.

Isaac Newton's law of gravity explained how the same physical laws govern motion both on earth and in the heavens.

Reading Check
Clarify Why was the law of gravitation important?

Newton Explains the Law of Gravity

By the mid-1600s, the accomplishments of Copernicus, Kepler, and Galileo had shattered the old views of astronomy and physics. Later, the great English scientist **Isaac Newton** helped to bring together their breakthroughs under a single theory of motion.

Newton studied mathematics and physics at Cambridge University. By the time he was 26, Newton was certain that all physical objects were affected equally by the same forces. Newton's great discovery was that the same force ruled motion of the planets and all matter on earth and in space. The key idea that linked motion in the heavens with motion on the earth was the law of universal gravitation. According to this law, every object in the universe attracts every other object. The degree of attraction depends on the mass of the objects and the distance between them.

In 1687, Newton published his ideas in a work entitled *The Mathematical Principles of Natural Philosophy* (sometimes known by its Latin title, *Principia Mathematica*). It was one of the most important scientific books ever written. The universe he described was like a giant clock. Its parts all worked together perfectly in ways that could be expressed mathematically. Newton believed that God was the creator of this orderly universe, the clockmaker who had set everything in motion. Many other scientists and philosophers during the Scientific Revolution, including Descartes, agreed with Newton's view of the role of God in the universe. This type of thinking was called **deism**, from the Latin word for God.

Changing Idea: Scientific Method

Old Science	New Science
Scholars generally relied on ancient authorities, church teachings, common sense, and reasoning to explain the physical world.	In time, scholars began to use observation, experimentation, and scientific reasoning to gather knowledge and draw conclusions about the physical world.

The Scientific Revolution Spreads

As astronomers explored the secrets of the universe, other scientists began to study the secrets of nature on earth. Careful observation and the use of the scientific method eventually became important in many different fields.

Scientific Instruments Scientists developed new tools and instruments to make the precise observations that the scientific method demanded. The first microscope was invented in 1590 by a Dutch maker of eyeglasses, Zacharias Janssen (YAHN•suhn). In the 1670s, a Dutch drapery merchant and amateur scientist named Anton van Leeuwenhoek (LAY•vuhn•huk) used a microscope to observe bacteria swimming in tooth scrapings. He also examined red blood cells for the first time.

In 1643, one of Galileo's students, Evangelista Torricelli (tawr•uh•CHEHL•ee), developed the first mercury barometer, a tool for measuring atmospheric pressure and predicting weather. In 1714, the German physicist Gabriel Fahrenheit (FAR•uhn•hyt) made the first thermometer to use mercury in glass. Fahrenheit's thermometer showed water freezing at 32°. A Swedish astronomer, Anders Celsius (SEHL•see•uhs), created another scale for the mercury thermometer in 1742. Celsius's scale showed freezing at 0°.

Medicine and the Human Body During the Middle Ages, European doctors had accepted as fact the writings of an ancient Greek physician named Galen. However, Galen had never dissected the body of a human being. Instead, he had studied the anatomy of pigs and other animals. Galen assumed that human anatomy was much the same. In the 1500s, a Flemish physician named Andreas Vesalius proved Galen's assumptions wrong. Vesalius dissected human corpses and published his observations. His book, *On the Structure of the Human Body* (1543), was filled with detailed drawings of human organs, bones, and muscles.

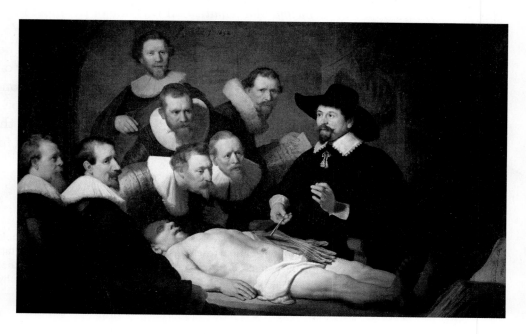

The famous Dutch artist Rembrandt painted *Anatomy Lesson of Dr. Nicolaes Tulp* in 1632 from an actual anatomy lesson. The corpse was that of a criminal.

In the late 1700s, British physician Edward Jenner introduced a vaccine to prevent smallpox. Inoculation using live smallpox germs had been practiced in Asia for centuries. While beneficial, this technique could also be dangerous. Jenner discovered that inoculation with germs from a cattle disease called cowpox gave permanent protection from smallpox for humans. Because cowpox was a much milder disease, the risks for this form of inoculation were much lower. Jenner used cowpox to produce the world's first vaccination.

Discoveries in Chemistry Robert Boyle pioneered the use of the scientific method in chemistry. Boyle had studied classical ideas about chemistry and medieval ideas including alchemy. Alchemists believed that base metals such as lead and copper could be transformed into silver and gold. Using both observations and experimentation, Boyle attempted to apply the principles and methods of chemistry to the study of the natural world and to medicine. He is considered the founder of modern chemistry. In a book called *The Sceptical Chymist (1661)*, Boyle challenged Aristotle's idea that the physical world consisted of four elements—earth, air, fire, and water. Instead, Boyle proposed that matter was made up of smaller primary particles that joined together in different ways. Boyle's most famous contribution to chemistry is Boyle's law. This law explains how the volume, temperature, and pressure of a gas affect each other.

The notions of reason and order, which spurred so many breakthroughs in science, soon moved into other fields of life. Philosophers and scholars across Europe began to rethink long-held beliefs about the human condition, most notably the rights and liberties of ordinary citizens. These thinkers helped to usher in a movement that challenged the age-old relationship between a government and its people and eventually changed forever the political landscape in numerous societies.

Reading Check
Make Inferences
Why were Galen's descriptions of human anatomy inaccurate?

Lesson 1 Assessment

1. **Organize Information** Which event or circumstance do you consider to be the most significant? Why?

Causes of the Scientific Revolution

2. **Key Terms and People** For each key term or person in the lesson, write a sentence explaining its significance.

3. **Analyze Issues** Why did the Catholic Church oppose the spreading of the heliocentric theory by scientists?

4. **Contrast** How did the scientific method differ from the approach generally followed by Medieval scholars?

5. **Draw Conclusions** "If I have seen farther than others," said Newton, "it is because I have stood on the shoulders of giants." Could this statement be said of most scientific accomplishments? Explain.

6. **Analyze Motives** Why might institutions of authority tend to reject new ideas developed by scientists and other thinkers?

7. **Form and Support Opinions** Do you agree with Galileo's actions during his Inquisition? Explain.

Enlightenment Thinkers

The Big Idea

A revolution in intellectual activity changed Europeans' view of government and society.

Why It Matters Now

The various freedoms enjoyed in many countries today are a result of Enlightenment thinking.

Key Terms and People

Enlightenment
social contract
John Locke
philosophe
rationalism
Voltaire
Montesquieu
Rousseau

Setting the Stage

In the wake of the Scientific Revolution and the new ways of thinking it prompted, scholars and philosophers began to reevaluate old notions about other aspects of society. They sought new insight into the underlying beliefs regarding government, religion, economics, and education. Their efforts spurred the **Enlightenment**, a new intellectual movement that stressed reason and thought and the power of individuals to solve problems. Known also as the Age of Reason, the movement reached its height in the mid-1700s and brought great change to many aspects of Western civilization.

Two Views on Government

The Enlightenment started from some key ideas put forth by two English political thinkers of the 1600s, Thomas Hobbes and John Locke. Both men experienced the political turmoil of England early in that century. However, they came to very different conclusions about government and human nature.

Hobbes's Social Contract

Thomas Hobbes expressed his views in a work called *Leviathan* (1651). The horrors of the English Civil War convinced him that all humans were naturally selfish and wicked. Without governments to keep order, Hobbes said, there would be "war . . . of every man against every man" and life would be "solitary, poor, nasty, brutish, and short."

Thomas Hobbes

Hobbes argued that to escape such a bleak life, people had to hand over their rights to a strong ruler. In exchange, they gained law and order. Hobbes called this agreement by which people created a government the **social contract**. Because people acted in their own self-interest, Hobbes said, the ruler needed total power to keep citizens under control. The best government was one that had the awesome power of a leviathan (sea monster). In Hobbes's view, such a government was an absolute monarchy, which could impose order and demand obedience.

Locke's Natural Rights The philosopher **John Locke** held a different, more positive view of human nature. He believed that people could learn from experience and improve themselves. As reasonable beings, they had the natural ability to govern their own affairs and to look after the welfare of society. Locke criticized absolute monarchy and favored the idea of self-government.

According to Locke, all people are born free and equal, with three natural or human rights—life, liberty, and property. The purpose of government, said Locke, is to protect these rights. If a government fails to do so, citizens have a right to overthrow it. Locke's theory had a deep influence on modern political thinking. His belief that a government's power comes from the consent of the people is the foundation of modern democracy. Locke's ideas of popular sovereignty, or government by popular consent, and the right to rebel against unjust rulers helped inspire struggles for liberty in Europe and the Americas.

Changing Idea: The Right to Govern	
Old Idea	**New Idea**
A monarch's rule is justified by divine right.	A government's power comes from the consent of the governed.

Locke's writings also led to new theories of education in Europe. Children are born with open minds, Locke wrote, and through education they can be taught society's important values. This type of thinking led some European rulers to issue edicts requiring young children to attend schools. Still, educational opportunities remained limited for girls or for those whose families did not belong to state churches.

Reading Check
Contrast How does Locke's view of human nature differ from that of Hobbes?

The Philosophes Advocate Reason

The Enlightenment reached its height in France in the mid-1700s. Paris became the meeting place for people who wanted to discuss politics and share ideas. The social critics of this period in France were known as **philosophes** (FIHL•uh•sahfs), the French word for "philosophers." The philosophes believed that people could apply reason to all aspects of life, just as Isaac Newton had applied reason to science. Five concepts formed the core of their beliefs:

1. **Reason** Enlightenment thinkers, building on ideas set forth earlier by Descartes, believed truth could be discovered through reason or logical thinking. This concept is sometimes called **rationalism**.
2. **Nature** The philosophes believed that what was natural was also good and reasonable. Enlightenment thinkers such as Locke focused on the rights that people have in their natural state as human beings in order to live in dignity. These rights cannot be taken away by any society or government.

3. **Happiness** The philosophes rejected the medieval notion that people should find joy in the hereafter and urged people to seek well-being on earth.
4. **Progress** The philosophes stressed that society and humankind could improve.
5. **Liberty** The philosophes called for the liberties that the English people had won in their Glorious Revolution and Bill of Rights.

Voltaire Combats Intolerance Probably the most brilliant and influential of the philosophes was François Marie Arouet. Using the pen name **Voltaire**, he published more than 70 books of political essays, philosophy, and drama.

Voltaire often used satire against his opponents. He made frequent targets of the clergy, the aristocracy, and the government. His sharp tongue made him enemies at the French court, and twice he was sent to prison. After his second jail term, Voltaire was exiled to England for more than two years.

Although he made powerful enemies, Voltaire never stopped fighting for tolerance, reason, freedom of religious belief, and freedom of speech. He used his quill pen as if it were a deadly weapon in a thinker's war against humanity's worst enemies—intolerance, prejudice, and superstition. He summed up his staunch defense of liberty in one of his most famous quotes: "I do not agree with a word you say but will defend to the death your right to say it."

Vocabulary
satire the use of irony, sarcasm, or wit to attack folly, vice, or stupidity

William Hogarth's painting *Canvassing for Votes* offers a satirical view of a corrupt British politician and his aides bribing voters ahead of an election.

Newton, Locke, and other major thinkers of the time were called deists. They believed that people should determine their religious beliefs mainly through reason instead of scripture. Some deists, such as Voltaire, harshly criticized the beliefs and practices of organized Christianity. They wanted to rid religious faith of superstition and fear and to promote tolerance of all religions.

Importance of the Individual Faith in science and in progress produced a third outcome, the rise of individualism. As people began to turn away from the church and royalty for guidance, they looked to themselves instead.

The philosophes encouraged people to use their own ability to reason in order to judge what was right or wrong. They also emphasized the importance of the individual in society. Government, they argued, was formed by individuals to promote their welfare. The British thinker Adam Smith extended the emphasis on the individual to economic thinking. He believed that individuals acting in their own self-interest created economic progress. Smith advocated the end of a system popular in Europe in the 1600s and 1700s known as mercantilism. In this system, countries believed they could increase their wealth by encouraging exports and discouraging imports. Smith called for freer trade practices and argued that countries could get wealthy and could keep more people employed by being both exporters and importers within a free market system.

During the Enlightenment, the greatest minds of Europe developed new ideas about reforming society. Some European kings and queens tried to apply these ideas to create progress in their countries. This influence also spread across the Atlantic. Inspired by Enlightenment ideas, colonial leaders in America decided to do the unthinkable: break away from their ruling country and found an independent republic.

Lesson 3 Assessment

1. **Organize Information** What are two generalizations you could make about the spread of Enlightenment ideas?

2. **Key Terms and People** For each key term or person in the lesson, write a sentence explaining its significance.

3. **Compare** What characteristics did classical music and neoclassical architecture have in common?

4. **Make Inferences** Why was the term "enlightened despot" appropriate to describe rulers such as Joseph II and Catherine the Great?

5. **Draw Conclusions** What advantages did salons have over earlier forms of communication in spreading ideas?

6. **Analyze Issues** Why might some women have been critical of the Enlightenment?

7. **Make Inferences** How did the *Encyclopedia* project reflect the age of Enlightenment?

The American Revolution

The Big Idea

Enlightenment ideas helped spur the American colonies to shed British rule and create a new nation.

Why It Matters Now

The revolution created a republic, the United States of America, that became a model for many nations of the world.

Key Terms and People

Declaration of Independence
Thomas Jefferson
checks and balances
federal system
Bill of Rights

Setting the Stage

Philosophes such as Voltaire considered England's government the most progressive in Europe. The Glorious Revolution of 1688 had given England a constitutional monarchy. In essence, this meant that various laws limited the power of the English king. Despite the view of the philosophes, however, a growing number of England's colonists in North America accused England of tyrannical rule. Emboldened by Enlightenment ideas, they would attempt to overthrow what was then the mightiest power on earth and create their own nation.

Britain and Its American Colonies

Throughout the 1600s and 1700s, British colonists had formed a large and thriving settlement along the eastern shore of North America. When George III became king of Great Britain in 1760, his North American colonies were growing by leaps and bounds. Their combined population soared from about 250,000 in 1700 to 2,150,000 in 1770, a nearly ninefold increase. Economically, the colonies thrived on trade with the nations of Europe.

Along with increasing population and prosperity, a new sense of identity was growing in the colonists' minds. By the mid-1700s, colonists had been living in America for nearly 150 years. Each of the 13 colonies had its own government, and people were used to a great degree of independence. Colonists saw themselves less as British and more as Virginians or Pennsylvanians. However, they were still British subjects and were expected to obey British law.

In 1651, the British Parliament passed a trade law called the Navigation Act. This and subsequent trade laws prevented colonists from selling their most valuable products to any country except Britain. In addition, colonists had to pay high taxes on imported French and Dutch goods. Despite the various trade restrictions, Britain's policies benefited both the colonies and the motherland. Britain bought American raw materials for low prices and sold manufactured goods to the colonists for a profit. Meanwhile, colonial merchants also made money when they sold British-made goods to the colonists.

The connection between American raw materials and British manufactured goods became even more important with the rise of industrialization in Britain in the 1700s. New inventions, such as spinning and weaving machines, made it possible for British textile manufacturers to greatly increase production of cloth. The availability of large supplies of American cotton, which the colonists were required to sell to Britain, helped to make Britain a worldwide leader in cotton textiles. In addition, the American colonies were a major market for British cloth.

Reading Check
Analyze Effects
In what ways did the American colonies help Britain's economy?

The Cloth Hall in Leeds, England, was a busy marketplace for British-made textiles.

Americans Win Independence

In 1754, war erupted on the North American continent between the English and the French. As you recall, the French had also colonized parts of North America throughout the 1600s and 1700s. The conflict was known as the French and Indian War. (The name stems from the fact that the French enlisted numerous Native American tribes to fight on their side.) The fighting lasted until 1763, when Britain and its colonists emerged victorious—and seized nearly all French land in North America.

The victory, however, only led to growing tensions between Britain and its colonists. In order to fight the war, Great Britain had run up a huge debt. Because American colonists benefited from Britain's victory, Britain expected the colonists to help pay the costs of the war. In 1765, Parliament passed the Stamp Act. According to this law, colonists had to pay a tax to have an official stamp put on wills, deeds, newspapers, and other printed material.

American colonists were outraged. They had never paid taxes directly to the British government before. Colonial lawyers argued that the stamp tax violated colonists' natural rights, and they accused the government of "taxation without representation." In Britain, citizens accepted taxes that their representatives in Parliament had passed. The colonists, however, had no representation in Parliament. Thus, they argued, they could not be taxed.

Growing Hostility Leads to War Over the next decade, hostilities between the two sides increased. Some colonial leaders favored independence from Britain. In 1773, to protest an import tax on tea, a group of colonists dumped a large load of British tea into Boston Harbor. George III, infuriated by the Boston Tea Party, as it was called, ordered the British navy to close the port of Boston.

Such harsh tactics by the British infuriated even moderate colonists. In September 1774, representatives from every colony except Georgia gathered in Philadelphia to form the First Continental Congress. This group protested the treatment of Boston. When the king paid little attention to their complaints, the colonies decided to form the Second Continental Congress to debate their next move.

On April 19, 1775, British soldiers and colonial militiamen exchanged gunfire on the village green in Lexington, Massachusetts. The fighting spread to nearby Concord. The Second Continental Congress voted to raise an army and organize for battle under the command of a Virginian named George Washington. The American Revolution had begun.

The Influence of the Enlightenment Colonial leaders used Enlightenment ideas to justify independence. The colonists had asked for the same political rights as people in Britain, they said, but the king had stubbornly refused. Therefore, the colonists were justified in rebelling against a tyrant who had wrongly restricted the liberty of those who are governed, as discussed by Locke and Rousseau. In July 1776, the Second Continental Congress issued the **Declaration of Independence**. This document, written by political leader **Thomas Jefferson**, was firmly based on Locke's ideas. The Declaration reflected these ideas in its eloquent argument for natural rights. "We hold these truths to be self-evident," states the beginning of the Declaration, "that all men are created equal, that they are endowed by their Creator with certain unalienable rights, that among these are life, liberty, and the pursuit of happiness."

Since Locke had asserted that people had the right to rebel against an unjust ruler, the Declaration of Independence included a long list of George III's abuses. The document ended by declaring the colonies' separation from Britain. The colonies, the Declaration said, "are absolved from all allegiance to the British crown."

BIOGRAPHY

Thomas Jefferson
(1743–1826)

The author of the Declaration of Independence, Thomas Jefferson of Virginia, was a true figure of the Enlightenment. As a writer and statesman, he supported free speech, religious freedom, and other civil liberties. At the same time, he was also a slave owner.

Jefferson was a man of many talents. He was an inventor as well as one of the great architects of early America. He designed the Virginia capitol building in Richmond and many buildings for the University of Virginia. Of all his achievements, Jefferson wanted to be most remembered for three: author of the Declaration of Independence, author of the Statute of Virginia for Religious Freedom, and founder of the University of Virginia.

Changing Idea: Colonial Attachment to Britain	
Old Idea	**New Idea**
American colonists considered themselves to be subjects of the British king.	After a long train of perceived abuses by the king, the colonists asserted their right to declare independence.

Success for the Colonists Britain was not about to let its colonies leave without a fight. Shortly after the publication of the Declaration of Independence, the two sides went to war. At first glance, the American colonists seemed destined to go down to quick defeat. Washington's ragtag, poorly trained army faced the well-trained forces of the most powerful country in the world. In the end, however, the colonists won their war for independence.

Several reasons explain the colonists' success. First, the Americans' motivation for fighting was much stronger than that of the British, as their army was defending their homeland. Second, the overconfident British generals made several mistakes. Third, time itself was on the side of the colonists. The British could win battle after battle, as they did, and still lose the war. Fighting an overseas war, 3,000 miles from London, was terribly expensive. After a few years, tax-weary British citizens called for peace.

Finally, the Americans did not fight alone. Louis XVI of France had little sympathy for the ideals of the American Revolution. However, he was eager to weaken Britain, France's rival. French entry into the war in 1778 was decisive.

In 1781, combined forces of about 9,500 Americans and 7,800 French trapped a British army commanded by Lord Cornwallis near Yorktown, Virginia. Unable to escape, Cornwallis eventually surrendered. The Americans had shocked the world and won their independence.

Reading Check
Analyze Causes
Why did the American colonists feel they were justified in rebelling against England?

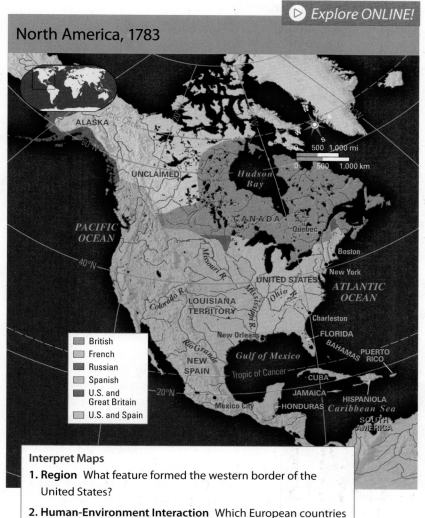

▶ *Explore ONLINE!*

North America, 1783

- British
- French
- Russian
- Spanish
- U.S. and Great Britain
- U.S. and Spain

Interpret Maps
1. **Region** What feature formed the western border of the United States?

2. **Human-Environment Interaction** Which European countries had claims on the North American continent in 1783?

Democracy

Ancient Greece and Rome were strong influences on the framers of the U.S. system of government. Democracy as it is practiced today, however, is different from the Greek and Roman models.

The most famous democracy today is the United States. The type of government the United States uses is called a federal republic. Federal means power is divided between the national and state governments. In a republic, the people vote for their representatives. Two key components of democracy in the United States are the Constitution and the ability to vote.

ENLIGHTENMENT IDEAS AND THE U.S. CONSTITUTION

Many of the ideas contained in the Constitution are built on the ideas of Enlightenment thinkers.

Enlightenment Idea	U.S. Constitution
Locke A government's power comes from the consent of the people	Preamble begins "We the people of the United States" to establish legitimacy. Creates representative government Limits government powers
Montesquieu Separation of powers	Federal system of government Powers divided among three branches System of checks and balances
Rousseau Direct democracy	Public election of president and Congress
Voltaire Free speech, religious tolerance	Bill of Rights provides for freedom of speech and religion.
Beccaria Accused have rights, no torture	Bill of Rights protects rights of accused and prohibits cruel and unusual punishment.

WHO VOTES?

Voting is an essential part of democracy. Universal suffrage means that all adult citizens can vote. Universal suffrage is part of democracy in the United States today, but that was not always the case. This chart shows how the United States gradually moved toward giving all citizens the right to vote.

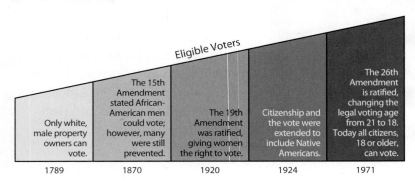

Eligible Voters

Only white, male property owners can vote. — 1789

The 15th Amendment stated African-American men could vote; however, many were still prevented. — 1870

The 19th Amendment was ratified, giving women the right to vote. — 1920

Citizenship and the vote were extended to include Native Americans. — 1924

The 26th Amendment is ratified, changing the legal voting age from 21 to 18. Today all citizens, 18 or older, can vote. — 1971

Critical Thinking

1. **Synthesize** If many of the concepts included in the U.S. Constitution are based upon European ideas, what key role did the framers of the U.S. Constitution play?

2. **Predict** Why is it important that every citizen has, and exercises, his or her right to vote?

Americans Create a Republic

Shortly after declaring their independence, the 13 individual states recognized the need for a national government. In establishing their government, they planned to build upon two ancient Greek ideas: constitutionalism (developing a written plan for running a state or country) and republicanism (establishing a system in which government is based on the consent of the people). In their new republic, the Americans wanted to make sure that the states retained many powers and the national government did not become too strong. They also feared establishing a democracy in which power was put directly in the hands of the people, many of whom were uneducated.

As victory became certain, all 13 states ratified a constitution in 1781. This plan of government was known as the Articles of Confederation. The Articles established the United States as a republic, a government in which citizens rule through elected representatives.

A Weak National Government To protect their authority, the 13 states created a loose confederation in which they held most of the power. Thus, the Articles of Confederation deliberately created a weak national government. There were no executive or judicial branches. Instead, the Articles established only one body of government, the Congress. Each state, regardless of size, had one vote in Congress. Congress could declare war, enter into treaties, and coin money. It had no power, however, to collect taxes or regulate trade. Passing new laws was difficult because laws needed the approval of 9 of the 13 states.

These limits on the national government soon produced many problems. Although the new national government needed money to operate, it could only request contributions from the states. Angry Revolutionary War veterans bitterly complained that Congress still owed them back pay for their services. Meanwhile, several states issued their own money. Some states even put tariffs on goods from neighboring states.

Global Patterns

Revolutionary Spirit

The American Revolution inspired a spirit of revolution in other countries. Across the Atlantic, a growing number of people in France began demanding reform in their own country. They saw the new government of the United States as the fulfillment of Enlightenment ideals and longed for such a government in France. The Declaration of Independence was widely circulated and admired in France, and the triumph of the colonies over Britain was cheered. In 1789, less than a decade after the American Revolution ended, an armed struggle to topple the government began in France.

The events of the French Revolution then inspired enslaved people in the French colony of Saint-Domingue in the Caribbean to begin a violent revolution of their own in 1791 led by Toussaint L'Ouverture. This revolution ended with the establishment of the Republic of Haiti in 1804.

A New Constitution Colonial leaders eventually recognized the need for a strong national government. In February 1787, Congress approved a Constitutional Convention to revise the Articles of Confederation. The Constitutional Convention held its first session on May 25, 1787. The 55 delegates were experienced statesmen who were familiar with the political theories of Locke, Montesquieu, and Rousseau.

Although the delegates shared basic ideas on government, they sometimes disagreed on how to put them into practice. For almost four months the delegates argued over important questions. Who should be represented in Congress? How many representatives should each state have? The delegates' deliberations produced not only compromises but also new approaches to governing. Using the political ideas of the Enlightenment, the delegates created a new system of government.

The Federal System Like Montesquieu, the delegates distrusted a powerful central government controlled by one person or group. They therefore established three separate branches—legislative, executive, and judicial. This setup provided a built-in system of **checks and balances**, with each branch checking the actions of the other two. For example, the president received the power to veto legislation passed by Congress. However, the Congress could override a presidential veto with the approval of two-thirds of its members. The Supreme Court could check that laws passed by Congress or actions taken by the president were constitutional.

Although the Constitution created a strong central government, it did not eliminate local governments. Instead, the Constitution set up a **federal system** in which power was divided between national and state governments.

Early copy of the U.S. Constitution

The Bill of Rights The convention delegates signed the new Constitution on September 17, 1787. In order to become law, however, the Constitution required approval by conventions in at least 9 of the 13 states. These conventions were marked by sharp debate. Supporters of the Constitution were called Federalists. They argued in their famous work, the **Federalist Papers**, that the new government would provide a better balance between national and state powers. Their opponents, the Antifederalists, feared that the Constitution gave the central government too much power. They also stressed the need for a bill of rights to protect the rights of individual citizens.

Finally, a compromise was reached. In order to gain support, the Federalists promised to add a bill of rights to the Constitution. This promise cleared the way for approval. Congress formally added to the Constitution the ten amendments known as the **Bill of Rights**. These amendments protected such basic rights as freedom of speech, press, assembly, and religion. Many of these rights had been advocated by Voltaire, Rousseau, and Locke.

The Constitution and Bill of Rights marked a turning point in people's ideas about government. Both documents put Enlightenment ideas into practice. They expressed an optimistic view that reason and reform could prevail and that progress was inevitable. Such optimism swept across the Atlantic. However, the monarchies and the privileged classes didn't give up power and position easily. Within a few years, the struggle to attain the principles of the Enlightenment would lead to violent revolution in France.

Main Idea
Analyze Issues
What were the opposing views regarding ratification of the Constitution?

Lesson 4 Assessment

1. **Organize Information** Use the organizer to record problems and solutions found in the lesson. Which of the solutions that you recorded represented a compromise?

Problem	Solution
1.	1.
2.	2.
3.	3.

2. **Key Terms and People** For each key term or person in the lesson, write a sentence explaining its significance.

3. **Analyze Causes** Why were the colonists so upset about passage of the Stamp Act?

4. **Analyze Effects** How did John Locke's notion of the social contract influence the American colonists?

5. **Make Inferences** Why might it be important to have a Bill of Rights that guarantees basic rights of citizens?

6. **Form and Support Opinions** Do you think the American Revolution would have happened if there had not been an Age of Enlightenment? Explain.

7. **Analyze Motives** Why do you think the colonists at first created such a weak central government?

Module 18 Assessment

Key Terms and People

For each term or name below, briefly explain its connection to European and American history between 1550 and 1789.

1. heliocentric theory
2. Isaac Newton
3. social contract
4. philosophe
5. salon
6. enlightened despot
7. Declaration of Independence
8. federal system

Main Ideas

Use your notes and the information in the module to answer the following questions.

The Scientific Revolution

1. According to Ptolemy, what was the earth's position in the universe? How did Copernicus's view differ?
2. What are the four steps in the scientific method?
3. What four new instruments came into use during the Scientific Revolution? What was the purpose of each one?

Enlightenment Thinkers

4. How did the ideas of Hobbes and Locke differ?
5. What did Montesquieu admire about the government of Britain?
6. What changes did Beccaria propose to correct abuses in the justice system?

The Enlightenment Spreads

7. What were three developments in the arts during the Enlightenment?
8. What were two changes for women that Mary Wollstonecraft advocated?
9. What types of reforms did the enlightened despots make?
10. How did the Enlightenment lead to a more secular outlook?

The American Revolution

11. Why did the Articles of Confederation result in a weak national government?
12. How did the writers of the U.S. Constitution put into practice the idea of separation of powers and a system of checks and balances?

Critical Thinking

1. **Evaluate** Make a two-column chart. In the left column, list important new ideas that arose during the Scientific Revolution and the Enlightenment. In the right column, briefly explain why each idea was revolutionary.

New Idea	Why Revolutionary?

2. **Analyze Effects** What role did technology play in the Scientific Revolution?

3. **Analyze Issues** How did the U.S. Constitution reflect the ideas of the Enlightenment? Refer to specific Enlightenment thinkers to support your answer.

4. **Clarify** How did the statement by Prussian ruler Frederick the Great that a ruler is only "the first servant of the state" highlight Enlightenment ideas about government?

5. **Predict** Explain how the day-to-day activities of scientists in Europe probably changed following the Scientific Revolution.

6. **Recognize Effects** What impact did the Scientific Revolution have on the church in European countries in the 1600s and 1700s?

7. **Evaluate Courses of Action** How did the decision by American leaders to replace the Articles of Confederation with the Constitution make the United States a stronger country?

8. **Evaluate** Did Catherine II of Russia deserve to be known as "Catherine the Great"?

9. **Analyze Motives** Why did European leaders imprison or exile satirists such as Voltaire?

10. **Make Inferences** While many European rulers sought to improve educational opportunities for their subjects, they offered little change for women and girls. Why not?

Engage with History

Think about the many different or revolutionary ideas or way of doing things you encountered in this module. Consider how such breakthroughs impacted society then and now. Discuss in a small group what you feel were the most significant new ideas or scientific developments and explain how they still impact our lives today.

Focus on Writing

Reexamine the material on the Scientific Revolution. Then write a three-paragraph **essay** summarizing the difference in scientific understanding before and after the various scientific breakthroughs. Focus on

• the ultimate authorities on many matters before the Scientific Revolution
• how and why that changed after the Scientific Revolution

Multimedia Activity

Writing an Internet-Based Research Paper

Use the Internet to explore a recent breakthrough in science or medicine. Look for information that will help you explain why the discovery is significant and how the new knowledge changes what scientists had thought about the topic.

In a well-organized paper, compare the significance of the discovery you are writing about with major scientific or medical discoveries of the Scientific Revolution. Be sure to

• apply a search strategy when using directories and search engines to locate web resources
• judge the usefulness of each website
• correctly cite your web resources
• revise and edit for correct use of language

THE *American* REVOLUTION

The American Revolution led to the formation of the United States of America in 1776. Beginning in the 1760s, tensions grew between American colonists and their British rulers when Britain started passing a series of new laws and taxes for the colonies. With no representation in the British government, however, colonists had no say in these laws, which led to growing discontent. After fighting broke out in 1775, colonial leaders met to decide what to do. They approved the Declaration of Independence, announcing that the American colonies were free from British rule. In reality, however, freedom would not come until after years of fighting.

Explore some of the people and events of the American Revolution online. You can find a wealth of information, video clips, primary sources, activities, and more through your online textbook.

> "I know not what course others may take; but as for me, give me liberty or give me death!"
>
> —Patrick Henry

"Give Me Liberty or Give Me Death!"
Read an excerpt from Patrick Henry's famous speech, which urged the colonists to fight against the British.

Seeds of Revolution
Watch the video to learn about colonial discontent in the years before the Revolutionary War.

Independence!
Watch the video to learn about the origins of the Declaration of Independence.

Victory!
Watch the video to learn how the American colonists won the Revolutionary War.

Module 19
The French Revolution and Napoleon

Essential Question
How did the French Revolution change the balance of power in Europe?

About the Painting: This painting shows some of the people who stormed the Bastille parading outside City Hall in Paris. They triumphantly display the keys to the Bastille, and one man is dragging the royal standard behind him, emphasizing the strong desire to end absolute monarchy. Others carry whatever they could find in the prison.

▷ *Explore ONLINE!*

HISTORY. VIDEOS, including...
- The French Revolution
- Napoleon Bonaparte: The Glory of France
- Battle of Waterloo

☑ Document Based Investigations

☑ Graphic Organizers

☑ Interactive Games

☑ Image with Hotspots: The Guillotine

☑ Image Compare: Europe Before and After the Congress of Vienna

In this module you will learn about the French Revolution, Napoleon Bonaparte's empire, and the Congress of Vienna.

What You Will Learn ...

Timeline of Events 1789–1815

▶ Explore ONLINE!

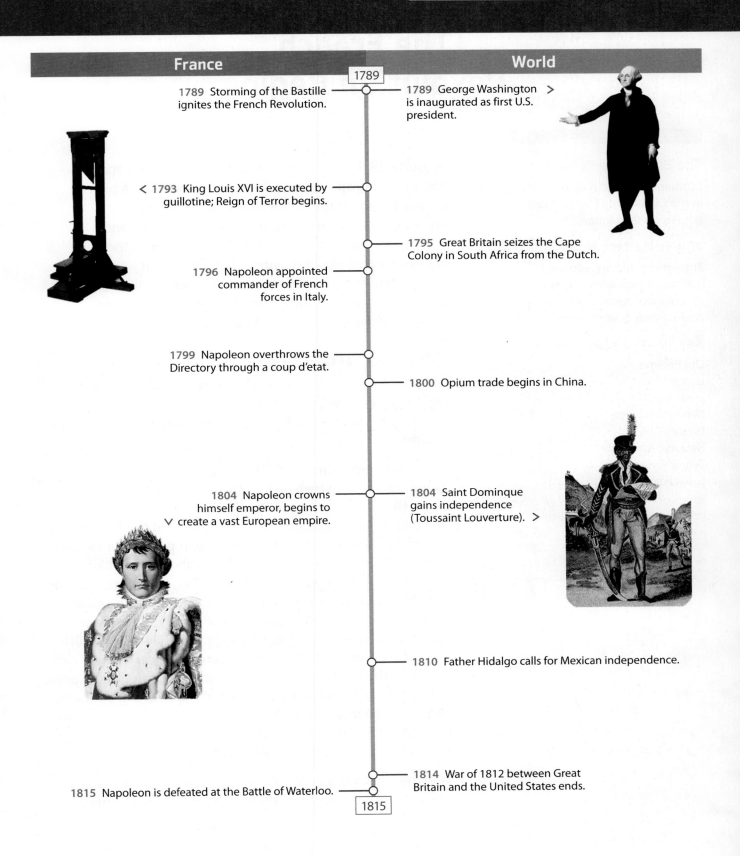

France

World

1789

1789 Storming of the Bastille ignites the French Revolution.

1789 George Washington is inaugurated as first U.S. president. >

< 1793 King Louis XVI is executed by guillotine; Reign of Terror begins.

1795 Great Britain seizes the Cape Colony in South Africa from the Dutch.

1796 Napoleon appointed commander of French forces in Italy.

1799 Napoleon overthrows the Directory through a coup d'etat.

1800 Opium trade begins in China.

1804 Napoleon crowns himself emperor, begins to ∨ create a vast European empire.

1804 Saint Dominque gains independence (Toussaint Louverture). >

1810 Father Hidalgo calls for Mexican independence.

1814 War of 1812 between Great Britain and the United States ends.

1815 Napoleon is defeated at the Battle of Waterloo.

1815

The French Revolution Begins

Setting the Stage

In the 1700s, France was considered the most advanced country of Europe. It had a large population and a prosperous foreign trade. It was the center of the Enlightenment, and France's culture was widely praised and imitated by the rest of the world. However, the appearance of success was deceiving. There was great unrest in France, caused by bad harvests, high prices, high taxes, and disturbing questions raised by the Enlightenment ideas of Locke, Rousseau, and Voltaire.

The Old Order

In the 1770s, the social and political system of France—the **Old Regime**—remained in place. Under this system, the people of France were divided into three large social classes, or **estates**.

The Privileged Estates Two of the estates had privileges, including access to high offices and exemptions from paying taxes, that were not granted to the members of the third. The Roman Catholic Church, whose clergy formed the First Estate, owned 10 percent of the land in France. It provided education and relief services to the poor and contributed about 2 percent of its income to the government. However, the Roman Catholic Church paid no taxes on the land it owned. At the same time, this land produced vast sums of money in rents and fees. Bishops and some other higher clergy controlled this wealth and became very rich. The Second Estate was made up of rich nobles. Although they accounted for just 2 percent of the population, the nobles owned 20 percent of the land and paid almost no taxes. The majority of the clergy and the nobility scorned Enlightenment ideas as radical notions that threatened their status and power as privileged persons.

The Third Estate About 97 percent of the people belonged to the Third Estate. The three groups that made up this estate differed greatly in their economic conditions. The first group—the bourgeoisie (BUR•zhwah•ZEE), or middle class—were bankers, factory owners, merchants, professionals, and skilled artisans. Often, they were well educated and believed strongly in the Enlightenment ideals of liberty and equality. Although some of the bourgeoisie were as rich as nobles, they paid high taxes and, like the rest of the Third Estate, lacked privileges. Many felt that their wealth entitled them to a greater degree of social status and political power.

The workers of France's cities formed the second, and poorest, group within the Third Estate. These urban workers included tradespeople, apprentices, laborers, and domestic servants. Paid low wages and frequently out of work, they often went hungry. If the cost of bread rose, mobs of these workers might attack grain carts and bread shops to steal what they needed.

DOCUMENT-BASED INVESTIGATION   Historical Source

The Three Estates

(A) FIRST ESTATE

- made up of clergy of Roman Catholic Church
- scorned Enlightenment ideas

(B) SECOND ESTATE

- made up of rich nobles
- held highest offices in government
- disagreed about Enlightenment ideas

(C) THIRD ESTATE

- included bourgeoisie, urban lower class, and peasant farmers
- had no power to influence government
- embraced Enlightenment ideas
- resented the wealthy First and Second Estates

A FAUT ESPERER Q'EU JEU LA FINIRA BEN TOT

Population of France, 1787

97% (Third Estate)

less than 1% (First Estate)

2% (Second Estate)

Percent of Income Paid in Taxes

2% (First Estate)

0% (Second Estate)

50% (Third Estate)

0%   20%   40%   60%   80%   100%

Analyze Historical Sources

How do the chart and the graphs help explain the political cartoon?

Why might the First and Second Estates be opposed to change?

Peasants formed the largest group within the Third Estate, more than 80 percent of France's 26 million people. Peasants paid about half their income in dues to nobles, tithes to the Church, and taxes to the king's agents. They even paid taxes on such basic staples as salt. Peasants and the urban poor resented the clergy and the nobles for their privileges and special treatment. The heavily taxed and discontented Third Estate was eager for change.

The Forces of Change

In addition to the growing resentment among the lower classes, other factors contributed to the revolutionary mood in France. New ideas about government, serious economic problems, and weak and indecisive leadership all helped to generate a desire for change.

Enlightenment Ideas New views about power and authority in government were spreading among the Third Estate. Members of the Third Estate were inspired by the success of the American Revolution. They began questioning long-standing notions about the structure of society. Quoting Rousseau and Voltaire, they began to demand equality, liberty, and democracy.

Economic Troubles By the 1780s, France's once prosperous economy was in decline. This caused alarm, particularly among the merchants, factory owners, and bankers of the Third Estate. On the surface, the economy appeared to be sound, because both production and trade were expanding rapidly. However, the heavy burden of taxes made it almost impossible to conduct business profitably within France. Further, the cost of living was rising sharply. In addition, bad weather in the 1780s caused widespread crop failures, resulting in a severe shortage of grain. The price of bread doubled in 1789, and many people faced starvation.

During the 1770s and 1780s, France's government sank deeply into debt. Part of the problem was the extravagant spending of **Louis XVI** and his queen, **Marie Antoinette**. Louis also inherited a considerable debt from previous kings. And he borrowed heavily in order to help the American revolutionaries in their war against Great Britain, France's chief rival. This nearly doubled the government's debt. In 1786, when bankers refused to lend the government any more money, Louis faced serious problems.

A Weak Leader Strong leadership might have solved these and other problems. Louis XVI, however, was indecisive and allowed matters to drift. He paid little attention to his government advisers, and had little patience for the details of governing. The queen only added to Louis's problems. She often interfered in the government, and frequently offered Louis poor advice. Further, since she was a member of the royal family of Austria, France's long-time enemy, Marie Antoinette had been unpopular from the moment she set foot in France. Her behavior only made the situation worse. As queen, she spent so much money on gowns, jewels, gambling, and gifts that she became known as "Madame Deficit."

Vocabulary
tithe a church tax, normally about one-tenth of a family's income

**Reading Check
Analyze Causes** Why were members of the Third Estate dissatisfied with life under the Old Regime?

**Vocabulary
deficit** debt

Rather than cutting expenses, Louis put off dealing with the emergency until he practically had no money left. His solution was to impose taxes on the nobility. However, the Second Estate forced him to call a meeting of the **Estates-General**—an assembly of representatives from all three estates—to approve this new tax. The meeting, the first in 175 years, was held on May 5, 1789, at Versailles.

--- BIOGRAPHY ---

Louis XVI
(1754–1793)

Louis XVI's tutors made little effort to prepare him for his role as king—and it showed. He was easily bored with affairs of state, and much preferred to spend his time in physical activities, particularly hunting. He also loved to work with his hands, and was skilled in several trades, including lockmaking, metalworking, and bricklaying.

Despite these shortcomings, Louis was well intentioned and sincerely wanted to improve the lives of the common people. However, he lacked the ability to make decisions and the determination to see policies through. When he did take action, it often was based on poor advice from ill-informed members of his court. As one politician of the time noted, "His reign was a succession of feeble attempts at doing good, shows of weakness, and clear evidence of his inadequacy as a leader."

--- BIOGRAPHY ---

Marie Antoinette
(1755–1793)

Marie Antoinette was a pretty, lighthearted, charming woman. However, she was unpopular with the French because of her spending and her involvement in controversial court affairs. She referred to Louis as "the poor man" and sometimes set the clock forward an hour to be rid of his presence.

Marie Antoinette refused to wear the tight-fitting clothing styles of the day and introduced a loose cotton dress for women. The elderly, who viewed the dress as an undergarment, thought that her clothing was scandalous. The French silk industry was equally angry.

In constant need of entertainment, Marie Antoinette often spent hours playing cards. One year she lost the equivalent of $1.5 million by gambling in card games.

Dawn of the Revolution

The clergy and the nobles had dominated the Estates-General throughout the Middle Ages and expected to do so in the 1789 meeting. Under the assembly's medieval rules, each estate's delegates met in a separate hall to vote, and each estate had one vote. The two privileged estates could always outvote the Third Estate.

The National Assembly The Third Estate delegates, mostly members of the bourgeoisie whose views had been shaped by the Enlightenment, were eager to make changes in the government. They insisted that all three estates meet together and that each delegate have a vote. This would give the advantage to the Third Estate, which had as many delegates as the other two estates combined.

Siding with the nobles, the king ordered the Estates-General to follow the medieval rules. The delegates of the Third Estate, however, became more and more determined to wield power. A leading spokesperson for their viewpoint was a clergyman sympathetic to their cause, Emmanuel-Joseph Sieyès (syay•YEHS). In a dramatic speech, Sieyès suggested that the Third Estate delegates name themselves the **National Assembly** and pass laws and reforms in the name of the French people.

After a long night of excited debate, the delegates of the Third Estate agreed to Sieyès's idea by an overwhelming majority. On June 17, 1789, they voted to establish the National Assembly, in effect proclaiming the end of absolute monarchy and the beginning of representative government. This vote was the first deliberate act of revolution.

Three days later, the Third Estate delegates found themselves locked out of their meeting room. They broke down a door to an indoor tennis court, pledging to stay until they had drawn up a new constitution. This pledge became known as the **Tennis Court Oath**. Their desire for constitutionalism, a government in which power is distributed and limited by a system of laws that the rulers must obey, stemmed from their belief that a constitutional government would prevent abuses of power and create a government that would benefit all. Soon after, nobles and members of the clergy who favored reform joined the Third Estate delegates. In response to these events, Louis stationed his mercenary army of Swiss guards around Versailles.

Storming the Bastille In Paris, rumors flew. Some people suggested that Louis was intent on using military force to dismiss the National Assembly. Others charged that the foreign troops were coming to Paris to massacre French citizens.

People began to gather weapons in order to defend the city against attack. On July 14, a mob searching for gunpowder and arms stormed the Bastille, a Paris prison. The mob overwhelmed the guard and seized

Vocabulary
mercenary army
a group of soldiers who will work for any country or employer that will pay them

The attack on the Bastille claimed the lives of about 100 people.

Bread

Bread was a staple of the diet of the common people of France. Most families consumed three or four 4-pound loaves a day. And the purchase of bread took about half of a worker's wages—when times were good. So, when the price of bread jumped dramatically, as it did in the fall of 1789, people faced a real threat of starvation.

On their march back from Versailles, the women of Paris happily sang that they were bringing "the baker, the baker's wife, and the baker's lad" with them. They expected the "baker"—Louis—to provide the cheap bread that they needed to live.

Reading Check
Analyze Motives
Why did the Third Estate propose a change in the Estates-General's voting rules?

control of the building. The angry attackers hacked the prison commander and several guards to death, and then paraded around the streets with the dead men's heads on pikes.

The fall of the Bastille became a great symbolic act of revolution to the French people. Ever since, July 14—Bastille Day—has been a French national holiday, similar to the Fourth of July in the United States.

Parisian women marching to the royal residence at Versailles.

A Great Fear Sweeps France

Before long, rebellion spread from Paris into the countryside. From one village to the next, wild rumors circulated that the nobles were hiring outlaws to terrorize the peasants. A wave of senseless panic called the **Great Fear** rolled through France. The peasants soon became outlaws themselves. Armed with pitchforks and other farm tools, they broke into nobles' manor houses and destroyed the old legal papers that bound them to pay feudal dues. In some cases, the peasants simply burned down the manor houses.

In October 1789, thousands of Parisian women rioted over the rising price of bread. Brandishing knives, axes, and other weapons, the women marched on Versailles. First, they demanded that the National Assembly take action to provide bread. Then they turned their anger on the king and queen. They broke into the palace, killing some of the guards. The women demanded that Louis and Marie Antoinette return to Paris. After some time, Louis agreed.

A few hours later the king, his family, and servants left Versailles, never again to see the magnificent palace. Their exit signaled the change of power and radical reforms about to overtake France.

Reading Check
Identify Effects
How did the women's march mark a turning point in the relationship between the king and the people?

Lesson 1 Assessment

1. **Organize Information** Complete the web to show the causes of Revolution. Select one of the causes and explain how it contributed to the French Revolution.

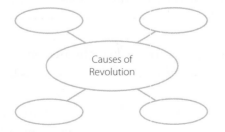

2. **Key Terms and People** For each key term or person in the lesson, write a sentence explaining its significance.
3. **Form and Support Opinions** Do you think that changes in the French government were inevitable? Support your interpretation with historical evidence.
4. **Analyze Motives** Why do you think some members of the First and Second Estates joined the National Assembly and worked to reform the government?
5. **Compare and Contrast** How were the storming of the Bastille and the women's march on Versailles similar? How were they different?

Revolution Brings Reform and Terror

The Big Idea

The revolutionary government of France made reforms but also used terror and violence to retain power.

Why It Matters Now

Some governments that lack the support of a majority of their people still use fear to control their citizens.

Key Terms and People

Legislative Assembly
émigré
sans-culotte
Jacobin
guillotine
Maximilien Robespierre
Reign of Terror

Setting the Stage

Peasants were not the only members of French society to feel the Great Fear. Nobles and officers of the Church were equally afraid. Throughout France, bands of angry peasants struck out against members of the upper classes, attacking and destroying many manor houses. In the summer of 1789, a few months before the women's march to Versailles, some nobles and members of clergy in the National Assembly responded to the uprisings in an emotional late-night meeting.

The Assembly Reforms France

Throughout the night of August 4, 1789, noblemen made grand speeches, declaring their love of liberty and equality. Motivated more by fear than by idealism, they joined other members of the National Assembly in sweeping away the feudal privileges of the First and Second Estates, thus making commoners equal to the nobles and the clergy. By morning, the Old Regime was dead.

The Rights of Man Three weeks later, the National Assembly adopted a statement of revolutionary ideals, the Declaration of the Rights of Man and of the Citizen. Reflecting the influence of the Declaration of Independence, the document stated that "men are born and remain free and equal in rights." These rights included "liberty, property, security, and resistance to oppression." Article 4 of the Declaration stated that "Liberty consists in the freedom to do everything which injures no one else; hence the exercise of the natural rights of each man has no limits, except those which assure to the other members of the society the enjoyment of the same rights. These limits can only be determined by law." This language emphasized the equality of all men, promoting the development of human rights. The Declaration also outlined civil rights in order to protect individuals' freedom. The document guaranteed citizens equal justice, freedom of speech, and freedom of religion.

In keeping with these principles, revolutionary leaders adopted the expression "Liberty, Equality, Fraternity" as their slogan. Such sentiments, however, did not apply to everyone. When writer Olympe de Gouges (aw•LIMP-duh-GOOZH) published a declaration of the rights of women, her ideas were rejected. Later, in 1793, she was declared an enemy of the Revolution and executed.

A State-Controlled Church Many of the National Assembly's early reforms focused on the Church. The assembly took over Church lands and declared that Church officials and priests were to be elected and paid as state officials. Thus, the Catholic Church lost both its lands and its political independence. The reasons for the assembly's actions were largely economic. Proceeds from the sale of Church lands helped pay off France's huge debt.

The assembly's actions alarmed millions of French peasants, who were devout Catholics. The effort to make the Church a part of the state offended them, even though it was in accord with Enlightenment philosophy. They believed that the pope should rule over a church independent of the state. From this time on, many peasants opposed the assembly's reforms.

Louis Tries to Escape As the National Assembly restructured the relationship between church and state, Louis XVI pondered his fate as a monarch. Some of his advisers warned him that he and his family were

One of the people who stopped Louis from escaping said that he recognized the king from his portrait on a French bank note.

Reading Check
Summarize What major reforms did the National Assembly introduce?

in danger. Many supporters of the monarchy thought France unsafe and left the country. Then, in June 1791, the royal family tried to escape from France to the Austrian Netherlands. As they neared the border, however, they were apprehended and returned to Paris under guard. Louis's attempted escape increased the influence of his radical enemies in the government and sealed his fate.

Divisions Develop

For two years, the National Assembly argued over a new constitution for France. By 1791, the delegates had made significant changes in France's government and society.

A Limited Monarchy In September 1791, the National Assembly completed the new constitution, which Louis reluctantly approved. The constitution created a limited constitutional monarchy. It stripped the king of much of his authority. It also created a new legislative body—the **Legislative Assembly**. This body had the power to create laws and to approve or reject declarations of war. However, the king still held the executive power to enforce laws.

Factions Split France Despite the new government, old problems, such as food shortages and government debt, remained. The question of how to handle these problems caused the Legislative Assembly to split into three general groups, each of which sat in a different part of the meeting hall. Radicals, who sat on the left side of the hall, opposed the idea of a monarchy and wanted sweeping changes in the way the government was run. Moderates sat in the center of the hall and wanted some changes in government, but not as many as the radicals. Conservatives sat on the right side of the hall. They upheld the idea of a limited monarchy and wanted few changes in government.

In addition, factions outside the Legislative Assembly wanted to influence the direction of the government, too. **Émigrés** (EHM•ih•GRAYZ), nobles and others who had fled France, hoped to undo the Revolution and restore the Old Regime. In contrast, some Parisian workers and small shopkeepers wanted the Revolution to bring even greater changes to France. They were called **sans-culottes** (SANZ kyoo•LAHTS), or "those

Now and Then

Left, Right, and Center

The terms generally used to describe where people stand politically derive from the factions that developed in the Legislative Assembly in 1791.

- People who want to radically change government are called left wing or are said to be on the left.

- People with moderate views often are called centrist or are said to be in the center.

- People who want few or no changes in government often are called right wing or are said to be on the right.

Reading Check
Recognize Effects
How did differences
of opinion on how to
handle such issues
as food shortages
and debt affect the
Legislative Assembly?

without knee breeches." Unlike the upper classes, who wore fancy knee-length pants, sans-culottes wore regular trousers. Although they did not have a role in the assembly, they soon discovered ways to exert their power on the streets of Paris.

War and Execution

Monarchs and nobles in many European countries watched the changes taking place in France with alarm. They feared that similar revolts might break out in their own countries. In fact, some radicals were keen to spread their revolutionary ideas across Europe. As a result, some countries took action. Austria and Prussia, for example, urged the French to restore Louis to his position as an absolute monarch. The Legislative Assembly responded by declaring war in April 1792.

France at War The war began badly for the French. By the summer of 1792, Prussian forces were advancing on Paris. The Prussian commander threatened to destroy Paris if the revolutionaries harmed any member of the royal family. This enraged the Parisians. On August 10, about 20,000 men and women invaded the Tuileries, the palace where the royal family was staying. The mob massacred the royal guards and imprisoned Louis, Marie Antoinette, and their children.

Shortly after, the French troops defending Paris were sent to reinforce the French army in the field. Rumors began to spread that supporters of the king held in Paris prisons planned to break out and seize control of the city. Angry and fearful citizens responded by taking the law into their own hands. For several days in early September, they raided the prisons and murdered over 1,000 prisoners. Many nobles, priests, and royalist sympathizers fell victim to the angry mobs in these September Massacres.

Under pressure from radicals in the streets and among its members, the Legislative Assembly set aside the Constitution of 1791. It declared the king deposed, dissolved the assembly, and called for the election of a new legislature. This new governing body, the National Convention, took office on September 21. It quickly abolished the monarchy and declared France a republic. This transition to republicanism meant that the people held popular sovereignty rather than being subjects of a king. Adult male citizens were granted the right to vote and hold office. Despite the important part they had already played in the Revolution, women were not given the vote.

----- BIOGRAPHY -----

Jean-Paul Marat (1743–1793)

Marat was a thin, high-strung, sickly man whose revolutionary writings stirred up the violent mood in Paris. Because he suffered from a painful skin disease, he often found comfort by relaxing in a cold bath—even arranging things so that he could work in his bathtub!

During the summer of 1793, Charlotte Corday, a supporter of a rival faction whose members had been jailed, gained an audience with Marat by pretending to have information about traitors. Once inside Marat's private chambers, she fatally stabbed him as he bathed. For her crime, Corday went to the guillotine.

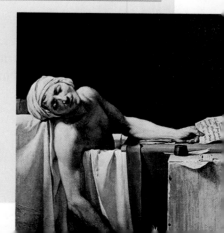

The Guillotine

If you think the guillotine was a cruel form of capital punishment, think again. Dr. Joseph Ignace Guillotin proposed a machine that satisfied many needs—it was efficient, humane, and democratic. A physician and member of the National Assembly, Guillotin claimed that those executed with the device "wouldn't even feel the slightest pain."

Prior to the guillotine's introduction in 1792, many French criminals had suffered through horrible punishments in public places. Although public punishments continued to attract large crowds, not all spectators were pleased with the new machine. Some witnesses felt that death by the guillotine occurred much too quickly to be enjoyed by an audience.

Once the executioner cranked the blade to the top, a mechanism released it. The sharp weighted blade fell, severing the victim's head from his or her body.

Before each execution, bound victims traveled from the prison to the scaffold in horse-drawn carts during a one and a half hour procession through city streets.

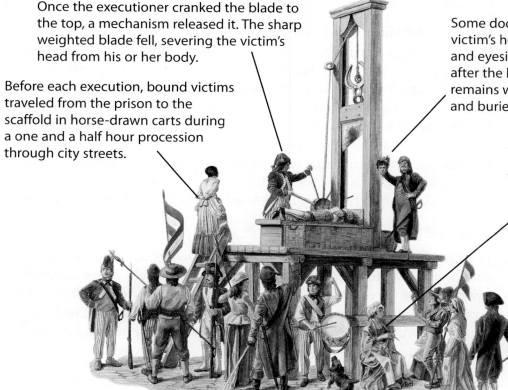

Some doctors believed that a victim's head retained its hearing and eyesight for up to 15 minutes after the blade's deadly blow. All remains were eventually gathered and buried in simple graves.

Tricoteuses, or "woman knitters," were regular spectators at executions and knitted stockings for soldiers as they sat near the base of the scaffold.

BEHEADING BY CLASS

More than 2,100 people were executed during the last 132 days of the Reign of Terror. This pie graph displays the breakdown of beheadings by class.

- ■ First Estate
- ■ Second Estate
- ■ Third Estate

Critical Thinking

1. **Synthesize** In what ways was the guillotine an efficient means of execution?

2. **Compare** France continued to use the guillotine until 1977. Four years later, France abolished capital punishment. Conduct research to identify countries where capital punishment is still used. Use your findings to create a map titled "Countries Using Capital Punishment."

Jacobins Take Control Most of the people involved in the governmental changes in September 1792 were members of a radical political organization, the **Jacobin** (JAK•uh•bihn) Club. One of the most prominent Jacobins, as club members were called, was Jean-Paul Marat (mah•RAH). During the Revolution, he edited a newspaper called *L'Ami du Peuple* (Friend of the People). In his fiery editorials, Marat called for the death of all those who continued to support the king. Georges Danton (zhawrzh dahn•TAWN), a lawyer, was among the club's most talented and passionate speakers. He also was known for his devotion to the rights of Paris's poor people.

The National Convention had reduced Louis XVI's role from that of a king to that of a common citizen and prisoner. Now, guided by radical Jacobins, it tried Louis for treason. The Convention found him guilty, and, by a very close vote, sentenced him to death. On January 21, 1793, the former king walked with calm dignity up the steps of the scaffold to be beheaded by the **guillotine** (GIHL•uh•teen).

The War Continues The National Convention also had to contend with the continuing war with Austria and Prussia. At about the time the Convention took office, the French army won a stunning victory against the Austrians and Prussians at the Battle of Valmy. Early in 1793, however, Great Britain, Holland, and Spain joined Prussia and Austria against France. Forced to contend with so many enemies, the French suffered a string of defeats. To reinforce the French army, Jacobin leaders in the Convention took an extreme step. At their urging, in February 1793 the Convention ordered a draft of 300,000 French citizens between the ages of 18 and 40. By 1794, the army had grown to 800,000 and included women.

Reading Check
Analyze Causes
What did the September Massacres show about the mood of the people?

The Terror Grips France

Foreign armies were not the only enemies of the French republic. The Jacobins had thousands of enemies within France itself. These included peasants who were horrified by the king's execution, priests who would not accept government control, and rival leaders who were stirring up rebellion in the provinces. How to contain and control these enemies became a central issue.

Robespierre Assumes Control In the early months of 1793, one Jacobin leader, **Maximilien Robespierre** (ROHBZ•peer), slowly gained power. Robespierre and his supporters set out to build a "republic of virtue" by wiping out every trace of France's past. Firm believers in reason, they changed the calendar, dividing the year into 12 months of 30 days and renaming each month. This calendar had no Sundays because the radicals considered religion old-fashioned and dangerous. They even closed all churches in Paris, and cities and towns all over France soon did the same.

In July 1793, Robespierre became leader of the Committee of Public Safety. For the next year, Robespierre governed France virtually as a dictator, and the period of his rule became known as the **Reign of Terror**. The Committee of Public Safety's chief task was to protect the Revolution from its enemies. Under Robespierre's leadership, the committee often had these "enemies" tried in the morning and guillotined in the afternoon. Robespierre justified his use of terror by suggesting that it enabled French citizens to remain true to the ideals of the Revolution. He also saw a connection between virtue and terror:

"The first maxim of our politics ought to be to lead the people by means of reason and the enemies of the people by terror. If the basis of popular government in time of peace is virtue, the basis of popular government in time of revolution is both virtue and terror: virtue without which terror is murderous, terror without which virtue is powerless. Terror is nothing else than swift, severe, indomitable justice; it flows, then, from virtue."

—Maximilien Robespierre, "On the Morals and Political Principles of Domestic Policy" (1794)

Historical Source

The French Revolution

Over time, people have expressed a wide variety of opinions about the French Revolution. The following quotes illustrate this diversity in opinion.

Edmund Burke

Burke, a British politician, was one of the earliest and most severe critics of the French Revolution. In 1790, he expressed his opinions.

Thomas Paine

In 1790, Paine—a strong supporter of the American Revolution—defended the French Revolution against Burke and other critics. He eventually went on to write *Rights of Man* where he continued to defend the revolution by saying it was the natural continuation of a new era in history, where men applied Enlightenment ideas into their governments.

Analyze Historical Sources
Contrast the different perspectives toward the French Revolution expressed by Burke and Paine.

"[The French have rebelled] against a mild and lawful monarch, with more fury, outrage, and insult, than ever any people has been known to rise against the most illegal usurper, or the most [bloodthirsty] tyrant. . . .

They have found their punishment in their success. Laws overturned; tribunals subverted . . . the people impoverished; a church pillaged, and . . . civil and military anarchy made the constitution of the kingdom. . . .

Were all these dreadful things necessary?"

"It is no longer the paltry cause of kings, or of this, or of that individual, that calls France and her armies into action. It is the great cause of ALL. It is the establishment of a new era, that shall blot despotism from the earth, and fix, on the lasting principles of peace and citizenship, the great Republic of Man."

"The scene that now opens itself to France extends far beyond the boundaries of her own dominions. Every nation is becoming her colleague, and every court is become her enemy. It is now the cause of all nations, against the cause of all courts."

At his trial, Georges Danton defended himself so skillfully that the authorities eventually denied him the right to speak.

The "enemies of the Revolution" who troubled Robespierre the most were fellow radicals who challenged his leadership. In 1793 and 1794, many of those who had led the Revolution received death sentences. Their only crime was that they were considered less radical than Robespierre. By early 1794, even Georges Danton found himself in danger. Danton's friends in the National Convention, afraid to defend him, joined in condemning him. On the scaffold, he told the executioner, "Don't forget to show my head to the people. It's well worth seeing."

The Terror claimed not only the famous, such as Danton and Marie Antoinette, the widowed queen. Thousands of unknown people were also sent to their deaths, often on the flimsiest of charges. For example, an 18-year-old youth was sentenced to die for cutting down a tree that had been planted as a symbol of liberty. Perhaps as many as 40,000 were executed during the Terror. About 85 percent were peasants or members of the urban poor or middle class—for whose benefit the Revolution had been launched.

Reading Check
Analyze Motives
How did Robespierre justify the use of terror?

End of the Terror

In July 1794, fearing for their own safety, some members of the National Convention turned on Robespierre. They demanded his arrest and execution. The Reign of Terror, the radical phase of the French Revolution, ended on July 28, 1794, when Robespierre went to the guillotine.

French public opinion shifted dramatically after Robespierre's death. People of all classes had grown weary of the Terror. They were also tired of the skyrocketing prices for bread, salt, and other necessities of life. In 1795, moderate leaders in the National Convention drafted a new plan of government, the third since 1789. It placed power firmly in the hands of the upper middle class and called for a two-house legislature and an executive body of five men, known as the Directory. These five were moderates, not revolutionary idealists. Some of them were corrupt and made themselves rich at the country's expense. Even so, they gave their troubled country a period of order. They also found the right general to command France's armies—Napoleon Bonaparte.

Reading Check
Summarize
Why did members of the National Assembly turn on Robespierre?

Lesson 2 Assessment

1. **Organize Information** Complete the chart to show the chain of events starting with Assembly Creates a Constitution. Do you think this chain of events could have been changed in any way? Explain.

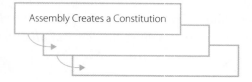

Assembly Creates a Constitution

2. **Key Terms and People** For each key term or person in the lesson, write a sentence explaining its significance.

3. **Synthesize** How did the slogan "Liberty, Equality, Fraternity" sum up the goals of the Revolution?

4. **Compare and Contrast** What similarities and differences do you see between the political factions in the Legislative Assembly and those in the U.S. government today?

5. **Identify Causes** What factors led to Robespierre becoming a dictator?

Napoleon's Empire

The Big Idea

Napoleon Bonaparte, a military genius, seized power in France and made himself emperor. His conquests aroused nationalistic feelings across Europe and contributed to his downfall.

Why It Matters Now

In times of political turmoil, military dictators often seize control of nations.

Key Terms and People

Napoleon Bonaparte
coup d'état
plebiscite
lycée
concordat
Napoleonic Code
Battle of Trafalgar
blockade
Continental System
guerrilla
Peninsular War
scorched-earth policy
Waterloo
Hundred Days

Setting the Stage

Napoleon Bonaparte would come to be recognized as one of the world's greatest military geniuses, along with Alexander the Great of Macedonia, Hannibal of Carthage, and Julius Caesar of Rome. In only four years, from 1795 to 1799, Napoleon rose from a relatively obscure position as an officer in the French army to become master of France. Napoleon worried that his vast empire would fall apart after his death if he didn't have a son and heir to succeed him. He divorced his wife, Josephine, for not bearing him a child and married Marie Louise, a member of the Austrian royal family. In 1811, she gave birth to a son, Napoleon II, whom Napoleon named king of Rome.

Napoleon Seizes Power

Napoleon Bonaparte was born in 1769 on the Mediterranean island of Corsica. When he was nine years old, his parents sent him to a military school. In 1785, at the age of 16, he finished school and became a lieutenant in the artillery. When the Revolution broke out, Napoleon joined the army of the new government.

Hero of the Hour In October 1795, fate handed the young officer a chance for glory. When royalist rebels marched on the National Convention, a government official told Napoleon to defend the delegates. Napoleon and his gunners greeted the thousands of royalists with a cannonade. Within minutes, the attackers fled in panic and confusion. Napoleon Bonaparte became the hero of the hour and was hailed throughout Paris as the savior of the French republic.

In 1796, the Directory appointed Napoleon to lead a French army against the forces of Austria and the Kingdom of Sardinia. He swept into Italy and won a series of remarkable victories. Next, in an attempt to protect French trade interests and to disrupt British trade with India, Napoleon led an expedition to Egypt. However, the British admiral Horatio Nelson defeated his naval forces, but Napoleon managed to keep his defeats out of the newspapers and thereby remained a great hero to the people of France.

Coup d'État By 1799, the Directory had lost control of the political situation and the confidence of the French people. When Napoleon returned from Egypt, his friends urged him to seize political power. In November 1799, his troops surrounded the national legislature and drove out most of its members. The remaining lawmakers voted to dissolve the Directory.

In its place, they established a group of three consuls, one of whom was Napoleon. Napoleon quickly took the title of first consul and assumed the powers of a dictator. A sudden seizure of power like Napoleon's is known as a *coup*—from the French phrase **coup d'état** (koo day•TAH), or "blow to the state."

At the time of Napoleon's coup, France was still at war. In 1799, Britain, Austria, and Russia joined forces with one goal in mind, to drive Napoleon from power. Once again, Napoleon rode from Paris at the head of his troops. Eventually, as a result of war and diplomacy, all three nations signed peace agreements with France. By 1802, Europe was at peace for the first time in ten years. Napoleon was free to focus his energies on restoring order in France.

Reading Check
Analyze Causes
How was Napoleon able to become a dictator?

Napoleon Rules France

At first, Napoleon pretended to be the constitutionally chosen leader of a free republic. In 1800, a **plebiscite** (PLEHB•ih•syt), or vote of the people, was held to approve a new constitution. Desperate for strong leadership, the people voted overwhelmingly in favor of the constitution. This gave all real power to Napoleon as first consul.

--- BIOGRAPHY ---

Napoleon Bonaparte
(1769–1821)

Because of his small stature and thick Corsican accent, Napoleon was mocked by his fellow students at military school. Haughty and proud, Napoleon refused to grace his tormentors' behavior with any kind of response. He simply ignored them, preferring to lose himself in his studies. He showed a particular passion for three subjects—classical history, geography, and mathematics.

In 1784, Napoleon was recommended for a career in the army and he transferred to the Ecole Militaire (the French equivalent of West Point) in Paris. There, he proved to be a fairly poor soldier, except when it came to artillery. His artillery instructor quickly noticed Napoleon's abilities: "He is most proud, ambitious, aspiring to everything. This young man merits our attention."

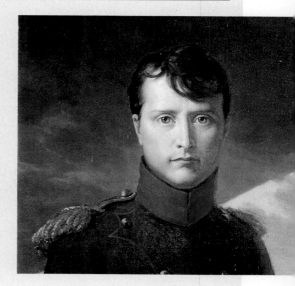

Restoring Order at Home Napoleon kept many of the changes that had come with the Revolution by supporting laws that would both strengthen the central government and achieve some of the goals of the Revolution.

Napoleon set up an efficient method of tax collection and established a national banking system in order to improve the economy. In addition to ensuring the government a steady supply of tax money, these actions promoted sound financial management and better control of the economy. Napoleon also took steps to end corruption and inefficiency in government. He dismissed corrupt officials and, in order to provide the government with trained officials, set up **lycées**, or government-run public schools. These lycées were open to male students of all backgrounds. Graduates were appointed to public office on the basis of merit rather than family connections.

One area where Napoleon disregarded changes introduced by the Revolution was religion. Both the clergy and many peasants wanted to restore the position of the Church in France. Responding to their wishes, Napoleon signed a **concordat**, or agreement, with Pope Pius VII. This established a new relationship between church and state. The government recognized the influence of the Church, but rejected Church control in national affairs. The concordat gained Napoleon the support of the organized Church as well as the majority of the French people.

Napoleon thought that his greatest work was his comprehensive system of laws, known as the **Napoleonic Code**. This gave the country a uniform set of laws and eliminated many injustices. However, it actually limited liberty and promoted order and authority over individual rights. For example, freedom of speech and of the press, established during the Revolution, were restricted under the code. The code also restored slavery in the French colonies of the Caribbean.

Napoleon Crowned as Emperor In 1804, Napoleon made himself emperor, and the French voters supported him. On December 2, 1804, dressed in a splendid robe of purple velvet, Napoleon walked down the long aisle of Notre Dame Cathedral in Paris. The pope waited for him with a glittering crown. As thousands watched, the new emperor took the crown from the pope and placed it on his own head. With this gesture, Napoleon signaled that he was more powerful than the Church, which had traditionally crowned the rulers of France.

Reading Check
Analyze Motives
Why do you think Napoleon crowned himself emperor?

Napoleon Creates an Empire

Napoleon was not content simply to be master of France. He wanted to control the rest of Europe and to reassert French power in the Americas. He envisioned his western empire including Louisiana, Florida, French Guiana, and the French West Indies. He knew that the key to this area was the sugar-producing colony of Saint Domingue (now called Haiti) on the island of Hispaniola.

Louisiana Purchase

After the Haitian Revolution, Napoleon gave up on building his empire in North America and focused on wars in Europe.

Loss of American Territories In 1789, the planters in Saint Domingue demanded that the National Assembly give them the same privileges as the people of France. Eventually, enslaved Africans in the colony demanded their freedom. A civil war erupted, and enslaved Africans under the leadership of Toussaint Louverture seized control of the colony. In 1801, Napoleon decided to take back the colony and restore its productive sugar industry. However, the French forces were devastated by disease. And the rebels proved to be fierce fighters.

After the failure of the expedition to Saint Domingue, Napoleon decided to cut his losses in the Americas. He offered to sell all of the Louisiana Territory to the United States, and in 1803 President Jefferson's administration agreed to purchase the land for $15 million. This became known as the Louisiana Purchase.

Conquering Europe Napoleon gave up ambitions in the New World and turned his attention to Europe. He had already annexed the Austrian Netherlands and parts of Italy to France and set up a puppet government in Switzerland. Now he looked to expand his influence further. Fearful of his ambitions, the British persuaded Russia, Austria, and Sweden to join them against France.

Napoleon met this challenge with a series of successful battles. After the Battle of Austerlitz in 1805, Napoleon issued a proclamation expressing his pride in his troops:

This painting by Jacques Louis David shows Napoleon in a heroic pose.

"Soldiers! I am pleased with you. On the day of Austerlitz, you justified everything that I was expecting of [you]. . . . In less than four hours, an army of 100,000 men, commanded by the emperors of Russia and Austria, was cut up and dispersed. . . . 120 pieces of artillery, 20 generals, and more than 30,000 men taken prisoner—such are the results of this day which will forever be famous. . . . And it will be enough for you to say, 'I was at Austerlitz' to hear the reply: 'There is a brave man!'"

—Napoleon, quoted in *Napoleon* by André Castelot

In time, Napoleon's battlefield successes forced the rulers of Austria, Prussia, and Russia to sign peace treaties. These successes also enabled him to build the largest European empire since that of the Romans. France's only major enemy left undefeated was the great naval power, Britain.

The Battle of Trafalgar In his drive for a European empire, Napoleon lost only one major battle, the **Battle of Trafalgar** (truh•FAL•guhr). This naval defeat, however, was more important than all of his victories on land. The battle took place in 1805 off the southwest coast of Spain. The British commander, Horatio Nelson, was as brilliant in warfare at sea as Napoleon was in warfare on land. In a bold maneuver, he split the larger French fleet, capturing many ships.

The destruction of the French fleet had two major results. First, it ensured the supremacy of the British navy for the next 100 years. Second, it forced Napoleon to give up his plans of invading Britain. He had to look for another way to control his powerful enemy across the English Channel. Eventually, Napoleon's extravagant efforts to crush Britain would lead to his own undoing.

The French Empire During the first decade of the 1800s, Napoleon's victories had given him mastery over most of Europe. By 1812, the only areas of Europe free from Napoleon's control were Britain, Portugal, Sweden, and the Ottoman Empire. In addition to the lands of the French Empire, Napoleon also controlled numerous supposedly independent countries. These included Spain, the Grand Duchy of Warsaw, and a number of German kingdoms in Central Europe. The rulers of these countries were Napoleon's puppets; some, in fact, were members of his family. Furthermore, the powerful countries of Russia, Prussia, and Austria were loosely attached to Napoleon's empire through alliances. Although not totally under Napoleon's control, they were easily manipulated by threats of military action.

The French Empire was huge but unstable. Napoleon was able to maintain it at its greatest extent for only five years—from 1807 to 1812. Then it quickly fell to pieces. Its sudden collapse was caused in part by Napoleon's actions.

Reading Check
Draw Conclusions
By 1805, how successful had Napoleon been in his efforts to build an empire?

Explore ONLINE!

■	French Empire
■	Controlled by Napoleon
✸	French victory
✴	French defeat
⬚	British blockade

KINGDOM OF SWEDEN

Moscow (1812)

KINGDOM OF DENMARK AND NORWAY

North Sea

Baltic Sea

REP. OF DANZIG

Borodino (1812)

Neman R.

Friedland (1807)

RUSSIAN EMPIRE

UNITED KINGDOM OF GREAT BRITAIN AND IRELAND

Elbe R.

PRUSSIA

London

Berlin

GRAND DUCHY OF WARSAW

Brussels
Amiens

CONFEDERATION OF THE RHINE

Leipzig (1813)
Jena (1806)

ATLANTIC OCEAN

Paris
Versailles

Seine R.

Rhine R.

Ulm (1805)

Austerlitz (1805)

Wagram (1809)
Aspern (1809)

AUSTRIAN EMPIRE

Loire R.

HELVETIC REPUBLIC

Vienna

La Coruña (1809)

Vitoria (1813)

Ebro R.

KINGDOM OF ITALY

Milan

ILLYRIAN PROVINCES

Talavera (1809)

Madrid (1808)

Tagus R.

SPAIN

Marseille

Po R.

Adriatic Sea

Danube R.

Black Sea

MONTENEGRO

PORTUGAL

Trafalgar (1805)

Valencia (1808)

CORSICA

Rome

Naples

OTTOMAN EMPIRE

Gibraltar

SARDINIA

KINGDOM OF NAPLES

Mediterranean Sea

SICILY

FRENCH EMPIRE

Battle of Trafalgar, Oct. 21, 1805

◯	British fleet
◯	French and Spanish fleet
→	British thrust

Villeneuve

Nelson

Álava

Collingwood

By dividing Villeneuve's formation, Admiral Nelson captured nearly two-thirds of the enemy fleet.

Battle of Austerlitz, Dec. 2, 1805

—	French forces
—	Allied Russian, Prussian, and Austrian forces
→	French thrust
→	Allied thrust

Lannes

Bagration

Bernadotte

Austerlitz

Soult

Pratzen Plateau

Kollowrat

NAPOLEON (About 70,000 troops)

Doctorov

CZAR ALEXANDER I (About 85,000 troops)

Davout

Goldbach Creek

N

0   2 Miles

0   4 Kilometers

By drawing an Allied attack on his right flank, Napoleon was able to split the Allied line at its center.

Interpret Maps

1. **Region** What was the extent of the lands under Napoleon's control?

Napoleon's Costly Mistakes

Napoleon's own personality proved to be the greatest danger to the future of his empire. His desire for power had raised him to great heights, and the same love of power led him to his doom. In his efforts to extend the French Empire and crush Great Britain, Napoleon made three disastrous mistakes.

A STOPPAGE to a STRIDE over the GLOBE

"Little Johnny Bull"—Great Britain—waves a sword at Napoleon as the emperor straddles the globe.

The Continental System In November 1806, Napoleon set up a **blockade**—a forcible closing of ports—to prevent all trade and communication between Great Britain and other European nations. Napoleon called this policy the **Continental System** because it was supposed to make continental Europe more self-sufficient. Napoleon also intended it to destroy Great Britain's commercial and industrial economy.

Napoleon's blockade, however, was not nearly tight enough. Aided by the British, smugglers managed to bring cargo from Britain into Europe. While the blockade weakened British trade, it did not destroy it. In addition, Britain responded with its own blockade. And because the British had a stronger navy, they were better able than the French to make the blockade work.

To enforce the blockade, the British navy stopped neutral ships bound for the continent and forced them to sail to a British port to be searched and taxed. American ships were among those stopped by the British navy. Angered, the U.S. Congress declared war on Britain in 1812. Even though the War of 1812 lasted two years, it was only a minor inconvenience to Britain in its struggle with Napoleon.

The Peninsular War In 1808, Napoleon made a second costly mistake. In an effort to get Portugal to accept the Continental System, he sent an invasion force through Spain. The Spanish people protested this action. In response, Napoleon removed the Spanish king and put his own brother, Joseph, on the throne. This outraged the Spanish people and inflamed their nationalistic feelings. The Spanish, who were devoutly Catholic, also worried that Napoleon would attack the Church. They had seen how the French Revolution had weakened the Catholic Church in France, and they feared that the same thing would happen to the Church in Spain.

For six years, bands of Spanish peasant fighters, known as **guerrillas**, struck at French armies in Spain. The guerrillas were not an army that Napoleon could defeat in open battle. Rather, they worked in small groups that ambushed French troops and then fled into hiding. The British added to the French troubles by sending troops to aid the Spanish. Napoleon lost about 300,000 men during this **Peninsular War**—so called because Spain lies on the Iberian Peninsula. These losses weakened the French Empire.

In Spain and elsewhere, nationalism, or loyalty to one's own country, was becoming a powerful weapon against Napoleon. People who had at first welcomed the French as their liberators now felt abused by a foreign conqueror. Like the Spanish guerrillas, Germans and Italians and other conquered peoples turned against the French.

The Invasion of Russia Napoleon's most disastrous mistake of all came in 1812. Even though Alexander I had become Napoleon's ally, the Russian *czar* refused to stop selling grain to Britain. In addition, the French and Russian rulers suspected each other of having competing designs on Poland. Because of this breakdown in their alliance, Napoleon decided to invade Russia.

In June 1812, Napoleon and his Grand Army of more than 420,000 soldiers marched into Russia. As Napoleon advanced, Alexander pulled back his troops, refusing to be lured into an unequal battle. On this retreat, the Russians practiced a **scorched-earth policy**. This involved burning grain fields and slaughtering livestock so as to leave nothing for the enemy to eat.

On September 7, 1812, the two armies finally clashed in the Battle of Borodino. After several hours of indecisive fighting, the Russians fell back, allowing Napoleon to move on Moscow. When Napoleon entered Moscow seven days later, the city was in flames. Rather than surrender Russia's "holy city" to the French, Alexander had destroyed it. Napoleon stayed in the ruined city until the middle of October, when he decided to turn back toward France.

Francisco Goya's painting *The Third of May, 1808* shows a French firing squad executing Spanish peasants suspected of being guerrillas.

Explore ONLINE!

422,000
June 1812 Napoleon and his troops march across the Neman River and into Russia.

50,000
Napoleon sends troops to Polotsk to protect his left flank.

175,000
Reduced by desertion, disease, starvation, and capture, an army of 175,000 arrives in Smolensk. Another 30,000 die there.

130,000
Sept. 7, 1812 Napoleon's army fights the Battle of Borodino and suffers 30,000 casualties.

Sept. 14, 1812 Napoleon enters Moscow to find it in ashes, torched by the czar. He waits, hoping to induce the czar to surrender.

Oct. 18, 1812 Frustrated and starving, having waited too long for the czar, the 100,000 survivors of the Grand Army begin their hellish retreat through the cruel Russia winter.

November 1812
The army returns to Smolensk and finds famine. The remaining 24,000 march on, abandoning their wounded.
37,000

Dec. 6, 1812 Troops march for the Neman River. Only 10,000 make it out of Russia.
28,000

The 30,000 in Polotsk join the 20,000 survivors. Thousands drown while crossing the Berezina River.
50,000

GRAND DUCHY OF WARSAW

Advancing troops
Retreating troops
= 10,000 soldiers
= 10,000 lost troops

Interpret Maps
Place Why was it a mistake for Napoleon to stay in Moscow until mid-October?

Reading Check
Recognize Effects
How could the growing feelings of nationalism in European countries hurt Napoleon?

As the snows—and the temperature—began to fall in early November, Russian raiders mercilessly attacked Napoleon's ragged, retreating army. Many soldiers were killed in these clashes or died of their wounds. Still more dropped in their tracks from exhaustion, hunger, and cold. Finally, in the middle of December, the last survivors straggled out of Russia. The retreat from Moscow had devastated the Grand Army—only 10,000 soldiers were left to fight.

Napoleon's Downfall

Napoleon's enemies were quick to take advantage of his weakness. Britain, Russia, Prussia, and Sweden joined forces against him. Austria also declared war on Napoleon, despite his marriage to Marie Louise. All of the main powers of Europe were now at war with France.

Napoleon Suffers Defeat In only a few months, Napoleon managed to raise another army. However, most of his troops were untrained and ill prepared for battle. By January of 1814, the allied armies were pushing steadily toward Paris. Some two months later, King Frederick William III of Prussia and Czar Alexander I of Russia led their troops in a triumphant parade through the French capital.

Napoleon wanted to fight on, but his generals refused. In April 1814, he accepted the terms of surrender and gave up his throne. The victors gave Napoleon a small pension and exiled, or banished, him to Elba, a tiny island off the Italian coast. The allies expected no further trouble from Napoleon, but they were wrong.

The Hundred Days Louis XVI's brother assumed the throne as Louis XVIII. (The executed king's son, Louis XVII, had died in prison in 1795.) However, the new king quickly became unpopular among his subjects, especially the peasants. They suspected him of wanting to undo the Revolution's land reforms.

The news of Louis's troubles was all the incentive Napoleon needed to try to regain power. He escaped from Elba and, on March 1, 1815, landed in France. Joyous crowds welcomed him on the march to Paris. And thousands of volunteers swelled the ranks of his army. Within days, Napoleon was again emperor of France.

In response, the European allies quickly marshaled their armies. The British army, led by the Duke of Wellington, prepared for battle near the village of **Waterloo** in Belgium. On June 18, 1815, Napoleon attacked. The British army defended its ground all day. Late in the afternoon, the Prussian army arrived. Together, the British and the Prussian forces attacked the French. Two days later, Napoleon's exhausted troops gave way, and the British and Prussian forces chased them from the field.

This defeat ended Napoleon's last bid for power, called the **Hundred Days**. Taking no chances this time, the British shipped Napoleon to St. Helena, a remote island in the South Atlantic. There, he lived in lonely exile for six years, writing his memoirs. He died in 1821 of a stomach ailment, perhaps cancer.

Without doubt, Napoleon was a military genius and a brilliant administrator. Yet all his victories and other achievements must be measured against the millions of lives that were lost in his wars. The French writer Alexis de Tocqueville summed up Napoleon's character by saying, "He was as great as a man can be without virtue." Napoleon's defeat opened the door for the freed European countries to establish a new order.

Reading Check
Analyze Motives
Why do you think the French people welcomed back Napoleon so eagerly?

Lesson 3 Assessment

1. **Organize Information** Make a list of Napoleon's mistakes and their effects on the empire. Explain which of his mistakes was the most serious. Why?

Napoleon's Mistakes	Effect on Empire

2. **Key Terms and People** For each key term or person in the lesson, write a sentence explaining its significance.

3. **Analyze Motives** Why did people in other European countries resist Napoleon's efforts to build an empire?

4. **Analyze Issues** Napoleon had to deal with forces both inside and outside the French Empire. In your judgment, which area was more important to control?

5. **Identify Causes** How did geography play a role in Napoleon's defeat?

The Congress of Vienna

The Big Idea

After exiling Napoleon, European leaders at the Congress of Vienna tried to restore order and reestablish peace.

Why It Matters Now

International bodies such as the United Nations play an active role in trying to maintain world peace and stability today.

Key Terms and People

Congress of Vienna
Klemens von Metternich
balance of power
legitimacy
Holy Alliance
Concert of Europe

Setting the Stage

European heads of government were looking to establish long-lasting peace and stability on the continent after the defeat of Napoleon. They had a goal of the new European order—one of collective security and stability for the entire continent. A series of meetings in Vienna, known as the **Congress of Vienna**, were called to set up policies to achieve this goal. Originally, the Congress of Vienna was scheduled to last for four weeks. Instead, it went on for eight months.

Metternich's Plan for Europe

Most of the decisions made in Vienna during the winter of 1814–1815 were made in secret among representatives of the five "great powers"—Russia, Prussia, Austria, Great Britain, and France. By far the most influential of these representatives was the foreign minister of Austria, Prince **Klemens von Metternich** (MEHT•uhr•nihk).

Metternich distrusted the democratic ideals of the French Revolution. Like most other European aristocrats, he felt that Napoleon's behavior had been a natural outcome of experiments with democracy. Metternich wanted to keep things as they were and remarked, "The first and greatest concern for the immense majority of every nation is the stability of laws—never their change." Metternich had three goals at the Congress of Vienna. First, he wanted to prevent future French aggression by surrounding France with strong countries. Second, he wanted to restore a **balance of power**, so that no country would be a threat to others. Third, he wanted to restore Europe's royal families to the thrones they had held before Napoleon's conquests.

The Containment of France The Congress took the following steps to make the weak countries around France stronger:

- The former Austrian Netherlands and Dutch Republic were united to form the Kingdom of the Netherlands.
- A group of 39 German states were loosely joined as the newly created German Confederation, dominated by Austria.
- Switzerland was recognized as an independent nation.
- The Kingdom of Sardinia in Italy was strengthened by the addition of Genoa.

These changes enabled the countries of Europe to contain France and prevent it from overpowering weaker nations.

Balance of Power Although the leaders of Europe wanted to weaken France, they did not want to leave it powerless. If they severely punished France, they might encourage the French to take revenge. If they broke up France, then another country might become so strong that it would threaten them all. Thus, the victorious powers did not exact a great price from the defeated nation. As a result, France remained a major but diminished European power. Also, no country in Europe could easily overpower another.

Legitimacy The great powers affirmed the principle of **legitimacy**—agreeing that as many as possible of the rulers whom Napoleon had driven from their thrones be restored to power. The ruling families of France, Spain, and several states in Italy and Central Europe regained their thrones. The participants in the Congress of Vienna believed that the return of the former monarchs would stabilize political relations among the nations.

Delegates at the Congress of Vienna study a map of Europe.

The Congress of Vienna was a political triumph in many ways. For the first time, the nations of an entire continent had cooperated to control political affairs. The settlements they agreed upon were fair enough that no country was left bearing a grudge. Therefore, the Congress did not sow the seeds of future wars. In that sense, it was more successful than many other peace meetings in history.

By agreeing to come to one another's aid in case of threats to peace, the European nations had temporarily ensured that there would be a balance of power on the continent. The Congress of Vienna, then, created a time of peace in Europe. It was a lasting peace. None of the five great powers waged war on one another for nearly 40 years, when Britain and France fought Russia in the Crimean War.

Reading Check
Draw Conclusions
In what ways was the
Congress of Vienna
a success?

Political Changes Beyond Vienna

The Congress of Vienna was a victory for conservatives. Kings and princes resumed power in country after country, in keeping with Metternich's goals. Nevertheless, there were important differences from one country to another. Britain and France now had constitutional monarchies. Generally speaking, however, the governments in Eastern and Central Europe were more conservative. The rulers of Russia, Prussia, and Austria were absolute monarchs.

Conservative Europe The rulers of Europe were very nervous about the legacy of the French Revolution. They worried that the ideals of liberty, equality, and fraternity might encourage revolutions elsewhere. Late in 1815, Czar Alexander I, Emperor Francis I of Austria, and King Frederick William III of Prussia signed an agreement called the **Holy Alliance**. In it, they pledged to base their relations with other nations on Christian principles in order to combat the forces of revolution. Finally, a series of alliances devised by Metternich, called the **Concert of Europe**, ensured that nations would help one another if any revolutions broke out.

Across Europe, conservatives held firm control of the governments, but they could not contain the ideas that had emerged during the French Revolution. France after 1815 was deeply divided politically. Conservatives were happy with the monarchy of Louis XVIII and were determined to make it last. Liberals, however, wanted the king to share more power with the legislature. And many people in the lower classes remained committed to the ideals of liberty, equality, and fraternity. Similarly, in other countries there was an explosive mixture of ideas and factions that would contribute directly to revolutions in 1830 and 1848.

Despite their efforts to undo the French Revolution, the leaders at the Congress of Vienna could not turn back the clock. The Revolution had given Europe its first experiment in democratic government. Although the experiment had failed, it had set new political ideas in motion. The major political upheavals of the early 1800s had their roots in the French Revolution.

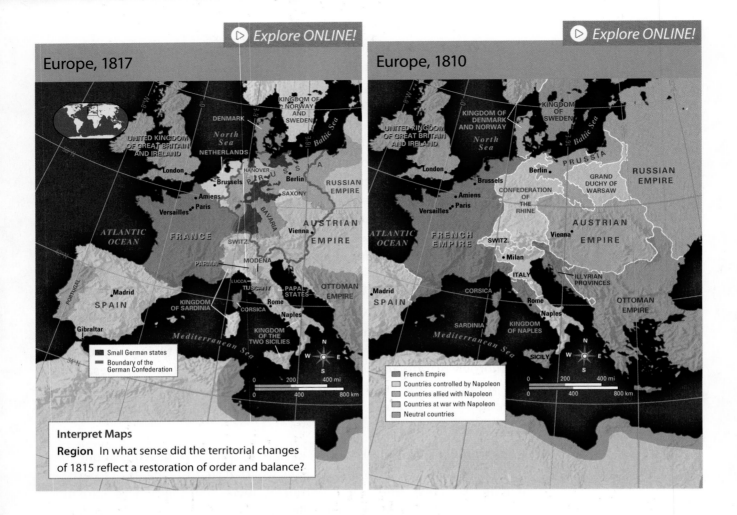

Europe, 1817

Europe, 1810

KINGDOM OF NORWAY AND SWEDEN

DENMARK

UNITED KINGDOM OF GREAT BRITAIN AND IRELAND

North Sea

NETHERLANDS

London

HANOVER

Brussels

Berlin

SAXONY

RUSSIAN EMPIRE

Amiens

Versailles Paris

BAVARIA

Vienna

ATLANTIC OCEAN

FRANCE

SWITZ

AUSTRIAN EMPIRE

PARMA

MODENA

LUCCA

TUSCANY

PAPAL STATES

OTTOMAN EMPIRE

Madrid

SPAIN

KINGDOM OF SARDINIA

Rome

CORSICA

Naples

Gibraltar

KINGDOM OF THE TWO SICILIES

Mediterranean Sea

■ Small German states
■ Boundary of the German Confederation

0   200   400 mi
0   400   800 km

Interpret Maps

Region In what sense did the territorial changes of 1815 reflect a restoration of order and balance?

KINGDOM OF DENMARK AND NORWAY

KINGDOM OF SWEDEN

UNITED KINGDOM OF GREAT BRITAIN AND IRELAND

North Sea

London

Brussels

Berlin

PRUSSIA

GRAND DUCHY OF WARSAW

RUSSIAN EMPIRE

CONFEDERATION OF THE RHINE

Amiens

Versailles Paris

ATLANTIC OCEAN

FRENCH EMPIRE

SWITZ

Vienna

AUSTRIAN EMPIRE

Milan

ITALY

ILLYRIAN PROVINCES

Madrid

SPAIN

CORSICA

Rome

Naples

OTTOMAN EMPIRE

SARDINIA

KINGDOM OF NAPLES

Mediterranean Sea

SICILY

■ French Empire
■ Countries controlled by Napoleon
■ Countries allied with Napoleon
■ Countries at war with Napoleon
■ Neutral countries

0   200   400 mi
0   400   800 km

Revolution in Latin America The actions of the Congress of Vienna had consequences far beyond events in Europe. When Napoleon deposed the king of Spain during the Peninsular War, liberal Creoles (colonists born in Spanish America) seized control of many colonies in the Americas. When the Congress of Vienna restored the king to the Spanish throne, royalist *peninsulares* (colonists born in Spain) tried to regain control of these colonial governments. The Creoles, however, attempted to retain and expand their power. In response, the Spanish king took steps to tighten control over the American colonies.

This action angered the Mexicans, who rose in revolt and successfully threw off Spain's control. Other Spanish colonies in Latin America also claimed independence. At about the same time, Brazil declared independence from Portugal.

Long-Term Legacy The Congress of Vienna left a legacy that would influence world politics for the next 100 years. The continent-wide efforts to establish and maintain a balance of power diminished the size and the power of France. At the same time, the power of Britain and Prussia increased.

Congress of Vienna and the United Nations

The Congress of Vienna and the Concert of Europe tried to keep the world safe from war. The modern equivalent of these agreements is the United Nations (UN), an international organization established in 1945 and continuing today, whose purpose is to promote world peace.

Like the Congress of Vienna, the United Nations was formed by major powers after a war—World War II. These powers agreed to cooperate to reduce tensions and bring greater harmony to international relations. Throughout its history, the United Nations has used diplomacy as its chief method of keeping the peace.

Reading Check
Identify Effects
How did the French Revolution affect not only Europe but also other areas of the world?

Nationalism began to spread in Italy, Germany, Greece, and to other areas that the Congress had put under foreign control. Eventually, the nationalistic feelings would explode into revolutions, and new nations would be formed. European colonies also responded to the power shift. Spanish colonies took advantage of the events in Europe to declare their independence and break away from Spain.

At the same time, ideas about the basis of power and authority had changed permanently as a result of the French Revolution. More and more, people saw democracy as the best way to ensure equality and justice for all. The French Revolution, then, changed the social attitudes and assumptions that had dominated Europe for centuries. A new era had begun.

Lesson 4 Assessment

1. **Organize Information** Create a chart listing the problems and their solutions under Metternich's Plan. Explain the overall effect of Metternich's plan on France.

Metternich's Plan	
Problem	Solution

2. **Key Terms and People** For each key term or person in the lesson, write a sentence explaining its significance.
3. **Draw Conclusions** From France's point of view, do you think the Congress of Vienna's decisions were fair?
4. **Form Opinions** What do you think about the role of nationalism in uniting and dividing citizens?
5. **Make Inferences** What do you think is meant by the statement that the French Revolution let the "genie out of the bottle"?

Module 19 Assessment

Key Terms and People

For each term or name below, write a sentence explaining its connection to the French Revolution or the rise and fall of Napoleon.

1. estate
2. Great Fear
3. guillotine
4. Maximilien Robespierre
5. coup d'état
6. Napoleonic Code
7. Waterloo
8. Congress of Vienna

Main Ideas

Use your notes and the information in the module to answer the following questions.

The French Revolution Begins

1. Why were the members of the Third Estate dissatisfied with their way of life under the Old Regime?
2. How did Louis XVI's weak leadership contribute to the growing crisis in France?
3. Why was the fall of the Bastille important to the French people?

Revolution Brings Reform and Terror

4. What political reforms resulted from the French Revolution?
5. What major reforms did the National Assembly introduce?
6. What are the main principles outlined in the French Declaration of the Rights of Man and the Citizen?
7. What did the divisions in the Legislative Assembly say about the differences in French society?
8. How did France evolve from a constitutional monarchy to Robespierre's democratic despotism (dictatorship)?

Napoleon's Empire

9. What reforms did Napoleon introduce?
10. What steps did Napoleon take to create an empire in Europe?
11. What factors led to Napoleon's defeat in Russia?
12. Why were the European allies able to defeat Napoleon in 1814 and again in 1815?

The Congress of Vienna

13. What were Metternich's three goals at the Congress of Vienna?
14. How did the Congress of Vienna ensure peace in Europe?

Module 19 Assessment, continued

Critical Thinking

1. **Identify Effects** Make a list of dates and events in Napoleon's career into your notebook. For each event, write whether Napoleon gained or lost power because of the event.
2. **Compare and Contrast** How were the economic conditions in France and the American colonies before their revolutions similar? How were they different?
3. **Analyze Issues** There is a saying: "Revolutions devour their own children." What evidence from this chapter supports that statement?
4. **Identify Effects** How did the Congress of Vienna affect power and authority in European countries after Napoleon's defeat? Consider who held power in the countries and the power of the countries themselves.

Engage with History

Explain your thoughts on how to change an unjust government. Was violent revolution justified? Effective? Would you have advised different actions? Discuss your opinions with a small group.

Focus on Writing

Identify Events Working in small teams, write a short report summarizing the important causes and events of the French Revolution. Include the following in your report:

- economic troubles
- rising middle class
- government corruption and incompetence
- Estates General
- storming of the Bastille
- beheading of Louis XIV
- Reign of Terror
- Napoleon's Empire

Multimedia Activity

NetExplorations: The French Revolution Plan a virtual field trip to sites in France related to the revolution. Be sure to include sites outside Paris. Include the following in your field trip plan:

- documents and other readings to help visitors prepare for each stop on the field trip
- topics to discuss at each site
- map highlighting the sites to be visited on the trip
- one or two sentences analyzing ways in which perspectives of the present shape interpretations of the past
- a list of websites used to create your virtual field trip

Module 20

Revolutions Sweep the West

Essential Question
What great shifts in thinking inspired revolutions in politics and the arts worldwide?

About the painting: From 1791 to 1824, revolutions took place in Haiti, Mexico, and Central and South America. By 1824, nearly all of Latin America had gained independence from European control. One of South America's great liberators was José de San Martín, shown.

▶ *Explore ONLINE!*

VIDEOS, including...
- Miguel Hidalgo's Call to Arms
- Ludwig Van Beethoven

☑ Document Based Investigations

☑ Graphic Organizers

☑ Interactive Games

☑ Chart: Bonds that Create a Nation-State

☑ Interactive Map: Unification of Germany, 1865–1871

In this module you will learn that nationalist revolutions, inspired by Enlightenment ideas, swept through Latin America and Europe.

What You Will Learn ...

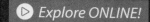
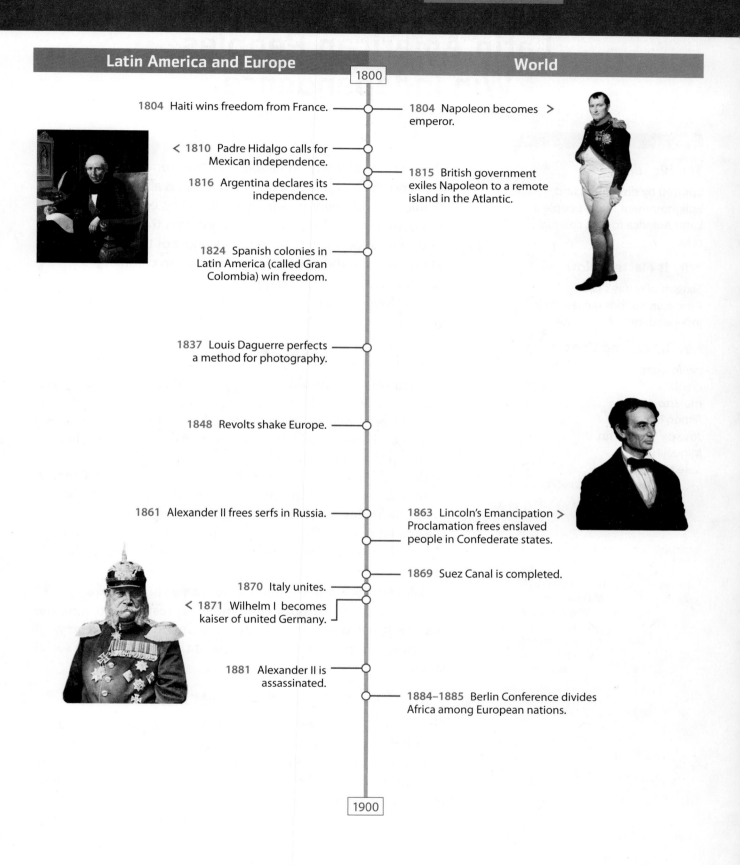

Latin America and Europe

World

1800

1804 Haiti wins freedom from France.

1804 Napoleon becomes emperor. >

< **1810** Padre Hidalgo calls for Mexican independence.

1816 Argentina declares its independence.

1815 British government exiles Napoleon to a remote island in the Atlantic.

1824 Spanish colonies in Latin America (called Gran Colombia) win freedom.

1837 Louis Daguerre perfects a method for photography.

1848 Revolts shake Europe.

1861 Alexander II frees serfs in Russia.

1863 Lincoln's Emancipation > Proclamation frees enslaved people in Confederate states.

1869 Suez Canal is completed.

1870 Italy unites.

< **1871** Wilhelm I becomes kaiser of united Germany.

1881 Alexander II is assassinated.

1884–1885 Berlin Conference divides Africa among European nations.

1900

Latin American Peoples Win Independence

The Big Idea

Spurred by discontent and Enlightenment ideas, people in Latin America fought colonial rule.

Why It Matters Now

Sixteen of today's Latin American nations gained their independence at this time.

Key Terms and People

peninsulare
creole
mulatto
Simón Bolívar
José de San Martín
Miguel Hidalgo
José María Morelos

Reading Check
Make Inferences
Why might the structure of Latin American colonial society have led to unrest?

Setting the Stage

The successful American Revolution, the French Revolution, and the Enlightenment changed ideas about who should control government. Ideas of liberty, equality, and democratic rule found their way across the seas to European colonies. In Latin America, most of the population resented the domination of European colonial powers. The time seemed right for the people who lived there to sweep away old colonial masters and gain control of the land.

Colonial Society Divided

In Latin American colonial society, class dictated people's place in society and jobs. At the top of Spanish-American society were the **peninsulares** (peh•neen•soo•LAH•rehs), people who had been born in Spain, which is on the Iberian peninsula. They formed a tiny percentage of the population. Only *peninsulares* could hold high office in Spanish colonial government. **Creoles**, Spaniards born in Latin America, were below the *peninsulares* in rank. Creoles could not hold high-level political office, but they could rise as officers in Spanish colonial armies. Together these two groups controlled land, wealth, and power in the Spanish colonies.

Below the *peninsulares* and creoles came the mestizos, persons of mixed European and Indian ancestry. Next were the **mulattos**, persons of mixed European and African ancestry, and enslaved Africans. Indians were at the bottom of the social ladder.

Revolutions in the Americas

By the late 1700s, colonists in Latin America, already aware of Enlightenment ideas, were electrified by the news of the American and French Revolutions. The success of the American Revolution encouraged them to try to gain freedom from their European masters.

The Divisions in Spanish Colonial Society, 1789

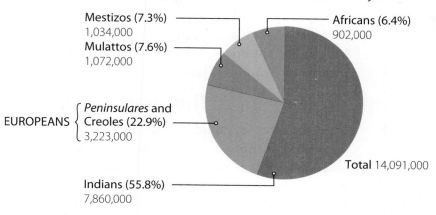

Mestizos (7.3%)
1,034,000

Mulattos (7.6%)
1,072,000

Africans (6.4%)
902,000

EUROPEANS {
Peninsulares and
Creoles (22.9%)
3,223,000

Total 14,091,000

Indians (55.8%)
7,860,000

Source: *Colonial Spanish America*, by Leslie Bethell

Interpret Graphs
1. **Synthesize** Which two groups made up the vast majority of the population in Spanish America?
2. **Make Inferences** Of the Europeans, which group—*peninsulares* or creoles—probably made up a larger percentage?

Toussaint Louverture led enslaved Africans in a revolt against the French that ended slavery and resulted in the new nation of Haiti.

Revolution in Haiti The French colony called Saint Domingue was the first Latin American territory to free itself from European rule. The colony, now known as Haiti, occupied the western third of the island of Hispaniola in the Caribbean Sea.

Nearly 500,000 enslaved Africans worked on French plantations, and they outnumbered their masters dramatically. White masters used brutal methods to terrorize them and keep them powerless.

While the French Revolution was taking place, oppressed people in the French colony of Haiti rose up against their French masters. In August 1791, 100,000 enslaved Africans rose in revolt. A leader soon emerged, Toussaint Louverture (too•SAN-loo•vair•TOOR). Formerly enslaved, Toussaint was unfamiliar with military and diplomatic matters. Even so, he rose to become a skilled general and diplomat. By 1801, Toussaint had taken control of the entire island and freed all the enslaved Africans.

In January 1802, 30,000 French troops landed in Saint Domingue to remove Toussaint from power. In May, Toussaint agreed to halt the revolution if the French would end slavery. Despite the agreement, the French soon accused him of planning another uprising. They seized him and sent him to a prison in the French Alps, where he died in April 1803.

Reading Check
Analyze Events
How did the American Revolution inspire the enslaved Africans of Saint Domingue to revolt?

Haiti's Independence Toussaint's lieutenant, Jean Jacques Dessalines (zhahn-ZHAHK-day•sah•LEEN), took up the fight for freedom. On January 1, 1804, General Dessalines declared the colony an independent country. It was the first black colony to free itself from European control. Dessalines called the country Haiti, which in the language of the Arawak natives meant "mountainous land."

Creoles Lead Independence

Even though they could not hold high public office, creoles were the least oppressed of those born in Latin America. They were also the best educated. In fact, many wealthy young creoles traveled to Europe for their education. In Europe, they read about and adopted Enlightenment ideas. When they returned to Latin America, they brought ideas of revolution with them.

Napoleon's conquest of Spain in 1808 triggered revolts in the Spanish colonies. Removing Spain's King Ferdinand VII, Napoleon made his brother Joseph king of Spain. Many creoles might have supported a Spanish king. However, they felt no loyalty to a king imposed by the French. Creoles, recalling Locke's idea of the consent of the governed, argued that when the real king was removed, power shifted to the people. In 1810, rebellion broke out in several parts of Latin America. The drive toward independence had begun.

The South American wars of independence rested on the achievements of two brilliant creole generals. One was **Simón Bolívar** (see•MAWN-boh•LEE•vahr), a wealthy Venezuelan creole. The other great liberator was **José de San Martín** (hoh•SAY-day-san-mahr•TEEN), an Argentinian.

BIOGRAPHY

Simón Bolívar
(1783–1830)

Called *Libertador* (Liberator), Bolívar was a brilliant general, a visionary, a writer, and a fighter. He is called the "George Washington of South America." Bolívar planned to unite the Spanish colonies of South America into a single country called Gran Colombia. The area of upper Peru was renamed Bolivia in his honor.

Discouraged by political disputes that tore the new Latin American nations apart, he is reported to have said, "America is ungovernable. Those who have served the revolution have ploughed the sea."

José de San Martín
(1778–1850)

Unlike the dashing Bolívar, San Martín was a modest man. Though born in Argentina, he spent much of his youth in Spain as a career military officer. He fought with Spanish forces against Napoleon. He returned to Latin America to be a part of its liberation from Spain. Fighting for 10 years, he became the liberator of Argentina, Chile, and Peru.

Discouraged by political infighting, San Martín sailed for Europe. He died, almost forgotten, on French soil in 1850.

Simón Bolívar

"The Jamaica Letter" is one of Simón Bolívar's most important political documents. In this excerpt, he discussed his political goals for South America after the revolution—and his fear that South Americans were not ready to achieve those goals.

Analyze Historical Sources
Why did Bolívar believe that South Americans were not ready for a republican form of government?

"The role of the inhabitants of the American hemisphere has for centuries been purely passive. Politically they were non-existent. . . . We have been harassed by a conduct which has not only deprived us of our rights but has kept us in a sort of permanent infancy with regard to public affairs. . . . Americans today, and perhaps to a greater extent than ever before, who live within the Spanish system occupy a position in society no better than that of serfs destined for labor. . . . Although I seek perfection for the government of my country, I cannot persuade myself that the New World can, at the moment, be organized as a great republic."

—Simón Bolívar,
from *"The Jamaica Letter"*

Bolívar's Route to Victory Simón Bolívar's native Venezuela declared its independence from Spain in 1811. But the struggle for independence had only begun. Bolívar's volunteer army of revolutionaries suffered numerous defeats. Twice Bolívar had to go into exile. A turning point came in August 1819. Bolívar led over 2,000 soldiers on a daring march through the Andes into what is now Colombia. (See map, "Latin America, 1830.") Coming from this direction, he took the Spanish army in Bogotá completely by surprise and won a decisive victory.

By 1821, Bolívar had won Venezuela's independence. He then marched south into Ecuador. In Ecuador, Bolívar finally met José de San Martín. Together they would decide the future of the Latin American revolutionary movement.

San Martín Leads Southern Liberation Forces San Martín's Argentina had declared its independence in 1816. However, Spanish forces in nearby Chile and Peru still posed a threat. In 1817, San Martín led an army on a grueling march across the Andes to Chile. He was joined there by forces led by Bernardo O'Higgins, son of a former viceroy of Peru. With O'Higgins's help, San Martín finally freed Chile.

Struggling Toward Democracy

Revolutions are as much a matter of ideas as they are of weapons. Simón Bolívar, the hero of Latin American independence, was both a thinker and a fighter. By 1800, Enlightenment ideas spread widely across the Latin American colonies. Bolívar combined Enlightenment political ideas, ideas from Greece and Rome, and his own original thinking. The result was a system of democratic ideas that would help spark revolutions throughout Latin America.

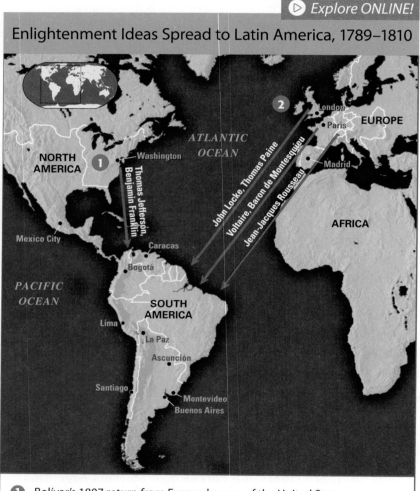

▶ *Explore ONLINE!*

Enlightenment Ideas Spread to Latin America, 1789–1810

NORTH AMERICA

Washington

Thomas Jefferson, Benjamin Franklin

Mexico City

Caracas

Bogotá

PACIFIC OCEAN

SOUTH AMERICA

Lima

La Paz

Ascunción

Santiago

Montevideo
Buenos Aires

ATLANTIC OCEAN

John Locke, Thomas Paine

Voltaire, Baron de Montesquieu

Jean-Jacques Rousseau

London

Paris

EUROPE

Madrid

AFRICA

❶ Bolívar's 1807 return from Europe by way of the United States allowed him to study the American system of government.

❷ In 1810, Bolívar went to London to seek support for the revolution in Latin America. At the same time, he studied British institutions of government.

▲ After winning South American independence, Simón Bolívar realized his dream of Gran Colombia, a sort of United States of South America.

Critical Thinking

1. **Make Inferences** How are Enlightenment thoughts and the successes of the American and French Revolutions reflected in Bolívar's thinking?

2. **Compare** What recent events in today's world are similar to Simón Bolívar's movement for Latin American independence?

In 1821, San Martín planned to drive the remaining Spanish forces out of Lima, Peru. But to do so, he needed a much larger force. San Martín and Bolívar discussed this when they met at Guayaquil, Ecuador, in 1822.

No one knows how the two men reached an agreement. But San Martín left his army for Bolívar to command. With unified revolutionary forces, Bolívar's army went on to defeat the Spanish at the Battle of Ayacucho (Peru) on December 9, 1824. In this last major battle of the war for independence, the Spanish colonies in Latin America won their freedom. The future countries of Venezuela, Colombia, Panama, and Ecuador were united into a country called Gran Colombia.

Mexico Ends Spanish Rule

In most Latin American countries, creoles led the revolutionary movements. But in Mexico, ethnic and racial groups mixed more freely. There, Indians and mestizos played the leading role.

A Cry for Freedom In 1810, Padre **Miguel Hidalgo** (mee•GEHL-ee•DAHL•goh), a priest in the small village of Dolores, took the first step toward independence. Hidalgo was a poor but well-educated man. He firmly believed in Enlightenment ideals. On September 16, 1810, he rang the bells of his village church. When the peasants gathered in the church, he issued a call for rebellion against the Spanish. Today, that call is known as the *grito de Dolores* (the cry of Dolores).

The very next day, Hidalgo's Indian and mestizo followers began a march toward Mexico City. This unruly army soon numbered 80,000 men. The uprising of the lower classes alarmed the Spanish army and creoles, who feared the loss of their property, control of the land, and their lives. The army defeated Hidalgo in 1811. The rebels then rallied around another strong leader, Padre **José María Morelos** (moh•RAY•lohs). Morelos led the revolution for four years. However, in 1815, a creole officer, Agustín de Iturbide (ah•goos•TEEN-day-ee•toor•BEE•day), defeated him.

Mexico's Independence Events in Mexico took yet another turn in 1820 when a revolution in Spain put a liberal group in power there. Mexico's creoles feared the loss of their privileges in the Spanish-controlled colony. So they united in support of Mexico's independence from Spain. Ironically, Agustín de Iturbide—the man who had defeated the rebel Padre Morelos—proclaimed independence in 1821.

Before the Mexican revolution, Central America was part of the viceroyalty of New Spain. It had been governed by the Spanish from the seat of colonial government in Mexico. In 1821, several Central American states declared their independence from Spain—and from Mexico as well. However, Iturbide (who had declared himself emperor), refused to recognize the declarations of independence. Iturbide was finally overthrown in 1823. Central America then declared its absolute independence from Mexico. It took the name United Provinces of Central America. The future countries of Nicaragua, Guatemala, Honduras, El Salvador, and Costa Rica would develop in this region.

Reading Check
Summarize
What factors caused the revolution in Latin America?

Miguel Hidalgo

Reading Check
Summarize
What was the *grito de Dolores*?

Symbolizing a Nation's Values

Artists can encourage national pride through the use of symbols.

Botswana

Industry and livestock are connected by water, the key to the nations' prosperity. *Pula* in the Setswana language means "rain." But to a Setswana speaker, it is also a common greeting meaning "luck, life, and prosperity."

Austria

The eagle was the symbol of the old Austrian Empire. The shield goes back to medieval times. The hammer and sickle symbolize agriculture and industry. The broken chains celebrate Austria's liberation from Germany at the end of World War II.

United States

The 13 original colonies are symbolized in the stars, stripes, leaves, and arrows. The Latin phrase *E pluribus unum* means "Out of many, one," expressing unity of the states. The American bald eagle holds an olive branch and arrows, which symbolize a desire for peace but a readiness for war.

Analyze Historical Sources

1. What role do symbols play in expressing a nation's view of itself and the world?
2. How do artists encourage national pride?

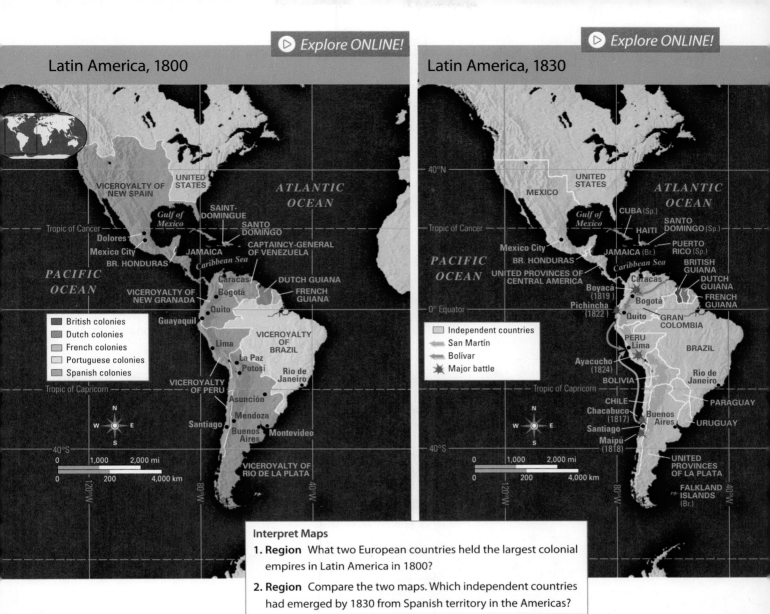

Latin America, 1800

Latin America, 1830

Map: Latin America, 1800

VICEROYALTY OF NEW SPAIN
UNITED STATES
ATLANTIC OCEAN
Gulf of Mexico
SAINT-DOMINGUE
SANTO DOMINGO
CAPTAINCY-GENERAL OF VENEZUELA
Tropic of Cancer
Dolores
Mexico City
BR. HONDURAS
JAMAICA
Caribbean Sea
PACIFIC OCEAN
Caracas
Bogotá
DUTCH GUIANA
FRENCH GUIANA
VICEROYALTY OF NEW GRANADA
Quito
Guayaquil
Lima
VICEROYALTY OF BRAZIL
La Paz
Potosí
Rio de Janiero
VICEROYALTY OF PERU
Asunción
Mendoza
Santiago
Buenos Aires
Montevideo
Tropic of Capricorn
VICEROYALTY OF RIO DE LA PLATA

Legend:
- British colonies
- Dutch colonies
- French colonies
- Portuguese colonies
- Spanish colonies

0 1,000 2,000 mi
0 200 4,000 km

Map: Latin America, 1830

40°N
UNITED STATES
MEXICO
ATLANTIC OCEAN
Gulf of Mexico
CUBA (Sp.)
SANTO DOMINGO (Sp.)
HAITI
PUERTO RICO (Sp.)
Tropic of Cancer
Mexico City
BR. HONDURAS
JAMAICA (Br.)
Caribbean Sea
BRITISH GUIANA
UNITED PROVINCES OF CENTRAL AMERICA
PACIFIC OCEAN
Boyacá (1819)
Pichincha (1822)
Caracas
Bogotá
DUTCH GUIANA
FRENCH GUIANA
0° Equator
Quito
GRAN COLOMBIA
PERU
Lima
BRAZIL
Ayacucho (1824)
BOLIVIA
Rio de Janeiro
Tropic of Capricorn
CHILE
Chacabuco (1817)
Santiago
Maipú (1818)
Buenos Aires
PARAGUAY
URUGUAY
UNITED PROVINCES OF LA PLATA
40°S
FALKLAND ISLANDS (Br.)

Legend:
- Independent countries
- San Martín
- Bolívar
- Major battle

0 1,000 2,000 mi
0 200 4,000 km

Interpret Maps

1. **Region** What two European countries held the largest colonial empires in Latin America in 1800?

2. **Region** Compare the two maps. Which independent countries had emerged by 1830 from Spanish territory in the Americas?

Brazil's Royal Liberator

Brazil's quest for independence was unique in this period of Latin American history because it occurred without violent upheavals or widespread bloodshed. In fact, a member of the Portuguese royal family actually played a key role in freeing Brazil from Portugal.

In 1807, Napoleon's armies invaded both Spain and Portugal. Napoleon's aim was to close the ports of these countries to British shipping. As French troops approached Lisbon, the Portuguese capital, Prince John (later King John VI) and the royal family boarded ships to escape capture. They took their court and royal treasury to Portugal's largest colony, Brazil. Rio de Janiero became the capital of the Portuguese empire. For 14 years, the Portuguese ran their empire from Brazil. After Napoleon's defeat in 1815, King John and the Portuguese government returned to Portugal six years later. Dom Pedro, King John's son, stayed behind in Brazil.

Reading Check
Make Inferences In what way did the presence of the royal family in Brazil help Portugal's largest colony?

King John planned to make Brazil a colony again. However, many Brazilians could not accept a return to colonial status. In 1822, creoles demanded Brazil's independence from Portugal. Eight thousand Brazilians signed a petition asking Dom Pedro to rule. He agreed. On September 7, 1822, he officially declared Brazil's independence. Brazil had won its independence in a bloodless revolution.

Meanwhile, the ideas of the French Revolution and the aftermath of the Napoleonic Wars were causing upheaval in Europe, as you will learn next.

Lesson 1 Assessment

1. **Organize Information** Make a table. Which independence movement was led by Toussaint Louverture?

Who	Where
When	Why

2. **Key Terms and People** For each key term or person in the lesson, write a sentence explaining its significance.

3. **Compare and Contrast** Compare and contrast the leadership of the South American revolutions to the leadership of Mexico's revolution.

4. **Form Opinions** Would creole revolutionaries tend to be democratic or authoritarian leaders? Explain.

5. **Analyze Causes** How were events in Europe related to the revolutions in Latin America?

Europe Faces Revolutions

The Big Idea

Liberal and nationalist uprisings challenged the old conservative order of Europe.

Why It Matters Now

The system of nation-states established in Europe during this period continues today.

Key Terms and People

conservative
liberal
radical
anarchism
nationalism
nation-state
Balkans
Louis-Napoleon
Alexander II

Setting the Stage

As revolutions shook the colonies in Latin America, Europe was also undergoing dramatic changes. Under the leadership of Prince Metternich of Austria, the Congress of Vienna had tried to restore the old monarchies and territorial divisions that had existed before the French Revolution. On an international level, this attempt to turn back history succeeded. For the next century, European countries seldom turned to war to solve their differences. Within countries, however, the effort failed. Revolutions erupted across Europe between 1815 and 1848.

Clash of Philosophies

In the first half of the 1800s, three schools of political thought struggled for supremacy in European societies. Each believed that its style of government would best serve the people. Each attracted a different set of followers. The following list identifies the philosophies, goals, and followers.

- **Conservative**: usually wealthy property owners and nobility. They argued for protecting the traditional monarchies of Europe.
- **Liberal**: mostly middle-class business leaders and merchants. They wanted to give more power to elected parliaments, but only the educated and the landowners would vote.
- **Radical**: favored drastic change to extend democracy to all people. They believed that governments should practice the ideals of the French Revolution—liberty, equality, and brotherhood. Some radicals believed in **anarchism**—a belief that government is harmful and not needed.

Reading Check
Make Inferences
How can people have such different philosophies?

Prince Clemens von Metternich shaped conservative control of Europe for almost 40 years.

Reading Check
Summarize
How did nationalism blur the line between philosophies?

Nationalism Develops

As conservatives, liberals, and radicals debated issues of government, a new movement called **nationalism** emerged. Nationalism is the belief that people's greatest loyalty should not be to a king or an empire but to a nation of people who share a common culture and history. The nationalist movement would blur the lines that separated the three political theories.

When a nation had its own independent government, it became a nation-state. A **nation-state** defends the nation's territory and way of life, and it represents the nation to the rest of the world. In Europe in 1815, only France, England, and Spain could be called nation-states. But soon that would change as nationalist movements achieved success.

Most of the people who believed in nationalism were either liberals or radicals. In most cases, the liberal middle class—teachers, lawyers, and businesspeople—led the struggle for constitutional government and the formation of nation-states. In Germany, for example, liberals wanted to gather the many different German states into a single nation-state. Other liberals in large empires, such as the Hungarians in the Austrian Empire, wanted to split away and establish self-rule.

Nationalists Challenge Conservative Power

Beginning in 1820, revolutions swept across Europe. Revolutions occurred in Spain, Portugal, Russia, and Italy that led to constitutional monarchies. In Greece, revolts led to Greek independence.

The first people to win self-rule during this period were the Greeks. For centuries, Greece had been part of the Ottoman Empire. The Ottomans controlled most of the **Balkans**. That region includes all or part of present-day Greece, Albania, Bulgaria, Romania, Turkey, and the former Yugoslavia. Greeks, however, had kept alive the memory of their ancient history and culture. Spurred on by the nationalist spirit, they demanded independence and rebelled against the Ottoman Turks in 1821.

Greeks Gain Independence The most powerful European governments opposed revolution. However, the cause of Greek independence was popular with people around the world. Russians, for example, felt a connection to Greek Orthodox Christians, who were ruled by the Muslim Ottomans. Educated Europeans and Americans loved and respected ancient Greek culture.

Nationalism

Nationalism—the belief that people should be loyal to their nation—was not widespread until the 1800s. The rise of modern nationalism is tied to the spread of democratic ideas and the growth of an educated middle class. People wanted to decide how they were governed.

Bonds That Create a Nation-State

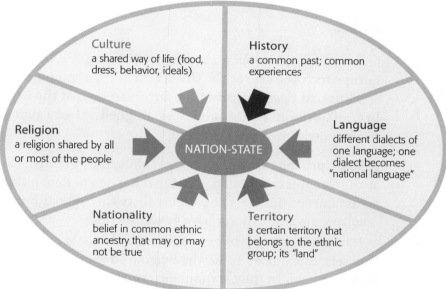

Culture a shared way of life (food, dress, behavior, ideals)

History a common past; common experiences

Religion a religion shared by all or most of the people

Language different dialects of one language; one dialect becomes "national language"

NATION-STATE

Nationality belief in common ethnic ancestry that may or may not be true

Territory a certain territory that belongs to the ethnic group; its "land"

Positive and Negative Results of Nationalism

Nationalism has not always been a positive influence. For example, strong nationalistic feelings sometimes lead a group to turn against outsiders. The chart lists positive and negative results of nationalism. Note how some results, such as competition, can be both positive and negative.

Positive Results	Negative Results
People within a nation overcoming differences for the common good	Forced assimilation of minority cultures
The overthrow of colonial rule	Ethnic cleansing, such as in Bosnia and Herzegovina in the 1990s
Democratic governments in nations worldwide	The rise of extreme nationalistic movements, such as Nazism
Competition among nations spurring scientific and technological advances	Competition between nations leading to warfare

Critical Thinking

1. **Form Opinions** Do you think nationalism has had more of a positive or negative impact on the world? Explain.

2. **Compare and Contrast** Which of the bonds used to create nation-states are found in the United States?

IMPACT OF NATIONALISM

- Between 1950 and 1980, 47 African countries overthrew colonial rulers and became independent nations.
- In the 1990s, the republics of Bosnia and Herzegovina, Croatia, Slovenia, and Macedonia broke away from Yugoslavia.
- In 2003, Yugoslavia changed its name to Serbia and Montenegro.
- Europe has about 50 countries. (Some of those lie partially in Europe, partially in Asia.) About 85 languages are spoken in the region.
- In most of Latin America, Spanish or Portuguese is the official language. However, many native languages are still spoken. For example, Bolivia has 37 official languages, including Spanish and the Indian languages of Aymara and Quechua.

Eventually, as popular support for Greece grew, the powerful nations of Europe took the side of the Greeks. In 1827, a combined British, French, and Russian fleet destroyed the Ottoman fleet at the Battle of Navarino. In 1830, Britain, France, and Russia signed a treaty guaranteeing an independent kingdom of Greece.

1830s Uprisings Crushed By the 1830s, the old order, carefully arranged at the Congress of Vienna, was breaking down. Revolutionary zeal swept across Europe. Liberals and nationalists throughout Europe were openly revolting against conservative governments.

Nationalist riots broke out against Dutch rule in the Belgian city of Brussels. In October 1830, the Belgians declared their independence from Dutch control. In Italy, nationalists worked to unite the many separate states on the Italian peninsula. Some were independent. Others were ruled by Austria, or by the pope. Eventually, Prince Metternich sent Austrian troops to restore order in Italy. The Poles living under the rule of Russia staged a revolt in Warsaw in late 1830. Russian armies took nearly an entire year to crush the Polish uprising. By the mid-1830s, the old order seemed to have reestablished itself. But the appearance of stability did not last long.

1848 Revolutions Fail to Unite In 1848, ethnic uprisings erupted throughout Europe. After an unruly mob in Vienna clashed with police, Metternich resigned and liberal uprisings broke out throughout the Austrian empire. In Budapest, nationalist leader Louis Kossuth called for a parliament and self-government for Hungary. Meanwhile in Prague, Czech liberals demanded Bohemian independence.

Louis Auguste Blanqui
(1805–1881)

A French revolutionary, Louis Auguste Blanqui, was jailed for more than 33 years for trying to overthrow the government. His followers, the Blanquists, advanced the workers' movement even after Blanqui's death.

Blanqui's main idea was that society could be changed only if workers controlled the wealth of the church and large property holders. He thought that the government should control industries and businesses. He wanted to establish industrial and agricultural worker groups, and improve education so that the nation's economy would run to benefit its workers.

Reading Check
Analyze Events
Why weren't the revolutions of 1830 and 1848 successful?

In *Combat Before the Hotel de Ville, July 28th, 1830*, Victor Schnetz portrays the riots in Paris that forced Charles X to flee to Great Britain.

European politics continued to seesaw. Many liberal gains were lost to conservatives within a year. In one country after another, the revolutionaries failed to unite themselves or their nations. Conservatives regained their nerve and their power. By 1849, Europe had practically returned to the conservatism that had controlled governments before 1848. These revolutions failed to achieve their nationalist and democratic objectives.

Radicals Change France

Radicals participated in many of the 1848 revolts. Only in France, however, was the radical demand for democratic government the main goal of revolution. In 1830, France's King Charles X tried to stage a return to absolute monarchy. The attempt sparked riots that forced Charles to flee to Great Britain. He was replaced by Louis-Philippe, who had long supported liberal reforms in France.

The Third Republic However, in 1848, after a reign of almost 18 years, Louis-Philippe fell from popular favor. Once again, a Paris mob overturned a monarchy and established a republic. The new republican government began to fall apart almost immediately. The radicals split into factions. One side wanted only political reform. The other side also wanted social and economic reform that would close up the differences in wealth between the "haves" and "have nots." The two sides set off bloody battles in Parisian streets. The violence turned French citizens away from the radicals. As a result, a moderate constitution was drawn up later in 1848. It called for a parliament and a strong president to be elected by the people.

Nationalistic Music

As the force of nationalism began to rise in Europe, ethnic groups recognized their music as a unique element of their culture. Composers used folk melodies in their works. For example, Czech composer Antonin Dvořák (DVAWR•zhahk), pictured, and the Norwegian composer Edvard Grieg incorporated popular melodies and legends into their works. These works became a source of pride and further encouraged the sense of nationalism. Richard Wagner created a cycle of four musical dramas called *Der Ring des Nibelungen*. His operas are considered the pinnacle of German nationalism.

France Accepts a Strong Ruler In December 1848, **Louis-Napoleon**, the nephew of Napoleon Bonaparte, won the presidential election. Four years later, Louis-Napoleon Bonaparte took the title of Emperor Napoleon III. A majority of French voters accepted this action without complaint. The French were weary of instability. They welcomed a strong ruler who would bring peace to France.

As France's emperor, Louis-Napoleon built railroads, encouraged industrialization, and promoted an ambitious program of public works. Gradually, because of Louis-Napoleon's policies, unemployment decreased in France, and the country experienced real prosperity.

Reading Check
Summarize
How would you describe the political swings occurring in France between 1830 and 1852?

Reform in Russia

Unlike France, Russia in the 1800s had yet to leap into the modern industrialized world. Under Russia's feudal system, serfs were bound to the nobles whose land they worked. Nobles enjoyed almost unlimited power over them. By the 1820s, many Russians believed that serfdom must end. In their eyes, the system was morally wrong. It also prevented the empire from advancing economically. The czars, however, were reluctant to free the serfs. Freeing them would anger the landowners, whose support the czars needed to stay in power.

Defeat Brings Change Eventually, Russia's lack of development became obvious to Russians and to the whole world. In 1853, Czar Nicholas I threatened to take over part of the Ottoman Empire in the Crimean War. However, Russia's industries failed to provide adequate supplies for the country's troops. As a result, in 1856, Russia lost the war against the combined forces of France, Great Britain, Sardinia, and the Ottoman Empire.

After the war, Nicholas's son, **Alexander II**, decided to move Russia toward modernization and social change. Alexander and his advisers believed that his reforms would allow Russia to compete with western Europe for world power.

History in Depth

Emancipation

In 1861, on the day before Abraham Lincoln became president of the United States, Czar Alexander II issued the Edict of Emancipation, freeing 20 million serfs. Less than two years later, President Lincoln issued the Emancipation Proclamation, freeing enslaved peoples living under the Confederacy.

The emancipation edicts did not entirely fulfill the hopes of Russian serfs or former slaves in the United States. Russian peasant communities, like the one pictured, were still tied to the land. And Lincoln did not free enslaved people in the border states.

Reform and Reaction The first and boldest of Alexander's reforms was a decree freeing the serfs in 1861. The abolition of serfdom, however, went only halfway. Peasant communities—rather than individual peasants—received about half the farmland in the country. Nobles kept the other half. The government paid the nobles for their land. Each peasant community, on the other hand, had 49 years to pay the government for the land it had received. So, while the serfs were legally free, the debt still tied them to the land.

Political and social reforms ground to a halt when terrorists assassinated Alexander II in 1881. His successor, Alexander III, tightened czarist control over the country. Alexander III and his ministers, however, encouraged industrial development to expand Russia's power. A major force behind Russia's drive toward industrial expansion was nationalism. Nationalism also stirred other ethnic groups. During the 1800s, such groups were uniting into nations and building industries to survive among other nation-states.

Reading Check
Analyze Issues Why did czars push for industrialization?

Lesson 2 Assessment

1. **Organize Information** Make a web. Why did most of the revolts fail?

   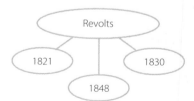

2. **Key Terms and People** For each key term or person in the lesson, write a sentence explaining its significance.

3. **Make Inferences** Why might liberals and radicals join together in a nationalist cause?

4. **Draw Conclusions** Why did some liberals disapprove of the way Louis-Napoleon ruled France after the uprisings of 1848?

5. **Evaluate** What consequences did Alexander's reforms have on Russia?

Revolutions Around the World

Each of the revolutions you studied had political, economic, and social causes, as shown in the tables. Use the table below to understand the causes of revolutions more fully.

Causes of Revolutions

	England	North America	France	Latin America
Political	King claimed divine right.	Colonists accused British leaders of tyranny.	Third Estate wanted greater representation.	French Revolution inspired political ideas.
	King dissolved Parliament.	Colonists demanded the same rights as English citizens.	Louis XVI was a weak ruler.	Royal officials committed injustices.
	Parliament sought guarantee of freedoms.		American Revolution inspired political ideas.	Napoleon's conquest triggered revolts.
Economic	King wanted money for wars.	Britain expected colonies to pay for defense.	Wars and royal extravagance created debt.	*Peninsulares* and creoles controlled wealth.
	King levied taxes and fines without Parliament's approval.	Colonies opposed taxation without representation.	Inflation and famine	Lower classes toiled as peasants with little income or as slaves.
			Peasants paid high taxes.	
Social	Early Stuart kings refused to make Puritan reforms.	Colonists began to identify as Americans.	Third Estate resented the First and Second estates' privileges.	Only *peninsulares* and creoles had power.
	Parliament feared James II would restore Catholicism.	Enlightenment ideas spread.	Enlightenment ideas spread.	Creoles spread Enlightenment ideas.

Interpret Tables

1. **Analyze Causes** What was the most frequent political cause of revolution? economic cause? social cause?

2. **Contrast** How did the causes of the revolutions in Latin America differ from those of the other three revolutions?

Use the table below to understand the effects of revolution more fully.

Effects of Revolutions

	England	North America	France	Latin America
Political	Constitutional monarchy established.	United States gained independence.	The Revolution led to a succession of governments.	Most colonial rule ended.
	The Bill of Rights guaranteed rights.	Constitution set up a republican government.	Expectations for equality and freedom sparked uprising.	Representative government was slow to develop.
	Overthrow of monarch inspired American revolutionaries.	Revolutionary ideals inspired groups seeking equality.	It inspired later revolutions.	The military or the wealthy controlled much of the region until the late 1900s.
Economic	Parliament encouraged trade.	Free enterprise developed.	Wars devastated France's economy.	Upper classes controlled wealth.
Social	England remained Protestant.	The ideals of Revolution inspired groups seeking social equality.	French feudal system abolished.	Much of Latin America continued to have a strong class system.

Interpret Tables

1. **Contrast** Which revolutions had positive economic effects, and which had negative? Explain.
2. **Analyze Effects** What common political effect did the revolutions in North America and Latin America achieve?

Historical Source

Thomas Paine

In this excerpt from the pamphlet *Common Sense*, Thomas Paine described the ideal government he wanted to see set up after the American Revolution.

> "But where, say some, is the king of America? I'll tell you, friend, . . . in America THE LAW IS KING. For as in absolute governments the king is law, so in free countries the law ought to BE king, and there ought to be no other."

Analyze Historical Sources
What did Paine believe should be the highest power in a new American government?

Nationalism

The Big Idea

Nationalism contributed to the formation of two new nations and a new political order in Europe.

Why It Matters Now

Nationalism is the basis of world politics today and has often caused conflicts and wars.

Key Terms and People

Russification
Camillo di Cavour
Giuseppe Garibaldi
Junker
Otto von Bismarck
realpolitik
kaiser

Setting the Stage

Nationalism was the most powerful idea of the 1800s. Its influence stretched throughout Europe and the Americas. It shaped countries by creating new ones or breaking up old ones. In Europe, it also upset the balance of power set up at the Congress of Vienna in 1815, affecting the lives of millions. Empires in Europe were made up of many different groups of people. Nationalism fed the desire of most of those groups to be free of the rule of empires and govern themselves in their traditional lands.

Nationalism: A Force for Unity or Disunity

During the 1800s, nationalism fueled efforts to build nation-states. Nationalists were not loyal to kings, but to their people—to those who shared common bonds. Nationalists believed that people of a single "nationality," or ancestry, should unite under a single government. However, people who wanted to restore the old order from before the French Revolution saw nationalism as a force for disunity.

Types of Nationalist Movements

Type	Characteristics	Example
Unification	Mergers of politically divided but culturally similar lands	19th-century Germany 19th-century Italy
Separation	Culturally distinct group resists being added to a state or tries to break away	Greeks in the Ottoman Empire
State-building	Culturally distinct groups form into a new state by accepting a single culture	United States Turkey

Interpret Charts

1. **Categorize** What types of nationalist movements can evolve in lands with culturally distinct groups?

2. **Draw Conclusions** What must be present for state-building to take place?

Reading Check
Summarize How can nationalism unify? How can it break groups apart?

Gradually, authoritarian rulers saw that nationalism could also unify people. They began to use nationalist feelings for their purposes. They built nation-states in areas where they remained in control.

In the table titled, "Types of Nationalist Movements," you can see three types of nationalist movements. In today's world, groups still use the spirit of nationalism to unify, separate, or build up nation-states.

Nationalism Shakes Aging Empires

Three aging empires—the Austrian Empire of the Hapsburgs, the Russian Empire of the Romanovs, and the Ottoman Empire of the Turks—contained a mixture of ethnic groups. Control moved back and forth between these empires, depending on victories or defeats in war and on royal marriages. When nationalism emerged in the 19th century, ethnic unrest threatened and eventually toppled these empires.

The Breakup of the Austrian Empire The Austrian Empire brought together Slovenes, Hungarians, Germans, Czechs, Slovaks, Croats, Poles, Serbs, and Italians. In 1866, Prussia defeated Austria in the Austro-Prussian War. With its victory, Prussia gained control of the newly organized North German Confederation, a union of Prussia and 21 smaller German political units. Then, pressured by the Hungarians, Emperor Francis Joseph of Austria split his empire in half, declaring Austria and Hungary independent states, with himself as ruler of both. The empire was now called Austria-Hungary or the Austro-Hungarian Empire. Nationalist disputes continued to weaken the empire for more than 40 years. Finally, after World War I, Austria-Hungary broke into several nation-states.

The Russian Empire Crumbles Nationalism also helped break up the 370-year-old empire of the czars in Russia. In addition to Russians, the czar ruled over 22 million Ukrainians, 8 million Poles, and smaller numbers of Lithuanians, Latvians, Estonians, Finns, Jews, Romanians, Georgians, Armenians, Turks, and others. Each group had its own culture.

The ruling Romanov dynasty of Russia was determined to maintain iron control over this diversity. They instituted a policy of **Russification**, forcing Russian culture on all the ethnic groups in the empire. This policy actually strengthened ethnic nationalist feelings and helped to disunify Russia. The weakened czarist empire finally could not withstand the double shock of World War I and the communist revolution. The last Romanov czar gave up his power in 1917.

Reading Check
Make Inferences Why might a policy like Russification produce results that are opposite of those intended?

The Ottoman Empire Weakens The ruling Turks of the Ottoman Empire controlled Greeks, Slavs, Arabs, Bulgarians, and Armenians. In 1856, under pressure from the British and French, the Ottomans granted citizenship to the people under their rule. That measure angered conservative Turks, who wanted no change in the situation, and caused tensions in the empire. In response to nationalism in Armenia, the Ottomans massacred and deported Armenians from 1894 to 1896 and again in 1915. Like Austria-Hungary, the Ottoman Empire broke apart soon after World War I.

Cavour Unites Italy

While nationalism destroyed empires, it also built nations. Italy was one of the countries to form from the territory of crumbling empires. Italians felt a strong cultural identity with others in Italy. Between 1815 and 1848, fewer and fewer Italians were content to live under foreign rulers.

Cavour Leads Italian Unification Italian nationalists looked for leadership from the kingdom of Piedmont-Sardinia, the largest and most powerful of the Italian states. The kingdom had adopted a liberal constitution in 1848. So, to the liberal Italian middle classes, unification under Piedmont-Sardinia seemed a good plan.

In 1852, Sardinia's king, Victor Emmanuel II, named Count **Camillo di Cavour** (kuh•VOOR) as his prime minister. Cavour was a cunning statesman who worked tirelessly to expand Piedmont-Sardinia's power. Using skillful diplomacy and well chosen alliances he set about gaining control of northern Italy for Sardinia.

▶ *Explore ONLINE!*

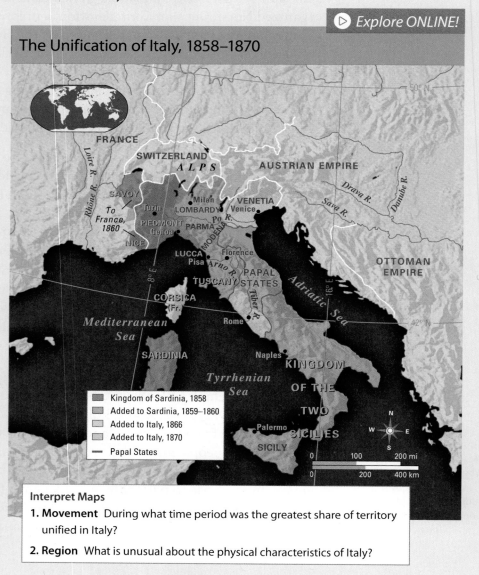

The Unification of Italy, 1858–1870

Kingdom of Sardinia, 1858
Added to Sardinia, 1859–1860
Added to Italy, 1866
Added to Italy, 1870
— Papal States

Interpret Maps

1. **Movement** During what time period was the greatest share of territory unified in Italy?

2. **Region** What is unusual about the physical characteristics of Italy?

"Right Leg in the Boot at Last"

In this 1860 British cartoon, the king of Sardinia is receiving control of lands taken by the nationalist Garibaldi. The act was one of the final steps in the unification of Italy.

Analyze Historical Sources
What symbol does the cartoonist use for the soon-to-be nation of Italy?

Cavour realized that the greatest roadblock to annexing northern Italy was Austria. In 1858, the French emperor Napoleon III agreed to help drive Austria out of the northern Italian provinces. Cavour then provoked a war with the Austrians. A combined French-Sardinian army won two quick victories. Sardinia succeeded in taking all of northern Italy, except Venetia.

Garibaldi Brings Unity As Cavour was uniting northern Italy, he secretly started helping nationalist rebels in southern Italy. In May 1860, a small army of Italian nationalists led by a bold and visionary soldier, **Giuseppe Garibaldi** (GAR•uh•BAWL•dee), captured Sicily. In battle, Garibaldi always wore a bright red shirt, as did his followers. As a result, they became known as the Red Shirts.

From Sicily, Garibaldi and his forces crossed to the Italian mainland and marched north. Eventually, Garibaldi agreed to unite the southern areas he had conquered with the kingdom of Piedmont-Sardinia. Cavour arranged for King Victor Emmanuel II to meet Garibaldi in Naples. "The Red One" willingly agreed to step aside and let the Sardinian king rule.

In 1866, the Austrian province of Venetia, which included the city of Venice, became part of Italy. In 1870, Italian forces took over the last part of a territory known as the Papal States. With this victory, the city of Rome came under Italian control. Soon after, Rome became the capital of the united kingdom of Italy. The pope, however, would continue to govern a section of Rome known as Vatican City.

Reading Check
Hypothesize
What reasons might Garibaldi have had to step aside and let the Sardinian king rule?

Bismarck Unites Germany

Like Italy, Germany also achieved national unity in the mid-1800s. Beginning in 1815, 39 German states formed a loose grouping called the German Confederation. The Austrian Empire dominated the confederation. However, Prussia was ready to unify all the German states.

Prussia Leads German Unification Prussia enjoyed several advantages that would eventually help it forge a strong German state. First of all, unlike the Austro-Hungarian Empire, Prussia had a mainly German population. As a result, nationalism actually unified Prussia. In contrast, ethnic groups in Austria-Hungary tore the empire apart. Moreover, Prussia's army was by far the most powerful in central Europe. In 1848, Berlin rioters forced a constitutional convention to write up a liberal constitution for the kingdom, paving the way for unification.

Bismarck Takes Control In 1861, Wilhelm I succeeded Frederick William to the throne. The liberal parliament refused him money for reforms that would double the strength of the army. Wilhelm saw the parliament's refusal as a major challenge to his authority. He was supported in his view by the **Junkers** (YUNG·kuhrz), strongly conservative members of Prussia's wealthy landowning class. In 1862, Wilhelm chose a conservative Junker named **Otto von Bismarck** as his prime minister. Bismarck was a master of what came to be known as **realpolitik**. This German term means "the politics of reality." The term is used to describe tough power politics with no room for idealism. With realpolitik as his style, Bismarck would become one of the commanding figures of German history.

With the king's approval, Bismarck declared that he would rule without the consent of parliament and without a legal budget. Those actions were

---

BIOGRAPHY

Otto von Bismarck
(1815–1898)

To some Germans, Bismarck was the greatest and noblest of Germany's statesmen. They say he almost single-handedly unified the nation and raised it to greatness. To others, he was nothing but a devious politician who abused his powers and led Germany into dictatorship.

His speeches, letters, and memoirs show him to be both crafty and deeply religious. At one moment, he could declare, "It is the destiny of the weak to be devoured by the strong."

At another moment he might claim, "We Germans shall never wage aggressive war, ambitious war, a war of conquest."

in violation of the constitution. In his first speech as prime minister, he told members of the Prussian parliament, "It is not by means of speeches and majority resolutions that the great issues of the day will be decided—that was the great mistake of 1848 and 1849—but by blood and iron."

Prussia Expands In 1864, Bismarck took the first step toward molding an empire. Prussia and Austria formed an alliance and went to war against Denmark to win two border provinces, Schleswig and Holstein.

A quick victory increased national pride among Prussians. It also won new respect from other Germans and lent support for Prussia as head of a unified Germany. After the victory, Prussia governed Schleswig, while Austria controlled Holstein.

Seven Weeks' War Bismarck purposely stirred up border conflicts with Austria over Schleswig and Holstein. The tensions provoked Austria into declaring war on Prussia in 1866. This conflict was known as the Seven Weeks' War. The Prussians used their superior training and equipment to win a devastating victory. They humiliated Austria. The Austrians lost the region of Venetia, which was given to Italy. They had to accept Prussian annexation of more German territory.

With its victory in the Seven Weeks' War, Prussia took control of northern Germany. For the first time, the eastern and western parts of the Prussian kingdom were joined. In 1867, the remaining states of the north joined the North German Confederation, which Prussia dominated completely.

The Franco-Prussian War By 1867, a few southern German states remained independent of Prussian control. The majority of southern Germans were Catholics. Many in the region resisted domination by a Protestant Prussia. However, Bismarck felt he could win the support of southerners if they faced a threat from outside. He reasoned that a war with France would rally the south.

Bismarck was an expert at manufacturing "incidents" to gain his ends. For example, he created the impression that the French ambassador had insulted the Prussian king. The French reacted to Bismarck's deception by declaring war on Prussia on July 19, 1870.

The Prussian army immediately poured into northern France. In September 1870, the Prussian army surrounded the main French force at Sedan. Among the 83,000 French prisoners taken was Napoleon III himself. Parisians withstood a German siege until hunger forced them to surrender.

The Franco-Prussian War was the final stage in German unification. Now the nationalistic fever also seized people in southern Germany. They finally accepted Prussian leadership. On January 18, 1871, at the captured French palace of Versailles, King Wilhelm I of Prussia was crowned **kaiser** (KY•zuhr), or emperor. Germans called their empire the Second Reich. (The Holy Roman Empire was the first.) Bismarck had achieved Prussian dominance over Germany and Europe "by blood and iron."

Reading Check
Analyze Motives
Bismarck ignored both the parliament and the constitution. How do you think this action would affect Prussian government?

The Unification of Germany, 1865–1871

Explore ONLINE!

DENMARK

North Sea

Baltic Sea

SCHLESWIG

HOLSTEIN

Memel

Neman R.

OLDENBURG

Hamburg

MECKLENBURG

EAST PRUSSIA

NETHERLANDS

HANOVER

BRANDENBURG

WEST PRUSSIA

Berlin

WESTPHALIA

Elbe R.

Oder R.

Vistula R.

Warsaw

BELGIUM

Rhine R.

HESSE

SAXONY

RUSSIAN EMPIRE

Sedan

Ems

Frankfurt

Prague

SILESIA

LUX.

BOHEMIA

50° N

LORRAINE

BAVARIA

AUSTRIAN EMPIRE

FRANCE

WÜRTTEMBURG

ALSACE

HOHENZOLLERN

Munich

Danube R.

SWITZERLAND

N

W E

S

ITALY

0   100   200 mi

0   200   400 km

Legend:
- Prussia, 1865
- Annexed by Prussia, 1866
- Joined Prussia in North German Confederation, 1867
- South German States (joined Prussia to form German Empire, 1871)
- Conquered from France, 1871
- German Empire, 1871

Interpret Maps

1. **Location** What was unusual about the territory of Prussia as it existed in 1865?

2. **Movement** After 1865, what year saw the biggest expansion of Prussian territory?

A Shift in Power

The 1815 Congress of Vienna had established five Great Powers in Europe—Britain, France, Austria, Prussia, and Russia. In 1815, the Great Powers were nearly equal in strength. The wars of the mid-1800s greatly strengthened one of the Great Powers, as Prussia joined with other German states to form Germany.

By 1871, Britain and Germany were clearly the most powerful, both militarily and economically. Austria and Russia lagged far behind. France struggled along somewhere in the middle. The European balance of power had broken down. This shift also found expression in the art of the period. In fact, during that century, artists, composers, and writers pointed to paths that they believed European society should follow.

Kaiser Wilhelm I of Germany

Reading Check
Summarize How did the European balance of power change from 1815 to 1871?

Lesson 3 Assessment

1. **Organize Information** Use a timeline to identify an event that made the unification of Italy or Germany possible.

   1800   1900

2. **Key Terms and People** For each key term or person in the lesson, write a sentence explaining its significance.

3. **Synthesize** How can nationalism be both a unifying and a disunifying force?

4. **Form Generalizations** Why did the Austrian, Russian, and Ottoman Empires face such great challenges to their control of land?

5. **Evaluate** Many liberals wanted government by elected parliaments. How was Bismarck's approach to achieving his goals different?

Revolutions in the Arts

Setting the Stage

During the first half of the 1800s, artists focused on ideas of freedom, the rights of individuals, and an idealistic view of history. After the great revolutions of 1848, political focus shifted to leaders who practiced realpolitik. Similarly, intellectuals and artists expressed a "realistic" view of the world. In this view, the rich pursued their selfish interests while ordinary people struggled and suffered. Newly invented photography became both a way to detail this struggle and a tool for scientific investigation.

The Romantic Movement

At the end of the 18th century, the Enlightenment idea of reason gradually gave way to another major movement in art and ideas: **romanticism**. This movement reflected deep interest both in nature and in the thoughts and feelings of the individual. In many ways, romantic thinkers and writers reacted against the ideals of the Enlightenment. They turned from reason to emotion, from society to nature. Romantics rejected the rigidly ordered world of the middle class. Nationalism also fired the romantic imagination. For example, George Gordon, Lord Byron, one of the leading romantic poets of the time, fought for Greece's freedom.

The Ideas of Romanticism Emotion, sometimes wild emotion, was a key element of romanticism. However, romanticism went beyond feelings. Romantics expressed a wide range of ideas and attitudes. In general, romantic thinkers and artists:

The Big Idea

Artistic and intellectual movements both reflected and fueled changes in Europe during the 1800s.

Why It Matters Now

Romanticism and realism are still found in novels, dramas, and films produced today.

Key Terms and People

romanticism
realism
deism
impressionism

buildings called **factories**. Factories needed waterpower, so the first ones were built near rivers and streams:

"A great number of streams . . . furnish water-power adequate to turn many hundred mills: they afford the element of water, indispensable for scouring, bleaching, printing, dyeing, and other processes of manufacture: and when collected in their larger channels, or employed to feed canals, they supply a superior inland navigation, so important for the transit of raw materials and merchandise."

—Edward Bains, *The History of Cotton Manufacture in Great Britain* (1835)

Global Patterns

Textiles Industrialize First

The Industrial Revolution that began in Britain was spurred by a revolution in technology. It started in the textile industry, where inventions in the late 1700s transformed the manufacture of cloth. The demand for clothing in Britain had greatly increased as a result of the population boom caused by the agricultural revolution. These developments, in turn, had an impact worldwide. For example, the consumption of cotton rose dramatically in Britain (see graph). This cotton came from plantations in the American South, where cotton production skyrocketed from 1820 to 1860 in response to demand from English textile mills.

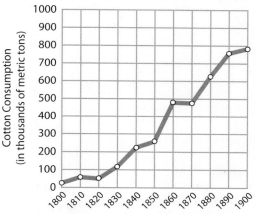

British Cotton Consumption, 1800–1900

Source: *European Historical Statistics, 1750–1975*

Flying shuttle

John Kay's flying shuttle speedily carried threads of yarn back and forth when the weaver pulled a handle on the loom. The flying shuttle greatly increased the productivity of weavers.

Critical Thinking

1. **Synthesize** How might the technological innovation and industrialization that took place in the textile industry during the Industrial Revolution have provided a model for other industries?

2. **Analyze Effects** Research the textile industry today to learn how it has been affected by new technology, including computerization. Prepare a two-paragraph summary on the effects of the new technology.

Inventions in America

In the United States, American inventors worked at making railroad travel more comfortable, inventing adjustable upholstered seats. They also revolutionized agriculture, manufacturing, and communications:

1831 Cyrus McCormick's reaper boosted American wheat production.

1837 Samuel F. B. Morse, a New England painter, first sent electrical signals over a telegraph.

1851 I. M. Singer improved the sewing machine by inventing a foot treadle (see photograph).

1876 Scottish-born inventor Alexander Graham Bell patented the telephone.

England's cotton came from plantations in the American South in the 1790s. Removing seeds from the raw cotton by hand was hard work. In 1793, an American inventor named Eli Whitney invented a machine to speed the chore. His cotton gin multiplied the amount of cotton that could be cleaned. American cotton production skyrocketed from 1.5 million pounds in 1790 to 85 million pounds in 1810.

Improvements in Transportation

Progress in the textile industry spurred other industrial improvements. New applications of steam energy would help bring about massive social, economic, and cultural change. The steam engine developed out of the search for a cheap, convenient source of power. As early as 1705, coal miners were using steam-powered pumps to remove water from deep mine shafts. But this early model of a steam engine gobbled great quantities of fuel, making it expensive to run.

Watt's Steam Engine James Watt, a mathematical instrument maker at the University of Glasgow in Scotland, thought about the problem for two years. In 1765, Watt figured out a way to make the steam engine work faster and more efficiently while burning less fuel. In 1774, Watt joined with a businessman named Matthew Boulton. Boulton was an **entrepreneur** (ahn•truh•pruh•NUR), a person who organizes, manages, and takes on the risks of a business. He paid Watt a salary and encouraged him to build better engines.

Reading Check
Summarize
What inventions transformed the textile industry?

Water Transportation Steam could also propel boats. An American inventor named Robert Fulton ordered a steam engine from Boulton and Watt. He built a steamboat called the *Clermont*, which made its first successful trip in 1807. The *Clermont* later ferried passengers up and down New York's Hudson River.

In England, water transportation improved with the creation of a network of canals, or human-made waterways. By the mid-1800s, 4,250 miles of inland channels slashed the cost of transporting both raw materials and finished goods.

Road Transportation British roads improved, too, thanks largely to the efforts of John McAdam, a Scottish engineer. Working in the early 1800s, McAdam equipped roadbeds with a layer of large stones for drainage. On top, he placed a carefully smoothed layer of crushed rock. Even in rainy weather, heavy wagons could travel over the new "macadam" roads without sinking in mud.

Private investors formed companies that built roads and then operated them for profit. People called the new roads turnpikes because travelers had to stop at tollgates (turnstiles or turnpikes) to pay tolls before traveling farther.

Reading Check
Find Main Ideas
How did steam-powered boats impact industry in England?

The Railway Age Begins

Steam-driven machinery powered English factories in the late 1700s. A steam engine on wheels—the railroad locomotive—drove English industry after 1820. It also triggered significant changes in British society and culture.

BIOGRAPHY

Henry Bessemer (1813–1898)

Henry Bessemer was a British engineer who invented a cheap way to mass-produce steel. The process he developed became known as the Bessemer Process. The process involved heating iron to a very high temperature and blowing air through it, which purified it and made it strong yet easy to pour. The resulting "mild steel" could be manipulated and worked into parts for building things usually made from heavy iron, such as ships, railroad rails, and train cars.

The Bessemer Process resulted in a massive economic change to Britain's manufacturing industries. Once steel could be mass-produced, its cost dropped. Soon steel was being used everywhere for building and construction.

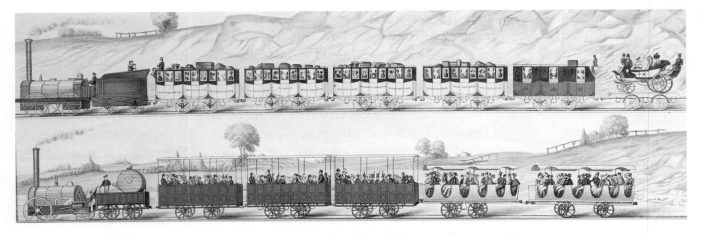

First-class passengers on the Liverpool-Manchester Railway in the 1830s rode in covered cars; all others rode in open cars.

Steam-Driven Locomotives In 1804, an English engineer named Richard Trevithick won a bet of several thousand dollars. He did this by hauling ten tons of iron over nearly ten miles of track in a steam-driven locomotive. Other British engineers soon built improved versions of Trevithick's locomotive. One of these early railroad engineers was George Stephenson. He had gained a solid reputation by building some 20 engines for mine operators in northern England. In 1821, Stephenson began work on the world's first railroad line. It was to run 27 miles from the Yorkshire coal fields to the port of Stockton on the North Sea. In 1825, the railroad opened. It used four locomotives that Stephenson had designed and built.

George Stephenson's *Rocket* powered the Liverpool-Manchester Railway. Eight of Stephenson's *Rocket* locomotives were used when the line opened in 1830.

The Liverpool-Manchester Railway News of this success quickly spread throughout Britain. The entrepreneurs of northern England wanted a railroad line to connect the port of Liverpool with the inland city of Manchester. The track was laid. In 1829, trials were held to choose the best locomotive for use on the new line. Five engines entered the competition. None could compare with the *Rocket*, designed by Stephenson and his son.

Smoke poured from the *Rocket*'s tall smokestack, and its two pistons pumped to and fro as they drove the front wheels. The locomotive hauled a 13-ton load at an unheard-of speed—more than 24 miles per hour. The Liverpool-Manchester Railway opened officially in 1830. It was an immediate success.

Railroads Revolutionize Life in Britain The invention and perfection of the steam-driven locomotive had at least four major economic—and social—effects. First, railroads spurred industrial growth by giving manufacturers a cheap way to transport materials and finished products. Second, the railroad boom created hundreds of thousands of new jobs for both railroad workers and miners. These miners provided iron for the tracks and coal for the steam engines. Third, the railroads boosted England's agricultural and fishing industries, which could transport their products to distant cities. Finally, by making travel easier, railroads encouraged country people to take distant city jobs.

Steam-powered railroads also signaled a cultural change as millions of British people (particularly members of the growing middle class) began taking train trips for leisure. By 1845, some 30 million passengers were riding Britain's railroads. Railroads lured city dwellers to resorts in the countryside. Rail excursions to the seashore were a common pleasure. Ordinary people had their horizons widened as they visited parts of the country they had never seen before. The British people were also able to see their monarch more often, as Queen Victoria made a point of traveling by train across the country. Like a locomotive racing across the country, the Industrial Revolution brought rapid changes to many aspects of people's lives.

Reading Check
Synthesize How did improvements in transportation promote industrialization in Britain?

Lesson 1 Assessment

1. **Organize Information** Create a timeline similar to the one shown and fill it in with the names and dates of nine key events or inventions from the period between 1700 and 1830. Which do you think was the most important? Explain.

   1700   1830

2. **Key Terms and People** For each key term or person in the lesson, write a sentence explaining its significance.

3. **Analyze Effects** How did rising population help the Industrial Revolution develop?

4. **Make Inferences** What effect did entrepreneurs have upon the Industrial Revolution?

5. **Develop Historical Perspective** It is the job of historians to develop theses to support or refute positions. Defend or refute this statement: "Without the steam engine, the Industrial Revolution would not have amounted to more than a pile of rickety machines." Support your position with evidence from the lesson as well as some additional research. Be sure to consider alternative explanations of why the steam engine was so significant and question its historical inevitability.

Industrialization

The Big Idea
The factory system changed the way people lived and worked, introducing a variety of problems.

Why It Matters Now
Many less developed countries are undergoing the difficult process of industrialization today.

Key Terms and People
urbanization
middle class

Setting the Stage
The Industrial Revolution affected every part of life in Great Britain, but proved to be a mixed blessing. Eventually, industrialization led to a better quality of life for most people. But the change to machine production initially caused human suffering. Rapid industrialization brought plentiful jobs, but it also caused unhealthy working conditions, air and water pollution, and the ills of child labor. It also led to rising class tensions, especially between the working class and the middle class.

Industrialization Changes Life
The pace of industrialization accelerated rapidly in Britain. By the 1800s, people could earn higher wages in factories than on farms. With this money, more people could afford to heat their homes with coal from Wales and dine on Scottish beef. They wore better clothing, too, woven on power looms in England's industrial cities. Cities swelled with waves of job seekers.

As cities grew, men, women, and children crowded into tenements and row houses such as these in London.

Industrial Cities Rise For centuries, most Europeans had lived in rural areas. After 1800, the balance shifted toward cities. This shift was caused by the growth of the factory system, where the manufacturing of goods was concentrated in a central location. Between 1800 and 1850, the number of European cities boasting more than 100,000 inhabitants rose from 22 to 47. Most of Europe's urban areas at least doubled in population; some even quadrupled. This period was one of **urbanization**—city building and the migration of people to cities.

The Day of a Child Laborer, William Cooper

Child labor was common in many industries during the Industrial Revolution. William Cooper began working in a textile factory at the age of ten. He had a sister who worked upstairs in the same factory. In 1832, Cooper was called to testify before a parliamentary committee about the conditions among child laborers in the textile industry. The following sketch of his day is based upon his testimony.

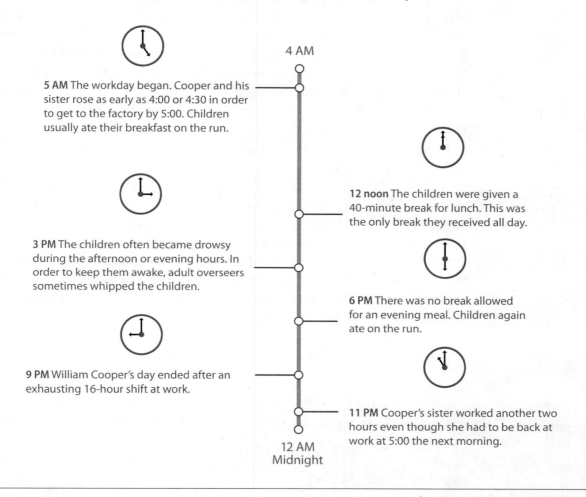

5 AM The workday began. Cooper and his sister rose as early as 4:00 or 4:30 in order to get to the factory by 5:00. Children usually ate their breakfast on the run.

3 PM The children often became drowsy during the afternoon or evening hours. In order to keep them awake, adult overseers sometimes whipped the children.

9 PM William Cooper's day ended after an exhausting 16-hour shift at work.

4 AM

12 noon The children were given a 40-minute break for lunch. This was the only break they received all day.

6 PM There was no break allowed for an evening meal. Children again ate on the run.

11 PM Cooper's sister worked another two hours even though she had to be back at work at 5:00 the next morning.

12 AM Midnight

Britain's natural resources and physical geography influenced industrialization and urbanization. For example, factories developed in clusters because entrepreneurs built them near sources of energy, such as water and coal. New uses for these forms of energy brought about massive economic change, as major new industrial centers sprang up between the coal-rich area of southern Wales and the Clyde River valley in Scotland. But the biggest of these centers developed in England.

Britain's capital, London, was the country's most important city. It had a population of about 1 million people by 1800. During the 1800s, its population exploded, providing a vast labor pool and market for new industry. London became Europe's largest city, with twice as many people as its closest rival (Paris). Newer cities challenged London's industrial leadership. Birmingham and Sheffield became iron-smelting centers. Leeds and Manchester dominated textile manufacturing. Along with the port of Liverpool, Manchester formed the center of Britain's bustling cotton industry. During the 1800s, Manchester experienced rapid growth from around 45,000 in 1760 to 300,000 by 1850.

Living Conditions Because England's cities grew rapidly, a variety of social, economic, and political problems arose. Often these problems affected many aspects of society all at once. For example, cities often had no development plans, sanitary codes, or building codes. Moreover, they lacked adequate housing, education, and police protection for the people who poured in from the countryside to seek jobs. Most of the unpaved streets had no drains, and garbage collected in heaps on them. Workers lived in dark, dirty shelters, with whole families—men, women, and children—crowding into one bedroom.

Public health became a major social, economic, and political concern as sickness was widespread. Epidemics of the deadly disease cholera regularly swept through the slums of Great Britain's industrial cities. In 1842, a British government study showed an average life span to be 17 years for working-class people in one large city, compared with 38 years in a nearby rural area. This level of poverty was clearly a social and economic issue. It was also a political problem because people expected solutions from their local authorities and agencies. But not everyone in urban areas lived miserably. Well-to-do merchants and factory owners often built luxurious homes in the suburbs.

Sheffield became a center of steel manufacturing. In fact, the Bessemer Process was used for the first time in a factory in Sheffield. The negative impact of being such a vital industrial center was terrible pollution.

Elizabeth Gaskell

Elizabeth Gaskell's *Mary Barton* (1848) is a work of fiction. But it presents a startlingly accurate portrayal of urban life experienced by many at the time. Gaskell provides a realistic description of the dank cellar dwelling of one family in a Manchester slum:

> *"You went down one step even from the foul area into the cellar in which a family of human beings lived. It was very dark inside. The window-panes many of them were broken and stuffed with rags. . . . the smell was so fetid [foul] as almost to knock the two men down. . . . they began to penetrate the thick darkness of the place, and to see three or four little children rolling on the damp, nay wet brick floor, through which the stagnant, filthy moisture of the street oozed up."*
>
> —Elizabeth Gaskell, *Mary Barton*

Elizabeth Gaskell (1810–1865) was a British writer who wrote about how ordinary people were impacted by poverty.

Analyze Historical Sources
How does Gaskell indicate her sympathy for the working class in this passage?

Working Conditions Poor living conditions were not the only social, economic, and political problems that resulted from the rise of cities during the Industrial Revolution. The conditions under which people worked presented new challenges as well.

To increase production, factory owners wanted to keep their machines running as many hours as possible. As a result, the average worker spent 14 hours a day at the job, 6 days a week. Work did not change with the seasons, as it did on the farm. Instead, work remained the same week after week, year after year.

Industry also posed new dangers for workers. Factories were seldom well lit or clean. Machines injured workers. A boiler might explode or a drive belt might catch an arm. This safety issue was also a political one, for there was no government program to provide aid in case of injury. The most dangerous conditions of all were found in coal mines. Frequent accidents, damp conditions, and the constant breathing of coal dust made the average miner's life span ten years shorter than that of other workers. Many women and children were employed in the mining industry because they were the cheapest source of labor.

Reading Check
Find Main Ideas
What is the main idea of the section titled "Working Conditions"?

Class Tensions Grow

Though poverty gripped Britain's working classes, the Industrial Revolution created enormous amounts of wealth in the nation. Most of this new money belonged to factory owners, shippers, and merchants. These people were part of a growing **middle class**, a social class made up of skilled workers, professionals, businesspeople, and wealthy farmers.

The Middle Class The new middle class transformed the social structure of Great Britain. In the past, landowners and aristocrats had occupied the top position in British society. With most of the wealth, they wielded the social and political power. Now some factory owners, merchants, and bankers grew wealthier than the landowners and aristocrats. Yet important social distinctions divided the two wealthy classes. Landowners looked down on those who had made their fortunes in the "vulgar" business world. Not until late in the 1800s were rich entrepreneurs considered the social equals of the lords of the countryside.

Gradually, a larger middle class—neither rich nor poor—emerged. The upper middle class consisted of government employees, doctors, lawyers, and managers of factories, mines, and shops. The lower middle class included factory overseers and such skilled workers as toolmakers, mechanical drafters, and printers. These people enjoyed a comfortable standard of living.

The Working Class During the years 1800 to 1850, however, laborers, or the working class, saw little improvement in their living and working conditions. They watched their livelihoods disappear as machines replaced them. Some working-class people became so frustrated that they smashed the machines they thought were putting them out of work.

One group of such workers was called the Luddites. They were named after Ned Ludd. Ludd, probably a mythical English laborer, was said to have destroyed weaving machinery around 1779. The Luddites attacked whole factories in northern England beginning in 1811, destroying laborsaving machinery. Outside the factories, mobs of workers rioted, mainly because of poor living and working conditions.

Daily Life New economic ideas were not the only effects of the Industrial Revolution and urbanization. Massive social changes occurred for men, women, and children, and each group found new roles.

The vast majority of industrial workers were men, as millions of farmers became factory workers. They developed a new work ethic that crossed over into daily life. Men were expected to be the breadwinners and the heads of their families. At the end of the workday, men found ways to socialize with one another. For example, they joined men's clubs, which were social organizations whose membership was limited to men only.

Industrialization and urbanization affected the lives of women in particular ways. Middle-class women were freed from chores because many could afford to hire domestic help. Some even began to attend college and

This image is of two British women (most likely from the middle or upper class) preparing for a game of tennis.

get jobs as teachers and nurses. Those who did work were often criticized by people who said that they should not work outside the home. Women who went to work in factories were separated from their families and earned low wages in low-skill jobs. Other working-class women found jobs as cooks, maids, and childcare workers because more families could afford to hire them. Others found some new educational and cultural opportunities in cities.

Both middle-class and working-class families became more tightly organized. Most men worked outside their homes and became the heads of their families, while women did domestic chores and raised the children. Middle-class children engaged in new leisure activities, like learning to play a musical instrument. Families joined together in various pastimes, such as reading. Wealthier families found time to attend public events, like circuses or symphony concerts.

Reading Check
Summarize
Describe the social classes in Britain.

Positive Effects of the Industrial Revolution

Despite the problems that followed industrialization, the Industrial Revolution had a number of positive effects. It created jobs for workers. It contributed to the wealth of the nation. It fostered technological progress and invention. It greatly increased the production of goods and raised the standard of living. Perhaps most important, it provided the hope of improvement in people's lives.

The Industrial Revolution produced a number of other benefits as well. These included healthier diets, better housing, and cheaper, mass-produced clothing. Because the Industrial Revolution created a demand for engineers as well as clerical and professional workers, it expanded educational opportunities.

The middle and upper classes prospered immediately from the Industrial Revolution. For the workers it took longer, but their lives gradually improved during the 1800s. Laborers eventually won higher wages, shorter hours, and better working conditions after they joined together to form labor unions.

Long-Term Effects The long-term effects of the Industrial Revolution are still evident. Most people today in industrialized countries can afford consumer goods that would have been considered luxuries 50 or 60 years ago. In addition, their living and working conditions are much improved over those of workers in the 19th century. Also, profits derived from industrialization produced tax revenues. These funds have allowed local, state, and federal governments to solve political problems by investing in urban improvements and raising the standard of living of most city dwellers.

The economic successes of the Industrial Revolution, and also the problems created by it, were clearly evident in one of Britain's new industrial cities in the 1800s—Manchester.

Reading Check
Find Main Ideas
In what way did the Industrial Revolution provide hope for people?

The Mills of Manchester

Manchester's unique advantages made it a leading example of the new industrial city. This northern English town had ready access to water-power. It also had available labor from the nearby countryside and an outlet to the sea at Liverpool.

"From this filthy sewer pure gold flows," wrote Alexis de Tocqueville (ah•lehk•SEE-duh-TOHK•vihl), the French writer, after he visited Manchester in 1835. Indeed, the industrial giant showed the best and worst of the Industrial Revolution. Manchester's rapid, unplanned growth made it an unhealthy place for the poor people who lived and worked there. But wealth flowed from its factories. It went first to the mill owners and the new middle class. Eventually, although not immediately, the working class saw their standard of living rise as well.

Manchester's business owners took pride in mastering each detail of the manufacturing process. They worked many hours and risked their own money. For their efforts, they were rewarded with high profits. Many erected gracious homes on the outskirts of town.

To provide the mill owners with high profits, workers labored under terrible conditions. Children as young as six joined their parents in the factories. There, for six days a week, they toiled from 6 a.m. to 7 or 8 p.m., with only half an hour for lunch and an hour for dinner. To keep the children awake, mill supervisors beat them. Tiny hands repaired broken threads in Manchester's spinning machines, replaced thread in the bobbins, or swept up cotton fluff. The dangerous machinery injured many children. The fluff filled their lungs and made them cough.

Until the first Factory Act passed in 1819, the British government exerted little control over child labor in Manchester and other factory cities. The act restricted working age and hours. For years after the act passed, young children still did heavy, dangerous work in Manchester's factories.

This engraving shows urban growth and industrial pollution in Manchester.

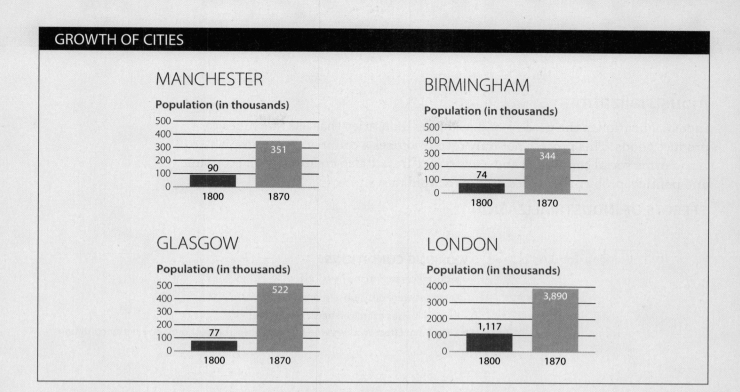

MANCHESTER
Population (in thousands)

- 90 (1800)
- 351 (1870)

BIRMINGHAM
Population (in thousands)

- 74 (1800)
- 344 (1870)

GLASGOW
Population (in thousands)

- 77 (1800)
- 522 (1870)

LONDON
Population (in thousands)

- 1,117 (1800)
- 3,890 (1870)

Interpret Graphs
How do the bar graphs help illustrate the effects of industrialization?

Putting so much industry into one place also changed the natural environment by polluting it. The coal that powered factories and warmed houses blackened the air. The iron smelting factories in one region of northwestern England emitted so much pollution that the region was nicknamed "black country." Because the iron-smelting required fires, one American visitor to the region called it "black by day and red by night." Textile dyes and other wastes poisoned Manchester's Irwell River. An eyewitness observer wrote the following description of the river in 1862:

"Steam boilers discharge into it their seething contents, and drains and sewers their fetid impurities; till at length it rolls on—here between tall dingy walls, there under precipices of red sandstone—considerably less a river than a flood of liquid manure."

— Hugh Miller, *The Old Red Sandstone*

Like other new industrial cities of the 19th century, Manchester produced consumer goods and created wealth on a grand scale. Yet it also stood as a reminder of the ills of rapid and unplanned industrialization. In the 1800s, the industrialization that began in Great Britain spread to the United States and to continental Europe.

Reading Check
Draw Conclusions
Whose interests did child labor serve?

Industrialization

Industrialization is the process of developing industries that use machines to produce goods. This process not only revolutionizes a country's economy, it also transforms social conditions and class structures. It also creates social, economic, and political problems as cities grow at a rapid rate.

EFFECTS OF INDUSTRIALIZATION

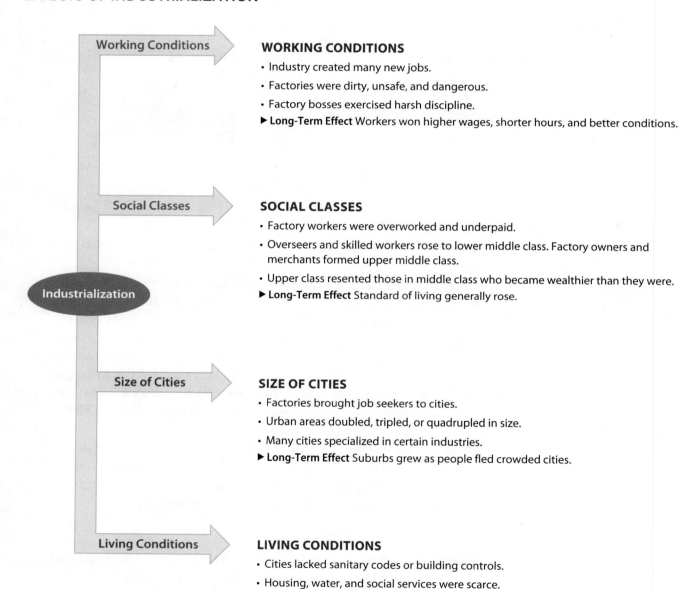

Working Conditions

WORKING CONDITIONS
- Industry created many new jobs.
- Factories were dirty, unsafe, and dangerous.
- Factory bosses exercised harsh discipline.
- ▶ **Long-Term Effect** Workers won higher wages, shorter hours, and better conditions.

Social Classes

SOCIAL CLASSES
- Factory workers were overworked and underpaid.
- Overseers and skilled workers rose to lower middle class. Factory owners and merchants formed upper middle class.
- Upper class resented those in middle class who became wealthier than they were.
- ▶ **Long-Term Effect** Standard of living generally rose.

Industrialization

Size of Cities

SIZE OF CITIES
- Factories brought job seekers to cities.
- Urban areas doubled, tripled, or quadrupled in size.
- Many cities specialized in certain industries.
- ▶ **Long-Term Effect** Suburbs grew as people fled crowded cities.

Living Conditions

LIVING CONDITIONS
- Cities lacked sanitary codes or building controls.
- Housing, water, and social services were scarce.
- Epidemics swept through the city.
- ▶ **Long-Term Effect** Housing, diet, and clothing improved.

Analyze Effects
What were some advantages and disadvantages of industrialization?

Child Labor Today

To save on labor costs, many corporations have moved their operations to developing countries, where young children work long hours under wretched conditions. In 2015, their number was estimated at 215 million children aged 5–17. They are unprotected by labor laws. For mere pennies per hour, children weave carpets, sort vegetables, or assemble expensive athletic shoes.

Several organizations are working to end child labor, including the Child Welfare League of America and the International Labor Rights Fund.

Lesson 2 Assessment

1. **Organize Information** Create an outline similar to the one shown and fill it in with facts and details from the chapter about industrialization and its effects. Add a third and fourth topic to the two that are given. Which change brought about by industrialization had the greatest impact?

   > I. Industrialization Changes Life
   >   A.
   >   B.
   > II. Class Tensions Grow

2. **Key Terms and People** For each key term or person in the lesson, write a sentence explaining its significance.

3. **Analyze Causes** Why did people flock to British cities and towns during the Industrial Revolution?

4. **Summarize** How did industrialization contribute to city growth?

5. **Evaluate** How were class tensions affected by the Industrial Revolution?

6. **Form Opinions** The Industrial Revolution has been described as a mixed blessing. Do you agree or disagree? Support your answer with text references.

Industrialization Spreads

The Big Idea

The industrialization that began in Great Britain spread to other parts of the world.

Why It Matters Now

The Industrial Revolution set the stage for the growth of modern cities and a global economy.

Key Terms and People

mass production
interchangeable parts
assembly line
division of labor
specialization
economic interdependence
stock
corporation

Setting the Stage

Great Britain's favorable geography and its financial systems, political stability, and natural resources sparked industrialization. British merchants built the world's first factories. When these factories prospered, more laborsaving machines and factories were built. Eventually, the Industrial Revolution that had begun in Britain spread both to the United States and to continental Europe. Countries that had conditions similar to those in Britain were ripe for industrialization.

Industrial Development in the United States

The United States possessed the same natural resources that allowed Britain to mechanize its industries. America's physical geography had fast-flowing rivers and rich deposits of coal and iron ore. Its resources included a supply of laborers made up of farm workers and immigrants. During the War of 1812, Britain blockaded the United States, trying to keep it from engaging in international trade. This blockade forced the young country to use its own natural resources to develop independent industries. Those industries would manufacture the goods the United States could no longer import.

Industrialization in the United States As in Britain, industrialization in the United States began in the textile industry. Eager to keep the secrets of industrialization to itself, Britain had forbidden engineers, mechanics, and toolmakers to leave the country. In 1789, however, a young British mill worker named Samuel Slater emigrated to the United States. There, Slater built a spinning machine from memory and a partial design. In 1793, he built what is known today as Slater's Mill in Pawtucket, Rhode Island. For his contribution, Slater became known as the Father of American Industry.

The following year, Moses Brown opened the first factory in the United States to house Slater's machines in Pawtucket, Rhode Island. But the Pawtucket factory mass-produced only one part of finished cloth, the thread.

In 1813, Francis Cabot Lowell of Boston and four other investors revolutionized the American textile industry. They mechanized every stage in the manufacture of cloth. Their weaving factory in Waltham, Massachusetts, earned them enough money to fund a larger operation in another Massachusetts town. Lowell took advantage of the area's physical geography and natural resources by using the power of a nearby waterfall to run his machinery. He also built his mills on a network of six miles of canals. When Lowell died, the remaining partners named the town after him. By the late 1820s, Lowell, Massachusetts, had become a booming manufacturing center and a model for other such industrial towns.

These factory towns needed people to work there, and Samuel Slater had a strategy of hiring entire families—not just able-bodied men. He also divided the factory work into simple tasks. Slater's approach, called the Rhode Island system, was emulated by mill owners throughout the Northeast. Owners advertised for "Men with growing families wanted." These advertisements impacted many families as well as individuals looking for opportunities to earn money and to learn a new skill.

Thousands of young single women flocked from their rural homes to work as mill girls in factory towns. There, they could make higher wages and have some independence. However, to ensure proper behavior, they were watched closely inside and outside the factory by their employers. The mill girls toiled more than 12 hours a day, 6 days a week, for decent wages. For some, the mill job was an alternative to being a servant and was often the only other job open to them:

"Country girls were naturally independent, and the feeling that at this new work the few hours they had of everyday leisure were entirely their own was a satisfaction to them. They preferred it to going out as 'hired help.' It was like a young man's pleasure in entering upon business for himself. Girls had never tried that experiment before, and they liked it."

—Lucy Larcom, *A New England Girlhood*

Textiles led the way, but clothing manufacture and shoemaking also underwent mechanization. Especially in the Northeast, skilled workers and farmers had formerly worked at home. Now they labored in factories in towns and cities such as Waltham, Lowell, and Lawrence, Massachusetts.

The Process of Mass Production The factory system transformed the workplace for many people. New processes changed how people worked and what they could produce.

Teenage mill girls at a Georgia cotton mill

Many changes in industry developed in the United States. One of these changes was the introduction of **mass production**—the system of manufacturing large numbers of identical items. Elements of mass production, including interchangeable parts and the assembly line, came to be known as the American system.

Interchangeable parts are identical machine-made parts. They made production and repair of factory-made goods more efficient. Before industrialization, one skilled worker might have made an entire gun, clock, or other product by himself. He or she would make or gather all the parts and assemble them. The process could be slow, and because the parts were all handmade, the finished products were often a little different from one another. With interchangeable parts, however, one worker could put together many identical products in a short time. Making repairs was easier, too, because replacement parts did not have to be custom-made to fit.

Another element of mass production related to movement within factories. In early workshops, the product stayed in one place and workers moved around it, adding parts and making refinements. The **assembly line** was an innovation that changed the way people worked in factories. In an assembly line, the product moves from worker to worker, as each person performs a step in the manufacturing process. Having different workers do different tasks is called **division of labor**. Division of labor allows workers to make many items quickly. Division of labor is a form of **specialization**. Specialization is an economic concept that refers to separating tasks. When people in a factory or company specialize, they work at one kind of job and learn to do it well.

Mass production had a great impact on industry. One big advantage was a dramatic increase in production. Businesses that made many items quickly could charge less per item. As a result, more people could afford to buy these mass-produced goods. For employees, however, mass production could lead to more repetitious jobs. At first, some workers protested, refusing to work quickly. But the changes could not be stopped, and mass production became the standard system in factories.

Another result of more efficient labor practices was an increase in **economic interdependence**. A society that is economically interdependent is one in which people rely on one another for the resources, goods, and services they need. Economic interdependence demonstrated that people did not have to make everything they needed or wanted themselves.

Economic interdependence was impacted by advances in technology, communication, and transportation. New technology helped produce goods, such as light bulbs and sewing machines, that brought more convenience to people's lives. New forms of communication and transportation helped connect places where different resources, goods, and services were available. In addition, advances in transportation allowed people and products to travel quickly from place to place.

Later Expansion of U.S. Industry The Northeast experienced much industrial growth in the early 1800s. Nonetheless, the United States remained primarily agricultural until the Civil War ended in 1865. During

The Growth of Railroads in the United States

Railroad System, 1840

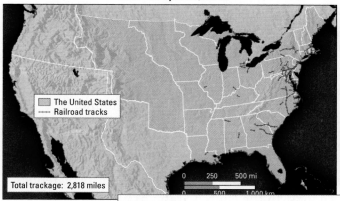

The United States
Railroad tracks

Total trackage: 2,818 miles

0   250   500 mi
0   500   1,000 km

Railroad System, 1890

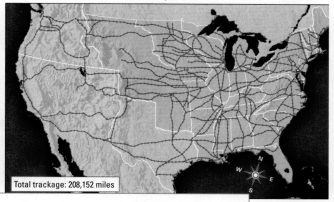

Total trackage: 208,152 miles

Interpret Maps

1. **Region** In what part of the country were the first railroads built? By 1890, what other part of the country was densely covered by railroad tracks?

2. **Movement** In what direction did the railroads help people move across the country?

the last third of the 1800s, the country experienced a technological boom. This period is sometimes referred to as the Second Industrial Revolution. As in Britain, a number of causes contributed to this boom. These included a wealth of natural resources, among them oil, coal, and iron; a burst of inventions, such as the electric light bulb and the telephone; and a swelling urban population that consumed the new manufactured goods.

An important factor that caused industrial cities to grow was immigration. The Industrial Revolution would have happened at a considerably slower rate had immigrants to the United States not provided much-needed labor. The 1880s saw the beginning of a wave of millions of immigrants coming from Europe. These new Americans were drawn by jobs in America's many factories. They had a powerful impact on American life. These immigrants, both skilled and unskilled, contributed to the nation's economic success and its cultural diversity.

Just like they did in Britain, railroads played a major role in America's industrialization. Cities like Chicago and Minneapolis expanded rapidly during the late 1800s. This was due to their location along the nation's expanding railroad lines. Chicago's stockyards and Minneapolis's grain industries prospered by selling products to the rest of the country. Indeed, the railroads themselves proved to be a profitable business. By the end of the 1800s, a limited number of large, powerful companies controlled more than two-thirds of the nation's railroads. Businesses of all kinds began to merge as the railroads had. Smaller companies joined together to form larger ones.

The Rise of Corporations Building large businesses like railroads required a great deal of money. To raise the money, entrepreneurs sold shares of **stock**, or certain rights of ownership. Thus people who bought stock became part owners of these businesses, which were called corporations. A **corporation** is a business owned by stockholders who share in its profits but are not personally responsible for its debts. Corporations are generally considered to be private economic institutions, since they are not part of the government. They are able to generate, distribute, and purchase goods and services. During the Industrial Revolution, corporations were able to raise the large amounts of capital needed to invest in industrial equipment.

In the late 1800s, large corporations such as Standard Oil (founded by John D. Rockefeller) and the Carnegie Steel Company (founded by Andrew Carnegie) sprang up. These institutions impacted a great number of individuals and groups as they sought to control every aspect of their own industries in order to make big profits. Big business—the giant corporations that controlled entire industries—also made big profits by reducing the cost of producing goods. In the United States as elsewhere, workers earned low wages for laboring long hours, while stockholders earned high profits and corporate leaders made fortunes.

Reading Check
Analyze Effects
How was economic interdependence impacted by advances in transportation?

Continental Europe Industrializes

European businesses yearned to adopt the "British miracle," the result of Britain's profitable new methods of manufacturing goods. But the troubles sparked by the French Revolution and the Napoleonic wars between 1789 and 1815 had halted trade, interrupted communication, and caused inflation in some parts of the continent. European countries watched the gap widen between themselves and Britain. Even so, industrialization eventually reached continental Europe.

Beginnings in Belgium Belgium led Europe in adopting Britain's new technology. It had rich deposits of iron ore and coal as well as fine waterways for transportation. As in the United States, British skilled workers played a key role in industrializing Belgium.

Industrialization spread to Denmark in the mid-1800s. People began to move to cities in large numbers. In 1847, the country built its first rail line. This 1885 painting by Peter Severin Kroyer shows Danish workers laboring in a steel mill.

Industrialization in Japan

With the beginning of the Meiji era in Japan in 1868, the central government began an ambitious program to transform the country into an industrialized state. It financed textile mills, coal mines, shipyards, and cement and other factories. It also asked private companies to invest in industry.

Some companies had been in business since the 1600s. But new companies sprang up too. Among them was the Mitsubishi company, founded in 1870 and still in business.

The industrializing of Japan produced sustained economic growth for the country. But it also led to strengthening the military and to Japanese imperialism in Asia.

In the years following World War II, Japan experienced an astonishing economic boom—

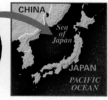

largely driven by its industrial sector. Today, Japan remains an industrial powerhouse. It manufactures automobiles, steel, and personal electronics, like smartphones. Japan is the world's third-largest economy, behind the United States and China.

Samuel Slater had smuggled the design of a spinning machine to the United States. Much like him, a Lancashire carpenter named William Cockerill illegally made his way to Belgium in 1799. He carried secret plans for building spinning machinery. His son John eventually built an enormous industrial enterprise in eastern Belgium. It produced a variety of mechanical equipment, including steam engines and railway locomotives. Carrying the latest British advances, more British workers came to work with Cockerill. Several then founded their own companies in Europe.

Germany Industrializes Germany was politically divided in the early 1800s. Economic isolation and scattered resources hampered countrywide industrialization. Instead, pockets of industrialization appeared, as in the coal-rich Ruhr Valley of west central Germany. Beginning around 1835, Germany began to copy the British model. Germany imported British equipment and engineers. German manufacturers also sent their children to England to learn industrial management.

Most important, Germany built railroads that linked its growing manufacturing cities, such as Frankfurt, with the Ruhr Valley's coal and iron ore deposits. In 1858, a German economist wrote, "Railroads and machine shops, coal mines and iron foundries, spinneries and rolling mills seem to spring up out of the ground, and smokestacks sprout from the earth like mushrooms." Germany's economic strength spurred its ability to develop as both an industrial and military power by the late 1800s.

Expansion Elsewhere in Europe In the rest of Europe, as in Germany, industrialization during the early 1800s proceeded by region rather than by country. Even in countries where agriculture dominated, pockets of industrialization arose. For example, Bohemia developed a spinning industry. Spain's Catalonia processed more cotton than Belgium. Northern Italy mechanized its textile production, specializing in silk spinning. Serf labor ran factories in regions around Moscow and St. Petersburg.

In France, sustained industrial growth occurred after 1830. French industrialization was more measured and controlled than in other countries because the agricultural economy remained strong. As a result, France avoided the great social and economic problems caused by industrialization. A thriving national market for new French products was created after 1850, when the government began railroad construction.

In Russia, nationalism played a key role in that country's move toward industrialization. At that time, Russia did not have the modern technology and industry necessary to build a military that could compete with Europe's powers. After the assassination of Czar Alexander II in 1881, his successor, Alexander III, promoted industrial expansion as a way for Russia to gain greater power in Europe.

For a variety of reasons, many European countries did not industrialize. In some nations, the social structure delayed the adoption of new methods of production. The accidents of geography held back others. In Austria-Hungary and Spain, transportation posed great obstacles. Austria-Hungary's mountains defeated railroad builders. Spain lacked both good roads and waterways for canals.

Reading Check
Analyze Causes
What factors slowed industrialization in Germany?

The Impact of Industrialization

The development of industrialization in places like Britain and the United States impacted the expanding market economy around the world. Put more succinctly, the Industrial Revolution shifted the world balance of power. It increased economic competition between industrialized nations and poverty in less-developed nations.

Rise of Global Inequality Industrialization widened the wealth gap between industrialized and nonindustrialized countries, even while it strengthened their economic ties via world markets. To keep factories running and workers fed, industrialized countries required a steady supply of raw materials from less-developed lands. In turn, industrialized countries viewed poor countries as markets for their manufactured products.

The Crystal Palace Exposition in London in 1851 celebrated the "works of industry of all nations."

Britain led in exploiting its overseas colonies for resources and markets. Soon other European countries, the United States, Russia, and Japan followed Britain's lead, seizing colonies for their economic resources. Imperialism, the policy of extending one country's rule over many other lands, gave even more power and wealth to these already wealthy nations. Imperialism was born out of the cycle of industrialization, the need for resources to supply the factories of Europe, and the development of new markets around the world.

Transformation of Society Between 1700 and 1900, revolutions in agriculture, production, transportation, and communication changed the lives of people in Western Europe and the United States. Industrialization gave Europe tremendous economic power. In contrast, the

How Technology Aided Imperialism

In this excerpt from his 1999 book *Guns, Germs, and Steel*, Jared Diamond related an incident to show how technological innovation helped Europeans conquer other lands.

As you read this secondary source, try to distinguish facts from the author's opinions. Also keep in mind that an author may have philosophical assumptions, beliefs, or biases about the subject—either implicit or explicit.

Analyze Historical Sources

1. Do you think the second sentence of the excerpt is a fact or an opinion? Explain. Would Jared Diamond be a credible authority on the relationship between technology and imperialism? Why or why not? Do you detect any philosophical assumptions, beliefs, or biases about the subject from Jared Diamond? Were they implicit or explicit? Explain your answer.

"In 1808 a British sailor named Charlie Savage equipped with muskets and excellent aim arrived in the Fiji Islands. [He] proceeded single-handedly to upset Fiji's balance of power. Among his many exploits, he paddled his canoe up a river to the Fijian village of Kasavu, halted less than a pistol shot's length from the village fence, and fired away at the undefended inhabitants. His victims were so numerous that . . . the stream beside the village was red with blood. Such examples of the power of guns against native peoples lacking guns could be multiplied indefinitely."

Reading Check
Summarize
Why did imperialism grow out of industrialization?

economies of Asia and Africa were still based on agriculture and small workshops. Industrialization revolutionized every aspect of society, from daily life to life expectancy. Despite the hardships early urban workers suffered, population, health, and wealth eventually rose dramatically in all industrialized countries. The development of a middle class created great opportunities for education and democratic participation. Greater democratic participation, in turn, fueled a powerful movement for social reform.

Lesson 3 Assessment

1. **Organize Information** Create a Venn diagram similar to the one shown, but instead of filling it with the given labels, fill it with details about how industrialization spread to the United States and continental Europe. Then, in the center, note details that they had in common. Which aspect of industrialization had the most impact in the United States? in continental Europe?

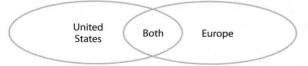

2. **Key Terms and People** For each key term or person in the lesson, write a sentence explaining its significance.

3. **Synthesize** What early industries mechanized in the United States?

4. **Analyze Effects** How did the Industrial Revolution shift the world balance of power?

5. **Make Inferences** Why was Britain unable to keep industrial secrets away from other nations?

6. **Form Opinions** What was the most significant effect of the Industrial Revolution?

Reforming the Industrial World

The Big Idea

The Industrial Revolution led to economic, social, and political reforms.

Why It Matters Now

Many modern social welfare programs developed during this period of reform.

Key Terms and People

laissez faire
Adam Smith
capitalism
utilitarianism
socialism
Karl Marx
communism
anarchism
union
strike

Setting the Stage

In industrialized countries in the 19th century, the Industrial Revolution opened a wide gap between the rich and the poor. Business leaders believed that governments should stay out of economic affairs. Reformers, however, felt that governments needed to play an active role to improve conditions for the poor. Workers also demanded more rights and protection. They formed labor unions to increase their influence.

The Philosophers of Industrialization

The term **laissez faire** (lehs•ay-FAIR) refers to the economic policy of letting owners of industry and business set working conditions without interference. This policy favors a free market unregulated by the government. The term is French for "let do," and by extension "let people do as they please."

Laissez-faire Economics French economic philosophers of the Enlightenment criticized the idea that nations grow wealthy by placing heavy tariffs on foreign goods. In fact, they argued, government regulations interfered with the production of wealth. These philosophers believed that if government allowed free trade—the flow of commerce without government regulation—the economy would prosper.

Adam Smith, a professor at the University of Glasgow, Scotland, defended the idea of a free economy, or free markets, in his 1776 book *The Wealth of Nations*. According to Smith, economic liberty guaranteed economic progress. As a result, government should not interfere. Smith's arguments rested on what he called the three natural laws of economics:

- law of self-interest—People work for their own good.
- law of competition—Competition forces people to make a better product.
- law of supply and demand—Enough goods would be produced at the lowest possible price to meet demand in a market economy.

Supply and Demand The laws of supply and demand impacted many individuals and groups during the Industrial Revolution. For example, during Britain's agricultural revolution, increased food supplies resulted in larger populations, and these people demanded more food and goods like cloth. This demand caused farmers and textile manufacturers to increase production so as to increase their supply. Another example of the impact of supply and demand occurred in America during its own Industrial Revolution. As the years progressed and manufacturing increased, there was a high demand for cheap labor. That caused groups of people to leave Europe and immigrate to America, looking for work.

The Economists of Capitalism Smith's basic ideas were supported by British economists Thomas Malthus and David Ricardo. Like Smith, they believed that natural laws governed economic life. Their important ideas were the foundation of laissez-faire capitalism. **Capitalism** is an economic system in which the factors of production are privately owned and money is invested in business ventures to make a profit. These ideas also helped bring about the Industrial Revolution.

In *An Essay on the Principle of Population*, written in 1798, Thomas Malthus argued that population tended to increase more rapidly than the food supply. Without wars and epidemics to kill off the extra people, most were destined to be poor and miserable. The predictions of Malthus seemed to be coming true in the 1840s.

David Ricardo, a wealthy stockbroker, took Malthus's theory one step further in his book, *Principles of Political Economy and Taxation* (1817). Like Malthus, Ricardo believed that a permanent underclass would always be poor. In a market system, if there are many workers and abundant resources, then labor and resources are cheap. If there are few workers and scarce resources, then they are expensive. Ricardo believed that wages would be forced down as population increased.

Laissez-faire thinkers such as Smith, Malthus, and Ricardo opposed government efforts to help poor workers. They thought that creating minimum wage laws and better working conditions would upset the free market system, lower profits, and undermine the production of wealth in society.

Reading Check
Summarize
What did Malthus and Ricardo say about the effects of population growth?

BIOGRAPHY

Adam Smith (1723–1790)

In his book *The Wealth of Nations*, Smith argued that if individuals freely followed their own self-interest, the world would be an orderly and progressive place. Social harmony would result without any government direction, "as if by an invisible hand."

Smith applied an invisible hand of his own. After his death, people discovered that he had secretly donated large sums of his income to charities.

The Rise of Socialism

Certain theorists had their own responses to both laissez-faire philosophy, which advised governments to leave business alone, and the rise of capitalism, which was emerging as the dominant economic system in the Western world. These thinkers believed that governments should intervene and that wealthy people or the government must take action to improve people's lives. The French writer Alexis de Tocqueville gave a warning:

> *"Consider what is happening among the working classes. . . . Do you not see spreading among them, little by little, opinions and ideas that aim not to overturn such and such a ministry, or such laws, or such a government, but society itself, to shake it to the foundations upon which it now rests?"*

> —Alexis de Tocqueville, 1848 speech

Utilitarianism English philosopher Jeremy Bentham modified the ideas of Adam Smith. In the late 1700s, Bentham introduced the philosophy of **utilitarianism**. Bentham wrote his most influential works in the late 1700s. According to Bentham's theory, people should judge ideas, institutions, and actions on the basis of their utility, or usefulness. He argued that the government should try to promote the greatest good for the greatest number of people. A government policy was only useful if it promoted this goal. Bentham believed that in general the individual should be free to pursue his or her own advantage without interference from the state.

John Stuart Mill, a philosopher and economist, led the utilitarian movement in the 1800s. Mill came to question unregulated capitalism. He believed it was wrong that workers should lead deprived lives that sometimes bordered on starvation. Mill wished to help ordinary working people with policies that would lead to a more equal division of profits. He also favored a cooperative system of agriculture and women's rights, including the right to vote. Mill called for the government to do away with great differences in wealth. Utilitarians also pushed for reforms in the legal and prison systems and in education.

Socialism French reformers such as Charles Fourier (FUR•ee•AY), Saint-Simon (san-see•MOHN), and others sought to offset the ill effects of industrialization with a new economic system called socialism. In **socialism**, the factors of production are owned by the public and operate for the welfare of all.

Socialism grew out of an optimistic view of human nature, a belief in progress, and a concern for social justice. Socialists argued that the government should plan the economy rather than depend on free-market capitalism to do the job. They argued that government control of factories, mines, railroads, and other key industries would end poverty and promote equality. Public ownership, they believed, would help workers, who were at the mercy of their employers. Some socialists—such as Louis Blanc—advocated change through extension of the right to vote.

Utopianism Other reformers took an even more active approach. Shocked by the misery and poverty of the working class and looking to demonstrate socialist ideas, a British factory owner named Robert Owen improved working conditions for his employees. Near his cotton mill in New Lanark, Scotland, Owen built houses, which he rented at low rates. He prohibited children under ten from working in the mills and provided free schooling.

Then, in 1824, Owen traveled to the United States. He founded a cooperative community called New Harmony in Indiana, in 1825. He intended this community to be a utopia, or perfect living place. The belief that such communities can solve society's problems is called utopianism.

New Harmony exhibited social reforms by offering such things as a kindergarten and a free library. New Harmony lasted only three years but inspired the founding of other communities. Utopianism existed in various forms in these communities. Some were religiously based, and others had a more political purpose.

The efforts of Robert Owen and other people who believed in socialism led to a movement called social democracy. Those who advocated social democracy wanted to move from capitalism to socialism by democratic means.

Reading Check
Find Main Ideas
How did Mill want to change the economic system?

Marxism: Radical Socialism

The writings of a German journalist named **Karl Marx** introduced the world to a radical type of socialism called Marxism. Marx and Friedrich Engels, a German whose father owned a textile mill in Manchester, outlined their ideas in a 23-page pamphlet called *The Communist Manifesto*.

BIOGRAPHY

Karl Marx
(1818–1883)

Karl Marx studied philosophy at the University of Berlin before he turned to journalism and economics. In 1849, Marx joined the flood of radicals who fled continental Europe for England. He had declared in *The Communist Manifesto* that "the working men have no country."

Marx's theories of socialism and the inevitable revolt of the working class made him little money. He earned a meager living as a journalist. His wealthy coauthor and fellow German, Friedrich Engels, gave Marx financial aid.

The Communist Manifesto In their manifesto, Marx and Engels argued that human societies have always been divided into warring classes. In their own time, these were the middle-class "haves" or employers, called the bourgeoisie (bur•zhwah•ZEE), and the "have-nots" or workers, called the proletariat (proh•lih•TAIR•ee•iht). While the wealthy controlled the means of producing goods, the poor performed backbreaking labor under terrible conditions. This situation resulted in conflict:

> *"Freeman and slave, patrician and plebeian, lord and serf, guild-master and journeyman, in a word, oppressor and oppressed, stood in constant opposition to one another, carried on an uninterrupted, now hidden, now open fight, a fight that each time ended, either in a revolutionary reconstitution of society at large, or in the common ruin of the contending classes."*
>
> —Karl Marx and Friedrich Engels, *The Communist Manifesto* (1848)

According to Marx and Engels, the Industrial Revolution had enriched the wealthy and impoverished the poor. The two writers predicted that the workers would overthrow the owners: "The proletarians have nothing to lose but their chains. They have a world to win. Workingmen of all countries, unite."

The Future According to Marx Marx believed that the capitalist system, which produced the Industrial Revolution, would eventually destroy itself in the following way. Factories would drive small artisans out of business, leaving a small number of manufacturers to control all the wealth. The large proletariat would revolt, seize the factories and mills from the capitalists, and produce what society needed. Workers, sharing in the profits, would bring about economic equality for all people. The workers would control the government in a "dictatorship of the proletariat." After a period of cooperative living and education, the state or government would wither away as a classless society developed.

Marx called this final phase pure communism. Marx described **communism** as a form of complete socialism in which the means of production—all land, mines, factories, railroads, and businesses—would be owned by the people. Private property would in effect cease to exist. All goods and services would be shared equally.

Published in 1848, *The Communist Manifesto* produced few short-term results. Though widespread revolts shook Europe during 1848 and 1849, Europe's leaders eventually put down the uprisings. Only after the turn of the century did the fiery Marxist pamphlet produce explosive results. In the 1900s, Marxism inspired revolutionaries such as Russia's Lenin, China's Mao Zedong, and Cuba's Fidel Castro. These leaders adapted Marx's beliefs to their own specific situations and needs.

Capitalism, Socialism, and Communism

The economic system called capitalism developed gradually over centuries, beginning in the late Middle Ages. Because of the ways industrialization changed society, some people began to think that capitalism led to certain problems, such as the abuse of workers. They responded by developing a new system of economic ideas called socialism. Communism was an even more radical form of socialism.

Capitalism	Socialism	Communism
Individuals and businesses own property and the means of production.	The public, in the form of the state, should own property and the means of production.	A community of workers controls the government, and the government controls the economy.
Progress results when individuals follow their own self-interest.	Progress results when a community of producers cooperate for the good of all.	Progress results when capitalism collapses and the people govern themselves. If capitalism is allowed to grow, eventually workers sink into poverty.
Government should not interfere in the economy because competition creates efficiency in business. Businesses follow their own self-interest by competing for the consumer's money. Each business tries to produce goods or services that are better and less expensive than those of competitors.	Socialists believe that capitalist employers take advantage of workers. The community or state must act to protect workers.	Communists seek to create a society based on cooperation and equal distribution of wealth.
Consumers compete to buy the best goods at the lowest prices. This competition shapes the market by affecting what businesses are able to sell.	Capitalism creates unequal distribution of wealth and material goods. A better system is to distribute goods according to each person's need.	A communist society is one that exists without class divisions.
Capitalism emerged in England out of the growth of that country's thriving, industrialized cloth industry.	Socialism thrived in France, where French thinkers expanded on optimistic Enlightenment ideals.	Communism first developed in Germany, where Marx and Engels criticized capitalism as it existed during the Industrial Revolution.

Interpret Charts

1. **Develop Historical Perspective** Consider the following people from 19th-century Britain: factory worker, shop owner, factory owner, unemployed artisan. Which of them would be most likely to prefer capitalism and which would prefer socialism? Why?

2. **Form Opinions** Which system of economic ideas seems most widespread today? Support your opinion.

In *The Communist Manifesto*, Marx and Engels stated their belief that economic forces alone dominated society. Time has shown, however, that religion, nationalism, ethnic loyalties, and a desire for democratic reforms may be as strong influences on history as economic forces. In addition, the gap between the rich and the poor within the industrialized countries failed to widen in the way that Marx and Engels predicted, mostly because of the various reforms enacted by governments.

Anarchism There was yet another political movement that gained traction during the Industrial Revolution, and that was anarchism. **Anarchism** argued that government actually hurt people and should be done away with entirely. Anarchists believed the people should be allowed to develop freely without any government interference whatsoever, and laws were, in and of themselves, oppressive and tyrannical.

Anarchism had a significant impact on European society in the late 19th century. There were major schools of anarchist thought in Britain, France, Russia, and Italy. An idealistic form of anarchism influenced some of the most prominent artists, writers, and thinkers of the age. However, some anarchist principles were taken too far. An alarming number of political assassinations and terrorist acts were carried out under the anarchist banner between 1890 and 1901, including the murders of King Umberto I of Italy and United States President William McKinley. These acts resulted in anarchism losing favor. In the early years of the 20th century, support for anarchism either moved into, or was destroyed by, rising communist and fascist movements.

Reading Check
Summarize
What were the ideas of Marx and Engels concerning relations between the owners and the working class?

Now and Then

Communism Today

Communism expanded to all parts of the world during the Cold War that followed the end of World War II. At the peak of Communist expansion in the 1980s, about 20 nations were Communist-controlled, including two of the world's largest—China and the Soviet Union. However, dissatisfaction with the theories of Karl Marx had been developing.

Eventually, most Communist governments were replaced. Today, there are only five Communist countries—China, North Korea, Vietnam, and Laos in Asia and Cuba in the Caribbean. Most of these nations, apart from North Korea, have largely abandoned communist economic principles.

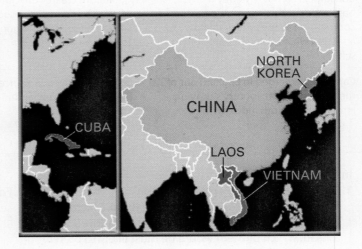

Industrialization

Industrialization raised the standard of living for many people, yet the process also brought suffering to countless workers who crowded into filthy cities to toil for starvation wages.

The following primary sources reveal multiple perspectives on this major historical movement. Interpretations of historical movements are, by their nature, tentative, limited, and diverse. They are tentative in that they change over time. They are limited and diverse in that they arise from different people's particular frames of reference.

Perspectives on history should always be interpreted based upon the historical, economic, political, social, and geographic context of the participants.

The credibility, or believability, of the participants must be considered as well. For example, you might question the credibility of someone whose writing betrays a clear political bias. On the other hand, you may be likely to trust the perspective of someone who lived during the historical period in question.

> "One great advantage which America will have in competing in the markets of the world is that her manufacturers will have the best home market. Upon this they can depend for a return upon capital, and the surplus product can be exported with advantage, even when the prices received for it do no more than cover actual cost, provided the exports be charged with their proportion of all expenses. The nation that has the best home market, especially if products are standardized, as ours are, can soon outsell the foreign producer."

> "Nobody troubles about the poor as they struggle helplessly in the whirlpool of modern industrial life. The working man may be lucky enough to find employment, if by his labor he can enrich some member of the middle classes. But his wages are so low that they hardly keep body and soul together. If he cannot find work, he can steal, unless he is afraid of the police; or he can go hungry and then the police will see to it that he will die of hunger in such a way as not to disturb the equanimity of the middle classes."

Andrew Carnegie

Andrew Carnegie was a multimillionaire industrialist who acquired his fortune in the American steel industry. In his autobiography, published in 1920, he viewed with optimism the growth of American industry.

Friedrich Engels

German-born Friedrich Engels coauthored *The Communist Manifesto* and managed a textile factory in Manchester, England. The above excerpt is from his 1844 book, *The Condition of the Working Class in England*.

Walter Crane

Walter Crane was born in Liverpool in 1845. His illustrations were often published in socialist periodicals. This political cartoon from 1886 shows the vampire bat of capitalism attacking a laborer. Socialism is pictured as an angel who is coming to the rescue.

Analyze Historical Sources
Why would Carnegie and Engels disagree about industrialization's effects? Consider their frames of reference, their own limitation s, and the different contexts in which they lived. Also, would Engels be a credible authority on the long-term effects of industrialization? Why or why not?

Labor Unions and Reform Laws

Factory workers faced long hours, dirty and dangerous working conditions, and the threat of being laid off. By the 1800s, working people became more active in politics. To press for reforms, workers joined together in voluntary labor associations called **unions**.

Unionization A union spoke for all the workers in a particular trade. Unions engaged in collective bargaining, negotiations between workers and their employers. They bargained for better working conditions and higher pay. If factory owners refused these demands, union members could **strike**, or refuse to work.

Skilled workers led the way in forming unions because their special skills gave them extra bargaining power. Management would have trouble replacing such skilled workers as carpenters, printers, and spinners. Thus, the earliest unions helped the lower middle class more than they helped the poorest workers.

The union movement underwent slow, painful growth in both Great Britain and the United States. For years, the British government denied workers the right to form unions. The government saw unions as a threat to social order and stability. Indeed, the Combination Acts of 1799 and 1800 outlawed unions and strikes. Ignoring the threat of jail or job loss, factory workers joined unions anyway. Parliament finally repealed the Combination Acts in 1824. After 1825, the British government unhappily tolerated unions.

Hungarian workers meet to plan their strategy before a strike.

British unions had shared goals of raising wages for their members and improving working conditions. By 1875, British trade unions had won the right to strike and picket peacefully. They had also built up a membership of about 1 million people.

In the United States, skilled workers had belonged to unions since the early 1800s. In 1886, several unions joined together to form the organization that would become the American Federation of Labor (AFL). A series of successful strikes won AFL members higher wages and shorter hours.

Reform Laws Eventually, reformers and unions forced political leaders to look into the abuses caused by industrialization. In both Great Britain and the United States, new laws reformed some of the worst abuses of industrialization. In the 1820s and 1830s, for example, Parliament began investigating child labor and working conditions in factories and mines. As a result of its findings, Parliament passed the Factory Act of 1833. The new law made it illegal to hire children under nine years old. Children from the ages of 9 to 12 could not work more than eight hours a day. Young people from 13 to 17 could not work more than 12 hours. In 1842, the Mines Act prevented women and children from working underground.

In 1847, the Parliament passed a bill that helped working women as well as their children. The Ten Hours Act of 1847 limited the workday to ten hours for women and children who worked in factories.

Reformers in the United States also passed laws to protect child workers. In 1904, a group of progressive reformers organized the National Child Labor Committee to end child labor. Arguing that child labor lowered wages for all workers, union members joined the reformers. Together they pressured national and state politicians to ban child labor and set maximum working hours.

In 1919, the U.S. Supreme Court objected to a federal child labor law, ruling that it interfered with states' rights to regulate labor. However, individual states were allowed to limit the working hours of women and, later, of men.

Reading Check
Summarize
What were some of the important reform bills passed in Britain during this period?

The Reform Movement Spreads

Almost from the beginning, reform movements rose in response to the negative impact of industrialization. These reforms included social reforms, such as improving the workplace, and democratic reforms, like extending the right to vote to working-class men. The same impulse toward reform, along with the ideals of the French Revolution, also helped to end slavery and promote new rights for women and children.

The Abolition of Slavery William Wilberforce, a highly religious man, was a member of Parliament who led the fight for abolition—the end of the slave trade and slavery in the British Empire. Parliament passed a bill to end the slave trade in the British West Indies in 1807. After he retired from Parliament in 1825, Wilberforce continued his fight to free the slaves. Britain finally abolished slavery in its empire in 1833.

British antislavery activists had mixed motives. Some, such as the abolitionist Wilberforce, were morally against slavery. Others viewed slave labor as an economic threat. Furthermore, a new class of industrialists developed who supported cheap labor rather than slave labor. They soon gained power in Parliament.

In the United States, the movement to fulfill the promise of the Declaration of Independence by ending slavery grew in the early 1800s. The enslavement of African people finally ended in the United States when the Union won the Civil War in 1865. Then, enslavement persisted in the Americas only in Puerto Rico, Cuba, and Brazil. In Puerto Rico, slavery was ended in 1873. Spain finally abolished slavery in its Cuban colony in 1886. Not until 1888 did Brazil's huge enslaved population win freedom.

The Fight for Women's Rights The Industrial Revolution—and its resulting urbanization—proved a mixed blessing for women. On the one hand, factory work offered higher wages than work done at home. Women spinners in Manchester, for example, earned much more money than women who stayed home to spin cotton thread. On the other hand, women factory workers usually made only one-third as much money as men did.

Women led reform movements to address this and other pressing social issues. During the mid-1800s, for example, women formed unions in the trades where they dominated. In Britain, some women served as safety inspectors in factories where other women worked. In the United States, college-educated women like Jane Addams ran settlement houses. These community centers served the poor residents of slum neighborhoods.

In both the United States and Britain, women who had rallied for the abolition of slavery began to wonder why their own rights should be denied on the basis of gender. The movement for women's rights began in the United States as early as 1848. Women activists around the world joined to found the International Council for Women in 1888. Delegates and observers from 27 countries attended the council's 1899 meeting.

Democratic Reforms in Britain As Britain's economy expanded and its cities grew, members of the British middle class expected to have more say in how their government operated. The policies of Parliament should reflect the people's interests, it was believed. Beginning in the 1830s, a series of democratic reforms expanded, or improved, voting in Britain. The 1832 Reform Bill expanded voting rights to middle-class men living in industrial towns. Another act in 1867 gave the vote to working-class men.

--- BIOGRAPHY ---

Jane Addams
(1860–1935)

After graduating from college, Jane Addams wondered what to do with her life:

"I gradually became convinced that it would be a good thing to rent a house in a part of the city where many primitive and actual needs are found, in which young women who had been given over too exclusively to study, might . . . learn of life from life itself."

Addams and her friend Ellen Starr set up Hull House in a working-class district in Chicago. Eventually the facilities included a nursery, a gym, a kitchen, and a boarding house for working women. Hull House not only served the immigrant population of the neighborhood, but it also trained social workers.

Voting by secret ballot was introduced in 1872, and a Third Reform Bill, in 1884–1885, brought agricultural workers into the democratic process. Full suffrage for men would come in 1918. However, full voting rights for British women over the age of 21 would not arrive until 1928.

Reforms Spread to Many Areas of Life In the United States and Western Europe, reformers tried to correct the problems troubling the newly industrialized nations. Public education and prison reform ranked high on the reformers' lists.

One of the most prominent U.S. reformers, Horace Mann of Massachusetts, favored free public education for all children. Mann, who spent his own childhood working at hard labor, warned, "If we do not prepare children to become good citizens . . . if we do not enrich their minds with knowledge, then our republic must go down to destruction." By the 1850s, many states were starting public school systems. In Western Europe, free public schooling became available in the late 1800s.

In 1831, French writer Alexis de Tocqueville had contrasted the brutal conditions in American prisons to the "extended liberty" of American society. Those who sought to reform prisons emphasized the goal of providing prisoners with the means to lead to useful lives upon release.

During the 1800s, democracy grew in industrialized countries even as foreign expansion increased. The industrialized democracies faced new challenges both at home and abroad.

Reading Check
Make Inferences
Why might women abolitionists have headed the movement for women's rights?

Lesson 4 Assessment

1. **Organize Information** Create a two-column graphic organizer similar to the one shown and fill it in with characteristics of capitalism and socialism. What characteristic do capitalism and socialism share?

Capitalism	Socialism
1. 2. 3.	1. 2. 3.

2. **Key Terms and People** For each key term or person in the lesson, write a sentence explaining its significance.

3. **Synthesize** What were Adam Smith's three natural laws of economics?

4. **Analyze Causes** Why did workers join together in unions?

5. **Identify Problems** What were the main problems faced by the unions during the 1800s and how did they overcome them?

6. **Make Inferences** Why did the labor reform movement spread to other areas of life?

Module 21 Assessment

Key Terms and People

For each term or name below, briefly explain its connection to the Industrial Revolution.

1. Industrial Revolution
2. enclosure
3. factory
4. urbanization
5. middle class
6. corporation
7. laissez faire
8. socialism
9. Karl Marx
10. union

Main Ideas

Use your notes and information in the module to answer the following questions.

The Beginnings of Industrialization

1. What were the four natural resources needed for British industrialization?
2. How did the enclosure movement change agriculture in England?
3. What were two important inventions created during the Industrial Revolution? Describe their impact.

Case Study: Industrialization

4. What were the living conditions like in Britain during industrialization?
5. How did the new middle class transform the social structure of Britain during industrialization?
6. How did industrialization affect Manchester's natural environment?

Industrialization Spreads

7. Why were other European countries slower to industrialize than Britain?
8. What might explain the rise of global inequality during the Industrial Revolution?

Reforming the Industrial World

9. What were the two warring classes that Marx and Engels outlined in *The Communist Manifesto*?
10. How did women fight for change during the Industrial Revolution?

Critical Thinking

1. **Synthesize** In a chart, list some of the major technological advances and their effects on society.

2. **Evaluate** How significant were the changes that the Industrial Revolution brought to the world? Explain your conclusion.

3. **Analyze Causes and Effects** How important were labor unions in increasing the power of workers? Give reasons for your opinion.

4. **Draw Conclusions** How did the Industrial Revolution help to increase Germany's military power? Support your answer with information from the module.

5. **Develop Historical Perspective** Would a non-industrialized or an industrialized nation more likely be an empire builder? Why?

6. **Synthesize** Use the Internet to find a recent news article or opinion piece about the working conditions of industrial workers today. Which primary source author does the perspective of the present-day writer support? How does the present-day writer's perspective shape your interpretation of the issue, generally?

Engage with History

Imagine that you are a 15-year-old living in Britain where the Industrial Revolution has spurred the growth of numerous factories. Would you attempt to change your working conditions in the factory? What working conditions would you change? What benefits and disadvantages might a union bring? Discuss these questions in small groups.

Focus on Writing

During and after the Industrial Revolution, capitalism emerged as the dominant economic system in the Western world. Write an **informative essay** analyzing how this occurred and how people responded to it, including such reform philosophies as utopianism, social democracy, socialism, and communism.

Multimedia Activity

Make a list of five major inventions or innovations of the Industrial Revolution. Research each to learn about the scientific, economic, and social changes that contributed to its development and the effects that it caused. Use the Internet, books, and other resources to conduct your research. Then use graphics software to create a chart, graph, or diagram depicting the relationship between the inventions and innovations, the changes, and the effects.

You may include some of the following:

- the plow
- the power loom
- the sewing machine
- the cotton gin
- the spinning jenny

Module 22

An Age of Democracy and Progress

Essential Question

How did democratic reforms, technological innovations, and scientific advancements impact Western society during the 19th century?

About the Photo: In this 1912 image, women marched down the streets of London demanding the right to vote.

 Explore ONLINE!

VIDEOS, including...
- Thomas Edison
- Independence for Texas
- Lincoln's Road Toward Emancipation
- Henry Ford and the Model T

☑ Document Based Investigations

☑ Graphic Organizers

☑ Interactive Games

☑ Carousel: Life in Early Australia

☑ Image Compare: Improving Public Health

In this module you will learn about the spread of democratic ideals and industrial and scientific progress in the 19th century.

What You Will Learn ...

Timeline of Events 1815–1915

▷ Explore ONLINE!

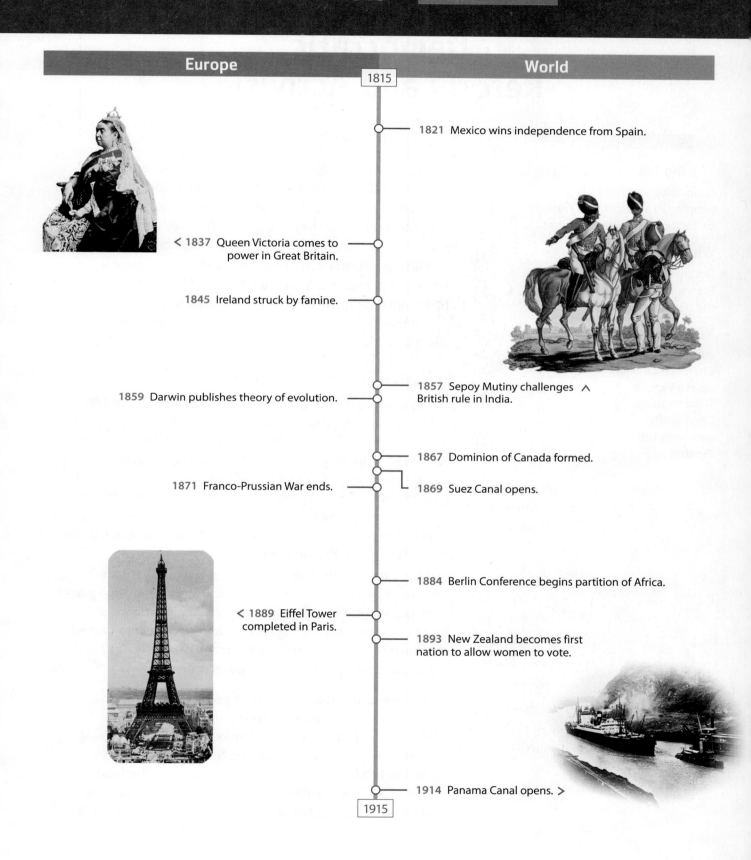

Europe

World

1815

1821 Mexico wins independence from Spain.

< 1837 Queen Victoria comes to power in Great Britain.

1845 Ireland struck by famine.

1857 Sepoy Mutiny challenges ∧ British rule in India.

1859 Darwin publishes theory of evolution.

1867 Dominion of Canada formed.

1871 Franco-Prussian War ends.

1869 Suez Canal opens.

1884 Berlin Conference begins partition of Africa.

< 1889 Eiffel Tower completed in Paris.

1893 New Zealand becomes first nation to allow women to vote.

1914 Panama Canal opens. >

1915

Democratic Reform and Activism

The Big Idea

Spurred by the demands of the people, Great Britain and France underwent democratic reforms.

Why It Matters Now

During this period, Britain and France were transformed into the democracies they are today.

Key Terms and People

suffrage
Chartist movement
Queen Victoria
Third Republic
Dreyfus affair
anti-Semitism
Zionism

Setting the Stage

Urbanization and industrialization brought sweeping changes to Western nations. People looking for solutions to the problems created by these developments began to demand reforms. They wanted to improve conditions for workers and the poor. Many people also began to call for political reforms. They demanded that more people be given a greater voice in government. Many different groups, including the middle class, workers, and women, argued that the right to vote be extended to groups that were excluded.

Britain Enacts Reforms

Britain became a constitutional monarchy in the late 1600s. Under this system, the monarch serves as the head of state, but Parliament holds the real power. The British Parliament consists of a House of Lords and a House of Commons. Traditionally, members of the House of Lords either inherited their seats or were appointed. However, this changed in 1999, when legislation was passed that abolished the right of hereditary peers to inherit their seats. Members of the House of Commons are elected by the British people.

In the early 1800s, the method of selecting the British government was not a true democracy. Only about five percent of the population had the right to elect the members of the House of Commons. Voting was limited to men who owned a substantial amount of land. Women could not vote at all. As a result, the upper classes ran the government.

The Reform Bill of 1832 The first group to demand a greater voice in politics was the wealthy, city-dwelling middle class—factory owners, bankers, and merchants—that had emerged as a result of the Industrial Revolution. Beginning in 1830, protests took place around England in favor of a bill in Parliament that would extend **suffrage**, or the right to vote. The Revolution of 1830 in France frightened parliamentary leaders. They feared that revolutionary violence would spread to Britain. Thus, Parliament passed the Reform Bill of 1832. This law expanded voting rights by easing property requirements so that well-to-do men in the middle class could vote. The Reform Bill also modernized the districts for electing members of Parliament and gave the thriving new industrial cities more representation.

Chartist Movement Although the Reform Bill expanded the number of British voters, only a small percentage of men were eligible to vote. A popular movement arose among the workers and other groups who still could not vote to press for more rights. It was called the **Chartist movement** because the group first presented its demands to Parliament in a petition called The People's Charter of 1838.

The People's Charter called for an expansion of Parliamentary government. It demanded suffrage for all men and annual Parliamentary elections. It also proposed to reform Parliament in other ways. In Britain at the time, eligible men voted openly. Since their vote was not secret, they could feel pressure to vote in a certain way. Members of Parliament had to own land and received no salary, so they needed to be wealthy. The Chartists wanted to make Parliament responsive to the lower classes. To do this, they demanded a secret ballot, an end to property requirements for serving in Parliament, and pay for members of Parliament.

Parliament rejected the Chartists' demands. However, their protests convinced many people that the workers had valid complaints. Over the years, workers continued to press for political reform, and Parliament responded. It gave the vote to working-class men in 1867 and to male rural workers in 1884. After 1884, most adult males in Britain had the right to vote. By the early 1900s, all the demands of the Chartists, except for annual elections, became law.

Expansion of Suffrage in Britain

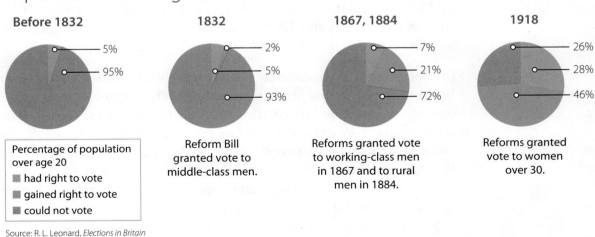

Before 1832
- 5%
- 95%

Percentage of population over age 20
- ■ had right to vote
- ■ gained right to vote
- ■ could not vote

1832
- 2%
- 5%
- 93%

Reform Bill granted vote to middle-class men.

1867, 1884
- 7%
- 21%
- 72%

Reforms granted vote to working-class men in 1867 and to rural men in 1884.

1918
- 26%
- 28%
- 46%

Reforms granted vote to women over 30.

Source: R. L. Leonard, *Elections in Britain*

Analyze Graphs
What percentage of the adults in Britain could vote in 1832? By how much did the percentage of voters increase after the reforms of 1867 and 1884?

Queen Victoria and Prince Albert

About two years after her coronation, Queen Victoria (1819–1901) fell in love with her cousin Albert (1819–1861), a German prince. She proposed to him and they were married in 1840. Together they had nine children. Prince Albert established a tone of politeness and correct behavior at court, and the royal couple presented a picture of loving family life that became a British ideal.

After Albert died in 1861, the queen wore black silk for the rest of her life in mourning. She once said of Albert, "Without him everything loses its interest."

Reading Check
Make Inferences
Why do you think the Chartists demanded a secret ballot rather than public voting?

The Victorian Age The figure who presided over all this historic change was **Queen Victoria**. Victoria came to the throne in 1837 at the age of 18. She was queen for nearly 64 years. During the Victorian Age, the British Empire reached the height of its wealth and power. Victoria was popular with her subjects, and she performed her duties capably. However, she was forced to accept a less powerful role for the monarchy.

The kings who preceded Victoria in the 1700s and 1800s had exercised great influence over Parliament. The spread of democracy in the 1800s shifted political power almost completely to Parliament, and especially to the elected House of Commons. Now the government was completely run by the prime minister and the cabinet.

Women Get the Vote

By 1890, several industrial countries had universal male suffrage (the right of all men to vote). No country, however, allowed women to vote. As more men gained suffrage, more women demanded the same.

Organization and Resistance During the 1800s, women in both Great Britain and the United States worked to gain the right to vote as the consequences of not participating in the electoral process were becoming truly apparent. Women were finding more opportunities for education and employment. For example, by 1870, about 20 percent of all college students in America were women. By 1900 that number had increased to more than one-third. With greater opportunities came a desire for greater involvement in the life of the community.

British women organized reform societies and protested unfair laws and customs. As women became more vocal, however, resistance to their demands grew. Many people, both men and women, thought that woman suffrage was too radical a break with tradition. Some claimed that women lacked the ability to take part in politics.

Militant Protests After decades of peaceful efforts to win the right to vote, some women took more drastic steps. In Britain, Emmeline Pankhurst formed the Women's Social and Political Union (WSPU) in 1903. The WSPU became the most militant organization for women's rights. Its goal was to draw attention to the cause of woman suffrage. When asked about why her group chose militant means to gain women's rights, Pankhurst replied:

"I want to say here and now that the only justification for violence, the only justification for damage to property, the only justification for risk to the comfort of other human beings is the fact that you have tried all other available means and have failed to secure justice."

—Emmeline Pankhurst, *Why We Are Militant*

Emmeline Pankhurst, her daughters Christabel and Sylvia, and other WSPU members were arrested and imprisoned many times. When they were jailed, the Pankhursts led hunger strikes to keep their cause in the public eye. British officials force-fed Sylvia and other activists to keep them alive.

Though the woman suffrage movement gained attention between 1880 and 1914, its successes were gradual. Women did not gain the right to vote in national elections in Great Britain until after World War I. In 1918, Parliament passed an act that allowed women older than 30 to vote. Another act, in 1928, extended voting rights to women over the age of 21.

Women's Suffrage in America The struggle for women's suffrage in the United States can be traced to the beginning of the 19th century. The movement really took hold, however, in the years following the American Civil War as suffragists, who had supported the abolition of slavery, called for granting women the vote as well as newly freed African American men.

In 1869, two pro-suffrage organizations were formed: the National Woman Suffrage Association (NWSA) and the American Woman Suffrage Association (AWSA). The groups had different approaches. NWSA campaigned for a constitutional amendment to give women the right to vote.

Global Patterns

The Women's Movement

By the 1880s, women were working internationally to win more rights. In 1888, women activists from the United States, Canada, and Europe met in Washington, D.C., for the International Council of Women. In 1893, delegates and observers from many countries attended a large congress of women in Chicago. They came from lands as far apart as New Zealand, Argentina, Iceland, Persia, and China.

The first countries to grant suffrage to women were New Zealand (1893) and Australia (1902). Only in two European countries—Finland (1906, then part of the Russian Empire) and Norway (1913)—did women gain voting rights before World War I. In the United States, the territory of Wyoming allowed women to vote in 1869. Several other Western states followed suit.

The AWSA focused on winning the right to vote on a state-by-state basis. In 1890, the two groups merged, forming the National American Woman Suffrage Association (NAWSA).

In the early part of the 20th century, the movement took some dramatic turns, highlighted by a split in the ranks of suffrage supporters over the best way to win the vote. Some leaders of the NAWSA, frustrated by its state-by-state approach, broke away and formed the Congressional Union for Woman Suffrage. Renamed the National Women's Party (NWP) in 1916, the group focused on passage of a federal constitutional amendment for women's suffrage.

The group learned new tactics from the British suffrage movement. Members of the NWP picketed the White House in January 1917, chaining themselves to the railings. Many were arrested. Some went on hunger strikes in prison. The dramatic efforts of the NWP protesters brought renewed attention to the suffrage cause.

Eventually, the work of suffragists convinced members of the United States Congress to support a constitutional amendment. Even the president at the time, Woodrow Wilson, lent his support. Proposed by Congress in 1919 and ratified in 1920, the Nineteenth Amendment finally gave American women over the age of 21 full voting rights. The presidential election of 1920 was the first in which women could vote in every state. The consequence of their participation was to help elect Ohio Senator Warren G. Harding as president.

Reading Check

Compare and Contrast How were the struggles for women's suffrage in Britain and America similar and different? Was the use of militant action effective in achieving the goal of woman suffrage? Explain.

France and Democracy

While Great Britain moved toward greater democracy in the late 1800s, democracy finally took hold in France.

The Third Republic In the aftermath of the Franco-Prussian War, France went through a series of crises. Between 1871 and 1914, France averaged a change of government almost yearly. A dozen political parties competed for power. Not until 1875 could the National Assembly agree on a new government. Eventually, the members voted to set up a republic. The **Third Republic** lasted over 60 years. However, France remained divided.

The Dreyfus Affair During the 1880s and 1890s, the Third Republic was threatened by monarchists, aristocrats, clergy, and army leaders. These groups wanted a monarchy or military rule. A controversy known as the **Dreyfus affair** became a battleground for these opposing forces. Widespread feelings of **anti-Semitism**, or prejudice against Jews, also played a role in this scandal.

In 1894, Captain Alfred Dreyfus, one of the few Jewish officers in the French army, was accused of selling military secrets to Germany. A court found him guilty, based on false evidence, and sentenced him to life in prison. In a few years, new evidence showed that Dreyfus had been framed by other army officers.

This engraving from an 1898 French magazine shows Émile Zola being surrounded by an anti-Semitic mob.

Public opinion was sharply divided over the scandal. Many army leaders, nationalists, leaders in the clergy, and anti-Jewish groups refused to let the case be reopened. They feared sudden action would cast doubt on the honor of the army. Dreyfus's defenders insisted that justice was more important. In 1898, the writer Émile Zola published an open letter titled *J'accuse!* (I accuse) in a popular French newspaper. In the letter, Zola denounced the army for covering up a scandal. Zola was sentenced to a year in prison for his views, but his letter gave strength to Dreyfus's cause. Eventually, the French government declared his innocence.

The Rise of Zionism The Dreyfus case showed the strength of anti-Semitism in France and other parts of Western Europe. However, persecution of Jews was even more severe in Eastern Europe. Russian officials permitted pogroms (puh•GRAHMS), organized campaigns of violence against Jews. From the late 1880s on, thousands of Jews fled Eastern Europe. Many headed for the United States.

For many Jews, the long history of exile and persecution convinced them to work to reestablish their ancient homeland. In the 1890s, a movement known as **Zionism** developed to pursue this goal. Its leader was Theodor Herzl (HEHRT•suhl), a writer in Vienna. It took many years, however, before the State of Israel was established.

Reading Check
Analyze Effects
What were two major effects of the Dreyfus affair?

Lesson 1 Assessment

1. **Organize Information** Create a two-column graphic organizer similar to the one shown and fill it in as you evaluate the ways in which the following events expanded democracy: Britain gradually extends suffrage to most adult males; women in many countries demand the right to vote. Which event was the greatest expansion of democracy?

Event	Evaluation

2. **Key Terms and People** For each key term or person in the lesson, write a sentence explaining its significance.
3. **Analyze Effects** What were some effects of the Reform Bill of 1832?
4. **Summarize** What was the goal of the WSPU in Britain?
5. **Compare** Why was the road to democracy more difficult for France than for England?
6. **Analyze Effects** What was the connection between anti-Semitism and Zionism?

Self-Rule for British Colonies

The Big Idea

Britain allowed self-rule in Canada, Australia, and New Zealand but delayed it for Ireland.

Why It Matters Now

Canada, Australia, and New Zealand are strong democracies today, while Ireland is divided.

Key Terms and People

dominion
Maori
Aborigine
penal colony
home rule
Irish Republican Army

Setting the Stage

By 1800, Great Britain had colonies around the world. These included outposts in Africa and Asia. In these areas, the British managed trade with the local peoples, but they had little influence over the population at large. In the colonies of Canada, Australia, and New Zealand, on the other hand, European colonists dominated the native populations. As Britain industrialized and prospered in the 1800s, so did these colonies. Some were becoming strong enough to stand on their own.

Canada Struggles for Self-Rule

Canada was originally home to many Native American peoples. The first European country to colonize Canada was France. The earliest French colonists, in the 1600s and 1700s, had included many fur trappers and missionaries. They tended to live among the Native Americans. Some French intermarried with Native Americans.

Great Britain took possession of the country in 1763 after it defeated France in the French and Indian War. The French who remained lived mostly in the lower St. Lawrence Valley. Many English-speaking colonists arrived in Canada after it came under British rule. Some came from Great Britain, and others were Americans who had stayed loyal to Britain after the American Revolution. They settled separately from the French along the Atlantic seaboard and the Great Lakes.

French and English Canada Religious and cultural differences between the mostly Roman Catholic French and the mainly Protestant English-speaking colonists caused conflict in Canada. Both groups pressed Britain for a greater voice in governing their own affairs. In 1791 the British Parliament tried to resolve both issues by creating two new Canadian provinces. Upper Canada (now Ontario) had an English-speaking majority. Lower Canada (now Quebec) had a French-speaking majority. Each province had its own elected assembly.

The Durham Report The division of Upper and Lower Canada temporarily eased tensions. In both colonies, the royal governor and a small group of wealthy British held most of the power. But during the early 1800s, middle-class professionals in both colonies began to demand political and economic reforms. In Lower Canada, these demands were also fueled by French resentment toward British rule. In the late 1830s, rebellions broke out in both Upper and Lower Canada. The British Parliament sent a reform-minded statesman, Lord Durham, to investigate.

In 1839, Durham sent a report to Parliament that urged two major reforms. First, Upper and Lower Canada should be reunited as the Province of Canada, and British immigration should be encouraged. In this way, the French would slowly become part of the dominant English culture. Second, colonists in the provinces of Canada should be allowed to govern themselves in domestic matters.

The Dominion of Canada By the mid-1800s, many Canadians believed that Canada needed a central government. A central government would be better able to protect the interests of Canadians against the United States, whose territory now extended from the Atlantic to the Pacific oceans. In 1867, Nova Scotia and New Brunswick joined the Province of Canada to form the Dominion of Canada. As a **dominion**, Canada was self-governing in domestic affairs but remained part of the British Empire.

Canada's Westward Expansion Canada's first prime minister, John MacDonald, expanded Canada westward by purchasing lands and persuading frontier territories to join the union. Canada stretched to the Pacific Ocean by 1871. MacDonald began the construction of a transcontinental railroad, completed in 1885.

Reading Check
Analyze Effects
How do you think Durham's report affected French-speaking Canadians?

History in Depth

Acadians to Cajuns

Colonists from France founded the colony of Acadia on the eastern coast of what is now Canada in 1604. Tensions flared between these settlers and later arrivals from England and Scotland.

In 1713, the British gained control of Acadia and renamed it Nova Scotia (New Scotland). They expelled thousands of descendants of the original Acadians. Many eventually settled in southern Louisiana. Today, their culture still thrives in the Mississippi Delta area, where the people are called Cajuns (an alteration of Acadian).

Explore ONLINE!

CANADA   Acadia

0   250   500 mi
0   500   1,000 km

Australia and New Zealand

The British sea captain James Cook claimed New Zealand in 1769 and part of Australia in 1770 for Great Britain. Both lands were already inhabited. In New Zealand, Cook was greeted by the **Maori**, a Polynesian people who had settled in New Zealand around AD 800. Maori culture was based on farming, hunting, and fishing.

When Cook reached Australia, he considered the land uninhabited. In fact, Australia was sparsely populated by **Aborigines**, as Europeans later called the native peoples. Aborigines are the longest ongoing culture in the world. These nomadic peoples fished, hunted, and gathered food.

Britain's Penal Colony Britain began colonizing Australia in 1788 with convicted criminals. The prisons in England were severely overcrowded. To solve this problem, the British government established a penal colony in Australia. A **penal colony** was a place where convicts were sent to serve their sentences. Many European nations used penal colonies as a way to prevent overcrowding of prisons. After their release, the newly freed prisoners could buy land and settle.

Free Settlers Arrive Free British settlers eventually joined the former convicts in both Australia and New Zealand. In the early 1800s, an Australian settler experimented with breeds of sheep until he found one that produced high quality wool and thrived in the country's warm, dry weather. Although sheep are not native to Australia, the raising and exporting of wool became its biggest business.

To encourage immigration, the government offered settlers cheap land. The population grew steadily in the early 1800s and then skyrocketed after a gold rush in 1851. The scattered settlements on Australia's east coast grew into separate colonies. Meanwhile, a few pioneers pushed westward across the vast dry interior and established outposts in western Australia.

Settling New Zealand European settlement of New Zealand grew more slowly. This was because Britain did not claim ownership of New Zealand, as it did Australia. Rather, it recognized the land rights of the Maori. In 1814, missionary groups began arriving from Australia seeking to convert the Maori to Christianity.

The arrival of more foreigners stirred conflicts between the Maori and the European settlers over land. Responding to the settlers' pleas, the British decided to annex New Zealand in 1839 and appointed a governor to negotiate with the Maori. In a treaty signed in 1840, the Maori accepted British rule in exchange for recognition of their land rights.

Self-Government Like Canadians, the colonists of Australia and New Zealand wanted to rule themselves yet remain in the British Empire. During the 1850s, the colonies in both Australia and New Zealand became self-governing and created parliamentary forms of government. In 1901, the Australian colonies were united under a federal constitution as the Commonwealth of Australia. During the early 1900s, both Australia and New Zealand became dominions.

Australia and New Zealand to 1850

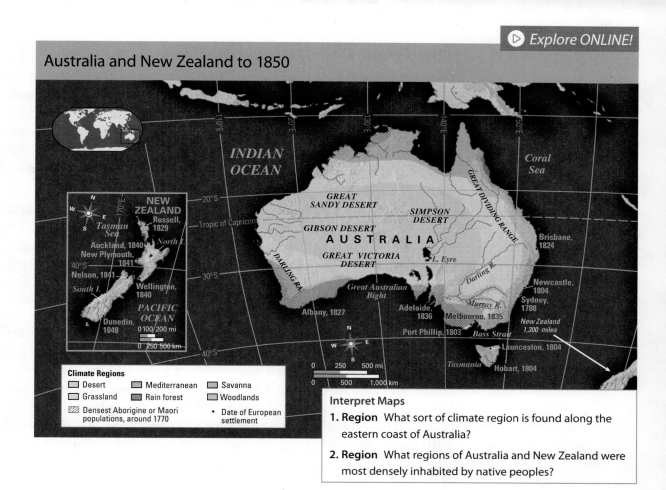

INDIAN OCEAN

NEW ZEALAND

Tasman Sea

Russell, 1829

Auckland, 1840
New Plymouth, 1841
Nelson, 1841
Wellington, 1840

North I.

South I.

PACIFIC OCEAN

Dunedin, 1848

0 100 200 mi

0 250 500 km

Tropic of Capricorn

GREAT SANDY DESERT

GIBSON DESERT

SIMPSON DESERT

AUSTRALIA

GREAT VICTORIA DESERT

DARLING RA.

L. Eyre

Great Australian Bight

Albany, 1827

Adelaide, 1836

Darling R.

Murray R.

Melbourne, 1835

Port Phillip, 1803

Bass Strait

Tasmania

Hobart, 1804

GREAT DIVIDING RANGE

Coral Sea

Brisbane, 1824

Newcastle, 1804
Sydney, 1788

New Zealand 1,300 miles

Launceston, 1804

0 250 500 mi

0 500 1,000 km

Climate Regions
- ☐ Desert
- ☐ Grassland
- ▨ Densest Aborigine or Maori populations, around 1770
- ☐ Mediterranean
- ☐ Rain forest
- • Date of European settlement
- ☐ Savanna
- ☐ Woodlands

Interpret Maps

1. **Region** What sort of climate region is found along the eastern coast of Australia?

2. **Region** What regions of Australia and New Zealand were most densely inhabited by native peoples?

The people of Australia and New Zealand pioneered a number of political reforms. For example, the secret ballot, sometimes called the Australian ballot, was first used in Australia in the 1850s. In 1893, New Zealand became the first nation in the world to give full voting rights to women. However, only white women gained these rights.

Status of Native Peoples

Native peoples and other non-Europeans were excluded from democracy and prosperity. Diseases brought by the Europeans killed Aborigines and Maori. As Australian settlement grew, the colonists displaced or killed many Aborigines.

In New Zealand, tensions between settlers and Maori continued to grow after it became a British colony. Between 1845 and 1872, the colonial government fought the Maori in a series of wars. Reduced by disease and outgunned by British weapons, the Maori were finally driven into a remote part of the country.

Reading Check
Contrast
How did the colonial settlement of Australia and New Zealand differ?

This photograph shows a Maori warrior with traditional dress and face markings.

The Irish Win Home Rule

English expansion into Ireland had begun in the 1100s, when the pope granted control of Ireland to the English king. English knights invaded Ireland, and many settled there to form a new aristocracy. The Irish, who had their own ancestry, culture, and language, bitterly resented the English presence. Laws imposed by the English in the 1500s and 1600s limited the rights of Catholics and favored the Protestant religion and the English language.

Over the years, the British government was determined to maintain its control over Ireland. It formally joined Ireland to Britain in 1801. Though a setback for Irish nationalism, this move gave Ireland representation in the British Parliament. Irish leader Daniel O'Connell persuaded Parliament to pass the Catholic Emancipation Act in 1829. This law restored many rights to Catholics.

The Great Famine In the 1840s, Ireland experienced one of the worst famines of modern history. For many years, Irish peasants had depended on potatoes as virtually their sole source of food. During the early years of Britain's agricultural revolution, better varieties of food crops, including potatoes, were developed. From 1845 to 1848, a plant fungus ruined nearly all of Ireland's potato crop. Out of a population of 8 million, about a million people died from starvation and disease over the next few years.

A traveler described what he saw on a journey through Ireland in 1847:

> "We entered a cabin. Stretched in one dark corner, scarcely visible, from the smoke and rags that covered them, were three children huddled together, lying there because they were too weak to rise, pale and ghastly, their little limbs—on removing a portion of the filthy covering—perfectly emaciated, eyes sunk, voice gone, and evidently in the last stage of actual starvation."
>
> —William Bennett, quoted in *Narrative of a Recent Journey of Six Weeks in Ireland*

During the famine years, about a million and a half people fled from Ireland. The famine is considered to be the primary reason for the enormous wave of Irish immigration to the United States that occurred during the 1840s. Between 1820 and 1860, over one-third of all U.S. immigrants were Irish, and in the 1840s, the Irish made up almost half of all U.S. immigrants.

A vast majority of these Irish immigrants lived in extremely impoverished neighborhoods in Northeastern cities like New York City. Irish men, many of whom were unskilled, entered the U.S. workforce at the lowest levels. They worked menial factory jobs for low wages. Irish women worked as domestic workers and servants. Nevertheless, Irish immigrants played a crucial role during the Industrial Revolution, working in coal mines and on railroads.

The Great Famine, 1845–1851

Analyze Historical Sources
What was the effect of the Great Famine on the population of Ireland? What was its effect on the development of other societies around the world?

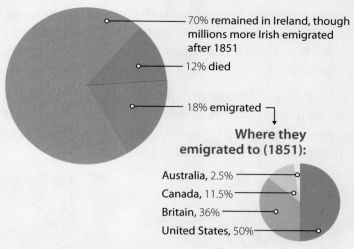

Fate of the Irish during the famine:

70% remained in Ireland, though millions more Irish emigrated after 1851

12% died

18% emigrated

Where they emigrated to (1851):

Australia, 2.5%
Canada, 11.5%
Britain, 36%
United States, 50%

Sources: R. F. Foster, *Modern Ireland, 1600–1972;* D. Fitzpatrick, *Irish Emigration, 1804–1921*

Other Irish immigrants went to Britain, Canada, and Australia. At home, in Ireland, the British government enforced the demands of the English landowners that the Irish peasants pay their rent. Many Irish lost their land and fell hopelessly in debt, while large landowners profited from higher food prices.

Demands for Home Rule During the second half of the 1800s, opposition to British rule over Ireland took two forms. Some Irish wanted independence for Ireland. A greater number of Irish preferred **home rule**, local control over internal matters only. The British, fearful of Irish moves toward independence, refused to consider either option.

One reason for Britain's opposition to home rule was concern for Ireland's Protestants. They feared being a minority in a country dominated by Catholics. Most Protestants lived in the northern part of Ireland, known as Ulster. Finally, in 1914, Parliament enacted a home rule bill for southern Ireland. Just one month before the plan was to take effect, World War I broke out in Europe. Irish home rule was put on hold.

Rebellion and Division Frustrated over the delay in gaining independence, a small group of Irish nationalists rebelled in Dublin during Easter week, 1916. British troops put down the Easter Rising and executed its leaders. Their fate, however, aroused wider popular support for the nationalist movement.

Life in Early Australia

European explorers located Australia long after they had begun colonizing other lands. Dutch explorers were probably the first Europeans to reach Australia around 1605. Australia was not claimed by a European power, however, until the British did so in 1770.

Early Australia had many groups of people with diverse interests, including a native population that had lived on the island for at least 40,000 years. On these pages you will discover the occupations, motivations, and interests of some Australians in the 17th and 18th centuries.

◀ ORIGINAL AUSTRALIANS
Aboriginal society and culture developed in close harmony with nature. There were between 200 and 300 Aboriginal languages, and most people were bilingual or multilingual. By 1900, half of Australia's original inhabitants had died fighting the British or from disease. The engraving depicts an Aboriginal man with ceremonial face paint and scars. The other image is an ancient Aboriginal rock painting.

CONVICTS ▶
Beginning in 1788, England sent both male and female prisoners to Australia—sometimes with their children. Convicts built public buildings, roads, and bridges. England stopped sending convicts to Australia in 1868. The prison ship shown here housed prisoners before they went to Australia.

◄ **FARMERS AND RANCHERS**
Free settlers made the journey to Australia willingly. Many went into farming and ranching. Farms provided much-needed food, and sheep ranching provided wool as a valuable export. Convicts were hired out to farmers and ranchers as cheap labor. Sheep ranching, shown in the picture, remains an important part of Australia's economy.

Critical Thinking
1. **Form Opinions** Of the groups represented on these pages, which do you believe had the highest quality of living? Why?
2. **Compare and Contrast** Use the Internet to research the issues that Australian Aborigines and Native Americans in the United States face today and compare them. How are they similar? How are they different?

GOLD MINERS ▼
In 1851, lured by the potential of striking it rich, thousands of people began prospecting for gold in Australia. Sometimes whole families moved to the gold fields, but life in the gold camps was hard and very few people struck it rich. Searching for gold was hard and dirty work, as this painting illustrates.

Northern Ireland Today

When Northern Ireland decided to stay united with Great Britain, many Catholics there refused to accept the partition, or division. In the late 1960s, Catholic groups began to demonstrate for more civil rights.

Their protests touched off fighting between Catholics and Protestants. Militant groups on both sides engaged in terrorism. This violent period, called the "troubles," continued into the 1990s.

In 1999, with a peace accord, Catholics and Protestants began sharing power in a new home-rule government. In May 2007, home rule returned under a new power-sharing government.

After World War I, the Irish nationalists won a victory in the elections for the British Parliament. To protest delays in home rule, the nationalist members decided not to attend Parliament. Instead, they formed an underground Irish government and declared themselves independent. The **Irish Republican Army** (IRA), an unofficial military force seeking independence for Ireland, staged a series of attacks against British officials in Ireland. The attacks sparked war between the nationalists and the British government.

In 1921, Britain divided Ireland and granted home rule to southern Ireland. Ulster, or Northern Ireland, remained a part of Great Britain. The south became a dominion called the Irish Free State. However, many Irish nationalists, led by Eamon De Valera, continued to seek total independence from Britain. In 1949, the Irish Free State declared itself the independent Republic of Ireland.

Reading Check
Draw Conclusions
Was Britain's policy in dividing Ireland successful? Why or why not?

Lesson 2 Assessment

1. **Organize Information** Create a two-column graphic organizer similar to the one shown and fill it in with key political events for each country that you read about in this module. In what ways was Ireland different from the other three colonies?

Country	Political Events
Canada	
Australia	
New Zealand	
Ireland	

2. **Key Terms and People** For each key term or person in the lesson, write a sentence explaining its significance.

3. **Form Generalizations** What was unusual about the first European settlers in Australia?

4. **Compare** How was Britain's policy toward Canada beginning in the late 1700s similar to its policy toward Ireland in the 1900s?

5. **Draw Conclusions** What impact did the Great Famine have on the population of Ireland?

6. **Synthesize** Why did Britain create Upper Canada and Lower Canada, and who lived in each colony?

War and Expansion in the United States

Setting the Stage

The United States won its independence from Britain in 1783. At the end of the Revolutionary War, the Mississippi River marked the western boundary of the new republic. As the original United States filled with settlers, land-hungry newcomers pushed beyond the Mississippi. The government helped them by acquiring new territory for settlement. Meanwhile, tensions between northern and southern states over the issues of states' rights and slavery continued to grow and threatened to reach a boiling point.

Americans Move West

In 1803, President Thomas Jefferson bought the Louisiana Territory from France. The Louisiana Purchase doubled the size of the new republic and extended its boundary to the Rocky Mountains. In 1819, Spain gave up Florida to the United States. In 1846, a treaty with Great Britain gave the United States part of the Oregon Territory. The nation now stretched from the Atlantic to the Pacific oceans.

Manifest Destiny Many Americans believed in **manifest destiny**, the idea that the United States had the right and duty to rule North America from the Atlantic Ocean to the Pacific Ocean. Government leaders used manifest destiny to justify evicting Native Americans from their tribal lands.

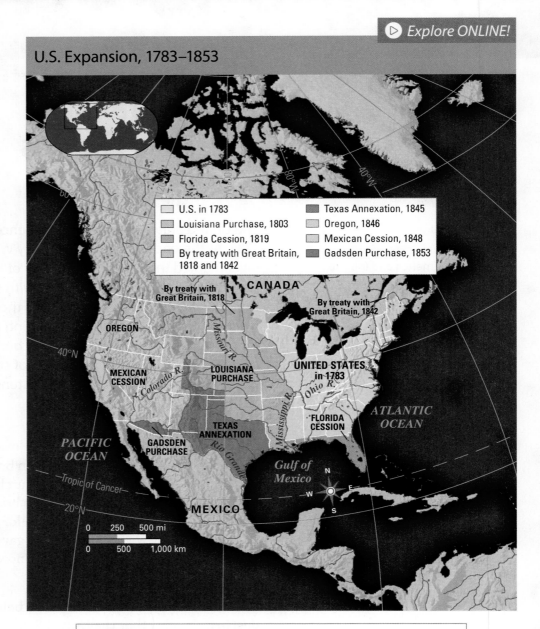

U.S. Expansion, 1783–1853

U.S. in 1783
Louisiana Purchase, 1803
Florida Cession, 1819
By treaty with Great Britain, 1818 and 1842
Texas Annexation, 1845
Oregon, 1846
Mexican Cession, 1848
Gadsden Purchase, 1853

By treaty with Great Britain, 1818

By treaty with Great Britain, 1842

CANADA

OREGON

MEXICAN CESSION

LOUISIANA PURCHASE

UNITED STATES in 1783

Missouri R.

Colorado R.

Ohio R.

Mississippi R.

ATLANTIC OCEAN

TEXAS ANNEXATION

FLORIDA CESSION

PACIFIC OCEAN

GADSDEN PURCHASE

Rio Grande

Gulf of Mexico

40°N

Tropic of Cancer

20°N

MEXICO

0   250   500 mi
0   500   1,000 km

Interpret Maps

1. **Movement** What was the first territory to be added to the United States after 1783?

2. **Region** What present-day states were part of the Mexican Cession?

The Indian Removal Act of 1830 made such actions official policy. This law enabled the federal government to force Native Americans living in the East to move to the West. Georgia's Cherokee tribe challenged the law before the Supreme Court. The Court, however, ruled that the suit was not valid. The Cherokees had to move. Most of them traveled 800 miles to Oklahoma, mainly on foot, on a journey later called the Trail of Tears. About a quarter of the Cherokees died on the trip. A survivor recalled how the journey began:

"The day was bright and beautiful, but a gloomy thoughtfulness was depicted in the lineaments of every face . . . . At this very moment a low sound of distant thunder fell on my ear . . . and sent forth a murmur, I almost thought a voice of divine indignation for the wrong of my poor and unhappy countrymen, driven by brutal power from all they loved and cherished in the land of their fathers."

—William Shorey Coodey, quoted in *The Trail of Tears*

When the Cherokees reached their destination, they ended up on land inferior to that which they had left. As white settlers moved west during the 19th century, the government continued to push Native Americans off their land.

Texas Joins the United States When Mexico had gained its independence from Spain in 1821, its territory included the lands west of the Louisiana Purchase. With Mexico's permission, American settlers moved into the Mexican territory of Texas. However, settlers were unhappy with Mexico's rule.

In 1836, Texans revolted against Mexican rule and won their independence. Then, in 1845, the United States annexed Texas. Since Mexico still claimed Texas, it viewed this annexation as an act of war.

War with Mexico Between May 1846 and February 1848, war raged between the two countries. Finally, Mexico surrendered. As part of the settlement of the Mexican-American War, Mexico ceded territory to the United States. The Mexican Cession included California and a huge area in the Southwest. In 1853, the Gadsden Purchase from Mexico brought the lower continental United States to its present boundaries.

Reading Check
Summarize
What territories did the United States acquire between 1803 and 1850?

Civil War Tests Democracy

America's westward expansion raised questions about what laws and customs should be followed in the West. Since the nation's early days, the northern and southern parts of the United States had followed different ways of life. Each section wanted to extend its own way of life to the new territories and states in the West.

North and South The North had a diversified economy, with both farms and industry. For both its factories and farms, the North depended on free workers. The South's economy, on the other hand, was based on just a few cash crops, mainly cotton. Southern planters relied on slave labor.

The economic differences between the two regions led to a conflict over slavery. Many northerners considered slavery morally wrong. They wanted to outlaw slavery in the new western states. Most white southerners believed slavery was necessary for their economy. They wanted laws to protect slavery in the West so that they could continue to raise cotton on the fertile soil there.

The disagreement over slavery fueled a debate about the rights of the individual states against those of the federal government. Southern politicians argued that the states had freely joined the Union, and so they could freely leave. Most northerners felt that the Constitution had established the Union once and for all.

Civil War Breaks Out Conflict between the North and South reached a climax in 1860, when **Abraham Lincoln** was elected president. Southerners fiercely opposed Lincoln, who had promised to stop the spread of slavery. One by one, southern states began to **secede**, or withdraw, from the Union. These states came together as the Confederate States of America.

On April 12, 1861, Confederate forces fired on Fort Sumter, a federal fort in Charleston, South Carolina. Lincoln ordered the army to bring the rebel states back into the Union. The **U.S. Civil War** had begun.

▶ *Explore ONLINE!*

Civil War in the United States, 1861–1865

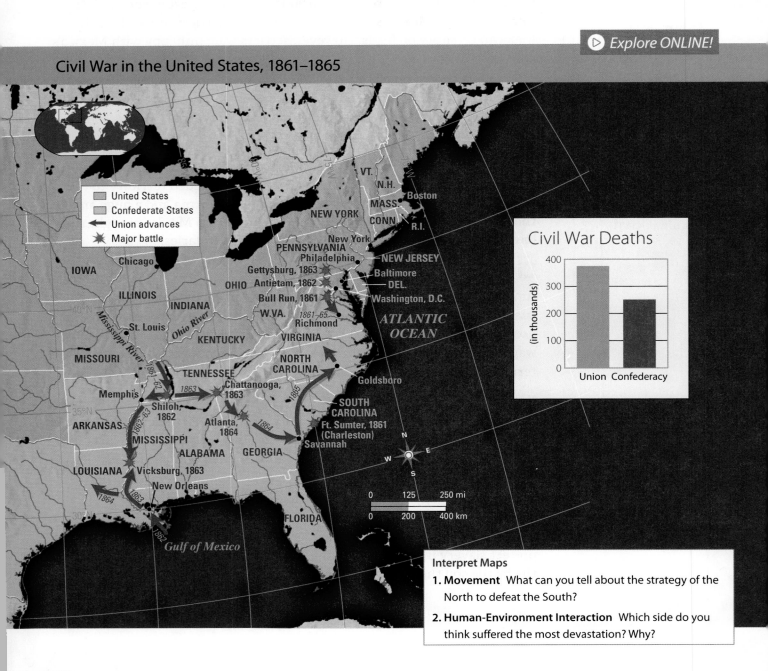

Civil War Deaths

Interpret Maps

1. **Movement** What can you tell about the strategy of the North to defeat the South?

2. **Human-Environment Interaction** Which side do you think suffered the most devastation? Why?

Abraham Lincoln (1809–1865)

Lincoln passionately believed in preserving the Union. His upbringing might help explain why. The son of rural, illiterate parents, he educated himself. After working as rail splitter, boatman, storekeeper, and surveyor, he taught himself to be a lawyer. This career path led eventually to the White House.

In Europe, people stayed at the level of society into which they had been born. Yet the United States had been founded on the belief that all men were created equal. Small wonder that Lincoln fought to preserve the democracy he described as the "last best hope of earth."

Four years of fighting followed, most of it in the South. Although the South had superior military leadership, the North had a larger population, better transportation, greater resources, and more factories. These advantages proved too much, and in April 1865, the South surrendered.

Abolition of Slavery Lincoln declared that the war was being fought to save the Union and not to end slavery. He eventually decided that ending slavery would help to save the Union. Early in 1863, he issued the **Emancipation Proclamation**, declaring that all slaves in the Confederate states were free.

At first, the proclamation freed no slaves, because the Confederate states did not accept it as law. As Union armies advanced into the South, however, they freed slaves in the areas they conquered. The Emancipation Proclamation also showed European nations that the war was being fought against slavery. As a result, these nations did not send the money and supplies that the South had hoped they would.

In the aftermath of the war, the U.S. Congress passed the Thirteenth Amendment to the Constitution, which abolished slavery in the United States. The Fourteenth and Fifteenth Amendments extended the rights of citizenship to all Americans and guaranteed former slaves the right to participatory citizenship. In other words, they finally had the right to vote.

Reconstruction From 1865 to 1877, Union troops occupied the South and enforced the constitutional protections. This period is called Reconstruction. After federal troops left the South, white southerners passed laws that limited African Americans' rights and made it difficult for them to vote. Such laws also encouraged **segregation**, or separation, of blacks and whites in the South. African Americans continued to face discrimination in the North as well.

Reading Check
Evaluate
Did the Emancipation Proclamation reflect a change in Lincoln's main goal for the war?

Beginning in 1892, Ellis Island in the New York Bay served as the main entry point for thousands of European immigrants to the United States.

The Postwar Economy

The need for mass production and distribution of goods during the Civil War speeded industrialization. After the war, the United States experienced industrial expansion unmatched in history. By 1914, it was a leading industrial power.

Immigration Industrialization could not have occurred so rapidly without immigrants. During the 1870s, immigrants arrived at a rate of nearly 2,000 a day. By 1914, more than 20 million people had moved to the United States from Europe and Asia. Many settled in the cities of the Northeast and Midwest. Others settled in the open spaces of the West.

The Railroads As settlers moved west, so did the nation's rail system. In 1862, Congress had authorized money to build a transcontinental railroad. For seven years, immigrants and other workers dug tunnels, built bridges, and laid track. When the railroad was completed in 1869, railroads linked California with the eastern United States.

By 1900, nearly 200,000 miles of track crossed the nation. This system linked farm to city and boosted trade and industry. The railroads bought huge quantities of steel. Also, trains brought materials such as coal and iron ore to factories and moved the finished goods to market. They carried corn, wheat, and cattle from the Great Plains to processing plants in St. Louis, Chicago, and Minneapolis. These developments helped to make the United States a world leader.

Reading Check
Analyze Effects
How did railroads affect the growth of the United States?

Lesson 3 Assessment

1. **Organize Information** Create a time line similar to the one shown and fill it in with the names and dates of seven events that contributed to U.S. expansion. Which event was the most significant?

2. **Key Terms and People** For each key term or person in the lesson, write a sentence explaining its significance.

3. **Contrast** What were some of the economic differences between the North and the South before the Civil War?

4. **Develop Historical Perspective** How did the Civil War speed up America's industrialization?

5. **Compare** What were the relative resources of the North and South in the U.S. Civil War?

6. **Make Inferences** How might the Mexican Cession have consequences today?

Nineteenth-Century Progress

The Big Idea

Breakthroughs in science and technology transformed daily life and entertainment.

Why It Matters Now

Electric lights, telephones, cars, and many other conveniences of modern life were invented during this period.

Key Terms and People

telegraph
assembly line
Charles Darwin
theory of evolution
radioactivity
psychology
mass culture

Setting the Stage

The Industrial Revolution happened because of inventions such as the spinning jenny and the steam engine. By the late 1800s, advances in both industry and technology were occurring faster than ever before. In turn, the demands of growing industries spurred even greater advances in technology. A surge of scientific discovery pushed the frontiers of knowledge forward. At the same time, in industrialized countries, economic growth produced many social changes.

Inventions Make Life Easier

In the early 1800s, coal and steam drove the machines of industry. By the late 1800s, new kinds of energy were coming into use. One was gasoline (made from oil), which powered the internal combustion engine. This engine would make the automobile possible. Another kind of energy was electricity.

Early Attempts at Electric Power For many centuries, scientists had known of and been interested in electricity. During the 1700s, Benjamin Franklin and other scientists had performed important experiments. Still, no one had developed a way to harness electricity and put it to use. In 1831, however, English chemist Michael Faraday discovered the connection between magnetism and electricity. His discovery led to the dynamo, a machine that generated electricity by moving a magnet through a coil of copper wire. Faraday used the electricity to power an electric motor, and his discoveries led to the development of electrical generators.

During the 1800s, other scientists also created devices that used electric power. For instance, in 1860 British chemist Joseph Swan developed a primitive electric light bulb that gave off light by passing heat through a small strip of paper. However, Swan's light bulb did not shine for very long, and its light was too dim. Swan's work was a beginning, but it was nearly 40 more years before the invention of a usable light bulb.

Edison the Inventor During his career, Thomas Edison patented more than 1,000 inventions, including the light bulb and the phonograph. Early in his career, Edison started a research laboratory in Menlo Park, New Jersey. Most of his important inventions were developed there, with help from the researchers he employed, such as Lewis H. Latimer, an African American inventor. Indeed, the idea of a research laboratory may have been Edison's most important invention.

The Telegraph Putting electricity to use made possible the invention of the **telegraph**, a machine that sent messages instantly over wires. American Samuel Morse is credited with inventing the telegraph in 1837. Morse also developed a "language," which became known as Morse code, for sending telegraph messages. Morse code is a series of long and short signals that represent letters and numbers. These telegraph messages were transmitted as electrical pulses of different lengths.

Historical Source

Impact of Scientific Research

This passage from *The Birth of the Modern: World Society, 1815–1830* by Paul Johnson discusses the far-reaching results of Michael Faraday's experiments with electromagnetism in the 1820s.

Synthesize
Paul Johnson wrote his book in 1991. Use the Internet to find a more recent news article, opinion piece, or data report that describes new—or highly impactful—scientific research being done in any field. Gather data, consider the multiple sources, and then analyze the way in which modern perspectives shape how past events are interpreted. In what way is electricity a good example of why scientific research is important?

"[By 1831, Faraday] had not only the first electric motor, but, in essence, the first dynamo: He could generate power.... What was remarkable about his work between 1820 and 1831 was that by showing exactly how mechanical could be transformed into electrical power, he made the jump between theoretical research and its practical application a comparatively narrow one. The electrical industry was the direct result of his work, and its first product, the electric telegraph, was soon in use. The idea of cause and effect was of great importance, for both industry and governments now began to appreciate the value of fundamental research and to finance it."

Thomas Edison moved to Menlo Park, New Jersey, in March 1876. It was there that he developed some of his most celebrated inventions, earning him the nickname "The Wizard of Menlo Park."

As the United States grew, the importance of the telegraph increased. By 1851, more than 50 telegraph companies were in operation in the United States. About ten years later, telegraph wires strung on poles along established railroad tracks linked much of the country. At railroad stations, passengers could send messages, or telegrams, to friends and family.

Communication between the United States and Europe also improved with the laying of a telegraph cable on the floor of the Atlantic Ocean in 1866. By 1870, telegraph wires stretched from England to India.

The telegraph revolutionized more than personal communication. In many countries, businesses could keep in close contact with suppliers and markets. News traveled around the world in hours instead of weeks. Newspapers sent correspondents to the front lines of wars, from where they telegraphed back vivid reports of victories and defeats. The reading public was very impressed by these timely reports. The reports were one way in which the telegraph globalized communication.

Other Advances in Communication As use of the telegraph spread around the world, inventors tried to improve on it. American Alexander Graham Bell, a teacher of hearing-impaired students, was one of the scientists working in sound technology. Bell tried to create a way to send multiple telegraph messages at the same time.

While working on that device, Bell made a remarkable discovery. One day in 1876, he was in one room and his assistant Thomas Watson was in another. Bell said, "Mr. Watson, come here, I want to see you!" Watson could hear Bell's voice not just through the air but also through the device's receiver. The telephone was born. Bell displayed his device at the Philadelphia Centennial Exposition of 1876.

Impact of the Telephone

By 1900, there were 1.4 million telephones in the United States. By 1912, there were 8.7 million. In this excerpt from "Thirty Years of the Telephone," published in September 1906, John Vaughn discussed how Alexander Graham Bell's invention affected life in the United States.

Analyze Historical Sources
What were some of the effects of the invention of the telephone?

"Various industries, unknown thirty years ago, but now sources of employment to many thousands of workers, depend entirely on the telephone for support. . . . The Bell Companies employ over 87,000 persons, and it may be added, pay them well. . . . These figures may be supplemented by the number of telephones in use (5,698,000), by the number of miles of wire (6,043,000) in the Bell lines, and by the number of conversations (4,479,500,000) electrically conveyed in 1905. The network of wire connects more than 33,000 cities, towns, villages, and hamlets."

The Italian inventor Guglielmo Marconi used theoretical discoveries about electromagnetic waves to create the first radio in 1895. This device was important because it sent messages (using Morse code) through the air, without the use of wires. Primitive radios soon became standard equipment for ships at sea.

Ford Sparks the Automobile Industry In the 1880s, German inventors used a gasoline engine to power a vehicle—the automobile. Automobile technology developed quickly, but since early cars were built by hand, they were expensive.

An American mechanic named Henry Ford decided to make cars that were affordable for most people. Ford used standardized, interchangeable parts. He also built them on an **assembly line**, a line of workers who each put a single piece on unfinished cars as they passed on a moving belt.

Assembly line workers could put together an entire Model T Ford in less than two hours. When Ford introduced this plain, black, reliable car in 1908, it sold for $850. As his production costs fell, Ford lowered the price. Eventually it dropped to less than $300. Other factories adopted Ford's ideas. By 1916, more than 3.5 million cars were traveling around on America's roads.

Edison's Inventions

Thomas Alva Edison was one of the greatest inventors in history. He held thousands of patents for his inventions in over 30 countries. The United States Patent Office alone issued Edison 1,093 patents. Among his inventions were an electric light bulb, the phonograph, and motion pictures.

Some scientists and historians, however, believe that Edison's greatest achievement was his development of the research laboratory. Edison worked with a team of specialists to produce his creations. His precise manner is illustrated by his famous quote: "Genius is 1 percent inspiration and 99 percent perspiration."

▲ **Motion pictures** The idea of "moving pictures" was not Edison's, but his "Kinetoscope" made movies practical.

◄ **Phonograph** Commonplace today, a device for recording sound did not exist until Thomas Edison invented it. He first demonstrated his phonograph in 1877.

Critical Thinking

1. **Make Inferences** What did Edison mean when he said, "Genius is 1 percent inspiration and 99 percent perspiration"?
2. **Form Opinions** Which of Edison's inventions do you think has had the most influence?

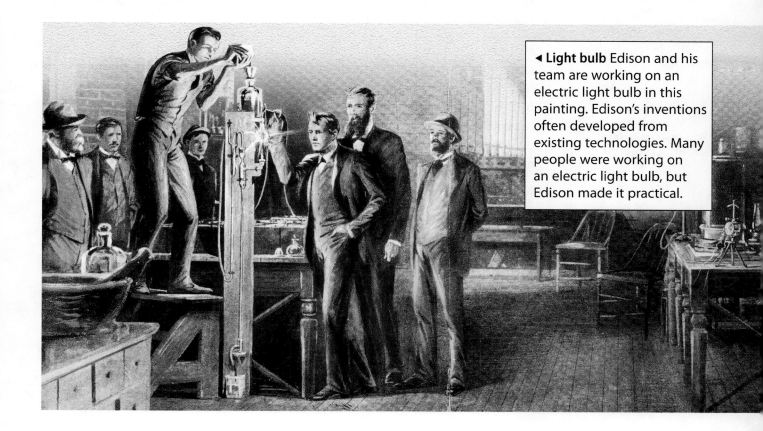

◄ **Light bulb** Edison and his team are working on an electric light bulb in this painting. Edison's inventions often developed from existing technologies. Many people were working on an electric light bulb, but Edison made it practical.

An Age of Inventions

▲ **Telephone**
Alexander Graham Bell demonstrated the first telephone in 1876. It quickly became an essential of modern life.

▲ **Airplane** Through trial and error, the Wright brothers designed wings that provided lift and balance in flight. Their design is based on principles that are still used in every aircraft.

▲ **Automobile assembly line** Ford's major innovation was to improve efficiency in his factory. By introducing the assembly line, he reduced the time it took to build a car from 12.5 to 1.5 worker-hours.

Analyze Historical Sources
Which has had the more lasting impact, the airplane or the automobile?

The Wright Brothers Fly Two bicycle mechanics from Dayton, Ohio, named Wilbur and Orville Wright, solved the age-old riddle of flight. On December 17, 1903, they flew a gasoline-powered flying machine at Kitty Hawk, North Carolina. The longest flight lasted only 59 seconds, but it started the aircraft industry.

Modern City Life Though innovations in technology, communication, and transportation improved lives, there were downsides to these changes as well. Many of the negative consequences of these new inventions related to urbanization. The telegraph, the phonograph, and the automobile may have offered convenience and pleasure, but they also contributed to new, urban problems like traffic jams, air pollution, and noise pollution. They all helped make modern city life hectic, noisy, and complicated.

Reading Check
Make Inferences
Why do you think Ford reduced the price of the Model T?

New Ideas in Medicine

Earlier centuries had established the scientific method. Now this method brought new insights into nature as well as practical results.

The Germ Theory of Disease An important breakthrough in the history of medicine was the germ theory of disease. It was developed by French chemist Louis Pasteur in the mid-1800s. While examining the fermentation process of alcohol, Pasteur discovered that it was caused by microscopic organisms he called bacteria. He also learned that heat killed bacteria. This led him to develop the process of pasteurization to kill germs in liquids such as milk. Soon, it became clear to Pasteur and others that bacteria also caused diseases.

Joseph Lister, a British surgeon, read about Pasteur's work. He thought germs might explain why half of surgical patients died of infections. In 1865, he ordered that his surgical wards be kept spotlessly clean. He insisted that wounds be washed in antiseptics, or germ-killing liquids. As a result, 85 percent of Lister's patients survived. Other hospitals adopted Lister's methods.

Public Health Public officials, too, began to understand that cleanliness helped prevent the spread of disease. Cities built plumbing and sewer systems and took other steps to improve public health. Meanwhile, medical researchers developed vaccines, or cures, for such deadly diseases as typhus, typhoid fever, cholera, diphtheria, and yellow fever. These advances helped people live longer, healthier lives.

Another improvement in public health was the building of more modern hospitals. More physicians, nurses, and other medical professionals were trained. Nursing schools trained large numbers of women as nurses or physicians' assistants. Some women even enrolled in medical school to become doctors. By 1900, 5 percent of American physicians were women.

A major consequence of these developments in medical care and public health was a shift in demographic trends. For example, there was a dramatic decline in infant mortality, or deaths in infancy. Statistics from Sweden provide a clear example. In 1800, Sweden reported 240 deaths of infants under one year old per 1,000 live births. By 1898, that figure had dropped to 91 deaths.

Reading Check
Find Main Ideas
What did pasteurization, antiseptics, and vaccines accomplish?

Historical Source

Improving Public Health

Industrialization, the growth of cities, and new ideas in medicine led to greater focus on improving public health.

A COURT FOR KING CHOLERA.

In this political cartoon called *A Court for King Cholera,* the artist shows details that cause epidemic disease.

This newspaper engraving shows a Board of Health doctor administering the smallpox vaccine to poor people at a police station in New York City.

Analyze Historical Sources
In what way or ways do the two primary source illustrations show different perspectives on the topic of public health? Evaluate and contrast the credibility and limitations of each illustration.

New Ideas in Science

No scientific idea of modern times aroused more controversy than the work of English naturalist **Charles Darwin**. The cause of the controversy was Darwin's answer to the question that faced biologists: How can we explain the tremendous variety of plants and animals on earth? A widely accepted answer in the 1800s was the idea of special creation—every kind of plant and animal had been created by God at the beginning of the world and had remained the same since then.

Darwin's Theory of Evolution Darwin challenged the idea of special creation. Based on his research as a naturalist on the voyage of the HMS *Beagle*, he developed a theory that all forms of life, including human beings, evolved from earlier living forms that had existed millions of years ago.

In 1859, Darwin published his thinking in a book titled *On the Origin of Species by Means of Natural Selection*. According to the idea of natural selection, populations tend to grow faster than the food supply and so must compete for food. The members of a species that survive are those that are fittest, or best adapted to their environment. These surviving members of a species produce offspring that share their advantages. Gradually, over many generations, the species may change. In this way, new species evolve. Darwin's idea of change through natural selection came to be called the **theory of evolution**.

Mendel and Genetics Although Darwin said that living things passed on their variations from one generation to the next, he did not know how they did so. In the 1850s and 1860s, an Austrian monk named Gregor Mendel discovered that there is a pattern to the way that certain traits are inherited. Although his work was not widely known until 1900, Mendel's work began the science of genetics.

--- BIOGRAPHY ---

Marie Curie
(1867–1934)

Marie Curie's original name was Marya Sklodowska. Born in Warsaw, Poland, she emigrated to Paris to study, where she changed her name to Marie.

She achieved a number of firsts in her career. She was the first woman to teach in the Sorbonne, a world-famous college that was part of the University of Paris. She was the first woman to win a Nobel Prize—two, in fact.

In 1911, she won the Nobel Prize for chemistry. In 1921, she journeyed to the United States. In 1934, she died from leukemia caused by the radiation she had been exposed to in her work.

Advances in Chemistry and Physics In 1803, the British chemist John Dalton theorized that all matter is made of tiny particles called atoms. Dalton showed that elements contain only one kind of atom, which has a specific weight. Compounds, on the other hand, contain more than one kind of atom.

In 1869, Dmitri Mendeleev (MEHN•duh•LAY•uhf), a Russian chemist, organized a chart on which all the known elements were arranged in order of weight, from lightest to heaviest. He left gaps where he predicted that new elements would be discovered. Later, his predictions proved correct. Mendeleev's chart, the Periodic Table, is still used today.

A husband and wife team working in Paris, Marie and Pierre Curie, discovered two of the missing elements, which they named radium and polonium. The elements were found in a mineral called pitchblende that released a powerful form of energy. In 1898, Marie Curie gave this energy the name **radioactivity**. In 1903, the Curies shared the Nobel Prize for physics for their work on radioactivity. In 1911, Marie Curie won the Nobel Prize for chemistry for the discovery of radium and polonium.

Physicists around 1900 continued to unravel the secrets of the atom. Earlier scientists believed that the atom was the smallest particle that existed. A British physicist named Ernest Rutherford suggested that atoms were made up of yet smaller particles. Each atom, he said, had a nucleus surrounded by one or more particles called electrons. Soon other physicists such as Max Planck, Niels Bohr, and Albert Einstein were studying the structure and energy of atoms.

Reading Check
Summarize
According to Darwin, how does natural selection affect evolution?

Social Sciences Explore Behavior

The scientific theories of the 1800s prompted scholars to study human society and behavior in a scientific way. Interest in these fields grew enormously during that century, as global expeditions produced a flood of new discoveries about ancient civilizations and world cultures. This led to the development of modern social sciences such as archaeology, anthropology, and sociology.

An important new social science was **psychology**, the study of the human mind and behavior. The Russian physiologist Ivan Pavlov believed that human actions were often unconscious reactions to experiences and could be changed by training.

Another pioneer in psychology, the Austrian doctor Sigmund Freud, also believed that the unconscious mind drives how people think and act. In Freud's view, unconscious forces such as suppressed memories, desires, and impulses shape behavior. He founded a type of therapy called psychoanalysis to deal with psychological conflicts created by these forces.

Freud's theories became very influential. However, his idea that the mind was beyond conscious control also shocked many people. The theories of Freud and Pavlov challenged the fundamental idea of the Enlightenment—that reason was supreme. The new ideas about psychology began to shake the 19th-century faith that humans could perfect themselves and society through reason.

Reading Check
Form Generalizations
Why was the work of Pavlov and Freud groundbreaking?

Social Darwinism

Charles Darwin (pictured at right) was a naturalist, but a number of 19th-century thinkers tried to apply his ideas to economics and politics. The leader in this movement was Herbert Spencer, an English philosopher.

Free economic competition, Spencer argued, was natural selection in action. The best companies make profits, while inefficient ones go bankrupt. He applied the same rules to individuals. Those who were fittest for survival enjoyed wealth and success, while the poor remained poor because they were unfit.

This idea became known as Social Darwinism. It also provided a rationalization for imperialism and colonialism.

The Rise of Mass Culture

In earlier periods, art, music, and theater were enjoyed by the wealthy. This group had the money, leisure time, and education to appreciate high culture. It was not until about 1900 that people could speak of **mass culture**—the appeal of art, writing, music, and other forms of entertainment to a larger audience.

Changes Produce Mass Culture There were several causes for the rise of mass culture. Their effects changed life in Europe and North America. Notice in the Rise of Mass Culture chart how working class people's lives were changed. The demand for leisure activities resulted in a variety of new pursuits for people to enjoy. People went to music performances, movies, and sporting events.

Rise of Mass Culture

Cause	Effect/Cause	Effect
Public education	Increase in literacy	Mass market for books and newspapers
Improvement in communications	Publications cheaper and more accessible	Mass market for books and newspapers
Invention of phonograph and records	More music directly in people's homes	Greater demand for musical entertainment
Shorter workday—10 hours shorter workweek—5-1/2 days	More leisure time	Greater demand for mass entertainment activities

Interpret Charts
According to the chart, what was the immediate cause for the increased demand for mass entertainment activities?

Music Halls, Vaudeville, and Movies A popular leisure activity was a trip to the local music hall. On a typical evening, a music hall might offer a dozen or more different acts. It might feature singers, dancers, comedians, jugglers, magicians, and acrobats. In the United States, musical variety shows were called vaudeville. Vaudeville acts traveled from town to town, appearing at theaters.

During the 1880s, several inventors worked at trying to project moving images. One successful design came from France. Another came from Thomas Edison's laboratory. The earliest motion pictures were black and white and lasted less than a minute.

By the early 1900s, filmmakers were producing the first feature films. Movies quickly became big business. By 1910, 5 million Americans attended some 10,000 theaters each day. The European movie industry experienced similar growth.

Sports Entertain Millions With time at their disposal, more people began to enjoy sports and outdoor activities. Spectator sports now became entertainment. In the United States, football and baseball soared in popularity. In Europe, the first professional soccer clubs formed and drew big crowds. Favorite English sports such as cricket spread to the British colonies of Australia, India, and South Africa.

As a result of the growing interest in sports, the International Olympic Games began in 1896. They revived the ancient Greek tradition of holding an athletic competition every four years. Fittingly, the first modern Olympics took place in Athens, Greece, the country where the games had originated.

Reading Check
Analyze Causes
Why might a young person living in the early 1900s think it possible to become— and earn a living at being—a professional entertainer?

Lesson 4 Assessment

1. **Organize Information** Create a web graphic organizer similar to the one shown and fill it in with inventions and breakthroughs in medicine, science, or social sciences. Include the name of a key person associated with each breakthrough.

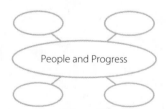

People and Progress

Which breakthrough helped people the most? Why?

2. **Key Terms and People** For each key term or person in the lesson, write a sentence explaining its significance.
3. **Analyze Effects** What effect did the assembly line have on production costs?
4. **Summarize** How did Joseph Lister improve the survival rate of his patients?
5. **Analyze Effects** What effect did the spread of public education have on culture?
6. **Analyze Causes** What changes led to the rise of mass culture around 1900?

Module 22 Assessment

Key Terms and People

For each term or name below, briefly explain its connection to the reforms, crises, or advances of Western nations from 1815 to 1914.

1. suffrage
2. anti-Semitism
3. dominion
4. home rule
5. manifest destiny
6. Emancipation Proclamation
7. assembly line
8. theory of evolution

Main Ideas

Use your notes and information in the module to answer the following questions.

Democratic Reform and Activism

1. What political reforms expanded democracy for men in Britain?
2. Why did the woman suffrage movement in Great Britain become more militant?

Self-Rule for British Colonies

3. What cultural conflict caused problems for Canada?
4. How did Australia's early history differ from that of other British colonies?
5. Why did the British pass a home rule bill for southern Ireland only?

War and Expansion in the United States

6. In what ways did the United States gain territory in the 1800s?
7. Why was the issue of slavery in the United States so divisive?

Nineteenth-Century Progress

8. What was Darwin's principle of natural selection?
9. What prompted the growth of the social sciences?
10. What were some of the effects of increased leisure time?

Critical Thinking

1. **Synthesize** Create a web diagram of the major political, economic, social and cultural, and scientific and technological changes of the 1800s and early 1900s.

2. **Recognize Effects** For a worker, what might be the advantages and disadvantages of an assembly line?

3. **Analyze Motives** What effect did the call for home rule in British colonies have on Ireland's desire for independence?

4. **Predict Effects** Imagine that circumstances had forced the North to surrender to the South in the Civil War, causing two countries to share the region now occupied by the United States. What economic effects might this have had on the North? the South? the region as a whole?

5. **Draw Conclusions** How did manifest destiny help shape the U.S. government's policies of land acquisition?

Engage with History

Using content from the module and your knowledge of events in the world today, consider what political ideals might be worth fighting and possibly even dying for. Discuss your opinions with a small group. During the discussion, think about some of the ideals that inspired American and French revolutionaries. What were the ideals that moved them to action? How did they try to change government to better reflect their ideals? Then, also consider your own:

- political ideals
- religious ideals
- family values

Focus on Writing

Write an **editorial** that might have appeared in a newspaper in 19th-century New Zealand. In the editorial, address the issue of British settlers' taking land from the Maori, and the Maori response.

Consider the following:

- the original inhabitants of New Zealand
- means for negotiating land disputes
- balancing the rights of native peoples and new settlers

Multimedia Activity

Use the Internet to learn more about the rise of mass culture and mass entertainment. Then research and write a newspaper article about spectators at one of the new forms of mass entertainment. Include in your article quotes from fictional visitors and their reactions to actual events and spectacles. You may want to mention one or more of the following:

- the Boston Pilgrims' victory over the Pittsburgh Pirates in baseball's first World Series
- the "Luna" ride at Coney Island
- a late 19th-century European appearance of Barnum & Bailey's circus
- a visit to the Palace of Electricity at the 1904 World's Fair in St. Louis

Henry Ford was a brilliant inventor and industrialist and founder of the Ford Motor Company. He helped bring about a time of rapid growth and progress that forever changed how people worked and lived. Henry Ford grew up on his family's farm near Dearborn, Michigan. As a child, he disliked life on the farm. He found the clicks and whirs of machinery much more exciting. When Ford was 16, he went to nearby Detroit to work in a machine shop. From there, he turned his ideas for how to make affordable and well-built cars into one of the world's largest automobile companies.

Explore the amazing life and career of Henry Ford online. You can find a wealth of information, video clips, primary sources, activities, and more through your online textbook.

> "My 'gasoline buggy' was the first and for a long time the only automobile in Detroit. It was considered . . . a nuisance, for it made a racket and it scared horses."
>
> —Henry Ford

 My Life and Work

Read the document to learn more about Henry Ford's life and career in his own words.

 Go online to view these and other **HISTORY**® resources.

Big Plans

Watch the video to learn more about Henry Ford's early career.

Taking the Low Road

Watch the video to explore Henry Ford's vision for his car company.

The Assembly Line

Watch the video to see how Henry Ford used the assembly line to produce cars more efficiently and cheaply.

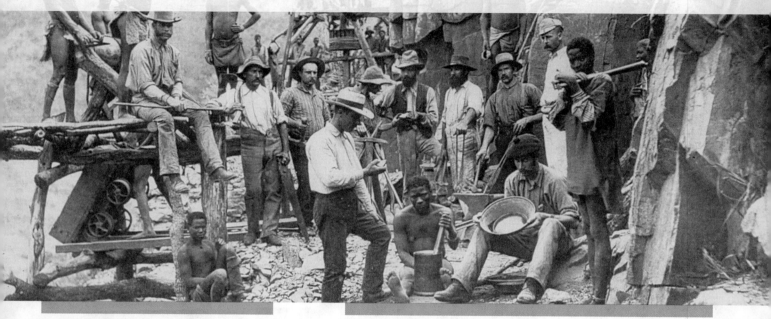

Module 23

The Age of Imperialism

Essential Question

What role did imperialism play in shaping the modern world?

About the Photo: In this photo, Europeans oversee the work of African migrant workers at a South African gold mine.

In this module, you will learn about the colonization by Western countries of large areas of Africa and Asia.

▷ *Explore ONLINE!*

H HISTORY.

VIDEOS, including...
• As It Happened
• In the Footsteps of Doctor Livingstone
• Ottoman Empire: The War Machine
• The Suez Canal
• The Conquest of Hawaii
• Inside the Panama Canal

☑ Document Based Investigations
☑ Graphic Organizers
☑ Interactive Games
☑ Image Compare: Imperialism in Africa, 1878 and 1913
☑ Animation: The Panama Canal

Timeline of Events 1850–1914

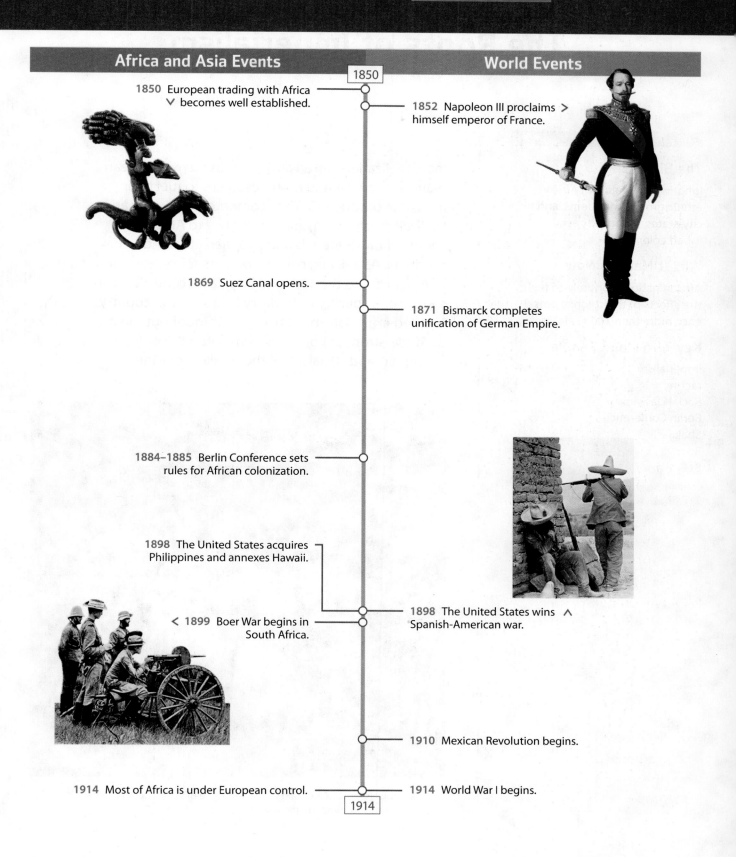

Africa and Asia Events

1850 European trading with Africa
∨ becomes well established.

1869 Suez Canal opens.

1884–1885 Berlin Conference sets
rules for African colonization.

1898 The United States acquires
Philippines and annexes Hawaii.

< **1899** Boer War begins in
South Africa.

1914 Most of Africa is under European control.

World Events

1852 Napoleon III proclaims >
himself emperor of France.

1871 Bismarck completes
unification of German Empire.

1898 The United States wins ∧
Spanish-American war.

1910 Mexican Revolution begins.

1914 World War I begins.

1850

1914

The Roots of Imperialism

The Big Idea

Ignoring the claims of African ethnic groups, kingdoms, and city-states, Europeans established colonies.

Why It Matters Now

African nations continue to feel the effects of the colonial presence more than 100 years later.

Key Terms and People

imperialism
racism
Social Darwinism
Berlin Conference
Shaka
Boer
Boer War

Setting the Stage

Industrialization stirred ambitions in many European nations. They wanted more resources to fuel their industrial production. They competed for new markets for their goods. Many nations looked to Africa as a source of raw materials and as a market for industrial products. As a result, colonial powers seized vast areas of Africa during the 19th and early 20th centuries. This seizure of a country or territory by a stronger country is called **imperialism**. As occurred throughout most of Africa, stronger countries dominated the political, economic, and social life of the weaker countries.

This painting shows Great Britain's Edward, Prince of Wales, being greeted by Indian princes during an official visit to India in 1875.

Africa Before European Domination

In the mid-1800s, on the eve of the European domination of Africa, African peoples were divided into hundreds of ethnic and linguistic groups. Most continued to follow traditional beliefs, while others converted to Islam or Christianity. These groups spoke more than 1,000 different languages. Politically, they ranged from large empires that united many ethnic groups to independent villages.

Europeans had established contacts with sub-Saharan Africans as early as the 1450s. However, powerful African armies were able to keep the Europeans out of most of Africa for 400 years. In fact, as late as 1880, Europeans controlled only 10 percent of the continent's land, mainly on the coast.

Furthermore, European travel into the interior on a large-scale basis was virtually impossible. Europeans could not navigate African rivers, which had many rapids, cataracts, and changing flows. The introduction of steam-powered riverboats in the early 1800s allowed Europeans to conduct major expeditions into the interior of Africa. Disease also discouraged European exploration.

Finally, Africans controlled their own trade networks and provided the trade items. These networks were specialized. The Chokwe, for example, collected ivory and beeswax in the Angolan highlands.

Africans had their own trade networks before the European invasion. One good, ivory, was often carved by artisans into pieces such as the one shown here.

Nations Compete for Overseas Empires Those Europeans who did penetrate the interior of Africa, which could be a challenging experience given its diverse terrain, climate, and cultures, were explorers, missionaries, or humanitarians who opposed the European and American slave trade. Europeans and Americans learned about Africa through travel books and newspapers. These publications competed for readers by hiring reporters to search the globe for stories of adventure, mystery, or excitement.

The Congo Sparks Interest In the late 1860s, David Livingstone, a missionary from Scotland who supported the rights and freedom of native peoples suppressed under European imperialism, traveled with a group of Africans deep into central Africa to promote Christianity. When several years passed with no word from him or his party, many people feared he was dead. An American newspaper hired reporter Henry Stanley to find Livingstone. In 1871, he found Dr. Livingstone on the shores of Lake Tanganyika. Stanley's famous greeting—"Dr. Livingstone, I presume?"—made headlines around the world.

Stanley set out to explore Africa himself and trace the course of the Congo River. His explorations sparked the interest of King Leopold II of Belgium, who commissioned Stanley to help him obtain land in the Congo. Between 1879 and 1882, Stanley signed treaties with local chiefs of the Congo River valley. The treaties gave King Leopold II of Belgium control of these lands.

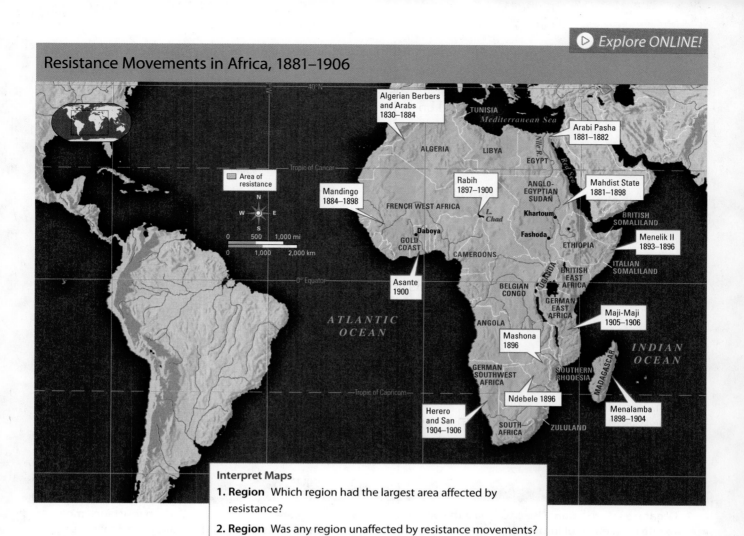

Resistance Movements in Africa, 1881–1906

▶ Explore ONLINE!

Map labels:
- Algerian Berbers and Arabs 1830–1884
- Arabi Pasha 1881–1882
- Mahdist State 1881–1898
- Rabih 1897–1900
- Mandingo 1884–1898
- Menelik II 1893–1896
- Asante 1900
- Maji-Maji 1905–1906
- Mashona 1896
- Ndebele 1896
- Herero and San 1904–1906
- Menalamba 1898–1904

Area of resistance

Interpret Maps

1. **Region** Which region had the largest area affected by resistance?

2. **Region** Was any region unaffected by resistance movements?

The Legacy of Colonial Rule

European colonial rule forever altered Africans' lives. In some cases, the Europeans brought benefits, but for the most part, the effects were negative.

Negative Effects On the negative side, Africans lost control of their land and their independence. Many died of new diseases such as smallpox. They also lost thousands of their people in resisting the Europeans. Famines resulted from the change to cash crops in place of subsistence agriculture. This practice would also impact Africa's economy after imperialism ended. Many Africans were forced to migrate for work, which altered their diets and caused them to neglect their food crops.

Africans also suffered from a breakdown of their traditional cultures. Traditional authority figures were replaced. Homes and property were transferred with little regard to their importance to the people. Men were forced to leave villages to find ways to support themselves and their families. Contempt for the traditional culture and admiration of European life undermined stable societies and caused identity problems for Africans.

The most harmful political legacy from the colonial period was the division of the African continent. Long-term rival chiefdoms were sometimes united, while at other times, kinship groups were split between colonies. The artificial boundaries combined or unnaturally divided groups, creating problems that plagued African colonies during European occupation. These boundaries continue to create problems for the nations that evolved from the former colonies.

Positive Effects On the positive side, colonialism reduced local warfare. Humanitarian efforts in some colonies improved sanitation and provided hospitals and schools. As a result, lifespans increased and literacy rates improved. Also positive was the economic expansion. African products came to be valued on the international market. To aid the economic growth, railroads, dams, and telephone and telegraph lines were built in African colonies. But for the most part, these benefited only European business interests, not Africans' lives.

The patterns of behavior of imperialist powers were similar, no matter where their colonies were located. Dealing with local traditions and peoples continued to cause problems in other areas of the world dominated by Europeans. Resistance to the European imperialists also continued, as you will see in Lesson 4.

Reading Check
Draw Conclusions
Why might the problems caused by artificial boundaries continue after the Europeans left?

Lesson 2 Assessment

1. **Organize Information** Use a scale like the one below to rate each effect of imperialism on Africa.

   Do you think the positive effects of imperialism outweighed the negative impact? Why or why not?

   positive   negative

2. **Key Terms and People** For each key term or person in the lesson, write a sentence explaining its significance.

3. **Make Inferences** Why were African resistance movements, such as those carried out by the Ashanti, usually unsuccessful?

4. **Analyze Effects** How did colonial rule cause a breakdown in traditional African culture?

5. **Evaluate** What important questions should be asked about the Industrial Revolution and how it related to European imperialism in Africa?

6. **Compare** How was the policy of paternalism like Social Darwinism?

Views of Imperialism

European imperialism extended to the continents beyond Africa. As imperialism spread, the colonizer and the colonized viewed the experience of imperialism in very different ways. Some Europeans were outspoken about the superiority they felt toward the peoples they conquered. Others thought imperialism was very wrong. Even the conquered had mixed feelings about their encounters with the Europeans.

J. A. HOBSON

Hobson's 1902 book, *Imperialism*, made a great impression on his fellow Britons.

"For Europe to rule Asia by force for purposes of gain, and to justify that rule by the pretence that she is civilizing Asia and raising her to a higher level of spiritual life, will be adjudged by history, perhaps, to be the crowning wrong and folly of Imperialism. What Asia has to give, her priceless stores of wisdom garnered from her experience of ages, we refuse to take; the much or little which we could give we spoil by the brutal manner of our giving. This is what Imperialism has done, and is doing, for Asia."

DADABHAI NAOROJI

Dadabhai Naoroji was the first Indian elected to the British Parliament. In 1871, he delivered a speech about the impact of Great Britain on India.

"To sum up the whole, the British rule has been—morally, a great blessing; politically peace and order on one hand, blunders on the other, materially, impoverishment. . . . The natives call the British system "Sakar ki Churi," the knife of sugar. That is to say there is no oppression, it is all smooth and sweet, but it is the knife, notwithstanding. I mention this that you should know these feelings. Our great misfortune is that you do not know our wants. When you will know our real wishes, I have not the least doubt that you would do justice. The genius and spirit of the British people is fair play and justice."

This 1882 American political cartoon, titled "The Devilfish in Egyptian Waters," depicts England as an octopus. Notice that Egypt is not yet one of the areas controlled by the British.

Analyze Issues

Choose two sources among the three sources shown (the two text excerpts and the political cartoon) to compare and contrast based on their frame of reference and how those affect the viewpoints expressed. Which sources are more credible? Do any of the sources have limitations? Explain.

Europeans Claim Muslim Lands

The Big Idea

European nations expanded their empires by seizing territories from Muslim states.

Why It Matters Now

Political events in this vital resource area are still influenced by actions from the imperialistic period.

Key Terms and People

geopolitics
Crimean War
Suez Canal

Setting the Stage

The European powers that carved up Africa also looked elsewhere for other lands to control. The Muslim lands that rimmed the Mediterranean had largely been claimed as a result of Arab and Ottoman conquests. As you have learned, the Ottoman Empire at its peak stretched from Hungary in the north, around the Black Sea, and across Egypt all the way west to the borders of Morocco. But during the empire's last 300 years, it had steadily declined in power. Europeans competed with each other to gain control of this strategically important area.

Ottoman Empire Loses Power

The declining Ottoman Empire had difficulties trying to fit into the modern world. However, the Ottomans made attempts to change before they finally were unable to hold back the European imperialist powers.

Reforms Fail When Suleyman I, the last great Ottoman sultan, died in 1566, he was followed by a succession of weak sultans. The palace government broke up into a number of quarreling, often corrupt factions. Weakening power brought other problems. Corruption and theft had caused financial losses. Coinage was devalued, causing inflation. Once the Ottoman Empire had embraced modern technologies, but now it fell further and further behind Europe.

When Selim III came into power in 1789, he attempted to modernize the army. However, the older janissary corps resisted his efforts. Selim III was overthrown, and reform movements were temporarily abandoned. Meanwhile, nationalist feelings began to stir among the Ottomans' subject peoples. In 1830, Greece gained its independence and Serbia gained self-rule. The Ottomans' weakness was becoming apparent to European powers, who were expanding their territories. They began to look for ways to take the lands away from the Ottomans.

Reading Check
Summarize
How did the Young
Turks unite people
against the Ottoman
sultan and consolidate
their power?

Meanwhile, in 1908 the Young Turks used nationalism to unite people against the Ottoman sultan, and after consolidating power helped modernize the empire. They proclaimed that every citizen would have equal rights regardless of nationality or religion and adopted a constitution, but they kept Turkish as the sole official language of the state. The Young Turks lost power before completing the reforms that they had planned.

Europeans Grab Territory

Geopolitics, an interest in or taking of land for its strategic location or products, played an important role in the fate of the Ottoman Empire. World powers were attracted to its strategic location. The Ottomans controlled access to the Mediterranean and the Atlantic sea trade. Merchants in landlocked countries that lay beyond the Black Sea had to go through Ottoman lands. Russia, for example, desperately wanted passage for its grain exports across the Black Sea and into the Mediterranean Sea. This desire strongly influenced Russia's relations with the Ottoman Empire. Russia attempted to win Ottoman favor, formed alliances with Ottoman enemies, and finally waged war against the Ottomans. Discovery of oil in Persia around 1900 and in the Arabian Peninsula after World War I focused even more attention on the area.

Russia and the Crimean War Each generation of Russian czars launched a war on the Ottomans to try to gain land on the Black Sea. The purpose was to give Russia a warm-weather port. In 1853, war broke out between the Russians and the Ottomans. The war was called the **Crimean War**, after a peninsula in the Black Sea where most of the war was fought. Britain and France wanted to prevent the Russians from gaining control of additional Ottoman lands. So they entered the war on the side of the Ottoman Empire. The combined forces of the Ottoman Empire, Britain, and France defeated Russia. The Crimean War was the first war in which women, led by Florence Nightingale, established their position as army nurses. It was also the first war to be covered by newspaper correspondents.

The Crimean War revealed the Ottoman Empire's military weakness. Despite the help of Britain and France, the Ottoman Empire continued to lose lands. The Russians came to the aid of Slavic people in the Balkans who rebelled against the Ottomans. The Ottomans lost control of Romania, Montenegro, Cyprus, Bosnia, Herzegovina, and an area that became Bulgaria. The Ottomans lost land in Africa, too. By the beginning of World War I, the Ottoman Empire was in deep decline.

The Great Game For much of the 19th century, Great Britain and Russia engaged in yet another geopolitical struggle, this time over Muslim lands in Central Asia. Known as the "Great Game," the war was waged over India, one of Britain's most profitable colonies. Russia sought to extend its empire and gain access to India's riches. Britain defended its colony and also attempted to spread its empire beyond India's borders. Afghanistan, which lay between the Russian and British empires, became the center of their struggle.

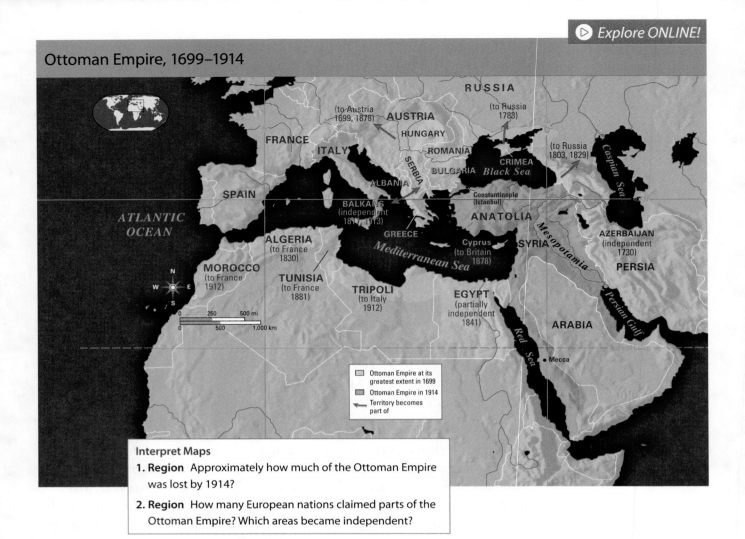

Ottoman Empire, 1699–1914

▶ Explore ONLINE!

Interpret Maps

1. **Region** Approximately how much of the Ottoman Empire was lost by 1914?

2. **Region** How many European nations claimed parts of the Ottoman Empire? Which areas became independent?

Reading Check
Make Inferences
How did the Crimean War help lead to the decline of the Ottoman Empire?

In the 1800s, Afghanistan was an independent Muslim kingdom. Its dry, mountainous terrain and determined people continually frustrated the invading imperial powers. After decades of fighting, Great Britain finally withdrew from Afghanistan in 1881. In 1921, Britain formally agreed that its empire would not extend beyond the Khyber Pass, which borders eastern Afghanistan. The newly formed Soviet Union, meanwhile, signed a nonaggression pact with Afghanistan. That agreement was honored until 1979, when the Soviet Union invaded Afghanistan.

Egypt Initiates Reforms

Observing the slow decline of the Ottoman Empire, some Muslim leaders decided that their countries would either have to adjust to the modern world or be consumed by it. Egypt initiated political and social reforms, in part to block European domination of its land.

Military and Economic Reforms Modernization came to Egypt as a result of the interest in the area created by the French occupation. Egypt's strategic location at the head of the Red Sea appeared valuable to France and Britain. After Napoleon failed to win Egypt, a new leader emerged:

Muhammad Ali. The Ottomans sent him as part of an expeditionary force to govern Egypt, but he soon broke away from Ottoman control. Beginning in 1831, he fought a series of battles in which he gained control of Syria and Arabia. Through the combined efforts of European powers, Muhammad Ali and his heirs were recognized as the hereditary rulers of Egypt.

Muhammad Ali began a series of reforms in the military and in the economy. Without foreign assistance, he personally directed a shift of Egyptian agriculture to a plantation cash crop—cotton. This brought Egypt into the international marketplace but at a cost to the peasants. They lost the use of lands they traditionally farmed and were forced to grow cash crops in place of food crops.

The Suez Canal Muhammad Ali's efforts to modernize Egypt were continued by his grandson, Isma'il. Isma'il supported the construction of the **Suez Canal**. The canal was a human-made waterway that cut through the Isthmus of Suez. It connected the Red Sea to the Mediterranean. It was built mainly with French money from private interest groups, using Egyptian labor. The Suez Canal opened in 1869 with a huge international celebration. However, Isma'il's modernization efforts, such as irrigation projects and communication networks, were enormously expensive. Egypt soon found that it could not pay its European bankers even the interest on its $450 million debt. The British insisted on overseeing financial control of the canal, and in 1882 the British occupied Egypt.

Reading Check
Analyze Effects
What two effects did raising cotton have on Egyptian agriculture?

Muhammad Ali was a common soldier who rose to leadership as a result of his military skill and political shrewdness.

Suez Canal

The Suez Canal was viewed as the "Lifeline of the Empire" because it allowed Britain quicker access to its colonies in Asia and Africa. In a speech to Parliament, Joseph Chamberlain explained that he believed Britain should continue its occupation of Egypt because of "the necessity for using every legitimate opportunity to extend our influence and control in that great African continent which is now being opened up to civilization and to commerce."

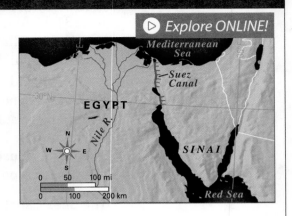

▷ Explore ONLINE!

This painting represents the opening celebration of the canal on November 17, 1869.

Interpret Maps
Place Approximately how long is the Suez Canal?

Persia Pressured to Change

Elsewhere in southwest Asia, Russia and Britain competed to exploit Persia commercially and to bring that country under their own spheres of influence. Russia was especially interested in gaining access to the Persian Gulf and the Indian Ocean. Twice Persia gave up territories to Russia, after military defeats in 1813 and 1828. Britain was interested in using Afghanistan as a buffer between India and Russia. In 1857, Persia resisted British demands but was forced to give up all claims to Afghanistan. Britain's interest in Persia increased greatly after the discovery of oil there in 1908.

Persia lacked the capital to develop its own resources. To raise money and to gain economic prestige, the Persian ruler began granting concessions to Western businesses. These concessions allowed businesses to buy the right to operate in a certain area or develop a certain product. For example, a British corporation, the AngloPersian Oil Company, began to develop Persia's rich oil fields in the early 1900s.

Nasir al-Din was killed by one of al-Afghani's followers a few years after the boycott.

Reading Check
Analyze Issues
Why did al-Afghani set up a tobacco boycott?

Battle over Tobacco Tension arose between the often corrupt rulers, who wanted to sell concessions to Europeans, and the people. The people were often backed by religious leaders who feared change or disliked Western influence in their nation. In 1890, Persian ruler Nasir al-Din sold a concession to a British company to export Persian tobacco. This action outraged Jamal al-Din al-Afghani, a leader who supported the modernization of Persia. He helped set up a tobacco boycott by the heavy-smoking Persians.

The tobacco boycott worked. Riots broke out, and the ruler was forced to cancel the concession. As unrest continued in Persia, however, the government was unable to control the situation. In 1906, a group of revolutionaries forced the ruler to establish a constitution. In 1907, Russia and Britain took over the country and divided it into spheres of influence. They exercised economic control over Persia.

In the Muslim lands, many European imperialists gained control by using economic imperialism and creating spheres of influence. Although some governments made attempts to modernize their nations, in most cases it was too little too late. In other areas of the globe, imperialists provided the modernization. India, for example, became a colony that experienced enormous change as a result of the occupation of the imperialist British. You will learn about India in Lesson 4.

Lesson 3 Assessment

1. **Organize Information** Make a chart to show imperialistic forms of control that the Europeans used to govern Muslim lands.

Muslim states failed to keep European imperialists out of their lands.

detail   detail   detail

2. **Key Terms and People** For each key term or person in the lesson, write a sentence explaining its significance.

3. **Draw Conclusions** Why did Great Britain want to control the Suez Canal?

4. **Form Generalizations** Why did the Persian people oppose their ruler's policy of selling business concessions to Europeans?

5. **Compare and Contrast** How were the reactions of African and Muslim rulers to imperialism similar? How were they different?

6. **Develop Historical Perspective** What does the quotation in the History in Depth feature suggest about Joseph Chamberlain's view of British imperialism in Africa? How do you think perspectives of British imperialism changed over time?

British Imperialism in India

The Big Idea

As the Mughal Empire declined, Britain seized Indian territory and soon controlled almost the whole subcontinent.

Why It Matters Now

India, the second most populated nation in the world, has its political roots in this colony.

Key Terms and People

sepoy
"jewel in the crown"
Sepoy Mutiny
Raj

Setting the Stage

British economic interest in India began in the 1600s, when the British East India Company set up trading posts at Bombay, Madras, and Calcutta. At first, India's ruling Mughal Dynasty kept European traders under control. By 1707, however, the Mughal Empire was collapsing. Dozens of small states, each headed by a ruler or maharajah, broke away from Mughal control. In 1757, Robert Clive led East India Company troops in a decisive victory over Indian forces allied with the French at the Battle of Plassey. From that time until 1858, the East India Company was the leading power in India.

British Expand Control over India

The area controlled by the East India Company grew over time. Eventually, it governed directly or indirectly an area that included modern Bangladesh, most of southern India, and nearly all the territory along the Ganges River in the north.

East India Company Dominates

Officially, the British government regulated the East India Company's efforts both in London and in India. Until the beginning of the 19th century, the company ruled India with little interference from the British government. The company even had its own army, led by British officers and staffed by **sepoys**, or Indian soldiers. The governor of Bombay, Mountstuart Elphinstone, referred to the sepoy army as "a delicate and dangerous machine, which a little mismanagement may easily turn against us."

A sepoy in uniform

Britain's "Jewel in the Crown" At first, the British treasured India more for its potential than its actual profit. The Industrial Revolution had turned Britain into the world's workshop, and India was a major supplier of raw materials for that workshop. Its 300 million people were also a large potential market for British-made goods. It is not surprising, then, that the British considered India the brightest "**jewel in the crown**," the most valuable of all of Britain's colonies.

The British set up restrictions that prevented the Indian economy from operating on its own. British policies called for India to produce raw materials for British manufacturing and to buy British goods. In addition, Indian competition with British goods was prohibited. For example, India's own handloom textile industry was almost put out of business by imported British textiles. Cheap cloth and ready-made clothes from England flooded the Indian market and drove out local producers.

British Transport Trade Goods India became increasingly valuable to the British after they established a railroad network there. Railroads transported raw products from the interior to the ports and manufactured goods back again. Most of the raw materials were agricultural products produced on plantations. Plantation crops included tea, indigo, coffee, cotton, and jute. Another crop was opium. The British shipped opium to China and exchanged it for tea, which they then sold in England.

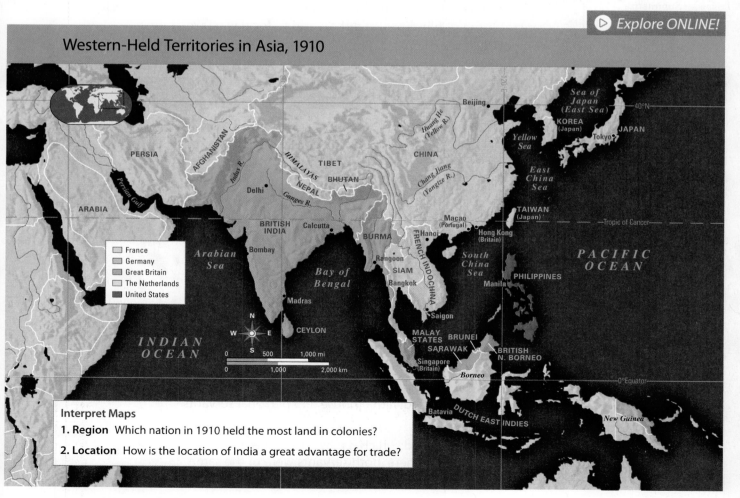

▶ *Explore ONLINE!*

Western-Held Territories in Asia, 1910

France
Germany
Great Britain
The Netherlands
United States

Interpret Maps

1. **Region** Which nation in 1910 held the most land in colonies?

2. **Location** How is the location of India a great advantage for trade?

Trade in these crops was closely tied to international events. For example, the Crimean War in the 1850s cut off the supply of Russian jute to Scottish jute mills. This boosted the export of raw jute from Bengal, a province in India. Likewise, cotton production in India increased when the Civil War in the United States cut off supplies of cotton for British textile mills.

Impact of Colonialism India both benefited from and was harmed by British colonialism. On the negative side, the British held much of the political and economic power. The British restricted Indian-owned industries such as cotton textiles. The emphasis on cash crops resulted in a loss of self-sufficiency for many villagers. The conversion to cash crops reduced food production, causing famines in the late 1800s. The British officially adopted a hands-off policy regarding Indian religious and social customs. Even so, the increased presence of missionaries and the racist attitude of most British officials threatened traditional Indian life.

On the positive side, the laying of the world's third largest railroad network was a major British achievement. When completed, the railroads enabled India to develop a modern economy and brought unity to the connected regions. Along with the railroads, a modern road network, telephone and telegraph lines, dams, bridges, and irrigation canals enabled India to modernize. Sanitation and public health improved. Schools and colleges were founded, and literacy increased. Also, British troops cleared central India of bandits and put an end to local warfare among competing local rulers.

Reading Check
Summarize
On which continents were Indian goods being traded?

SOCIAL HISTORY

Social Class in India

In the photograph at right, a British officer is waited on by Indian servants. This reflects the class system in India.

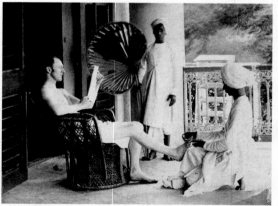

BRITISH ARMY
Social class determined the way of life for the British Army in India. Upper-class men served as officers. Lower-class British served at lesser rank and did not advance past the rank of sergeant. Only men with the rank of sergeant and above were allowed to bring their wives to India.

Each English officer's wife attempted to re-create England in the home setting. Like a general, she directed an army of 20 to 30 servants.

INDIAN SERVANTS
Caste determined Indian occupations. Castes were divided into four broad categories called varna. Indian civil servants were of the third varna. House and personal servants were of the fourth varna.

Even within the varna, jobs were strictly regulated, which is why such large servant staffs were required. For example, in the picture here, both servants were of the same varna. Although the two servants were from the same varna, they had different jobs.

This engraving shows sepoys attacking the British infantry at the Battle of Cawnpore in 1857.

The Sepoy Mutiny

By 1850, the British controlled most of the Indian subcontinent. However, there were many pockets of discontent. Many Indians believed that in addition to controlling their land, the British were trying to convert them to Christianity. The Indian people also resented the constant racism that the British expressed toward them.

Indians Rebel As economic problems increased for Indians, so did their feelings of resentment and nationalism. In 1857, gossip spread among the sepoys, the Indian soldiers, that the cartridges of their new Enfield rifles were greased with beef and pork fat. To use the cartridges, soldiers had to bite off the ends. Both Hindus, who consider the cow sacred, and Muslims, who do not eat pork, were outraged by the news.

A garrison commander was shocked when 85 of the 90 sepoys refused to accept the cartridges. The British handled the crisis badly. The soldiers who had disobeyed were jailed. The next day, on May 10, 1857, the sepoys rebelled. They marched to Delhi, where they were joined by Indian soldiers stationed there. They captured the city of Delhi. From Delhi, the rebellion spread to northern and central India.

Some historians have called this outbreak the **Sepoy Mutiny**. The uprising spread over much of northern India. Fierce fighting took place. Both British and sepoys tried to slaughter each other's armies. The East India Company took more than a year to regain control of the country. The British government sent troops to help them.

The Indians could not unite against the British due to weak leadership and serious splits between Hindus and Muslims. Hindus did not want the Muslim Mughal Empire restored. Indeed, many Hindus preferred British

The Sepoy Mutiny

The Sepoy Mutiny fueled the racist attitudes of the British. Lord Kitchener, British commander in chief of the army in India, illustrated these attitudes.

Analyze Historical Sources
What attitude do you think the native people had toward the British?

"It is this consciousness of the inherent superiority of the European which has won for us India. However well educated and clever a native may be, and however brave he may prove himself, I believe that no rank we can bestow on him would cause him to be considered an equal of the British officer."

—Lord Kitchener, quoted in K. M. Panikkar, *Asia and Western Dominance*

rule to Muslim rule. Most of the princes and maharajahs who had made alliances with the East India Company did not take part in the rebellion. The Sikhs, a religious group that had been hostile to the Mughals, also remained loyal to the British. Indeed, from then on, the bearded and turbaned Sikhs became the mainstay of Britain's army in India.

Turning Point The mutiny marked a turning point in Indian history. As a result of the mutiny, in 1858 the British government took direct command of India. The term **Raj** refers to British rule after India came under the British crown during the reign of Queen Victoria. A cabinet minister in London directed policy, and a British governor-general in India carried out the government's orders. After 1877, this official held the title of viceroy.

To reward the many princes who had remained loyal to Britain, the British promised to respect all treaties the East India Company had made with them. They also promised that the Indian states that were still free would remain independent. Unofficially, however, Britain won greater and greater control of those states.

The mutiny increased distrust between the British and the Indians. A political pamphlet suggested that both Hindus and Muslims "are being ruined under the tyranny and oppression of the . . . treacherous English."

Reading Check
Analyze Effects
In what ways did the Sepoy Mutiny change the political climate of India?

Lesson 4 Assessment

1. **Organize Information** Using your notes, make a list of the key events of British imperialism in India. Then organize the events on a timeline like the one below.

2. **Key Terms and People** For each key term or person in the lesson, write a sentence explaining its significance.

3. **Draw Conclusions** Why didn't Indians unite against the British in the Sepoy Mutiny?

4. **Summarize** What form did British rule take under the Raj?

5. **Make Inferences** How did economic imperialism lead to India's becoming a British colony?

6. **Synthesize** How did imperialism contribute to unity and to the growth of nationalism in India?

European Claims in Southeast Asia

The Big Idea

Demand for Asian products drove Western imperialists to seek possession of Southeast Asian lands.

Why It Matters Now

Southeast Asian independence struggles in the 20th century have their roots in this period of imperialism.

Key Terms and People

Pacific Rim
King Mongkut

Setting the Stage

Just as the European powers rushed to divide Africa, they also competed to carve up the lands of Southeast Asia. These lands form part of the **Pacific Rim**, the countries that border the Pacific Ocean. Western nations desired the Pacific Rim lands for their strategic location along the sea route to China. Westerners also recognized the value of the Pacific colonies as sources of tropical agriculture, minerals, and oil. As the European powers began to appreciate the value of the area, they challenged each other for their own parts of the prize.

European Powers Invade the Pacific Rim

Early in the 18th century, the Dutch East India Company established control over most of the 3,000-mile-long chain of Indonesian islands. The British established a major trading port at Singapore. The French took over Indochina on the Southeast Asian mainland. The Germans claimed the Marshall Islands and parts of New Guinea and the Solomon islands.

The lands of Southeast Asia were perfect for plantation agriculture. The major focus was on sugar cane, coffee, cocoa, rubber, coconuts, bananas, and pineapple. As these products became more important in the world trade markets, European powers raced each other to claim lands.

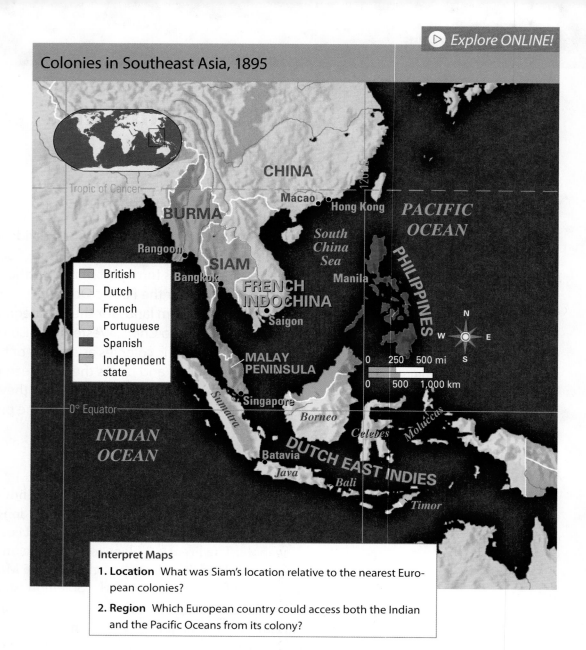

Colonies in Southeast Asia, 1895

▷ Explore ONLINE!

CHINA

BURMA

Rangoon

SIAM

Bangkok

Macao

Hong Kong

South
China
Sea

Manila

PACIFIC
OCEAN

PHILIPPINES

FRENCH
INDOCHINA

Saigon

Tropic of Cancer

Legend:

- British
- Dutch
- French
- Portuguese
- Spanish
- Independent state

MALAY
PENINSULA

Singapore

Borneo

Celebes

Moluccas

0° Equator

INDIAN
OCEAN

Sumatra

Batavia

Java

Bali

DUTCH EAST INDIES

Timor

N
W   E
S

0   250   500 mi

0   500   1,000 km

Interpret Maps

1. **Location** What was Siam's location relative to the nearest European colonies?

2. **Region** Which European country could access both the Indian and the Pacific Oceans from its colony?

Dutch Expand Control The Dutch East India Company, chartered in 1602, actively sought lands in Southeast Asia. It seized Malacca from the Portuguese and fought the British and Javanese for control of Java. The discovery of oil and tin on the islands and the desire for more rubber plantations prompted the Dutch to gradually expand their control over Sumatra, part of Borneo, Celebes, the Moluccas, and Bali. Finally the Dutch ruled the whole island chain of Indonesia, then called the Dutch East Indies.

Management of plantations and trade brought a large Dutch population to the islands. In contrast to the British, who lived temporarily in India but retired in Britain, the Dutch thought of Indonesia as their home. They moved to Indonesia and created a rigid social class system there. The Dutch were on top, wealthy and educated Indonesians came next, and plantation workers were at the bottom. The Dutch also forced farmers to plant one-fifth of their land in specified export crops.

British Take the Malayan Peninsula To compete with the Dutch, the British sought a trading base that would serve as a stop for their ships that traveled the India-China sea routes. They found a large, sheltered harbor on Singapore, an island just off the tip of the Malay Peninsula. The opening of the Suez Canal and the increased demand for tin and rubber combined to make Singapore one of the world's busiest ports.

Britain also gained colonies in Malaysia and in Burma (modern Myanmar). Malaysia had large deposits of tin and became the world's leading rubber exporter. Needing workers to mine the tin and tap the rubber trees, Britain encouraged Chinese to immigrate to Malaysia. Chinese flocked to the area. As a result of such immigration, the Malays soon became a minority in their own country. Conflict between the resident Chinese and the native Malays remains unresolved today.

French Control Indochina The French had been active in Southeast Asia since the 17th century. They even helped the Nguyen (nuh•WIN) dynasty rise to power in Vietnam. In the 1840s, during the rule of an anti-Christian Vietnamese emperor, seven French missionaries were killed. Church leaders and capitalists who wanted a larger share of the overseas market demanded military intervention. Emperor Napoleon III ordered the French army to invade southern Vietnam. Later, the French added Laos, Cambodia, and northern Vietnam to the territory. The combined states would eventually be called French Indochina.

Using direct colonial management, the French themselves filled all important positions in the government bureaucracy. They did not encourage local industry. Four times as much land was devoted to rice production. However, the peasants' consumption of rice decreased because much of the rice was exported. Anger over this reduction set the stage for Vietnamese resistance against the French.

Colonial Impact In Southeast Asia, colonization brought mixed results. Economies grew based on cash crops or goods that could be sold on the world market. Roads, harbors, and rail systems improved communication and transportation but mostly benefited European business. However, education, health, and sanitation did improve.

Unlike other colonial areas, millions of people from other areas of Asia and the world migrated to work on plantations and in the mines in Southeast Asia. The region became a melting pot of Hindus, Muslims, Christians, and Buddhists. The resulting cultural changes often led to racial and religious clashes that are still seen today.

Reading Check
Analyze Motives
Why do you think so many Chinese moved to Malaysia?

The King on Progress

Siam modernized itself under the guidance of **King Mongkut** and his son Chulalongkorn (pictured here). In a royal proclamation, King Chulalongkorn showed his understanding of the importance of progress.

> *"As the times and the course of things in our country have changed, it is essential to promote the advancement of all our academic and technical knowledge and to prevent it from succumbing [giving in] to competition from the outside. In order to achieve this, it is imperative to make haste in education so that knowledge and ability will increase."*
>
> —King Chulalongkorn, "Royal Proclamation in Education"

Analyze Historical Sources
Why do you think King Chulalongkorn believed that education could prevent competition from foreigners?

Siam Remains Independent

While its neighbors on all sides fell under the control of imperialists, Siam (present-day Thailand) maintained its independence throughout the colonial period. Siam lay between British-controlled Burma and French Indochina. France and Britain each aimed to prevent the other from gaining control of Siam. Knowing this, Siamese kings skillfully promoted Siam as a neutral zone between the two powers.

To accomplish the changes, Siam started schools, reformed the legal system, and reorganized the government. The government built its own railroads and telegraph systems and ended slavery. Because the changes came from their own government, the Siamese people escaped the social turmoil, racist treatment, and economic exploitation that occurred in other countries controlled by foreigners.

Reading Check
Summarize
How did Siam keep Britain and France at bay?

Lesson 5 Assessment

1. **Organize Information** Which Western power do you think had the most negative impact on its colonies in Southeast Asia?

   Western powers in Southeast Asia

2. **Key Terms and People** For each key term or person in the lesson, write a sentence explaining its significance.

3. **Compare** How were the Dutch East India Trading Company and the British East India Company similar?

4. **Analyze Effects** What changes took place in Southeast Asia as a result of colonial control?

5. **Draw Conclusions** How did the reforms of the Siamese kings help Siam remain independent?

U.S. Economic Imperialism

The Big Idea

The United States followed an imperialist policy in the Pacific Islands and also put increasing economic and political pressure on Latin America during the 19th century.

Why It Matters Now

This policy set the stage for 20th-century relations between Latin America and the United States and encouraged U.S. imperialism in the Pacific Islands.

Key Terms and People

Emilio Aguinaldo
annexation
Queen Liliuokalani
caudillo
Monroe Doctrine
José Martí
Spanish-American War
Panama Canal
Roosevelt Corollary

Setting the Stage

Western nations desired the Pacific Rim lands for their strategic location along the sea route to China. Westerners also recognized the value of the Pacific colonies as sources of tropical agriculture, minerals, and oil. Latin America's long struggle to gain independence from colonial domination between the late 18th and the mid-19th centuries left the new nations in shambles. Farm fields had been neglected and were overrun with weeds. Buildings in many cities bore the scars of battle. Some cities had been left in ruins. The new nations of Latin America faced a struggle for economic and political recovery that was every bit as difficult as their struggle for independence had been.

A Brazilian plantation at the roadstead of Rio de Janeiro (1830)

U.S. Imperialism in the Pacific Islands

Because Americans had fought for their independence from Britain, most of them disliked the idea of colonizing other nations. However, two groups of Americans were outspoken in their support of imperialism. One group of ambitious empire builders felt the United States should fulfill its destiny as a world power, colonizing like the Europeans. The other group, composed of business interests, welcomed the opening of new markets and trade possibilities.

This photograph shows American soldiers fighting the Filipino nationalists in the early years of the war.

The Philippines Change Hands The United States acquired the Philippine Islands, Puerto Rico, and Guam as a result of the Spanish-American War in 1898. Gaining the Philippines touched off a debate in the United States over imperialism. President McKinley's views swayed many to his side. He told a group of Methodist ministers his intention to "educate Filipinos, and uplift and Christianize them."

Filipino nationalists were not happy to trade one colonizer—the Spanish—for another, the Americans. **Emilio Aguinaldo** (eh•MEE•lyoh-AH•gee•NAHL•doh), leader of the Filipino nationalists, claimed that the United States had promised immediate independence after the Spanish-American War ended. The nationalists declared independence and established the Philippine Republic.

The United States plunged into a fierce struggle with the Filipino nationalists in 1899 and defeated them in 1902. The United States promised the Philippine people that it would prepare them for self-rule. To achieve this goal, the United States built roads, railroads, and hospitals, and set up school systems. However, as with other Southeast Asian areas, businessmen encouraged growing cash crops such as sugar at the expense of basic food crops. This led to food shortages for the Filipinos.

Hawaii Becomes a Republic U.S. interest in Hawaii began around the 1790s when Hawaii was a port on the way to China and East India. Beginning about the 1820s, sugar trade began to change the Hawaiian economy. Americans established sugarcane plantations and became highly

Queen Liliuokalani
(1838–1917)

Liliuokalani was Hawaii's only queen and the last monarch of Hawaii. She bitterly regretted her brother's loss of power to American planters and worked to regain power for the Hawaiian monarchy. As queen, she refused to renew a treaty signed by her brother that would have given commercial privileges to foreign businessmen. It was a decision that would cost her the crown.

successful. By the mid-19th century, American sugar plantations accounted for 75 percent of Hawaii's wealth. At the same time, American sugar planters also gained great political power in Hawaii.

Then in 1890, the McKinley Tariff Act passed by the U.S. government set off a crisis in the islands. The act eliminated the tariffs on all sugar entering the United States. Now, sugar from Hawaii was no longer cheaper than sugar produced elsewhere. That change cut into the sugar producers' profits. Some U.S. business leaders pushed for **annexation** of Hawaii, or the adding of the territory to the United States. Making Hawaii a part of the United States meant that Hawaiian sugar could be sold for greater profits because American producers got an extra two cents a pound from the U.S. government.

About the same time, the new Hawaiian ruler, **Queen Liliuokalani** (luh•LEE•uh•oh•kuh•LAH•nee), took the throne. In 1893, she called for a new constitution that would increase her power. It would also restore the political power of Hawaiians at the expense of wealthy planters. To prevent this from happening, a group of American businessmen hatched a plot to overthrow the Hawaiian monarchy. In 1893, Queen Liliuokalani was removed from power.

In 1894, Sanford B. Dole, a wealthy plantation owner and politician, was named president of the new Republic of Hawaii. The president of the new republic asked the United States to annex it. At first, President Cleveland refused. In 1898, however, the Republic of Hawaii was annexed by the United States.

The period of imperialism was a time of great power and domination of others by mostly European powers. As the 19th century closed, the lands of the world were all claimed. The European powers now faced each other with competing claims. Their battles would become the focus of the 20th century.

Reading Check
Compare and Contrast How were the independence movements in the Pacific Islands similar to and different from the struggle for independence in the United States?

Argentine reformer Domingo Sarmiento

Latin America After Independence

Political independence meant little for most citizens of the new Latin American nations. The majority remained poor laborers caught up in a cycle of poverty.

Colonial Legacy Both before and after independence, most Latin Americans worked for large landowners. The employers paid their workers with vouchers that could be used only at their own supply stores. Since wages were low and prices were high, workers went into debt. Their debt accumulated and passed from one generation to the next. In this system known as peonage, "free" workers were little better than slaves.

Landowners, on the other hand, only got wealthier after independence. Many new Latin American governments took over the lands owned by native peoples and by the Catholic Church. Then they put those lands up for sale. Wealthy landowners were the only people who could afford to buy them, and they snapped them up. But as one Argentinean newspaper reported, "Their greed for land does not equal their ability to use it intelligently." The unequal distribution of land and the landowners' inability to use it effectively combined to prevent social and economic development in Latin America.

Political Instability Political instability was another widespread problem in 19th-century Latin America. Many Latin American army leaders had gained fame and power during their long struggle for independence. They often continued to assert their power. They controlled the new nations as military dictators, or **caudillos** (kaw•DEEL•yohz). They were able to hold on to power because they were backed by the military. By the mid-1800s, nearly all the countries of Latin America were ruled by caudillos. One typical caudillo was Juan Vicente Gómez.

Workers unload coffee beans at a plantation in Brazil. Until recently, Brazil's economy depended heavily on the export of coffee.

He was a ruthless man who ruled Venezuela for nearly 30 years after seizing power in 1908. "All Venezuela is my cattle ranch," he once boasted.

There were some exceptions, however. Reform-minded presidents, such as Argentina's Domingo Sarmiento, made strong commitments to improving education. During Sarmiento's presidency, between 1868 and 1874, the number of students in Argentina doubled. But such reformers usually did not stay in office long. More often than not, a caudillo, supported by the army, seized control of the government.

The caudillos faced little opposition. The wealthy landowners usually supported them because they opposed giving power to the lower classes. In addition, Latin Americans had gained little experience with democracy under European colonial rule. So, the dictatorship of a caudillo did not seem unusual to them. But even when caudillos were not in power, most Latin Americans still lacked a voice in the government. Voting rights—and with them, political power—were restricted to the relatively few members of the upper and middle classes who owned property or could read.

Reading Check
Identify Problems
What difficulties did lower-class Latin Americans continue to face after independence?

Economies Grow Under Foreign Influence

When colonial rule ended in Latin America in the early 1800s, the new nations were no longer restricted to trading with colonial powers. Britain and, later, the United States became Latin America's main trading partners.

Old Products and New Markets Latin America's economies continued to depend on exports, no matter whom they were trading with. As during the colonial era, each country concentrated on one or two products. With advances in technology, however, Latin America's exports grew. The development of the steamship and the building of railroads in the 19th century, for example, greatly increased Latin American trade. Toward the end of the century, the invention of refrigeration helped increase Latin America's exports. The sale of beef, fruits and vegetables, and other perishable goods soared.

But foreign nations benefited far more from the increased trade than Latin America did. In exchange for their exports, Latin Americans imported European and North American manufactured goods. As a result, they had little reason to develop their own manufacturing industries. And as long as Latin America remained unindustrialized, it could not play a leading role on the world economic stage.

Outside Investment and Interference Furthermore, Latin American, including South American, countries used little of their export income to build roads, schools, or hospitals. Nor did they fund programs that would help them become self-sufficient. Instead, they often borrowed money at high interest rates to develop facilities for their export industries. Countries such as Britain, France, the United States, and Germany were willing lenders. The Latin American countries often were unable to pay back their loans, however. In response, foreign lenders sometimes threatened to collect the debt by force. At other times, they threatened to take over the facilities they had funded. In this way, foreign companies gained control of many Latin American industries. This began a new age of economic colonialism in Latin America.

Reading Check
Analyze Effects
How did technology affect Latin American and South American economies?

A Latin American Empire

Long before the United States had any economic interest in Latin American countries, it realized that it had strong links with its southern neighbors. Leaders of the United States were well aware that their country's security depended on the security of Latin America.

The Monroe Doctrine Most Latin American colonies had gained their independence by the early 1800s. But their position was not secure. Many Latin Americans feared that European countries would try to reconquer the new republics. The United States, a young nation itself, feared this, too. So, in 1823, President James Monroe issued what came to be called the **Monroe Doctrine**. This document stated that "the American continents . . . are henceforth not to be considered as subjects for future

José Martí
(1853–1895)

José Martí was only 15 in 1868 when he first began speaking out for Cuban independence. In 1871, the Spanish colonial government punished Martí's open opposition with exile. Except for a brief return to his homeland in 1878, Martí remained in exile for about 20 years. For most of this time, he lived in New York City. There he continued his career as a writer and a revolutionary. "Life on earth is a hand-to-hand combat . . . between the law of love and the law of hate," he proclaimed.

While in New York, Martí helped raise an army to fight for Cuban independence. He died on the battlefield only a month after the war began. But Martí's cry for freedom echoes in his essays and poems and in folk songs about him that are still sung throughout the world.

colonization by any European powers." Until 1898, though, the United States did little to enforce the Monroe Doctrine. Cuba provided a real testing ground.

Cuba Declares Independence The Caribbean island of Cuba was one of Spain's last colonies in the Americas. In 1868, Cuba declared its independence and fought a ten-year war against Spain. In 1878, with the island in ruins, the Cubans gave up the fight. But some Cubans continued to seek independence from Spain. In 1895, **José Martí**, a writer who had been exiled from Cuba by the Spanish, returned to launch a second war for Cuban independence. Martí was killed early in the fighting, but the Cubans battled on.

By the mid-1890s, the United States had developed substantial business holdings in Cuba. Therefore it had an economic stake in the fate of the country. In addition, the Spanish had forced many Cuban civilians into concentration camps. Americans objected to the Spanish brutality. In 1898, the United States joined the Cuban war for independence. This conflict, which became known as the **Spanish-American War**, lasted about four months. U.S. forces launched their first attack not on Cuba but on the Philippine Islands, a Spanish colony thousands of miles away in the Pacific. Unprepared for a war on two fronts, the Spanish military quickly collapsed.

In 1901, Cuba became an independent nation, at least in name. However, the United States installed a military government and continued to exert control over Cuban affairs. This caused tremendous resentment among many Cubans, who had assumed that the United States' aim in

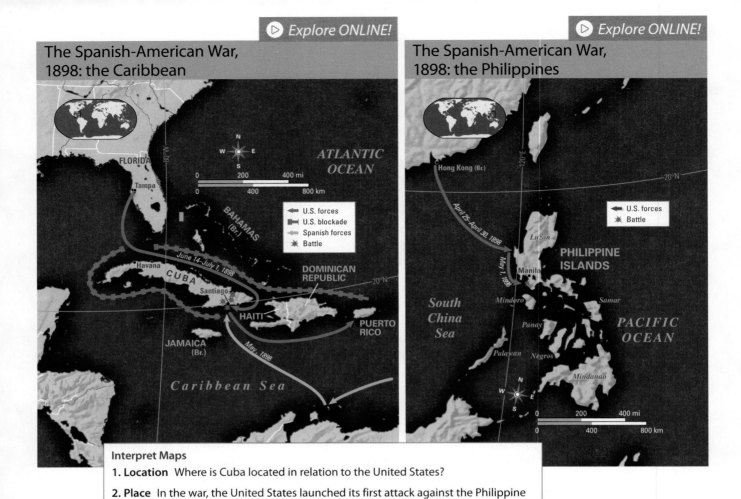

The Spanish-American War, 1898: the Caribbean

The Spanish-American War, 1898: the Philippines

Interpret Maps

1. **Location** Where is Cuba located in relation to the United States?

2. **Place** In the war, the United States launched its first attack against the Philippine Islands. Why might this have surprised the Spanish?

intervening was to help Cuba become truly independent. The split that developed between the United States and Cuba at this time continues to keep these close neighbors miles apart more than a century later.

Connecting the Oceans After Spain's defeat in the Spanish-American War, the United States was the dominant imperial power in Latin America and next set its sights on Panama. Latin Americans were beginning to regard the United States as the political and economic "Colossus of the North." The United States was a colossus in geographic terms, too. By the 1870s, the transcontinental railroad connected its east and west coasts. But land travel still was time consuming and difficult. And sea travel between the coasts involved a trip of about 13,000 miles around the tip of South America. If a canal could be dug across a narrow section of Central America, however, the coast-to-coast journey would be cut in half.

The United States had been thinking about such a project since the early 19th century. In the 1880s, a French company tried—but failed—to build a canal across Panama. Despite this failure, Americans remained enthusiastic about the canal. And no one was more enthusiastic than President Theodore Roosevelt, who led the nation from 1901 to 1909. In 1903, Panama was a province of Colombia. Roosevelt offered that country $10 million plus a yearly payment for the right to build a canal. When the Colombian government demanded more money, the United States responded by encouraging a revolution in Panama. The Panamanians had been trying to break away from Colombia for almost a century. In 1903, with help from the United States Navy, they won their country's independence. In gratitude, Panama gave the United States a ten-mile-wide zone in which to build a canal.

For the next decade, American engineers contended with floods and withering heat to build the massive waterway. However, their greatest challenge was the disease-carrying insects that infested the area. The United States began a campaign to destroy the mosquitoes that carried yellow fever and malaria and the rats that carried bubonic plague. The effort to control these diseases was eventually successful. Even so, thousands of workers died during construction of the canal. The **Panama Canal** finally opened in 1914. Ships from around the world soon began to use it. Latin America had become a crossroads of world trade. And the United States controlled the tollgate.

The Roosevelt Corollary The building of the Panama Canal was only one way that the United States expanded its influence in Latin America in the early 20th century. Its presence in Cuba and its large investments in

THE BIG STICK IN THE CARIBBEAN SEA

This cartoon suggests that the Roosevelt Corollary turned the Caribbean into a U.S. wading pool.

Panama Canal

The Panama Canal is considered one of the world's greatest engineering accomplishments. Its completion changed the course of history by opening a worldwide trade route between the Atlantic and Pacific Oceans. As shown in the diagram, on entering the canal, ships are raised about 85 feet in a series of three locks. On leaving the canal, ships are lowered to sea level by another series of three locks.

The canal also had a lasting effect on other technologies. Since the early 1900s, ships have been built to dimensions that will allow them to pass through the canal's locks.

Ships passing through the Pedro Miguel Locks

Panama Canal Cross-section

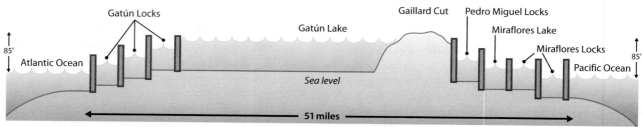

This cross-section shows the different elevations and locks that a ship moves through on the trip through the canal.

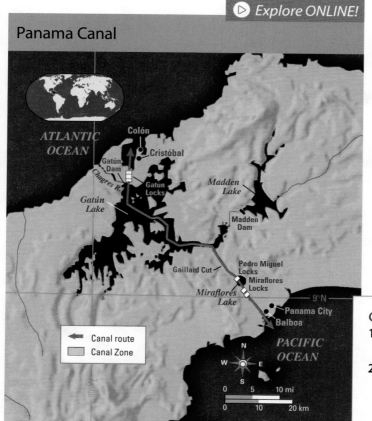

Canal Facts

- The canal took ten years to build (1904–1914) and cost $380 million.
- During the construction of the canal, workers dug up more than 200 million cubic yards of earth.
- Thousands of workers died from diseases while building the canal.
- The trip from San Francisco to New York City via the Panama Canal is about 9,000 miles shorter than the trip around South America.
- The 51-mile trip through the canal takes 8 to 10 hours.
- The canal now handles more than 13,000 ships a year from around 70 nations carrying 192 million short tons of cargo.
- Panama took control of the canal on December 31, 1999 and began expanding it in 2007.

Critical Thinking

1. **Identify Problems** What difficulties did workers face in constructing the canal?

2. **Evaluate** In the more than 100 years since it was built, do you think that the benefits of the Panama Canal to world trade have outweighed the costs in time, money, and human life? Explain your answer.

many Central and South American countries strengthened its foothold. To protect those economic interests, in 1904, President Roosevelt issued a corollary, or extension, to the Monroe Doctrine. The **Roosevelt Corollary** gave the United States the right to be "an international police power" in the Western Hemisphere.

The United States used the Roosevelt Corollary many times in the following years to justify U.S. intervention in Latin America. U.S. troops occupied some countries for decades. Many Latin Americans protested this intervention, but they were powerless to stop their giant neighbor to the north. The U.S. government simply turned a deaf ear to their protests. It could not ignore the rumblings of revolution just over its border with Mexico, however.

Reading Check
Analyze Motives
Why was the United States so interested in building the Panama Canal?

Lesson 6 Assessment

1. **Organize Information** Write the events that you think were most beneficial to Latin America on the timeline.

| 1823 | 1898 | 1903 | 1914 |

2. **Key Terms and People** For each key term or person in the lesson, write a sentence explaining its significance.

3. **Summarize** Why did the gap between rich and poor in Latin America grow after independence?

4. **Analyze Effects** What economic gains and setbacks did Latin American countries experience after independence?

5. **Make Inferences** Why was the United States so interested in the security of Latin America?

6. **Contrast** How was the principle of the Roosevelt Corollary different from that of the Monroe Doctrine?

Module 23 Assessment

Key Terms and People

For each term or name below, briefly explain its connection to the imperialism of 1850–1914.

1. imperialism
2. Berlin Conference
3. Menelik II
4. Social Darwinism
5. Shaka
6. Suez Canal
7. Raj
8. Queen Liliuokalani
9. Monroe Doctrine
10. Spanish-American War

Main Ideas

Use your notes and the information in the module to answer the following questions.

The Roots of Imperialism

1. What motivated the nations of Europe to engage in imperialist activities? Cite specific text evidence to support your answer.
2. What effect did the Boer War have on Africans?

Imperialism in Africa

3. What are the forms of imperial rule?
4. How did Ethiopia successfully resist European rule?

Europeans Claim Muslim Lands

5. Why were the European nations interested in controlling the Muslim lands?
6. What methods did the Muslim leaders use to try to prevent European imperialism?

British Imperialism in India

7. How was the economy of India transformed by the British?
8. What caused the Sepoy Mutiny?

European Claims in Southeast Asia

9. How did Siam manage to remain independent while other countries in the area were being colonized?
10. Why did Southeast Asia become an ethnically diverse region during the colonial era?

U.S. Economic Imperialism

11. How were Latin American caudillos able to achieve power and hold on to it?
12. What effects did the Monroe Doctrine and the Roosevelt Corollary have on Latin America?

Critical Thinking

1. **Summarize** How did the local people in Africa, India, and Southeast Asia resist the demands of the Europeans?

2. **Analyze Effects** What effects did imperialism have on the economic life of the lands and people colonized by the European imperialists?

3. **Draw Conclusions** Why do you think the British viewed the Suez Canal as the lifeline of their empire?

4. **Synthesize** What positive and negative impact did inventions such as the railroad and the steamship have on the land and people conquered by the imperialists?

5. **Develop Historical Perspectives** What economic, political, and social conditions encouraged the growth of imperialism in Africa and Asia?

6. **Evaluate** How did the decline of the Ottoman Empire contribute to the increasing power of European nations?

7. **Compare and Contrast** Investigate the resistance in the Sudan, and compare it to the resistance by the Ashanti. How were they similar or different?

Engage with History

In the feature Views of Imperialism, you read different primary sources that revealed distinct perspectives on European imperialism. Analyze the evolution of perspectives into contemporary times by researching and examining one or two secondary sources on the topic. Consider the following questions:

- Does the author make implicit or explicit philosophical assumptions?
- What beliefs does the author express or assert?
- Does the author show a bias on the topic?
- What is the nature of the author's historical interpretation of the topic?
- Does the author use facts and evidence to support his or her argument?
- Does the author use facts and evidence to refute another argument?

Discuss these questions in a small group. Then evaluate the authors' interpretations of European imperialism, considering their use of fact versus opinion, multiple perspectives, and causes and effects.

Focus on Writing

Write a magazine **feature article** about the effects of colonization. Be sure to address the following points:

- Provide some background and facts on the country you're writing about.
- Tell where the colonizers have come from.
- Describe how the colonizers treat the colonized people.
- Include quotations from both the colonizers and the colonized.
- Draw conclusions about each side's opinion of the other.

Read your feature article aloud while a partner or small group is listening. Ask them to call out any word, phrases, or concepts that are unfamiliar to them. Provide clarifications as needed.

Multimedia Activity

Compare British and French imperialism in Africa and Asia by examining

- the influence of geography;
- natural resources;
- their policies.

Write interview questions for both British and French political leaders of the time.

Module 24

Transformations Around the Globe

Essential Question

How did imperialism, economic instability, and revolution affect China, Japan, and Mexico?

About the Photo: This painting from the 18th century shows Canton, known today as Guangzhou, a busy Chinese port on the Pearl River.

▶ *Explore ONLINE!*

HISTORY.

VIDEOS, including...
- Guns of the Revolution (Tales of the Gun)
- Chinatown: Strangers in a Strange Land

☑ Document Based Investigations

☑ Graphic Organizers

☑ Interactive Games

☑ Interactive Map: Colonial Powers Carve Up China, 1850–1910

☑ Image Compare: The Mexican Revolution

In this module, you will learn how China and Japan responded to European powers. You will also learn about the Mexican Revolution.

What You Will Learn ...

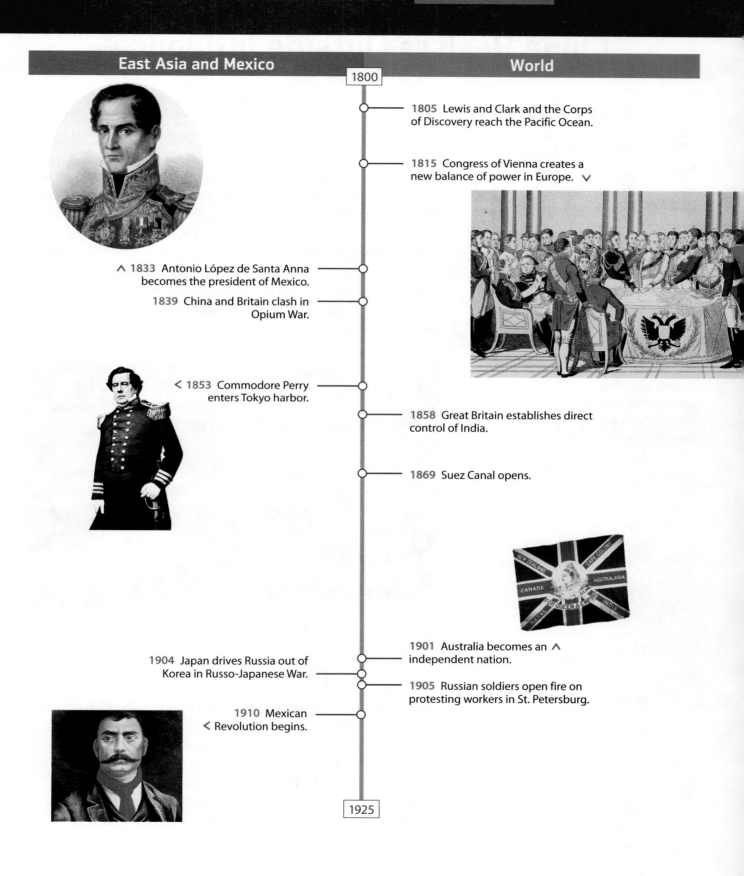

Timeline of Events 1800–1925

▶ Explore ONLINE!

East Asia and Mexico

World

1800

1805 Lewis and Clark and the Corps of Discovery reach the Pacific Ocean.

1815 Congress of Vienna creates a new balance of power in Europe. ∨

∧ **1833** Antonio López de Santa Anna becomes the president of Mexico.

1839 China and Britain clash in Opium War.

< **1853** Commodore Perry enters Tokyo harbor.

1858 Great Britain establishes direct control of India.

1869 Suez Canal opens.

1901 Australia becomes an ∧ independent nation.

1904 Japan drives Russia out of Korea in Russo-Japanese War.

1905 Russian soldiers open fire on protesting workers in St. Petersburg.

1910 Mexican < Revolution begins.

1925

China Resists Outside Influence

The Big Idea

Western economic pressure forced China to open to foreign trade and influence.

Why It Matters Now

China has become an increasingly important member of the global community.

Key Terms and People

Opium War
extraterritorial rights
Taiping Rebellion
sphere of influence
Open Door Policy
Boxer Rebellion

Setting the Stage

Out of pride in their ancient culture, the Chinese looked down on all foreigners. In 1793, however, the Qing emperor agreed to receive an ambassador from England. The Englishman brought gifts of the West's most advanced technology—clocks, globes, musical instruments, and even a hot-air balloon. The emperor was not impressed. In a letter to England's King George III, he stated that the Chinese already had everything they needed. They were not interested in the "strange objects" and gadgets that the West was offering them.

Finely made lanterns were among the Chinese goods favored by the Western merchants.

China and the West

China was able to reject these offers from the West because it was largely self-sufficient. The basis of this self-sufficiency was China's healthy agricultural economy. During the 11th century, China had acquired a quick-growing strain of rice from Southeast Asia. By the time of the Qing Dynasty, the rice was being grown throughout the southern part of the country. Around the same time, the 17th and 18th centuries, Spanish and Portuguese traders brought maize, sweet potatoes, and peanuts from the Americas as part of the Columbian Exchange. These new crops helped China increase the productivity of its existing farmland, and the crops also could be grown throughout the nation. Therefore, new farms and settlements emerged throughout China. The resulting increase in agriculture allowed China to effectively feed its huge population. In the Americas, however, the Columbian Exchange had the opposite effect—it devastated indigenous populations as diseases killed an unprecedented number of people.

China also had extensive mining and manufacturing industries. Rich salt, tin, silver, and iron mines produced great quantities of ore. The mines provided work for tens of thousands of people. The Chinese also produced beautiful silks, high-quality cottons, and fine porcelain.

The Tea-Opium Connection Because of their self-sufficiency, the Chinese had little interest in trading with the West. For decades, the only place they would allow foreigners to do business was at the southern port of Guangzhou (gwahng•joh). And the balance of trade at Guangzhou was clearly in China's favor. This means that China earned much more for its exports than it spent on imports.

European merchants were determined to find a product the Chinese would buy in large quantities. Eventually they found one—opium. Opium is a habit-forming narcotic made from the poppy plant. Chinese doctors had been using it to relieve pain for hundreds of years. In the late 18th century, however, British merchants smuggled opium into China for nonmedical use. It took a few decades for opium smoking to catch on, but by 1835, as many as 12 million Chinese people were addicted to the drug.

War Breaks Out This growing supply of opium caused great problems for China. The Qing emperor was angry about the situation. In 1839, one of his highest advisers wrote a letter to England's Queen Victoria about the problem:

> "By what right do they [British merchants] . . . use the poisonous drug to injure the Chinese people? . . . I have heard that the smoking of opium is very strictly forbidden by your country; that is because the harm caused by opium is clearly understood. Since it is not permitted to do harm to your own country, then even less should you let it be passed on to the harm of other countries."
>
> —Lin Zexu, quoted in *China's Response to the West*

The pleas went unanswered, and Britain refused to stop trading opium. The result was an open clash between the British and the Chinese—the **Opium War** of 1839. The battles took place mostly at sea. China's outdated ships were no match for Britain's steam-powered gunboats. As a result, the Chinese suffered a humiliating defeat. In 1842, they signed a peace treaty, the Treaty of Nanjing.

This painting depicts the British iron steam ship *Nemesis* defeating Chinese warships during the Opium Wars.

Reading Check
Analyze Issues
What conflicting
British and Chinese
positions led to the
Opium War?

This treaty gave Britain the island of Hong Kong. After signing another treaty in 1844, U.S. and other foreign citizens also gained **extraterritorial rights**. Under these rights, foreigners were not subject to Chinese law at Guangzhou and four other Chinese ports. Many Chinese greatly resented the foreigners and the bustling trade in opium they conducted.

Growing Internal Problems

Foreigners were not the greatest of China's problems in the mid-19th century, however. The country's own population provided an overwhelming challenge. The number of Chinese grew to 430 million by 1850, a 30 percent gain in only 60 years. Yet, in the same period of time, food production barely increased. As a result, hunger was widespread, even in good years. Many people became discouraged, and opium addiction rose steadily. As their problems mounted, the Chinese began to rebel against the Qing Dynasty.

The Taiping Rebellion During the late 1830s, Hong Xiuquan (hung-shee•oo•choo•ahn), a young man from Guangdong province in southern China, began recruiting followers to help him build a "Heavenly Kingdom of Great Peace." In this kingdom, all Chinese people would share China's vast wealth and no one would live in poverty. Hong's movement was called the **Taiping Rebellion**, from the Chinese word *taiping,* meaning "great peace."

By the 1850s, Hong had organized a massive peasant army of some one million people. Over time, the Taiping army took control of large areas of southeastern China. Then, in 1853, Hong captured the city of Nanjing and

---

Now and Then

Special Economic Zones

Today, as in the late 1800s, the Chinese government limits foreign economic activity to particular areas of the country. Most of these areas, called special economic zones (SEZs), are located on the coast and waterways of southeastern China. First established in the late 1970s, the SEZs are designed to attract, but also control, foreign investment.

One of the most successful SEZs is Shanghai. Dozens of foreign companies—including IBM of the United States, Hitachi of Japan, Siemens of Germany, and Unilever of Great Britain—had invested over $73 billion in the building and operating of factories, stores, and other businesses. This investment had a huge impact. Shanghai's per capita GDP grew from around $1200 in 1990 to over $15,00 in 2014.

Shanghai today

declared it his capital. Hong soon withdrew from everyday life and left family members and his trusted lieutenants in charge of the government of his kingdom.

The leaders of the Taiping government, however, constantly feuded among themselves. Also, Qing imperial troops and British and French forces all launched attacks against the Taiping. By 1864, this combination of internal fighting and outside assaults had brought down the Taiping government. But China paid a terrible price. At least 20 million—and possibly twice that many—people died in the rebellion.

Reading Check
Recognize Effects
What were the results of the Taiping Rebellion?

A Taiping force surrounds and destroys an enemy village.

Foreign Influence Grows

The Taiping Rebellion and several other smaller uprisings put tremendous internal pressure on the Chinese government. And, despite the Treaty of Nanjing, external pressure from foreign powers was increasing. At the Qing court, stormy debates raged about how best to deal with these issues. Some government leaders called for reforms patterned on Western ways. Others, however, clung to traditional ways and accepted change very reluctantly.

Resistance to Change During the last half of the 19th century, one person was in command at the Qing imperial palace. The Dowager Empress Cixi (tsoo•shee) held the reins of power in China from 1862 until 1908 with only one brief gap. Although she was committed to traditional values, the Dowager Empress did support certain reforms. In the 1860s,

Vocabulary
dowager a widow who holds a title or property from her deceased husband

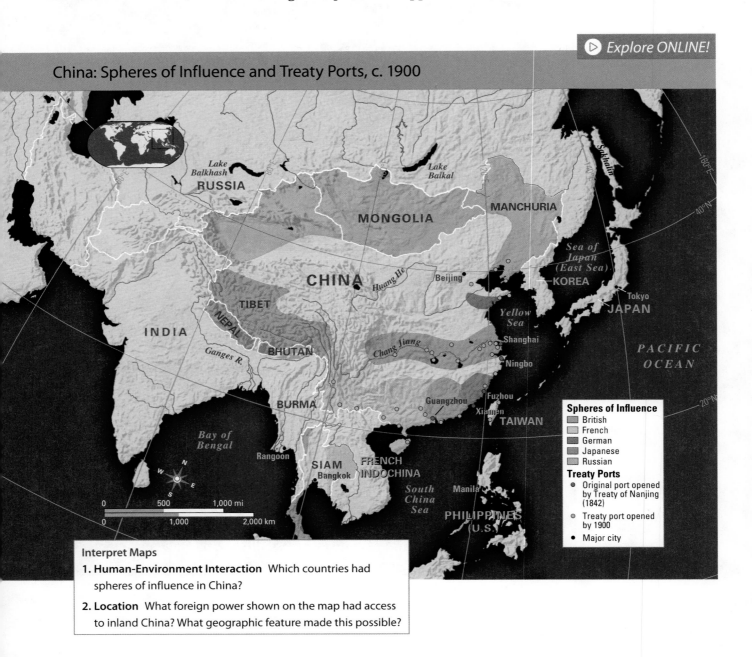

▷ *Explore ONLINE!*

China: Spheres of Influence and Treaty Ports, c. 1900

Spheres of Influence
- ▨ British
- ▨ French
- ▨ German
- ▨ Japanese
- ▨ Russian

Treaty Ports
- ● Original port opened by Treaty of Nanjing (1842)
- ○ Treaty port opened by 1900
- ● Major city

Interpret Maps

1. **Human-Environment Interaction** Which countries had spheres of influence in China?

2. **Location** What foreign power shown on the map had access to inland China? What geographic feature made this possible?

The Dowager Empress Cixi

for example, she backed the self-strengthening movement. This program aimed to update China's educational system, diplomatic service, and military. Under this program, China set up factories to manufacture steam-powered gunboats, rifles, and ammunition. The self-strengthening movement had mixed results, however.

Other Nations Step In Other countries were well aware of China's continuing problems. Throughout the late 19th century, many foreign nations took advantage of the situation and attacked China. Treaty negotiations after each conflict gave these nations increasing control over China's economy. Many of Europe's major powers and Japan gained a strong foothold in China. This foothold, or **sphere of influence**, was an area in which the foreign nation controlled trade and investment.

The United States was a long-time trading partner with China. Americans worried that other nations would soon divide China into formal colonies and shut out American traders. To prevent this occurrence, in 1899 the United States declared the **Open Door Policy**. This proposed that China's "doors" be open to merchants of all nations. Britain and the other European nations agreed. The policy thus protected both U.S. trading rights in China and China's freedom from colonization. But the country was still at the mercy of foreign powers.

Reading Check
Recognize Effects
What importance did spheres of influence have for China?

An Upsurge in Chinese Nationalism

Humiliated by their loss of power, many Chinese pressed for strong reforms. Among those demanding change was China's young emperor, Guangxu (gwahng•shoo). In June 1898, Guangxu introduced measures to modernize China. These measures called for reorganizing China's educational system, strengthening the economy, modernizing the military, and streamlining the government.

Most Qing officials saw these innovations as threats to their power. They reacted with alarm, calling the Dowager Empress back to the imperial court. On her return, she acted with great speed. She placed Guangxu under arrest and took control of the government. She then reversed his reforms. Guangxu's efforts brought about no change whatsoever. The Chinese people's frustration with their situation continued to grow.

The Boxer Rebellion This widespread frustration finally erupted into violence. Poor peasants and workers resented the special privileges granted to foreigners. They also resented Chinese Christians, who had adopted a foreign faith. To demonstrate their discontent, they formed a secret organization called the Society of Righteous and Harmonious Fists. They soon came to be known as the Boxers. Their campaign against the Dowager Empress's rule and foreigner privilege was called the **Boxer Rebellion**.

A gang of Boxers attacks Chinese Christians.

In the spring of 1900, the Boxers descended on Beijing. Shouting "Death to the foreign devils," the Boxers surrounded the European section of the city. They kept it under siege for several months. The Dowager Empress expressed support for the Boxers but did not back her words with military aid. In August, a multinational force of 19,000 troops marched on Beijing and quickly defeated the Boxers.

Despite the failure of the Boxer Rebellion, a strong sense of nationalism had emerged in China. The Chinese people realized that their country must resist more foreign intervention. Even more important, they felt that the government must become responsive to their needs.

The Beginnings of Reform At this point, even the Qing court realized that China needed to make profound changes to survive. In 1905, the Dowager Empress sent a select group of Chinese officials on a world tour to study the operation of different governments. The group traveled to Japan, the United States, Britain, France, Germany, Russia, and Italy. On their return in the spring of 1906, the officials recommended that China restructure its government. They based their suggestions on the constitutional monarchy of Japan. The empress accepted this recommendation and began making reforms. Although she convened a national assembly within a year, change was slow. In 1908, the court announced that it would establish a full constitutional government by 1917.

However, the turmoil in China did not end with these progressive steps. China experienced unrest for the next four decades as it continued to face internal and external threats. China's neighbor Japan also faced pressure from the West during this time. But it responded to this influence in a much different way.

Reading Check
Analyze Causes
Why did the Boxer Rebellion fail?

Lesson 1 Assessment

1. **Organize Information** List China's problems in a chart. Were internal or external problems the most trouble for China? Why?

China's Problems	
Internal	External

2. **Key Terms and People** For each key term or person in the lesson, write a sentence explaining its significance.

3. **Summarize** Why did the Chinese have little interest in trading with the West?

4. **Identify Problems** What internal problems did China face prior to the Taiping Rebellion?

5. **Analyze Motives** Why do you think European powers established spheres of influence in China rather than colonies, as they did in Africa and other parts of Asia?

6. **Compare and Contrast** What were the similarities and differences between the Taiping Rebellion and the Boxer Rebellion?

7. **Synthesize** What would you show on an annotated map of the special economic zones in China?

Modernization in Japan

Setting the Stage

In the early 17th century, Japan had shut itself off from almost all contact with other nations. Under the rule of the Tokugawa shoguns, Japanese society was very tightly ordered. The shogun parceled out land to the daimyo, or lords. The peasants worked for and lived under the protection of their daimyo and his small army of samurai, or warriors. This rigid feudal system kept the country free of civil war. Peace and relative prosperity reigned in Japan for two centuries.

The Big Idea

Japan followed the model of Western powers by industrializing and expanding its foreign influence.

Why It Matters Now

Japan's continued development of its own way of life has made it a leading world power.

Key Terms and People

Treaty of Kanagawa
Meiji era
Russo-Japanese War
annexation

This woodblock print by Katsushika Hokusai shows rural life in Japan.

Japan Ends Its Isolation

The Japanese had almost no contact with the industrialized world during this time of isolation. They continued, however, to trade with China and with Dutch merchants from Indonesia. They also had diplomatic contact with Korea. However, trade was growing in importance, both inside and outside Japan.

The Demand for Foreign Trade Beginning in the early 19th century, Westerners tried to convince the Japanese to open their ports to trade. British, French, Russian, and American officials occasionally anchored off the Japanese coast. Like China, however, Japan repeatedly refused to receive them. Then, in 1853, U.S. Commodore Matthew Perry took four ships into what is now Tokyo Harbor. These massive wooden ships powered by steam astounded the Japanese. The ships' cannons also shocked them. The Tokugawa shogun realized he had no choice but to receive Perry and the letter Perry had brought from U.S. president Millard Fillmore.

Fillmore's letter asked the shogun to allow free trade between the United States and Japan. Perry delivered it with a threat, however. He would come back with a larger fleet in a year to receive Japan's reply. That reply was the **Treaty of Kanagawa** of 1854. Under its terms, Japan opened two ports at which U.S. ships could take on supplies. After the United States had pushed open the door, other Western powers followed. By 1860, Japan, like China, had granted foreigners permission to trade at several treaty ports. It had also extended extraterritorial rights to many foreign nations.

Meiji Era The Japanese were angry that the shogun had given in to the foreigners' demands. They turned to Japan's young emperor, Mutsuhito (moot•soo•HEE•toh), who seemed to symbolize the country's sense of pride and nationalism. In 1867, the Tokugawa shogun stepped down, ending the military dictatorships that had lasted since the 12th century. Mutsuhito took control of the government. He chose the name *Meiji* for his reign, which means "enlightened rule." Mutsuhito's reign, which lasted 45 years, is known as the **Meiji era**. The emperor realized that the best way to counter Western influence was to modernize. He sent diplomats to Europe and North America to study Western ways.

Meiji Reform and Modernization The Japanese chose what they believed to be the best that Western civilization had to offer and adapted it. They admired Germany's strong centralized government, so they used its constitution as a model for their own. The Japanese also admired the discipline of the German army and the skill of the British navy. They imitated these European powers as they modernized their military. They also instituted a military draft. Japan adopted the American system of universal public education and required that all Japanese children attend school, resulting in greater literacy in Japan. Their teachers often included foreign experts. Students could go abroad to study as well. The government also established medical schools that taught German and other Western medical practices. These new medical practices changed the way doctors were educated, the way patients were treated, and the medicine people were given. It also led to changes in the testing and making of medicine.

The emperor supported following the Western path of industrialization. By the early 20th century, the Japanese economy had become as modern as any in the world. The country built its first railroad line in 1872. The track connected Tokyo, the nation's capital, with the port of Yokohama, 20 miles to the south. By 1914, Japan had more than 7,000 miles of railroad.

Japanese Emperor Mutsuhito

Telegraph and telephone lines opened communication across the nation. In addition, coal production grew from half a million tons in 1875 to more than 21 million tons in 1913. Meanwhile, large, state-supported companies built thousands of factories. Traditional Japanese industries, such as tea processing and silk production, expanded to give the country unique products to trade. Developing modern industries, such as shipbuilding, made Japan competitive with the West.

Japanese society and culture changed as the nation modernized. Many Japanese people adopted Western cultural trends, such as fashion and sports like baseball. Even drinking tea changed. As more tea could be manufactured, tea was served more frequently.

Japanese Nationalism As Japanese leaders modernized the country, they fostered a national identity in the people. This was accomplished by establishing a mandatory educational system that taught loyalty to the government and to the emperor. The end of feudalism and its legal class distinctions, along with the institution of universal military service for all men, also unified the Japanese people. People now shared more commonalties and were united under the emperor. However, this path to nationalism was very different from the paths other nations followed. For example, Otto von Bismarck orchestrated the unification of Germany very differently. He unified the country not through "enlightened rule" and unifying systems as Emperor did, but through strengthening the military and forming alliances that supported his agenda of unification, including prompting countries into war with Austria. Bismarck unified the nation by "blood" and "iron," terms he used in a speech to the Prussian legislature.

Reading Check **Compare and Contrast** How was Japan's rise to nationalism different from Germany's?

SOCIAL HISTORY

Effects of Industrialization on Nations

Industrialization had common effects in many nations. In England and Japan, for example, many people moved from rural areas to cities to work in factories. Communication improved as newspapers and telegraph lines proliferated and people traveled on railways. In addition, people of all classes—not just the aristocracy—could now own land and start companies. Both nations also faced similar challenges. Pollution increased, especially in growing cities, and economies depended more on natural resources. Working conditions in factories were harsh, and workers lived in terrible conditions.

The industrialization of England and Japan had differences, too. Citizens in England invented many technologies used in new industrial processes, but Japan imported them. Entrepreneurship and private capital financed much industrialization in England, but Japan's government financed the new industries. Once established, the companies were often sold to wealthy citizens.

Critical Thinking

1. **Compare and Contrast** How was industrialization similar and different in England and Japan?

2. **Form Opinions** Which nation do you think faced the most challenges?

Imperial Japan

Japan's race to modernize paid off. By 1890, the country had several dozen war ships and 500,000 well-trained, well-armed soldiers. It had become the strongest military power in Asia.

Japan had gained military, political, and economic strength. It then sought to eliminate the extraterritorial rights of foreigners. The Japanese foreign minister assured foreigners that they could rely on fair treatment in Japan. This was because its constitution and legal codes were similar to those of European nations, he explained. His reasoning was convincing, and in 1894, foreign powers accepted the abolition of extraterritorial rights for their citizens living in Japan. Japan's feeling of strength and equality with the Western nations rose.

As Japan's sense of power grew, the nation also became more imperialistic. As in Europe, national pride played a large part in Japan's imperial plans. The Japanese were determined to show the world that they were a powerful nation.

Japan Attacks China The Japanese first turned their sights to their neighbor, Korea. In 1876, Japan forced Korea to open three ports to Japanese trade. But China also considered Korea to be important, both as a trading partner and a military outpost. Recognizing their similar interests in Korea, Japan and China signed a hands-off agreement. In 1885, both countries pledged that they would not send their armies into Korea.

In June 1894, however, China broke that agreement. Rebellions had broken out against Korea's king. He asked China for military help in putting them down. Chinese troops marched into Korea. Japan protested and sent its troops to Korea to fight the Chinese. This Sino-Japanese War lasted just a few months. In that time, Japan drove the Chinese out of Korea, destroyed the Chinese navy, and gained a foothold in Manchuria.

Vocabulary
Sino a prefix meaning "Chinese"

China and Japan Confront the West and Imperialism

China	Both	Japan
Remains committed to traditional values	Have well-established traditional values	Considers modernization to be necessary
Loses numerous territorial conflicts	Initially resist change	Borrows and adapts Western ways
Grants other nations spheres of influence within China	Oppose Western imperialism	Strengthens its economic and military power
Finally accepts necessity for reform		Becomes an empire builder

Interpret Charts

1. **Contrast** According to the chart, in what ways did China and Japan deal differently with Western influence?

2. **Compare** What similar responses did each country share despite the different paths they followed? Were these responses similar to how other countries, such as India, responded to outside influence?

Warlike Japan

Cartoonists often use symbols to identify the countries, individuals, or even ideas featured in their cartoons. Russia has long been symbolized as a bear by cartoonists. Here, the cartoonist uses a polar bear.

Prior to the Meiji era, cartoonists usually pictured Japan as a fierce samurai. Later, however, Japan often was symbolized by a caricature of Emperor Mutsuhito. Here, the cartoonist has exaggerated the emperor's physical features to make him look like a bird of prey.

Analyze Historical Sources
1. How does the cartoonist signify that Japan is warlike?
2. In their fight, Russia and Japan appear to be crushing someone. Who do you think this might be?

In 1895, China and Japan signed a peace treaty. This treaty gave Japan its first colonies, Taiwan and the neighboring Pescadores Islands. Shortly after the war, Japan renewed its focus to build an even stronger military. Japan wanted a military that could defend the nation from Western powers.

Russo-Japanese War Japan's victory over China changed the world's balance of power. Russia and Japan emerged as the major powers—and enemies—in East Asia. The two countries soon went to war over Manchuria. In 1903, Japan offered to recognize Russia's rights in Manchuria if the Russians would agree to stay out of Korea. But the Russians refused.

In February 1904, Japan launched a surprise attack on Russian ships anchored off the coast of Manchuria. In the resulting **Russo-Japanese War**, Japan drove Russian troops out of Korea and captured most of Russia's Pacific fleet. It also destroyed Russia's Baltic fleet, which had sailed all the way around Africa to participate in the war.

In 1905, Japan and Russia began peace negotiations. U.S. president Theodore Roosevelt helped draft the treaty, which the two nations signed on a ship off Portsmouth, New Hampshire. This agreement, the Treaty of Portsmouth, gave Japan the captured territories. It also forced Russia to withdraw from Manchuria and to stay out of Korea.

Japanese Occupation of Korea After defeating Russia, Japan attacked Korea with a vengeance. In 1905, it made Korea a protectorate. Japan sent in "advisers," who grabbed more and more power from the Korean government. The Korean king was unable to rally international support for his regime. In 1907, Japan forced him to give up control of the country. Within

Vocabulary
protectorate
a country under the partial control and protection of another nation

Western Views of the East

The Japanese victory over the Russians in 1905 exploded a strong Western myth. Many Westerners believed that white people were a superior race. The overwhelming success of European colonialism and imperialism in the Americas, Africa, and Asia had reinforced this belief. But the Japanese had shown Europeans that people of other races were their equal in modern warfare.

Unfortunately, Japan's military victory led to a different form of Western racism. Influenced by the ideas of Germany's Emperor Wilhelm II, the West imagined the Japanese uniting with the Chinese and conquering Europe. The resulting racist Western fear of what was called the *yellow peril* influenced world politics for many decades.

two years, the Korean Imperial Army was disbanded. In 1910, Japan officially imposed **annexation** on Korea, or brought that country under Japan's control.

The Japanese were harsh rulers. They shut down Korean newspapers and took over Korean schools. There they replaced the study of Korean language and history with Japanese subjects. They took land away from Korean farmers and gave it to Japanese settlers. They encouraged Japanese businessmen to start industries in Korea, but forbade Koreans from going into business. Resentment of Japan's repressive rule grew, helping to create a strong Korean nationalist movement.

The rest of the world clearly saw the brutal results of Japan's imperialism. Nevertheless, the United States and other European countries largely ignored what was happening in Korea. They were too busy with their own imperialistic aims.

Reading Check
Summarize How did Japan treat the Koreans after it annexed the country?

Lesson 2 Assessment

1. **Organize Information** Do you think that Japan could have become an imperialistic power if it had not modernized? Why or why not?

Modernization
Imperialism

2. **Key Terms and People** For each key term or person in the lesson, write a sentence explaining its significance.

3. **Compare** How was the Treaty of Kanagawa similar to the treaties that China signed with various European powers?

4. **Summarize** What steps did the Meiji emperor take to modernize Japan?

5. **Find Main Ideas** How did Japan begin its quest to build an empire?

6. **Analyze Causes** What influences do you think were most important in motivating Japan to build its empire?

7. **Analyze Effects** How did Japan's victory in the Russo-Japanese War both explode and create stereotypes?

Japanese Woodblock Printing

Woodblock printing in Japan evolved from black-and-white prints created by Buddhists in the 700s. By the late 1700s, artists developed methods to create multicolor prints.

Woodblock prints could be produced quickly and in large quantities, so they were cheaper than paintings. In the mid-1800s, a Japanese person could buy a woodblock print for about the same price as a bowl of noodles. As a result, woodblock prints like those shown here became a widespread art form. The most popular subjects included actors, beautiful women, urban life, and landscapes.

▲ **NANIWAYA OKITA**
The artist Kitagawa Utamaro created many prints of attractive women. This print shows Naniwaya Okita, a famous beauty of the late 1700s. Her long face, elaborate hairstyle, and many-colored robes were all considered part of her beauty.

▲ **CARVING THE BLOCK**
These photographs show a modern artist carving a block for the black ink. (The artist must carve a separate block for each color that will be in the final print.)

Carving the raised image requires precision and patience. For example, David Bull, the artist in the photographs, makes five cuts to create each strand of hair. One slip of the knife, and the block will be ruined.

▲ UNDER THE WAVE OFF KANAGAWA

Katsushika Hokusai was one of the most famous of all Japanese printmakers. This scene is taken from his well-known series *Thirty-Six Views of Mount Fuji*. Mount Fuji, which many Japanese considered sacred, is the mountain peak in the background of this scene.

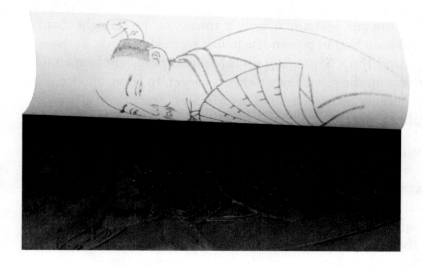

◄ PRINTING

After the carved block is inked, the artist presses paper on it, printing a partial image. He or she repeats this stage for each new color. The artist must ensure that every color ends up in exactly the right place, so that no blocks of color extend beyond the outlines or fall short of them.

Critical Thinking

1. **Make Inferences** What personal qualities and skills would an artist need to be good at making woodblock prints?

2. **Form Opinions** Hokusai's print of the wave remains very popular today. Why do you think this image appeals to modern people?

Turmoil and Change in Mexico

The Big Idea

Political, economic, and social inequalities in Mexico triggered a period of revolution and reform.

Why It Matters Now

Mexico has moved toward political democracy and is a strong economic force in the Americas.

Key Terms and People

Antonio López de Santa Anna
Benito Juárez
La Reforma
Porfirio Díaz
Francisco Madero
"Pancho" Villa
Emiliano Zapata

Setting the Stage

The legacy of Spanish colonialism and long-term political instability that plagued the newly emerging South American nations caused problems for Mexico as well. Mexico, however, had a further issue to contend with—a shared border with the United States. The "Colossus of the North," as the United States was known in Latin America, wanted to extend its territory all the way west to the Pacific Ocean. But most of the lands in the American Southwest belonged to Mexico.

Santa Anna and the Mexican War

During the early 19th century, no one dominated Mexican political life more than **Antonio López de Santa Anna**. Santa Anna played a leading role in Mexico's fight for independence from Spain in 1821. In 1829, he fought against Spain again as the European power tried to regain control of Mexico. Then, in 1833, Santa Anna became Mexico's president.

One of Latin America's most powerful caudillos, or military dictators, Santa Anna was a clever politician. He would support a measure one year and oppose it the next if he thought that would keep him in power. His policy seemed to work. Between 1833 and 1855, Santa Anna was Mexico's president four times. He gave up the presidency twice, however, to serve Mexico in a more urgent cause—leading the Mexican army in an effort to retain the territory of Texas.

The Texas Revolt In the 1820s, Mexico encouraged American citizens to move to the Mexican territory of Texas to help populate the country. Thousands of English-speaking colonists, or Anglos, answered the call. In return for inexpensive land, they pledged to follow the laws of Mexico. As the Anglo population grew, though, tensions developed between the colonists and Mexico over several issues, including slavery and religion. As a result, many Texas colonists wanted greater self-government. But when Mexico refused to grant this, Stephen Austin, a leading Anglo, encouraged a revolt against Mexico in 1835.

Mexican leader Santa Anna

Santa Anna led Mexican forces north to try to hold on to the rebellious territory. He won a few early battles, including a bitter fight at the Alamo, a mission in San Antonio. However, his fortunes changed at the Battle of San Jacinto. His troops were defeated, and he was captured. Texan leader Sam Houston released Santa Anna after he promised to respect the independence of Texas. When Santa Anna returned to Mexico in 1836, he was quickly ousted from power.

War and the Fall of Santa Anna Santa Anna regained power, though, and fought against the United States again. In 1845, the United States annexed Texas. Outraged Mexicans considered this an act of aggression. In a dispute over the border, the United States invaded Mexico. Santa Anna's army fought valiantly, but U.S. troops defeated them after two years of war. In 1848, the two nations signed the Treaty of Guadalupe Hidalgo. The United States received the northern third of what was then Mexico, including California and the American Southwest. Santa Anna went into exile. He returned as dictator one final time, however, in 1853. After his final fall, in 1855, he remained in exile for almost 20 years. When he returned to Mexico in 1874, he was poor, blind, powerless, and essentially forgotten.

Reading Check
Analyze Causes
What led to the Anglos call for greater self-government?

Santa Anna's army met with strong resistance from the defenders of the Alamo.

Juárez and *La Reforma*

During the mid-19th century, as Santa Anna's power rose and fell, a liberal reformer, **Benito Juárez** (HWAHR•ehz), strongly influenced the politics of Mexico. Juárez was Santa Anna's complete opposite in background as well as in goals. Santa Anna came from a well-off Creole family. Juárez was a poor Zapotec Indian who was orphaned at the age of three. While Santa Anna put his own personal power first, Juárez worked primarily to serve his country.

Juárez Rises to Power Ancestry and racial background were important elements of political power and economic success in 19th-century Mexico. For that reason, the rise of Benito Juárez was clearly due to his personal leadership qualities. Juárez was raised on a small farm in the Mexican state of Oaxaca. When he was 12, he moved to the city of Oaxaca. He started going to school at age 15, and in 1829, he entered a newly opened state-run university. He received a law degree in 1831.

He then returned to the city of Oaxaca, where he opened a law office. Most of his clients were poor people who could not otherwise have afforded legal assistance. Juárez gained a reputation for honesty, integrity, hard work, and good judgment. He was elected to the city legislature and then rose steadily in power. Beginning in 1847, he served as governor of the state of Oaxaca.

Juárez Works for Reform Throughout the late 1840s and early 1850s, Juárez worked to start a liberal reform movement. He called this movement *La Reforma*. Its major goals were redistribution of land, separation of church and state, and increased educational opportunities for the poor. In 1853, however, Santa Anna sent Juárez and other leaders of *La Reforma* into exile.

Just two years later, a rebellion against Santa Anna brought down his government. Juárez and other exiled liberal leaders returned to Mexico to deal with their country's tremendous problems. As in other Latin American nations, rich landowners kept most other Mexicans in a cycle of debt and poverty. In a speech to the Constitutional Convention, liberal leader Ponciano Arriaga described how these circumstances led to great problems for both poor farmers and the government. He argued that people would not have equal rights until the majority of the nation was given opportunities to make better lives for themselves.

Not surprisingly, Arriaga's ideas and those of the other liberals in government threatened most conservative, upper-class Mexicans. Many conservatives responded by launching a rebellion against the liberal government in 1858. They enjoyed some early successes in battle and seized control of Mexico City. The liberals kept up the fight from their headquarters in the city of Veracruz. Eventually the liberals gained the upper hand and, after three years of bitter civil war, they defeated the rebels. Juárez became president of the reunited country after his election in 1861.

The French Invade Mexico The end of the civil war did not bring an end to Mexico's troubles, though. Exiled conservatives plotted with some Europeans to reconquer Mexico. In 1862, French ruler Napoleon III responded by sending a large army to Mexico. Within 18 months, France had taken over the country. Napoleon appointed Austrian Archduke Maximilian to rule Mexico as emperor. Juárez and other Mexicans fought against French rule. After five years under siege, the French decided that the struggle was too costly. In 1867, Napoleon ordered the army to withdraw from Mexico. Maximilian was captured and executed.

Juárez was reelected president of Mexico in 1867. He returned to the reforms he had proposed more than ten years earlier. He began rebuilding the country, which had been shattered during years of war. He promoted trade with foreign countries, the opening of new roads, the building of railroads, and the establishment of a telegraph service. He set up a national education system separate from that run by the Catholic Church. In 1872, Juárez died of a heart attack. But after half a century of civil strife and chaos, he left his country a legacy of relative peace, progress, and reform.

Reading Check
Contrast In what ways did Benito Juárez differ from Santa Anna?

Mexican painter José Clemente Orozco celebrated Benito Juárez in the fresco *Juárez, the Church and the Imperialists*. The supporters of Emperor Maximilian, carrying his body, are shown below Juárez. To either side of Juárez, the soldiers of Mexican independence prepare to attack these representatives of imperialism.

Porfirio Díaz and "Order and Progress"

Juárez's era of reform did not last long, however. In the mid-1870s, a new caudillo, **Porfirio Díaz**, came to power. Like Juárez, Díaz was a mestizo from Oaxaca. He rose through the army and became a noted general in the civil war and the fight against the French. Díaz expected to be rewarded with a government position for the part he played in the French defeat. Juárez refused his request, however. After this, Díaz opposed Juárez. In 1876, Díaz took control of Mexico by ousting the president. He had the support of the military, whose power had been reduced during and

Porfirio Díaz
(1830–1915)

To control all the various groups in Mexican society, Porfirio Díaz adopted an approach called *pan o palo*— "bread or the club." The "bread" he provided took many forms. To potential political opponents, he offered positions in his government. To business leaders, he gave huge subsidies or the chance to operate as monopolies in Mexico. And he won the support of the Church and wealthy landowners simply by promising not to meddle in their affairs. Those who turned down the offer of bread and continued to oppose Díaz soon felt the blow of the club. Thousands were killed, beaten, or thrown into jail.

His use of the club, Díaz admitted, was harsh and cruel—but also necessary if Mexico was to have peace. That peace, Díaz argued, enabled the country to progress economically. "If there was cruelty," he said, "results have justified it."

after the Juárez years. Indians and small landholders also supported him because they thought he would work for more radical land reform.

During the Díaz years, elections became meaningless. Díaz offered land, power, or political favors to anyone who supported him. He terrorized many who refused to support him, ordering them to be beaten or put in jail. Using such strong-arm methods, Díaz managed to remain in power until 1911. Over the years, Díaz used a political slogan adapted from a rallying cry of the Juárez era. Juárez had called for "Liberty, Order, and Progress." Díaz, however, wanted merely "Order and Progress."

Díaz's use of dictatorial powers ensured that there was order in Mexico. But the country saw progress under Díaz, too. Railroads expanded, banks were built, the currency stabilized, and foreign investment grew. Mexico seemed to be a stable, prospering country. Appearances were deceiving, however. The wealthy acquired more and more land, which they did not put to good use. As a result, food costs rose steadily. Most Mexicans remained poor farmers and workers, and they continued to grow poorer.

Reading Check
Recognize Effects
What effects did Díaz's rule have on Mexico?

Revolution and Civil War

In the early 1900s, Mexicans from many walks of life began to protest Díaz's harsh rule. Like those who fought to break away from Britain in the American Revolution, Mexican liberals hungered for liberty. They, too, wanted a say in their government. Farm laborers hungered for land. Workers hungered for fairer wages and better working conditions. Even some of Díaz's handpicked political allies spoke out for reform. A variety of political parties opposed to Díaz began to form. Among the most powerful was a party led by Francisco Madero.

Madero Begins the Revolution Born into one of Mexico's ten richest families, **Francisco Madero** was educated in the United States and France. He believed in democracy and wanted to strengthen its hold in Mexico. Madero announced his candidacy for president of Mexico early in 1910. Soon afterward, Díaz had him arrested. From exile in the United States, Madero called for an armed revolution against Díaz.

The Mexican Revolution began slowly. Leaders arose in different parts of Mexico and gathered their own armies. In the north, Francisco **"Pancho" Villa** became immensely popular. He had a bold Robin Hood policy of taking money from the rich and giving it to the poor. South of Mexico City, another strong, popular leader, **Emiliano Zapata**, raised

---

BIOGRAPHY

Emiliano Zapata
(1879–1919)

Shortly after Francisco Madero took office, he met with Emiliano Zapata, one of his leading supporters. However, Madero's reluctance to quickly enact real land reform angered Zapata. He left the meeting convinced that Madero was not the man to carry through the Mexican Revolution.

A few days later, Zapata issued the Plan of Ayala. This called for the removal of Madero and the appointment of a new president. The plan also demanded that the large landowners give up a third of their land for redistribution to the peasants. Zapata's rallying cry, "Land and Liberty," grew out of the Plan of Ayala.

When Venustiano Carranza ordered Zapata's assassination, he expected Zapata's revolutionary ideas on land reform to die with him. However, they lived on and were enacted by Alvaro Obregón, a follower of Zapata, who seized power from Carranza in 1920.

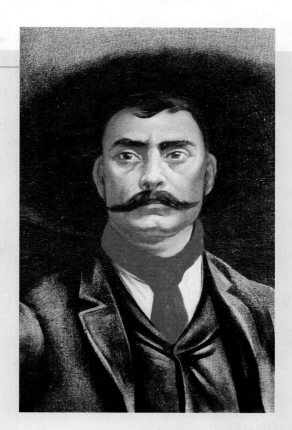

a powerful revolutionary army. Like Villa, Zapata came from a poor family. He was determined to see that land was returned to peasants and small farmers. He wanted the laws reformed to protect their rights. *"Tierra y Libertad"* ("Land and Liberty") was his battle cry. Villa, Zapata, and other armed revolutionaries won important victories against Díaz's army. By the spring of 1911, Díaz agreed to step down. He called for new elections.

Mexican Leaders Struggle for Power Madero was elected president in November 1911. However, his policies were seen as too liberal by some and not revolutionary enough by others. Some of those who had supported Madero, including Villa and Zapata, took up arms against him. In 1913, realizing that he could not hold on to power, Madero resigned. The military leader General Victoriano Huerta then took over the presidency. Shortly after, Madero was assassinated, probably on Huerta's orders.

Huerta was unpopular with many people, including Villa and Zapata. These revolutionary leaders allied themselves with Venustiano Carranza, another politician who wanted to overthrow Huerta. Their three armies advanced, seizing the Mexican countryside from Huerta's forces and approaching the capital, Mexico City. They overthrew Huerta only 15 months after he took power.

Carranza took control of the government and then turned his army on his former revolutionary allies. Both Villa and Zapata continued to fight. In 1919, however, Carranza lured Zapata into a trap and murdered him. With Zapata's death, the civil war also came to an end. More than a million Mexicans had lost their lives.

The New Mexican Constitution Carranza began a revision of Mexico's constitution. It was adopted in 1917. A revolutionary document, that constitution is still in effect today. The constitution promoted education, land reforms, and workers' rights. Carranza did not support the final

Reforms of Mexican Constitution of 1917			
Land	**Religion**	**Labor**	**Social Issues**
Breakup of large estates	State takeover of land owned by the Church	Minimum wage for workers	Equal pay for equal work
Restrictions on foreign ownership of land		Right to strike	State to provide free, secular elementary education for all
Government control of resources (oil)		Institution of labor unions	

Interpret Charts
1. **Make Inferences** Which reforms do you think landowners resented?
2. **Recognize Effects** Which reforms benefited workers?

version of the constitution, however, and in 1920, he was overthrown by one of his generals, Alvaro Obregón.

Although Obregón seized power violently, he did not remain a dictator. Instead, he supported the reforms the constitution called for, particularly land reform. He also promoted public education. Mexican public schools taught a common language—Spanish—and stressed nationalism. In this way, his policies helped unite the various regions and peoples of the country. Nevertheless, Obregón was assassinated in 1928.

The next year, a new political party, the Institutional Revolutionary Party (PRI), arose. Although the PRI did not tolerate opposition, it initiated an ongoing period of peace and political stability in Mexico. While Mexico was struggling toward peace, however, the rest of the world was on the brink of war.

Reading Check
Summarize
What were Obregón's accomplishments?

Lesson 3 Assessment

1. **Organize Information** Which leader do you think benefited Mexico most? Why?

Leader	Major Accomplishment

2. **Key Terms and People** For each key term or person in the lesson, write a sentence explaining its significance.

3. **Analyze Effects** How did Porfirio Díaz change the direction of government in Mexico?

4. **Draw Conclusions** What is the significance of the Battle of San Jacinto?

5. **Summarize** What does Ponciano Arriaga think is Mexico's greatest problem?

6. **Contrast** In the fresco of Juárez, how is the portrayal of the imperialists different from the portrayal of the forces of independence? What bias does the artist show in his work?

7. **Form Opinions** The revision of Mexico's constitution is considered revolutionary. Do you agree with this characterization? Why or why not?

Module 24 Assessment

Key Terms and People

For each term or name below, briefly explain its connection to the changes in global power between 1800 and 1914.

1. Opium War
2. sphere of influence
3. Boxer Rebellion
4. Meiji era
5. Russo-Japanese War
6. annexation
7. Benito Juárez
8. *La Reforma*
9. Porfirio Díaz
10. "Pancho" Villa

Main Ideas

Use your notes and the information in the module to answer the following questions.

China Resists Outside Influence

1. How did the Dowager Empress's perspective on reform evolve?
2. Although Emperor Guangxu's effort at reform failed, what changes did it finally set in motion?
3. What were the different schools of thought on how China should deal with internal and external pressures after the Taiping Rebellion?

Modernization in Japan

4. What events caused Japan to end its isolation and begin to westernize?
5. What were the results of Japan's growing imperialism at the end of the 19th century?

Turmoil and Change in Mexico

6. What were the major causes of tension between the Mexicans and the American colonists who settled in Texas?
7. In what ways was Santa Anna a typical caudillo?
8. What roles did Francisco "Pancho" Villa and Emiliano Zapata play in the Mexican Revolution?
9. In what ways was the Mexican Revolution similar to the American Revolution?

Critical Thinking

1. **Analyze Events** Use a timeline continuum like the one below to indicate the major events of Santa Anna's military and political career in Mexico.

Fights for independence from Spain

1820s

2. **Compare and Contrast** How were the effects of the Columbian Exchange in China similar to and different from its effects in the Americas?

3. **Make Inferences** Would Emperor Guangxu have been able to put his reforms into practice if the Dowager Empress Cixi had not intervened? Explain your position.

4. **Analyze Issues** How do Lin Zexu's beliefs about harming others differ from the beliefs of the British merchants?

5. **Form Opinions** Think about what you know about Japan's, Germany's, and Italy's path to nationalism. How were the paths similar or different?

6. **Compare** How do Japan's modernization efforts in the late 1800s compare with Japan's cultural borrowing of earlier times?

7. **Compare and Contrast** Consider what you have learned in this module and what you know about the industrialization of England. Compare and contrast the social, political, and economic effects industrialization had on Japan with those felt in England. Include positive and negative effects.

8. **Form Opinions** In your view, was Japan's aggressive imperialism justified? Support your answer with information from the text.

9. **Make Inferences** Why might Benito Juárez's rise to power be considered surprising?

10. **Evaluate** Recall what you have learned about Mexican history and about how countries undergo change. What are the pros and cons of using both military strategies and peaceful political means to improve a country's economic, social, and political conditions?

Engage with History

Now that you have learned how several countries dealt with foreign influence and what the results were, would you seek out or resist foreign influence? Discuss your ideas in a small group.

Focus on Writing

Write a **dialogue** that might have taken place between a conservative member of the Dowager Empress Cixi's court and an official in Emperor Mutsuhito's Meiji government. In the dialogue, have the characters discuss

- the kinds of foreign intervention their countries faced;
- the actions their leaders took to deal with this foreign intervention.

Multimedia Activity

On May 5, 1862, badly outnumbered Mexican forces defeated the French at the Battle of Puebla. Mexicans still celebrate their country's triumph on the holiday Cinco de Mayo. Working in a group with two other students, conduct research and plan a television news special on how Cinco de Mayo is celebrated by Mexicans today. Focus on celebrations in Mexico or in Mexican communities in the United States. As you review both primary and secondary sources in your research, note what makes them credible or if they are limited in any way. Consider including the following in your news special:

- information on the Battle of Puebla
- an explanation of how and why Cinco de Mayo became a national holiday
- images of any special activities or traditions that have become part of the celebration
- interviews with participants discussing how they feel about Cinco de Mayo

MEXICO

Teotihuacán, established around 200 BC, was the first great civilization of ancient Mexico. At its height around the middle of the first millennium AD, the "City of the Gods" was one of the largest cities in the world. It covered 12 square miles and was home to some 200,000 people. The Pyramid of the Sun, above, was the largest building in Teotihuacán.

For centuries after the fall of Teotihuacán, present-day Mexico was home to a number of great empires, including the highly sophisticated Aztec civilization. The arrival of the Spanish in the early 1500s forever changed life for Mexico's ancient peoples, and Mexican culture today is dominated by a blend of indigenous and Spanish cultures.

Explore the history of Mexico from ancient to modern times online. You can find a wealth of information, video clips, primary sources, activities, and more through your online textbook.

◼ The Arrival of the Spanish

Watch the video to learn how the arrival of the conquistadors led to the fall of the Aztec Empire.

◼ Miguel Hidalgo's Call to Arms

Watch the video to learn about Miguel Hidalgo's path from priest to revolutionary leader.

◼ Mexico in the Modern Era

Watch the video to learn about the role of oil in the industrialization of Mexico's economy.

◼ Mexico's Ancient Civilizations

Watch the video to learn about the great civilizations that arose in ancient Mexico.

Module 25
World War I

Essential Question
Why did World War I last so long?

About the Painting: This painting by François Flameng shows French soldiers crossing a river on pontoon bridges.

In this module you will learn about the factors that led to World War I, a conflict that devastated Europe and had a major impact on the world.

▶ *Explore ONLINE!*

HISTORY

VIDEOS, including...
• Dear Home: Letters From World War I

☑ Document Based Investigations

☑ Graphic Organizers

☑ Interactive Games

☑ Interactive Map: World War I in Europe, 1914–1918

☑ Carousel: The New Weapons of War

Timeline of Events 1914–1918

▶ *Explore ONLINE!*

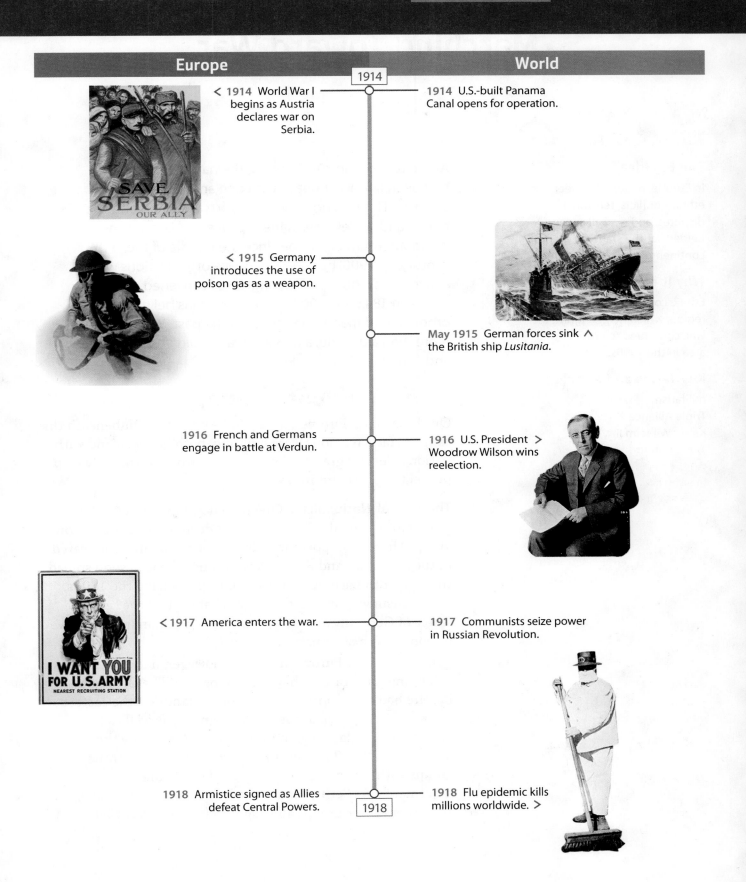

Europe	1914	World
‹ 1914 World War I begins as Austria declares war on Serbia.		**1914** U.S.-built Panama Canal opens for operation.
‹ 1915 Germany introduces the use of poison gas as a weapon.		
		May 1915 German forces sink ∧ the British ship *Lusitania*.
1916 French and Germans engage in battle at Verdun.		**1916** U.S. President › Woodrow Wilson wins reelection.
‹ 1917 America enters the war.		**1917** Communists seize power in Russian Revolution.
1918 Armistice signed as Allies defeat Central Powers.	1918	**1918** Flu epidemic kills millions worldwide. ›

Marching Toward War

The Big Idea

In Europe, nationalistic feelings, ethnic conflicts, territorial disputes, and rival alliances helped set the stage for a continental war.

Why It Matters Now

Ethnic conflict in the Balkan region, which helped ignite the war, continued to erupt in that area in the 1990s.

Key Terms and People

militarism
Triple Alliance
Kaiser Wilhelm II
Triple Entente

Setting the Stage

At the turn of the 20th century, the nations of Europe had been largely at peace with one another for nearly 30 years. This was no accident. Efforts to put an end to war and achieve permanent peace had been gaining momentum in Europe since the middle of the 19th century. By 1900, hundreds of peace organizations were active. In addition, peace congresses convened regularly between 1843 and 1907. Some Europeans believed that progress had made war a thing of the past. Yet in a little more than a decade, a massive war would engulf Europe and spread across the globe.

Rising Tensions in Europe

On the surface, Europe seemed to be peaceful. But beneath this calm surface, tensions were building, both between and within nations. Several gradual developments would ultimately help propel the continent into war.

The Rise of Nationalism One such development was the growth of nationalism, or a sense of devotion to one's national group. The first important examples of nationalism appeared in the American and French revolutions. The idea soon spread through both Latin America and Europe. During the 1800s, nationalism was among the forces that unified the separate states of Germany and Italy, transforming them into cohesive nations with a clear national identity.

In some other European powers, however, nationalism was a dividing force rather than a unifying one. The Ottoman Empire had once controlled most of the lands on the eastern and southern shores of the Mediterranean, as well as the Balkan peninsula, a region in southeast Europe. By the beginning of the 20th century, some of the many ethnic groups within the empire had formed nationalist movements. As Serbs, Albanians, Bulgarians, Romanians, and other ethnic groups all sought independence, other powers in the region hoped to seize them, thus increasing their territory. Eventually, Serbia, Albania, Bulgaria, Greece, Macedonia, Montenegro, and Romania emerged as independent nations. Other Ottoman territories in Europe were annexed by Russia and Austria-Hungary.

Economic Rivalry Europe's Great Powers—Germany, Austria-Hungary, Great Britain, Russia, Italy, and France—were also rivals in other areas. This increasing rivalry stemmed from several sources. One source was industrialization. Germany and Great Britain led Europe in industrial growth, which gave them economic power, especially compared to less industrialized nations. This caused increased competition for materials and markets. The other nations of Europe struggled to build their own industrial bases in order to catch up economically with Germany and Great Britain.

Political Rivalry Another source was political rivalry and territorial disputes. France, for example, had never gotten over the loss of Alsace-Lorraine to Germany in the Franco-Prussian War (1870). Austria-Hungary and Russia both tried to dominate in the Balkans as the Ottoman Empire crumbled.

Imperialism and Militarism Another force that helped set the stage for war in Europe was imperialism. The nations of Europe competed fiercely for colonies in Africa and Asia. The quest for colonies sometimes pushed European nations to the brink of war. As European countries continued to compete for overseas empires, their rivalry and mistrust of one another deepened.

Yet another troubling development throughout the early years of the 20th century was the rise of a dangerous European arms race. The nations of Europe believed that to be truly great, they needed to have a powerful military. By 1914, all the Great Powers except Britain had large standing armies. In addition, military experts stressed the importance of being able to quickly mobilize, or organize and move troops in case of a war. Generals in each country developed highly detailed plans for such a mobilization.

The policy of glorifying military power and keeping an army prepared for war was known as **militarism**. Having a large and strong standing army made citizens feel patriotic. However, it also frightened some people. As early as 1895, Frédéric Passy, a prominent peace activist, expressed the concern that a minor incident could ignite a devastating war throughout Europe.

Reading Check
Draw Conclusions
How do imperialism and militarism work together to promote war?

Tangled Alliances

Growing rivalries and mutual mistrust had led to the creation of several military alliances among the Great Powers as early as the 1870s. This alliance system had been designed to keep peace in Europe. But it would instead help push the continent into war.

Military Aviation

World War I introduced airplane warfare—and by doing so, ushered in an era of tremendous progress in the field of military aviation. Although the plane itself was relatively new and untested by 1914, the warring nations quickly recognized its potential as a powerful weapon. Throughout the conflict, countries on both sides built faster and stronger aircraft, and designed them to drop bombs and shoot at one another in the sky. Between the beginning and end of the war, the total number of planes in use by the major combatants soared from around 850 to nearly 10,000. After the war, countries continued to maintain a strong and advanced air force, as they realized that supremacy of the air was a key to military victory.

A World War I pilot shows off an early air-to-ground communication device.

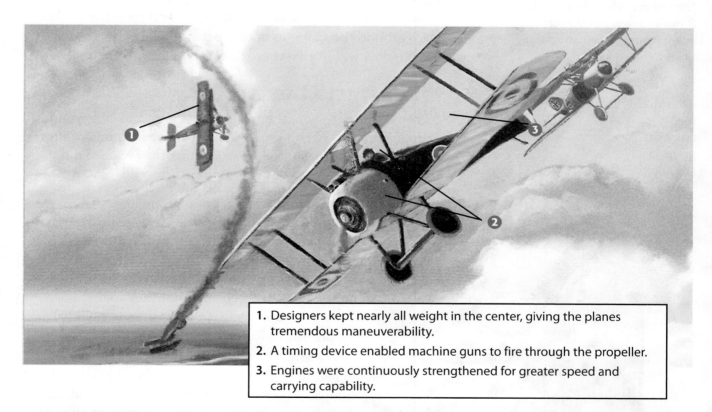

1. Designers kept nearly all weight in the center, giving the planes tremendous maneuverability.
2. A timing device enabled machine guns to fire through the propeller.
3. Engines were continuously strengthened for greater speed and carrying capability.

Two Top Fighter Planes: A Comparison

	Fokker D VII (German)	Sopwith F1 Camel (British)
Length	23 feet	18 feet 8 inches
Wingspan	29 feet 3 inches	28 feet
Maximum Speed	116 mph	122 mph
Maximum Height	22,900 feet	24,000 feet
Maximum Flight Time	1.5 hours	2.5 hours

Critical Thinking

1. **Draw Conclusions** Why would communication with someone outside the plane be important for pilots in World War I and today?
2. **Compare** Using the Internet and other resources, find out more about a recent innovation with regard to fighter planes and explain its significance.

A Global Conflict

Setting the Stage

World War I was much more than a European conflict. Australia and Japan, for example, entered the war on the Allies' side, while India supplied troops to fight alongside their British rulers. Meanwhile, the Ottoman Turks and later Bulgaria allied themselves with Germany and the Central Powers. As the war promised to be a grim, drawn-out affair, all the Great Powers looked for other allies around the globe to tip the balance. They also sought new war fronts where they might achieve victory.

War Affects the World

As the war dragged on, the main combatants looked beyond Europe for a way to end the stalemate. However, none of the alliances they formed or new battlefronts they opened did much to end the slow and grinding conflict.

The Gallipoli Campaign A promising strategy for the Allies seemed to be to attack a region in the Ottoman Empire known as the Dardanelles. This narrow sea strait was the gateway to the Ottoman capital, Constantinople. By securing the Dardanelles, the Allies believed that they could take Constantinople, defeat the Turks, and establish a supply line to Russia.

The effort to take the Dardanelles strait began in February 1915. It was known as the Gallipoli campaign. British, Australian, New Zealand, and French troops made repeated assaults on the Gallipoli Peninsula on the western side of the strait. Turkish troops, some commanded by German officers, vigorously defended the region. By May, Gallipoli had turned into another bloody stalemate. Both sides dug trenches, from which they battled for the rest of the year. In December, the Allies gave up the campaign and began to evacuate. They had suffered about 250,000 casualties.

Gallipoli Campaign

▶ **Explore ONLINE!**

Black Sea

Bosporus

GREECE

Gallipoli Peninsula

Constantinople

Sea of Marmara

OTTOMAN EMPIRE

Dardanelles

Aegean Sea

N
W E
S

0   50   100 mi
0   100   200 km

Battles in Africa and Asia In various parts of Asia and Africa, Germany's colonial possessions came under assault. The Japanese quickly overran German outposts in China. They also captured Germany's Pacific island colonies. English and French troops attacked Germany's four African possessions. They seized control of three.

Elsewhere in Asia and Africa, the British and French recruited subjects in their colonies for the struggle. Fighting troops as well as laborers came from India, South Africa, Senegal, Egypt, Algeria, and Indochina. Many fought and died on the battlefield. Others worked to keep the front lines supplied. To be sure, some colonial subjects wanted nothing to do with their European rulers' conflicts. Others volunteered in the hope that service would lead to their independence. This was the view of Indian political leader Mohandas Gandhi, who supported Indian participation in the war. "If we would improve our status through the help and cooperation of the British," he wrote, "it was our duty to win their help by standing by them in their hour of need."

America Joins the Fight In 1917, the focus of the war shifted to the high seas. That year, the Germans intensified the submarine warfare that had raged in the Atlantic Ocean since shortly after the war began. In January 1917, the Germans announced that their submarines would sink without warning any ship in the waters around Britain. This policy was called **unrestricted submarine warfare**.

▶ *Explore ONLINE!*

The World at War, 1914–1918

War rages in Southwest Asia as Arab nationalists battle their Turkish rulers.

Main fighting of the war occurs on Western and Eastern Fronts.

Japan declares war on Germany in 1914; seizes German colonies in China and the Pacific.

The United States enters the war on the side of the Allies in 1917.

Brazil is the only South American country to enter the war. It supports the Allies with warships and personnel.

The European colonies throughout Africa become a battlefield as the warring parties strike at one another's colonial possessions.

India provides about 1.3 million men to fight and labor alongside their British rulers throughout Europe.

Both countries fight on the side of the Allies and contribute many troops to the 1915 Gallipoli campaign in Southwest Asia.

Interpret Maps

1. **Region** Which countries were aligned with the European Allies?

2. **Location** Outside of Europe, where was World War I fought?

The Germans had tried this policy before. On May 7, 1915, a German submarine, or U-boat, had sunk the British passenger ship *Lusitania*. The attack left 1,198 people dead, including 128 U.S. citizens. Germany claimed that the ship had been carrying ammunition, which turned out to be true. Nevertheless, the American public was outraged. President Woodrow Wilson sent a strong protest to Germany. After two further attacks, the Germans finally agreed to stop attacking neutral and passenger ships.

Desperate for an advantage over the Allies, however, the Germans returned to unrestricted submarine warfare in 1917. They knew it might lead to war with the United States. They gambled that their naval blockade would starve Britain into defeat before the United States could mobilize. Ignoring warnings by President Wilson, German U-boats sank three American ships.

In February 1917, another German action pushed the United States closer to war. Officials intercepted a telegram written by Germany's foreign secretary, Arthur Zimmermann, stating that Germany would help Mexico "reconquer" the land it had lost to the United States if Mexico would ally itself with Germany.

The Zimmermann note simply proved to be the last straw. A large part of the American population already favored the Allies. In particular, America felt a bond with England. The two nations shared a common ancestry and language, as well as similar democratic institutions and legal systems. More important, America's economic ties with the Allies were far stronger than those with the Central Powers. On April 2, 1917, President Wilson asked Congress to declare war so that the United States could enter World War I. This excerpt from his speech gives some of his reasons.

> *"The world must be made safe for democracy. Its peace must be planted upon the tested foundations of political liberty. We have no selfish ends to serve. We desire no conquest, no dominion. We seek no indemnities for ourselves, no material compensation for the sacrifice we shall freely make. We are but one of the champions of the rights of mankind. We shall be satisfied when those rights have been made as secure as the faith and the freedom of nations can make them."*
>
> –Woodrow Wilson, Speech to Congress, April 2, 1917

Reading Check
Contrast How was the experience of war different for the subjects of European colonies in Africa and India?

Days later, the United States entered the war on the side of the Allies.

War Affects the Home Front

By the time the United States joined the Allies, the war had been raging for nearly three years. In those three years, Europe had lost more men in battle than in all the wars of the previous three centuries. The war had claimed the lives of millions and had changed countless lives forever. The Great War, as the conflict came to be known, affected everyone. It touched not only the soldiers in the trenches but civilians as well.

Governments Wage Total War World War I soon became a **total war**. This meant that countries devoted all their resources to the war effort. In Britain, Germany, Austria, Russia, and France, the entire force of government was dedicated to winning the conflict. In each country, the wartime government took control of the economy. Governments told factories what to produce and how much.

Numerous facilities were converted to munitions factories. Nearly every able-bodied civilian was put to work. Unemployment in many European countries all but disappeared.

So many goods were in short supply that governments turned to **rationing**. Under this system, people could buy only small amounts of those items that were also needed for the war effort. Eventually, rationing covered a wide range of goods, from butter to shoe leather.

Governments also suppressed antiwar activity, sometimes forcibly. In addition, they censored news about the war. Many leaders feared that honest reporting of the war would turn people against it. Governments also used **propaganda**, one-sided information designed to persuade, to keep up morale and support for the war.

Women and the War Total war meant that governments turned to help from women as never before. Thousands of women replaced men in factories, offices, and shops. Women built tanks and munitions, plowed fields, paved streets, and ran hospitals. They also kept troops supplied with food, clothing, and weapons. Although most women left the work force when the war ended, they changed many people's views of what women were capable of doing.

Women also saw the horrors of war firsthand, working on or near the front lines as nurses. Here, American nurse Shirley Millard describes her experience with a soldier who had lost his eyes and feet:

A woman relief worker writes a letter home for a wounded soldier.

> *"He moaned through the bandages that his head was splitting with pain. I gave him morphine. Suddenly aware of the fact that he had [numerous] wounds, he asked: 'Sa-ay! What's the matter with my legs?' Reaching down to feel his legs before I could stop him, he uttered a heartbreaking scream. I held his hands firmly until the drug I had given him took effect."*

Shirley Millard, *I Saw Them Die*

Reading Check
Summarize How did the governments of the warring nations fight a total war?

The Allies Win the War

With the United States finally in the war, it seemed that the balance was about to tip in the Allies' favor. Before that happened, however, events in Russia gave Germany a victory on the Eastern Front and new hope for winning the conflict.

The Influenza Epidemic

In the spring of 1918, a powerful new enemy emerged, threatening nations on each side of World War I. This "enemy" was a deadly strain of influenza. The Spanish flu, as it was popularly known, hit England and India in May. By the fall, it had spread through Europe, Russia, Asia, and to the United States.

The influenza epidemic killed soldiers and civilians alike. In India, at least 12 million people died of influenza. In Berlin, on a single day in October, 1,500 people died. In the end, this global epidemic was more destructive than the war itself, killing 20 million people worldwide.

City officials and street cleaners in Chicago guard against the Spanish flu.

Russia Withdraws In March 1917, civil unrest in Russia—due in large part to war-related shortages of food and fuel—forced Czar Nicholas to step down. In his place a provisional government was established. The new government pledged to continue fighting the war. However, by 1917, nearly 5.5 million Russian soldiers had been wounded, killed, or taken prisoner. As a result, the war-weary Russian army refused to fight any longer.

Eight months after the new government took over, a revolution shook Russia. In November 1917, Communist leader Vladimir Ilyich Lenin seized power. Lenin insisted on ending his country's involvement in the war. One of his first acts was to offer Germany a truce. In March 1918, Germany and Russia signed the Treaty of Brest-Litovsk, which ended the war between them.

The Central Powers Collapse Russia's withdrawal from the war at last allowed Germany to send nearly all its forces to the Western Front. In March 1918, the Germans mounted one final, massive attack on the Allies in France. As in the opening weeks of the war, the German forces crushed everything in their path. By late May 1918, the Germans had again reached the Marne River. Paris was less than 40 miles away. Victory seemed within reach.

By this time, however, the German military had been weakened. The effort to reach the Marne had exhausted men and supplies alike. Sensing this weakness, the Allies—with the aid of nearly 140,000 fresh U.S. troops—launched a counterattack. In July 1918, the Allies and Germans clashed at the Second Battle of the Marne. Leading the Allied attack were some 350 tanks that rumbled slowly forward, smashing through the German lines. With the arrival of 2 million more American troops, the Allied forces began to advance steadily toward Germany.

Soon, the Central Powers began to crumble. First the Bulgarians and then the Ottoman Turks surrendered. In October, revolution swept through Austria-Hungary. In Germany, soldiers mutinied, and the public turned on the kaiser.

Allied View of Armistice

News of the armistice affected the Allied and Central powers differently. Here, a U.S. soldier named Harry Truman, who would go on to become president, recalls the day the fighting stopped.

> "Every single one of them [the French soldiers] had to march by my bed and salute and yell, 'Vive President Wilson, Vive le capitaine d'artillerie américaine!' No sleep all night. The infantry fired Very pistols, sent up all the flares they could lay their hands on, fired rifles, pistols, whatever else would make noise, all night long."
>
> —Harry Truman, quoted in *The First World War*

German Reaction to Armistice

On the other side of the fighting line, German officer Herbert Sulzbach struggled to inform his troops of the war's end.

> "'Hostilities will cease as from 12 noon today.' This was the order which I had to read out to my men. The war is over. . . . How we looked forward to this moment; how we used to picture it as the most splendid event of our lives; and here we are now, humbled, our souls torn and bleeding, and know that we've surrendered. Germany has surrendered to the Entente!"
>
> —Herbert Sulzbach, *With the German Guns*

Analyze Historical Sources
1. What is the main difference between these two excerpts?
2. How did Herbert Sulzbach's vision of the armistice differ from what actually occurred?

Reading Check
Compare How was the Second Battle of the Marne similar to the first?

On November 9, 1918, Kaiser Wilhelm II stepped down. Germany declared itself a republic. A representative of the new German government met with French Commander Marshal Foch in a railway car near Paris. The two signed an **armistice**, or an agreement to stop fighting. On November 11, World War I came to an end.

The Legacy of the War

World War I was, in many ways, a new kind of war. It involved the use of new technologies. It ushered in the notion of war on a grand and global scale. It also left behind a landscape of death and destruction such as was never before seen.

Both sides in World War I paid a tremendous price in terms of human life. About 8.5 million soldiers died as a result of the war. Another 21 million were wounded. In addition, the war led to the death of countless civilians by way of starvation, disease, and slaughter. Taken together, these figures spelled tragedy—an entire generation of Europeans wiped out. The war also had a devastating economic impact on Europe. The great conflict drained the treasuries of European countries. One account put the total

World War I Statistics

Total Number of Troops Mobilized

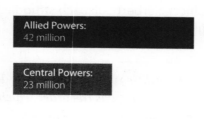

Allied Powers:
42 million

Central Powers:
23 million

Source:
Encyclopaedia Britannica

Battlefield Deaths of Major Combatants

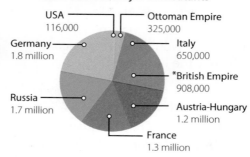

USA
116,000

Ottoman Empire
325,000

Germany
1.8 million

Italy
650,000

*British Empire
908,000

Russia
1.7 million

Austria-Hungary
1.2 million

France
1.3 million

* Includes troops from Britain, Canada, Australia, New Zealand, India, and South Africa

Interpret Graphs

1. **Compare** Which Allied nation suffered the greatest number of battlefield deaths?

2. **Analyze Issues** Which four nations accounted for about 75 percent of all battlefield deaths?

---

cost of the war at $338 billion, a staggering amount for that time. The war also destroyed acres of farmland as well as homes, villages, and towns.

The enormous suffering that resulted from the Great War left a deep mark on Western society as well. A sense of disillusionment settled over the survivors. The insecurity and despair that many people experienced are reflected in the art and literature of the time.

Another significant legacy of the war lay in its peace agreement. The treaties to end World War I were forged after great debate and compromise. And while they sought to bring a new sense of security and peace to the world, they prompted mainly anger and resentment.

Reading Check
Analyze Effects
How did total war affect the warring nations' economies?

Lesson 3 Assessment

1. **Organize Information** Use a web like the one below to show the effects of World War I.

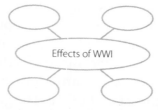

Effects of WWI

Which effect do you think was most significant? Why?

2. **Key Terms and People** For each key term or person in the lesson, write a sentence explaining its significance.

3. **Analyze Causes** What factors helped prompt the United States to join the war on the Allies' side?

4. **Analyze Issues** In what ways was World War I truly a global conflict?

5. **Draw Conclusions** Which of the non-European countries had the greatest impact on the war effort? Explain.

A Flawed Peace

The Big Idea

After winning the war, the Allies dictated a harsh peace settlement that left many nations feeling betrayed.

Why It Matters Now

Hard feelings left by the peace settlement helped cause World War II.

Key Terms and People

Woodrow Wilson
Georges Clemenceau
Fourteen Points
self-determination
Treaty of Versailles
League of Nations

Setting the Stage

World War I was over. The killing had stopped. The terms of peace, however, still had to be worked out. On January 18, 1919, a conference to establish those terms began at the Palace of Versailles, outside Paris. Attending the talks, known as the Paris Peace Conference, were delegates representing 32 countries. For one year, this conference would be the scene of vigorous, often bitter debate. The Allied powers struggled to solve their conflicting aims in various peace treaties.

The Allies Meet and Debate

Although the conference included representatives from many countries, the major decisions were hammered out by a group known as the Big Four: **Woodrow Wilson** of the United States, **Georges Clemenceau** of France, David Lloyd George of Great Britain, and Vittorio Orlando of Italy. Russia, in the grip of civil war, was not represented. Neither were Germany and its allies.

Wilson's Plan for Peace In January 1918, while the war was still raging, President Wilson had drawn up a series of peace proposals. Known as the **Fourteen Points**, they outlined a plan for achieving a just and lasting peace.

The first four points included an end to secret treaties, freedom of the seas, free trade, and reduced national armies and navies. The fifth goal was the adjustment of colonial claims with fairness toward colonial peoples. The sixth through thirteenth points were specific suggestions for changing borders and creating new nations. The guiding idea behind these points was **self-determination**. This meant allowing people to decide for themselves under what government they wished to live.

Finally, the fourteenth point proposed a "general association of nations" that would protect "great and small states alike." This reflected Wilson's hope for an organization that could peacefully negotiate solutions to world conflicts.

The Versailles Treaty As the Paris Peace Conference opened, Britain and France showed little sign of agreeing to Wilson's vision of peace. Both nations were concerned with national security. They also wanted to strip Germany of its war-making power.

The differences in French, British, and U.S. aims led to heated arguments among the nations' leaders. Finally a compromise was reached. **The Treaty of Versailles** between Germany and the Allied powers was signed on June 28, 1919, five years to the day after Franz Ferdinand's assassination in Sarajevo. Adopting Wilson's fourteenth point, the treaty created a **League of Nations**. The league was to be an international association whose goal would be to keep peace among nations.

The treaty also punished Germany. The defeated nation lost substantial territory and had severe restrictions placed on its military operations. As tough as these provisions were, the harshest was Article 231. It was also known as the "war guilt" clause. It placed sole responsibility for the war on Germany's shoulders. As a result, Germany had to pay reparations to the Allies.

All of Germany's territories in Africa and the Pacific were declared mandates, or territories to be administered by the League of Nations. Under the peace agreement, the Allies would govern the mandates until they were judged ready for independence.

Vocabulary
reparations
payments made by a defeated nation to compensate for damage or injury during a war

Reading Check
Analyze Causes
How did the different goals of the negotiators affect the treaty?

BIOGRAPHY

Woodrow Wilson
(1856–1924)

Wilson was tall and thin and often in poor health. He suffered from terrible indigestion and sometimes had to use a stomach pump on himself. A scholarly man, Wilson once served as president of Princeton University in New Jersey.

Passionate about international peace, he took on the U.S. Senate after it vowed to reject the Treaty of Versailles. During the political battle, he suffered a stroke that disabled him for the rest of his term.

Georges Clemenceau
(1841–1929)

The near opposite of Wilson, Clemenceau had a compact physique and a combative style that earned him the nickname "Tiger." He had worked as a physician and journalist before entering the political arena.

Determined to punish Germany, Clemenceau rarely agreed with Wilson and his larger quest for world peace. He once remarked of Wilson, "He thinks he is another Jesus Christ come upon earth to reform men."

A Troubled Treaty

The Versailles treaty was just one of five treaties negotiated by the Allies. In the end, these agreements created feelings of bitterness and betrayal among both the victors and the defeated.

New Nations and Mandates The Western powers signed separate peace treaties in 1919 and 1920 with each of the other defeated nations: Austria-Hungary, Bulgaria, and the Ottoman Empire. These treaties, too, led to huge land losses for the Central Powers. Several new countries were created out of the Austro-Hungarian Empire. Austria, Hungary, Czechoslovakia, and Yugoslavia were all recognized as independent nations.

The Ottoman Turks were forced to give up almost all of their former empire. They retained only the territory that is today the country of Turkey. The Allies carved up the lands that the Ottomans lost in Southwest Asia into mandates rather than independent nations. Britain received the mandates for Palestine (including Transjordan) and Iraq; France was assigned the mandates for Syria and Lebanon.

Russia, which had left the war early, suffered land losses as well. Romania and Poland both gained Russian territory. Finland, Estonia, Latvia, and Lithuania, formerly part of Russia, became independent nations.

Initial Successes of the Peace Agreement The League of Nations held its first meeting in January 1920. Some agencies under the League's supervision were able to successfully introduce important changes. For example, the International Labour Organization (ILO) introduced restrictions on lead in paint and convinced several nations to adopt standards for work days and weeks. The League made progress in ending legal slavery around the world and set up a Commission for Refugees to help some of the millions displaced by the war.

"A Peace Built on Quicksand" In the end, the Treaty of Versailles did little to build a lasting peace. For one thing, the United States—considered after the war to be the dominant nation in the world—ultimately rejected the treaty. Many Americans objected to the settlement and especially to President Wilson's League of Nations. Americans believed that the United States' best hope for peace was to stay out of European affairs. The United States worked out a separate treaty with Germany and its allies several years later.

In addition, the treaty with Germany, in particular the war-guilt clause, left a legacy of bitterness and hatred in the hearts of the German people. Other countries also felt cheated and betrayed by the peace settlements. Throughout Africa and Asia, people in the mandated territories were angry at the way the Allies disregarded their desire for independence. The European powers, it seemed to them, merely talked about the principle of national self-determination. European colonialism, disguised as the mandate system, continued in Asia and Africa.

Europe Pre–World War I

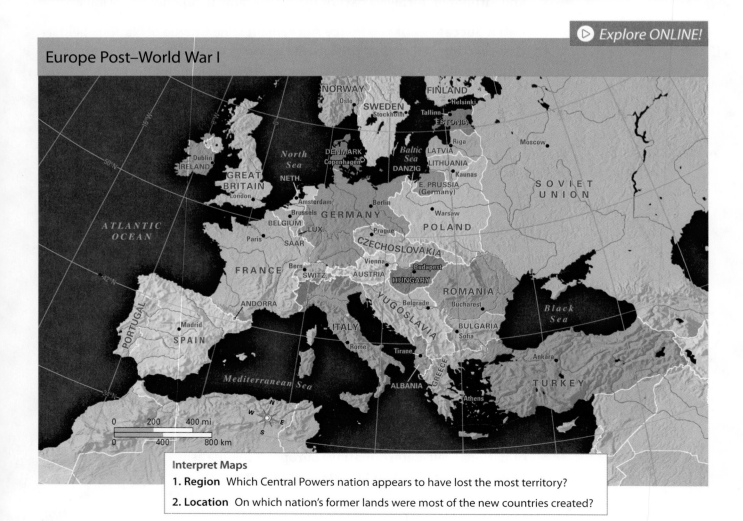

Europe Post–World War I

Interpret Maps

1. Region Which Central Powers nation appears to have lost the most territory?

2. Location On which nation's former lands were most of the new countries created?

The Treaty of Versailles: Major Provisions

League of Nations	Territorial Losses	Military Restrictions	War Guilt
International peace organization; enemy and neutral nations initially excluded	Germany returns Alsace-Lorraine to France; French border extended to west bank of Rhine River	Limits set on the size of the German army	Sole responsibility for the war placed on Germany's shoulders
Germany and Russia excluded	Germany surrenders all of its overseas colonies in Africa and the Pacific	Germany prohibited from importing or manufacturing weapons or war material	Germany forced to pay the Allies $33 billion in reparations over 30 years
		Germany forbidden to build or buy submarines or have an air force	

Interpreting Charts

1. **Analyze Issues** In what ways did the treaty punish Germany?
2. **Analyze Effects** What region was returned to France as a result of the treaty?

Reading Check
Analyze Issues
What complaints did various mandated countries voice about the Treaty of Versailles?

Some Allied powers, too, were embittered by the outcome. Both Japan and Italy, which had entered the war to gain territory, had gained less than they wanted. Lacking the support of the United States, and later other world powers, the League of Nations was in no position to take action on these and other complaints. The settlements at Versailles represented, as one observer noted, "a peace built on quicksand." Indeed, that quicksand eventually would give way. In a little more than two decades, the treaties' legacy of bitterness would help plunge the world into another catastrophic war.

Lesson 4 Assessment

1. **Organize Information** Create a chart like the one below to show how different groups reacted to the Treaty of Versailles.

Reaction to Treaty	
Germany	
Africans & Asians	
Italy & Japan	

Which group was most justified in its reaction to the treaty? Why?

2. **Key Terms and People** For each key term or person in the lesson, write a sentence explaining its significance.
3. **Summarize** What was the goal of Woodrow Wilson's Fourteen Points?
4. **Analyze causes** Why did the United States reject the Treaty of Versailles?
5. **Form opinions** Were the Versailles treaties fair? Consider all the nations affected.

Module 25 Assessment

Key Terms and People

For each term or name below, write a sentence explaining its connection to World War I.

1. Triple Alliance
2. Triple Entente
3. Central Powers
4. Allies
5. total war
6. armistice
7. Fourteen Points
8. Treaty of Versailles

Main Ideas

Marching Toward War

1. How did nationalism, imperialism, and militarism help set the stage for World War I?
2. Why was the Balkan Peninsula known as "the powder keg of Europe"?

Europe Plunges into War

3. Why was the First Battle of the Marne considered so significant?
4. Where was the Western Front? the Eastern Front?

A Global Conflict

5. What factors prompted the United States to enter the war?
6. In what ways was World War I a total war?

A Flawed Peace

7. What was the purpose of the League of Nations?
8. What was the mandate system, and why did it leave many groups feeling betrayed?

Module 25 Assessment, continued

Critical Thinking

1. **Organize Information** Trace the formation of the two major alliance systems that dominated Europe on the eve of World War I by providing the event that corresponds with each date on the chart.

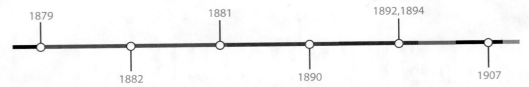

2. **Evaluate Decisions** How did the Treaty of Versailles reflect the different personalities and agendas of the men in power at the end of World War I?

3. **Synthesize** How did the war have both a positive and negative impact on the economies of Europe?

4. **Analyze issues** One British official commented that the Allied victory in World War I had been "bought so dear [high in price] as to be indistinguishable from defeat." What did he mean by this statement? Use examples from the text to support your answer.

5. **Draw Conclusions** What was the social and cultural impact of World War I?

Engage with History

In the feature "The Armenian Genocide," you read about the deaths of hundreds of thousands of Armenians in the Ottoman Empire. One hundred years later this is still a controversial issue. Members of the Armenian community say the killings were a deliberate attempt to destroy the Armenian people and should be considered genocide. The Turkish government says the deaths were an unfortunate part of the war but do not constitute genocide. Think about human rights violations and genocide. Were the Armenian massacres genocide? Discuss your opinions with a small group.

Focus on Writing

Write a paragraph explaining how the concept of total war affected the warring nations' economies.

Multimedia Activity

In many countries, nationalism was used in propaganda designed to show the enemy in a negative light, to encourage support from other countries, and to increase civilian support for the war. Work with a group to create an electronic presentation about propaganda during World War I. Have each member choose one of the six members of the Triple Alliance and the Triple Entente to research in terms of the propaganda produced before and during the war. Next, create an electronic presentation about propaganda, including the agencies responsible, the focus of the propaganda effort, and examples of different materials.

You may want to include the following types of media:

- posters
- newspaper articles
- leaflets
- movies

Dear home:
LETTERS FROM
WWI

When U.S. troops arrived in Europe in 1917 to fight in World War I, the war had been dragging on for nearly three years. The American soldiers suddenly found themselves in the midst of chaos. Each day, they faced the threats of machine-gun fire, poison gas, and aerial attacks. Still, the arrival of American reinforcements had sparked a new zeal among the Allies, who believed the new forces could finally turn the tide in their favor. The letters soldiers wrote to their families back home reveal the many emotions they felt on the battlefield: confusion about their surroundings, fear for their own safety, concern for friends and loved ones, and hope that the war would soon be over.

Explore World War I online through the eyes of the soldiers who fought in it. You can find a wealth of information, video clips, primary sources, activities, and more through your online textbook.

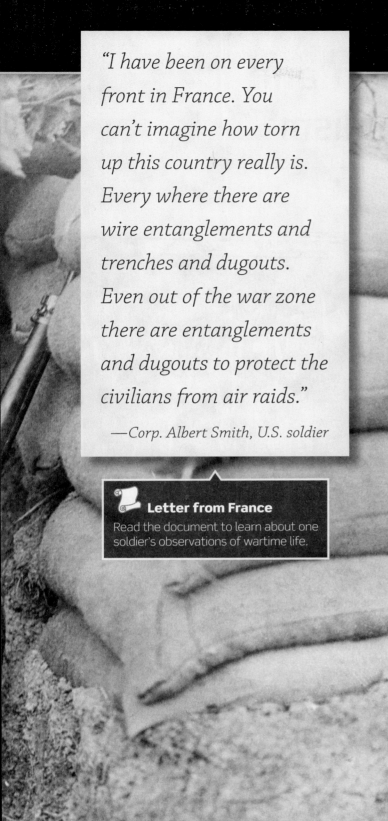

"I have been on every front in France. You can't imagine how torn up this country really is. Every where there are wire entanglements and trenches and dugouts. Even out of the war zone there are entanglements and dugouts to protect the civilians from air raids."

—Corp. Albert Smith, U.S. soldier

Letter from France
Read the document to learn about one soldier's observations of wartime life.

Over There
Watch the video to learn about the experiences of American soldiers on the way to Europe and upon their arrival.

War on the Western Front
Watch the video to hear one soldier's vivid account of battle and its aftermath.

Surrender!
Watch the video to experience soldiers' reactions to the news that the war was finally over.

Revolution and Nationalism

Essential Question
Does nationalism unite or divide?

About the Photo: Students gather in Tiananmen Square in Bejing to protest the Versailles Treaty on May 4, 1919. This event sparked widespread protests and marked the beginning of Chinese nationalism.

In this chapter you will learn that the political upheavals that swept through Russia, China, and the Ottoman Empire resulted in Russia forming a totalitarian state, China undergoing a civil war, and the collapse of the Ottoman Empire into the present-day country of Turkey.

▷ *Explore ONLINE!*

HISTORY

VIDEOS, including...
• The Romanovs
• The Trans-Siberian Railroad
• Stalin's Purges
• Ottoman Empire: The War Machine

☑ Document Based Investigations
☑ Graphic Organizers
☑ Interactive Games
☑ Chart: Totalitarianism
☑ Carousel: Propaganda

Timeline of Events 1900–1940

▶ Explore ONLINE!

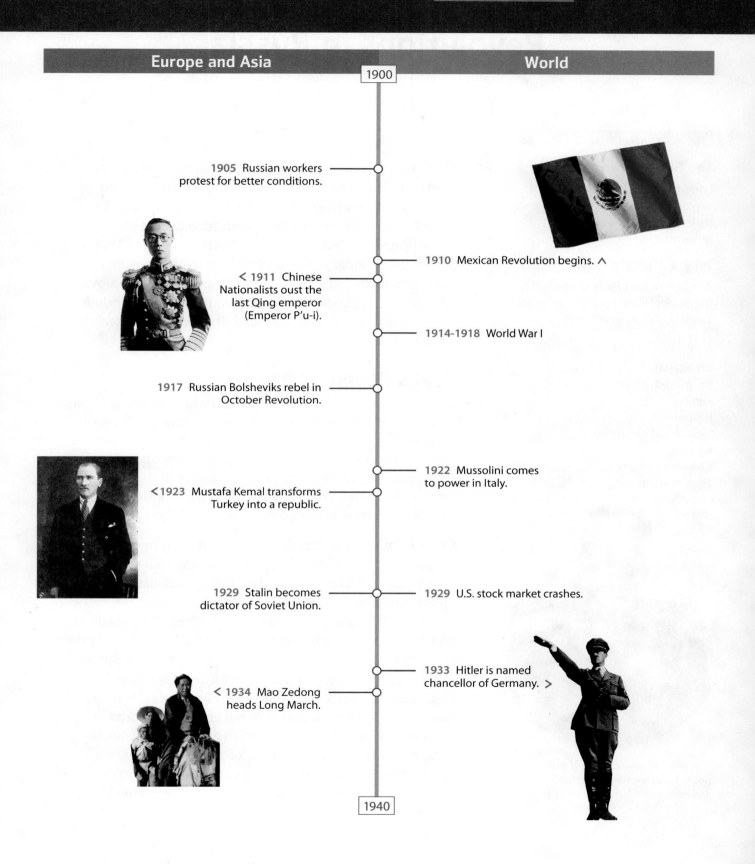

Europe and Asia

World

1900

1905 Russian workers protest for better conditions.

1910 Mexican Revolution begins. ∧

< 1911 Chinese Nationalists oust the last Qing emperor (Emperor P'u-i).

1914-1918 World War I

1917 Russian Bolsheviks rebel in October Revolution.

1922 Mussolini comes to power in Italy.

<1923 Mustafa Kemal transforms Turkey into a republic.

1929 Stalin becomes dictator of Soviet Union.

1929 U.S. stock market crashes.

1933 Hitler is named chancellor of Germany. >

< 1934 Mao Zedong heads Long March.

1940

Revolutions in Russia

The Big Idea

Long-term social unrest in Russia exploded in revolution and ushered in the first communist government.

Why It Matters Now

The Communist Party controlled the Soviet Union until the country's breakup in 1991.

Key Terms and People

proletariat
Bolsheviks
Lenin
Rasputin
provisional government
soviet
Communist Party
Joseph Stalin

Alexander III turned Russia into a police state, teeming with spies and informers.

Setting the Stage

The Russian Revolution was like a firecracker with a very long fuse. The explosion came in 1917, yet the fuse had been burning for nearly a century. The cruel, oppressive rule of most 19th-century czars caused widespread social unrest for decades. Army officers revolted in 1825. Secret revolutionary groups plotted to overthrow the government. In 1881, revolutionaries angry over the slow pace of political change assassinated the reform-minded czar, Alexander II. Russia was heading toward a full-scale revolution.

Czars Resist Change

In 1881, Alexander III succeeded his father, Alexander II, and halted all reforms in Russia. Like his grandfather Nicholas I, Alexander III clung to the principles of autocracy, a form of government in which he had total power. Anyone who questioned the absolute authority of the czar, worshiped outside the Russian Orthodox Church, or spoke a language other than Russian was labeled dangerous.

Czars Continue Autocratic Rule To wipe out revolutionaries, Alexander III used harsh measures. He imposed strict censorship codes on published materials and written documents, including private letters. His secret police carefully watched both secondary schools and universities. Teachers had to send detailed reports on every student. Political prisoners were sent to Siberia, a remote region of eastern Russia.

To establish a uniform Russian culture, Alexander III oppressed other national groups within Russia. He made Russian the official language of the empire and forbade the use of minority languages, such as Polish, in schools. Alexander made Jews the target of persecution. A wave of pogroms—organized violence against Jews—broke out in many parts of Russia. Police and soldiers stood by

Reading Check
Synthesize
What measures did Alexander III use to wipe our revolutionary threats?

Vocabulary
minister person in charge of an area of government, such as finance

and watched Russian citizens loot and destroy Jewish homes, stores, and synagogues.

When Nicholas II became czar in 1894, he continued the tradition of Russian autocracy. Unfortunately, it blinded him to the changing conditions of his times.

Russia Industrializes

Rapid industrialization changed the face of the Russian economy. The number of factories more than doubled between 1863 and 1900. Still, Russia lagged behind the industrial nations of western Europe. In the 1890s, Nicholas's most capable minister launched a program to move the country forward. To finance the buildup of Russian industries, the government sought foreign investors and raised taxes. These steps boosted the growth of heavy industry, particularly steel. By around 1900, Russia had become the world's fourth-ranking producer of steel. Only the United States, Germany, and Great Britain produced more steel.

With the help of British and French investors, work began on the world's longest continuous rail line—the Trans-Siberian Railway. Begun in 1891, the railway was not completed until 1916. It connected European Russia in the west with Russian ports on the Pacific Ocean in the east.

The Revolutionary Movement Grows Rapid industrialization stirred discontent among the people of Russia. The growth of factories brought new problems, such as grueling working conditions, miserably low wages, and child labor. The government outlawed trade unions. To try to improve their lives, workers unhappy with their low standard of living and lack of political power organized strikes.

As a result of all of these factors, several revolutionary movements began to grow and compete for power. A group that followed the views of Karl Marx successfully established a following in Russia. The Marxist revolutionaries believed that the industrial class of workers would overthrow the czar. These workers would then form "a dictatorship of the proletariat." This meant that the **proletariat**—the workers—would rule the country.

In 1903, Russian Marxists split into two groups over revolutionary tactics. The more moderate Mensheviks (MEHN·shuh·vihks) wanted a broad base of popular support for the revolution. The more radical **Bolsheviks** (BOHL·shuh·vihks) supported a small number of committed revolutionaries willing to sacrifice everything for change.

The major leader of the Bolsheviks was Vladimir Ilyich Ulyanov (ool·YAH·nuhf). He adopted the name of **Lenin**. He had an engaging personality and was an excellent organizer. He was also ruthless. These traits would ultimately help him gain command of the Bolsheviks. In the early 1900s, Lenin fled to western Europe to avoid arrest by the czarist regime. From there he maintained contact with other Bolsheviks. Lenin then waited until he could safely return to Russia.

Reading Check
Analyze Causes
Why did industrialization in Russia lead to unrest?

V. I. Lenin
(1870–1924)

In 1887, when he was 17, Lenin's brother, Alexander, was hanged for plotting to kill the czar. Legend has it that this event turned Lenin into a revolutionary.

Though Alexander's execution influenced Lenin, he already harbored ill feelings against the government. By the early 1900s, he planned to overthrow the czar. After the revolution in 1917, Russians revered him as the "Father of the Revolution."

Following Lenin's death in 1924, the government placed his tomb in Red Square in Moscow. His preserved body, encased in a bulletproof, glass-topped coffin, is still on display. Many Russians today, though, favor moving Lenin's corpse away from public view.

Crises at Home and Abroad

The revolutionaries would not have to wait long to realize their visions. Between 1904 and 1917, Russia faced a series of crises. These events showed the czar's weakness and paved the way for revolution.

The Russo-Japanese War In the late 1800s, Russia and Japan competed for control of Korea and Manchuria. The two nations signed a series of agreements over the territories, but Russia broke them. Japan retaliated by attacking the Russians at Port Arthur, Manchuria, in February 1904. News of repeated Russian losses sparked unrest at home and led to a revolt in the midst of the war.

Bloody Sunday: The Revolution of 1905 On January 22, 1905, about 200,000 workers and their families approached the czar's Winter Palace in St. Petersburg. They carried a petition asking for better working conditions, more personal freedom, and an elected national legislature. Nicholas II's generals ordered soldiers to fire on the crowd. More than 1,000 were wounded, and several hundred were killed. Russians quickly named the event "Bloody Sunday."

Bloody Sunday provoked a wave of strikes and violence that spread across the country. In October 1905, Nicholas reluctantly promised more freedom. He approved the creation of the Duma (Doo•muh)—Russia's first parliament. The first Duma met in May 1906. Its leaders were moderates who wanted Russia to become a constitutional monarchy similar to Britain. But because he was hesitant to share his power, the czar dissolved the Duma after ten weeks.

Vocabulary
constitutional monarchy a form of government in which a single ruler heads the state and shares authority with elected lawmakers

▼ ALTERED PHOTOGRAPHS

Stalin attempted to enhance his legacy and erase his rivals from history by extensively altering photographs as this series shows.

1. The original photograph was taken in 1926 and showed, from left to right, Nikolai Antipov, Stalin, Sergei Kirov, and Nikolai Shvernik.

2. This altered image appeared in a 1949 biography of Stalin. Why Shvernik was removed is unclear—he was head of the Central Committee of the Communist Party until Stalin's death in 1954. Antipov, however, was arrested during Stalin's purge and executed in 1941.

3. This heroic oil painting by Isaak Brodsky is based on the original photograph, but only Stalin is left. Kirov was assassinated in 1934 by a student, but the official investigation report has never been released. Stalin did fear Kirov's popularity and considered him a threat to his leadership.

Critical Thinking

1. **Analyze Visuals** Of the examples, which do you think would have been most effective as propaganda? Why?

2. **Compare and Contrast** What are the similarities and differences between propaganda and modern advertising campaigns? Support your answer with examples.

Totalitarianism

Totalitarianism is a form of government in which the national government takes control of all aspects of both public and private life. Thus, totalitarianism seeks to erase the line between government and society. It has an ideology, or set of beliefs, that all citizens are expected to approve. It is often led by a dynamic leader and a single political party. It is similar to an authoritarian regime, but the primary difference is that a totalitarian government controls all aspects of life including control over social and economic institutions as well as government institutions.

Mass communication technology helps a totalitarian government spread its aims and support its policies. Also, surveillance technology makes it possible to keep track of the activities of many people. Finally, violence, such as police terror, discourages those who disagree with the goals of the government.

FEAR OF TOTALITARIANISM ▶

George Orwell illustrated the horrors of a totalitarian government in his novel *1984*. The novel depicts a world in which personal freedom and privacy have vanished. It is a world made possible through modern technology. Even citizens' homes have television cameras that constantly survey their behavior.

KEY TRAITS OF TOTALITARIANISM ▼

Ideology
- sets goals of the state
- glorifies aims of the state
- justifies government actions

State Control of Individuals
- demands loyalty
- denies basic liberties
- expects personal sacrifice for the good of the state

Dynamic Leader
- unites people
- symbolizes government
- encourages popular support through force of will

Methods of Enforcement
- police terror
- indoctrination
- censorship
- persecution

TOTALITARIANISM

Dictatorship and One-Party Rule
- exercises absolute authority
- dominates the government

State Control of Society
- business
- labor
- housing
- education
- religion
- the arts
- personal life
- youth groups

Modern Technology
- mass communication to spread propaganda
- advanced military weapons

TOTALITARIAN LEADERS IN THE 20TH CENTURY

- Adolf Hitler (Germany) 1933–1945
- Benito Mussolini (Italy) 1925–1943
- Joseph Stalin (Soviet Union) 1929–1953
- Kim Il Sung (North Korea) 1948–1994
- Saddam Hussein (Iraq) 1979–2003

STATE TERROR

- The two most infamous examples of state terror in the 20th century were in Nazi Germany and Stalinist Russia.
- An estimated 12.5–20 million people were killed in Nazi Germany.
- An estimated 8–20 million people were killed in Stalinist Russia.

TOTALITARIANISM TODAY

- There are many authoritarian regimes in the world, but there are very few actual totalitarian governments. In 2000, one monitoring agency identified five totalitarian regimes—Afghanistan, Cuba, North Korea, Laos, and Vietnam.

Critical Thinking

1. **Synthesize** How does a totalitarian state attempt to make citizens obey its rules?

2. **Predict** How would your life change if you lived in a totalitarian state?

Stalin Seizes Control of the Economy

As Stalin began to gain complete control of society, he was setting plans in motion to overhaul the economy. He announced, "We are fifty or a hundred years behind the advanced countries. We must make good this distance in ten years." In 1928 Stalin's plans called for a **command economy**, a system in which the government made all economic decisions. Under this system, political leaders identify the country's economic needs and determine how to fulfill them.

Under Stalin, women were expected to perform the same jobs as men.

An Industrial Revolution Stalin outlined the first of several **Five-Year Plans** for the development of the Soviet Union's economy. The Five-Year Plans set impossibly high quotas, or numerical goals, to increase the output of steel, coal, oil, and electricity. To reach these targets, the government limited production of consumer goods. As a result, people faced severe shortages of housing, food, clothing, and other necessary goods.

Stalin's tough methods produced impressive economic results. Although most of the targets of the first Five-Year Plan fell short, the Soviets made substantial gains in coal and steel production. A second plan, launched in 1933, proved equally successful. From 1928 to 1937, industrial production of steel increased more than 25 percent.

An Agricultural Revolution In 1928, the government began to seize over 25 million privately owned farms in the USSR. It combined them into large, government-owned farms, called **collective farms**, a process called collectivization. Hundreds of families worked on the collectives. The government expected that the collectives' modern machinery would boost food production and reduce the number of workers. However, many peasants actively resisted the government's attempt to take their land. Some killed livestock and destroyed crops in protest. In response, Soviet secret police herded peasants onto collective farms by force. In Ukraine, the kulaks, a class of wealthy peasants, resisted collectivization fiercely. Stalin organized a mass starvation of the kulaks as a means to crush their resistance to forced collectivization. Soviet military confiscated food and blocked borders to cut off food supply, sentencing the kulaks to death by hunger. The government essentially carried out genocide against the kulaks, thousands of whom were executed or sent to labor camps. Disease, starvation, and bad harvests took more lives. In the early 1930s, between 4 million and 10 million peasants died as a direct result of Stalin's agricultural revolution. After the disaster earlier in the decade, agricultural production of some crops increased. By 1938, more than 90 percent of all peasants lived on collectives. That year the country produced almost twice the wheat it had before collectivization.

In areas where farming was more difficult, the government set up state farms. These state farms operated like factories. The workers received wages instead of a share of the profits. These farms were much larger than collectives and mostly produced wheat.

Reading Check
Summarize
What methods did Stalin use to bring agriculture under state control?

Daily Life Under Stalin

Stalin's totalitarian rule revolutionized Soviet society. Women's roles greatly expanded. People became better educated and mastered new technical skills. The dramatic changes in people's lives came at great cost. Soviet citizens found their personal freedoms limited, consumer goods in short supply, and dissent prohibited.

Stalin's economic plans created a high demand for many skilled workers. University and technical training became the key to a better life. As one young man explained, "If a person does not want to become a collective farmer or just a cleaning woman, the only means you have to get something is through education."

Women Gain Rights The Bolshevik Revolution of 1917 declared men and women equal. Laws were passed to grant women equal rights. After Stalin became dictator, women helped the state-controlled economy prosper. Under his Five-Year Plans, they had no choice but to join the labor force. The state provided child care for all working mothers. Some young women performed the same jobs as men. Millions of women worked in factories and in construction. However, men continued to hold the best jobs.

Given new educational opportunities, women prepared for careers in engineering and science. Medicine, in particular, attracted many women. By 1950, they made up 75 percent of Soviet doctors.

Soviet women paid a heavy price for their rising status in society. Besides having full-time jobs, they were responsible for housework and child care. Motherhood is considered a patriotic duty in totalitarian regimes. Soviet women were expected to provide the state with future generations of loyal, obedient citizens.

Reading Check
Summarize
How did daily life under Stalin's rule change the lives of women in the Soviet Union?

The Buildup of the Soviet Economy, 1928–1938

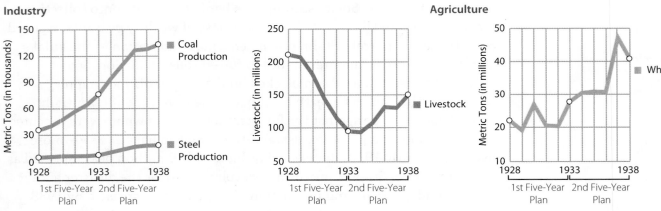
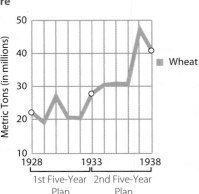

Source: *European Historical Statistics*

Interpret Graphs
1. **Synthesize** How many more metric tons of coal were produced in 1938 than in 1928?
2. **Draw Conclusions** What do the graphs show about the contrast between the progress of industry and agriculture production under Stalin's first Five-Year Plan?

Ukrainian Kulaks

The kulaks in Ukraine fiercely resisted collectivization. They murdered officials, torched the property of the collectives, and burned their own crops and grain in protest.

Recognizing the threat kulaks posed to his policies, Stalin declared that they should "liquidate kulaks as a class." The state took control of kulak land and equipment, and confiscated stores of food and grain. More than 3 million Ukrainians were shot, exiled, or imprisoned. Some 6 million people died in the government-engineered famine, known as the Ukrainian Holodomor, which resulted from the destruction of crops and animals. By 1935, the kulaks had been eliminated.

Total Control Achieved

By the mid-1930s, Stalin had forcibly transformed the Soviet Union into a totalitarian regime and an industrial and political power. He stood unopposed as dictator and maintained his authority over the Communist Party. Stalin would not tolerate individual creativity. He saw it as a threat to the conformity and obedience required of citizens in a totalitarian state. He ushered in a period of total social control and rule by terror rather than constitutional government.

Like Russia, China would fall under the influence of Karl Marx's theories and communist beliefs. The dynamic leader Mao Zedong would pave the way for transforming China into a totalitarian communist state.

Lesson 2 Assessment

1. **Organize Information** List methods of control that Stalin used and provide examples. Explain which method you think was most influential in maintaining Stalin's power.

Methods of control	Example
1.	
2.	
3.	
4.	

2. **Key Terms and People** For each key term or person in the lesson, write a sentence explaining its significance.

3. **Contrast** How do totalitarian states and constitutional governments differ?

4. **Analyze Effects** How did Stalin use communication and technology to change the government's relationship with its citizens and empower his regime?

5. **Evaluate** Were the Five-Year Plans the best way to move the Soviet economy forward? Explain.

Imperial China Collapses

The Big Idea

After the fall of the Qing dynasty, nationalist and Communist movements struggled for power.

Why It Matters Now

The seeds of China's late-20th-century political thought, communism, were planted at this time.

Key Terms and People

Kuomintang
Sun Yixian
May Fourth Movement
Mao Zedong
Jiang Jieshi
Long March

Setting the Stage

In the early 1900s, China was ripe for revolution. China had faced years of humiliation at the hands of outsiders. Foreign countries controlled its trade and economic resources. Many Chinese believed that modernization and nationalism held the country's keys for survival. They wanted to build up the army and navy, to construct modern factories, and to reform education. Yet others feared change. They believed that China's greatness lay in its traditional ways.

Temple of Heaven, Beijing, China

Nationalists Overthrow Qing Dynasty

Among the groups pushing for modernization and nation-alization was the **Kuomintang** (KWOH•mihn•TANG), or the Nationalist Party. Its first great leader was **Sun Yixian** (soon-yee•shyahn). In 1911, the Revolutionary Alliance, a forerunner of the Kuomintang, succeeded in overthrowing the last emperor of the Qing dynasty during the Xinhai Revolution.

Shaky Start for the New Republic In 1912, Sun became president of the new Republic of China. Sun hoped to establish a modern government based on the "Three Principles of the People":

1. nationalism—an end to foreign control
2. people's rights—democracy, and
3. people's livelihood—economic security for all Chinese.

Sun Yixian considered nationalism vital. He said, "The Chinese people . . . do not have national spirit. Therefore even though we have four hundred million people gathered together in one China, in reality, they are just a heap of loose sand." Despite his lasting influence as a revolutionary leader, Sun lacked the authority and military support to secure national unity.

Without an established national army, Sun utilized regional armies. However, the most powerful army was controlled by General Yuan Shikai. Unable to defeat Yuan, Sun turned over the presidency to him in order to reunify China. Yuan quickly betrayed the democratic ideals of the revolution. After the general died in 1916, civil war broke out. Real authority fell into the hands of provincial warlords, the military leaders who headed various regional armies. This Warlord Era (1916–27) broke China into a jigsaw of regions controlled by the regional warlords. By 1928, the country was reunified but faced a series of other looming problems.

Sun Yixian led the overthrow of the last Chinese emperor.

World War I Spells More Problems In 1917, the government in Beijing, hoping for an Allied victory, declared war against Germany. Some leaders mistakenly believed that for China's participation the thankful Allies would return control of Chinese territories that had previously belonged to Germany. However, under the Treaty of Versailles, the Allied leaders gave Japan those territories.

When news of the Treaty of Versailles reached China, outrage swept the country. On May 4, 1919, over 3,000 angry students gathered in the center of Beijing. The demonstrations spread to other cities and exploded into a national movement. It was called the **May Fourth Movement**. Workers, shopkeepers, and professionals joined the cause. Though not officially a revolution, these demonstrations showed the Chinese people's commitment to the goal of establishing a strong, modern nation. Sun Yixian and members of the Kuomintang also shared the aims of the movement. But they could not strengthen central rule on their own. Many young Chinese intellectuals turned against Sun Yixian's belief in Western democracy in favor of Lenin's brand of Soviet communism. The protestors during the May Fourth Movement saw the early success of communism in Russia and believed they could apply the theoretical writings of Lenin and his beliefs of communism to China. This was the beginning of the growth of the communist movement in China.

Reading Check
Identify Problems
What problems did the new Republic of China face?

Tiananmen Square

In Tiananmen Square, the Gate of Heavenly Peace was the site of many political activities during the 20th century. Early in the century, May 4, 1919, thousands of students gathered there to protest the terms of the Versailles Treaty. The May Fourth Movement was born that day. The movement marks the beginning of Chinese nationalism.

Seventy years later, in 1989, students once again gathered at the square to demand political reforms. Shortly after the anniversary of the May 4 event, thousands—and perhaps a million people—gathered at the square. On June 3, 1989, the Chinese army was ordered to clear the square of all protesters. Thousands were killed or injured.

The Communist Party in China

In 1921, a group met in Shanghai to organize the Chinese Communist Party. **Mao Zedong** (mow-dzuh•dahng), an assistant librarian at Beijing University, was among its founders. Later he would become China's greatest revolutionary leader.

Mao Zedong had already begun to develop his own brand of communism. Lenin had based his Marxist revolution on his organization in Russia's cities. Mao envisioned a different setting. He believed he could bring revolution to a rural country where the peasants could be the true revolutionaries. He argued his point passionately in 1927:

> "The force of the peasantry is like that of the raging winds and driving rain. It is rapidly increasing in violence. No force can stand in its way. The peasantry will tear apart all nets which bind it and hasten along the road to liberation. They will bury beneath them all forces of imperialism, militarism, corrupt officialdom, village bosses and evil gentry."

—Mao Zedong, quoted in *Chinese Communism and the Rise of Mao*

Lenin Befriends China While the Chinese Communist Party was forming, Sun Yixian and his Nationalist Party set up a government in southern China. Like the Communists, Sun became disillusioned with the Western democracies that refused to support his struggling government. Sun decided to ally the Kuomintang with the newly formed Communist Party. He hoped to unite all the revolutionary groups for common action.

Lenin seized the opportunity to help China's Nationalist government. In 1923, he sent military advisers and equipment to the Nationalists in return for allowing the Chinese Communists to join the Kuomintang.

Jiang Jieshi and the Nationalist forces united China under one government in 1928.

Peasants Align with the Communists After Sun Yixian died in 1925, **Jiang Jieshi** (jee•ahng-jee•shee), formerly called Chiang Kai-shek, headed the Kuomintang. Jiang was the son of a middle-class merchant. Many of Jiang's followers were bankers and businesspeople. Like Jiang, they feared the Communists' goal of creating a socialist economy modeled after the Soviet Union's.

Jiang had promised democracy and political rights to all Chinese. Yet his government became steadily less democratic and more corrupt. Most peasants believed that Jiang was doing little to improve their lives. As a result, many peasants threw their support to the Chinese Communist Party. To enlist the support of the peasants, Mao divided land that the Communists won among the local farmers.

Nationalists and Communists Clash At first, Jiang put aside his differences with the Communists. Together Jiang's Nationalist forces and the Communists successfully fought the warlords. Soon afterward, though, he turned against the Communists.

In April 1927, Nationalist troops and armed gangs moved into Shanghai. They killed many Communist leaders and trade union members in the city streets. Similar killings took place in other cities. The Nationalists nearly wiped out the Chinese Communist Party.

In 1928, Jiang became president of the Nationalist Republic of China. Great Britain and the United States both formally recognized the new government. Because of the slaughter of Communists at Shanghai, the Soviet Union did not. Jiang's treachery also had long-term effects. The Communists' deep-seated rage over the massacre erupted in a civil war that would last until 1949.

Reading Check
Analyze Primary Sources What forces does Mao identify as those that the peasants will overcome?

Civil War Rages in China

By 1930, Nationalists and Communists were fighting a bloody civil war. Mao and other Communist leaders established themselves in the hills of south-central China. Mao referred to this tactic of taking his revolution to the countryside as "swimming in the peasant sea." He recruited the peasants to join his Red Army. He then trained them in guerrilla warfare. Nationalists attacked the Communists repeatedly but failed to drive them out.

The Long March

The Long March of the Chinese Communists from the south of China to the caves of Shaanxi [shahn•shee] in the north is a remarkable story. The march covered 6,000 miles, about the distance from New York to San Francisco and back again. They crossed miles of swampland. They slept sitting up, leaning back-to-back in pairs, to keep from sinking into the mud and drowning. In total, the Communists crossed 18 mountain ranges and 24 rivers in their yearlong flight from the Nationalist forces.

▷ *Explore ONLINE!*

The Long March, 1934–1935

Route of march
Communist base 1934
Communist base 1935
Mountains
Pass

Beijing
Huang He
Yan'an
Songpan Plateau
Snowy Mts. (Jiajin Shan)
Tatu R.
Luding
Shanghai
Chang Jiang
Loushan Pass
Ruijin (Juichin)
Taiwan
Tropic of Cancer
South China Sea
Hainan

0 200 400 mi
0 300 600 km

Interpret Maps

1. **Movement** What was the course of the Long March, in terms of direction, beginning in Ruijin and ending near Yan'an?

2. **Movement** Why didn't Mao's forces move west or south?

In one of the more daring and difficult acts of the march, the Red Army crossed a bridge of iron chains whose planks had been removed.

The Red Army had to cross the Snowy Mountains, some of the highest in the world. Every man carried enough food and fuel to last for ten days. They marched six to seven hours a day.

After finally arriving at the caves in Shaanxi, Mao declared, "If we can survive all this, we can survive everything. This is but the first stage of our Long March. The final stage leads to Peking [Beijing]!"

A Japanese landing party approaches the Chinese mainland. The invasion forced Mao and Jiang to join forces to fight the Japanese.

The Long March In 1933, Jiang gathered an army of at least 700,000 men. Jiang's army then surrounded the Communists' mountain stronghold. Outnumbered, the Communist Party leaders realized that they faced defeat. In a daring move, 100,000 Communist forces fled. They began a hazardous, 6,000-mile-long journey called the **Long March**. Between 1934 and 1935, the Communists kept only a step ahead of Jiang's forces. Thousands died from hunger, cold, exposure, and battle wounds.

Finally, after a little more than a year, Mao and the seven or eight thousand Communist survivors settled in caves in northwestern China. There they gained new followers. Meanwhile, as civil war between Nationalists and Communists raged, Japan invaded China.

Civil War Suspended In 1931, as Chinese fought Chinese, the Japanese watched the power struggles with rising interest. Japanese forces took advantage of China's weakening situation. They invaded Manchuria, an industrialized province in the northeast part of China.

In 1937, the Japanese launched an all-out invasion of China. Massive bombings of villages and cities killed thousands of Chinese. The destruction of farms caused many more to die of starvation. By 1938, Japan held control of a large part of China.

The Japanese threat forced an uneasy truce between Jiang's and Mao's forces. The civil war gradually ground to a halt as Nationalists and Communists temporarily united to fight the Japanese. The National Assembly further agreed to promote changes outlined in Sun Yixian's "Three Principles of the People"—nationalism, democracy, and people's livelihood. At the same time, similar principles also were serving as a guiding force in southwest Asia.

Reading Check
Analyze Effects
What were the results of the Long March?

Lesson 3 Assessment

1. **Organize Information** Make a chart that lists the reforms of Jiang and Mao. Explain whose reforms had a greater appeal to the peasants.

Jiang	Mao
1.	1.
2.	2.
3.	3.

2. **Key Terms and People** For each key term or person in the lesson, write a sentence explaining its significance.

3. **Analyze Effects** What influence did foreign nations have on China from 1912 to 1938?

4. **Analyze Causes** What caused the Communist revolutionary movement in China to gain strength?

5. **Predict** If the Long March had failed, do you think the Nationalist party would have been successful in uniting the Chinese? Why or why not?

Nationalism in Southwest Asia

The Big Idea

Nationalism triggered independence movements to overthrow colonial powers.

Why It Matters Now

These independent nations—Turkey, Iran, and Saudi Arabia—are key players on the world stage today.

Key Terms and People

Ottoman Empire
Central Powers
Mustafa Kemal

Setting the Stage

The Ottoman Empire was broken up as a result of World War I. The weakening of the empire stirred nationalist activity in Turkey and other southwest Asian countries. Many groups within in the region began to work to gain independence and establish new forms of governments. The discovery of oil also focused attention on the region.

Turkish Nationalism

The origins of modern-day Turkey trace back more than 600 years, when it was part of the vast and powerful **Ottoman Empire**. Constantinople, the city at the heart of the empire, is present-day Istanbul, Turkey. Although reformers called for change in the 1800s, the sultans who ruled the Ottoman Empire dominated. As a result of war and the influx of new ideas, the empire dissolved in 1922, which spurred the rise of nationalism in this region.

The Young Turk Revolution The Ottoman Empire was ruled by a sultan as an absolute monarchy, but in the late 19th century various political factions began to challenge the ruling form of government. The dissent started as a conspiracy by military medical students to overthrow the Ottoman Empire's ruler. When the plot was discovered, several leaders fled abroad, where they continued to agitate for revolution. Differences arose within the groups; however, they unified behind the common goal of restoring the Constitution of 1876. This document was the first constitution in any Islamic country. Under intense political pressure in the 1870s, the sultan had reluctantly agreed to it, but he maintained most of the power. The constitution provided for a two-house parliament, although one tightly controlled by the sultan. The sultan had dissolved parliament in 1877 after only one year, and had jailed, exiled, or executed the opposition. But times had changed. The efforts of these new political groups led to the Young Turk Revolution of 1908.

Sultan Abdul Hamid II (1842–1918), was Ottoman sultan from 1876 to 1909.

This time, sultan Abdul Hamid II was unable to suppress the uprising, and rebellion spread rapidly throughout the empire. As a result, the sultan restored the constitution and stepped down from power. The new government faced many internal and external problems as well as political challenges. It seemed as if the Ottoman Empire would dissolve, especially as war loomed.

Ottoman Involvement in World War I The Ottoman Empire officially entered World War I on October 29, 1914, when the Allied Powers—France, Russia, and Great Britain—declared war in response to the Ottoman bombardment of Russian ports located on the Black Sea. The Ottoman Empire joined the **Central Powers'** war effort. Ottoman forces suffered a significant setback when Bulgaria surrendered to the Allied Powers in 1918. Shortly thereafter, the Ottoman Empire signed the Armistice of Mudros on October 30, 1918. As a result, a series of wartime agreements led to the partitioning of the Ottoman Empire into many countries. This partitioning created the modern Arab world and the Republic of Turkey. European powers governed a number of the new nations: Britain controlled modern-day Iraq and Palestine, while France governed Lebanon and Syria, to name a few. The borders for these new nations were drawn by foreign countries and mostly disregarded this region's rich ethnic history. This oversight contributed to subsequent wars, civil wars, political revolutions, and the formation of terrorist groups that are still in existence today.

Turkey Becomes a Republic At the end of World War I, the Ottoman Empire was forced to give up all its territories except Turkey. Turkish lands included the old Turkish homeland of Anatolia and a small strip of land around Istanbul.

In 1919, Greek soldiers invaded Turkey and threatened to conquer it. The Turkish sultan was powerless to stop the Greeks. However, in 1922, a brilliant commander, **Mustafa Kemal** (keh•MAHL), successfully led Turkish nationalists in fighting back the Greeks and their British backers. After winning a peace, the nationalists overthrew the last Ottoman sultan.

In 1923, Kemal became the president of the new Republic of Turkey, the first republic in southwest Asia. To achieve his goal of transforming Turkey into a modern nation, he ushered in these sweeping reforms:

- separated the laws of Islam from the laws of the nation
- abolished religious courts and created a new legal system based on European law
- granted women the right to vote and to hold public office
- launched government-funded programs to industrialize Turkey and to spur economic growth

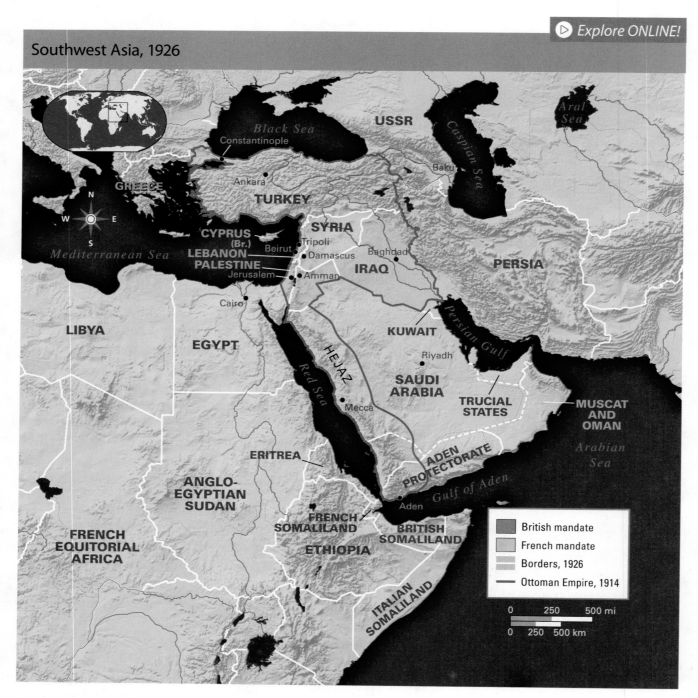

Southwest Asia, 1926

■	British mandate
■	French mandate
—	Borders, 1926
—	Ottoman Empire, 1914

0   250   500 mi
0   250   500 km

New nations appeared during the 1920s and 1930s in the former Ottoman Empire in southwest Asia. These nations adopted a variety of government styles, from republics to monarchies.

Reading Check
Synthesize How did the rise of nationalism contribute to the decline of the Ottoman Empire?

Kemal died in 1938. From his leadership, Turkey gained a new sense of its national identity. His influence was so strong that the Turkish people gave him the name Ataturk—"father of the Turks."

Mustafa Kemal
(1881–1938)

As president of Turkey, Mustafa Kemal campaigned vigorously to mold the new republic into a modern nation. His models were the United States and European countries.

Kemal believed that even the clothing of the Turks should be changed to reflect a civilized, international dress. To reach this goal, Kemal set rules for clothing. He required government workers to wear Western-style business suits and banned the fez, a brimless red felt hat that was part of traditional Turkish clothing.

Changes in Southwest Asia

The aftermath of World War I was important in shaping the development of modern southwest Asia. European countries were in ruin after the Great War, and this created the perfect situation for nationalist leaders in southwest Asia to establish their territories as new countries. Some leaders espoused new philosophies and ideals that were not embraced by the total population. This region is facing modern-day civil wars and continues to suffer from other acts of violence.

Government did not play a major role in Iran's education in the early twentieth century. Before Shah's educational reform, both private and state schools barely reached an enrollment of 50,000 students including the small class shown here.

Persia Becomes Iran Before World War I, both Great Britain and Russia had established spheres of influence in the ancient country of Persia. After the war, when Russia was still reeling from the Bolshevik Revolution, the British tried to take over all of Persia. This maneuver triggered a nationalist revolt in Persia. In 1921, a Persian army officer seized power. In 1925 he deposed the ruling shah.

Persia's new leader, Reza Shah Pahlavi (PAL•uh•vee), ruled until 1941. Reza Shah, like Kemal in Turkey, set out to modernize his country. He established public schools, built roads and railroads, promoted industrial growth, and extended women's rights. Unlike Kemal, Reza Shah Pahlavi kept all power in his own hands. In 1935, he changed the name of the country from the Greek name Persia to the traditional name Iran.

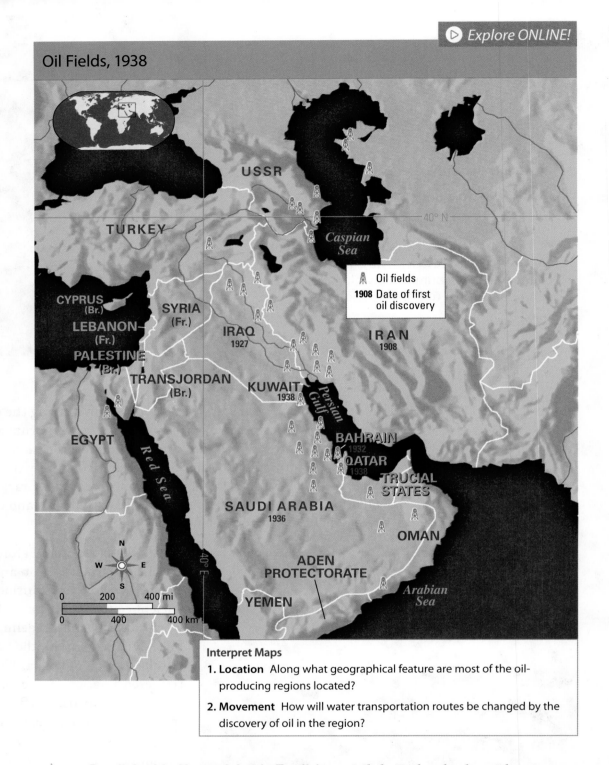

Oil Fields, 1938

▶ *Explore ONLINE!*

USSR

TURKEY

CYPRUS (Br.)

LEBANON (Fr.)

PALESTINE (Br.)

SYRIA (Fr.)

IRAQ 1927

IRAN 1908

Caspian Sea

40° N

Oil fields
1908 Date of first oil discovery

TRANSJORDAN (Br.)

KUWAIT 1938

Persian Gulf

BAHRAIN 1932

QATAR 1938

TRUCIAL STATES

EGYPT

Red Sea

SAUDI ARABIA 1936

OMAN

N W E S

0   200   400 mi
0   400   400 km

40° E

ADEN PROTECTORATE

Arabian Sea

YEMEN

Interpret Maps

1. **Location** Along what geographical feature are most of the oil-producing regions located?

2. **Movement** How will water transportation routes be changed by the discovery of oil in the region?

Saudi Arabia Keeps Islamic Traditions While Turkey broke with many Islamic traditions, another new country held strictly to Islamic law. In 1902, Abd al-Aziz Ibn Saud (sah•OOD), a member of a once-powerful Arabian family, began a successful campaign to unify Arabia. In 1932, he renamed the new kingdom Saudi Arabia after his family.

Ibn Saud carried on Arab and Islamic traditions. Loyalty to the Saudi government was based on custom, religion, and family ties. Like Kemal and Reza Shah, Ibn Saud brought some modern technology, such as telephones and radios, to his country. However, modernization in Saudi Arabia was limited to religiously acceptable areas. There also were no efforts to begin to practice democracy.

Oil Drives Development While nationalism steadily emerged as a major force in southwest Asia, the region's economy was also taking a new direction. The rising demand for petroleum products in industrialized countries brought new oil explorations to southwest Asia. During the 1920s and 1930s, European and American companies discovered enormous oil deposits in Iran, Iraq, Saudi Arabia, and Kuwait. Foreign businesses invested huge sums of money to develop these oil fields. For example, the Anglo-Persian Oil Company, a British company, started developing the oil fields of Iran. Geologists later learned that the land around the Persian Gulf has nearly two-thirds of the world's known supply of oil.

This important resource led to rapid and dramatic economic changes and development. Because oil brought huge profits, Western nations tried to dominate this region. Meanwhile, these same Western nations were about to face a more immediate crisis as power-hungry leaders seized control in Italy and Germany.

Reading Check
Compare How were Kemal's leadership and Reza Shah Pahlavi's leadership similar?

Lesson 4 Assessment

1. **Organize Information** Make a graphic organizer. Why do you think the nations in this section adopted different styles of government?

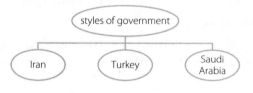

2. **Key Terms and People** For each key term or person in the lesson, write a sentence explaining its significance.

3. **Compare and Contrast** Compare the tensions between modernization and traditional culture in Turkey under the rule of Kemal.

4. **Analyze Effects** How did World War I create an atmosphere for political change in Southwest Asia?

5. **Evaluate** Explain the role nationalism played in shaping the identity and character of the people of southwest Asia.

Module 26 Assessment

Key Terms and People

For each term or name below, write a sentence explaining its importance in Russia, China, or the Ottoman Empire.

1. Bolsheviks
2. Lenin
3. soviet
4. Joseph Stalin
5. totalitarianism
6. Mao Zedong
7. Young Turks
8. Ottoman Empire
9. Mustafa Kemal

Main Ideas

Use your notes and the information in the module to answer the following questions.

Revolutions in Russia

1. How did World War I lead to the downfall of Czar Nicholas II?
2. Why did Russia's provisional government fail?
3. Explain the causes of Russia's civil war and its outcome.

Totalitarianism
CASE STUDY: Stalinist Russia

4. What are the key traits of totalitarianism?
5. What individual freedoms are denied in a totalitarian state?
6. How did Joseph Stalin create a totalitarian state in the Soviet Union?

Imperial China Collapses

7. Why did the peasants align themselves with the Chinese communists?
8. Why did Mao Zedong undertake the Long March?

Nationalism in Southwest Asia

9. How did Southwest Asia change as a result of nationalism?
10. What steps did Kemal take to modernize Turkey?
11. How did newly found petroleum deposits change the new nations in Southwest Asia?

Critical Thinking

1. **Summarize** In a diagram, show the causes of changes in government in the countries listed.

2. **Form Opinions** Which of the weapons of totalitarian governments do you think is most effective in maintaining control of a country? Explain.

3. **Analyze Causes** What role did World War I play in the revolutions and nationalistic uprisings discussed in this module?

4. **Predict** Why were the empires discussed in this chapter unable to remain in control of all of their lands?

5. **Recognize Effects** **Power and Authority** How did women's roles change under Stalin in Russia and Kemal in Turkey?

Engage with History

Some groups resort to violence as a tactic for change. Now that you have read the module, how would you assess the violent uprisings that occurred in the revolutions of Russia, China, and the Ottoman Empire? What role did violence play in the Russian and Chinese revolutions? Discuss your opinions in a small group.

Focus on Writing

Write an essay analyzing the similarities and differences among the political systems of socialism, communism, and democracy. Use multiple sources when writing the essay.

Multimedia Activity

Writing a Documentary Film Script

Write a documentary film script profiling a country where nationalistic revolutionary movements are currently active. Consider the following:

- What type of government is currently in power? (constitutional monarchy, single-party dictatorship, theocracy, republic) How long has it been in power?
- Who are the top political leaders, and how are they viewed inside and outside the country?
- Do citizens have complaints about their government? What are they?
- What nationalist revolutionary groups are active? What are their goals and strategies?

The script should also include narration, locations, sound, and visuals.

Years of Crisis

Essential Question

How did the world come to the brink of a second world war?

About the Photo: This photo shows a soldier distributing food to hungry Germans in 1931 during a severe economic depression. Germany's economic problems soon helped lead to the rise of a powerful dictator.

▶ Explore ONLINE!

HISTORY.

VIDEOS, including...
- The Year That Everything Changed
- Conspiracy for Change
- 1929: The Stock Market Crash
- A Rising Threat

☑ Document Based Investigations

☑ Graphic Organizers

☑ Interactive Games

☑ Chart: Characteristics of Fascism

☑ Image Compare: Guernica

In this module, you will read about the economic crisis and the political and social changes that brought societies to the brink of another world war.

What You Will Learn ...

Timeline of Events 1919–1939

▶ Explore ONLINE!

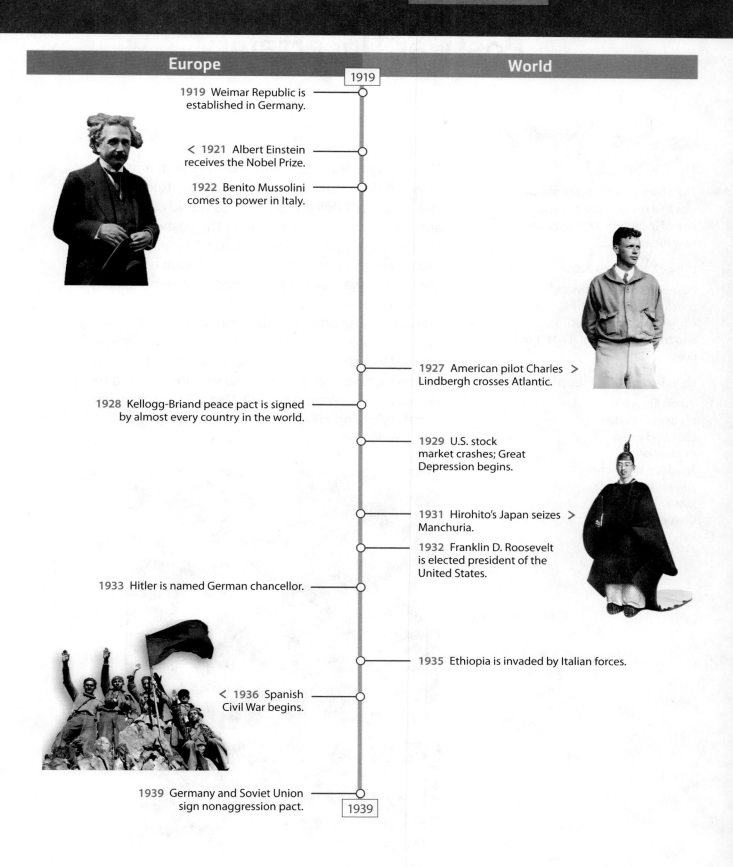

Europe		World
	1919	

1919 Weimar Republic is established in Germany.

< 1921 Albert Einstein receives the Nobel Prize.

1922 Benito Mussolini comes to power in Italy.

1927 American pilot Charles **>** Lindbergh crosses Atlantic.

1928 Kellogg-Briand peace pact is signed by almost every country in the world.

1929 U.S. stock market crashes; Great Depression begins.

1931 Hirohito's Japan seizes **>** Manchuria.

1932 Franklin D. Roosevelt is elected president of the United States.

1933 Hitler is named German chancellor.

1935 Ethiopia is invaded by Italian forces.

< 1936 Spanish Civil War begins.

1939 Germany and Soviet Union sign nonaggression pact.

1939

Postwar Uncertainty

The Big Idea

The postwar period was one of loss and uncertainty but also one of invention, creativity, and new ideas.

Why It Matters Now

Postwar trends in physics, psychiatry, art, literature, communication, music, and transportation still affect our lives.

Key Terms and People

Albert Einstein
theory of relativity
Sigmund Freud
existentialism
Friedrich Nietzsche
surrealism
jazz
Charles Lindbergh

Setting the Stage

There were many short-term and long-term effects of World War I. The horrors of the war shattered the Enlightenment belief that progress would continue and reason would prevail. During the postwar period, people began questioning traditional beliefs. Some found answers in new scientific developments, which challenged the way people looked at the world. Many enjoyed the convenience of technological improvements in transportation and communication. As society became more open, young people adopted new values and women demanded more rights. Great Britain had recognized women's right to vote in 1918, and the United States followed in 1920. Meanwhile, unconventional styles and ideas in literature, philosophy, and music reflected the uncertain times.

Life magazine cover, 1926

A New Revolution in Science

The ideas of Albert Einstein and Sigmund Freud had an enormous impact on the 20th century. These Jewish thinkers were part of a scientific revolution as important as that brought about centuries earlier by Copernicus and Galileo.

Impact of Einstein's Theory of Relativity German-born physicist **Albert Einstein** offered startling new ideas on space, time, energy, and matter. Scientists had found that light travels at exactly the same speed no matter what direction it moves in relation to Earth. In 1905, Einstein theorized that while the speed of light is constant, other things that seem constant, such as space and time, are not. Space and time can change when measured relative to an object moving near the speed of light—about 186,000 miles per second. Since relative motion is the key to Einstein's idea, it is called the **theory of relativity**. Einstein's ideas had implications not only for science but also for how people viewed the world. Now uncertainty and relativity replaced Isaac Newton's comforting belief of a world operating according to absolute laws of motion and gravity.

Influence of Freudian Psychology The ideas of Austrian physician **Sigmund Freud** were as revolutionary as Einstein's. Freud treated patients with psychological problems. From his experiences, he constructed a theory about the human mind. He believed that much of human behavior is irrational, or beyond reason. He called the irrational part of the mind the unconscious. In the unconscious, a number of drives existed, especially pleasure-seeking drives, of which the conscious mind was unaware. Freud's ideas weakened faith in reason. Even so, by the 1920s, Freud's theories had developed widespread influence.

Reading Check
Analyze Effects
What were some of the effects of World War I?

Literature in the 1920s

The brutality of World War I caused philosophers and writers to question accepted ideas about reason and progress. Disillusioned by changes brought on by the war, many people also feared the future and expressed doubts about traditional religious beliefs. Some writers and thinkers expressed their anxieties by creating disturbing visions of the present and the future, leaning more toward a modernist view of society. They became a part of new philosophical movements, such as modernism and expressionism.

In 1922, T. S. Eliot, an American poet living in England, wrote that Western society had lost its spiritual values. He described the postwar world as a barren "wasteland," drained of hope and faith. In 1921, the Irish poet William Butler Yeats conveyed a sense of dark times ahead in the poem "The Second Coming": "Things fall apart; the centre cannot hold; / Mere anarchy is loosed upon the world."

Writers of the "Lost Generation"

During the 1920s, many American writers, musicians, and painters left the United States to live in Europe. These expatriates, people who left their native country to live elsewhere, often settled in Paris. American writer Gertrude Stein called them the "Lost Generation." They were trying to find meaning in life. Life empty of meaning is the fate of Dexter Green, the main character in F. Scott Fitzgerald's short story "Winter Dreams" (1922).

> "*The dream was gone. Something had been taken from him. . . . For the first time in years the tears were streaming down his face. But they were for himself now. . . . He wanted to care, and he could not care. For he had gone away and he could never go back any more. The gates were closed, the sun was gone down, and there was no beauty but the gray beauty of steel that withstands all time. Even the grief he could have borne was left behind in the country of illusion, of youth, of the richness of life, where his winter dreams had flourished.*
>
> *'Long ago,' he said, 'long ago, there was something in me, but now that thing is gone. Now that thing is gone, that thing is gone. I cannot cry. I cannot care. That thing will come back no more.'*"
>
> —F. Scott Fitzgerald, *Winter Dreams*

A 1920s photo of F. Scott Fitzgerald

Analyze Historical Sources
What seems to be the narrator's attitude toward the future?

Writers Reflect Society's Concerns The horror of war made a deep impression on many writers. The Czech-born Jewish author Franz Kafka wrote eerie novels such as *The Trial* (1925) and *The Castle* (1926). His books feature people caught in threatening situations they can neither understand nor escape. The books struck a chord among readers in the uneasy postwar years.

Many novels showed the influence of Freud's theories on the unconscious. The Irish-born author James Joyce gained widespread attention with his stream-of-consciousness novel *Ulysses* (1922). This book focuses on a single day in the lives of three people in Dublin, Ireland. Joyce broke with normal sentence structure and vocabulary in a bold attempt to mirror the workings of the human mind.

Thinkers React to Uncertainties In their search for meaning in an uncertain world, some thinkers turned to the philosophy known as **existentialism**. A major leader of this movement was the philosopher Jean Paul Sartre (SAHR•truh) of France. Existentialists believed that there is no universal meaning to life. Each person creates his or her own meaning in life through choices made and actions taken.

The existentialists were influenced by the German philosopher **Friedrich Nietzsche** (NEE•chuh). In the 1880s, Nietzsche wrote that Western ideas such as reason, democracy, and progress had stifled people's creativity and actions. Nietzsche urged a return to the ancient heroic values of pride, assertiveness, and strength. He also championed nihilism, a philosophy that rejects moral principles and values and suggests that life is meaningless. His ideas attracted growing attention in the 20th century and had a great impact on politics in Italy and Germany in the 1920s and 1930s.

Reading Check
Make Inferences
What context clues help you to determine the meaning of existentialism?

Revolution in the Arts

Although many of the new directions in painting and music began in the prewar period, they evolved after the war.

Artists Rebel Against Tradition Artists rebelled against earlier realistic and romantic styles of painting and moved toward modernism and expressionism. Their work was a symbolic response to political and economic changes that were taking place on a global scale. Artists of this period wanted to turn against tradition and depict the inner world of emotion

The Persistence of Memory (1931), a surrealist work by Spanish artist Salvador Dali, shows watches melting in a desert.

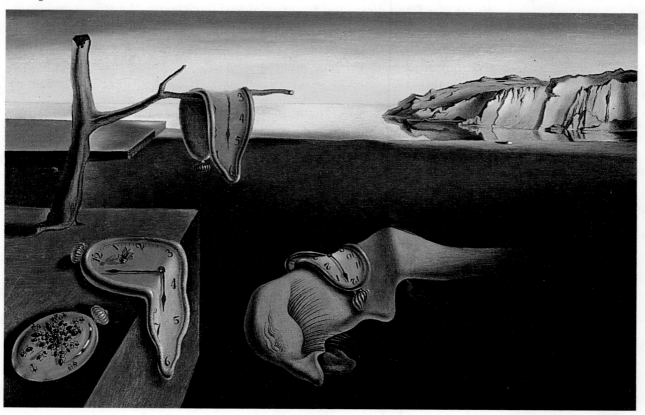

and imagination, rather than show realistic representations of objects. Expressionist painters like Paul Klee and Wassily Kandinsky used bold colors and distorted or exaggerated forms.

Inspired by traditional African art, Georges Braque of France and Pablo Picasso of Spain founded Cubism in 1907. Cubism transformed natural shapes into geometric forms. Objects were broken down into different parts with sharp angles and edges. Often several views were depicted at the same time.

Surrealism, an art movement that sought to link the world of dreams with real life, was inspired by Freud's ideas. The term *surreal* means "beyond or above reality." Surrealists tried to call on the unconscious part of their minds. Many of their paintings have an eerie, dreamlike quality and depict objects in unrealistic ways.

Composers Try New Styles In both classical and popular music, composers moved away from traditional to more modern and abstract styles. In his ballet masterpiece, *The Rite of Spring*, the Russian composer Igor Stravinsky used irregular rhythms and dissonances, or harsh combinations of sound. The Austrian composer Arnold Schoenberg rejected traditional harmonies and musical scales.

A new popular musical style called **jazz** emerged in the United States. It was developed by musicians, mainly African Americans, in New Orleans, Memphis, and Chicago. It swept the United States and Europe. The lively, loose beat of jazz seemed to capture the new freedom of the age.

Reading Check
Find the Main Idea
What was the major trend in postwar art and music?

Society Challenges Convention

World War I had disrupted traditional social patterns. New ideas and ways of life led to a new kind of individual freedom during the 1920s. Young people especially were willing to break with the traditional values, norms, and romanticism of the past and experiment with modernism and modernist values.

Women's Roles Change The independent spirit of the times showed clearly in the changes women were making in their lives. The war had allowed women to take on new roles. Their work in the war effort was decisive in helping them win the right to vote. After the war, women's suffrage became law in many countries, including the United States, Britain, Germany, Sweden, and Austria.

Women abandoned restrictive clothing and hairstyles. They wore shorter, looser garments and had their hair "bobbed," or cut short. They also wore makeup, drove cars, and drank and smoked in public. Although most women still followed traditional paths of marriage and family, a growing number spoke out for greater freedom in their lives. Margaret Sanger and Emma Goldman risked arrest by speaking in favor of birth control. As women sought new careers, the numbers of women in medicine, education, journalism, and other professions increased.

Women like these marching in a 1912 suffrage parade in New York City helped gain American women's right to vote in 1920.

Reading Check
Summarize How did the changes of the postwar years affect women and African Americans like Mrs. J. H. Adams?

The Great Migration Before the end of World War I, many African Americans left the South and migrated north to cities such as Chicago, Detroit, Philadelphia, and Pittsburgh. They were searching for new economic opportunities and trying to escape from job discrimination. In the 1920s, about 800,000 African Americans left the South. About half as many migrated north in the 1930s. This first wave of the Great Migration was followed by a second wave after World War II.

DOCUMENT-BASED INVESTIGATION   Historical Source

A Plea from the South

In 1918, Mrs. J. H. Adams of Macon, Georgia, wrote a letter to the Bethlehem Baptist Association in Chicago in hopes of leaving the South for a new life in the North.

"To the Bethlehem Baptist Association reading in the Chicago Defender of your help securing positions I want to know if it is any way you can oblige me by helping me to get out there as I am anxious to leave here and everything so hard here. I hope you will oblige in helping me to leave here [answer] at once. . . ."

—Mrs. J. H. Adams of Macon, Georgia, 1918, Library of Congress, Holograph Carter G. Woodson Papers

Analyze Historical Sources
Why does Adams seem to be in a hurry to get help?

Technological Advances Improve Life

During World War I, scientists developed new drugs and medical treatments that helped millions of people in the postwar years. The war's technological advances were put to use to improve transportation and communication after the war.

The Automobile Alters Society The automobile benefited from a host of wartime innovations and improvements—electric starters, air-filled tires, and more powerful engines. Cars were now sleek and brightly polished, complete with headlights and chrome-plated bumpers. In prewar Britain, autos were owned exclusively by the rich. British factories produced 34,000 autos in 1913. After the war, prices dropped, and the middle class could afford cars. By 1937, the British were producing 511,000 autos per year.

Increased auto use by the average family led to lifestyle changes. More people traveled for pleasure. In Europe and the United States, new businesses opened to serve the mobile tourist. The auto also affected where people lived and worked. People moved to suburbs and commuted to work in the cities.

Airplanes Transform Travel International air travel became an objective after the war. In 1919, two British pilots made the first successful flight across the Atlantic, from Newfoundland to Ireland. In 1927, an American pilot named **Charles Lindbergh** captured world attention with a 33-hour solo flight from New York to Paris. Most of the world's major passenger airlines were established during the 1920s. At first only the rich were able to afford air travel. Still, everyone enjoyed the exploits of the aviation pioneers, including those of Amelia Earhart. She was an American pilot who, in 1932, became the first woman to fly solo across the Atlantic.

Radio and Movies Dominate Popular Entertainment Media expanded during the interwar period with new technologies. It also became an important tool in advertising. Before the invention of the radio, people relied mostly on newspapers and print for news, sports, and entertainment. New media influenced culture, politics, and the economy. It brought people together and connected the world. Media such as radio and motion pictures were used to advertise new products and technologies, which influenced consumer spending. The media also provided an opportunity for the spreading of political propaganda and ideas.

Dressed in a ragged suit and oversized shoes, Charlie Chaplin's little tramp used gentle humor to get himself out of difficult situations.

Guglielmo Marconi had conducted his first successful experiments with radio in 1895. However, the real push for radio development came during World War I. In 1920, the world's first commercial radio station—KDKA in Pittsburgh, Pennsylvania—began broadcasting. Almost overnight, radio mania swept the United States. Every major city had stations broadcasting news, plays, and even live sporting events. Soon most families owned a radio.

Other forms of media, such as motion pictures, became a major industry in the 1920s. Many countries, from Cuba to Japan, produced movies. In Europe, film was a serious art form. However, in the Hollywood district of Los Angeles, where 90 percent of all films were made, movies were entertainment.

The king of Hollywood's silent screen was the English-born Charlie Chaplin, a comic genius best known for his portrayal of the lonely little tramp bewildered by life. In the late 1920s, the addition of sound transformed movies.

The advances in transportation and communication that followed the war had brought the world in closer touch. Global prosperity came to depend on the economic well-being of all major nations, especially the United States.

Reading Check
Analyze Effects
What were the results of the peacetime adaptations of war technology?

Lesson 1 Assessment

1. **Organize Information** Make a chart to show the contributions that had the most lasting impact by field.

Field	Contributors
science	
technology	
literature and philosophy	

2. **Key Terms and People** For each key term or person in the lesson, write a sentence explaining its significance.

3. **Make Inferences** Why were the ideas of Einstein and Freud revolutionary?

4. **Summarize** How did literature and art in the 1920s reflect the uncertainty of the period?

5. **Analyze Effects** How did the increased use of the automobile affect average people?

6. **Develop Historical Perspective** Why did some women begin demanding more political and social freedom?

7. **Make Inferences** Why were new medical treatments and inventions developed during World War I?

Labor-Saving Devices in the United States

Several changes that took place during the 1920s made the use of electrical household appliances more widespread.

- Wiring for electricity became common. In 1917, only 24 percent of U.S. homes had electricity. By 1930, that figure was almost 70 percent.
- Merchants offered the installment plan, which allowed buyers to make payments over time. That way, people could purchase appliances even if they couldn't pay the entire price at once.
- The use of advertising grew. Ads praised appliances, claiming that they would shorten tasks and give women more free time.

Ironically, the new labor-saving devices generally did not decrease the amount of time women spent doing housework. Because the tasks became less physically difficult, many families stopped hiring servants and relied on the wife to do all the work herself.

WASHING MACHINE ▲

To do laundry manually, women had to carry and heat about 50 gallons of water for each load. They rubbed the clothes on ridged washboards, rinsed them in tubs, and wrung them out by hand.

This early electric washing machine, photographed in 1933, made the job less strenuous. The casters on the legs made it easier to move tubs of water. The two rollers at the top of the machine squeezed water from clothes. That innovation alone saved women's wrists from constant strain.

▲ REFRIGERATOR

People used to keep perishable food in iceboxes cooled by large chunks of ice that gradually melted and had to be replaced. Electric refrigerators, like the one in this 1929 advertisement, kept the food at a fairly constant temperature, which reduced spoilage. Because food kept longer, housewives could shop less frequently.

◄ COFFEE POT

The electric coffee pot shown in this 1933 photograph was a vacuum pot. The water in the bottom chamber would come to a boil and bubble up into the top chamber, where the grounds were. The resulting vacuum in the lower chamber pulled the liquid back through the grounds and into the lower chamber.

Stop This! What an iron fails to supply in heat, a woman must furnish in arm-aching pressure.

Start This! If your iron KEEPS hot regardless of damp things, you can do nearly all pieces sitting down.

Five women's magazine editors agree that women would sit to iron if they could

▲ IRON
Before electrical appliances, women heated irons on a stove. The irons cooled quickly, and as they did so, women had to push down harder to press out wrinkles. Early electric irons also had inconsistent heat. This 1926 ad offered an electric iron that stayed evenly hot, so women didn't have to put so much force into their ironing. Therefore, they could iron sitting down.

Twice the cleaning... *twice* the leisure!

Premier Duplex

▲ VACUUM CLEANER
This 1920 ad promised "Twice as many rooms cleaned. . . . twice as much leisure left for you to enjoy." However, women rarely experienced that benefit. Because the new appliances made housework easier, people began to expect homes to be cleaner. As a result, many women vacuumed more often and generally used their newfound "leisure" time to do even more household chores than before.

APPLIANCES IN THE HOME

- In 1929, a survey of 100 Ford employees showed that 98 of them had electric irons in their homes.
- The same survey showed that 49 of the 100 had washing machines at home.

Mechanical Washing Machines Shipped

Numbers in Thousands

1500, 1300, 1100, 900, 700, 500

1927 1931 1935 1939

Source: *Historical Statistics of the United States*

Persons Employed as Private Laundress

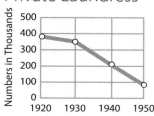

Numbers in Thousands

500, 400, 300, 200, 100, 0

1920 1930 1940 1950

Source: *Historical Statistics of the United States*

Critical Thinking
1. **Analyze Issues** What benefits did advertisers promise that the new electrical appliances would provide for women? Explain whether women actually received those benefits.
2. **Evaluate** Do you think that advertising of these new household technologies influenced buyers to purchase them? Did it promote consumerism to individual or different groups of Americans? How do you think advertising was different in the 1930s compared to today?

A Worldwide Depression

The Big Idea

An economic depression in the United States spread throughout the world and lasted for a decade.

Why It Matters Now

Many social and economic programs introduced worldwide to combat the Great Depression are still operating.

Key Terms and People

coalition government
Weimar Republic
Great Depression
recession
Franklin D. Roosevelt
New Deal
John Maynard Keynes

Setting the Stage

By the late 1920s, European nations were rebuilding war-torn economies. They were aided by loans from the more prosperous United States. Only the United States and Japan came out of the war in better financial shape than before. In the United States, Americans seemed confident that the country would continue on the road to even greater economic prosperity. One sign of this was the booming stock market and booming economy. Yet the American economy had serious weaknesses that would soon bring about the most severe economic downturn the world had yet known.

People waiting for a free lunch for the unemployed, 1930

Postwar Europe

In both human suffering and economic terms, the cost of World War I was immense. The Great War left every major European country nearly bankrupt. In addition, Europe's domination in world affairs declined after the war.

Unstable New Democracies The war's end saw the sudden rise of new democracies. From 1914 to 1918, Europe's last absolute rulers had been overthrown. The first of the new governments was formed in Russia in 1917. The Provisional Government, as it was called, hoped to establish constitutional and democratic rule. However, within months it had fallen to a Communist dictatorship. Even so, for the first time, most European nations had democratic governments.

Many citizens of the new democracies had little experience with representative government. For generations, kings and emperors had ruled Germany and the new nations formed from Austria-Hungary. Even in France and Italy, whose parliaments had existed before World War I, the large number of political parties made effective government difficult. Some countries had a dozen or more political groups. In these countries, it was almost impossible for one party to win enough support to govern effectively. When no single party won a majority, a **coalition government**, or temporary alliance of several parties, was needed to form a parliamentary majority. Because the parties disagreed on so many policies, coalitions seldom lasted very long.

Frequent changes in government made it hard for democratic countries to develop strong leadership and move toward long-term goals. The weaknesses of a coalition government became a major problem in times of crisis. Voters in several countries were then willing to sacrifice democratic government for strong, authoritarian leadership.

Reading Check
Make Inferences
Why were coalition governments ineffective after the war ended?

The Weimar Republic

Germany's new democratic government was set up in 1919. Known as the **Weimar** (WY•MAHR) **Republic**, it was named after the city where the national assembly met. The Weimar Republic had serious weaknesses from the start. First, Germany lacked a strong democratic tradition. Furthermore, postwar Germany had several major political parties and many minor ones. Worst of all, millions of Germans blamed the Weimar government, not their wartime leaders, for the country's defeat and postwar humiliation caused by the Versailles Treaty.

Inflation Causes Crisis in Germany Germany also faced enormous economic problems that had begun during the war. Unlike Britain and France, Germany had not greatly increased its wartime taxes. To pay the expenses of the war, the Germans had simply printed money. After Germany's defeat, this paper money steadily lost its value. Burdened with war debt and heavy reparations payments to the Allies, Germany printed even more money. As a result, the value of the mark, as Germany's currency was called, fell sharply. Severe and high inflation, or hyperinflation, set in. Germans needed more and more money to buy even the most basic goods. For example, in Berlin a loaf of bread cost less than a mark in 1918, more than 160 marks in 1922, and some 200 billion marks by late 1923. People took wheelbarrows full of money to buy food. As a result, many Germans questioned the value of their new democratic government.

Attempts at Economic Stability Germany recovered from the 1923 inflation thanks largely to the work of an international committee. The committee was headed by Charles Dawes, an American banker. The Dawes Plan provided for a $200 million loan from American banks to stabilize German currency and strengthen its economy. The plan also set a more realistic schedule for Germany's reparations payments.

Put into effect in 1924, the Dawes Plan helped slow inflation. As the German economy began to recover, it attracted more loans and investments from the United States. By 1929, German factories were producing as much as they had before the war.

German children use stacks of paper money, which had lost much of its value, as building blocks during the 1923 inflation.

Efforts at a Lasting Peace As prosperity returned, Germany's foreign minister, Gustav Stresemann (STRAY•zuh•mahn), and France's foreign minister, Aristide Briand (bree•AHND), tried to improve relations between their countries. In 1925, the two ministers met in Locarno, Switzerland, with officials from Belgium, Italy, and Britain. They signed a treaty promising that France and Germany would never again make war against each other. Germany also agreed to respect the existing borders of France and Belgium. It then was admitted to the League of Nations.

In 1928, the hopes raised by the "spirit of Locarno" led to the Kellogg-Briand peace pact. Frank Kellogg, the U.S. Secretary of State, arranged this agreement with France's Briand. Almost every country in the world, including the Soviet Union, signed. They pledged "to renounce war as an instrument of national policy."

Reading Check
Identify Problems
What political and economic problems did the Weimar Republic face?

Unfortunately, the treaty had no means to enforce its provisions. The League of Nations, the obvious choice as enforcer, had no armed forces. The refusal of the United States to join the League also weakened it. Nonetheless, the peace agreements seemed like a good start.

Financial Collapse

In the late 1920s, American economic prosperity largely sustained the world economy. If the U.S. economy weakened, the whole world's economic system was at risk of collapse. In 1929, it did.

A Flawed U.S. Economy Despite prosperity, several weaknesses in the U.S. economy caused serious problems. These included uneven distribution of wealth, overproduction by business and agriculture, and the fact that many Americans were buying less.

By 1929, American factories were turning out nearly half of the world's industrial goods. The rising productivity led to enormous profits. However, this new wealth was not evenly distributed. The richest 5 percent of the population received 33 percent of all personal income in 1929. Yet 60 percent of all American families earned less than $2,000 per year. Thus, most families were too poor to buy the goods being produced. Unable to sell all their goods, store owners eventually cut back their orders from factories. Factories in turn reduced production and laid off workers. A downward economic spiral began. As more workers lost their jobs, families bought even fewer goods. In turn, factories made further cuts in production and laid off more workers.

During the 1920s, overproduction affected American farmers as well. Scientific farming methods and new farm machinery had dramatically increased crop yields. American farmers were producing more food. Meanwhile, they faced new competition from farmers in Australia, Latin America, and Europe. As a result, a worldwide surplus of agricultural products drove prices and profits down.

Unable to sell their crops at a profit, many farmers could not pay off the bank loans that kept them in business. Their unpaid debts weakened banks and forced some to close. The danger signs of overproduction by factories and farms should have warned people against gambling on the stock market. Yet no one heeded the warning.

The Stock Market Crashes In 1929, New York City's Wall Street was the financial capital of the world. Banks and investment companies lined its sidewalks. At Wall Street's New York Stock Exchange, optimism about the booming U.S. economy showed in soaring prices for stocks. To get in on the boom, many middle-income people began buying stocks on margin. This meant that they paid a small percentage of a stock's price as a down payment and borrowed the rest from a stockbroker. The system worked well as long as stock prices were rising. However, if they fell, investors had no money to pay off the loan.

In September 1929, some investors began to think that stock prices were unnaturally high. They started selling their stocks, believing the prices would soon go down. By Thursday, October 24, the gradual lowering of stock prices had become an all-out slide downward. A panic resulted. Everyone wanted to sell stocks, and no one wanted to buy. Prices plunged to a new low on Tuesday, October 29. A record 16 million stocks were sold. Then the market collapsed.

Reading Check
Identify Problems
What major weaknesses had appeared in the American economy by 1929?

History in Depth

Investing in Stocks

Stocks are shares of ownership in a company. Businesses get money to operate by selling shares of stock to investors, or buyers. Companies pay interest on the invested money in the form of dividends to the shareholders. Dividends rise or fall depending on a company's profits.

Investors do not buy stocks directly from the company. Instead, stock brokers transact the business of buying and selling.

Investors hope to make more money on stocks than if they put their money elsewhere, such as in a savings account with a fixed rate of interest. However, if the stock price goes down, investors lose money when they sell their stock at a lower price than they paid for it.

Stock Prices, 1925–1933

Source: *Historical Statistics of the United States*

Interpret Graphs
Why do you think stock prices continued to plummet after the stock market crashed in 1929?

SOCIAL HISTORY

Life in the Depression

During the Great Depression of 1929 to 1939, millions of people worldwide lost their jobs or their farms. At first the unemployed had to depend on the charity of others for food, clothing, and shelter. Many, like the men in this photo taken in New York City, made their home in makeshift shacks. Local governments and charities opened soup kitchens to provide free food. Applicants formed long lines for whatever work was available, and these jobs usually paid low wages. American culture changed as a result of mass migrations to the West in search of jobs and new opportunities. Americans began to focus inward and revisit their roots. An interest in traditional folk culture flourished.

Analyze Visuals
Why do you think the line is made up of men only? Explain your response.

The Great Depression

People could not pay the money they owed on margin purchases. Stocks they had bought at high prices were now worthless. Within months of the crash, unemployment rates began to rise as industrial production, prices, and wages declined. A long business slump, which would come to be called the **Great Depression**, followed. An economic depression is a long period of economic decline when there is low production, a shrinking of the economy, high unemployment, and loss of businesses. The stock market crash alone did not cause the Great Depression, but it quickened the collapse of the economy and made the Depression more difficult. By 1932, factory production had been cut in half. Thousands of businesses failed, and banks closed. As a result, around 9 million people lost the money in their savings accounts when banks had no money to pay them. When banks closed, people and businesses could no longer get loans. Many farmers lost their lands when they could not make mortgage payments. By 1933, one-fourth of all American workers had no jobs. During this wave of "bad times," the Hoover administration did little to help Americans or provide relief during the Great Depression. Many newly homeless people found themselves living in "Hoovervilles" with little relief in sight.

Isolationist Policy The United States had generally followed a policy of isolation after World War I, but after the Great Depression hit, the country turned inward even more. The U.S. government's focus was on recovery and relief for Americans. Even with the rise of fascism in Japan and the Japanese invasion of Manchuria in 1931, U.S. policy did not shift toward intervention. The United States remained committed to isolationism, but it did assert that the United States would not recognize or support any territory that was taken aggressively by another nation. Only after President Franklin D. Roosevelt's election into office did the United States slowly move toward intervention in foreign affairs.

A Global Depression The collapse of the American economy sent shock waves around the world. Worried American bankers demanded repayment of their overseas loans, and American investors withdrew their money from Europe. The American market for European goods dropped sharply as the U.S. Congress placed high tariffs on imported goods so that American dollars would stay in the United States and pay for American goods. This policy backfired. Conditions worsened for the United States. Many countries that depended on exporting goods to the United States also suffered. Moreover, when the United States raised tariffs, it set off a chain reaction. Other nations imposed their own higher tariffs. World trade dropped by 65 percent. This contributed further to the economic downturn. Unemployment rates soared.

Unemployment Rate, 1928–1938

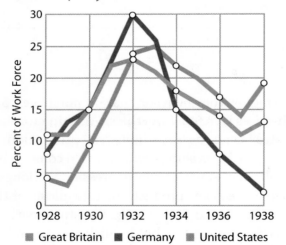

Great Britain   Germany   United States

Sources: *European Historical Statistics: 1750–1970;*
Historical Statistics of the United States: Colonial Times to 1970.

World Trade, 1929–1933

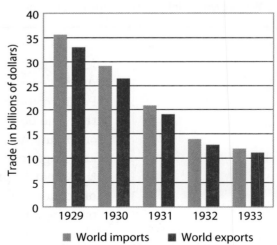

World imports   World exports

Source: Kenneth Oye, *Economic Discrimination and Political Exchange*

Interpret Graphs
1. **Compare** What nation had the highest rate of unemployment? How high did it reach?
2. **Contrast** Between 1929 and 1933, how much did world exports drop? What about world imports?

Reading Check
Analyze Effects
What effect
did private and
government
institutions have on
people and businesses
during the Great
Depression?

Effects Throughout the World Because of war debts and dependence on American loans and investments, Germany and Austria were particularly hard hit. In 1931, Austria's largest bank failed. In Asia, both farmers and urban workers suffered as the value of exports fell by half between 1929 and 1931. The crash was felt heavily in Latin America as well. As European and U.S. demand for such Latin American products as sugar, beef, and copper dropped, prices collapsed.

The World Confronts the Crisis

The Depression confronted democracies with a serious challenge to their economic and political systems. Each country met the crisis in its own way.

This photograph shows a soldier distributing food to hungry Germans in 1931 during the country's economic depression.

Britain Takes Steps to Improve Its Economy

The Depression hit Britain severely. To meet the emergency, British voters elected a multiparty coalition known as the National Government. It passed high protective tariffs, increased taxes, and regulated the currency. It also lowered interest rates to encourage industrial growth. These measures brought about a slow but steady recovery. By 1937, unemployment had been cut in half, and production had risen above 1929 levels. Britain avoided political extremes and preserved democracy.

France Responds to the Economic Crisis

Unlike Britain, France had a more self-sufficient economy. In 1930, it was still heavily agricultural and less dependent on foreign trade. Nevertheless, by 1935, one million French workers were unemployed.

The economic crisis contributed to political instability. In 1933, five coalition governments formed and fell. Many political leaders were frightened by the growth of antidemocratic forces both in France and in other parts of Europe. So in 1936, moderates, socialists, and communists formed a coalition. The Popular Front, as it was called, passed a series of reforms to help the workers. Unfortunately, price increases quickly offset wage gains. Unemployment remained high. Yet France also preserved democratic government.

Socialist Governments Find Solutions

The socialist governments in the Scandinavian countries of Denmark, Sweden, and Norway also met the challenge of economic crisis successfully. They built their recovery programs on an existing tradition of cooperative community action. In Sweden, the government sponsored massive public works projects that kept people employed and producing. All the Scandinavian countries raised pensions for the elderly and increased unemployment insurance, subsidies for housing, and other welfare benefits. To pay for these benefits, the governments taxed all citizens. Democracy remained intact.

Addressing the Nation

On March 4, 1933, President Roosevelt sought to restore Americans' faith in their nation:

Analyze Historical Sources
Based on this excerpt, what motive did Roosevelt have when he delivered his First Inaugural Address?

> *"This great Nation will endure as it has endured, will revive and will prosper. . . . [L]et me assert my firm belief that the only thing we have to fear is fear itself—nameless, unreasoning, unjustified terror which paralyzes needed efforts to convert retreat into advance."*
>
> —Franklin Roosevelt, First Inaugural Address

Stricken with polio in 1921, Roosevelt vowed he would not allow bodily disability to defeat his will.

Recovery in the United States

Herbert Hoover and his administration were unsuccessful at helping Americans during the Great Depression. They tried to stop the **recession**, or period of low or reduced economic activity, but conditions worsened. However, in 1932, U.S. voters elected **Franklin D. Roosevelt**. His confident manner appealed to millions of Americans who felt bewildered by the Depression.

Roosevelt immediately began a program of government reform that he called the **New Deal**. Large public works projects helped to provide jobs for the unemployed. New government agencies gave financial help to businesses and farms. Large amounts of public money were spent on welfare and relief programs. Roosevelt and his advisers believed that government spending would create jobs and start a recovery. Regulations were imposed to reform the stock market and the banking system.

The New Deal did eventually reform the American economic system. Roosevelt's leadership preserved the country's faith in its democratic political system. It also established him as a leader of democracy in a world threatened by ruthless dictators, as you will read about in Lesson 3.

Keynesian Economics In 1936, British economist **John Maynard Keynes** published the *General Theory of Employment, Interest, and Money*. Even though he had advocated for government action to be taken in the 1920s to help cure unemployment, it was not until the publication of the *General Theory* that he provided a full approach and solution (better known as Keynesian economics) to the Great Depression. He argued that the government should provide full employment through government job programs, changing tax policies, and modifying spending for public funding. This economic thinking was a new approach to capitalist economic theory, which had been driven by Adam Smith's economic philosophy in the late 1700s that government should be *laissez-faire* and that the people, not the government, should drive a capitalist economy and regulate themselves. President Roosevelt adopted Keynesian economics in some of his administration's policy after the recession of 1936–1937.

Reading Check
Summarize What was the major theme in Keynes's *General Theory of Employment, Interest, and Money*?

Lesson 2 Assessment

1. **Organize Information** Make a chart to show what President Roosevelt did to try to counter the effects of the Great Depression.

The Great Depression

2. **Key Terms and People** For each key term or person in the lesson, write a sentence explaining its significance.

3. **Summarize** How did World War I change the balance of economic power in the world?

4. **Analyze Causes** What economic and political problems did the collapse of the American economy cause in other countries?

5. **Analyze Effects** How did Europe respond to the economic crisis?

6. **Make Inferences** What did the weakness of the League of Nations in 1928 suggest about its future effectiveness?

Fascism Rises in Europe

The Big Idea

In response to political turmoil and economic crises, Italy and Germany turned to totalitarian dictators.

Why It Matters Now

These dictators changed the course of history, and the world is still recovering from their abuse of power.

Key Terms and People

fascism
Benito Mussolini
Adolf Hitler
Nazism
Mein Kampf
lebensraum

Setting the Stage

Many democracies, including the United States, Britain, and France, remained strong despite the economic crisis caused by the Great Depression. However, millions of people lost faith in democratic government and became open to new economic movements and ideologies to stimulate the economy such as socialism and communism. These movements and ideologies were in conflict with those of democratic societies.

Some turned to an extreme system of government called **fascism** (FASH•ihz•uhm), a new, militant political movement that emphasized loyalty to the state and obedience to its leader. Fascists promised to revive the economy, punish those responsible for hard times, and restore order and national pride. Their message attracted many people who felt frustrated and angered by the peace treaties that followed World War I and the Great Depression.

Fascism's Rise in Italy

Unlike communism, fascism had no clearly defined theory or program. Nevertheless, most fascists shared several ideas. They preached an extreme form of nationalism, or loyalty to one's country. Fascists believed that nations must struggle—peaceful states were doomed to be conquered. They pledged loyalty to an authoritarian leader who guided and brought order to the state. In each nation, fascists wore uniforms of a certain color, used special salutes, and held mass rallies.

Fascism

Fascism is a political movement that promotes an extreme form of nationalism and militarism. It also includes a denial of individual rights and dictatorial one-party rule. Nazism was the fascist movement that developed in Germany in the 1920s and 1930s. It included a belief in the racial superiority of the German people. The fascists in Italy were led by Benito Mussolini.

CHARACTERISTICS OF FASCISM

Cultural
- censorship
- indoctrination
- secret police

Social
- supported by middle class, industrialists, and military

Economic
- economic functions controlled by state corporations or state

Chief Examples
- Italy
- Spain
- Germany

Political
- nationalist
- racist (Nazism)
- one-party rule
- supreme leader

Basic Principles
- authoritarianism
- state more important than the individual
- charismatic leader
- action oriented

Interpret Charts

1. **Analyze** Which political, cultural, and economic characteristics helped make fascism an authoritarian system?

2. **Make Inferences** What characteristics of fascism might make it attractive to people during times of crisis such as the Great Depression?

In some ways, fascism was similar to communism. Both systems were ruled by dictators who allowed only their own political party (one-party rule). Both denied individual rights. In both, the state was supreme. Neither practiced any kind of democracy. However, unlike communists, fascists did not seek a classless society. Rather, they believed that each class had its place and function. In most cases, fascist parties were made up of aristocrats and industrialists, war veterans, and the lower middle class. Also, fascists were nationalists, but communists were internationalists, hoping to unite workers worldwide.

Mussolini Takes Control Fascism's rise in Italy was fueled by bitter disappointment over the failure to win large territorial gains at the 1919 Paris Peace Conference. Rising inflation and unemployment also contributed to widespread social unrest. To growing numbers of Italians, their democratic government seemed helpless to deal with the country's problems. They wanted a leader who would take action.

A newspaper editor and politician named **Benito Mussolini** boldly promised to rescue Italy by reviving its economy and rebuilding its armed forces. He vowed to give Italy strong leadership. Mussolini had founded the Fascist Party in 1919. As economic conditions worsened, his popularity rapidly increased. Finally, Mussolini publicly criticized Italy's government. Groups of fascists wearing black shirts attacked communists and socialists on the streets. Because Mussolini played on the fear of a workers' revolt, he began to win support from the middle classes, the aristocracy, and industrial leaders.

In October 1922, about 30,000 fascists marched on Rome. They demanded that King Victor Emmanuel III put Mussolini in charge of the government. The king decided that Mussolini was the best hope for his dynasty to survive. After widespread violence and a threatened uprising, Mussolini took power "legally."

─── BIOGRAPHY ───

Benito Mussolini (1883–1945)

Because Mussolini was of modest height, he usually chose a location for his speeches where he towered above the crowds—often a balcony high above a public square. He then roused audiences with his emotional speeches and theatrical gestures and body movements.

Vowing to lead Italy "back to her ways of ancient greatness," Mussolini peppered his speeches with aggressive words such as *war* and *power*.

Reading Check
Summarize
What promises did
Mussolini make to the
Italian people?

IL Duce's Leadership Mussolini was now IL Duce (ihl-DOO•chay), or the leader. He abolished democracy and outlawed all political parties except the Fascist Party. He used terror and violence to enforce his policies. Secret police jailed his opponents. Government censors forced radio stations and publications to broadcast or publish only fascist doctrines. Mussolini outlawed strikes. He sought to control the economy by allying the fascists with the industrialists and large landowners. However, Mussolini never had the total control achieved by Joseph Stalin in the Soviet Union or Adolf Hitler in Germany.

— BIOGRAPHY —

Adolf Hitler (1889–1945)

Like Mussolini, Hitler could manipulate huge audiences with his fiery oratory. Making speeches was crucial to Hitler. He believed: "All great world-shaking events have been brought about . . . by the spoken word!"

Because he appeared awkward and unimposing, Hitler rehearsed his speeches. Usually he began a speech in a normal voice. Suddenly, he spoke louder as his anger grew. His voice rose to a screech, and his hands flailed the air. Then he would stop, smooth his hair, and look quite calm.

Hitler Rises to Power in Germany

When Mussolini became dictator of Italy in the mid-1920s, **Adolf Hitler** was a little-known political leader whose early life had been marked by disappointment. When World War I broke out, Hitler found a new beginning. He volunteered for the German army and was twice awarded the Iron Cross, a medal for bravery.

The Rise of the Nazis At the end of the war, Hitler settled in Munich. In 1919, he joined a tiny right-wing political group. This group shared his belief that Germany had to overturn the Treaty of Versailles and combat communism. The group later named itself the National Socialist German Workers' Party, called Nazi for short. Its policies formed the German brand of fascism known as **Nazism**. The party adopted the swastika, or hooked cross, as its symbol. The Nazis also set up a private militia called the storm troopers or Brown Shirts.

Within a short time, Hitler's success as an organizer and speaker led him to be chosen *der Führer* (duhr-FYUR•uhr), or the leader, of the Nazi party. Inspired by Mussolini's march on Rome, Hitler and the Nazis plotted to seize power in Munich in 1923. The attempt failed, and Hitler was arrested. He was tried for treason but was sentenced to only five years in prison. He served less than nine months.

While in jail, Hitler wrote **Mein Kampf** (*My Struggle*). This book set forth his beliefs and his goals for Germany. Hitler asserted that the Germans, whom he incorrectly called "Aryans," were a "master race." He declared that non-Aryan "races," such as Jews, Slavs, and Gypsies, were inferior. He called the Versailles Treaty an outrage and vowed to regain German lands.

After leaving prison in 1924, Hitler revived the Nazi Party. Most Germans ignored him and his angry message until the Great Depression ended the nation's brief postwar recovery. The economic effects of the Great Depression helped Hitler's cause, as the German people were also desperate for a strong leader who would improve their lives. When American loans stopped, the German economy collapsed. Civil unrest broke out. Frightened and confused, Germans now turned to Hitler, hoping for security and firm leadership. Hitler also declared that Germany was overcrowded and needed more **lebensraum**, or living space. He promised to get that space through imperialism, by rebuilding Germany's military and conquering eastern Europe and Russia.

Reading Check
Make Inferences
Why did Germans at first support Hitler?

Hitler Becomes Chancellor

The Nazis had become the largest political party by 1932. Conservative leaders mistakenly believed they could control Hitler and use him for their purposes. In January 1933, they advised President Paul von Hindenburg to name Hitler chancellor. Thus Hitler came to power legally.

Vocabulary
chancellor the prime minister or president in certain countries

Once in office, Hitler called for new elections, hoping to win a parliamentary majority. Six days before the election, a fire destroyed the Reichstag building, where the parliament met. The Nazis blamed the communists. By stirring up fear of the communists, the Nazis and their allies won by a slim majority.

DOCUMENT-BASED INVESTIGATION   Historical Source

A Prediction About Hitler

Soon after Hitler came to power, General Erich Ludendorff, a former ally of Hitler's, wrote to Hindenburg:

> "By naming Hitler as Reichschancellor, you have delivered up our holy Fatherland to one of the greatest [rabblerousers] of all time. I solemnly [predict] that this accursed man will plunge our Reich into the abyss and bring our nation into inconceivable misery."
>
> —Erich Ludendorff,
> letter to President Hindenburg,
> February 1, 1933

Analyze Historical Sources
How do you think Ludendorff made such an accurate prediction?

At a 1933 rally in Nuremberg, Germany, storm troopers carried flags bearing the swastika.

Hitler used his new power to turn Germany into a totalitarian state. He banned all other political parties and had opponents arrested. Meanwhile, an elite, black-uniformed unit called the SS (*Schutzstaffel*, or protection squad) was created. It was loyal only to Hitler. In 1934, the SS arrested and murdered hundreds of Hitler's enemies. This brutal action and the terror applied by the Gestapo, the Nazi secret police, shocked most Germans into total obedience.

The Nazis quickly took command of the economy, including transportation and technology. New laws banned strikes, dissolved independent labor unions, and gave the government authority over business and labor. Hitler put millions of Germans to work. They constructed factories, built highways, manufactured weapons, and served in the military. As a result, the number of unemployed dropped from about 6 million to 1.5 million in 1936.

The Führer Is Supreme Hitler wanted more than just economic and political power—he wanted control over every aspect of German life. To shape public opinion and to win praise for his leadership, Hitler, like Mussolini, turned the press, radio, literature, painting, and film into propaganda tools. Books that did not conform to Nazi beliefs were burned in huge bonfires. Churches were forbidden to criticize the Nazis or the government. Schoolchildren had to join the Hitler Youth (for boys) or the League of German Girls. Hitler believed that continuous struggle brought victory to the strong. He twisted the philosophy of Friedrich Nietzsche to support his use of brute force.

Hitler Makes War on the Jews Hatred of Jews, or anti-Semitism, was a key part of Nazi ideology and had a long, unfortunate tradition in Europe. So-called "scientific" racism, which focused on the belief that Jews were inferior to the Aryan race, both mentally and physically, emerged in Germany in the 19th century, notably among Social Darwinists. Although Jews were less than 1 percent of the population, the Nazis used them as scapegoats for all of Germany's troubles since the war. This led to a wave of anti-Semitism across Germany. Beginning in 1933, the Nazis passed laws depriving Jews of most of their rights. Violence against Jews mounted. On the night of November 9, 1938, Nazi mobs attacked Jews in their homes and on the streets and destroyed thousands of Jewish-owned buildings. This rampage, called *Kristallnacht* (Night of the Broken Glass), signaled the real start of the process of eliminating the Jews from German life. Hitler's "Final Solution" plan was to eliminate and exterminate the Jewish population in Europe, which later became known as the Holocaust (*Shoah* in Hebrew). Eventually, six million Jews perished during the Holocaust.

Reading Check
Summarize
How did Hitler create
a totalitarian state?

Global Patterns

Fascism in Argentina

Juan Perón served as Argentina's president from 1946 to 1955 and again in 1973 and 1974. The two years he spent in Europe before World War II greatly influenced his strong-man rule.

A career army officer, Perón went to Italy in 1939 for military training. He then served at the Argentine embassy in Rome. A visit to Berlin gave Perón a chance to see Nazi Germany. The ability of Hitler and Mussolini to manipulate their citizens impressed Perón.

When Perón himself gained power, he patterned his military dictatorship on that of the European fascists.

Other Countries Fall to Dictators

While fascists took power in Italy and Germany, the nations formed in eastern Europe after World War I were also falling to dictators. In Hungary in 1919, after a brief Communist regime, military forces and wealthy landowners joined to make Admiral Miklós Horthy the first European postwar dictator. In Poland, Marshal Jozef Pilsudski (pihl·SOOT·skee) seized power in 1926. In Yugoslavia, Albania, Bulgaria, and Romania, kings turned to strong-man rule. They suspended constitutions and silenced foes. In 1935, only one democracy, Czechoslovakia, remained in eastern Europe.

Only in European nations with strong democratic traditions—Britain, France, and the Scandinavian countries—did democracy survive. With no democratic experience and severe economic problems, many Europeans saw dictatorship as the only way to prevent instability.

By the mid-1930s, the powerful nations of the world were split into two antagonistic camps—democratic and totalitarian. And to gain their ends, the fascist dictatorships had indicated a willingness to use military aggression. Although all of these dictatorships restricted civil rights, none asserted control with the brutality of the Russian Communists or the Nazis.

Reading Check
Analyze Causes
Why do you think that many countries in Europe were falling to dictators?

Lesson 3 Assessment

1. **Organize Information** Do you think Hitler and Mussolini were more alike or different? Create a table to show your response.

	Rise	Goals
Hitler		
Mussolini		

2. **Key Terms and People** For each key term or person in the lesson, write a sentence explaining its significance.

3. **Analyze Effects** What factors led to the rise of fascism in Italy?

4. **Summarize** How did Hitler maintain power, and what was his plan to eliminate the Jews?

5. **Make Inferences** Why did the leadership of Italy and Germany fall to dictators?

6. **Compare and Contrast** What techniques did Hitler and Mussolini use to appear powerful to their listeners?

Aggressors Invade Nations

The Big Idea

As Germany, Italy, and Japan conquered other countries, the rest of the world did nothing to stop them.

Why It Matters Now

Many nations today take a more active and collective role in world affairs, as in the United Nations.

Key Terms and People

Hirohito
appeasement
Axis Powers
Francisco Franco
isolationism
Third Reich
Munich Conference

Setting the Stage

By the mid-1930s, Germany and Italy seemed bent on military conquest. The major democracies—Britain, France, and the United States—were distracted by economic problems at home and longed to remain at peace. With the world moving toward war, many nations pinned their hopes for peace on the League of Nations. As fascism spread in Europe, however, a powerful nation in Asia moved toward a similar system. Following a period of reform and progress in the 1920s, Japan fell under military rule.

Japan Seeks an Empire

During the 1920s, the Japanese government became more democratic. In 1922, Japan signed an international treaty agreeing to respect China's borders. In 1928, it signed the Kellogg-Briand Pact renouncing war. Japan's parliamentary system had several weaknesses, however. Its constitution put strict limits on the powers of the prime minister and the cabinet. Most importantly, civilian leaders had little control over the armed forces. Military leaders reported only to the emperor.

Militarists Take Control of Japan As long as Japan remained prosperous, the civilian government kept power. But when the Great Depression struck in 1929, many Japanese blamed the government. Military leaders gained support and soon won control of the country. Unlike the Fascists in Europe, the militarists in Japan did not try to establish a new system of government. They wanted to restore traditional control of the government to the military. Instead of a forceful leader like Mussolini or Hitler, the militarists made the emperor the symbol of state power, but had total control over all aspects of life in the country, including the government, economy, and transportation.

Keeping Emperor **Hirohito** as head of state won popular support for the army leaders who ruled in his name. Like Hitler and Mussolini, Japan's militarists were extreme nationalists. They wanted to solve the country's economic problems, which stemmed from the depression that was being felt around the world. Japan's population was growing, and more resources and land were needed. The Japanese militarists chose imperialism, or foreign expansion, as the solution to their problem. They planned a Pacific empire that included a conquered China. The empire would provide Japan with raw materials and markets for its goods. It would also give Japan room for its rising population. Nationalism, combined with militarism, drove the Japanese to turn their eyes westward to China, their traditional political and economic rival.

Japan Invades Manchuria Japanese businesses had invested heavily in China's northeast province, Manchuria. It was an area rich in iron and coal. In 1931, the Japanese army seized Manchuria, despite objections from the Japanese parliament. The army then set up a puppet government. Japanese engineers and technicians began arriving in large numbers to build mines and factories.

The Japanese attack on Manchuria was the first direct challenge to the League of Nations. In the early 1930s, the League's members included all major democracies except the United States. The League also included the three countries that posed the greatest threat to peace—Germany, Japan, and Italy. When Japan seized Manchuria, many League members vigorously protested. Japan ignored the protests and withdrew from the League in 1933.

Japan Invades China Four years later, a border incident touched off a full-scale war between Japan and China. Japanese forces swept into northern China. Despite having a million soldiers, China's army led by Jiang Jieshi was no match for the better equipped and trained Japanese.

Beijing and other northern cities as well as the capital, Nanjing, fell to the Japanese in 1937. Japanese troops killed tens of thousands of captured soldiers and civilians in what became known by the Chinese as the "Rape of Nanjing." Forced to retreat westward, Jiang Jieshi set up a new capital at Chongqing. At the same time, Chinese guerrillas led by China's Communist leader, Mao Zedong, continued to fight the Japanese in the conquered area.

Reading Check
Make Inferences
What was the major weakness of the League of Nations?

A Chinese city burns after a devastating Japanese attack.

European Aggressors on the March

The League's failure to stop the Japanese encouraged European Fascists to plan aggression of their own. The Italian leader Mussolini dreamed of building a colonial empire in Africa like those of Britain and France.

Mussolini Attacks Ethiopia Mussolini set out to make Italy a strong military power and to carry out an imperialist policy. Ethiopia was one of Africa's three independent nations. The Ethiopians had successfully resisted an Italian attempt at conquest during the 1890s. To avenge that defeat, Mussolini ordered a massive invasion of Ethiopia in October 1935. The spears and swords of the Ethiopians were no match for Italian airplanes, tanks, guns, and poison gas.

The Ethiopian emperor, Haile Selassie, urgently appealed to the League for help. Although the League condemned the attack, its members did nothing. Britain continued to let Italian troops and supplies pass through the British-controlled Suez Canal on their way to Ethiopia. By giving in to Mussolini in Africa, Britain and France hoped to keep peace in Europe.

Aggression in Europe, Asia, and Africa, 1931–1939

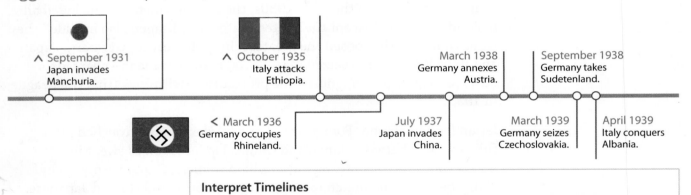

September 1931 Japan invades Manchuria.

October 1935 Italy attacks Ethiopia.

March 1938 Germany annexes Austria.

September 1938 Germany takes Sudetenland.

March 1936 Germany occupies Rhineland.

July 1937 Japan invades China.

March 1939 Germany seizes Czechoslovakia.

April 1939 Italy conquers Albania.

> **Interpret Timelines**
> How did actions taken by aggressor nations in the early 1930s affect later events?

Hitler Defies Versailles Treaty Hitler had long pledged to undo the Versailles Treaty. Among its provisions, the treaty limited the size of Germany's army. In March 1935, the Führer announced that Germany would not obey these restrictions. The League issued only a mild condemnation.

The League's failure to stop Germany from rearming convinced Hitler to take even greater risks. The treaty had forbidden German troops to enter a 30-mile-wide zone on either side of the Rhine River. Known as the Rhineland, the zone formed a buffer between Germany and France. It was also an important industrial area. On March 7, 1936, German troops moved into the Rhineland. Stunned, the French were unwilling to risk war. The British urged **appeasement**, giving in to an aggressor to keep peace.

Hitler later admitted that he would have backed down if the French and British had challenged him. The German reoccupation of the Rhineland marked a turning point in the march toward war. First, it strengthened Hitler's power and prestige within Germany. Second, the balance of power changed in Germany's favor. France and Belgium were now open to attack from German troops. Finally, the weak response by France and Britain encouraged Hitler to speed up his expansion.

Comparing Ideologies

Ideology	Description	Practices and Examples
socialism	an economic system in which the factors of production are owned by the public and operate for the welfare of all	Karl Marx's socialist ideas became popular in Russia in the late 1800s; they led to the revolutions in Russia, which became the Soviet Union in 1917. Vladimir Lenin led the communist government.
communism	an economic system in which all means of production—land, mines, factories, railroads, and businesses—are owned by the people, private property does not exist, and all goods and services are shared equally	Stalin became the totalitarian dictator of the Soviet Union in 1924. He took a different approach to communism and made the Soviet Union a totalitarian state. Stalin controlled every aspect of Soviet life.
fascism	a political movement that promotes an extreme form of nationalism, a denial of individual rights, and a dictatorial one-party rule	Italy: Benito Mussolini came to power and ruled as a dictator. He ran Italy as a police state. Spain: When Francisco Franco came to power, a civil war erupted between Nationalists who supported Franco and Republicans. The Nationalists won and Franco ruled as dictator.
liberalism	the belief in individual freedom and the protection of political and civil liberties	Liberalism developed during the Industrial Revolution in the 1800s. Proponents of liberalism believed that the government should take away restrictions that blocked or inhibited individual freedoms.
nationalism	the belief that people should be loyal mainly to their nation—that is, to the people with whom they share a culture and history—rather than to a king or empire	The unifications of Germany and of Italy were achieved and driven by nationalism. Hitler and Mussolini used extreme forms of nationalism to gain support.
imperialism	a policy in which a strong nation seeks to dominate other countries politically, economically, or socially	In the late 1800s, industrialization caused European nations to compete for resources in Africa and Asia, where they seized countries and territories.

Interpret Charts
Compare and Contrast Which ideologies did most of the aggressors in Europe adhere to in the 1930s?

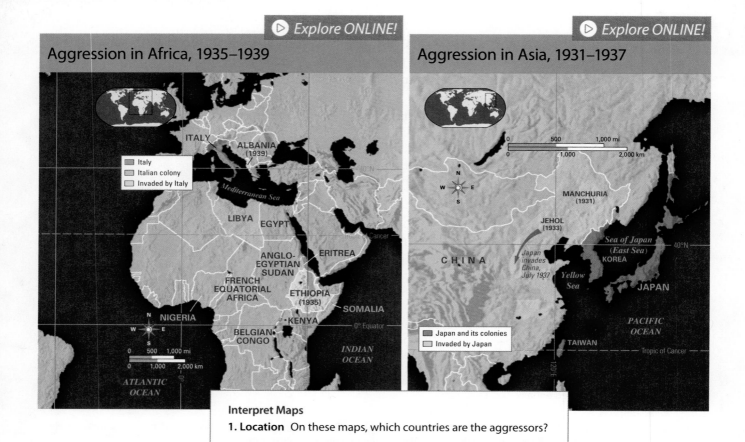

Aggression in Africa, 1935–1939

Explore ONLINE!

Legend:
- Italy
- Italian colony
- Invaded by Italy

ITALY, ALBANIA (1939), Mediterranean Sea, LIBYA, EGYPT, ANGLO-EGYPTIAN SUDAN, FRENCH EQUATORIAL AFRICA, ERITREA, ETHIOPIA (1935), SOMALIA, NIGERIA, KENYA, BELGIAN CONGO, INDIAN OCEAN, ATLANTIC OCEAN

Aggression in Asia, 1931–1937

Explore ONLINE!

Legend:
- Japan and its colonies
- Invaded by Japan

MANCHURIA (1931), JEHOL (1933), CHINA, Japan invades China, July 1937, Sea of Japan (East Sea), KOREA, Yellow Sea, JAPAN, PACIFIC OCEAN, TAIWAN, Tropic of Cancer

Interpret Maps

1. **Location** On these maps, which countries are the aggressors?

2. **Movement** On what two continents did the aggression occur?

Hitler's growing strength convinced Mussolini that he should seek an alliance with Germany. In October 1936, the two dictators reached an agreement that became known as the Rome-Berlin Axis. A month later, Germany also made an agreement with Japan. Germany, Italy, and Japan came to be called the **Axis Powers**.

Civil War Erupts in Spain Hitler and Mussolini again tested the will of the democracies of Europe in the Spanish Civil War. Spain had been a monarchy until 1931, when a republic was declared. The government, run by liberals and socialists, held office amid many crises. In July 1936, army leaders, favoring a fascist-style government, joined General **Francisco Franco** in a revolt. Thus began a civil war that dragged on for three years.

Hitler and Mussolini sent troops, tanks, and airplanes to help Franco's forces, which were called the Nationalists. The armed forces of the Republicans, as supporters of Spain's elected government were known, received little help from abroad. The Western democracies remained neutral. Only the Soviet Union sent equipment and advisers. An international brigade of volunteers fought on the Republican side. Early in 1939, Republican resistance collapsed. Franco became Spain's fascist dictator. Like Hitler and Mussolini, Franco also established a totalitarian regime.

Reading Check
Summarize
How did totalitarian governments in Europe gain power and influence?

Guernica

On April 26, 1937, Franco's German allies bombed the ancient Basque city of Guernica in Spain. The photograph (right) shows the city reduced to rubble by the bombing. Spanish artist Pablo Picasso captured the human horror of the event with his painting *Guernica* (below).

Using the geometric forms of Cubism, Picasso showed societal changes, including a city and people that have been torn to pieces. Using unnatural angles, overlapping images of people, severed limbs, and distorted animals in his art, Picasso reflected the suffering and chaos caused by the attack. At left, a mother cries over her dead child. In the center, a horse screams and a soldier lies dead. At right, a woman falls from a burning house.

Critical Thinking
1. **Analyze Motives** What were Picasso's probable motives for painting *Guernica*?
2. **Hypothesize** What feelings do you think *Guernica* stirred in the public in the late 1930s?

Democratic Nations Try to Preserve Peace

Instead of taking a stand against Fascist aggression in the 1930s, Britain and France repeatedly made concessions, hoping to keep peace. Both nations were dealing with serious economic problems as a result of the Great Depression. In addition, the horrors of and lessons learned from World War I had created a deep desire to avoid war.

United States Follows an Isolationist Policy Many Americans supported **isolationism**, the belief that political ties to other countries should be avoided. Isolationists argued that entry into World War I had been a costly error. Beginning in 1935, Congress passed three Neutrality Acts. These laws banned loans and the sale of arms to nations at war.

The German Reich Expands On November 5, 1937, Hitler announced to his advisers his plans to absorb Austria and Czechoslovakia into the **Third Reich** (ryk), or German Empire. The Treaty of Versailles prohibited *Anschluss* (AHN•SHLUS), or a union between Austria and Germany. However, Hitler knew that many ethnic Germans lived in Austria. Many Austrians supported unity with Germany. In March 1938, Hitler sent his army into Austria and annexed it. France and Britain ignored their pledge to protect Austrian independence.

Hitler next turned to Czechoslovakia. About three million German-speaking people lived in the western border regions of Czechoslovakia called the Sudetenland. Hitler wanted to expand Germany's borders where a large majority of the population was ethnically German. This heavily fortified area formed the Czechs' main defense against Germany. The Anschluss raised pro-Nazi feelings among Sudeten Germans. In September 1938, Hitler demanded that the Sudetenland be given to Germany. The Czechs refused and asked France for help.

Britain and France Again Choose Appeasement France and Britain were preparing for war when Mussolini proposed a meeting of Germany, France, Britain, and Italy in Munich, Germany. The **Munich Conference** was held on September 29, 1938. The Czechs were not invited. British prime minister Neville Chamberlain believed that he could preserve peace by giving in to Hitler's demand. Britain and France agreed that Hitler could take the Sudetenland. In exchange, Hitler pledged to respect Czechoslovakia's new borders. When Chamberlain returned to London, he told cheering crowds, "I believe it is peace for our time." Chamberlain had his critics.

Less than six months after the Munich meeting, Hitler took Czechoslovakia. Soon after, Mussolini seized Albania. Then Hitler demanded that Poland return the former German port of Danzig. The Poles refused and turned to Britain and France for aid. But appeasement had convinced Hitler that neither nation would risk war.

Peace with Honor

In this photograph, Chamberlain waves the statement he read following the Munich Conference. Winston Churchill, a member of the British Parliament, strongly disagreed with Chamberlain. He opposed the appeasement policy and sternly warned of its consequences.

Analyze Historical Sources
Why do you think Chamberlain waved the statement he read at the Munich Conference?

Reading Check
Analyze Issues
Why did Churchill believe that Chamberlain's policy of appeasement was a defeat for the British?

Nazis and Soviets Sign Nonaggression Pact Britain and France asked the Soviet Union to join them in stopping Hitler's aggression. As Stalin talked with Britain and France, he also bargained with Hitler. The two dictators reached an agreement. Once bitter enemies and political and economic rivals, fascist Germany and communist Russia now publicly pledged never to attack each other. On August 23, 1939, their leaders signed a nonaggression pact. As the Axis Powers moved unchecked at the end of the decade, war appeared inevitable.

Lesson 4 Assessment

1. **Organize Information** Create a time line to show the key events described in this lesson. Explain which event was the most significant, and why.

2. **Key Terms and People** For each key term or person in the lesson, write a sentence explaining its significance.

3. **Compare** How did the government of the militarists in Japan compare with those of Italy and Germany?

4. **Analyze Effects** How did the Allied countries respond to the aggressor actions of Italy and Germany?

5. **Synthesize** What similar goals did Hitler, Mussolini, and Hirohito share?

6. **Make Inferences** Do you think the fascist nations of the Axis Powers could have been stopped? Explain.

Module 27 Assessment

Key Terms and People

For each term or name below, briefly explain its connection to world history from 1919 to 1939.

1. Albert Einstein
2. Sigmund Freud
3. Weimar Republic
4. New Deal
5. fascism
6. Benito Mussolini
7. Adolf Hitler
8. appeasement
9. Francisco Franco
10. Munich Conference

Main Ideas

Use your notes and the information in the module to answer the following questions.

Postwar Uncertainty

1. What effect did Einstein's theory of relativity and Freud's theory of the unconscious have on the public?
2. What advances were made in transportation and communication in the 1920s and 1930s?

A Worldwide Depression

3. Why was the Weimar Republic considered weak?
4. What caused the stock market crash of 1929?

Fascism Rises in Europe

5. For what political and economic reasons did the Italians turn to Mussolini?
6. What beliefs and goals did Hitler express in *Mein Kampf*?

Aggressors Invade Nations

7. How did Japan plan to solve its economic problems?
8. Why was Germany's reoccupation of the Rhineland a significant turning point toward war?

Critical Thinking

1. **Analyze Causes** What events led to the Great Depression?

2. **Make Inferences** What were the advantages and disadvantages of being under fascist rule?

3. **Draw Conclusions** What weaknesses made the League of Nations an ineffective force for peace in the 1920s and 1930s?

4. **Synthesize** How did the scientific and technological revolutions of the 1920s help set the stage for transportation in the United States today?

5. **Hypothesize** What might have been the outcome if Great Britain, France, and other European nations had not chosen to appease German, Italian, and Japanese aggression?

6. **Compare and Contrast** How were the German, Italian, and Japanese drives to expand their empires in the 1930s, including atrocities in China, the Italian invasion of Ethiopia, German militarism, and the Stalin-Hitler Pact of 1939 similar and different?

7. **Compare and Contrast** How was Japanese imperialist policy in Asia similar to and different from British imperialist policy in South Africa and India and French imperialist policy in Indochina?

8. **Compare and Contrast** What were the short-term and long-term effects of World War I?

9. **Analyze Causes** What were the long-term causes of World War II? Were any of them also long-term effects of World War I? Explain.

Engage with History

In the Comparing Ideologies table, you learned about the main ideas and practices of fascism, communism, socialism, liberalism, nationalism, and imperialism. Now that you have read the module, you have learned about how these ideologies were adopted by different people, groups, and countries. Consider the following questions:

- How are the ideologies and their practices similar?
- How are the ideologies and their practices different?
- How did economic instability lead to the rise of some of these ideologies?

Discuss these questions in the form of a debate. Consult additional print and electronic sources if needed. Use audiovisual equipment to record the debate.

Focus on Writing

Write an advertisement that might have appeared in a 1920s newspaper, magazine, radio ad, or motion picture for one of the technological innovations discussed in Lesson 1. Consider your audience when creating your advertisement. Exchange advertisements with a partner. Evaluate the effectiveness of your partner's ad.

Multimedia Activity

Use the Internet and other sources of media to create a Web page on the influence of World War I on the arts. Consult both primary and secondary sources in your research, and be aware of facts versus opinions in your analysis. Include in your Web page how the war influenced literature, art, and intellectual life, as well as content about the following topics:

- Pablo Picasso
- the Lost Generation
- the rise of jazz music

World War II

Essential Question
Why did the Allies win World War II?

About the Illustration: A German bombing raid on London during the Battle of Britain.

In this module you will learn that, during World War II, the Allied forces defeated the Axis powers, the Jewish people suffered through the Holocaust, and Europe and Japan were left devastated.

What You Will Learn ...

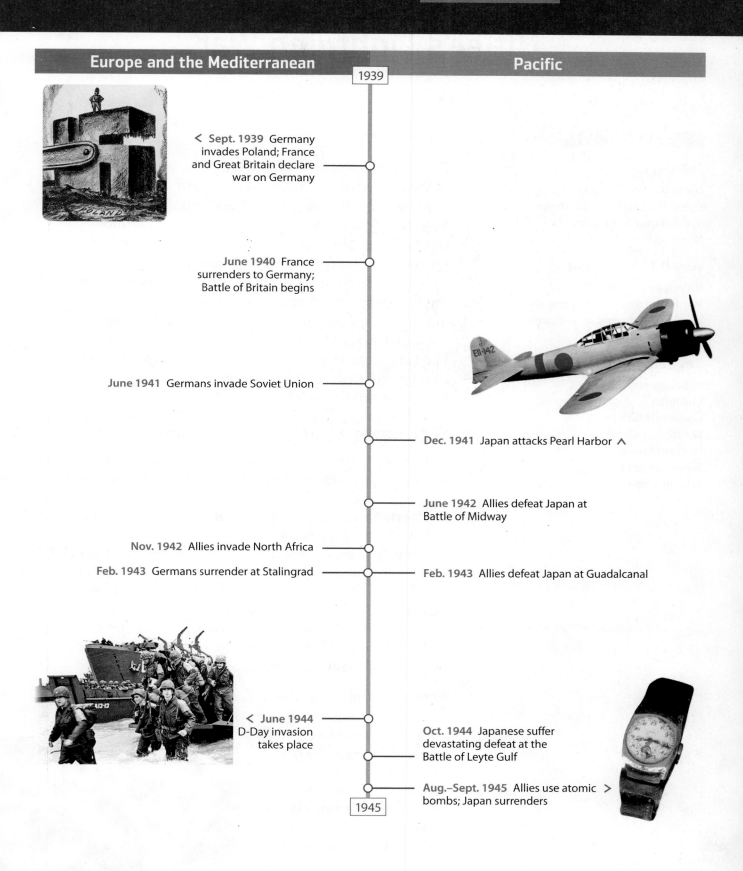

Europe and the Mediterranean	1939	Pacific

< Sept. 1939 Germany invades Poland; France and Great Britain declare war on Germany

June 1940 France surrenders to Germany; Battle of Britain begins

June 1941 Germans invade Soviet Union

Dec. 1941 Japan attacks Pearl Harbor ∧

June 1942 Allies defeat Japan at Battle of Midway

Nov. 1942 Allies invade North Africa

Feb. 1943 Germans surrender at Stalingrad

Feb. 1943 Allies defeat Japan at Guadalcanal

< June 1944 D-Day invasion takes place

Oct. 1944 Japanese suffer devastating defeat at the Battle of Leyte Gulf

Aug.–Sept. 1945 Allies use atomic > bombs; Japan surrenders

1945

Hitler's Lightning War

The Big Idea

Using the sudden mass attack called the blitzkrieg, Germany overran much of Europe and North Africa.

Why It Matters Now

Hitler's actions set off World War II. The results of the war still affect the politics and economics of today's world.

Key Terms and People

nonaggression pact
blitzkrieg
Charles de Gaulle
Winston Churchill
Battle of Britain
Erwin Rommel
Atlantic Charter

Setting the Stage

During the 1930s, Hitler played on the hopes and fears of the Western democracies, and acted on his promise to restore Germany to greatness and expand its territory. Each time the Nazi dictator grabbed new territory, he would declare an end to his demands. Peace seemed guaranteed—until Hitler moved again. Germany's expansionism and Britain and France's policy of appeasement were on a crash course toward war. After his moves into the Rhineland, Austria, and Czechoslovakia, Hitler turned his eyes to Poland. After World War I, the Allies had cut out the Polish Corridor from German territory to give Poland access to the sea. In 1939, Hitler demanded that the Polish Corridor be returned to Germany.

Germany Sparks a New War in Europe

In August of 1939, Soviet dictator Joseph Stalin signed a ten-year **nonaggression pact** with Hitler. After being excluded from the Munich Conference, Stalin was not eager to join with the West. Also, Hitler had promised him territory. In a secret part of the pact, Germany and the Soviet Union agreed to divide Poland between them. They also agreed that the USSR could take over Finland and the Baltic countries of Lithuania, Latvia, and Estonia. It was an unlikely alliance between the fascist and communist leaders of two traditionally enemy countries, and it shocked Britain and France, who had been discussing an alliance with Stalin. His pact with Hitler indicated that war with Germany was inevitable.

Germany's Lightning Attack

After the nonaggression pact with the Soviets was revealed, Hitler quickly moved ahead with plans to conquer Poland. His surprise attack took place at dawn on September 1, 1939. German tanks and troop

German soldiers invading Poland, September 1939

trucks rumbled across the Polish border. At the same time, German aircraft and artillery began a merciless bombing of Poland's capital, Warsaw.

France and Great Britain declared war on Germany on September 3. But Poland fell some time before those nations could make any military response. After his victory, Hitler annexed the western half of Poland. That region had a large German population.

The German invasion of Poland was the first test of Germany's newest military strategy—the **blitzkrieg** (BLIHTS·kreeg), or "lightning war." The massive rearmament and conscription programs that Hitler began in the mid-1930s had produced thousands of state-of-the-art fighter and bomber planes, tanks, and a greatly expanded infantry force. The blitzkrieg involved using air strikes, fast tanks, and artillery, followed by soldiers sped into battle on trucks, to take enemy defenders by surprise and quickly overwhelm them. It was a mobile assault quite advanced from the limited air power and slower tanks available in World War I. In the case of Poland, the strategy worked.

The Soviets Make Their Move On September 17, Stalin sent Soviet troops to occupy the eastern half of Poland. Stalin then moved to annex countries to the north of Poland. Lithuania, Latvia, and Estonia fell without a struggle, but Finland resisted. In November, Stalin sent nearly one million Soviet troops into Finland. The Soviets expected to win a quick victory, so they were not prepared for winter fighting. This was a crucial mistake.

The Finns were outnumbered and outgunned, but they fiercely defended their country. In the freezing winter weather, soldiers on skis swiftly attacked Soviet positions. In contrast, the Soviets struggled to make progress through the deep snow. The Soviets suffered heavy losses, but they finally won through sheer force of numbers. By March 1940, Stalin had forced the Finns to accept his surrender terms.

The Phony War After they declared war on Germany, the French and British had mobilized their armies. They stationed their troops along the Maginot (MAZH·uh·noh) Line, a system of fortifications along France's border with Germany. There they waited for the Germans to attack—but nothing happened. With little to do, the bored Allied soldiers stared eastward toward the enemy. Equally bored, German soldiers stared back from their Siegfried Line a few miles away. Germans jokingly called it the *sitzkrieg*, or "sitting war." Some newspapers referred to it simply as "the phony war."

Suddenly, on April 9, 1940, the calm ended. Hitler launched a surprise invasion of Denmark and Norway. In just four hours after the attack, Denmark fell. Two months later, Norway surrendered as well. The Germans then began to build bases along the Norwegian and Danish coasts from which they could launch strikes on Great Britain.

Reading Check
Analyze Motives
What were Stalin's goals in Europe at the beginning of World War II?

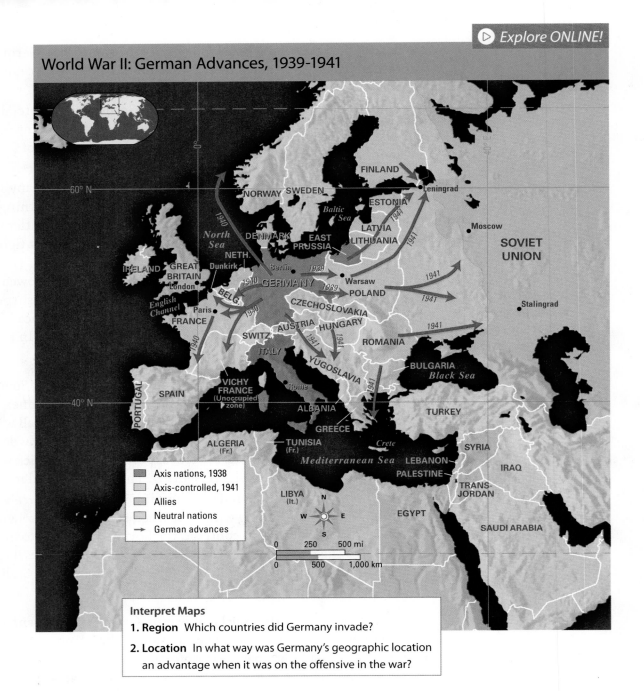

World War II: German Advances, 1939-1941

Axis nations, 1938
Axis-controlled, 1941
Allies
Neutral nations
→ German advances

0   250   500 mi
0   500   1,000 km

Interpret Maps

1. **Region** Which countries did Germany invade?

2. **Location** In what way was Germany's geographic location an advantage when it was on the offensive in the war?

The Fall of France

In May of 1940, Hitler began a dramatic sweep through the Netherlands, Belgium, and Luxembourg. This was part of a strategy to strike at France. Keeping the Allies' attention on those countries, Hitler then sent an even larger force of tanks and troops south to slice through the Ardennes (ahr•DEHN). This was a heavily wooded area in northern France, Luxembourg, and Belgium. The Allies considered the forest, hills, and poor roads of the Ardennes a hindrance to the heavily armored Nazi offensive, and so it was lightly defended. German forces moved steadily through the forest, and fought their way around the Maginot Line. From there, they moved across France and reached the country's northern coast in ten days.

Rescue at Dunkirk After reaching the French coast, the German forces swung north again and joined with German troops in Belgium. By the end of May 1940, the Germans had trapped the Allied forces around the northern French city of Lille (leel). Outnumbered, outgunned, and pounded from the air, the Allies retreated to the beaches of Dunkirk, a French port city near the Belgian border. They were trapped with their backs to the sea.

In one of the most heroic acts of the war, Great Britain set out to rescue the army. It sent a fleet of about 850 ships across the English Channel to Dunkirk. Along with Royal Navy ships, civilian craft—yachts, lifeboats, motorboats, paddle steamers, and fishing boats—joined the rescue effort. From May 26 to June 4, this amateur armada, under heavy fire from German bombers, sailed back and forth from Britain to Dunkirk. The boats carried some 338,000 battle-weary soldiers to safety.

France Falls Following Dunkirk, resistance in France began to crumble. By June 14, the Germans had taken Paris. Accepting the inevitable, French leaders surrendered on June 22, 1940. The Germans took control of the northern part of the country. They left the southern part to a puppet government headed by Marshal Philippe Pétain (pay•TAN), a French hero from World War I. The headquarters of this government was in the city of Vichy (VEESH•ee).

After France fell, **Charles de Gaulle** (duh-GOHL), a French general, set up a government-in-exile in London. He committed all his energy to reconquering France. In a radio broadcast from England, de Gaulle called on the people of France to join him in resisting the Germans:

> *"It is the bounden [obligatory] duty of all Frenchmen who still bear arms to continue the struggle. For them to lay down their arms, to evacuate any position of military importance, or agree to hand over any part of French territory, however small, to enemy control would be a crime against our country."*
>
> —General Charles De Gaulle, quoted in *Charles de Gaulle: A Biography*

De Gaulle went on to organize the Free French military forces that battled the Nazis until France was liberated in 1944.

The Battle of Britain

With the fall of France, Great Britain stood alone against the Nazis. **Winston Churchill**, the new British prime minister, had already declared that his nation would never give in. In a rousing speech, he proclaimed, "We shall fight on the beaches, we shall fight on the landing grounds, we shall fight in the fields and in the streets . . . we shall never surrender." Hitler now turned his mind to an invasion of Great Britain. His plan was first to knock out the Royal Air Force (RAF) and then to land more than 250,000 soldiers on England's shores. In the summer of 1940, the Luftwaffe (Looft•VAHF•uh), Germany's air force, began bombing Great Britain. At first, the Germans targeted British airfields and aircraft

Reading Check
Analyze Effects
How was Hitler's attack through the Ardennes forest a bold strike and an early turning point in the war?

Vocabulary
Luftwaffe the German word for "air weapon"

Winston Churchill
(1874–1965)

Possibly the most powerful weapon the British had as they stood alone against Hitler's Germany was the nation's prime minister—Winston Churchill. "Big Winnie," Londoners boasted, "was the lad for us."

Although Churchill had a speech defect as a youngster, he grew to become one of the greatest orators of all time. He used all his gifts as a speaker to rally the people behind the effort to crush Germany. In one famous speech he promised that Britain would

". . . wage war, by sea, land and air, with all our might and with all the strength that God can give us . . . against a monstrous tyranny."

factories. Then, on September 7, 1940, they began focusing on the cities, especially London, to break British morale. Despite the destruction and loss of life, the British did not waver. The RAF, although badly outnumbered, began to hit back hard. Two technological devices helped turn the tide in the RAF's favor. One was an electronic tracking system known as radar. Developed in the late 1930s, radar could tell the number, speed, and direction of incoming warplanes. The other device was a German code-making machine named Enigma. A complete Enigma machine had been smuggled into Great Britain in the late 1930s. Enigma enabled the British to decode German secret messages. With information gathered by these devices, RAF fliers could quickly launch attacks on the enemy. To avoid the RAF's attacks, the Germans gave up daylight raids in October 1940 in favor of night bombing. At sunset, the wail of sirens filled the air as Londoners flocked to the subways, which served as air-raid shelters. Some rode out the bombing raids at home in smaller air-raid shelters or basements. This **Battle of Britain** continued until May 10, 1941. Stunned by British resistance, Hitler decided to call off his attacks. Instead, he focused on the Mediterranean and Eastern Europe. The Battle of Britain taught the Allies a crucial lesson. Hitler's attacks could be blocked.

Reading Check
Analyze Effects
Why was the outcome of the Battle of Britain important for the Allies?

A London bus is submerged in a bomb crater after a German air raid.

The Mediterranean and the Eastern Front

The stubborn resistance of the British in the Battle of Britain caused a shift in Hitler's strategy in Europe. He decided to deal with Great Britain later. He then turned his attention east to the Mediterranean area and the Balkans—and to the ultimate prize, the Soviet Union.

Axis Forces Attack North Africa Germany's first objective in the Mediterranean region was North Africa, mainly because of Hitler's partner, Mussolini. Despite its alliance with Germany, Italy had remained neutral at the beginning of the war. With Hitler's conquest of France, however, Mussolini knew he had to take action. After declaring war on France and Great Britain, Mussolini moved into France.

Mussolini took his next step in North Africa in September 1940. While the Battle of Britain was raging, he ordered his army to attack British-controlled Egypt. Egypt's Suez Canal was key to reaching the oil fields of the Middle East from the Mediterranean, so it was a crucial colonial interest for both the Allies and Axis powers. Within a week, Italian troops had pushed 60 miles inside Egypt, forcing British units back. Then both sides dug in and waited.

Britain Strikes Back Finally, in December, the British forces—including troops from its colony, India, and Commonwealth nations Canada, Australia, New Zealand, and South Africa—struck back. The result was a disaster for the Italians. By February 1941, the British had swept 500 miles across North Africa and had taken 130,000 Italian prisoners. Hitler had to step in to save his Axis partner. To reinforce the Italians, Hitler sent a crack German tank force, the Afrika Korps, under the command of General **Erwin Rommel**. In late March 1941, Rommel's Afrika Korps attacked. Caught by surprise, British forces retreated east to Tobruk, Libya.

After fierce fighting for Tobruk, the British began to drive Rommel back. By mid-January 1942, Rommel had retreated to where he had started. By June 1942, the tide of battle turned again. Rommel regrouped, pushed the British back across the desert, and seized Tobruk—a shattering loss for the Allies. Rommel's successes in North Africa earned him the nickname "Desert Fox."

The War in the Balkans While Rommel campaigned in North Africa, other German generals were active in the Balkans. Hitler had begun planning to attack his ally, the Soviet Union, as early as the summer of 1940. The Balkan countries of southeastern Europe were the key to Hitler's plan. Hitler wanted to build bases there for the attack on the Soviet Union. He also wanted to make sure that the British did not interfere.

To prepare for his invasion, Hitler moved to expand his influence in the Balkans. By early 1941, through the threat of force, he had persuaded Bulgaria, Romania, and Hungary to join the Axis powers. Yugoslavia and Greece, which had pro-British governments, resisted. In early April 1941, Hitler invaded both countries. Yugoslavia fell in 11 days. Greece surrendered in 17. In Athens, the Nazis celebrated their victory by raising swastikas on the Acropolis.

Vocabulary
Middle East
region that includes the countries of Southwest Asia and northeast Africa

Russian soldiers prepare to attack German lines outside Leningrad.

Hitler Invades the Soviet Union With the Balkans firmly in control, Hitler could move ahead with Operation Barbarossa, his plan to invade the Soviet Union. Early in the morning of June 22, 1941, the roar of German tanks and aircraft announced the beginning of the invasion. The Soviet Union was not prepared for this attack. Although it had the largest army in the world, its troops were neither well equipped nor well trained.

The invasion rolled on week after week until the Germans had pushed 500 miles inside the Soviet Union. As the Soviet troops retreated, they burned and destroyed everything in the enemy's path. The Russians had used this scorched-earth strategy against Napoleon.

On September 8, German forces put Leningrad under siege. By early November, the city was completely cut off from the rest of the Soviet Union. To force a surrender, Hitler was ready to starve the city's more than 2.5 million inhabitants. German bombs destroyed warehouses where food was stored. Desperately hungry, people began eating cattle and horse feed, as well as cats and dogs and, finally, crows and rats. Nearly one million people died in Leningrad during the winter of 1941–1942. Yet the city refused to fall.

Impatient with the progress in Leningrad, Hitler looked to Moscow, the capital and heart of the Soviet Union. A Nazi drive on the capital began on October 2, 1941. By December, the Germans had advanced to the outskirts of Moscow. Soviet General Georgi Zhukov (ZHOO•kuhf) counterattacked. As temperatures fell, the Germans, in summer uniforms, retreated. Ignoring Napoleon's winter defeat 130 years before, Hitler sent his generals a stunning order: "No retreat!" German troops dug in about 125 miles west of Moscow. They held the line against the Soviets until March 1943. Hitler's advance on the Soviet Union gained nothing but cost the Germans 500,000 lives.

Reading Check
Make Inferences
What does the fact that German armies were not prepared for the Russian winter indicate about Hitler's expectations for the Soviet campaign?

The United States Aids Its Allies

Most Americans felt that the United States should not get involved in the war. Between 1935 and 1937, Congress passed a series of Neutrality Acts. The laws made it illegal to sell arms or lend money to nations at war. But President Roosevelt knew that if the Allies fell, the United States would be drawn into the war. In September 1939, he asked Congress to allow the Allies to buy American arms. The Allies would pay cash and then carry the goods on their own ships.

Under the Lend-Lease Act, passed in March 1941, the president could lend or lease arms and other supplies to any country vital to the United States. By the summer of 1941, the U.S. Navy was escorting British ships carrying U.S. arms. In response, Hitler ordered his submarines to sink any cargo ships they met.

Although the United States had not yet entered the war, Roosevelt and Churchill met secretly and issued a joint declaration called the **Atlantic Charter**, which outlined their purpose for the war. It stated that they sought no territorial gain in the war, and it upheld the principles of free trade among nations and the right of people to choose their own government.

On September 4, a German U-boat fired on a U.S. destroyer in the Atlantic. In response, Roosevelt ordered navy commanders to shoot German submarines on sight. The United States was now involved in an undeclared naval war with Hitler. To almost everyone's surprise, however, the attack that actually drew the United States into the war did not come from Germany. It came from Japan.

Reading Check
Find Main Ideas
Why did President Franklin Roosevelt want to offer help to the Allies?

Lesson 1 Assessment

1. **Organize Information** Which of the listed events might be considered a turning point for the Allies? Why?

Cause	Effect
First blitzkrieg	
Allies stranded at Dunkirk	
Lend-Lease Act	

2. **Key Terms and People** For each key term or person in the lesson, write a sentence explaining its significance.

3. **Compare and Contrast** Review the events that led directly to World War I. Then compare and contrast them with the events that led directly to World War II.

4. **Synthesize** What do you think is meant by the statement that Winston Churchill was possibly Britain's most powerful weapon against Hitler's Germany?

5. **Make Inferences** What factors do you think a country's leaders consider when deciding whether to surrender or fight?

6. **Compare** In what ways were the consequences of Hitler's decisions on the Eastern Front similar to those of Napoleon when he invaded Russia?

Japan's Pacific Campaign

The Big Idea

Japan attacked Pearl Harbor in Hawaii and brought the United States into World War II.

Why It Matters Now

World War II established the United States as a leading player in international affairs.

Key Terms and People

Isoroku Yamamoto
Pearl Harbor
Battle of Midway
Douglas MacArthur
Battle of Guadalcanal

Setting the Stage

Like Hitler, Japan's military leaders also had dreams of empire. Japan's expansion had begun in 1931. That year, Japanese troops took over Manchuria in northeastern China. Six years later, Japanese armies swept into the heartland of China. They expected quick victory. Chinese resistance, however, caused the war to drag on. This placed a strain on Japan's economy. To increase their resources, Japanese leaders looked toward the rich European colonies of Southeast Asia, signaling a confrontation with the West.

Surprise Attack on Pearl Harbor

By October 1940, Americans had cracked one of the codes that the Japanese used in sending secret messages. Therefore, they were well aware of Japanese plans for Southeast Asia. If Japan conquered European colonies there, it could also threaten the American-controlled Philippine Islands and Guam. To stop the Japanese advance, the U.S. government sent aid to strengthen Chinese resistance. And when the Japanese overran French Indochina—Vietnam, Cambodia, and Laos—in July 1941, Roosevelt cut off oil shipments to Japan.

Despite an oil shortage, the Japanese continued their conquests. They hoped to catch the European colonial powers and the United States by surprise. So they planned massive attacks on British and Dutch colonies in Southeast Asia and on American outposts in the Pacific—at the same time. Admiral **Isoroku Yamamoto** (ih•soh•ROO•koo-yah•muh•MOH•toh), Japan's greatest naval strategist, also called for an attack on the U.S. fleet in Hawaii. It was, he said, "a dagger pointed at [Japan's] throat" and must be destroyed.

The *U.S.S. West Virginia* is engulfed by flames after taking a direct hit during the Japanese attack on Pearl Harbor.

Day of Infamy Early in the morning of December 7, 1941, American sailors at **Pearl Harbor** in Hawaii awoke to the roar of explosives. A Japanese attack was under way. U.S. military leaders had known from a coded Japanese message that an attack might come. But they did not know when or where it would occur. Within two hours, the Japanese had sunk or damaged 19 ships, including 8 battleships, moored in Pearl Harbor. More than 2,300 Americans were killed—with over 1,100 wounded. News of the attack stunned the American people. The next day, President Roosevelt addressed Congress, which quickly accepted his request for a declaration of war on Japan and its allies.

"Yesterday, December 7th, 1941—a date which will live in infamy— the United States of America was suddenly and deliberately attacked by naval and air forces of the Empire of Japan. . . . As Commander in Chief of the Army and Navy, I have directed that all measures be taken for our defense. But always will we remember the character of the onslaught against us. . . . I believe that I interpret the will of the Congress and of the people when I assert that we will not only defend ourselves to the uttermost, but will make it very certain that this form of treachery shall never again endanger us."

—President Franklin Delano Roosevelt, *Address to Congress, Dec. 8, 1941*

Reading Check
Analyze Causes and Effects What were the causes and effects of Japan's attack on the United States?

Almost at the same time as the Pearl Harbor attack, the Japanese launched bombing raids on the British colony of Hong Kong and American-controlled Guam and Wake Island. (See the map World War II in Asia and the Pacific, 1941–1945.) They also landed an invasion force in Thailand. The Japanese drive for a Pacific empire was under way.

Japanese Victories

Lightly defended, Guam and Wake Island quickly fell to Japanese forces. The Japanese then turned their attention to the Philippines, controlled by the United States with several military bases there. In January 1942, they marched into the Philippine capital of Manila. American and Filipino forces took up a defensive position on the Bataan (buh•TAN) Peninsula on the northwestern edge of Manila Bay. At the same time, the Philippine government moved to the island of Corregidor just to the south of Bataan. After about three months of tough fighting, the Japanese took the Bataan Peninsula in April. Corregidor fell the following month.

The Japanese also continued their strikes against British possessions in Asia. After seizing Hong Kong, they invaded Malaya from the sea and overland from Thailand. By February 1942, the Japanese had reached Singapore, strategically located at the southern tip of the Malay Peninsula. After a fierce pounding, the colony surrendered. Within a month, the Japanese had conquered the resource-rich Dutch East Indies (now Indonesia), including the islands of Java, Sumatra, Borneo, and Celebes (SEHL•uh•beez). These British and Dutch colonies in Southeast Asia held much-needed oil, rubber, and other raw materials needed to defend Japan's expansion. The Japanese also moved westward, taking Burma. From there, they planned to launch a strike against India, the largest of Great Britain's colonies.

By the time Burma fell, Japan had taken control of more than 1 million square miles of Asian land. About 150 million people lived in this vast area. Before these conquests, the Japanese had tried to win the support of Asians with the anticolonialist idea of "East Asia for the Asiatics." After victory, however, the Japanese quickly made it clear that they had come as conquerors. They often treated the people of their new colonies with extreme cruelty.

However, the Japanese reserved the most brutal treatment for Allied prisoners of war. The Japanese considered it dishonorable to surrender, and they had contempt for the prisoners of war in their charge. On the Bataan Death March—a forced march of more than 50 miles up the peninsula—the Japanese subjected their captives to terrible cruelties. 500 Americans and approximately 2,500 Filipino prisoners died on the march. Thousands more later perished at the inhumane prison camp. Of the approximately 76,000 prisoners who started the Bataan Death March, only 54,000 survived.

Reading Check
Find Main Ideas How did the Japanese often treat the native people of East Asia and their prisoners of war in territory they conquered?

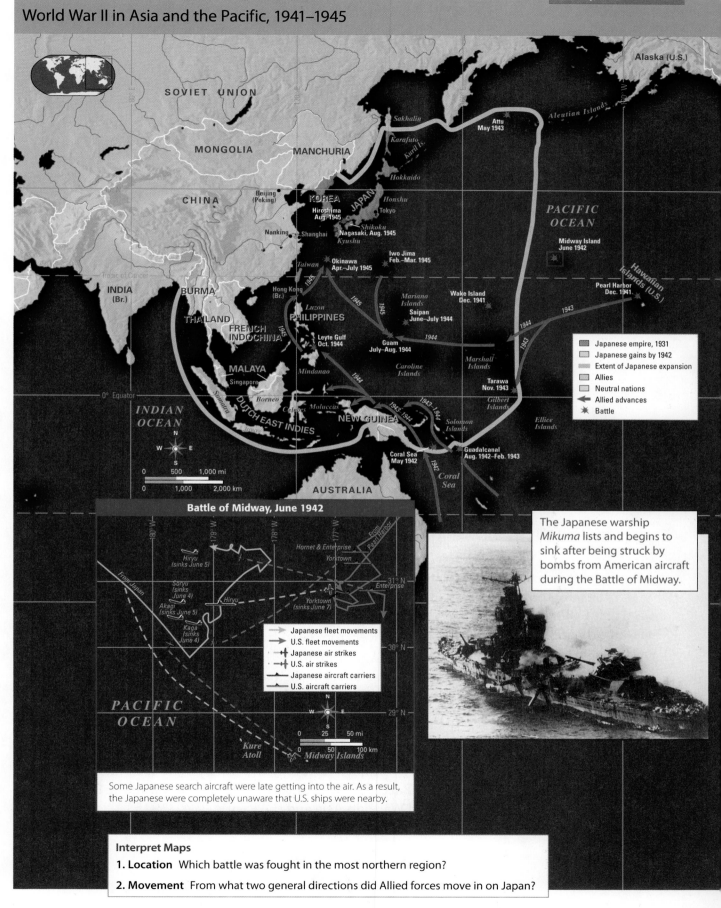

World War II in Asia and the Pacific, 1941–1945

▶ *Explore ONLINE!*

Alaska (U.S.)

SOVIET UNION

MONGOLIA   MANCHURIA

Sakhalin

Karafuto Is.

Attu
May 1943

Aleutian Islands

Kuril Is.

Hokkaido

CHINA

Beijing
(Peking)

KOREA   JAPAN   Honshu

Hiroshima
Aug. 1945   Tokyo

PACIFIC
OCEAN

Nanking   Shanghai   Shikoku

Nagasaki, Aug. 1945

Kyushu

Midway Island
June 1942

Taiwan

Okinawa
Apr.–July 1945

Iwo Jima
Feb.–Mar. 1945

INDIA
(Br.)

BURMA

Hong Kong
(Br.)

1945

Wake Island
Dec. 1941

Pearl Harbor
Dec. 1941

Hawaiian Islands (U.S.)

THAILAND

Luzon

PHILIPPINES

Mariana
Islands

1945   1945

Saipan
June–July 1944

FRENCH
INDOCHINA

1945

Leyte Gulf
Oct. 1944

Guam
July–Aug. 1944

1944

1944   1943

MALAYA

Singapore

Mindanao

Caroline
Islands

Marshall
Islands

1943

Sumatra

Borneo

Celebes   Moluccas

1944

Tarawa
Nov. 1943

0° Equator

DUTCH EAST INDIES

NEW GUINEA

1943 1944

1943–1944

Gilbert
Islands

INDIAN
OCEAN

N
W   E
S

0   500   1,000 mi

0   1,000   2,000 km

Solomon
Islands

Ellice
Islands

Coral Sea
May 1942

Guadalcanal
Aug. 1942–Feb. 1943

1942

Coral
Sea

AUSTRALIA

Legend:
- Japanese empire, 1931
- Japanese gains by 1942
- Extent of Japanese expansion
- Allies
- Neutral nations
- ← Allied advances
- ✳ Battle

Battle of Midway, June 1942

180° W   178° W   178° W   177° W

From Pearl Harbor

Hornet & Enterprise
Yorktown

Hiryu
(sinks June 5)

31° N
Enterprise

Soryu
(sinks
June 4)

Hiryu

From Japan

Akagi
(sinks June 5)

Yorktown
(sinks June 7)

Kaga
(sinks
June 4)

30° N

Legend:
- → Japanese fleet movements
- → U.S. fleet movements
- ⊬ Japanese air strikes
- ⊬ U.S. air strikes
- ⊢ Japanese aircraft carriers
- ⊢ U.S. aircraft carriers

PACIFIC
OCEAN

29° N

N
W   E
S

0   25   50 mi

0   50   100 km

Kure
Atoll

Midway Islands

Some Japanese search aircraft were late getting into the air. As a result, the Japanese were completely unaware that U.S. ships were nearby.

The Japanese warship *Mikuma* lists and begins to sink after being struck by bombs from American aircraft during the Battle of Midway.

Interpret Maps

1. Location Which battle was fought in the most northern region?

2. Movement From what two general directions did Allied forces move in on Japan?

The Allies Strike Back

After a string of victories, the Japanese seemed unbeatable. Nonetheless, the Allies—mainly Americans and Australians—were anxious to strike back in the Pacific. The United States in particular wanted revenge for Pearl Harbor. In April 1942, a squadron of 16 B-25 bombers under the command of Lieutenant Colonel James H. Doolittle bombed Tokyo and several other Japanese cities. The bombs did little damage. The raid, however, made an important psychological point to both Americans and Japanese: Japan was vulnerable to attack.

The Allies Turn the Tide Doolittle's raid on Japan raised American morale and shook the confidence of some in Japan. As one Japanese citizen noted, "We started to doubt that we were invincible." In addition, some Japanese worried that defending and controlling a vast empire had caused them to spread their resources too thin.

Slowly, the Allies began to turn the tide of war. Early in May 1942, an American fleet with Australian support intercepted a Japanese strike force headed for Port Moresby in New Guinea. This city housed a critical Allied air base. Control of the air base would put the Japanese in easy striking distance of Australia.

In the battle that followed—the Battle of the Coral Sea—both sides used a new kind of naval warfare. The opposing ships did not fire a single shot. In fact, they often could not see one another. Instead, airplanes taking off from huge aircraft carriers attacked the ships. The Allies suffered more losses in ships and troops than did the Japanese. However, the Battle of the Coral Sea was something of a victory, for the Allies had stopped Japan's southward advance.

The Battle of Midway Japan next targeted Midway Island, some 1,500 miles west of Hawaii, the location of a key American airfield. Thanks to Allied code breakers, Admiral Chester Nimitz, commander in chief of the U.S. Pacific Fleet, knew that a huge Japanese force was heading toward Midway. Admiral Yamamoto himself was in command of the Japanese fleet. He hoped that the attack on Midway would draw the whole of the U.S. Pacific Fleet from Pearl Harbor to defend the island.

On June 4, with American forces hidden beyond the horizon, Nimitz allowed the Japanese to begin their assault on the island. As the first Japanese planes got into the air, American planes swooped in to attack the Japanese fleet. Many Japanese planes were still on the decks of the aircraft carriers. The strategy was a success. American pilots destroyed 332 Japanese planes, all four aircraft carriers, and one support ship. Yamamoto ordered his crippled fleet to withdraw. By June 7, 1942, the battle was over. The **Battle of Midway** turned the tide of war in the Pacific. (See the map World War II in Asia and the Pacific, 1941–1945.)

Vocabulary
invincible
unable to be overcome by force

Reading Check
Analyze Motives
Why might the Americans send their entire Pacific Fleet to defend Midway Island?

An Allied Offensive

With morale high after their victory at Midway, the Allies took the offensive. The war in the Pacific involved vast distances. Japanese troops had dug in on hundreds of islands across the ocean. General **Douglas MacArthur**, the commander of the Allied land forces in the Pacific, developed a plan to handle this problem.

MacArthur believed that storming each island would be a long, costly effort. Instead, he wanted to "island-hop" past Japanese strongholds. His strategy was to capture weaker Japanese-controlled islands, then use these bases to seize islands closer to Japan. In the process, the Allies would cut off supply lines needed to keep the Japanese navy afloat.

MacArthur's first target soon presented itself. U.S. military leaders had learned that the Japanese were building a huge air base on the island of Guadalcanal in the Solomon Islands. The Allies had to strike fast before the base was completed and became another Japanese stronghold. At dawn on August 7, 1942, several thousand U.S. Marines, with Australian support, landed on Guadalcanal and the neighboring island of Tulagi.

U.S. Marines storm ashore at Guadalcanal.

BIOGRAPHY

General Douglas MacArthur
(1880–1964)

Douglas MacArthur's qualities as a leader and a fighting soldier emerged in France during World War I. Showing incredible dash and courage on the battlefield, he received several decorations for bravery. And he won promotion from the rank of major to brigadier general.

After serving in several positions in the United States, MacArthur received a posting to the Philippines in 1935. He remained there until shortly before the islands fell in 1941. But he left very reluctantly. In a message to the troops who remained behind, he vowed, "I shall return." As you will read later, MacArthur kept his promise.

The marines had little trouble seizing Guadalcanal's airfield. But the battle for control of the island turned into a savage struggle as both sides poured in fresh troops. In February 1943, after six months of fighting on land and at sea, the **Battle of Guadalcanal** finally ended. After losing more than 24,000 of a force of 36,000 soldiers, the Japanese abandoned what they came to call "the Island of Death."

To American war correspondent Ralph Martin and the U.S. soldiers who fought there, Guadalcanal was simply "hell":

> *"Hell was red furry spiders as big as your fist, . . . enormous rats and bats everywhere, and rivers with waiting crocodiles. Hell was the sour, foul smell of the squishy jungle, humidity that rotted a body within hours. . . . Hell was an enemy . . . so fanatic that it used its own dead as booby traps."*
>
> —Ralph G. Martin, *The GI War*

As Japan worked to establish a new order in Southeast Asia and the Pacific, the Nazis moved ahead with Hitler's design for a new order in Europe. This design included plans for dealing with those Hitler considered unfit for the Third Reich. You will learn about these plans in the next lesson.

Reading Check
Identify Problems
If the vast distances of the Pacific caused problems for the Allies, how might they have caused military problems for the Japanese also?

Lesson 2 Assessment

1. **Organize Information** Which event was most important in turning the tide of the war in the Pacific against the Japanese? Why?

Event	Effect

2. **Key Terms and People** For each key term or person in the lesson, write a sentence explaining its significance.

3. **Evaluate** Did Admiral Yamamoto make a wise decision in bombing Pearl Harbor? Why or why not?

4. **Analyze Motives** Why do you think the Japanese changed their approach from trying to win the support of the colonized peoples to acting as conquerors?

5. **Identify Problems** What problems did Japan face in building an empire in the Pacific?

The Holocaust

The Big Idea

During the Holocaust, Hitler's Nazis killed six million Jews and five million other "non-Aryans."

Why It Matters Now

The violence against Jews during the Holocaust led to the founding of Israel after World War II.

Key Terms and People

Aryan
Holocaust
Kristallnacht
ghetto
Final Solution
genocide

Setting the Stage

As part of their vision for Europe, the Nazis proposed a new racial order. They proclaimed that the Germanic peoples, or **Aryans**, were a "master race." (This was a misuse of the term *Aryan*. The term actually refers to the Indo-European peoples who began to migrate into the Indian subcontinent around 1500 BC.) The Nazis claimed that all non-Aryan peoples, particularly Jewish people, were inferior. This racist message would eventually lead to the **Holocaust**, the systematic mass slaughter of Jews. In addition, the Nazis murdered millions of other people they deemed inferior.

The Holocaust Begins

To gain support for his racist ideas, Hitler knowingly tapped into a hatred for Jews that had deep roots in European history. Anti-Semitism, a hostility toward or prejudice against Jews, had existed in Christian Europe since the Middle Ages. For generations, many Germans, along with other Europeans, had targeted Jews as the cause of their failures. Some Germans even blamed Jews for their country's defeat in World War I and for its economic problems after that war.

In time, Hitler made the targeting of Jews a government policy. The Nuremberg Laws, passed in 1935, deprived Jews of their rights to German citizenship and forbade marriages between Jews and non-Jews. Laws passed later also limited the kinds of work that Jews could do.

"Night of Broken Glass" Worse was yet to come. Early in November 1938, 17-year-old Herschel Grynszpan (GRIHN•shpahn), a Jewish youth from Germany, was visiting an uncle in Paris. While Grynszpan was there, he received a postcard. It said that after living in Germany for 27 years, his father had been deported to Poland. On November 7, wishing to avenge his father's deportation, Grynszpan shot a German diplomat living in Paris.

When Nazi leaders heard the news, they used this pretext to launch a violent attack on the Jewish community. On November 9, Nazi storm troopers attacked Jewish homes, businesses, and synagogues across Germany and Austria and murdered close to 100 Jews. Using the practice of ethnic cleansing, they rounded up 30,000 Jews and sent them to concentration camps, where many died. An American in Leipzig wrote, "Jewish shop windows by the hundreds were systematically . . . smashed. . . . The main streets of the city were a positive litter of shattered plate glass." The night of November 9 became known as **Kristallnacht** (krih•STAHL•nahkt), or "Night of Broken Glass." A 14-year-old boy described his memory of that awful night:

> *"All the things for which my parents had worked for eighteen long years were destroyed in less than ten minutes. Piles of valuable glasses, expensive furniture, linens—in short, everything was destroyed. . . . The Nazis left us, yelling, "Don't try to leave this house! We'll soon be back again and take you to a concentration camp to be shot."*
>
> —M. I. Libau, quoted in *Never to Forget: The Jews of the Holocaust*

Kristallnacht marked a major step-up in the Nazi policy of Jewish persecution. The future for Jews in Germany looked truly grim.

A Flood of Refugees After *Kristallnacht*, some Jews realized that violence against them was bound to increase. By the end of 1939, a number of German Jews had fled to other countries. Many, however, remained in Germany. Later, Hitler's forces conquered territories in which millions more Jews lived.

At first, Hitler favored emigration as a solution to what he called "the Jewish problem." Getting other countries to continue admitting Germany's Jews became an issue, however. After admitting tens of thousands of Jewish refugees, such countries as France, Britain, and the United States abruptly closed their doors to further immigration. Germany's foreign minister observed, "We all want to get rid of our Jews. The difficulty is that no country wishes to receive them."

Isolating the Jews When Hitler found that he could not get rid of Jews through emigration, he put another plan into effect. He ordered Jews in all countries under his control to be moved to designated cities. In those cities, the Nazis herded the Jews into dismal, overcrowded **ghettos**, or segregated Jewish areas. The Nazis then sealed off the ghettos with barbed wire and stone walls. They hoped that the Jews inside would starve to death or die from disease.

Even under these horrible conditions, the Jews hung on. Some, particularly the Jews in Warsaw, Poland, formed resistance organizations within the ghettos. They also struggled to keep their traditions. Ghetto theaters produced plays and concerts. Teachers taught lessons in secret schools. Scholars kept records so that one day people would find out the truth.

After 1941, all Jews in German-controlled areas had to wear a yellow Star of David patch.

Reading Check
Find Main Ideas
What steps did Hitler take to rid Germany of Jews?

The "Final Solution"

Hitler soon grew impatient and decided to take more direct action. His plan was called the **Final Solution**. It was actually a program of **genocide**, the systematic murder of an entire people.

Hitler believed that his plan of conquest depended on the purity of the Aryan race. He had adopted the view of late 19th-century European anti-Semites that Jews constituted not only a separate religion, but a separate race, one intent on polluting Aryan blood. To protect racial purity, the Nazis had to eliminate other races, nationalities, or groups they viewed as inferior—as "subhumans." These included the Roma (gypsies), who were regarded as nomadic outsiders of mixed race, as well as Poles, Russians, homosexuals, the insane, the disabled, and the incurably ill. But the Nazis focused especially on the Jews.

The Mass Killings Begin As Nazi troops swept across Eastern Europe and the Soviet Union, the mass killings began. Units from the SS (Hitler's elite security force) moved from town to town to hunt down Jews. The SS and their collaborators rounded up men, women, children, and even babies and took them to isolated spots. They then shot their prisoners in pits that became the prisoners' graves.

German soldiers round up Jews in the Warsaw ghetto.

Jews in communities not reached by the killing squads were rounded up and taken to concentration camps, or slave-labor prisons. These camps were located mainly in Germany and Poland. Hitler hoped that the horrible conditions in the camps would speed the total elimination of the Jews.

The prisoners worked seven days a week as slaves for the SS or for German businesses. Guards severely beat or killed their prisoners for not working fast enough. With meals of thin soup, a scrap of bread, and potato peelings, most prisoners lost 50 pounds in the first few months. Hunger was so intense, recalled one survivor, "that if a bit of soup spilled over, prisoners would . . . dig their spoons into the mud and stuff the mess in their mouths."

The Final Stage Hitler's war on the Jews turned toward the Final Solution in 1942. The Nazis built extermination camps equipped with huge gas chambers that could kill as many as 6,000 human beings in a day.

When prisoners arrived at Auschwitz (OUSH•vihts), the largest of the extermination camps, they paraded before a committee of SS doctors. With a wave of the hand, these doctors separated the strong—mostly men—from the weak—mostly women, young children, the elderly, and the sick. Those labeled as weak would die that day. They were told to undress for a shower and then led into a chamber with fake showerheads. After the doors were closed, cyanide gas poured from the showerheads or holes in the ceiling. All inside were killed in a matter of minutes. Later, the Nazis installed crematoriums, or ovens, to burn the bodies.

▶ Explore ONLINE!

Nazi Labor and Death Camps

Interpret Maps

1. **Location** In which country were most death camps located?

Jewish Resistance

Even in the extermination camps, Jews rose up and fought against the Nazis. At Treblinka in August 1943, and at Sobibor in October 1943, small groups of Jews revolted. They killed guards, stormed the camp armories, stole guns and grenades, and then broke out. In both uprisings, about 300 prisoners escaped. Most were killed soon after. Of those who survived, many joined up with partisan groups and continued to fight until the end of the war.

Late in 1944, prisoners at Auschwitz revolted, too. Like the escapees at Treblinka and Sobibor, most were caught and killed. Young women like Ella Gartner and Roza Robota made the Auschwitz uprising possible. Gartner smuggled gunpowder into the camp from the munitions factory where she worked. Robota helped organize resistance in the camp. Gartner and Robota were executed on January 6, 1945. Less than a month later, Auschwitz was liberated.

Ella Gartner

Roza Robota

Critical Thinking
Form Generalizations What do you think Gartner, Robota, and other Jews who revolted had in common?

Jews Murdered Under Nazi Rule*

	Original Jewish Population	Jews Murdered	Percent Surviving
Poland	3,300,000	2,800,000	15%
Soviet Union (area occupied by Germans)	2,100,000	1,500,000	29%
Hungary	404,000	200,000	49%
Romania	850,000	425,000	50%
Germany/Austria	270,000	210,000	22%

*Estimates

Source: Hannah Vogt, *The Burden of Guilt*

Response from the Allies Reports of the deportation and mass executions of Jews reached Allied leaders as early as 1942. The Allies officially condemned the Nazi's extermination of Jews in Europe and promised punishment, but it is not clear that they truly believed or understood the full ramifications of the Final Solution. In 1944, the War Refugee Board was created in the U.S., and this helped rescue some 200,000 European Jews. No military action, however, was undertaken to disrupt the transport and murder of Jews during the war.

The Survivors Some six million European Jews died in the extermination camps and in Nazi massacres. Fewer than four million survived. Some escaped the horrors of the extermination camps with help from non-Jewish people. These rescuers, at great risk to their own lives, hid Jews in their homes or helped them escape to neutral countries.

The Roma of Europe were also exterminated in the Nazi death camps. It is estimated that 25% of the one million Roma in Europe did not survive the Holocaust. Millions of others – including Poles, Slavs, homosexuals, and the disabled – died in the camps.

Those who survived the camps were changed forever by what they had experienced. Elie Wiesel, a Jew who was nearly 15 years old when he entered Auschwitz, wrote:

"Never shall I forget the small faces of the children whose bodies I saw transformed into smoke under a silent sky. Never shall I forget those flames that consumed my faith forever. . . . Never shall I forget those moments that murdered my God and my soul and turned my dreams to ashes. . . . Never."

—Elie Wiesel, quoted in *Night*

Lesson 3 Assessment

1. **Organize Information** What Nazi actions were part of the Final Solution?

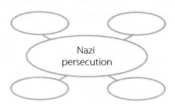

Nazi persecution

2. **Key Terms and People** For each key term or person in the lesson, write a sentence explaining its significance.

3. **Analyze Motives** Why might people want to blame a minority group for most of their country's problems?

4. **Draw Conclusions** Why do you think the Allies did not respond to the forced removal, or ethnic cleansing, and genocide of Jews in countries under Nazi control?

5. **Make Inferences** Why do you think German people were bystanders, and went along with the Nazi policy of persecution of the Jews?

6. **Identify Effects** What impact did the Holocaust have on the Jewish and Roma population of Europe?

The Allied Victory

The Big Idea
Led by the United States, Great Britain, and the Soviet Union, the Allies scored key victories and won the war.

Why It Matters Now
The Allies' victory in World War II set up conditions for both the Cold War and today's post-Cold War world.

Key Terms and People
Dwight D. Eisenhower
Battle of Stalingrad
D-Day
Battle of the Bulge
kamikaze

Setting the Stage

On December 22, 1941, just after Pearl Harbor, Winston Churchill and President Roosevelt met at the White House to develop a joint war policy. Stalin had asked his allies to relieve German pressure on his armies in the east. He wanted them to open a second front in the west. This would split the Germans' strength by forcing them to fight major battles in two regions instead of one. Churchill agreed with Stalin's strategy. The Allies would weaken Germany on two fronts before dealing a deathblow. At first, Roosevelt was torn, but ultimately he agreed.

The Tide Turns on Two Fronts

Churchill wanted Britain and the United States to strike first at North Africa and southern Europe. The strategy angered Stalin. He wanted the Allies to open the second front in France. The Soviet Union, therefore, had to hold out on its own against the Germans. All Britain and the United States could offer in the way of help was supplies. Nevertheless, late in 1942, the Allies began to turn the tide of war both in the Mediterranean and on the Eastern Front.

The North African Campaign General Erwin Rommel took the key Libyan port city of Tobruk in June 1942. With Tobruk's fall, London sent General Bernard Montgomery— "Monty" to his troops—to take control of British forces in North Africa. These included British, Indian, and British Commonwealth troops from Canada, Australia, South Africa, and New Zealand. By the time Montgomery arrived, however, the Germans had advanced to an Egyptian village called El Alamein (al•uh•MAYN), west of Alexandria. (See the map World War II: Allied Advances, 1942–1945.) They were dug in so well that British forces could not go around them. The only way to dislodge them, Montgomery decided, was with a massive frontal attack. The Battle of El Alamein began on the night of October 23. The roar of approximately

1,000 British guns took the Axis soldiers totally by surprise. They fought back fiercely and held their ground for several days. By November 4, however, Rommel's army had been beaten. He and his forces fell back.

As Rommel retreated west, the Allies launched Operation Torch. On November 8, an Allied force of more than 100,000 troops—mostly Americans— landed in Morocco and Algeria. American general **Dwight D. Eisenhower** led this force. Caught between Montgomery's and Eisenhower's armies, Rommel's Afrika Korps was finally crushed in May 1943.

The Battle for Stalingrad As Rommel suffered defeats in North Africa, German armies also met their match in the Soviet Union. The German advance had stalled at Leningrad and Moscow late in 1941. The bitter winter made the situation worse. When the summer of 1942 arrived, however, Hitler sent his Sixth Army, under the command of General Friedrich Paulus, to seize the oil fields in the Caucasus Mountains. The army was also to capture Stalingrad (now Volgograd), a major industrial center on the Volga River. (See the map World War II: Allied Advances, 1942–1945.)

The **Battle of Stalingrad** began on August 23, 1942. The Luftwaffe went on nightly bombing raids that set much of the city ablaze and reduced the rest to rubble. The situation looked desperate. Nonetheless, Stalin had already told his commanders to defend the city named after him to the death.

By early November 1942, Germans controlled 90 percent of the ruined city. Then another Russian winter set in. On November 19, Soviet troops outside the city launched a counterattack. Closing in around Stalingrad, they trapped the Germans inside and cut off their supplies. General Paulus begged Hitler to order a retreat. But Hitler refused, saying the city was "to be held at all costs."

On February 2, 1943, some 90,000 frostbitten, half-starved German troops surrendered to the Soviets. These pitiful survi-

Soviet troops launch an attack during the battle for Stalingrad.

vors were all that remained of an army of 330,000. Stalingrad's defense had cost the Soviets over one million soldiers. The city was 99 percent destroyed. However, the Germans were now on the defensive, with the Soviets pushing them steadily westward.

World War II: Allied Advances, 1942–1945

Legend:
- Axis nations, 1938
- Axis-controlled, 1942
- Allies
- Neutral nations
- Allied advances
- Major Battles

Interpret Maps

1. **Region** Which European countries remained neutral during World War II?

2. **Movement** What seems to be the destination for most of the Allied advances that took place in Europe during 1943–1944?

The Invasion of Italy As the Battle of Stalingrad raged, Stalin continued to urge the British and Americans to invade France. However, Roosevelt and Churchill decided to attack Italy first. On July 10, 1943, Allied forces landed on Sicily and captured it from Italian and German troops about a month later.

Reading Check
Make Inferences
What advantages
might a weaker
army fighting on
its home soil have
over a stronger
invading army?

The conquest of Sicily toppled Mussolini from power. On July 25, King Victor Emmanuel III had the dictator arrested. On September 3, Italy surrendered. But the Germans seized control of northern Italy and put Mussolini back in charge. Finally, the Germans retreated northward, and the victorious Allies entered Rome on June 4, 1944. Fighting in Italy, however, continued until Germany fell in May 1945. On April 27, 1945, Italian resistance fighters ambushed some German trucks near the northern Italian city of Milan. Inside one of the trucks, they found Mussolini disguised as a German soldier. They shot him the next day and later hung his body in downtown Milan for all to see.

The Allied Home Fronts

Wherever Allied forces fought, people on the home fronts rallied to support them. In war-torn countries like the Soviet Union and Great Britain, civilians endured extreme hardships. Many lost their lives. Except for a few of its territories, such as Hawaii, the United States did not suffer invasion or major bombing. Nonetheless, Americans at home made a crucial contribution to the Allied war effort. Americans produced the weapons and equipment that would help win the war.

Mobilizing for War Defeating the Axis powers required mobilizing for total war. In this feature of warfare in the 20th century, entire national economies were directed toward the war effort. Increased armament production in the United States provided an indispensable boost to the Allied war effort. In 1939, the United States manufactured 3,000 military aircraft. From 1941–1945, the United States produced 300,000 more, as well as 61,000 tanks; 200 submarines; 27 aircraft carriers; and much more military weaponry and materials. Factories converted their peacetime operations to wartime production and made everything from machine guns to boots. Automobile factories produced tanks. A typewriter company made armor-piercing shells. By 1944, between 17 and 18 million U.S. workers had jobs in war industries. Production boomed as citizens—many of them women entering the work force for the first time—flocked to meet the labor demand, working long hours to help win the war.

With factories turning out products for the war, a shortage of consumer goods hit the United States. From meat and sugar to tires and gasoline, from nylon stockings to laundry soap, the American government rationed scarce items. Setting the speed limit at 35 miles per hour also helped to save gasoline and rubber. In European countries directly affected by the war, rationing was even more drastic.

To inspire their people to greater efforts, Allied governments conducted highly effective propaganda campaigns, in which citizens were asked to do their part to conserve and contribute resources to the war effort. In the Soviet Union, a Moscow youngster collected enough scrap metal to produce 14,000 artillery shells. A Russian family used its life savings to buy a tank for the Red Army. Other propaganda campaigns used nationalistic sentiment to request money to support the troops fighting for freedom.

American school children helped the war effort by recycling scrap metal and rubber and by buying war bonds.

In the United States, youngsters saved their pennies and bought government war stamps and bonds to help finance the war.

War Limits Civil Rights Government propaganda also had a negative effect. After Pearl Harbor, a wave of prejudice arose in the United States against Japanese Americans. Most lived in Hawaii and on the West Coast. The bombing of Pearl Harbor frightened Americans. This fear, encouraged by government propaganda, was turned against Japanese Americans. They were suddenly seen as "the enemy." On February 19, 1942, President Roosevelt issued an executive order calling for the internment of Japanese Americans because they were considered a threat to the country.

In March, the military began rounding up "aliens" and shipping them to relocation camps. The camps were restricted military areas located far away from the coast. Such locations, it was thought, would prevent these "enemy aliens" from assisting a Japanese invasion. However, two-thirds of those interned were Nisei, native-born American citizens whose parents were Japanese. Many of them volunteered for military service and fought bravely for the United States, even though their families remained in the camps.

Reading Check
Analyze Issues
What were some costs and benefits for workers and businesses in converting factories to wartime production?

Victory in Europe

While the Allies were dealing with issues on the home front, they also were preparing to push toward victory in Europe. In 1943, the Allies began secretly building an invasion force in Great Britain. Their plan was to launch an attack on German-held France across the English Channel.

The D-Day Invasion By May 1944, the invasion force was ready. Thousands of planes, ships, tanks, and landing craft and more than three million troops awaited the order to attack. General Dwight D. Eisenhower, the commander of this enormous force, planned to strike on the coast of Normandy, in northwestern France. The Germans knew that an attack was coming. But they did not know where it would be launched. To keep Hitler guessing, the Allies set up a huge dummy army with its own headquarters and equipment. This make-believe army appeared to be preparing to attack the French seaport of Calais (ka•LAY).

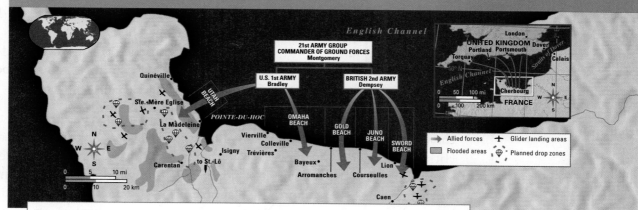

The D-Day Invasion, June 6, 1944

Explore ONLINE!

21st ARMY GROUP COMMANDER OF GROUND FORCES Montgomery

U.S. 1st ARMY Bradley

BRITISH 2nd ARMY Dempsey

English Channel

Quinéville
Ste.-Mère Eglise
UTAH BEACH
La Madeleine
POINTE-DU-HOC
OMAHA BEACH
Vierville
Colleville
Isigny
Trévières
Carentan
to St.-Lô
Bayeux
Arromanches
GOLD BEACH
JUNO BEACH
SWORD BEACH
Courseulles
Lion
Caen

UNITED KINGDOM
London
Portland
Portsmouth
Dover
Torquay
Strait of Dover
Calais
English Channel
Cherbourg
FRANCE

Allied forces — Glider landing areas
Flooded areas — Planned drop zones

Interpret Maps

1. **Human-Environment Interaction** What environmental problem might have been encountered by 1st Army soldiers landing at Utah Beach?

2. **Movement** Looking at the map, what might have been the Allied strategy behind parachuting troops into France?

Code-named Operation Overlord, the invasion of Normandy was the largest land and sea attack in history. The invasion began on June 6, 1944—known as **D-Day**. At dawn on that day, British, American, French, and Canadian troops fought their way onto a 60-mile stretch of beach in Normandy. (See the map The D-Day Invasion, June 6, 1944.) The Germans had dug in with machine guns, rocket launchers, and cannons. They sheltered behind concrete walls three feet thick. Not surprisingly, the Allies took heavy casualties. Among the American forces alone, more than 2,700 men died on the beaches that day.

BIOGRAPHY

General Dwight D. Eisenhower
(1890–1969)

In his career, U.S. General Dwight Eisenhower had shown an uncommon ability to work with all kinds of people—even competitive Allies. His chief of staff said of Eisenhower, "The sun rises and sets on him for me." He was also wildly popular with the troops, who affectionately called him "Uncle Ike."

So it was not a surprise when, in December 1943, U.S. Army Chief of Staff George Marshall named Eisenhower as supreme commander of the Allied forces in Europe. The new commander's "people skills" enabled him to join American and British forces together to put a permanent end to Nazi aggression.

Vocabulary
beachheads enemy
shoreline captured
just before invading
forces move inland

Despite heavy losses, the Allies held the beachheads. Within a month of D-Day, more than one million additional troops had landed. Then, on July 25, the Allies punched a hole in the German defenses near Saint-Lô (san•LOH), and the United States Third Army, led by General George Patton, broke out. A month later, the Allies marched triumphantly into Paris. By September, they had liberated France, Belgium, and Luxembourg. They then set their sights on Germany.

The Battle of the Bulge As Allied forces moved toward Germany from the west, the Soviet army was advancing toward Germany from the east. Hitler now faced a war on two fronts. In a desperate gamble, he decided to counterattack in the west. Hitler hoped a victory would split American and British forces and break up Allied supply lines. Explaining the reasoning behind his plan, Hitler said, "This battle is to decide whether we shall live or die. . . . All resistance must be broken in a wave of terror."

On December 16, German tanks broke through weak American defenses along a 75-mile front in the Ardennes. The push into Allied lines gave the campaign its name—the **Battle of the Bulge**. Although caught off guard, the Allies eventually pushed the Germans back. The Germans had little choice but to retreat, since there were no reinforcements available.

Germany's Unconditional Surrender After the Battle of the Bulge, the war in Europe rapidly drew to a close. In late March 1945, the Allies rolled across the Rhine River into Germany. By the middle of April, a noose was closing around Berlin. About three million Allied soldiers approached Berlin from the southwest. Another six million Soviet troops approached from the east. By April 25, 1945, the Soviets had surrounded the capital and were pounding the city with artillery fire.

While Soviet shells burst over Berlin, Hitler prepared for his end in an underground headquarters beneath the crumbling city. On April 29, he married his long-time companion, Eva Braun. The next day, Hitler and Eva Braun committed suicide. Their bodies were then carried outside and burned.

Reading Check
Find Main Ideas
How did the Allies
try to conceal the
true location for the
D-Day landings?

On May 7, 1945, General Eisenhower accepted the unconditional surrender of the Third Reich from the German military. President Roosevelt, however, did not live to witness the long-awaited victory. He had died suddenly on April 12, as Allied armies were advancing toward Berlin. Roosevelt's successor, Harry Truman, received the news of the Nazi surrender. On May 9, the surrender was officially signed in Berlin. The United States and other Allied powers celebrated V-E Day—Victory in Europe Day. After nearly six years of fighting, the war in Europe had ended.

Victory in the Pacific

Although the war in Europe was over, the Allies were still fighting the Japanese in the Pacific. With the Allied victory at Guadalcanal, however, the Japanese advances in the Pacific had been stopped. For the rest of the war, the Japanese retreated before the counterattack of the Allied powers.

The Japanese in Retreat By the fall of 1944, the Allies were moving in on Japan. In October, Allied forces landed on the island of Leyte (LAY•tee) in the Philippines. General Douglas MacArthur, who had been ordered to leave the islands before their surrender in May 1942, waded ashore at Leyte with his troops. On reaching the beach, he declared, "People of the Philippines, I have returned."

U.S. marines raise the Stars and Stripes after their victory at Iwo Jima.

Actually, the takeover would not be quite that easy. The Japanese had devised a bold plan to halt the Allied advance. They would destroy the American fleet, thus preventing the Allies from resupplying their ground troops. This plan, however, required risking almost the entire Japanese fleet. They took this gamble on October 23, in the Battle of Leyte Gulf. Within four days, the Japanese navy had lost disastrously—eliminating it as a fighting force in the war. Now, only the Japanese army and the feared kamikaze stood between the Allies and Japan. The **kamikazes** were Japanese suicide pilots. They would sink Allied ships by crash-diving their bomb-filled planes into them.

In March 1945, after a month of bitter fighting and heavy losses, American Marines took Iwo Jima (EE•wuh-JEE•muh), an island 760 miles from Tokyo. On April 1, U.S. troops moved onto the island of Okinawa, only about 350 miles from southern Japan. The Japanese put up a desperate fight. Nevertheless, on June 21, one of the bloodiest land battles of the war ended. The Japanese lost over 100,000 troops, and the Americans 12,000.

The Japanese Surrender After Okinawa, the next stop for the Allies had to be Japan. President Truman's advisers had informed him that an invasion of the Japanese homeland might cost the Allies half a million lives. Truman had to make a decision whether to use a powerful new weapon called the atomic bomb, or A-bomb. Most of his advisers felt that using it would bring the war to the quickest possible end. The bomb had been developed by the top-secret Manhattan Project, headed by General Leslie Groves and Jewish scientist J. Robert Oppenheimer. Truman first learned of the new bomb's existence when he became president.

Vocabulary
kamikaze Japanese word for "divine wind"; the term was originally applied to a storm that saved Japan from a Mongol invasion in 1281

The Atomic Bomb

On the eve of World War II, scientists in Germany succeeded in splitting the nucleus of a uranium atom, releasing a huge amount of energy. Albert Einstein wrote to President Franklin Roosevelt and warned him that Nazi Germany might be working to develop atomic weapons. Roosevelt responded by giving his approval for an American program, later code-named the Manhattan Project, to develop an atomic bomb. In 1942, a Nobel Prize-winning Italian physicist at the University of Chicago, Enrico Fermi, produced the first nuclear chain reaction. In 1945, the Manhattan Project completed its goal of creating the world's first atomic bomb.

▼ On the morning of August 6, 1945, the B-29 bomber *Enola Gay*, flown by Colonel Paul W. Tibbets, Jr., took off from Tinian Island in the Mariana Islands.

▶ At precisely 8:16 a.m., the atomic bomb exploded above Hiroshima, a city on the Japanese island of Honshu.

Nagasaki citizens trudge through the still smoldering ruins of their city in this photograph by Yosuke Yamahata. ▼

Hiroshima: Day of Fire

Impact of the Bombing	
Ground temperatures	7,000 °F
Catastrophic winds	980 miles per hour
Energy released	20,000 tons of TNT
Buildings destroyed	62,000 buildings
Killed immediately	70,000 people
Dead by the end of 1945	140,000 people
Total deaths related to A-bomb	210,000 people

The overwhelming destructive power of the Hiroshima bomb, and of the bomb dropped on Nagasaki three days later, changed the nature of war forever. Nuclear destruction also led to questions about the ethics of scientists and politicians who chose to develop and use the bomb.

Critical Thinking
1. **Develop Historical Perspective** If you were to design a memorial to the victims of the Hiroshima and Nagasaki bombings, what symbol would you use? Make a sketch of your memorial.

The first atomic bomb was exploded in a desert in New Mexico on July 16, 1945. President Truman then warned the Japanese. He stated that unless they surrendered, they could expect a "rain of ruin from the air." The Japanese did not reply. So, on August 6, 1945, the United States dropped an atomic bomb on Hiroshima, a Japanese city of nearly 350,000 people. Between 70,000 and 80,000 people died in the attack. Three days later, on August 9, a second bomb was dropped on Nagasaki, a city of 270,000. More than 70,000 people were killed immediately. Radiation fallout from the two explosions killed many more.

The Japanese finally surrendered to General Douglas MacArthur on September 2. The ceremony took place aboard the United States battleship *Missouri* in Tokyo Bay. With Japan's surrender, the war had ended. Now, countries faced the task of rebuilding a war-torn world.

J. Robert Oppenheimer (left) and General Leslie Groves inspect the site of the first atomic bomb test near Alamogordo, New Mexico.

Reading Check
Find Main Ideas
What brought about Japan's surrender?

Lesson 4 Assessment

1. **Organize Information** Which battle do you think was most important in turning the war in favor of the Allies? Why?

Battle	Outcome
Battle of El Alamein	
Battle of Stalingrad	
D-Day Invasion	

2. **Key Terms and People** For each key term or person in the lesson, write a sentence explaining its significance.

3. **Synthesize** How do governments gather support for a war effort on the home front?

4. **Analyze Issues** Should governments have the power to limit the rights of their citizens during wartime? Explain your answer.

5. **Form Opinions** Did President Truman make the correct decision in using the atomic bomb? What would the consequences have been if he had chosen not to drop the bomb?

Europe and Japan in Ruins

The Big Idea

World War II cost millions of human lives and billions of dollars in damages. It left Europe and Japan in ruins.

Why It Matters Now

The United States survived World War II undamaged, allowing it to become a world leader.

Key Terms and People

Nuremberg Trials
demilitarization
democratization

Setting the Stage

After six long years of war, the Allies finally were victorious. However, their victory had been achieved at a very high price. World War II had caused more death and destruction than any other conflict in history. It left over 60 million dead. About one-third of these deaths occurred in one country, the Soviet Union. Another 50 million people had been uprooted from their homes and wandered the countryside in search of somewhere to live. Property damage ran into billions of U.S. dollars.

Devastation in Europe

By the end of World War II, Europe lay in ruins. Close to 40 million Europeans had died, two-thirds of them civilians. Constant bombing and shelling had reduced hundreds of cities to rubble. The ground war had destroyed much of the country-side. Displaced persons from many nations were left homeless.

A Harvest of Destruction A few of the great cities of Europe—Paris, Rome, and Brussels—remained largely undamaged by war. Many, however, had suffered terrible destruction. The Battle of Britain left huge areas of London little more than blackened ruins. Warsaw, the capital of Poland, was almost completely destroyed. In 1939, Warsaw had a population of nearly 1.3 million. When Soviet soldiers entered the city in January 1945, only 153,000 people remained. Thousands of tons of Allied bombs had demolished 95 percent of the central area of Berlin. One U.S. officer stationed in the German capital reported, "Wherever we looked we saw desolation. It was like a city of the dead." Civilians had died by the millions as a result of military operations, concentration camps, the bombing of towns and cities, and starvation and disease.

Many of the surviving civilians stayed where they were and tried to get on with their lives. Some lived in partially destroyed homes or apartments. Others huddled in cellars or caves made from rubble. They had no water, no electricity, and very little food. Most no longer had a workplace to provide income or a farm that supplied food.

A large number of people did not stay where they were. Rather, they took to the roads. These displaced persons included the survivors of concentration camps, prisoners of war, and refugees who found themselves in the wrong country when postwar treaties changed national borders. They wandered across Europe, hoping to find their families or to find a safe place to live.

Simon Weisenthal, a prisoner at Auschwitz, described the search made by Holocaust survivors:

> "Across Europe a wild tide of frantic survivors was flowing. . . . Many of them didn't really know where to go. . . . And yet the survivors continued their pilgrimage of despair. . . . 'Perhaps someone is still alive. . . .' Someone might tell where to find a wife, a mother, children, a brother—or whether they were dead. . . . The desire to find one's people was stronger than hunger, thirst, fatigue."

—Simon Weisenthal, quoted in *Never to Forget: The Jews of the Holocaust*

Costs of World War II: Allied Powers and Axis Powers

	Direct War Costs	Military Killed/Missing	Civilians Killed
United States	$288.0 billion*	292,131**	—
Great Britain	$117.0 billion	272,311	60,595
France	$111.3 billion	205,707***	173,260†
Soviet Union	$93.0 billion	13,600,000	7,720,000
Germany	$212.3 billion	3,300,000	2,893,000††
Japan	$41.3 billion	1,140,429	953,000
China	unknown	1,310,224†††	unknown

* In 1945 dollars
** An additional 115,187 servicemen died from nonbattle causes.
*** Before surrender to Nazis
† Includes 65,000 murdered Jews
†† Includes about 170,000 murdered Jews and 56,000 foreign civilians in Germany
††† Includes China's war with Japan beginning in 1937

Interpret Charts
1. Draw Conclusions Which of the nations listed in the chart suffered the greatest human costs?

Reading Check
Analyze Effects
What were some immediate after-effects of the war in Europe?

Misery Continues After the War The misery in Europe continued for years after the war. The fighting had ravaged Europe's countryside, and agriculture had been completely disrupted. Most able-bodied men had served in the military, and the women had worked in war production. Few remained to plant the fields. With the transportation system destroyed, the meager harvests often did not reach the cities. Thousands died as famine and disease spread through the bombed-out cities. The first postwar winter brought more suffering as people went without shoes and coats.

Postwar Governments and Politics

Despairing Europeans often blamed their leaders for the war and its aftermath. Once the Germans had lost, some prewar governments—like those in Belgium, Holland, Denmark, and Norway—returned quickly. In countries like Germany, Italy, and France, however, a return to the old leadership was not desirable. Hitler's Nazi government had brought Germany to ruins. Mussolini had led Italy to defeat. The Vichy government had collaborated with the Nazis. Much of the old leadership was in disgrace. Also, in Italy and France, many resistance fighters were communists.

After the war, the Communist Party promised change, and millions were ready to listen. In both France and Italy, Communist Party membership skyrocketed. The communists made huge gains in the first postwar elections. Anxious to speed up a political takeover, the communists staged a series of violent strikes. Alarmed French and Italians reacted by voting for anticommunist parties. Communist Party membership and influence began to decline. And they declined even more as the economies of France and Italy began to recover.

The Nuremberg Trials While nations were struggling to recover politically and economically, they also tried to deal with the issue of war crimes. During 1945 and 1946, an International Military Tribunal representing 23 nations put Nazi war criminals on trial in Nuremberg, Germany. In the first of these **Nuremberg Trials**, 22 Nazi leaders were charged with waging a war of aggression. They were also accused of committing "crimes against humanity"—the murder of 11 million people.

Adolf Hitler, SS chief Heinrich Himmler, and Minister of Propaganda Joseph Goebbels had committed suicide long before the trials began. However, Hermann Göring, the commander of the Luftwaffe; Rudolf Hess, Hitler's former deputy; and other high-ranking Nazi leaders remained to face the charges.

Hess was found guilty and was sentenced to life in prison. Göring received a death sentence, but cheated the executioner by committing suicide. Ten other Nazi leaders were hanged on October 16, 1946. Hans Frank, the "Slayer of Poles," was the only convicted Nazi to express remorse: "A thousand years will pass," he said, "and still this guilt of Germany will not have been erased." The bodies of those executed were burned at the concentration camp of Dachau (DAHK•ow). They were cremated in the same ovens that had burned so many of their victims.

Reading Check
Identify Problems
Why might it have been difficult to find democratic government leaders in post-Nazi Germany?

A New War Crimes Tribunal

In 1993, the UN established the International Criminal Tribunal for the former Yugoslavia (ICTY) to prosecute war crimes committed in the Balkan conflicts of the 1990s. This was the first international war crimes court since those held in Nuremberg and Tokyo after World War II.

The ICTY, located in The Hague, Netherlands, issued its first indictment in 1994 and began trial proceedings in 1996. By mid-2007, a total of 161 defendants had been indicted. The most prominent of these, Slobodan Milosevic (shown), the former president of Yugoslavia, was charged with 66 counts of genocide, crimes against humanity, and other war crimes. On March 11, 2006, Milosevic, who had suffered from poor health, was found dead in his cell. Radovan Karadzic and Ratko Mladic, the leaders of the Bosnian Serbs, were arrested in 2008 and 2011, respectively. Both were put on trial in The Hague, charged with multiple war crimes.

Postwar Japan

The defeat suffered by Japan in World War II left the country in ruins. Two million lives had been lost. The country's major cities, including the capital, Tokyo, had been largely destroyed by bombing raids. The atomic bomb had turned Hiroshima and Nagasaki into blackened wastelands. The Allies had stripped Japan of its colonial empire.

Occupied Japan General Douglas MacArthur, who had accepted the Japanese surrender, took charge of the U.S. occupation of Japan. MacArthur was determined to be fair and not to plant the seeds of a future war. Nevertheless, to ensure that peace would prevail, he began a process of **demilitarization**, or disbanding the Japanese armed forces. He achieved this quickly, leaving the Japanese with only a small police force. MacArthur also began bringing Japan's major war criminals to trial. The Tokyo Trials took place from 1946 to 1948, prosecuting the same war crimes as those introduced at Nuremberg. All of the 25 surviving defendants were found guilty. Former Premier Hideki Tojo and six others were condemned to hang. The Nuremberg and Tokyo Trials were the first international criminal tribunals to prosecute high-level political and military leaders for war crimes.

MacArthur then turned his attention to **democratization**, the process of creating a government elected by the people. In February 1946, he and his American political advisers drew up a new constitution. It changed the empire into a constitutional monarchy like that of Great Britain. The Japanese accepted the constitution. It went into effect on May 3, 1947.

MacArthur was not told to revive the Japanese economy. However, he was instructed to broaden land ownership and increase the participation of workers and farmers in the new democracy. To this end, MacArthur put forward a plan that required absentee landlords with huge estates to sell land to the government. The government then sold the land to tenant farmers at reasonable prices. These land reforms, as well as government agricultural subsidies and price supports, quickly led to a prosperous agricultural economy. This, in turn, contributed to Japan's growth as a consumer economy. Other reforms pushed by MacArthur gave workers the right to create independent labor unions.

Occupation Brings Deep Changes

The new constitution was the most important achievement of the occupation. It brought deep changes to Japanese society. A long Japanese tradition had viewed the emperor as divine. He was also an absolute ruler whose will was law. The emperor now had to declare that he was not divine. That admission was as shocking to the Japanese as defeat. His power was also dramatically reduced. Like the ruler of Great Britain, the emperor became largely a figurehead—a symbol of Japan.

Reading Check
Make Inferences
How would demilitarization and a revived economy help Japan achieve democracy?

Emperor Hirohito and U.S. General Douglas MacArthur look distant and uncomfortable as they pose here. Although Hirohito's power was greatly reduced after the war, MacArthur felt retaining him as the head of a constitutional monarchy would help the Japanese accept the changes imposed upon them.

The new constitution guaranteed that real political power in Japan rested with the people. The people elected a two-house parliament, called the Diet. All citizens over the age of 20, including women, had the right to vote. The government was led by a prime minister chosen by a majority of the Diet. A constitutional bill of rights protected basic freedoms. One more key provision of the constitution—Article 9—stated that the Japanese could no longer make war. They could fight only if attacked.

In September 1951, the United States and 47 other nations signed a formal peace treaty with Japan. The treaty officially ended the war. Some six months later, the U.S. occupation of Japan was over. However, with no armed forces, the Japanese agreed to a continuing U.S. military presence to protect their country. The United States and Japan, once bitter enemies, were now allies.

In the postwar world, enemies not only became allies. Sometimes, allies became enemies. World War II had changed the political landscape of Europe. The Soviet Union and the United States emerged from the war as the world's two major powers. They also ended the war as allies. However, it soon became clear that their postwar goals were very different. This difference stirred up conflicts that would shape the modern world for decades.

Reading Check
Analyze Causes
Why did the Americans choose the British system of government for the Japanese, instead of the American system?

Lesson 5 Assessment

1. **Organize Information** How did the aftermath of the war in Europe differ from the aftermath of the war in Japan?

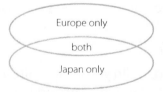

2. **Key Terms and People** For each key term or person in the lesson, write a sentence explaining its significance.

3. **Analyze Causes** Why do you think that many Europeans favored communism after World War II?

4. **Form Opinions** Do you think it was right for the Allies to try only Nazi and Japanese leaders for war crimes? Why or why not?

5. **Make Inferences** How do you think MacArthur's reforms impacted Japan culturally?

6. **Compare and Contrast** Compare and contrast how life in Europe was affected in the immediate aftermath of World War I and World War II.

Module 28 Assessment

Key Terms and People

For each term or name below, write a sentence explaining its connection to World War II.

1. blitzkrieg
2. Battle of Britain
3. Atlantic Charter
4. Battle of Midway
5. Douglas MacArthur
6. Holocaust
7. genocide
8. D-Day
9. Battle of the Bulge
10. Nuremberg Trials
11. demilitarization

Main Ideas

Use your notes and the information in the module to answer the following questions.

Hitler's Lightning War

1. How was Hitler's pact with Stalin and Germany's invasion of Poland a direct cause of World War II?
2. How did German blitzkrieg tactics rely on new military technology?
3. Why were the early months of World War II referred to as the "phony war"?
4. Why was capturing Egypt's Suez Canal so important to the Axis powers?
5. What was the Atlantic Charter and what did it state?

Japan's Pacific Campaign

6. What was Yamamoto's objective at Pearl Harbor?
7. How did Japan try to win support from other Asian countries?
8. In what way was the Battle of the Coral Sea a new kind of naval warfare?
9. What was General Douglas MacArthur's island-hopping strategy?

The Holocaust

10. What was the new racial order proposed by the Nazis?
11. Name two tactics that Hitler used to rid Germany of Jews before creating his Final Solution.
12. What Nazi action marked the final stage of the Final Solution?
13. How did some non-Jews oppose Hitler's war on the Jews?

The Allied Victory

14. Why did Stalin want the United States and Britain to launch a second front in the west?
15. Why were consumer goods rationed during the war?
16. What was Operation Overlord?

Europe and Japan in Ruins

17. Why did so many Europeans take to the roads and wander the countryside after the war?
18. How did the governments of non-Axis nations respond to the issue of genocidal war crimes in Europe?
19. What were two of the most important steps that MacArthur took in Japan following the war?

Critical Thinking

1. **Organize Information** Copy the chart into your notebook and specify for each listed battle or conflict whether the Axis powers or the Allied powers gained an advantage.

Battle/ Conflict	Allied or Axis Powers?
Battle of Britain	
War in the Balkans	
Pearl Harbor	
Battle of the Coral Sea	
Battle of Midway	

2. **Draw Conclusions** Consider the personalities, tactics, and policies of Hitler, Rommel, MacArthur, and Churchill. What qualities make a good war leader?

3. **Compare And Contrast** Compare and contrast Japan's and Germany's goals in World War II. What actions did they take in pursuit of these goals that caused Britain, France, and then the United States to declare war?

4. **Evaluate** Why do you think the governments of the United States and other countries encouraged people on the home front to organize programs for such activities as scrap collection?

Engage with History

Reread the quotation from Elie Wiesel's *Night* in Lesson 3. Then find other sources of personal reflections on the Holocaust from survivors, as well as from non-Jews living in Germany during World War II. Determine how these writings help contribute to an understanding of the Holocaust. What kind of voice and perspective is apparent? How are events interpreted? Consider how these reflections may help shape your interpretation of the past.

Focus on Writing

Conduct research on the scientific and technological developments used in the Allied war effort. Use your findings to create several **information cards** for a card series titled "Science and Technology During World War II." Organize the information on your cards in the following categories:

- name of invention or development
- country
- year
- use in the war
- use today

Multimedia Activity

During World War II, many consumer-goods manufacturers switched to the production of military goods. Many of these companies still exist. Working with a partner, use the Internet to research one such company. Find out what products the company made before and during the war, and how the company's wartime role affected its reputation.

Present the results of your research in a well-organized paper. Be sure to

- apply a search strategy when using directories and search engines to locate web resources
- judge the usefulness and reliability of each website
- correctly cite your web sources
- edit for organization and correct use of language

Memories of WORLD WAR II

A global conflict, World War II shaped the history of both the United States and the world. Americans contributed to the war effort in numerous ways. Many enlisted in the military and served in Africa, Europe, and the Pacific. Others contributed by working in factories to produce the massive amounts of ships, planes, guns, and other supplies necessary to win the war. In the process, these Americans left behind firsthand accounts of their experiences during the war, both at home and abroad. Explore some of the personal stories and recollections of World War II online. You can find a wealth of information, video clips, primary sources, activities, and more through your online textbook.

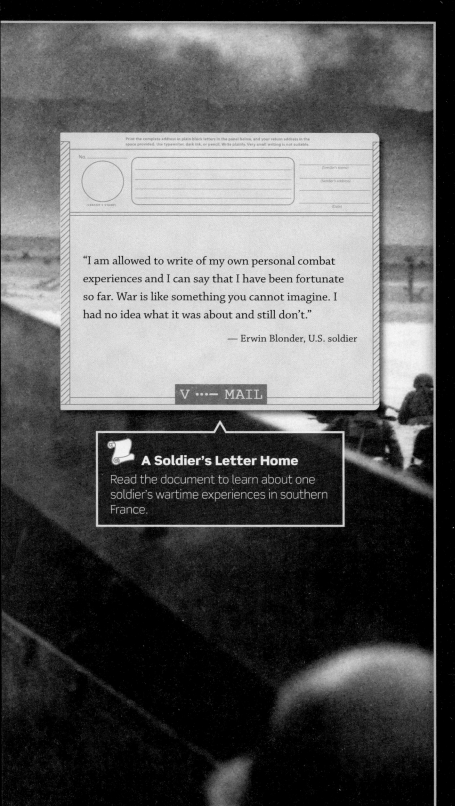

> "I am allowed to write of my own personal combat experiences and I can say that I have been fortunate so far. War is like something you cannot imagine. I had no idea what it was about and still don't."
>
> — Erwin Blonder, U.S. soldier

V ···· — MAIL

A Soldier's Letter Home

Read the document to learn about one soldier's wartime experiences in southern France.

America Mobilizes for War

Watch the video to see how the United States mobilized its citizens for war and how society changed as a result.

Air War Over Germany

Watch the video to see how the P-51 Mustang helped the Allies win the air war over Germany.

The Pacific Islands

Watch the video to hear veterans describe their experiences fighting in the Pacific theater.

Cold War Conflicts

Essential Question

Why did the Cold War never develop into a direct military conflict between the United States and the Soviet Union?

About the Photo: South Korean citizens wave flags to cheer on U.S. First Cavalry Division soldiers on their way to battle Communist troops during the Korean War.

> ▷ *Explore ONLINE!*

HISTORY.

VIDEOS, including...
- Korea: The Forgotten War
- Arriving in Vietnam
- Ayatollah Khomeini

✓ Document Based Investigations

✓ Graphic Organizers

✓ Interactive Games

✓ Image Compare: Political Boundaries Before and After World War II

✓ Carousel: War in Vietnam

In this module you will learn that the United States and the Soviet Union competed for dominance in the post–World War II world, with important consequences for other nations.

What You Will Learn ...

Timeline of Events 1945–Present

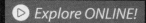 *Explore ONLINE!*

World

1945

< **1945** United Nations formed.

1947 Independent India partitioned into India and Pakistan.

1949 Communists take control of China.

< **1957** Ghana achieves independence from Great Britain.

1957 Soviets launch *Sputnik.*

1959 Cuba becomes Communist > under Fidel Castro.

< **1969** U.S. lands astronauts on the moon.

1973 Arab forces attack Israel in Yom Kippur War.

1975 Vietnam War ends.

1989 Berlin Wall in Germany is knocked down. >

1990 Communists voted out of power in Nicaragua.

1994 First all-race election in South Africa is held. (Nelson Mandela) ∨

2000 South Korea and North Korea meet to improve relations.

2006 North Korea tests a nuclear weapon.

2010

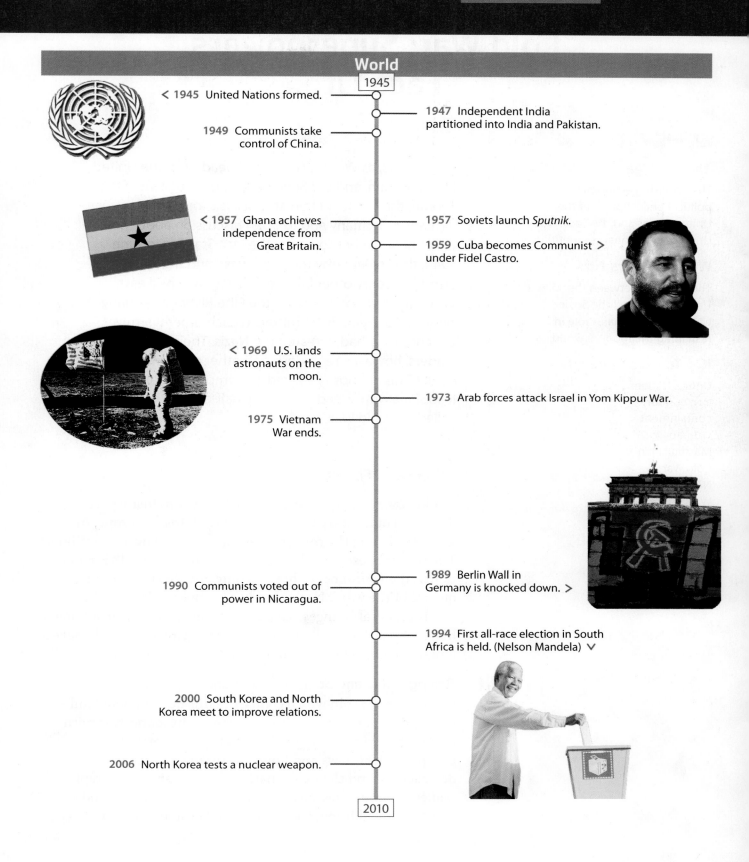

Cold War: Superpowers Face Off

The Big Idea

The opposing economic and political philosophies of the United States and the Soviet Union led to global competition.

Why It Matters Now

The conflicts between the United States and the Soviet Union played a major role in reshaping the modern world.

Key Terms and People

United Nations
iron curtain
containment
Truman Doctrine
Marshall Plan
Cold War
NATO
Warsaw Pact
brinkmanship

Setting the Stage

In late 1943, as World War II raged, leaders of the United States, Britain, and the Soviet Union met together at Tehran, the capital of Iran, to discuss a joint strategy for defeating Germany and to open discussion about how to set national borders after the war. Starting in June 1944, the Soviet army marched west, and the American army, joined by other European allies, marched east. When the two forces met at the Elbe River in Germany on April 25, 1945, they embraced each other warmly because they had defeated the Nazis. Their national leaders, however, regarded each other much more coolly. This animosity caused by competing political philosophies would lead to a nearly half-century of conflict called the Cold War.

Long-term Consequences of World War II

World War II was the most destructive war in history. The death toll of military personnel and civilians in Europe, Africa, and Asia during the conflict may have reached over 60 million. The total represented almost 3 percent of the world's population at the time. Loss of life was only one short-term consequence of the war. Massive land and property destruction, environmental changes, social issues, and problems involving hunger and disease also occurred. These problems would have a long-term impact on the continent.

Demographic and Social Consequences World War II was the first war in which civilian deaths outnumbered military ones. Many civilian deaths occurred in connection with battles, bombings, or enemy occupations. Several ethnic groups, such as Jews and Roma, were singled out for destruction, and their elimination changed the demographic makeup of countries such as Poland, Czechoslovakia, and Hungary. In addition, the fighting and destruction as well as changes in national borders caused millions of civilians to abandon their homes and property and move to new areas. Families were often split up, and many fathers died. Hunger and disease also took their toll on populations in the long term. Medical experts noted increased incidences of diabetes, depression, and heart disease following the war. Many soldiers and civilians also suffered adverse health effects as a result of exposure to chemical, biological, and atomic weapons.

Economic and Environmental Consequences Tank battles and bombing raids during the war caused a great deal of destruction both to the infrastructure (buildings, bridges, and roads) of countries and to the physical environment. Forests were depleted, and farmland was destroyed. It would take several years for crop production to reach prewar levels again. Countries began rebuilding soon after the war, and economies improved in most Western European nations. Countries under Soviet control took longer to rebound during the Cold War, as you will read below.

Reading Check
Analyze Effects
What demographic changes did Europe undergo as a result of World War II?

Allies Become Enemies

Even before World War II ended, the U.S. alliance with the Soviet Union had begun to unravel. The United States was upset that Joseph Stalin, the Soviet leader, had signed a nonaggression pact with Germany in 1939. Later, Stalin blamed the Allies for not invading German-occupied Europe earlier than 1944. Driven by these and other disagreements, the two allies began to pursue opposing goals.

Yalta Conference: A Postwar Plan The war was not yet over in February 1945. But the leaders of the United States, Britain, and the Soviet Union met again at the Soviet Black Sea resort of Yalta. There, they agreed to divide Germany into zones of occupation controlled by the Allied military forces. Germany also would have to pay the Soviet Union to compensate for its loss of life and property during the war. Stalin agreed to join the war against Japan once Germany surrendered. He also promised that Eastern Europeans would have free elections. A skeptical Winston Churchill predicted that Stalin would keep his pledge only if the Eastern Europeans followed "a policy friendly to Russia." Events after the war proved Churchill right, as the Soviet Union under Stalin never permitted free elections.

Winston Churchill, Franklin D. Roosevelt, and Joseph Stalin meet at Yalta in 1945.

Creation of the United Nations and Geneva Conventions In June 1945, the United States and the Soviet Union temporarily set aside their differences. They joined 48 other countries in forming the **United Nations** (UN). This international organization was intended to protect the members against aggression. It was to be based in New York.

The new peacekeeping organization included a large General Assembly, in which each UN member nation could vote on a broad range of issues. An 11-member body called the Security Council had the real power to investigate and settle disputes, though. Its five permanent members were Britain, China, France, the United States, and the Soviet Union (now Russia). Each could veto any council action. This provision was intended to prevent any members of the council from voting as a bloc to override the others.

Many nations also joined together after the war in adopting a series of treaties on the treatment of civilians, prisoners of war (POWs), and those injured during wartime. Known as the Geneva Conventions, the treaties were adopted in 1949, added to in later years, and are still in force today.

Differing U.S. and Soviet Philosophy and Goals Despite agreement at Yalta and their presence on the UN Security Council, the United States and the Soviet Union split sharply after the war. The two "superpowers" were leaders both in military strength and in political and economic influence among the world's nations. The United States promoted the capitalist economic philosophy, while the Soviet Union promoted communism.

The war had affected the two superpowers very differently. The United States suffered 400,000 deaths, but its cities remained intact. The Soviet Union had at least 50 times as many fatalities. Also, many Soviet cities were demolished. These contrasting situations, as well as political and economic differences, affected the two countries' postwar goals and decisions.

Reading Check
Summarize
Why did the United States and the Soviet Union split after the war?

Superpower Aims in Europe

United States	Soviet Union
Encourage democracy in other countries to help prevent the rise of Communist governments	Encourage communism in other countries as part of a worldwide workers' revolution
Gain access to raw materials and markets to fuel booming industries	Rebuild its war-ravaged economy using Eastern Europe's industrial equipment and raw materials
Rebuild European governments to promote stability and create new markets for U.S. goods	Control Eastern Europe to protect Soviet borders and balance the U.S. influence in Western Europe
Reunite Germany to stabilize it and increase the security of Europe	Keep Germany divided to prevent its waging war again

Analyze Charts
Contrast Which U.S. and Soviet aims in Europe conflicted?

Eastern Europe's Iron Curtain

A major goal of the Soviet Union was to shield itself from another invasion from the west. Centuries of history had taught the Soviets to fear invasion. Because it lacked natural western borders, Russia fell victim to each of its neighbors in turn. In the 17th century, the Poles captured the Kremlin. During the next century, the Swedes attacked. Napoleon overran Moscow in 1812. The Germans invaded Russia during World Wars I and II.

Soviets Build a Buffer As World War II drew to a close, the Soviet troops pushed the Nazis back across Eastern Europe. At war's end, these troops occupied a strip of countries along the Soviet Union's own western border. Stalin regarded these countries as a necessary buffer, or wall of protection. He ignored the Yalta agreement and installed or secured Communist governments in Albania, Bulgaria, Hungary, Czechoslovakia, Romania, Poland, and Yugoslavia.

The Soviet leader's American partner at Yalta, Franklin D. Roosevelt, had died on April 12, 1945. To Roosevelt's successor, Harry S. Truman, Stalin's reluctance to allow free elections in Eastern European nations was a clear violation of those countries' rights. Truman, Stalin, and Churchill met at Potsdam, Germany, in July 1945. There, Truman pressed Stalin to permit free elections in Eastern Europe. The Soviet leader refused. In a speech in early 1946, Stalin declared that communism and capitalism could not exist in the same world.

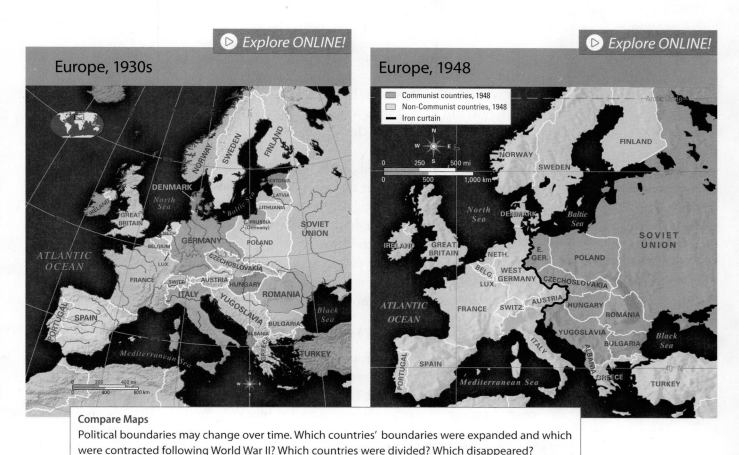

Compare Maps

Political boundaries may change over time. Which countries' boundaries were expanded and which were contracted following World War II? Which countries were divided? Which disappeared?

An Iron Curtain Divides East and West Europe now lay divided between East and West. Germany had been split into two sections. The Soviets controlled the eastern part, including half of the capital, Berlin. Under a Communist government, East Germany was named the German Democratic Republic. The western zones were occupied by forces and supporting personnel from the United States, Britain, and France. The population in West Germany, devastated by the war, relied on the Allies for goods and services. The Allies soon became concerned about the costs of continuing to support their German sectors and slowly began withdrawing from the country. In 1949, the united West German sectors officially became the Federal Republic of Germany.

Winston Churchill described the division of Europe following the war by referring to Soviet efforts to take control of its neighbors as establishing an "**iron curtain**." Churchill's phrase came to represent Europe's division into mostly democratic Western Europe and Communist Eastern Europe.

"From Stettin in the Baltic to Trieste in the Adriatic, an iron curtain has descended across the continent. Behind that line lie all the capitals of the ancient states of Central and Eastern Europe. . . . All these famous cities and the populations around them lie in the Soviet sphere and all are subject in one form or another, not only to Soviet influence but to a very high and increasing measure of control from Moscow."

—Winston Churchill,
"Iron Curtain" speech, March 5, 1946

Reading Check
Draw Conclusions
What meanings do Churchill and Stalin hope to convey in using the phrases *iron curtain* and *firebrand of war*? Discuss this question with several classmates before writing your answer.

Nine days after Churchill's speech, Stalin responded angrily in an interview with the Soviet press. He said, "Mr. Churchill now stands as a firebrand of war." The Soviet Union suffered much greater losses than either Great Britain or the United States, Stalin explained. "One can ask, therefore, what can be surprising in the fact that the Soviet Union, in a desire to ensure its security for the future, tries to achieve that these countries should have governments whose relations to the Soviet Union are loyal?"

The Iron Curtain is shown dropping on Czechoslovakia in this 1948 political cartoon.

United States Tries to Contain Soviets

U.S.-Soviet relations continued to worsen in 1946 and 1947. An increasingly worried United States tried to offset the growing Soviet threat to Eastern Europe. President Truman adopted a foreign policy called **containment**. It was a policy directed at blocking Soviet influence and stopping the expansion of communism. Containment policies included forming alliances and helping weak countries resist Soviet advances.

The Truman Doctrine In a speech asking Congress for foreign aid for Turkey and Greece, Truman contrasted democracy with communism:

"One way of life is based upon the will of the majority, and is distinguished by free institutions . . . free elections . . . and freedom from political oppression. The second way of life is based upon the will of a minority forcibly imposed upon the majority. It relies upon terror and oppression . . . fixed elections, and the suppression of personal freedoms. I believe it must be the policy of the United States to support free people . . . resisting attempted subjugation [control] by armed minorities or by outside pressures."

—President Harry S. Truman,
speech to Congress, March 12, 1947

Truman's support for countries that rejected communism was called the **Truman Doctrine**. It caused great controversy. Some opponents objected to American interference in other nations' affairs. Others argued that the United States could not afford to carry on a global crusade against communism. Congress, however, immediately authorized more than $400 million in aid to Turkey and Greece. The Truman Doctrine established an ongoing U.S. commitment to offer assistance to protect other democratic countries when it was deemed to be in the best interest of the United States.

The Marshall Plan Much of Western Europe lay in ruins after the war. There was also economic turmoil—a scarcity of jobs and food. In 1947, U.S. Secretary of State George Marshall proposed that the United States give aid to needy European countries. This assistance program, called the **Marshall Plan**, would provide food, machinery, and other materials to rebuild Western Europe. As Congress debated the $12.5 billion program in 1948, the Communists seized power in Czechoslovakia. Congress immediately voted approval. The plan was a spectacular success. Even Communist Yugoslavia received aid after it broke away from Soviet domination.

The Berlin Airlift While Europe began rebuilding, the United States and its allies clashed with the Soviet Union over Germany. The Soviets wanted to keep their former enemy weak and divided. But in 1948, France, Britain, and the United States decided to withdraw their forces from Germany and allow their occupation zones to form one nation. The Soviet Union responded by holding West Berlin hostage.

Although Berlin lay well within the Soviet occupation zone of Germany, it too had been divided into four zones. The Soviet Union cut off highway, water, and rail traffic into Berlin's western zones. The city faced starvation. Stalin gambled that the Allies would surrender West Berlin or give up their idea of reunifying Germany. But American and British officials flew food and supplies into West Berlin for nearly 11 months. In May 1949, the Soviet Union admitted defeat and lifted the blockade.

Reading Check
Make Inferences
What was Truman's major reason for offering aid to other European countries?

The Berlin Airlift

From June 1948 to May 1949, Allied planes took off and landed every three minutes in West Berlin. On 278,000 flights, pilots brought in 2.3 million tons of food, fuel, medicine, and even Christmas gifts to West Berliners.

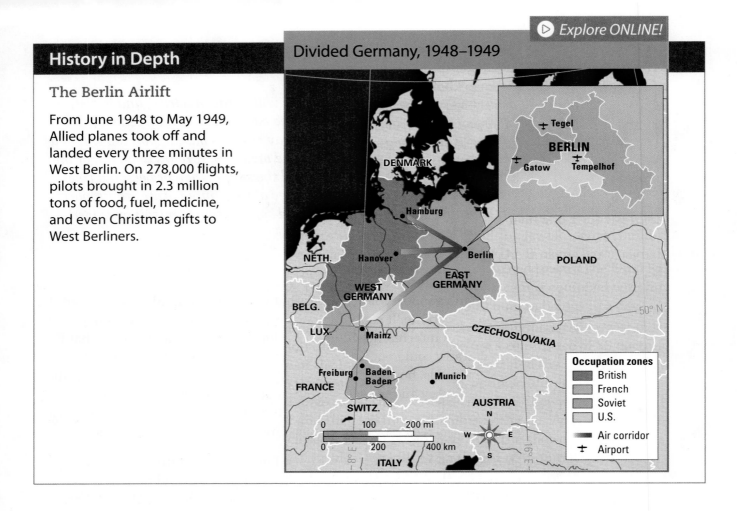

Divided Germany, 1948–1949

▶ Explore ONLINE!

Assistance to Asian Nations The Marshall Plan was designed to help European nations recover from the war. President Truman also initiated a similar program to provide technical assistance for non-European nations, such as those in Southeast Asia as well as Pakistan, Israel, and Iran, which had been impacted by the war. The Point Four program provided technical expertise to help build up agriculture, public health, and education within affected countries. It gave rise to other assistance programs administered by an agency of the UN but funded largely by the United States.

The Cold War Divides the World

These conflicts marked the start of the **Cold War** between the United States and the Soviet Union. A cold war is a struggle over political differences carried on by means short of military action or war. Beginning in 1949, the superpowers used spying, propaganda, diplomacy, and secret operations in their dealings with each other. Much of the world allied with one side or the other. In fact, until the Soviet Union finally broke up in 1991, the Cold War not only dictated U.S. and Soviet foreign policy but influenced world alliances as well.

Superpowers Form Rival Alliances The Berlin blockade heightened Western Europe's fears of Soviet aggression. As a result, in 1949, ten western European nations joined with the United States and Canada to form a defensive military alliance. It was called the North Atlantic Treaty

Reading Check
Summarize
What Soviet action led to the Berlin airlift?

Countries Aided by the Marshall Plan, 1948–1951

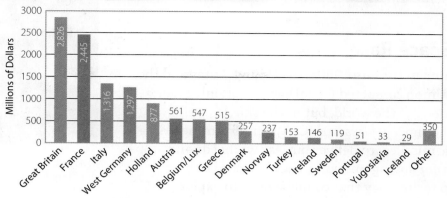

Source: *Problèmes Économiques No. 306*

Interpret Charts
1. **Draw Conclusions** Which country received the most aid from the United States?
2. **Make Inferences** Why do you think Great Britain and France received so much aid?

Organization (**NATO**). An attack on any NATO member would be met with armed force by all member nations.

The Soviet Union saw NATO as a threat and formed its own alliance in 1955. It was called the **Warsaw Pact** and included the Soviet Union, East Germany, Czechoslovakia, Poland, Hungary, Romania, Bulgaria, and Albania. In 1961, the East Germans built a wall to separate East and West Berlin. The Berlin Wall symbolized a world divided into rival camps. However, not every country joined the new alliances. Some, like India, chose not to align with either side. And China, the largest Communist country, came to distrust the Soviet Union. It remained nonaligned.

In the Western Hemisphere, the United States pushed for the formation of an organization of countries in North, Central, and South America and the Caribbean. Formed in 1948, the Organization of American States (OAS) hoped to bring peace and security to its member nations and to increase economic and social cooperation.

The Threat of Nuclear War As these alliances were forming, the Cold War threatened to heat up enough to destroy the world. The United States already had atomic bombs, thanks to the work of scientists in America such as Italian-born Enrico Fermi, who directed early experiments in splitting atoms in the early 1940s. Fermi was one of the architects of the nuclear age. In 1949, the Soviet Union exploded its own atomic weapon. President Truman was determined to develop a more deadly weapon before the Soviets did. He authorized work on a thermonuclear weapon in 1950.

The hydrogen or H-bomb would be much more powerful than the A-bomb. Its power came from the fusion, or joining together, of atoms rather than the splitting of atoms, as in the A-bomb. Edward Teller, a Hungarian-born American nuclear physicist, was a leading proponent of the H-bomb and played an important role in its design. The team that

The Space Race

Beginning in the late 1950s, the United States and the Soviet Union competed for influence not only among the nations of the world, but in the skies as well. Once the superpowers had ICBMs (intercontinental ballistic missiles) to deliver nuclear warheads and aircraft for spying missions, they both began to develop technology that could be used to explore—and ultimately control—space. However, after nearly two decades of costly competition, the two superpowers began to cooperate in space exploration.

In a major technological triumph, the United States put human beings on the moon on July 20, 1969. Astronaut Buzz Aldrin is shown on the lunar surface with the lunar lander spacecraft.

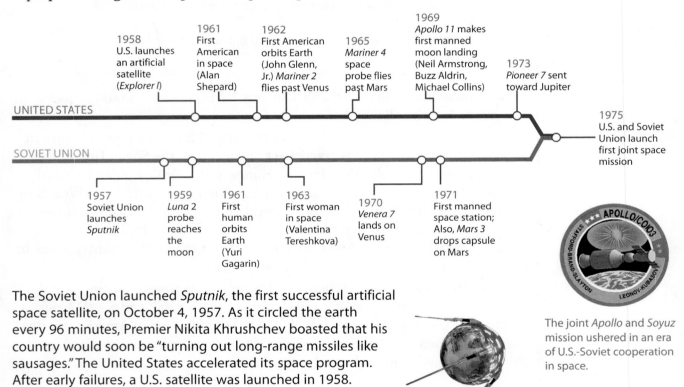

1958 U.S. launches an artificial satellite (*Explorer I*)

1961 First American in space (Alan Shepard)

1962 First American orbits Earth (John Glenn, Jr.) *Mariner 2* flies past Venus

1965 *Mariner 4* space probe flies past Mars

1969 *Apollo 11* makes first manned moon landing (Neil Armstrong, Buzz Aldrin, Michael Collins)

1973 *Pioneer 7* sent toward Jupiter

UNITED STATES

SOVIET UNION

1975 U.S. and Soviet Union launch first joint space mission

1957 Soviet Union launches *Sputnik*

1959 *Luna 2* probe reaches the moon

1961 First human orbits Earth (Yuri Gagarin)

1963 First woman in space (Valentina Tereshkova)

1970 *Venera 7* lands on Venus

1971 First manned space station; Also, *Mars 3* drops capsule on Mars

The Soviet Union launched *Sputnik*, the first successful artificial space satellite, on October 4, 1957. As it circled the earth every 96 minutes, Premier Nikita Khrushchev boasted that his country would soon be "turning out long-range missiles like sausages." The United States accelerated its space program. After early failures, a U.S. satellite was launched in 1958.

The joint *Apollo* and *Soyuz* mission ushered in an era of U.S.-Soviet cooperation in space.

Critical Thinking
1. **Compare** Which destinations in space did both the United States and the Soviet Union explore?
2. **Make Inferences** What role might space continue to play in achieving world peace?

---

developed the new weapon was based in Los Alamos, New Mexico. In 1952, the United States tested the first H-bomb on a group of coral islands in the Pacific. It yielded an explosion equivalent to 10 million tons (10 megatons) of TNT, more than 600 times more powerful than the atomic bomb dropped on Hiroshima, Japan. The Soviets were also hard at work on their own H-bomb and exploded one in 1953.

Dwight D. Eisenhower became the U.S. president in 1953. He appointed the firmly anti-Communist John Foster Dulles as his secretary of state. If the Soviet Union or its supporters attacked U.S. interests, Dulles threatened, the United States would "retaliate instantly, by means and at places of our own choosing." This willingness to go to the brink, or edge, of war became known as **brinkmanship**. Brinkmanship required a reliable source of nuclear weapons and airplanes to deliver them. So, the United States strengthened its air force and began producing stockpiles of nuclear weapons. The Soviet Union responded with its own military buildup, beginning an arms race that would go on for four decades.

The Cold War in the Skies The Cold War also affected the science and education programs of the two countries. In August 1957, the Soviets announced the development of a rocket that could travel great distances—an intercontinental ballistic missile, or ICBM. On October 4, the Soviets used an ICBM to push *Sputnik*, the first unmanned satellite, above the earth's atmosphere. Americans felt they had fallen behind in science and technology, and the government poured money into science education. In 1958, the United States launched its own satellite. A German-born rocket scientist named Wehrner von Braun was the driving force behind the U.S. ballistic missile program. He would play a major role in the American space program for more than 30 years.

In 1960, the skies again provided the arena for a superpower conflict. Five years earlier, Eisenhower had proposed that the United States and the Soviet Union be able to fly over each other's territory to guard against surprise nuclear attacks. The Soviet Union said no. In response, the U.S. Central Intelligence Agency (CIA) started secret high-altitude spy flights over Soviet territory in planes called U-2s. In May 1960, the Soviets shot down a U-2 plane, and its pilot, Francis Gary Powers, was captured. This U-2 incident heightened Cold War tensions.

While Soviet Communists were squaring off against the United States, Communists in China were fighting a civil war for control of that country.

Reading Check
Analyze Effects
How did the U.S. policy of brinkmanship contribute to the arms race?

Lesson 1 Assessment

1. **Organize Information** Which action or event of the Cold War was the most significant? Explain.

2. **Key Terms and People** For each key term or person in the lesson, write a sentence explaining its significance.

3. **Analyze Causes** How was formation of the United Nations a response to World War II?

4. **Evaluate** Do you consider the Marshall Plan and Berlin Airlift to have been successful? Explain.

5. **Compare and Contrast** What factors help to explain why the United States and the Soviet Union became rivals instead of allies?

6. **Analyze Motives** What were Stalin's objectives in supporting Communist governments in Eastern Europe?

7. **Analyze Issues** Why might Berlin have been a likely spot for trouble to develop during the Cold War?

Communists Take Power in China

The Big Idea
After World War II, Chinese Communists defeated Nationalist forces, and two separate Chinas emerged.

Why It Matters Now
China remains a Communist country and a major power in the world.

Key Terms and People
Mao Zedong
Jiang Jieshi
commune
Red Guards
Cultural Revolution

Setting the Stage

In World War II, China fought on the side of the victorious Allies. But the victory proved to be a hollow one for China. During the war, Japan's armies had occupied and devastated most of China's cities. China's civilian death toll alone was estimated to be between 10 and 22 million persons. This vast country suffered casualties second only to those of the Soviet Union. However, conflict did not end with the defeat of the Japanese. In 1945, opposing Chinese armies faced one another.

Communists vs. Nationalists

A bitter civil war was raging between the Nationalists and the Communists when the Japanese invaded China in 1937. During World War II, the political opponents temporarily united to fight the Japanese. But they continued to jockey for position within China.

World War II in China Under their leader, **Mao Zedong** (mow-dzuh•dahng), the Communists had a stronghold in northwestern China. From there, they mobilized peasants for guerrilla war against the Japanese in the northeast. Thanks to their efforts to promote literacy and improve food production, the Communists won the peasants' loyalty. By 1945, they controlled much of northern China.

Meanwhile, the Nationalist forces under **Jiang Jieshi** (jee•ahng-jee•shee) dominated southwestern China. Protected from the Japanese by rugged mountain ranges, Jiang gathered an army of 2.5 million men. From 1942 to 1945, the United States sent the Nationalists at least $1.5 billion in aid to fight the Japanese. Instead of benefiting the army, however, these supplies and money often ended up in the hands of a few corrupt officers. Jiang's army actually fought few battles against the Japanese. Instead, the Nationalist army saved its strength for the coming battle against Mao's Red Army. After Japan surrendered, the Nationalists and Communists resumed fighting.

Civil War Resumes The renewed civil war lasted from 1946 to 1949. At first, the Nationalists had the advantage. Their army outnumbered the Communists' army by as much as three to one. And the United States continued its support by providing nearly $2 billion in military aid. The Nationalist forces, however, did little to win popular support. With China's economy collapsing, thousands of Nationalist soldiers deserted to join the Communists. In spring 1949, China's major cities fell to the well-trained Red forces. Mao's troops were also enthusiastic about his promise to return land to the peasants. The remnants of Jiang's shattered army fled south. In October 1949, Mao Zedong gained control of the country. He proclaimed it the People's Republic of China. Jiang and other Nationalist leaders retreated to the island of Taiwan, which Westerners called Formosa.

Mao Zedong's victory fueled U.S. anti-Communist feelings. Those feelings grew stronger after the Chinese and Soviets signed a treaty of friendship in 1950. Many people in the United States viewed the takeover of China as another step in a Communist campaign to conquer the world.

Reading Check
Recognize Effects
How did the outcome of the Chinese civil war contribute to Cold War tensions?

The Chinese Revolution had several things in common with earlier and later social revolutions. For example, like the French Revolution that began in 1789, the Russian Revolution of 1917, and the Cuban Revolution that began in 1959, a central purpose of the Chinese Revolution was to break down the existing class structure and provide more economic and political opportunity for those other than the ruling class, including land ownership. In all of the revolutions, peasants played a key role.

Chinese Political Opponents, 1945

Nationalists		Communists
Jiang Jieshi	**Leader**	Mao Zedong
Southern China	**Area Ruled**	Northern China
United States	**Foreign Support**	Soviet Union
Defeat of Communists	**Domestic Policy**	National liberation
Weak due to inflation and failing economy	**Public Support**	Strong due to promised land reform for peasants
Ineffective, corrupt leadership and poor morale	**Military Organization**	Experienced, motivated guerrilla army

Interpret Charts
1. **Draw Conclusions** Which party's domestic policy might appeal more to Chinese peasants? Why?

2. **Form and Support Opinions** Which aspect of the Communist approach do you think was most responsible for Mao's victory? Explain.

The Two Chinas Affect the Cold War

China had split into two nations. One was the island of Taiwan, or Nationalist China, with an area of 13,000 square miles. The mainland, or People's Republic of China, had an area of more than 3.5 million square miles. The existence of two Chinas, and the conflicting international loyalties they inspired, intensified the Cold War.

The Superpowers React After Jiang Jieshi fled to Taiwan, the United States helped him set up a Nationalist government on that small island. It was called the Republic of China. The Soviets gave financial, military, and technical aid to Communist China. In addition, the Chinese and the Soviets pledged to come to each other's defense if either was attacked. The United States tried to halt Soviet expansion in Asia. For example, when Soviet forces occupied the northern half of Korea after World War II and set up a Communist government there, the United States supported a separate state in the south.

China Expands Under the Communists In the early years of Mao's reign, Chinese troops expanded into Tibet, India, and southern, or Inner, Mongolia. Northern, or Outer, Mongolia, which bordered the Soviet Union, remained in the Soviet sphere.

In a brutal assault in 1950 and 1951, China took control of Tibet. The Chinese promised autonomy to Tibetans, who followed their religious leader, the Dalai Lama. When China's control over Tibet tightened in the late 1950s, the Dalai Lama fled to India. India welcomed many Tibetan refugees after a failed revolt in Tibet in 1959. As a result, resentment between India and China grew. In 1962, they clashed briefly over the two countries' unclear border. The fighting stopped but resentment continued.

--- BIOGRAPHY ---

Mao Zedong
(1893–1976)

Born into a peasant family, Mao embraced Marxist socialism as a young man. Though he began as an urban labor organizer, Mao quickly realized the revolutionary potential of China's peasants. In 1927, Mao predicted:

The force of the peasantry is like that of the raging winds and driving rain. . . . They will bury beneath them all forces of imperialism, militarism, corrupt officialdom, village bosses and evil gentry.

Mao's first attempt to lead the peasants in revolt failed in 1927. But during the Japanese occupation, Mao and his followers won widespread peasant support by reducing rents and promising to redistribute land.

The Communists Transform China

For decades, China had been in turmoil, engaged in civil war or fighting with Japan. So, when the Communists took power, they moved rapidly to strengthen their rule over China's 550 million people. They also aimed to restore China as a powerful nation.

Communists Consolidate Power After taking control of China, the Communists began to tighten their hold. The party's 4.5 million members made up just 1 percent of the population. But they were a disciplined group. Like the Soviets, the Chinese Communists set up two parallel organizations, the Communist Party and the national government. Mao headed both until 1959.

Mao's Brand of Marxist Socialism Mao was determined to reshape China's economy based on Marxist socialism. Eighty percent of the people lived in rural areas, but most owned no land. Instead, 10 percent of the rural population controlled 70 percent of the farmland. Under the Agrarian Reform Law of 1950, Mao seized the holdings of these landlords. His forces killed more than a million landlords who resisted. He then divided the land among the peasants. Later, to further Mao's socialist principles, the government forced peasants to join collective farms. Each of these farms was comprised of 200 to 300 households.

Mao's changes also transformed industry and business. Gradually, private companies were nationalized, or brought under government ownership. In 1953, Mao launched a five-year plan that set high production goals for industry. By 1957, China's output of coal, cement, steel, and electricity had increased dramatically.

"The Great Leap Forward" To expand the success of the first Five-Year Plan, Mao proclaimed the "Great Leap Forward" in early 1958. This plan called for still larger collective farms, or **communes**. By the end of 1958, about 26,000 communes had been created. The average commune sprawled over 15,000 acres and supported more than 25,000 people. In the strictly controlled life of the communes, peasants worked the land together. They ate in communal dining rooms, slept in communal dormitories, and raised children in communal nurseries. And they owned nothing. The peasants had no incentive to work hard when only the state profited from their labor.

The Great Leap Forward was a giant step backward. Poor planning and inefficient "backyard," or home, industries hampered growth. The program was ended in 1961 after crop failures caused a famine that killed about 20 million people.

Soviet Competition and Global Politics China was facing external problems as well as internal ones in the late 1950s. The spirit of cooperation that had bound the Soviet Union and China together began to fade. The two countries clashed several times in territorial disputes along their long shared border. They also were involved in political clashes as each sought to be viewed as the leader of a worldwide Communist movement.

Mao's revolution had an impact on global politics from the 1950s through the 1970s. Close to home, the Chinese provided military, advisory, and financial support to Communist leaders in Korea and Vietnam. Farther away, Mao took a particular interest in Communist expansion in Latin American countries such as Cuba, Peru, and Bolivia. Latin American Communist leaders came to China to learn from Mao about political organization and guerilla fighting, which they put into practice during periods of unrest in their own countries during the 1960s and 1970s. African revolutionaries also took lessons from the Chinese Communist leaders and then employed what they learned in their own countries.

The Cultural Revolution After the failure of the Great Leap Forward and the split with the Soviet Union, Mao reduced his role in China's government. Other leaders moved away from Mao's strict socialist ideas. For example, farm families were permitted to live in their own homes and could sell crops they grew on small private plots. Factory workers could compete for wage increases and promotions.

Mao thought China's new economic policies weakened the Communist goal of social equality. He was determined to revive the revolution. In 1966, he urged China's young people to "learn revolution by making revolution." Millions of high school and college students responded. They left their classrooms and formed militia units called **Red Guards**.

The Red Guards led a major uprising known as the **Cultural Revolution**. Its goal was to establish a society of peasants and workers in which all were equal. The new hero was the peasant who worked with his hands.

History in Depth

The Red Guards

The Red Guards were students, mainly teenagers. They pledged their devotion to Chairman Mao and the Cultural Revolution. From 1966 to 1968, 20 to 30 million Red Guards roamed China's cities and countryside, causing widespread chaos. To smash the old, non-Maoist way of life, they destroyed buildings and beat and even killed Mao's alleged enemies. They lashed out at professors, government officials, factory managers, and even parents.

Eventually, even Mao turned on them. Most were exiled to the countryside. Others were arrested and some executed.

The life of the mind—intellectual and artistic activity—was considered useless and dangerous. To stamp out this threat, the Red Guards shut down colleges and schools. They targeted anyone who resisted the regime. Intellectuals had to "purify" themselves by doing hard labor in remote villages. Thousands were executed or imprisoned.

Chaos threatened farm production and closed down factories. Civil war seemed possible. By 1968, even Mao admitted that the Cultural Revolution had to stop. The army was ordered to put down the Red Guards. Zhou Enlai (joh-ehn•leye), Chinese Communist party founder and premier since 1949, began to restore order. While China was struggling to become stable, the Cold War continued to rage. In addition, two full-scale "hot" wars broke out—in Korea and in Vietnam.

Reading Check
Analyze Issues
What aspects of Marxist socialism did Mao try to bring to China?

Lesson 2 Assessment

1. **Organize Information** Which effect of the Communist Revolution in China do you think had the most permanent impact? Explain.

Cause	Effect
1.	1.
2.	2.
3.	3.

2. **Key Terms and People** For each key term or person in the lesson, write a sentence explaining its significance.

3. **Analyze Issues** What policies or actions enabled the Communists to defeat the Nationalists in the Chinese civil war?

4. **Make Inferences** Why did the United States support the Nationalists in the civil war in China?

5. **Identify Problems** What circumstances prevented Mao's Great Leap Forward from bringing economic prosperity to China in the late 1950s and early 1960s?

6. **Analyze Effects** Why was the Cultural Revolution led by the Red Guards a failure?

Wars in Korea and Vietnam

The Big Idea

In Asia, the Cold War flared into actual wars supported mainly by the superpowers.

Why It Matters Now

Today, Vietnam is a Communist country, and Korea is split into Communist and non-Communist nations.

Key Terms and People

38th parallel
Douglas MacArthur
Ho Chi Minh
domino theory
Ngo Dinh Diem
Vietcong
Vietnamization
Khmer Rouge

Setting the Stage

When World War II ended, Korea became a divided nation. North of the **38th parallel**, a line that crosses Korea at 38 degrees north latitude, Japanese troops surrendered to Soviet forces. South of this line, the Japanese surrendered to American troops. As in Germany, two nations developed. One was the Communist industrial north, whose government had been set up by the Soviets. The other was the non-Communist rural south, supported by the Western powers.

War in Korea

By 1949, both the United States and the Soviet Union had withdrawn most of their troops from Korea. The Soviets gambled that the United States would not defend South Korea. So they supplied North Korea with tanks, airplanes, and money in an attempt to take over the peninsula.

Standoff at the 38th Parallel On June 25, 1950, North Koreans swept across the 38th parallel in a surprise attack on South Korea. Within days, North Korean troops had penetrated deep into the south. President Truman was convinced that the North Korean aggressors were repeating the types of actions that Hitler, Mussolini, and the Japanese had taken in the 1930s. Truman's policy of containment was being put to the test. And Truman resolved to help South Korea resist communism.

South Korea also asked the United Nations to intervene. When the matter came to a vote in the Security Council, the Soviets were absent. They had refused to take part in the council to protest admission of Nationalist China (Taiwan), rather than Communist China, into the UN. As a result, the Soviet Union could not veto the UN's plan to send an international force to Korea to stop the invasion. A total of 15 nations, including the United States and Britain, participated under the command of General **Douglas MacArthur**.

Meanwhile, the North Koreans continued to advance. By September 1950, they controlled the entire Korean peninsula except for a tiny area around Pusan in the far southeast. That month, however, MacArthur launched a surprise attack. Troops moving north from Pusan met with forces that had made an amphibious landing at Inchon. Caught in this "pincer action," about half of the North Koreans surrendered. The rest retreated.

The Fighting Continues The UN troops pursued the retreating North Koreans across the 38th parallel into North Korea. They pushed them almost to the Yalu River at the Chinese border. The UN forces were mostly from the United States. The Chinese felt threatened by these troops and by an American fleet off their coast. In October 1950, they sent 300,000 troops into North Korea.

The Chinese greatly outnumbered the UN forces. By January 1951, they had pushed UN and South Korean troops out of North Korea. The Chinese then moved into South Korea and captured the capital, Seoul. "We face an entirely new war," declared MacArthur. He called for a nuclear attack against China. Truman viewed MacArthur's proposals as reckless. "We are trying to prevent a world war, not start one," he said. MacArthur tried to go over the president's head by taking his case to Congress and the press. In response, Truman removed him from his command.

Over the next two years, UN forces fought to drive the Chinese and North Koreans back. By 1952, UN troops had regained control of South Korea. Finally, in July 1953, the UN forces and North Korea signed a cease-fire agreement. The border between the two Koreas was set near the 38th parallel, almost where it had been before the war. In the meantime, 4 million soldiers and civilians had died.

Aftermath of the War After the war, Korea remained divided. A demilitarized zone, which still exists, separated the two countries. In North Korea, the Communist dictator Kim Il Sung established collective farms, developed heavy industry, and built up the military. At Kim's death in

UN forces landing at Inchon in South Korea in 1950

1994, his son Kim Jong Il took power. Under his rule, Communist North Korea developed nuclear weapons but had serious economic problems.

On the other hand, South Korea prospered, thanks partly to massive aid from the United States and other countries. In the 1960s, South Korea concentrated on developing its industry and expanding foreign trade. A succession of dictatorships ruled the rapidly developing country. With the 1987 adoption of a democratic constitution, however, South Korea established free elections. During the 1980s and 1990s, South Korea had one of the highest economic growth rates in the world.

Political differences have kept the two Koreas apart, despite periodic discussions of reuniting the country. North Korea's possession of nuclear weapons is a major obstacle. The United States still keeps troops in South Korea.

Reading Check
Recognize Effects
What effects did the Korean War have on the Korean people and nation?

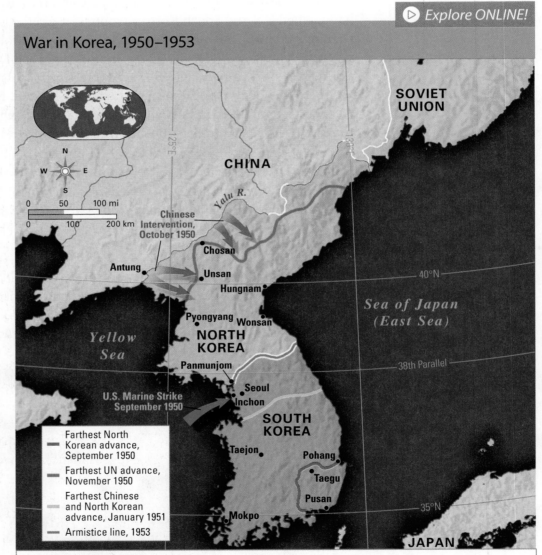

▷ *Explore ONLINE!*

War in Korea, 1950–1953

SOVIET UNION

CHINA

Yalu R.

Chinese Intervention, October 1950

Chosan

Antung

Unsan

Hungnam

40°N

Sea of Japan (East Sea)

Pyongyang   Wonsan

Yellow Sea

NORTH KOREA

Panmunjom

38th Parallel

U.S. Marine Strike September 1950

Seoul
Inchon

SOUTH KOREA

Taejon

Pohang

Taegu

Pusan

35°N

Mokpo

JAPAN

Farthest North Korean advance, September 1950

Farthest UN advance, November 1950

Farthest Chinese and North Korean advance, January 1951

Armistice line, 1953

0   50   100 mi

0   100   200 km

Interpret Maps

1. **Movement** What was the northernmost Korean city UN troops had reached by November 1950?

2. **Changing Boundaries** If the war had ended in January 1951, where would the southern border of North Korea have been located?

War Breaks Out in Vietnam

Much like its involvement in the Korean War, the involvement of the United States in Vietnam stemmed from its Cold War containment policy. After World War II, stopping the spread of communism was the principal goal of U.S. foreign policy.

The Road to War In the early 1900s, France controlled most of resource-rich Southeast Asia. (French Indochina included what are now Vietnam, Laos, and Cambodia.) But nationalist independence movements had begun to develop. A young Vietnamese nationalist, **Ho Chi Minh**, turned to the Communists for help in his struggle. During the 1930s, Ho's Indochinese Communist Party led revolts and strikes against the French.

The French responded by jailing Vietnamese protesters. They also sentenced Ho to death. He fled into exile but returned to Vietnam in 1941, a year after the Japanese seized control of his country during World War II. Ho and other nationalists founded the Vietminh (Independence) League. The Japanese were forced out of Vietnam after their defeat in 1945. Ho Chi Minh believed that independence would follow, but France intended to regain its colony.

The Fighting Begins Vietnamese Nationalists and Communists joined to fight the French armies. The French held most major cities, but the Vietminh had widespread support in the countryside. The Vietminh used hit-and-run tactics to confine the French to the cities. In France the people began to doubt that their colony was worth the lives and money the struggle cost. In 1954, the French suffered a major military defeat at Dien Bien Phu. They surrendered to Ho.

The United States had supported France. With France's defeat, the United States saw a rising threat to the rest of Asia. President Eisenhower described this threat in terms of the **domino theory**. The Southeast Asian nations were like a row of dominos, he said. The fall of one to communism would lead to the fall of its neighbors. This theory became a major justification for U.S. foreign policy during the Cold War era.

Vietnam: A Divided Country After France's defeat, an international peace conference met in Geneva, Switzerland, to discuss the future of Indochina. Based on these talks, Vietnam was divided at 17° north latitude. This is similar to the way Korea was divided at the 38th parallel. North of that line, Ho Chi Minh's Communist forces governed. To the south, the United States and France set up an anti-Communist government under the leadership of **Ngo Dinh Diem** (NOH dihn D'YEM).

Diem ruled the south as a dictator. Opposition to his government grew. Communist guerrillas, called **Vietcong**, began to gain strength in the south. While some of the Vietcong were trained soldiers from North Vietnam, most were South Vietnamese who hated Diem. Gradually, the Vietcong won control of large areas of the countryside. In 1963, a group of South Vietnamese generals had Diem assassinated. But the new leaders were no more popular than Diem had been. It appeared that a takeover by the Communist Vietcong, backed by North Vietnam, was inevitable.

Reading Check
Make Inferences
What actions might the United States have justified by the domino theory?

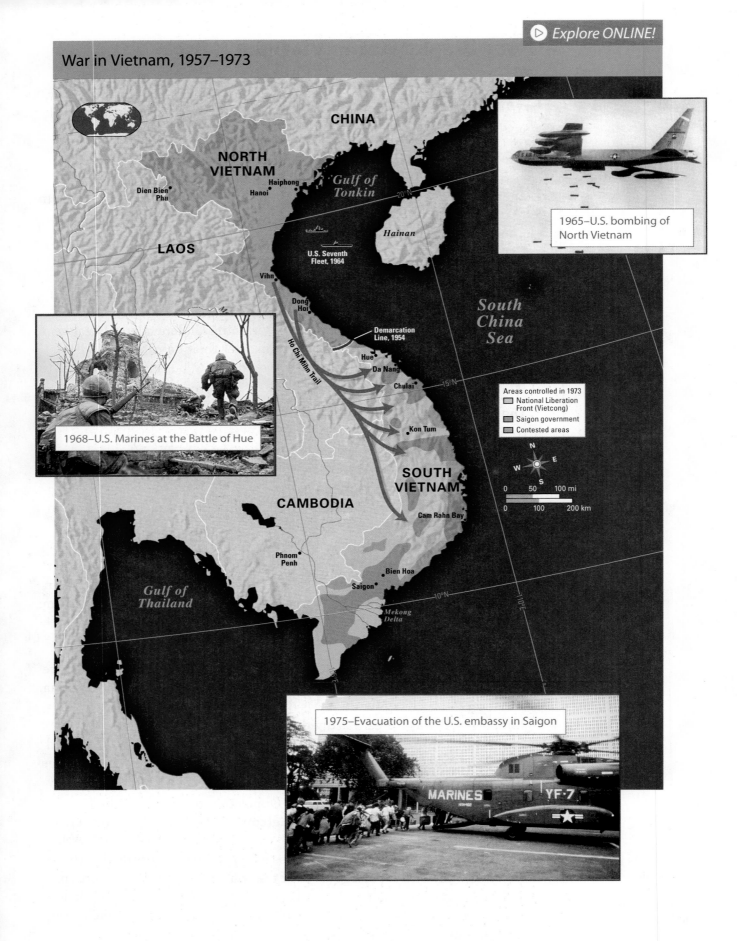

War in Vietnam, 1957–1973

CHINA

NORTH VIETNAM

Dien Bien Phu

Haiphong
Hanoi

Gulf of Tonkin

Hainan

20°N

LAOS

U.S. Seventh Fleet, 1964

Vihn

Dong Hoi

Ho Chi Minh Trail

Demarcation Line, 1954

Hue

Da Nang

Chulai

15°N

Kon Tum

SOUTH VIETNAM

CAMBODIA

South China Sea

1965–U.S. bombing of North Vietnam

1968–U.S. Marines at the Battle of Hue

Areas controlled in 1973
National Liberation Front (Vietcong)
Saigon government
Contested areas

N
W   E
S

0   50   100 mi
0   100   200 km

Cam Rahn Bay

Phnom Penh

Bien Hoa

Saigon

Gulf of Thailand

10°N

Mekong Delta

1975–Evacuation of the U.S. embassy in Saigon

MARINES   YF·7

Ho Chi Minh
(1890–1969)

When he was young, the poor Vietnamese Nguyen Tat Thanh (WEE•un tat thawn) worked as a cook on a French steamship. In visiting U.S. cities where the boat docked, he learned about American culture and ideals. He later took a new name— Ho Chi Minh, meaning "He who enlightens." In proclaiming Vietnam's independence from France in 1945, he declared, "All men are created equal," echoing the words of the American Declaration of Independence.

His people revered him, calling him Uncle Ho. However, Ho Chi Minh did not put his democratic ideals into practice. He ruled North Vietnam by crushing all opposition.

The United States Gets Involved

Faced with the possibility of a Communist victory, the United States decided to escalate, or increase, its involvement. Some U.S. troops had been serving as advisers to the South Vietnamese since the late 1950s. But their numbers steadily grew, as did the numbers of planes and other military equipment sent to South Vietnam.

U.S. Troops Enter the Fight In August 1964, U.S. President Lyndon Johnson told Congress that North Vietnamese patrol boats had attacked two U.S. destroyers in the Gulf of Tonkin. As a result, Congress authorized the president to send U.S. troops to fight in Vietnam. By late 1965, more than 185,000 U.S. soldiers were in combat on Vietnamese soil. U.S. planes had also begun to bomb North Vietnam. By 1968, more than half a million U.S. soldiers were in combat there.

The United States had the best equipped, most advanced army in the world. Yet it faced two major difficulties. First, U.S. soldiers were fighting a guerrilla war in unfamiliar jungle terrain. Second, the South Vietnamese government that they were defending was becoming more unpopular. At the same time, support for the Vietcong grew, with help and supplies from Ho Chi Minh, the Soviet Union, and China. Unable to win a decisive victory on the ground, the United States turned to air power.

The United States began widespread "carpet bombing" of millions of acres of farmland and forests in an attempt to destroy enemy hideouts and deter guerilla attacks. The bombers spread two deadly chemicals, napalm (a jellied oil product) and Agent Orange (a powerful weed killer). Both had terrible side effects. Napalm killed vegetation but also stuck to humans, burning their skin. Agent Orange did clear the jungles but also destroyed cropland and caused sickness in some farm animals. This bombing strengthened peasants' opposition to the South Vietnamese government and to the American forces inside their country.

The United States Withdraws During the late 1960s, the war grew increasingly unpopular in the United States. Dissatisfied young people began to protest the tremendous loss of life in a conflict on the other side of the world. Bowing to intense public pressure, President Richard Nixon began withdrawing U.S. troops from Vietnam in 1969.

Nixon had a plan called **Vietnamization**. It allowed for U.S. troops to gradually pull out, while the South Vietnamese increased their combat role. To pursue Vietnamization while preserving the South Vietnamese government, Nixon authorized a massive bombing campaign against North Vietnamese bases and supply routes. He also authorized bombings in neighboring Laos and Cambodia to destroy Vietcong hiding places.

In response to protests and political pressure at home, Nixon kept withdrawing U.S. troops. The last left in 1973. Two years later, the North Vietnamese overran South Vietnam. The war ended, but more than 1.5 million Vietnamese and 58,000 Americans had lost their lives.

Reading Check
Analyze Causes
What were two reasons U.S. troops had trouble fighting the war on Vietnamese soil?

Postwar Southeast Asia

War's end did not bring an immediate halt to bloodshed and chaos in Southeast Asia. Cambodia (also known as Kampuchea) was under siege by Communist rebels. During the war, it had suffered U.S. bombing when it was used as a sanctuary by North Vietnamese and Vietcong troops.

Cambodia in Turmoil In 1975, Communist rebels known as the **Khmer Rouge** set up a brutal Communist government under the leadership of Pol Pot. In a ruthless attempt to transform Cambodia into a Communist society, Pol Pot's followers carried out mass killings of 2 million people. This was almost one quarter of the nation's population. The Vietnamese invaded in 1978. They overthrew the Khmer Rouge and installed a less repressive government. But fighting continued. The Vietnamese withdrew in 1989. In 1993, under the supervision of UN peacekeepers, Cambodia adopted a democratic constitution and held free elections.

Vietnam After the War After 1975, the victorious North Vietnamese imposed tight controls over the South. Officials sent thousands of people to "reeducation camps" for training in Communist thought. They nationalized industries and strictly controlled businesses. They also renamed Saigon, the South's former capital, Ho Chi Minh City. Communist oppression caused 1.5 million people to flee Vietnam. Most escaped in dangerously overcrowded ships. More than 200,000 "boat people" died at sea. The survivors often spent months in refugee

The skulls and bones of Cambodian citizens form a haunting memorial to the brutality of its Communist government in the 1970s.

Vietnam Today

Vietnam remains a Communist country. But, like China, it has introduced elements of capitalism into its economy. The changes prompted a Western travel magazine in 1997 to claim that Hanoi, the capital of Vietnam, "jumps with vitality, its streets and shops jammed with locals and handfuls of Western tourists and businesspeople." The photo on the right shows two executives touring the city.

Along Hanoi's shaded boulevards, billboards advertise U.S. and Japanese motorcycles, copiers, video recorders, and soft drinks. On the streets, enterprising Vietnamese business people offer more traditional services. These include bicycle repair, a haircut, a shave, or a tasty snack.

Reading Check
Recognize Effects
What was one of the effects of Pol Pot's efforts to turn Cambodia into a Communist peasant society?

camps in Southeast Asia. About 70,000 eventually settled in the United States or Canada. Although Communists still govern Vietnam, the country now welcomes foreign investment. The United States normalized relations with Vietnam in 1995.

While the superpowers were struggling for advantage during the Korean and Vietnam wars, they also were seeking influence in other parts of the world.

Lesson 3 Assessment

1. **Organize Information** In what ways were the causes and effects of the wars in Korea and Vietnam similar?

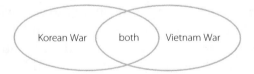

2. **Key Terms and People** For each key term or person in the lesson, write a sentence explaining its significance.

3. **Make Inferences** When President Truman told General MacArthur, "We are trying to prevent a world war, not start one," what did he mean?

4. **Analyze Motives** What role did the policy of containment play in the involvement of the United States in wars in Korea and Vietnam?

5. **Identify Causes** How might imperialism be one of the causes of the Vietnam War?

6. **Form Opinions** Do you think U.S. involvement in Vietnam was justified? Why or why not?

7. **Analyze Motives** Why did the North Vietnamese change the name of Saigon to Ho Chi Minh City?

The Cold War Divides the World

The Big Idea

The superpowers supported opposing sides in Latin American and Middle Eastern conflicts.

Why It Matters Now

Many of these areas today are troubled by political, economic, and military conflict and crisis.

Key Terms and People

Third World
nonaligned nations
Fidel Castro
Anastasio Somoza
Daniel Ortega
Ayatollah Ruholla Khomeini

Setting the Stage

Following World War II, the world's nations were grouped politically into three "worlds." The first was the industrialized capitalist nations, including the United States and its allies. The second was the Communist nations led by the Soviet Union. The **Third World** consisted of developing nations, often newly independent, who were not aligned with either superpower. These nonaligned countries provided yet another arena for competition between the Cold War superpowers.

Fighting for the Third World

The Third World nations were located in Latin America, Asia, and Africa. They were economically poor and politically unstable. This was largely due to a long history of colonialism. They also suffered from ethnic conflicts and lack of technology and education. Each needed a political and economic system around which to build its society. Soviet-style communism and U.S.-style free-market democracy were the main choices.

Cold War Strategies The United States, the Soviet Union, and, in some cases, China, used a variety of techniques to gain influence in the Third World. They backed wars of revolution, liberation, or counterrevolution. The U.S. and Soviet intelligence agencies—the CIA and the KGB—engaged in various covert, or secret, activities, ranging from spying to assassination attempts. The United States also gave military aid, built schools, set up programs to combat poverty, and sent volunteer workers to many developing nations. The Soviets offered military and technical assistance as well as economic aid, mainly to India, Egypt, and newly independent countries in central and west Africa, such as Congo, Angola, and Mozambique.

Association of Nonaligned Nations Other developing nations also needed assistance. They became important

How the Cold War Was Fought

During the Cold War, the United States and the Soviet Union both believed that they needed to stop the other side from extending its power. What differentiated the Cold War from other 20th-century conflicts was that the two enemies did not engage in a shooting war. Instead, they pursued their rivalry by using the strategies shown below.

Egypt built the Aswan High Dam with Soviet aid.

▶ *Explore ONLINE!*

European Alignments, 1955

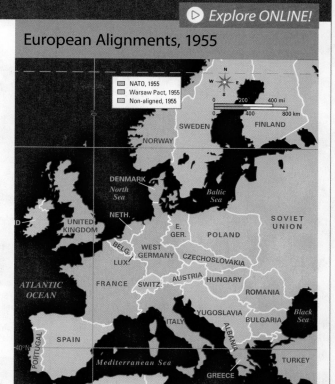

- NATO, 1955
- Warsaw Pact, 1955
- Non-aligned, 1955

MAJOR STRATEGIES OF THE COLD WAR

FOREIGN AID

The two superpowers tried to win allies by giving financial aid to other nations. For instance, Egypt took aid from the Soviet Union to build the Aswan High Dam.

ESPIONAGE

Fearing the enemy might be gaining the advantage, each side spied on the other. One famous incident was the Soviet downing of a U.S. U-2 spy plane in 1960.

MULTINATIONAL ALLIANCES

To gain the support of other nations, both the Soviet Union and the United States entered into alliances. Two examples of this were NATO and the Warsaw Pact (shown on map above).

PROPAGANDA

Both superpowers used propaganda to try to win support overseas. For example, Radio Free Europe broadcast radio programs about the rest of the world into Eastern Europe.

BRINKMANSHIP

The policy of brinkmanship meant going to the brink of war to make the other side back down. One example was the Cuban Missile Crisis.

SURROGATE OR PROXY WARS

The word *surrogate* means "substitute" and *proxy* means "representing someone else." Although the United States and the Soviet Union did not fight each other directly, they fought indirectly by backing opposing sides in many smaller conflicts.

Interpret Visuals

1. **Generalize** Judging from the map, how would you describe the effect on Europe of multinational alliances?

2. **Analyze Motives** What motive did the two superpowers have for fighting surrogate or proxy wars?

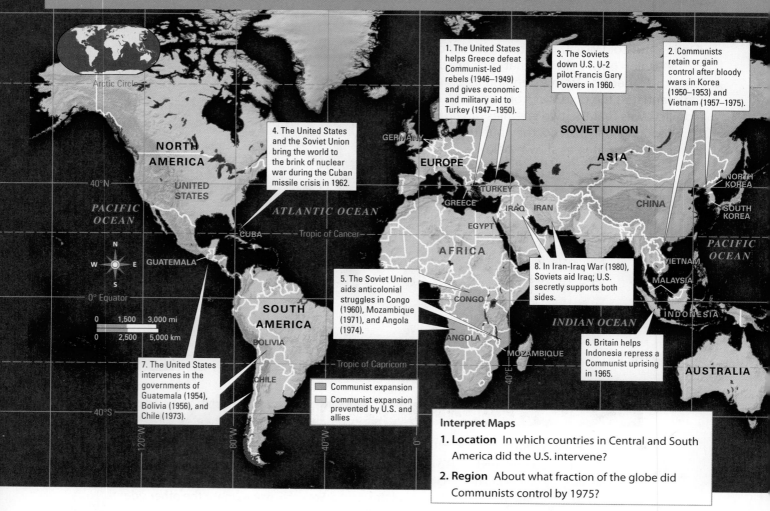

1. The United States helps Greece defeat Communist-led rebels (1946–1949) and gives economic and military aid to Turkey (1947–1950).

2. Communists retain or gain control after bloody wars in Korea (1950–1953) and Vietnam (1957–1975).

3. The Soviets down U.S. U-2 pilot Francis Gary Powers in 1960.

4. The United States and the Soviet Union bring the world to the brink of nuclear war during the Cuban missile crisis in 1962.

5. The Soviet Union aids anticolonial struggles in Congo (1960), Mozambique (1971), and Angola (1974).

6. Britain helps Indonesia repress a Communist uprising in 1965.

7. The United States intervenes in the governments of Guatemala (1954), Bolivia (1956), and Chile (1973).

8. In Iran-Iraq War (1980), Soviets aid Iraq; U.S. secretly supports both sides.

Communist expansion

Communist expansion prevented by U.S. and allies

Interpret Maps

1. **Location** In which countries in Central and South America did the U.S. intervene?

2. **Region** About what fraction of the globe did Communists control by 1975?

players in the Cold War competition between the United States, the Soviet Union, and later, China. But not all Third World countries wished to play a role in the Cold War. For example, India vowed to remain neutral. Indonesia, a populous island nation in Southeast Asia, also struggled to stay uninvolved. In 1955, it hosted many leaders from Asia and Africa at the Bandung Conference. They met to form what they called a "third force" of independent countries, or **nonaligned nations**. Some nations, such as India and Indonesia, maintained their neutrality. Others took sides with the superpowers or played competing sides against each other. For example, Egypt first accepted Soviet aid to help build the Aswan High Dam and Soviet weapons for its conflicts with Israel. Later, Egypt switched allegiance to the United States following the 1973 Yom Kippur War.

Reading Check
Analyze Motives
Why did some nations choose to be nonaligned?

Confrontations in Latin America

After World War II, rapid industrialization, population growth, and a lingering gap between the rich and the poor led Latin American nations to seek aid from both superpowers. At the same time, many of these countries alternated between short-lived democracy and harsh military rule. U.S. involvement in Latin America began long before World War II.

American businesses backed leaders who protected U.S. interests but who also often oppressed their people. After the war, communism and nationalistic feelings inspired revolutionary movements. These found enthusiastic Soviet support. In response, the United States provided military and economic assistance to anti-Communist dictators.

Fidel Castro and the Cuban Revolution In the 1950s, Cuba was ruled by an unpopular dictator, Fulgencio Batista, who had U.S. support. Cuban resentment led to a popular revolution, which overthrew Batista in January 1959. A young lawyer named **Fidel Castro** led that revolution. At first, many people praised Castro for bringing social reforms to Cuba and improving the economy. Yet Castro was a harsh dictator. He suspended elections, jailed or executed his opponents, and tightly controlled the press.

Castro nationalized U.S.-owned sugar mills and refineries. In response, President Eisenhower ordered an embargo on all trade with Cuba. Castro then turned to the Soviets for economic and military aid.

In 1960, the CIA began to train anti-Castro Cuban exiles. In April 1961, they invaded, landing in southwestern Cuba at the Bay of Pigs. However, the United States did not provide the hoped-for air support. Castro's forces easily defeated the invaders, humiliating the United States.

Nuclear Face-off: The Cuban Missile Crisis The failed Bay of Pigs invasion convinced Soviet leader Nikita Khrushchev that the United States would not resist Soviet expansion in Latin America. So, in July 1962, Khrushchev secretly began to build 42 missile sites in Cuba. In October, an American spy plane discovered the sites. President John F. Kennedy declared that missiles so close to the U.S. mainland were a threat. He demanded their removal and also announced a naval blockade of Cuba. Kennedy explained his actions to the American people and the rest of the world in a televised address:

> *"Our policy has been one of patience and restraint, as befits a peaceful and powerful nation which leads a worldwide alliance. We have been determined not to be diverted from our central concerns by mere irritants and fanatics. But now further action is required, and it is under way; and these actions may only be the beginning. We will not prematurely or unnecessarily risk the costs of worldwide nuclear war in which even the fruits of victory would be ashes in our mouth; but neither will we shrink from that risk at any time it must be faced."*
>
> —John F. Kennedy, October 22, 1962

Castro protested that his country was being used as a pawn and that he did not intend for Cuba to get involved in the Cold War. But Castro and Cuba were deeply involved. Kennedy's demand for the removal of Soviet missiles put the United States and the Soviet Union on a collision course. People around the world feared nuclear war. Fortunately, Khrushchev agreed to remove the missiles in return for a U.S. promise not to invade Cuba.

Fidel Castro
(1926–2016)

The son of a wealthy Spanish-Cuban farmer, Fidel Castro became involved in politics at the University of Havana. He first tried to overthrow the Cuban dictator, Batista, in 1953. He was imprisoned but made this vow to continue the struggle for independence:

"Personally, I am not interested in power, nor do I envisage assuming it at any time. All that I will do is to make sure that the sacrifices of so many compatriots should not be in vain."

Despite this declaration, Castro ruled Cuba as a dictator for nearly 50 years. In 2008, his younger brother, Raul Castro, succeeded him as president.

The resolution of the Cuban Missile Crisis left Castro completely dependent on Soviet support. In exchange for this support, Castro backed Communist revolutions in Latin America and Africa. Soviet aid to Cuba, however, ended abruptly with the breakup of the Soviet Union in 1991. This loss dealt a crippling blow to the Cuban economy. Eventually, Castro loosened state control of Cuba's economy and sought better relations with other countries.

Civil War in Nicaragua Just as the United States had supported Batista in Cuba, it had also funded the Nicaraguan dictatorship of **Anastasio Somoza** and his family since 1933. In 1979, Communist Sandinista rebels toppled Somoza's son. Both the United States and the Soviet Union initially gave aid to the Sandinistas and their leader, **Daniel Ortega** (awr•TAY•guh). The Sandinistas, however, gave assistance to other Marxist rebels in nearby El Salvador. To help the El Salvadoran government fight those rebels, the United States supported Nicaraguan anti-Communist forces called the Contras or *contrarevolucionarios*.

The civil war in Nicaragua lasted more than a decade and seriously weakened the country's economy. In 1990, President Ortega agreed to hold free elections, the first in the nation's history. Violeta Chamorro, a reform candidate, defeated him. The Sandinistas also lost elections in 1996 and 2001. However, Ortega won the election once again in 2006 and returned to power.

Reading Check
Analyze Motives
Why did the U.S. switch its support from the Sandinistas to the Contras in Nicaragua?

Coup in Guatemala In 1950, the people of Guatemala elected a new president, Jacobo Arbenz, who promised economic reforms. When Arbenz began a land reform program and nationalized foreign industries in his country, the United States became concerned that his government might turn Communist. President Eisenhower and CIA director Allen Dulles devised a two-part strategy to overthrow Arbenz. First, the CIA began a propaganda campaign that turned the people and the army against their leader. Then, in June 1954, a group of CIA-backed troops led a rebellion and forced Arbenz to flee the country. The U.S.-chosen leader of the military coup, Carlos Castillo Armas, assumed control of the government and promoted American interests in Guatemala.

Confrontations in the Middle East

As the map on page 1146 shows, Cold War confrontations continued to erupt around the globe. The oil-rich Middle East attracted both superpowers.

Religious and Secular Values Clash in Iran Throughout the Middle East, oil industry wealth fueled a growing clash between traditional Islamic values and modern Western materialism. In no country was this cultural conflict more dramatically shown than in Iran (Persia before 1935). After World War II, Iran's leader, Shah Mohammed Reza Pahlavi (PAH•luh•vee), embraced Western governments and wealthy Western oil companies. Iranian nationalists resented these foreign alliances and united under Prime Minister Muhammed Mossadeq (moh•sah•DEHK). They nationalized a British-owned oil company and, in 1953, forced the shah to flee. Fearing Iran might turn to the Soviets for support, the United States helped restore the shah to power.

The United States Supports Secular Rule With U.S. support, the shah westernized his country. By the end of the 1950s, Iran's capital, Tehran, featured gleaming skyscrapers, foreign banks, and modern factories. Millions of Iranians, however, still lived in extreme poverty. The shah tried to weaken the political influence of Iran's conservative Muslim leaders, known as ayatollahs (eye•uh•TOH•luhz), who opposed Western influences. The leader of this religious opposition, **Ayatollah Ruholla Khomeini** (koh•MAY•nee), was living in exile. Spurred by his tape-recorded messages, Iranians rioted in every major city in late 1978. Faced with overwhelming opposition, the shah fled Iran in 1979. A triumphant Khomeini returned to establish an Islamic state and to export Iran's militant form of Islam.

Khomeini's Anti-U.S. Policies Strict adherence to Islam was at the core of Khomeini's domestic policies. But hatred of the United States, because of U.S. support for the shah, was at the heart of his foreign policy. In 1979, with the ayatollah's blessing, young Islamic revolutionaries seized the U.S. embassy in Tehran. They took more than 60 Americans hostage and demanded the United States force the shah to face trial. Most hostages remained prisoners for 444 days before being released in January 1981.

Ayatollah Khomeini (inset) supported the taking of U.S. hostages by Islamic militants in Tehran in 1979.

Khomeini encouraged Muslim radicals elsewhere to overthrow their secular governments. Intended to unify Muslims, this policy heightened tensions between Iran and its neighbor and territorial rival, Iraq. A military leader, Saddam Hussein (hoo•SAYN), governed Iraq as a secular state.

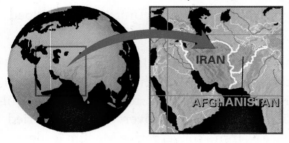

War broke out between Iran and Iraq in 1980. The United States secretly gave aid to both sides because it did not want the balance of power in the region to change. The Soviet Union, on the other hand, had long been a supporter of Iraq. A million Iranians and Iraqis died in the war before the United Nations negotiated a ceasefire in 1988.

The Superpowers Face Off in Afghanistan For several years following World War II, Afghanistan maintained its independence from both the neighboring Soviet Union and from the United States. In the 1950s, however, Soviet influence in the country began to increase. In the late 1970s, a Muslim revolt threatened to topple Afghanistan's Communist regime. This revolt led to a Soviet invasion in 1979.

The Soviets expected to prop up the Afghan Communists and quickly withdraw. Instead, just like the United States in Vietnam, the Soviets found themselves stuck. And like the Vietcong in Vietnam, rebel forces outmaneuvered a military superpower. Supplied with American weapons, the Afghan rebels, called *mujahideen*, or holy warriors, fought on.

Timeline of Events 1920–2005

▶ Explore ONLINE!

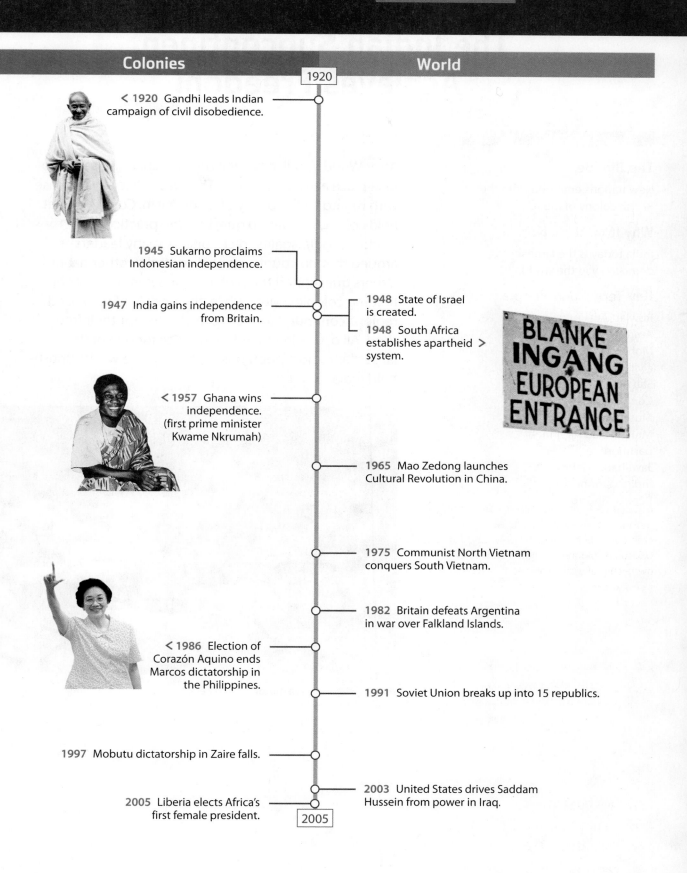

Colonies	World

1920

< **1920** Gandhi leads Indian campaign of civil disobedience.

1945 Sukarno proclaims Indonesian independence.

1947 India gains independence from Britain.

1948 State of Israel is created.

1948 South Africa establishes apartheid > system.

< **1957** Ghana wins independence. (first prime minister Kwame Nkrumah)

1965 Mao Zedong launches Cultural Revolution in China.

1975 Communist North Vietnam conquers South Vietnam.

1982 Britain defeats Argentina in war over Falkland Islands.

< **1986** Election of Corazón Aquino ends Marcos dictatorship in the Philippines.

1991 Soviet Union breaks up into 15 republics.

1997 Mobutu dictatorship in Zaire falls.

2003 United States drives Saddam Hussein from power in Iraq.

2005 Liberia elects Africa's first female president.

2005

BLANKE INGANG EUROPEAN ENTRANCE

The Indian Subcontinent Achieves Freedom

The Big Idea

New nations emerged from the British colony of India.

Why It Matters Now

India today is the largest democracy in the world.

Key Terms and People

Rowlatt Acts
Amritsar Massacre
Mohandas K. Gandhi
civil disobedience
Salt March
Congress Party
Muslim League
Muhammad Ali Jinnah
partition
Jawaharlal Nehru
Indira Gandhi
Benazir Bhutto

Setting the Stage

After World War II, dramatic political changes began to take place across the world. This was especially the case with regard to the policy of colonialism. Countries that held colonies began to question the practice. After the world struggle against dictatorship, many leaders argued that no country should control another nation. Others questioned the high cost and commitment of holding colonies. Meanwhile, the people of colonized regions continued to press even harder for their freedom. All of this led to independence for one of the largest and most populous colonies in the world: British-held India.

Modern-day India is a mix of old and new.

Nationalism Surfaces in India

Growing nationalism led to the founding of two nationalist groups, the primarily Hindu Indian National Congress, or Congress Party, in 1885 and the Muslim League in 1906. At first, such groups concentrated on specific concerns for Indians. By the early 1900s, however, they were calling for self-government. Though deep divisions existed between Hindus and Muslims, they found common ground. They shared the heritage of British rule and an understanding of democratic ideals. These two groups both worked toward the goal of independence from the British.

The nationalists were further inflamed in 1905 by the partition of Bengal. The province was too large for administrative purposes, so the British divided it into a Hindu section and a Muslim section. Keeping the two religious groups apart made it difficult for them to unite in calling for independence. In 1911, the British took back the order and divided the province in a different way.

World War I Increases Nationalist Activity Until World War I, the vast majority of Indians had little interest in nationalism. The situation changed as over a million Indians enlisted in the British army. In return for their service, the British government promised reforms that would eventually lead to self-government.

In 1918, Indian troops returned home from the war. They expected Britain to fulfill its promise. Instead, they were once again treated as second-class citizens. Radical nationalists carried out acts of violence to show their hatred of British rule. To curb dissent, in 1919 the British passed the **Rowlatt Acts**. These laws allowed the government to jail protesters without trial for as long as two years. To Western-educated Indians, denial of a trial by jury violated their individual rights.

BIOGRAPHY

Ram Mohun Roy
(1772–1833)

In the early 1800s, some Indians began demanding more modernization and a greater role in governing themselves. Ram Mohun Roy, a modern-thinking, well-educated Indian, began a campaign to move India away from traditional practices and ideas. Ram Mohun Roy saw arranged child marriages and the rigid caste separation as parts of Indian life that needed to be changed. He believed that if the practices were not changed, India would continue to be controlled by outsiders. Roy's writings inspired other Indian reformers to call for adoption of Western ways. Roy also founded a social reform movement that worked for change in India.

Besides modernization and Westernization, nationalist feelings started to surface in India. Indians hated a system that made them second-class citizens in their own country. They were barred from top posts in the Indian Civil Service. Those who managed to get middle-level jobs were paid less than Europeans. A British engineer on the East India Railway, for example, made nearly 20 times as much money as an Indian engineer.

Amritsar Massacre To protest the Rowlatt Acts, around 10,000 Hindus and Muslims flocked to Amritsar, a major city in the Punjab, in the spring of 1919. At a huge festival in an enclosed square, they intended to fast and pray and to listen to political speeches. The demonstration, viewed as a nationalist outburst, alarmed the British. They were especially concerned about the alliance of Hindus and Muslims.

Most people at the gathering were unaware that the British government had banned public meetings. However, the British commander at Amritsar believed they were openly defying the ban. He ordered his troops to fire on the crowd without warning. The shooting in the enclosed courtyard continued for ten minutes. Official reports showed nearly 400 Indians died and about 1,200 were wounded. Others estimate the numbers were higher.

Reading Check
Recognize Effects
What changes resulted from the Amritsar Massacre?

News of the slaughter, called the **Amritsar Massacre**, sparked an explosion of anger across India. Almost overnight, millions of Indians changed from loyal British subjects into nationalists. These Indians demanded independence.

Gandhi's Tactics of Nonviolence

The massacre at Amritsar set the stage for **Mohandas K. Gandhi** (GAHN·dee) to emerge as the leader of the independence movement. Gandhi's strategy for battling injustice evolved from his deeply religious approach to political activity. His teachings blended ideas from all of the major world religions, including Hinduism, Jainism, Buddhism, Islam, and Christianity. Gandhi attracted millions of followers. Soon they began calling him the Mahatma (muh·HAHT·muh), meaning "great soul."

Noncooperation When the British failed to punish the officers responsible for the Amritsar Massacre, Gandhi urged the Indian National Congress to follow a policy of noncooperation with the British government. In 1920, the Congress Party endorsed **civil disobedience**, the deliberate and public

Gandhi adopted the spinning wheel as a symbol of Indian resistance to British rule. The wheel was featured on the Indian National Congress flag, a forerunner of India's national flag.

refusal to obey an unjust law, and nonviolence as the means to achieve independence. Gandhi then launched his campaign of civil disobedience to weaken the British government's authority and economic power over India.

Boycotts Gandhi called on Indians to refuse to buy British goods, attend government schools, pay British taxes, or vote in elections. Gandhi staged a successful boycott of British cloth, a source of wealth for the British. He urged all Indians to weave their own cloth. Gandhi himself devoted two hours each day to spinning his own yarn on a simple handwheel. He wore only homespun cloth and encouraged Indians to follow his example. As a result of the boycott, the sale of British cloth in India dropped sharply.

DOCUMENT-BASED INVESTIGATION   Historical Sources

Satyagraha

A central element of Gandhi's philosophy of nonviolence was called *satyagraha*, often translated as "soul-force" or "truth-force."

> *"Passive resistance is a method of securing rights by personal suffering; it is the reverse of resistance by arms. When I refuse to do a thing that is repugnant to my conscience, I use soul-force. For instance, the government of the day has passed a law which is applicable to me: I do not like it, if, by using violence, I force the government to repeal the law, I am employing what may be termed body-force. If I do not obey the law and accept the penalty for its breach, I use soul-force. It involves sacrifice of self."*
>
> —Gandhi, Chapter XVII, *Hind Swaraj*

Nonviolence

In *Pledge of Resistance in Transvaal Africa,* 1906, Gandhi offered a warning to those who were contemplating joining the struggle for independence.

> *"[I]t is not at all impossible that we might have to endure every hardship that we can imagine, and wisdom lies in pledging ourselves on the understanding that we shall have to suffer all that and worse. If some one asks me when and how the struggle may end, I may say that if the entire community manfully stands the test, the end will be near. If many of us fall back under storm and stress, the struggle will be prolonged. But I can boldly declare, and with certainty, that so long as there is even a handful of men true to their pledge, there can only be one end to the struggle, and that is victory."*
>
> —Gandhi, *Pledge of Resistance in Transvaal Africa,* 1906

Analyze Historical Sources
1. How is soul-force different from body-force?
2. What do Gandhi's writings suggest about his view of suffering? Give examples from each document.

Strikes and Demonstrations Gandhi's weapon of civil disobedience took an economic toll on the British. They struggled to keep trains running, factories operating, and overcrowded jails from bursting. Throughout 1920, the British arrested thousands of Indians who had participated in strikes and demonstrations. But despite Gandhi's pleas for nonviolence, protests often led to riots.

The Salt March In 1930, Gandhi organized a demonstration to defy the hated Salt Acts. According to these British laws, Indians could buy salt from no other source but the government. They also had to pay sales tax on salt. To show their opposition, Gandhi and his followers walked about 240 miles to the seacoast. There they began to make their own salt by collecting seawater and letting it evaporate. This peaceful protest was called the **Salt March**.

Soon afterward, some demonstrators planned a march to a site where the British government processed salt. They intended to shut this salt-works down. Police officers with steel-tipped clubs attacked the demonstrators. An American journalist was an eyewitness to the event. He described the "sickening whacks of clubs on unprotected skulls" and people "writhing in pain with fractured skulls or broken shoulders." Still the people continued to march peacefully, refusing to defend themselves against their attackers. Newspapers across the globe carried the journalist's story, which won worldwide support for Gandhi's independence movement.

More demonstrations against the salt tax took place throughout India. Eventually, about 60,000 people, including Gandhi, were arrested.

Reading Check
Make Inferences
How did the Salt March represent Gandhi's methods for change?

Britain Grants Limited Self-Rule

Gandhi and his followers gradually reaped the rewards of their civil disobedience campaigns and gained greater political power for the Indian people. In 1935, the British Parliament passed the Government of India Act. It provided local self-government and limited democratic elections but not total independence.

However, the Government of India Act also fueled mounting tensions between Muslims and Hindus. These two groups had conflicting visions of India's future as an independent nation. Indian Muslims, outnumbered by Hindus, feared that Hindus would control India if it won independence.

A Movement Toward Independence The British had ruled India for almost two centuries. Indian resistance to Britain intensified in 1939, when Britain committed India's armed forces to World War II without first consulting the colony's elected representatives. The move left Indian nationalists stunned and humiliated. Indian leader Mohandas Gandhi launched a nonviolent campaign of noncooperation with the British. Officials imprisoned numerous nationalists for this action. In 1942, the British tried to gain the support of the nationalists by promising governmental changes after the war. But the offer did not include Indian independence.

Muhammad Ali Jinnah

As they intensified their struggle against the British, Indians also struggled with each other. The Indian National Congress, or the **Congress Party**, was India's national political party. Most members of the Congress Party were Hindus, but the party at times had many Muslim members.

In competition with the Congress Party was the **Muslim League**, an organization founded to protect Muslim interests. Members of the league felt that the mainly Hindu Congress Party looked out primarily for Hindu interests. The leader of the Muslim League, **Muhammad Ali Jinnah** (mu•HAM•ihd-ah•LEE-JIHN•uh), insisted that all Muslims resign from the Congress Party. The Muslim League stated that it would never accept Indian independence if it meant rule by the Hindu-dominated Congress Party. Jinnah stated, "The only thing the Muslim has in common with the Hindu is his slavery to the British."

Reading Check
Summarize What were the two main political parties and two main religions in India during this period?

Freedom Brings Turmoil

When World War II ended, Britain found itself faced with enormous war debts. As a result, British leaders began to rethink the expense of maintaining and governing distant colonies. With India continuing to push for independence, the stage was set for the British to hand over power. However, a key problem emerged: Who should receive the power—Hindus or Muslims?

Partition and Bloodshed Muslims resisted attempts to include them in an Indian government dominated by Hindus. Rioting between the two groups broke out in several Indian cities. In August 1946, four days of clashes in Calcutta left more than 5,000 people dead and more than 15,000 hurt.

British officials soon became convinced that partition, an idea first proposed by India's Muslims, would be the only way to ensure a safe and secure region. **Partition** was the term given to the division of India into separate Hindu and Muslim nations. The northwest and eastern regions of India, where most Muslims lived, would become the new nation of Pakistan. Pakistan comprised two separate states in 1947: West Pakistan and East Pakistan. (See map, The Indian Subcontinent, 1947.)

The British House of Commons passed an act on July 16, 1947, that granted two nations, India and Pakistan, independence in one month's time. In that short period, more than 500 independent native princes had to decide which nation they would join. The administration of the courts, the military, the railways, and the police—the whole of the civil service—had to be divided down to the last paper clip. Most difficult of all, millions of Indian citizens—Hindus, Muslims, and yet another significant religious group, the Sikhs—had to decide where to go.

During the summer of 1947, 10 million people were on the move in the Indian subcontinent. As people scrambled to relocate, violence among the different religious groups erupted. Muslims killed Sikhs who were

The Indian Subcontinent, 1947

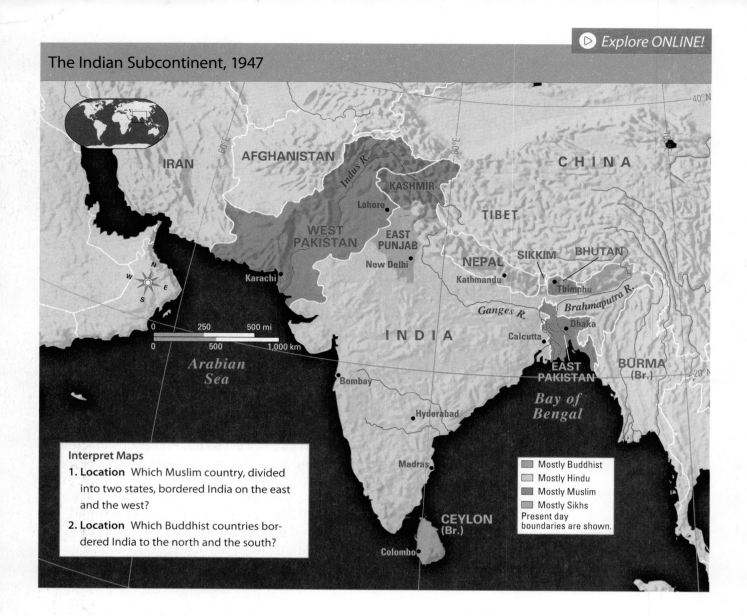

IRAN

AFGHANISTAN

CHINA

Indus R.

KASHMIR

Lahore

TIBET

WEST PAKISTAN

EAST PUNJAB

New Delhi

NEPAL

SIKKIM

BHUTAN

Kathmandu

Thimphu

Brahmaputra R.

Karachi

Ganges R.

Dhaka

I N D I A

Calcutta

EAST PAKISTAN

BURMA (Br.)

Arabian Sea

Bombay

Bay of Bengal

Hyderabad

Madras

CEYLON (Br.)

Colombo

Interpret Maps

1. **Location** Which Muslim country, divided into two states, bordered India on the east and the west?

2. **Location** Which Buddhist countries bordered India to the north and the south?

Mostly Buddhist
Mostly Hindu
Mostly Muslim
Mostly Sikhs
Present day boundaries are shown.

moving into India. Hindus and Sikhs killed Muslims who were headed into Pakistan. In all, an estimated 1 million died.

"What is there to celebrate?" Gandhi mourned. "I see nothing but rivers of blood." Gandhi personally went to the Indian capital of Delhi to plead for fair treatment of Muslim refugees. While there, he himself became a victim of the nation's violence. A Hindu extremist who thought Gandhi too protective of Muslims shot and killed him on January 30, 1948.

The Battle for Kashmir As if partition itself didn't result in enough bloodshed between India's Muslims and Hindus, the two groups quickly squared off over the small region of Kashmir. Kashmir lay at the northern point of India next to Pakistan. Although its ruler was Hindu, Kashmir had a majority Muslim population. Shortly after independence, India and Pakistan began battling each other for control of the region. The fighting continued until the United Nations arranged a ceasefire in 1949. The ceasefire left a third of Kashmir under Pakistani control and the rest under Indian control. The two countries continue to fight over the region today.

Reading Check
Analyze Causes
What was the cause of the conflict between India and Pakistan over Kashmir?

The Coldest War

No part of Kashmir is beyond a fight for India and Pakistan—including the giant Siachen glacier high above the region. The dividing line established by the 1949 cease-fire did not extend to the glacier because officials figured neither side would try to occupy such a barren and frigid strip of land.

They figured wrong. In 1984, both sides sent troops to take the glacier, and they have been dug in ever since. At altitudes nearing 21,000 feet, Indian and Pakistani soldiers shoot at each other from trenches in temperatures that reach 70 degrees below zero. This bitterly cold war was interrupted in 2003 when Pakistan and India declared a cease-fire.

Modern India

With the granting of its independence on August 15, 1947, India became the world's largest democracy. As the long-awaited hour of India's freedom approached, **Jawaharlal Nehru** became the independent nation's first prime minister.

Nehru Leads India Nehru served as India's leader for its first 17 years of independence. He had been one of Gandhi's most devoted followers. Educated in Britain, Nehru won popularity among all groups in India. He emphasized democracy, unity, and economic modernization. Unlike Gandhi, he promoted industrialization as the key to improving India's economy. After independence, he worked to enhance India's heavy manufacturing industries.

Nehru used his leadership to move India forward. He led other newly independent nations of the world in forming an alliance of countries that were neutral in the Cold War conflicts between the United States and the Soviet Union. On the home front, Nehru called for a reorganization of the states by language. He also pushed for industrialization and sponsored social reforms. He tried to elevate the status of the lower castes, or those at the bottom of society, and help women gain the rights promised by the constitution.

Vocabulary
neutralism/ nonalignment a policy in which a nation does not side with any major powers

— BIOGRAPHY —

Jawaharlal Nehru
(1889–1964)

Nehru's father was an influential attorney, and so the first prime minister of India grew up amid great wealth. As a young man, he lived and studied in England. "In my likes and dislikes I was perhaps more an Englishman than an Indian," he once remarked.

Upon returning to India, however, he became moved by the horrible state in which many of his fellow Indians lived. "A new picture of India seemed to rise before me," he recalled, "naked, starving, crushed, and utterly miserable." From then on, he devoted his life to improving conditions in his country.

A Turbulent History

< 1977
Ali Bhutto
Prime Minister Ali Bhutto of Pakistan is deposed in a coup led by General Zia. Bhutto is later hanged for having ordered the assassination of a political opponent.

1988
General Zia, president of Pakistan, dies in a mysterious plane crash.

< 2007
Benazir Bhutto
Ali Bhutto's daughter also comes to a violent end, the victim of a suicide bomber while campaigning for parliamentary elections.

1999
General Pervez Musharraf seizes control of government in a military coup.

Pakistan   1970   1980   1990   2000   2010

India

< 1984
Indira Gandhi
Indira Gandhi is gunned down by two of her Sikh bodyguards. Her murder is in retaliation for an attack she ordered on a Sikh temple.

< 1991
Rajiv Gandhi
Rajiv Gandhi is killed by a bomb while campaigning. The bomb is carried by a woman opposed to Gandhi's policies.

2008
Ten gunmen attack the Indian city of Mumbai; more than 170 are killed. The attack was planned in and staged from Pakistan, which raises tensions between the two nations.

Troubled Times Nehru died in 1964. His death left the Congress Party with no leader strong enough to hold together the many political factions that had emerged with India's independence. Then, in 1966, Nehru's daughter, **Indira Gandhi**, was chosen prime minister. After a short spell out of office, she was reelected in 1980.

Although she ruled capably, Gandhi faced many challenges, including the growing threat from Sikh extremists who themselves wanted an independent state. The Golden Temple at Amritsar stood as the religious center for the Sikhs. From there, Sikh nationalists ventured out to attack symbols of Indian authority. In June 1984, Indian army troops overran the Golden Temple. They killed about 500 Sikhs and destroyed sacred property. In retaliation, Sikh bodyguards assigned to Indira Gandhi gunned her down. This violent act was met by a murderous frenzy that led to the deaths of thousands of Sikhs.

In the wake of the murder of Indira Gandhi, her son, Rajiv (rah•JEEV) Gandhi, took over as prime minister. His party, however, lost its power in 1989 because of accusations of widespread corruption. In 1991, while campaigning again for prime minister near the town of Madras, Rajiv was killed by a bomb. Members of a group opposed to his policies claimed responsibility.

Twenty-first Century Challenges India's prime minister, Manmohan Singh, is a Sikh—the first non-Hindu to hold the job. He and his nation face a number of problems. Simmering religious tensions still occasionally boil over in episodes of violence and reprisal. Also, India's population continues to increase and is expected to surpass that of China by 2035. More acutely, Maoist rebels in the nation's eastern states continue to pose a serious military threat to the government's authority.

Even more troubling are India's tense relations with its neighbor Pakistan and the fact that both have become nuclear powers. In 1974, India exploded a "peaceful" nuclear device. For the next 24 years, the nation quietly worked on building up its nuclear capability. In 1998, Indian officials conducted five underground nuclear tests. Meanwhile, the Pakistanis had been building their own nuclear program. Shortly after India conducted its nuclear tests, Pakistan demonstrated that it too had nuclear weapons. The presence of these weapons in the hands of such bitter enemies and neighbors has become a matter of great international concern, especially in light of their continuing struggle over Kashmir.

In 2002, the two nations came close to war over Kashmir. However, in 2003 a peace process began to ease tension. From 2004 to 2014, the Congress Party led the nation. The Congress Party focused on jobs and the economy, but still the economy worsened. When this happened, voters deserted the Congress Party. In 2014, two-thirds of the people voted for the Bharatiya Janata Party (BJP) candidate, Narenda Modi. The BJP is a pro-Hindu party.

Reading Check
Analyze Challenges
What are some of the issues modern-day India must face?

Pakistan Copes with Freedom

The history of Pakistan since independence has been no less turbulent than that of India. Pakistan actually began as two separate and divided states, East Pakistan and West Pakistan. East Pakistan lay to the east of India, West Pakistan to the northwest. These regions were separated by more than 1,000 miles of Indian territory. In culture, language, history, geography, economics, and ethnic background, the two regions were very different. Only the Islamic religion united them.

Civil War From the beginning, the two regions of Pakistan experienced strained relations. While East Pakistan had the larger population, it was often ignored by West Pakistan, home to the central government. In 1970, a giant cyclone and tidal wave struck East Pakistan and killed an estimated 266,000 residents. While international aid poured into Pakistan, the government in West Pakistan did not quickly transfer that aid to East Pakistan. Demonstrations broke out in East Pakistan, and protesters called for an end to all ties with West Pakistan.

On March 26, 1971, East Pakistan declared itself an independent nation called Bangladesh. A civil war followed between Bangladesh and Pakistan. Eventually, Indian forces stepped in and sided with Bangladesh. Pakistani forces surrendered. More than 1 million people died in the war. Pakistan lost about one-seventh of its area and about one-half of its population to Bangladesh.

A Pattern of Instability Muhammad Ali Jinnah, the first governor-general of Pakistan, died shortly after independence. Beginning in 1958, Pakistan went through a series of military coups. Ali Bhutto took control of the country following the civil war. A military coup in 1977 led by General Zia removed Bhutto, who was later executed for crimes allegedly committed while in office.

After Zia's death, Bhutto's daughter, **Benazir Bhutto**, was twice elected prime minister. However, she was removed from office in 1996. Nawaz Sharif became prime minister after the 1997 elections. In 1999, army leaders led by General Pervez Musharraf ousted Sharif in yet another coup and imposed military rule over Pakistan. By 2007, however, he faced growing political opposition at home. Meanwhile, Benazir Bhutto had returned from exile abroad, only to be assassinated in December 2007. By August 2008, Musharraf had resigned, with Bhutto's widower, Asif Ali Zardari, winning the presidency the following month.

In 2010, Pakistan endured the worst floods in recorded history. The disaster led to food and water shortages, disease, looting, and transportation and communications problems. Pakistan is a nation that relies on agriculture. The floods destroyed farmland and killed farm animals, which led to shortages of food and raw materials.

In 2011, U.S. forces located the leader of the al-Qaeda network, Osama bin Laden, in a city near Islamabad in Pakistan. On May 2, the U.S. military staged an operation in which bin Laden was killed. Before the operation, Pakistani officials had denied that bin Laden was living in Pakistan. The U.S. military action increased distrust between the United States and Pakistan. In 2013, Nawaz Sharif entered his third term as prime minister.

Bangladesh and Sri Lanka Struggle

Meanwhile, the newly created nations of Bangladesh and Sri Lanka struggled with enormous problems of their own in the decades following independence.

Bangladesh Faces Many Problems The war with Pakistan had ruined the economy of Bangladesh and fractured its communications system. Rebuilding the shattered country seemed like an overwhelming task. Sheik Mujibur Rahman became the nation's first prime minister. He soon took over all authority and declared Bangladesh a one-party state. In August 1975, military leaders assassinated him.

Over the years Bangladesh has attempted with great difficulty to create a more democratic form of government. Charges of election fraud and government corruption are common. In recent years, however, the government has become more stable.

Reading Check
Compare How does the history of Pakistan in 1971 parallel the history of India in 1947?

Poverty Levels in Asia

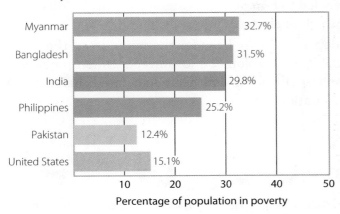

Country	Percentage
Myanmar	32.7%
Bangladesh	31.5%
India	29.8%
Philippines	25.2%
Pakistan	12.4%
United States	15.1%

Percentage of population in poverty

Source: *The World Factbook* 2013–14. Washington, DC: Central Intelligence Agency, 2013.

Overcrowded and poor villages are a common sight throughout Bangladesh.

Bangladesh also has had to cope with crippling natural disasters. Bangladesh is a low-lying nation that is subject to many cyclones and tidal waves. Massive storms regularly flood the land, ruin crops and homes, and take lives. A cyclone in 1991 killed approximately 139,000 people. Such catastrophes, along with a rapidly growing population, have put much stress on the country's economy. Bangladesh is one of the poorest nations in the world. The per capita income there is about $360 per year. About half the workers are employed in agriculture and fishing jobs.

This emblem of the separatist group Liberation Tigers of Tamil Eelam represents the struggle for independence of the Tamils.

Civil Strife Grips Sri Lanka Another newly freed and deeply troubled country on the Indian subcontinent is Sri Lanka, a small, teardrop-shaped island nation just off the southeast coast of India. Formerly known as Ceylon, Sri Lanka gained its independence from Britain in February 1948. Two main ethnic groups dominate the nation. Three-quarters of the population are Sinhalese, who are Buddhists. One-fifth are Tamils, a Hindu people of southern India and northern Sri Lanka.

Sri Lanka's recent history has also been one of turmoil. A militant group of Tamils has long fought an armed struggle for a separate Tamil nation. Since 1981, thousands of lives have been lost. In an effort to end the violence, Rajiv Gandhi and the Sri Lankan president tried to reach an accord in 1987. The agreement called for Indian troops to enter Sri Lanka and help disarm Tamil rebels. This effort was unsuccessful, and Indian troops left in 1990. But in 2009, a government military offensive decisively defeated Tamil separatist forces.

Sri Lanka began to recover from its long civil war. The economy grew, and at first the government had strong support. The parliament amended Sri Lanka's constitution to give the president greater powers. Over time, however, these greater powers led to human rights abuses against Tamils. In an upset victory in 2015, voters elected a new president.

As difficult as postindependence has been for the countries of the Indian subcontinent, other former colonies encountered similar problems. A number of formerly held territories in Southeast Asia faced challenges as they became independent nations.

Reading Check
Compare and Contrast What issues do Bangladesh and Sri Lanka face?

Lesson 1 Assessment

1. **Organize Information** Make a timeline, similar to the one shown, that lists the leaders of India and Pakistan. What tragic connection did many of the leaders share?

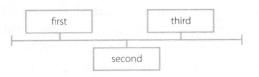

2. **Key Terms and People** For each key term or person in the lesson, write a sentence explaining its significance.

3. **Draw Conclusions** Why did British officials partition India into India and Pakistan?

4. **Synthesize** Why might India's political and economic success be so crucial to the future of democracy in Asia?

5. **Analyze Issues** How did religious and cultural differences create problems for newly emerging nations?

6. **Draw Conclusions** What is the main cause today of civil strife in Sri Lanka?

7. **Synthesize** How did imperialism contribute to unity and to the growth of nationalism in India?

Southeast Asian Nations Gain Independence

The Big Idea

Former colonies in Southeast Asia worked to build new governments and economies.

Why It Matters Now

The power and influence of the Pacific Rim nations are likely to expand during the next century.

Key Terms and People

Ferdinand Marcos
Corazón Aquino
Aung San Suu Kyi
Sukarno
Suharto

Setting the Stage

World War II had a significant impact on the colonized groups of Southeast Asia. During the war, the Japanese seized much of Southeast Asia from the European nations that had controlled the region for many years. The Japanese conquest helped the people of Southeast Asia see that the Europeans were far from invincible. When the war ended and the Japanese themselves had been forced out, many Southeast Asians refused to live again under European rule. They called for and won their independence, and a series of new nations emerged.

A floating market in Bangkok, Thailand

The Philippines Achieves Independence

The Philippines became the first of the world's colonies to achieve independence following World War II. The United States granted the Philippines independence in 1946, on the anniversary of its own Declaration of Independence, the Fourth of July.

The United States and the Philippines The Filipinos' immediate goals were to rebuild the economy and to restore the capital of Manila. The city had been badly damaged in World War II. The United States had promised the Philippines $620 million in war damages. However, the U.S. government insisted that Filipinos approve the Bell Act in order to get the money. This act would establish free trade between the United States and the Philippines for eight years, to be followed by gradually increasing tariffs. Filipinos were worried that American businesses would exploit the resources and environment of the Philippines. In spite of this concern, Filipinos approved the Bell Act and received their money.

The United States also wanted to maintain its military presence in the Philippines. With the onset of the Cold War, the United States needed to protect its interests in Asia. Both China and the Soviet Union were rivals of the United States at the time. Both were Pacific powers with bases close to allies of the United States and to resources vital to U.S. interests. Therefore, the United States demanded a 99-year lease on its military and naval bases in the Philippines. The bases, Clark Air Force Base and Subic Bay Naval Base near Manila, proved to be critical to the United States later in the staging of the Korean and Vietnam wars.

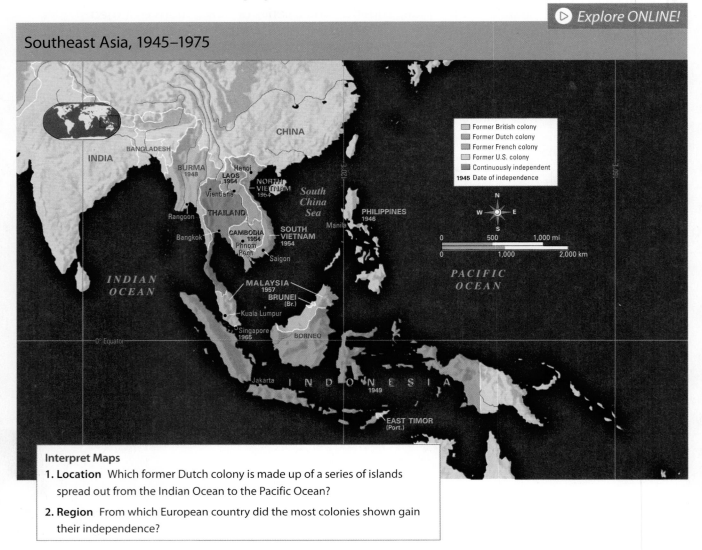

▷ *Explore ONLINE!*

Southeast Asia, 1945–1975

Interpret Maps

1. **Location** Which former Dutch colony is made up of a series of islands spread out from the Indian Ocean to the Pacific Ocean?

2. **Region** From which European country did the most colonies shown gain their independence?

These military bases also became the single greatest source of conflict between the United States and the Philippines. Many Filipinos regarded the bases as proof of American imperialism. Later agreements shortened the terms of the lease, and the United States gave up both bases in 1992.

After World War II, the Philippine government was still almost completely dependent on the United States economically and politically. The Philippine government looked for ways to lessen this dependency. It welcomed Japanese investments. It also broadened its contacts with Southeast Asian neighbors and with nonaligned nations.

From Marcos to Ramos **Ferdinand Marcos** was elected president of the Philippines in 1965. The country suffered under his rule from 1966 to 1986. Marcos imposed an authoritarian regime and stole millions of dollars from the public treasury. Although the constitution limited Marcos to eight years in office, he got around this restriction by imposing martial law from 1972 to 1981. Two years later, his chief opponent, Benigno Aquino, Jr., was assassinated as he returned from the United States to the Philippines, lured by the promise of coming elections.

In the elections of 1986, Aquino's widow, **Corazón Aquino**, challenged Marcos. Aquino won decisively, but Marcos refused to acknowledge her victory. When he declared himself the official winner, a public outcry resulted. He was forced into exile in Hawaii, where he later died. In 1995, the Philippines succeeded in recovering $475 million Marcos had stolen from his country and deposited in Swiss banks.

During Aquino's presidency, the Philippine government ratified a new constitution. It also negotiated successfully with the United States to end the lease on the U.S. military bases. In 1992, Fidel V. Ramos succeeded Aquino as president. Ramos was restricted by the constitution to a single six-year term. The single-term limit is intended to prevent the abuse of power that occurred during Marcos's 20-year rule.

As she took the oath of office, Aquino promised to usher in a more open and democratic form of government:

Reading Check
Use context clues to explain the meaning of the word *vigilance* in the quotation by Corazón Aquino.

Historical Source

"I pledge a government dedicated to upholding truth and justice, morality and decency in government, freedom and democracy. I ask our people not to relax, but to maintain more vigilance in this, our moment of triumph. The Motherland can't thank them enough, yet we all realize that more is required of each of us to achieve a truly just society for our people. This is just the beginning."

—Corazón Aquino, *inaugural speech, Feb. 24, 1986*

Analyze Sources
According to Aquino, what is needed to achieve a just society?

This cartoon is showing the political situation in the Philippines as a mess that Corazón Aquino needed to clean up when she was elected president.

The Government Battles Rebels

Since gaining its independence, the Philippines has had to battle its own separatist group. For centuries, the southern part of the country has been a stronghold of Muslims known as the Moros. In the early 1970s, a group of Moros formed the Moro National Liberation Front (MNLF). They began an armed struggle for independence from Philippine rule.

In 1996, the government and rebels agreed to a cease-fire, and the Moros were granted an autonomous region in the southern Philippines. The agreement, however, did not satisfy a splinter group of the MNLF called Abu Sayyaf. These rebels have continued fighting the government, often using terror tactics to try to achieve their goals. In 2000, they kidnapped 21 people including foreign tourists. While the group eventually was freed, subsequent kidnappings and bombings by Abu Sayyaf have killed and injured hundreds of people. President Gloria Macapagal Arroyo launched an all-out military response to this group. The United States provided military assistance to the government's efforts.

Arroyo faced widespread crime, including kidnappings. She was accused of corruption, which led to two attempted coups in 2003 and 2006. After the 2006 coup attempt, Arroyo banned public demonstrations. Many people looked upon this action as evidence of her authoritarian rule.

In 2010, the people elected as president Benigno S. Aquino III, son of Corazón Aquino. He faced many issues, including a powerful typhoon in 2013, which killed thousands of people and left hundreds of thousands homeless.

British Colonies Gain Independence

Britain's timetable for granting independence to its Southeast Asian colonies depended on local circumstances. Burma had been pressing for independence from Britain for decades. It became a sovereign republic in 1948. In 1989, Burma was officially named Myanmar (mee•AHN•mahr), its name in the Burmese language.

Burma Experiences Turmoil After gaining freedom, Burma suffered one political upheaval after another. Its people struggled between repressive military governments and prodemocracy forces. Conflict among Communists and ethnic minorities also disrupted the nation. In 1962, General Ne Win set up a military government, with the goal of making Burma a socialist state. Although Ne Win stepped down in 1988, the military continued to rule repressively.

Reading Check
Make Inferences
Why might the United States have been interested in maintaining military bases in the Philippines?

In 1988, **Aung San Suu Kyi** (owng sahn soo chee) returned to Burma after many years abroad. Her father was Aung San, a leader of the Burmese nationalists' army killed years before by political rivals. Aung San Suu Kyi became active in the newly formed National League for Democracy (NLD). For her prodemocracy activities, she was placed under house arrest for six years by the government. In the 1990 election—the country's first multiparty election in 30 years—the National League for Democracy won 80 percent of the seats. The military government refused to recognize the election, and it kept Aung San Suu Kyi under house arrest. She was finally released in 1995, only to be placed under house arrest again in 2000. Freed in 2002, she was detained again in 2003. In June 2007, Aung San Suu Kyi's house arrest was extended.

In 2010, Burma passed new laws. Among other things, the laws said that people married to foreign nationals could not run for political office. This law disqualified Aung San Suu Kyi, who was married to a British citizen, from running for office. Most international groups, including the United Nations, thought that the 2010 election was not fair. Aung San Suu Kyi was released from house arrest six days after the election.

On February 4, 2011, members of the legislature elected Thein Sein, a former general, president of Myanmar. Thein Sein made many reforms. He removed restrictions on the press and released many political prisoners. He allowed unions to form, and people to demonstrate peacefully. He even relaxed the restrictions on Aung San Suu Kyi.

In December, the NLD became an official party. In 2012, Aung San Suu Kyi ran for office. She and other NLD candidates won 43 of 45 seats. Since the elections, the United States and European Union have lifted restrictions on Myanmar. In addition, Myanmar officials are working to increase investment in the nation and to attract tourists.

> **Vocabulary**
> **house arrest**
> confinement to one's quarters, or house, rather than to prison

---

Aung San Suu Kyi
(1945–)

Aung San Suu Kyi won the Nobel Peace Prize in 1991 for her efforts to establish democracy in Myanmar. She could not accept the award in person, however, because she was still under house arrest.

The Nobel Prize committee said that in awarding her the peace prize, it intended the following:

to show its support for the many people throughout the world who are striving to attain democracy, human rights, and ethnic conciliation by peaceful means. Suu Kyi's struggle is one of the most extraordinary examples of civil courage in Asia in recent decades.

Malaysia and Singapore During World War II, the Japanese conquered the Malay Peninsula, formerly ruled by the British. The British returned to the peninsula after the Japanese defeat in 1945. They tried, unsuccessfully, to organize the different peoples of Malaya into one state. They also struggled to put down a Communist uprising. Ethnic groups resisted British efforts to unite their colonies on the peninsula and in the northern part of the island of Borneo. Malays were a slight majority on the peninsula, while Chinese were the largest group on the southern tip, the island of Singapore.

In 1957, officials created the Federation of Malaya from Singapore, Malaya, Sarawak, and Sabah. The two regions—on the Malay Peninsula and on northern Borneo—were separated by 400 miles of ocean. In 1965, Singapore separated from the federation and became an independent city-state. The federation, consisting of Malaya, Sarawak, and Sabah, became known as Malaysia. A coalition of many ethnic groups maintained steady economic progress in Malaysia.

Singapore, which has one of the busiest ports in the world, has become an extremely prosperous nation. Lee Kuan Yew ruled Singapore as prime minister from 1959 to 1990. Under his guidance, Singapore emerged as a banking center as well as a center of trade. It had a standard of living far higher than any of its Southeast Asian neighbors. In 2011, the Geneva World Economic Forum listed the world's strongest economies. Singapore's economy ranked third, behind Switzerland and Sweden and ahead of the United States, Germany, and Japan.

In addition, efforts are underway in Singapore to make health care, public housing, and education more affordable for all of its people. A national health care plan went into effect at the end of 2015.

Reading Check
Make Inferences
What do the top economies listed by the Geneva World Economic Forum have in common?

Indonesia Gains Independence from the Dutch

Like members of other European nations, the Dutch, who ruled the area of Southeast Asia known as Indonesia, saw their colonial empire crumble with the onset of World War II. The Japanese conquered the region and destroyed the Dutch colonial order. When the war ended and the defeated Japanese were forced to leave, the people of Indonesia moved to establish a free nation.

Sukarno Leads the Independence Movement Leading the effort to establish an independent Indonesia was **Sukarno** (soo•KAHR•noh), known only by his one name. In August 1945, two days after the Japanese surrendered, Sukarno proclaimed Indonesia's independence and named himself president. A guerrilla army backed him. The Dutch, supported initially by Britain and the United States, attempted to regain control of Indonesia. But after losing the support of the United Nations and the United States, the Dutch agreed to grant Indonesia its independence in 1949.

The new Indonesia became the world's fourth most populous nation. It consisted of more than 13,600 islands, with 300 different ethnic groups, 250 languages, and most of the world's major religions. It contained the world's largest Islamic population. Sukarno, who took the official title of "life-time president," attempted to guide this diverse nation in a parliamentary democracy.

Vocabulary
coup the sudden overthrow of a government by a small group of people

Instability and Turmoil Sukarno's efforts to build a stable democratic nation were unsuccessful. He was not able to manage Indonesia's economy, and the country slid downhill rapidly. Foreign banks refused to lend money to Indonesia, and inflation occasionally soared as high as 1,000 percent. In 1965, a group of junior army officers attempted a coup. A general named **Suharto** (suh•HAHR•toh) put down the rebellion. He then seized power for himself and began a bloodbath in which 500,000 to 1 million Indonesians were killed.

Suharto, officially named president in 1967, turned Indonesia into a police state and imposed frequent periods of martial law. Outside observers heavily criticized him for his annexation of nearby East Timor in 1976 and for human rights violations there. Suharto's government also showed little tolerance for religious freedoms.

Bribery and corruption became commonplace. The economy improved under Suharto for a while, but from 1997 through 1998 the nation suffered one of the worst financial crises in its history. Growing unrest over both government repression and a crippling economic crisis prompted Suharto to step down in 1998. While turmoil continued to grip the country, it moved slowly toward democracy. The daughter of Sukarno, Megawati Sukarnoputri, was elected to the presidency in 2001.

Upon taking office, the new president hailed the virtues of democracy:

DOCUMENT-BASED INVESTIGATION Historical Source

Excerpt from Megawati Sukarnoputri's Inaugural Speech

"Democracy requires sincerity and respect for the rules of the game. Beginning my duty, I urge all groups to sincerely and openly accept the outcome of the democratic process . . . . In my opinion, respect for the people's voice, sincerity in accepting it, and respect for the rules of game are the main pillars of democracy which we will further develop. I urge all Indonesians to look forward to the future and unite to improve the life and our dignity as a nation."

—Megawati Sukarnoputri, July 23, 2001

Analyze Historical Sources
According to Sukarnoputri, what are the cornerstones of democracy?

Changing Times in Southeast Asia

As you have read, many countries in Southeast Asia have undergone revolutionary changes in their political and social organization. The region continues to struggle with its past and to face new challenges, but democratic reforms are becoming more common.

The past and present exist side by side throughout much of Southeast Asia. For an increasing number of Southeast Asians, housing, transportation, even purchasing food are a mixture of old and new. These images explore the differences between traditional and modern, rich and poor, past and present.

▲ HOUSING

The luxury apartment building (background) in Jakarta, Indonesia, towers over the shabby and polluted slum of Muarabaru (foreground). Indonesia declared its independence in 1945 but was not recognized by the United Nations until 1950. Since independence, Indonesians have enjoyed relative economic prosperity, but bridging the gap between rich and poor is an issue that faces Indonesia and much of Southeast Asia.

TRANSPORTATION

The water buffalo-drawn cart (above) is a common sight in rural Thailand. It is a mode of transport that reaches deep into the past.

In Bangkok, Thailand (right)—with its cars, motorcycles, and public buses—transportation is very different. These distinctly past and present modes of transportation symbolize the changes many Southeast Asian countries are facing.

SOUTHEAST ASIA

GEOGRAPHY

- Eleven countries are generally referred to as Southeast Asia: Brunei, Cambodia, East Timor, Indonesia, Laos, Malaysia, Myanmar, the Philippines, Singapore, Thailand, and Vietnam.

POPULATION

- About 9 percent of the world's population lives in Southeast Asia.
- Indonesia is the world's fourth most populous country, behind China, India, and the United States.

ECONOMICS

- Ten Southeast Asian nations— Indonesia, Malaysia, the Philippines, Singapore, Brunei, Cambodia, Laos, Vietnam, Myanmar, and Thailand—make up a trading alliance known as the Association of South-East Asian Nations (ASEAN).

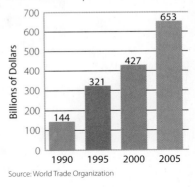

ASEAN Exports, 1990–2005

Source: World Trade Organization

MARKETS

As the postcolonial economies of Southeast Asia grow, traditional markets, like the floating market in Thailand (above), give way to the modern convenience of stores with prepackaged foods, like this street-side store (below) in Vietnam.

Critical Thinking

1. **Draw Conclusions** Why might some countries in Southeast Asia have more successful economies than others?

2. **Form and Support Opinions** Are the issues facing Southeast Asians discussed here also a concern for Americans? Why or why not?

An earthquake off the coast of Indonesia on December 26, 2004, triggered a devastating tsunami. The tidal waves and floods killed more than 150,000 people.

Indonesia's next president, Susilo Bambang Yudhoyono, faced enormous challenges, including ethnic strife and government corruption. In 2004, an earthquake caused a large tsunami that flooded Indonesia's western coast. The tsunami caused many deaths and great damage. In spite of this disaster, Yudhoyono improved the nation's economy. In 2009, he was elected to a second term.

Soon after the election, however, Yudhoyono faced more natural disasters. These natural disasters included a major earthquake, tsunamis, and a volcanic eruption. Despite this, Yudhoyono led Indonesia to continued prosperity and peace. Economic growth slowed in 2013, however, and inflation rose. In 2014, Joko Widodo became Indonesia's new president.

East Timor Wins Independence As Indonesia worked to overcome its numerous obstacles, it lost control of East Timor. Indonesian forces had ruled the land with brutal force since Suharto had seized it in the 1970s. The East Timorese, however, never stopped pushing to regain their freedom. Jose Ramos-Horta, an East Timorese independence campaigner, won the 1996 Nobel Peace Prize (along with East Timor's Roman Catholic bishop) for his efforts to gain independence for the region without violence. In a United Nations-sponsored referendum held in August 1999, the East Timorese voted for independence. The election angered pro-Indonesian forces. They ignored the referendum results and went on a bloody rampage. They killed hundreds and forced thousands into refugee camps in West Timor, which is a part of Indonesia. UN intervention forces eventually brought peace to the area. In 2002, East Timor celebrated independence. In May 2007, Jose Ramos-Horta won the presidency, but in 2008, he was injured in an assassination attempt. Ramos-Horta recovered, but he lost his second bid for president. Ramos-Horta appointed Xanana Gusmão to be prime minister.

During Gusmão's first term, the economy grew. But many people still lived in poverty. The government did little to improve their condition. In February 2015, Gusmão stepped down as prime minister. He was succeeded by Rui Maria de Araújo.

As on the Indian subcontinent, violence and struggle were part of the transition in Southeast Asia from colonies to free nations. The same would be true in Africa, where numerous former colonies shed European rule and created independent countries in the wake of World War II.

Reading Check
Summarize
How did East Timor achieve independence?

Lesson 2 Assessment

1. **Organize Information** Use a table to show challenges nations faced following independence. Which nation faced the greatest challenges? Why?

Nation	Challenges Following Independence
The Philippines	
Burma	
Indonesia	

2. **Key Terms and People** For each key term or person in the lesson, write a sentence explaining its significance.

3. **Draw Conclusions** Why did the retention of U.S. military bases in the Philippines so anger Filipinos?

4. **Synthesize** What was the outcome of the 1990 Myanmar election? How did the government respond?

5. **Clarify** How did World War II play a role in the eventual decolonization of Southeast Asia?

6. **Make Inferences** Why do you think that the United States demanded a 99-year lease on military and naval bases in the Philippines?

7. **Compare and Contrast** What was similar and different about the elections that brought defeat to the ruling governments in the Philippines and in Burma?

New Nations in Africa

Setting the Stage

Throughout the first half of the 20th century, Africa resembled little more than a European outpost. As you recall, the nations of Europe had marched in during the late 1800s and colonized much of the continent. Like the diverse groups living in Asia, however, the many different peoples of Africa were unwilling to return to colonial domination after World War II. And so, in the decades following the great global conflict, they too won their independence from foreign rule and went to work building new nations.

Achieving Independence

The African push for independence actually began in the decades before World War II. French-speaking Africans and West Indians began to express their growing sense of black consciousness and pride in traditional Africa. They formed the **Negritude movement**, a movement to celebrate African culture, heritage, and values.

When World War II erupted, African soldiers fought alongside Europeans to "defend freedom." This experience made them unwilling to accept colonial domination when they returned home. The war had changed the thinking of Europeans too. Many began to question the cost, as well as the morality, of maintaining colonies abroad. These and other factors helped African colonies gain their freedom throughout the 1950s and 1960s.

The Big Idea

After World War II, African leaders threw off colonial rule and created independent countries.

Why It Matters Now

Today, many of those independent countries are engaged in building political and economic stability.

Key Terms and People

Negritude movement
Kwame Nkrumah
Jomo Kenyatta
Ahmed Ben Bella
Mobutu Sese Seko

The ways in which African nations achieved independence, however, differed across the continent. European nations employed two basic styles of government in colonial Africa—direct and indirect. Under indirect rule, local officials did much of the governing and colonists enjoyed limited self-rule. As a result, these colonies generally experienced an easier transition to independence. For colonies under direct rule, in which foreigners governed at all levels and no self-rule existed, independence came with more difficulty. Some colonies even had to fight wars of liberation, as European settlers refused to surrender power to African nationalist groups.

No matter how they gained their freedom, however, most new African nations found the road to a strong and stable nation to be difficult. They had to deal with everything from creating a new government to establishing a postcolonial economy. Many new countries were also plagued by great ethnic strife. In colonizing Africa, the Europeans had created artificial borders that had little to do with the areas where ethnic groups actually lived. While national borders separated people with similar cultures, they also enclosed traditional enemies who began fighting each other soon after the Europeans left. For many African nations, all of this led to instability, violence, and an overall struggle to deal with their newly gained independence.

Reading Check
Recognize Effects
How were the struggles of newly independent nations in Africa and Southeast Asia similar?

Ghana Leads the Way

The British colony of the Gold Coast became the first African colony south of the Sahara to achieve independence. Following World War II, the British in the Gold Coast began making preparations. For example, they allowed more Africans to be nominated to the Legislative Council. However, the Africans wanted full freedom. The leader of their largely nonviolent movement was **Kwame Nkrumah** (KWAH•mee-uhn•KROO•muh). Starting in 1947, he worked to liberate the Gold Coast from the British. Nkrumah organized strikes and boycotts and was often imprisoned by the British government. Ultimately, his efforts were successful.

On receiving its independence in 1957, the Gold Coast took the name Ghana. This name honored a famous West African kingdom of the past. Nkrumah became Ghana's first prime minister and later its president-for-life. Nkrumah pushed through new roads, new schools, and expanded health facilities. These costly projects soon crippled the country. His programs for industrialization, health and welfare, and expanded educational facilities showed good intentions. However, the expense of the programs undermined the economy and strengthened his opposition.

Vocabulary
Pan-African refers to a vision of strengthening all of Africa, not just a single country

In addition, Nkrumah was often criticized for spending too much time on Pan-African efforts and neglecting economic problems in his own country. He dreamed of a "United States of Africa." In 1966, while Nkrumah was in China, the army and police in Ghana seized power. Since then, the country has shifted back and forth between civilian and military rule and has struggled for economic stability. In 2000, Ghana held its first open elections.

In 2001, the people elected a new president: Agyekum Kufuor. This transition was the first peaceful transfer of power between elected governments since 1957. In 2004, the people reelected Kufuor.

In Ghana's 2008 presidential elections, the people elected John Evans Atta Mills, and there was again a peaceful transfer of power. In 2012, Mills died. He was succeeded by his vice president, John Dramani Mahama. In the next election, Mahama ran against seven other candidates and narrowly won reelection.

Reading Check
Analyze Causes
How did Nkrumah's policies undermine Ghana's economy?

Fighting for Freedom

In contrast to Ghana, nations such as Kenya and Algeria had to take up arms against their European rulers to win their freedom.

Kenya Claims Independence The British ruled Kenya, and many British settlers resisted Kenyan independence—especially those who had taken over prize farmland in the northern highlands of the country. They were forced to accept African self-government as a result of two developments. One was the strong leadership of Kenyan nationalist **Jomo Kenyatta**. The second was the rise of a group known as the Mau Mau (MOW mow). This was a secret society made up mostly of native Kenyan farmers forced out of the highlands by the British.

Using guerrilla war tactics, the Mau Mau sought to push the white farmers into leaving the highlands. Kenyatta claimed to have no connection to the Mau Mau. However, he refused to condemn the organization. As a result, the British imprisoned him for nearly a decade. By the time the British granted Kenya independence in 1963, more than 10,000 Africans and 100 settlers had been killed.

BIOGRAPHY

Jomo Kenyatta
(1891–1978)

A man willing to spend years in jail for his beliefs, Kenyatta viewed independence as the only option for Africans.

The African can only advance to a "higher level" if he is free to express himself, to organize economically, politically and socially, and to take part in the government of his own country.

On the official day that freedom came to Kenya, December 12, 1963, Kenyatta recalls watching with delight as the British flag came down and the new flag of Kenya rose up. He called it "the greatest day in Kenya's history and the happiest day in my life."

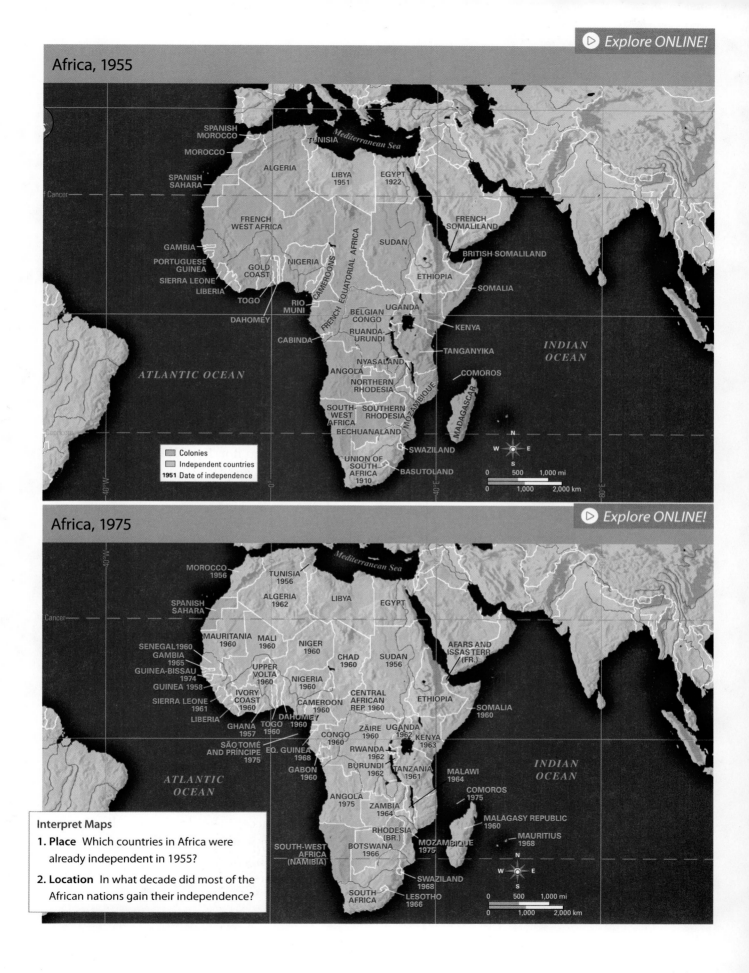

Africa, 1955

SPANISH MOROCCO
MOROCCO
SPANISH SAHARA
ALGERIA
TUNISIA
Mediterranean Sea
LIBYA 1951
EGYPT 1922
FRENCH WEST AFRICA
FRENCH SOMALILAND
GAMBIA
PORTUGUESE GUINEA
SIERRA LEONE
LIBERIA
GOLD COAST
NIGERIA
SUDAN
BRITISH SOMALILAND
TOGO
DAHOMEY
RIO MUNI
CAMEROONS
FRENCH EQUATORIAL AFRICA
ETHIOPIA
SOMALIA
CABINDA
BELGIAN CONGO
RUANDA-URUNDI
UGANDA
KENYA
TANGANYIKA
INDIAN OCEAN
NYASALAND
ANGOLA
NORTHERN RHODESIA
COMOROS
MADAGASCAR
SOUTH-WEST AFRICA
SOUTHERN RHODESIA
MOZAMBIQUE
BECHUANALAND
ATLANTIC OCEAN
of Cancer
Capricorn
SWAZILAND
UNION OF SOUTH AFRICA 1910
BASUTOLAND

Colonies
Independent countries
1951 Date of independence

N W E S
0   500   1,000 mi
0   1,000   2,000 km

Africa, 1975

MOROCCO 1956
TUNISIA 1956
Mediterranean Sea
SPANISH SAHARA
ALGERIA 1962
LIBYA
EGYPT
Cancer
MAURITANIA 1960
MALI 1960
NIGER 1960
SENEGAL 1960
GAMBIA 1965
GUINEA-BISSAU 1974
GUINEA 1958
UPPER VOLTA 1960
CHAD 1960
SUDAN 1956
AFARS AND ISSAS TERR. (FR.)
SIERRA LEONE 1961
IVORY COAST 1960
NIGERIA 1960
CAMEROON 1960
CENTRAL AFRICAN REP. 1960
ETHIOPIA
SOMALIA 1960
LIBERIA
GHANA 1957
TOGO 1960
DAHOMEY 1960
ZAÏRE 1960
UGANDA 1962
KENYA 1963
SÃO TOMÉ AND PRÍNCIPE 1975
EQ. GUINEA 1968
CONGO 1960
RWANDA 1962
GABON 1960
BURUNDI 1962
TANZANIA 1961
MALAWI 1964
INDIAN OCEAN
ATLANTIC OCEAN
ANGOLA 1975
ZAMBIA 1964
COMOROS 1975
MALAGASY REPUBLIC 1960
MAURITIUS 1968
RHODESIA (BR.)
MOZAMBIQUE 1975
SOUTH-WEST AFRICA (NAMIBIA)
BOTSWANA 1966
SWAZILAND 1968
SOUTH AFRICA
LESOTHO 1966

N W E S
0   500   1,000 mi
0   1,000   2,000 km

Interpret Maps

1. **Place** Which countries in Africa were already independent in 1955?

2. **Location** In what decade did most of the African nations gain their independence?

Kenyatta became president of the new nation. He worked to unite the country's many cultures and language groups. Kenyatta died in 1978. His successor, Daniel arap Moi, had a more difficult time running the nation. Some people disagreed with his one-party rule and accused his government of corruption. Ethnic conflicts killed hundreds and left thousands homeless. Moi stepped down in 2002. A new party gained power through free elections.

A record high number of voters turned out for the 2007 presidential elections. It was one of the closest elections in Kenya's history. Disputes over the close results led to violence. More than 1,000 people were killed and more than 600,000 injured in the violence that followed the election.

In August 2010, Kenyan voters adopted a new constitution. This constitution gave more control to local governments and limited the president's power.

Although many people feared the worst, the presidential election of 2013 was mostly peaceful. The people elected Uhuru Kenyatta, Jomo Kenyetta's son, with 50.07 percent of the vote.

In 2011, Kenyan troops joined a fight against an Islamic militant group, al-Shabaab, in Somalia. In retaliation, the group began to attack Kenya. One attack occurred in 2013, when al-Shabaab gunmen attacked a shopping mall in Nairobi. At least 65 people were killed. In late 2014, al-Shabaab killed dozens of non-Muslims in northern Kenya. On April 2, 2015, al-Shabaab attacked a Kenyan university, killing more than 140 people.

Algeria Struggles with Independence France's principal overseas colony, Algeria, had a population of 1 million French colonists and 9 million Arabs and Berber Muslims. After World War II, the French colonists refused to share political power with the native Algerians. In 1954, the Algerian National Liberation Front, or FLN, announced its intention to fight for independence. The French sent about half a million troops into Algeria to fight the FLN. Both sides committed atrocities. The FLN prevailed, and Algeria gained its independence in July 1962.

The leader of the FLN, **Ahmed Ben Bella**, became first president of the newly independent Algeria. He attempted to make Algeria a socialist state but was overthrown in 1965 by his army commander. From 1965 until 1988, Algerians tried unsuccessfully to modernize and industrialize the nation. Unemployment and dissatisfaction with the government contributed to the rise of religious fundamentalists who wanted to make Algeria an Islamic state. The chief Islamic party, the Islamic Salvation Front (FIS), won local and parliamentary elections in 1990 and 1991. However, the ruling government and army refused to accept the election results. As a result, a civil war broke out between Islamic militants and the government. The war continues, on and off, to this day.

Reading Check
Contrast How did the granting of independence to the British colonies of Ghana and Kenya differ?

Civil War in Congo and Angola

Civil war also plagued the new nations of Congo and Angola. Congo's problems lay in its corrupt dictatorship and hostile ethnic groups. Meanwhile, Angola's difficulties stemmed from intense political differences.

Freedom and Turmoil for Congo Of all the European possessions in Africa, one of the most exploited was the Belgian Congo. Belgium had ruthlessly plundered the colony's rich resources of rubber and copper. In addition, Belgian officials ruled with a harsh hand and provided the population with no social services. They also had made no attempt to prepare the people for independence. Not surprisingly, Belgium's granting of independence in 1960 to the Congo (known as Zaire from 1971 to 1997) resulted in upheaval.

In 1960, **Patrice Lumumba** became the Congo's first prime minister. He worked for a united Congo because he didn't want to divide the nation along ethnic or regional lines. Like many other African leaders, he supported Pan-Africanism, neutralism, and an end to colonial territories. Soon after he came to power, however, he was murdered. People throughout Africa mourned his death.

Mobuto Sese Seko

After years of civil war, an army officer, Colonel Joseph Mobutu, later known as **Mobutu Sese Seko** (moh•BOO•too-SAY•say-SAY•koh), seized power in 1965. For 32 years, Mobutu ruled the country that he renamed Zaire. He maintained control though a combination of force, one-party rule, and gifts to supporters. Mobutu successfully withstood several armed rebellions. He was finally overthrown in 1997 by rebel leader Laurent Kabila after months of civil war. Shortly thereafter, the country was renamed the Democratic Republic of the Congo.

On becoming president, Kabila promised a transition to democracy and free elections by April 1999. Such elections never came. By 2000 the nation endured another round of civil war, as three separate rebel groups sought to overthrow Kabila's autocratic rule. In January 2001, a bodyguard assassinated Kabila.

His son, Joseph Kabila, took power and began a quest for peace. In 2002, the government signed peace deals with rebel groups and neighboring countries. In 2006, Kabila was elected president under a new constitution. In 2008, the government and more than 20 rebel groups signed a peace agreement. They wanted to end the fighting in the eastern part of the nation. Later in the year, however, rebels attacked. The truce broke down. Tens of thousands of people were displaced.

Eleven candidates ran for election in 2011. Kabila, with 49 percent of the vote, was declared the winner. Former prime minister Etienne Tshisekedi, with 32 percent of the vote, was second. The Supreme Court later confirmed the results, but Tshisekedi's party rejected the results. Tshisekedi declared himself the nation's rightful president. Kabila's party, however, had won more than half of the seats in the National Assembly.

War Tears at Angola To the southwest of Congo lies Angola, a country that not only had to fight to gain its freedom but to hold itself together after independence. The Portuguese had long ruled Angola and had no desire to stop. When an independence movement broke out in the colony, Portugal sent in 50,000 troops. The cost of the conflict amounted to almost half of Portugal's national budget. The heavy cost of fighting, as well as growing opposition at home to the war, prompted the Portuguese to withdraw from Angola in 1975.

Almost immediately, the Communist-leaning MPLA (Popular Movement for the Liberation of Angola) declared itself the new nation's rightful government. This led to a prolonged civil war, as various rebel groups fought the government and each other for power. Each group received help from outside sources. The MPLA was assisted by some 50,000 Cuban troops and by the Soviet Union. The major opposition to the MPLA was UNITA (National Union for the Total Independence of Angola),

History in Depth

Genocide in East Africa

In East Africa, both Rwanda and Darfur, a region in Sudan, have suffered from campaigns of genocide.

In the spring of 1994, the Rwandan president, a Hutu, died in a suspicious plane crash. In the months that followed, Hutus slaughtered about 1 million Tutsis before Tutsi rebels put an end to the killings. The United Nations set up a tribunal to punish those responsible for the worst acts of genocide.

In 2004, Sudanese government forces and progovernment militias began killing villagers in Darfur as part of a campaign against rebel forces. In 2007, President Bush announced fresh sanctions against Sudan.

In 2009 an International Criminal Court (ICC) issued an arrest warrant for president Omar al-Bashir, president of Sudan. The ICC accused Bashir of genocide, war crimes, and crimes against humanity. The Sudan government said that Bashir was innocent.

In spite of the presence of United Nations troops, terror in Darfur continues. In 2014, the UN stated that more than 3,000 villages in Darfur had been burned down. It said also that there was widespread violence against the people there.

to which South Africa and the United States lent support. For decades, the two sides agreed to and then abandoned various cease-fire agreements. In 2002, the warring sides agreed to a peace accord, and the 27-year-long civil war ended.

The Angolan government had to rebuild the country, which had been destroyed by warfare. Epidemics and cholera outbreaks occurred because of poor sanitation. The civil war left more than 4 million people homeless. Hundreds of thousands of refugees outside the nation wanted to return home.

Thousands of land mines buried across the country limited farmers' ability to farm again. The Angolan government had to work with separatist groups, who demanded independence. When the government and the main separatist group reached an agreement in 2006, Angolans hoped that peace had finally come to their nation.

In 2008, Angola held elections. The MPLA won about four-fifths of the vote. A new constitution let the president be elected by the party with the most votes. The MPLA party selected José dos Santos to be president. In the 2012 elections, the MPLA easily won a majority, and dos Santos became president again.

As the colonies of Africa worked to become stable nations, the new nation of Israel was emerging in the Middle East. However, its growth upset many in the surrounding Arab world and would prompt one of the longest-running conflicts in modern history.

Reading Check
Recognize Effects
Why was the Congo vulnerable to turmoil after independence?

Lesson 3 Assessment

1. **Organize Information** Use a two-column table to list important items in the history of African nations. Which item had the greatest impact on its country? Why?

Ghana	
Kenya	
Zaire	
Algeria	
Angola	

2. **Key Terms and People** For each key term or person in the lesson, write a sentence explaining its significance.

3. **Draw Conclusions** Who were the Mau Mau of Kenya? What was their goal?

4. **Synthesize** What ignited the genocide in Rwanda, and how was the issue resolved by the United Nations?

5. **Draw Conclusions** How did the way in which European colonialists carved up Africa in the 1800s lead to civil strife in many new African nations?

6. **Analyze Motives** What prompted Portugal to grant Angola its freedom? Why do you think the United States and the Soviet Union participated in Angola's civil war?

7. **Analyze Issues** Why do you think revolution swept so many African nations following their independence from European rule?

Conflicts in the Middle East

The Big Idea

Division of the Palestine Mandate after World War II made the Middle East a hotbed of competing nationalist movements.

Why It Matters Now

The Arab-Israeli conflict is one of several conflicts in the region today.

Key Terms and People

Anwar Sadat
Golda Meir
PLO
Yasir Arafat
Menachem Begin
Camp David Accords
intifada
Oslo Peace Accords
Yitzhak Rabin

Vocabulary

Pan-Arabism refers to the idea of cultural and political unity among Arab nations

Setting the Stage

In the years following World War II, the Jewish people won their own state. The gaining of their ancient homeland along the eastern coast of the Mediterranean Sea, however, came at a heavy price. A Jewish state was unwelcome in this mostly Arab region, where Arab nationalism, or Pan-Arabism, was a common sentiment. The resulting Arab hostility led to a series of wars. Perhaps no Arab people, however, have been more opposed to a Jewish state than the Palestinian Arabs who claim that the entire Jewish land belongs to them.

Israel Becomes a State

The former Palestine Mandate now consists of Israel, the West Bank, and the Gaza Strip. To Jews, their claim to the land dates back 3,000 years, when Jewish kings ruled the region from Jerusalem. To Palestinian Arabs, the land has belonged to them since their conquest of the area in the 7th century.

After being forced out of Jerusalem during the second century AD, many Jews were dispersed throughout the world. Those who remained in the newly named Roman province of Palestinia were unable to establish their own state. The global dispersal of the Jews, which had begun many centuries before, is known as the Diaspora. During the late 19th and early 20th centuries, a Jewish nationalist movement began supporting the return of Jews to the region. Known as Zionists, they planned to reestablish the Jewish national homeland. At this time, the region known as Palestine was still part of the Ottoman Empire, ruled by Islamic Turks. After the Ottomans' defeat in World War I, the League of Nations gave Britain a mandate to oversee Palestine until it was ready for independence.

Both Jews and Arabs had moved to the area in large numbers, and the Jews were pressing for their own nation in the territory. The Arabs living in the region strongly opposed such a move. In a 1917 letter to Zionist leaders, British Foreign Secretary Sir Arthur Balfour promoted the idea of creating a Jewish homeland in Palestine while protecting the "rights of existing non-Jewish communities." The British also promised the Arabs a state and gave part of the Palestine Mandate—Transjordan—to Abdullah for a kingdom in 1921.

At the end of World War II, the United Nations took action. In 1947, the UN General Assembly voted to partition the Palestine Mandate into an Arab state and a Jewish state. Jerusalem was to be an international city owned by neither side. The terms of the partition gave Jews and Arabs land according to their population centers. In the wake of the war and the Holocaust, the United States and many European nations felt great sympathy for the Jews.

All of the Islamic countries voted against partition, and the Palestinian Arabs rejected it outright. They argued that the UN did not have the right to partition a territory without considering the wishes of the majority of its people. Finally, the date was set for the formation of Israel, May 14, 1948. On that date, David Ben-Gurion, long-time leader of the Jews residing in Palestine, announced the creation of an independent Israel.

Reading Check
Summarize What recommendations did the UN make for the Palestine Mandate?

Israel and Arab States in Conflict

The new nation of Israel got a hostile greeting from its neighbors. The day after it proclaimed itself a state, six Islamic states—Egypt, Iraq, Jordan, Lebanon, Saudi Arabia, and Syria—invaded Israel. The first of many Arab-Israeli wars, this one ended within months in a victory for Israel. Full-scale war broke out again in 1956, 1967, and 1973. Arab governments forced out 700,000 Jews living in Arab lands. Most moved to Israel.

The state that the UN had set aside for Arabs never came into being because the Arabs rejected it. Israel gained part of the land in the 1948–1949 fighting. Meanwhile, Egypt took control of the Gaza Strip, and Jordan annexed the West Bank of the Jordan River and the Old City of Jerusalem. (See map, The Middle East, 1947–present.) While the fighting raged, at least 600,000 Arab Palestinians fled, migrating from the areas under Israeli control. They settled in refugee camps in the areas designated for the Arab state and in neighboring Arab countries.

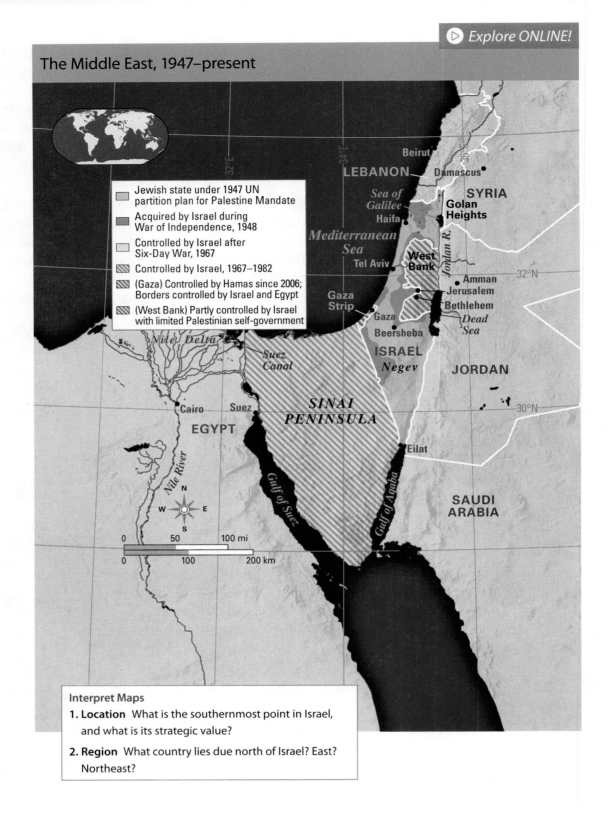

The Middle East, 1947–present

▶ Explore ONLINE!

Legend:
- Jewish state under 1947 UN partition plan for Palestine Mandate
- Acquired by Israel during War of Independence, 1948
- Controlled by Israel after Six-Day War, 1967
- Controlled by Israel, 1967–1982
- (Gaza) Controlled by Hamas since 2006; Borders controlled by Israel and Egypt
- (West Bank) Partly controlled by Israel with limited Palestinian self-government

Map labels: Beirut, LEBANON, Damascus, SYRIA, Sea of Galilee, Golan Heights, Haifa, Mediterranean Sea, West Bank, Tel Aviv, Jordan R., Amman, Jerusalem, Bethlehem, Dead Sea, Gaza Strip, Gaza, Beersheba, ISRAEL, Negev, JORDAN, Nile Delta, Suez Canal, SINAI PENINSULA, Cairo, Suez, EGYPT, Nile River, Gulf of Suez, Gulf of Aqaba, Eilat, SAUDI ARABIA

Scale: 0 50 100 mi / 0 100 200 km

32°E, 34°E, 36°E, 32°N, 30°N

Interpret Maps

1. **Location** What is the southernmost point in Israel, and what is its strategic value?

2. **Region** What country lies due north of Israel? East? Northeast?

The 1956 Suez Crisis The second Arab-Israeli war followed in 1956. That year, Egypt seized control of the Suez Canal, which ran along Egypt's eastern border between the Gulf of Suez and the Mediterranean Sea. Egyptian president Gamal Abdel Nasser blockaded Israeli shipping and took the canal, which was controlled by British interests. The military action was prompted in large part by Nasser's anger over the loss of U.S. and British financial support for the building of Egypt's Aswan Dam.

Outraged, the British made an agreement with France and Israel to retake the canal. With air support provided by their European allies, the Israelis marched on the Suez Canal and quickly defeated the Egyptians. However, pressure from the world community, including the United States and the Soviet Union, forced Israel and the Europeans to withdraw from Egypt. This left Egypt in charge of the canal and thus ended the Suez Crisis.

Arab-Israeli Wars Continue Tensions between Israel and the Arab states began to build again in the years following the resolution of the Suez Crisis. By early 1967, Nasser and his Arab allies, equipped with Soviet tanks and aircraft, felt ready to confront Israel. "We are eager for battle in order to force the enemy to awake from his dreams," Nasser announced, "and meet Arab reality face to face." He moved to close off the Gulf of Aqaba, Israel's outlet to the Red Sea.

Arab armies massed on Israel's borders. The Israelis struck airfields in Egypt, Iraq, Jordan, and Syria. Safe from air attack, Israeli ground forces struck like lightning on three fronts. Israel defeated the Arab states in what became known as the Six-Day War, because it was over in six days. Israel lost 800 troops in the fighting, while Arab losses exceeded 15,000.

As a consequence of the Six-Day War, Israel gained control of the old city of Jerusalem, the Sinai Peninsula, the Golan Heights, and the West Bank. Israelis saw these new holdings as a key buffer zone against further Arab attacks and expected to exchange the land for peace agreements. Arabs who lived in Jerusalem were given the choice of Israeli or Jordanian citizenship. Most chose the latter. People who lived in the other areas came under Israel's control pending a peace treaty.

A fourth Arab-Israeli conflict erupted in October 1973. Nasser's successor, Egyptian president **Anwar Sadat** (AHN•wahr-suh•DAT), planned a joint Arab attack on the date of Yom Kippur, the holiest of Jewish holidays. This time the Israelis were caught by surprise. Arab forces inflicted heavy casualties and recaptured some of the territory lost in 1967. The Israelis, under their prime minister, **Golda Meir** (MY•uhr), launched a counter attack and regained most of the lost territory. Both sides agreed to a truce after several weeks of fighting, and the Yom Kippur war came to an end.

Anwar Sadat

Golda Meir (1898–1978)

Meir was born in Kiev, Russia, but grew up in the American heartland. Although a skilled carpenter, Meir's father could not find enough work in Kiev. So he sold his tools and other belongings and moved his family to Milwaukee, Wisconsin. Meir would spend more than a decade in the United States before moving to the Palestine Mandate.

The future Israeli prime minister exhibited strong leadership qualities early on. When she learned that many of her fellow fourth-grade classmates could not afford textbooks, she created the American Young Sisters Society, an organization that succeeded in raising the necessary funds.

The Palestine Liberation Organization As Israel fought for its existence, the Palestinians struggled for recognition. While the United Nations had granted both Jews and Arabs their own states, the Arabs rejected their state and the Arab countries launched a war to destroy Israel. The Arabs refused to negotiate peace with Israel.

In 1964, Palestinian officials formed the Palestine Liberation Organization (**PLO**) to push for the formation of an Arab Palestinian state that would include all of Israel. Originally, the PLO was an umbrella organization made up of different groups—laborers, teachers, lawyers, and guerrilla fighters. Soon, guerrilla groups came to dominate the organization and insisted that the only way to achieve their goal was through armed struggle. In 1969 **Yasir Arafat** (YAH·sur-AR·uh·FAT) became chairman of the PLO. Throughout the 1960s and 1970s the group carried out numerous terrorist attacks against Israel. Some of Israel's Arab neighbors supported the PLO's goals by allowing PLO guerrillas to operate from their lands.

Reading Check
Recognize Effects
What were some of the effects of the Arab-Israeli conflicts?

Efforts at Peace

In November 1977, just four years after the Yom Kippur war, Anwar Sadat stunned the world by extending a hand to Israel. No Arab country up to this point had recognized Israel's right to exist. In a dramatic gesture, Sadat went before the Knesset, the Israeli parliament, and invited his one-time enemies to join him in a quest for peace.

Sadat emphasized that in exchange for peace Israel would have to recognize the rights of Palestinians. Furthermore, it would have to withdraw from territory captured in 1967 from Egypt, Jordan, and Syria.

Excerpt from Sadat's Knesset Speech

"Today, through my visit to you, I ask you why don't we stretch our hands with faith and sincerity and so that together we might . . . remove all suspicion of fear, betrayal, and bad intention? Why don't we stand together with the courage of men and the boldness of heroes who dedicate themselves to a sublime [supreme] aim? Why don't we stand together with the same courage and daring to erect a huge edifice [building] of peace? An edifice that . . . serves as a beacon for generations to come with the human message for construction, development, and the dignity of man."

—Anwar Sadat, Knesset speech, November 20, 1977

Analyze Historical Sources
What conditions for peace did Sadat request?

U.S. President Jimmy Carter recognized that Sadat had created a historic opportunity for peace. In 1978, Carter invited Sadat and Israeli prime minister **Menachem Begin** (mehn•AHK•hehm-BAY•gihn) to Camp David, the presidential retreat in rural Maryland. Isolated from the press and from domestic political pressures, Sadat and Begin worked to reach an agreement. After 13 days of negotiations, Carter triumphantly announced that Egypt recognized Israel as a legitimate state. In exchange, Israel agreed to return the Sinai Peninsula to Egypt. Signed in 1978, the **Camp David Accords** ended 30 years of hostilities between Egypt and Israel and became the first signed agreement between Israel and an Arab country.

President Sadat (left), President Carter, and Prime Minister Begin celebrate the signing of the Camp David Accords.

The Israeli-Arab Struggle

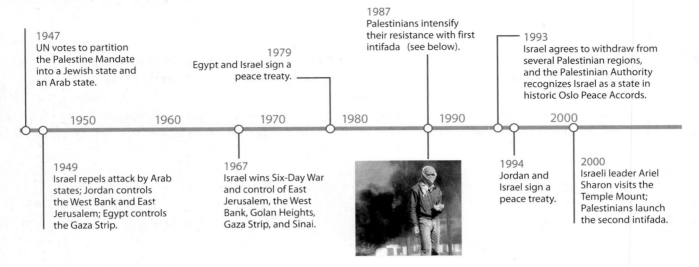

1947
UN votes to partition the Palestine Mandate into a Jewish state and an Arab state.

1979
Egypt and Israel sign a peace treaty.

1987
Palestinians intensify their resistance with first intifada (see below).

1993
Israel agrees to withdraw from several Palestinian regions, and the Palestinian Authority recognizes Israel as a state in historic Oslo Peace Accords.

1950   1960   1970   1980   1990   2000

1949
Israel repels attack by Arab states; Jordan controls the West Bank and East Jerusalem; Egypt controls the Gaza Strip.

1967
Israel wins Six-Day War and control of East Jerusalem, the West Bank, Golan Heights, Gaza Strip, and Sinai.

1994
Jordan and Israel sign a peace treaty.

2000
Israeli leader Ariel Sharon visits the Temple Mount; Palestinians launch the second intifada.

While world leaders praised Sadat, his peace initiative enraged many Arab countries. In 1981, a group of Muslim extremists assassinated him. However, Egypt's next leader, Hosni Mubarak (HAHS•nee-moo•BAHR•uhk), worked to maintain peace with Israel.

Israeli-Palestinian Tensions Increase One Arab group that continued to clash with the Israelis were the Palestinians, a large number of whom lived in the West Bank and Gaza Strip—lands controlled by Israel. During the 1970s and 1980s, the military wing of the PLO conducted a campaign against Israel. Israel responded forcefully, bombing suspected rebel bases in Palestinian towns. In 1982, the Israeli army invaded Lebanon in an attempt to destroy strongholds in Palestinian villages. The Israelis became involved in Lebanon's civil war and were forced to withdraw.

In 1987, Palestinians began to express their frustrations in a widespread **intifada**, or "uprising." The intifada took the form of boycotts, demonstrations, violent attacks on Israelis, rock throwing, shootings, and use of explosives. The intifada continued into the 1990s, with little progress made toward a solution. However, the intifada affected world opinion, which, in turn, put pressure on Israel and the Palestinians to negotiate. Finally, in October 1991, Israeli and Palestinian delegates met for a series of peace talks.

The Oslo Peace Accords Negotiations between the two sides made little progress, as the status of the Palestinian

Yitzhak Rabin, Bill Clinton, and Yasir Arafat at the Oslo Peace Accords.

History in Depth

Signs of Hope

Amid the cycle of violence and disagreement in the Middle East, there are small but inspiring efforts to bring together Israelis and Palestinians. One is Seeds of Peace, a summer camp that hosts teenagers from opposing sides of world conflicts in the hopes of creating lasting friendships. Another is the West-Eastern Divan, an orchestra made up of Jewish and Arab musicians—the creation of famous Jewish conductor Daniel Barenboim and prominent Palestinian writer Edward Said.

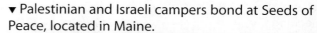

▼ Palestinian and Israeli campers bond at Seeds of Peace, located in Maine.

Edward Said and Daniel Barenboim (left) talk about their orchestra (right).

territories proved to be a bitterly divisive issue. In 1993, secret talks in Oslo, Norway, produced a surprise agreement: the **Oslo Peace Accords**. Israel agreed to grant the Palestinians self-rule in the Gaza Strip and the West Bank, beginning with Jericho. The Palestinians agreed to end violence and recognize Israel. Prime Minister **Yitzhak Rabin** (YIHTS•hahk-rah•BEEN) and Arafat signed the agreement in 1993. In 1994, Jordan and Israel signed a peace treaty.

Reading Check
Clarify What was the significance of the Camp David Accords?

Continuing Palestinian terrorist attacks against Israelis and the assassination of Rabin in 1995 by a right-wing Jewish extremist demonstrated the difficulty of making the agreement work. Rabin was succeeded as prime minister by Benjamin Netanyahu (neh•tan•YAH•hoo), who had opposed the Oslo Accords. Still, Netanyahu made efforts to keep to the agreement. In January 1997, Netanyahu met with Arafat to work out plans for a partial Israeli withdrawal from the West Bank.

Peace Slips Away

In 1999, the slow and difficult peace negotiations between Israel and the Palestinians seemed to get a boost. Ehud Barak won election as Israeli prime minister. Many observers viewed him as a much stronger supporter of the peace plan than Netanyahu had been. The world community, led by the United States, was determined to take advantage of such a development.

In July of 2000, U.S. President Bill Clinton hosted a 15-day summit meeting at Camp David between Ehud Barak and Yasir Arafat. Arafat rejected American and Israeli proposals and offered no alternatives, so the peace process once again stalled. Just two months later, Israeli political leader Ariel Sharon visited Jerusalem's Temple Mount, a site holy to both Jews and Muslims. The next day, the Voice of Palestine, the Palestinian Authority's official radio station, called upon Palestinians to protest the visit. Riots broke out in Jerusalem and the West Bank, and a second intifada, sometimes called the Al-Aqsa intifada, was launched.

The Conflict Intensifies The second intifada began much like the first with demonstrations, attacks on Israeli soldiers, and rock throwing. Palestinian groups also used suicide bombers as a weapon against Israelis. Their attacks on Jewish settlements and on civilian locations throughout Israel significantly raised the level of bloodshed. As the second intifada continued through 2007, thousands of Israelis and Palestinians had died in the conflict.

In response to the uprising, Israeli forces moved into Palestinian refugee camps and clamped down on terrorists. Troops destroyed buildings in which they suspected extremists were hiding and bulldozed entire areas of Palestinian towns and camps. The Israeli army bombed Arafat's headquarters, trapping him inside his compound for many days.

Arab-Israeli relations did not improve with Israel's next prime minister, Ariel Sharon. Sharon, a former military leader, refused to negotiate with the Palestinians until attacks on Israelis stopped. Eventually, under intense pressure from the world community, Arafat agreed to take a less prominent role in peace talks.

In early 2003, the Palestinian Authority appointed its first-ever prime minister, PLO official Mahmoud Abbas. Shortly afterward, U.S. President George W. Bush brought together Sharon and Abbas to begin working on a new peace plan known as the "road map." But violence increased again in 2003, and talks stalled.

Shifting Power and Alliances In the summer of 2005, Israel unilaterally evacuated all its settlers and military from the Gaza Strip. Then in 2006, Hamas, a militant terrorist group intent on replacing Israel with an Islamic state, won majority control in Palestinian Authority elections.

Israel refused to recognize the new Hamas government. However, in August 2007, Israeli Prime Minister Ehud Olmert began talks with Palestinian leader Mahmoud Abbas. In 2010, Olmert was replaced as prime minister by Benjamin Netanyahu and, after three weeks, the talks broke down when Israel refused to stop building Jewish housing in the West Bank.

In 2012, Abbas asked the UN General Assembly to recognize Palestinian statehood. He requested that the UN upgrade the status of Palestine to "nonmember observer state." This status, which is less than full UN membership, allowed Palestinians to become members of international groups, such as the International Criminal Court. The resolution passed.

In 2014, Netanyahu's governing coalition collapsed and early elections were held. However, Netanyahu's Likud party (a nationalist party that is against a Palestinian state) won more seats than any other party and Netanyahu remained as prime minister.

Reading Check
Evaluate What do you think it will take to achieve peace between Palestinians and Israelis?

Lesson 4 Assessment

1. **Organize Information** Make notes about the major events of the Arab-Israeli conflict. What is the significance of the 1967 war to Jews and Palestinians?

Suez Crisis

2. **Key Terms and People** For each key term or person in the lesson, write a sentence explaining its significance.

3. **Analyze Issues** What historic claim do both Palestinians and Jews make to the same land?

4. **Summarize** What land did Israel gain from the wars against its Arab neighbors?

5. **Synthesize** What were the terms of the Oslo Accords?

6. **Compare** How was the creation of Israel similar to the establishment of an independent India?

7. **Draw Conclusions** Why do you think all of the Israeli-Palestinian accords ultimately have failed? Some have said that this conflict represents the struggle of right against right. Explain why you agree or disagree.

Central Asia Struggles

The Big Idea

Lands controlled or influenced by the Soviet Union struggled with the challenges of establishing new nations.

Why It Matters Now

The security issues in these nations pose a threat to world peace and security.

Key Terms and People

Transcaucasian Republics
Central Asian Republics
mujahideen
Taliban

Setting the Stage

For thousands of years, the different peoples of Central Asia suffered invasions and domination by powerful groups such as the Mongols, Byzantines, Ottomans, and finally the Communist rulers of the Soviet Union. While such occupation brought many changes to this region, its various ethnic groups worked to keep alive much of their culture. They also longed to create nations of their own, a dream they realized in the early 1990s with the collapse of the Soviet Union. In the decade since then, however, these groups have come to know the challenges of building strong and stable independent nations.

Freedom Brings New Challenges

In 1991, the Soviet Union collapsed, and the republics that it had conquered emerged as 15 independent nations. Among them were those that had made up the Soviet empire's southern borders. Geographers often group these new nations into two geographic areas.

Armenia, Azerbaijan, and Georgia make up the **Transcaucasian Republics**. These three nations lie in the Caucasus Mountains between the Black and Caspian seas. East of the Caspian Sea and extending to the Tian Shan and Pamir mountains lie the five nations known as the **Central Asian Republics**. They are Uzbekistan, Turkmenistan, Tajikistan, Kazakhstan, and Kyrgyzstan.

Economic Struggles Since gaining independence, these nations have struggled economically and are today some of the poorest countries in the world. Much of the problem stems from their heavy reliance on the Soviet Union for economic help. As a result, they have had a difficult time standing on their own. Economic practices during the Soviet era have created additional problems. The Soviets, for example, converted much of the available farmland in the Central Asian Republics to grow "white gold"—cotton. Dependence on a single crop has hurt the development of a balanced economy in these nations.

Azerbaijan, which is located among the oil fields of the Caspian Sea, has the best chance to build a solid economy based on the income from oil and oil products. Meanwhile, Kazakhstan and Turkmenistan are working hard to tap their large reserves of oil and natural gas.

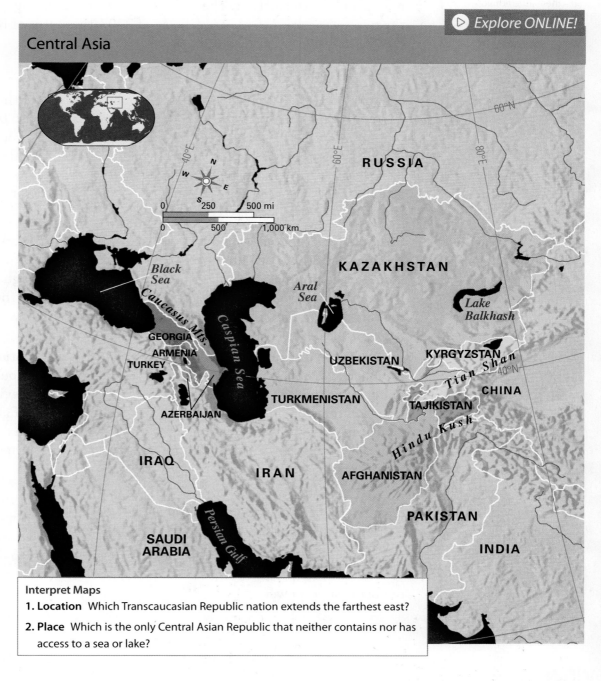

▷ *Explore ONLINE!*

Central Asia

Interpret Maps

1. **Location** Which Transcaucasian Republic nation extends the farthest east?

2. **Place** Which is the only Central Asian Republic that neither contains nor has access to a sea or lake?

Ethnic and Religious Strife Fighting among various ethnic and religious groups has created another obstacle to stability for many of the newly independent countries of Central Asia. The region is home to a number of different peoples, including some with long histories of hostility toward each other. With their iron-fisted rule, the Soviets kept a lid on these hostilities and largely prevented any serious ethnic clashes. After the breakup of the Soviet Union, however, long-simmering ethnic rivalries erupted into fighting. Some even became small regional wars.

Such was the case in Azerbaijan. Within this mostly Muslim country lies Nagorno-Karabakh, a small region of mainly Armenian Christians. In the wake of the Soviet Union's collapse, the people of this area declared their independence. Azerbaijan had no intention of letting go of this land, and fighting quickly broke out. Neighboring Armenia rushed to aid the Armenian people in the district. The war raged from 1991 through 1994, when the two sides agreed to a cease-fire. As of 2007, the status of Nagorno-Karabakh remained unresolved.

Reading Check Clarify Why was there little ethnic or religious strife in Central Asia during Soviet rule?

Afghanistan and the World

Just to the south of the Central Asian Republics lies one of the region's more prominent nations. Afghanistan is a small nation with both mountainous and desert terrain. It is one of the least-developed countries in the world, as most of its inhabitants are farmers or herders. And yet, over the past several decades, this mostly Muslim nation has grabbed the world's attention with two high-profile wars—one against the Soviet Union and the other against the United States.

Struggle for Freedom Afghanistan has endured a long history of struggle. During the 1800s, both Russia and Britain competed for control of its land. Russia wanted access to the Indian Ocean through Afghanistan, while Britain wanted control of the land in order to protect the northern borders of its Indian Empire. Britain fought three separate wars with the Afghanis before eventually leaving in 1919.

That year, Afghanistan declared itself an independent nation and established a monarchy. The government implemented various reforms and tried to modernize the country. In 1964, the country devised a constitution that sought to establish a more democratic style of government. However, officials could not agree on a reform program and most people showed little interest in the effort to transform the government. As a result, a democratic system failed to develop.

Pushing Back the Soviets Nonetheless, Afghanistan had grown stable enough to establish good relations with many Western European nations and to hold its own on the world stage. When the Cold War conflict between the United States and Soviet Union broke out, Afghanistan chose to remain neutral. However, over the years, it received aid from both of the opposing superpowers.

Situated so close to the Soviet Union, however, Afghanistan could not hold out against the force of communism forever. In 1973, military leaders overthrew the government. Five years later, in 1978, a rival group with strong ties to the Soviet Union seized control of the country. Much of the population opposed the group and its strong association with communism. Many Afghanis felt that Communist policies conflicted with the teachings of Islam.

The opposition forces banded together to form a group known as the **mujahideen** (moo•JAH•heh•DEEN), or holy warriors. These rebels took up arms and fought fiercely against the Soviet-supported government. The rebellion soon prompted the Soviet Union to step in. In 1979 and 1980, Soviet troops rolled into Afghanistan to conquer the country and add it to their Communist empire.

With the Soviets' superior military force and advanced weaponry, the war had all the makings of a quick and lopsided affair. But the Afghan rebels used the land and guerrilla tactics to their advantage. In addition, the United States provided financial and military assistance. After nearly 10 years of bloody and fruitless fighting, the Soviet Union withdrew its troops. The Afghanis had taken on the world's Communist superpower and won.

Rise and Fall of the Taliban With the Soviets gone, various Afghan rebel groups began battling each other for control of the country. A conservative Islamic group known as the **Taliban** emerged as the victor. By 1998, it controlled 90 percent of the country. Another rebel group, the Northern Alliance, held the northwest corner of the country. Observers initially viewed the Taliban as a positive force, as it brought order to the war-torn nation, rooted out corruption, and promoted the growth of business.

History in Depth

Destroying the Past

Among the Taliban's extreme policies that stemmed from their interpretation of Islam, one in particular shocked and angered historians around the world. In the years after gaining power, Taliban leaders destroyed some of Afghanistan's most prized artifacts—two centuries-old Buddhas carved out of cliffs in the Bamiyan Valley.

The Taliban deemed the giant statues offensive to Islam. Ignoring pleas from scholars and museums, they demolished the ancient figures with dynamite and bombs. One of the two statues was thought to have dated back to the third century AD.

The terrain of Central Asia varies widely, from mountains to plains.

However, the group followed an extreme interpretation of Islamic law and applied it to nearly every aspect of Afghan society. Taliban leaders restricted women's lives by forbidding them to go to school or hold jobs. They banned everything from television and movies to modern music. Punishment for violating the rules included severe beatings, amputation, and even execution.

Even more troubling to the world community was the Taliban's role in the growing problem of world terrorism. Western leaders accused the Taliban of allowing terrorist groups to train in Afghanistan. The Taliban also provided refuge for terrorist leaders, including Osama bin Laden, whose al-Qaeda organization is thought to be responsible for numerous attacks on the West—including the attacks on the World Trade Center in New York and the Pentagon in Washington, D.C., on September 11, 2001.

In the wake of the September 11 attacks, the U.S. government demanded that the Taliban turn over bin Laden. After its leaders refused, the United States took military action. In October 2001, U.S. forces began bombing Taliban air defense, airfields, and command centers, as well as al-Qaeda training camps. On the ground, the United States provided assistance to anti-Taliban forces, such as the Northern Alliance. By December, the United States had driven the Taliban from power.

Challenges Ahead While the Taliban regrouped in remote parts of Afghanistan and Pakistan, Afghan officials selected a new government under the leadership of Hamid Karzai. Later, in 2004, he was elected president for a five-year term. His government faced the task of rebuilding a country that had endured more than two decades of warfare. However, in 2006, the Taliban appeared resurgent, and NATO troops took

In the Afghanistan elections, the ballot included photographs of the candidates and symbols for each party.

over military operations in the South. Heavy fighting continued. In 2008, civilian casualties reached the highest levels since the war began.

On August 20, 2009, Afghanistan held a presidential election. Karzai won, and later that year he was inaugurated as president for a second term.

By 2012, NATO forces in Afghanistan had reached nearly 150,000. President Barack Obama sent U.S. troops, too. This increase in troops had mixed results. Although NATO troops removed the Taliban from some areas, Taliban fighters attacked military and civilian targets in other areas.

NATO withdrew all troops by 2014. Then Afghanistan held a presidential election. Under Afghanistan's constitution, Karzai could not run again. Two leading candidates, Abdullah Abdullah and Ashraf Ghani, emerged. Because of voter fraud, both candidates declared victory.

On September 21, 2014, Ghani and Abdullah worked out a compromise. Ghani would become president. But Abdullah (or someone from his party) would become chief executive officer, which was a newly created role.

The challenge before Afghanistan is neither unique nor new. Over the past 60 years, countries around the world have attempted to shed their old and often repressive forms of rule and implement a more democratic style of government.

Reading Check
Draw Conclusions
Why do you think the Soviets finally decided to leave Afghanistan?

Lesson 5 Assessment

1. **Organize Information** Make a list like the one shown. Which challenge for the Central Asian nations is most difficult to overcome?

   > Freedom Brings New Challenges
   > A.
   > B.
   >
   > Afghanistan and the World
   > A.
   > B.

2. **Key Terms and People** For each key term or person in the lesson, write a sentence explaining its significance.

3. **Summarize** What countries make up the Central Asian Republics?

4. **Draw Conclusions** Why did Afghanis oppose the idea of Communist rule? Why might Afghanis have been willing to accept Taliban rule by 1998?

5. **Analyze Causes** Why did the United States take military action against the Taliban?

6. **Make Inferences** Some historians call the Soviet-Afghan war the Soviet Union's "Vietnam." What do they mean by this reference? Do you agree with it?

7. **Identify Problems** Why did the new nations of Central Asia experience such economic difficulties?

Module 30 Assessment

Key Terms and People

For each term or name below, briefly explain its connection to colonial independence or other international developments after World War II.

1. partition
2. Jawaharlal Nehru
3. Indira Gandhi
4. Corazón Aquino
5. Jomo Kenyatta
6. Anwar Sadat
7. PLO
8. mujahideen

Main Ideas

The Indian Subcontinent Achieves Freedom

1. What two nations emerged from the British colony of India in 1947?
2. How did Jawaharlal Nehru spur India's economic growth after India became an independent nation?
3. In what way did Pakistan undergo a partition?
4. Briefly explain the reason for the civil disorder in Sri Lanka.

Southeast Asian Nations Gain Independence

5. What were some concerns the Filipinos had regarding the Bell Act?
6. Who is Sukarno, and what did he accomplish in Indonesia?

New Nations in Africa

7. Why were Kwame Nkrumah's politics criticized?
8. Why did Zaire face such difficulty upon gaining independence?
9. What sparked the present-day civil struggle in Algeria?

Conflicts in the Middle East

10. What was the Suez Crisis?
11. What were the Camp David Accords?

Central Asia Struggles

12. Which nations comprise the Transcaucasian Republics?
13. What was the Taliban?

Critical Thinking

1. Use a web diagram to show some of the challenges that newly independent nations have faced.

Challenges for Newly
Independent Nations

2. **Support Opinions** Do you think there should be a limit to the methods revolutionaries use? Explain your opinion.

3. **Analyze Issues** Why have so many of the new nations that emerged over the past half-century struggled economically?

4. **Draw Conclusions** In your view, was religion a unifying or destructive force as colonies around the world became new nations?
   Support your answer with specific examples from the text.

5. **Contrast** Describe the nature of totalitarianism and the police state that existed in Russia, and how it differed from some authoritarian governments you learned about in this lesson.

6. **Compare** Compare the rise of nationalism in Turkey, India, and China.

7. **Analyze** Compare and contrast the methods used by African and Asian nations to achieve independence.

8. **Infer** Use a globe to make a chart that shows the distance from Moscow and Washington, D.C., to Afghanistan, Ghana, the Philippines, and India. What do these distances tell you about the influences of the United States and the Soviet Union on these new nations?

9. With a partner, take turns reading, listening to, summarizing, and discussing the quotation by Anwar Sadat in lesson 4.

Analyze Historical Accuracy

Examine websites, documentaries, movies, newspaper articles, and biographies about one of the leaders in these lessons. Based on what you know, critique the historical accuracy of at least two sources. What specifically can you find that is biased or inaccurate? What is most fair and impartial?

Interact with History

Now that you have read about the efforts by so many former colonies to forge new countries, identify the main factors that determine whether a new nation struggles or thrives. Be sure to cite specific examples from the text.

Focus on Writing

Select one of the leaders discussed in this module. Review the decisions the leader made while in power. Write an evaluation of the leader's decisions and his or her impact on the country. Consider the following:

- the leader's views on government and democracy
- the leader's handling of the economy
- the leader's accomplishments and failures

Multimedia Activity

Creating a Database

Use the Internet, library resources, and other reference materials to create a database showing the economic growth of any four countries discussed in this module. Create one table for each country, with column headings for each measure of economic growth you choose to record and row headings for each 10-year period. Then insert the most current data you can find. Consider the following questions to get started.

- Which statistics will be most useful in making comparisons between nations?
- Which nations have capitalist economies? What other types of economies did you discover?
- Which nations have "one-crop" economies?

Module 31

Struggles for Democracy

Essential Question

Have the attempts at democracy in China and nations in Latin America, Africa, and the former Soviet bloc been worthwhile?

About the Photo: Protesters march in Caracas, Venezuela, in favor of democracy.

In this module, you will learn about the struggles for change in Latin America, Africa, the former Soviet bloc, and China.

What You Will Learn ...

Timeline of Events 1945–Present

▶ Explore ONLINE!

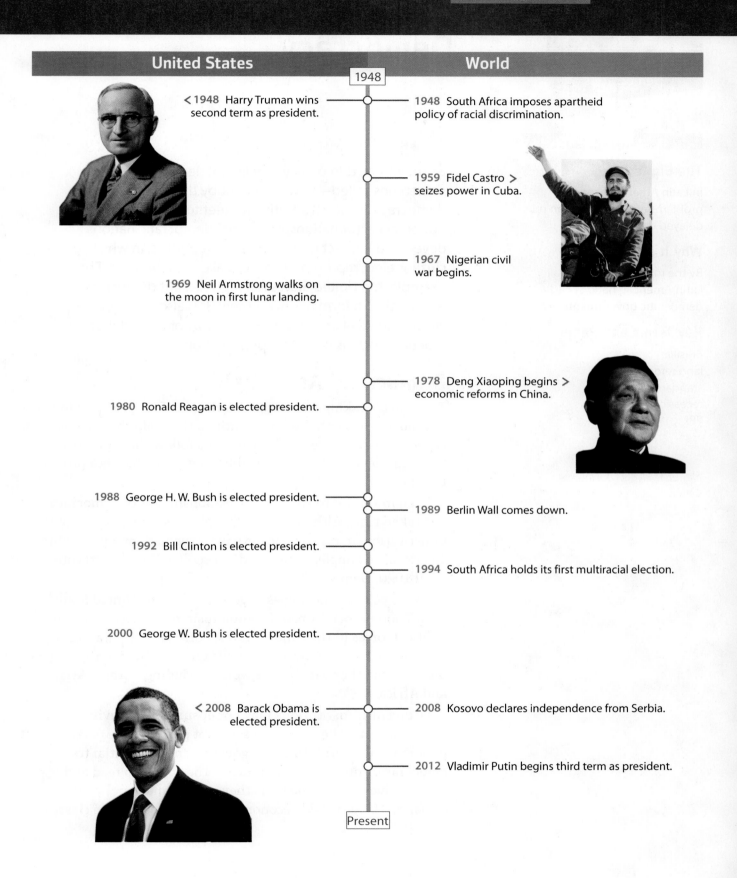

United States	World

1948

< 1948 Harry Truman wins second term as president.

1948 South Africa imposes apartheid policy of racial discrimination.

1959 Fidel Castro > seizes power in Cuba.

1967 Nigerian civil war begins.

1969 Neil Armstrong walks on the moon in first lunar landing.

1978 Deng Xiaoping begins > economic reforms in China.

1980 Ronald Reagan is elected president.

1988 George H. W. Bush is elected president.

1989 Berlin Wall comes down.

1992 Bill Clinton is elected president.

1994 South Africa holds its first multiracial election.

2000 George W. Bush is elected president.

< 2008 Barack Obama is elected president.

2008 Kosovo declares independence from Serbia.

2012 Vladimir Putin begins third term as president.

Present

Democracy

The Big Idea

In Latin America, economic problems and authoritarian rule delayed democracy.

Why It Matters Now

By the mid-1990s, almost all Latin American nations had democratic governments.

Key Terms and People

Brasília
land reform
standard of living
recession
PRI

Setting the Stage

By definition, democracy—or liberal democracy as it is sometimes called—is government by the people. Direct democracy, in which all citizens meet to pass laws, is not practical for nations. Therefore, democratic nations developed indirect democracies, or republics, in which citizens elect representatives to make laws for them. For example, the United States is a republic. But democracy is more than a form of government. It is also a way of life and an ideal goal. A democratic way of life includes practices such as free and open elections.

Democracy As a Goal

The chart "Making Democracy Work" lists four practices in a democracy, together with conditions that help these democratic practices succeed. Many nations follow these practices to a large degree. However, establishing democracy is a process that takes years.

Even in the United States, the establishment of democracy has taken time. Although the principle of equality is part of the Constitution, many Americans have struggled for equal rights. To cite one example, women did not receive the right to vote until 1920. Democracy is always a "work in progress."

Other political ideologies have existed in the United States as well. Though socialism and communism never became strong political forces in the United States, both have maintained a presence here. The movements have remained a much stronger presence in other parts of the world, including Europe, Asia, and Africa.

Democratic institutions may not ensure stable, civilian government if other conditions are not present. The participation of a nation's citizens in government is essential to democracy. Education and literacy—the ability to read and write—give citizens the tools they need to make political decisions. Also, a stable economy with a strong middle class and opportunities for advancement help democracy. It does so by giving citizens a stake in the future of their nation.

Other conditions advance democracy. First, a firm belief in the rights of the individual promotes the fair and equal treatment of citizens. Second, rule by law helps prevent leaders from abusing power without fear of punishment. Third, a sense of national identity helps encourage citizens to work together for the good of the nation. In contrast, a citizen of an authoritarian system receives few or no rights while their rulers demand loyalty and service to the government.

The struggle to establish democracy and to build stable economies continued into the twenty-first century as many nations abandoned authoritarian rule for democratic institutions. As the cold war has faded, nations have worked to establish a New World Order, in which countries work together to promote peace rather than conflict. The Organization of American States (OAS) is one such way the countries of the Americas work together to promote democracy and defend human rights. A United Nations study released in July 2002 warned that the spread of democracy around the world could be derailed if free elections in poor countries are not followed by economic growth. The United Nations Development Program's annual report warned particularly about Latin America.

Reading Check
Make Inferences
Why would democracy suffer if citizens didn't participate?

Making Democracy Work

Common	Conditions That Foster Those Practices
Free elections	Having more than one political party Universal suffrage—all adult citizens can vote
Citizen participation	High levels of education and literacy Economic security Freedoms of speech, press, and assembly
Majority rule, minority rights	All citizens equal before the law Shared national identity Protection of such individual rights as freedom of religion Representatives elected by citizens to carry out their will
Constitutional government	Clear body of traditions and laws on which government is based Widespread education about how government works National acceptance of majority decisions Shared belief that no one is above the law

Interpret Charts
How might economic security foster citizen participation?

Dictators and Democracy

Many Latin American nations won their independence from Spain and Portugal in the early 1800s. However, three centuries of colonial rule left many problems. These included powerful militaries, economies that were too dependent on a single crop, and large gaps between rich and poor. These patterns persisted in the modern era. Citizens of many Latin American countries worked to gain more rights. Women, indigenous people, and other groups fought for both civil rights—the rights of citizens to political and social freedoms, and for human rights—the basic rights belonging to every person.

After gaining independence from Portugal in 1822, Brazil became a monarchy. This lasted until 1889, when Brazilians established a republican government, which a wealthy elite controlled. Then, in the 1930s, Getulio Vargas became dictator. Vargas suppressed political opposition. At the same time, however, he promoted economic growth and helped turn Brazil into a modern industrial nation.

Kubitschek's Ambitious Program After Vargas, three popularly elected presidents tried to steer Brazil toward democracy. Juscelino Kubitschek (zhoo•suh•LEE•nuh-KOO•bih•chehk), who governed from 1956 to 1961, continued to develop Brazil's economy. Kubitschek encouraged foreign investment to help pay for development projects. He built a new capital city, **Brasília** (bruh•ZIHL•yuh), in the country's interior. Kubitschek's dream proved expensive. The nation's foreign debt soared and inflation shot up.

Kubitschek's successors proposed reforms to ease economic and social problems. Conservatives resisted this strongly. They especially opposed the plan for **land reform**—breaking up large estates and distributing that land to peasants. In 1964, with the blessing of wealthy Brazilians, the army seized power in a military coup.

Military Dictators For two decades military dictators ruled Brazil. Emphasizing economic growth, the generals fostered foreign investment. They began huge development projects in the Amazon jungle. The economy boomed.

The boom had a downside, though. The government froze wages and cut back on social programs. This caused a decline in the **standard of living**, or level of material comfort, which is judged by the amount of goods people have. When Brazilians protested, the government imposed censorship. It also jailed, tortured, and sometimes killed government critics. Nevertheless, opposition to military rule continued to grow.

The Road to Democracy By the early 1980s, a **recession**, or slowdown in the economy, gripped Brazil. At that point, the generals decided to open up the political system. They allowed direct elections of local, state, and national officials.

Explore ONLINE!

Latin America

UNITED STATES
Rio Grande
Gulf of Mexico
Tropic of Cancer
MEXICO
Mexico City
BAHAMAS
WEST INDIES
DOMINICAN REPUBLIC
HAITI
CUBA
JAMAICA
BELIZE
HONDURAS
GUATEMALA
EL SALVADOR
NICARAGUA
Caribbean Sea
ATLANTIC OCEAN
COSTA RICA
PANAMA
GUYANA
SURINAME
FRENCH GUIANA
Orinoco R.
VENEZUELA
COLOMBIA
0° Equator
ECUADOR
Amazon River
PACIFIC OCEAN
BRAZIL
PERU
ANDES MOUNTAINS
Brasília
BOLIVIA
Paraná River
N
W
E
S
0
500
1,000 mi
0
1,000
2,000 km
Tropic of Capricorn
PARAGUAY
CHILE
URUGUAY
Buenos Aires
ARGENTINA
40°S
FALKLAND IS. (Br.)
120°W
80°W
40°W

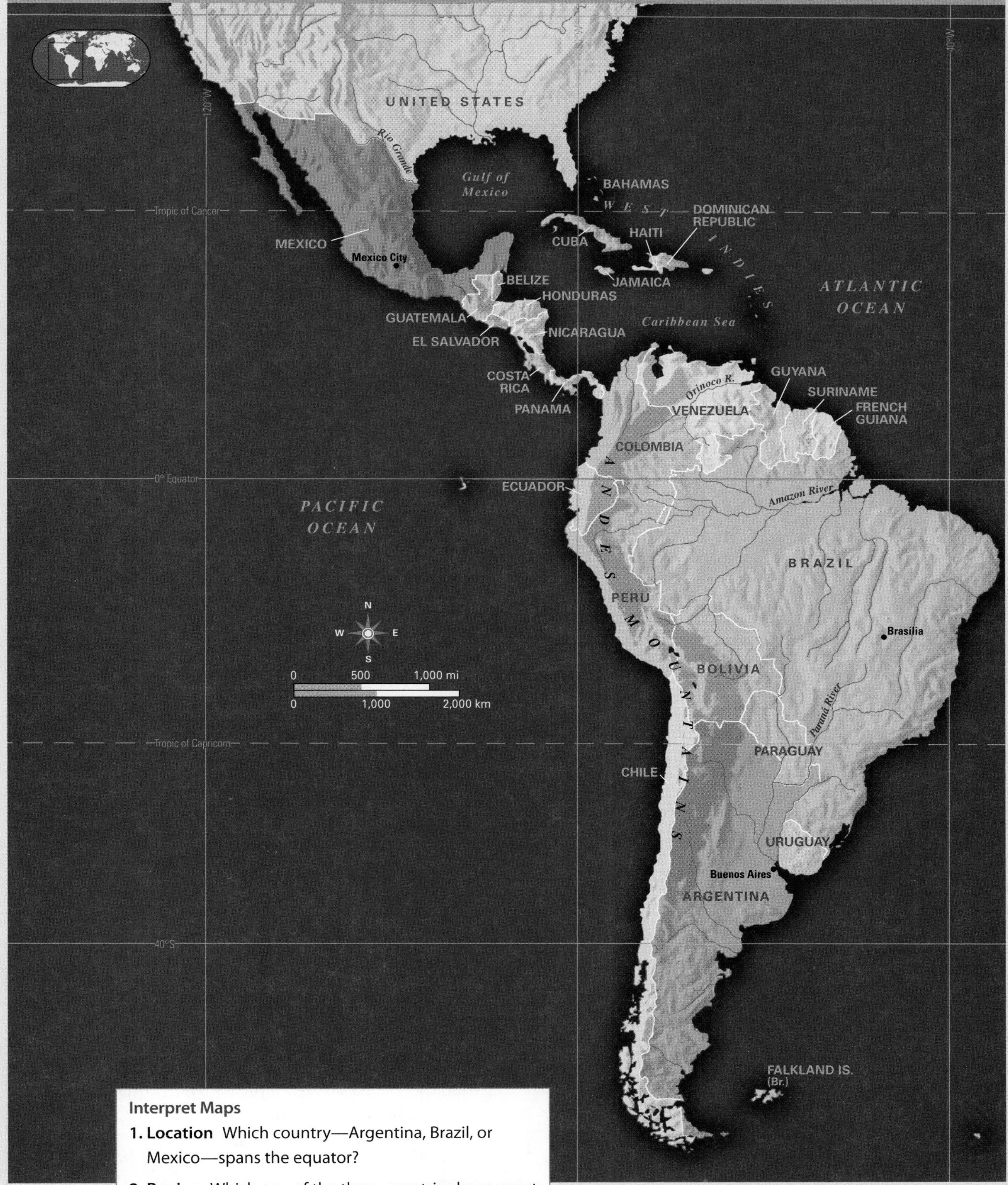

Interpret Maps

1. **Location** Which country—Argentina, Brazil, or Mexico—spans the equator?
2. **Region** Which one of the three countries has a coast on the Caribbean Sea?

In 1985, a new civilian president, José Sarney (zhoh•ZAY-SAHR•nay), took office. Sarney inherited a country in crisis because of foreign debt and inflation. He proved unable to solve the country's problems and lost support. The next elected president fared even worse. He resigned because of corruption charges.

In 1994 and again in 1998, Brazilians elected Fernando Henrique Cardoso, who achieved some success in tackling the nation's economic and political problems. Although trained as a Marxist scholar, Cardoso became a strong advocate of free markets. One of his main concerns was the widening income gap in Brazil. He embarked on a program to promote economic reform.

The 2002 Presidential Election In the presidential election of October 2002, Cardoso's handpicked successor to lead his centrist coalition was José Serra. Serra faced two candidates who proposed a sharp break with Cardoso's pro-business policies. These candidates included Luiz Inácio Lula da Silva, a candidate of the leftist Workers Party.

An economic crisis hit many countries in South America, including Brazil, in 2002. Because of stalled economic growth, rising unemployment, and poverty, there was a backlash against free-market economic policies. This made the election of 2002 a close contest. Da Silva, the leftist candidate, won the hotly disputed election, defeating the ruling party candidate, Serra. The election was part of the trend toward socialist governments in Latin America. By 2005, approximately three out of four Latin Americans were living under leftist administrations. This marked a change from the previous era when leaders ruled governments supported by the United States, a country seeking to end the spread of communism.

Da Silva, who was reelected in 2006, proved a more moderate president than his supporters and opponents had expected. In 2010, Dilma Rousseff became the first woman president elected in Brazil. She has faced many challenges, including natural disasters and political scandals. Demonstrators at widespread protests have called for her impeachment. Despite these challenges, Brazil continues on the path of democracy.

Reading Check
Analyze Motives
Why might the wealthy have preferred military rule to land reform?

Brazilian Economy, 1955–2000

Debt

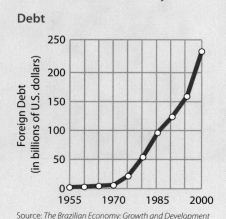

Inflation

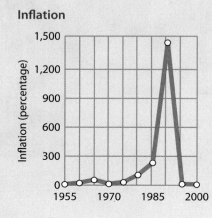

Interpret Graphs
Of the years shown on the line graph, which was the worst year for inflation?

Source: *The Brazilian Economy: Growth and Development*

State-Sponsored Terror

In 1970, Chileans elected the leftist Salvador Allende as president. Allende spent huge amounts of money in efforts to improve the lives of the working class and stimulate the economy. The government broke up large estates and distributed the land to peasants. It also nationalized foreign-owned companies. For a time, Allende's measures were successful and widely popular.

Allende's Fall Allende soon ran into trouble. Industrial and farm production fell, prices rose, and food shortages spread. In addition, Allende's Communist policies alienated business owners and worried the U.S. government, which feared that Allende had developed close ties with the Soviet Union. The U.S. Central Intelligence Agency (CIA) began providing secret funding and military training to opposition groups in Chile in hopes of triggering an anti-Allende revolt. As the economy failed, more and more people turned against Allende. On September 11, 1973, the military rebelled. Allende and more than 3,000 others died in the bloodshed.

The Pinochet Regime Several weeks before the coup, Allende had appointed a new commander in chief of the army, Augusto Pinochet (peen•oh•SHAY). General Pinochet was closely involved in the rebellion. He took command of the new military regime and became president in 1974.

Pinochet moved quickly to destroy the opposition. He disbanded congress, suspended the constitution, and banned opposition parties. He also censored the media. His plan to cement his control of the Chilean government can best be described as politically motivated mass murder. Within three years, an estimated 130,000 people were arrested for opposing the government. Thousands of people disappeared, were tortured, killed, or fled into exile.

Despite the political crackdown, Chile's economy experienced rapid growth. Pinochet's government privatized state-owned businesses, slashed government budgets, cut tariffs, and eased government regulations. Exports grew and the economy took off. The cost of living, however, exploded and the gap between rich and poor got wider and wider. Even with a 30 percent unemployment rate, Chile became the fastest-growing economy in Latin America.

Government Reform Under international pressure, Augusto Pinochet agreed to mild reforms in 1980. That year, he allowed for a new constitution. Under the agreement, Pinochet would remain president until 1989 and receive immunity for any crimes he may have committed. However, courts in Europe and Chile continued to seek justice for victims of the Pinochet regime. Pinochet was eventually charged with kidnapping and murder, but the court was not able to convict him before his death in 2006. Today, Chile's government is once again a democracy.

Reading Check
Find Main Ideas State the main idea of the section "The Pinochet Regime." Then cite at least two details that support the main idea.

One-Party Rule

Unlike Brazil, Mexico enjoyed relative political stability for most of the 20th century. Following the Mexican Revolution, the government passed the Constitution of 1917. The new constitution outlined a democracy and promised reforms.

Beginnings of One-Party Domination From 1920 to 1934, Mexico elected several generals as president. However, these men did not rule as military dictators. They did create a ruling party—the National Revolutionary Party, which dominated Mexico under various names for the rest of the 20th century. From 1934 to 1940, President Lázaro Cárdenas (KAHR·day·nahs) tried to improve life for peasants and workers. He carried out land reform and promoted labor rights. He nationalized the Mexican oil industry, kicking out foreign oil companies and creating a state-run oil industry. After Cárdenas, however, a series of more conservative presidents turned away from reform.

The Party Becomes the PRI In 1946, the main political party changed its name to the Institutional Revolutionary Party, or **PRI**. In the half-century that followed, the PRI became the main force for political stability in Mexico. Although stable, the government was an imperfect democracy. The PRI controlled the congress and won every presidential election. The government allowed opposition parties to compete, but fraud and corruption tainted the elections.

Even as the Mexican economy rapidly developed, Mexico continued to suffer severe economic problems. Lacking land and jobs, millions of Mexicans struggled for survival. In addition, a huge foreign debt forced the government to spend money on interest payments. In the late 1960s, students and workers began calling for economic and political change. On October 2, 1968, protesters gathered at the site of an ancient Aztec market in Mexico City. Soldiers hidden in the ruins opened fire on the protesters. The massacre claimed several hundred lives.

People also called for change in the United States as the civil rights movement there grew in strength. Between 1942 and 1964, more than four million Mexicans moved to the United States as part of the bracero program. Braceros worked as farm laborers in California and other states. Migrant workers often faced very poor working conditions and received little pay. Labor leaders such as Cesar Chavez worked to improve the rights of these workers.

Chavez effected change by organizing boycotts and encouraging migrant farmers to form labor unions. As the movement grew, Chavez's opponents tried to stop it. When a large grape grower named Schenley sprayed its vineyard workers with pesticides, Chavez and the National Farm Workers Association fought back harder. They organized a massive march that resulted in Schenley agreeing to a bargain with the union.

Military Rule and Democracy

Throughout the 20th century, many Latin American countries were ruled by military dictators or political bosses. Most typically, the dictator's support came from the wealthy and the military. But sometimes the dictator's support came from the people.

Analyze Historical Sources
Do dictators typically take into account the opinions of the people they rule? What does this cartoon suggest about the dictator's attitude toward the opinion of the people he rules?

"My goodness, if I'd known how badly you wanted democracy I'd have given it to you ages ago."

Another critical episode occurred during the early 1980s. By that time, huge new oil and natural gas reserves had been discovered in Mexico. The economy had become dependent on oil and gas exports. In 1981, world oil prices fell, cutting Mexico's oil and gas revenues in half. Mexico went into an economic decline.

Economic and Political Crises The 1980s and 1990s saw Mexico facing various crises. In 1988, opposition parties challenged the PRI in national elections. The PRI candidate, Carlos Salinas, won the presidency. Even so, opposition parties won seats in the congress and began to force a gradual opening of the political system.

Latin Americans Living in Poverty, 2006–2007

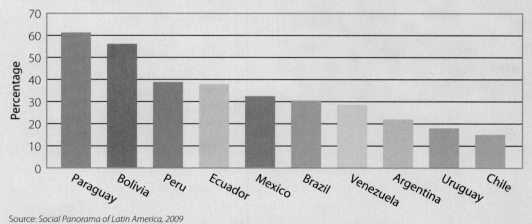

Source: *Social Panorama of Latin America, 2009*

Interpret Graphs
In which three countries of Latin America is the percentage of people living in poverty the lowest? In which three countries is the poverty rate the highest?

The Collapse of the Soviet Union

The Big Idea

Democratic reforms brought important changes to the Soviet Union.

Why It Matters Now

Russia continues to struggle to establish democracy.

Key Terms and People

Politburo
Mikhail Gorbachev
glasnost
perestroika
Boris Yeltsin
CIS
"shock therapy"

Setting the Stage

After World War II, the Soviet Union and the United States engaged in a cold war. Each tried to increase its worldwide influence. The Soviet Union extended its power over much of Eastern Europe. By the 1960s, it appeared that communism was permanently established in the region. During the 1960s and 1970s, the Soviet Union's Communist leadership kept tight control over the Soviet people. But big changes, including democratic reforms, were on the horizon.

Gorbachev Moves Toward Democracy

Soviet premier Leonid Brezhnev and the **Politburo**—the ruling committee of the Communist Party—crushed all political disagreement. Censors decided what writers could publish. The Communist Party also restricted freedom of speech and worship. After Brezhnev's death in 1982, the aging leadership of the Soviet Union tried to hold on to power. However, each of Brezhnev's two successors died after only about a year in office. Who would succeed them?

A Younger Leader To answer that question, the Politburo debated between two men. One was **Mikhail Gorbachev** (mih·KYL-GAWR·buh·chawf). Gorbachev's supporters praised his youth, energy, and political skills. With their backing, Gorbachev became the party's new general secretary. In choosing him, Politburo members did not realize they were unleashing another Russian Revolution.

The Soviet people welcomed Gorbachev's election. At 54, he was the youngest Soviet leader since Stalin. Gorbachev was only a child during Stalin's ruthless purge of independent-minded party members. Unlike other Soviet leaders, Gorbachev decided to pursue new ideas.

Glasnost

Mikhail Gorbachev's policies of glasnost and perestroika shook up the traditional way of doing things in the Soviet economy and in the society at large.

Analyze Historical Sources

1. One arrow points down the road toward stagnation. Where is the other arrow, pointing in the opposite direction, likely to lead?
2. Why might the Soviet Union look different to the figure in the cartoon?

Glasnost Promotes Openness

Past Soviet leaders had created a totalitarian state. It rewarded silence and discouraged individuals from acting on their own. As a result, Soviet society rarely changed, and the Soviet economy stagnated. Gorbachev realized that economic and social reforms could not occur without a free flow of ideas and information. In 1985, he announced a policy known as **glasnost** (GLAHS·nuhst), or openness.

Glasnost brought remarkable changes. The government allowed churches to open. It released dissidents from prison and allowed the publication of books by previously banned authors. Reporters investigated problems and criticized officials. These changes helped to improve human rights for the Soviet people by giving them more freedom to do and say what they wanted.

Reading Check
Draw Conclusions
What effect would glasnost likely have on the public's opinion of Gorbachev?

Reforming the Economy and Politics

The new openness allowed Soviet citizens to complain about economic problems. Consumers protested that they had to stand in lines to buy food and other basics.

Economic Restructuring Gorbachev blamed these problems on the Soviet Union's inefficient system of central planning. Under central planning, party officials told farm and factory managers how much to produce. They also told them what wages to pay and what prices to charge. Because individuals could not increase their pay by producing more, they had little motive to improve efficiency.

In 1985, Gorbachev introduced the idea of **perestroika** (pehr·ih·STROY·kuh), or economic restructuring. In 1986, he made changes to revive the Soviet economy. Local managers gained greater authority over their farms and factories, and people were allowed to open small private businesses. Gorbachev's goal was not to throw out communism, but to make the economic system more efficient and productive.

Democratization Opens the Political System Gorbachev knew that for the economy to improve, the Communist Party would have to loosen its grip on Soviet society. In 1987, he unveiled a third new policy called democratization which was a gradual opening of the political system.

The plan called for the election of a new legislative body. In the past, voters had merely approved candidates who were handpicked by the Communist Party. Now, voters could choose from a list of candidates for each office. The election produced many surprises. In several places, voters chose lesser-known candidates and reformers over powerful party bosses.

Foreign Policy Soviet foreign policy also changed, in part due to President Ronald Reagan's strong anti-Soviet views. Reagan famously called the Soviet Union "an evil empire" during a speech in 1983. To compete militarily with the Soviet Union, Reagan had begun the most expensive military buildup in peacetime history, costing more than $2 trillion. Under pressure from U.S. military spending, Gorbachev realized that the Soviet economy could not afford the costly arms race. Arms control became one of Gorbachev's top priorities. In December 1987, he and Reagan signed the Intermediate-Range Nuclear Forces (INF) Treaty. This treaty banned nuclear missiles with ranges of 300 to 3,400 miles.

Reading Check
Make Inferences
Why would it be inefficient for the central government to decide what should be produced all over the country?

The Soviet Union Faces Turmoil

Gorbachev's new thinking led him to support movements for change in both the economic and political systems within the Soviet Union. Powerful forces for democracy were building in the country, and Gorbachev decided not to oppose reform. Glasnost, perestroika, and democratization were all means to reform the system. However, the move to reform the Soviet Union ultimately led to its breakup.

Various nationalities in the Soviet Union began to call for their freedom. More than 100 ethnic groups lived in the Soviet Union. Russians were the largest, most powerful group. However, non-Russians formed a majority in the 14 Soviet republics other than Russia.

Ethnic tensions brewed beneath the surface of Soviet society. As reforms loosened central controls, unrest spread across the country. Nationalist groups in Georgia, Ukraine, and Moldavia (now Moldova) demanded self-rule. The Muslim peoples of Soviet Central Asia called for religious freedom.

Lithuania Defies Gorbachev The first challenge came from the Baltic nations of Lithuania, Estonia, and Latvia. These republics had been independent states between the two world wars until the Soviets annexed them in 1940. Fifty years later, in March 1990, Lithuania declared its independence. To try to force it back into the Soviet Union, Gorbachev ordered an economic blockade of the republic.

Although Gorbachev was reluctant to use stronger measures, he feared that Lithuania's example might encourage other republics to secede. In January 1991, Soviet troops attacked unarmed civilians in Lithuania's capital. The army killed 14 and wounded hundreds.

Mikhail Gorbachev
(1931–)

Mikhail Gorbachev's background shaped the role he would play in history. Both of his grandfathers were arrested during Stalin's purges. Both were eventually freed. However, Gorbachev never forgot his grandfathers' stories.

After working on a state farm, Gorbachev studied law in Moscow and joined the Communist Party. As an official in a farming region, Gorbachev learned much about the Soviet system and its problems.

He advanced quickly in the party. When he became general secretary in 1985, he was the youngest Politburo member and a man who wanted to bring change. He succeeded. Although he pursued reform to save the Soviet Union, ultimately he triggered its breakup.

Boris Yeltsin
(1931–2007)

Boris Yeltsin was raised in poverty. For ten years, his family lived in a single room.

As a youth, Yeltsin earned good grades but behaved badly. Mikhail Gorbachev named him party boss and mayor of Moscow in 1985. Yeltsin's outspokenness got him into trouble. At one meeting, he launched into a bitter speech criticizing conservatives for working against perestroika. Gorbachev fired him for the sake of party unity.

Yeltsin made a dramatic comeback and won a seat in parliament in 1989. Parliament elected him president of Russia in 1990, and voters reelected him in 1991. Due at least in part to his failing health (heart problems), Yeltsin resigned in 1999.

Yeltsin Denounces Gorbachev The assault in Lithuania and the lack of economic progress damaged Gorbachev's popularity. People looked for leadership to **Boris Yeltsin**. He was a member of parliament and former mayor of Moscow. Yeltsin criticized the crackdown in Lithuania and the slow pace of reforms. In June 1991, voters chose Yeltsin to become the Russian Federation's first directly elected president.

In spite of their rivalry, Yeltsin and Gorbachev faced a common enemy in the old guard of Communist officials. Hardliners—conservatives who opposed reform—were furious that Gorbachev had given up the Soviet Union's role as the dominant force in Eastern Europe. They also feared losing their power and privileges. These officials vowed to overthrow Gorbachev and undo his reforms.

The August Coup On August 18, 1991, the hardliners detained Gorbachev at his vacation home on the Black Sea. They demanded his resignation as Soviet president. Early the next day, hundreds of tanks and armored vehicles rolled into Moscow. However, the Soviet people had lost their fear of the party. They were willing to defend their freedoms. Protesters gathered at the Russian parliament building, where Yeltsin had his office.

Around midday, Yeltsin emerged and climbed atop one of the tanks. As his supporters cheered, he declared, "We proclaim all decisions and decrees of this committee to be illegal. . . . We appeal to the citizens of Russia to . . . demand a return of the country to normal constitutional developments."

On August 20, the hardliners ordered troops to attack the parliament building, but they refused. Their refusal turned the tide. On August 21, the military withdrew its forces from Moscow. That night, Gorbachev returned to Moscow.

End of the Soviet Union The coup attempt sparked anger against the Communist Party. Gorbachev resigned as general secretary of the party. The Soviet parliament voted to stop all party activities. Having first seized power in 1917 in a coup that succeeded, the Communist Party now collapsed because of a coup that failed.

The coup also played a decisive role in accelerating the breakup of the Soviet Union. Estonia and Latvia quickly declared their independence. Other republics soon followed. Although Gorbachev pleaded for unity, no one was listening. By early December, all 15 republics had declared independence.

Reading Check
Analyze Motives
Why do you think the Soviet troops refused the order to attack the parliament building?

Yeltsin met with the leaders of other republics to chart a new course. They agreed to form the Commonwealth of Independent States, or **CIS**, a loose federation of former Soviet territories. Only the Baltic republics (also called states) and Georgia declined to join. The formation of the CIS meant the death of the Soviet Union. It also signaled the end of the Cold War. On Christmas Day 1991, Gorbachev announced his resignation as president of the Soviet Union, a country that ceased to exist. Fifteen new countries, including Ukraine, Kazakhstan, and the Baltic States, formed in its place.

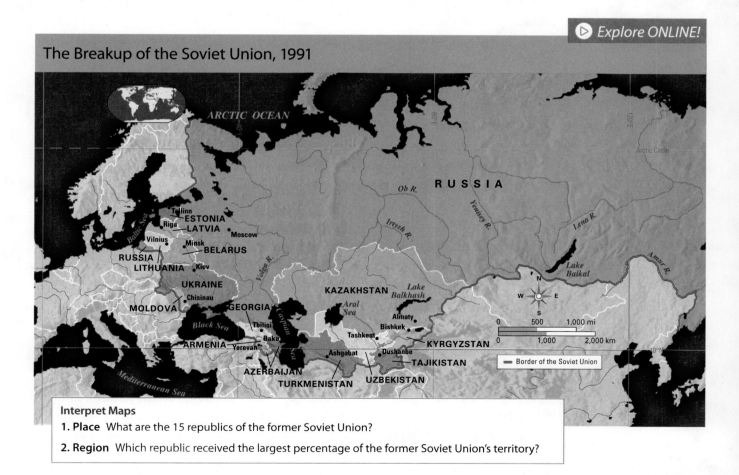

▶ Explore ONLINE!

The Breakup of the Soviet Union, 1991

Interpret Maps

1. **Place** What are the 15 republics of the former Soviet Union?

2. **Region** Which republic received the largest percentage of the former Soviet Union's territory?

A Russian soldier throws away a spent shell case near the Chechnyan capital of Grozny.

Russia Under Boris Yeltsin

As president of the large Russian Federation, Boris Yeltsin was now the most powerful figure in the CIS. He would face many problems, including an ailing economy, tough political opposition, and an unpopular war.

Yeltsin Faces Problems One of Yeltsin's goals was to reform the Russian economy. He adopted a bold plan known as **"shock therapy,"** an abrupt shift to free-market economics. Yeltsin lowered trade barriers, removed price controls, and ended subsidies to state-owned industries.

Initially, the plan produced more shock than therapy. Prices soared; from 1992 to 1994, the inflation rate averaged 800 percent. Many factories dependent on government money had to cut production or shut down entirely. This forced thousands of people out of work. By 1993 most Russians were suffering economic hardship.

Economic problems fueled a political crisis. In October 1993, legislators opposed to Yeltsin's policies shut themselves inside the parliament building. Yeltsin ordered troops to bombard the building, forcing hundreds of rebel legislators to surrender. Many were killed. Opponents accused Yeltsin of acting like a dictator.

Vocabulary
subsidies
government funds given in support of industries

Impact on the World The breakup of the Soviet Union created challenges in many parts of the world. Tensions between Russia and the United States grew as Yeltsin and other Russian leaders worried about U.S. dominance. Leaders in Moscow strengthened relations with China and India in an attempt to challenge the United States. Hostility grew further as the two nations disagreed over issues in Iraq.

Dozens of countries had chosen to stay nonaligned, or neutral, during the Cold War. These nations were also impacted by the collapse of the Soviet Union. Some feared the nonaligned countries that had banded together during the Cold War had lost their purpose to protect nations of the developing world. Internal conflicts among the many diverse members of the movement also presented problems.

Chechnya Rebels Yeltsin's troubles included war in Chechnya (CHEHCH•nee•uh), a largely Muslim area in southwestern Russia. In 1991, Chechnya declared its independence, but Yeltsin denied the region's right to secede. In 1994, he ordered 40,000 Russian troops into the breakaway republic. Russian forces reduced the capital city of Grozny (GROHZ•nee) to rubble. News of the death and destruction sparked anger throughout Russia.

With an election coming, Yeltsin sought to end the war. In August 1996, the two sides signed a ceasefire. That year, Yeltsin won reelection. War soon broke out again between Russia and Chechnya, however. In 1999, as the fighting raged, Yeltsin resigned and named Vladimir Putin as acting president.

Reading Check
Compare Compare Yeltsin's action here to his actions during the August Coup. Which were more supportive of democracy?

Russia Under Vladimir Putin

Putin forcefully dealt with the rebellion in Chechnya—a popular move that helped him win the presidential election in 2000. Nonetheless, violence in the region continues.

— BIOGRAPHY —

Vladimir Putin (1952–)

Vladimir Putin worked for 15 years as an intelligence officer in the KGB (Committee for State Security). Six of those years were spent in East Germany. In 1990, at the age of 38, he retired from the KGB with the rank of lieutenant colonel.

In 1996, he moved to Moscow where he joined the presidential staff. Eventually, Boris Yeltsin appointed Putin prime minister. When Yeltsin resigned at the end of 1999, he appointed Putin acting president. In 2000 and 2004, Putin won election as president. In 2008, he took the post of prime minister. He returned to the office of president for a third term in 2012.

Putin Struggles with Chechnya Putin's war in Chechnya helped draw terrorism into the Russian capital itself. In October 2002, Chechens seized a theater in Moscow, and more than 150 people died in the rescue attempt by Russian forces.

As the war in Chechnya dragged on, Russian popular support faded, and Putin moved to suppress his critics. The 2005 Chechen elections helped restore order, and as of 2010, under current Russian president, Dmitry Medvedev, the rebels had been largely quieted. But rebellion still simmers.

Economic, Political, and Social Problems Since the collapse of the Soviet Union, Russia has seen growth in homelessness, domestic violence, and unemployment, and a decrease in life expectancy. Concerns over Russia's nuclear weapons have grown. Experts worry that security at nuclear storage sites in Russia is lacking. In addition, several former Soviet republics have stockpiles of nuclear weapons that some worry could get in the hands of rogue states and terrorist organizations.

Observers have wondered whether Russian democracy could survive. Putin's presidency has not settled the question. Russia has been moving toward greater participation in world trade by modernizing banking, insurance, and tax codes. Putin also worked to improve the economy by increasing exports in oil and natural gas. At the same time, attacks on democratic institutions such as a free press have not built the world's confidence.

The histories of Russia and its European neighbors have always been intertwined. Unrest in the Soviet Union had an enormous impact on Central and Eastern Europe as well.

Reading Check
Make Inferences
Why do you think some critics have wondered whether Russian democracy will survive?

Lesson 3 Assessment

1. **Organize Information** Add major events from the lesson to a timeline like the one shown here.

2. **Key Terms and People** For each key term or person in the lesson, write a sentence explaining its significance.

3. **Evaluate** Describe the weaknesses of the Soviet command economy.

4. **Synthesize** How did Gorbachev's reforms help to move the Soviet Union toward democracy?

5. **Evaluate** What were some of the consequences of the breakup of the Soviet Union?

6. **Compare** In what ways were the policies of Gorbachev, Yeltsin, and Putin similar?

Changes in Central and Eastern Europe

Setting the Stage

The Soviet reforms of the late 1980s brought high hopes to the people of Central and Eastern Europe. For the first time in decades, they were free to make choices about the economic and political systems governing their lives. However, they discovered that increased freedom sometimes challenges the social order. Mikhail Gorbachev's new thinking in the Soviet Union led him to urge Central and Eastern European leaders to open up their economic and political systems.

The Big Idea

Changes in the Soviet Union led to changes throughout Central and Eastern Europe.

Why It Matters Now

Many Eastern European nations that overthrew Communist governments are still struggling with reform.

Key Terms and People

Solidarity
Lech Walesa
reunification
ethnic cleansing

Poland and Hungary Reform

The aging Communist rulers of Europe resisted reform. However, powerful forces for democracy were building in their countries. In the past, the threat of Soviet intervention had kept such forces in check. Now, Gorbachev was saying that the Soviet Union would not oppose reform.

Poland and Hungary were among the first countries in Eastern Europe to embrace the spirit of change. In 1980, Polish workers at the Gdansk shipyard went on strike, demanding government recognition of their union, **Solidarity**. When millions of Poles supported the action, the government gave in to the union's demands. Union leader **Lech Walesa** (lehk-vah•WEHN•sah) became a national hero.

Solidarity Defeats Communists The next year, however, the Polish government banned Solidarity again and declared martial law. The Communist Party discovered that military rule could not revive Poland's failing economy. In the 1980s, industrial production declined, while foreign debt rose to more than $40 billion.

Public discontent deepened as the economic crisis worsened. In August 1988, defiant workers walked off their jobs. They demanded raises and the legalization of Solidarity. The military leader, General Jaruzelski (yar•uh•ZEHL•skee), agreed to hold talks with Solidarity leaders. In April 1989,

Jaruzelski legalized Solidarity and agreed to hold Poland's first free election since the Communists took power.

In elections during 1989 and 1990, Polish voters voted against Communists and overwhelmingly chose Solidarity candidates. They elected Lech Walesa president.

Poland Votes Out Walesa After becoming president in 1990, Lech Walesa tried to revive Poland's bankrupt economy. Like Boris Yeltsin, he adopted a strategy of shock therapy to move Poland toward a free-market economy. As in Russia, inflation and unemployment shot up. By the mid-1990s, the economy was improving.

Nevertheless, many Poles remained unhappy with the pace of economic progress. In the elections of 1995, they turned Walesa out of office in favor of a former Communist, Aleksander Kwasniewski (kfahs•N'YEHF•skee).

Poland Under Kwasniewski President Kwasniewski led Poland in its drive to become part of a broader European community. In 1999, Poland became a full member of NATO. As a NATO member, Poland provided strong support in the war against terrorism after the attack on the World Trade Center in New York on September 11, 2001.

In 2005, Lech Kaczynski of the conservative Law and Justice party won the presidency. The following year Kaczynski's twin brother Jaroslaw became prime minister. The Kaczynskis fought Poland's pervasive corruption, opposed rapid reforms of the free market, and supported the American-led campaign in Iraq. After Lech Kaczynski was killed in a plane crash in 2010, Bronislaw Komorowski of the Civic Platform party was elected president. Political scandals lowered support of Komorowski's party, however, and Polish citizens elected Andrzej Duda to replace him in 2015.

Hungarian Communists Disband Inspired by the changes in Poland, Hungarian leaders launched a sweeping reform program. To stimulate economic growth, reformers encouraged private enterprise and allowed a small stock market to operate. A new constitution permitted a multiparty system with free elections.

The pace of change grew faster when radical reformers took over a Communist Party congress in October 1989. The radicals deposed the party's leaders and then dissolved the party itself. Here was another first: a European Communist Party had voted itself out of existence. A year later, in national elections, the nation's voters put a non-Communist government in power.

In 1994, a socialist party—largely made up of former Communists—won a majority of seats in Hungary's parliament. The socialist party and a democratic party formed a coalition, or alliance, to rule.

In parliamentary elections in 1998, a liberal party won the most seats in the National Assembly. In 1999, Hungary joined the North Atlantic Treaty Organization as a full member. In the year 2001, there was a general economic downturn in Hungary. This was due to weak exports, a

Vocabulary
deposed removed from power

decline in foreign investment, excessive spending on state pensions, and increased minimum wages. Economic crises continued through the early part of the twenty-first century, leading to broad legislative actions by the Fidesz administration. In 2012, Hungary adopted a new constitution that emphasized conservative, Christian morals. Many in Hungary protested this constitution, and foreign criticism rose as well.

Reading Check
Analyze Causes
How did Solidarity affect Communist rule in Poland?

Germany Reunifies

While Poland and Hungary were moving toward reform, East Germany's 77-year-old party boss, Erich Honecker, dismissed reforms as unnecessary. Then, in 1989, Hungary allowed vacationing East German tourists to cross the border into Austria. From there they could travel to West Germany. Thousands of East Germans took this new escape route to the west.

Fall of the Berlin Wall In response, the East German government closed its borders entirely. By October 1989, huge demonstrations had broken out in cities across East Germany. The protesters demanded the right to travel freely, and later added the demand for free elections. Honecker lost his authority with the party and resigned on October 18.

In June 1987, President Reagan had stood before the Berlin Wall and demanded, "Mr. Gorbachev, tear down this wall!" Two years later, the wall was indeed about to come down. The new East German leader, Egon Krenz, boldly gambled that he could restore stability by allowing people to leave East Germany. On November 9, 1989, he opened the Berlin Wall. The long-divided city of Berlin erupted in joyous celebration. Krenz's dramatic gamble to save communism did not work. By the end of 1989, the East German Communist Party had ceased to exist.

The fall of the Berlin Wall, November 10, 1989

Reunification With the fall of communism in East Germany, many Germans began to speak of **reunification**—the merging of the two Germanys. However, the movement for reunification worried many people who feared a united Germany.

The West German chancellor, Helmut Kohl, assured world leaders that Germans had learned from the past. They were now committed to democracy and human rights. Kohl's assurances helped persuade other European nations to accept German reunification. Germany was officially reunited on October 3, 1990.

Germany's Challenges The newly united Germany faced serious problems. More than 40 years of Communist rule had left eastern Germany in ruins. Its railroads, highways, and telephone system had not been modernized since World War II. East German industries produced goods that could not compete in the global market.

Rebuilding eastern Germany's bankrupt economy was going to be a difficult, costly process. To pay these costs, Kohl raised taxes. As taxpayers tightened their belts, workers in eastern Germany faced a second problem—unemployment. Inefficient factories closed, depriving millions of workers of their jobs.

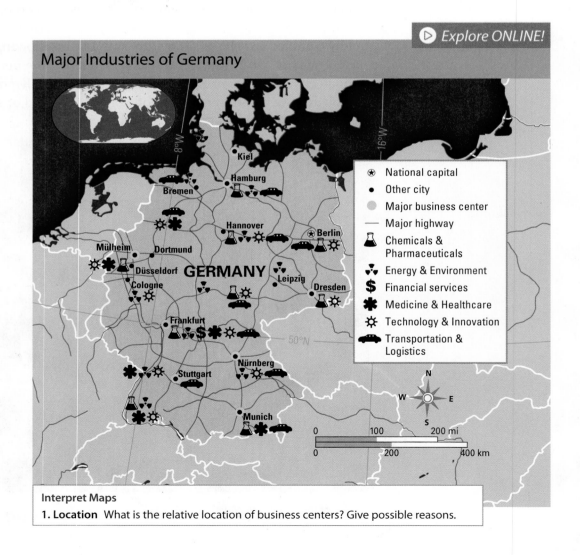

▷ Explore ONLINE!

Major Industries of Germany

Legend:
- ⊛ National capital
- • Other city
- ● Major business center
- — Major highway
- ⚗ Chemicals & Pharmaceuticals
- Energy & Environment
- $ Financial services
- ✳ Medicine & Healthcare
- ☼ Technology & Innovation
- Transportation & Logistics

Interpret Maps

1. **Location** What is the relative location of business centers? Give possible reasons.

Economic Challenges In 1998, voters turned Kohl out of office and elected a new chancellor, Gerhard Schroeder, of the Socialist Democratic Party (SDP). Schroeder started out as a market reformer, but slow economic growth made the task of reform difficult. Although Germany had the world's third largest economy, it had sunk to fifth by 2005. Germany's unemployment rate was among the highest in Europe, and rising inflation was a problem. However, in 2006, a year after Angela Merkel of the Christian Democratic Union (CDU) was elected chancellor, unemployment fell below 4 million, and Germany's budget deficit was kept to within EU limits. In 2013, Merkel became only the third chancellor in Germany since World War II to win three elections, and her international popularity remained high.

Reunification has also forced Germany—as Central Europe's largest country—to rethink its role in international affairs.

Reading Check
Synthesize Why would Europeans fear the reunification of Germany?

Democracy Spreads in Czechoslovakia

Changes in East Germany affected other European countries, including Czechoslovakia and Romania.

Czechoslovakia Reforms While huge crowds were demanding democracy in East Germany, neighboring Czechoslovakia remained quiet. A conservative government led by Milos Jakes resisted all change. In 1989, the police arrested several dissidents. Among those was the Czech playwright Václav Havel (VAH•tslahv-HAH•vehl), a popular critic of the government.

On October 28, 1989, about 10,000 people gathered in Wenceslas Square in the center of Prague. They demanded democracy and freedom. Hundreds were arrested. Three weeks later, about 25,000 students inspired by the fall of the Berlin Wall gathered in Prague to demand reform. Following orders from the government, the police brutally attacked the demonstrators and injured hundreds.

The government crackdown angered the Czech people. Huge crowds gathered in Wenceslas Square. They demanded an end to Communist rule. On November 25, about 500,000 protesters crowded into downtown Prague. Within hours, Milos Jakes and his entire Politburo resigned. One month later, a new parliament elected Václav Havel president of Czechoslovakia.

Czechoslovakia Breaks Up In Czechoslovakia, reformers also launched an economic program based on "shock therapy." The program caused a sharp rise in unemployment. It especially hurt Slovakia, the republic occupying the eastern third of Czechoslovakia.

Unable to agree on economic policy, the country's two parts—Slovakia and the Czech Republic—drifted apart. In spite of President Václav Havel's pleas for unity, a movement to split the nation gained support among the people. Havel resigned because of this. Czechoslovakia split into two countries on January 1, 1993.

Havel was elected president of the Czech Republic. He won reelection in 1998. Then, in 2003, Havel stepped down as president, in part because of ill health. The Czech parliament chose Václav Klaus, a right-wing economist and former prime minister, to succeed him. The economy of the Czech Republic has steadily improved in the face of some serious problems, aided by its becoming a full member of the European Union (EU) in 2004. In 2012, the Czech government passed a constitutional amendment to allow direct presidential elections. The following year Milos Zeman was elected in the first presidential election in the country.

Slovakia, too, proceeded on a reformist, pro-Western path. It experienced one of the highest economic growth rates in the region in 2002. In 2004, it elected Ivan Gasparovic president and joined both NATO and the EU. Andrej Kiska, an entrepreneur, became president in 2014.

Reading Check
Analyze Causes
What was the main cause of the breakup of Czechoslovakia?

Overthrow in Romania

By late 1989, only Romania seemed unmoved by the calls for reform. Romania's ruthless Communist dictator Nicolae Ceausescu (chow•SHES•koo) maintained a firm grip on power. His secret police enforced his orders brutally. Nevertheless, Romanians were aware of the reforms in other countries. They began a protest movement of their own.

A Popular Uprising In December, Ceausescu ordered the army to fire on demonstrators in the city of Timisoara (tee•mee•SHWAH•rah). The army killed and wounded hundreds of people. The massacre in Timisoara ignited a popular uprising against Ceausescu. Within days, the army joined the people. Shocked by the collapse of his power, Ceausescu and his wife attempted to flee. They were captured, however, and then tried and executed on Christmas Day, 1989. Elections have been held regularly since then. In 2014, Klaus Iohannis was elected president.

SOCIAL HISTORY

The Romanian Language

The Romanians are the only people in Eastern Europe whose ancestry and language go back to the ancient Romans. Romanian is the only Eastern European language that developed from Latin. For this reason, Romanian is very different from the other languages spoken in the region.

Today's Romanians are descended from the Dacians (the original people in the region), the Romans, and tribes that arrived later, such as the Goths, Huns, and Slavs.

Romanian remains the official language today. Minority groups within Romania (such as Hungarians, Germans, Gypsies, Jews, Turks, and Ukrainians) sometimes speak their own ethnic languages among themselves. Nonetheless, almost all the people speak Romanian as well.

A view of downtown Sarajevo through a bullet-shattered window

The Romanian Economy Throughout the 1990s, Romania struggled with corruption and crime as it tried to salvage its economy. In 2001, overall production was still only 75 percent of what it had been in 1989, the year of Ceausescu's overthrow. In the first years of the twenty-first century, two-thirds of the economy was still state owned.

However, the government made economic reforms to introduce elements of capitalism. The government also began to reduce the layers of bureaucracy in order to encourage foreign investors. In 2007, Romania joined the European Union as the Romanian government began to move away from a state controlled economy. Much of Iohannis's campaign focused on ending corruption and raising living standards for Romanians. The nation is the second poorest in the European Union.

Reading Check
Contrast Contrast the democratic revolutions in Czechoslovakia and Romania.

The Breakup of Yugoslavia

Ethnic conflict plagued Yugoslavia. This country, formed after World War I, had eight major ethnic groups—Serbs, Croats, Bosniaks, Slovenes, Macedonians, Albanians, Hungarians, and Montenegrins. Ethnic and religious differences dating back centuries caused many people to develop prejudiced views of other groups, based on long-held stereotypes. After World War II, Yugoslavia became a federation of six republics. Each republic had a mixed population.

A Bloody Breakup Josip Tito, who led Yugoslavia from 1945 to 1980, held the country together. After Tito's death, ethnic resentments boiled over. Serbian leader Slobodan Milosevic (mee•LOH•sheh•vihch) asserted leadership over Yugoslavia. Many Serbs opposed Milosevic and his policies and fled the country.

Two republics, Slovenia and Croatia, declared independence. In June 1991, the Serbian-led Yugoslav army invaded both republics. After months of bloody fighting, both republics freed themselves from Serbian rule. Early in 1992, Bosnia-Herzegovina joined Slovenia and Croatia in declaring independence. (In April, Serbia and Montenegro formed a new Yugoslavia.) Bosnia's population included Bosniaks (44 percent), Serbs (31 percent), and Croats (17 percent). While Bosniaks and Croats backed independence, Bosnian Serbs strongly opposed it. Supported by the country of Serbia, the Bosnian Serbs launched a war in March 1992.

During the war, Serbian military forces used violence and forced emigration against Bosniaks living in Serb-held lands. Called **ethnic cleansing**, this policy was intended to rid Bosnia of its Bosniak population. The international response focused on providing humanitarian aid to those affected by the war. Critics argue that many nations, including the United States and those in the European Union, could have done more to end the human rights abuses taking place in Bosnia. By 1995, the Serbian military controlled 70 percent of Bosnia. In December of that year, leaders of the three factions involved in the war signed a UN- and U.S.-brokered peace treaty. In September 1996, Bosnians elected a three-person presidency, one leader from each ethnic group. By 2001, Bosnia and Herzegovina began to stand on its own without as much need for supervision by the international community.

Rebellion in Kosovo The Balkan region descended into violence and bloodshed again in 1998, this time in Kosovo, a province in southern Serbia made up almost entirely of ethnic Albanians. As an independence movement in Kosovo grew increasingly violent, Serbian military forces invaded the province. In response to growing reports of atrocities—and the failure of diplomacy to bring peace—NATO began a bombing campaign against Yugoslavia in the spring of 1999. After enduring more than two months of sustained bombing, Yugoslav leaders finally withdrew their troops from Kosovo. In 2007, talks continued over the status of Kosovo.

The Region Faces Its Problems In the early years of the twenty-first century, there were conflicting signs in Yugoslavia. Slobodan Milosevic was extradited to stand trial for war crimes but died in 2006, while his trial was continuing. A large portion of the country's foreign debt was erased. Despite an independence movement in Kosovo, parliamentary elections under UN supervision took place in November 2001 without violence.

Ethnic Groups in the Former Yugoslavia

Many ethnic and religious groups lived within Yugoslavia, which was a federation of six republics. The map shows how the ethnic groups were distributed. Some of those groups held ancient grudges against one another. The chart summarizes some of the cultural differences among the groups.

Ethnic Groups in the Former Yugoslavia, 1992

▷ Explore ONLINE!

Differences Among the Ethnic Groups

Group	Language (slavic unless noted)	Religion
Albanians	Albanian (not Slavic)	mostly Bosniak
Croats	dialect of Serbo-Croatian*	mostly Roman Catholic
Hungarians	Magyar (not Slavic)	many types of Christians
Macedonians	Macedonian	mostly Eastern Orthodox
Montenegrins	dialect of Serbo-Croatian*	mostly Eastern Orthodox
Bosniak	dialect of Serbo-Croatian*	Muslim (converted under Ottoman rule)
Serbs	dialect of Serbo-Croatian*	mostly Eastern Orthodox
Slovenes	Slovenian	mostly Roman Catholic

Interpret Visuals

Use the chart to find out information about the various groups that lived in Bosnia and Herzegovina (as shown on the map). What were some of the differences among those groups?

*Since Yugoslavia broke apart, many residents of the former republics have started to refer to their dialects as separate languages: Croatian for Croats, Bosnian for Bosniaks, Serbian for Serbs and Montenegrins.

In Montenegro (which together with Serbia made up Yugoslavia), an independence referendum in May 2006 revealed that most voters wanted to separate from Serbia. As the Montenegrins declared independence in 2006, Serbia accepted the new situation peacefully. In 2007, Serbia held a parliamentary election in which the ultra-nationalist Radical Party made some gains, but it could not win enough seats to form a new government.

The nations of Central and Eastern Europe made many gains in the early years of the twenty-first century. Even so, they continued to face serious obstacles to democracy. Resolving ethnic conflicts remained crucial, as did economic progress. If the nations of Central and Eastern Europe and the former Soviet Union can improve their standard of living, democracy may have a better chance to grow.

Reading Check
Identify Problems
Why did Bosnia's mixed population cause a problem after Bosnia declared independence?

Lesson 4 Assessment

1. **Organize Information** Which nation seems to have done best since the breakup? Explain.

Former nations	Reasons for breakup
Yugoslavia	
Czechoslovakia	

2. **Key Terms and People** For each key term or person in the lesson, write a sentence explaining its significance.

3. **Evaluate** What effect did reunification have on Germany's international role?

4. **Analyze Causes** Why did ethnic tension become such a severe problem in the Soviet Union and Yugoslavia?

5. **Draw Conclusions** What are some of the problems faced in Central and Eastern Europe in the twenty-first century?

6. **Analyze Effects** What effect did economic reform have on Slovakia?

China: Reform and Reaction

Setting the Stage

The trend toward democracy around the world also affected China to a limited degree. A political reform movement arose in the late 1980s. It built on economic reforms begun earlier in the decade. However, although the leadership of the Communist Party in China generally supported economic reform, it opposed political reform. China's Communist government clamped down on the political reformers. At the same time, it maintained a firm grip on power in the country.

The Legacy of Mao

After the Communists came to power in China in 1949, Mao Zedong set out to transform China. Mao believed that peasant equality, revolutionary spirit, and hard work were all that was needed to improve the Chinese economy.

However, lack of modern technology damaged Chinese efforts to increase agricultural and industrial output. In addition, Mao's policies stifled economic growth. He eliminated incentives for higher production. He tried to replace

Mao's Attempts to Change China

Mao's Programs	Program Results
First Five-Year Plan 1953–1957	Industry grew 15 percent a year. Agricultural output grew very slowly.
Great Leap Forward 1958–1961	China suffered economic disaster—industrial declines and food shortages. Mao lost influence.
Cultural Revolution 1966–1976	Mao regained influence by backing radicals. Purges and conflicts among leaders created economic, social, and political chaos.

Interpret Charts
Which of Mao's programs do you think had the greatest impact on China?

Zhou Enlai, a translator, Mao Zedong, President Nixon, and Henry Kissinger meet in Beijing in 1972.

family life with life in the communes. These policies took away the peasants' motive to work for the good of themselves and their families.

Facing economic disaster, some Chinese Communists talked of modernizing the economy. Accusing them of "taking the capitalist road," Mao began the Cultural Revolution in 1966 to cleanse China of antirevolutionary influences.

Instead of saving radical communism, however, the Cultural Revolution turned many people against it. In the early 1970s, China entered another moderate period under **Zhou Enlai** (joh-ehn•ly). Zhou had been premier since 1949. During the Cultural Revolution, he had tried to restrain the radicals.

Reading Check
Analyze Effects
What was the ultimate result of Mao's radical Communist policies?

China and the West

Throughout the Cultural Revolution, China played almost no role in world affairs. In the early 1960s, China had split with the Soviet Union over the leadership of world communism. In addition, China displayed hostility toward the United States because of U.S. support for the government on Taiwan.

China Opened Its Doors China's isolation worried Zhou. He began to send out signals that he was willing to form ties to the West. In 1971, Zhou startled the world by inviting an American table-tennis team to tour China. It was the first visit by an American group to China since 1949.

The visit began a new era in Chinese-American relations. In 1971, the United States reversed its policy and endorsed UN membership for the People's Republic of China. The next year, President Nixon made a state visit to China. He met with Mao and Zhou. The three leaders agreed to begin cultural exchanges and a limited amount of trade. In 1979, the United States and China established diplomatic relations.

Economic Reform Both Mao and Zhou died in 1976. Soon, moderates took control of the Communist Party. They jailed several of the radicals who had led the Cultural Revolution. By 1980, **Deng Xiaoping** (duhng-show•pihng) had emerged as the most powerful leader in China. He was the last of the "old revolutionaries" who had ruled China since 1949.

Although a lifelong Communist, Deng boldly supported moderate economic policies. Unlike Mao, he was willing to use capitalist ideas to help China's economy. He embraced a set of goals known as the **Four Modernizations**. These called for progress in agriculture, industry, defense, and science and technology. Deng launched an ambitious program of economic reforms.

First, Deng eliminated Mao's communes and leased the land to individual farmers. The farmers paid rent by delivering a fixed quota of food to the government. They could then grow crops and sell them for a profit. Under this system, food production increased by 50 percent in the years 1978 to 1984.

Deng extended his program to industry. The government permitted private businesses to operate. It gave the managers of state-owned industries more freedom to set production goals. Deng also welcomed foreign technology and investment.

Deng's economic policies produced striking changes in Chinese life. As incomes increased, people began to buy appliances and televisions. Chinese youths now wore stylish clothes and listened to Western music. Gleaming hotels filled with foreign tourists symbolized China's new policy of openness.

Reading Check
Synthesize What were some of Deng Xiaoping's economic reforms?

Massacre in Tiananmen Square

Deng's economic reforms produced a number of unexpected problems. As living standards improved, the gap between the rich and poor widened. Increasingly, the public believed that party officials profited from their positions.

Furthermore, the new policies admitted not only Western investments and tourists but also Western political ideas. Increasing numbers of Chinese students studied abroad and learned about the West. In Deng's view, the benefits of opening the economy exceeded the risks. Nevertheless, as Chinese students learned more about democracy, they began to question China's lack of political freedom.

Students Demand Democracy In 1989, students sparked a popular uprising that stunned China's leaders. Beginning in April of that year, more than 100,000 students occupied **Tiananmen** (tyahn•ahn•mehn) **Square**, a huge public space in the heart of Beijing. The students mounted a protest for democracy.

The student protest won widespread popular support. When thousands of students began a hunger strike to highlight their cause, people poured into Tiananmen Square to support them. Many students called for Deng Xiaoping to resign.

Deng Orders a Crackdown Instead of considering political reform, Deng declared martial law. He ordered about 100,000 troops to surround Beijing. Although many students left the square after martial law was declared, about 5,000 chose to remain and continue their protest.

Training the Chinese Army

After the massacre in Tiananmen Square, Xiao Ye (a former Chinese soldier living in the United States) explained how Chinese soldiers are trained to obey orders without complaint.

Analyze Historical Sources

1. For whom did the soldiers seem to believe they were making their physical sacrifices?

2. What attitude toward obeying orders did their training seem to encourage in the soldiers?

"We usually developed bleeding blisters on our feet after a few days of . . . hiking. Our feet were a mass of soggy peeling flesh and blood, and the pain was almost unbearable. . . . We considered the physical challenge a means of tempering [hardening] ourselves for the sake of the Party. . . . No one wanted to look bad. . . ."

"And during the days in Tiananmen, once again the soldiers did not complain. They obediently drove forward, aimed, and opened fire on command. In light of their training, how could it have been otherwise?"

—Xiao Ye, "Tiananmen Square: A Soldier's Story"

The students revived their spirits by defiantly erecting a 33-foot statue that they named the "Goddess of Democracy."

On June 4, 1989, the standoff came to an end. Thousands of heavily armed soldiers stormed Tiananmen Square. Tanks smashed through barricades and crushed the Goddess of Democracy. Soldiers sprayed gunfire into crowds of frightened students. They also attacked protesters elsewhere in Beijing. The assault killed hundreds and wounded thousands.

The attack on Tiananmen Square marked the beginning of a massive government campaign to stamp out protest. Police arrested thousands of people. The state used the media to announce that reports of a massacre were untrue. Officials claimed that a small group of criminals had plotted against the government. Television news, however, had already broadcast the truth to the world.

Reading Check
Analyze Causes How did economic reform introduce new political ideas to China?

China Enters the New Millennium

The brutal repression of the prodemocracy movement left Deng firmly in control of China. During the final years of his life, Deng continued his program of economic reforms.

Although Deng moved out of the limelight in 1995, he remained China's leader. In February 1997, after a long illness, Deng died. Communist Party General Secretary Jiang Zemin (jee•ahng-zeh•meen) assumed the presidency.

China Under Jiang Many questions arose after Deng's death. What kind of leader would Jiang be? Would he be able to hold on to power and ensure political stability? A highly intelligent and educated man, Jiang had served as mayor of Shanghai. He was considered skilled, flexible, and practical. However, he had no military experience. Therefore, Jiang had few allies among the generals. He also faced challenges from rivals, including hard-line officials who favored a shift away from Deng's economic policies.

Other questions following Deng's death had to do with China's poor human rights record, its occupation of Tibet, and relations with the United States. During the 1990s, the United States pressured China to release political prisoners and ensure basic rights for political opponents. China remained hostile to such pressure. Its government continued to repress the prodemocracy movement. Nevertheless, the desire for freedom still ran through Chinese society. If China remained economically open but politically closed, tensions seemed bound to surface.

In late 1997, Jiang paid a state visit to the United States. During his visit, U.S. protesters demanded more democracy in China. Jiang admitted that China had made some mistakes but refused to promise that China's policies would change.

President Jiang Zemin and Premier Zhu Rongji announced their retirement in late 2002. Jiang's successor was Hu Jintao. However, Jiang was expected to wield influence over his successor behind the scenes. Hu became president of the country and general secretary of the Communist Party. Jiang remained political leader of the military. Both supported China's move to a market economy.

Jiang Zemin
(1926–)

Jiang Zemin was trained as an engineer. After working as an engineer, heading several technological institutes, and serving as minister of the electronics industry, he moved up in politics.

In 1982, he joined the Central Committee of the Communist Party in China. He became mayor of Shanghai in 1985, in which post he proved to be an effective administrator. In 1989, he became general secretary of the Chinese Communist Party. This promotion was largely due to his support for the government's putdown of the prodemocracy demonstrations in that year. In 1993, he became president. In 2003, he stepped down and was replaced by Hu Jintao; however, Jiang retained power behind the scenes.

Reading Check
Summarize
What challenges did Jiang Zemin face when he became president?

Transfer of Hong Kong Another major issue for China was the status of **Hong Kong**. Hong Kong was a thriving business center and British colony on the southeastern coast of China. On July 1, 1997, Great Britain handed Hong Kong over to China, ending 155 years of colonial rule. As part of the transfer, China promised to respect Hong Kong's economic system and political liberties for 50 years.

Many of Hong Kong's citizens worried about Chinese rule and feared the loss of their freedoms. Others, however, saw the transfer as a way to reconnect with their Chinese heritage. In the first four or five years after the transfer, the control of mainland China over Hong Kong tightened.

China Beyond 2000

The case of China demonstrates that the creation of democracy can be a slow, fitful, and incomplete process. Liberal reforms in one area, such as the economy, may not lead immediately to political reforms.

People celebrate in Tiananmen Square after Beijing won the bid for the 2008 Olympic Games.

Economics and Politics In China, there has been a dramatic reduction in poverty. Some experts argue that China managed to reform its economy and reduce poverty because it adopted a gradual approach to selling off state industries and privatizing the economy rather than a more abrupt approach. China's strategy has paid off; by 2007, the country had the world's fourth largest economy, after the United States, Japan, and Germany. Cheap consumer goods from China are filling shops and department stores worldwide.

But China's economic strength has come with a cost. The wealth gap between urban and rural areas has widened, with inequality leading to social unrest. In addition, rapid industrialization has caused pollution and severe environmental problems.

As countries are increasingly linked through technology and trade, they will have more opportunity to influence each other politically. When the U.S. Congress voted to normalize trade with China, supporters of such a move argued that the best way to prompt political change in China is through greater engagement rather than isolation. Another sign of China's increasing engagement with the world was its successful hosting of the 2008 Summer Olympics in Beijing. Two years later China hosted the Expo 2010, a world exposition in Shanghai that was one of the largest world fairs ever hosted.

In recent years, China's economy has begun to slow. Decreased global demand has caused traditional sources of growth in China, such as investment and manufacturing, to decline. A new five-year plan introduced in 2015 has promised to better balance the economy by focusing on the service and technology industries. The plan also officially ends the controversial one-child policy in China to help increase the future labor supply.

Reading Check
Make Inferences
Why has technology led to an increase in political influence among China and other countries?

Lesson 5 Assessment

1. **Organize Information** Other than the demonstration in Tiananmen Square, which events in the lesson were most important? Explain.

2. **Key Terms and People** For each key term or person in the lesson, write a sentence explaining its significance.

3. **Analyze Effects** What effect did Mao's policies have on economic growth?

4. **Form Opinions** How would you describe China's record on human rights?

5. **Predict** Judging from what you have read about the Chinese government, do you think Hong Kong will keep its freedoms under Chinese rule? Explain.

6. **Summarize** What were some of the events that followed the demonstration in Tiananmen Square?

7. **Compare and Contrast** Has there been greater progress in political or economic reform in China?

Photojournalism

From the earliest days of photography, media such as magazines and newspapers have used photographs to convey the news. Today, websites are a common source of news journalism. Photojournalists must respond quickly to recognize a history-making moment and to record that moment before it passes. As these photographs demonstrate, photojournalists have captured many of the democratic struggles that have occurred in the last few decades. In some cases, news photographs have helped protesters or oppressed people gain the support of the world.

FLIGHT FROM SREBRENICA ▶
During the conflicts in Bosnia and Herzegovina, the United Nations declared the city of Srebrenica a safe area. Even so, the Bosnian Serb army invaded in July 1995 and expelled more than 20,000 Muslims—nearly all of them women, children, or elderly people. In addition, the soldiers held more than 7,000 men and boys prisoner and over a five-day period massacred them.

▲ MAN DEFYING TANKS
A single Chinese man blocked tanks on their way to crush prodemocracy protests in Tiananmen Square in June 1989. No one knows for sure what happened to the man afterward—or even who he was. Even so, this image has become one of the enduring photographs of the 20th century; it has come to stand for one man's courage in defying tyranny.

▲ ABUELAS DE PLAZA DE MAYO
From 1976 to 1983, the military government of Argentina tortured and killed thousands of political dissidents and sometimes stole their children. In this demonstration in December 1979, the *Abuelas de Plaza de Mayo* (Grandmothers of the Plaza de Mayo) demanded to know the fate of their relatives. The banner they carried reads "Disappeared Children."

▲ FALL OF THE WALL
When the East German government opened the Berlin Wall in November 1989, a huge celebration broke out. Some people began to use pickaxes to demolish the wall entirely. Others danced on top of the wall.

▲ VOTING LINE
When South Africa held its first all-race election in April 1994, people were so eager to vote that they stood in lines that sometimes stretched nearly a kilometer (0.62 mile).

Critical Thinking
1. **Form Opinions** Choose one of the photographs, and evaluate its impact on human behavior.
2. **Evaluate** Use the Internet to find a news photograph that you think effectively shows a recent historic event. Bring a copy of the photograph to class, and explain orally or in writing what it conveys about the event. Be sure to carefully evaluate the website you choose for accuracy.

Module 31 Assessment

Key Terms and People

For each term or name below, write a sentence explaining its connection to the democratic movements that took place from 1945 to the present.

1. PRI
2. apartheid
3. Nelson Mandela
4. Mikhail Gorbachev
5. glasnost
6. Lech Walesa
7. Deng Xiaoping
8. Tiananmen Square

Main Ideas

Use your notes and the information in the module to answer the following questions.

Democracy

1. What are four common democratic practices?
2. What group held up democratic progress in both Brazil and Argentina until the 1980s?

The Challenge of Democracy in Africa

3. What brought about the civil war in Nigeria?
4. What were three significant steps toward democracy taken by South Africa in the 1990s?

The Collapse of the Soviet Union

5. What were the main reforms promoted by Soviet leader Mikhail Gorbachev?
6. What was the August Coup, and how did it end?

Changes in Central and Eastern Europe

7. Which nations overthrew Communist governments in 1989?
8. What led to the breakup of Yugoslavia?

China: Reform and Reaction

9. What changes took place in China during the 1970s?
10. How did the Chinese government react to demands for democratic reform?

Critical Thinking

1. **Evaluate** List several leaders who helped their nations make democratic progress. For each, cite one positive action.

2. **Analyze Issues** What are some examples from this chapter in which the negative impact of one culture on another blocked democratic progress?

3. **Synthesize** Consider what conditions helped democratic movements succeed and what conditions caused difficulties for them. What do you think were their hardest challenges?

4. **Draw Conclusions** How does a nation's economy affect its democratic progress?

5. **Summarize** It has been said that Gorbachev's reforms led to another Russian Revolution. In your opinion, what did this revolution overthrow? Support your opinion in a two-paragraph essay.

6. **Compare** Choose a revolutionary or independence movement you have read about in this module. Compare and contrast the movement with a revolutionary or independence movement from a previous era. What were people trying to achieve in each movement? Were they successful?

Engage with History

A government official has asked you to evaluate the following three systems: free market capitalism, communism, and socialism. Go through the module and gather information to create a chart comparing the three systems. Then, compile a report to recommend which system you think is the most successful. Consider the following issues:

- unemployment
- inflation
- political effects
- social upheaval

Focus on Writing

Working in small teams, write biographies of South African leaders who were instrumental in the revolutionary overturn of apartheid. Use at least one existing biography and one newspaper article in your research. Include a brief critique of each source's accuracy before writing your own biography.

Multimedia Activity

With two other classmates, plan a two-week virtual field trip to explore the sights in China, including the Forbidden City and the sites of the 2008 Summer Olympics. After selecting and researching the sites you'd like to visit, use maps to determine your itinerary. Consider visiting the following places and enjoying these excursions:

- sites of the 2008 Summer Olympic Games
- sites around Beijing
- Great Wall
- a cruise along the Chang Jiang or Huang He Rivers
- Three Gorges Dam
- Shanghai

For each place or excursion, give one reason why it is an important destination on a field trip to China. Include pictures and sound in your presentation.

Module 32

Global Interdependence

Essential Question
Do the benefits of globalization outweigh the problems it causes?

About the Photo: This photo taken from the Old City in Shanghai features one of the tallest buildings in the world (Shanghai Tower) and reflects the changes seen in China as the world grew increasingly interconnected.

▶ Explore ONLINE!

VIDEOS, including...
- A World Without Oil
- Battle for Baghdad
- History of Terrorism
- 100 Years of Terror
- A World Without Water

☑ Document Based Investigations

☑ Graphic Organizers

☑ Interactive Games

☑ Image Compare: Evolution of Computers

☑ Carousel: The Reality of War: Ethnic and Religious Conflicts

In this module, you will learn how technology, economics, and diplomacy have helped make the world a more interconnected place.

What You Will Learn ...

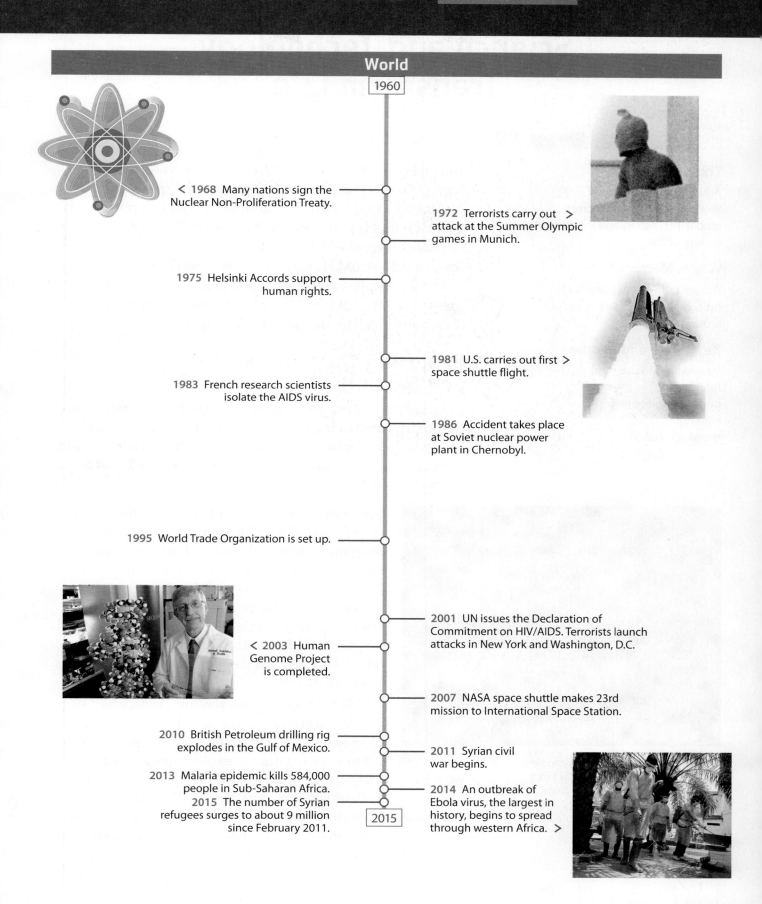

Timeline of Events 1960–2015

▷ Explore ONLINE!

World

1960

< 1968 Many nations sign the Nuclear Non-Proliferation Treaty.

1972 Terrorists carry out **>** attack at the Summer Olympic games in Munich.

1975 Helsinki Accords support human rights.

1981 U.S. carries out first **>** space shuttle flight.

1983 French research scientists isolate the AIDS virus.

1986 Accident takes place at Soviet nuclear power plant in Chernobyl.

1995 World Trade Organization is set up.

2001 UN issues the Declaration of Commitment on HIV/AIDS. Terrorists launch attacks in New York and Washington, D.C.

< 2003 Human Genome Project is completed.

2007 NASA space shuttle makes 23rd mission to International Space Station.

2010 British Petroleum drilling rig explodes in the Gulf of Mexico.

2011 Syrian civil war begins.

2013 Malaria epidemic kills 584,000 people in Sub-Saharan Africa.

2014 An outbreak of Ebola virus, the largest in history, begins to spread through western Africa. **>**

2015 The number of Syrian refugees surges to about 9 million since February 2011.

2015

Science and Technology Transform Life

The Big Idea

Advances in technology after World War II led to increased global interaction and improved quality of life.

Why It Matters Now

Advances in science and technology affect the lives of people around the world.

Key Terms and People

International Space Station
Internet
genetic engineering
cloning
green revolution

Setting the Stage

Beginning in the late 1950s, the United States and the Soviet Union competed in the exploration of space. The Soviets launched Earth's first artificial satellite and put the first human in orbit around the planet. By the late 1960s, however, the United States had surpassed the Soviets. U.S. astronauts landed on the moon in 1969. The heavy emphasis on science and technology that the space race required led to the development of products that changed life for people across the globe.

Exploring the Solar System and Beyond

In its early years, competition between the United States and the Soviet Union in the space race was intense. Eventually, however, space exploration became one of the world's first and most successful arenas for cooperation between U.S. and Soviet scientists.

This grand design spiral galaxy can be found about twelve million light-years away in the Ursa Major constellation.

Cooperation in Space In 1972, years before the end of the Cold War, the U.S. and Soviet space programs began work on a cooperative project— the docking of U.S. and Soviet spacecraft in orbit. This goal was achieved on July 17, 1975, when spacecraft from the two countries docked some 140 miles above Earth. Television viewers across the globe watched as the hatch between the space vehicles opened and crews from the rival countries greeted each other.

This first cooperative venture in space between the United States and the Soviet Union was an isolated event. People from different countries, however, continued to work together to explore space. The Soviets were the first to send an international crew into space. The crew of *Soyuz 28*, which orbited Earth in 1978, included a Czech cosmonaut. Since the mid-1980s, crews on U.S. space missions have included astronauts from Saudi Arabia, France, Germany, Canada, Italy, Japan, Israel, and Mexico.

The **International Space Station** (ISS) project came together in 1993 when the United States and Russia agreed to merge their individual space station programs. The European Space Agency (ESA) and Japan also became part of the effort. Beginning in 1998, U.S. shuttles and Russian spacecraft transported sections of the ISS to be assembled in space. In 2011, the ISS was completed, covering an area larger than a six-bedroom home and four times larger than *Mir*, the Russian Space Station. It weighs almost one million pounds. Ongoing experiments aboard the ISS helped lead to advances in medicine and technology and have allowed scientists to study the long-term effects of weightlessness on the human body.

Space Exploration The U.S. space shuttle program began in 1981 with the launch of *Columbia*. Over the next 30 years, space shuttles hosted great numbers of scientific experiments in orbit around Earth and deployed satellites from their enormous cargo bays. The space shuttle program ended on July 21, 2011, when the shuttle *Atlantis* landed at the Kennedy Space Center in Florida.

In 1990, the United States' National Aeronautics and Space Administration (NASA) and the ESA developed and launched the Hubble Space Telescope. More than 20 years later, this orbiting telescope continues

DOCUMENT-BASED INVESTIGATION   Historical Source

The Tranquility Module

In February, 2010, the crew of the space shuttle *Endeavor* delivered Tranquility, one of the last pieces of the space station. To mark the occasion, President Obama hosted a video conference with the crew of the shuttle and of the ISS.

> *THE PRESIDENT: "...The amazing work that's being done on the International Space Station not only by our American astronauts but also our colleagues from Japan and Russia is just a testimony to the human ingenuity; a testimony to extraordinary skill and courage . . . ; and is also a testimony to why continued space exploration is so important. . . . I wanted you guys to maybe let us know what this new Tranquility Module will help you accomplish. . . .*
>
> *COMMANDER WILLIAMS: . . . The Tranquility Module . . . is going to serve as a gym, as a hygiene area, as a place a crew can maintain themselves for a long duration. And a long duration living and working in space is what the Space Station is all about—to do the research and the science necessary to take us beyond Earth orbit. That was the ultimate purpose of the Space Station, and the arrival of this module will enable us to do that."*
>
> —from Remarks by the President in Conversation with the ISS Crew and the Space Shuttle *Endeavor* Crew, February 10, 2010

Analyze Historical Sources
What common goals are the Americans and their Japanese and Russian colleagues working toward on the ISS?

This view of the ISS was taken from the space shuttle *Endeavor*.

to record and send back images of objects many millions of light-years from Earth.

Other NASA programs focus on neighbors in Earth's solar system. In 2004, NASA successfully landed two robotic rovers on Mars. Their mission was to study the planet for signs of water or life (now or in the past). Both rovers, *Spirit* and *Opportunity,* found evidence of water in Mars's past. *Spirit* stopped operating in 2010, while *Opportunity* continues to explore Mars, taking panoramic images. In September 2015, NASA announced that a satellite orbiting Mars found evidence that liquid water exists on Mars under certain conditions. In July 2015, NASA made history when *New Horizons,* a U.S. space probe, flew by Pluto and one of its moons. This was the first time that a space probe had flown by Pluto.

Reading Check
Analyze Motives Why might rival nations cooperate in space activities but not on Earth?

Expanding Global Communications

Since the 1960s, artificial satellites launched into orbit around Earth have aided worldwide communications. With satellite communication, the world has been transformed into a global village. Today, political and cultural events occurring in one part of the world often are witnessed live by people thousands of miles away. This linking of the globe through worldwide communications is made possible by the miniaturization of the computer.

Smaller, More Powerful Computers In the 1940s, when computers first came into use, they took up a huge room. In the years since then, however, the circuitry that runs the computer has become smaller and more powerful. By the late 1950s, the much smaller transistor had replaced the bulky vacuum tubes used earlier. Today, tiny silicon chips, also called microchips, can contain a billion or more transistors, and that number doubles about every two years.

Tablet computer users have books, newspapers, music, games, and movies at their fingertips.

In light of these developments, industries began to use computers and silicon chips to run assembly lines. Today a variety of consumer products such as microwave ovens, keyboard instruments, smartphones, household thermostats, and cars use computers and chips. Computers have become essential in many industries, and millions of people around the globe have computers in their homes.

Communications Networks Starting in the 1990s, businesses and individuals began using a worldwide network of linked computers known as the **Internet**. The Internet is a voluntary network that began in the late 1960s as a method of linking scientists so they could exchange information about research. Through wired or wireless links, business

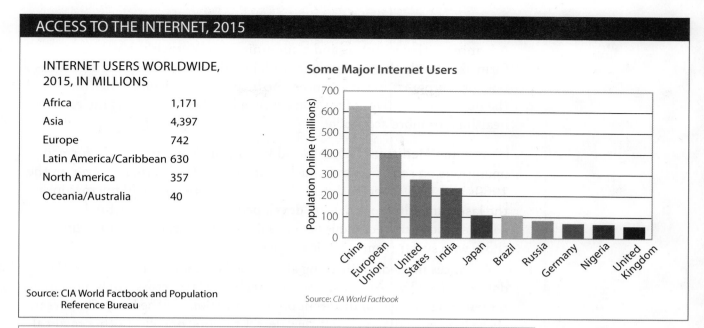

ACCESS TO THE INTERNET, 2015

INTERNET USERS WORLDWIDE, 2015, IN MILLIONS

Africa	1,171
Asia	4,397
Europe	742
Latin America/Caribbean	630
North America	357
Oceania/Australia	40

Source: CIA World Factbook and Population Reference Bureau

Some Major Internet Users

Source: *CIA World Factbook*

Interpret Visuals

1. **Compare** In which world region do most Internet users live?

2. **Draw Conclusions** How would you describe most of the nations with large percentages of their populations online?

and personal computers can connect to these computer networks. These networks allow users to communicate with people across the nation and around the world. The rapid exchange of information over these networks has become so integral to economic activity that this period of human history has come to be known as the Information Age. Between 2000 and the end of 2015, the number of worldwide Internet users soared from 394 million to more than 3 billion.

Conducting business on the Internet has become a way of life, and the Internet has increased personal and business electronic communications to create a global culture. Because it transmits information electronically to remote locations, the Internet paved the way for home offices and telecommuting—working at home using a computer connected to a business network. Once again, as it has many times in the past, technology has changed how and where people work.

It has also changed how people live, affecting not only traditional cultures but also people's values. The ability for one culture to connect electronically with another culture enables cultures to influence one another more easily and rapidly than ever before. This influence can be positive or negative depending on how different cultural values and traditions are perceived and adopted among cultures.

The Internet has also changed social interactions. Social networks allow users to connect with people with similar interests or backgrounds regardless of geographic locations. Social networking services allow people to communicate their ideas, pictures, posts, events, and interests with others in their network.

Reading Check
Summarize What types of technology have recently changed the workplace?

Transforming Human Life

Advances with computers and communications networks have transformed not only the ways people work but also standards of living. Technological progress in the sciences, medicine, and agriculture has improved the quality of the lives of millions of people, whether making life easier, healthier, or more accessible.

Health and Medicine Before World War II, surgeons seldom performed operations on sensitive areas such as the eye or the brain. However, in the 1960s and 1970s, new technologies, such as more powerful microscopes, the laser, and ultrasound, were developed. Many of these technologies advanced surgical techniques to save lives and improve quality of life for those who suffer from chronic disease.

Advances in medical imaging also helped to improve health care. Using data provided by CAT scans and MRI techniques, doctors can build three-dimensional images of different organs or regions of the body. Doctors use these images to diagnose injuries, detect tumors, or collect other medical information. Advanced imaging with MRIs has helped detect neurological injuries and aided neurological studies.

In the 1980s, genetics, the study of heredity through research on genes, became a fast-growing field of science. Found in the cells of all organisms, genes are hereditary units that cause specific traits, such as eye color, in every living organism. Technology allowed scientists to isolate and examine individual genes that are responsible for different traits. Through **genetic engineering**, scientists were able to modify the traits of an organism by changing its genes.

Another aspect of genetic engineering is **cloning**. This is the creation of identical copies of DNA, the chemical chains of genes that determine heredity. Cloning allows scientists to reproduce both plants and animals that are identical to existing plants and animals. The application of genetics has led to many breakthroughs, especially in agriculture.

Mapping the human genome

The Green Revolution In the 1960s, agricultural scientists around the world started a campaign known as the **green revolution**. It was an attempt to increase food production worldwide. Scientists promoted the use of irrigation, fertilizers, pesticides, and high-yield, disease-resistant strains of a variety of crops. The green revolution helped avert famine, which can be caused by natural disasters, armed conflicts, and overused soil, and increased crop yields in many parts of the world.

However, the green revolution had its negative side. Fertilizers and pesticides often contain dangerous chemicals that may cause cancer and pollute the environment. Also, the cost of the chemicals and the equipment to harvest more crops was far too expensive for an average peasant farmer. Consequently, owners of small farms received little benefit from the advances in agriculture. In some cases, farmers were forced off the land by larger agricultural businesses.

Molecular Medicine

In 2003, scientists employed on the Human Genome Project completed work on a map of the thousands of genes contained in human DNA—human genetic material. The information provided by this map has helped in the development of a new field of medicine. Called molecular medicine, it focuses on how genetic diseases develop and progress.

Researchers in molecular medicine are working to identify the genes that cause various diseases. This will help scientists detect diseases in early stages of development and find new ways to treat the diseases. Another area of interest to researchers is gene therapy. This involves using genes to treat disease either by replacing a patient's mutated genes with healthy ones, deactivating a mutated gene, or adding a gene that can fight disease. The ultimate aim of workers in this field is to create customizable drugs based on a person's genetic makeup.

Reading Check
Analyze Effects
What are some of the positive and negative effects of genetic engineering?

Advances in genetics research seem to be helping to fulfill some of the goals of the green revolution. In this new "gene revolution," resistance to pests is bred into plant strains, reducing the need for pesticides. Plants being bred to tolerate poor soil conditions also reduce the need for fertilizers. The gene revolution involves some risks, including the accidental creation of disease-causing organisms. However, the revolution holds great promise for increasing food production in a world with an expanding population.

Science and technology have changed the lives of millions of people. What people produce and even their jobs have changed. These changes have altered the economies of nations. Not only have nations become linked through communications networks but they are also linked in a global economic network, as you will see in lesson 2.

Lesson 1 Assessment

1. **Organize Information** List the effects of changes in communications, health and medicine, and agriculture on the chart. Explain which of the three developments you think has had the greatest global effect.

Developments	Effects
Communications	
Health and Medicine	
Agriculture	

2. **Key Terms and People** For each key term or person in the lesson, write a sentence explaining its significance.

3. **Make Inferences** Why do you think that space exploration became an area of cooperation between the Soviet Union and the United States?

4. **Predict** How do you think the Internet will affect the world of work in the future? Create a graph that shows your prediction.

5. **Form Opinions** How do you think scientific and technological advances have changed the quality of life?

Global Economic Development

The Big Idea

The economies of the world's nations have been so tightly linked that the actions of one nation have affected others.

Why It Matters Now

Every individual is affected by the global economy and the environment.

Key Terms and People

developed nation
emerging nation
gross domestic product
global economy
globalization
free trade
ozone layer
sustainable development

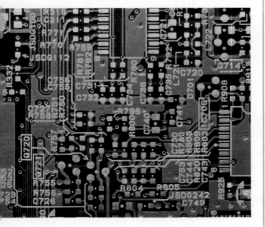

An integrated circuit such as this one was first developed in the 1950s. It was smaller than other circuits and easier to manufacture.

Setting the Stage

At the end of World War II, much of Europe and Asia lay in ruins, with many of the major cities leveled by bombing. The devastation of the war was immense. However, with aid from the United States, the economies of Western European nations and Japan began expanding rapidly within a decade. Their growth continued, long after the United States ceased supplying aid. Advances in science and technology contributed significantly to this ongoing economic growth.

Economic Opportunities and Challenges

In both Asia and the Western world, an explosion in scientific knowledge prompted great progress that led to new industries. Technological advances in plastics, robotics, and computer science changed industrial and business processes, lowered costs, improved quality, and led to large productivity gains. For example, robotic arms on automobile assembly lines made possible the fast and safe manufacture of high-quality cars, and the Internet enabled companies to reach new markets around the world. But these developments did not eliminate economic challenges. Nations routinely monitor their economies and take action to promote growth and reduce risks.

Information Industries Change Economies Technological advances in manufacturing have reduced the need for factory workers, but in other areas of the economy new demands are emerging. Computerization and communications advances changed the processing of information. By the 1980s, people could transmit information quickly and cheaply. Information industries such as financial services, insurance, market research, and communications services boomed. Those industries depended on "knowledge workers," or people whose jobs focus on working with information.

Nigeria, an emerging nation, produces about 2.2 million barrels of crude oil each day. Its annual petroleum exports are worth about $77 billion.

The Effects of New Economies In the post-World War II era, the expansion of the world's economies led to an increase in the production of goods and services so that many nations benefited. The economic base of some nations shifted. Manufacturing jobs began to move out of **developed nations**, those nations with the industrialization, transportation, and business facilities for advanced production of manufactured goods, into **emerging nations**, those nations in the process of becoming industrialized. Overall there are far more emerging countries in the world than developed countries.

Emerging nations became prime locations for new manufacturing operations. Some economists believe these areas were chosen because they had many eager workers whose skills fit manufacturing-type jobs. Also, these workers would work for less money than those in developed nations. On the other hand, information industries that require better-educated workers who demand higher wages multiplied in the economies of developed nations. Thus the changes brought by technology changed the workplace, resources, and labor of both developed and emerging nations.

Wealth and Inequality Nations measure the strength and stability of their economies in many ways. **Gross domestic product (GDP)** is one key indicator of a country's economic health. GDP is a measure of the total market value of all goods and services produced by a country in a given period of time. Many factors affect GDP, including natural resources, governmental institutions, market structures, technological capabilities, and labor skills. Ongoing changes to these factors may impact the economy in multiple ways.

Developed countries have the highest GDPs. They include the world's wealthiest and most powerful nations and are found mostly in Europe, North America, and parts of Asia. People in developed countries generally have access to good health care, education, and technology. Their standard of living is high compared to that of developing countries. The world's poorest countries, those with the lowest GDP, are sometimes called the least developed countries. Most of these countries are located in Africa and southern Asia. They suffer from high levels of poverty, a lack of political and social stability, and often, ongoing war or other conflicts. These challenges make it difficult for the least developed countries to compete in a global economy.

Even within the developed economies, however, there are inequities in the distribution of wealth and income that result in different economic outcomes for individuals, ranging from poverty to extreme wealth. These imbalances present very real challenges and suffering to the people at the lower end of the economic scale. Governments, charitable organizations, and sometimes even businesses design and implement programs to address the suffering that results from poverty. Governments use redistributive measures (such as taxing those with higher incomes and distributing the funds to those with lower incomes) and social programs (such as subsidized health care and housing). An example of how business and charitable organizations work together to address poverty in the United States and in many other countries are the food banks that collect and redistribute excess food to those in need.

Economic Stability The most common factors that contribute to the successful development of an economy are strong legal and judicial institutions, free markets, and economic freedom. Less developed countries tend to have weak political institutions and low rates of participation in the economy, as well as markets that offer fewer products. Countries with a high concentration of governmental control—North Korea, Venezuela, and Cuba, for example—exhibit some of the worst economic outcomes and the greatest political and economic inequality. A lack of educational opportunity and poor-quality infrastructure (roads, bridges, sanitation systems, and so forth) can also contribute to poor economic results.

Most developing countries aim to create stable political, economic, and social conditions for their people. Factors such as affordable health care, educational opportunity, and low levels of crime contribute to social stability, or the well-being of a country's population. Countries that enjoy social stability tend to attract increased investment, leading to the expansion of their economies. A stable society can also promote political order and democratic governance. Political stability and the rule of law, which protects private property, contracts, and other legal agreements, can further foster the growth of the economy. A strong economy leads to the creation of wealth, more jobs, and expanding consumer markets. In the United States and many other nations, economic strength helps enlarge the middle class, which forms the backbone of a stable society. However, in many developing nations in Latin America, Africa, and southern Asia, instability is common. In such situations, investors are unwilling to make the investments that would lead to a stronger economy.

Politics and Inequity

Former Philippine president Gloria Macapagal Arroyo discusses the importance of the rule of law in government:

Analyze Historical Sources
According to Arroyo, how does traditional politics promote poverty? What do you think she means by "patronage"?

> *"Politics and political power as traditionally practiced and used in the Philippines are among the roots of the social and economic inequities that characterize our national problems. Thus, to achieve true reforms, we need to outgrow our traditional brand of politics based on patronage and personality. Traditional politics is the politics of the status quo. It is a structural part of our problem. We need to promote a new politics of true party programs and platforms, of an institutional process of dialogue with our citizenry. This new politics is the politics of genuine reform. It is a structural part of the solution."*

—Gloria Macapagal Arroyo
Inauguration Speech, 2001

Managing Economies Monetary authorities control the money supply in a country. Monetary policy can include taking short-term actions, such as raising or lowering interest rates, to try to ensure an adequate money supply and to sustain and expand a country's economy. Monetary policy also manages or limits the effects of recessions and inflation.

Many developing countries struggle with poor monetary policies. In some of these countries, the central bank places the government's financial interests above the health of the country's economy. This can result in a weak financial system and an unstable money supply.

Governments can regulate the economy toward different goals, whether to maintain a competitive environment for businesses, increase consumer spending, or to spur economic growth. Governments can use price ceilings (upper limits) and floors (lower limits) on goods and services. Such regulations mean that businesses can only charge prices for a good or service within these limits.

Price ceilings and floors are generally understood to create negative distortions in the economy, resulting in surpluses or shortages of the price-controlled commodity. For example, when the U.S. government tried to control the maximum price of gasoline, shortages appeared, resulting in long lines at gas stations. A minimum wage is an example of a price floor. The government sets a minimum price for labor, and businesses must pay this minimum to workers even if it is higher than what the business can afford to pay. In this situation, some businesses may downsize, or reduce their number of employees, in order to pay the higher wage. Thus, a surplus of labor would enter the economy and could cause unemployment to rise. However, those who support a minimum wage argue that paying workers a higher wage causes those earners to spend more as consumers, which can spur economic growth.

Reading Check
Find Main Ideas
What are some ways that emerging nations can improve their economies?

Economic Globalization

Economies in different parts of the world have been linked for centuries through trade and through national policies, such as colonialism. However, a true global economy did not begin to take shape until well into the second half of the 1800s. The **global economy** includes all the economic interactions—among people, businesses, and governments—that cross international borders. In recent decades, several factors hastened the process of **globalization**. Huge cargo ships could inexpensively carry enormous supplies of fuels and other goods from one part of the world to another. Technology such as the telephone and computer linkages made global financial transactions quick and easy. In addition, multinational corporations developed around the world.

In order to foster global monetary cooperation, the International Monetary Fund (IMF) was created to facilitate international trade, promote employment and sustainable economic growth, and reduce poverty around the world. The IMF pursues its goals by monitoring financial and economic policy in member countries; providing technical assistance and training, especially for countries with lower and middle income; and providing loans with the expectation that the country receiving the money will put into action IMF policies to improve its economy for sustainable growth.

Multinational Corporations Companies that operate in a number of countries are called multinational or transnational corporations. U.S. companies such as Exxon Mobil and Ford, European companies such as BP and Royal Dutch/Shell, and Japanese companies such as Toyota and Mitsui are all multinational giants.

All of these companies have established manufacturing plants, offices, or stores in many countries. For their manufacturing plants, they select spots where the raw materials or labor are cheapest. This enables them to produce components of their products on different continents. They ship the various components to another

Multinational Corporations, 2014

Based on a comparison of revenues with GDP, some of the top multinationals have economies bigger than those of several countries.

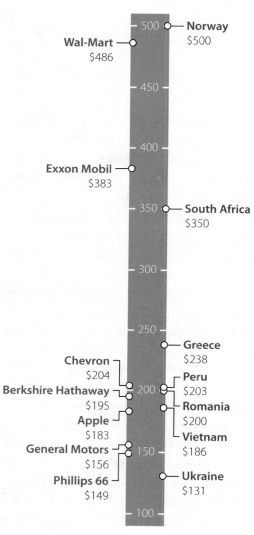

Sources: *Fortune Magazine* and *CIA World Factbook*

Interpret Graphs

1. **Compare** Which has the larger economy, Vietnam or General Motors?

2. **Compare** Which countries have an economy greater than the annual revenue of Chevron but smaller than that of Wal-Mart?

location to be assembled. This level of economic integration is beneficial because it allows such companies to view the whole world as the market for their goods. Goods or services are distributed throughout the world as if there were no national boundaries.

Multinational corporations create jobs when they open new locations in host countries. They may increase profits and productivity (the rate of output per unit of input). They often bring technology to an area, which helps to improve production and the area's economy in general. At the same time, multinational corporations face challenges such as management across multiple countries where processes and standards differ. Critics accuse multinational corporations of widening the gap between developed and emerging countries and contributing to economic exploitation, human rights abuses, and the loss of traditional industries in emerging countries.

Expanding Free Trade Opening up the world's markets to trade is a key aspect of globalization. In fact, a major goal of globalization is **free trade**, or the elimination of trade barriers, such as tariffs, among nations. As early as 1947, nations began discussing ways to open trade. The result of these discussions was the General Agreement on Tariffs and Trade (GATT). Over the years, meetings among the nations that signed the GATT have brought about a general lowering of protective tariffs and considerable expansion of free trade. Since 1995, the World Trade Organization (WTO) has overseen the GATT to ensure that trade among nations flows smoothly and freely.

Global flows, which include the movement of goods, services, finances, and people, have driven global economic growth. They play an important role in creating new international economic relations. In 2014, the value of all exports and imports made up about half of global GDP, and some experts expect this value to increase. Several factors cause global flows growth, including rising prosperity, emerging world markets, regional trade blocs, and the increased use of the Internet.

Regional Trade Blocs A European organization set up in 1951 promoted tariff-free trade among member countries. This experiment in economic cooperation was so successful that six years later, a new organization, the European Economic Community (EEC), was formed. Over time, most of the other Western European countries joined the organization, which has been known as the European Union (EU) since 1992. By 2015, twenty-eight European nations were EU members, and many had adopted the common European currency—the euro (symbol: €). The EU is an economic and political union and is now the largest trading bloc in the world. It acts as a single economic unit but also advocates a united foreign and security policy and works to promote peace and equality.

The success of the EU inspired countries in other regions to make trade agreements with each other. The North American Free Trade Agreement (NAFTA), put into effect in 1994, called for the gradual elimination of tariffs and trade restrictions among Canada, the United States, and Mexico. All three countries received a small positive economic benefit as seen in each country's GDP. Organizations in Asia, Africa, Latin America, and the

Vocabulary
tariff a tax on goods imported from another country

World Trading Blocs, 2015

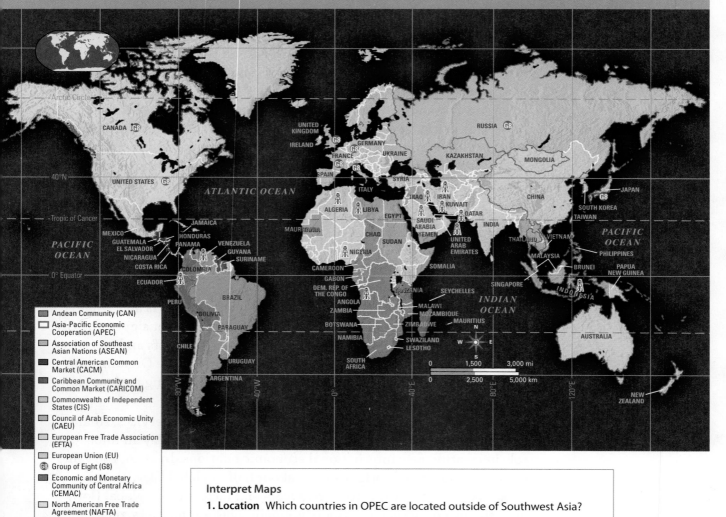

Legend:
- Andean Community (CAN)
- Asia-Pacific Economic Cooperation (APEC)
- Association of Southeast Asian Nations (ASEAN)
- Central American Common Market (CACM)
- Caribbean Community and Common Market (CARICOM)
- Commonwealth of Independent States (CIS)
- Council of Arab Economic Unity (CAEU)
- European Free Trade Association (EFTA)
- European Union (EU)
- Group of Eight (G8)
- Economic and Monetary Community of Central Africa (CEMAC)
- North American Free Trade Agreement (NAFTA)
- Organization of the Petroleum Exporting Countries (OPEC)
- Southern Common Market (MERCOSUR)
- Southern African Development Community (SADC)

Interpret Maps

1. **Location** Which countries in OPEC are located outside of Southwest Asia?

2. **Location** To which world trade organization does the United States belong?

Vocabulary

scarcity in economics, having unlimited wants and resources too limited to meet all of the wants

South Pacific have also created regional trade policies. In 2013, the United States began negotiating a free trade agreement, called the Transatlantic Trade and Investment Partnership (T-TIP), with the EU.

These trade agreements, along with other global economic trends, have made nations economically interdependent, or mutually dependent. Nations depend on other nations for the goods and services that scarcity prevents them from being able to produce themselves. Nations produce those goods or services for which they have a comparative advantage, or an ability to produce at a relatively low cost. They are then able to sell their product or service to other nations that cannot produce it efficiently, at the same time acquiring items they are unable to produce. For example, a nation with extensive forests but no iron ore may harvest timber to export but need to import steel from nations who have the iron ore needed to create it.

Asia in the G20

The Group of Twenty, known as the G20, is an international group that was founded in 1999 with the goal of promoting discussion of policy affecting the global economy. It forms strategic communications between political leaders and central bank governors. The G20 is comprised of 19 countries, many of which are Asian—China, Japan, India, Indonesia, and the Republic of Korea—and the European Union.

The Asian economies of China, India, Vietnam, and Indonesia have been emerging from the mid- to late 20th and early 21st centuries. The G20 issued a working paper in 2011 predicting that large Asian economies, such as those of China and India, would play a more prominent role in the global economy over time. The G20 works to promote sustainable, balanced growth within an Asian intraregional trade market while also encouraging domestic demand.

Vocabulary
Keynesian relating to the theories of economist John Maynard Keynes, who advocated use of government deficit spending to stimulate commerce and decrease unemployment

A Global Economic Crisis Beginning in 2007, after a long period of relative worldwide prosperity, several factors combined to cause an economic downturn, which later became known as the "Great Recession." Housing prices in the United States and in parts of Europe had increased dramatically over a short time, driven up by lax lending policies that offered mortgage loans to almost anyone and monetary policies that supported the growth of the money supply. The financial industry found it could bundle groups of these mortgages into an investment vehicle called a mortgage-backed security (MBS), which it sold to investors despite hidden risks. When housing prices in the United States and parts of Europe began to plummet, banks and financial institutions across the globe were not prepared to deal with the loss of value in their portfolios of mortgages and mortgage-backed securities. As these entities began to fail, governments around the world stepped in to attempt to stabilize the situation. Meanwhile, unemployment rates skyrocketed.

When economic crises occur, governments enact programs in the hopes of improving economic outcomes. These programs are often based on competing models of how the economy works and what governments can do to address the issues. When the financial crisis hit the U.S. economy in 2007, a Keynesian program of fiscal stimulus was enacted. It consisted of a combination of new government spending (road construction, extended unemployment benefits) and tax cuts (tax rebates). The bulk of the stimulus was implemented in 2008 and 2009. As the economic crisis continued, the U.S. government tried a different approach. It allowed the tax cuts to expire, reduced government spending, and attempted to restrain growth of the federal deficit. Whether despite or in response to these competing programs, the U.S. economy stabilized in the second half of 2009 and began to slowly grow out of the recession, with unemployment declining beginning in 2010.

By 2010, the world economy had stabilized, but it remained weak, as seen especially in the economies of Greece, Spain, Portugal, Italy, and Ireland. In May 2010, the IMF, the European Commission, and the

Globalization

Globalization can be described in broad terms as a process that makes something worldwide in its reach or operation. Currently, globalization is most often used in reference to the spread and diffusion of economic or cultural influences. The graphics below focus on economic globalization. The first shows a global corporation. The second lists some arguments for and against economic globalization.

Global Corporation

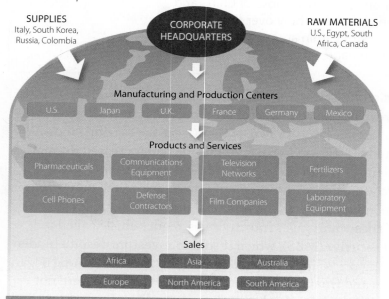

SUPPLIES
Italy, South Korea, Russia, Colombia

CORPORATE HEADQUARTERS

RAW MATERIALS
U.S., Egypt, South Africa, Canada

Manufacturing and Production Centers

U.S. | Japan | U.K. | France | Germany | Mexico

Products and Services

Pharmaceuticals | Communications Equipment | Television Networks | Fertilizers

Cell Phones | Defense Contractors | Film Companies | Laboratory Equipment

Sales

Africa | Asia | Australia

Europe | North America | South America

Arguments for and Against Economic Globalization

For	Against
promotes peace through trade	creates conflict because of an inherently unfair system
raises the standard of living around the world	benefits developed nations disproportionately
creates jobs in emerging countries	takes jobs from high-paid laborers in developed countries
promotes investment in less developed countries	benefits those who already have money
creates a sense of world community	erodes local cultures

INTERNATIONAL REGULATION

Many countries have joined international organizations to help regulate and stimulate the global economy. Such groups face the same criticisms against globalization in general.

WORLD TRADE ORGANIZATION (WTO)

- Stated goal: "Help trade flow smoothly, freely, fairly, and predictably"
- About 160 member nations; around 25 nations negotiating for admission
- WTO members account for about 95 percent of world trade.

INTERNATIONAL MONETARY FUND (IMF)

- Stated goal: "Promote international monetary cooperation; to foster economic growth and high levels of employment; and to provide temporary financial assistance to countries"
- 188 member countries
- In September 2015, IMF total resources were $334 billion.

THE WORLD BANK GROUP

- Stated goal: "A world free of poverty"
- 5 organizations
- In 2015, this group provided $42.5 billion to emerging countries.

Critical Thinking

1. **Make Inferences** How do developed countries influence culture around the world?
2. **Predict** How will increased globalization impact the 21st century?

European Central Bank provided a loan of 110 billion euro to help finance Greece's debt. This was followed a year later with an additional loan of 130 billion euro and the restructuring of private bank debt. The World Bank also provided financial support and partnered with the IMF and EU on assistance programs.

Impact of Global Development

The development of the global economy has had a notable impact on the use of energy and other resources. Worldwide demand for resources has led to both political and environmental problems.

Political Impacts Manufacturing requires the processing of raw materials. Trade requires the transport of finished goods. These activities, essential for development, require the use of much energy. For the past 50 years, one of the main sources of energy used by developed and emerging nations has been oil. For nations with little of this resource available in their own land, disruption of the distribution of oil causes economic and political problems.

On the other hand, nations possessing oil reserves have the power to affect economic and political situations in countries all over the world. For example, in the 1970s the Arab members of the Organization of Petroleum Exporting Countries (OPEC) declared an oil embargo—a restriction of trade. This contributed to a significant economic decline in many developed nations during that decade. The OPEC crisis also caused a shift in international relations and changes in foreign policies. For example, as a result of the embargo, many developed countries changed their policies toward the Arab-Israeli conflict.

In 1990, Iraq invaded Kuwait and seized the Kuwaiti oil fields. Fears began to mount that Iraq would also invade Saudi Arabia, another major source of oil. This would have destabilized Saudi Arabia and put most of

During the 1991 Persian Gulf War, the Iraqis set hundreds of Kuwaiti oil wells ablaze. Smoke from these fires clouded the skies more than 250 miles away.

the world's petroleum supplies under Iraqi control. Economic sanctions imposed by the UN failed to persuade Iraq to withdraw from Kuwait. Then, in early 1991, a coalition of some 39 nations declared war on Iraq. After several weeks of fighting, the Iraqis left Kuwait and accepted a cease-fire. This Persian Gulf War showed the extent to which the economies of nations are globally linked.

Environmental Impacts Economic development has had a major impact on the environment. The burning of coal and oil as an energy source releases carbon dioxide and other gases into the atmosphere, causing health-damaging pollution and acid rain. The buildup of carbon dioxide in the atmosphere also contributes to global warming.

The release of chemicals called chlorofluorocarbons (CFCs), used in refrigerators, air conditioners, and manufacturing processes, has destroyed the ozone layer in Earth's upper atmosphere. The **ozone layer** is our main protection against the sun's damaging ultraviolet rays. With the increase in ultraviolet radiation reaching Earth's surface, the incidence of skin cancer continues to rise in many parts of the world. Increased ultraviolet radiation also may result in damage to populations of plants and plankton at the bases of the food chains, which sustain all life on Earth.

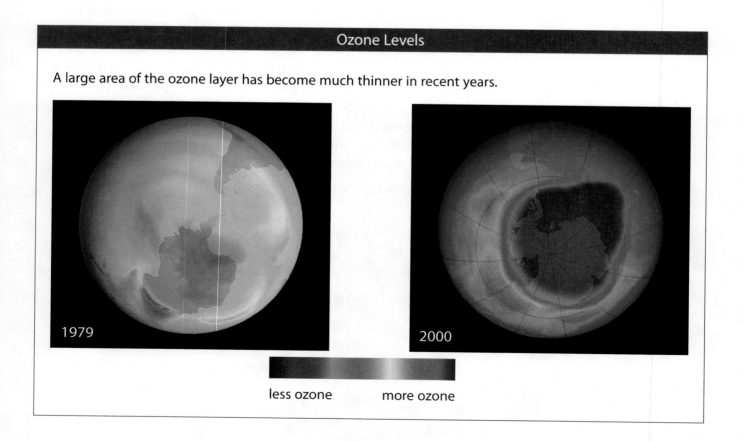

Ozone Levels

A large area of the ozone layer has become much thinner in recent years.

1979

2000

less ozone   more ozone

Economic development has also led to problems with the land. Large-scale soil erosion is a worldwide problem due to damaging farming techniques. The habitat destruction that comes from land development has also led to shrinking numbers of wildlife around the world. At present, the extinction rate of plants and animals is about a thousand times greater than it would naturally be, and it appears to be increasing. This high extinction rate means that certain species can no longer serve as an economic resource. The resulting loss of wildlife could endanger complex and life-sustaining processes that keep Earth in balance.

Sustainable Development Working together, economists and scientists are looking for ways to reduce the negative effect that development has on the environment. Their goal is to manage development so that growth can occur without destroying air, water, and land resources. The concept is sometimes called "green growth." Many people feel that the negative impact of economic growth on the environment will not be completely removed.

But "green growth," also known as **sustainable development**, is possible. This involves creating economic growth while preserving the environment. Making such plans and putting them into practice have proved to be difficult. Because the economies of nations are tied to their political institutions, such development plans will depend on the efforts of nations in both economic and political areas.

Reading Check
Analyze Issues
Explain the influence and importance of the petroleum industry in world politics and in the global economy.

Lesson 2 Assessment

1. **Organize Information** Create a web to list the forces that shape the global economy. Explain which of these forces has had the greatest impact on the development of a global economy.

Forces that shape a global economy

2. **Key Terms and People** For each key term or person in the lesson, write a sentence explaining its significance.

3. **Analyze Effects** In what ways has technology changed the workplace of people across the world?

4. **Draw Conclusions** Describe the impact of the European Union on member nations and non-member nations.

5. **Form Opinions** Do you think that sustainable development is possible? Why or why not?

6. **Form Opinions** Do you think that the euro has provided economic unity and stability among EU members? Use reasoning and evidence in your response.

7. **Evaluate** Do you agree with the actions taken by the IMF and the World Bank during the world economic crisis in 2007? Explain your response.

Global Security Issues

The Big Idea

Since 1945, nations have used collective security efforts to solve problems.

Why It Matters Now

Personal security of the people of the world is tied to security within and between nations.

Key Terms and People

supranational union
refugee
proliferation
Universal Declaration of
    Human Rights
nonbinding agreement
political dissent
gender inequality
AIDS
refugees

Setting the Stage

World War II was one of history's most devastating conflicts. More than 55 million people died as a result of bombings, the Holocaust, combat, starvation, and disease. Near the end of the war, one of humankind's most destructive weapons, the atomic bomb, killed more than 100,000 people in Hiroshima and Nagasaki in a matter of minutes. Perhaps because of these horrors, world leaders look for ways to make the earth a safer, more secure place to live.

Issues of War and Peace

In the years after World War II, the Cold War created new divisions and tensions among the world's nations. This uneasy situation potentially threatened the economic, environmental, and personal security of people across the world. So, nations began to work together to pursue collective security.

Nations Unite and Take Action Many nations consider that having a strong military is important to their security. After World War II, nations banded together to create military alliances. They formed the North Atlantic Treaty Organization (NATO), the Southeast Asia Treaty Organization (SEATO), the Warsaw Pact, and others. The member nations of each of these alliances generally pledged military aid for their common defense.

In addition to military alliances to increase their security, some world leaders also took steps to reduce the threat of war and promote political and economic unity through the creation of **supranational unions**. *Supranational* refers to something extending beyond national boundaries. One such supranational union was the European Economic Community (EEC), created in 1957 to unify its member states' economies. In 1993 the EEC became part of the European Union, which carried on the EEC's mission and pursued additional goals related to justice, foreign policy, and security. Other unions, such as the African Union (AU), pursue similar goals for their member nations. The United Nations (UN) also works in a variety of ways toward increasing collective global security. The Organization of Ibero-American States (OEI) works to advance science, culture, and education in its member countries.

Peacekeeping Activities One of the major aims of the UN is to promote world peace. The UN provides a public forum, private meeting places, and skilled mediators to help nations try to resolve conflicts at any stage of their development. At the invitation of the warring parties, the UN also provides peacekeeping forces. These forces are made up of soldiers from different nations. They work to carry out peace agreements, monitor cease-fires, or end fighting to allow peace negotiations to go forward. They also help to move **refugees**, deliver supplies, and operate hospitals. A refugee is a person who leaves his or her country to find safety in another country.

As of October 2015, the UN had more than 100,000 soldiers, military observers, and police in 16 peacekeeping operations around the world. Some forces, such as those in India, Pakistan, and Cyprus, have been in place for decades.

Weapons of Mass Destruction Nations not only have worked to prevent and contain conflicts, but they also have forged treaties to limit the manufacturing, testing, and trade of weapons. The weapons of most concern are those that cause mass destruction. These include nuclear, chemical, and biological weapons that can kill thousands, even millions of people.

In 1968, many nations signed a Nuclear Non-Proliferation Treaty to help prevent the **proliferation**, or spread, of nuclear weapons to other nations. In the 1970s, the United States and the Soviet Union signed the Strategic Arms Limitation Treaties. In the 1980s, both countries talked about deactivating some of their nuclear weapons. Many nations also signed treaties promising not to produce biological or chemical weapons. Still, at least nine countries are known to possess nuclear weapons, while others are believed to be trying to develop them.

One difficulty in controlling nuclear weapons is that nuclear technology can be used for legitimate purposes, such as generating energy. Many countries and international organizations try to ensure that nuclear technology is used safely. For example, the International Atomic Energy Agency (IAEA) routinely monitors countries suspected of developing nuclear weapons. In addition, countries may sanction other nations they consider to be nuclear threats.

War in Iraq Other nations, however, have tried to develop weapons of mass destruction (WMD). Iraq, for example, used chemical weapons in conflicts during the 1980s. Many people suspected that the Iraqi leader, Saddam Hussein, had plans to develop biological and nuclear weapons too. As part of the cease-fire arrangements in the Persian Gulf War, Iraq agreed to destroy its weapons of mass destruction. UN inspectors were sent to monitor this disarmament process. However, in 1998, the Iraqis ordered the inspectors to leave.

Vocabulary
sanction to impose an economic or political penalty on another country in order to force a change in that country's policy

In central Baghdad, a U.S. Marine watches as a statue of Saddam Hussein is pulled down.

In 2002, analysts once again suspected that Hussein might be developing WMD. UN weapons inspectors returned, but Hussein seemed reluctant to cooperate. U.S. President George W. Bush argued that Hussein might be close to building powerful weapons to use against the United States or its allies. In March 2003, Bush ordered American troops to invade Iraq. Troops from Great Britain and other countries supported the attack. After four weeks of fighting, Hussein's government fell.

However, violence in Iraq continued. Factions of Iraqis battled one another for power in the new government. Iraqis angered by the presence of foreign troops in their country fought American soldiers. By the end of 2011, untold thousands of Iraqis and more than 4,486 Americans had been killed. No WMD were ever found.

Chaos in Somalia From 1969 to 1991, a dictator named Mohamed Siad Barre ruled Somalia. Barre banned political parties and arrested or executed political rivals. In 1973, he signed a treaty with the Soviet Union and then enacted Soviet-style economic reforms. The state took control of banks and many businesses. Barre also increased the size of Somalia's military. Beginning in the late 1970s, various clans challenged Barre's rule. In 1991, Barre fled when clan-based militias defeated his military. Those militias then began to fight each other. They killed thousands of civilians in their attempt to gain control of the country. Fighting and mass killings continued for years.

Between 1991 and 2004, there were multiple attempts to negotiate a government. In 2004, the Transitional Federal Government (TFG) was created. Around that time, Somali Islamist groups, including the Islamic Courts Union (ICU) and other affiliated militias, emerged. Concerned about terrorist activity in Somalia, the United States began helping the TFG. In 2006, U.S.-backed Ethiopian troops invaded Somalia to support the TFG against the Islamist militias. In 2009, Ethiopian troops withdrew from Somalia. As a result, the TFG lost territory and agreed to a power-sharing deal with Islamist splinter groups. One such group, al Shabaab, separated from the ICU and rejected the peace deal. It continues to operate as a militant group that commits acts of terrorism. Somalia's government is still transitional.

Ethnic and Religious Conflicts Violence caused by ethnic and religious hatred is a threat to people in many parts of the world. Some conflicts among people of different ethnic or religious groups have roots centuries old. Such conflicts include those between Protestants and Catholics in Ireland, between Palestinians and Israelis in the Middle East, and among Serbs, Bosnians, and Croats in southeastern Europe.

These conflicts have led to terrible violence. The Kurds of southwest Asia have also been the victims of such violence. For decades, Kurds have wanted their own country. But their traditional lands cross the borders of three countries—Turkey, Iran, and Iraq. In the past, the Turks responded to Kurdish nationalism by forbidding Kurds to speak their native language. The Iranians also persecuted the Kurds, attacking them over religious issues. In the late 1980s, the Iraqis dropped poison gas on the Kurds, killing 5,000. Several international organizations, including the UN, worked to end the human rights abuses inflicted upon the Kurds.

South Sudanese refugees

In Rwanda, people of the Hutu ethnic group massacred nearly 1 million people of the Tutsi group. They also killed thousands of Hutus who opposed the killings. Another 2 million Tutsi and Hutu refugees fled to neighboring countries, where food shortages and disease killed thousands more, despite international humanitarian aid. As part of a peacekeeping mission, French and UN troops worked to maintain a ceasefire in Rwanda until a new government could establish order and end the violence. In 1998, some of the people involved in the conflict were tried by the International Criminal Tribunal for Rwanda (ICTR). They were charged with genocide, crimes against humanity, and war crimes. Many were convicted and sentenced to life in prison or executed for their crimes.

A similar situation occurred in the 2000s in the Darfur region of Sudan. There, Arab militias supported by the government attacked African villagers and looted and destroyed their homes. The African Union sent a peacekeeping force to Sudan to try to end the killings, but the violence continued. By 2006, some 400,000 people had been killed in Darfur, and more than 2 million others had fled to refugee camps. In 2011, the southern region of Sudan became a separate state, South Sudan. Unfortunately, a civil war erupted in South Sudan in 2013, and thousands died before a tentative peace agreement was reached in August 2015. Ethnic and religious violence continues in Sudan and South Sudan today.

Vocabulary
transitional government a temporary government that prepares the way for elections to establish a permanent government

Reading Check
Analyze Motives
Why did nations join supranational organizations in the decades after World War II?

Universal Declaration of Human Rights

The Universal Declaration of Human Rights contains thirty articles that explain the political, economic, and cultural rights of all people.

> "**Article 1**: All human beings are born free and equal in dignity and rights. They are endowed with reason and conscience and should act towards one another in a spirit of brotherhood.
>
> **Article 2**: Everyone is entitled to all the rights and freedoms set forth in this Declaration, without distinction of any kind, such as race, colour, sex, language, religion, political or other opinion, national or social origin, property, birth or other status. Furthermore, no distinction shall be made on the basis of the political, jurisdictional or international status of the country or territory to which a person belongs, whether it be independent, trust, non-self-governing or under any other limitation of sovereignty.
>
> **Article 3**: Everyone has the right to life, liberty and security of person.
>
> **Article 4**: No one shall be held in slavery or servitude; slavery and the slave trade shall be prohibited in all their forms.
>
> **Article 5**: No one shall be subjected to torture or to cruel, inhuman or degrading treatment or punishment. . . ."
>
> —quoted from *The Universal Declaration of Human Rights*

Analyze Historical Sources
How are some of the words and ideas expressed in the Universal Declaration of Human Rights similar to other historical declarations?

Human Rights Issues

In 1948, the UN issued the **Universal Declaration of Human Rights**, which set human rights standards for all nations. The declaration listed specific rights, such as the right to liberty and the right to work, that all human beings should have. Later, in the Helsinki Accords of 1975, the UN addressed the issues of freedom of movement and freedom to publish and exchange information.

Both the declaration and the accords are **nonbinding agreements**. A nonbinding agreement means that a nation does not suffer a penalty if it does not meet the terms of the declaration. However, the sentiments in these documents inspired many people around the world. They made a commitment to ensuring that basic human rights are respected. The UN and other private international agencies, such as Amnesty International, identify and publicize human rights violations. They also encourage people to work toward a world in which liberty and justice are guaranteed for all.

Some of the greatest human rights successes have come in the area of political rights and freedoms. In Europe, most countries that were once

Human Rights Movements

Human rights movements resisting colonialism, imperialism, slavery, racism, apartheid, patriarchy, and other abuses have reshaped political, social, and economic life around the world. A human rights movement is a social movement that responds to human rights issues. Many national and international government organizations and NGOs have been dedicated to such movements, and the most successful campaigns usually involve a number of organizations working together for a common goal.

Recognizing this, the National Economic and Social Rights Initiative (NESRI) decided to work with many community organizations across the United States. Founded in 2004, NESRI organizes and supports initiatives to integrate social and economic rights into American laws and political culture. Economic and social rights include access to safe work with fair wages; affordable, quality health care; education; nutritious food; and safe, affordable housing.

Analyze Issues
Which human rights does NESRI promote in the United States?

Vocabulary
nongovernmental organization
a nonprofit group set up by private citizens, businesses, or groups

part of the Soviet bloc have opened up their political systems to allow for democratic elections and the free expression of ideas. There have been similar successes in South Africa, where the apartheid system of racial separation came to an end in the early 1990s. Free elections held in South Africa in 1994 finally brought a multiracial government to power.

Combatting Human Rights Abuses Many multinational organizations combat human rights abuses. Non-governmental organizations (NGOs) like Amnesty International and Human Rights Watch research and publicize abuses and campaign to end them. Human Rights Watch's annual world reports detail human rights issues and policy developments around the globe, and the organization works with governments and institutions to promote human rights in more than 90 countries and territories. These and other NGOs have played key roles in the fights against slavery, violence against women, and apartheid. Other groups such as the International Red Cross and Red Crescent are charitable NGOs that offer free assistance to people in times of crisis.

Intergovernmental organizations also play a role. The International Criminal Court (ICC), housed in the Netherlands, prosecutes individuals for genocide, crimes against humanity, and war crimes. By 2015, the ICC had investigated nine situations, including the human rights violations in Darfur.

Continuing Rights Violations Despite the best efforts of various human rights organizations, protecting human rights remains an uphill battle. Serious violations of fundamental rights continue to occur around the world.

Mother Teresa (1910–1997)

Mother Teresa was one of the great champions of human rights for all people. Born Agnes Gonxha Bojaxhiu in what today is Macedonia, Mother Teresa joined a convent in Ireland at the age of 18. A short time later, she headed to India to teach at a girls' school. Over time, she noticed many sick and homeless people in the streets. She soon vowed to devote her life to helping India's poor.

In 1948, she established the Order of the Missionaries of Charity in Calcutta, which committed itself to serving the sick, needy, and unfortunate. In recognition of her commitment to the downtrodden, Mother Teresa received the Nobel Peace Prize in 1979.

One type of violation occurs when governments try to stamp out **political dissent**, or the difference of opinion over political issues. In many countries around the world, from Cuba to Iran to Myanmar, individuals and groups have been persecuted for holding political views that differ from those of the people in power. In some countries, like Sudan, ethnic or racial hatreds lead to human rights abuses.

Women's Status Improves In the past, when women in Western nations entered the workforce, they often faced discrimination in employment and salary. In non-Western countries, many women not only faced discrimination in jobs, they were denied access to education. In regions torn by war or ethnic conflict, women have often been victims of violence and abuse. As women suffered, so have their family members, especially children.

In the 1970s, a heightened awareness of human rights encouraged women in many countries to work to improve their lives. They pushed for new laws and government policies that gave them greater equality. In 1975, the UN held the first of several international conferences on women's status in the world. The UN also sponsored a movement toward gender equality, and most countries signed the Convention on the Elimination of All Forms of Discrimination Against Women (1979). In Southeast Asia, all but a few nations, such as Vietnam and Laos, have ratified the treaty. The fourth conference was held in Beijing, China, in 1995. It addressed such issues as preventing violence against women and empowering women to take leadership roles in politics and in business.

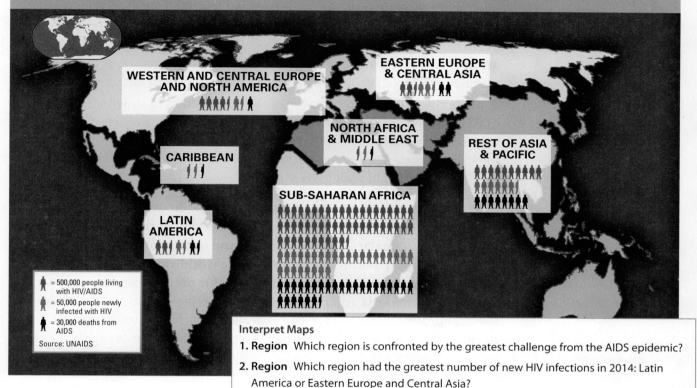

World AIDS Situation, 2014

▶ Explore ONLINE!

WESTERN AND CENTRAL EUROPE AND NORTH AMERICA

EASTERN EUROPE & CENTRAL ASIA

NORTH AFRICA & MIDDLE EAST

REST OF ASIA & PACIFIC

CARIBBEAN

SUB-SAHARAN AFRICA

LATIN AMERICA

⬤ = 500,000 people living with HIV/AIDS
⬤ = 50,000 people newly infected with HIV
⬤ = 30,000 deaths from AIDS
Source: UNAIDS

Interpret Maps

1. **Region** Which region is confronted by the greatest challenge from the AIDS epidemic?

2. **Region** Which region had the greatest number of new HIV infections in 2014: Latin America or Eastern Europe and Central Asia?

Reading Check
Analyze Issues
What responsibilities do nations have for protecting human rights in other countries?

In its report *Progress of the World's Women 2015–2016,* the UN found that women had made notable gains in many parts of the world, especially in the areas of education and work. Even so, the report concluded that **gender inequality**—the difference between men and women in terms of wealth and status—still very much exists. It cites discrimination in health care, political representation, employment, and education as reasons for the continued imbalance between men and women.

Health Issues

In recent decades, the enjoyment of a decent standard of health has become recognized as a basic human right. However, for much of the world, poor health is the norm. World health faced a major threat in 2003, with the outbreak of severe acute respiratory syndrome (SARS). This pneumonia-like disease emerged in China and spread worldwide. Afraid of infection, many people canceled travel to Asia. The resulting loss of business hurt Asian economies.

Vocabulary
pandemic an infectious disease that spreads through a human population in a widespread geographic area

The AIDS Epidemic One of the greatest global health issues is a disease known as **AIDS**, or acquired immune deficiency syndrome. It attacks the immune system, leaving sufferers open to deadly infections. The disease was first detected in the early 1980s. Since that time, AIDS has become a global pandemic: it has claimed the lives of nearly 39 million people worldwide. By the end of 2014, there were almost 37 million people across the world living with HIV (the virus that causes AIDS) or AIDS. And in 2014, two million people were newly infected with HIV.

While AIDS is a worldwide problem, sub-Saharan Africa has suffered most from the epidemic. About 70 percent of all persons infected with HIV live in this region. And in 2014, more than 1.1 million Africans died of AIDS. Many of the people dying are young adults—the age when people are at their most productive economically. AIDS, therefore, is reducing the number of people available as workers, managers, and entrepreneurs.

Since the '90s the world has made some progress in slowing the spread of AIDS. In response to the devastating impact of the disease, the UN issued the Declaration of Commitment on HIV/AIDS in 2001. This document set targets for halting the spread of AIDS and provided guidelines on how countries could pool their efforts.

Other Health Issues Other diseases also threaten world health. For example, in 2015, there were about 214 million malaria cases and an estimated 438,000 malaria deaths. The UN and other global organizations are working to reduce outbreaks of the disease worldwide. As a result, there has been an increase in resources available for prevention and treatment. Cases of tuberculosis are increasing in some regions, and the ability of medical professionals to cure this disease and others caused by bacteria is in jeopardy, as some antibiotics have lost their effectiveness against drug-resistant bacteria.

Reading Check
Synthesize Why are health issues considered a threat to global security?

SOCIAL HISTORY

Syrian Civil War

In 2011, Syrian prodemocracy protesters demanded the resignation of President Bashar al-Assad. In response, the government used military force to end the protests and silence opposition. Violence soon escalated, and a civil war broke out as rebel groups formed to fight against government forces for control of cities and towns. After years of fighting, the conflict has grown into a struggle between the Sunni Muslim majority and the president's Shia Muslim sect. The growth of insurgent groups, such as the Islamic State of Iraq and the Levant (ISIL), have furthered the conflict.

This Syrian refugee family left their home in November 2015 and fled to Turkey along with many other refugee families. The refugee families live in tents, storehouses and rental properties in many different countries as they try to find safety.

As a result of the civil war, more than 220,000 Syrians have lost their lives and more than 11 million have been forced to leave their homes. According to human rights organizations, at least 7 million Syrians have been displaced within Syria, and more than 4 million have fled as refugees to neighboring countries, mostly Turkey, Lebanon, Jordan, and Iraq.

Two Afghan girls quietly wait for food at a refugee camp on the Afghanistan-Iran border.

Population Movement

The global movement of people has increased dramatically in recent years. This migration has taken place for both negative and positive reasons.

Push-Pull Factors People often move because they feel pushed out of their homelands. Lack of food due to drought, natural disasters, and political oppression are examples of push factors of migration. At the end of 2014, the number of **refugees** stood at 19.5 million. Millions more were displaced within their home countries.

Not only negative events push people to migrate. Most people have strong connections to their home countries and do not leave unless strong positive attractions pull them away. They hope for a better life for themselves and for their children, and thus migrate to developed nations. For example, hundreds of thousands of people migrate from Africa to Europe and from Latin America to the United States every year. Many of these people eventually become citizens. Others do not, perhaps because they entered the country illegally. Although their rights are limited, even noncitizens have responsibilities in civic participation, such as paying taxes.

Effects of Migration Everyone has the right to leave his or her country. However, the country to which a migrant wants to move may not accept that person. The receiving country might have one policy about accepting refugees from political situations, and another about migrants coming for economic reasons. Because of the huge volume of people migrating from war-torn, famine-stricken, and politically unstable regions, millions of people have no place to go. Crowded into refugee camps, often under squalid conditions, these migrants face a very uncertain future.

Those accepted into new countries face many challenges and opportunities. In their adopted countries, they often have more services and opportunities available to them, such as health care, education, and jobs. However, it may be difficult to obtain those services due to language barriers, cost, or lack of knowledge about how to access services. If immigrants don't speak the adopted country's language or if job training obtained in their home country isn't considered valid in the receiving country, they may struggle to find work. Once they do, however, they can sometimes reduce the economic struggles of family and friends still in their home country by sending money to them. At the same time, immigrants bring their home cultures to their adopted countries, helping to create a rich, diverse blended culture.

Immigrants often help offset labor shortages in a variety of industries. Nevertheless, some citizens in receiving countries believe that immigrants take more than they give, a belief that can lead to policies intended to reduce immigration. For example, in Canada, where about 250,000 immigrants arrive each year, government policies enacted in 2015 made it more difficult to obtain Canadian citizenship. Some believe this change is a reaction to recent economic difficulties and job scarcity, because in the past Canada has served as a model for immigration.

Reading Check
Analyze Causes
What push and pull factors cause people to migrate?

Lesson 3 Assessment

1. Use a table to note the methods of global security and examples of each method. Explain which methods have resulted in the greatest contribution to global security.

Method	Examples
Form military alliances	NATO, SEATO, Warsaw Pact

2. **Key Terms and People** For each key term or person in the lesson, write a sentence explaining its significance.

3. **Make Inferences** Why might nations want to retain or develop an arsenal of nuclear, biological, and chemical weapons?

4. **Analyze Effects** How have conflict and cooperation among groups impacted the control of limited resources in the world?

5. **Evaluate** What strategies have been used to resolve conflicts in society and government? Do you think they have been effective?

6. **Identify Problems** How are ethnic and religious conflicts related to problems of global security?

7. **Recognize Effects** How can individuals affect social conditions around the world? Consider the example of Mother Teresa when writing your answer.

🌐 Terrorism

The Big Idea

Terrorism has threatened the safety of people all over the world.

Why It Matters Now

People and nations must work together against the dangers posed by terrorism.

Key Terms and People

terrorism
cyberterrorism
Department of Homeland
  Security

USA PATRIOT Act

Setting the Stage

Wars are not the only threat to international peace and security. **Terrorism**, the use of violence against noncombatants to force changes in societies or governments, strikes fear in the hearts of people everywhere. Recently, terrorist incidents have increased dramatically around the world. Because terrorists often cross national borders to commit their acts or to escape to countries friendly to their cause, most people consider terrorism an international problem.

What Is Terrorism?

Terrorism is not new. Throughout history, individuals, small groups, and governments have used terror tactics to try to achieve political or social goals, whether to bring down a government, eliminate opponents, or promote a cause. In recent times, however, terrorism has changed.

Modern Terrorism Since the late 1960s, tens of thousands of terrorist attacks have occurred worldwide. International terrorist groups have carried out increasingly destructive, high-profile attacks to call attention to their goals and to gain major media coverage. Many countries also face domestic terrorists who oppose their governments' policies or have special interests to promote.

The reasons for modern terrorism are many. The traditional motives, such as gaining independence, expelling foreigners, or changing society, still drive various terrorist groups. These groups use violence to force concessions from their enemies, usually the governments in power. But other kinds of terrorists, driven by radical religious and cultural motives, began to emerge in the late 20th century.

The goal of these terrorists is the destruction of what they consider to be evil. This evil might be located in their own countries or in other parts of the world. These terrorists are willing to die to ensure the success of their attacks.

The sarin gas attack in the Tokyo subway in 1995 is the most notorious act of biochemical terrorism.

Terrorist Methods Terrorist acts involve violence against noncombatants. The weapons most frequently used by terrorists are the bomb and the bullet. The targets of terrorist attacks often are crowded places where people normally feel safe—subway stations, bus stops, restaurants, or shopping malls, for example. Or terrorists might target something that symbolizes what they are against, such as a government building or a religious site. Such targets are carefully chosen in order to gain the most attention and to achieve the highest level of intimidation.

Recently, some terrorist groups have used biological and chemical agents in their attacks. These actions involved the release of bacteria or poisonous gases into the atmosphere. While both biological and chemical attacks can inflict terrible casualties, they are equally powerful in generating great fear among the public. This development in terrorism is particularly worrisome, because biochemical agents are relatively easy to acquire. Laboratories all over the world use bacteria and viruses in the development of new drugs. And the raw materials needed to make some deadly chemical agents can be purchased in many stores or online.

Cyberterrorism is another recent development. This involves politically motivated attacks on information systems, such as hacking into computer networks or spreading computer viruses. Many governments and businesses now use computers and networks to store data and run operations. Cyberattacks have increased accordingly.

Responding to Terrorism Governments take various steps to stamp out terrorism. Most adopt a very aggressive approach in tracking down and punishing terrorist groups. This approach includes infiltrating the groups to gather information on membership and future plans. It also includes striking back harshly after a terrorist attack, even to the point of assassinating known terrorist leaders.

Another approach governments use is to make it more difficult for terrorists to act. This involves eliminating extremists' sources of funds, persuading governments not to protect or support terrorist groups, and tightening security measures.

Reading Check
Draw Conclusions
Why do terrorists tend to target crowded places?

Terrorism Around the World

The problem of modern international terrorism first came to world attention in a shocking way during the 1972 Summer Olympic Games in Munich, Germany (then West Germany). Members of a Palestinian terrorist group killed two Israeli athletes and took nine others hostage, later killing them. Palestinian terrorists also used airplane hijackings and suicide bombers. Since then, few regions of the world have been spared from terrorist attacks.

Islamist Movements Some Muslims believe that society's laws should be based on what they hold is God's law as written in the Qur'an. In the mid- to late-twentieth century, some Islamic scholars turned to a strict interpretation of the Qur'an. They felt that Western influences were corrupting Muslim countries. They called for all true Muslims to join a global *jihad*, or struggle, against Western societies and governments.

Many young men radicalized by fundamentalist teachings answered that call. These men, and some women, became the foot soldiers for fundamentalist organizations such as Al-Qaeda, Hamas, Hezbollah, and the Taliban. They have been responsible for numerous acts of terrorism.

The Middle East Many terrorist organizations have roots in the Israeli-Palestinian conflict over land in the Middle East. Groups such as the Palestine Islamic Jihad, Hamas, and Hezbollah have sought to prevent a peace settlement between Israel and the Palestinians. They want a homeland for the Palestinians on their own terms, deny Israel's right to exist, and seek Israel's destruction. In a continual cycle of violence, the Israelis retaliate after most terrorist attacks, and the terrorists strike again. Moderates in the region believe that the only long-term solution is a compromise between Israel and the Palestinians over the issue of land. However, the violence has continued with only occasional breaks.

The Iran-backed Lebanese terrorist group Hezbollah formed after the 1982 Israeli invasion of Lebanon to fight the Israeli occupation of South Lebanon. One of the group's primary goals is the destruction of the state of Israel. In July 2006, Hezbollah kidnapped two Israeli soldiers and fired rockets into Israel, triggering a month-long conflict between Israel and Lebanon.

In 2002, Israel began building a security barrier to prevent Palestinian suicide bombers from entering Israel. This Palestinian protest took place in 2007.

Europe Many countries in Europe have been targets of domestic terrorists who oppose government policies. For decades the mostly Catholic Irish Republican Army (IRA) engaged in terrorist attacks against Britain because it opposed British control of Northern Ireland. Since 1998, however, the British, the IRA, and representatives of Northern Ireland's Protestants have been negotiating a peaceful solution to the situation. An agreement was reached in 2005.

Other European terrorist groups include the ETA, a militant separatist group that sought independence for the Basque region of Spain, and the left-wing Red Brigades in Italy, which sought to destabilize the Italian government in the 1970s and 1980s before collapsing after many members were arrested. In 2011 the ETA announced a permanent cease-fire.

Asia Afghanistan, in Southwest Asia, became a haven for international terrorists after the Taliban came to power in 1996. In that year, Osama bin Laden, a Saudi Arabian millionaire involved in terrorist activities, moved to Afghanistan. There he began using mountain hideouts as a base of operations for his global network of Muslim terrorists known as al-Qaeda.

Terrorist groups have arisen in East Asia, as well. One, known as Aum Shinrikyo ("Supreme Truth"), is a religious cult that wants to control Japan. In 1995, cult members released sarin, a deadly nerve gas, in subway stations in Tokyo. Twelve people were killed and more than 5,700 injured. This attack brought global attention to the threat of biological and chemical agents as terrorist weapons.

In South Asia, the Tamil Tigers (LTTE) in Sri Lanka have used suicide bombings and other terrorist tactics in their fight for an independent state. In 1983, after the LTTE ambushed 13 Sinhalese soldiers, a civil war erupted. Even though a cease-fire agreement was signed with the LTTE and the government in 2002, violence continued. In 2008 the government broke the agreement to pursue and eliminate the leadership of the LTTE, which it achieved the following year.

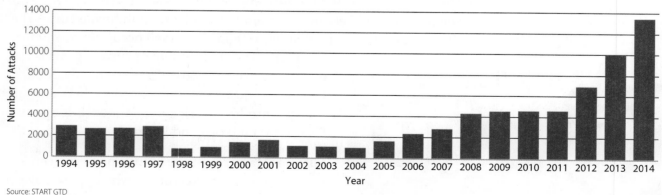

Total Worldwide Terror Attacks, 1994–2014

Source: START GTD

Interpret Graphs
1. **Compare** When did the global total of terrorist incidents begin to rise above 5,000?

Africa Civil unrest and regional wars were the root causes of most terrorist activity in Africa at the end of the 20th century. But al-Qaeda cells operated in many African countries, and several major attacks against U.S. personnel and facilities in Africa were linked to al-Qaeda. In 1998, for example, bombings at the U.S. embassies in Kenya and Tanzania left more than 200 people dead and more than 5,000 have injured. The United States responded to these attacks with missile strikes on suspected terrorist facilities in Afghanistan and in Sudan, where bin Laden was based from 1991 to 1996.

Latin America Narcoterrorism, or terrorism linked to drug trafficking, is a major problem in Latin America, particularly in Colombia. The powerful groups that control that country's narcotics trade have frequently turned to violence. The Revolutionary Armed Forces of Colombia (FARC) is a left-wing guerrilla group that has links with these drug traffickers. The FARC has attacked Colombian political, military, and economic targets, as well as those with American ties.

Other Latin American groups were motivated by political ideologies rather than the economics of the drug trade. Shining Path, a militant Communist group founded in 1970 in Peru, sought to overthrow the Peruvian government to replace it with a Communist government. Its 20-year campaign of violence caused tens of thousands of deaths and disrupted the country's economy.

Reading Check
Analyze Causes
What are some reasons for terrorism in various regions of the world?

History in Depth

Drug Trafficking

Drug trafficking is an illegal trade that includes producing, distributing, and selling illegal drugs. From the 1970s to the 1990s, Colombia served as the dominant location in the distribution of cocaine. Criminal organizations known as drug cartels controlled the distribution and sale of cocaine. In recent years, the United States has been working with the Colombian government as part of the Plan Colombia program. The Plan Colombia program provided hundreds of millions of dollars per year for military aid, training, and equipment to fight the FARC and other guerrilla forces involved in drug trafficking.

At the height of Colombian drug trafficking and cartel control, illegal gang and criminal activity related to drug trafficking arose. These activities, as well as economic opportunities, drove local residents to migrate to other countries, including the United States. Once working in their new countries, many of these immigrant workers sent their salaries back to family members in their home country. Once economic conditions and security improve in their home country, they often return.

Attack on the United States

On the morning of September 11, 2001, nineteen Arab terrorists hijacked four airliners heading from East Coast airports to California. In a series of coordinated strikes, the hijackers crashed two of the jets into the twin towers of the World Trade Center in New York City and a third into the Pentagon outside Washington, D.C. The fourth plane crashed in an empty field in Pennsylvania.

The Destruction The planes, loaded with fuel, became destructive missiles when they crashed into the World Trade Center and the Pentagon. The explosions and fires so weakened the damaged skyscrapers that they crumbled to the ground less than two hours after impact. The fire and raining debris caused nearby buildings to collapse as well. The damage at the Pentagon, though extensive, was confined to one section of the building.

The toll in human lives was great. Nearly 3,000 people died in the attacks. All passengers on the four planes were killed, as well as workers and visitors in the World Trade Center and the Pentagon. The dead

DOCUMENT-BASED INVESTIGATION   Historical Source

President George W. Bush

Two months after the 9/11 attacks, U.S. President George W. Bush addressed the United Nations General Assembly to discuss terrorism.

Analyze Historical Sources
Describe the global security responsibilities of all United Nations members.

> *"The most basic obligations in this new conflict have already been defined by the United Nations.... Every United Nations member has a responsibility to crack down on terrorist financing. We must pass all necessary laws in our own countries to allow the confiscation of terrorist assets. We must apply those laws to every financial institution in every nation.*
>
> *We have responsibility to share intelligence and coordinate the efforts of law enforcement. If you know something, tell us. If we know something, we'll tell you. And when we find the terrorists, we must work together to bring them to justice.... We have a responsibility to deny weapons to terrorists...."*
>
> —George W. Bush

included more than 340 New York City firefighters and 60 police officers who rushed to the scene to help and were buried in the rubble when the skyscrapers collapsed.

The Impact of the Attack September 11 had a devastating impact on the way Americans looked at life. Many reported feeling that everything had changed—that life would never be the same. Before, Americans had viewed terrorism as something that happened in other countries. Now they felt vulnerable and afraid.

This sense of vulnerability was underscored just a few days after September 11, when terrorism struck the United States again. Letters containing spores of a bacterium that causes the disease anthrax were sent to people in the news media and to members of Congress in Washington, D.C. Anthrax bacteria, when inhaled, can damage the lungs and cause death. Five people who came in contact with spores from the tainted letters died of inhalation anthrax. Two were postal workers.

Investigators did not find a link between the September 11 attacks and the anthrax letters. Some of them believed that the letters might be the work of a lone terrorist rather than an organized group. Regardless of who was responsible for the anthrax scare, it caused incredible psychological damage. Many Americans were now fearful of an everyday part of life—the mail.

Reading Check
Make Inferences
Why were the specific targets of the September 11 attacks selected by the terrorists?

History in Depth

Destruction in New York City and the Pentagon

▲ Stunned bystanders look on as smoke billows from the twin towers of the World Trade Center.

▲ The strike on the Pentagon left a charred, gaping hole in the southwest side of the building.

▶ A hazardous materials team prepares to enter a congressional building during the anthrax scare.

The United States Responds

Immediately after September 11, the United States called for an international effort to combat terrorist groups. President George W. Bush declared, "This battle will take time and resolve. But make no mistake about it: we will win."

The Hunt for Osama bin Laden As a first step in this battle, the U.S. government organized a massive effort to identify those responsible for the attacks. Officials concluded that Osama bin Laden directed the terrorists. The effort to bring him to justice led the United States to begin military action against Afghanistan. In spite of this military action, bin Laden managed to elude justice for nearly 10 years. But in 2011, U.S. efforts finally paid off when intelligence experts located his hideout in Abbottabad, Pakistan. On May 2, 2011, U.S. Navy commandos raided bin Laden's fortified compound and killed the terrorist leader.

Homeland Security Alert uses a color-coded alert system to communicate effectively with the American public about terrorist threats. The colors begin with green and blue for low and guarded risk of attacks. Yellow and orange are elevated and high risk of terrorist attacks. Red signifies a severe risk of terrorist attacks.

Antiterrorism Measures The federal government warned Americans that additional terrorist attacks were likely. It then took action to prevent such attacks. The **Department of Homeland Security** was created in 2002 to coordinate national efforts against terrorism. Antiterrorism measures included a search for terrorists in the United States and the passage of antiterrorism laws. Officials began detaining and questioning other Arabs and other Muslims whose behavior was considered suspicious or who had violated immigration regulations.

Some critics charged that detaining these men was unfair to the innocent and violated their civil rights. However, the government held that the actions were justified because the hijackers had been Arabs. The government further argued that it was not unusual to curtail civil liberties during wartime in order to protect national security. This argument was also used to justify a proposal to try some terrorist suspects in military tribunals rather than in criminal courts. On October 26, 2001, President Bush signed an antiterrorism bill into law. The law, known as the **USA PATRIOT Act**, allowed the government to

- detain foreigners suspected of terrorism for seven days without charging them with a crime
- tap all phones used by suspects and monitor their e-mail and Internet use
- make search warrants valid across states
- order U.S. banks to investigate sources of large foreign accounts
- prosecute terrorist crimes without any time restrictions or limitations

Again, critics warned that these measures allowed the government to infringe on people's civil rights.

Aviation Security The federal government also increased its involvement in aviation security. The Federal Aviation Administration (FAA) ordered airlines to install bars on cockpit doors to prevent passengers from gaining control of planes, as the hijackers had done. Sky marshals—trained security officers—were assigned to fly on planes, and National Guard troops began patrolling airports.

The Aviation and Transportation Security Act, which became law in November 2001, made airport security the responsibility of the federal government. Previously, individual airports had been responsible. The law provided for a federal security force that would inspect passengers and carry-on bags. It also required the screening of checked baggage.

Airline and government officials debated these and other measures for making air travel more secure. Major concerns were long delays at airports and respect for passengers' privacy. It has also become clear that public debate over security measures will continue as long as the United States fights terrorism and tries to balance national security with civil rights.

Global Effects of Terrorism

For the past 15 years, terrorism has been a pressing global issue. The September 11, 2001, attacks in the United States and subsequent attacks around the world have heightened focus on the issue and its effects.

Global Security Many countries have faced security issues since 9/11. Bomb attacks on trains and buses in Madrid, London, and Jerusalem spurred Spain, Great Britain, and Israel to investigate ways to use technology to improve security for their transportation systems. Officials hoped that these measures would help to prevent future terrorist attacks.

Many countries have also increased security in other public spaces and at public events, including government buildings, tourist attractions, and public gatherings during festivals, celebrations, and holidays. Many Western countries and some Middle Eastern countries started working together to share intelligence about possible terrorists and terrorist activities. They use surveillance technology to track and record the actions of suspicious people or groups.

In July 2005, four suicide bombers attacked central London with backpacks full of explosives. A total of 52 people were killed and hundreds more were injured as the bombers detonated devices on the London Underground and another on a double-decker bus.

Impacts on Economy, Society, and Politics Terrorist attacks have ripple effects through various aspects of society. The economic effects include loss of property, loss of lives, and costs of additional security measures. The insecurity that the population feels after an attack or in anticipation of an attack affects the stock market and international investments. This was a major factor after the 9/11 attacks. Terrorist groups such as al-Qaeda want to disrupt financial institutions worldwide as this builds fear and can lead to financial and economic insecurity. In 2007, al-Qaeda developed a new strategy for attacking the United States by cutting off its energy supply. The attack failed, but had it been successful it would have crippled transportation industries globally and world economies would have been paralyzed. Militants of the terrorist group called Islamic State of Iraq and the Levant (ISIL), also known as ISIS, attacked two separate sites

Passengers wait to go through a security check at La Guardia Airport in New York.

in Tunisia in March and June 2015 and killed 60 people. These terrorist incidents affected the country's tourism industry, a mainstay of its economy. Many people who had planned to visit Tunisia canceled their plans because they feared another attack.

Political effects of terrorism include the destabilization of the government, especially when political leaders are assassinated and new leaders replace them. This could result in a change in a government's policies related to combatting terrorism. However, governments may cooperate with other governments or form military agreements in order to stop terrorism or terrorist activity. This form of global cooperation to fight terrorism has been effective. For example, coalition forces, including the United States military, launched a successful airstrike against several ISIS leaders in September 2015. Yet combatting terrorism causes financial strain. Government leaders must weigh cutting domestic programs in order to fund programs and military spending to fight terrorism.

Reading Check
Compare
What issues must a government address when combatting terrorism?

Lesson 4 Assessment

1. Complete a chart to compare and contrast world terrorist incidents and the September 11 terrorist attacks. Explain how the September 11 attacks were unique and how they were similar to other terrorist incidents.

World Terrorist Incidents

September 11 Attacks

2. **Key Terms and People** For each key term or person in the lesson, write a sentence explaining its significance.
3. **Analyze Motives** What might cause individuals to use terror tactics to bring about change?
4. **Form Opinions** Is it important for the U.S. government to respect peoples' civil rights as it wages a war against terrorism? Why or why not?
5. **Draw Conclusions** What are the wider international consequences of terrorist attacks?

Environmental Challenges

The Big Idea
Technology, population growth, and industrialization have created environmental challenges that have affected the entire world.

Why It Matters Now
Failure to solve environmental problems will threaten the health of the planet.

Key Terms and People
desertification
greenhouse effect
conservation

Setting the Stage

As the world's population increases, so do people's demands on the environment. Technology and industrialization have helped to raise standards of living for many people. But they have also affected the global environment. For two centuries, industrialization has increased the demands for energy and natural resources. In addition, industry and technology have increased the amount of pollution on the planet. Pollution and the potential shortage of natural resources have prompted everyone from world leaders to ordinary citizens to look for ways to better protect our natural surroundings.

Development and Population Pressures

The environment has been altered greatly by industrialization and human population growth. As societies have became more sophisticated and developed, populations have increased, resulting in a greater need for resources. As the global population increases, so have industrialization and technology, which have had negative effects on the environment.

Industrialization The Industrial Revolution, which began in Great Britain in the late 1700s, changed human life and greatly impacted the relationship that humans have with the environment. In the process of industrialization, the use of machines replaced human labor in Europe and later North America and other parts of the world. Industrialization affected many aspects of basic human needs, such as food, housing, and clothing. Industrialization produced products faster and in greater quantities. However, this new standard of living took a toll on the environment. Industries relied on fossil fuels for energy sources, including coal, natural gas, and oil. Because of this reliance on the burning of fossil fuels, industrialization caused pollution and many other

DEPLETION OF THE BRAZILIAN AMAZON RAINFOREST

Extent of Deforestation, 1970–2013

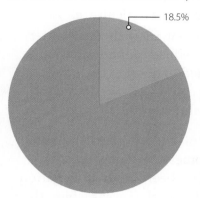

18.5%

Total area: 4.1 million square miles

Sources: Mongabay.com; Brazilian National Institute of Space Research; United Nations Food and Agriculture Organization

Interpret Graphs

1. **Clarify** How many square miles of the Brazilian Amazon rainforest were deforested from 1970 to 2013?

Brazilian government is to improve the social and economic conditions of its poor population and the indigenous people who live in the rainforests of Brazil. Unlike the United States and other developed countries, Brazil does not have the financial resources or economic strength to put into place environmental policies regarding resource management. In order to diminish deforestation in the Amazon region, the government would have to use substantial financial resources. As one American diplomat explained, "Environmental concerns are a luxury of the rich, and this is not a rich country. Brazilians are not going to just preserve the Amazon. They are going to develop it. The question is, how."

Many other developing nations face the same problem as Brazil. They need to achieve sustainable development, the process of creating economic growth while preserving the environment. The United Nations Economic and Social Council (ECOSOC) has been working with other organizations and countries on sustainable development. In September 2015 the ECOSOC hosted a UN Conference on Sustainable Development to share sustainable development initiatives. In some areas, sustainable development initiatives are seeing positive results The UN estimates that over the past 25 years, the deforestation rate has slowed. It attributes this improvement to better management of forest resources.

Distribution of Natural Resources Resources are not distributed equally around the world, which gives some countries and regions economic advantages over others. Many different organizations such as the International Union for Conservation of Nature and the Hague Institute for Global Justice work to improve and narrow the inequitable distribution of resources. Such organizations have pointed out that conservation efforts to manage natural resources have unfairly affected indigenous peoples, who often practice and rely on subsistence agriculture.

Developed nations have other advantages that allow them to better access their natural resources. Many industrialized countries have the financial resources and the technology needed to develop their natural resources. Even though some developing countries have abundant resources, they may not have comparable technology or financial means.

As more resources become depleted, people often look to other areas where natural resources can be obtained. Sometimes this affects settlement patterns. For example, if a lake has been used for irrigation and its water is depleted, people may migrate to other areas where they can find water for irrigation, which can cause population shifts. Another example is if people clear a forested area for agriculture but experience high population growth in their village or town, they may need to migrate to new areas in search of more potential cropland. In addition, countries that have larger and increasing populations often use a higher percentage of natural resources than other countries and regions with smaller populations.

A Growing Appetite for Energy

Sustainable development depends on using energy sources wisely. Energy sources can be defined as renewable or nonrenewable. Renewable energy sources, such as wind, water, and solar power, can be replenished. Nonrenewable energy sources, such as oil and coal, cannot. Although nonrenewable sources are generally cheaper to use, supplies are limited. Also, their use can cause environmental damage.

U.S. Coast Guard fireboat response crews battle the blazing remnants of the off-shore oil rig Deepwater Horizon in the Gulf of Mexico on April 21, 2010, near New Orleans, Louisiana.

As population growth increases in urban and suburban areas, demand for energy also rises. Larger populations often require the use of more energy for light, heat, and power. Urban and suburban areas are increasingly centers of population growth and economic activity, both of which fuel energy consumption. As more and more shopping malls and fast-food restaurants are constructed to meet the needs of growing suburban populations around the world, some argue that this will negatively impact the environment. Others assert that this development will strengthen economies and provide more opportunities for globalization.

Energy Use and Its Challenges Eighty percent of the earth's energy supply now comes from nonrenewable sources. Developed countries consume most of this energy. North America, Europe, and China are the biggest consumers.

The petroleum industry has contributed greatly to industrialization, but it also contributes to the world's climate change crisis. The extraction and use of petroleum and petroleum products releases harmful toxins into the environment. As much of the global community relies on petroleum to meet its energy needs, it must manage the effects on the environment and practice sustainable development. Other nonrenewable energy sources also have environmental effects. Like petroleum, the burning of coal also contributes to greenhouse gases. Cutting down trees for fuel leads to soil erosion and the expansion of deserts in some areas. Nuclear power plants produce radioactive wastes that can remain hazardous for many years.

The Gulf Oil Spill Oil spills are another example of energy-related pollution. Every year, several serious oil spills take place around the world. They foul water and shorelines and kill sea life. Although oil companies take precautions to prevent spills, spills appear to be an inevitable result of oil use.

The largest oil spill in U.S. history occurred in April 2010 when a drilling rig owned by British Petroleum (BP) exploded in the Gulf of Mexico. The accident spilled millions of gallons of oil along the Gulf coast,

Now and Then

Alternative Fuel Cars

Automobiles, most of which run on gasoline, use a great deal of the world's nonrenewable energy. But perhaps not for long. Automakers have begun creating cars fueled by alternative power, such as hydrogen—one of the most abundant natural elements on earth.

The trend toward environmentally safer vehicles is growing. California, for example, recently required the production of millions of low-emission vehicles—which use a combination of gas and electric power—over the next two decades.

However, some scientists are questioning the environmental hazards of electric cars. Electric cars do not emit hazardous gases as do conventional cars, but the manufacture of electric cars impacts global warming. The use of raw materials and the energy needed to build the lithium ion batteries also affect the environment. The power used to charge the battery contributes to global warming if it comes from a nonrenewable energy source such as coal. Energy is produced differently in countries where electric cars are made, and electricity produced from coal is the most polluting way to generate power. Even though no zero-emission vehicle currently exists, many scientists are working toward building the most environmentally friendly alternative.

seriously damaging marine habitats and fishing and tourism industries. BP managed to contain the spill after several months and promised to pay all cleanup costs.

Solutions for the 21st Century Government action and stronger regulations may provide solutions to the world's environmental problems in the 21st century. In the long run, however, improved technology might stand as the best hope for a cleaner environment. More inexpensive ways to use renewable energy sources, such as wind and solar power, may reduce air pollution and global warming. In any event, the nations of the world will need to agree on how to achieve sustainable development in this new millennium.

Some governments have taken action against pollution and global warming by passing laws to protect Earth's air and water. Still, many nations do not have strict pollution controls in place, or even if they have enacted laws they continue to be among the world's largest polluters of the environment. The United States, for example, fits into this category. In the United States and elsewhere, politicians often have difficulty agreeing on a course of action because of differing ideologies. Some nations fear that placing strict limits on the emission of carbon dioxide and other greenhouse gases that contribute to global warming might harm economic development. Preventing and reducing pollution while protecting businesses and economies is a major political and international challenge for governments around the globe.

Reading Check
Identify Problems
What are some problems associated with the use of nonrenewable energy?

Lesson 5 Assessment

1. **Organize Information** Use the web diagram below to list environmental problems. Which set of problems do you consider to be the most serious?

2. **Key Terms and People** For each key term or person in the lesson, write a sentence explaining its significance.
3. **Analyze Issues** How are population growth and urbanization connected to global warming?
4. **Form Opinions** Should developing nations have to meet the same environmental standards as developed nations? Why or why not?
5. **Compare** What are the environmental arguments for and against globalization?
6. **Predict** What impact will increased globalization in the 20th and 21st centuries have?

Cultures Blend in a Global Age

The Big Idea

Technology has increased contact among the world's people, changing their cultures.

Why It Matters Now

Globalization of culture has changed the ways people live, their perceptions, and their interactions.

Key Terms and People

popular culture
consumerism

Setting the Stage

Since the beginnings of civilization, people have blended ideas and ways of doing things from other cultures into their own culture. The same kind of cultural sharing and blending continues today. But, because of advances in technology, it occurs at a much more rapid pace and over much greater distances. Twenty-first-century technologies allow people from all over the world to have increasing interaction with one another. Such contacts promote widespread sharing of cultures.

Cultural Exchange Accelerates

Cultural elements that reflect a group's common background and changing interests are called **popular culture**. Popular culture involves music, sports, movies, the Internet, clothing fashions, foods, and hobbies or leisure activities. Popular culture around the world incorporates features from many different lands. Of all the technologies that contribute to such cultural sharing, television, movies, the Internet, and other mass media have been the most powerful.

Mass Media In the United States, 99 percent of American households have at least one television set. In Western Europe, too, most households have one or more televisions. Access to television is less widespread in the emerging nations, but it is growing. The speed at which television can present information helps create an up-to-the-minute shared experience of global events. Wars, natural disasters, and political drama in faraway places have become a part of everyday life.

However, no mass media does more to promote a sense of a globally shared experience than does the Internet. In a matter of minutes, a political demonstration in South America can be captured on a camera phone and uploaded

Rock 'n' Roll

In the middle of the 1950s, a new style of music emerged on the American scene. It was called rock 'n' roll. The music explored social and political themes. Rock music, which seemed to adults to reflect a youth rebellion, soon became the dominant popular music for young people across the world. As the influence of rock music spread, international artists added their own traditions, instruments, and musical styles to the mix called rock.

"The King" ▶

"Rock and roll music, if you like it and you feel it, you just can't help but move to it. That's what happens to me, I can't help it."—Elvis Presley, called the "King of Rock 'n' Roll" by many.

▲ U2

U2, led by singer Bono, is one of the world's most popular and influential rock bands. Over a career spanning nearly 40 years, this Irish band has kept its music vibrant and fresh by absorbing and reworking all manner of musical styles. The band has drawn on the blues, gospel, 1950s rock 'n' roll, 1960s protest songs, and hip-hop to create a very distinctive kind of music.

"World Pop" ▶

Youssou N'Dour, a singer from the West African country of Senegal, blends traditional African styles with American rock to create a new form that has been called "world-pop fusion."

Critical Thinking

1. **Make Inferences** How have improvements in technology and global communications aided in the blending of musical styles?

2. **Analyze Events** Write a brief analysis of a major musical development that occurred in the past century.

to an online video community for all the world to see. Blogs, social networking sites, and real-time information networks also transmit the most current news, information, entertainment, and opinions worldwide in the blink of an eye.

Television, the Internet, and other mass media, including radio and movies, are among the world's most popular forms of entertainment. But they also show how people in other parts of the world live and what they value. Mass media is the major way popular culture spreads to all parts of the globe.

International Elements of Popular Culture The entertainment field, especially television, has a massive influence on popular culture. People from around the world are avid viewers of American TV programs. For example, in Bhutan, a tiny country high in the Himalayas, ESPN, HBO, Cartoon Network, and CNN are among the most-watched channels. CNN is a global channel, since it reaches more than 250 million households in more than 200 countries.

Television broadcasts of sporting events provide a front-row seat for sports fans all over the globe. Basketball and soccer are among the most popular televised sports. National Basketball Association (NBA) games are televised in more than 200 countries. In China, for example, broadcasts of NBA games of the week regularly attract an audience in the millions. One of the most-watched international sporting events is the soccer World Cup. Hundreds of millions of viewers worldwide watched the 2014 World Cup final.

Music is another aspect of popular culture that has become international. As the equipment for listening to music has become more portable, there are only a few places in the world that do not have access to music from other cultures. People from around the world dance to reggae bands from the Caribbean, chant rap lyrics from the United States, play air guitar to rowdy European bands, and enjoy the fast drumming of Afropop tunes. And the performers who create this music often gain international fame.

Reading Check
Analyze Effects
What effects have television and mass media had on popular culture?

Now and Then

International Baseball

The sport of baseball is an example of global popular culture. When American missionaries and teachers arrived in Japan in the 1870s, they introduced the game of baseball. Over the years the game gained popularity there. Today, some Major League teams have Japanese players and several American players play in the Japanese league.

Baseball spread to Mexico, Cuba, Puerto Rico, Panama, and the Dominican Republic in the late 19th and early 20th centuries. Today, baseball is a popular game in these and other Latin American countries. About 25 percent of the players in Major League Baseball come from Latin America.

World Culture Blends Many Influences

Greater access to the ideas and customs of different cultures often results in cultural blending. As cultural ideas move with people among cultures, some beliefs and habits seem to have a greater effect than others. In the 20th century, ideas from the West have been very dominant in shaping cultures in many parts of the globe.

Westernizing Influences on Different Cultures Western domination of the worldwide mass media helps explain the huge influence the West has on many different cultures today. However, heavy Western influence on the rest of the world's cultures is actually rooted in the 19th century. Western domination of areas all over the globe left behind a legacy of Western customs and ideas. Western languages are spoken throughout the world, mainly because of Europe's history of colonization in the Americas, Asia, and Africa.

Over the past 50 years, English has emerged as the premier international language. English is spoken by about 500 million people as their first or second language. Although more people speak Mandarin Chinese than English, English speakers are more widely distributed. English is the most common language used on the Internet and at international conferences. The language is used by scientists, diplomats, doctors, and businesspeople around the world. The widespread use of English is responsible, in part, for the emergence of a dynamic global culture.

Western influence can be seen in other aspects of popular culture. For example, blue jeans are the clothes of choice of most of the world's youth. Western business suits are standard uniforms among many people. American-style hamburgers and soft drinks can be purchased in many countries of the world. Mickey Mouse and other Disney characters are almost universally recognized.

Some people believe that these changes are largely negative. They argue that mass media and advertising impact group behavior by encouraging the growth of **consumerism**, or the preoccupation with the buying of consumer goods. For example, as individuals in developing countries gain more wealth, many begin to spend their new money on consumer goods from clothing to technological devices to automobiles. This market for consumer goods, some opponents say, is shaped by the media and advertising, rather than by actual needs. Thus, they suggest that globalization is beginning to create a common world culture and is encouraging traditional cultures to lose some of their uniqueness.

Non-Western Influences Cultural ideas are not confined to moving only from the West to other lands. Non-Western cultures also influence people in Europe and the United States. From music and clothing styles to ideas about art and architecture, to religious and ethical systems, non-Western ideas are incorporated into Western life. And cultural blending of Western and non-Western elements opens communications channels for the further exchange of ideas throughout the globe. This cross-fertilization

Bollywood

Bollywood is the largest component of the Indian film industry. Bollywood films are influenced by ancient Indian epics, ancient Sanskrit dramas, traditional folk theatre of India, Parsi theatre, and Hollywood. In the 2000s, Bollywood played a key role in reviving the American musical film genre. The musical film *Moulin Rouge!* was inspired by Bollywood musicals as well as many other musical films.

As a result of globalization, Bollywood films are popular not only with Indians, but also with Nigerians, Egyptians, Senegalese, and Russians. Generations of non-Indian fans have grown up with Bollywood and have witnessed the cross-cultural appeal of Indian movies. Towards the end of the twentieth century and into the twenty-first century, Bollywood has expanded its popularity with Western audiences and music and movie producers.

between cultures can be seen in the Brazilian martial art capoeira. Capoeira combines elements of dance, acrobatics, and music. It originated in West Africa, but West Africans brought it to Brazil during the slave trade in the sixteenth century. Currently, capoeira is practiced around the world.

The Arts Become International Modern art, like popular culture, has become increasingly international. Advances in transportation and technology have facilitated the sharing of ideas about art and the sharing of actual works of art. Shows and museums throughout the world exhibit art of different styles and from different places. It became possible to see art from other cultures that had not previously been available to the public.

Literature, too, has become internationally appreciated. Well-known writers routinely have their works translated into dozens of languages, resulting in truly international audiences. The list of Nobel Prize winners in literature over the last 20 years reflects a broad variety of nationalities, including Turkish, Egyptian, Mexican, South African, West Indian, Japanese, Polish, Chinese, and Hungarian.

Reading Check
Summarize Name three advances that allow a greater sharing of the arts

Inside the Villaggio shopping mall in Doha, Qatar

Future Challenges and Hopes

Many people view with alarm the development of a global popular culture heavily influenced by Western, and particularly American, ways of life. They fear that this will result in the loss of their unique identity as a people or nation. As a result, many countries have adopted policies that reserve television broadcast time for national programming. For example, France requires that 40 percent of broadcast time be set aside for French-produced programs. South Korea also places significant limits on the amount of foreign programming that can be broadcast.

Kenzaburo Oe of Japan was awarded the Nobel literature prize in 1994. Oe studied Western literature in college, and he has used Western literary styles to tell stories about his personal life and the myths and history of his country.

South African writer Nadine Gordimer won the Nobel Prize for Literature in 1991. Many of her novels and stories published prior to 1991 focused on the evils of the apartheid system. As a result, much of her work was censored or banned by the South African government.

Some countries take a different approach to protecting cultural diversity in the media. Television programmers take American shows and rework them according to their own culture and traditions. As an Indian media researcher noted, "We really want to see things our own way." Other countries take more drastic steps to protect their cultural identity. They strictly censor the mass media to keep unwanted ideas from entering their nation.

Sometimes people respond to perceived threats to their culture by trying to return to traditional ways. Cultural practices and rites of passage may receive even more emphasis as a group tries to preserve its identity. In some countries, native groups take an active role in preserving the traditional ways of life. For example, the Maori in New Zealand have revived ancestral customs rather than face cultural extinction. Many Maori cultural activities are conducted in a way that preserves Maori ways of thinking and behaving. In 1987, the New Zealand government recognized the importance of this trend by making the Maori language one of the country's official languages.

Global Interdependence Despite the fear and uncertainty accompanying global interdependence, economic, political, and environmental issues do bring all nations closer together. Nations have begun to recognize that they are dependent on other nations and deeply affected by the actions of others far away. As elements of everyday life and expressions of culture become more international in scope, people across the world gain a sense of connectedness with people in other areas of the world. For example, the response to the events of September 11, 2001, was international in scope. People from around the world expressed their concern and support for the United States. It was as if this act of terrorism had struck their own countries.

Throughout history, human beings have faced challenges to survive and to live better. In the 21st century, these challenges will be faced by people who are in increasing contact with one another. They have a greater stake in learning to live together in harmony and with the physical planet.

Reading Check
Analyze Effects
How do people react against greater global interdependence?

Lesson 6 Assessment

1. **Organize Information** Create a web listing aspects of international popular culture. Explain which of the aspects has the greatest effect on your life.

International popular culture

2. **Key Terms and People** For each key term or person in the lesson, write a sentence explaining its significance.
3. **Synthesize** Why are the mass media such an effective means of transmitting culture?
4. **Analyze Effects** Do you think that limiting the amount of foreign television programming is an effective way to protect cultural diversity? Why or why not?
5. **Form Opinions** "Ethnocentrism— the belief in the superiority of one's own ethnic group—has taken hold in the world." Do you agree or disagree? Explain.

Module 32 Assessment

Key Terms and People

For each term or name below, write a sentence explaining its connection to global interdependence from 1960 to the present.

1. Internet
2. genetic engineering
3. global economy
4. free trade
5. political dissent
6. refugee
7. terrorism
8. USA Patriot Act
9. popular culture
10. consumerism

Main Ideas

Science and Technology Transform Life

1. In what ways have science and technology changed the lives of people today?
2. What was the goal of the green revolution?

Global Economic Development

3. How are a developed nation and an emerging nation different?
4. What is the function of the World Trade Organization?

Global Security Issues

5. What methods has the world community used to resolve conflicts since World War II?
6. What efforts have been made to guarantee basic human rights?

Terrorism

7. What methods do terrorists employ?
8. How did the United States respond to the terrorist attacks of September 11, 2001?

Environmental Challenges

9. What natural resources does the world community fear are becoming scarce?
10. How do rain forests benefit the environment?

Cultures Blend in a Global Age

11. Which technologies have had the most powerful impact on cultural sharing?
12. Why have Western influences had a major impact all over the world?

Critical Thinking

1. **Summarize** How is the UN working to address the unresolved problems of the world?

2. **Analyze Issues** How does globalization affect relationships and economic development among developed and developing countries?

3. **Identify Solutions** Imagine you are the culture minister of a small country. What steps would you take to ensure that your country's cultural identity is protected? Explain why you think these steps would be effective.

4. **Recognize Effects** How are individuals affected by the global economy?

Engage with History

Imagine that you are a U.S. economics analyst preparing for a group discussion on the United States' economic system and its impact on society. You may use print and electronic resources to help you gather information. Address the following topics in your discussion:

- GDP
- supply and demand
- competition
- consumer price index (CPI)
- income
- elasticity
- the role of government in the economy

Focus on Writing

Work in groups of four to create a report describing how private enterprises affect politics, the economy, and social life in countries within one of these regions: Africa, Latin America, Europe, or the United States. Each group member should research a different region. Consider the following questions as you research:

- What is a private enterprise?
- How do private enterprises interact with the government?
- Which laws affect private companies?
- Do private enterprises improve economies? How?
- In what ways do private enterprises change the lives of people who work for them or of people in the community?

Multimedia Activity

Work in groups of three to create a multimedia presentation showing how urbanization and industrialization have changed the roles of social institutions such as family, religion, education, and government in many societies. Each group should choose a region, and each person should choose one of the countries listed for that region.

- Africa: Zimbabwe, Kenya, Nigeria, Sierra Leone
- Latin America: Brazil, Argentina, Chile, Mexico
- Asia: China, India, Indonesia, South Korea

Each person should then select one social institution to research for their chosen country. Use the Internet, periodicals, and other sources to research your presentation.

Your presentation should feature historical, literary, musical, and visual materials that relate to your topic.

References

References

Available Online:

- Reading Like a Historian
- World History Themes
- Biographical Dictionary
- Close-Read Screencasts
- Economics Handbook
- Geography and Map Skills Handbook
- Skillbuilder Handbook

A Global View

Religion is defined as an organized system of beliefs, ceremonies, practices, and worship that centers on one or more gods. As many modules in this book explain, religion has had a significant impact on world history. Throughout the centuries, religion has guided the beliefs and actions of millions around the globe. It has brought people together. But it has also torn them apart.

Religion continues to be a dominant force throughout the world, affecting everything from what people wear to how they behave. There are thousands of religions in the world. The following pages concentrate on six major religions and on Confucianism, an ethical system. They examine some of the characteristics and practices that make these religions and systems similar as well as unique. They also present some of each religion's sects and denominations.

North America

1%
1%
5%
13%
80%

Latin America

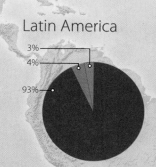

3%
4%
93%

World Population's Religious Affiliations

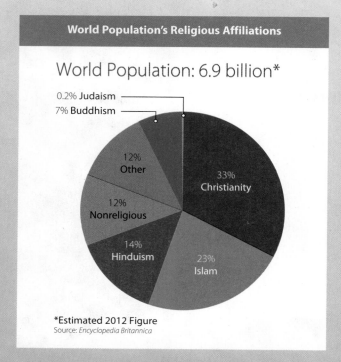

World Population: 6.9 billion*

0.2% Judaism
7% Buddhism
12% Other
12% Nonreligious
14% Hinduism
23% Islam
33% Christianity

*Estimated 2012 Figure
Source: *Encyclopedia Britannica*

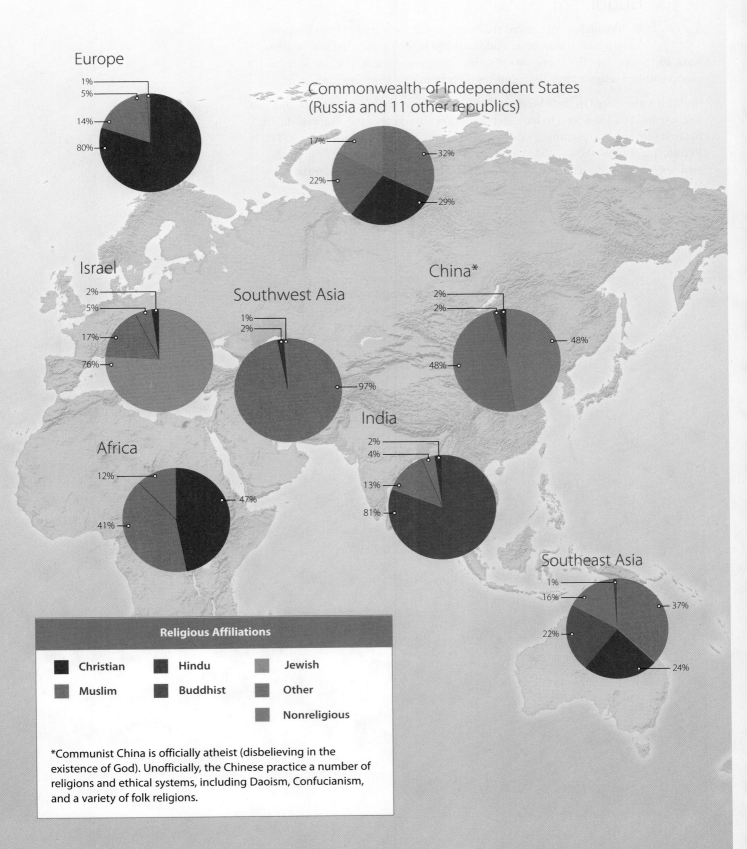

Europe
- 1%
- 5%
- 14%
- 80%

Commonwealth of Independent States
(Russia and 11 other republics)
- 17%
- 32%
- 22%
- 29%

Israel
- 2%
- 5%
- 17%
- 76%

Southwest Asia
- 1%
- 2%
- 97%

China*
- 2%
- 2%
- 48%
- 48%

India
- 2%
- 4%
- 13%
- 81%

Africa
- 12%
- 47%
- 41%

Southeast Asia
- 1%
- 16%
- 37%
- 22%
- 24%

Religious Affiliations
- Christian
- Muslim
- Hindu
- Buddhist
- Jewish
- Other
- Nonreligious

*Communist China is officially atheist (disbelieving in the existence of God). Unofficially, the Chinese practice a number of religions and ethical systems, including Daoism, Confucianism, and a variety of folk religions.

Buddhism

Buddhism has influenced Asian religion, society, and culture for over 2,500 years. Today, most Buddhists live in Sri Lanka, East and Southeast Asia, and Japan. Buddhism consists of several different sects. A religious sect is a group within a religion that distinguishes itself by one or more unique beliefs.

Buddhists are united in their belief in the Buddha's teachings, known as the dharma. Because the Buddha is said to have "set in motion the wheel of the dharma" during his first sermon, his teaching is often symbolized by a wheel, as shown above. The Buddha taught that the key to happiness was detachment from all worldly goods and desires. This was achieved by following the Noble Eightfold Path, or the Middle Way, a life between earthly desires and extreme forms of self-denial.

LEADERSHIP

Those who dedicate their entire life to the teachings of the Buddha are known as Buddhist monks and nuns. In many Buddhist sects, monks are expected to lead a life of poverty, meditation, and study. Here, Buddhist monks file past shrines in Thailand. To learn humility, monks must beg for food and money.

RITUAL

Women in Rangoon, Myanmar, sweep the ground so that monks can avoid stepping on and killing any insects. Many Buddhists believe in rebirth, the idea that living beings, after death, are reborn and continue to exist. Buddhists believe that all living beings possess the potential for spiritual growth—and the possibility of rebirth as humans.

WORSHIP PRACTICES

Statues of the Buddha, such as this one in China, appear in shrines throughout Asia. Buddhists strive to follow the Buddha's teachings through meditation, a form of religious contemplation. They also make offerings at shrines, temples, and monasteries.

Major Buddhist Sects

Theravada   Mahayana

Buddhism

Mantrayana

THE THREE CARDINAL FAULTS

This image depicts what Buddhists consider the three cardinal faults of humanity: greed (the pig); hatred (the snake); and delusion (the rooster).

DHAMMAPADA

PRIMARY SOURCE

One of the most well-known Buddhist scriptures is the *Dhammapada*, or *Verses of Righteousness*. The book is a collection of sayings on Buddhist practices. In this verse, Buddhists are instructed to avoid envying others:

> *"Let him not despise what he has received, nor should he live envying the gains of others. The disciple who envies the gains of others does not attain concentration."*
>
> —Dhammapada *365*

CELEBRATION

During the sacred month known as Ramadan, Muslims fast, or abstain from food and drink, from dawn to sunset. The family shown here is ending their fast. The most important night of Ramadan is called the Night of Power. This is believed to be the night the angel Gabriel first spoke to Muhammad.

WORSHIP PRACTICES

Five times a day Muslims throughout the world face Mecca and pray to Allah. Pictured here are Muslims praying at a mosque in Turkey.

There are no priests or other clergy in Islam. However, a Muslim community leader known as the imam conducts the prayers in a mosque. Islam also has a scholar class called the ulama, which includes religious teachers.

Major Islamic Sects

Sunni

↑

Islam

↓

Shi'a

PRAYER RUG

Muslims often pray by kneeling on a rug. The design of the rug includes a pointed or arch-shaped pattern. The rug must be placed so that the arch points toward Mecca.

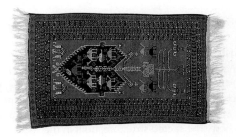

THE QUR'AN

PRIMARY SOURCE

The Qur'an, the sacred book of Muslims, consists of verses grouped into 114 chapters, or suras. The book is the spiritual guide on matters of Muslim faith. It also contains teachings for Muslim daily life. In the following verse, Muslims are instructed to appreciate the world's physical and spiritual riches:

"Do you not see that God has subjected to your use all things in the heavens and on earth, and has made His bounties flow to you in exceeding measure, both seen and unseen?"

—Qur'an, sura 31:20

Judaism

Judaism is the religion of the more than 14 million Jews throughout the world. Judaism was the first major religion to teach the existence of only one God. The basic laws and teachings of Judaism come from the Torah, the first five books of the Hebrew Bible. Judaism teaches that a person serves God by studying the Torah and living by its teachings. Orthodox Jews closely observe the laws of the Torah. Conservative and Reform Jews interpret the Torah less strictly and literally. The Star of David (shown above), also called the Shield of David, is the universal symbol of Judaism. The emblem refers to King David, who ruled the kingdom of Israel from about 1000–962 BC.

RITUAL

Major events in a Jew's life are marked by special rites and ceremonies. When Jewish children reach the age of 12 (girls) or 13 (boys), for example, they enter the adult religious community. The event is marked in the synagogue with a ceremony called a bar mitzvah for a boy and a bat mitzvah for a girl, shown here.

WORSHIP PRACTICES

The synagogue is the Jewish house of worship and the center of Jewish community life. Services in the synagogue are usually conducted by a rabbi, the congregation's teacher and spiritual leader. Many Jews make the pilgrimage to the Western Wall, shown here. The sacred structure, built in the second century BC, formed the western wall of the courtyard of the Second Temple of Jerusalem. The Romans destroyed the Temple in AD 70.

Major Jewish Sects

Reform   **Orthodox**

Judaism

Conservative

CELEBRATION

Jews celebrate a number of holidays that honor their history as well as God. Pictured here are Jews celebrating the holiday of Purim. Purim is a festival honoring the survival of the Jews who, in the fifth century BC, were marked for death by their Persian rulers.

Jews celebrate Purim by sending food and gifts. They also dress in costumes and hold carnivals and dances.

YARMULKE

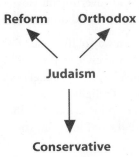

Out of respect for God, Jewish men are not supposed to leave their head uncovered. Therefore, many Orthodox and Conservative Jews wear a skullcap known as a yarmulke, or kippah.

THE TORAH

PRIMARY SOURCE

During a synagogue service, the Torah scroll is lifted, while the congregation declares: "This is the Law which Moses set before the children of Israel." The following verse from the Torah makes clear Moses's law regarding belief in one God:

"Hear O Israel: the Lord our God, the Lord is One."

—Deuteronomy 6:4

Confucianism

With no clergy and with no gods to worship, Confucianism is not a religion in the traditional sense. Rather, it is an ethical system that provides direction for personal behavior and good government. However, this ancient philosophy guides the actions and beliefs of millions of Chinese and other peoples of the East. Thus, many view it as a religion.

Confucianism is a way of life based on the teachings of the Chinese scholar Confucius. It stresses social and civic responsibility. Over the centuries, however, Confucianism has greatly influenced people's spiritual beliefs as well. While East Asians declare themselves to follow any one of a number of religions, many also claim to be Confucian. The yin and yang symbol shown above represents opposite forces in the world working together. It symbolizes the social order and harmony that Confucianism stresses.

CELEBRATION

While scholars remain uncertain of Confucius's date of birth, people throughout East Asia celebrate it on September 28. In Taiwan, it is an official holiday, known as Teachers' Day. The holiday also pays tribute to teachers. Confucius himself was a teacher, and he believed that education was an important part of a fulfilled life. Here, dancers take part in a ceremony honoring Confucius.

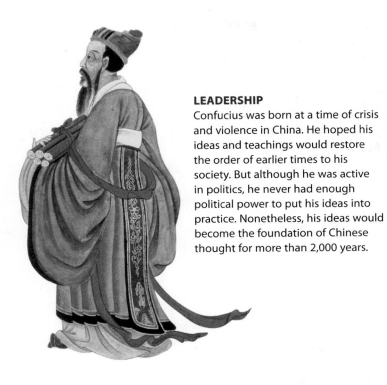

LEADERSHIP

Confucius was born at a time of crisis and violence in China. He hoped his ideas and teachings would restore the order of earlier times to his society. But although he was active in politics, he never had enough political power to put his ideas into practice. Nonetheless, his ideas would become the foundation of Chinese thought for more than 2,000 years.

RITUAL

A key aspect of Confucianism is filial piety, the respect children owe their parents. Traditionally, filial piety meant complete obedience to one's parents during their lifetime. It also required the performance of certain rituals after their death. In this 12th-century Chinese painting, a sage instructs a pupil on the virtue of filial piety.

The Five Relationships

Confucius believed society should be organized around five basic relationships between the following:

1. ruler ⬅➡ subject
2. father ⬅➡ son
3. husband ⬅➡ wife
4. older brother ⬅➡ younger brother
5. friend ⬅➡ friend

CONFUCIUS'S GOLDEN RULE

"Do not do unto others what you would not want others to do unto you."

THE ANALECTS

PRIMARY SOURCE

The earliest and most authentic record of Confucius's ideas was collected by his students. Around 400 BC, they compiled Confucius's thoughts in a book called the *Analects*. In the following selections from the *Analects*, Confucius (the Master) gives advice regarding virtue and pride:

"The Master said: "Don't worry if people don't recognize your merits; worry that you may not recognize theirs."

—*Analects 1.16*

"The Master said: "Do not be concerned that others do not recognize you; be concerned about what you are yet unable to do."

—*Analects 14.30*

Sikhism

Today an estimated 25 million people identify themselves as Sikhs, making Sikhism the world's fifth-largest religion. The majority of Sikhs live in the Punjab region of India, where more than 500 years ago a young spiritual teacher named Guru Nanak founded the faith. Guru Nanak wrote his teachings as poems. These poems, along with the teachings of four other gurus, or prophets, now form part of the holy scripture for Sikhs.

Sikhs strive to live according to these teachings, which they believe to be the living word of a single, all-powerful God. Serving others, living a truthful life, and the view that all people are equal, regardless of gender, race, or social class, are core to Sikh beliefs.

CELEBRATION

Sikhism's most popular holiday is Visakhi, which is held on April 14. For Sikhs, it is a cultural and spiritual day of celebration. Culturally, it is celebrated as a harvest festival in Punjab. Spiritually, it marks the day that Guru Gobind Singh, the tenth Guru, established the Khalsa, the community of people who have been initiated into the Sikh religion. The daylong celebration includes religious services, parades. music, and dancing.

Here young Sikhs dance to the beat of a dhol—an Indian drum—at a Visakhi celebration in Vancouver, Canada. In the years after World War II, Sikhs began to leave the Punjab in search of better economic opportunities. Initially, most headed for Britain. In recent years, Sikhs have moved farther afield. Today, there are large Sikh communities in Britain, Canada, Australia, East Asia, East Africa, and the United States.

ARTICLES OF FAITH

People who have been initiated into the Khalsa wear a "uniform" that binds them together as a community and reminds them of their commitment to Sikhism. This uniform includes the five Sikh articles of faith that should be worn every day:

Kesh—uncut hair, which is kept covered by a distinctive turban

Kirpan—a religious sword, which represents readiness to protect the weak and fight against injustice

Kara—a metal bracelet, which represents strength

Kanga—a wooden comb, which represents cleanliness

Kachera—cotton undergarments, which represents self-discipline

GURDWARAS—SIKH HOUSES OF WORSHIP

The Harmandir Sahib, or Golden Temple, in Armritsar, is one of the most popular gurdwaras in the world. The original gurdwara was built in the 1580s by Guru Arjan Dev, the fifth Guru, who wanted Sikhs to a have a central place of worship. The gurdwara has four doors, signifying that it is open to all, regardless of religion.

THE TEN GURUS

Guru Nanak	born 1469
Guru Angad	1504
Guru Amar Dass	1479
Guru Ram Das	1534
Guru Arjun Dev	1563
Guru Har Gobind	1595
Guru Har Rai	1630
Guru Har Krishan	1656
Guru Teg Bahadur	1621
Guru Gobind Singh	1666

Guru Gobind Singh was the last guru in human form. He appointed the Guru Granth Sahib, the Sikh holy scripture, as his successor, saying "The Word is the Guru now."

THE GURU GRANTH SAHIB

PRIMARY SOURCE

The Guru Granth Sahib, a collection of hymns and poems, is unique among holy scriptures, as it contains not only writings by Sikhs but also the words of saints and prophets of other religions. This acceptance of all humanity as children of God is exemplified by the following composition:

*"The One God is the [parent] of all
We are all [the children of God];
O Guru, a Friend, I dedicate my heart to [you],
If [you let] me but have a glimpse of God . . .
Free [yourself] of pride, take refuge in [God],
Accept with joy what [God does],
Hearken, my friend,
Give [your] body, mind, [your] whole self unto [God],
And thus, have glimpse of the Divine."*

—Rag Sorath, page 611

A Comparison

	Buddhism	Christianity	Hinduism	Islam	Judaism	Confucianism	Sikhism
Followers Worldwide (estimated)	462.6 million	2.3 billion	942.9 million	1.6 billion	14.8 million	6.5 million	25 million
Name of Deity	no god	God	Brahman	Allah	God	no god	God
Founder	The Buddha	Jesus	No one founder	No founder, but spread by Muhammad	Abraham	Confucius	Guru Nanak
Holy Book	Many sacred texts, including the *Dhammapada*	Christian Bible	Many sacred texts, including the Upanishads	Qur'an	Hebrew Bible, including the Torah	the *Analects* the Five Classics	Guru Granth Sahib
Leadership	Buddhist monks and nuns	Priests, ministers, monks, and nuns	Brahmin priests, monks, and gurus	No clergy but a scholar class called the ulama, and the imams, who may lead prayers	Rabbis	No clergy	No clergy but Granthis, people learned in Sikh scripture, who act as teachers.
Basic Beliefs	•Persons achieve complete peace and happiness (nirvana) by eliminating their attachment to worldly things. •Nirvana is reached by following the Noble Eightfold Path: Right views; Right resolve; Right speech; Right conduct; Right livelihood; Right effort; Right mindfulness; Right concentration.	•There is only one God, who watches over and cares for his people. •Jesus Christ is the son of God. He died to save humanity from sin. His death and resurrection made eternal life possible for others.	•The soul never dies, but is continually reborn. •Persons achieve happiness and enlightenment after they free themselves from their earthly desires. •Freedom from earthly desires comes from a life-time of worship, knowledge, and virtuous acts.	•Persons achieve salvation by following the Five Pillars of Islam and living a just life. These pillars are: faith; prayer; almsgiving, or charity to the poor; fasting, which Muslims perform during Ramadan; pilgrimage to Mecca.	•There is only one God, who watches over and cares for all people. •God loves and protects his people, but also holds people accountable for their sins and shortcomings. •Persons serve God by studying the Torah and living by its teachings.	•Social order, harmony, and good government should be based on strong family relationships. •Respect for parents and elders is important to a well-ordered society. •Education is important both to the welfare of the individual and to society.	•There is only one God, the God of all people of all religions. •All people, regardless of sex, race, religion, or class, are equal in the eyes of God. •The path to God requires daily devotion, honest living, charity, and service to others.

Main Ideas

Buddhism

1. According to the Buddha, how does one achieve happiness and fulfillment?
2. Why do Buddhists take special care to avoid killing any living being?

Christianity

3. Why is Jesus central to the Christian religion?
4. What do Christians hope to achieve by following the teachings of Jesus?

Hinduism

5. What is the importance of the Ganges River in Hinduism?
6. Who are the three main gods of Hinduism?

Islam

7. What is the most important night of Ramadan? Why?
8. What are the Five Pillars of Islam?

Judaism

9. Why do Jews consider the Western Wall to be sacred?
10. In the Jewish tradition, how do people serve God?

Confucianism

11. Around what five relationships did Confucius believe society should be organized?
12. According to tradition, what does filial piety require of children?

Sikhism

13. What are the historical origins and central ideas of Sikhism?
14. How has Sikhism spread beyond the Punjab region?

Critical Thinking

1. **Synthesizing** What basic principles do all of the world religions have in common?
2. **Drawing Conclusions** What role does religion play in people's everyday lives?
3. **Making Inferences** Why do you think ritual and celebrations are an important part of all world religions?
4. **Forming Opinions** What do you think people hope to gain from their religion?

Engage with History

Imagine that you could meet one of the founders discussed in this section. What questions would you ask about his life and beliefs? What views of your own would you share? Take turns role-playing your conversation with a partner. Be sure to use the correct religious terminology in your conversation.

Focus on Writing

Research to learn more about one of the celebrations you read about in this section. Then write a three-paragraph **essay** about its origins. Discuss the celebration's history, symbolism, and meaning.

United States: Political

Strait of Juan de Fuca
Puget Sound
Franklin D. Roosevelt Lake
Pend Oreille
45°N
WASHINGTON
Seattle
Tacoma
Olympia ★
Spokane
Portland
Salem ★
Columbia River
Eugene
OREGON
Flathead Lake
Great Falls
Helena ★
MONTANA
Billings
Fort Peck Lake
Missouri River
Yellowstone River
NORTH DAKOTA
Lake Sakakawea
Bismarck

IDAHO
Boise ★
Sun Valley
Snake River
Pocatello
Yellowstone Lake
WYOMING
Cheyenne ★
Lake Oahe
SOUTH DAKOTA
Pierre ★
Rapid City

40°N
Cape Mendocino
Goose Lake
Shasta Lake
Sacramento River
Pyramid Lake
125°W
Reno
Berkeley
Carson City ★
Lake Tahoe
Oakland
San Francisco
San Francisco Bay
Sacramento
San Joaquin River
San Jose
Monterey Bay
Fresno
35°N
CALIFORNIA
NEVADA
Ogden
Great Salt Lake
Salt Lake City ★
Provo
Utah Lake
UTAH
Green River
Lake Powell
Las Vegas
NEBRASKA
Platte River
Boulder
Vail
Aspen
Denver ★
Colorado Springs
COLORADO
Pueblo
Arkansas River
KANSAS

PACIFIC OCEAN
Santa Barbara
Ventura
Channel Islands
Long Beach
Los Angeles
Riverside
Palm Springs
Anaheim
Santa Ana
San Diego
Salton Sea
Colorado River
Lake Mead
120°W
30°N
Flagstaff
ARIZONA
Phoenix
Casa Grande
Gila River
Tucson
Taos
Santa Fe ★
Albuquerque
NEW MEXICO
Las Cruces
El Paso
OKLAHOMA
Canadian River
Oklahoma City ★
Lawton
Amarillo
Lubbock
Brazos River
Abilene
Fort Worth
Midland
Odessa
TEXAS
Colorado River
Pecos River
Austin
San Antonio
Corpus Christi
Laredo
Padre Island

To understand the relative locations of Alaska and Hawaii, as well as the vast distances separating them from the rest of the United States, see the world map.

Kauai
Niihau
Oahu
HAWAII
Honolulu ★
Molokai
Maui
22°N
N
160°W
PACIFIC OCEAN
Lanai
Kahoolawe
W — E
S
155°W
Hilo
Hawaii
19°N
0   75   150 mi
0   75   150 km
Projection: Mercator

ARCTIC OCEAN
Arctic Circle
RUSSIA
Bering Strait
St. Lawrence Island
St. Matthew Island
Nunivak Island
Nome
Yukon River
Fairbanks
CANADA
ALASKA
Anchorage
Valdez
Skagway
Juneau
Kodiak Island
Alexander Archipelago
Bering Sea
55°N
Gulf of Alaska
170°W
160°W
150°W
55°N
0   250   500 mi
0   250   500 km
Projection: Albers Equal Area

Gulf of California
MEXICO
Rio Grande
Amistad Reservoir

Atlas **R21**

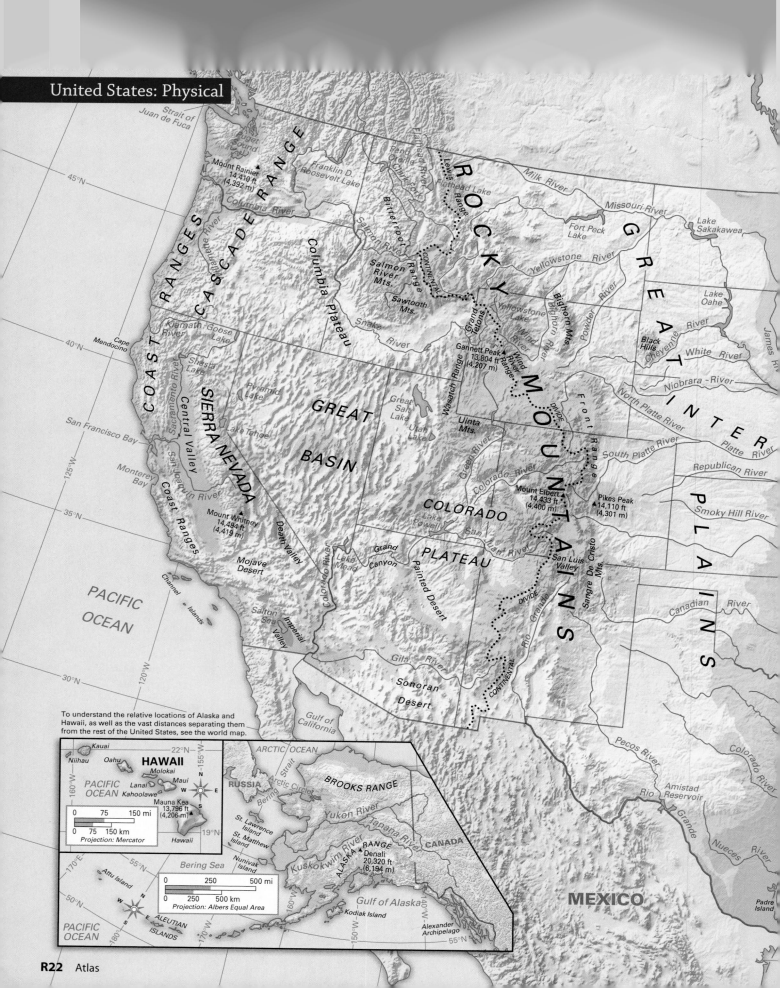

Strait of
Juan de Fuca

Puget
Sound

Mount Rainier
14,410 ft
(4,392 m)

COAST RANGES

CASCADE RANGE

Columbia River

Willamette River

Franklin D.
Roosevelt Lake

Pend
Oreille Lake

Flathead
Lake

Flathead River

Clark Fork

Bitterroot Range

Salmon River

Salmon River

ROCKY

Lewis Range

CONTINENTAL

Milk River

Missouri River

Fort Peck
Lake

GREAT

Lake
Sakakawea

Yellowstone River

Columbia Plateau

Salmon
River
Mts.

Sawtooth
Mts.

Snake River

Klamath River

Goose
Lake

Cape
Mendocino

40°N

45°N

Shasta
Lake

Sacramento River

Pyramid
Lake

Lake Tahoe

Great Salt Lake

Utah
Lake

Wasatch Range

Grand
Tetons

MOUNTAINS

Yellowstone
Lake

Wind River Range

Bighorn River

Bighorn Mts.

Powder River

Black
Hills

Lake
Oahe

Cheyenne River

White River

James River

Gannett Peak
13,804 ft
(4,207 m)

INTER

125°W

San Francisco Bay

Monterey
Bay

SIERRA NEVADA

Central Valley

San Joaquin River

Coast Ranges

GREAT

BASIN

Green River

Uinta
Mts.

DIVIDE

Front Range

North Platte River

Niobrara River

South Platte River

Platte River

Republican River

35°N

120°W

Mount Whitney
14,494 ft
(4,419 m)

Death Valley

Mojave
Desert

Lake
Mead

Grand
Canyon

COLORADO

Colorado River

Lake
Powell

San Juan River

PLATEAU

Painted Desert

Mount Elbert
14,433 ft
(4,400 m)

Pikes Peak
14,110 ft
(4,301 m)

San Luis
Valley

Sangre De Cristo Mts.

Smoky Hill River

PLAINS

PACIFIC

OCEAN

Channel
Islands

Salton
Sea

Imperial
Valley

Colorado River

Gila River

Sonoran

Desert

DIVIDE

CONTINENTAL

Rio Grande

Canadian River

30°N

To understand the relative locations of Alaska and
Hawaii, as well as the vast distances separating them
from the rest of the United States, see the world map.

Gulf of
California

Pecos River

Colorado River

Amistad
Reservoir

Rio Grande

Nueces River

MEXICO

Padre
Island

Kauai

Niihau

Oahu

Molokai

HAWAII

22°N

155°W

ARCTIC OCEAN

Arctic Circle

Bering Strait

BROOKS RANGE

PACIFIC
OCEAN

Lanai

Maui

Kahoolawe

Mauna Kea
13,796 ft
(4,206 m)

19°N

RUSSIA

Yukon River

Tanana River

CANADA

St. Lawrence
Island

St. Matthew
Island

Nunivak
Island

Kuskokwim River

ALASKA RANGE

Denali
20,320 ft
(6,194 m)

160°W

0   75   150 mi

0   75   150 km

Projection: Mercator

Hawaii

0   250   500 mi

0   250   500 km

Projection: Albers Equal Area

170°E

55°N

50°N

Bering Sea

Attu Island

ALEUTIAN

ISLANDS

180°

PACIFIC
OCEAN

Kodiak Island

Gulf of Alaska

Alexander
Archipelago

55°N

160°W

150°W

CANADA

Isle
Royale
Mesabi Range
Lake Superior

Minnesota River
Mississippi River
Wisconsin River
Des Moines River
Missouri River

Lake Michigan
Lake Huron
Lake Ontario
Lake Erie

St. Lawrence River
St. Lawrence Seaway
St. John River
Penobscot River
Longfellow Mts.
Lake Champlain
White Mts.
Green Mts.
Adirondack Mts.
Hudson R.
Connecticut River
Cape Cod
Long Island Sound
Long Island

PLAINS

Illinois River
Wabash River
Scioto River
Ohio River

ALLEGHENY PLATEAU
Allegheny R.
Catskill Mts.
Susquehanna River
Delaware River
Delaware Bay

MOUNTAINS

Monongahela R.
Potomac River
Kanawha River
James River
Roanoke River
Chesapeake Bay

ATLANTIC
OCEAN

Pamlico Sound
Cape Hatteras

Sas R.
Lake of the Ozarks
OZARK PLATEAU
Keystone Lake
Arkansas River
White River
Kentucky Lake
Lake Barkley
Cumberland River
Cumberland Plateau
Great Smoky Mts.
APPALACHIAN
BLUE RIDGE MOUNTAINS
PIEDMONT
Tennessee River

Ouachita Mts.
oma
Saline River
Red River
Toledo Bend Reservoir
Mississippi
Pearl River
Tombigbee River
Alabama R.
Coosa River
Chattahoochee River
Oconee River
Ocmulgee River
Savannah River
Altamaha River
Sea Islands

COASTAL PLAIN

Chandeleur Islands
Mississippi Delta

Okefenokee Swamp

FLORIDA PENINSULA

Cape Canaveral

Gulf of Mexico

BAHAMAS

Lake Okeechobee
The Everglades
Cape Sable
Florida Keys
Straits of Florida

ELEVATION

Feet	Meters
13,120	4,000
6,560	2,000
1,640	500
656	200
(Sea level) 0	0 (Sea level)
Below sea level	Below sea level

0   100   200 mi
0   100   200 km

Projection: Albers Equal Area

40°N
35°N
25°N
70°W
75°W
80°W
85°W
90°W
95°W

N
W   E
S

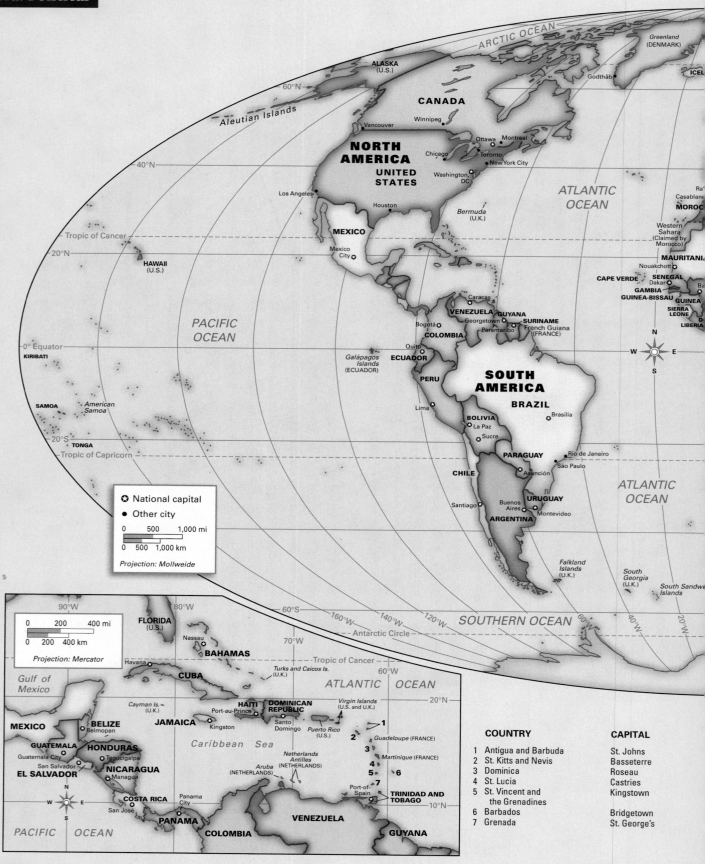

ARCTIC OCEAN

Greenland
(DENMARK)

Godthåb

ICEL

60°N

ALASKA
(U.S.)

CANADA

Winnipeg

Vancouver

Ottawa Montreal

Chicago Toronto

NORTH
AMERICA

40°N

UNITED
STATES

New York City

Washington,
DC

ATLANTIC
OCEAN

Ra

Casablan

MOROC

Los Angeles

Houston

Bermuda
(U.K.)

Tropic of Cancer

MEXICO

Western
Sahara
(Claimed by
Morocco)

20°N

Mexico
City

MAURITANI

Nouakchott

HAWAII
(U.S.)

CAPE VERDE

SENEGAL
Dakar

Ba

GAMBIA
GUINEA-BISSAU GUINEA

Caracas

PACIFIC
OCEAN

VENEZUELA GUYANA

SIERRA
LEONE

Bogotá

Georgetown SURINAME

LIBERIA

COLOMBIA

Paramaribo French Guiana
(FRANCE)

N

Quito

W ✦ E

0° Equator

ECUADOR

S

KIRIBATI

Galápagos
Islands
(ECUADOR)

PERU

SOUTH
AMERICA

SAMOA

*American
Samoa*

Lima

BRAZIL

Brasília

BOLIVIA
La Paz

20°S

TONGA

Sucre

Tropic of Capricorn

PARAGUAY

Rio de Janeiro

São Paulo

ATLANTIC
OCEAN

CHILE

Asunción

✪ National capital

● Other city

0   500   1,000 mi

0 500 1,000 km

Projection: Mollweide

Santiago

URUGUAY

Buenos
Aires

Montevideo

ARGENTINA

*Falkland
Islands*
(U.K.)

*South
Georgia*
(U.K.)

*South Sandw
Islands*

60°S

SOUTHERN OCEAN

160°W 140°W 120°W

Antarctic Circle

40°W

20°W

90°W   80°W

FLORIDA
(U.S.)

70°W

60°W

0   200   400 mi

Nassau

Tropic of Cancer

0   200   400 km

BAHAMAS

20°N

Projection: Mercator

Havana

Turks and Caicos Is.
(U.K.)

ATLANTIC   OCEAN

Gulf of
Mexico

CUBA

Cayman Is.
(U.K.)

HAITI
Port-au-Prince

DOMINICAN
REPUBLIC

Virgin Islands
(U.S. and U.K.)

20°N

1

MEXICO

BELIZE
Belmopan

JAMAICA

Kingston

Santo
Domingo

Puerto Rico
(U.S.)

Guadeloupe (FRANCE)

2

GUATEMALA HONDURAS

Caribbean Sea

3

Guatemala City Tegucigalpa

Martinique (FRANCE)

San Salvador

*Netherlands
Antilles*
(NETHERLANDS)

4

EL SALVADOR NICARAGUA

Aruba
(NETHERLANDS)

5

6

Managua

N

7

W ✦ E

Port-of-
Spain

TRINIDAD AND
TOBAGO

S

COSTA RICA

Panama
City

10°N

San Jose

PANAMA

PACIFIC   OCEAN

VENEZUELA

COLOMBIA

GUYANA

	COUNTRY	CAPITAL
1	Antigua and Barbuda	St. Johns
2	St. Kitts and Nevis	Basseterre
3	Dominica	Roseau
4	St. Lucia	Castries
5	St. Vincent and the Grenadines	Kingstown
6	Barbados	Bridgetown
7	Grenada	St. George's

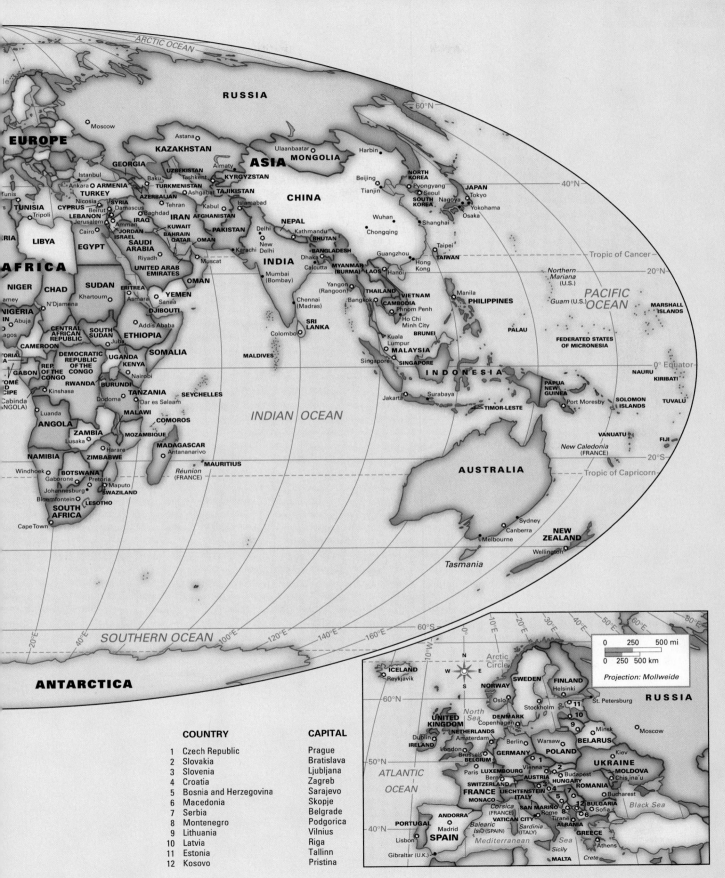

ARCTIC OCEAN

RUSSIA

EUROPE

Moscow

KAZAKHSTAN

Astana

ASIA

MONGOLIA

Ulaanbaatar

Harbin

60°N

GEORGIA
UZBEKISTAN
Almaty
KYRGYZSTAN
Istanbul
Ankara ARMENIA
Baku
Tashkent
Beijing
Tianjin
NORTH
KOREA
Pyongyang
Seoul
JAPAN
Tokyo
40°N

TURKEY
AZERBAIJAN
TURKMENISTAN
TAJIKISTAN
CHINA
SOUTH
KOREA
Nagoya
Yokohama

Nicosia
CYPRUS
SYRIA
Damascus
Ashgabat
Tehran
Wuhan
Shanghai
Osaka

Beirut
LEBANON
IRAQ
Baghdad
Kabul
Islamabad
Chongqing

Jerusalem
JORDAN
Amman
IRAN
AFGHANISTAN
Delhi
Taipei
TAIWAN

Cairo
ISRAEL
KUWAIT
BAHRAIN
QATAR
OMAN
PAKISTAN
NEPAL
Kathmandu
BHUTAN
Guangzhou
Hong
Kong
Tropic of Cancer

LIBYA
EGYPT
SAUDI
ARABIA
Riyadh
Karachi
New
Delhi
BANGLADESH
Dhaka
Calcutta
MYANMAR
(BURMA)
LAOS
Hanoi
Northern
Mariana
(U.S.)
20°N

AFRICA
UNITED ARAB
EMIRATES
Muscat
Mumbai
(Bombay)
INDIA
Yangon
(Rangoon)
THAILAND
VIETNAM
Manila
PHILIPPINES
Guam (U.S.)
PACIFIC
OCEAN
MARSHALL
ISLANDS

NIGER
CHAD
SUDAN
ERITREA
YEMEN
OMAN
Chennai
(Madras)
Bangkok
CAMBODIA
Phnom Penh
PALAU
FEDERATED STATES
OF MICRONESIA

NIGERIA
Khartoum
Asmara
Sanaa
DJIBOUTI
SRI
LANKA
Ho Chi
Minh City
BRUNEI

Abuja
N'Djamena
CENTRAL
AFRICAN
REPUBLIC
SOUTH
SUDAN
ETHIOPIA
Addis Ababa
Colombo
MALDIVES
Kuala
Lumpur
MALAYSIA
Equator 0°

CAMEROON
Juba
SOMALIA
Singapore
SINGAPORE
NAURU
KIRIBATI

GABON
DEMOCRATIC
REPUBLIC
OF THE
CONGO
UGANDA
KENYA
Nairobi
INDONESIA
PAPUA
NEW
GUINEA
Port Moresby
SOLOMON
ISLANDS
TUVALU

REP.
OF THE
CONGO
RWANDA
BURUNDI
Dodoma
SEYCHELLES
Jakarta
Surabaya
TIMOR-LESTE

Kinshasa
TANZANIA
Dar es Salaam
VANUATU
FIJI

Luanda
MALAWI
COMOROS
New Caledonia
(FRANCE)
20°S

ANGOLA
ZAMBIA
MOZAMBIQUE
INDIAN OCEAN
AUSTRALIA
Tropic of Capricorn

Lusaka
Harare
MADAGASCAR
Antananarivo

NAMIBIA
ZIMBABWE
MAURITIUS
Réunion
(FRANCE)

Windhoek
BOTSWANA
Gaborone
Pretoria
Maputo
SWAZILAND
Sydney
Canberra
NEW
ZEALAND

Johannesburg
LESOTHO
Melbourne
Wellington

Bloemfontein
SOUTH
AFRICA

Cape Town
Tasmania

100°E
120°E
140°E
160°E
60°S
SOUTHERN OCEAN

20°E
40°E

ANTARCTICA

	COUNTRY	CAPITAL
1	Czech Republic	Prague
2	Slovakia	Bratislava
3	Slovenia	Ljubljana
4	Croatia	Zagreb
5	Bosnia and Herzegovina	Sarajevo
6	Macedonia	Skopje
7	Serbia	Belgrade
8	Montenegro	Podgorica
9	Lithuania	Vilnius
10	Latvia	Riga
11	Estonia	Tallinn
12	Kosovo	Pristina

0   250   500 mi
0   250   500 km
Projection: Mollweide

ICELAND
Reykjavik
Arctic
Circle
SWEDEN
FINLAND
Helsinki
RUSSIA

NORWAY
Oslo
St. Petersburg
60°N

UNITED
KINGDOM
North
Sea
Stockholm
11
10
Minsk

Dublin
IRELAND
DENMARK
Copenhagen
9
Moscow

London
NETHERLANDS
Amsterdam
Berlin
Warsaw
BELARUS

ATLANTIC
OCEAN
BELGIUM
Brussels
GERMANY
POLAND
Kiev
UKRAINE
50°N

Paris
LUXEMBOURG
Vienna
1
2
Budapest
MOLDOVA
Chisinau

SWITZERLAND
Bern
AUSTRIA
3
HUNGARY
7
ROMANIA

FRANCE
LIECHTENSTEIN
4
5
Bucharest

MONACO
ITALY
8
12
BULGARIA
Black Sea

ANDORRA
Corsica
(FRANCE)
SAN MARINO
Rome
8
6
Sofia

PORTUGAL
VATICAN CITY
Tirane
ALBANIA

Madrid
Balearic
Isl. (SPAIN)
Sardinia
(ITALY)
GREECE
40°N

Lisbon
SPAIN
Mediterranean
Sicily
Athens

Gibraltar (U.K.)
MALTA
Crete

Atlas   **R25**

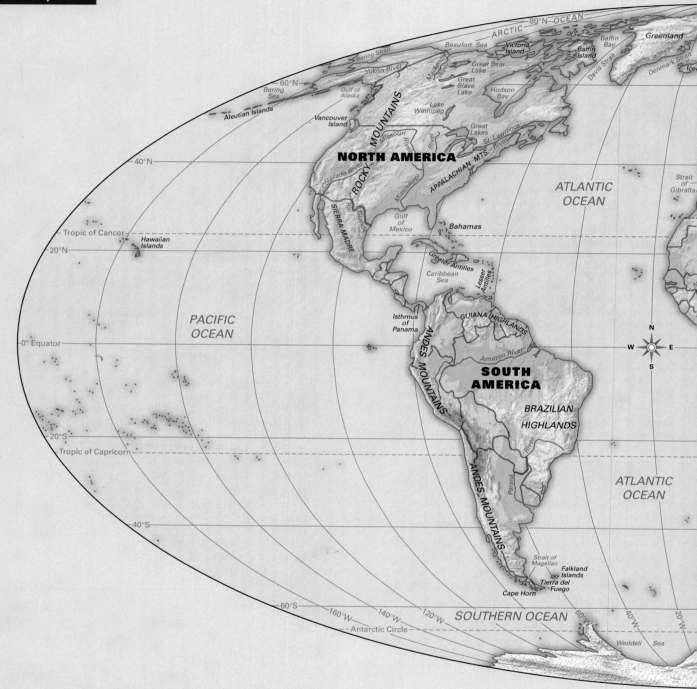

ARCTIC — 80°N — OCEAN
Beaufort Sea
Victoria Island
Baffin Island
Baffin Bay
Greenland
Bering Strait
Yukon River
Mackenzie River
Great Bear Lake
Davis Strait
Denmark Strait
Ice
60°N
Gulf of Alaska
Great Slave Lake
Hudson Bay
Aleutian Islands
Vancouver Island
Lake Winnipeg
MOUNTAINS
Missouri River
Great Lakes
St. Lawrence River
40°N
NORTH AMERICA
ROCKY
Colorado River
Mississippi
APPALACHIAN MTS.
ATLANTIC OCEAN
Strait of Gibraltar
SIERRA MADRE
Rio Grande
Gulf of Mexico
Bahamas
Tropic of Cancer
Hawaiian Islands
20°N
Greater Antilles
Caribbean Sea
Lesser Antilles
PACIFIC OCEAN
Isthmus of Panama
GUIANA HIGHLANDS
N
W   E
S
0° Equator
ANDES
Amazon River
SOUTH AMERICA
MOUNTAINS
BRAZILIAN HIGHLANDS
20°S
Tropic of Capricorn
River
ANDES MOUNTAINS
Paraná
ATLANTIC OCEAN
40°S
Strait of Magellan
Falkland Islands
Tierra del Fuego
Cape Horn
160°W   140°W   120°W
60°S
SOUTHERN OCEAN
60
40°W
20°W
Antarctic Circle
Weddell Sea

ELEVATION

Feet		Meters
13,120		4,000
6,560		2,000
1,640		500
656		200
(Sea level) 0		0 (Sea level)
Below sea level		Below sea level

Ice cap

```
0          1,000          2,000 mi
0     1,000     2,000 km
```

Projection: Mollweide

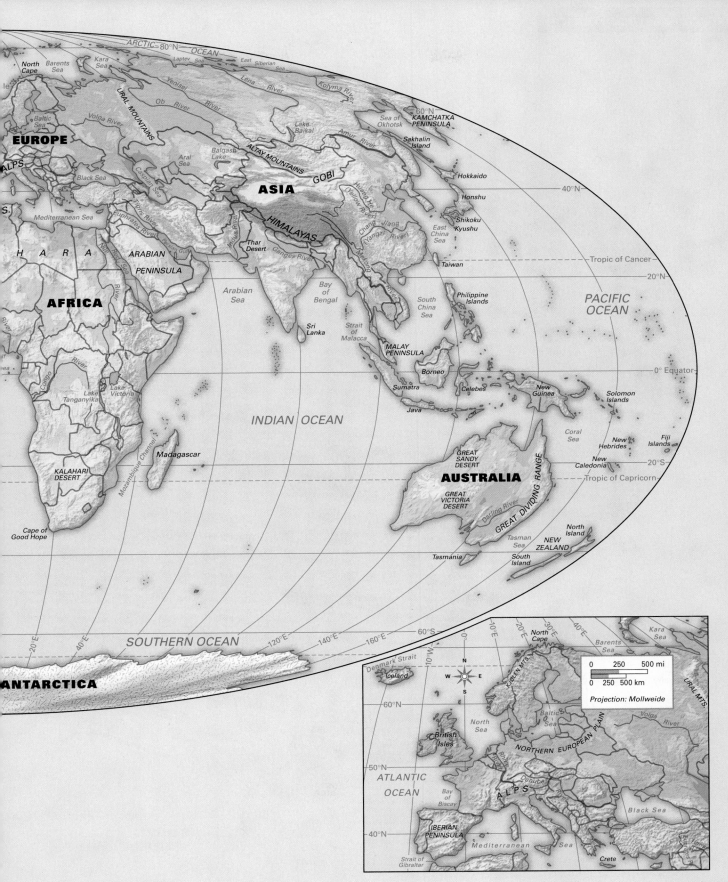

EUROPE

ALPS

S.

Black Sea

Mediterranean Sea

S   A   H   A   R   A

AFRICA

Congo River

Lake Tanganyika

Lake Victoria

KALAHARI DESERT

Cape of Good Hope

ANTARCTICA

ARCTIC 80°N OCEAN

North Cape

Barents Sea

Kara Sea

Laptev Sea

East Siberian Sea

Baltic Sea

URAL MOUNTAINS

Volga River

Ob River

Yenisei River

Lena River

Kolyma River

60°N

Caspian Sea

Aral Sea

Balqash Lake

ALTAY MOUNTAINS

Lake Baikal

Amur River

Sea of Okhotsk

KAMCHATKA PENINSULA

Sakhalin Island

Euphrates River

Tigris River

Persian Gulf

ASIA

GOBI

Hokkaido

40°N

ARABIAN PENINSULA

Indus River

Thar Desert

HIMALAYAS

Huang He (Yellow River)

Chang Jiang (Yangzi) River

East China Sea

Honshu

Shikoku

Kyushu

Ganges River

Mekong River

Tropic of Cancer

Arabian Sea

Bay of Bengal

Taiwan

20°N

Sri Lanka

Strait of Malacca

South China Sea

Philippine Islands

PACIFIC OCEAN

MALAY PENINSULA

Borneo

0° Equator

Sumatra

Celebes

New Guinea

Solomon Islands

INDIAN OCEAN

Java

Madagascar

Mozambique Channel

GREAT SANDY DESERT

AUSTRALIA

Coral Sea

New Hebrides

New Caledonia

Fiji Islands

20°S

GREAT VICTORIA DESERT

GREAT DIVIDING RANGE

Tropic of Capricorn

Darling River

Tasman Sea

North Island

NEW ZEALAND

Tasmania

South Island

SOUTHERN OCEAN

20°E   40°E   120°E   140°E   160°E   60°S

Denmark Strait

Iceland

North Cape

Kara Sea

Barents Sea

URAL MTS.

10°E   20°E   30°E   40°E

N
W   E
S

0   250   500 mi
0   250   500 km

Projection: Mollweide

KJÖLEN MTS.

60°N

British Isles

North Sea

Baltic Sea

NORTHERN EUROPEAN PLAIN

Volga River

50°N

ATLANTIC OCEAN

Bay of Biscay

Danube

ALPS

Black Sea

40°N

IBERIAN PENINSULA

Strait of Gibraltar

Mediterranean Sea

Crete

ASIA

EUROPE

ARCTIC OCEAN

+ North Pole

ICELAND

ALASKA (U.S.)

Queen Elizabeth Islands

Ellesmere Island

Greenland (DENMARK)

Bering Strait

St. Lawrence Island

Nunivak Island

Bering Sea

Point Barrow

Beaufort Sea

Banks Island

Victoria Island

Baffin Bay

Baffin Island

Hudson Strait

Davis Strait

Denmark Strait

Arctic Circle

Cape Farewell

Anchorage

Gulf of Alaska

Kodiak Island

Alexander Archipelago

Juneau

Queen Charlotte Islands

Great Bear Lake

Great Slave Lake

Southampton Island

Coats Island

Mansel Island

Labrador Sea

PACIFIC OCEAN

Vancouver Island

Edmonton

CANADA

Hudson Bay

Anticosti Island

Newfoundland

St. Pierre and Miquelon (FRANCE)

Vancouver

Calgary

Lake Winnipeg

Prince Edward Island

Cape Breton Island

Gulf of St. Lawrence

Seattle

Winnipeg

Lake Superior

Portland

Quebec

Montreal

Lake Huron

Ottawa

Toronto

Lake Ontario

Lake Erie

Boston

Cape Cod

Minneapolis

Lake Michigan

Milwaukee

Detroit

Cleveland

New York City

Philadelphia

San Francisco

San Jose

Salt Lake City

Great Salt Lake

Chicago

Columbus

Baltimore

Washington, DC

ATLANTIC OCEAN

Denver

Indianapolis

St. Louis

Norfolk

Kansas City

UNITED STATES

Bermuda (U.K.)

Los Angeles

San Diego

Memphis

Tijuana

Phoenix

Atlanta

Birmingham

Dallas

Jacksonville

Austin

San Antonio

Houston

New Orleans

Tropic of Cancer

Gulf of Mexico

Miami

BAHAMAS

Florida Keys

Nassau

Turks and Caicos Islands (U.K.)

DOMINICAN REPUBLIC

Puerto Rico (U.S.)

ST. KITTS & NEVIS

ANTIGUA & BARBUDA

Gulf of California

Monterrey

Havana

Straits of Florida

San Juan

Guadeloupe (FRANCE)

DOMINICA

MEXICO

CUBA

HAITI

Santo Domingo

Virgin Is. (U.S., U.K.)

Guadalajara

Mexico City

Mérida

Cayman Is. (U.K.)

Kingston

Port-au-Prince

JAMAICA

Martinique (FRANCE)

ST. LUCIA

BARBADOS

Puebla

Belmopan

BELIZE

Caribbean Sea

ST. VINCENT AND THE GRENADINES

Netherlands Antilles (NETHERLANDS)

GRENADA

GUATEMALA

HONDURAS

Tegucigalpa

Aruba (NETHERLANDS)

Guatemala City

NICARAGUA

TRINIDAD AND TOBAGO

San Salvador

Managua

EL SALVADOR

Panama Canal

San José

Panama City

COSTA RICA

PANAMA

SOUTH AMERICA

0° Equator

N
W E
S

Legend

⊛ National capital

● Other city

| 0 | 300 | 600 mi |

| 0 | 300 | 600 km |

Projection: Azimuthal Equal-Area

North America: Physical

ASIA

ARCTIC OCEAN

+ North Pole

POLAR ICE PACK

EUROPE

Arctic Circle

St. Lawrence Island
Bering Sea
Nunivak Island

BROOKS RANGE
Denali 20,320 ft (6,194 m)
ALASKA RANGE
Yukon River
ALASKA
Kodiak Island
Gulf of Alaska
Alexander Archipelago
Queen Charlotte Islands
Vancouver Island

YUKON PLATEAU
Mackenzie River
Great Bear Lake
Great Slave Lake
Peace River
Lake Athabasca
Athabasca River
Saskatchewan River
Nelson River
Lake Winnipeg

Beaufort Sea
Banks Island
Victoria Island

Queen Elizabeth Islands

Ellesmere Island
Greenland
Baffin Bay
Baffin Island
Davis Strait
Cape Farewell
Denmark Strait

Southampton Island
Coats Island
Mansel Island
Hudson Strait
Hudson Bay

CANADIAN SHIELD

Labrador Sea

Anticosti Island
Newfoundland
Prince Edward Island
Cape Breton Island
Gulf of St. Lawrence

PACIFIC OCEAN

Cape Mendocino

Mount Rainier 14,410 ft (4,392 m)
COAST RANGES
CASCADE RANGE
Columbia River
Snake River
SIERRA NEVADA
CENTRAL VALLEY
GREAT BASIN
Great Salt Lake
DEATH VALLEY
Mount Whitney 14,494 ft (4,419 m)
Colorado River
COLORADO PLATEAU

ROCKY MOUNTAINS
GREAT PLAINS
Missouri River
BLACK HILLS
Platte River
Arkansas River
Red River
Rio Grande

INTERIOR PLAINS
Mississippi River
OZARK PLATEAU
Ohio River
Tennessee River
Cumberland R.

Lake Superior
Lake Michigan
Lake Huron
Lake Erie
Lake Ontario
St. Lawrence River

APPALACHIAN MOUNTAINS
PIEDMONT
ATLANTIC COASTAL PLAIN
Cape Cod
Long Island
Cape Hatteras

ATLANTIC OCEAN

Bermuda

Tropic of Cancer

Guadalupe Island

BAJA CALIFORNIA
Gulf of California
SIERRA MADRE OCCIDENTAL
SIERRA MADRE ORIENTAL
Brazos River

GULF COASTAL PLAIN
Gulf of Mexico

FLORIDA PENINSULA
Cape Canaveral
Florida Keys
Straits of Florida

Bahamas
Cuba
Greater Antilles
Jamaica
Hispaniola
Puerto Rico
Lesser Antilles
Trinidad
Caribbean Sea

Popocatépetl 17,887 ft (5,452 m)
YUCATÁN PENINSULA
SIERRA MADRE DEL SUR
Lake Nicaragua

CENTRAL AMERICA
ISTHMUS OF PANAMA

SOUTH AMERICA

0° Equator

ELEVATION

Feet	Meters
13,120	4,000
6,560	2,000
1,640	500
656	200
(Sea level) 0	0 (Sea level)
Below sea level	Below sea level

Ice cap

0   300   600 mi
0   300   600 km

Projection: Azimuthal Equal Area

W N E S

South America: Political

CENTRAL AMERICA

Caribbean Sea

Barranquilla
Cartagena

Caracas

VENEZUELA

Lake Maracaibo

Georgetown
Paramaribo

GUYANA

Cayenne

Medellín

SURINAME

French Guiana (FRANCE)

Bogotá

COLOMBIA

Malpelo Island (COLOMBIA)

Cali

Quito

ECUADOR

Guayaquil

0° Equator

0° Equator

Galápagos Islands (ECUADOR)

Belém

PERU

BRAZIL

Trujillo

Recife

10°S

Callao Lima

Salvador

PACIFIC OCEAN

Arequipa

Lake Titicaca

La Paz

Brasília

Lake Poopó

BOLIVIA

Sucre

Belo Horizonte

20°S

PARAGUAY

São Paulo

Rio de Janeiro

Asunción

Tropic of Capricorn

Tropic of Capricorn

San Félix Island (CHILE)

San Ambrosio Island (CHILE)

Curitiba

CHILE

Pôrto Alegre

Juan Fernández Islands (CHILE)

Córdoba

30°S

Valparaíso
Santiago

Rosario

URUGUAY

ATLANTIC OCEAN

Buenos Aires

Montevideo

ARGENTINA

N
W   E
S

ATLANTIC OCEAN

○ National capital
● Other city

0   250   500 mi
0   250   500 km

Projection: Azimuthal Equal-Area

Strait of Magellan

Falkland Islands (U.K.)

South Georgia Island (U.K.)

Tierra del Fuego

CENTRAL
AMERICA

Caribbean Sea

Panama
Canal

Gulf
of
Panama

Margarita
Island
Tobago
Trinidad

Orinoco River
Delta

Lake
Maracaibo

LLANOS

Cauca
River

Meta
River

Orinoco River

Orinoco
River

Angel Falls

GUIANA
HIGHLANDS

Devil's Island
Cape Orange

ATLANTIC
OCEAN

Malpelo
Island

Mount Tolima
18,425 ft
(5,616 m)

Magdalena River

Caquetá
River

Rio   Negro

Amazon
River Delta

Galápagos
Islands

0° Equator

Mount Chimborazo
20,561 ft
(6,267 m)

Japurá
River

Amazon

River

AMAZON
BASIN

Amazon

River

Tapajós River

Tocantins

River

0° Equator

Gulf of Guayaquil

ANDES

Marañón River

Amazon
River

Juruá

River

Ucayali

River

Purus

Madeira

River

Xingu

River

Araguaia

River

Parnaíba

River

River

São Francisco

River

BRAZILIAN
HIGHLANDS

Mount Huascarán
22,205 ft
(6,768 m)

River

PACIFIC
OCEAN

Lake
Titicaca

Ancohuma Peak
20,958 ft
(6,388 m)

Beni   River

Mamoré

River

MATO GROSSO
PLATEAU

10°S

Lake
Poopó

Pilcomayo

River

BRAZILIAN
PLATEAU

San Ambrosio
Island

San Félix Island

ATACAMA DESERT

ANDES

CHACO

Salado

River

Paraná

River

Paraguay

River

Uruguay River

Tropic of Capricorn

20°S

Tropic of Capricorn

Juan Fernández
Islands

Mount Aconcagua
22,834 ft
(6,960 m)

Salado River

River

PAMPAS

Rio de la Plata

ATLANTIC
OCEAN

30°S

Colorado

River

Gulf of San Matías

Chiloé
Island

Chonos
Archipelago

Gulf of
San Jorge

Cape Tres Puntas

PATAGONIA

40°S

Bahía
Grande

Strait of
Magellan

Falkland
Islands

South
Georgia
Islands

Tierra del
Fuego

Cape Horn

50°S

ELEVATION

Feet		Meters
13,120		4,000
6,560		2,000
1,640		500
656		200
(Sea level) 0		0 (Sea level)
Below
sea level		Below
sea level

0   250   500 mi

0   250   500 km

Projection: Azimuthal Equal Area

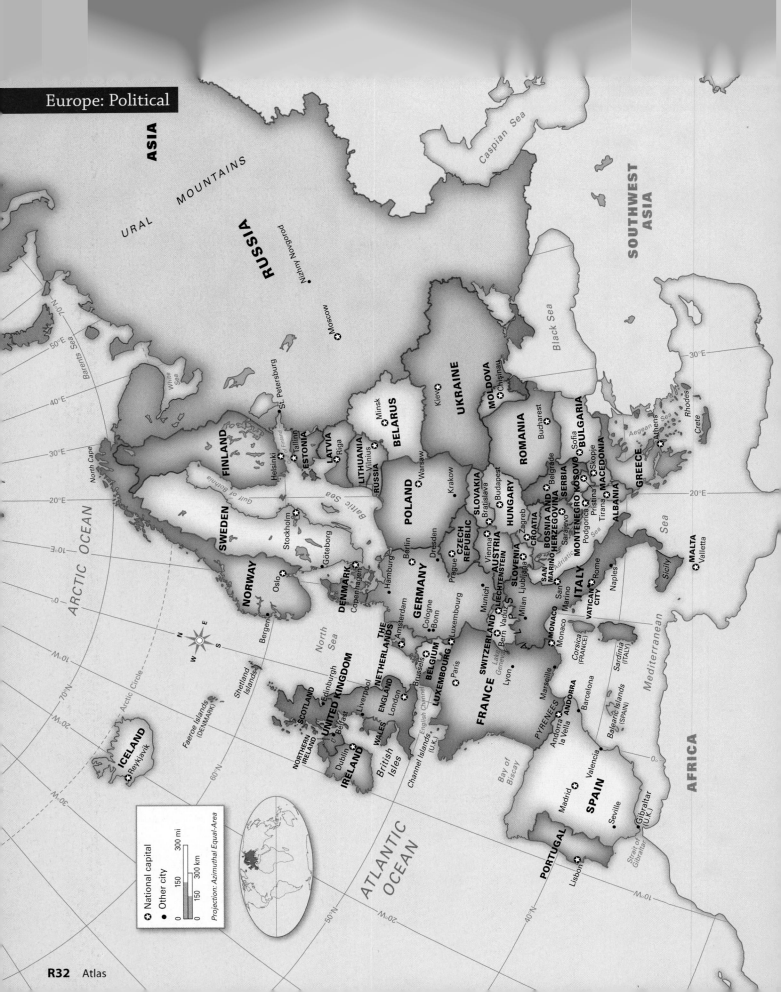

Europe: Political

ASIA

URAL MOUNTAINS

RUSSIA

Caspian Sea

SOUTHWEST ASIA

Nizhny Novgorod

Moscow ✪

Barents Sea

White Sea

North Cape

ARCTIC OCEAN

St. Petersburg

FINLAND

Helsinki ✪

Gulf of Finland

Tallinn
ESTONIA

LATVIA
Riga ✪

LITHUANIA
Vilnius ✪

RUSSIA

BELARUS
Minsk ✪

Warsaw ✪

POLAND

Krakow •

UKRAINE

Kiev ✪

MOLDOVA
Chişinău ✪

Black Sea

ROMANIA
Bucharest ✪

Sofia ✪
BULGARIA

SERBIA
Belgrade ✪

KOSOVO
Pristina ✪

Skopje ✪
MACEDONIA

Tirana ✪
ALBANIA

GREECE

Athens ✪

Aegean Sea

Rhodes

Crete

SWEDEN
Stockholm ✪

Göteborg •

Baltic Sea

Gulf of Bothnia

NORWAY
Oslo ✪

Bergen •

DENMARK
Copenhagen ✪

Hamburg •

Berlin ✪
Dresden •

GERMANY

Prague ✪
CZECH REPUBLIC

SLOVAKIA
Bratislava ✪

Vienna ✪
AUSTRIA

Budapest ✪
HUNGARY

SLOVENIA
Ljubljana ✪

Zagreb ✪
CROATIA

BOSNIA AND HERZEGOVINA
Sarajevo ✪

MONTENEGRO
Podgorica ✪

SAN MARINO
San Marino ✪

ITALY
Rome ✪

Naples •

VATICAN CITY

MALTA
Valletta ✪

Sicily

Mediterranean Sea

Cologne •
Bonn •
Amsterdam ✪
THE NETHERLANDS

Brussels ✪
BELGIUM
LUXEMBOURG
Luxembourg ✪

Munich •
LIECHTENSTEIN
Vaduz ✪
SWITZERLAND
Bern ✪
Lake Geneva
Milan •
MONACO
Monaco ✪

Lyon •

Marseille •

ANDORRA
Andorra la Vella ✪

Corsica (FRANCE)

Sardinia (ITALY)

ICELAND
Reykjavik ✪

Faeroe Islands (DENMARK)

Shetland Islands

SCOTLAND
Edinburgh ✪
Liverpool •
UNITED KINGDOM
NORTHERN IRELAND
Belfast •
Dublin ✪
IRELAND

WALES
ENGLAND
London ✪

British Isles

Channel Islands (U.K.)

English Channel

FRANCE

Paris ✪

Bay of Biscay

PYRENEES

Barcelona •

Balearic Islands (SPAIN)

ATLANTIC OCEAN

PORTUGAL
Lisbon ✪

SPAIN
Madrid ✪

Valencia •

Seville •

Gibraltar (U.K.)

Strait of Gibraltar

AFRICA

N E W S

✪ National capital
• Other city

0   150   300 mi
0   150   300 km

Projection: Azimuthal Equal-Area

Arctic Circle

70°N
60°N
50°N

40°E
30°E
20°E
10°E
0°
10°W
20°W
30°W

70°N
50°E
40°E
30°E

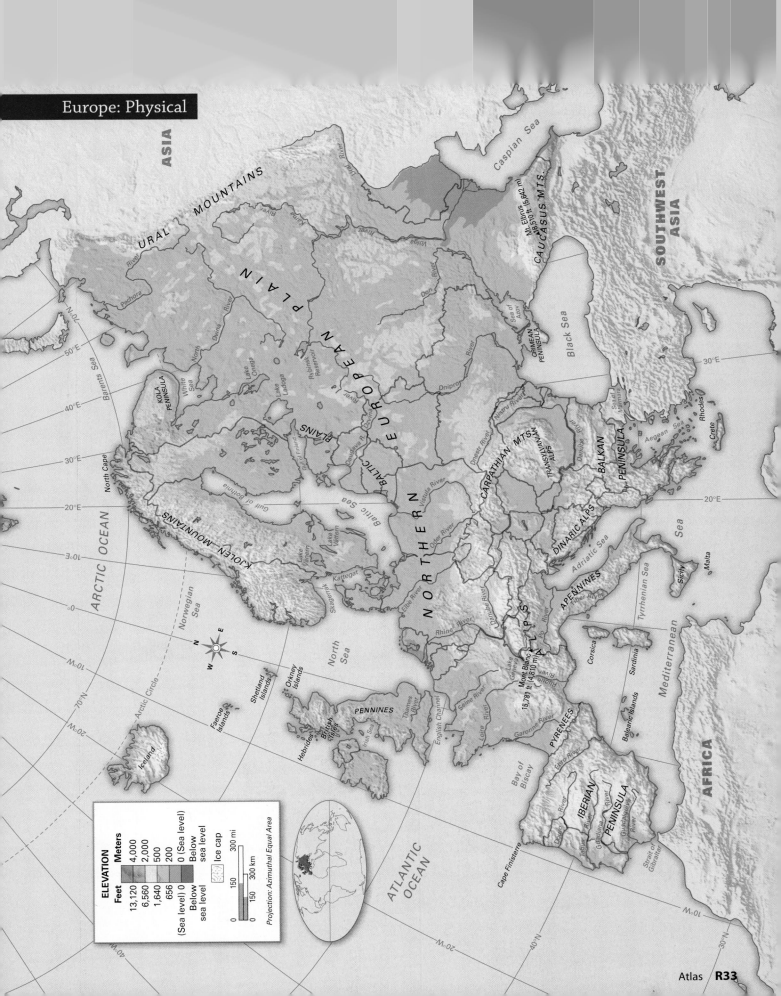

Europe: Physical

ASIA

URAL MOUNTAINS

NORTHERN EUROPEAN PLAIN

BALTIC PLAINS

KOLA PENINSULA

Caspian Sea

CAUCASUS MTS.
Mt. Elbrus 18,510 ft 5,642 m

SOUTHWEST ASIA

Barents Sea

White Sea

Lake Onega
Lake Ladoga
Rybinsk Reservoir

Pechora River
Dvina River
North Dvina River
Ural River
Kama River
Volga River
Don River
Dnipro River

Sea of Azov
CRIMEAN PENINSULA

Black Sea

Sea of Marmara
Aegean Sea
Rhodes
Crete

North Cape

ARCTIC OCEAN

KJOLEN MOUNTAINS

Norwegian Sea

Gulf of Bothnia
Gulf of Finland
Lake Vänern
Lake Vättern
Baltic Sea
Kattegat
Skagerrak

Daugava R.

Vistula River
Oder River
Elbe River

CARPATHIAN MTS.
TRANSYLVANIAN ALPS
BALKAN PENINSULA
DINARIC ALPS

Nistru River
Danube River

Adriatic Sea

APENNINES

Tyrrhenian Sea

Sicily

Malta

Mediterranean Sea

North Sea

PENNINES

British Isles

Hebrides
Inish Sea
Orkney Islands
Shetland Islands
Faeroe Islands

Iceland

Thames River
English Channel
Seine River
Loire River

ALPS
Lake Geneva
Mont Blanc 15,781 ft 4,810 m
Rhône River

Rhine River
Danube River

Corsica
Sardinia
Balearic Islands

Bay of Biscay

PYRENEES
Garonne River
Ebro River

IBERIAN PENINSULA
Douro River
Tagus River
Guadiana River
Guadalquivir River

Cape Finisterre

Strait of Gibraltar

AFRICA

ATLANTIC OCEAN

Arctic Circle

N E W S

ELEVATION

Feet	Meters
13,120	4,000
6,560	2,000
1,640	500
656	200
(Sea level) 0	0 (Sea level)
Below sea level	Below sea level

Ice cap

0   150   300 mi
0   150   300 km

Projection: Azimuthal Equal Area

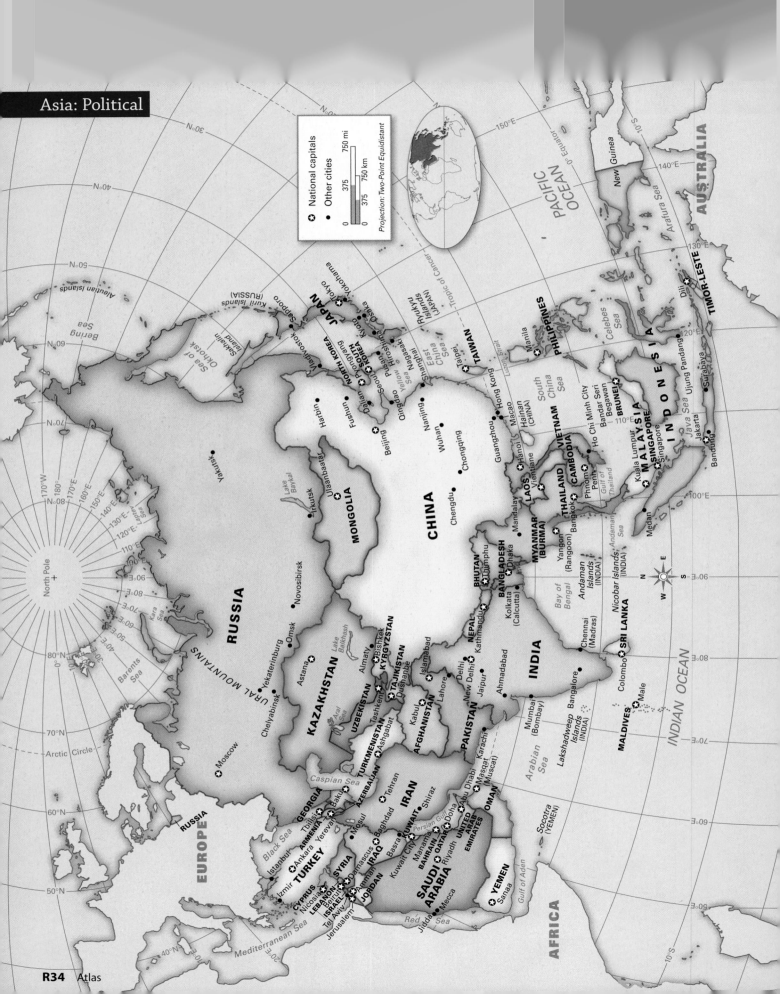

Asia: Political

National capitals
Other cities

750 mi
375
750 km
375

Projection: Two-Point Equidistant

PACIFIC OCEAN

AUSTRALIA

New Guinea

TIMOR-LESTE

Dili

PHILIPPINES

Manila

INDONESIA

Ujung Pandang

Surabaya

Jakarta

Bandung

Java Sea

Celebes Sea

Arafura Sea

BRUNEI

Bandar Seri Begawan

MALAYSIA

SINGAPORE

Kuala Lumpur

Singapore

Medan

VIETNAM

Ho Chi Minh City

Hanoi

CAMBODIA

Phnom Penh

LAOS

Vientiane

THAILAND

Bangkok

MYANMAR (BURMA)

Yangon (Rangoon)

Mandalay

Luzon Strait

South China Sea

Hainan (CHINA)

Macao

Hong Kong

Guangzhou

TAIWAN

Taipei

East China Sea

Ryukyu Islands (JAPAN)

Tropic of Cancer

JAPAN

Tokyo

Yokohama

Osaka

Kyoto

Hiroshima

Nagasaki

Sapporo

Kuril Islands (RUSSIA)

Sakhalin Island

Sea of Okhotsk

Bering Sea

Aleutian Islands

Vladivostok

NORTH KOREA

Pyongyang

SOUTH KOREA

Seoul

Pusan

Yellow Sea

Shanghai

Nanjing

Qingdao

Dalian

Fushun

Beijing

Harbin

CHINA

Wuhan

Chongqing

Chengdu

MONGOLIA

Ulaanbaatar

Lake Baykal

Irkutsk

Yakutsk

RUSSIA

Novosibirsk

Omsk

Yekaterinburg

Chelyabinsk

URAL MOUNTAINS

Moscow

EUROPE

RUSSIA

Barents Sea

Kara Sea

Arctic Circle

North Pole

KAZAKHSTAN

Astana

Aral Sea

Lake Balkhash

Almaty

UZBEKISTAN

Tashkent

KYRGYZSTAN

Bishkek

TAJIKISTAN

Dushanbe

TURKMENISTAN

Ashgabat

AFGHANISTAN

Kabul

Caspian Sea

Tehran

IRAN

Shiraz

GEORGIA

Tbilisi

ARMENIA

Yerevan

AZERBAIJAN

Baku

Black Sea

Istanbul

TURKEY

Ankara

Izmir

CYPRUS

Nicosia

LEBANON

Beirut

ISRAEL

Tel Aviv

Jerusalem

SYRIA

Damascus

JORDAN

Amman

Mediterranean Sea

IRAQ

Mosul

Baghdad

Basra

KUWAIT

Kuwait City

BAHRAIN

Manama

QATAR

Doha

UNITED ARAB EMIRATES

Abu Dhabi

OMAN

Masqat (Muscat)

SAUDI ARABIA

Riyadh

Mecca

Jidda

Persian Gulf

YEMEN

Sanaa

Gulf of Aden

Red Sea

AFRICA

Socotra (YEMEN)

Arabian Sea

PAKISTAN

Islamabad

Lahore

Karachi

Kabul

AFGHANISTAN

INDIA

New Delhi

Delhi

Jaipur

Ahmadabad

Mumbai (Bombay)

Bangalore

Chennai (Madras)

Kolkata (Calcutta)

NEPAL

Kathmandu

BHUTAN

Thimphu

BANGLADESH

Dhaka

Bay of Bengal

Andaman Islands (INDIA)

Andaman Sea

Gulf of Thailand

Nicobar Islands (INDIA)

SRI LANKA

Colombo

MALDIVES

Male

Lakshadweep Islands (INDIA)

INDIAN OCEAN

Equator

N
W   E
S

R34 Atlas

ELEVATION

Feet	Meters
13,120	4,000
6,560	2,000
1,640	500
656	200
(Sea level) 0	0 (Sea level)
Below sea level	Below sea level

Ice cap

750 mi
0   375   750 km

Projection: Two-Point Equidistant

PACIFIC OCEAN

AUSTRALIA

New Guinea

MAOKE MOUNTAINS

Arafura Sea

Banda Sea

Molucca

Celebes Sea

Celebes

Borneo

Java Sea

Java

Sumatra

Bangka

Mentawai Islands

MALAY PENINSULA

South China Sea

Hainan

INDOCHINA PENINSULA

Gulf of Tonkin

Mekong River

Xi River

Chang Jiang (Yangtze River)

Chao Phraya River

Gulf of Thailand

Andaman Sea

Nicobar Islands

Andaman Islands

Bay of Bengal

Sri Lanka

INDIAN OCEAN

Maldives

Lakshadweep Islands

Socotra Island

Gulf of Aden

AFRICA

Red Sea

SINAI PENINSULA

Gulf of Oman

Arabian Sea

RUB' AL-KHALI

AN-NAFUD

Persian Gulf

Strait of Hormuz

SYRIAN DESERT

ZAGROS MTS.

Euphrates River

Tigris River

Mount Ararat 16,945 ft (5,165 m)

CAUCASUS MTS.

ANATOLIAN PLATEAU

Cyprus

Mediterranean Sea

Black Sea

Bosporus

EUROPE

Caspian Sea

USTYURT PLATEAU

GREAT SALT DESERT

Ural River

Aral Sea

KARA KUM

KYZYL KUM

TURAN LOWLAND

Amu Darya

Syr Darya

HINDU KUSH

Indus River

THAR DESERT

INDO-GANGETIC PLAIN

Ganges River

Brahmaputra River

Godavari River

DECCAN PLATEAU

EASTERN GHATS

WESTERN GHATS

H I M A L A Y A S

Mount Everest 29,035 ft (8,850 m)

Sutlej River

PLATEAU OF TIBET

Nu River

KUNLUN MOUNTAINS

TAKLIMAKAN DESERT

TARIM BASIN

TIAN SHAN

Balqash Lake

KAZAKH UPLANDS

Irtysh River

Ob River

ALTAY MOUNTAINS

SAYAN MOUNTAINS

G O B I

MONGOLIAN PLATEAU

GREATER KHINGAN RANGE

QIN LING

Huang He (Yellow River)

NORTH CHINA PLAIN

Yellow Sea

BOHEA HILLS

East China Sea

Ryukyu Islands

Okinawa

Taiwan

Luzon Strait

Luzon

Mindanao

Philippines

Tropic of Cancer

URAL MOUNTAINS

WEST SIBERIAN PLAIN

Lower Tunguska River

Yenisey River

Angara River

Lake Baykal

YABLONOVY RANGE

Shilka River

Amur River

STANOVOY MOUNTAINS

Aldan River

S I B E R I A

CENTRAL SIBERIAN PLATEAU

Lena River

VERKHOYANSK RANGE

CHERSKIY RANGE

KOLYMA MTS.

TAYMYR PENINSULA

North Land

Laptev Sea

New Siberian Islands

Wrangel Island

CENTRAL RANGE

KAMCHATKA PENINSULA

Sea of Okhotsk

Sakhalin Island

Kuril Islands

Hokkaido

Sea of Japan (East Sea)

Honshu

Shikoku

Kyushu

Korea Strait

Japan

Bering Sea

Aleutian Islands

Arctic Circle

North Pole

Franz Josef Land

Novaya Zemlya

Kara Sea

Barents Sea

Ob River

Africa: Political

EUROPE

SOUTHWEST ASIA

Mediterranean Sea

Azores (PORTUGAL)

Madeira (PORTUGAL)

Strait of Gibraltar

Casablanca ● Rabat
Algiers ✪   Tunis ✪
MOROCCO   **TUNISIA**   ✪ Tripoli
Alexandria ●
Giza ● ✪ Cairo

Canary Islands (SPAIN)

El Aaiún ●
WESTERN SAHARA (Claimed by Morocco)

Tropic of Cancer

ALGERIA   **LIBYA**   **EGYPT**

Red Sea

CAPE VERDE

● Praia

MAURITANIA   ✪ Nouakchott
MALI

SENEGAL   **NIGER**   **SUDAN**   **ERITREA**
Dakar ✪   Niamey ●   **CHAD**   Khartoum ●   Asmara ●
Banjul ✪ **GAMBIA**   Bamako ●   **BURKINA FASO**   Gulf of Aden
Bissau ✪   Ouagadougou ●   N'Djamena ●   **DJIBOUTI**
GUINEA-BISSAU   **GUINEA**   **BENIN**   Djibouti ●
Conakry ✪   **CÔTE D'IVOIRE** **TOGO**   **NIGERIA**   **ETHIOPIA**
Freetown ●   **GHANA**   ● Abuja   **CENTRAL AFRICAN REPUBLIC**   Addis Ababa ●
SIERRA LEONE   Yamoussoukro ●   Lomé   **SOUTH SUDAN**
Monrovia ●   Accra ●   Porto-   Lagos ●   Bangui ●   **SOMALIA**
LIBERIA   Abidjan ●   Novo   Lake Chad   Juba ●
Gulf of Guinea   **CAMEROON**
Malabo ✪   Yaoundé ●
EQUATORIAL GUINEA   Mogadishu ●
SÃO TOMÉ AND PRÍNCIPE   **UGANDA**   **KENYA**
São Tomé ●   Libreville ✪   **REPUBLIC OF THE CONGO**   Kampala ●   Nairobi ●
0° Equator   **GABON**   Kisangani ●   **RWANDA**   Kigali ●   0° Equator
DEMOCRATIC REPUBLIC OF THE CONGO   Bujumbura ●   **INDIAN OCEAN**
Brazzaville ✪   **BURUNDI**   Mombasa ●   Victoria ●
CABINDA (ANGOLA)   Kinshasa   Lake Victoria   **TANZANIA**   *Pemba* **SEYCHELLES**
Dodoma ●   *Zanzibar*
Lake Tanganyika   Dar es Salaam ●
ATLANTIC OCEAN
Luanda ●   Lake Malawi (Nyasa)   **COMOROS**
10°S   Lubumbashi ●   Moroni ●   10°S
ANGOLA   **MALAWI**
ZAMBIA   Lilongwe ●
St. Helena (U.K.)   Lusaka ●   Antananarivo ●
Harare ●   **MOZAMBIQUE**   **MAURITIUS**
ZIMBABWE   **MADAGASCAR**   Port Louis ●
Bulawayo ●   *Réunion (FRANCE)*
NAMIBIA   **BOTSWANA**   Tropic of Capricorn
Windhoek ●   Gaborone ●   Pretoria ●   Maputo ●
Johannesburg ●   Mbabane ●
Bloemfontein ●   **SWAZILAND**
Maseru ●
LESOTHO
SOUTH AFRICA
Cape Town ●

✪ National capital
● Other city

0   250   500 mi
0   250   500 km

Projection: Azimuthal Equal-Area

R36 Atlas

EUROPE

SOUTHWEST ASIA

Azores

Madeira Islands

Strait of Gibraltar

Mediterranean Sea

Gulf of Sidra

Suez Canal

Persian Gulf

ATLAS MOUNTAINS

QATTARA DEPRESSION

Canary Islands

Tropic of Cancer

Cape Blanc

EL DJOUF

S A H A R A

AHAGGAR MOUNTAINS

LIBYAN DESERT

Nile River

Lake Nasser

Red Sea

NUBIAN DESERT

TIBESTI MOUNTAINS

AIR MTS.

S A H E L

Cape Verde Islands

Cape Verde

Senegal R.

Niger River

S U D A N

CHAD BASIN

Lake Chad

Gulf of Aden

FOUTA DJALLON

Black R.

White Volta R.

Volta R.

Lake Volta

Benue River

SUDAN BASIN

Blue Nile

White Nile

Lake Tana

ETHIOPIAN HIGHLANDS

HORN OF AFRICA

SOMALI PENINSULA

Cape Palmas

Gulf of Guinea

ADAMAWA MTS.

Ubangi River

Lake Turkana

RIFT VALLEY

Mount Kenya 17,058 ft (5,199 m) ▲

Cape Lopez

Congo River

CONGO BASIN

Lake Albert

Lake Edward

Lake Victoria

Mount Kilimanjaro 19,340 ft (5,895 m) ▲

INDIAN OCEAN

0° Equator

Kasai River

Lake Kivu

SERENGETI PLAIN

MASAI STEPPE

Zanzibar

Seychelles

ATLANTIC OCEAN

Ascension

MITUMBA MOUNTAINS

WESTERN RIFT VALLEY

EASTERN RIFT VALLEY

Lake Tanganyika

Lake Rukwa

Cuanza River

Lake Mweru

Lake Malawi (Nyasa)

Cape Delgado

Comoro Islands

Madagascar

Mauritius

Réunion

Lake Kariba

Zambezi River

Mozambique Channel

NAMIB DESERT

Okavango Delta

Victoria Falls

KALAHARI BASIN

Impopo River

KALAHARI DESERT

Vaal River

Orange River

DRAKENSBERG MOUNTAINS

GREAT KARROO

Cape of Good Hope

Tropic of Capricorn

ELEVATION

Feet	Meters
13,120	4,000
6,560	2,000
1,640	500
656	200
(Sea level) 0	0 (Sea level)
Below sea level	Below sea level

0   250   500 mi

0   250   500 km

Projection: Azimuthal Equal-Area

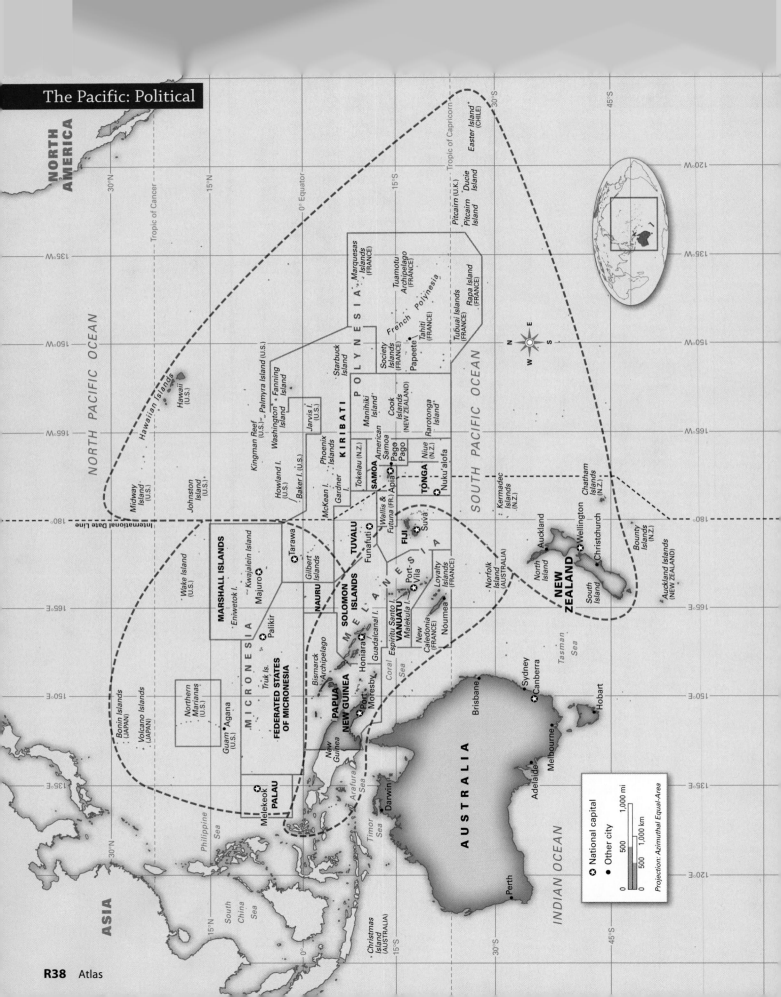

NORTH
AMERICA

NORTH PACIFIC OCEAN

ASIA

Tropic of Cancer

Equator

Tropic of Capricorn

International Date Line

Hawaiian Islands
Hawaii (U.S.)

Midway Island (U.S.)

Johnston Island (U.S.)*

Wake Island (U.S.)

Bonin Islands (JAPAN)

Volcano Islands (JAPAN)

Northern Marianas (U.S.)

Guam (U.S.) • Agana

MARSHALL ISLANDS
Eniwetok I. • Kwajalein Island ✪ Majuro

Palikir ✪
FEDERATED STATES OF MICRONESIA

M I C R O N E S I A

Truk Is.

PALAU
Melekeok ✪

New Guinea

PAPUA NEW GUINEA
Port Moresby ✪

Bismarck Archipelago

Arafura Sea

Timor Sea

Philippine Sea

South China Sea

Kingman Reef
Palmyra Island (U.S.)
Washington Fanning Island (U.S.) Island

Jarvis I. (U.S.)

Howland I. (U.S.)
Baker I. (U.S.)

Tarawa ✪

Gilbert Islands

NAURU

SOLOMON ISLANDS
Honiara ✪
Guadalcanal I.

Coral Sea

Starbuck Island

Phoenix Islands

McKean I.
Gardner

KIRIBATI

Tokelau (N.Z.)

Manihiki

American Samoa
Pago Pago

SAMOA
Apia ✪

Wallis & Futuna (FR.)

TUVALU
Funafuti ✪

FIJI
Suva ✪

Espiritu Santo I.
Malekula I.

VANUATU
Port Vila ✪

New Caledonia (FRANCE)
Noumea

Loyalty Islands (FRANCE)

M E L A N E S I A

P O L Y N E S I A

Marquesas Islands (FRANCE)

Tuamotu Archipelago (FRANCE)

French Polynesia

Society Islands (FRANCE)
Papeete

Tahiti (FRANCE)

Tubuai Islands (FRANCE)

Rapa Island (FRANCE)

Cook Islands (NEW ZEALAND)

Rarotonga Island

Niue (N.Z.)

TONGA
Nuku'alofa ✪

Kermadec Islands (N.Z.)

Norfolk Island (AUSTRALIA)

Pitcairn (U.K.)
Pitcairn Island

Ducie Island

Easter Island (CHILE)

SOUTH PACIFIC OCEAN

Auckland

NEW ZEALAND
North Island
Wellington ✪
South Island
Christchurch

Chatham Islands (N.Z.)

Bounty Islands (N.Z.)

Auckland Islands (NEW ZEALAND)

Tasman Sea

AUSTRALIA

Brisbane
Sydney
Canberra ✪
Melbourne
Hobart
Adelaide

Darwin

Perth

INDIAN OCEAN

Christmas Island (AUSTRALIA)

N
E
S
W

National capital ✪
Other city •

0   500   1,000 mi
0   500   1,000 km

Projection: Azimuthal Equal-Area

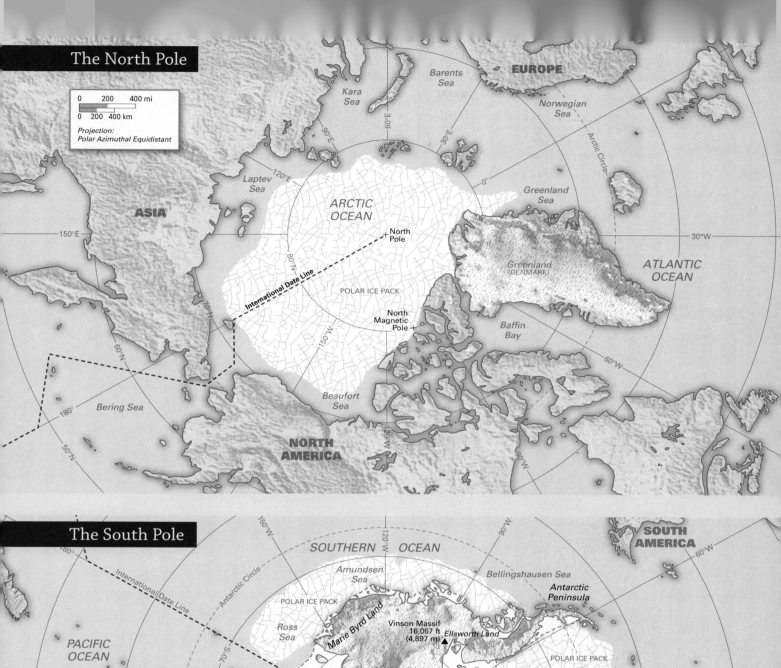

The North Pole

Projection:
Polar Azimuthal Equidistant

0   200   400 mi
0   200   400 km

EUROPE

Barents Sea

Norwegian Sea

Kara Sea

ASIA

Laptev Sea

ARCTIC OCEAN

North Pole

POLAR ICE PACK

International Date Line

North Magnetic Pole

Greenland Sea

Greenland (DENMARK)

Arctic Circle

ATLANTIC OCEAN

Baffin Bay

Beaufort Sea

Bering Sea

NORTH AMERICA

90°E
120°E
150°E
60°E
30°E
0°
30°W
60°W
80°N
70°N
60°N
50°N
180°
150°W
120°W
90°W
60°W

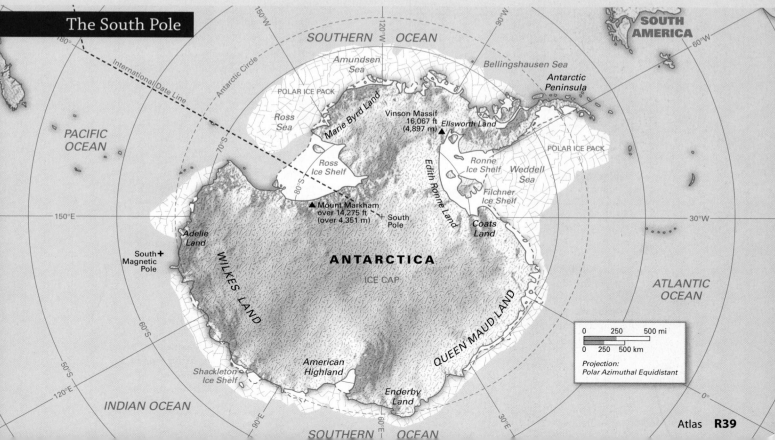

The South Pole

Projection:
Polar Azimuthal Equidistant

0   250   500 mi
0   250   500 km

SOUTHERN OCEAN

SOUTH AMERICA

International Date Line

Antarctic Circle

Amundsen Sea

Bellingshausen Sea

Antarctic Peninsula

POLAR ICE PACK

Ross Sea

Marie Byrd Land

Vinson Massif 16,067 ft (4,897 m)

Ellsworth Land

PACIFIC OCEAN

Ross Ice Shelf

Edith Ronne Land

Ronne Ice Shelf

Weddell Sea

POLAR ICE PACK

Mount Markham over 14,275 ft (over 4,351 m)

South Pole

Filchner Ice Shelf

Coats Land

Adelie Land

South Magnetic Pole

WILKES LAND

ANTARCTICA

ICE CAP

QUEEN MAUD LAND

ATLANTIC OCEAN

Shackleton Ice Shelf

American Highland

Enderby Land

INDIAN OCEAN

SOUTHERN OCEAN

150°W
120°W
90°W
60°W
30°W
0°
30°E
60°E
90°E
120°E
150°E
180°
70°S
80°S
60°S
50°S

English and Spanish Glossary

The Glossary is an alphabetical listing of many of the key terms from the modules, along with their meanings. The definitions listed in the Glossary are the ones that apply to the way the words are used in this textbook. The Glossary gives the part of speech of each word. The following abbreviations are used:

adj. adjective   *n.* noun   *v.* verb

Pronunciation Key

Some of the words in this book are followed by respellings that show how the words are pronounced. The following key will help you understand what sounds are represented by the letters used in the respellings.

SYMBOL	EXAMPLES	SYMBOL	EXAMPLES
a	apple [AP•uhl], catch [kach]	oh	road, [rohd], know [noh]
ah	barn [bahrn], pot [paht]	oo	school [skool], glue [gloo]
air	bear [bair], dare [dair]	ow	out [owt], cow [kow]
aw	bought [bawt], horse [hawrs]	oy	coin [koyn], boys [boyz]
ay	ape [ayp], mail [mayl]	p	pig [pihg], top [tahp]
b	bell [behl], table [TAY•buhl]	r	rose [rohz], star [stahr]
ch	chain [chayn], ditch [dihch]	s	soap [sohp], icy [EYE•see]
d	dog [dawg], rained [raynd]	sh	share [shair], nation [NAY•shuhn]
ee	even [EE•vuhn], meal [meel]	t	tired [tyrd], boat [boht]
eh	egg [ehg], ten [tehn]	th	thin [thihn], mother [MUH•thuhr]
eye	iron [EYE•uhrn]	u	pull [pul], look [luk]
f	fall [fawl], laugh [laf]	uh	bump [buhmp], awake [uh•WAYK],
g	gold [gohld], big [bihg]		happen [HAP•uhn], pencil [PEHN•suhl],
h	hot [haht], exhale [ehks•HAYL]		pilot [PY•luht]
hw	white [hwyt]	ur	earth [urth], bird [burd], worm [wurm]
ih	into [IHN•too], sick [sihk]	v	vase [vays], love [luhv]
j	jar [jahr], badge [baj]	w	web [wehb], twin [twihn]
k	cat [kat], luck [luhk]	y	As a consonant: yard [yahrd], mule [myool]
l	load [lohd], ball [bawl]		As a vowel: ice [ys], tried [tryd], sigh [sy]
m	make [mayk], gem [jehm]	z	zone [zohn], reason [REE•zuhn]
n	night [nyt], win [wihn]	zh	treasure [TREHZH•uhr],
ng	song [sawng],		garage [guh•RAHZH]
	anger [ANG•guhr]		

Syllables that are stressed when the words are spoken appear in CAPITAL LETTERS in the respellings. For example, the respelling of *patterns* (PAT•uhrnz) shows that the first syllable of the word is stressed.

A

Abbasids [uh•BAS•ihdz] *n.* a dynasty that ruled much of the Muslim Empire from AD 750 to 1258. (p. 281)
abasidas *s.* dinastía que gobernó gran parte del imperio musulmán entre 750 y 1258 d.C. (pág. 281)

Aborigine [ab•uh•RIHJ•uh•nee] *n.* a member of any of the native peoples of Australia. (p. 868)
aborigen *s.* miembro de cualquiera de los pueblos nativos de Australia. (pág. 868)

absolute monarch [MAHN•uhrk] *n.* a king or queen who has unlimited power and seeks to control all aspects of society. (p. 674)
monarca absoluto *s.* rey o reina que tiene poder ilimitado y que procura controlar todos los aspectos de la sociedad. (pág. 674)

globalization *n.* the spread of economic and cultural influences around the world. (p. 1276)
globalización *s.* la propagación de las influencias económicas y culturales de todo el mundo. (pág. 1276)

Glorious Revolution *n.* the bloodless overthrow of the English king James II and his replacement by William and Mary. (p. 704)
Revolución Gloriosa *s.* derrocamiento incruento del rey Jacobo II de Inglaterra, quien fue reemplazado por Guillermo y María. (pág. 704)

glyph [glihf] *n.* a symbolic picture, especially one used as part of a writing system for carving messages in stone. (p. 512)
glifo *s.* dibujo simbólico, especialmente el usado como parte de un sistema de escritura para tallar mensajes en piedra. (pág. 512)

Gothic [GAHTH•ihk] *adj.* relating to a style of church architecture that developed in medieval Europe, featuring ribbed vaults, stained glass windows, flying buttresses, pointed arches, and tall spires. (p. 401)
gótico *adj.* relacionado con un nuevo estilo de arquitectura religiosa surgido en la Europa medieval, caracterizado por bóvedas de nervadura, vitrales emplomados, contrafuertes volantes, arcos ojivales y altas agujas. (pág. 401)
gobierno *s.* cun sistema que controla la sociedad. (pág. 401)

Great Depression *n.* the severe economic slump that followed the collapse of the U.S. stock market in 1929. (p. 1053)
Gran Depresión *s.* crisis económica aguda que siguió a la caída del mercado de valores en 1929. (pág. 1053)

Great Famine *n.* (1315-1317) a prolonged period of major crop failures that led to mass starvation in Northern Europe. (p. 424)
Gran hambruna *s.* un período prolongado de grandes pérdidas de cosechas que provocaron una hambruna masiva en el norte de Europa. (pág. 424)

Great Fear *n.* a wave of senseless panic that spread through the French countryside after the storming of the Bastille in 1789. (p. 752)
Gran Miedo *s.* ola de temor insensato que se extendió por las provincias francesas después de la toma de la Bastilla en 1789. (pág. 752)

Great Purge *n.* a campaign of terror in the Soviet Union during the 1930s, in which Joseph Stalin sought to eliminate all Communist Party members and other citizens who threatened his power. (p. 1014)
Gran Purga *s.* campaña de terror en la Unión Soviética durante la década de 1930, en la cual José Stalin trató de eliminar a todos los miembros del Partido Comunista y ciudadanos que amenazaban su poder. (pág. 1014)

Great Schism [SIHZ•uhm] *n.* a division in the medieval Roman Catholic Church, during which rival popes were established in Avignon and in Rome. (p. 423)
Gran Cisma *s.* división de la Iglesia Católica Romana medieval, durante la cual había dos Papas rivales, uno en Avignon y el otro en Roma. (pág. 423)

Great Zimbabwe *n.* a southern African city that grew rich from controlling trade between the interior goldfields and Sofala and established an empire from the 1200s into the 1400s. (p. 476)
Gran Zimbabue *s.* una ciudad del sur de África que se enriqueció por el control del comercio entre las minas de oro interiores y Sofala, y estableció un imperio durante las décadas de 1200 a 1400. (pág. 476)

Greco-Roman culture *n.* an ancient culture that developed from a blending of Greek, Hellenistic, and Roman cultures. (p. 229)
cultura grecorromana *s.* cultura antigua que se desarrolló a partir de la combinación de las culturas griega, helénica y romana. (pág. 229)

green revolution *n.* a 20th-century attempt to increase food resources worldwide, involving the use of fertilizers and pesticides and the development of disease-resistant crops. (p. 1270)
revolución verde *s.* esfuerzo en el siglo 20 de aumentar los alimentos en el mundo entero, a través del uso de fertilizantes y pesticidas, y de la creación de cultivos resistentes a enfermedades. (pág. 1270)

Greenhouse Effect *n.* the warming of Earth's surface and lower atmosphere that results from energy being absorbed by certain gases such as carbon dioxide, water vapor, and methane. (p. 1310)

Efecto invernadero *s.* el calentamiento de la superficie terrestre y la atmósfera inferior que resulta de la energía que se absorbe por ciertos gases como el dióxido de carbono, vapor de agua y metano. (pág. 1310)

griot [gree•OH] n. a West African storyteller. (p. 439)
griot *s.* narrador de África occidental. (pág. 439)

gross domestic product *n.* GDP; total market value of all goods and services produced by a country in a given period of time. (p. 1273)
producto interno bruto *s.* PIB; una medida del valor total del mercado de todos los bienes y servicios producidos por un país en un período determinado de tiempo. (pág. 1273)

guerrilla [guh•RIHL•uh] *n.* a member of a loosely organized fighting force that makes surprise attacks on enemy troops occupying his or her country. (p. 767)
guerrillero *s.* miembro de una unidad de combate informal que ataca por sorpresa las tropas enemigas que ocupan su país. (pág. 767)

guild [gihld] *n.* a medieval association of people working at the same occupation, which controlled its members' wages and prices. (p. 409)
gremio *s.* asociación medieval de personas que laboraban en lo mismo; controlaba salarios y precios. (pág. 409)

guillotine [GIHL•uh•teen] *n.* a machine for beheading people, used as a means of execution during the French Revolution. (p. 758)
guillotina *s.* máquina para decapitar con que se hicieron ejecuciones durante la Revolución Francesa. (pág. 758)

Gupta Empire [GUP•tuh] *n.* the second empire in India, founded by Chandra Gupta I in AD 320. (p. 245)
Imperio Gupta *s.* segundo imperio de la India, fundado por Chandra Gupta I en el año 320 d. C. (pág. 245)

H

habeas corpus [HAY•bee•uhs KAWR•puhs] *n.* a document requiring that a prisoner be brought before a court or judge so that it can be decided whether his or her imprisonment is legal. (p. 703)

habeas corpus *s.* documento que requiere que un detenido comparezca ante un tribunal o juez para que se determine si su detención es legal. (pág. 703)

Hagia Sophia [HAY•ee•uh soh•FEE•uh] *n.* the Cathedral of Holy Wisdom in Constantinople, built by order of the Byzantine emperor Justinian. (p. 350)
Santa Sofía *s.* catedral de la Santa Sabiduría en Constantinopla, construida por orden del emperador bizantino Justiniano. (pág. 350)

haiku [HY•koo] *n.* a Japanese form of poetry, consisting of three unrhymed lines of five, seven, and five syllables. (p. 629)
haiku *s.* poema japonés que tiene tres versos no rimados de cinco, siete y cinco sílabas. (pág. 629)

hajj [haj] *n.* a pilgrimage to Mecca, performed as a duty by Muslims. (p. 275)
hajj *s.* peregrinación a la Meca realizada como deber por los musulmanes. (pág. 275)

Han [hahn] Dynasty *n.* Chinese dynasty that ruled from 202 BC to AD 9 and again from AD 23 to 220. (p. 256)
dinastía Han *s.* dinastía china que gobernó desde el año 202 a. C. hasta el 9 d. C., y luego otra vez desde el 23 hasta el 220 d. C. (pág. 256)

Harappan civilization *n.* another name for the Indus Valley civilization that arose along the Indus River, possibly as early as 7000 BC; characterized by sophisticated city planning. (p. 64)
civilización Harappa *s.* nombre alternativo de la civilización del valle del Indo que surgió a lo largo del río Indo, posiblemente ya desde el año 7000 a. C.; se caracterizaba por su sofisticada planificación urbana. (pág. 64)

Hausa [HOW•suh] *n.* a West African people who lived in several city-states in what is now northern Nigeria. (p. 467)
hausa *s.* pueblo de África occidental que vivía en varias ciudades Estado en el actual norte de Nigeria. (pág.467)

heliocentric theory [hee•lee•oh•SEHN•trihk] *n.* the idea that the earth and the other planets revolve around the sun. (p. 711)
teoría heliocéntrica *s.* idea de que la Tierra y los otros planetas giran en torno al Sol. (pág. 711)

Hellenistic [hehl•uh•NIHS•tihk] *adj.* relating to the civilization, language, art, science, and literature of the Greek world from the death of Alexander the Great to the late second century BC. (p. 182)

helénico *adj.* relacionado con la civilización, el idioma, el arte, la ciencia y la literatura del mundo griego desde la muerte de Alejandro Magno hasta fines del siglo II a. C. (pág. 182)

helot [HEHL•uht] *n.* in the society of ancient Sparta, a peasant bound to the land. (p. 157)

ilota *s.* en la sociedad de la Antigua Esparta, campesino ligado a la tierra. (pág. 157)

heresy [HEHR•uh•see] *n.* a denial of Church teachings. (p. 590)

herejía *s.* una negación de las enseñanzas de la Iglesia. (pág. 590)

heretic *n.* a person who is accused of having a religious belief that is contrary to the official teachings of the Church. (p. 587)

hereje *s.* una persona a quien se acusa de tener una creencia religiosa que es contraria a las enseñanzas oficiales de la Iglesia. (pág. 587)

hieroglyphics [HY•uhr•uh•GLIHF•ihks] *n.* an ancient Egyptian writing system in which pictures were used to represent ideas and sounds. (p. 57)

jeroglíficos *s.* sistema de escritura del Antiguo Egipto en el que se usaban dibujos para representar ideas y sonidos. (pág. 57)

Hijrah [HIHJ•ruh] *n.* Muhammad's migration from Mecca to Yathrib (Medina) in AD 622. (p. 273)

Hijrah *s.* migración de Mahoma de la Meca a Yathrib (Medina) en el 622 d.C. (pág. 273)

historiography *n.* the study and writing of history with an emphasis on the careful examination of information or data, often from the analysis of evidence. (p. 4)

historiografía *s.* el estudio y la escritura de la historia, con especial énfasis en el examen cuidadoso de la información o los datos, generalmente a través del análisis de la evidencia. (pág. 4)

Hittites [HIHT•yts] *n.* an Indo-European people who settled in Anatolia around 2000 BC. (p. 83)

hititas *s.* pueblo indoeuropeo que se estableció en Anatolia alrededor del año 2000 a. C. (pág. 83)

Holocaust [HAHL•uh•kawst] *n.* a mass slaughter of Jews and other civilians, carried out by the Nazi government of Germany before and during World War II. (p.1093)

Holocausto *s.* matanza en masa de judíos ejecutada por el gobierno de la Alemania nazi, antes y durante la II Guerra Mundial. (pág. 1093)

Holy Alliance *n.* a league of European nations formed by the leaders of Russia, Austria, and Prussia after the Congress of Vienna. (p. 773)

Alianza Sagrada *s.* liga de naciones europeas formada por los dirigentes de Rusia, Austria y Prusia después del Congreso de Viena. (pág. 773)

Holy Land *n.* a region that included Jerusalem and the area around it, considered holy by Jews, Christians, and Muslims. (p. 401)

Tierra Santa *s.* una región que incluía Jerusalén y el área alrededor de ella, considerada sagrada por judíos, cristianos y musulmanes. (pág. 401)

Holy Roman Empire *n.* an empire established in Europe in the 10th century AD, originally consisting mainly of lands in what is now Germany and Italy. (p. 394)

Sacro Imperio Romano *s.* imperio establecido en Europa en el siglo 10, que inicialmente se formó con tierras de lo que hoy es Alemania e Italia. (pág. 394)

home rule *n.* a control over internal matters granted to the residents of a region by a ruling government. (p. 871)

autogobierno *s.* control sobre asuntos internos que da el gobierno a los residentes de una región. (pág. 871)

hominid [HOM•uh•NIHD] *n.* A human and other creatures that walk upright. (p. 13)

homínido *s.* ser humano u otra criatura que camina erguida. (pág. 13)

Homo sapiens [homo•SAY•pee•uhnz] *n.* the species name for modern humans. (p. 16)

Homo sapiens *s.* nombre de la especie a la que pertenece el ser humano moderno. (pág. 16)

Hong Kong *n.* a former British colony on the southeastern coast of China that was returned to China in 1997. (p. 1258)

Hong Kong *s.* una antigua colonia británica en la costa sureste de China que fue devuelta a China en 1997. (pág. 1258)

English and Spanish Glossary

house arrest *n.* confinement to one's quarters, or house, rather than to prison. (p. 1179)
arresto domiciliario *s.* confinamiento en alojamiento o casa, en lugar de a la cárcel. (pág. 1179)

House of Wisdom *n.* a center of learning established in Baghdad in the 800s. (p. 286)
Casa de la Sabiduría *s.* centro de enseñanza en Bagdad en el siglo 9. (pág. 286)

Huguenot [HYOO•guh•naht] *n.* followers of John Calvin; French Protestants. (p. 593)
Hugonotes *s.* seguidores de Juan Calvino; Protestantes franceses. (pág. 593)

humanism [HYOO•muh•nihz•uhm] *n.* a Renaissance intellectual movement in which thinkers studied classical texts and focused on human potential and achievements. (p. 543)
humanismo *s.* movimiento intelectual del Renacimiento que estudió los textos clásicos y se enfocó en el potencial y los logros humanos. (pág. 543)

Hundred Days *n.* the brief period during 1815 when Napoleon made his last bid for power, deposing the French king and again becoming emperor of France. (p. 770)
Cien Días *s.* corto período de 1815 en que Napoleón hizo su último intento de recuperar el poder, depuso al rey francés y de nuevo se proclamó emperador de Francia. (pág. 770)

Hundred Years' War *n.* a conflict in which England and France battled on French soil on and off from 1337 to 1453. (p. 427)
Guerra de los Cien Años *s.* conflicto en el cual Inglaterra y Francia lucharon en territorio francés de 1337 a 1453, con interrupciones. (pág. 427)

hunter-gatherer *n.* nomadic groups whose food supply depends on hunting animals and collecting plant foods. (p. 22)
cazadores y recolectores *s.* grupos nómadas cuya provisión de alimentos depende de la caza de animales y la recolección de frutos y vegetales. (pág. 22)

Hyksos [HIHK•sohs] *n.* people from Western Asia, who settled in Egypt, in about 1650 BC. (p. 118)
hicsos *s.* pueblo del este de Asia que se estableció en Egipto alrededor del año 1650 a. C. (pág. 118)

I

I Ching [ee jihng] *n.* a Chinese book of oracles, consulted to answer ethical and practical problems. (p. 140)
I Ching *s.* libro de oráculos chino que se consulta para obtener respuestas a problemas éticos y prácticos. (pág. 140)

icon [EYE•kahn] *n.* a religious image used by eastern Christians. (p. 355)
icono *s.* imagen religiosa usada por los cristianos de Oriente. (pág. 355)

imperialism [ihm•PEER•ee•uh•lihz•uhm] *n.* a policy in which a strong nation seeks to dominate other countries politically, economically, or socially. (p. 896)
imperialismo *s.* política en que una nación fuerte buscar dominar la vida política, económica y social de otros países. (pág. 896)

impressionism [ihm•PREHSH•uh•nihz•uhm] *n.* a movement in 19th-century painting, in which artists reacted against realism by seeking to convey their impressions of subjects or moments in time. (p. 810)
impresionismo *s.* movimiento de la pintura del siglo 19 en reacción al realismo, que buscaba dar impresiones personales de sujetos o momentos. (pág. 810)

indentured servitude *n.* a system of labor by which a person could work to pay off the cost of coming to the Americas. (p. 652)
trabajador no abandonado *s.* un sistema de trabajo por el cual una persona puede trabajar para pagar el costo de venir a las Américas. (pág. 652)

Indo-Europeans [ihn•doh•yur•uh•PEE•uhnz] *n.* a group of seminomadic peoples who, about 1700 BC, began to migrate from what is now southern Russia to the Indian subcontinent, Europe, and Southwest Asia. (p. 82)
indoeuropeos *s.* grupo de pueblos seminómadas que, alrededor del año 1700 a. C., comenzó a migrar desde lo que en la actualidad pertenece al sur de Rusia hacia el subcontinente indio, Europa y el suroeste asiático. (pág. 82)

indulgence [ihn•DUHL•juhns] *n.* a pardon releasing a person from punishments due for a sin. (p. 571)
indulgencia *s.* perdón que libera al pecador de la penitencia por un pecado. (pág. 571)

Industrial Revolution *n.* the shift, beginning in England during the 18th century, from making goods by hand to making them by machine. (p. 818)
Revolución Industrial *s.* cambio, que comenzó en Inglaterra durante el siglo 18, de la producción manual a la producción con máquinas. (pág. 818)

industrialization [ihn•duhs•tree•uh•lih•ZAY• shuhn] *n.* the development of industries for the machine production of goods. (p. 819)
industrialización *s.* desarrollo de industrias para la producción con máquinas. (pág. 819)

inflation *n.* a decline in the value of money, accompanied by a rise in the prices of goods and services. (p. 223)
inflación *s.* baja del valor de la moneda, acompañada de un alza de precios de bienes y servicios. (pág. 223)

Inquisition [ihn•kwih•ZIHSH•uhn] *n.* a Roman Catholic tribunal for investigating and prosecuting charges of heresy—especially the one active in Spain during the 1400s. (p. 590)
Inquisición *s.* tribunal de la Iglesia Católica para investigar y juzgar a los acusados de herejía, especialmente el establecido en España durante el siglo 15. (pág. 590)

institution *n.* a long-lasting pattern of organization in a community. (p. 39)
institución *s.* modelo de organización perdurable de una comunidad. (pág. 39)

intendant [ihn•TEHN•duhnt] *n.* a French government official appointed by the monarch to collect taxes and administer justice. (p. 679)
intendente *s.* funcionario del gobierno francés nombrado por el monarca para recaudar impuestos e impartir justicia. (pág. 679)

interchangeable parts *n.* identical machine-made parts, the use of which made factory work more efficient. (p.838)
piezas intercambiables *s.* piezas idénticas hechas a máquina, las cuales hicieron el trabajo más eficiente en las fábricas. (pág. 838)

International Space Station *n.* cooperative venture sponsored by the United States, Russia, and 14 other nations to establish and maintain a working laboratory for scientific experimentation in space. (p. 1267)

Estación Espacial Internacional *s.* colaboración patrocinada por Estados Unidos, Rusia y otras 14 naciones para establecer y mantener un laboratorio activo para realizar experimentos científicos en el espacio. (pág. 1267)

Internet *n.* a linkage of computer networks that enables people around the world to exchange information and communicate with one another. (p. 1268)
Internet *s.* vinculación de redes de computadora que permite a gente de todo el mundo comunicarse e intercambiar información. (pág. 1268)

intifada *n.* literally, "shaking off"; Palestinian campaigns of violence and nonviolent resistance against Israel. Violence during the 1980s intifada targeted the Israeli army; violence during the 2000s intifada targeted Israeli civilians. (p. 1200)
intifada *s.* literalmente, "quitarse de encima"; campaña palestina de resistencia violenta y no violenta contra los israelíes. La primera *intifada* o alzamiento ocurrió en 1987 ; la segunda, en el 2000. (pág. 1200)

Irish Republican Army (IRA) *n.* an unofficial nationalist military force seeking independence for Ireland from Great Britain. (p. 874)
Ejército Republicano Irlandés (el IRA) *s.* fuerza paramilitar nacionalista que lucha porque Gran Bretaña dé la independencia la Irlanda del Norte. (pág. 874)

iron curtain *n.* during the Cold War, the boundary separating the Communist nations of Eastern Europe from the mostly democratic nations of Western Europe. (p. 1124)
cortina de hierro *s.* durante la Guerra Fría, división que separaba las naciones comunistas de Europa oriental de las naciones democráticas de Europa occidental. (pág. 1124)

Iroquois [IHR•uh•kwoy] *n.* a group of Native American peoples who spoke related languages, lived in the eastern Great Lakes region of North America, and formed an alliance in the late 1500s. (p. 506)
iroqueses *s.* grupo de pueblos amerindios que hablaban lenguas relacionadas, vivían en la parte este de la región de los Grandes Lagos en Norteamérica y formaron una alianza a fines del siglo 16. (pág. 506)

English and Spanish Glossary

isolationism *n.* a policy of avoiding political or military involvement with other countries. (p. 1072)

aislacionismo *s.* política de evitar lazos políticos o militares con otros países. (pág. 1072)

Israel [IHZ•ree•uhl] *n.* a kingdom of the united Israelites lasting from about 1020 to 922 BC; later, the northernmost of the two Israelite kingdoms; now, the Jewish nation that was established in the ancient homeland in 1948. (p. 111)

Israel *s.* reino de israelitas unidos que duró aproximadamente desde el año 1020 a. C. hasta el 922 a. C.; posteriormente, esa unidad se dividió en dos reinos, e Israel estuvo constituida solo por el que se encontraba más al norte; en la actualidad, se trata de la nación judía que se estableció en su antigua tierra natal en 1948. (pág. 111)

J

Jacobin *n.* member of a radical political organization during the French Revolution. (p. 758)

Jacobino *s.* miembro de una organización política radical durante la Revolución Francesa. (pág. 758)

Jainism [JY•nihz•uhm] *n.* a religion founded in India in the sixth century BC, whose members believe that everything in the universe has a soul and therefore should not be harmed. (p. 91)

jainismo *s.* religión fundada en la India en siglo VI a. C., cuyos miembros creen que todo lo que existe en el universo tiene un alma y, por lo tanto, no debe ser dañado. (pág. 91)

Jamestown *n.* the first permanent English settlement in North America. (p. 645)

Jamestown *s.* el primer asentamiento permanente Inglés en América del Norte. (pág. 645)

janissary [JAN•ih•sehr•ee] *n.* a member of an elite force of soldiers in the Ottoman Empire. (p. 298)

janísero *s.* miembro de una fuerza élite de soldados del imperio otomano. (pág. 298)

jazz *n.* a 20th-century style of popular music developed mainly by African-American musicians. (p. 1042)

jazz *s.* estilo de música popular del siglo 20 concebido principalmente por músicos afroamericanos. (pág. 1042)

Jesuits [JEHZH•oo•ihts] *n.* members of the Society of Jesus, a Roman Catholic religious order founded by Ignatius of Loyola. (p. 586)

jesuitas *s.* miembros de la Sociedad de Jesús, orden católica romana fundada por Ignacio de Loyola. (pág. 586)

"jewel in the crown" *n.* the British colony of India—so called because of its importance in the British Empire, both as a supplier of raw materials and as a market for British trade goods. (p. 921)

"joya de la corona" *s.* coloniam británica de India, así llamada por su importancia para el imperio británico, tanto como proveedor de materia prima como mercado para sus productos. (pág. 921)

joint-stock company *n.* a business in which investors pool their wealth for a common purpose, then share the profits. (p. 661)

sociedad de capitales *s.* negocio en el que los inversionistas reúnen capital para un propósito común y después comparten las ganancias. (pág. 661)

Judah [JOO•duh] *n.* an Israelite kingdom in Canaan, established around 922 BC. (p. 112)

Judá *s.* reino israelita de la región de Canaán, establecido alrededor del año 922 a. C. (pág. 112)

Junker [YUNG•kuhr] *n.* strongly conservative member of Prussia's wealthy landowning class. (p. 802)

Junker *s.* miembro sumamente conservador de la nobleza terrateniente de Prusia. (pág. 802)

Justinian Code [juh•STIHN•ee•uhn] *n.* the body of Roman civil law collected and organized by order of the Byzantine emperor Justinian around AD 534. (p. 349)

Código Justiniano *s.* cuerpo del derecho civil romano recopilado y organizado por órdenes del emperador bizantino Justiniano hacia el 534 d.C. (pág. 349)

K

kabuki [kuh·BOO·kee] *n.* a type of Japanese drama in which music, dance, and mime are used to present stories. (p. 630)
kabuki *s.* forma de teatro japonés en que se representa una historia con música, danza y mímica. (pág. 630)

kaiser [KY·zuhr] *n.* a German emperor (from the Roman title Caesar). (p. 803)
kaiser *s.* emperador alemán (del título romano Caesar). (pág. 803)

kamikaze [kah·mih·KAH·zee] *n.* during World War II, Japanese suicide pilots trained to sink Allied ships by crashing bomb-filled planes into them. (p. 1107)
kamikaze *s.* durante la II Guerra Mundial, pilotos suicidas japoneses entrenados para hundir barcos de los Aliados lanzándose sobre ellos con aviones llenos de bombas. (pág. 1107)

karma [KAHR·muh] *n.* in Hinduism and Buddhism, the totality of the good and bad deeds performed by a person, which is believed to determine his or her fate after rebirth. (p. 90)
karma *s.* para el hinduismo y el budismo, la totalidad de las acciones buenas y malas que una persona realiza y que, se cree, determinan el destino de esa persona luego de su reencarnación. (pág. 90)

Khmer Empire [kmair] *n.* a Southeast Asian empire, centered in what is now Cambodia, that reached its peak of power around AD 1200. (p.342)
imperio Khmer *s.* imperio del sureste asiático, centrado en la actual Camboya, que alcanzó su mayor auge hacia 1200 d.C. (pág. 342)

Khmer Rouge [roozh] *n.* a group of Communist rebels who seized power in Cambodia in 1975. (p. 1142)
Khmer Rouge *s.* grupo de rebeldes comunistas que tomaron el poder en Camboya en 1975. (pág. 1142)

knight *n.* in medieval Europe, an armored warrior who fought on horseback. (p. 376)
caballero *s.* en Europa medieval, guerrero con armadura y cabalgadura. (pág. 376)

Knossos [kuh·nuh·SOS] *n.* capital city of ancient Minoan civilization on the island of Crete. (p. 99)
Cnosos *s.* ciudad capital de la antigua civilización minoica que floreció en la isla de Creta. (pág. 99)

Koryo Dynasty [KAWR·yoo] *n.* a dynasty that ruled Korea from AD 935 to 1392. (p. 332)
dinastía koryu *s.* dinastía coreana del 935 a 1392 d.C. (pág. 332)

Kristallnacht [krih·STAHL·nahkt] *n.* "Night of Broken Glass"—the night of November 9, 1938, on which Nazi storm troopers attacked Jewish homes, businesses, and synagogues throughout Germany. (p. 1094)
Kristallnacht *s.* "Noche de cristales rotos": noche del 9 de noviembre de 1938, en que milicianos nazis atacaron hogares, negocios y sinagogas judíos en toda Alemania. (pág. 1094)

Kuomintang [KWOH·mihn·tang] *n.* the Chinese Nationalist Party, formed in 1912. (p. 1022)
Kuomintang *s.* Partido Nacionalista de China, formado en 1912. (pág. 1022)

Kush [KOOSH] *n.* an ancient Nubian kingdom whose rulers controlled Egypt between 2000 and 1000 BC. (p. 123)
Kush *s.* antiguo reino de Nubia cuyos gobernantes controlaron Egipto entre los años 2000 y 1000 a. C. (pág. 123)

L

laissez faire [lehs·ay FAIR] *n.* the idea that government should not interfere with or regulate industries and businesses. (p. 844)
laissez faire *s.* idea de que el gobierno no debe regular ni interferir en las industrias y empresas. (pág. 844)

land reform *n.* a redistribution of farmland by breaking up large estates and giving the resulting smaller farms to peasants. (p. 1216)
reforma agraria *s.* redistribución de tierras agrícolas con división de grandes latifundios y reparto de fincas a campesinos. (pág. 1216)

***La Reforma* [lah reh·fawr·mah]** *n.* a liberal reform movement in 19th-century Mexico, led by Benito Juárez. (p. 962)
La Reforma s. movimiento de reforma liberal en el siglo 19 en México fundado por Benito Juárez. (pág. 962)

English and Spanish Glossary

lay investiture [ihn•VEHS•tuh•chur] *n.* the appointment of religious officials by kings or nobles. (p. 395)
investidura seglar *s.* nombramiento de funcionarios de la Iglesia por reyes y nobles. (pág. 395)

League of Nations *n.* an international association formed after World War I with the goal of keeping peace among nations. (p. 994)
Liga de las Naciones *s.* organización internacional formada después de la I Guerra Mundial cuyo propósito era mantener la paz entre las naciones. (pág. 994)

***lebensraum* [LAY•buhns•rowm]** *n.* "living space"—the additional territory that, according to Adolf Hitler, Germany needed because it was overcrowded. (p. 1062)
lebensraum *s.* "espacio vital": territorio adicional que, según Adolfo Hitler, Alemania necesitaba porque estaba sobrepoblada. (pág. 1062)

Legalism *n.* a Chinese political philosophy based on the idea that a highly efficient and powerful government is the key to social order. (p. 140)
legalismo *s.* filosofía política china basada en la idea de que un gobierno eficiente y poderoso es la clave para mantener el orden social. (pág. 140)

legion *n.* a military unit of the ancient Roman army, made up of about 5,000 foot soldiers and a group of soldiers on horseback; the term also means a multitude. (p. 196)
legión *s.* unidad militar del ejército de la Antigua Roma compuesta por aproximadamente 5,000 soldados de a pie y un grupo de soldados a caballo; el término también hace referencia a una multitud. (pág. 196)

Legislative Assembly [LEHJ•ih•slay•tihv] *n.* a French congress with the power to create laws and approve declarations of war, established by the Constitution of 1791. (p. 755)
Asamblea Legislativa *s.* congreso creado por la Constitución francesa de 1791, con poder para emitir leyes y aprobar declaraciones de guerra. (pág. 755)

legitimacy [luh•JIHT•uh•muh•see] *n.* the hereditary right of a monarch to rule. (p. 772)
legitimidad *s.* derecho hereditario de un monarca a gobernar. (pág. 772)

letter of credit *n.* a document issued by a bank allowing the bearer to withdraw a specific amount of money from the bank or its branches. (p. 411)
carta de crédito *s.* un documento emitido por un banco que permite al portador retirar una cantidad específica de dinero del banco o de sus sucursales. (pág. 411)

liberal *n.* in the first half of the 19th century, a European—usually a middle-class business leader or merchant—who wanted to give more political power to elected parliaments. (p. 789)
liberale *s.* en la primera mitad del siglo 19, europeo—principalmente empresarios y comerciantes de clase media—que deseaba darle más poder político a los parlamentos elegidos. (pág. 789)

lineage [LIHN•ee•ihj] *n.* the people who are descended from a common ancestor. (p. 438)
linaje *s.* individuos que descienden de un antepasado común. (pág. 438)

loess [LOH•uhs] *n.* a fertile deposit of windblown soil. (p. 70)
loess *s.* depósito fértil de sedimentos transportados por el viento. (pág. 70)

Long March *n.* a 6,000-mile journey made in 1934–1935 by Chinese Communists fleeing from Jiang Jieshi's Nationalist forces. (p. 1027)
Larga Marcha *s.* viaje de 6,000 millas que realizaron en 1934–35 las fuerzas comunistas de China para escapar de las fuerzas nacionalistas de Jiang Jieshi. (pág. 1027)

lord *n.* in feudal Europe, a person who controlled land and could therefore grant estates to vassals. (p. 376)
señor *s.* en la Europa feudal, persona que controlaba tierras y por lo tanto podía dar feudos a vasallos. (pág. 376)

Lutheran [LOO•thuhr•uhn] *n.* a member of a Protestant church founded on the teachings of Martin Luther. (p. 573)
luterano *s.* miembro de una iglesia protestante basada en las enseñanzas de Martín Lutero. (pág. 573)

lycée [lee•SAY] *n.* a government-run public school in France. (p. 763)
liceo *s.* escuela pública en Francia. (pág. 763)

lyric poetry *n.* poetry that describes emotions and desires, rather than tells stories. (p. 170)
poesía lírica *s.* poesía que, más que contar una historia, describe emociones y deseos. (pág. 170)

M

Macedonia [mas·ih·DOH·nee·uh] *n.* an ancient kingdom north of Greece, whose ruler Philip II conquered Greece in 338 BC. (p. 176)
Macedonia *s.* reino antiguo que estaba ubicado al norte de Grecia y cuyo gobernante, Filipo II, conquistó Grecia en el año 338 a. C. (pág. 176)

Maghrib [MUHG·ruhb] *n.* a region of western North Africa, consisting of the Mediterranean coastlands of what is now Morocco, Tunisia, and Algeria. (p. 456)
Maghreb *s.* región del norte de África que abarca la costa del Mediterráneo de lo que en la actualidad es Marruecos, Túnez y Argelia. (pág. 456)

Magna Carta [MAG·nuh KAHR·tuh] *n.* a document, written by English nobles, as a way to present their demands to the king. It was a contract between the king and nobles of England. (p. 418)
Carta Magna *s.* "Gran Carta": documento de Inglaterra que garantiza derechos políticos elementales, elaborado por nobles ingleses y aprobado por el rey Juan en 1215 d.C. (pág. 418)

Mahabharata [muh·huh·BAH·ruh·tuh] *n.* an Indian epic poem reflecting the struggles of the Aryans as they moved south into India. (p. 87)
Mahabharata *s.* poema épico de la India que refleja las luchas de los arios a medida que se dirigían hacia el sur e ingresaban a la India. (pág. 87)

Mahayana [mah·huh·yah·nuh] *n.* A sect of Buddhism that offers salvation to all and allows popular worship. (p. 248)
Mahayana *s.* secta budista que ofrece la salvación para todas las personas y permite el culto popular. (pág. 248)

maize [mayz] *n.* a cultivated cereal grain that bears its kernels on large ears; usually called corn in the United States. (p. 488)
maíz *s.* cereal cultivado cuyos granos se encuentran en grandes espigas, o mazorcas. (pág. 488)

Mali [MAH·lee] *n.* a West African empire that flourished from 1235 to the 1400s and grew rich from trade. (p. 462)
Mali *s.* imperio de África occidental que floreció entre 1235 y el siglo 15, y se enriqueció con el comercio. (pág. 462)

Manchus [MAN·chooz] *n.* a people, native to Manchuria, who ruled China during the Qing Dynasty (1644–1912). (p. 623)
manchú *s.* pueblo originario de Manchuria que gobernó en China durante la dinastía Qing (1644–1912). (pág. 623)

Mandate of Heaven *n.* in Chinese history, the divine approval thought to be the basis of royal authority. (p. 75)
Mandato del Cielo *s.* en la historia china, la aprobación divina que se consideraba el fundamento de la autoridad real. (pág. 75)

manifest destiny *n.* the idea, popular among mid-19th-century Americans, that it was the right and the duty of the United States to rule North America from the Atlantic Ocean to the Pacific Ocean. (p. 875)
destino manifiesto *s.* idea popular en el siglo 19 en Estados Unidos de que era su derecho y obligación regir Norteamérica, desde el océano Atlántico hasta el Pacífico. (pág. 875)

manor *n.* a lord's estate in feudal Europe. (p. 377)
señorío *s.* dominios de un señor en la Europa feudal. (pág. 377)

Maori [MOW·ree] *n.* a member of a Polynesian people who settled in New Zealand around AD 800. (p. 868)
maorí *s.* miembro de un pueblo polinesio establecido en Nueva Zelanda hacia 800 d.C. (pág. 868)

Marshall Plan *n.* a U.S. program of economic aid to European countries to help them rebuild after World War II. (p. 1125)
Plan Marshall *s.* programa estadounidense de ayuda económica a países europeos para su reconstrucción después de la II Guerra Mundial. (pág. 1125)

martial law [MAHR·shuhl] *n.* a temporary rule by military authorities over a civilian population, usually imposed in times of war or civil unrest. (p. 1229)
ley marcial *s.* gobierno militar temporal impuesto a la población civil, normalmente en época de guerra o de trastornos civiles. (pág. 1229)

English and Spanish Glossary

mass culture *n.* the production of works of art and entertainment designed to appeal to a large audience. (p. 890)
cultura de masas *s.* producción de obras de arte y diversión concebidas con el fin de atraer a un amplio público. (pág. 890)

mass production *n.* the system of manufacturing large numbers of identical items. (p. 838)
producción a gran escala *s.* el sistema de fabricación de un gran número de artículos idénticos. (pág. 838)

matriarchal [may·tree·AHR·kuhl] *adj.* relating to a social system in which the mother is the head of the family. (p. 246)
matriarcal *adj.* relacionado con un sistema social en el que la madre es la jefa o cabeza de la familia. (pág. 246)

matrilineal [mat·ruh·LIHN·ee·uhl] *adj.* relating to a social system in which family descent and inheritance rights are traced through the mother. (p. 438)
matrilineal *adj.* relacionado con un sistema social en el que la descendencia familiar y los derechos de herencia se trasmiten a través de la madre. (pág. 438)

Mauryan Empire [MAH·ur·yuhn] *n.* the first empire in India, founded by Chandragupta Maurya in 321 BC. (p. 242)
Imperio Maurya *s.* primer imperio de la India, fundado por Chandragupta Maurya en el año 321 a. C. (pág. 242)

May Fourth Movement *n.* a national protest in China in 1919, in which people demonstrated against the Treaty of Versailles and foreign interference. (p. 1023)
Movimiento del 4 de Mayo *s.* protesta nacional china en 1919 con manifestaciones contra el Tratado de Versalles y la interferencia extranjera. (pág. 1023)

Medes [meedz] *n.* a Southwest Asian people who helped to destroy the Assyrian Empire. (p. 128)
medos *s.* pueblo del suroeste asiático que ayudó a destruir el Imperio asirio. (pág. 128)

Meiji era [MAY·jee] *n.* the period of Japanese history from 1867 to 1912, during which the country was ruled by Emperor Mutsuhito. (p. 953)

era Meiji *s.* período de la historia japonesa entre 1867 y 1912, cuando gobernó el emperador Mutshito. (pág. 953)

Mein Kampf [myn KAHMPF] *n.* "My Struggle"—a book written by Adolf Hitler during his imprisonment in 1923–1924, in which he set forth his beliefs and his goals for Germany. (p. 1062)
Mi lucha *s.* libro escrito por Adolfo Hitler en prisión (1923–1924), en el cual expone sus creencias y sus ideales para Alemania. (pág. 1062)

mercantilism [MUR·kuhn·tee·lihz·uhm] *n.* an economic policy under which nations sought to increase their wealth and power by obtaining large amounts of gold and silver and by selling more goods than they bought. (p. 662)
mercantilismo *s.* política económica de aumentar la riqueza y poder de una nación obteniendo grandes cantidades de oro y plata, y vendiendo más bienes de los que se compran. (pág. 662)

mercenary [MUR·suh·nehr·ee] *n.* a soldier who is paid to fight in a foreign army. (p. 224)
mercenario *s.* soldado que recibe sueldo por pelear en un ejército extranjero. (pág. 224)

Meroë [MEHR·oh·ee] *n.* center of the Kush dynasty from about 250 BC to AD 150; known for its manufacture of iron weapons and tools. (p. 125)
Meroë *s.* centro de la dinastía Kush desde el año 250 a. C. hasta el año 150 d. C., aproximadamente; conocida por la fabricación de armas y herramientas de hierro. (pág. 125)

Mesoamerica [mehz·oh·uh·MEHR·ih·kuh] *n.* an area extending from central Mexico to Honduras, where several of the ancient complex societies of the Americas developed. (p. 490)
Mesoamérica *s.* región que se extiende desde el centro de México hasta Honduras, donde se desarrollaron varias de las antiguas sociedades complejas de América. (pág. 490)

Mesopotamia [MEHS·uh·puh·TAY·mee·uh] *n.* part of the land making up the Fertile Crescent, meaning "land between the rivers" in Greek. (p. 44)
Mesopotamia *s.* parte de las tierras que forman el Creciente Fértil; significa "tierra entre ríos" en griego. (pág. 44)

mestizo [mehs•TEE•zoh] *n.* a person of mixed Spanish and Native American ancestry. (p. 640)

mestizo *s.* mezcla de español y amerindio. (pág. 640)

Middle Ages *n.* the era in European history that followed the fall of the Roman Empire, lasting from about 500 to 1500—also called the medieval period. (p. 366)

Edad Media *s.* era en la historia europea posterior a la caída del imperio romano, que abarca aproximadamente desde el 500 hasta 1500, también llamada época medieval. (pág. 366)

middle class *n.* a social class made up of skilled workers, professionals, businesspeople, and wealthy farmers. (p. 830)

clase media *s.* clase social formada por trabajadores especializados, profesionales, comerciantes y granjeros acaudalados. (pág. 830)

Middle Passage *n.* the voyage that brought captured Africans to the West Indies, and later to North and South America, to be sold as slaves—so called because it was considered the middle leg of the triangular trade. (p. 655)

travesía intermedia *s.* viaje que trajo a africanos capturados al Caribe y, posteriormente, a América del Norte y del Sur, para venderlos como esclavos; recibió este nombre porque era considerada la porción media del triángulo comercial trasatlántico. (pág. 655)

migration *n.* the act of moving from one place to settle in another. (p. 444)

migración *s.* acto de trasladarse de un lugar para establecerse en otro. (págs. 444)

militarism [MIHL•ih•tuh•rihz•uhm] *n.* a policy of glorifying military power and keeping a standing army always prepared for war. (p. 973)

militarismo *s.* política de glorificar el poder militar y de mantener un ejército permanente, siempre preparado para luchar. (pág. 973)

Ming Dynasty *n.* a Chinese dynasty that ruled from 1368 to 1644. (p. 617)

dinastía Ming *s.* dinastía que reinó en China desde 1368 hasta 1644. (pág. 617)

Minoans [mih•NOH•uhnz] *n.* a seafaring and trading people that lived on the island of Crete from about 2000 to 1400 BC. (p. 99)

minoicos *s.* pueblo de navegantes y comerciantes que vivió en la isla de Creta desde el año 2000 a. C. hasta el año 1400 a. C., aproximadamente. (pág. 99)

Mississippian [mihs•ih•SIHP•ee•uhn] *adj.* relating to a Mound Builder culture that flourished in North America between AD 800 and 1500. (p. 506)

misisipiense *adj.* relacionado con una cultura constructora de túmulos que floreció en Norteamérica entre el 800 y 1500 d.C. (pág. 506)

mita [MEE•tuh] *n.* in the Inca Empire, the requirement that all able-bodied subjects work for the state a certain number of days each year. (p. 527)

mita *s.* en el imperio inca, obligación de todo súbdito de trabajar ciertos días al año para el Estado. (pág. 527)

Moche [MOH•chay] *n.* a civilization that flourished on what is now the northern coast of Peru from about AD 100 to 700. (p. 501)

moche *s.* civilización que floreció en la actual costa norte de Perú de aproximadamente 100 a 700 d.C. (pág. 501)

monarchy [MAHN•uhr•kee] *n.* a government in which power is in the hands of a single person. (p. 154)

monarquía *s.* gobierno en que el poder está en manos de una sola persona. (pág. 154)

monastery [MAHN•uh•stehr•ee] *n.* a religious community of men (called monks) who have given up their possessions to devote themselves to a life of prayer and worship. (p. 369)

monasterio *s.* comunidad religiosa de hombres, llamados monjes, que ceden todas sus posesiones y se dedican a la oración y veneración. (pág. 369)

monopoly *n.* a government in which power is concentrated in a central authority to which local governments are subject (p. 261)

monopolio *s.* gobierno en el que el poder está concentrado en una autoridad central y los gobiernos locales están subordinados a esta. (pág. 261)

English and Spanish Glossary

monotheism [MAHN·uh·thee·ihz·uhm] *n.* a belief in a single god. (p. 106)
monoteísmo *s.* creencia en un solo dios. (pág. 106)

Monroe Doctrine *n.* a U.S. policy of opposition to European interference in Latin America, announced by President James Monroe in 1823. (p. 934)
doctrina Monroe *s.* política estadounidense de oposición a la interferencia europea en Latinoamérica, anunciada por el presidente James Monroe en 1823. (pág. 934)

monsoon [mahn·SOON] *n.* a wind that shifts in direction at certain times of each year. (p. 63)
monzón *s.* viento que cambia de dirección en ciertas épocas del año. (pág. 63)

Monte Albán *n.* the first real urban center, built by the Zapotec in about 500 B.C. in the Oaxaca Valley, Mesoamerica. (p. 494)
Monte Albán *s.* el primer centro urbano de bienes, construido por los zapotecas aproximadamente 500 a. C. en el Valle de Oaxaca, Mesoamérica. (pág. 494)

mosque [mahsk] *n.* an Islamic place of worship. (p. 275)
mezquita *s.* lugar de veneración islámica. (pág. 275)

movable type *n.* blocks of metal or wood, each bearing a single character, that can be arranged to make up a page for printing. (p. 313)
tipo móvil *s.* bloques de metal o de madera, cada uno con caracteres individuales, que pueden distribuirse para formar una página de impresión. (pág. 313)

Mughal [MOO·guhl] *n.* one of the nomads who invaded the Indian subcontinent in the 16th century and established a powerful empire there. (p. 598)
mogol *s.* uno de los nómadas que invadieron el subcontinente de India en el siglo 16 y establecieron un poderoso imperio. (pág. 598)

mujahideen [moo·jah·heh·DEEN] *n.* in Afghanistan, holy warriors who banded together to fight the Soviet-supported government in the late 1970s. (p. 1207)
muyahidin *s.* guerreros religiosos afganos que se unieron para luchar contra el gobierno apoyado por los soviéticos a fines de la década de 1970. (pág. 1207)

mulatto [muh·LAT·oh] *n.* a person of mixed European and African ancestry. (p. 780)
mulato *s.* persona de ascendencia europea y africana. (pág. 780)

mummification [MUHM·uh·fih·KAY·shuhn] *n.* a process of embalming and drying corpses to prevent them from decaying. (p. 55)
momificación *s.* proceso de embalsamar y secar cadáveres para evitar su descomposición. (pág. 55)

Munich Conference [MYOO·nihk] *n.* a 1938 meeting of representatives from Britain, France, Italy, and Germany, at which Britain and France agreed to allow Nazi Germany to annex part of Czechoslovakia in return for Adolf Hitler's pledge to respect Czechoslovakia's new borders. (p. 1072)
Conferencia de Munich *s.* reunión en 1938 de Inglaterra, Francia, Italia y Alemania, en la cual Gran Bretaña y Francia aceptaron que la Alemania nazi anexara parte de Checoslovaquia, a cambio de la promesa de Adolfo Hitler de respetar las nuevas fronteras checas. (pág. 1072)

Muslim [MUHZ·luhm] *n.* a follower of Islam. (p. 272)
musulmán *s.* devoto del islam. (pág. 272)

Muslim League *n.* an organization formed in 1906 to protect the interests of India's Muslims, which later proposed that India be divided into separate Muslim and Hindu nations. (p. 1167)
Liga Musulmana *s.* organización formada en 1906 para proteger los intereses de los musulmanes de India; después propuso la división del país en dos naciones: una musulmana y una hindú. (pág. 1167)

Mutapa [moo·TAHP·uh] *adj.* relating to a southern African empire established by Mutota in the 15th century AD. (p. 478)
mutapa *adj.* con un imperio de África del sur establecido por Mutota en el siglo 15 a.D. (pág. 478)

Mycenaean [my·suh·nee·uhn] *n.* a people who settled on the Greek mainland around 2000 BC. (p. 149)
micénicos *s.* pueblo que se estableció en Grecia continental alrededor del año 2000 a. C. (pág. 149)

myth *n.* a traditional story about gods, ancestors, or heroes, told to explain the natural world or the customs and beliefs of a society. (p. 152)
mito *s.* relato tradicional sobre dioses, ancestros o héroes que se narra para explicar el mundo natural o las costumbres y creencias de una sociedad. (pág. 152)

N

Napoleonic Code [nuh·poh·lee·AHN·ihk] *n.* a comprehensive and uniform system of laws established for France by Napoleon. (p. 763)
código napoleónico *s.* sistema extenso y uniforme de leyes establecido para Francia por Napoleón. (pág. 763)

National Assembly *n.* a French congress established by representatives of the Third Estate on June 17, 1789, to enact laws and reforms in the name of the French people. (p. 750)
Asamblea Nacional *s.* congreso francés establecido el 17 de junio de 1789 por representantes del Tercer Estado para promulgar leyes y reformas en nombre del pueblo. (pág. 750)

nationalism *n.* the belief that people should be loyal mainly to their nation—that is, to the people with whom they share a culture and history—rather than to a king or empire. (p. 790)
nacionalismo *s.* creencia de que la principal lealtad del pueblo debe ser a su nación—es decir, a la gente con quien comparte historia y cultura—y no al rey o al imperio. (pág. 790)

nation-state *n.* an independent geopolitical unit of people having a common culture and identity. (p. 589, 790)
nación Estado *s.* nación independiente de gente que tiene una cultura e identidad común. (pág. 589, 790)

NATO [NAY·toh] *n.* the North Atlantic Treaty Organization—a defensive military alliance formed in 1949 by ten Western European nations, the United States, and Canada. (p. 1127)
OTAN *s.* Organización del Tratado del Atlántico Norte: alianza militar defensiva formada en 1949 por diez naciones de Europa occidental, Estados Unidos y Canadá. (pág. 1127)

Nazca [NAHS·kah] *n.* a civilization that flourished on what is now the southern coast of Peru from about 200 BC to AD 600. (p. 501)
nazca *s.* civilización que floreció en la actual costa sur de Perú de 200 a.C. a 600 d.C. (pág. 501)

Nazism [NAHT·sihz·uhm] *n.* the fascist policies of the National Socialist German Workers' party, based on totalitarianism, a belief in racial superiority, and state control of industry. (p. 1061)
nazismo *s.* políticas fascistas del Partido Nacional socialista de los Trabajadores de Alemania, basadas en el totalitarismo, la creencia en superioridad racial y el control estatal de la industria. (pág. 1061)

Negritude movement [NEE·grih·tood] *n.* a movement in which French-speaking Africans and West Indians celebrated their heritage of traditional African culture and values. (p. 1186)
movimiento de negritud *s.* movimiento de africanos de lengua francesa que celebra el legado de la cultura tradicional africana y sus valores. (pág. 1186)

neoclassical [nee·oh·KLAS·ih·kuhl] *adj.* relating to a simple, elegant style (based on ideas and themes from ancient Greece and Rome) that characterized the arts in Europe during the late 1700s. (p. 726)
neoclásico *adj.* relacionado con un estilo sencillo y elegante (inspirado en ideas y temas de la antigua Grecia y Roma) que caracterizó las artes en Europa a fines del siglo 18. (pág. 726)

Neolithic Age [nee·oh·LIH·thick] *n.* the New Stone Age, lasting from about 8000 BC to as early as 3000 BC. (p. 14)
Neolítico *s.* la Nueva Edad de Piedra, que duró desde el año 8000 a. C. hasta principios del año 3000 a. C., aproximadamente. (pág. 14)

English and Spanish Glossary

Neolithic Revolution *n.* the agricultural revolution—the far-reaching changes in human life resulting from the beginnings of farming. (p. 23)

Revolución neolítica *s.* revolución agrícola; los cambios trascendentales en el modo de vida del ser humano como resultado del comienzo de la agricultura. (pág. 23)

neutralism *n.* a policy of siding with none of the major powers. The policy was pursued by many new nations in Asia and Africa after World War II. (p. 1169)

neutralismo *n.* una política que no apoya ninguna de las grandes potencias. La política fue acogida por muchas nuevas naciones de Asia y África después de la Segunda Guerra Mundial. (pág. 1169)

New Deal *n.* U.S. president Franklin Roosevelt's economic reform program designed to solve the problems created by the Great Depression. (p. 1056)

New Deal *s.* programa de reformas económicas del presidente Franklin D. Roosevelt ideado para solucionar los problemas creados por la Gran Depresión. (pág. 1056)

New France *n.* France's colonial empire in North America. (p. 645)

Nueva Francia *s.* imperio colonial francés en América del Norte. (pág. 645)

New Kingdom *n.* Egypt's third period of glory, after the overthrow of the Hyksos in about 1570 BC. (p. 119)

Reino Nuevo *s.* tercer período de gloria de Egipto, tras el derrocamiento de los hicsos alrededor del año 1570 a. C. (pág. 119)

New Netherland *n.* Dutch colonial holdings in North America. (p. 647)

Nuevos Países Bajos *s.* territorios coloniales holandeses en América del Norte. (pág. 647)

Nineveh [NINH•uh•vuh] *n.* a large walled city, the capital of Assyria, located on the Tigris River. (p. 128)

Nínive *s.* gran ciudad amurallada, capital de Asiria, ubicada a orillas del río Tigris. (pág. 128)

nirvana [neer•VAH•nuh] *n.* in Buddhism, the release from pain and suffering achieved after enlightenment. (p. 95)

nirvana *s.* para el budismo, la liberación de todo dolor y sufrimiento que se alcanza luego de la iluminación. (pág. 95)

Nok [nahk] *n.* an African people who lived in what is now Nigeria between 500 BC and AD 200. (p. 440)

nok *s.* pueblo africano que vivió en lo que es hoy Nigeria entre 500 a.C. y 200 d.C. (pág. 440)

nomad [NOH•mhad] *n.* highly mobile people who moved from place to place foraging, or searching, for new sources of food. (p. 22)

nómadas *s.* pueblos de marcada tendencia migratoria, que se trasladaban de un lugar a otro en busca de nuevas fuentes de alimento. (pág. 22)

nonaggression pact [nahn•uh•GRESH•uhn] *n.* an agreement in which nations promise not to attack one another. (p. 1078)

pacto de no agresión *s.* acuerdo en que dos o más naciones prometen no atacarse. (pág. 1078)

nonaligned nations *n.* the independent countries that remained neutral in the Cold War competition between the United States and the Soviet Union. (p. 1146)

países no alineados *s.* naciones independientes que permanecieron neutrales durante la Guerra Fría entre Estados Unidos y la Unión Soviética. (pág. 1146)

nonbinding agreement *n.* an agreement that does not carry a penalty for noncompliance. (p. 1288)

acuerdo no vinculante *s.* un acuerdo que no tiene sanciones por no cumplirse. (pág. 1288)

Nubia [NU•bee•uh] *n.* a region of Africa that straddled the upper Nile River. (p. 120)

Nubia *s.* región de África que se extiende a ambas orillas de la parte alta del río Nilo. (pág. 120)

Nuremberg Trials [NUR•uhm•burg] *n.* a series of court proceedings held in Nuremberg, Germany, after World War II, in which Nazi leaders were tried for aggression, violations of the rules of war, and crimes against humanity. (p. 1112)

juicios de Nuremberg *s.* serie de juicios realizados en Nuremberg, Alemania, tras la II Guerra Mundial a líderes nazis por agresión, violación a las leyes de guerra y crímenes contra la humanidad. (pág. 1112)

O

obsidian [ahb·SIHD·ee·uhn] *n.* a hard, glassy volcanic rock used by early peoples to make sharp weapons. (p. 517)
obsidiana *s.* roca volcánica dura y vítrea con que los primeros seres humanos elaboraban herramientas de piedra. (pág. 517)

Old Regime [ray·ZHEEM] *n.* the political and social system that existed in France before the French Revolution. (p. 746)
antiguo régimen *s.* sistema político y social que existía en Francia antes de la Revolución Francesa. (pág. 746)

oligarchy [AHL·ih·gahr·kee] *n.* a government in which power is in the hands of a few people—especially one in which rule is based upon wealth. (p. 154)
oligarquía *s.* gobierno en que el poder está en manos de pocas personas, particularmente un gobierno que se basa en la riqueza. (pág. 154)

Olmec [AHL·mehk] *n.* the earliest-known Mesoamerican civilization, which flourished around 1200 BC and influenced later societies throughout the region. (p. 490)
olmeca *s.* civilización mesoamericana más antigua que se conoce, que floreció hacia 1200 a.C. e influyó sobre las posteriores sociedades de la región. (pág. 490)

Open Door Policy *n.* a policy, proposed by the United States in 1899, under which all nations would have equal opportunities to trade in China. (p. 949)
política de puertas abiertas *s.* política propuesta por E.U.A. en 1899, que postulaba que todas las naciones tuvieran las mismas oportunidades de comerciar con China. (pág. 949)

Opium War *n.* a conflict between Britain and China, lasting from 1839 to 1842, over Britain's opium trade in China. (p. 945)
Guerra del Opio *s.* conflicto entre Inglaterra y China, de 1839 a 1842, por el comercio inglés de opio en China. (pág. 945)

oracle bone *n.* one of the animal bones or tortoise shells used by ancient Chinese priests to communicate with the gods. (p. 73)
hueso oracular *s.* uno de los huesos de animales o caparazones de tortuga que usaban los antiguos sacerdotes chinos para comunicarse con los dioses. (pág. 73)

Oslo Peace Accords *n.* an agreement in 1993 in which Israeli prime minister Rabin granted Palestinian self-rule in the Gaza Strip and the West Bank. (p. 1201)
Acuerdos de Paz de Oslo *s.* acuerdos de 1993 cuando el primer ministro israelí, Rabin, otorgó autonomía a Palestina en la Franja de Gaza y Cisjordania. (pág. 1201)

Ottoman *n.* follower of Osman, the leader who founded a small Muslim state in Anatolia between 1299 and 1326. (p. 293)
Otomano *s.* seguidor de Osman, el líder que fundó un pequeño estado musulmán en Anatolia entre 1299 y 1326. (pág. 293)

Ottoman Empire *n.* an empire founded in 1299 and dissolved in 1922. (p. 1028)
Imperio otomano *s.* un imperio fundado en 1299 y fue abolido en 1922. (pág. 1028)

ozone layer *n.* a layer of Earth's upper atmosphere, which protects living things from the sun's damaging ultraviolet rays. (p. 1282)
capa de ozono *s.* capa de la atmósfera superior de la Tierra que protege a los seres vivos de los rayos ultravioleta de la luz solar. (pág. 1282)

P

Pacific Rim *n.* the lands that border the Pacific Ocean, especially those in Asia. (p. 925)
Cuenca del Pacífico *s.* tierras que bordean el océano Pacífico, especialmente las de Asia. (pág. 925)

Pagan [puh·GAHN] *n.* a Southeast Asian kingdom, located in what is now Myanmar, that flourished between the 11th and 13th centuries. (p. 341)
Reino de Pagan *s.* un reino del sudeste asiático, que se encuentra en lo que hoy es Myanmar, que creció entre los siglos 11 y 13. (pág. 341)

Paleolithic Age [PAY·lee·oh·LIH·thick] *n.* the Old Stone Age, lasting from about 2.5 million years ago to 8000 BC. (p. 14)
Paleolítico *s.* la Vieja Edad de Piedra, que duró desde unos 2.5 millones de años atrás hasta el año 8000 a. C., aproximadamente. (pág. 14)

English and Spanish Glossary

Pan-African *n.* a vision of strengthening all of Africa, not just a single country. (p. 1187)
Panafricanismo *s.* una visión de fortalecimiento de toda África, no de solo un país.(pág. 1187)

Pan-Arabism *n.* the idea of cultural and political unity among Arab nations. (p. 1194)
Panarabismo *s.* la idea de unidad cultural y política entre las naciones árabes. (pág. 1194)

Panama Canal *n.* a human-made waterway connecting the Atlantic and Pacific oceans, built in Panama by the United States and opened in 1914. (p. 937)
canal de Panamá *s.* vía marítima que une al océano Atlántico con el Pacífico, construida en Panamá por Estados Unidos y terminada en 1914. (pág. 937)

papyrus [puh•PY•ruhs] *n.* a tall reed that grows in the Nile delta, used by the ancient Egyptians to make a paper-like material for writing on. (p. 58)
papiro *s.* junco alto que crece en el delta del Nilo, usado por los antiguos egipcios para fabricar un material similar al papel sobre el cual poder escribir. (pág. 58)

parliament [PAHR•luh•muhnt] *n.* a body of representatives that makes laws for a nation. (p. 418)
parlamento *s.* cuerpo de representantes que promulga las leyes de una nación. (pág. 418)

partition *n.* a division into parts, like the 1947 division of the British colony of India into the two nations of India and Pakistan. (p. 1167)
partición *s.* división en partes, como la división en 1947 de la colonia británica de India en dos naciones: India y Paquistán. (pág. 1167)

pastoralist [PAS•tuhr•uh•lihst] *n.* a member of a nomadic group that herds domesticated animals. (p. 321)
pastor *s.* miembro de un grupo nómada que pastorea rebaños de animales domesticados. (pág. 321)

paterfamilias *n.* the oldest living male of a Roman family who served as the powerful head of the family. (p. 210)

paterfamilias *s.* el hombre de mayor edad de una familia romana, quien cumplía el rol de jefe o cabeza de la familia. (pág. 210)

paternalism [puh•TUR•nuh•lihz•uhm] *n.* a policy of treating subject people as if they were children, providing for their needs but not giving them rights. (p.905)
paternalismo *s.* política de tratar a los gobernados como si fueran niños, atendiendo a sus necesidades pero sin darles derechos. (pág. 905)

patriarch [PAY•tree•ahrk] *n.* a principal bishop in the eastern branch of Christianity. (p.355)
patriarca *s.* obispo principal de la rama oriental de la cristiandad. (pág. 355)

patriarchal [pay•tree•AHR•kuhl] *adj.* relating to a social system in which the father is the head of the family. (p. 246)
patriarcal *adj.* relacionado con un sistema social en el que el padre es el jefe o cabeza de la familia. (pág. 246)

patrician [puh•TRIHSH•uhn] *n.* in ancient Rome, a member of the wealthy, privileged upper class. (p. 194)
patricio *s.* en la antigua Roma, miembro de la clase alta, privilegiada y rica. (pág. 194)

patrilineal [pat•ruh•LIHN•ee•uhl] *adj.* relating to a social system in which family descent and inheritance rights are traced through the father. (p. 438)
patrilineal *adj.* relacionado con un sistema social en el que la descendencia y los derechos de herencia se trasmiten a través del padre. (pág. 438)

patron [PAY•truhn] *n.* a person who supports artists, especially financially. (p. 545)
mecenas *s.* persona que apoya a los artistas, especialmente en el aspecto financiero. (pág. 545)

Pax Mongolica [paks mahng•GAHL•ih•kuh] *n.* the "Mongol Peace"—the period from the mid-1200s to the mid-1300s when the Mongols imposed stability and law and order across much of Eurasia. (p. 325)
Paz Mongólica *s.* período de mediados de 1200 a mediados de 1300 d.C., cuando los mongoles impusieron estabilidad y orden público en casi toda Eurasia. (pág. 325)

Pax Romana [PAHKS roh•MAH•nah] *n.* a period of peace and prosperity throughout the Roman Empire lasting from 27 BC to AD 180. (p. 204)

Pax romana *s.* período de paz y prosperidad durante el Imperio romano que duró desde el año 27 a. C. hasta el año 180 d. C. (pág. 204)

Peace of Augsburg [AWGZ•burg] *n.* a 1555 agreement declaring that the religion of each German state would be decided by its ruler. (p. 575)

Paz de Augsburgo *s.* acuerdo realizado en 1555 que declaró que la religión de cada Estado alemán sería decidida por su gobernante. (pág. 575)

Pearl Harbor *n.* U.S. naval base in Hawaii attacked by the Japanese, Dec. 7, 1941, precipitating U.S. entry into World War II. (p. 1087)

Pearl Harbor *s.* la base naval estadounidense en Hawái atacada por los japoneses el 7 de diciembre de 1941, lo que precipitó Estados Unidos a la Segunda Guerra Mundial. (pág. 1087)

Peloponnesian [pehl•uh•puh•NEE•zhuhn] War *n.* a war, lasting from 431 to 404 BC, in which Athens and its allies were defeated by Sparta and its allies. (p. 165)

Guerra del Peloponeso *s.* guerra que duró desde el año 431 hasta el año 404 a. C., en la que Esparta y sus aliados vencieron a Atenas y sus aliados. (pág. 165)

penal colony [PEE•nuhl] *n.* a colony to which convicts are sent as an alternative to prison. (p. 868)

colonia penal *s.* colonia a donde se mandan convictos como alternativa a una prisión. (pág. 868)

Peninsular War [puh•NIHN•syuh•luhr] *n.* a conflict, lasting from 1808 to 1813, in which Spanish rebels, with the aid of British forces, fought to drive Napoleon's French troops out of Spain. (p. 767)

Guerra Peninsular *s.* conflicto de 1808–1813 en que los rebeldes españoles lucharon con la ayuda de Gran Bretaña para expulsar de España las tropas de Napoleón. (pág. 767)

***peninsulares* [peh•neen•soo•LAH•rehs]** *n.* in Spanish colonial society, colonists who were born in Spain. (p. 780)

peninsulares *s.* en la sociedad española colonial, colonos nacidos en España. (pág. 780)

perestroika [pehr•ih•STROY•kuh] *n.* a restructuring of the Soviet economy to permit more local decision making, begun by Mikhail Gorbachev in 1985. (p. 1236)

perestroika *s.* reestructuración de la economía soviética para permitir mayor poder de decisión local, iniciada por Mijail Gorbachev en 1985. (pág. 1236)

Persian Wars *n.* a series of wars in the fifth century BC, in which Greek city-states battled the Persian Empire. (p. 160)

guerras médicas *s.* serie de guerras que tuvieron lugar en el siglo V a. C. en las que las ciudades-estado griegas lucharon contra el Imperio persa. (pág. 160)

perspective [puhr•SPEHK•tihv] *n.* an artistic technique that creates the appearance of three dimensions on a flat surface. (p. 546)

perspectiva *s.* técnica artística que crea la apariencia de tres dimensiones en una superficie plana. (pág. 546)

phalanx [FAY•langks] *n.* a military formation of foot soldiers armed with spears and shields. (p. 159)

falange *s.* formación militar de soldados de a pie armados con lanzas y escudos. (pág. 159)

pharaoh [FAIR•oh] *n.* a king of ancient Egypt, considered a god as well as a political and military leader. (p. 54)

faraón *s.* rey del Antiguo Egipto, considerado un dios y un líder político-militar. (pág. 54)

philosophe [FIHL•uh•sahf] *n.* one of a group of social thinkers in France during the Enlightenment. (p. 719)

philosophe *s.* miembro de un grupo de pensadores sociales de la Ilustración en Francia. (pág. 719)

philosopher *n.* a thinker who uses logic and reason to investigate the nature of the universe, human society, and morality. (p. 173)

filósofo *s.* pensador que usa la lógica y la razón para investigar la naturaleza del universo, las sociedades humanas y la moral. (pág. 173)

English and Spanish Glossary

Phoenicians [fih•NIHSH•uhnz] *n.* a seafaring people of Southwest Asia, who around 1100 BC began to trade and established colonies throughout the Mediterranean region. (p. 101)
fenicios *s.* pueblo de navegantes del suroeste asiático que, alrededor del año 1100 a. C., comenzó a comerciar y estableció colonias en toda la región mediterránea. (pág. 101)

Pilgrims *n.* a group of people who, in 1620, founded the colony of Plymouth in Massachusetts to escape religious persecution in England. (p. 646)
peregrinos *s.* grupo que en 1620 fundó la colonia de Plymouth en Massachusetts para escapar de persecución religiosa en Inglaterra. (pág. 646)

plebeian [plih•BEE•uhn] *n.* in ancient Rome, one of the common farmers, artisans, and merchants who made up most of the population. (p. 194)
plebeyo *s.* en la antigua Roma, uno de los agricultores, artesanos o comerciantes comunes que conformaban la mayoría de la población. (pág. 194)

plebiscite [PLEHB•ih•syt] *n.* a direct vote in which a country's people have the opportunity to approve or reject a proposal. (p. 762)
plebiscito *s.* voto directo mediante el cual la población de un país tiene la oportunidad de aceptar o rechazar una propuesta. (pág. 762)

PLO *n.* the Palestine Liberation Organization—dedicated to the establishment of an independent state for Palestinian Arabs and the elimination of Israel. (p. 1198)
OLP *s.* Organización de Liberación Palestina, dedicada a establecer un estado independiente para los árabes palestinos y a la eliminación de Israel. (pág. 1198)

polis [poh•lihs] *n.* a Greek city-state—the fundamental political unit of ancient Greece after about 750 BC. (p. 153)
polis *s.* ciudad-estado griega; unidad política fundamental de la Antigua Grecia después del año 750 a. C., aproximadamente. (pág. 153)

Politburo [PAHL•iht•byoor•oh] *n.* the ruling committee of the Communist Party in the Soviet Union. (p. 1235)
Politburó *s.* comité dirigente del Partido Comunista en la Unión Soviética. (pág. 1235)

political dissent *n.* the difference of opinion over political issues. (p. 1290)
disidencia política *s.* diferencia de opiniones sobre asuntos políticos. (pág. 1290)

polytheism [PAHL•ee•thee•IHZ•uhm] *n.* a belief in many gods. (p. 47)
politeísmo *s.* creencia en varios dioses. (pág. 47)

Pompeii *n.* Roman town that was buried in ash after the eruption of Mount Vesuvius and thereby preserved for thousands of years. (p. 230)
Pompeya *s.* ciudad romana que quedó sepultada bajo las cenizas luego de la erupción del monte Vesubio y, por lo tanto, se mantuvo intacta por miles de años. (pág. 230)

pope *n.* the bishop of Rome, head of the Roman Catholic Church. (p. 221)
papa *s.* obispo de Roma, cabeza de la Iglesia católica romana. (pág. 221)

***Popol Vuh* [POH•pohl VOO]** *n.* a book containing a version of the Mayan story of creation. (p. 512)
Popol Vuh *s.* libro que narra una versión de la historia maya de la creación. (pág. 512)

popular culture *n.* the cultural elements—sports, music, movies, clothing, and so forth—that reflect a group's common background and changing interests. (p. 1319)
cultura popular *s.* elementos culturales—deportes, música, cine, ropa, etc.—que muestran los antecedentes comunes de un grupo y sus intereses cambiantes. (pág. 1319)

potlatch [PAHT•lach] *n.* a ceremonial feast used to display rank and prosperity in some Northwest Coast tribes of Native Americans. (p. 503)
potlatch *s.* fiesta ceremonial celebrada para mostrar rango y prosperidad en varias tribus del Noroeste de Norteamérica. (pág. 503)

predestination [pree•dehs•tuh•NAY•shuhn] *n.* the doctrine that God has decided all things beforehand, including which people will be eternally saved. (p. 580)
predestinación *s.* doctrina que postula que Dios ha decidido todo de antemano, incluso quiénes obtendrán la salvación eterna. (pág.580)

Presbyterian [prehz·bih·TEER·ee·uhn] *n.* a member of a Protestant church governed by presbyters (elders) and founded on the teachings of John Knox. (p. 581)
presbiteriano *s.* miembro de una iglesia protestante gobernada por presbíteros conforme a las enseñanzas de John Knox. (pág. 581)

PRI *n.* the Institutional Revolutionary Party—the main political party of Mexico. (p. 1220)
PRI *s.* Partido Revolucionario Institucional: principal partido político en México. (pág. 1220)

proletariat [proh·lih·TAIR·ee·iht] *n.* in Marxist theory, the group of workers who would overthrow the czar and come to rule Russia. (p. 1003)
proletariado *s.* según la teoría marxista, el grupo de trabajadores que derrocaría al zar y gobernaría a Rusia. (pág. 1003)

proliferation [pruh·lihf·uh·RAY·shuhn] *n.* a growth or spread—especially the spread of nuclear weapons to nations that do not currently have them. (p. 1285)
proliferación *s.* crecimiento o expansión, especialmente la expansión de armas nucleares a naciones que actualmente no las tienen. (pág. 1285)

propaganda [prahp·uh·GAN·duh] *n.* information or material spread to advance a cause or to damage an opponent's cause. (p.989)
propaganda *s.* información o material distribuido para apoyar una causa o socavar una causa opuesta. (pág. 989)

protectorate *n.* a dependent territory granted some independence but usually accepting specified obligations. (p. 956)
protectorado *s.* un territorio dependiente otorgado con cierta independencia que generalmente acepta algunas obligaciones especificadas. (pág. 956)

Protestant [PRAHT·ih·stuhnt] *n.* a member of a Christian church founded on the principles of the Reformation. (p. 573)
protestante *s.* miembro de una iglesia cristiana fundada de acuerdo a los principios de la Reforma. (pág. 573)

provisional government *n.* a temporary government. (p. 1006)
gobierno provisional *s.* gobierno temporal. (pág. 1006)

psychology [sy·KAHL·uh·jee] *n.* the study of the human mind and human behavior. (p. 889)
psicología *s.* estudio de la mente y la conducta humanas. (pág. 889)

pueblo [PWEHB·loh] *n.* a village of large apartment-like buildings made of clay and stone, built by the Anasazi and later peoples of the American Southwest. (p. 505)
pueblos *s.* aldeas similares a complejos departamentales hechos de adobe, construidas por los anasazi y pueblos posteriores en el Suroeste de lo que hoy es Estados Unidos. (pág. 505)

Punic Wars *n.* a series of three wars between Rome and Carthage (264–146 BC); resulted in the destruction of Carthage and Rome's dominance over the western Mediterranean; "Punic" is an adjective that comes from the Latin word for Phoenician. (p. 198)
guerras púnicas *s.* serie de tres guerras entre Roma y Cartago (264–146 a. C.); el resultado fue la destrucción de Cartago y el domino de Roma sobre el Mediterráneo occidental; "púnico" es un adjetivo que proviene del término "fenicio" en latín. (pág. 198)

Puritans *n.* a group of people who sought freedom from religious persecution in England by founding a colony at Massachusetts Bay in the early 1600s. (p. 646)
puritanos *s.* grupo que, para liberarse de la persecución religiosa en Inglaterra, fundó una colonia en la bahía de Massachusetts a principios del siglo 17. (pág. 646)

push-pull factors *n.* conditions that draw people to another location (pull factors) or cause people to leave their homelands and migrate to another region (push factors). (p. 444)
factores de empuje y de atracción *s.* factores que hacen que la gente abandone sus hogares y emigre a otra región (factores de empuje); o factores que atraen a la gente a otros lugares (factores de atracción). (pág. 444)

pyramid [PIHR•uh•mihd] *n.* a massive structure with a rectangular base and four triangular sides, like those that were built in Egypt as burial places for Old Kingdom pharaohs. (p. 54)

pirámide *s.* estructura enorme con una base rectangular y cuatro lados triangulares, como las que se construyeron en Egipto como tumbas para los faraones del Reino Antiguo. (pág. 54)

Q

Qin Dynasty [chihn] *n.* a short-lived Chinese dynasty that replaced the Zhou Dynasty in the third century BC. (p. 141)

dinastía Qin *s.* dinastía china breve que reemplazó a la dinastía Zhou en el siglo III a. C. (pág. 141)

Qing Dynasty [chihng] *n.* China's last dynasty, which ruled from 1644 to 1912. (p. 623)

dinastía Qing *s.* última dinastía china; reinó de 1644 a 1912. (pág. 623)

Quetzalcoatl [keht•sahl•koh•AHT•uhl] *n.* "the Feathered Serpent"—a god of the Toltecs and other Mesoamerican peoples. (p. 517)

Quetzalcóatl *s.* serpiente emplumada: dios de los toltecas y otros pueblos de Mesoamérica. (pág. 517)

quipu [KEE•poo] *n.* an arrangement of knotted strings on a cord, used by the Inca to record numerical information. (p. 528)

quipu *s.* cuerda con nudos usadas para registrar información numérica por los incas. (pág. 528)

Qur'an [kuh•RAN] *n.* the holy book of Islam. (p. 276)

Corán *s.* libro sagrado del islam. (pág. 276)

R

racism [RAY•sihz•uhm] *n.* in the first half the belief that one race is superior to others. (p. 898)

racismo *s.* creencia de que una raza es superior a otras. (pág. 898)

radical *n.* in the first half of the 19th century, a European who favored drastic change to extend democracy to all people. (p. 789)

radicale *s.* en la primera mitad del siglo 19, el europeo a favor de cambios drásticos para extender la democracia a toda la población. (pág. 789)

radioactivity *n.* a form of energy released as atoms decay. (p. 889)

radioactividad *s.* forma de energía liberada mediante la descomposición de átomos. (pág. 889)

Raj [rahj] *n.* the British-controlled portions of India in the years 1757–1947. (p. 924)

Raj *s.* la autoridad británica despues que India estaba bajo el dominio del la Corona británica durante el reino de la reina Victoria. (pág. 924)

rationalism [RASH•nuh•lihz•uhm] *n.* a belief held by Enlightenment thinkers that truth could be discovered through reason or logical thinking. (p. 719)

racionalismo *s.* una creencia de los filósofos de la Ilustración que la verdad puede ser descubierta a través de la razón o el pensamiento lógico. (pág. 719)

rationing [RASH•uh•nihng] *n.* the limiting of the amounts of goods people can buy—often imposed by governments during wartime, when goods are in short supply. (p. 989)

racionamiento *s.* limitación de la cantidad de bienes que la población puede comprar, generalmente impuesta por un gobierno durante una guerra debido a escasez. (pág. 989)

realism *n.* a 19th-century artistic movement in which writers and painters sought to show life as it is rather than life as it should be. (p. 809)

realismo *s.* movimiento artístico del siglo 19 en que los escritores y pintores trataron de mostrar la vida como es, no como debiera ser. (pág. 809)

realpolitik [ray•AHL•poh•lih•teek] *n.* "the politics of reality"—the practice of tough power politics without room for idealism. (p. 802)

realpolitik *s.* "política de la realidad"; posición política dura que no da lugar al idealismo. (pág. 802)

recession *n.* a slowdown in a nation's economy. (p. 1056, 1216)

recesión *s.* descenso de la economía de una nación. (pág. 1056, 1216)

Red Guards *n.* militia units formed by young Chinese people in 1966 in response to Mao Zedong's call for a social and cultural revolution. (p. 1134)

Guardias Rojos *s.* unidades de milicianos formadas por jóvenes chinos en 1966 en respuesta al llamado de Mao Zedong a llevar a cabo una revolución social y cultural. (pág. 1134)

Reformation [rehf•uhr•MAY•shuhn] *n.* a 16th-century movement for religious reform, leading to the founding of Christian churches that rejected the pope's authority. (p. 572, 585)

Reforma *s.* movimiento del siglo 16 para realizar cambios religiosos que llevó a la fundación de iglesias cristianas que rechazaron la autoridad del Papa. (pág. 572, 585)

refugee *n.* a person who leaves his or her country to move to another to find safety. (p. 1285, 1293)

refugiado *s.* persona que sale de su país a otro país para buscar seguridad. (pág. 1285, 1293)

Reign of Terror [rayn] *n.* the period, from mid-1793 to mid-1794, when Maximilien Robespierre ruled France nearly as a dictator and thousands of political figures and ordinary citizens were executed. (p. 758)

Régimen del Terror *s.* período entre 1793–1794 en que Maximilien Robespierre gobernó a Francia casi como dictador, durante el cual fueron ejecutados miles de personajes políticos y de ciudadanos comunes. (pág. 758)

reincarnation [ree•ihn•kahr•NAY•shuhn] *n.* in Hinduism and Buddhism, the process by which a soul is reborn continuously until it achieves perfect understanding. (p. 90)

reencarnación *s.* para el hinduismo y el budismo, el proceso por el cual un alma renace continuamente hasta que alcanza el conocimiento perfecto. (pág. 90)

religious toleration *n.* a recognition of people's right to hold differing religious beliefs. (p. 244)

tolerancia religiosa *s.* reconocimiento del derecho que tienen las personas a profesar diversas creencias religiosas. (pág. 244)

Renaissance [rehn•ih•SAHNS] *n.* a period of European history, lasting from about 1300 to 1600, during which renewed interest in classical culture led to far-reaching changes in art, learning, and views of the world. (p. 538)

Renacimiento *s.* período de la historia europea de aproximadamente 1300 a 1600, durante el cual renació un interés en la cultura clásica que generó importantes cambios en el arte, la educación y la visión del mundo. (pág. 538)

republic *n.* a form of government in which power is in the hands of representatives and leaders are elected by citizens who have the right to vote. (p. 194)

república *s.* forma de gobierno en que el poder está en manos de representantes y líderes elegidos por los ciudadanos. (pág. 194)

Restoration [rehs•tuh•RAY•shuhn] *n.* the period of Charles II's rule over England, after the collapse of Oliver Cromwell's government. (p. 703)

Restauración *s.* en Inglaterra, período del reinado de Carlos II, después del colapso del gobierno de Oliver Cromwell. (pág. 703)

reunification [ree•yoo•nuh•fih•KAY•shuhn] *n.* a bringing together again of things that have been separated, like the reuniting of East Germany and West Germany in 1990. (p. 1246)

reunificación *s.* proceso de unir dos elementos que estaban separados, como la reunificación de Alemania oriental y Alemania occidental en 1990. (pág.1246)

romanticism [roh•MAN•tih•sihz•uhm] *n.* an early-19th-century movement in art and thought, which focused on emotion and nature rather than reason and society. (p. 806)

romanticismo *s.* movimiento de principios del siglo 19 en el arte y las ideas que recalca la emoción y la naturaleza, más que la razón y la sociedad. (pág. 806)

Roosevelt Corollary [ROH·zuh·vehlt KAWR·uh·lehr·ee] *n.* President Theodore Roosevelt's 1904 extension of the Monroe Doctrine, in which he declared that the United States had the right to exercise "police power" throughout the Western Hemisphere. (p. 939)
corolario Roosevelt *s.* ampliación de la doctrina Monroe, emitida por el presidente Theodore Roosevelt en 1904, en que declaró que Estados Unidos tenía el derecho de ejercer "poderes policiales" en el hemisferio occidental. (pág. 939)

Rowlatt Acts *n.* laws passed in 1919 that allowed the British government in India to jail anti-British protesters without trial for as long as two years. (p. 1163)
Leyes Rowlatt *s.* leyes, ratificadas en 1919, que los permitían al gobierno británico en India encarcelar a manifestantes por dos años sin juicio. (pág. 1163)

Royal Road *n.* a road in the Persian Empire, stretching over 1,600 miles from Susa in Persia to Sardis in Anatolia. (p. 134)
Camino Real *s.* ruta perteneciente al Imperio persa que se extendía por más de 1,600 millas, desde Susa, en Persia, hasta Sardis, en Anatolia. (pág. 134)

Russification [ruhs·uh·fih·KAY·shuhn] *n.* the process of forcing Russian culture on all ethnic groups in the Russian Empire. (p. 799)
rusificación *s.* proceso que obliga a todos los grupos étnicos a adoptar la cultura rusa en el imperio ruso. (pág. 799)

Russo-Japanese War *n.* a 1904–1905 conflict between Russia and Japan, sparked by the two countries' efforts to dominate Manchuria and Korea. (p. 956)
Guerra Ruso-Japonesa *s.* conflicto de 1904–1905 entre Rusia y Japón, causada por el interés de los dos países de dominar Manchuria y Corea. (pág. 956)

S

sacrament [SAK·ruh·muhnt] *n.* one of the Christian ceremonies in which God's grace is transmitted to people. (p. 393)
sacramento *s.* una de las ceremonias cristianas en que se trasmite la gracia de Dios a los creyentes. (pág. 393)

Safavid [suh·FAH·vihd] *n.* a member of a Shi'a Muslim dynasty that built an empire in Persia in the 16th–18th centuries. (p. 301)
safávido *s.* miembro de una dinastía musulmana shi'a que construyó un imperio en Persia del siglo 16 al 18. (pág. 301)

Sahara *n.* North African desert that stretches from the Atlantic Ocean east to the Red Sea and from the Mediterranean Sea south to the Sahel. (p. 434)
El Sahara *s.* Desierto del norte de África que se extiende desde el océano Atlántico al este del Mar Rojo, y desde el Mar Mediterráneo al sur de la región del Sahel. (pág. 434)

Sahel [suh·HAYL] *n.* the African region along the southern border of the Sahara. (p. 434)
Sahel *s.* región africana a lo largo de la frontera sur del Sahara. (pág. 434)

salon [suh·LAHN] *n.* a social gathering of intellectuals and artists, like those held in the homes of wealthy women in Paris and other European cities during the Enlightenment. (p. 725)
salón *s.* reunión social de intelectuales y artistas, como las que celebraban en sus hogares señoras acaudaladas de París y otras ciudades europeas durante la Ilustración. (pág. 725)

SALT *n.* the Strategic Arms Limitation Talks—a series of meetings in the 1970s, in which leaders of the United States and the Soviet Union agreed to limit their nations' stocks of nuclear weapons. (p. 1155, 1166)
SALT *s.* Conversaciones para la Limitación de Armas Estratégicas: serie de reuniones durante la década de 1970 en que líderes de Estados Unidos y la Unión Soviética acordaron limitar el número de armas nucleares de sus países. (pág. 1155, 1166)

Salt March *n.* a peaceful protest against the Salt Acts in 1930 in India in which Mohandas Gandhi led his followers on a 240-mile walk to the sea, where they made their own salt from evaporated seawater. (p. 1166)
Marcha de la Sal *s.* manifestación pacífica en 1930 en India ocasionada por las Leyes de la Sal; Mohandas Gandhi condujo a sus seguidores, caminando 240 millas al mar, donde hicieron su propia sal del agua de mar evaporada. (pág. 1166)

samurai [SAM•uh•ry] *n.* one of the professional warriors who served Japanese feudal lords. (p. 337)
samurai *s.* guerrero profesional que servía a los nobles en el Japón feudal. (pág. 337)

sans-culottes [sans•kyoo•LAHTS] *n.* in the French Revolution, a radical group made up of Parisian wage-earners and small shopkeepers who wanted a greater voice in government, lower prices, and an end to food shortages. (p. 755)
sans-culottes *s.* en la Revolución Francesa, grupo político radical de parisienses asalariados y pequeños comerciantes que anhelaban más voz en el gobierno, bajas de precios y fin a la escasez de alimentos. (pág. 755)

satrap [SAY•trap] *n.* a provincial governor of ancient Persia under Darius. (p. 134)
sátrapa *s.* gobernador provincial de la Antigua Persia durante el reinado de Darío. (pág. 134)

savanna [suh•VAN•uh] *n.* a flat, grassy plain. (p. 436)
sabana *s.* planicie con pastizales. (pág. 436)

Schlieffen Plan [SHLEE•fuhn] *n.* Germany's military plan at the outbreak of World War I, according to which German troops would rapidly defeat France and then move east to attack Russia. (p. 979)
Plan Schlieffen *s.* plan militar alemán al comienzo de la I Guerra Mundial, que preveía que Alemania derrotaría rápidamente a Francia y después atacaría a Rusia en el este. (pág. 979)

scholastics [skuh•LAS•tihks] *n.* scholars who gathered and taught at medieval European universities. (p. 415)
escolásticos *s.* académicos que se reunían y enseñaban en las universidades medievales de Europa. (pág. 415)

scientific method *n.* a logical procedure for gathering information about the natural world, in which experimentation and observation are used to test hypotheses. (p. 713)
método científico *s.* procedimiento lógico para reunir información sobre el mundo natural, en que se usa experimentación y observación para poner a prueba hipótesis. (pág. 713)

Scientific Revolution *n.* a major change in European thought, starting in the mid-1500s, in which the study of the natural world began to be characterized by careful observation and the questioning of accepted beliefs. (p. 711)
Revolución Científica *s.* profundo cambio en el pensamiento europeo que comenzó a mediados del siglo 16, en que el estudio del mundo natural se caracterizó por cuidadosa observación y cuestionamiento de teorías aceptadas. (pág. 711)

scorched-earth policy *n.* the practice of burning crops and killing livestock during wartime so that the enemy cannot live off the land. (p. 768)
política de arrasamiento de campos *s.* práctica de quemar campos de cultivo y de matar ganado durante la guerra para que el enemigo no pueda vivir de las tierras. (pág. 768)

scribe *n.* one of the professional record keepers in early civilizations. (p. 40)
escriba *s.* uno de los profesionales encargados de registrar información por escrito en las primeras civilizaciones. (pág. 40)

secede [sih•SEED] *v.* to withdraw formally from an association or alliance. (p. 878)
seceder *v.* retirarse formalmente de una asociación o alianza. (pág. 878)

secular [SEHK•yuh•luhr] *adj.* concerned with worldly rather than spiritual matters. (p. 370, 543)
secular *adj.* relacionado con lo mundano más que con los asuntos espirituales. (pág. 370, 543)

segregation [sehg•rih•GAY•shuhn] *n.* the legal or social separation of people of different races. (p. 879)
segregación *s.* separación legal o social de gente de diferentes razas. (pág. 879)

English and Spanish Glossary

self-determination [sehlf·dih·tur·muh· NAY·shuhn] *n.* the freedom of a people to decide under what form of government they wish to live. (p. 993)
autodeterminación *s.* libertad de un pueblo para decidir libremente la forma de gobierno que desea. (pág. 993)

senate *n.* in ancient Rome, the supreme governing body, originally made up only of aristocrats. (p. 196)
senado *s.* en la antigua Roma, organismo supremo de gobierno formado inicialmente sólo por aristócratas. (pág. 196)

sepoy [SEE·poy] *n.* an Indian soldier serving under British command. (p. 920)
cipayo *s.* soldado hindú bajo el mando británico. (pág. 920)

Sepoy Mutiny [MYOOT·uh·nee] *n.* an 1857 rebellion of Hindu and Muslim soldiers against the British in India. (p. 923)
Motín de Cipayos *s.* rebelión de 1857 de soldados hindúes y musulmanes contra los británicos en India. (pág. 923)

serf *n.* a medieval peasant legally bound to live on a lord's estate. (p. 377)
siervo *s.* campesino medieval legalmente obligado a vivir en los dominios de un señor. (pág. 377)

Seven Years' War *n.* a conflict in Europe, North America, and India, lasting from 1756 to 1763, in which the forces of Britain and Prussia battled those of Austria, France, Russia, and other countries. (p. 691)
Guerra de los Siete Años *s.* conflicto en Europa, Norteamérica e India de 1756 a 1763, en que las fuerzas de Inglaterra y Prusia lucharon con las de Austria, Francia, Rusia y otros países. (pág. 691)

shah [shah] *n.* hereditary monarch of Iran. (p. 303, 304)
sha *s.* monarca hereditario de Irán. (pág. 303, 304)

shari'a [shah·REE·ah] *n.* a body of law governing the lives of Muslims. (p. 276)
shari'a *s.* conjunto de leyes que rigen la vida de los musulmanes. (pág. 276)

Shi'a [SHEE·uh] *n.* the branch of Islam whose members acknowledge Ali and his descendants as the rightful successors of Muhammad. (p. 281)
shi'a *s.* rama del islam que reconoce a los primeros cuatro califas como legítimos sucesores de Mahoma. (pág. 281)

Shinto [SHIHN·toh] *n.* the native religion of Japan. (p. 335)
shintoísmo *s.* religión oriunda de Japón. (pág. 335)

Shiva [shee·vuh] *n.* a Hindu god considered the destroyer of the world. (p. 249)
Shiva *s.* dios hindú que es considerado el destructor del mundo. (pág. 249)

"shock therapy" *n.* an economic program implemented in Russia by Boris Yeltsin in the 1990s, involving an abrupt shift from a command economy to a free-market economy. (p. 1240)
terapia de shock *s.* programa económico implementado en Rusia por Boris Yeltsin en la década de 1990, que implicó un cambio abrupto de una economía de mando a una economía de Mercado libre. (pág. 1240)

shogun [SHOH·guhn] *n.* in feudal Japan, a supreme military commander who ruled in the name of the emperor. (p. 339)
shogún *s.* en el Japón feudal, jefe militar supremo que regía en nombre del emperador. (pág. 339)

Sikh [seek] *n.* a member of a nonviolent religious group whose beliefs blend elements of Buddhism, Hinduism, and Sufism. (p. 602)
sikh *s.* miembro de un grupo religioso no violento cuyas creencias combinaban elementos del budismo, el hinduismo y el sufismo. (pág. 602)

Silla Dynasty [SHIL·uh] *n.* a dynasty that unified Korea and ruled from AD 668 to 935. (p. 332)
Dinastía Silla *s.* una dinastía que unificó Corea y gobernó desde 668-935 d. C. (pág. 332)

simony [SY·muh·nee] *n.* the selling or buying of a position in a Christian church. (p. 398)
simonía *s.* venta o compra de una posición en una iglesia cristiana. (pág. 398)

sistrum [SIS·truhm] *n.* a hand-held percussion instrument, usually of metal, that includes a frame with rods or loops attached to it. (p. 453)
sistro *s.* un instrumento de percusión de mano, por lo general de metal, que incluye un marco con varillas o aros conectados a él. (pág. 453)

skepticism [SKEHP·tih·sihz·uhm] *n.* a philosophy based on the idea that nothing can be known for certain. (p. 565, 677)
escepticismo *s.* filosofía basada en la noción de que nada puede saberse con certeza. (pág. 565, 677)

slash-and-burn farming *n.* a farming method in which people clear fields by cutting and burning trees and grasses, the ashes of which serve to fertilize the soil. (p. 24)
agricultura de tala y quema *s.* método agrícola de desbrozar terrenos talando y quemando árboles y pastos, cuyas cenizas sirven como fertilizante. (pág. 24)

Slavs [slahvz] *n.* a people from the forests north of the Black Sea, ancestors of many peoples in Eastern Europe today. (p. 357)
eslavos *s.* pueblo de los bosques al norte del mar Negro, origen de muchos pueblos de la Europa oriental de nuestros días. (pág. 357)

social contract *n.* the agreement by which people define and limit their individual rights, thus creating an organized society or government. (p. 718)
contrato social *s.* acuerdo mediante el cual el pueblo define y limita sus derechos individuales, creando así una sociedad o gobierno organizados. (pág. 718)

Social Darwinism [DAHR·wih·nihz·uhm] *n.* the application of Charles Darwin's ideas about evolution and "survival of the fittest" to human societies—particularly as justification for imperialist expansion. (p. 898)
darvinismo social *s.* aplicación de las teorías de Charles Darwin sobre la evolución y la "sobrevivencia del más apto" a las sociedades humanas, particularmente como justificación para la expansión imperialista. (pág. 898)

socialism *n.* an economic system in which the factors of production are owned by the public and operate for the welfare of all. (p. 846)

socialismo *s.* sistema económico en el cual los factores de producción son propiedad del pueblo y se administran para el bienestar de todos. (pág. 846)

Solidarity [sahl·ih·DAR·ih·tee] *n.* a Polish labor union that during the 1980s became the main force of opposition to Communist rule in Poland. (p. 1243)
Solidaridad *s.* sindicato polaco de trabajadores que presentó la principal fuerza de oposición al gobierno comunista en Polonia en la década de 1980. (pág. 1243)

Songhai [SAWNG·hy] *n.* a West African empire that conquered Mali and controlled trade from the 1400s to 1591. (p. 465)
Songhai *s.* imperio de África occidental que conquistó Malí y controló el comercio desde el siglo 15 hasta 1591. (pág. 465)

soviet [SOH·vee·eht] *n.* one of the local representative councils formed in Russia after the downfall of Czar Nicholas II. (p. 1006)
soviet *s.* consejo local de representantes formado en Rusia después de la caída del zar Nicolás II. (pág. 1006)

Spanish-American War *n.* an 1898 conflict between the United States and Spain, in which the United States supported Cubans' fight for independence. (p. 935)
Guerra Hispano-Americana *s.* conflicto de 1898 entre Estados Unidos y España, en que Estados Unidos apoyó la lucha de independencia cubana. (pág. 935)

specialization *n.* an economic concept that refers to separating tasks in which people in a factory or company work at one kind of job and learn to do it well. (p. 39, 838)
especialización *s.* un concepto económico que se refiere a la separación de tareas en que las personas en una fábrica o empresa trabajan en un tipo de trabajo y aprenden a hacerlo bien. (pág. 39, 838)

sphere of influence *n.* a foreign region in which a nation has control over trade and other economic activities. (p. 949)
esfera de influencia *s.* concepto económico que hace referencia a la separación de tareas y según el cual las personas que trabajan en una fábrica o una empresa realizan un solo tipo de trabajo y aprenden a hacerlo bien. (pág. 949)

English and Spanish Glossary

standard of living *n.* the quality of life of a person or a population, as indicated by the goods, services, and luxuries available to the person or people. (p. 1216)
  nivel de vida *s.* calidad de la vida de una persona o población que se mide conforme a los bienes, servicios y lujos que tiene a su disposición. (pág. 1216)

stateless society *n.* cultural group in which authority is shared by lineages of equal power instead of being exercised by a central government. (p. 438)
  sociedades sin Estado *s.* grupos culturales en los que la autoridad es compartida por linajes de igual poder, en vez de ser ejercida por un gobierno central. (pág. 438)

steppes [stehps] *n.* dry, grass-covered plains. (p. 82)
  estepas *s.* llanuras secas cubiertas de hierba. (pág. 82)

stock *n.* certain rights of ownership of a corporation. (p. 839)
  acciones *s.* ciertos derechos de propiedad de una corporación. (pág. 839)

strike *v.* to refuse to work in order to force an employer to meet certain demands. (p. 852)
  huelga *s.* paro de trabajo para obligar al patrón a acceder a ciertas demandas. (pág.852)

stupa [STOO-puh] *n.* mounded stone structures built over Buddhist holy relics. (p. 249)
  estupas *s.* estructuras de piedra con forma de montículo construidas sobre reliquias sagradas budistas. (pág. 249)

subcontinent *n.* a large landmass that forms a distinct part of a continent. (p. 62)
  subcontinente *s.* gran masa de tierra que ocupa un lugar bien diferenciado dentro de un continente. (pág. 62)

Suez Canal [soo•EHZ] *n.* a human-made waterway, which was opened in 1869, connecting the Red Sea and the Mediterranean Sea. (p. 917)
  canal de Suez *s.* canal marítimo que une al mar Rojo y al golfo de Suez con el mar Mediterráneo, cuya construcción terminó en 1869. (pág. 917)

suffrage [SUHF•rihj] *n.* the right to vote. (p. 860)
  sufragio *s.* derecho al voto. (pág. 860)

Sufi [SOO•fee] *n.* a Muslim who seeks to achieve direct contact with God through mystical means. (p. 281)
  sufí *s.* musulmán que busca contacto directo con Dios por medio del misticismo. (pág. 281)

sultan *n.* "overlord," or "one with power"; title for Ottoman rulers during the rise of the Ottoman Empire. (p. 294)
  sultán *s.* "jefe supremo" o "el que tiene poder"; título de los gobernantes otomanos durante el auge del imperio otomano. (pág. 294)

Sunna [SOON•uh] *n.* an Islamic model for living, based on the life and teachings of Muhammad. (p. 276)
  sunna *s.* modelo islámico de vida que se basa en las enseñanzas y vida de Mahoma. (pág. 276)

Sunni [SOON•ee] *n.* the branch of Islam whose members acknowledge the first four caliphs as the rightful successors of Muhammad. (p. 281)
  sunni *s.* rama del islam que reconoce a Alí y a sus descendientes como sucesores legítimos de Mahoma. (pág. 281)

supranational union *n.* an organization that stretches across national boundaries, such as the European Union. (p. 1284)
  supranacionalidad *s.* una organización que se extiende a través de las fronteras nacionales, como la Unión Europea. (pág. 1284)

surrealism [suh•REE•uh•lihz•uhm] *n.* a 20th-century artistic movement that focuses on the workings of the unconscious mind. (p. 1042)
  surrealismo *s.* movimiento artístico del siglo 20 que se concentra en el inconsciente. (pág. 1042)

sustainable development *n.* the process of creating economic growth while preserving the environment. (p. 1283)
  desarrollo sostenible *s.* el proceso de crear crecimiento económico, preservando el medio ambiente. (pág. 1283)

Swahili [swah•HEE•lee] *n.* an Arabic-influenced Bantu language that is spoken widely in eastern and central Africa. (p. 472)
  suahili *s.* lengua bantú con influencias árabes que se usa en África oriental y central. (pág. 472)

T

Taiping Rebellion [ty•pihng] *n.* a mid-19th century rebellion against the Qing Dynasty in China, led by Hong Xiuquan. (p. 946)
Rebelión Taiping *s.* rebelión a media-dos del siglo 19 contra la dinastía Qing en China, encabezada por Hong Xiuquan. (pág. 946)

Taj Mahal [tahzh muh•HAHL] *n.* a beautiful tomb in Agra, India, built by the Mughal emperor Shah Jahan for his wife Mumtaz Mahal. (p. 603)
Taj Mahal *s.* bella tumba en Agra, India, construida por el emperador mogol Shah Jahan para su esposa Mumtaz Mahal. (pág. 603)

Taliban *n.* conservative Islamic group that took control of Afghanistan after the Soviet Union withdrew its troops; driven from power by U.S. forces in December 2001 because of its harboring of suspected terrorists. (p. 1207)
Talibán *s.* grupo musulmán conservador que tomó el poder en Afganistán después de que la Unión Soviética retiró sus tropas; expulsado por el ejército estadounidense en diciembre de 2001 por darles amparo a sospechosos de terrorismo. (pág. 1207)

Tamil [TAM•uhl] *n.* a language of southern India; also, the people who speak that language. (p. 244)
tamil *s.* lengua del sur de la India; también, pueblo que habla esa lengua. (pág. 244)

technology [tek•NAH•loh•gee] *n.* ways of applying knowledge, tools, and inventions to meet people's needs. (p. 15)
tecnología *s.* distintas maneras de utilizar conocimientos, herramientas e inventos para satisfacer las necesidades de las personas. (pág. 15)

telegraph *n.* a machine that sent messages instantly over wires. (p. 882)
telégrafo *s.* una máquina que envió mensajes al instante a través de cables. (pág. 882)

Tennis Court Oath *n.* a pledge made by the members of France's National Assembly in 1789, in which they vowed to continue meeting until they had drawn up a new constitution. (p. 750)
Juramento de la Cancha de Tenis *s.* promesa hecha por los miembros de la Asamblea Nacional de Francia en 1789 de permanecer reunidos hasta que elaboraran una nueva constitución. (pág.750)

terraces *n.* a new form of agriculture in Aksum, in which stepped ridges constructed on mountain slopes help retain water and reduce erosion. (p.454)
cultivos en andenes/cultivos en terrazas *s.* en Aksum, una técnica nueva para cultivar la tierra, utilizando campos horizontales a manera de peldaños, cortados en laderas o pendientes de montañas, para retener agua y reducir la erosión. (pág. 454)

terrorism *n.* the use of force or threats to frighten people or governments to change their policies. (p. 1295)
terrorismo *s.* uso de la fuerza o de amenazas para presionar a personas o gobiernos a que cambien sus políticas. (pág. 1295)

theocracy [thee•AHK•ruh•see] *n.* a government controlled by religious leaders. (p. 54, 580)
teocracia *s.* gobierno controlado por líderes religiosos. (pág. 54, 580)

theory of evolution *n.* the idea, proposed by Charles Darwin in 1859, that species of plants and animals arise by means of a process of natural selection. (p. 888)
teoría de la evolución *s.* concepto propuesto por Charles Darwin en 1859 de que las especies de plantas y animales surgen debido a un proceso de selección natural. (pág. 888)

theory of relativity [rehl•uh•TIHV•ih•tee] *n.* Albert Einstein's ideas about the interrelationships between time and space and between energy and matter. (p. 1039)
teoría de la relatividad *s.* ideas de Albert Einstein acerca de la interrelación entre el tiempo y el espacio, y entre la energía y la materia. (pág. 1039)

Theravada [thehr•uh•VAH•duh] *n.* a sect of Buddhism focusing on the strict spiritual discipline originally advocated by the Buddha. (p. 249)
theravada *s.* secta budista que se enfoca en la estricta disciplina espiritual que originalmente predicaba Buda. (pág. 249)

Third Reich [ryk] *n.* the Third German Empire, established by Adolf Hitler in the 1930s. (p. 1072)
Tercer Reich *s.* Tercer Imperio Alemán establecido por Adolfo Hitler en la década de 1930. (pág. 1072)

Third Republic *n.* the republic that was established in France after the downfall of Napoleon III and ended with the German occupation of France during World War II. (p. 864)
Tercera República *s.* república establecida en Francia después de la caída de Napoleón III; acabó con la ocupación alemana de Francia durante la II Guerra Mundial. (pág. 864)

Third World *n.* during the Cold War, the developing nations not allied with either the United States or the Soviet Union. (p. 1144)
Tercer Mundo *s.* durante la Guerra Fría, naciones que no se aliaron ni con Estados Unidos ni con la Unión Soviética. (pág. 1144)

38th parallel *n.* a line of latitude that crosses Korea. When World War II ended, Korea was divided into two nations at this line. North of the parallel a communist government was installed; south of the parallel, a non-communist government. (p. 1136)
paralelo 38 *s.* una línea de latitud que atraviesa Corea. Cuando terminó la Segunda Guerra Mundial, Corea fue dividida en dos naciones en esta línea. Se instaló un gobierno comunista al Norte del paralelo; y al sur del paralelo, un gobierno no comunista. (pág. 1136)

Thirty Years' War *n.* a European conflict over religion and territory and for power among ruling families, lasting from 1618 to 1648. (p. 686)
Guerra de los Treinta Años *s.* conflicto europeo de 1618 a 1648 por cuestiones religiosas, territoriales y de poder entre familias reinantes. (pág. 686)

three-field system *n.* a system of farming developed in medieval Europe, in which farmland was divided into three fields of equal size and each of these was successively planted with a winter crop, planted with a spring crop, and left unplanted. (p. 409)

sistema de tres campos *s.* sistema agrícola de la Europa medieval en que las tierras de cultivo se dividían en tres campos de igual tamaño y cada uno se sembraba sucesivamente con un cultivo de invierno, un cultivo de primavera y el tercero se dejaba sin cultivar. (pág. 409)

Tiananmen Square [tyahn·ahn·mehn] *n.* a huge public space in Beijing, China; in 1989, the site of a student uprising in support of democratic reforms. (p. 1255)
Plaza Tiananmen *s.* plaza pública en Beijing, China; sede en 1989 de un enorme levantamiento estudiantil en favor de reformas democráticas. (pág. 1255)

Tikal *n.* a major center in present-day northern Guatemala that was once home to the Maya civilization. (p. 509)
Tikal *s.* un centro importante en el territorio actual del norte de Guatemala que una vez fue el hogar de la civilización maya. (pág. 509)

tithe [tyth] *n.* a family's payment of one-tenth of its income to a church. (p. 378)
diezmo *s.* pago de una familia a la Iglesia de la décima parte de sus ingresos. (pág. 378)

Tokugawa Shogunate [toh·koo·GAH·wah SHOH·guh·niht] *n.* a dynasty of shoguns that ruled a unified Japan from 1603 to 1867. (p. 628)
shogunato Tokugawa *s.* dinastía de shogúns que gobernó un Japón unificado de 1603 a 1867. (pág.628)

Torah [TAWR·uh] *n.* the first five books of the Hebrew Bible—the most sacred writings in the Jewish tradition. (p. 105)
Torah *s.* cinco primeros libros de la Biblia hebrea, los más sagrados de la tradición judía. (pág. 105)

totalitarianism [toh·tal·ih·TAIR·ee·uh·nihz·uhm] *n.* government control over every aspect of public and private life. (p. 1012)
totalitarismo *s.* gobierno que controla todo aspecto de la vida pública y privada. (pág. 1012)

total war *n.* a conflict in which the participating countries devote all their resources to the war effort. (p. 989)
guerra total *s.* conflicto en el que los países participantes dedican todos sus recursos a la guerra. (pág. 989)

totem [TOH·tuhm] *n.* an animal or other natural object that serves as a symbol of the unity of clans or other groups of people. (p. 508)
tóteme *s.* la animale u otro objeto natural que sirven de símbolo de unidad de clanes u otros grupos. (pág. 508)

tournament *n.* a mock battle between groups of knights. (p. 383)
torneo *s.* justa deportiva entre grupos de caballeros. (pág. 383)

tragedy *n.* a serious form of drama dealing with the downfall of a heroic or noble character. (p. 171)
tragedia *s.* género teatral serio que trata sobre la caída en desgracia de un personaje heroico o noble. (pág. 171)

Transcaucasian Republics *n.* three nations (Armenia, Azerbaijan, and Georgia) in the Caucasus Mountains between the Black and Caspian seas. (p. 1204)
Repúblicas transcaucasias *s.* tres naciones (Armenia, Azerbaiyán y Georgia) en las montañas del Cáucaso entre los mares Negro y Caspio. (pág. 1204)

Treaty of Kanagawa [kah·NAH·gah·wah] *n.* an 1854 agreement between the United States and Japan, which opened two Japanese ports to U.S. ships and allowed the United States to set up an embassy in Japan. (p. 953)
Tratado de Kanagawa *s.* acuerdo de 1854 entre Estados Unidos y Japón, que abrió dos puertos japoneses a los barcos de Estados Unidos y le permitió abrir una embajada en Japón. (pág. 953)

Treaty of Tordesillas [tawr·day·SEEL·yahs] *n.* a 1494 agreement between Portugal and Spain, declaring that newly discovered lands to the west of an imaginary line in the Atlantic Ocean would belong to Spain and newly discovered lands to the east of the line would belong to Portugal. (p. 613)
Tratado de Tordesillas *s.* acuerdo de 1494 entre Portugal y España que estableció que las tierras descubiertas al oeste de una línea imaginaria en el océano Atlántico pertenecerían a España y las tierras al este pertenecerían a Portugal. (pág. 613)

Treaty of Versailles [vuhr·SY] *n.* the peace treaty signed by Germany and the Allied powers after World War I. (p. 994)

Tratado de Versalles *s.* acuerdo de paz firmado por Alemania y los Aliados después de la I Guerra Mundial. (pág. 994)

trench warfare *n.* a form of warfare in which opposing armies fight each other from trenches dug in the battlefield. (p. 980)
guerra de trincheras *s.* forma de guerra en la que dos ejércitos contrincantes luchan detrás de trincheras cavadas en el campo de batalla. (pág. 980)

triangular trade *n.* the transatlantic trading network along which slaves and other goods were carried between Africa, England, Europe, the West Indies, and the colonies in the Americas. (p. 654)
triángulo comercial *s.* red comercial trasatlántica que transportaba esclavos y productos entre África, Inglaterra, Europa continental, el Caribe y las colonias de Norteamérica. (pág. 654)

tribune [TRIHB·yoon] *n.* in ancient Rome, an official elected by the plebeians to protect their rights. (p. 194)
tribuno *s.* en la Antigua Roma, funcionario elegido por los plebeyos para proteger sus derechos. (pág. 194)

tribute *n.* a payment made by a weaker power to a stronger power to obtain an assurance of peace and security. (p. 113)
tributo *s.* pago que un poder más débil realizaba a un poder mayor a fin de garantizar la paz y seguridad. (pág. 113)

Triple Alliance *n.* 1. an association of the city-states of Tenochtitlán, Texcoco, and Tlacopan, which led to the formation of the Aztec Empire. (p. 289) 2. a military alliance between Germany, Austria-Hungary, and Italy in the years preceding World War I. (p. 519, 974)
Triple Alianza *s.* 1. asociación de las ciudades Estado de Tenochtitlan, Texcoco y Tlacopan, que dio origen al imperio azteca (pág. 289). 2. alianza military establecida entre Alemania, Austro-Hungría e Italia antes de la I Guerra Mundial. (pág. 519, 974)

Triple Entente [ahn·TAHNT] *n.* a military alliance between Great Britain, France, and Russia in the years preceding World War I. (p. 974)
Triple Entente *s.* alianza militar entre Gran Bretaña, Francia y Rusia establecida antes de la I Guerra Mundial. (pág. 974)

English and Spanish Glossary

triumvirate [try·UHM·vuhr·iht] *n.* in ancient Rome, a group of three leaders sharing control of the government. (p. 201)
triunvirato *s.* en la Antigua Roma, grupo de tres líderes que compartían el control del gobierno. (pág. 201)

Trojan War *n.* a war, fought during the 1200s BC, in which the Mycenaeans attacked the independent trading city of Troy in Anatolia. (p. 150)
Guerra de Troya *s.* guerra que se libró durante el siglo XIII a. C., en la que los micénicos atacaron la ciudad independiente de Troya, dedicada al comercio y ubicada en Anatolia. (pág. 150)

troubadour [TROO·buh·dawr] *n.* a medieval poet and musician who traveled from place to place, entertaining people with songs of courtly love. (p. 385)
trovador *s.* poeta y músico medieval que viajaba de un lugar a otro para divertir con sus cantos de amor cortesano. (pág. 385)

Truman Doctrine *n.* announced by President Harry Truman in 1947, a U.S. policy of giving economic and military aid to free nations threatened by internal or external opponents. (p. 1125)
Doctrina Truman *s.* política estadounidense de dar ayuda económica y militar a las naciones libres amenazadas por oponentes internos o externos, anunciada por el presidente Harry Truman en 1947. (pág. 1125)

tyrant [TY·ruhnt] *n.* in ancient Greece, a powerful individual who gained control of a city-state's government by appealing to the poor for support. (p. 154)
tirano *s.* en la Antigua Grecia, persona poderosa que obtenía el control del gobierno de una ciudad-estado apelando al apoyo de los sectores más pobres. (pág. 154)

U

U.S. Civil War *n.* a conflict between Northern and Southern states of the United States over the issue of slavery, lasting from 1861 to 1865. (p. 878)
Guerra Civil de E.U.A. *s.* conflicto entre los estados del Norte y el Sur de Estados Unidos desde 1861 a 1865, sobre el asunto de la esclavitud. (pág. 878)

U.S.A. Patriot Act *n.* an antiterrorism bill of 2001 that strengthened governmental rights to detain foreigners suspected of terrorism and prosecute terrorist crimes. (p. 1302)
Ley Patriota de E.U.A. *s.* proyecto de ley antiterrorista de 2001 que hizo más fuerte los derechos gubernamentales para detener a extranjeros sospechosos de terrorismo y para procesar crímenes terroristas. (pág. 1302)

Umayyads [oo·MY·adz] *n.* a dynasty that ruled the Muslim Empire from AD 661 to 750 and later established a kingdom in al-Andalus. (p. 281)
omeyas *s.* dinastía que gobernó el imperio musulmán del 661 al 750 d.C. y después estableció un reino en al-Andalus. (pág. 281)

union *n.* an association of workers, formed to bargain for better working conditions and higher wages. (p. 852)
sindicato *s.* asociación de trabajadores formada para negociar mejores salarios y condiciones de trabajo. (pág. 852)

United Nations *n.* an international peacekeeping organization founded in 1945 to provide security to the nations of the world. (p. 1122)
Organización de las Naciones Unidas (ONU) *s.* organización internacional fundada en 1945 con el propósito de ofrecer seguridad a las naciones del mundo. (pág. 1122)

Universal Declaration of Human Rights *n.* a 1948 statement in which the United Nations declared that all human beings have rights to life, liberty, and security. (p. 1288)
Declaración Universal de Derechos Humanos *s.* declaración en que la ONU proclamó en 1948 que todos los seres humanos tienen derecho a la vida, la libertad y la seguridad. (pág. 1288)

unrestricted submarine warfare *n.* the use of submarines to sink without warning any ship (including neutral ships and unarmed passenger liners) found in an enemy's waters. (p. 987)
guerra submarina irrestricta *s.* uso de submarinos para hundir sin alerta previa cualquier barco (incluso barcos neutrales y de pasajeros sin armamento) que se encuentre en aguas enemigas. (pág. 987)

urbanization [ur·buh·nih·ZAY·shuhn] *n.* the growth of cities and the migration of people into them. (p. 826)

urbanización *s.* crecimiento de ciudades y migración hacia ellas. (pág. 826)

utilitarianism [yoo•tihl•ih•TAIR•ee•uh•nihz •uhm] *n.* the theory, proposed by Jeremy Bentham in the late 1700s, that government actions are useful only if they promote the greatest good for the greatest number of people. (p. 846)
utilitarismo *s.* teoría, propuesta por Jeremy Bentham a fines del siglo 18, de que las acciones del gobierno sólo son útiles si promueven el mayor bien para el mayor número de personas. (pág. 846)

utopia [yoo•TOH•pee•uh] *n.* an imaginary land described by Thomas More in his book *Utopia*—hence, an ideal place. (p. 556)
utopía *s.* tierra imaginaria descrita por Tomás Moro en su libro del mismo nombre; lugar ideal. (pág. 556)

V

vassal [VAS•uhl] *n.* in feudal Europe, a person who received a grant of land from a lord in exchange for a pledge of loyalty and services. (p. 376)
vasallo *s.* en la Europa feudal, persona que recibía un dominio (tierras) de un señor a cambio de su promesa de lealtad y servicios. (pág. 376)

Vedas [VAY•duhz] *n.* four collections of sacred writings produced by the Aryans during an early stage of their settlement in India. (p. 84)
Vedas *s.* las cuatro colecciones de textos sagrados producidos por los arios durante la primera etapa de asentamiento en la India. (pág. 84)

vernacular [vuhr•NAK•yuh•luhr] *n.* the everyday language of people in a region or country. (p.414, 563)
vernacular *s.* lenguaje común y corriente de la gente de una región o país. (págs. 414, 563)

Vietcong [vee•eht•KAHNG] *n.* a group of Communist guerrillas who, with the help of North Vietnam, fought against the South Vietnamese government in the Vietnam War. (p. 1139)
Vietcong *s.* grupo de guerrilleros comunistas que, con la ayuda de Vietnam del Norte, pelearon contra el gobierno de Vietnam del Sur durante la Guerra de Vietnam. (pág. 1139)

Vietnamization [vee•eht•nuh•mih•ZAY•shuhn] *n.* President Richard Nixon's strategy for ending U.S. involvement in the Vietnam War, involving a gradual withdrawal of American troops and replacement of them with South Vietnamese forces. (p. 1142)
vietnamización *s.* estrategia del presidente de E.U.A. Richard Nixon para terminar con la participación en la Guerra de Vietnam, mediante el retiro gradual de tropas estadounidenses y su reemplazo con fuerzas survietnamitas. (pág. 1142)

villa *n.* a country home owned by wealthy Roman citizens. (p. 208)
villa *s.* vivienda rural que poseían los ciudadanos adinerados de Roma. (pág. 208)

Vishnu [VIHSH•noo] *n.* a Hindu god considered the preserver of the world. (p. 249)
Visnú *s.* dios hindú considerado el preservador del mundo. (pág. 249)

W

War of the Spanish Succession *n.* a conflict, lasting from 1701 to 1713, in which a number of European states fought to prevent the Bourbon family from controlling Spain as well as France. (p. 683)
Guerra de Sucesión Española *s.* conflicto de 1701 a 1713 en que varios Estados europeos lucharon para impedir que la familia Borbón controlara a España, como a Francia. (pág. 683)

Warsaw Pact *n.* a military alliance formed in 1955 by the Soviet Union and seven Eastern European countries. (p. 1127)
Pacto de Varsovia *s.* alianza militar formada en 1955 por la Unión Soviética y siete países de Europa oriental. (pág. 1127)

Waterloo *n.* village in Belgium where European forces defeated Napoleon in 1815. (p. 770)
Waterloo *s.* pueblo en Bélgica donde las fuerzas europeas derrotaron a Napoleón en 1815. (pág. 770)

Weimar Republic [WY•mahr] *n.* the republic that was established in Germany in 1919 and ended in 1933. (p. 1049)
República de Weimar *s.* república establecida en Alemania en 1919 que acabó en 1933. (pág. 1049)

English and Spanish Glossary

Western Front *n.* in World War I, the region of northern France where the forces of the Allies and the Central Powers battled each other. (p. 979)

Frente Occidental *s.* en la I Guerra Mundial, región del norte de Francia donde peleaban las fuerzas de los Aliados y de las Potencias Centrales. (pág. 979)

westernization *n.* an adoption of the social, political, or economic institutions of Western—especially European or American—countries. (p. 695)

occidentalización *s.* adopción de las instituciones sociales, políticas o económicas del Occidente, especialmente de Europa o Estados Unidos. (pág. 695)

X Y Z

yin and yang *n.* In Chinese thought, the two powers that govern the natural rhythms of life. (p. 141)

yin y yang *s.* según el pensamiento chino, los dos poderes que gobiernan los ritmos naturales de la vida. (pág. 141)

Yoruba [YAWR•uh•buh] *n.* a West African people who formed several kingdoms in what is now Benin and southern Nigeria. (p. 468)

yoruba *s.* pueblo del África occidental que formó varios reinos en lo que hoy es Benin y el sur de Nigeria. (pág. 468)

Zapotec [zah•puh•TEHK] *n.* an early Mesoamerican civilization that was centered in the Oaxaca Valley of what is now Mexico. (p. 493)

zapoteca *s.* civilización mesoamericana centrada en el valle de Oaxaca de lo que hoy es México. (pág. 493)

ziggurat [ZIHG•uh•RAT] *n.* a temple, which literally means "mountain of god." (p. 42)

zigurat *s.* un tipo de templo; literalmente, significa "montaña de dios". (pág. 42)

Zionism [ZY•uh•nihz•uhm] *n.* a movement founded in the 1890s to promote Jewish self-determination and the establishment of a Jewish state in the ancient Jewish homeland. (p. 865)

sionismo *s.* movimiento fundado en la década de 1890 para promover la autodeterminación judía y el establecimiento de un estadso judío en la antigua patria judía. (pág. 865)

Index

Index

English in, 645–647
European claims to, 644–645
European exploration of, m636
European settlement of, 644–650
European struggles over colonization of, 647–648, m648
in Ice Age, 485
land bridge to Asia, 485
Native American response to colonization, 649–650
slavery in, 653, 656
North American Free Trade Agreement (NAFTA), 1222, 1277
North American societies, 503–508
characteristics of, 503–506
cultural connections among, 507–508
culture areas, c. 1400, m504
Mound Builders, 506
woodland cultures, 506
North Atlantic Treaty Organization (NATO), 1127, m1145, 1208–1209, 1244, 1248, 1250, 1284
Northern Alliance, 1207, 1208
Northern Ireland (Ulster), 871, 874, 1297
Northern Renaissance, 554–561
artistic ideas in, 555–556
beginning of, 554
Elizabethan Age and, 557
printing and, 558, 559
writing in, 556–557
North German Confederation, 799, 803
North Korea, 259, 260, 332, 850, 1136–1138
Northmen. *See* Vikings
North Vietnam, 1139–1142
Norway
post–World War I depression and, 1055
in World War II, 1079
Notre Dame, Cathedral of, 401
Nova Scotia, 867, m867
Novellae, The **(Justinian),** 349
Novgorod, Russia, 358

Now and Then
acupuncture, 313
alternative fuel cars, 1317
Bantu languages: Swahili, 449
baseball, 1321
Bollywood, 250, i250, c250
Buddhism in the West, 97
Chad discovery, 19
child labor today, 835, i835
communism today, 850, m850
conditions contributing to Reformation, 584
democracy in United States, 705
global trade, 616
Hinduism today, 89, m89
impact of nationalism, 792
International Criminal Tribunal for the Former Yugoslavia, 1113
kabuki theater, 630
Kashmir, 1169
modern marathons, 161
North and South Korea, 332
Northern Ireland, 874
online encyclopedias, 726
plague, 426
political factions, 755
Scorpion King, 54
Shakespeare's popularity, 558
special economic zones, 946
Taliban, 1151
Tiananmen Square, 1024
United Nations and Congress of Vienna, 775
Vietnam, 1143
women leaders of Indian subcontinent, 602
Nubia
Egyptian armies in, 120
interaction of Egypt and, 123, 124
trade with Egypt, i119
Nubian Empire, 120, 123–125
Nuclear Non-Proliferation Treaty, 1285
nuclear war, Cold War and threat of, 1127–1129, 1154–1155
nuclear weapons
in former Soviet Union, 1242
in India and Pakistan, 1171
proliferation of, 1285

numbers, 58–59, 235
numina, 212
nuns, 369, 588
Buddhist, 96–98, 263
Daoist, 263
Jain, 92
Nuremberg Trials, 1112
Nur Jahan, 601–603
NWP (National Women's Party), 864
NWSA (National Woman Suffrage Association), 863, 864

O

OAS (Organization of American States), 1127, 1215
Oaxaca Valley, 493–495
Obama, Barack, 1209, 1267
Obasanjo, Olusegun, 1230
Obregón, Alvaro, 965, 967
observatories, 287, 290, 342, 494
obsidian, 27, 517
O'Connell, Daniel, 870
Octavian, 202, 203. *See also* Augustus
Odyssey **(Homer),** 152, 170
Oe, Kenzaburo, i1324
Ogoni people, 1230
O'Higgins, Bernardo, 783
oil, 1281–1282
in Persia, 918
in Southwest Asia, m1032, 1033
oil fields, m1032
oil spills, 1317, 1318
Okita, Naniwaya, 958
Old Kingdom (Egypt), 53–55, 59
"Old Red Sandstone" (Miller), 833
Old Regime (French), 746–748, 753
Old Stone Age. *See* Paleolithic Age
Old Testament, 221
Olduvai Gorge, Tanzania, 10, 15
Oleg, 358
Olga, princess of Russia, 359
oligarchy, 154, c155

silk, 261, 262, *i264*
Silk Roads, 252, 262, *i262,* 314, 327
 and Arabian trade routes, 271
 and Muslim Empire, 282
Silla Dynasty, 332
Silla Kingdom, 331
Sima Qian, 258, 263
simony, 398, 399
Sinan, 299
Singapore, 1180
 imperialism in, 927
 independence in, 1180
Singh, Manmohan, 1171
Sino (term), 955
Sino-Japanese War, 955
sistrum, 453
Six-Day War, 1197
Skara Brae, 30, 31, *i31*
skepticism, 565, 677–678
sky marshals, 1303
slash-and-burn farming, 24
Slater, Samuel, 836, 837, 841
Slater's Mill (Pawtucket, Rhode Island), 836–837
slavery, 209, 210
 abolition of, 853
 in ancient Athens, 155, 156
 in Brazilian colonies, 640
 causes of, 651–653
 class of slaves in Muslim society, 285
 in Egypt, 57
 emancipation, 795, 879
 Enlightenment views of, 732
 Magyar invasions and, 376
 in North and South America, 653, 656
 in Roman Republic, 200
 in Saint Domingue, 781
 in Spanish colonies, 643
 in United States, 879
 and U.S. Civil War, 877–879
slave trade
 African, 475, *i475,* 476
 Atlantic, 651–657
 trans-Saharan, 459
 by Zazzau, 467, 468
Slavs, 357
 Christian conversion of, 356
 Constantinople attacked by, 353

 in Serbia, 975
 Vikings and, 359
Slovakia, 1247, 1248
Slovenia, 1250
Smith, Adam, 733, 844, 845, *i845*
Sobibor, 1097
social changes
 after World War II, 1120–1121
 in ancient China, 316–317
 in early villages, 39
 as foundation for Renaissance, 538–539
 during Industrial Revolution, 830–831
 in nineteenth century, 881–891
 in Russia, 1242
social classes
 in ancient Athens, 155
 ancient China, 316–317
 in Aztec society, 519
 in Egypt, 55, 57, 60
 in feudal system, 377
 and growth of cities, 39
 in India, 922
 Industrial Revolution and, 830–831
 in Latin American colonies, 780, *c781*
 Mayan, 510–511
 in Muslim society, 285–286
 in Roman Empire, 208–210
 Sumerian, 47
 in Ur, 41
social contract, 718, 723
 Hobbes' idea of, 718
Social Contract, The **(Rousseau),** 722, 723
Social Darwinism, 890, 898, 899
Social History
 age of superstition (Middle Ages), 394, *i394*
 ancient Chinese technology, 318–319
 bread, 751
 bull leapers of Knossos, 100, *i100*
 China's population, 625
 Chinese society, 259, *c259*
 city life in Renaissance Europe, *i560,* 560–561, *i561*

 class system in India, 922
 collecting water, 439
 dangers and rewards of Crusades, 403
 effects of industrialization, 954
 Islam in West Africa, 466
 Kyoto Protocol, 1311
 labor-saving devices in the United States, *i1046,* 1046–1047, *i1047*
 life in early Australia, *i872,* 872–873, *i873*
 life in the Depression, 1053, *i1053*
 life in a Roman villa, 214–215, *i214–i215*
 molecular medicine, 1271
 Muslim prayer, 277
 nationalistic music, 794
 negotiating conflict in stateless societies, 438
 revolutionary change in Southeast Asia, 1182–1183
 Romanian language, 1248
 Russian winters, 698–699
 surnames, 409
 Syrian civil war, 1292
 Ukrainian kulaks, 1021
 work and play in ancient Egypt, *i60,* 60–61, *i61*
socialism, 846–847
 comparing other ideologies and, *c1069*
 defined, 846
 industrialization and, 846–847, 849, *c849*
 Marxist, 1133
 post-World War I depression and, 1055
 radical, 847–848, 850
social networking, 1269
social order
 under Confucianism, 137–138
 in Empire of Ghana, 460
 under feudalism, 376–377, 379, 381–387
 in medieval western Europe, 408–415
 merchant class and, 413
 in Roman Republic, 194
 Spartan, 157

Text Acknowledgments

Excerpt from "1973 Statement to the Knesset" by President Sadat. Text copyright © November 20, 1977 by Anwar Sadat. Reprinted by permission of Israel Ministry of Foreign Affairs.

Excerpts from *The Analects of Confusicous* translated by Simon Leys. Text copyright © 1997 by Pierre Ryckmans. Reprinted by permission of W. W. Norton & Company Inc.

Excerpt from "Article 6, The Ten Abominations" from *The T'ang Code*, Vol. 1, translated with an Introduction by Wallace Johnson. Text copyright © 1979 by Princeton University Press. Reprinted by permission of Princeton University Press.

Excerpts from "The Big Picture" by Peter Stearns from *Human Legacy*. Text copyright © 2008 by Houghton Mifflin Harcourt. Reprinted by permission of Houghton Mifflin Harcourt Publishing Company.

Excerpt from *The Birth of the Modern: World Society 1815-1830* by Paul Johnson. Text copyright © 1991 by Paul Johnson. Reprinted by permission of HarperCollins Publishers and Orion Publishing Group

Excerpt from "The Prologue" from *The Canterbury Tales* by Geoffrey Chaucer, translated by Nevill Coghill. Text copyright ©1951, 1958, 1960, 1975, 1977 by Nevill Coghill. Reprinted by permission of Penguin Group UK and Curtis Brown Ltd., London, on behalf of the Estate of Nevill Coghill.

Excerpts from "Daily Routine Peasant Woman" from *Women in Medieval Times* by Fiona Macdonald. Text copyright © 2000 by Fiona Macdonald. Reprinted by permission of McGraw-Hill Education.

Excerpt from "Eco-Economy: Building an Economy for the Earth," by Lester Brown. Speech, *Colloquium on Global Partnerships for Sustainable Development: Harnessing Action for the 21st Century; 24 March 2002*. Reprinted by permission of the Earth Policy Institute.

Exodus 20:2-14 (Ten Commandments) from *Tanakh: A New Translation of the Holy Scriptures According to the Traditional Hebrew Text* by the Jewish Publication Society. Text copyright © 1985 by the Jewish Publication Society. Reprinted by permission of University of Nebraska Press.

Excerpt from *The Gathering Storm* speech to the House of Commons by Winston S. Churchill. Text copyright 1940 by Winston Churchill. Reproduced with permission of Curtis Brown, London, on behalf of the Estate of Sir Winston Churchill. Copyright © The Estate of Winston Churchill.

Excerpt from Chapter XVII, *Hind Swaraj* (Home Rule) by M. K. Gandhi. Reprinted by permission of The Navajivan Trust.

From *Hymn to Aphrodite* by Sappho from www.stoa.org/diotima, translated by Elizabeth Vandiver. Copyright © 1997 by Elizabeth Vandiver. Reproduced by permission of the author.

"An Iron Curtain has Descended" speech from *The Sinews of Peace* by Winston Churchill. Text copyright © March 5, 1946 by Winston Churchill. Reprinted by permission of Curtis Brown, London on behalf of The Estate of Winston S. Churchill.

Excerpt from "Ly Thai To: Edict on Moving the capital (1010)" from *Sources of Vietnamese Tradition*, edited by George E. Dutton, Jayne S. Werner, and John K. Whitmore. Text copyright © 2012 by George E. Dutton, Jayne S. Werner and John K. Whitmore. Reprinted by permission of Columbia University Press.

Excerpt from *A Month and a Day: A Detention Diary* by Ken Saro-Wiwa. Text copyright © 1996 by Ken Saro-Wiwa. Reprinted by permission of Penguin Books Ltd.

"Moonlight Night" by Tu Fu from *The Columbia Book of Chinese Poetry*, translated and edited by Burton Watson. Text copyright © 1984 Columbia University Press. Reprinted by permission of Columbia University Press.

M.I. Libau quote from *Never to Forget: The Jews of the Holocaust* by Milton Meltzer. Text copyright © 1991 by Milton Meltzer. Reprinted by permission of HarperCollins Publishers.

Simon Weisenthal quote from *Never to Forget: The Jews of the Holocaust* by Milton Meltzer. Text copyright © 1991 by Milton Meltzer. Reprinted by permission of HarperCollins Publishers.

Excerpt from *Night* by Elie Wiesel. Text copyright © 1972, 1985 by Elie Wiesel. English translation copyright © 2006 by Marion Wiesel. Orginially published as *La Nuit* by Les Editions de Minuit. Text copyright © 1958 by Les Editions de Minuit. Reprinted by permission of Farrar Straus and Giroux, Georges Borchardt, Inc. for Les Editions de Minuit and Recorded Books.

"On a Journey" from *Matsuo Basho* by Makoto Ueda. Text copyright © 1970 by Twayne Publishers Inc. Reprinted by permission of Kodansha America, Inc.

Excerpt from "Overview" from CII-ITC Centre of Excellence for Sustainable Development. Text copyright © Reprinted by permission of the CII-ITC Centre of Excellence for Sustainable Development, the Confederation of Indian Industry, New Delhi.

Excerpt from *Piers Plowman* by William Langland, translated by George Economou. Text copyright © 1996 by George Economou. Reprinted by permission of the University of Pennsylvania Press.

Excerpt from "Pledge of Resistance in Transvaal Africa, 1906" by M. K. Gandhi from *The Collected Works of Mahatma Gandhi*. Reprinted by permission of The Navajivan Trust.

Excerpt from "The Prologue," from *The Canterbury Tales* by Geoffrey Chaucer, translated by Nevill Coghill. Text copyright © 1951 by Nevill Coghill. Copyright © 1958, 1960, 1975, 1977 by the Estate of Neveill Coghill. Reprinted by permission of Penguin Books Ltd.

Excerpts from "Reading Like a Historian" by Sam Wineburg from *Human Legacy*. Text copyright © 2008 by Houghton Mifflin Harcourt. Reprinted by permission of Houghton Mifflin Harcourt Publishing Company.

Excerpt from "Samurai's Instructions to His Son," from *A History of Japan to 1334* by George Sansom. Copyright © 1958 by the Board of Trustees of the Leland Stanford Junior University. Reprinted by permission of Stanford University Press.

Excerpt from *The Song of Roland* translated by Frederick Goldin. Text copyright © 1978 by W. W. Norton & Company, Inc. Reprinted by permission of W. W. Norton & Company, Inc.

Excerpt from *Sundiata: An Epic of Old Mali* by D. T. Niane, translated by G. D. Pickett. Original French text Copyright ©1960 by Presence Africaine, English text copyright © 1965 by Longman Group Ltd. Reprinted by permission of Pearson Education and Presence Africaine.

From "This Old House" from *The Leopard's Tale: Revealing the Mysteries of Çatalhöyük* by Ian Hodder. Copyright © 2006 by Thames & Hudson. Reproduced by permission of the publisher.

Excerpt from "Tienanmen Square: A Soldier's Story" by Xiao Ye from *Teenage Soldiers, Adult Wars* edited by Roger Rosen and Patra McSharry. Text copyright © 1991 by The Rosen Publishing Group, Inc. Reprinted by permission of the Rosen Publishing Group, Inc.

 Illustration and Photo Credits

Unless otherwise indicated, all video reference screens are © 2010 A&E Television Networks, LLC. All rights reserved.

Maps: Atlas maps by Houghton Mifflin Harcourt; maps on page 211, 233, 391, 800 by Maps.com LLC. Other maps, locators, and globe locators by Mapping Specialists.

Table of Contents

Signing U.S. Constitution ©Art Resource, NY; **Machu Picchu** ©Tim Hursley/SuperStock; **Orville Wright plane** The Granger Collection, NY; **trench warfare** ©Corbis

MODULE 1

Archaeologist ©Denzil Maregele/ Foto24/Gallo Images/Getty Images; **hominid footprint** ©John Reader/Photo Researchers; **Paleolithic engraving of a lunar calendar on a reindeer antler**, (38,000 b.c.) Dordogne, France. Photo ©Réunion des Musées Nationaux/Art Resource, New York; **Cro-Magnon skull** ©John Reader/SPL/Photo Researchers; **archaeologist** ©Sebastian Castaeda/ Anadolu Agency/Getty Images; **White Cliffs of Dover** ©Joan van Hurck/ Alamy; **cave excavation** ©RIA Novosti/ Science Source; **forensic anthropology** ©Evrim Aydin/Anadolu Agency/Getty Images; **Rising Star cave** ©University Of The Witwatersrand / Barcroft Media via Getty Images; **Leakey family** ©Des Bartlett/Photo Researchers; **Toumai skull** ©AFP/Getty Images; **Algerian cave painting** Paintings at Tassili n'Ajer, Algeria, Musée de l'Homme, Paris. Henri Lhote Collection. Photo ©Erich Lessing/ Art Resource, New York; **Argentinian cave painting** Paintings at Cuevas de las manos, Argentina ©Alberto Gandsas, Buenos Aires, Argentina, www.gandsas. com; **French cave painting** Replica of Lascaux Cave Painting, France ©Sissie Brimberg/National Geographic Image Collection/Getty Images; **Australian Aboriginal cave painting** ©Pam Gardner, Frank Lane Picture Agency/ Corbis; **Ice Man at site** ©Paul Hanny/ GAMMA/ZUMA/Press; **Ice Man in lab** ©Getty Images/The Bridgeman Art Library/South Tyrol Museum of Archaeology, Bolzano, Italy; **tool and sheath** ©Photo Archives, South Tyrol Museum of Archaeology; **grindstone** ©Gianni Dagli Orti/Corbis; **clay figurine** ©Sonia Halliday Photographs; **gold stag** ©Ann Ronan Pictures/Print Collector/ Getty Images; **Skara Brae** ©KEENPRESS/ National Geographic Creative; **Stonehenge** ©Moment/Getty Images; **stone monument at Stonehenge** ©Rex Features via AP Images.

MODULE 2

Ceramic tile painting Two gentlemen engrossed in conversation while two others look on, a painting on a ceramic tile from a tomb near Luoyang, Henan province, dated to the Eastern Han Dynasty (25-220 AD)/Pictures from History/Bridgeman Images; **Sargon** Head of Sargon the Great. (2300-2200 b.c.). Nineveh. Iraq Museum, Baghdad. Photo ©Scala/Art Resource, New York; **scribe** Seated Scribe. Saqqara, Egypt, (5th dynasty). Painted limestone. Louvre, Paris. Photo ©Erich Lessing/Art Resource, New York; **vase** Fragment of a vase depicting ibex, from Onengo-Daro. Indus Valley. Pakistan. National Museum of Karachi, Karachi, Pakistan. Photo ©The Bridgeman Art Library; **cooking vessel** Fandang (rectangular cooking vessel), Shang dynasty (1600-1100b.c.). Bronze. From Ningxian, China. Photo ©Giraudon/ Art Resource, New York; **cuneiform** ©The British Museum,London. Photo ©The Bridgeman Art Library; **aerial of Ur** ©Courtesy of University of Pennsylvania Museum, Philadelphia (Neg.# S4-139540); **Ziggurat at Ur** ©DEA Picture Library/Art Resource, NY; **figure** Itur-Shamagen, King of Mari, in prayer. Sumerian. National Museum, Damascus, Syria. Photo ©Giraudon/Art Resource, New York; **gold ram** ©The British Museum; **Code of Hammurabi** ©Gianni Dagli Orti/ Corbis; **Hammurabi** Royal head, perhaps depicting Hammurabi (1792-1740 b.c.), from Susa. Diorite, 15 cm high. Louvre, Paris, France. Photo ©Erich Lessing/Art Resource, New York; **Nile River** Jacques Descloitres, MODIS Land Science Team/ NASA; **mummy** ©Bettmann/Corbis; **sarcophagus** Canopic sarcophagus containing the organs of Pharaoh Tutankhamen. Egypt, (18th dynasty). Egyptian Museum, Cairo, Egypt. Photo ©Scala/Art Resource, New York; **Canopic jars** ©The British Museum; **pyramids** ©David Sutherland/ Getty Images; **Herodotus** Portrait bust of Herodotus, copy of Greek (300s b.c.). Museo Archeologico Nazional, Naples, Italy. Photo ©The Bridgeman Art Library; **Rosetta Stone** The Granger Collection, New York; **farmers** Victor R. Boswell, Jr./ National Geographic Image Collection; **games** ©Gianni Dagli Orti/Corbis; **game board** ©The British Museum; **cosmetics** ©Werner Forman/Universal Images Group/Getty Images; **illustration of Karnak** ©Corbis; **Karnak** ©De Agostini/G. Sioen/Getty Images; **map of citadel** ©1994 West Publishing Company; **plumbing** Illustration by Tom Jester; **elephant** Seal depicting elephant and monograms, steatite (2500-200 b.c.). Indus Civilization, from Mohenjo Daro. National Museum, Karachi, Pakistan. Photo ©Alfredo Dagli Orti/The Art Archive; **rhinoceros** Seal depicting armor plated rhinoceros and monograms, steatite (2500-2000 b.c.). Indus Civilization, from Mohenjo Daro. National Museum Karachi, Pakistan. Photo ©Alfredo Dagli Orti/The Art Archive; **zebu** Seal depicting zebu and monograms, steatite (2500-200 b.c.). Indus Civilization, from Mohenjo Daro. National Museum Karachi, Pakistan. Photo ©Alfredo Dagli Orti/The Art Archive; **bearded figure** ©Archivo Iconografico, S.A./Corbis; **Huang He** ©Julia Waterlow/Eye Ubiquitous/Corbis; **oracle bone** ©Royal Ontario Museum/ Corbis; **Chinese coins** ©Lowell Georgia/ Corbis; **bronze mask** Bronze Mask inlaid with gold in the Hall of Masks, Sanxingdui Archaeological Museum, Guanghan, China. Photo ©Nik Wheeler/ Getty Images.

MODULE 3

Caravan Illustration by Terence J. Gabbey; **stele** Funerary stele of merchant holding weighing scales, (700s b.c.), Hittite culture. Musée du Louvre, Paris. Photo ©Gianni Dagli Orti/The Art Archive; **Olmec head** Colossal Head No. 1, (1200-400 b.c.), Olmec culture. Archaeological garden of La Venta in Villahermosa, Mexico. Photo ©Gianni Dagli Orti/The Art Archive; **Harappan god** Bearded head pendant, (200s b.c.), Phoenician. National Museum of Carthage, Carthage, Tunisia. Photo ©Erich Lessing/Art Resource, New York; **bat god** Jade mask of bat god (about 500 b.c.-800 a.d.), Zapotec culture. Museo Nacional de Antropologica, Mexico City. Photo ©Michel Zabe/Art Resource, New York; **reclining Buddha** ©Scala/Art Resource, New York; **Brahma** Five-headed Brahma on his Vahana, the Cosmic Goose (1800s), Southern India. Photo ©Victoria and Albert Museum, London/Art Resource, New York; **Krishna** The Granger Collection, New York; **Vishnu** Vishnu Visvarrupa, preserver of the universe, represented as the whole world, (early 1800s), Jaipur, India. Victoria and Albert Museum, London. Photo ©Sally Chappell/ The Art Archive; **Siddhartha Gautama** ©Reuters/Bazuki Muhammad; **reclining Buddha** ©Scala/Art Resource, New York; **Buddhist monks** ©Glen Allison/ Stone/Getty Images; **bull leapers** Bull dancing (1700-1400 b.c.). Minoan fresco from Knossos, Crete. Heraklion (Crete) Museum. Photo ©Gianni Dagli Orti/The Art Archive; **Phoenician Inscription 76** Detail of the inscription from the sarcophagus of Eshmunazar recounting how he and his mother Amashtarte built temples to the gods of Sidon, (3000-1200 b.c.), Phoenician. Louvre, Paris. Photo ©Lauros-Giraudon/The Bridgeman Art Library; **Moses** The Santa Croce Altarpiece (1324-1325), Ugolino di Nerio. Tempera on wood, 54.4 cm x 31.4 cm. Bought, 1983 (NG6484). National Gallery, London. Photo ©National Gallery, London/Art Resource, New York; **Torah** Keter Torah. ©Zev Radovan, Jerusalem, Israel; Mezuzah, (mid-late 1900s), Bezalel school. The Jewish Museum, New York, gift of Mrs. William Minder, 1987-57. Photo by John Parnell ©The Jewish Museum of New York/Art Resource, New York; **King Solomon** (1400s), Pedro Berruguete. Galleria Nazionale delle Marche, Urbino, Italy. Photo ©Alinari/Art Resource, New York.

MODULE 4

Assyrian lion ©Bartosz Hadyniak/ Getty Images, Inc.; **Temple at Karnak** ©Andrea Jemolo/Corbis; **Mask of Agamemnon**, (1500s b.c.), Mycenaean. National Archaeological Museum, Athens. Photo ©Gianni Dagli Orti/ The Art Archive; **Ceramic jar from Grave 566**, Meroitic Period, Karanog, Nubia. Courtesy of University of Pennsylvania Museum, Philadelphia (Neg. #T4-55OC.2); **Alexander III**, King of Macedonia, (338 b.c.), Roman, copied from Greek statue by Eufranor. Staatliche Glypothek, Munich. Photo ©Alfredo Dagli Orti/The Art Archive; **Hatshepsut**. Egyptian; from Deir el-Bahri, western Thebes, New Kingdom, Dynasty 18, reign of Hatshepsut, ca. 1473-1458 b.c. Indurated limestone, H. 76.75 in. (195 cm). The Metropolitan Museum of Art, Rogers Fund, 1929 (29.3.2). Photo ©1997 The Metropolitan Museum of Art; **temple** Temple of Pharaoh Ramses II at Abu Simbel (1279-1213 b.c.). Photo ©Alfredo Dagli Orti /The Art Archive; **Nubian Pyramid** Photo by Derek A. Welsby ©Derek A. Welsby; **Stone Ram** ©Paul Almasy/Corbis; **Shawabits of King Taharka**, (690-664 b.c.), Nubian, Napatan Period. Museum of Fine Arts, Boston. Harvard University Museum-Museum of Fine Arts Expedition. Photo ©2008 Museum of Fine Arts, Boston; **gold shield** Gold ring shield from Queen Amanishakheto's pyramid. Staatliche Museen zu Berlin, Preussischer Kulturbesitz, Aegyptisches Museum, Berlin. Photo ©Margarete Buesing/Art Resource, New York; **Assyrian sculpture** Warriors scaling walls with ladders fighting hand-to-hand. Ashurnazirpal's assault on a city. Stone bas-relief from the palace of Ashurnazirpal II in Nimrud. The British Museum, London. Photo ©Erich Lessing/Art Resource, New York; **Hanging Gardens of Babylon** ©Bettmann/Corbis; **reliefs at Persepolis** ©Corbis; **chariot** ©The British Museum; **Confucius** The British Library HIP/The Image Works; **Laozi** The Granger Collection, New York; **Yin-and-Yang** ©Photodisc/Getty Images; **Shi Huang-Di of the Qin Dynasty.** By permission of the British Library; **wall ruins** ©Zoonar GmbH/Alamy Stock Photo; **general view of wall** ©VCG/VCG via Getty Images.

MODULE 5

Temple of Neptune ©John Heseltine/Corbis/Getty Images; **vase** Vase from Palaikastro, Minoan. Archaeological Museum, Heraklion, Crete. Photo ©Nimatallah/Art Resource, New York; **Hatshepsut** (18th dynasty), from the temple of Hatshepsut. Deir el Bahari, West Thebes. Egyptian Museum, Cairo, Egypt. Photo ©Scala/Art Resource, New York; **animal mask** (about 1100–771 b.c.), Chinese, Western Zhou dynasty. Musée des Arts Asiatiques-Guimet, Paris. Photo by Richard Lambert ©Werner Forman/Art Resource, New York; **shield** Breastplate, Mixtec, Postclassic Monte Alban V, Yanhuitlan, Oaxaca. Museo Nacional de Antropologia, Mexico City. Photo ©Réunion des Musées Nationaux/Art Resource, New York; **Trojan Horse** ©Bettmann/Corbis; **Head of Polyphemos** (about 150 b.c. or later), Hellenistic or Roman Period, Greece. Marble from Thasos, 15 1/8" (38.3 cm). Gift in Honor of Edward W. Forbes from his friends. Photo ©Museum of Fine Arts, Boston; **Acropolis** ©DEA Picture Library/De Agostini/Getty Images; **stele** Funeral stele of Ktesileos and Theano (about 420). Greek, Attic, Classical. Marble, 93 cm H x 50 cm W. Found in Athens, 1921.

National Archaeological Museum, Athens. Photo ©Herve Champollion/akg-images, London; **Black-figured hydria** (500s), Painter of Micali. Museo Gregoriano Etrusco, Vatican Museums, Rome. Photo ©Scala/Art Resource, New York; **discus thrower** ©Scala/Art Resource, NY; **Mount Olympus** ©Vanni Archive/Corbis; **vase** Detail of warriors on Chigi vase, Greek. Museo Nazionale di Villa Giulia, Rome, Italy. Photo ©Scala/Art Resource, New York; **Boston Marathon** ©AFP/Getty; **Bust of Pericles** (100s), Roman. Photo ©British Museum, London/Bridgeman Art Library; **Greek sculpture** ©Erich Lessing/Art Resource, NY; **Athena statue** ©Reunion des Musees Nationaux/Hervé Lewandowski/Art Resource, New York; **Parthenon** ©Werner Forman/Art Resource, New York; **dish** Red-figure dish depicting Theseus slaying the Minotaur (400s b.c.). The British Museum, London. Photo ©The Bridgeman Art Library; **Medea Poster** ©Christie's Images/Corbis; **theater mask** ©Tarker/Bridgeman Images; **Socrates death** *The Death of Socrates* (1780), Francois-Louis Joseph Watteau. Musée des Beaux-Arts, Lille, France. Photo by P. Bernard ©Réunion des Musées Nationaux/Art Resource, New York; **Socrates** ©Museo Capitolino, Rome/SuperStock; **Plato** ©Museo Capitolino, Rome/SuperStock; **Aristotle** ©SuperStock; **Alexander the Great** Detail of Alexander, from the Battle of Issus mosaic, House of the Faun, Pompeii (about 80 b.c.). Museo Archeologico Nazionale, Naples, Italy. Photo ©Scala/Art Resource, New York; **Alexander the Great statue** ©Yiannis Papadimitriou/Alamy Stock Photo; **Pharos of Alexandria** ©Bettmann/Getty Images; **Hipparchus** The Granger Collection, New York; **Arabic Pythagorean Theorem** The Granger Collection, New York; **Chinese Pythagorean Theorem** Smith Collection, Rare Book and Manuscript Library, Columbia University, New York; **Winged Victory** ©Erich Lessing/Art Resource, New York.

MODULE 6

Senate *Cicero Denouncing Catalina Before the Senate* (1800s), Cesare Maccari. Wallpainting. Palazzo Madama, Rome. Photo ©Scala/Art Resource, New York; **Han Dynasty** Funerary figure (206 b.c.–220 a.d.), Han dynasty. Private Collection. Photo ©Werner Forman/Art Resource, New York; **Cleopatra** ©Ancient Art & Architecture Collection Ltd.; **Gold Toucan** Small gold figure studded with turquoises in the form of a toucan (about 1400–1534 a.d.), Moche Culture. Private Collection. Photo ©Werner Forman/Art Resource, New York; **horseman** Roman horseman (Soldier). Musée des Antiquites Nationales, Saint Germain-en-Laye, France. Photo ©Erich Lessing/Art Resource, New York; **Romulus and Remus** Wolf Mosaic, Aldborough Roman Town, Yorkshire, 300 AD (mosaic) ©Leeds Museums and Art Galleries (City Museum) UK/The Bridgeman Art Library; **Roman Forum ruins** Caesar's Forum and

Temple of Venus Genetrix, Rome, Italy. Photo ©Gianni Dagli Orti/The Art Archive; **Hannibal** *Hannibal* (about 1508–1513). Museo Capitolino, Rome. Photo ©Gianni Dagli Orti/The Art Archive; **Caesar** *The Death of Julius Caesar* (1793), Vincenzo Camuccini. Galleria d'Arte Moderna, Rome. Photo ©Alfredo Dagli Orti/The Art Archive; **Augustus** Roman Emperor Augustus with laurel wreath (about 1000), German. Cameo from Lothair cross. Cathedral Treasury Aachen. Photo ©Alfredo Dagli Orti/The Art Archive; **Caligula** ©Charles & Josette Lenars/Corbis; **Trajan** The Granger Collection, New York; **slave mosaic** ©De Agostini Picture Library/Getty Images; **gladiators** Gladiators fighting wild beasts (300s). Roman mosaic from Terranova, Italy. Galleria Borghese, Rome. Photo ©Alfredo Dagli Orti/The Art Archive; **Roman bath** ©Greg Balfour Evans/Alamy Stock Photo; **Lares** ©DEA Picture Library/De Agostini/Getty Images; **Roman Villa** Illustration by John James/Temple Rogers; **fresco** ©Mimmo Jodice/Corbis; **Vesuvius bodies** ©Dorling Kindersley; **bread** ©DK Images; **St. Peter** *Christ's Charge to Saint Peter*, Raphael. Photo ©Victoria and Albert Museum, London/Art Resource, New York; **St. Paul** ©Universal Images Group/Getty Images; **Augustine** *Saint Augustine of Hippo, Bishop and Doctor of the Church* (1400s), Swiss. Musée des Beaux Arts, Dijon, France. Photo ©Gianni Dagli Orti/The Art Archive; **Germanic skull** ©Carlos Muñoz-Yagüe/Science Source; **Trajan Column** ©Vittoriano Rastelli/Corbis; **mosaic portrait of woman** ©Alfredo Dagli Orti/The Art Archive/Corbis; **Roman aqueduct** ©Dennis Degnan/Corbis; **Colosseum** ©John Heseltine/Corbis.

MODULE 7

Bronze horse carriage National Museum, Beijing, China. Photo ©Erich Lessing/Art Resource, New York; **bronze galloping horse** ©Giraudon/Bridgeman Images; **head of Buddha** ©Bridgeman Images; **Kuba mask** ©Gianni Dagli Orti/Art Resource, New York; **Shiva** Shiva Nataraja (bronze), Indian School, (13th century)/Museum of Fine Arts, Houston, Texas, USA/Gift of Carol and Robert Straus/Bridgeman Images; **Asoka's Edicts on pillar** Column of Asoka (200s b.c.). Photo ©Borromeo/Art Resource, New York; **Asoka's Lions** Pillar of Asoka. Photo ©Borromeo/Art Resource, New York; **Terracotta tile** Terracotta tile with a musician (400s a.d.), Central India, Gupta period. ©The British Museum; **Gandharan Buddha** National Museum, New Delhi, India. Photo ©Scala/Art Resource, New York; **Bollywood** ©Monopole–Pathe/Photofest; **Buddha** Buddha (500s) Bronze. Gupta period. National Museum of India, New Delhi, India. Photo ©The Bridgeman Art Library; **The Great Stupa** Stupe no. 3, Early Andhra dynasty. Sandhi, India. Photo ©Scala/Art Resource, New York; **Devi Jagadambi Temple** ©David Cumming/Eye Ubiquitous/Corbis; **Ganesha (car** Ganesa (400s a.d.). Gupta dynasty Itar. Museum and Picture Library

©Borromeo/Art Resource, New York; **Ganesha (colorful)** ©Arvind Garg/Corbis; **Emperor Liu Bang** By permission of the British Library; **papermaking** ©Bettmann/Corbis; **camel caravan** The Granger Collection, New York; **traded gold** The Granger Collection, New York; **silk fabric** ©Robert Harding Picture Library.

MODULE 8

Charles Martel ©Bettmann/Corbis; **Charlemagne.** Louvre, Paris. Photo ©Erich Lessing/Art Resource, New York; **eye** Anatomy of the Eye (592), Arabian manuscript. Of the *Hegira* (1214), Al-Mutadibih. Egyptian Museum, Cairo. Photo ©Gianni Dagli Orti/The Art Archive; **Genghis Khan** ©Stapleton Collection/Corbis; **Zheng He Serpent** ©Werner Forman/Art Resource, NY; **Gutenberg Bible** Bridgeman Art Library; **Osman I** ©Sonia Halliday Photographs; **Muslim Prayer** ©Murat Ayranci/SuperStock; **elephants charging under the Ka'Bah** (1368). From the Apostles Biography. Illuminated manuscript. Topkapi Museum, Istanbul, Turkey. Photo ©Eileen Tweedy/The Art Archive; **Dome of the Rock** ©Rostislav Glinsky/Shutterstock; **Interior of Dome of the Rock** ©Hanan Isachar/Corbis; **Interior of Dome of the Rock** ©Ted Spiegel/Corbis; **Qu'ran Ju/XXVII.** Mamluk (1300s). Arabic School. Private Collection. Photo ©Bonhams, London/The Bridgeman Art Library; **manuscript** *Battle of the tribes.* Illumination from Add. Or 25900, f. 121v. By permission of the British Library; **Arab traders** ©Sonia Halliday Photographs; **Persian garden party** ©Bodleian Library, Oxford/Art Resource, NY; **Turkish astronomers** The Granger Collection, NY; **astrolabe** The Granger Collection, NY; **armillary sphere** ©Gianni Dagli Orti/Art Resource, NY; **The Thousand and One Nights** The Granger Collection, NY; **calligraphy** ©Peter Sanders; **Arabesque** ©Arthur Thévenart/Corbis; **geometric patterns** ©Arthur Thévenart/Corbis; **Jami Masjid Mosque** ©Arthur Thévenart/Corbis; **Cordoba Mosque** ©Jaume Balanya/Getty Images; **Hagia Sophia** ©James L. Stanfield/Getty Images; **Conquest of Constantinople** Taking of Constantinople by the Turks, MS Fr. 9087 f. 207. *Voyage d-Outremer de Bertrand de la Broquiere* Bibliotheque Nationale, Paris. Photo ©Sonia Halliday Photographs; **Suleyman the Lawgiver** *Sulieman the Magnificent.* Galleria degli Uffizi, Florence, Italy. Photo ©Dagli Orti/The Art Archive; **Sinan's Mosque** ©Sonia Halliday Photographs; **Shah Abbas** Shah Abbas I (1640s). Safavid mural. Chihil Sutun, Isfahan, Iran. Photo ©SEF/Art Resource, New York; **Masjid-e-Imam Mosque** Dome of south Iwan (1611–1638). Safavid dynasty. Majid-i Shah, Isfahan, Iran. Photo ©SEF/Art Resource, New York.

MODULE 9

City life in China ©Werner Forman/Universal Images Group/Getty Images; **Mayan sculpture** ©Art Resource, NY; **Tang horse** ©RMN-Grand Palais/Art Resource, NY; **Pope excommunicates** ©Gianni Dagli Orti/Art Resource, NY; **Ariwara-no-Narihara** ©Gianni Dagli Orti/Art Resource, NY; **Temple** ©Kelly-Mooney Photography/Corbis; **Emperor Tang Taizong.** National Palace Museum, Taipei. Photo ©Wan-go Weng; **Empress Wu Zetian** (1700s). Tang dynasty. Chinese. British Library. Photo ©The Art Archive; **Acupuncture** ©William Whitehurst/Corbis; **Tu Fu** (1700s). Chinese. The British Museum, London. Photo ©The Art Archive; **Song Painting** ©Burstein Collection/Corbis; **small plate.** Northern Sung dynasty, China. Musée Guimet, Paris. Photo ©Gianni Dagli Orti/The Art Archive; **Chinese arrow launcher** Wubeizhi ('On Warfare') (woodblock print), Chinese School/British Library, London, UK/Bridgeman Images; **printing press** Illustration by Peter Dennis; **Genghis Khan** James L. Stanfield/National Geographic Image Collection; **Mongol Soldiers** Illustration by Patrick Whelan; **Mongol warship** The Granger Collection, New York; **Kublai Khan** William H. Boyd/National Geographic Image Collection; **Marco Polo** ©Biblioteca Nazionale, Turin, Italy/SilvioFiore/SuperStock; **Dangun** The man god Dangun, Korean School. Natural pigment on paper, 52 cm x 80 cm. Gahoe Museum, Jongnogu, South Korea. ©The Bridgeman Art Library; **Tale of Genji** ©Laurie Platt Winfrey, Inc.; **female samurai** Tomoe, a brave woman of the Genji and Heishi period (about 900 A.D.). Photo ©The Art Archive; **Japanese Samurai** Illustration by Peter Dennis; **temple** ©Kelly-Mooney Photography/Corbis; **Angkor Wat** ©Dave G. Houser/Corbis; **Buddha** ©Steve Vidler/SuperStock.

MODULE 10

Justinian mosaic ©Ancient Art & Architecture Collection Ltd.; **Martel** Feats of the noble prince Charles Martel. Musée Goya, Castres, France. Photo ©Giraudon/Art Resource, New York; **silk** *The Genies Gathering Over the Sea.* Poem by Ma Lin on silk. (a.d. 960–1279), Chinese, Song dynasty. Calligraphy. Musée des Arts, Asiatiques–Guimet. Paris. Inv.: EG 2146. Photo by Michel Urtado. Photo ©Réunion des Musées Nationaux/Art Resource, New York; **peasants** Month of June from the Grimani Breviary (1500s). Biblioteca Marciana, Venice. Photo ©Scala/Art Resource, New York; **Archangel Michael** The Archangel Michael (2nd half 1300s). Russian Byzantine icon. Tretyakov Gallery, Moscow. Photo ©Scala/Art Resource, New York; **cross** Greek cross (1000s). Byzantine. Museo della Civilta Romana, Rome. Photo ©Gianni Dagli Orti/The Art Archive; **Theodora** ©R. Sheridan/Ancient Art & Architecture Collection Ltd.; **St. Basil** ©Jonathan Blair/Corbis; **Patriarch Bartholomew** ©Alessandro Bianchi/Reuters/Corbis; **Pope Francis** ©Franco Origlia/Getty Images; **chalice** Chalice (1000s). Byzantine. Basilica San Marco, Venice. Photo ©Gianni Dagli Orti/The Art Archive; **Hagia Sofia** ©Mehmet Cetin/Shutterstock; **Ivan III** ©Archive Images/Kean Collection/Getty Images; **Archangel Gabriel** ©Archivo Iconografico, S.A./Corbis; **scribe** Scribe writing out the Gospel (late 1400s). Hermitage, St. Petersburg, Russia. Photo ©The Bridgeman Art Library; **ivory cross** ©Massimo Listri/Corbis; **silver chest** ©Elio Ciol/Corbis; **Italian manuscript** The army leaves after sack of town (1300s). Manuscript. Biblioteca Nazionale Marciana, Venice. Photo ©Alfredo Dagli Orti/The Art Archive; **German manuscript** Illuminated decoration, from 'Vita Christi' by Ludolph of Saxony, printed 1472 (printed text & woodcut with hand colouring), German School, (15th century)/By permission of the Governors of Stonyhurst College/Bridgeman Images; **Saint Benedict,** Hans Memling. Uffizi, Florence, Italy. Photo ©Scala/Art Resource, New York; **St. Scholastica** ©National Gallery Collection; By kind permission of the trustees of the National Gallery, London/Corbis; **Charlemagne** *Portrait of Charlemagne*, Albrecht Durer. ©Germanisches Nationalmuseum, Nuremberg, Germany. Photo ©Lauros–Giraudon, Paris/SuperStock; **Viking boat** ©Dorling Kindersley; **European feudalism** Illustration by Terry Gabbey; **medieval manor** ©North Wind Picture Archives; **beating corn** Two men beating corn with flails (about 1320). From *The Luttrell Psalter.* The British Library, London. Photo ©HIP/Art Resource, New York; **caltrops** Royal Armouries; **St. George** *St. George and the Dragon* (about 1460), Paolo Uccello. National Gallery, London. Photo ©The Bridgeman Art Library; **castle and siege weapons** Illustration by Wood Ronsaville Harlin, Inc.; **noblewoman** ©Archivo Iconografico, S.A./Corbis; **peasant woman** *Peasant Woman With Scythe and Rake,* Alexei Venetsianov. Photo ©The State Russian Museum/Corbis; **women defending castle** MS Bruxelles, B.R. 9961-62, fol. 91v. Photo ©Bibliotheque Royal Albert ler, Brussels, Belgium.

MODULE 11

Toltec figurine ©Gianni Dagli Orti/Corbis; **William I** *William the Conqueror* (1289). Cloister of the Church of the Annunciation, Florence, Italy. Photo ©Gianni Dagli Orti/The Art Archive; **Genghis Khan** Portrait of Genghis Khan. National Palace Museum, Taipei, Taiwan. Photo ©The Bridgeman Art Library; **manuscript** Hours of Marguerite de Coetivy: The Final Moments (1400s). Ms. 74/1088 f. 90. Musée Conde, Chantilly, France. Photo ©Giraudon/Art Resource, New York; **Notre Dame** ©Viacheslav Lopatin/Shutterstock; **Pope's tiara** Museo Tesoro di San Pietro, Vatican State. Photo ©Scala/Art Resource, New York; **Full Moon** ©Aaron Horowitz/Corbis; **Frederick I** *Frederick I Barbarossa and his Sons* (1100s). German School. Landes Bibliothek, Fulda, Germany.

Photo ©Alinari/The Bridgeman Art Library; **gothic architecture illustration** Harry Bliss/National Geographic Image Collection; **Chartres Cathedral** ©Bruce Yuanyue Bi/Lonely Planet Images/Getty Images; **stained glass** *Portrait of the Good Samaritan* (1200s). Stained glass. Chartres Cathedral, France. Photo ©Giraudon/Art Resource, New York (both); **crusader** Mary Evans Picture Library; **Richard I** *Richard Coeur de Lion on his way to Jerusalem,* James William Glass. Phillips, The International Fine Art Auctioneers, United Kingdom. Photo ©The Bridgeman Art Library; **Luttrell Psalter** By permission of the British Library; **Richard the Lion-Hearted** ©Bettmann/Corbis; **Saladin** *Portrait of Saladin, Sultan of Egypt.* Museo di Andrea del Castagno, Uffizi, Florence. Photo ©SEF/Art Resource, New York; **craft guild (all)** Illustration by Peter Dennis/Linda Rogers Associates; **fish market** *Fish Market,* Joachim Beuklelaer. Museo Nazionale de Capodimonte, Naples, Italy. Photo ©Alinari/Art Resource, New York; **Ibn Sina** *Imaginary portrait of Avicenna.* Ibn Sina. French School. Bibliotheque de la Faculte de Medecine, Paris. Photo ©Archives Charmet/The Bridgeman Art Library; **St. Thomas Aquinas** St. Thomas Aquinas from the Demidoff Altarpiece, Carlo Crivelli. Photo ©National Gallery Collection/By kind permission of the Trustees of the National Gallery, London/Corbis; **Eleanor of Aquitaine** *Eleanor of Aquitaine* (1800s), French School. Bibliotheque Nationale, Paris. Photo ©The Bridgemann Art Library; **Magna Carta** National Archives; **Coronation of Phillip II** MS francais 6465, f. 212 v. Bibliotheque Nationale, Paris. Photo by AKG London; **church ceiling** ©Corbis; **plague** *The Triumph of Death* (late 1400s). Flemish. Musée du Berry, Bourges, France. Photo ©Bridgeman- Giraudon/Art Resource, New York; **skeleton** ©Morphart Creations Inc./Shutterstock; **rat** ©Hein Nouwens/Shutterstock; **longbow (all)** Illustration by Peter Dennis/Linda Rogers Associates.

MODULE 12

Nok head ©Werner Forman/Art Resource, NY; **Aksum crown** ©Jane Taylor/Sonia Halliday Photographs; **bronze head** ©Paul Almasy/Corbis; **First Crusade** ©Bettmann/Corbis; **Mansu Musa, King of Mali.** The Granger Collection, New York; **Roman soldier** ©The British Museum; **death** *Death strangling a victim of the plague* (1300s), Czechoslovakia. From the Stitny Codex. University Library, Prague, Czech Republic. Photo ©Werner Forman/Art Resource, New York; **rock painting** Cave painting of Tassili n'Ajjer, (2nd millennium B.C.). Musée de l'Homme, Paris. Henri Lhote Collection. Photo ©Erich Lessing/Art Resource, New York; **Masai herder** ©David Turnley/Corbis; **Tsetse fly** ©Martin Dohrn/Photo Researchers, **Sahara** ©Photowood Inc./Corbis, **savanna** ©Mary Ann McDonald/Corbis, **rain forest** ©Nordic Photos/SuperStock; **collecting water** ©Liba

Taylor/Corbis; **Nok terracotta figure** ©Bridgeman Images; **African ironworking** Illustration by Terry Gabbey; **Kuba mask** Mask, Kuba culture, Zaire. Private Collection. Photo ©Aldo Tutino/Art Resource, New York; **woman with basket** ©Staffan Widstrand/Corbis; **Kuba mask** Ngady Amwaash. Kuba Culture of Central Zaire. National Museum, Ghana. Photo ©Werner Forman/Art Resource, New York; **mural in Aksum** ©George Gerster/Rapho/Eyedea; **Pillars of Aksum** Stela at Axum. Axum, Ethiopia. Photo ©Werner Forman/Art Resource, New York; **Marrakech carpet market** ©Richard Bickel/Corbis; **Mansu Musa, King of Mali.** The Granger Collection, New York; **Yoruba Crown** ©North Carolina Museum of Art/Corbis; **Benin ivory mask** ©Universal History Archive/Universal Images Group/Getty Images; **Benin, Queen Mother head.** Photo ©The British Museum; **Benin plaque** ©Werner Forman/Art Resource, New York; **horn blower** Bronze figure of a horn blower (late 1500s–early 1600s a.d.), Edo. Benin Kingdom, Nigeria. Photo ©The British Museum; **Benin figure** Benin, cast figure, bronze aquamanile. Benin Kingdom, Nigeria. Photo ©The British Museum; **lost-wax process** Illustration by Yuan Lee; **city** ©Michele Burgess/SuperStock; **Muslim caravan** The Granger Collection, New York; **Arab slave market** The Granger Collection, New York; **Great Zimbabwe** ©Robert Preston/Alamy Ltd; **Great Enclosure walls** ©Colin Hoskins/Alamy Stock Photo; **Great Zimbabwe tower** ©Victor Watts/Alamy Stock Photo.

MODULE 13

Olmec wrestler ©DEA Picture Library/Getty Images; **sphinx** The Giza Sphinx with the pyramid of Chephren (Old Kingdom, Fourth dynasty). Pyramid of Chefren, Giza, Egypt. Photo ©Werner Forman/Art Resource, New York; **Hadrian** Bust of Emperor Hadrian (100s a.d.), Roman. Galleria degli Uffizi, Florence, Italy. Photo ©Alinari/The Bridgeman Art Library; **monkey** Gold monkey-head bead (100–600 a.d.), Mochia, La Mina, Jequetepeque Valley, north coast of Peru. Photo ©Werner Forman/Art Resource, New York; **crown** Crown of the Holy Roman Empire (about 962). Kunsthistorisches Museum, Vienna, Austria. Photo ©Erich Lessing/Art Resource, New York; **mask from Teotihuacan** ©Charles & Josette Lenars/Corbis; **goddess figure** Fertility goddess (pre-Columbian), Aztec. The British Museum, London. Photo ©Werner Forman/Art Resource, New York; **David** ©David Lees/Corbis; **mammoth hunt** ©Chase Studio/Photo Researchers; **Alaska** Kenneth Garrett/National Geographic Image Collection; **Meadowcroft Blades** J. M. Adovasio, Mercyhurst Archaeological Institute; **archaeologists** Kenneth Garrett/National Geographic Image Collection; **Bison Kill site (all)** Dale Walde/University of Calgary; **Olmec Head** ©DeAgostini / SuperStock; **Monte Alban** ©JuanSalvador/Shutterstock;

Olmec head ©Gerardo Borbolla/Fotolia; **Jaguar figure** ©De Agostini Picture Library / Bridgeman Images; **altar** Altar no. 4 with Olmec lord in niche beneath jaguar pelt (about a.d. 500–1000), Pre-Columbian. Archaeological garden of La Venta in Villahermosa, Mexico. Photo ©Gianni Dagli Orti/The Art Archive; **head** Julio Donoso/Corbis Sygma; **Olmec region** ©Jonathan Blair/Corbis; **Andes** ©SuperStock; **Nazca spider** William Allard/National Geographic Image Collection; **Nazca hummingbird** ©Philip Baird/ www.anthroarcheart.org; **Nazca wedge** ©Yann Arthus-Berthand/Corbis; **headdress** ©Werner Forman/Bridgeman Images; **Mesa Verde cliff palace** ©Getty Images; **Great Serpent Mound** ©Richard A. Cooke/Corbis; **mask** Jade mask used in burial rituals (600s), Classic Maya. Excavated from the Temple of Inscriptions at Palenque. Museo Nacional de Antropologia, Mexico City. Photo ©Werner Forman/Art Resource, New York; **codex** (Detail of) Prisoners marching as a result of destruction of the land of Mu from Maya codex Troano or Tro-Cortesianus. Antochiw Collection, Mexico. Photo ©Mireille Vautier/The Art Archive; **jaguar** Two-headed jaguar throne from Uxmal, Yucatan, Maya. Photo ©Danielle Gustafson/Art Resource, New York; **Maya Stele** The Granger Collection, New York; **Mayan Pyramid** ©Alison Wright/Corbis; **ball court** Ball court at Chichen Itza, Maya, Yucatan, Mexico. Photo ©Dagli Orti/The Art Archive; **ball court hoop** ©Ludovic Maisant/Corbis; **Machu Picchu** ©Tim Hursley/SuperStock; **Aztec sun stone** ©SuperStock; **Quetzalcoatl** Quetzalcoatl (900s), Toltec. Western Yucatan, Mexico. Photo ©Dagli Orti/The Art Archive at Art Resource, New York; **Pyramid of the Sun** ©Angelo Hornak/Corbis; **warrior** Eagle Warrior (pre-Columbian), Aztec. Mueseo del Templo Mayor, Mexico City. Photo ©Michel Zabe/Art Resource, New York; **mural** Detail of *The Aztec World* (1929), Diego Rivera. Mural. National Palace Museum, Mexico City. ©Banco de Mexico Trust. Photo ©Schalkwijk/Art Resource, New York; **calendar** Solar calendar (reconstruction), Aztec, Mexica culture. National Anthropological Museum, Mexico. Photo ©Dagli Orti/The Art Archive; **Sun God, Tonatiuh** ©et de Trianon, Versailles, France; **Aztec sun stone** ©AZA/Archive Zabé / Art Resource, NY; **Pachacutic** Pachacutic Inca IX, detail from Geneaology (1700s), Cuzco School. Museo Pedro de Osma, Lima, Peru. Photo ©Mireille Vautier/The Art Archive; **Machu Picchu** Machu Picchu, Peru, seen from royal quarters and House of the Inca. Photo ©Gianni Dagli Orti/The Art Archive; **royal treatment** Parading a sacred Inca mummy on a litter (1565), Felipe Guanman Poma de Ayala. From *El Primer Nueva Coronica y buen Gobierno,* Perus codex facsimile. Royal Library, Copenhagen, Denmark. Photo ©Nick Saunders Barbara Heller Photo Library, London/Art Resource, New York; **Incan mummy** Stephen Alvarez/National Geographic Image

Collection; **mummy bundle** ©2003 Ira Block; **mummy bundle (illus)** Illustration by John Dawson/National Geographic Image Collection; **Gifts for the Dead** The Granger Collection, NY.

MODULE 14

Lorenzo de Medici Bust of Lorenzo de Medici (1400s or 1500s). Museo di Andrea del Castagno, Uffizi, Florence, Italy. Photo ©Scala/Art Resource, New York; **bible** Gutenberg Bible (about 1455). Volume II, f. 45v–46. PML 818 ch1 ff1. The Pierpont Morgan Library, New York. Photo ©The Pierpont Morgan Library/Art Resource, New York; **Madonna** *The Madonna of Chancellor Rolin* (about 1434), Jan van Eyck. Louvre, Paris. Photo ©Scala/Art Resource, New York; **Lorenzo de Medici** (Detail of) *Lorenzo de Medici and the Arts in Florence* (about 1634) Giovanni da Sangiovanni. Palazzo Pitti, Florence, Italy. Photo ©Alfredo Dagli Orti/The Art Archive; **Castiglione** *Portrait of Baldassare Castiglione,* Raphael. Louvre, Paris. ©Scala/ Art Resource, New York; **Isabella D'Este** The Granger Collection, New York; **Cordoba** ©nito/Shutterstock; **Ferdinand and Isabella** ©The Catholic King and Queen with an Embassy from the King of Fez, Lopez y Portana, Vicente (1772-1850)/ Real Academia de Bellas Artes de San Fernando, Madrid, Spain/ Bridgeman Images; **Venice** ©In Green/ Shutterstock; **portrait of female** *Portrait of Cecilia Gallerani, Lady with an Ermine',* c1490. Cecilia Gallerani was an influential mistress of the ruler of Milan, Ludovico Sforza. ©Art Media/Print Collector/Getty Images; **marriage** *Marriage of the Virgin* (1504), Raphael. Pinocoteca di Brera, Milan, Italy. Photo ©Scala/Art Resource, New York; **Leonardo da Vinci** Stephano Bianchetti/Corbis; **Michelangelo Buonarroti** The Granger Collection, New York; **Machiavelli** *Portrait of Niccolo Machiavelli,* Santi di Tito. Palazzo Vecchio, Florence, Italy. Photo ©Erich Lessing/Art Resource, New York; **Mona Lisa** *Mona Lisa* (1503–1506), Leonardo da Vinci. Louvre, Paris. Photo by R. G. Ojeda. Photo ©Réunion des Musées Nationaux/Art Resource, New York; **David** ©SuperStock; **Athens** *The School of Athens* (1400s), Raphael. Stanza della Segnatura, Vatican Palace, Vatican State. Photo ©Scala/Art Resource, New York; **Leonardo's Helicopter** ©Bettmann/Corbis; **wedding** *Peasant Wedding* (1568), Peter Bruegel the Elder. Kunsthistorisches Museum, Vienna, Austria. Photo ©Saskia Ltd./Art Resource, New York; **Thomas More** *Thomas More, Lord Chancellor* (late 1400s). Private Collection. Photo ©The Stapleton Collection/The Bridgeman Art Library; **Christine de Pizan** Christine de Pizan teaches her son (about 1430). Harley MS 4431, f. 26 ff. The British Library, London. Photo by AKG London/British Library; *Othello* ©Castle Rock/Dakota Films/The Kobal Collection; *Ran* ©Touchstone/The Kobal Collection; *Romeo and Juliet* ©Merick Morton/20th Century Fox/The Kobal Collection; *10 Things I Hate about You* ©Herald Ace/Nippon Herald/Greenwich/The Kobal Collection; **printing**

press Illustration by Peter Dennis/Linda Rogers Associates; **joblessness** By permission of the Folger Shakespeare Library, Washington, D.C.; **performance of a play** KMSKA Antwerp-Image courtesy of Reproductiefonds; **Pomander** Musée de la Parfumerie Fragonard, Paris. Photo ©Gianni Dagli Orti/ The Art Archive; **table prayer** *A Family Saying Grace Before the Meal* (1585), Anthuenis (Antoon) Claeissins or Claeissens. Oil on panel, 96.5 cm x 142 cm. Private Collection. Photo ©Bridgeman Art Library; **London** MS Sloane 2596, f. 52. British Library. Photo by AKG London/British Library; **Botticelli's** *Primavera* ©Photodisc/Getty Images; **Martin Luther** *Portrait of Martin Luther* (1529) Lucas Cranach the Elder. Museo Poldi Pezzoli, Milan, Italy. Photo ©The Bridgeman Art Library; **Renaissance architecture** ©Fotolia.

MODULE 15

Martin Luther Martin Luther Attaching Theses ©SuperStock; **bible** *Gutenberg Bible* (about 1455). Volume II, f. 45v–46. PML 818 ch1 ff1. The Pierpont Morgan Library, New York. Photo ©The Pierpont Morgan Library/Art Resource, New York; **dancers** Detail of Nobles entertained in garden by musicians and dancers (about 1590), Mughal. Photo ©British Library/The Art Archive; **Martin Luther** *Portrait of Martin Luther* (1529) Lucas Cranach the Elder. Museo Poldi Pezzoli, Milan, Italy. Photo ©The Bridgeman Art Library; **Council of Trent** *Pope Paul III Farnese at the Council of Trent* (1560-1566), Taddeo and Federico Zuccari. Farnese Palace, Caprarola, Italy. Photo ©Alfredo Dagli Orti/The Art Archive; **Martin Luther** *Portrait of Martin Luther* (1529) Lucas Cranach the Elder. Museo Poldi Pezzoli, Milan, Italy. Photo ©The Bridgeman Art Library; **Henry VIII** *Portrait of Henry VIII, King of England* (1540), Hans Holbein the Younger. Galleria Nazionale d'Arte Antica, Rome. Photo ©Scala/Art Resource, New York; **Anne Boleyn** *Anne Boleyn* (about 1530), unknown artist. Oil on wood panel. National Portrait Gallery, London. ©National Portrait Gallery/SuperStock; **Catherine Howard** ©Stapleton Collection/Corbis; **Mary I** *Mary I Tudor* (1554), Antonis Moro or Mor. Museo del Prado, Madrid. Photo ©Gianni Dagli Orti/The Art Archive; **Elizabeth I** *Elizabeth I, Queen of England,* Federico Zuccari. Pinacoteca Nazionale di Siena. Photo ©Gianni Dagli Orti/The Art Archive; **Elizabeth I** *Elizabeth I* (about 1588), George Gower. Oil on wood panel. National Portrait Gallery, London. ©National Portrait Gallery/SuperStock; **John Calvin** John Calvin as a young man, Flemish School. Bibliotheque Publique et Universitaire, Geneva, Switzerland. Photo ©Erich Lessing/Art Resource, New York; **Queen of Navarre** *Marguerite d'Angouleme, Queen of Navarre* (1500s). Musée Condé, Chantilly, France. Photo ©Réunion des Musées Nationaux/Art Resource, New York; **Council of Trent** *Pope Paul III Farnese at the Council of Trent* (1560-1566), Taddeo and Federico Zuccari. Farnese Palace, Caprarola,

Italy. Photo ©Alfredo Dagli Orti/The Art Archive; **Georgetown University** ©Orhan Cam/Shutterstock; **court** *Scene at Court* (1710–1720), Alessandro Magnasco. Kunthistorisches Museum, Vienna. Photo ©Erich Lessing/Art Resource, New York.

MODULE 16

Tokugawa *Portrait of Tokugawa Ieyasu* (1600s), Japanese. Private Collection. Photo ©The Bridgeman Art Library; **Cortés** Album/Oronoz/SuperStock; **Champlain** The Granger Collection, New York; **Shah Jahan** ©Burstein Collection/Corbis; **George Washington** *Washington Crossing the Delaware* (1851), Eastman Johnson. Copy after the Emmanuel Leutze painting in the Metropolitan Museum, New York. Private collection. Photo ©Art Resource, New York; **Akbar** Portrait of Akbar and Prince Salim (1800s) (detail). India, Mughal. Gift of Sally Sample Aal, 1997. Inv. 97.19.16. The Newark Museum, Newark, New Jersey. Photo ©The Newark Museum/Art Resource, New York; **Pratibha Patil, Chandrika Bandaranaike Kumaratunga, Khaleda Zia** AP/Wide World Photos; **Indira Gandhi** ©Bettmann/Corbis; **Taj Mahal** ©Steve Vidler/SuperStock; **dagger** Dagger handle (in the form of a horse's head). Mughal. India. Victoria and Albert Museum, London. ©Victoria and Albert Museum, London/The Bridgeman Art Library; **Tomb** ©Abbie Enock/Travel Ink/Corbis; **Mughal painting** Akbar on the elephant Hawai pursuing the elephant rau Bagha (about 1590). Double page miniature from the Akbarnama. Mughal. Photo ©Victoria and Albert Museum, London/Art Resource, New York; **tapestry** Tent hanging (early 1700s). Mughal dynasty. Victoria and Albert Museum, London. Photo ©Victoria and Albert Museum, London/Art Resource, New York; **early globe** Globe (about 1492), Martin Behaim. Bibliotheque Nationale, Paris. Photo ©Giraudon/Art Resource, New York; **Prince Henry** Detail of *St. Vincent Polyptych* (1400s), Nuno Goncalves. Museu Nacional de Arte Antiga, Lisbon, Portugal. Photo ©Scala/Art Resource, New York; **caravel** ©Bettmann/Corbis; **mariner using sextant** ©Bridgeman-Giraudon/Art Resource, NY; **sextant** ©Dave King/DK Images (Dorling Kindersley); **compass** *sextant* ©V&A Images, London/Art Resource, NY; **man rolling barrel** ©Bettman/Corbis; **Afonso de Albuquerque** ©Stapleton Collection/Corbis; **Hong Kong** ©Morton Beebe/Corbis; **Ming vase** ©Musee Guimet, Paris, France/The Bridgeman Art Library; **Great Wall of China** ©Corbis; **Hall of Supreme Harmony** ©TAO Images Limited/Alamy; **Hall of Central Harmony** ©John T. Young/Corbis; **Nine Dragon Wall** ©Harvey Lloyd/Getty Images; **Emperor Kangxi** ©Hu Weibiao/Image Works, Inc.; **marriage** Marriage ceremony (1800s), China. Victoria and Albert Museum, London. Photo ©Eileen Tweedy/The Art Archive; **making silk** The Granger Collection, New York; **Samurai warrior** The Granger Collection, NY;

Himeji castle ©B.S.P.I./Corbis; **Matsuo Basho** ©Asian Art & Archeology/Corbis; **Kabuki theater (samurai)** ©Asian Art & Archaeology/Corbis; **Kabuki theater (warrior)** Charles & Josette Lenars/Corbis; **Jesuit missionaries** ©1995 Christie's Images Limited; **Zen Buddhism** Monk Tokiyori. Musée des Arts, Asiatiques-Guimet, Paris. Photo by Richard Lambert. Photo ©Réunion des Musées Nationaux/Art Resource, New York; **Columbus** Christopher Columbus (1400s), Sebastiano del Piombo. Metropolitan Museum of Art, New York. Photo ©The Bridgeman Art Library; **Francisco Pizarro** The Granger Collection, New York; **Atahualpa** South American Pictures; **U.S. postage stamp** The Granger Collection, New York; **smallpox** The Granger Collection, New York; **letter** (Detail of) Letter from Christopher Columbus to his son Diego (February 5, 1505). General Archive of the Indies, Seville, Spain. Photo ©Gianni Dagli Orti/The Art Archive; **Henry Hudson Arrives in New York** The Granger Collection, New York; **pirate** North Carolina Collection, University of North Carolina, Chapel Hill; **slavery** The Granger Collection, New York; **Olaudah Equiano** The Granger Collection, New York; **slave ship diagram** The Newberry Library, Chicago; **slaves on sugar plantation** The Granger Collection, New York.

MODULE 17

Philip II Philip II, King of Spain and Portugal (1500s), Alonso Sanchez Coello. Museo del Prado, Madrid, Spain. Photo ©Erich Lessing/Art Resource, New York; **Pizarro** Francisco Pizarro (1835), Amable-Paul Coutan. Chateau de Versailles et de Trianon, Versailles, France. Photo by Franck Raux. Photo ©Réunion des Musées Nationaux/Art Resource, New York; **Oliver Cromwell** The Granger Collection, New York; **Taj Mahal** ©Pallava Bagla/Corbis; **Louis XIV** Louis XIV, King of France (1701), Hyacinthe Rigaud. Louvre, Paris. Photo ©Erich Lessing/Art Resource, New York; **statue of Louis XIV** ©Todd A. Gipstein/Corbis; **marriage** Marriage of Louis XIV, 1638-1715. King of France and Marie Thérèse of Austria (detail). ©Gianni Dagli Orti/Art Resource, NY; **Spanish Armada** The Granger Collection, NY; **family portrait** Las Meninas or The Family of Philip IV (about 1656), Diego Rodriguez de Silva y Velasquez. Prado, Madrid, Spain. Photo ©The Bridgeman Art Library; **The Night Watch** The Granger Collection, New York; **Richelieu** Cardinal Richelieu (1636), Phillippe de Champaigne. Musée Condé, Chantilly, France. Photo ©Erich Lessing/Art Resource, New York; **Louis XIV** Louis XIV, King of France (1600s), follower of Pierre Mignard. Contemporary copy after a lost portrait by Mignard. Oil on canvas, 105 cm x 90 cm. Cat. 2299. Museo del Prado, Madrid. Photo ©Erich Lessing/Art Resource, New York; **aerial of Versailles** ©Archivo Iconografico, S.A./Corbis; **Hall of Mirrors** ©Massimo Listri/Corbis; **Versailles fountains** ©Adam Woolfitt/Corbis; **Versailles gardens** ©Ben Mangor/SuperStock; **battle** Battle of Denain, 24th July 1712 (1839), Jean Alaux. Chateau de Versailles, France. Photo ©Giraudon/The Bridgeman Art Library; **Hapsburg** Hapsburg dynasty (about 1700). Heeresgeschichtliches Museum, Vienna, Austria. ©The Bridgeman Art Library; **silver samovar** ©Dorling Kindersley; **traditional dress** Costumes of Crimean tribes (1888), A. Racinet. From Historical Costumes vol, V. Musée des Arts Décoratifs, Paris. Photo ©Dagli Orti/The Art Archive; **Troika** ©Historical Picture Archive/Corbis; **Russian painting** Shrovetide (1919), Boris Kustidiev. The I. Brodsky Museum, St. Petersburg, Russia. Photo Courtesy of the Smithsonian Institution Traveling Exhibition Service; **wooden house** ©Scheufler Collection/Corbis; **statue of Louis XIV** ©Todd A. Gipstein/Corbis; **Beheading of Charles I** The Granger Collection, New York.

MODULE 18

Hogarth painting The Granger Collection, New York; **princess** Portrait of a Princess Holding a Wine Cup (1600s-1700s), Mughal. India. The Newark Museum, Newark, New Jersey. Photo ©The Newark Museum/Art Resource, New York; **telescope** Isaac Newton's reflecting telescope (1672) Royal Society. Photo ©Eileen Tweedy/The Art Archive; **Lohan** Statuette of a Lohan, Ching dynasty. Musée des Arts Asiatiques-Guimet, Paris. Photo ©Giraudon/Art Resource, New York; **Liberty Bell** ©Leif Skoogfors/Corbis; **Galileo** Galileo before the Holy Office of the Vatican. John Nicolas Robert-Fleury. Oil on canvas. Louvre, Paris. Photo by Gerard Blot. Photo ©Réunion des Musées Nationaux/Art Resource, New York; **Nicolaus Copernicus** ©Bettmann/Corbis; **telescope** Isaac Newton's reflecting telescope (1672). Royal Society. Photo ©Eileen Tweed/The Art Archive; **Isaac Newton** ©Bettmann/Corbis; **anatomy lesson** The Anatomy Lesson of Dr. Tulp (1632), Rembrandt van Rijn. Mauritshuis, The Hague, The Netherlands. Photo ©Scala/Art Resource, New York; **Voltaire** The Granger Collection, New York; **Hogarth painting** The Granger Collection, NY; **Joseph II** Joseph II, Emperor of Austria and of the Holy Roman Empire, King of Hungary and Bohemia (1700s), Austrian. Musée du Château de Versailles. Photo ©Gianni Dagli Orti/The Art Archive; **Catherine the Great** ©Anatoly Sapronenkov, Tomsk Regional Arts Museum/SuperStock; **Mary Wollstonecraft** Mary Evans Picture Library; **flags in speech bubble** ©hobbit/Shutterstock; **Baroque building** ©Goran Bogicevic/Shutterstock; **Neoclassical building** ©PLRANG ART/Shutterstock; **Constitution, Toussaint L'Ouverture** The Granger Collection, NY; **Cloth Hall** ©duncan1890/iStock/Getty Images.

MODULE 19

George Washington George Washington, George Healy. Musée du Château de Versailles. Photo ©Gianni Dagli Orti/The Art Archive; **guillotine** Reduced model of a guillotine. Musée de la Ville de Paris, Musée Carnavalet, Paris. Photo ©Bridgeman-Giraudon/Art Resource, New York; **Napoleon** Napoleon Bonaparte, Emperor of France. Musée du Château de Versailles. Photo ©Gianni Dagli Orti/The Art Archive; **Toussaint L'Ouverture** The Granger Collection, New York; **storming the Bastille** The Conquerors of the Bastille Before the Hotel de Ville (1839), Paul Delaroche. Musée du Petit Palais, Paris. Photo ©Erich Lessing/Art Resource, New York; **Three Estates** Detail of Caricature of the three estates: A faut esperer que jeu la finira bientot (1700s). Color engraving, Musée de la Ville de Paris, Musée Carnavalet, Paris. Photo by Bulloz. Photo ©Réunion des Musées Nationaux/Art Resource, New York; **Louis XVI** Louis XVI, King of France. Musée de Château de Versailles. Photo ©Dagli Orti/The Art Archive; **Marie Antoinette** Marie Antoinette, Queen of France (replica of work painted in 1778) Musée du Château de Versailles. Photo ©Gianni Dagli Orti/The Art Archive; **storming the Bastille** The Taking of the Bastille, July 14, 1789, Anonymous French painter. Chateaux de Versailles et de Trianon, Versailles, France. Photo ©Erich Lessing/Art Resource, New York; **arrest** Arrest of Louis XVI, King of France and his family attempting to flee the country at Varennes, France June 21-22, 1791. Musée Carnavalet, Paris. Photo ©Gianni Dagli Orti/The Art Archive; **guillotine** Illustration by Patrick Whelan; **Robespierre** Portrait of Robespierre, Louis L. Boilly. Musée des Beaux-Arts, Lille, France. Photo R. G. Ojeda. Photo ©Réunion des Musées Nationaux/Art Resource, New York; **Danton** Portrait of Danton (1700s), Anonymous. Musée de la Ville de Paris, Musée Carnavalet, Paris. Photo by Bulloz. Photo ©Réunion des Musées Nationaux/Art Resource, New York; **Napoleon** Portrait of Bonaparte, premier consul (1803), Francois Gerard. Oil on canvas. Musée Conde, Chantilly, France. Photo by Harry Breja. Photo ©Réunion des Musées Nationaux./Art Resource, New York; **crossing Alps** Detail of Napoleon Crossing the Alps (1800s), Jacques Louis David. Chateau de Malmaison et bois–Preau, Rueil–Malmaison, France. Photo ©Erich Lessing/Art Resource, New York; **globe caricature** A Stoppage to a Stride over the Globe (1803). English School. Color lithograph. Private collection. Photo ©The Bridgeman Art Library; **firing squad** ©Archivo Iconografico, S.A./Corbis; **Congress of Vienna** ©Christel Gerstenberg/Corbis.

MODULE 20

Padre Manuel Hidalgo Portrait of Miguel Gregorio Antonio Ignacio Hidalgo-Costilla y Gallaga Mandarte Villasenor (1753-1811) revolutionary and Mexican priest, considered the instigator of the Mexican War of Independence. Painting by Serrano. Mexico, 18th-19th century. De Agostini Picture Library/G. Dagli Orti/Bridgeman Images; **Napoleon** *Napoleon in his study at the Tuileries* (1812). Jacques Louis David. Collection of Prince and Princess Napoleon, Paris. Photo ©Bridgeman- Giraudon/Art Resource, New York; **Wilhelm I** ©Hulton-Deutsch Collection/Corbis; **Lincoln** ©Francis G. Mayer/Corbis; **Jose de San Martin** The Granger Collection, New York; **Toussaint L'ouverture** *Portrait of Francois-Dominique Toussaint, known as Toussaint Louverture*, Anonymous. Musée du Quai Branly, Paris. Photo J. G. Berizzi. Photo ©Réunion des Musées Nationaux/Art Resource, New York; **Simon Bolivar** ©Christie's Images/Corbis; **Jose de San Martin** The Granger Collection, New York; **Simon Bolivar** ©Bettmann/Corbis; **Thomas Paine, Simon Bolivar** The Granger Collection, New York; **Shields of Botswana, Austria, United States** Courtesy of the Flag Institute; **Prince Metternich** *Klemens Metternich, Austrian prince and statesman.* Museo Glauco, Lombardi, Parma, Italy. Photo ©Gianni Dagli Orti/The Art Archive; **Antonin Dvorak** ©Archivo Iconografico, S.A./Corbis; **Hotel de Ville** *Combat Before the Hotel de Ville, July 28th, 1830*, Victor Schnetz. Musée du Petit Palais, Paris. Photo by Bulloz. Photo ©Réunion des Musées Nationaux/Art Resource, New York; **King of Sardinia and Garibaldi** The Granger Collection, New York; **Otto von Bismarck** ©Bettmann/Corbis; **Lord Byron** ©Bettmann/Corbis; **Beethoven** *Portrait of Ludwig von Beethoven* (1819), Anonymous. Beethoven House, Bonn, Germany. Photo ©Snark/Art Resource, New York; **Muybridge's Horses** racing ©Hulton-Deutsch Collection/Corbis; **poppies** *Poppy Field* by Claude Monet ©Corbis; **lions** *Lion Hunt* (1860/1861) Eugene Delacroix. Potter Palmer Collection, 1922.404, Reproduction. The Art Institute of Chicago, Chicago, Illinois; **field work** *The Stone Breakers* (1849), Gustave Courbet. Gemaldegalerie, Dresden, Germany. Photo ©The Bridgeman Art Library; **palace** *Ducal Palace* by Claude Monet ©Francis G. Mayer/Corbis.

MODULE 21

Seed drill The Granger Collection, New York; **cotton gin** ©Bettmann/Corbis; **Karl Marx** ©akg-images, London; **Hall of Supreme Harmony** ©TAO Images Limited/Alamy; **boy in a factory** ©Corbis; **man using seed drill** ©Hulton Archive/Getty Images; **Flying shuttle** ©Michael St. Maur Sheil/Corbis; **man using loom** *Blind man using a loom*, plate 17 from *Essai su l'Instruction des Aveugles* (1817) Dr. Sebastien Guillie. Colored engraving Julie Ribault. Bibliotheque de l'Institut d'Ophtalmologie, Paris, Archives Charmet. Photo ©The Bridgeman Art Library; **sewing machine** ©Bettmann/Corbis; **Sir Henry Bessemer** Edward Gooch/Getty Images; **train** Liverpool and Manchester passenger train (about 1830). National Railway Museum, York, North Yorkshire, United Kingdom. Photo ©The Bridgeman Art Library; **George Stephenson's Rocket** ©Hulton Archive/Getty Images; **row houses** The Granger Collection, New York; **Elizabeth Gaskell** The Granger Collection, New York; **Manchester** The Granger Collection, New York; **child labor** ©Steve Raymer/Corbis; **mill girls** ©Corbis; **worker** *Workers at Biermeister and Wain* (1885), Peter Severin Kroyer. Statens Museum for Kunst, Copenhagen, Denmark. Photo ©Snark/Art Resource, New York; **The Crystal Palace** Mary Evans Picture Library; **Adam Smith** ©Bettmann/Corbis; **Karl Marx** ©Archivo Iconografico, S.A./Corbis; **capitalism caricature** The Capitalist Vampire (1885) by Walter Crane; **worker strike** *Strike* (1895), Mihaly Munkacsy. Magyar Nemzeti Galeria, Budapest, Hungary. Photo ©The Bridgeman Art Library; **Jane Addams** *Jane Addams* (about 1920), George de Forest Brush. Photo ©National Portrait Gallery, Smithsonian Institution/Art Resource, New York.

MODULE 22

Queen Victoria ©Victoria & Albert Museum/Art Resource, NY; **Eiffel Tower** The Granger Collection, NY; **soldiers on horses** ©The Stapleton Collection/The Bridgeman Art Library; **Panama Canal** ©Corbis; **suffragettes** ©Hulton-Deutsch Collection/Corbis; **Queen Victoria and Prince Albert** ©Bettmann/Corbis; **Zola** ©Gianni Dagli Orti/Art Resource, NY; **Maori man** ©Sean Sexton Collection/Corbis; **Aboriginal fish painting** ©Charles & Josette Lenars/Corbis; **Australia gold mining** ©Art Resource, NY; **Aborigine** Nouvelle-Hollande. Cour-Rou-Bari-Gal., Plate XVIII from Atlas historique: du Voyage de decouvertes aux terres australes, by Charles Alexandre Leseur and Nicolas-Martin Petit. Image Courtesy of State Library of South Australia; **prison ship** The Granger Collection, NY; **Abraham Lincoln** Library of Congress Prints & Photographs Division, Washington, D.C.

[LC-USZ62-12950]; **Thomas Edison** ©Bettmann/Corbis; **Thomas Edison and team** The Granger Collection, NY; **Kinetoscope** Library of Congress Prints & Photographs Division, Washington, D.C. [200033635]; **Edison phonograph** Phonograph, by Thomas Alva Edison (1847-1931), USA, 19th century. De Agostini Picture Library/Bridgeman Images; **Orville Wright plane** The Granger Collection, NY; **woman holding phone** ©Bettmann/Corbis; **Ford Model-T factory** ©Bettmann/Corbis; **cholera cartoon** ©Bridgeman Art Library; **smallpox vaccinations** The Granger Collection, NY; **Marie Curie** The Granger Collection, NY; **Darwin painting** ©Bettmann/Corbis.

MODULE 23

Asante sculpture Brass weight for weighing gold dust in the form of a horse and rider. Ashanti, Ghana. British Museum, London. ©Werner Forman/Art Resource, New York; **Napoleon III** *Portrait of Napoleon III, Emperor of France*, Franz Xavier (after). Oil on canvas, Photo ©Chateau de Versailles, France/The Bridgeman Art Library; **Boer War** ©Bettmann/Corbis; **Mexican Revolution** ©Bettmann/Corbis; **South African mines** ©Robert Harris/Hulton Archive/Getty Images; **stamp** The Granger Collection, New York; **Cecil Rhodes** The Granger Collection, New York; **King Cetshwayo** The Granger Collection, New York; **Winston Churchill** ©Hulton-Deutsch Collection/Corbis; **Menelik II** ©Culver Pictures; **Devilfish cartoon** The Granger Collection, New York; **Muhammad Ali** *Mehemet Ali, Viceroy of Egypt* (1800s), Louis Charles Auguste Couder. Château de Versailles, France. Photo ©Lauros-Giraudon/The Bridgeman Art Library; **Suez Canal** *Shipping on the Suez Canal* (1869), Edouard Riou. Château de Compiegne, Oise, France. Photo ©Lauros-Giraudon/The Bridgeman Art Library; **Nasir al-Din** *Portrait of Nasir Al-Din Shah* (1800s), unknown artist. Louvre, Paris. Photo ©Réunion des Musées Nationaux/Art Resource, New York; **Sepoy** *A Sepoy (an Indian Soldier in the French Battalion) at Pondicherry* (1800s), Racinet. Photo ©The Stapleton Collection/The Bridgeman Art Library; **British officer in India** ©Hulton Archive/ Getty Images; **Battle of Cawnpore** The Granger Collection, New York; **American soldiers in the Philippines** ©Corbis; **Queen Liliuokalani** The Granger Collection, New York; **plantation** *A Brazilian Plantation at the Roadstead of Rio de Janeiro* (Johann Lorenz Rugendas), 1830. Color lithograph. Photo by Hermann Buresch ©Bildarchiv Preussischer Kulturbesitz/Art Resource, New York; **Domingo Sarmiento** ©Bettmann/Corbis; **workers unload coffee beans** ©Underwood & Underwood/Corbis; **José Martí** The Granger Collection, New York; **Pedro Míguel Locks** ©Danny Lehman/Corbis; **Roosevelt cartoon** The Granger Collection, New York.

MODULE 24

View of Canton, China ©DEA/G. DAGLI ORTI/Getty Images; **Commodore Perry** ©Bettmann/Corbis; **Queen Victoria** Union Flag with portrait of Queen Victoria and British Colonies. The Bodleian Library, Oxford, England, John Johnson Collection (Printed Fabrics 1). Photo ©The Bodleian Library/The Art Archive; **Zapata** *Emiliano Zapata* (1800s-1900s), unknown artist. National History Museum, Mexico City. Photo ©Gianni Dagli Orti/The Art Archive; **Chinese goods** ©Historical Picture Archive/Corbis; **Shanghai, China** Blackstation/Getty Images; **Taiping forces** The Granger Collection, New York; **Boxer Rebellion** ©SuperStock; **woodblock landscape** ©Alfredo Dagli Orti/Art Resource, NY; **Russo-Japanese cartoon** Mary Evans Picture Library, London; **Carving the Block (all)** Photo by Fumi Bull. Courtesy David Bull; **Naniway Okita** ©Sakamoto Photo Research Laboratory/Corbis; **wave painting** *Under the Wave off Kanagawa* ©Historical Picture Archive/Corbis; **printing** Photo by Fumi Bull. Courtesy David Bull; **Santa Anna** The Granger Collection, New York; **Defending the Alamo** ©Bettmann/Corbis; **Juárez mural** The Granger Collection, New York; **Porfirio Diaz** Interim Archives/Getty Images; **Zapata** *Emiliano Zapata* (1800s-1900s), unknown artist. National History Museum, Mexico City. Photo ©Gianni Dagli Orti/The Art Archive.

MODULE 25

WWI Soldier ©The Image Bank/Getty Images; **Lusitania** ©Bettmann/Corbis; **Uncle Sam** ©Bettmann/Corbis; **Woodrow Wilson** Mary Evans Picture Library; **clean up worker** ©Bettmann/Corbis; **frozen troops** ©Hulton-Deutsch Collection/Corbis; **Kaiser Wilhelm II** Mary Evans Picture Library; **Allied troops** ©Corbis; **machine gun** ©pop-perfoto.com/Classicstock; **tank** Hulton Archive/Getty Images; **frozen troops** ©Hulton-Deutsch Collection/Corbis; **pilot** ©Hulton-Deutsch Collection/Corbis; **planes in dogfight** ©Fraser May; **flu** Spanish Flu in Chicago ©Bettmann/Corbis; **female relief worker** ©Corbis; **Woodrow Wilson** *Thomas Woodrow Wilson* (1921), Edmund Charles Tarbell. Photo ©National Portrait Gallery, Smithsonian Institution/Art Resource, New York; **Clemenceau** *Portrait of George Clemenceau* (1879-1880), Edouard Manet. Musée d'Orsay, Paris. Photo ©Erich Lessing/Art Resource, New York.

MODULE 26

Emperor P'u-i ©Bettmann/Corbis; **Mexican flag** ©The Flag Institute; **Mao Zedong** ©AFP/Getty Images; **Hitler** ©Hulton Archive/Getty Images; **Kemal** ©Hulton-Deutsch Collection/Corbis; **Tiananaman (1919)** ©Duke University Rare Book, Manuscript & Special Collections; **Alexander III** ©Archivo Iconografico, S.A./Corbis; **V.I. Lenin** ©Bettmann/Corbis; **massacre** *Bloody Sunday* ©Tass/Sovfoto; **Red Army** ©TASS/Sovfoto; **Marx** ©Archivo Iconografico, S.A./Corbis; **Lenin** ©Bettmann/Corbis; **young communists** ©Bettmann/Corbis; **1984 book cover** illustration by Mark Wiener; **Joseph Stalin** David King Collection, London; **Ukrainian Kulaks** ©TASS/Sovfoto; **Soviet factory poster** Heritage/SuperStock; **Glory to Great Stalin** ©CTK/Sovfoto/Eastfoto; **Stalin altered photos (all)** David King Collection, London; **Temple of Heaven** ©Patrick Field/Eye Ubiquitous/Corbis; **Sun Yixian** ©Hulton Archive/Getty Images; **Tiananmen Square** ©Peter Turnley/Corbis; **Tiananaman (1919)** ©Duke University Rare Book, Manuscript & Special Collections; **Jiang Jieshi** ©Corbis; **bridge of iron chains** From *Chinese Communists Sketches and Autobiographies of the Old Guard: Red Dust* by Nym Wales. June 1972. Greenwood Publishing Group; **Red Army** ©Rene Burri/Magnum Photos; **Shaanxi caves** AP/Wide World Photos; **Japanese landing party** ©Hulton Archive/Getty Images; **Abdul Hamid II** ©Ann Ronan Pictures/Hulton Archive/Getty Images; **Kemal** ©Hulton-Deutsch Collection/Corbis; **Reza Shah** ©J.W. Cook/National Geographic Creative/Corbis.

MODULE 27

Einstein ©Hulton Archive/Getty Images; **Charles Lindbergh** ©Bettmann/Corbis; **Spanish Civil War** ©Hulton-Deutsch Collection/Corbis; **Hirohito** ©General Photographic Agency/Getty Images; **crowd** George Marks/Getty Images; **Life Magazine cover** ©The Advertising Archives/Alamy Stock Photo; **F. Scott Fitzgerald** AP/Wide World Photos; **Dali painting** *The Persistence of Memory* (1931), Salvador Dali. Oil on canvas, 9 1/2" x 13" (162.1934). The Museum of Modern Art, New York. Given anonymously. ©2000 Foundation Gala-Salvador Dali/VEGAP ©2007 Salvador Dali, Gala-Salvador Dali Foundation/Artists Rights Society (ARS), New York Digital Image ©The Museum of Modern Art/Licensed by Scala/Art Resource, New York; **suffrage parade** The Granger Collection, New York; **Charlie Chaplin** ©Bettmann/Corbis; **Frigidaire ad** The Granger Collection, New York; **washing machine** ©Schenectady Museum/ Hall of Electrical History Foundation/Corbis; **iron ad** The Granger Collection, New York; **coffee pot** ©Schenectady Museum/ Hall of Electrical History Foundation/Corbis; **vacuum ad** The Granger Collection, New York; **Depression lunch room** Getty Images; **money as building blocks** ©Hulton Archive/Getty Images; **Depression** ©Bettmann/Corbis; **Franklin Roosevelt** The Granger Collection, New York; **Benito Mussolini** ©Hulton Archive/Getty Images; **Adolph Hitler** ©Hulton Archive/Getty Images; **Nazi rally** ©Getty Images; **Juan Peron** ©Bettmann/Corbis; **Guernica** ©Corbis; **Picasso painting** *Guernica*, Pablo Picasso The Granger Collection, New York; **Neville Chamberlain** ©Getty Images.

MODULE 28

Nazi cartoon The Granger Collection, New York; **airplane** ©Museum of Flight/Corbis; **German surrender** ©Bettmann/Corbis; **watch** U.S. Air Force; **air raid** German planes bombing London, England (1940), *La Domenica del Corriere*. Photo ©Alfredo Dagli Orti/Art Archive; **Winston Churchill** The Granger Collection, New York; **London bus** ©William Vandivert/Getty Images; **Russian soldiers** ©The Art Archive; **U.S.S. West Virginia** ©Bettmann/Corbis; **Japanese warship** *Mikuma* The Granger Collection, New York; **General MacArthur** ©Bettmann/Corbis; **U.S. marines at Guadalcanal** ©AP/Wide World Photos; **Star of David patch** Courtesy of the Spertus Museum, Spertus Institute of Jewish Studies, Chicago; **Warsaw ghetto** ©Hulton-Deutsch Collection/Corbis; **Ella Gartner and Roza Robota** Courtesy of the United States Holocaust Memorial Museum Photo Archives; **Soviet troops** ©Hulton Archive/Getty Images; **Schools at War poster** Image courtesy of The Advertising Archives; **Eisenhower** ©Bettmann/Corbis; **Iwo Jima flag raising** ©Hulton Archive/Getty Images; **Nagasaki citizens** ©Yosuke Yamahata. Photo restoration by TX Unlimited, San Francisco. Courtesy Shogo Yamahata; **Enola Gay** ©UPI/Bettmann/Corbis; **atomic bomb** U.S. Air Force; **Oppenheimer and Groves** ©Bettmann/Corbis; **War Crimes Tribunal** ©AFP/Corbis; **Hirohio and MacArthur** ©AP/Wide World Photos.

MODULE 29

Korean 38th Parallel ©Everett Collection/ Alamy; **United Nations symbol** ©United Nations; **Fidel Castro** ©Wally McNamee/Corbis; **Ghana flag** ©Flag Institute Enterprises, Ltd.; **Berlin Wall graffiti** ©Peter Turnley/Corbis; **man on moon** NASA; **Nelson Mandela voting** ©Peter Turnley/Corbis; **Yalta conference** ©Art Resource, NY; **Czech political cartoon** ©Tom Little/Nashville Tennessean; **Sputnik** ©TASS/Sovfoto/ Eastfoto; **Apollo/Soyuz Mission symbol** NASA; **walking on moon** NASA; **Chiang Kai-Shek** ©Corbis; **Mao Zedong** ©Roman Soumar/Corbis; **Mao Zedong** ©Hulton Archive/Getty Images; **China Red Guards** ©Bettmann/Corbis; **Korean War at sea** ©Bert Hardy/Picture Post/ Getty Images; **Ho Chi Minh** ©Hulton Archive/Getty Images; **Vietnam Battle at Hue** ©Bettmann/Corbis; **plane dropping bombs** AP Images; **withdrawal from Vietnam** ©Nik Wheeler/Black Star Picture Collection; **girl playing with skulls** ©Les Stone/Sygma/Corbis; **men on rickshaws** ©Catherine Karnow/ Corbis; **dam builders** ©Bettmann/ Corbis; **Fidel Castro** ©Wally McNamee/ Corbis; **U.S. hostages** ©Alain Mingam/ Getty Images; **Taliban** ©Zaheeruddin Abdullah/AP Images; **Imre Nagy** Apic/Getty Images; **Prague (1968)** ©AP Images; **Nixon in China** ©Wally McNamee/Corbis; **Ronald Reagan button** ©David J. & Janice L. Frent Collection/Corbis.

MODULE 30

European entrance AP/Wide World Photos; **Kwame Nkrumah** ©Black Star; **Corazon Aquino** AP/Wide World Photos; **Gandhi** ©Hulton-Deutsch/ Getty Images; **voting rights** ©Firdia Lisnawati/AP Images; **Indian delivery cart** ©Brent Winebrenner/Lonely Planet Images/Getty Images; **Gandhi at spinning wheel** ©Margaret Bourke-White/ Time & Life Pictures/Getty Images; **Ali Bhutto** ©Romano Cagnoni/Black Star Picture Collection; **Rajiv Gandhi** ©Alain Nogues/Corbis; **Benazir Bhutto** ©Wally McNamee/Corbis; **Indira Gandhi** ©Imagno/Hulton Archive/Getty Images; **Bangladeshi Village** ©Nik Wheeler/ Corbis; **Tamil Tigers** ©Nokelsberg/ Getty News Images; **floating flower market** ©Steve Vidler/SuperStock; **Indonesian Tsunami** AP/Wide World Photos; **water buffalo cart** ©Jack Fields/Corbis; **Jakarta slum** AP/Wide World Photos; **Southeast Asian market** ©Steve Raymer/Corbis; **floating market** ©ML Sinibaldi/Corbis; **Mobuto Sese Seko** ©Reuters NewMedia Inc./Corbis; **Palestinian protester** ©Peter Turnley/ Corbis; **Oslo Peace Accords** AP/Wide World Photos; **Signs of Hope** (all) AP/ Wide World Photos; **Asian mountains** ©Dean Conger/Corbis; **Yaks on the plains** ©Tiziana and Gianni Baldizzone/ Corbis; **Afghan election ballot** ©Ahmad Masood/Reuters/Corbis.

MODULE 31

Fidel Castro ©Bettmann/Corbis; **Harry Truman** Getty Images; **Deng Xiaoping** ©Wally McNamee/Corbis; **Barack Obama** ©Brooks Craft/Corbis; **Protest in Venezuela** AP/Wide World Photos; **political cartoon** ©2001 The New Yorker Collection from cartoonbank.com. All Rights Reserved; **Vicente Fox** AP/Wide World Photos; **Eva Peron** ©Bettmann/ Corbis; **Ken Saro-Wiwa** ©Greenpeace; **South African poll worker** ©David Turnley/Corbis; **Nelson Mandela** ©David Turnley/Corbis; **F.W. De Klerk** AP/Wide World Photos; **Glasnost cartoon** Jeff Stahler. Reprinted by permission of Newspaper Enterprise Association, Inc.; **Mikhail Gorbachev** ©Peter Turnley/ Corbis; **Boris Yeltsin** ©Peter Turnley/ Corbis; **Russian tank** AP/Wide World Photos; **Vladimir Putin** ©Ron Sachs/ Corbis; **fall of the Berlin Wall** The Granger Collection, New York; **Sarajevo** ©Chris Rainier/Corbis; **Zhou, Mao Nixon and Kissinger** ©Bettmann/Corbis; **Chinese soldiers** AP/Wide World Photos; **Jiang Zemin** ©Reuters NewMedia Inc./ Corbis; **Olympic bid in Beijing** AP/ Wide World Photos; **Bosnian refugees** ©Str Old/Reuters; **man in Tiananmen Square** AP/Wide World Photos; **Abuelas de Plaza de Mayo** AP/Wide World Photos; **fall of Berlin Wall** ©Gilles Peress/ Magnum Photos; **voting line in South Africa** ©Peter Turnley/Corbis.

MODULE 32

Shanghai Tower ©bpperry/Getty Images; **Atomic Energy Symbol** ©Photodisc/Getty Images; **masked terrorist** ©Bettmann/Corbis; **space shuttle** ©AFP/Getty Images; **refugee camp** ©Ratib Al Safadi/Anadolu Agency/ Getty Images; **international space station** ©Corbis/Sygma; **tablet computer** Manu Fernandez/AP Photo; **mapping DNA** ©Jean-Christian Bourcart/ Hulton Archive/Getty Images; **cargo ship** ©Getty Images; **Persian Gulf War** ©Peter Turnley/Corbis; **ozone levels** (all) NASA; **Baghdad** AP/Wide World Photos; **Mother Teresa** AP/Wide World Photos; **Syrian refugees** ©Cem Genco/Anadolu Agency/Getty Images; **Afghan Refugees** ©Reuters NewMedia Inc./Corbis; **Sarin gas attack** ©Tokyo Shimbum/ Corbis Sygma; **Israeli security barrier** ©Kevin Frayer/AP Images; **Homeland Security alert** ©Joshua Roberts/AFP/ Getty Images; **World Trade Center** AP/ Wide World Photos; **Pentagon** ©Reuters NewMedia Inc./Corbis; **anthrax scare** ©Stephen Jaffe/AFP/Getty Images; **airport security** AP/Wide World Photos; **trees** ©Will & Deni McIntyre/Corbis; **deforestation** ©Getty Images; **hydrogen car** ©Mark Wilson/Getty Images News/ Getty Images; **Elvis** AP/Wide World Photos; **Youssou N'Dour** AP/Wide World Photos; **Nadine Gordimer** AP/Wide World Photos; **Kenzaburo Oe** ©Reuters NewMedia Inc./Corbis.